Russell Pizzuto
Sales Representative
716 430 2111
rpizzuto@roadrunner.com

PHYSICAL SCIENCE

Exploring Matter and Energy

Dr. Gustavo Loret de Mola

McGraw Hill Wright Group

The McGraw-Hill Companies

Author

Dr. Gustavo Loret de Mola is a science educator with more than 35 years of teaching and administrative experience at the middle school, high school, and college levels. He holds a BS degree in education from the University of Miami, an MS degree in science from Nova University, and an EdD in Educational Leadership from Nova University. Dr. Loret de Mola taught high school science for 11 years before serving as a project manager in science and a middle school assistant principal for Dade County Public Schools. Dr. Loret de Mola then served 20 years as District Science Supervisor for Dade County Public Schools. As a committee member, Dr. Loret de Mola helped develop the Teacher Certification Tests in Science for the State of Florida. He also served as State Chairperson for the State of Florida Life Sciences Instructional Materials Council. Currently, Dr. Loret de Mola continues to work in the sciences as adjunct professor at the University of Miami, where he teaches science and science methodology courses for graduate students in education.

Series Consultants

Richard Audet, EdD
  Roger Williams University

Matthew Marino, PhD
  Washington State University

Barbara Scott, MD
  Los Angeles Unified School District

Lisa Soll, BS
  San Antonio Independent School District

Content Reviewers

Valerie Amen, BS, Genoa, Illinois
Brian Howes, MA, Dubuque, Iowa
Janie Martin, MA, San Antonio, Texas
Sarah Schlussel, MA, Bakersfield, California
Marilyn Zaragoza, EdD, Pembroke Pines, Florida

ELL Consultants

Mary Smith, MA, Merced, California
Brian Silva, MS, Long Beach, California

Laboratory Reviewer

Garrett Hall, BA, Pleasant Hill, Iowa

Laboratory Safety Consultant

Jeff Vogt, MED, West Virginia University at Parkersburg

About the Cover

Photo credits are on pages 491–492.

www.WrightGroup.com

 **Wright Group**

Printed in the United States of America.

Send all inquiries to:
Wright Group/McGraw-Hill
P.O. Box 812960
Chicago, IL 60681

ISBN 978-0-07-704140-3
MHID 0-07-704140-2

1 2 3 4 5 6 7 8 9 QWV 13 12 11 10 09 08 07

The **McGraw·Hill** Companies

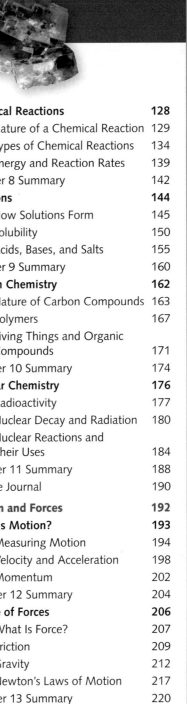

Contents

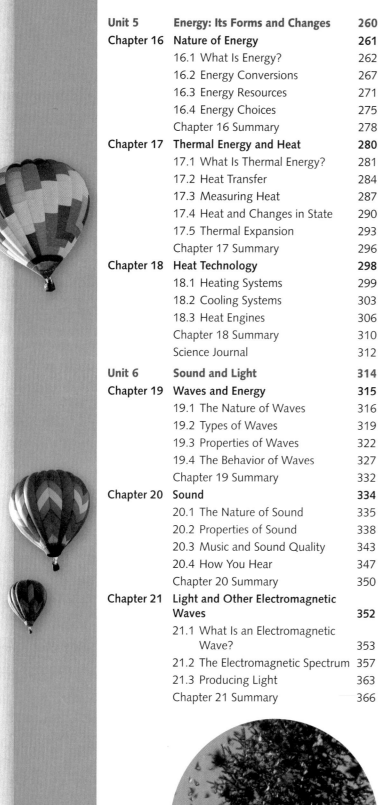

Physical Science: Exploring Matter and Energy invites students to enter a wonderfully exciting and important world. The Student Edition is a valuable tool for students as they gain knowledge about matter and energy, appreciate the scientific process, and become scientifically literate citizens. To achieve those ends, students should become familiar with the organization and features of the textbook and use the textbook effectively. The following pages illustrate the features that were designed with student and teacher success in mind.

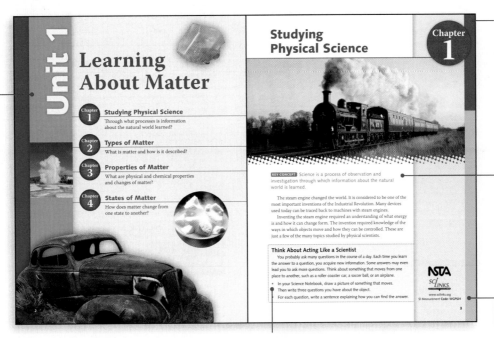

UNIT OPENER

The **Unit Opener** provides a preview of the material students will learn in upcoming chapters. Through striking visuals and thought-provoking questions representative of each chapter in the unit, students are encouraged to begin thinking about the content of the unit and making connections among its chapters.

CHAPTER OPENER

This **introduction to the chapter** puts the content in context and reflects the relevance of physical science to today's world. The introductory story captures student interest and motivates continued reading.

KEY CONCEPT

The **Key Concept** identifies the "big idea" of the chapter and connects the various concepts within the chapter. Combined, the Key Concepts of the textbook represent the basic principles of physical science.

SCILINKS CODES

SciLinks codes direct students to NSTA-approved Web sites.

THINK ABOUT . . .

A strategy for activating prior knowledge, the **Think About . . .** feature relates directly to the Chapter Opener story and to the chapter content. Encouraging students to identify previously acquired information and/or skills, the feature presents a brief set of questions or activities for students to complete using that information or skill. Students can practice expressing their knowledge, experiences, and ideas by recording their answers in their **Science Notebooks.**

BEFORE YOU READ

One of a trio of literacy activities, **Before You Read** is a prereading exercise that incorporates appropriate reading comprehension and literacy skills strategies. Each Before You Read activity is closely integrated with the As You Read and After You Read activities within a lesson, providing introduction, reinforcement, and assessment of essential literacy skills.

LEARNING GOALS

Each chapter is divided into lessons of manageable length. Each lesson begins with **Learning Goals,** which help students focus on the cognitive outcomes they should achieve as a result of reading the lesson. The Learning Goals are further used at the end of the chapter to help students prepare for the Chapter Test.

NEW VOCABULARY

New Vocabulary is a list of the important terms in the lesson that appear in boldface type upon initial reference. The list serves as a preview for students, identifying both familiar and unfamiliar terms.

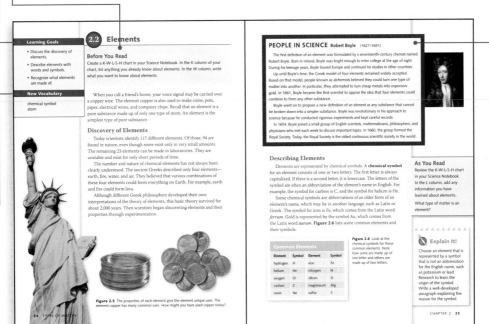

PEOPLE IN SCIENCE

The study of physical science is essentially the story of individual and group contributions to the understanding of matter and energy. The **People in Science** feature highlights a figure or figures of historical or current importance in the field by providing biographical information and emphasizing the contribution to scientific knowledge and/or research.

NARRATIVE AND VISUALS

Most important to students' understanding of physical science and their appreciation of the scientific process is content presentation that makes learning easier and more accessible. Great care has been taken to write and present the concepts of physical science in a way that motivates students and guarantees their success. Both the **narrative** and the **visuals** support English language learners and struggling readers. Visuals are functional, interesting, and understandable. Narrative is clear, concise, logically sequenced, and is presented in an outline-style format. Consideration of a range of reading levels and learning styles is evident in the friendly, engaging, and appropriate prose.

AS YOU READ

This during-reading literacy activity focuses on both the science content that has been presented in the lesson and the literacy activity introduced in Before You Read. **As You Read** poses a content-related question that incorporates the literacy skill and encourages students to work collaboratively.

FIGURE IT OUT

An essential skill for student success, reading and interpreting visuals is practiced and reinforced by the **Figure It Out** feature. Important tables, graphs, diagrams, and photos are highlighted in the lessons and accompanied by questions that assess student comprehension of the visuals.

CONNECTION

The relevance of physical science to other areas of science and to other disciplines is emphasized by the **Connection** feature. Students are made aware of the ways in which scientific concepts and thinking skills can be applied to other areas of learning. Although they are studying physical science, students will become more scientifically literate as they understand the interconnections presented in this feature.

EXTEND IT!

Providing an opportunity to go beyond the content of the textbook, **Extend It!** activities encourage students to research related topics and report their findings in an appropriate way.

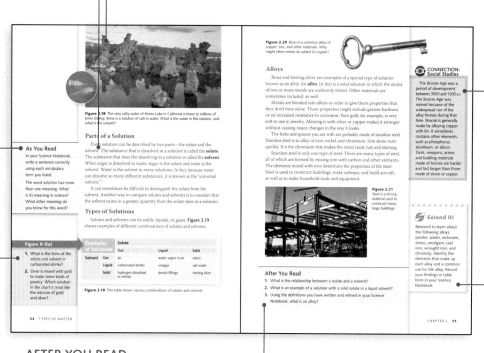

AFTER YOU READ

The final part of the literacy skill strategy and an assessment tool, **After You Read** poses content-related questions that correspond to the lesson's Learning Goals. The questions range from recall to higher-level thinking skills, and one question utilizes the literacy activity introduced in Before You Read and supplemented in As You Read.

DID YOU KNOW?

Information about the role of physical science in students' lives is presented in a lively, engaging manner in the Did You Know? feature. These intriguing and often humorous stories address common misconceptions, provide additional content, and present fun factoids—all for the purpose of stimulating student thinking and class discussion.

EXPLAIN IT!

Students can practice expressing their knowledge, ideas, and experiences by completing the activities contained in Explain It! These writing activities assess students' understanding of the content by providing practice in analyzing and applying concepts.

EXPLORE IT!

The quick and effective hands-on activities that comprise Explore It! can be done by students in class with partners or in groups, or at home as a homework assignment. Requiring easily obtained materials, the activities support content by providing students with an active-learning experience. They help students experience science as a process as well as a body of knowledge, and they reinforce the scientific approach to problem-solving.

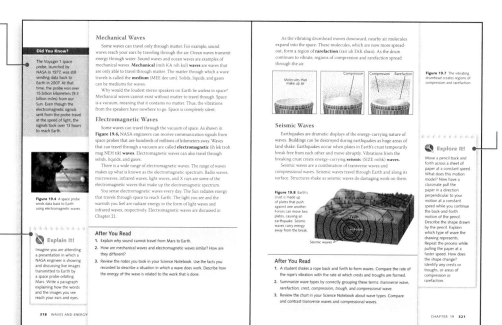

CHAPTER SUMMARY

The **Chapter Summary** provides concept review, vocabulary review and assessment, and content and concept evaluation.

KEY CONCEPTS

The key concepts in each lesson are listed in **Key Concepts** to help students review the chapter content. Students should be encouraged to make sure they understand each concept and its relationship to other concepts in the chapter, to the main idea of the chapter, and to the basic principles of physical science.

VOCABULARY REVIEW

Vocabulary terms are essential to students' understanding of science. The key terms listed in Vocabulary Review are those students should be especially familiar with. Students are encouraged to demonstrate their understanding of the terms by defining them in complete, well-developed sentences or paragraphs.

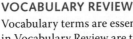

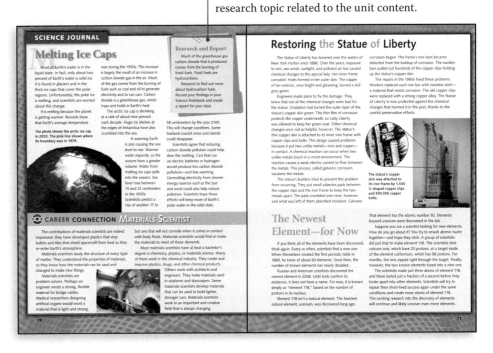

MASTERING CONCEPTS

Students can test their knowledge of the facts, evaluate their understanding of the concepts, and apply their factual knowledge and conceptual understanding by answering the various types of assessments contained in **Mastering Concepts.** Assessment forms include modified true or false, short answer, and critical thinking. Also included is a standardized test question, which helps familiarize students with this test format, and a Test-Taking Tip.

PREPARE FOR CHAPTER TEST

To help students prepare for the chapter test, this self-assessment activity integrates the lesson Learning Goals with the chapter Key Concept. As students convert the Learning Goals into questions that they answer, they evaluate their understanding of the chapter's main ideas. As students then use those answers to write a well-developed essay summarizing the chapter content, they demonstrate their ability to support the Key Concept with pertinent facts and vocabulary.

RESEARCH AND REPORT

Research and Report provides students a research topic related to the unit content.

SCIENCE JOURNAL

This end-of-unit enrichment feature is designed to extend chapter content with motivating articles that address connections, breakthroughs, and issues in physical science. All of the concepts of a unit are integrated in articles that demonstrate the relevance and role of science in students' lives and the lives of others. Science Journal contains several case studies and a career connection, which highlights how the study of physical science can be applied to a variety of interesting and important vocations.

The Teacher's Edition is designed to support and supplement teaching efforts and knowledge of physical science as well as maximize the opportunities for both student and teacher success. Organization tools, teaching strategies, background information, and suggestions for reaching all students are provided within a user-friendly and visually concise wraparound format.

UNIT AND CHAPTER FEATURES

The **Unit Opener** copy offers strategies for introducing the unit content and suggestions for Unit Projects in the areas of career research, hands-on research, and technology research. Each project is intended to address the main ideas of the unit and to extend over the duration of the unit coverage. For each Unit Project, students are encouraged to use the Student Presentation Builder on the Student CD-ROM to display their results.

The **End-of-Unit** copy addresses each of the unit case studies by suggesting research activities and providing background information. It also connects the Unit Opener career research activity with the selected unit career.

The **Chapter Opener** and **Chapter Planning Guide** provide an overview of the chapter's organization. The Chapter Opener also includes a reference to the Getting Started! activity in the Lab Manual, a strategy for introducing the chapter content, and suggestions for the Think About . . . feature. The Chapter Planning Guide identifies the various print and computer ancillaries designed to be used with each lesson, as well as the National Standards covered by the lesson content. The Chapter Planning Guide also includes suggested numbers of instructional periods needed for the lessons.

LESSON CYCLE

A **three-step lesson cycle** based on current educational methodology—INTRODUCE, TEACH, ASSESS—incorporates the **five Es** of effective science teaching: Engage, Explore, Explain, Evaluate, and Extend.

Point-of-use support for text and margin features, including answers to lesson and chapter assessment questions, is found in the side columns. This support is designed to enhance the teacher's ability to maximize student learning. Also included in the side columns are features that extend vocabulary, reinforce visual learning, encourage student writing, and assess understanding: **Vocabulary, Use the Visual, Science Notebook Extra,** and **Alternative Assessment.**

The bottom margins of wraparound copy contain information to support, supplement, and extend teacher resources. Included here are **Background Information, Differentiate Instruction, ELL Strategy, Teacher Alert, Field Study,** and **Reading Links.**

LABORATORY MANUAL TEACHER'S EDITION

This two-page spread found at the end of a chapter provides important information and guidance for each of the three chapter laboratory activities found in the Laboratory Manual. Activity teaching notes include **Objectives, Skill Set, Planning, Materials, Advance Preparation, Answers to Observations, Answers to Analysis and Conclusions,** and **Going Further.**

A complete **Lab Materials List** is found on pages 492A–492B of the Teacher's Edition. The easily accessible materials are referenced by lab activity and reported in total for the program to help the teacher in ordering yearly supplies. It is assumed that safety goggles, laboratory aprons, laboratory manuals, paper, pencils, and pens are available for all activities. The Lab Materials List is followed by a list of **Equipment Suppliers.**

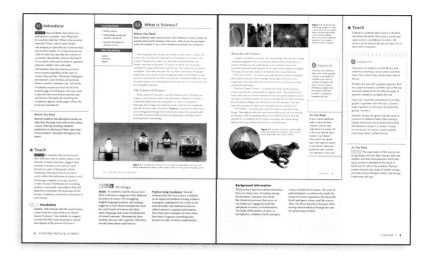

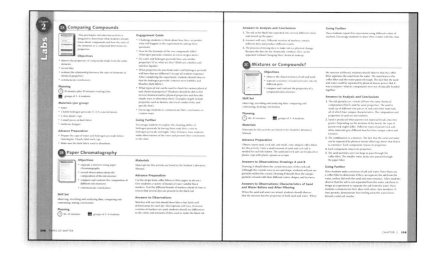

The Student Edition and Teacher's Edition of *Physical Science: Exploring Matter and Energy* are supplemented by the **Workbook, Laboratory Manual, Blackline Master Assessment Packet,** and **Electronic Material.**

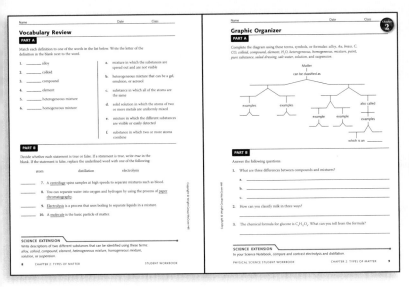

Chapter content is reviewed, reinforced, and extended by **Workbook** activities of the following kind: **Key Concept Review, Vocabulary Review, Interpreting Diagrams, Graphic Organizer, Reading Comprehension, Curriculum Connection,** and **Science Challenge.** Answers to all Workbook activities are found in the Teacher's Edition. The **Laboratory Manual** provides three opportunities for students to engage in hands-on learning for each chapter.

Lab A is a one-page, 15- to 20-minute activity that activates prior knowledge and introduces the chapter concepts in an innovative, motivating, and fun-to-do way. It uses limited materials and can be done as a classroom demonstration or homework assignment. **Lab B** and **Lab C** are scaffolded according to difficulty level. Both are two- to three-page activities designed to be completed in a class period of 45 to 50 minutes.

Information about preparation and implementation of all Laboratory Manual activities, as well as answers to all Observations and Analysis and Conclusions questions, are found in the Teacher's Edition.

ABOUT THE STUDENT SOFTWARE

The Student Software contains several instructional tools:

Student Electronic Material (CD-ROM)

The entire Student Edition is available in e-book PDF format with links to audio, animation, searches, glossary, laboratory activities, Spanish introductions and activities, and instructional interactivities.

Student Presentation Builder

The Student Presentation Builder utilizes PowerPoint technology with graphics from the Student Edition.

Interactive Laboratory Activities

The interactive laboratory activities will provide students with: 1) activities that are a higher level in difficulty and more complicated to conduct in a school setting; 2) activities that are lower in difficulty but more efficient to conduct on the computer; and 3) activities that will trigger and build prior knowledge.

Spanish Introductions and Activities

Research has shown that English Language Learners benefit from first generating prior knowledge verbally about a given topic in their first language. Also, by writing about a concept in their first language, students increase comprehension and are better prepared for content acquisition in English.

Graphic Organizer Software

This component will provide printable PDF graphic organizers, electronic graphic organizer templates that can export to and from an outline format, and a template for students to complete lab reports with nonprintable prompts.

TEACHER'S RESOURCES

Teacher's Electronic Manual (CD-ROM)

The entire teacher's edition is available via e-book, along with links to all related ancillaries. This CD-ROM also includes instructional interactivities, a Teacher Presentation Builder, interactive library activities, electronic graphic organizer software, Spanish introductions and activities, and links to PDFs of ELL Blackline Masters, Overhead Transparencies, the Student Workbook Answer Key, and the Laboratory Manual.

Blackline Masters

The Blackline Masters are designed to enhance the curriculum.

Test Question Generator (CD-ROM)

Question-bank development can be used to create various book assessments. The questions are cross-correlated to National Science Standards.

Overhead Transparencies

This 48-page component provides teachers with key graphics related to the curriculum.

Correlation to the National Science Education Standards

Content Standard	Chapters
(UCP) Unifying Concepts and Processes (Grades 5–8, 9–12)	
1. Systems, order, and organization	1, 2, 3, 4, 5, 6, 7, 8, 9, 10, 11, 12, 13, 14, 15, 16, 17, 18, 19, 20, 21, 22, 23, 24, 25, 26
2. Evidence, models, and explanation	1, 2, 3, 4, 5, 6, 7, 8, 9, 10, 11, 12, 13, 14, 15, 16, 17, 18, 19, 20, 21, 22, 23, 24, 25, 26
3. Constancy, change, and measurement	1, 2, 3, 4, 5, 6, 7, 8, 9, 10, 11, 12, 13, 14, 15, 16, 17, 18, 19, 20, 21, 22, 23, 24, 25, 26
4. Evolution and equilibrium	2, 8, 9, 10, 11, 12, 13, 14, 15, 16, 17, 18, 19, 20, 23, 24, 26
5. Form and function	2, 4, 5, 6 ,7, 9, 10, 11, 12, 13, 14, 15, 16, 17, 18, 19, 20, 21, 22, 23, 24, 25, 26
(A) Science as Inquiry (Grades 5–8, 9–12)	
1. Abilities necessary to do scientific inquiry	1, 2, 3, 5, 6, 7, 8, 9, 10, 11, 12, 13, 14, 15, 16, 17, 18, 20, 22, 23, 24, 26
2. Understandings about scientific inquiry	1, 2, 4, 5, 6, 7, 8, 9, 10, 11, 12, 13, 14, 15, 16, 17, 18, 19, 20, 21, 22, 23, 24, 25, 26
(B) Physical Science (Grades 5–8)	
1. Properties and changes of properties in matter	1, 2, 3, 4, 5, 6, 7, 8, 9, 10, 11, 12, 14, 16, 17, 23, 24, 26
2. Motions and forces	9, 11, 12, 13, 14, 15, 17, 19, 20, 23, 24, 25
3. Transfer of energy	8, 9, 11, 12, 13, 14, 15, 16, 17, 19, 20, 21, 22, 23, 25, 26
(B) Physical Science (Grades 9–12)	
1. Structure of atoms	5, 7, 9, 10, 11, 16, 17
2. Structure and properties of matter	1, 2, 3, 4, 5, 6, 7, 8, 9, 10, 11, 14, 16, 17, 23, 24, 26
3. Chemical reactions	3, 8, 9, 10, 16, 17, 18
4. Motions and forces	11, 12, 13, 14, 15, 17, 19, 20, 23, 24, 25
5. Conservation of energy and increase in disorder	4, 9, 11, 12, 13, 15, 16, 17, 18, 19, 20, 21, 22, 25, 26
6. Interactions of energy and matter	12
(C) Life Science (Grades 5–8)	
1. Structure and function in living systems	3, 9, 12, 13, 14, 16, 19, 20, 22, 23, 24
3. Regulation and behavior	9, 12, 16, 17
5. Diversity and adaptations of organisms	2, 3, 4, 5, 8, 10, 11, 12, 13, 14, 15, 17, 18, 20
(C) Life Science (Grades 9–12)	
1. The cell	23
2. Molecular basis of heredity	10
5. Matter, energy, and organization in living systems	11, 14, 16, 20, 22
6. Behavior of organisms	12, 13, 14, 17, 19

Correlation to the National Science Education Standards (continued)

Content Standard	Chapters
(D) Earth and Space Science (Grades 5–8)	
1. Structure of the earth system	2, 11, 13, 14
3. Earth in the solar system	12, 13, 20
(D) Earth and Space Science (Grades 9–12)	
1. Energy in the earth system	13, 16, 20, 24
(E) Science and Technology (Grades 5–8, 9–12)	
1. Abilities of technological design	6, 9, 10, 13, 14, 15, 16, 17, 18, 20, 21, 22, 23, 24, 25, 26
2. Understandings about science and technology	1, 5, 10, 11, 13, 14, 15, 16, 17, 18, 19, 20, 21, 22, 23, 24, 25, 26
(F) Science in Personal and Social Perspectives (Grades 5–8)	
1. Personal health	6, 9, 10, 11, 16, 17, 20, 21, 22, 23
2. Populations, resources, and environments	14, 16
3. Natural hazards	6, 11, 21, 23, 24
4. Risks and benefits	6, 11, 16, 18, 20, 21
5. Science and technology in society	1, 10, 13, 14, 15, 16, 17, 18, 19, 20, 21, 22, 23, 24, 25, 26
(F) Science in Personal and Social Perspectives (Grades 9–12)	
1. Personal and community health	6, 9, 11, 16, 20, 21, 22, 23, 24
3. Natural resources	16, 24
4. Environmental quality	16
5. Natural and human-induced hazards	7, 8, 17, 25
6. Science and technology in local, national, and global challenges	1, 10, 11, 13, 14, 15, 16, 17, 18, 19, 20, 21, 22, 23, 24, 25, 26
(G) History and Nature of Science (Grades 5–8)	
1. Science as a human endeavor	1, 2, 4, 5, 6, 7, 8, 10, 11, 13, 14, 15, 16, 18, 19, 20, 21, 22, 24, 25, 26
2. Nature of science	1, 2, 4, 5, 6, 7, 8, 10, 11, 12, 13, 14, 15, 16, 17, 18, 20, 21, 22, 23, 24, 25, 26
3. History of science	2, 4, 5, 6, 7, 8, 10, 11, 13, 15, 16, 18, 20, 21, 22, 24, 25, 26
(G) History and Nature of Science (Grades 9–12)	
1. Science as a human endeavor	1, 2, 4, 5, 6, 7, 8, 10, 11, 13, 15, 16, 18, 19, 20, 21, 22, 24, 25, 26
2. Nature of scientific knowledge	1, 2, 4, 5, 6, 7, 8, 10, 11, 12, 13, 14, 15, 16, 17, 18, 20, 21, 22, 23, 24, 25, 26
3. Historical perspectives	2, 4, 5, 6, 7, 8, 10, 11, 13, 15, 16, 18, 20, 21, 22, 24, 25, 26

Unit 1

Introduce Unit 1

Explain to students that the topic of this unit is studying physical science. Help students understand that physical science is in part the study of matter.

Have students write in their Science Notebooks some facts they already know about matter. As they read the chapters in this unit, have them add to and revise this information.

Unit Projects

For each Unit Project, have students use the Presentation Builder on the Student CD-ROM to display their results.

Career Research Have each student choose a career in physical science. Have each student research what the job entails and record this information in his or her Science Notebook. Students may want to create a special section in their Science Notebooks for career research. When students have completed their research, have them present brief oral reports about the careers they chose to research.

Hands-On Research Have students work in groups to explore the physical dimensions and properties of their classroom. Encourage students to map, measure, weigh, and otherwise observe the room and its contents. Provide some basic tools: a metric ruler, balance, thermometer, and graduated cylinder. Tell students to describe the room in as much detail as possible, including the state(s) of matter found there. Finished reports should include data sets and drawings.

Technology Research Have students consider the data they gathered in the hands-on activity. Ask: *What information were you unable to collect because of your limited tools?* As a class, brainstorm technologies that would enable students to conduct a more thorough investigation of the room.

Unit 1

Learning About Matter

Chapter 1 — Studying Physical Science
Through what processes is information about the natural world learned?

Chapter 2 — Types of Matter
What is matter and how is it described?

Chapter 3 — Properties of Matter
What are physical and chemical properties and changes of matter?

Chapter 4 — States of Matter
How does matter change from one state to another?

 Software Summary

Student CD-ROM
—Interactive Student Book
—Vocabulary Review
—Key Concept Review
—Lab Report Template
—ELL Preview and Writing Activities
—Presentation Digital Library
—Graphic Organizing Software
—Spanish Cognate Dictionary

Interactive Labs
Chapter 2C—Mixtures or Compounds?

Studying Physical Science

KEY CONCEPT Science is a process of observation and investigation through which information about the natural world is learned.

The steam engine changed the world. It is considered to be one of the most important inventions of the Industrial Revolution. Many devices used today can be traced back to machines with steam engines.

Inventing the steam engine required an understanding of what energy is and how it can change form. The invention required knowledge of the ways in which objects move and how they can be controlled. These are just a few of the many topics studied by physical scientists.

Think About Acting Like a Scientist

You probably ask many questions in the course of a day. Each time you learn the answer to a question, you acquire new information. Some answers may even lead you to ask more questions. Think about something that moves from one place to another, such as a roller coaster car, a soccer ball, or an airplane.

- In your Science Notebook, draw a picture of something that moves. Then write three questions you have about the object.
- For each question, write a sentence explaining how you can find the answer.

www.scilinks.org
SI Measurement **Code: WGPS01**

3

Introduce Chapter 1

As a starting activity, use Lab 1A on page 1 of the Laboratory Manual.

ENGAGE Ask students to describe what they know about steam engines. Direct them to look at the photograph of the steam engine. Discuss the impact that the steam engine's invention had on this country. Ask students to think about different forms of energy and how those forms affect our everyday lives.

Think About Acting Like a Scientist

ENGAGE Ask students to give examples of some of the questions they ask themselves or others in a day. Encourage students to think about both complex and simple questions. Discuss the different ways in which they might find answers to their questions. Give an example of a scientific question, such as *What are all substances made of?* Remind students that when scientists first asked this question, they didn't have many tools to find the answer. Ask students to suggest ways in which scientists might have tried to answer that question when it was first asked, and how scientists might answer the question now. Encourage students to recognize that although the tools for finding answers are different today, the method of asking questions and searching for answers remains the same.

Direct students to complete each bulleted activity. As a class, discuss students' results. On the board, record students' ideas about how they might find answers to their questions.

Chapter 1 Planning Guide

Instructional Periods	National Standards	Lab Manual	Workbook
1.1 2 Periods	A.1, A.2, G.1, G.2; A.1, A.2, G.1, G.2; UCP.1	**Lab 1A: p. 1** Accuracy in Measurement	Key Concept Review p. 1 Vocabulary Review p. 2 Graphic Organizer p. 3
1.2 2 Periods	A.1, B.1, E.2, F.5, G.2; A.1, B.1, E.2, F.5, G.2; UCP.2	**Lab 1B: pp. 2–4** Counting Your Money **Lab 1C: pp. 5–6**	Reading Comprehension p. 4 Curriculum Connection p. 5 Science Challenge p. 6
1.3 2 Periods	A.1, A.2, G.1, G.2; A.1, A.2, G.1, G.2; UCP.3	Calculating Density Using SI Units	

Middle School Standard; High School Standard; Unifying Concept and Principle

1.1 Introduce

ENGAGE Have students close their eyes and picture a scientist. Ask: *What does the scientist look like? What is the scientist wearing? What is the scientist doing?*

Ask students to describe the scientists they saw in their minds. As a class, brainstorm a list of verbs that describe the actions of a scientist. Record the verbs on the board. Try to elicit verbs such as *observe, question, measure, predict, test,* and *study.*

Tell students that all scientists perform these actions regardless of the type of science they practice. Physicists, biologists, astronomers, and chemists all question, observe, predict, measure, test, and study.

Vocabulary terms are listed on the first student page of each lesson. You may wish to preview the terms before introducing each lesson. Strategies for teaching the vocabulary appear on the pages where the terms are introduced.

Before You Read

Remind students that descriptive words are adjectives that give more information about a noun. Start by recording students' predictions on the board if they need help. Check students' examples throughout the lesson.

● Teach

EXPLAIN to students that in this lesson, they will learn how to define science and identify its many branches. Suggest that students visualize a tree and see each branch as a part of the greater whole. Emphasize that each branch of science exists within the definition of science itself.

Encourage students to set up a section in their Science Notebooks for recording prefixes, root words, and suffixes that will help them remember the meanings of the science vocabulary terms they encounter in each lesson.

◎ Vocabulary

science Tell students that the word *science* comes from the Latin word *scire,* which means "to know." Ask students to suggest reasons why this Latin meaning is a good description of the process of science.

Learning Goals

- Define science.
- Differentiate among the branches of science.
- Examine the topics of physical science.

New Vocabulary

science
chemistry
physics

1.1 What Is Science?

Before You Read

Make predictions about what you think is the definition of science. Preview the Learning Goals and the headings in this lesson. Write at least five descriptive words and examples in your Science Notebook to describe your predictions.

There's going to be a racing-car contest at your school. It's part of a science fair. You and your classmates are building cars to enter in the contest. The goal is to make a car that will travel the farthest and fastest—and also be the safest. To make a winning car, your group members try large wheels and small wheels. They make the car heavier and lighter. They sand and paint the car. After each action, the group studies the car to decide if each change has made it travel faster. It may surprise you to know that when you and your classmates follow this type of organized process of learning about the movement of a racing car, you are acting like scientists.

The Nature of Science

What comes to mind when you think about science? Perhaps you imagine a set of books packed with information. Maybe you think of a laboratory filled with colored liquids in a variety of containers. Although these images are related to science, they do not completely describe the true nature of science. **Science** is a process of observation and investigation through which information about the natural world is learned. Science is both the process of gaining knowledge and the resulting body of knowledge.

Figure 1.1 Learning how energy can be changed to make things move and how design influences the speed at which objects move are two goals of studying science.

ⒺⓁⓁ Strategy

Model As students read the lesson, have them each draw a diagram of the different branches of science. For struggling English language learners, one strategy might be to have them translate the word for each branch of science into their native language and create a bulleted list of related concepts. Alternatively, have students discuss with a partner what they already know about each branch.

Practice Using Vocabulary Remind students that the term *science* is defined as an organized method of using evidence to propose explanations for events in the natural world. Ask students to discuss what it means to organize information. Have them give examples of times when they had to organize something they learned in order to better understand it.

Figure 1.2 Understanding what keeps people in a roller coaster when it turns upside-down and how information can be carried without wires is the work of physical scientists. So is creating brilliant fireworks displays.

Teach

Explain to students that science is divided into three branches: life science, Earth and space science, and physical science. All science as we know it fits into at least one of these three branches.

Explain It!

Have pairs of students use the library and Internet to develop a list of several scientific tasks, from which they should select one to discuss.

Provide each pair with a graphic organizer that has a place to record a scientific task at the top and space below to list the different types of scientists needed to complete the task.

Have pairs share the information from their graphic organizers with the class. Create a large organizer on the board to record the groups' answers.

Students should recognize that the work of scientists in different fields often overlaps. Explain that most natural phenomena lend themselves to study in a variety of ways, so one branch of science cannot explore everything about a phenomenon.

Branches of Science

Imagine yourself as a scientist. Are you wearing a lab coat and mixing substances together? Are you looking at photos of the newest spot on Jupiter? Perhaps you are scuba diving to see animals in the ocean. A specific scientist's work depends on the topics that scientist investigates. The topics of scientific study are divided into three main branches.

Physical Science Scientists who study physical science investigate such topics as motion, forces, energy, sound, light, electricity, and magnetism. They also study the interactions that occur between types of particles and matter.

Earth and Space Science Scientists who study Earth and space science examine the characteristics of planet Earth. They study Earth's water, land, and air as well as weather events and natural disasters. Earth and space scientists consider the process through which Earth developed, how the planet changes, and where it fits into the universe. They also study the processes by which stars and galaxies form and function.

Life Science Scientists who study life science work with living things. This might include the more obvious life forms, such as animals and plants, or the living things that are too small to be seen with the unaided eye. In addition, life scientists investigate how living things interact with one another and with their environments.

Figure 1.3 An Earth and space scientist might study the eruptions of volcanoes. Life scientists study living things such as this cheetah.

Explain It!

Scientists from different fields often work together. Choose an example of a scientific task, such as sending astronauts into space. In your Science Notebook, explain how the input of different scientists is needed to complete the task.

As You Read

In your Science Notebook, make a chart with three columns—one for each major branch of science. Fill in the chart with the topics studied in each branch. Then predict two specific topics that might be studied in each branch. Share your predictions with a partner and write them in the chart.

As You Read

[ANSWER] The main topics of life science are living things and how they interact with one another and their environments. Earth and space science is devoted to the study of Earth and its role in the universe. Physical science includes the study of matter, energy, and interactions between matter and energy. Predictions will vary.

Background Information

While science has three distinct branches, there are many cases of overlap among the branches. Scientists who study the chemical processes that occur in our bodies are engaged in both life and physical science, or biochemistry. The study of the physics of stars, or astrophysics, combines Earth and space science and physical science. The work of paleontologists, scientists who study the fossils of extinct organisms, fits into both Earth and space science and life science. Thus, the three branches of science often overlap when looked at through the eyes of a practicing scientist.

Teach

Emphasize the fact that almost every job requires the use or knowledge of science. Ask students to brainstorm a list of professions. Record that list on the board. Then have students look at the jobs on the list and discuss the role of science in each one.

Figure It Out: Figure 1.4

ANSWER 1. chemistry 2. Both scientists might be investigating the properties of a material. However, the chemist might study the particles in the material, while the physicist might study how the material behaves in different conditions and when exposed to forces.

 Vocabulary

chemistry Review with students the definition of this term (the study of matter). Then write the terms *chemist* (noun) and *chemical* (noun and adjective) on the board and discuss the meaning and part(s) of speech of each term. Have students use each term in a sentence.

physics Review with students the definition of this term (the study of energy and how it changes matter). Have students list and describe the various forms of energy (heat, light, sound, electricity, magnetism, atomic interactions).

Assess

Use the After You Read questions and Alternative Assessment to help you evaluate students' understanding of this lesson.

After You Read

1. Science is an action because it involves asking questions and learning about the world. It is also the knowledge learned, which makes it a thing.
2. Earth and space scientist (meteorologist)
3. life scientist
4. The life scientist might study how germs affect the human body. The physical scientist might be a chemist investigating the properties of a drug developed to combat the germs or the drug's effects on the chemical balance of the human body.

Branches of Physical Science

Each branch of science is further divided into more specific fields. This textbook explores the world of physical science. Physical science can be divided into two major branches: chemistry and physics. **Chemistry** is the study of matter. **Physics** is the study of energy and how it changes matter.

Figure It Out

1. A scientist purifying water through a process known as distillation works in which branch of physical science?
2. How might the work of a chemist and the work of a physicist be related?

Questions in the Branches of Physical Science

Chemistry	Physics
What are things made of?	What is force and how does it relate to motion?
What are the different types of matter?	What is energy and how can it change form?
How does matter change into other types of matter?	What are electric charges and what happens when they move?

Figure 1.4 The table lists some of the questions that might be studied within each branch of physical science.

Did You Know?

While many physical scientists work in a laboratory or out in the field, others rarely leave their desks. A theoretical physicist attempts to explain the world through complex ideas and models that involve high-level mathematics. Theoretical physicists seldom perform laboratory experiments. The progress of physics depends on the interaction between theoretical physicists and physicists who conduct experiments, known as experimental physicists.

Who Studies Science?

Perhaps after learning about science and its branches, you are thinking that science is only for scientists in laboratories. How wrong you are! Many people working in other fields study science or use the work of scientists.

For example, people who work in government need an understanding of many science topics in order to make useful decisions. They need to know the properties of waste from nuclear power plants in order to decide how this waste should be disposed of. They should understand how living things interact with their environments in order to make decisions about water conservation. Almost every job imaginable requires some understanding of scientific topics.

After You Read

1. Describe how science can be considered both an action and a thing. Refer to the predictions you recorded in your Science Notebook.
2. Which type of scientist is most likely to study weather patterns?
3. Which type of scientist is most likely to study the migration of birds?
4. The work of a physical scientist can be related to the work of a life scientist. Suppose a life scientist studies germs. Predict how the research of the life scientist might be related to the research of a physical scientist.

Alternative Assessment

Have students look at and refine their lists of scientific tasks. Lists should include the scientific process skills: observation, classification, comparison, organization, evaluation, prediction, experimentation, and application. To help students understand these tasks, have them draw pictures to illustrate the terms' meanings.

Differentiated Instruction

Interpersonal Have students reach out to scientists in their community. As a class, brainstorm a list of questions that students might ask a local scientist. Students might visit a local hospital, lab, water-treatment plant, or zoo to discover what the life of a scientist is like on a daily basis. English language learners should write out their questions. After the visit to observe the scientist's life, they should write a description of what they observed.

- Describe the steps of the scientific method.

- Identify safe practices in the science laboratory.

- Distinguish between a hypothesis and a theory.

New Vocabulary

scientific method
observation
hypothesis
experiment
variable
controlled experiment
independent variable
dependent variable
control group
experimental group
safety symbol
data
conclusion
theory
prediction

Before You Read

Create a sequence chart in your Science Notebook. Imagine that your teacher gives you a topic to research. You are not familiar with the topic, but your teacher would like you to prepare a report. In your sequence chart, write the steps that you might follow to learn about the topic.

The process through which scientists attempt to answer questions about the natural world is generally known as the **scientific method**. Although there is no single series of steps that is always followed in the scientific method, all scientific investigations follow an orderly approach.

Making Observations

The process of science often begins with an observation. An **observation** is information you gather by using your senses. Your senses involve seeing, hearing, smelling, tasting, and touching. Maybe you see that rust has formed on an iron shovel. It could be that you hear static in a radio broadcast. Perhaps you smell the rotten-egg odor of stagnant water. Can you think of other examples of observations that can be made using your senses?

Asking Questions

Suppose you step outside one morning and smell smoke in the air. The first thing you might do is ask yourself what is burning. The scientific process happens in a similar way. A scientist asks a question about an observation. A scientific question can be answered through observation, experimental design, testing, and analysis.

Figure 1.5 A scientist studying how objects float on water makes many observations. What are some observations that can be made about this boat?

ENGAGE Encourage students to draw upon prior knowledge about things they do in a particular sequence. Ask: *What are some activities that you have to do in a particular order?*

As a class, brainstorm examples. Choose one example and have students describe the steps involved in completing that task. Help students recognize that scientists go about finding answers to their questions in an organized and orderly process known as the scientific method.

Before You Read

Draw a blank sequence chart on the board. If students need help, fill out the first few steps of the chart with the whole class. Check students' sequence charts throughout the lesson.

● Teach

EXPLAIN to students that scientists carefully record their observations and usually observe something on more than one occasion in order to compare their findings.

Use the Visual: Figure 1.5

EXTEND Ask students to examine the figure and make some observations about the boat and how it floats. Have students share their observations with the class.

Vocabulary

scientific method Explain to students that the term *scientific method* encompasses all of the other vocabulary terms in this lesson. It describes the process scientists use to answer questions about the natural world.

observation Tell students that scientific observation uses all five senses. Scientists attempt to be as detailed as possible when recording observations.

E L L   Strategy

Relate to Personal Experience As students read the lesson, encourage them to think about their own experiences of observing and questioning their observations.

Encourage struggling English language learners to discuss their experiences in their native language and then translate into English.

Practice Using Vocabulary If time permits, have students create crossword puzzles using the vocabulary terms. Allow students to trade and complete one another's puzzles.

Field Study

Take students outside to practice their observation skills. Have each student find something outside to observe. They should record their observations in their Science Notebooks. Encourage students to use all appropriate senses to describe their observations.

● Teach

Emphasize the difference between guessing and hypothesizing. Explain that a hypothesis must be based on observations, previous knowledge, and research.

As You Read

ANSWER A hypothesis describes how one thinks the dependent variable will respond to changes in the independent variable.

Use the Visual: Figure 1.6

ANSWER Starting height is the independent variable. How high the ball bounces is the dependent variable.

 Vocabulary

hypothesis Explain that the word *hypothesis* is derived from an ancient Greek word meaning "to place under."

experiment Tell students the meaning of this term when used as both a noun (an investigation in which information is collected under controlled conditions) and a verb (plan and conduct an investigation).

variable Tell students that variables are factors that can be changed in an experiment. Have students list all of the variables that can be changed in order to grow the tallest bean plant (examples: amount of sunlight, quality of soil).

controlled experiment Explain to students that in a controlled experiment, only one variable is changed at a time to determine which has the greatest effect on the result. Have students discuss the common meaning of the term *controlled* and relate it to the definition.

independent variable Tell students it is called independent because it does not rely on anything else in order to be changed. Have students suggest common meanings of the term *independent* and relate those meanings to the use of the term in the definition.

dependent variable Ask students to identify the relationship between the terms *independent* and *dependent* (they are antonyms, or opposites). Then, have them apply that relationship to the meaning of the term *dependent variable.*

Did You Know?

When a person attempts to explain an observation based on what he or she already knows, that person is inferring. The explanation is called an inference. An inference is not a fact and therefore, can be wrong.

As You Read

Review the sequence chart you created in your Science Notebook. Work with a partner to make changes or additions so that your chart describes the steps of the scientific method.

How does the hypothesis relate the dependent variable to the independent variable?

Figure 1.6 Every variable must remain constant except for the independent variable. What is the independent variable in this experiment? What is the dependent variable?

Developing a Hypothesis

When wondering about the source of the smoke, you guess that it might be a brush fire in a nearby forest. This is your hypothesis. A **hypothesis** (hi PAH thuh sus, plural: hypotheses) is a proposed explanation for an observation. A hypothesis is not a random guess. It must be based on observations, previous knowledge, and research.

A good hypothesis must be proposed in such a way that it can be tested to find out if it is supported. Some hypotheses are tested by making more observations. Others are tested through experiments. An **experiment** is an investigation in which information is collected under controlled conditions.

Designing an Experiment

All experiments involve **variables**, which are factors that can be changed. For example, suppose you want to conduct an experiment to find out how the height from which you drop a ball affects how high the ball bounces. Variables include the type of ball, the surface on which the ball bounces, and the starting height of the ball. Even temperature can be a variable. If you change all of the variables throughout the experiment, you will not be able to determine which variable affected the bounce.

Instead, you must perform a **controlled experiment**, or an experiment in which you change only one variable at a time. The variable that is changed is called the **independent variable**. In the bouncing ball experiment, starting height is the independent variable. Something that is independent does not rely on other factors. Each time you drop the ball, it is called a trial. The starting height changes during each trial.

The variable that is observed to find out if it changes as a result of the independent variable is called the **dependent variable**. Something that is dependent relies on another factor. How high the ball bounces is the dependent variable. All other variables must remain unchanged. That means you need to drop the same type of ball onto the same surface under the same conditions.

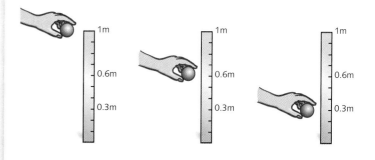

control group Have students relate the meaning of this term (part of an experiment used as a comparison to the group that is being tested) to the idea of a controlled experiment.

experimental group Have students compare and contrast this term and the term *control group.*

E L L Strategy

Model Have students work in groups to make diagrams that represent the scientific method. For struggling English language learners, be sure to clarify all terms that have multiple meanings. When introducing and explaining new concepts and terms, direct students' attention to vocabulary, syntax, grammar, and context clues. Identifying cognates may also help English language learners.

Control Group Some experiments are performed with two groups of variables. In the **control group**, all the variables are kept the same. In the **experimental group**, the independent variable is changed. These groups are tested at the same time. The control group is used for comparison. It shows what would have happened if nothing was changed. Having information from the control group makes it easier to see the effects of changing an independent variable.

CONNECTION: Astronomy

High in the sky, a huge telescope orbits Earth every 97 minutes. Known as the Hubble Space Telescope, this instrument has changed astronomy by forming amazing images of the solar system and beyond. It is the largest and most complex telescope ever sent into orbit. The telescope was named after Edwin Hubble, who was the first person to show that the universe is expanding.

The Hubble telescope, which is a reflecting telescope, wasn't always such a success. A reflecting telescope, or reflector, uses a mirror to gather light. The Hubble's main mirror is 2.4 m across. When the mirror was being made, it was attached to a device that tested its curve. Unfortunately, this device was set to the wrong measurement. When the device indicated that the mirror was essentially perfect, it was mistaken.

Shortly after the Hubble was launched in 1990, it began sending images to astronomers on Earth. To everyone's surprise and disappointment, the images were blurry! The difference in shape that resulted from the incorrect measurement caused the mirror to focus less light than expected. Most of the light the mirror gathered was spread out into a fuzzy region of light.

How big was the mistake on the mirror for it to have caused so much trouble? Was it off by a few meters, or maybe by several centimeters? Actually, the error on the measuring device was estimated to be only 1.3 mm. On a mirror as smooth as the Hubble telescope's, however, a tiny error in measurement can lead to tremendous problems in results. The Hubble serves as an excellent example of the importance of careful measurements in science.

Astronauts repaired the telescope by installing a set of special corrective lenses to change the focus of the mirror. So it can actually be said that the Hubble telescope wears glasses to see clearly! The Hubble now provides spectacular images of objects in space that allow astronomers to learn more about the universe.

Explore It!

Design an experiment to find out how the shape of a sheet of foil affects the foil's ability to float. Propose a hypothesis. Identify the independent and dependent variables. Describe the control and experimental groups. Share your experiment design with a partner.

● Teach

Discuss with students examples of experiments that can and cannot be controlled. Make two lists on the board and record students' examples. Ask students to discuss the advantages and disadvantages of being able to control an experiment.

CONNECTION: Astronomy

Find and share images from the Hubble Space Telescope. Images may be found on the NASA Web site.

Have students look at several images and discuss their observations in small groups.

Since that initial error, the Hubble telescope has been upgraded several times. Astronauts have installed components to improve the telescope's function. The telescope was scheduled for an upgrade in 2006, but the mission was canceled because of concerns for the safety of the astronauts after the 2003 Space Shuttle *Columbia* disaster.

EXTEND Have students write about their observations in their Science Notebooks. Ask each student to describe the photograph that he or she likes best and explain its appeal.

Explore It!

Suggest that students list all of the steps in the scientific method in their Science Notebooks and fill in their plans for each step.

Before students begin work on their own, provide an example of an experiment to the whole class. Students should note that the independent variable in this experiment is the shape of the foil, and the dependent variable is the foil's ability to float or sink.

Background Information

Scientists adhere to the strict guidelines of the scientific method to eliminate bias and prejudice in their conclusions. Before a scientist's conclusions are accepted, the experiment must be replicated by other scientists with the same results. Scientists keep careful records of their procedures so that their experiments can be precisely repeated and confirmed by others.

Key Concept Review
Workbook, p. 1

Teach

Emphasize the importance of safety in a lab setting. Remind students that when they are working with dangerous substances, it is essential that they follow all safety instructions. Point out the safety features of the lab, such as the eye-wash station and shower, if available.

 Vocabulary

safety symbol Tell students that scientists use easily recognizable symbols to provide information about the hazards associated with an experiment. Emphasize that it is extremely important to heed these warnings, as not doing so could result in a serious injury.

data Explain to students that the word *data* is the plural of the Latin word *datum*, which means "something given." In a scientific experiment, the data are the information "given" to scientists by their observations.

conclusion Explain that the word *conclusion* has many common usages. It is often used to describe the ending of a book or a piece of music. Have students compare these meanings with the scientific meaning of *conclusion* as a statement that uses evidence from an experiment to indicate whether a hypothesis is supported.

Figure It Out: Figure 1.8

ANSWER **1.** temperature and time **2.** the thermostat in Classroom A

Figure 1.7 These and other safety symbols indicate the possible dangers of a laboratory experiment.

Safety An important aspect of every scientific experiment is working safely. Scientists and students alike must take precautions to protect themselves from possible dangers. In the experiments you will be doing as you study physical science, you will see **safety symbols** that warn you about a possible danger. **Figure 1.7** describes the meaning of some of the major safety symbols. Appendix A on page 462 provides more information about laboratory safety.

Most important, be sure to read the instructions for every experiment in advance. Make sure you understand what you need to do. Let your teacher know if you have questions. Immediately report any accident that occurs in the laboratory.

Collecting and Analyzing Data

The information obtained through observation is called **data** (singular: datum). Some experiments produce huge amounts of data. To make sense of all the information, scientists organize the data into forms that are easier to read and analyze. One way to organize data is in a table. A table has rows and columns with headings that describe the information. **Figure 1.8** shows a data table produced during a test of three different thermostats.

Another way to organize data is to create a graph. Line graphs are best for data that change continuously, such as temperatures or the distances traveled by an object. **Figure 1.8** also shows a line graph for the data described in the table. Note that there is a break in the vertical axis between 0 and 15. This break means that numbers are left out. This leaves room to spread the scale where the data points lie, which makes the graph easier to read.

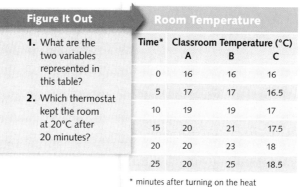

Figure It Out

1. What are the two variables represented in this table?
2. Which thermostat kept the room at 20°C after 20 minutes?

Room Temperature

Time*	Classroom Temperature (°C)		
	A	B	C
0	16	16	16
5	17	17	16.5
10	19	19	17
15	20	21	17.5
20	20	23	18
25	20	25	18.5

* minutes after turning on the heat

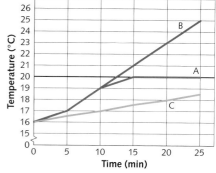

Figure 1.8 For this experiment, thermostats in different classrooms were each set to 20°C. The classroom temperature was then recorded every five minutes.

ELL Strategy

Illustrate Invite students to use the chart in **Figure 1.7** to make posters for the lab that illustrate each safety symbol and its meaning. For struggling English language learners, translate the meaning of each safety symbol into the students' native languages. Students might choose to include multiple languages on their posters.

Not all data are best represented by line graphs. Circle graphs and bar graphs are also used to present data. Circle graphs are best for analyzing data that are divided into parts of a whole, such as the elements in Earth's crust shown at the right in **Figure 1.9**. Bar graphs are especially useful for comparing data. The table in **Figure 1.9** at the bottom of the page shows data for the number of students in different classrooms. The bar graph displaying this data makes it easy to quickly compare the sizes of the classes.

Drawing Conclusions

Once the experiment has been conducted and the data have been collected, a scientist tries to determine if the hypothesis is supported. A **conclusion** is a statement that uses evidence from an experiment to indicate whether the hypothesis is supported.

A conclusion is not necessarily the end of the investigation. If the conclusion indicates that the hypothesis is not supported, the scientist may develop a new hypothesis and design a new experiment to test it. If the conclusion indicates that the hypothesis is supported, the scientist needs to repeat the experiment many times to make sure that the conclusion is valid. The scientist also needs to share his or her results with the scientific community. In this way, other scientists can repeat the experiment to confirm the results.

Figure 1.9 Data can be presented in a variety of formats, including circle graphs (right) and bar graphs (bottom).

Elements in Earth's Crust

Element	Percent by Mass
oxygen (O)	46.6
silicon (Si)	27.7
aluminum (Al)	8.1
iron (Fe)	5.0
calcium (Ca)	3.6
sodium (Na)	2.8
potassium (K)	2.6
magnesium (Mg)	2.1
others	1.5

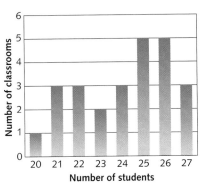

Circle graph labels:
2.6% Potassium (K)
2.1% Magnesium (Mg)
2.8% Sodium (Na)
1.5% Others
3.6% Calcium (Ca)
5.0% Iron (Fe)
8.1% Aluminum (Al)
46.6% Oxygen (O)
27.7% Silicon (Si)

Classroom Size

Number of Students	Number of Classrooms
20	1
21	3
22	3
23	2
24	3
25	5
26	5
27	3

Bar graph: y-axis "Number of classrooms" (0–6), x-axis "Number of students" (20–27).

● Teach

EXPLAIN to students that in addition to using tables to organize data, scientists also use many types of graphs. Ask students to list the different kinds of graphs that they have used to organize data.

Take some time to discuss with students the nature of a conclusion—especially the fact that a conclusion is not necessarily the end of an investigation and that many conclusions turn out to be "wrong" (that is, they indicate that the hypotheses are not supported). Emphasize that if a conclusion indicates that a hypothesis is not supported, the scientist must develop a new hypothesis and design a new experiment to test it. If the conclusion indicates that the hypothesis is supported, the scientist needs to repeat the experiment many times to make sure that the conclusion is valid. The scientist also needs to share results with the scientific community so that other scientists can repeat the experiment to confirm the results.

Impress upon students that in addition to knowledge, curiosity, and essential skills, a scientist must also have a great deal of patience.

Differentiated Instruction

Kinesthetic Have students collect data on the heights of their classmates. Then have each student create a bar graph to represent the data. Convert the individual bar graphs into a class bar graph recorded on the board. With that bar graph as a background, have students assemble themselves into a corresponding "human bar graph" for a hands-on experience of the way that data can be organized.

Graphic Organizer
Workbook, p. 3

Teach

EXPLAIN to students that a hypothesis becomes part of a theory only after it has been supported by many separate investigations over a long period of time. Ask students to think about scientific theories that they have heard about, such as the Big Bang theory or the theory of relativity.

 Vocabulary

theory Tell students that the word *theory* is derived from the Greek word *theōríā*, meaning "a looking-at." A theory is an explanation for a broad range of observations, or "things looked-at." Explain that a theory is distinguished from a hypothesis by the amount of data that support it. A hypothesis is a tentative explanation of the data, while a theory is derived from a larger body of scientific evidence.

prediction Explain to students that the prefix *pre-* in the word *prediction* means "before." A prediction is a statement that suggests what a person thinks will happen "before" completing an experiment.

Assess

Use the After You Read questions and Alternative Assessment to help you evaluate students' understanding of this lesson.

After You Read

1. The hypothesis is a possible explanation for an observation.

2. If many experiments conducted over a long period of time continuously support the same hypothesis, the hypothesis might become part of a theory. A theory is a broad explanation for a set of related observations.

3. The independent variable is changed during the experiment. The dependent variable is observed to find out if and how it changes in response to the independent variable.

4. The symbol indicates that the experiment will involve materials, such as chemicals, that may spill on or stain clothing.

5. The conclusion might cause a scientist to propose a new hypothesis and design a new experiment.

Communicating the Results

Throughout an experiment, a scientist should keep careful records that describe everything about the research. These records include not only the data, but also information about the experiment's design, possible sources of error, unexpected results, and any remaining questions.

Scientists share their results with one another by communicating through written reports and journal articles, as well as through oral presentations. Sharing information in this way not only adds to the body of scientific knowledge, it also gives other scientists an opportunity to repeat the experiment. The results of an investigation can only be considered valid if they are achieved during repeated trials of the same procedure.

Scientific Theories

If a hypothesis is supported by many separate investigations over a long period of time, it may become part of a theory. A **theory** is an explanation for a broad range of observations that is supported by a body of scientific evidence. A theory is not the same as a scientific law. A scientific law is a rule that describes an observed pattern in nature.

Scientists can use a theory to make predictions about new situations. A **prediction** is a statement that suggests what a person thinks will happen in the future based on past experience and evidence.

A theory is not considered absolute truth, but it is supported by a vast amount of scientific evidence. Scientists continually analyze the strengths and weaknesses of a theory. If new evidence is discovered, a theory can be revised or replaced.

Figure 1.10 One theory in physical science suggests that all light waves can bend when they move near a large object, such as Jupiter.

After You Read

1. How is a hypothesis related to an observation?

2. Describe how a hypothesis might become part of a theory.

3. What is the difference between the independent and dependent variables in a controlled experiment?

4. You see a symbol of an apron in a laboratory procedure. What does this symbol tell you about the experiment you will be conducting?

5. Review the sequence chart you completed in your Science Notebook. In a well-developed paragraph, explain how the last step might lead back to the first step.

Alternative Assessment

Have students create sequence charts to describe the steps they would follow when designing an experiment. Struggling ELLs should be encouraged to include the vocabulary words and their definitions in the sequence chart.

Teacher Alert

Students often confuse the definition of *hypothesis* with the definition of *theory*. Emphasize to students that a hypothesis contributes to the development of a theory only after other scientists have experimentally supported it many times over an extended period of time.

1.3 Measurements in Science

Before You Read

Look at the headings in the lesson to find the measurements that are discussed. In your Science Notebook, create a chart with three columns. Label one column *Quantity*, the next column *Units*, and the third column *Examples*. Include a row for each measurement you find.

The shelves of the supermarket are lined with colorful packages of assorted foods. Many of the foods are produced by machines in factories. Huge numbers of items can be produced in a very short amount of time. How many items and how fast they can be produced are examples of measurements. A **measurement** is quantity, dimension, or amount. Scientists rely on measurements to gather and analyze data.

Units of Measurements

Would you say that it takes you 15 to get to school? Probably not. You would say that it takes you 15 minutes to get to school. That description would help another person know how long it takes for you to get from your home to school. Minutes are an example of units. A unit is a precise quantity that does not change. All measurements must be described with the appropriate unit.

During the 1700s, people used all sorts of different units to describe measurements. To describe the length of an object, a person could use any one of more than ten different units. In addition, because many of the units were based on body parts such as feet and hands, the size of a unit could vary significantly, depending on who was making the measurement. The variety of units not only made it confusing to talk about measurements, it also made it difficult to buy and sell goods.

To put an end to the confusion, the French government asked the Academy of Sciences to develop a standard system of measurement. The organization produced a system, known as the metric system, based on the number ten. This makes it very simple to convert from one unit to another by dividing or multiplying by ten. You can learn more about the metric system in Appendix B in the back of the book.

In 1960, parts of the metric system were incorporated into the **International System of Units (SI)**. This system of measurement is used by most countries throughout the world and in almost all scientific activities.

Learning Goals

- Identify the SI units of several scientific measurements.
- Recognize how prefixes indicate the magnitude of a unit.
- Describe how common measurement tools are used.
- Apply conversion factors and scientific notation.

New Vocabulary

measurement
International System of Units (SI)
mass
volume
meniscus
derived unit
density
dimensional analysis
conversion factor
scientific notation

Figure 1.11 This factory can produce thousands of ice cream bars every day. What are some other measurements related to making foods?

ELL Strategy

Act Out Have students pretend to play baseball. As they are playing, ask them to call out possible measurements. For struggling English language learners, pair students with peer tutors who can explain the game if it is unfamiliar.

Practice Using Vocabulary If time permits, have students create a poster for each unit of measurement that includes a picture of something being measured. For example, the poster with the word *mass* might show something being massed on a balance.

1.3 Introduce

EXPLORE Provide pairs of students with measuring tapes, and have them measure each other's height and arm span (from middle finger to middle finger with arms outstretched). These measurements should be close to equal for each person. Ask: *How does your arm span compare to your height?* Have each student divide his or her height by his or her arm span. As a class, collect height-to-arm-span ratio data. Help students recognize that this ratio is close to one.

As a class, brainstorm ways to measure height and arm span without a tape measure. Help students see that if the units change, the ratio will remain the same as long as the measuring tool remains constant.

Before You Read

As a class, have students look through the headings in the lesson. Write each measurement on the board. Have students fill in the chart with each measurement. Check students' charts throughout the lesson.

Teach

EXPLAIN Have students work in pairs to measure the length and width of the classroom using the length of their feet, the span of their hands, or the length of their strides. Have students compare their results. Help them recognize that the variety of hand, foot, and stride sizes makes it difficult to collect accurate data.

Use the Visual: Figure 1.11

ANSWER Other measurements might include the amounts of ingredients, item size and packaging, and the time it takes for the item to cook, freeze, or become solid.

Vocabulary

measurement Have students note the presence of the word *measure* and the suffix *-ment*. Explain that *-ment* can mean "the act of" or "the result of."

International System of Units Discuss with students the importance of having a common system of measurement for all scientific observations.

Teach

Point out to students that all SI measurements use the same prefixes. Emphasize the importance of remembering the meanings of these prefixes. Remind students that the prefixes *milli-* and *centi-* indicate measurements less than one, and the prefix *kilo-* indicates a measurement greater than one.

Use the Visual: Figure 1.12

ANSWER 1 million

 CONNECTION: Math

Have students practice using this shortcut for multiplying and dividing by multiples of ten. Ask them to use their Science Notebooks to record the answers to 145 ÷ 10; 145 ÷ 100; 145 × 10; and 145 × 100. (Answers: 14.5, 1.45, 1,450, 14,500.)

 Extend It!

Resistance to the metric system has left America as a minority in the world of measurement. The majority of the world has been metric since 1975. The United States, however, adopted a voluntary approach to the change.

In 1991, President George H. W. Bush issued an executive order mandating the transition to the use of metric measurement for all federal agencies. When use of the system will become widespread has yet to be determined. Discuss with students the advantages and disadvantages of mandating the use of the metric system nationwide.

 Vocabulary

mass Discuss with students the various parts of speech and meanings of the term *mass* (noun: a lump, the majority, a large quantity; adjective: of or by many people; verb: to gather together). Have students use each meaning in a correctly written sentence.

volume Ask students if they know of other meanings of the term *volume*. Based on their responses, discuss volume as it relates to the loudness of a sound and a book that is part of a set or series.

Figure 1.12 You can use the prefix of an SI unit to figure out how large or small a measurement is. How many millimeters are in one kilometer?

Metric Prefixes	
Prefix	**Meaning**
kilo-	1,000
hecto-	100
deka-	10
base unit	1
deci-	0.1 (one tenth)
centi-	0.01 (one hundredth)
milli-	0.001 (one thousandth)

 Extend It!

The United States is the only major industrialized nation in the world that does not use the metric system. Work in a small group to research the history of the metric system. Prepare a poster or time line showing the major developments in the system and the laws governing its use. Then separate into teams and debate the topic of whether the United States should adopt this system.

meniscus Tell students that the word *meniscus* is derived from a Greek word that means "moon." The meniscus resembles the shape of a waxing or waning moon.

derived unit Tell students that a derived unit is obtained by combining other units. Compare the concept of derived units to the concept of primary and secondary colors.

Length

When you describe how far you throw a ball, how long a table is, or how tall a building is, you are describing length. The base SI unit of length is the meter (m). A baseball bat is about one meter long. An average doorknob is about one meter above the floor.

A meter is divided into smaller units called centimeters (cm) and millimeters (mm). The prefix *centi-* means "one-hundredth." There are 100 centimeters in a meter. The prefix *milli-* means "one-thousandth." There are 1,000 millimeters in a meter. A millimeter is about the thickness of one dime.

For longer lengths, scientists use a unit called a kilometer (km). The prefix *kilo-* means "one thousand." There are 1,000 meters in a kilometer. The distance from San Diego, CA to New York, NY is 3,909 km. The world's tallest mountain, Mt. Everest, has a height of almost 9 km.

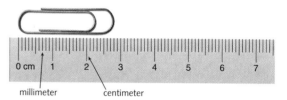

Figure 1.13 Length can be measured with a metric ruler. Line up one end of an object with the first mark on the ruler. Find the line closest to the other end of the object. The longer lines show centimeters, and the shorter lines show millimeters.

Mass

The amount of matter in an object is that object's **mass**. The base unit of mass in the SI system is the kilogram (kg). A kilogram consists of 1,000 smaller units called grams (g). The mass of a paper clip is about one gram. Even smaller masses are measured in milligrams (mg). There are 1,000 milligrams in one gram. The mass of many objects is measured on a balance, such as a triple-beam balance.

 **CONNECTION: Math**

All number systems have a base number. The number system you use every day has a base of 10. This makes it convenient to multiply or divide by multiples of 10. To multiply a number by a multiple of 10, move the decimal point of the number to the right the same number of places as there are zeros. For example, to multiply a number by 100, move the decimal point of the number two places to the right. You can follow a similar process to divide by multiples of 10 by moving the decimal point to the left instead.

Teacher Alert

It is important to distinguish mass from weight, which measures the pull of gravity on an object and changes based on where the object is. An object on the Moon will have the same mass as it does on Earth. However, its weight will be different.

Volume

Have you ever tried to pour all of the liquid from a large container into a smaller container? If so, you probably made a mess! That's because the liquid takes up a certain amount of space. If the smaller container does not have enough space, the liquid spills over the sides.

The amount of space an object takes up is its **volume**. How volume is measured depends on the sample being measured. The sample being measured also determines the units used for the measurement.

Finding the Volume of a Liquid The volume of a liquid, such as water, is measured in units called liters (L). A liter is not an SI unit, but because it is important and widely used, it is accepted for use with the SI. You may have seen one-liter and two-liter bottles of drinks at the supermarket. Smaller volumes can be measured in milliliters. Recall that the prefix *milli-* means "one-thousandth." There are 1,000 milliliters in a liter.

One way to measure the volume of a liquid is by pouring the liquid into a container that has measured markings on it. Perhaps you have poured water or milk into a measuring cup to find a specific amount for a recipe. Scientists often use a graduated cylinder to measure liquid volumes.

Figure 1.14 shows a liquid being measured in a graduated cylinder marked in one-milliliter intervals. You can see that the top surface of the liquid is slightly curved. The curve is known as the **meniscus** (meh NIHS cus). To find the volume of the liquid, you must read the measurement of the marking at the bottom of the meniscus.

Finding the Volume of a Solid Solids such as a number cube and a shoebox are called rectangular solids. The volume of a rectangular solid can be found by multiplying its length by its width by its height.

$$\text{volume} = \text{length} \times \text{width} \times \text{height}$$

If the measurements are made in centimeters, the unit of volume is cubic centimeters (cm^3: $cm \times cm \times cm$). If the measurements are made in meters, the unit of volume is cubic meters (m^3: $m \times m \times m$). A unit that consists of more than one base unit is called a **derived unit**. Volume is a derived unit.

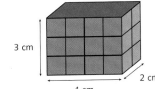

Figure 1.15 The volume of this solid is 4 cm × 2 cm × 3 cm = 24 cm³.

3 cm
2 cm
4 cm

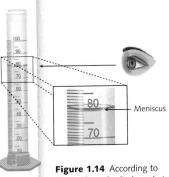

Meniscus

Figure 1.14 According to the graduated cylinder, what is the volume of this liquid?

As You Read

In your chart of measurements, fill in the second column with the units in which each measurement can be described. Provide at least two examples of each measurement in the third column.

Explore It!

Find three rectangular solids in your home or classroom. Examples include a book, an eraser, a cereal box, and a tissue box. Work alone or with a partner to find the volume of each solid.

● Teach

Ask students to give some examples of liquids, rectangular solids, and irregular solids. Make three columns on the board and write each example in the proper column. Discuss with students the challenges of measuring the amount of space taken up by each substance. Explain that there are different methods for measuring the volume of each type of substance.

Use the Visual: Figure 1.14
ANSWER 79 mL

Explore It!

Collect a variety of rectangular solids to bring to the classroom. Solids might include empty food boxes, books, shoeboxes, gift or jewelry boxes, number cubes, or a deck of playing cards in the package.

Place different solids at different stations around the room. Pair students and provide them with rulers or measuring tape. Have pairs rotate around the room, recording the length, width, and height of each object and finding its volume. Allow students to use calculators to compute volume. Remind students to include the correct units.

Have each student pair share one volume measurement with the class. Record these measurements on the board. Then have pairs compare their results with those of the class. Students should understand that their answers might vary because of inaccurate measurement or incorrect multiplication.

As You Read

Remind students that the units for measuring volume depend upon the type of substance being measured.

Background Information

Since the 1890s, the U.S. Congress has attempted to change the U.S. system of measurement to the metric system, but it has never been successful in doing so. Congress passed the Metric Conversion Act in 1975, which called for a voluntary conversion to the metric system. By the early 2000s, scientists and engineers had complied, but the average U.S. citizen is not yet fully comfortable with this system of measurement.

● Teach

Ask students to give examples of some irregular solids. Have students suggest ways to find the volume of these objects. Discuss with students the difficulties of finding the volume of solids that are not easily measured.

Figure It Out: Figure 1.17

ANSWER **1.** about 37°C **2.** No, the temperature scales do not use the same size intervals. On the Fahrenheit scale, the range is 180 degrees. On the Celsius scale, the range is 100 degrees.

Figure 1.16 The water rises from the 26-mL mark to the 32-mL mark after the stone is placed in it. Therefore, the volume of the stone is 6 mL.

Figure It Out

1. Normal human body temperature is 98.6°F. What is this temperature on the Celsius scale?

2. Is the range of temperature between the freezing point of water and the boiling point of water the same on all temperature scales? Explain your answer.

Not all solids are rectangular solids. Some solids have an irregular shape, and their volumes cannot be found by using a formula. One method for finding the volume of an irregular solid is to place the object in water. Once the object is completely submerged (under water), the level of the water will rise. Subtracting the original water level from the new water level will give the volume of the solid.

Density

If you place a table-tennis ball in water, it will float. If you place a golf ball in water, it will sink. Even though the balls have about the same volume, they have different masses. The amount of mass in a given volume is an object's **density**. You can find the density of an object by dividing its mass by its volume.

$$density = \frac{mass}{volume}$$

Density is a derived unit. The unit of density is made up of a unit of mass divided by a unit of volume. If mass is measured in grams and volume is measured in cubic centimeters, the unit of density is grams per cubic centimeter (g/cm^3). If volume is measured in milliliters, the unit of density is grams per milliliter (g/mL).

Time and Temperature

Time is the interval between two events. The second (s) is the SI base unit of time. Temperature is a measure of the energy associated with the movement of the particles in an object. Temperature can be measured on different scales. A scale commonly used in science is the Celsius scale, on which temperature is measured in degrees Celsius (°C). Water freezes at 0°C and boils at 100°C. These temperatures are known as the freezing point and boiling point.

The SI base unit of temperature is the kelvin. Units on the Kelvin scale are the same size as those on the Celsius scale. However, each value on the Kelvin scale is 273 degrees more than on the Celsius scale.

Fahrenheit measurements are generally not used in science.

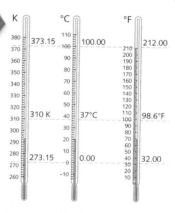

Figure 1.17 The diagram compares the Celsius, Fahrenheit, and Kelvin scales. A thermometer is used to measure temperature.

Background Information

A substance that has a density greater than the density of water (1g/mL) will sink. A substance that has a density less than the density of water will float. Finding the density of an unknown substance can help scientists identify the substance.

Dimensional Analysis

Scientists often need to convert from one unit of measurement to another. **Dimensional analysis** is a process of using a conversion factor to change from one unit to another. A **conversion factor** is a ratio of equal values used to express the same quantity in different units. A conversion factor is always equal to one. For example, the relationship between meters and kilometers can be expressed as a pair of conversion factors.

$$\frac{1,000 \text{ meters}}{1 \text{ kilometer}} = \frac{1 \text{ kilometer}}{1,000 \text{ meters}} = 1$$

To convert units, you multiply a given measurement by the appropriate conversion factor. Use the conversion factor with the desired unit in the numerator and the given unit in the denominator.

Scientific Notation

To work with very large and very small numbers, scientists use scientific notation. **Scientific notation** involves writing a number as a decimal number multiplied by 10 raised to an exponent.

To write a number in scientific notation, find the first digit. For the speed of light, 300,000,000 m/s, the first digit is 3. Place a decimal after the 3. Write any other digits after the decimal point. If there are no other digits, write a zero. The resulting decimal number is known as the coefficient. The coefficient must be a number between 1 and 10. For the speed of light, the coefficient is 3.0.

Next, count the number of places the decimal has moved from its original position. The decimal moved eight places to the left, so the exponent is 8. The speed of light in scientific notation is 3.0×10^8 m/s.

The mass of a dust particle is 0.000 000 000 753 kg. The coefficient is 7.53. The decimal has moved ten places to the right from its original position to its new position between 7 and 5. The exponent is 10. Because the decimal moves to the right, the exponent is negative, or −10. The mass of a dust particle in scientific notation is 7.53×10^{-10} kg.

3.00,000,000

The decimal moved eight places to the left.

0.000 000 000 753

The decimal moved ten places to the right.

After You Read

1. Which type of measurement can be made using a triple-beam balance?

2. How many milliseconds are in 5 seconds? How is this quantity written in scientific notation?

3. Review the chart of measurements you made in your Science Notebook. Explain which units are base units and which units are derived units.

Background Information

The sundial's first recorded use was in Babylon in the year 2000 B.C. Modern clocks were not invented until 1400 A.D. A sundial has two parts: the plane (or dial face) and the gnomon (or style). The gnomon is a flat piece of metal that points toward the north or south pole, depending on the hemisphere in which it is used. It is shaped such that the upper edge slants away from the dial face at an angle equal to the latitude of the sundial's location.

Alternative Assessment

Provide students with several different items, including liquids and rectangular and irregular solids. Have students calculate the volume, mass, and density of each item.

● Teach

Ask students to think about which would take longer: 9,000 seconds or two hours. Explain to students that it is easier to compare quantities when the units are the same. Scientists use dimensional analysis to change from one unit to another. To change from seconds to hours, you would use a conversion factor of 3,600. 9,000 seconds is equal to 2.5 hours, so it is longer.

Vocabulary

density Explain to students that density is a derived unit calculated by comparing an object's mass to its volume. This is a ratio. Discuss the meaning of a ratio with students, and have them provide other examples (speed, electric energy).

dimensional analysis Explain to students that the word *dimension* comes from the Latin prefix *dis-*, meaning "out," and the root *mētīrī*, meaning "to measure." The word *analysis* comes from the Greek word meaning "a breaking-up." Dimensional analysis is converting from one unit of measure to another by "breaking it up" using a conversion factor.

conversion factor Tell students that the prefix *con-* means "around," and the root *vertere* means "turn." A conversion factor is used to "turn around" one unit of measure into another.

scientific notation Explain to students that our number system is based on powers of ten. Scientific notation is used to simplify very large and very small numbers to numbers between 1 and 10. Doing so makes it much easier to use, manipulate, and compare these numbers.

● Assess

Use the After You Read questions and Alternative Assessment to help you evaluate students' understanding of this lesson.

After You Read

1. A triple-beam balance measures mass.

2. 5,000 ms, or 5.0×10^3 ms

3. base units: meter (length), kilogram (mass), kelvin (temperature), second (time); derived units: liter (volume) and grams/milliliter or grams/cubic centimeter (density)

Chapter 1 Summary

VOCABULARY REVIEW

Check students' sentences or paragraphs to make sure that they understand the meaning of each vocabulary term.

Before students begin their essays, review the process for writing explanatory or descriptive paragraphs. Go over the elements of paragraph structure, including main idea/topic sentence, supporting sentences, and concluding sentence.

Evaluate students' essays using the following criteria:

1. The topic sentence, or main idea, should restate the Key Concept.

2. The supporting paragraphs should incorporate the answers to the Learning Goal questions students have written and include details, facts, and examples they have recorded in their Science Notebooks.

3. The concluding sentence should summarize the main idea of the chapter and restate the Key Concept.

MASTERING CONCEPTS

True or False

1. True
2. False, hypothesis
3. False, independent
4. False, data
5. False, volume
6. False, meniscus

Short Answer

7. They are alike because scientists in all three branches attempt to learn about the natural world. They are different in that they focus on different aspects of the natural world, such as living things for life scientists, features of Earth and the universe for Earth and space scientists, and motion, forces, energy, and matter for physical scientists.

8. A hypothesis needs to be testable in order to find out whether it is supported. If it is not supported, the hypothesis can be discarded and a new one established. If it is not proved unsupportable, additional tests can be designed to test it in different ways or learn more about the topic.

KEY CONCEPTS

1.1 What Is Science?

- Science is a process of observation and investigation through which information about the natural world is learned. Science is both the process of gaining knowledge and the resulting body of knowledge.

- The branches of science are physical science, Earth and space science, and life science.

- Physical science is divided into chemistry, which focuses on matter, and physics, which focuses on energy and forces.

1.2 How Is Science Studied?

- The scientific method is an organized process of obtaining evidence to learn about the natural world.

- Scientists make observations, ask questions, develop hypotheses, design and conduct experiments, analyze data, and draw conclusions.

- The steps of the scientific method are not always followed in the same order or in the same way.

- A hypothesis is a proposed answer to a scientific question.

1.3 Measurements in Science

- SI base units include the meter for length, the kilogram for mass, the kelvin for temperature, and the second for time. The liter, for volume, is a non-SI unit.

- Derived units are made up of two or more base units. Volume is a derived unit. Density is a derived unit made up of a unit of mass divided by a unit of volume.

- Dimensional analysis is a process of using a conversion factor to change from one unit to another. A conversion factor is a ratio of equal values used to express the same quantity in different units. It is always equal to one.

- Very large or very small numbers can be written in scientific notation, which consists of a coefficient multiplied by 10 raised to an exponent.

VOCABULARY REVIEW

Write each term in a complete sentence or write a paragraph relating several terms.

1.1
science, p. 4
chemistry, p. 6
physics, p. 6

1.2
scientific method, p. 7
observation, p. 7
hypothesis, p. 8
experiment, p. 8
variable, p. 8
controlled experiment, p. 8
independent variable, p. 8
dependent variable, p. 8
control group, p. 9
experimental group, p. 9
safety symbol, p. 10
data, p. 10
conclusion, p. 11
theory, p. 12
prediction, p. 12

1.3
measurement, p. 13
International System of Units (SI), p. 13
mass, p. 14
volume, p. 15
meniscus, p. 15
derived unit, p. 15
density, p. 16
dimensional analysis, p. 17
conversion factor, p. 17
scientific notation, p. 17

PREPARE FOR CHAPTER TEST

To prepare for the chapter test, create a question from each Learning Goal and answer each question. Then use these answers to write a well-developed essay about the chapter. Use the Key Concept on the first page of this chapter as your topic sentence.

Reading Comprehension Workbook, p. 4

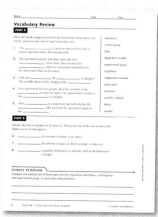

Vocabulary Review Workbook, p. 2

MASTERING CONCEPTS

True or False
If the statement is true, write "true." If it is false, change the underlined word or words to make the statement true.

1. The amount of salt in ocean water is a topic of study in <u>Earth and space</u> science.

2. A <u>conclusion</u> is an educated guess that attempts to explain an observation.

3. The variable that a scientist changes during an experiment is called the <u>dependent</u> variable.

4. The facts, figures, and other evidence obtained during an experiment make up the <u>hypothesis</u>.

5. A graduated cylinder is used to measure the <u>length</u> of an object.

6. The curve that can be seen at the top surface of a liquid is called the <u>variable</u>.

Short Answer
Answer each of the following in a sentence or brief paragraph.

7. Describe how the three branches of science are alike. Describe how they are different.

8. Explain why a hypothesis needs to be testable.

9. What are the two types of variables in a controlled experiment? Explain how they are different.

10. Discuss why using a common system of measurement is useful to scientists.

11. A student pours 14.2 mL of water into a graduated cylinder. She then places a stone in the cylinder. The meniscus of the water rises to 18.8 mL. Calculate the volume of the stone.

Critical Thinking
Use what you have learned in this chapter to answer each of the following.

12. **Calculate** At liftoff, Space Shuttle *Discovery* has a mass of about 2.04×10^6 kg. How would you write this number in standard notation?

13. **Compare and Contrast** Compare the measurements of each figure. Which object has a greater volume?

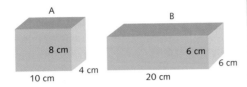

A 8 cm 10 cm 4 cm

B 6 cm 20 cm 6 cm

14. **Sequence** List and describe the steps you could follow to find the density of a marble.

Standardized Test Question
Choose the letter of the response that correctly answers the question.

15. The driving distance from New York, New York to Denver, Colorado, is 2,859.85 kilometers. What is this distance in meters?

   A. 2.85985 m
   B. 2,859.85 m
   C. 2,859,850 m
   D. 2,859,850,000 m

> **Test-Taking Tip**
>
> Quickly look over the entire test so you know how to use your time wisely. Allow more time for sections of the test that look the most difficult.

9. Controlled experiments involve an independent variable, which is purposefully changed during the experiment. They also involve a dependent variable, which is observed to find out if and how it changes as a result of changes in the independent variable.

10. Using a common system of measurement enables scientists all over the world to use the same values when describing quantities.

11. 4.6 mL

Critical Thinking

12. 2,040,000 kg

13. The volume of Object A is 320 cm³, and the volume of Object B is 720 cm³. Object B has the greater volume.

14. The marble can first be placed on a balance to find its mass and be placed in a graduated cylinder partially-filled with water to find its volume. Dividing the mass by the volume will give its density.

Standardized Test Question

15. C

Reading Links

Portraits of Great American Scientists

This unusual collection presents a series of 15 biographies of American scientists written by high school students from the Illinois Mathematics and Science Academy. The project, directed by Nobel Prize-winning physicist Leon M. Lederman, resulted in a book that is sure to engage readers and promote scientific literacy. Portraits include photographs, anecdotes, and valuable discussion of scientific careers.

Leon M. Lederman and Judith Scheppler, eds. Prometheus Books. 308 pp. Illustrated. Trade ISBN 978-1-57392-932-5.

Ink Sandwiches, Electric Worms, and 37 Other Experiments for Saturday Science

For more advanced or curious students, this book provides a set of activities that use common, affordable materials to illustrate and extend the physics topics that will be explored throughout the year. The quirky experiments are also ideal for more elaborate teacher demonstrations.

Neil A. Downie. Johns Hopkins University Press. 352 pp. Illustrated. Trade ISBN 978-0-8018-7410-9.

Curriculum Connection
Workbook, p. 5

Science Challenge
Workbook, p. 6

1A Accuracy in Measurement

This prechapter introduction activity is designed to determine what students already know about measurement by having them measure volume using a graduated cylinder. The activity also allows students to infer that different sizes of graduated cylinders have different accuracies.

Objectives

- measure the volume of colored water using different sizes of graduated cylinders
- record data
- compare and analyze data from other groups
- communicate conclusions about which graduated cylinders are the most accurate

Planning

 20–30 minutes   groups of 3–4 students

Materials (per group)

- 10-mL, 25-mL, 50-mL, and 100-mL graduated cylinders
- water
- food coloring

Advance Preparation

- Review with students the proper technique for reading a graduated cylinder.
- Prepare the colored water in advance and add it to the graduated cylinders before the students begin the activity.
- For reference, accurately read and record the volume of colored water added to each graduated cylinder. Use this data when evaluating the accuracy of student measurements.
- Place at least two graduated cylinders of different sizes at each lab table. Give the students three to four minutes at

each lab table to read the graduated cylinders and record their data. Have students move to each lab table until they have read every graduated cylinder.

- Make a blank data table on the board where students can record their measurements.

Engagement Guide

- Challenge students to think about measurements and accuracy by asking these questions:
  - *Is it easier to measure the diameter of a penny using a meter stick or a centimeter ruler? Will the measurements be the same?* (The centimeter ruler is much easier to use because its size is more appropriate and it has smaller divisions marked on it. The results will likely differ because of errors in estimating the diameter when using the larger divisions marked on the meterstick. Emphasize the importance of using an appropriately sized measuring device.)
  - *Which graduated cylinder do you think will be the most accurate? Why?* (Students should recognize that the 10-mL graduated cylinder is likely to be the most accurate because it has smaller divisions marked on it.)
  - *What might make students have different readings from the same graduated cylinder?* (The major source of error is related to estimating the value of a reading that falls between the marked unit divisions.)
- Encourage students to communicate their conclusions in creative ways.

Going Further

Encourage students to repeat this activity using 250-mL and 1,000-mL graduated cylinders. Have students present their findings to the class.

1B Counting Your Money

Objectives

- develop measuring skills using a metric ruler and a balance
- create graphs to interpret data
- compare relationships among mass, length, and the number of coins in a roll

Skill Set

observing, recording and analyzing data, graphing, comparing and contrasting, stating conclusions

Planning

 40–45 minutes   groups of 3–4 students

Materials

Materials for this activity are listed in the Student Laboratory Manual.

Advance Preparation

- Place a balance, centimeter ruler, ten pennies, and a roll of 50 pennies at each lab station. Be sure to use only post-1982 pennies; mixing pre- and post-1982 pennies will result in inconsistent data.

Answers to Observations: Data Table 1

Students' values might vary slightly. Check that the data is consistent. The graphs should reflect the information shown in Data Table 1. The line on each graph should be straight; that is, it should have a constant slope.

Answers to Analysis and Conclusions

1. The lines in Graph 1 and Graph 2 are both straight, with a positive slope.
2. Pennies are mass-produced. Due to variables in the manufacturing process, newly minted coins have slight differences in thickness and mass. Also, coins in longer circulation become worn, causing changes in their thickness and mass.

3. The average thickness and mass of a coin can be determined. Those average values can be multiplied by the number of coins in the roll to determine the thickness and mass of a roll of coins.
4. The slope of Graph 1 should be about 1.55 mm/penny, the average thickness of a penny. The slope of Graph 2 should be about 2.5 g/penny, the average mass of a penny.

Going Further

Create rolls of coins that have either too many or too few coins in the rolls. Have students measure the thicknesses and masses of these rolls. Based on their measurements, have students infer how many coins they think are in each roll.

IC Calculating Density Using SI Units

Objectives

- develop measuring skills using a graduated cylinder and a balance
- compare the density of one marble to the average density of three marbles
- communicate conclusions

Skill Set

measuring, recording and analyzing data, drawing conclusions

Planning

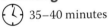

35–40 minutes   groups of 3–4 students

Materials

Materials for this activity are listed in the Student Laboratory Manual.

Advance Preparation

- Provide a 100-mL graduated cylinder, water, paper towels, marbles, and a balance for each group.
- Review students on the proper techniques for measuring the mass and volume of the marbles.
- If students use a triple-beam balance, suggest that they place a piece of paper towel on the balance and find its mass before they place the marble on the towel. The paper towel will keep the marble from rolling off the balance. The mass of the paper towel can be subtracted from the total mass to find the mass of the marble.

Answers to Observations: Data Table 1

Answers will vary due to variations in the size and mass of the marbles used. Assuming very similar marbles are used, students should observe that the average density of the three marbles is nearly the same as the density of a single marble. Students' calculations should be recorded in Data Table 1.

Answers to Analysis and Conclusions

1. As the number of marbles tripled, the total mass and the total volume also tripled.
2. The graduated cylinder had an initial volume of 50 mL. Thus, 50 mL must be subtracted from the measured volumes to obtain the volumes of the marbles alone.
3. Density is a property of a substance that does not depend on the amount of the substance present. Regardless of the amount, the density is constant. Mass, however, is a measured quantity that does depend on the amount of substance present.
4. The kilogram of feathers would take up more space because it has a lower density. It takes a larger volume of feathers than iron to reach a mass of 1 kilogram.

Going Further

The density of water is 1 g/mL. Objects with a density of less than 1 g/mL float on water, whereas objects with a density of more than 1 g/mL sink. Have students calculate the density of classroom objects such as pencils, pens, paper clips, and wadded paper. Have students use their calculated densities to predict whether each object will float or sink in water. Then have students test their predictions by placing the objects in water.

Introduce Chapter 2

As a starting activity, use Lab 2A on page 7 of the Laboratory Manual.

ENGAGE Ask students to think about the rivers they have seen. Refer them to the photo of the Grand Canyon. Ask if anyone has seen a canyon like this one and if so, to share their experiences. Explain that wind, water, and air help carve canyons.

Think About Making Comparisons

Choose one object and draw a sketch of the object on the board. Ask: *What are the distinguishing features of this object? What words help distinguish this object from other objects in the classroom?* Write students' responses on the board. Encourage students to be specific. Ask students to choose three other objects in the room and write at least three adjectives underneath each object.

Chapter 2 Types of Matter

KEY CONCEPT Matter, which is anything that has mass and takes up space, can be described by its composition.

The interaction of wind, water, air, and rock make the Grand Canyon one of the wonders of the world. This chapter describes the different things you might see in the Grand Canyon and elsewhere, and how these things are alike and different.

Think About Making Comparisons

Many different objects surround you every day. They are made of different types of materials and have different characteristics and uses. Some objects are made of one material, whereas others are a combination of materials. Identify three different objects in your classroom or in a room at home.

- Look carefully at the objects. Observe how they look and feel, and think about what they are used for.

- In your Science Notebook, draw a picture of each object and write several words describing it. Tell what substance or substances you think make up each object. After you complete this chapter, determine if the words you have used to describe each object are correct. Then write a carefully developed sentence about each object.

NSTA
SCI LINKS.
THE WORLD'S A CLICK AWAY
www.scilinks.org
Matter **Code: WGPS02**

20

Chapter 2 Planning Guide

Instructional Periods	National Standards	Lab Manual	Workbook
2.1 1 Period	A.1, B.1; A.2, B.2; UCP.1	**Lab 2A: p. 7** Comparing Compounds	Key Concept Review p. 7
2.2 2 Periods	A.2, B.1, G.1, G.2, G.3; A.2, B.2, G.1, G.2, G.3; UCP.3		Vocabulary Review p. 8
2.3 2 Periods	A.1, B.1; A.1, B.2; UCP.1, UCP.5	**Lab 2B: pp. 8–9** Paper Chromatography	Graphic Organizer p. 9 Reading Comprehension p. 10
2.4 2 Periods	A.1, B.1; A.1, B.2; UCP.1, UCP.3		
2.5 2 Periods	A.1, B.1, G.1, G.3; A.1, B.2, G.1, G.3; UCP.3	**Lab 2C: pp. 10–12** Mixtures or Compounds?	Curriculum Connection p. 11
2.6 2 Periods	B.1; B.2, D.1; UCP.3, UCP.4		Science Challenge p. 12

Middle School Standard; High School Standard; Unifying Concept and Principle

2.1 Classifying Matter

Before You Read

Preview the headings in this lesson. Write each heading in your Science Notebook, leaving space below each one to write examples. Name two objects that you predict are examples of each type of matter. Record your predictions.

A busy bakery produces many appealing smells. The breads, cookies, and cakes baked there are made from combinations of ingredients such as eggs, milk, sugar, and flour. Everything you see in a bakery is a type of matter. **Matter** is anything that has mass and takes up space.

A loaf of bread is matter, and so is the dish it might be placed on or the paper it might be wrapped in. The money a person might use to buy the bread is also matter. Not all matter is visible, however. Air is matter, although it cannot be seen.

To decide if something is matter, think about the definition of the term. Matter has mass and takes up space. The aromas in a bakery do not have mass or take up space. Therefore, they are not matter. For the same reason, light, heat, and sounds are also not matter.

Figure 2.1 There are many different types of matter in a market. Although all of the matter has mass and takes up space, there are important differences that allow the matter to be described as elements, compounds, or mixtures.

Learning Goals

- Define *matter*.
- Differentiate among the types of matter.
- Identify examples of elements, compounds, and mixtures.

New Vocabulary

matter
molecule
pure substance
element
compound
mixture
heterogeneous mixture
homogeneous mixture
solution

Differentiate Instruction

Artistic, Linguistic Have students write the adjectives they used to describe the three objects in the room on separate pieces of paper. Collect all of the pieces, fold them in half, and put them in a bowl or a bag. Ask each student to reach into the bowl or bag and pull out four or five words. Tell each student to write a poem using all of the words that he or she picked. Have students illustrate their poems.

2.1 Introduce

ENGAGE Have students create three-column charts in their Science Notebooks. Ask students to label the columns *Solid*, *Liquid*, and *Gas*. Ask them the following questions: *What solids would you find in a bakery? What liquids would you find in a bakery? What gases would you find in a bakery?* Have students work in pairs to fill in their columns. Draw three columns on the board. Ask pairs to share what they have written. Record students' answers on the board.

Vocabulary terms are listed on the first student page of each lesson. You may wish to preview the terms before introducing each lesson. Strategies for teaching the vocabulary appear on the pages where the terms are introduced.

Before You Read

Ask students to identify the first three headings in this lesson. Draw a three-column chart on the board. Label the columns *Pure Substances*, *Elements*, and *Compounds*. Ask students to think of two examples for each column heading. Have students copy the columns into their Science Notebooks and continue to fill in examples as they read.

Teach

EXPLAIN to students that in this lesson they will learn to define matter, to differentiate among the types of matter, and to identify examples of elements, compounds, and mixtures.

 Vocabulary

matter Explain to students that the word *matter* comes from the Latin word *māteria*, which means "substance." Everything of substance is made up of matter.

● Teach

 EXPLAIN to students that they will learn about the differences among pure substances, elements, and compounds.

 Vocabulary

molecule Explain to students that the word *molecule* comes from the Latin word *mōlé,* meaning "mass."

pure substance Tell students the prefix *sub-* in the word *substance* comes from the Latin word *substāre,* meaning "to stand firm." A pure substance is made of one kind of particle and "stands firmly" together.

element Explain to students that the word *element* comes from the Latin *elementum,* meaning "rudiment" or "beginning." Have students apply this to the term *element.*

compound Tell students that the prefix *com-* in the word *compound* means "together," and the root *pound* comes from the Latin *pōnere,* which means "put."

mixture Remind students that the word *mix* means "to put together." A mixture is a group of substances that are mixed together but can be separated by physical means.

heterogeneous mixture Tell students that the word *heterogenous* comes from a combination of the Greek words *héteros,* which means "different," and *génos,* which means "kind." Have students relate these meanings to the definition of the term.

homogeneous mixture Explain to students that the prefix *homo-* comes from the Greek word *homós,* meaning "same." Ask students to use that meaning and the meaning of *génos* to define a homogeneous mixture.

solution Tell students that the word *solution* comes from the Latin *solvere,* which means "loosen" or "dissolve."

Use the Visual: Figure 2.3

ANSWER There are two hydrogen atoms to every one oxygen atom.

CONNECTION: **Math**

ANSWER The ratio of carbon atoms to oxygen atoms is 1:2, or 1 to 2.

EXTEND Have students find the ratio of the atoms in each of these compounds: NaCl (salt), H_2O_2 (hydrogen peroxide), and NH_3 (ammonia).

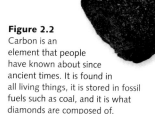

Figure 2.2 Carbon is an element that people have known about since ancient times. It is found in all living things, it is stored in fossil fuels such as coal, and it is what diamonds are composed of.

As You Read

In your Science Notebook, write another example of an element and a compound. Check to see if your original predictions were correct, and replace them as necessary.

In what way are elements and compounds similar?

 CONNECTION: **Math**

A ratio describes a relationship between two numbers. For example, a water molecule can be described by the ratio of two hydrogen atoms to one oxygen atom. You can write a ratio as 2:1 or as 2 to 1. Both forms describe the same relationship.

Carbon dioxide contains one carbon atom and two oxygen atoms. What is the ratio of carbon to oxygen in this compound?

Pure Substances

All matter is made up of small particles called atoms. There are more than 100 different kinds of atoms, and most can combine with other atoms of the same kind or with different atoms to form larger particles called molecules. A **molecule** (MAH lih kyewl) is formed when two or more atoms combine.

A **pure substance**, generally just called a substance, is a type of matter made up of only one kind of particle. Every sample of a pure substance has the same properties and the same composition. A pure substance can be either an element or a compound.

Elements A substance in which all of the atoms are the same is called a chemical **element**. Gold, silver, and iron are examples of elements. So, too, are mercury, neon, and uranium. All matter can be described in terms of the elements from which it is made.

Compounds Few elements are found uncombined in nature. Instead, most elements combine with other elements to form compounds. A **compound** is a pure substance in which the atoms of two or more elements combine. Examples of compounds include carbon dioxide, ammonia, table salt, and rust.

The elements in a compound always combine in a specific ratio. For example, water is a compound in which two atoms of hydrogen combine with one atom of oxygen. No matter where on Earth you find the water, every water molecule always exists in this ratio of two hydrogen atoms to one oxygen atom.

Figure 2.3 Water is a compound made up of the elements hydrogen and oxygen. What is the ratio of these elements in a molecule of water?

As You Read

ANSWER Elements and compounds are both pure substances, and they are both made up of atoms.

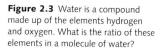 **Strategy**

Illustrate Have students draw pictures of an element and a compound using different colors and shapes to represent the different forms of matter. Students should label their drawings on the back. Collect the drawings and redistribute them throughout the class. Ask students to identify the drawings and then check their answers by turning over the pictures.

Mixtures

A fruit salad might contain grapes, watermelon, strawberries, kiwi, and cantaloupe. Even though the fruits are tossed together, they do not actually combine or change. Thus they could easily be separated from the salad with fingers or a spoon.

A fruit salad is an example of a mixture. A **mixture** is made up of substances that can be separated by physical means. Unlike compounds, mixtures do not always contain the same ratio of the substances that make them up. For example, granite is a mixture of different minerals, such as feldspar and mica. Some granite has a greater amount of feldspar and appears pink. Other samples of granite have more mica and appear black. The same combination of minerals always forms granite, but the minerals may exist in different ratios.

Heterogeneous Mixtures   A mixture in which the different materials can be distinguished easily is called a **heterogeneous** (he tuh roh JEE nee us) **mixture**. Granite is a heterogeneous mixture. The different minerals in granite can be observed by looking at a sample under a microscope. Sand and soil are other heterogeneous mixtures.

Homogeneous Mixtures   In some mixtures, the particles are spread out so evenly that they cannot be seen even with a microscope. A mixture in which the substances are uniformly spread out is called a **homogeneous** (hoh mo JEE nee us) **mixture**. Another name for a homogeneous mixture is a **solution**. Examples of homogeneous mixtures include air, ocean water, antifreeze, and tea.

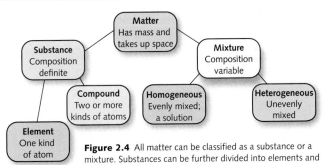

Figure 2.4 All matter can be classified as a substance or a mixture. Substances can be further divided into elements and compounds. Mixtures can be heterogeneous or homogeneous.

After You Read

1. How is a compound different from an element?
2. Compare the ratio of substances in a mixture to that in a compound.
3. How should lemonade made from a powdered mix be classified? Use the examples in your Science Notebook to help you answer the question.

Explore It!

1. Put equal amounts of soil, clay, sand, gravel, and pebbles in a clear plastic container. Add water until the container is almost full. (Wash your hands after handling the materials.)

2. Put the lid on the container and shake the mixture thoroughly. Predict the order in which the materials will settle. Observe what happens. Compare your observations to your predictions.

What kind of mixture did you make? How do you know? In what order did the materials settle? Suggest reasons why.

Figure It Out

1. Which type of matter is made up of only one kind of atom?
2. How would you classify a sample of vinegar?

Teach

EXPLAIN to students that they will learn about two different types of mixtures: heterogeneous and homogeneous.

Figure It Out: Figure 2.4
ANSWER 1. Elements are made up of only one kind of atom. 2. Vinegar would be classified as a homogeneous mixture, or a solution.

Explore It!

Pair students and distribute the same amount of each material to each pair. Use small jars or plastic containers. Remind students to make sure the tops are on tightly before shaking. If running water is not available, provide students with containers of water at each station. Students should find that it is a heterogeneous mixture because particles keep their identity and settle out. The materials settle out in order of particle size.

Assess

Use the After You Read questions and the Alternative Assessment to help you evaluate students' understanding of the lesson.

After You Read

1. A compound contains more than one kind of element.
2. The ratio in a compound is always the same, but the ratio in a mixture can vary.
3. homogeneous mixture, or solution

Differentiate Instruction

Kinesthetic, Artistic Provide students with sand, salt, and water. Have them mix the salt with the water, the sand with the water, and the salt with the sand. Ask students to draw a picture of each type of mixture and label each picture as a heterogeneous or homogeneous mixture.

Alternative Assessment

Have students share their lists of examples in small groups. Ask students to add additional examples to their Science Notebooks. Have them discuss points of uncertainty. Check that students' examples are in the correct columns.

2.2 Introduce

ENGAGE Ask students to look at the photographs in **Figure 2.5.** Ask them to think about other places they have seen copper used. Remind students that an element is a pure substance. Ask students if they know how to determine whether something is made of pure copper or is a mixture of copper and other materials. Have students discuss this question in small groups and then share their ideas with the class.

Before You Read

Model a K-W-L-S-H chart on the board. Ask students to volunteer some of the things they already know about elements. Have students turn to a partner and share something they still want to know about elements. Direct students to draw a similar chart in their Science Notebooks and write what they know and want to know about elements.

● Teach

EXPLAIN to students that in this lesson, they will be learning about the discovery of elements. They will be able to describe elements with words and symbols and recognize what elements are made of.

Use the Visual: Figure 2.5

ANSWER Answers will vary but might include using coins, home telephones (wiring), pots and pans, or plumbing (pipes).

Learning Goals
• Discuss the discovery of elements.
• Describe elements with words and symbols.
• Recognize what elements are made of.

New Vocabulary
chemical symbol
atom

2.2 Elements

Before You Read

Create a K-W-L-S-H chart in your Science Notebook. In the *K* column of your chart, list anything you already know about elements. In the *W* column, write what you want to know about elements.

When you call a friend's home, your voice signal may be carried over a copper wire. The element copper is also used to make coins, pots, pipes, electrical wires, and computer chips. Recall that an element is a pure substance made up of only one type of atom. An element is the simplest type of pure substance.

Discovery of Elements

Today scientists identify 117 different elements. Of those, 94 are found in nature, even though some exist only in very small amounts. The remaining 23 elements can be made in laboratories. They are unstable and exist for only short periods of time.

The number and nature of chemical elements has not always been clearly understood. The ancient Greeks described only four elements—earth, fire, water, and air. They believed that various combinations of these four elements could form everything on Earth. For example, earth and fire could form lava.

Although different Greek philosophers developed their own interpretations of the theory of elements, this basic theory survived for about 2,000 years. Then scientists began discovering elements and their properties through experimentation.

Figure 2.5 The properties of each element give the element unique uses. The element copper has many common uses. How might you have used copper today?

Background Information

Pennies were made of pure copper from 1793–1837. From 1837–1857 and from 1864–1962, they were made from bronze, which is 95% copper and 5% tin and zinc. In between, from 1857–1864, they were made from 88% copper and 12% nickel. In 1962, the tin was removed, which left pennies with 95% copper and 5% zinc. Since 1982, pennies have been made from 97.5% zinc and 2.5% copper.

The first definition of an element was formulated by a seventeenth-century chemist named Robert Boyle. Born in Ireland, Boyle was bright enough to enter college at the age of eight. During his teenage years, Boyle toured Europe and continued his studies in other countries.

Up until Boyle's time, the Greek model of four elements remained widely accepted. Based on that model, people known as alchemists believed they could turn one type of matter into another. In particular, they attempted to turn cheap metals into expensive gold. In 1661, Boyle became the first scientist to oppose the idea that four elements could combine to form any other substance.

Boyle went on to propose a new definition of an element as any substance that cannot be broken down into a simpler substance. Boyle was revolutionary in his approach to science because he conducted rigorous experiments and kept careful records.

In 1654, Boyle joined a small group of English scientists, mathematicians, philosophers, and physicians who met each week to discuss important topics. In 1660, the group formed the Royal Society. Today, the Royal Society is the oldest continuous scientific society in the world.

Describing Elements

Elements are represented by chemical symbols. A **chemical symbol** for an element consists of one or two letters. The first letter is always capitalized. If there is a second letter, it is lowercase. The letters of the symbol are often an abbreviation of the element's name in English. For example, the symbol for carbon is C, and the symbol for helium is He.

Some chemical symbols are abbreviations of an older form of an element's name, which may be in another language, such as Latin or Greek. The symbol for iron is Fe, which comes from the Latin word *ferrum*. Gold is represented by the symbol Au, which comes from the Latin word *aurum*. **Figure 2.6** lists some common elements and their symbols.

Common Elements

Element	Symbol	Element	Symbol
hydrogen	H	iron	Fe
helium	He	nitrogen	N
oxygen	O	silicon	Si
carbon	C	magnesium	Mg
neon	Ne	sulfur	S

Figure 2.6 Look at the chemical symbols for these common elements. Note how some are made up of one letter and others are made up of two letters.

As You Read

Review the K-W-L-S-H chart in your Science Notebook. In the *L* column, add any information you have learned about elements.

What type of matter is an element?

Explain It!

Choose an element that is represented by a symbol that is not an abbreviation for the English name, such as potassium or lead. Research to learn the origin of the symbol. Write a well-developed paragraph explaining the reason for the symbol.

Teach

EXPLAIN to students that in this section of the lesson, they will learn how to describe elements using symbols. Ask students if they know of any symbols that are used to describe elements.

 Vocabulary

chemical symbol Explain to students that a symbol is something that stands for something else; for example, a lion often symbolizes courage. Ask students to give examples of other symbols. Encourage them to think about road symbols.

PEOPLE IN SCIENCE

Explain to students that Robert Boyle's ideas were not popular when he introduced them. His ideas contradicted what the scientific community had believed for many years. Ask students if they know of any other scientists who went against popular opinion and were later found to be correct. Lead students to remember that before Copernicus and Galileo, scientists believed that the Sun and planets revolved around Earth.

EXTEND Ask students to think about how it would feel to propose a theory that contradicted the beliefs of a majority of scientists. Tell students to think about the characteristics a person needs to have to take that kind of risk. Have students write about their ideas in their Science Notebooks.

 Explain It!

Explain to students that many of the symbols used to describe elements come from the Latin words for those elements. Suggest that students conduct library or internet research to find examples of this naming convention.

As You Read

Have students share their K-W-L-S-H charts with partners. Allow them time to add new information gained from the discussion.
ANSWER An element is a pure substance.

Background Information

The periodic table lists all of the known elements using their chemical symbols. The elements are arranged based on their atomic numbers. Elements listed horizontally all have similar properties. The periodic table also provides information about the atomic mass of each element and the arrangement of electrons in its electron shells. There are also classes of elements that are grouped together, such as the transition metals.

ELL Strategy

Prepare Presentations Have each student make a presentation to the class about a chosen element he or she has researched. Encourage students to make diagrams, include pictures, and/or provide samples of the elements to support and reinforce their presentations. If possible, provide time for English language learners to practice giving their presentations with a peer tutor to clarify terms and pronunciation.

● Teach

Tell students that in this section of the lesson, they will be learning about the makeup of elements. Note: Chapter 5 presents more in-depth coverage of modern atomic theory and the structure of the atom.

 Vocabulary

atom Tell students that the word *atom* comes from the Greek *átomos*, which means "indivisible." There was a time when scientists believed that the atom was the smallest particle of matter and was indivisible. Discuss with students the three major subatomic particles: neutrons, protons, and electrons.

Figure It Out: Figure 2.7
ANSWER **1.** protons and neutrons
2. helium

 CONNECTION: **Economics**

Ask students to think about other elements that might have a high economic value. Distribute copies of the periodic table (or use the one on pp. 94–95 of this textbook) and have students work in groups to make a list of these elements. Under each element, have students list the reasons why they think the element might be valuable. Invite groups to share their lists with the class. Students' lists should include other precious metals, such as silver, platinum, and titanium. Radioactive elements such as uranium and plutonium are also quite valuable because of their nuclear applications. Radioactive elements are also important in medicine.

● Assess

Use the After You Read questions and Alternative Assessment to help you evaluate students' understanding of this lesson.

After You Read

1. neon
2. All atoms of the same element have the same number of protons.
3. Elements are made up of identical atoms.

CONNECTION: Economics

Some elements have high economic value. One such element is gold. Some of the properties that make gold useful are its rarity, its durability, and the fact that it resists corrosion. In addition, gold can be divided into parts, and it is easily identified by its color and density.

Figure It Out

1. Which particles are in the nucleus of an atom?

2. Which element is made up of atoms with two protons?

The Makeup of Elements

You read earlier than an element is made up of atoms. An **atom** is the basic particle of matter. Atoms are extremely small. One atom is less than one-millionth of a millimeter across (0.000001 mm). You cannot see an atom with your eye or even with a simple microscope.

As small as an atom is, every atom is made up of even smaller particles. Two of these particles are found in the nucleus—which is located in the center of an atom. These particles are called protons and neutrons. The nucleus is surrounded by a cloud of particles called electrons.

Every kind of atom has a different number of protons. But all of the atoms of an element have the same number of protons. That means that every single hydrogen atom has 1 proton, every magnesium atom has 12 protons, every oxygen atom has 8 protons, and every copper atom has 29 protons.

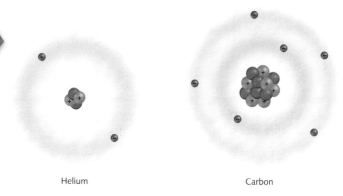

Helium   Carbon

Figure 2.7 An element is made up of atoms with the same number of protons. These models represent atoms of helium and carbon. The orange balls represent protons, the blue balls represent neutrons, and the red balls represent electrons.

After You Read

1. What element is represented by the symbol Ne?
2. Why can't a sample of gold have atoms with different numbers of protons?
3. Using information you have recorded in the *L* column of your K-W-L-S-H chart, describe the relationship between atoms and elements. Complete your chart by indicating in the *S* column what you would still like to know about elements. Then, in the *H* column, describe how you might go about getting this information.

Alternative Assessment

Provide each student with a blank K-W-L-S-H chart. Ask students to fill in as much as they know about elements and their composition.

Differentiate Instruction

Linguistic, Musical Have small groups of students write songs that include at least ten elements and some information about each one. Ask each group to perform its song for the class. Distribute copies of the lyrics to the entire class for each of the songs.

2.3 Compounds

Before You Read

Look at the photos presented in this lesson. Based on the photos, formulate a description of what a compound is. In your Science Notebook, write a definition of the term *compound* in your own words. Include examples you found in the photos.

You take your seat at the movie theater with a large container of popcorn. As you begin to eat it, your friend informs you that the popcorn has been sprinkled with a chemical compound. Should you panic? No, this compound is ordinary table salt. Table salt, or sodium chloride, is a compound of the elements sodium and chlorine. Recall that a compound is a pure substance formed when atoms of two or more elements combine. You use many such compounds every day. This particular compound can add flavor to your food.

Properties of Compounds

The properties of compounds are different from the properties of the elements from which they form. For example, sodium chloride is a salty solid that is safe to eat. By contrast, sodium is a highly reactive silvery solid and chlorine is a green, poisonous gas. When these two elements combine, there is a basic change in their properties.

The properties of a specific compound are also different from the properties of other compounds, even if they are made up of the same elements. The compound water, for example, is made up of two hydrogen atoms and one oxygen atom. Water is an odorless compound that can be used for cooking, cleaning, and drinking. Hydrogen peroxide is also made up of hydrogen and oxygen. However, it has two hydrogen atoms and two oxygen atoms. The different ratio gives hydrogen peroxide properties different from those of water. It has a strong odor, can be used for cleaning wounds, and can cause harm if eaten or spilled into the eyes.

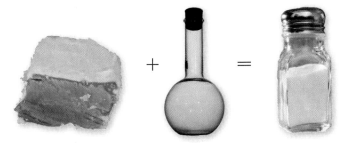

Figure 2.8 The properties of a compound such as sodium chloride are different from the properties of the individual elements that make it up.

Learning Goals

- Define *compound* and identify examples of compounds.
- Relate molecules to compounds.
- Understand how chemical formulas are used to name compounds.
- Recognize how compounds can be broken down into elements.

New Vocabulary

chemical formula
subscript
electrolysis

2.3 Introduce

ENGAGE Explain to students that there are compounds all around. Ask students to look around the room and identify some of the compounds that they see. Encourage students to notice the wood, plastic, water, paint, and glass in the room. Challenge students to identify a compound in the air around them.

Before You Read

Have students look through the lesson and identify the compounds found in the photos. Ask students to write these in their Science Notebooks. In pairs, have students check that they have included all of the compounds. Ask students to share two or three of these with the class. Write the names on the board. Ask students to describe each of the compounds. Suggest that their descriptions will help them write a definition of the term *compound*.

● Teach

EXPLAIN that in this lesson, students will be learning to define compounds and identify examples. They will also be learning to relate molecules to compounds and to understand how chemical formulas are used to name compounds. Finally, they will be learning how compounds can be broken down into elements.

Teacher Alert

Students often confuse solutions and compounds. It is important for students to realize that a compound can only be broken apart by chemical means, while a solution can be separated through distillation or evaporation.

Field Study

Take students for a walk through the school and around the school grounds. Have students look for examples of compounds that they see. Ask students to record their observations in their Science Notebooks.

● Teach

EXPLAIN to students that in this lesson, they will learn about and chemical formulas and the composition of compounds.

Use the Visual: Figure 2.9

[ANSWER] 1:1:3 (calcium to carbon to oxygen)

Figure It Out: Figure 2.10

[ANSWER] **1.** 1:4 (carbon to hydrogen)
2. *Mono-* means "one," and *di-* means "two."

Science Notebook EXTRA

Provide students with the following analogy: *Chemical symbols are like letters of the alphabet, and chemical formulas are like words.* Then list the following formulas on the board and have students copy some or all into their Science Notebooks: H_2O, H_2O_2, C_2H_6, SO_2, $NaCl$, $MgBr_2$, $C_6H_{12}O_6$. Instruct students to write a sentence for each formula identifying the elements (letters) that have been put together to form each compound (word). Make appropriate resource material available to students.

As You Read

Ask students to volunteer some of the definitions for the term *compound* that they have recorded in their Science Notebooks. Write these definitions on the board. Have students work together to refine and combine the definitions. Ask students to record this final version in their Science Notebooks.

[ANSWER] A compound is represented by a chemical formula made up of chemical symbols and subscripts. The symbols tell the elements in the compound, and the subscripts tell the ratio of atoms.

As You Read

Compare the definition of the term *compound* that you wrote in your Science Notebook with a partner's definition. Revise your definition as necessary based on what you have read. Add examples of compounds to your list.

How is a compound represented by a chemical formula?

Figure It Out

1. What ratio describes a molecule of methane?
2. A prefix can change the meaning of a word. Look at the formulas for carbon monoxide and carbon dioxide. Which prefixes indicate the number of oxygen atoms in these compounds?

Composition of Compounds

Whether you have a single drop, a full bottle, or a poolful of it, all water has the same composition, or makeup. This is also true if the water is in the solid, liquid, or gaseous state. Hydrogen and oxygen are always present in the same ratio. Each atom of oxygen combines with two atoms of hydrogen to form a molecule of water. Recall that a molecule is a particle formed when two or more atoms join together.

In a similar way, every molecule of carbon dioxide has one atom of carbon and two atoms of oxygen. Every molecule of ammonia has one atom of nitrogen and three atoms of hydrogen. These compounds will always be made of atoms in these same ratios.

Figure 2.9 Chalk is a compound formed when one atom of calcium combines with one atom of carbon and three atoms of oxygen. How can the ratio of elements in chalk be expressed?

Chemical Formulas

Just as elements can be represented by chemical symbols, compounds can be represented by chemical formulas. A **chemical formula** shows the elements in a compound and the ratio of their atoms.

Figure 2.10 shows the chemical formulas of some common compounds, including ones you have just read about. The chemical formula for carbon dioxide, for example, is CO_2. The formula includes the chemical symbol for carbon, C, and the chemical symbol for oxygen, O—the two elements that make up the compound. The number 2 below the symbol for oxygen is called a subscript. A **subscript** below an element's symbol indicates the number of atoms of that element present in the compound. The subscript below the symbol for oxygen indicates that there are two atoms of oxygen. If there is no subscript, as in the case of the carbon atom, it is understood to be 1. So the ratio of carbon to oxygen in carbon dioxide is 2 to 1.

Common Compounds	
Compound	**Chemical Formula**
ammonia	NH_3
carbon dioxide	CO_2
carbon monoxide	CO
hydrogen peroxide	H_2O_2
methane	CH_4
sodium chloride	$NaCl$
water	H_2O

Figure 2.10 The table lists several common compounds and their chemical formulas.

ELL Strategy

Compare and Contrast Have students refer back to the definitions of *compound*, *molecule*, and *element*. Ask each student to draw a Venn diagram using three circles. Have students use these charts to record the similarities and differences among the three concepts. Examples of each type of substance should be included in the outer parts of the circle.

Key Concept Review Workbook, p. 7

Separating Compounds

Compounds cannot be decomposed, or separated into individual elements, by physical means such as evaporation or filtering. Instead, a more complex chemical process is required. One such process is used to change water (H_2O) into hydrogen and oxygen. The process is known as **electrolysis** (eh lek TRAH luh sus).

During the electrolysis of water, electricity from a battery or a power supply is passed through a sample of water. Hydrogen gas bubbles up at one part of the electric circuit, called the cathode. Oxygen gas bubbles up at another part of the electric circuit, called the anode. The hydrogen and oxygen gases can then be collected in containers.

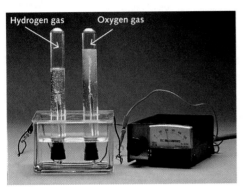

Hydrogen gas   Oxygen gas

Figure 2.11 A portion of the hydrogen used to make fertilizers and to convert petroleum, or crude oil, into more useful forms is produced through electrolysis.

Other compounds can be broken down in a similar way. However, for some the process requires several steps. When chalk, $CaCO_3$, is heated, it decomposes into lime, CaO, and carbon dioxide, CO_2. Neither of these products are elements. They are still compounds. Through electrolysis, lime can be broken down into calcium, Ca, and oxygen, O. Carbon dioxide can then be broken down into carbon, C, and oxygen, O.

After You Read

1. How is a compound different from an element?
2. How are molecules related to compounds?
3. The chemical formula for table sugar is $C_{12}H_{22}O_{11}$. What does this tell you about the chemical composition of table sugar?
4. Review the notes in your Science Notebook. Based on your notes, explain how the formation and decomposition of compounds are opposite processes.

Differentiate Instruction

Artistic, Kinesthetic Provide students with materials such as paint, toothpicks, and marshmallows or clay. Ask students to create models of some common compounds, such as H_2O, CO_2, CH_4, and NH_3.

Did You Know?

All compounds are made up of molecules. A molecule is a combination of two or more atoms. However, not all molecules are compounds. Some molecules are made up of combinations of the same kind of atom. For example, hydrogen (H_2), oxygen (O_2), and nitrogen (N_2) can form molecules when two atoms join together. These molecules are not compounds because they are each composed of only one element.

● Teach

 EXPLAIN to students that they will learn how some compounds are separated.

Vocabulary

chemical formula Explain to students that chemical formulas are similar to mathematical formulas. Both use symbols to show how variables or elements are put together.

subscript Tell students that the prefix *sub-* means "under" and the root *script* means "to write." A subscript is the writing that goes under a symbol.

electrolysis Explain to students that the root of the word *electrolysis* comes from the Greek *lýsis*, which means "a loosening." Electrolysis uses electricity to "loosen" the bonds between elements.

● Assess

Use the After You Read questions and the Alternative Assessment to help you evaluate students' understanding of the lesson.

After You Read

1. A compound is made up of more than one element.
2. Compounds are made up of molecules.
3. It has 12 atoms of carbon, 22 atoms of hydrogen, and 11 atoms of oxygen.
4. When compounds are formed, elements combine. When compounds are broken down, elements are separated from one another.

Alternative Assessment

Provide each student with a blank Venn diagram with two circles labeled *Compound* and *Element*. Have students fill out the diagrams by properly comparing and contrasting the two concepts. Instruct students to use the terms *atom* and *molecule* in their diagrams.

students by asking them to picture themselves on a sandy beach. Ask: *If you were to reach down and pick up a handful of sand, what would it look like? How would it feel?* Have students share their thoughts with the class. Encourage students to talk about colors and textures. Explain that sand is a mixture of different types of rocks and minerals. Tell students that sand can be separated out into its components by physical means, such as filtering for different-sized particles.

Before You Read

Ask students to look through the lesson and record the headings and subheadings in their Science Notebooks. Have students share with partners one question that they have about the topics covered in the lesson. Ask students to share their questions with the class. Record their questions on the board. Then have students record their own questions in their Science Notebooks.

Teach

EXPLAIN to students that in this lesson, they will learn to identify mixtures and their properties and to classify mixtures as heterogeneous or homogeneous. They will also learn how to describe methods of separating mixtures into their components.

Learning Goals

- Identify mixtures and their properties.
- Classify mixtures as heterogeneous or homogeneous.
- Describe methods of separating mixtures into their components.

New Vocabulary

distillation
filtering
centrifuge
paper chromatography

Before You Read

Preview the lesson, noting the headings and subheadings. In your Science Notebook, write at least three questions you have about the topics. Then add any information you might already know that will help you answer the questions. As you read, add to these notes.

There are sandy beaches all over the world. Depending on the location, the sand may look and feel very different. Some beaches have smooth, white sand. Other beaches have rough, pink sand. Still others have thick, brown sand. The sand in a desert may be very fine, whereas the sand on a beach might be coarse and grainy.

Sand is made up of broken pieces of rock that have been smoothed by water and wind over time. Sand usually contains a material called quartz, along with other materials. Sand is a mixture. Recall that a mixture is made up of substances that can be separated by physical means.

Mixtures Versus Compounds

Although both mixtures and compounds are made up of different elements, mixtures are different from compounds in several ways. Unlike in compounds, the ratio of substances in a mixture can change from one sample to the next and even within a sample. Handfuls of sand gathered from two different beaches will show different combinations of materials. Even handfuls of sand from different parts of the same beach may vary. In addition, each substance in a mixture keeps its own identity. That means that if the mixture is separated, the substances will be the same as they were before the mixture was made.

The characteristics of a mixture are evident in salt water, which is a mixture of water and salt. The amount of salt in water can vary from one body of water to another. Water from the Dead Sea, for example, has more salt than water from the Atlantic Ocean. The amount of salt can also vary based on location in the same ocean. When a mixture of salt water is separated, the original substances—water and salt—are the same as they were before being combined.

Air is another mixture. It is a mixture of different gases, including nitrogen, oxygen, and small amounts of other gases. The ratio of these gases can change with location or altitude.

Figure 2.12 Sand, salt water, and air are mixtures of different substances. The materials in each mixture can vary from one sample to the next.

Background Information

Small pieces of rocks and minerals are classified as sand if they are larger than 0.06 mm and smaller than 2.1 mm. Quartz is the most common mineral found in sand. Sand can also be made up of feldspar, broken-down coral or shells, and rocks formed from hardened volcanic lava known as basalt. Sand has many industrial uses. Different forms of sand can be used to manufacture concrete, glass, abrasives, and scientific molds.

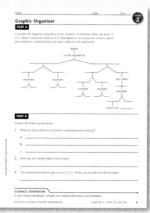

Graphic Organizer
Workbook, p. 9

Types of Mixtures

As discussed earlier, there are different types of mixtures. Some mixtures are heterogeneous and others are homogeneous. Classifying a mixture depends on the types of materials that make up the mixture.

Heterogeneous Mixtures A recipe calls for sprinkling a mixture of cinnamon and sugar onto a cake. No matter how well the cinnamon and the sugar are mixed together, the different particles are visible. Fine brown cinnamon particles can be distinguished from the larger white grains of sugar. The cinnamon and sugar mixture is a heterogeneous mixture because it is not uniform throughout.

Any mixture in which the different substances can be detected is considered to be heterogeneous. The rocks and soil in a garden are mixtures. Fruit and vegetable salads, hamburgers, and tacos are heterogeneous mixtures of foods. Piles of books, games, and tools are also heterogeneous mixtures.

Homogeneous Mixtures Brass is a mixture of copper and zinc. Particles of copper or particles of zinc cannot be distinguished in a sample of brass because they are blended together so well. Brass is an example of a homogeneous mixture. Unlike the particles in a heterogeneous mixture, the particles in a homogeneous mixture will not settle out. The mixture stays uniformly mixed.

Homogeneous mixtures can exist as solids, liquids, or gases. Brass is a solid mixture. Vinegar is an example of a liquid. It is a homogeneous mixture of acetic acid and water. Air is an example of a homogeneous mixture that is a gas.

Figure 2.14 Vinegar is a homogeneous mixture. So is brass. How are they different from heterogeneous mixtures?

⬡ CONNECTION: Art

Look through magazines for examples of mixtures. Gather a collection of pictures of heterogeneous and homogeneous mixtures. Arrange the pictures into a collage that demonstrates the difference between the two types of mixtures. Glue the collage into place on a poster to display for your classmates.

Figure 2.13 Blood is a heterogeneous mixture. The different parts can settle into layers. Cinnamon and sugar also form a heterogeneous mixture. What is a heterogeneous mixture?

As You Read

Review the questions you wrote in your Science Notebook. Write the answers to any questions you can, based on what you have learned so far.

How can you identify a heterogeneous mixture?

● Teach

EXPLAIN to students that in this section of the lesson, they will learn to identify different types of mixtures.

Use the Visual:

Figure 2.13 [ANSWER] A heterogeneous mixture is one that is not uniform throughout.

Figure 2.14 [ANSWER] The substances in a homogeneous mixture are uniformly mixed and cannot be distinguished from one another.

As You Read

Encourage students to look back through their Science Notebooks to find the answers to their questions. Suggest that students also turn to a partner to discuss their questions and possible answers.

[ANSWER] The different substances in a heterogeneous mixture can be seen.

CONNECTION: Art

If time is limited, you might want to cut out examples of different kinds of mixtures ahead of time and then distribute them. Suggest that students divide their posters in to two sections and label them *Heterogeneous* and *Homogeneous*. Tell students to divide their pictures into two piles and glue the corresponding pictures on the appropriate section of the poster.

Differentiate Instruction

Kinesthetic Place small jars containing heterogeneous and homogeneous mixtures around the room. Label each jar with a number or letter. Have pairs of students rotate around the room, looking at each jar and identifying it as either heterogeneous or homogeneous.

When students have finished, ask them to share their observations with the class. Draw two columns on the board. Label one *Heterogeneous* and the other *Homogeneous*. Show students the correct classification for each jar. Discuss with students any questions they might have.

Teach

 EXPLAIN that in this last section of the lesson, students will learn how to separate different types of mixtures.

Figure It Out: Figure 2.15

ANSWER **1.** paper chromatography **2.** the sizes of the particles

 **Vocabulary**

distillation Tell students that the prefix in the word *distillation* comes from the Latin *dē-*, meaning "down." The root of the word *distillation* comes from the Latin *stīlla,* which means "drop." During distillation, different liquids that have been boiled off are cooled so that they condense and "drop down."

filtering Explain to students that this word comes from the Latin *filtrum,* a piece of felt cloth used to separate solids from liquids.

centrifuge Tell students that the prefix *centri-* means "center," and the root *fuge* comes from the Latin *fugere,* meaning "flee from." A centrifuge separates mixtures by spinning so that parts "flee from the center."

paper chromatography Explain to students that the prefix *chroma-* comes from the Greek *chrôma,* meaning "color." The suffix comes from the Greek *-graphos,* which means "to draw or write." Paper chromatography separates color mixtures, which are "drawn" or "written" on paper.

Assess

Use the After You Read questions and the Alternative Assessment to help you evaluate students' understanding of the lesson.

After You Read

1. In a mixture, the substances do not combine. They can be separated, and they retain their individual identities.
2. The salt and water are uniformly mixed throughout.
3. filtering, distillation, use of centrifuge

Figure It Out

1. Which method of separation is best for liquids that travel at different speeds through paper?
2. What characteristic of substances is used to separate mixtures using a filter?

Figure 2.15 Mixtures can be separated in different ways. The method used depends on the properties of the substances in the mixture.

Separating Mixtures

Mixtures can be separated into their individual components in different ways. Some mixtures can be separated by removing components by hand or by using an instrument such as tweezers.

Other mixtures can be separated by using a liquid. For example, if you add water to a mixture of sugar and sand, the sugar dissolves, or breaks apart, in the water. If the mixture is then poured through a filter, the sugar water will pass through the filter. The sand will be left behind.

The remaining mixture of sugar and water can then be separated through boiling or evaporation. During these processes, liquid water changes into water vapor and the solid sugar remains behind.

A similar process known as **distillation** (dihs tuh LAY shun) is used to separate mixtures of different liquids. The individual liquids boil at different temperatures. As each liquid changes into a gas, it is collected and then cooled so it changes back into a liquid in a separate container.

Filtering, or straining, can separate the components of some mixtures. A mixture of marbles, pebbles, and sand can be separated by pouring it through smaller and smaller filters.

A **centrifuge** (SEN trih fyewj) is a device that spins samples at high speeds. Blood and other mixtures can be separated into their components using a centrifuge.

A technique known as **paper chromatography** (kroh muh TAH gruh fee) can separate mixtures of dyes or pigments. The paper is dipped into the mixture, and as the substances are absorbed into the paper, they move at different rates. Over time, they separate into layers.

After You Read

1. How is a mixture different from a compound?
2. Why is a sample of salt water classified as a homogeneous mixture?
3. Using the answers to the questions in your Science Notebook, identify three ways of separating mixtures into their components.

Explore It!

Make a mixture of sawdust and iron filings. Devise two different ways to separate the mixture. Test your plans.

In your Science Notebook, describe how you separated this mixture.

 Explore It!

Students should work in pairs. Have each member of the pair get one substance. Provide a variety of tools for students to use for separating the materials. One way to separate the two substances is to use a magnet to remove the iron. Another way is to add water, which will cause the sawdust to float.

ELL Strategy

Practice Using Vocabulary Have students write each vocabulary term in this chapter on an index card. In pairs, have students take turns explaining what they know about each term. Alternatively, students can explain what they know about a term and have peers guess the vocabulary term.

2.5 Solutions

Before You Read

In your Science Notebook, write each of the vocabulary terms in this lesson. Leave some space below each term. Using your own words, write what you think each term means. As you come across each term in the lesson, modify or replace your definition if needed.

Learning Goals

- Describe the properties of a solution.
- Identify the different types of solutions.
- Define *alloy*. Recognize the applications of alloys.

New Vocabulary

dissolve
solute
solvent
alloy

Some of the world's most colorful fish live in salt water. Salt water is a homogeneous mixture, or a solution, of salt and water. This means that the salt and water are uniformly mixed. Even if a container of salt water is left undisturbed, the salt will not settle to the bottom of the container.

Forming a Solution

What happens when a spoonful of sugar is poured into a cup of hot water? Gradually, the sugar seems to disappear. The sugar **dissolves**, or breaks apart, in the water. The molecules of sugar separate and mix with the water molecules. In time, they become uniformly mixed. Any part of the mixture tastes equally sweet, and the sugar can no longer be seen.

When other solutions are formed, particles break apart. Table salt, for example, breaks into parts called ions. Sodium and chloride ions then mix uniformly with water molecules.

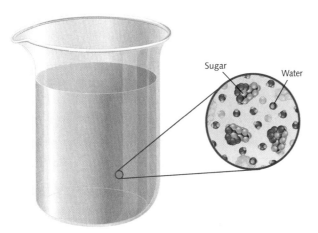

Figure 2.16 The salt water in which these fish live is a solution of salt and water.

Figure 2.17 In a homogeneous mixture, particles of both substances become uniformly mixed. In this example of sugar and water, molecules of sugar mix uniformly with molecules of water. What is another name for a homogeneous mixture?

Differentiate Instruction

Kinesthetic Provide students with two glasses of cold water, one glass of hot water, three tablespoons of salt, and a spoon. Direct students to add a tablespoon of salt to each glass. Students should label the glasses *A (cold)*, *B (cold)*, and *C (hot)*. After they add the salt to each glass, tell students to leave glasses A and C alone, but to stir glass B for 30 seconds and then observe the three glasses. Students should record their observations in their Science Notebooks. Students should find that both stirring and heating the water speed up the rate at which the salt dissolves.

2.5 Introduce

ENGAGE students by asking them to again picture themselves on a sandy ocean beach. Ask: *If you were to reach down and scoop up some water, what would it look like? How would it feel? How would it smell?* Have students share their thoughts with the class. Encourage students to engage all of their senses in the description. Explain that ocean water is a special kind of mixture called a solution. Salts are dissolved in the water, forming a homogeneous mixture. Like all mixtures, ocean water can be separated by physical means.

Before You Read

Have students count the number of vocabulary terms in this lesson. They should find that there are four terms. Suggest that each student divide a page in his or her Science Notebook into four quadrants. Students should write one term in each quadrant and then write their own definition under each term.

Teach

EXPLAIN to students that in this lesson they will learn to describe the properties of a solution and identify the different types of solutions. They will also learn to define alloys and recognize their applications.

Vocabulary

dissolve Tell students that the Latin roots of the term *dissolve* mean "to loosen apart." Ask students how this meaning corresponds to the definition of the term. Also tell students that there are other meanings of the verb *dissolve*, including "to terminate," "to fade away," and "to be overcome emotionally." Ask if students are familiar with any of these meanings and if they can use them in a sentence.

Use the Visual: Figure 2.17

ANSWER Another name for a homogeneous mixture is a solution.

Teach

 EXPLAIN to students that in this section of the lesson, they will learn to identify different types of solutions and the parts of a solution.

Use the Visual: Figure 2.18

(ANSWER) Salt is the solute and water is the solvent.

Vocabulary

solute Explain to students that the word *solute* is the past tense of the root *solvere,* meaning "loosened." A solute is a substance that is dissolved.

solvent Tell students that the word *solvent* is the present tense of the root *solvere,* meaning "loosen." A solvent dissolves a solute.

alloy Explain to students that the word *alloy* comes from the Latin *alligāre,* which means "to bind." An alloy is a solution in which two metals are bound together.

Figure It Out: Figure 2.19

(ANSWER) **1.** gas solute in liquid solvent
2. sterling silver

As You Read

Have students write their sentences underneath the words in each quadrant of the page in their Science Notebooks.

(ANSWER) In science, a solution is a homogenous mixture. A solution can also be an answer to a problem or calculation.

Figure 2.18 The very salty water of Mono Lake in California is home to millions of brine shrimp. Brine is a solution of salt in water. What is the solute in this solution, and what is the solvent?

As You Read

In your Science Notebook, write a sentence correctly using each vocabulary term you listed.

The word *solution* has more than one meaning. What is its meaning in science? What other meaning do you know for this word?

Parts of a Solution

Every solution can be described by two parts—the solute and the solvent. The substance that is dissolved in a solution is called the **solute**. The substance that does the dissolving in a solution is called the **solvent**. When sugar is dissolved in water, sugar is the solute and water is the solvent. Water is the solvent in many solutions. In fact, because water can dissolve so many different substances, it is known as the "universal solvent."

It can sometimes be difficult to distinguish the solute from the solvent. Another way to compare solutes and solvents is to consider that the solvent exists in a greater quantity than the solute does in a solution.

Types of Solutions

Solutes and solvents can be solids, liquids, or gases. **Figure 2.19** shows examples of different combinations of solutes and solvents.

Figure It Out

1. What is the form of the solute and solvent in carbonated drinks?

2. Silver is mixed with gold to make some kinds of jewelry. Which solution in the chart is most like the mixture of gold and silver?

Examples of Solutions		Solute		
		Gas	Liquid	Solid
Solvent	Gas	air	water vapor in air	odors
	Liquid	carbonated drinks	vinegar	salt water
	Solid	hydrogen dissolved in metals	dental fillings	sterling silver

Figure 2.19 This table shows various combinations of solutes and solvents.

Teacher Alert

Students often confuse the terms *solute* and *solvent*. It is important to stress the difference between the two terms: a solute is dissolved in a solvent. Students also often think of solutions as only involving a solid in a liquid. It is important to stress that all states of matter can be both solutes and solvents.

 Strategy

Illustrate Have students make posters illustrating the concepts of solute and solvent. Hang these posters on the wall to help solidify students' understanding of the terms.

Figure 2.20 Brass is a common alloy of copper, zinc, and other materials. Why might other metals be added to copper?

Alloys

Brass and sterling silver are examples of a special type of solution known as an alloy. An **alloy** (A loy) is a solid solution in which the atoms of two or more metals are uniformly mixed. Other materials are sometimes included, as well.

Metals are blended into alloys in order to give them properties that they don't have alone. These properties might include greater hardness or an increased resistance to corrosion. Pure gold, for example, is very soft to use in jewelry. Alloying it with silver or copper makes it stronger without causing major changes in the way it looks.

The forks and spoons you eat with are probably made of stainless steel. Stainless steel is an alloy of iron, nickel, and chromium. Iron alone rusts quickly. It is the chromium that makes the metal resist rust and staining.

Stainless steel is only one type of steel. There are many types of steel, all of which are formed by mixing iron with carbon and other elements. The elements mixed with iron determine the properties of the steel. Steel is used to construct buildings, make railways, and build aircraft, as well as to make household tools and equipment.

Figure 2.21 Steel is a strong material used to construct many large buildings.

After You Read

1. What is the relationship between a solute and a solvent?
2. What is an example of a solution with a solid solute in a liquid solvent?
3. Using the definitions you have written and refined in your Science Notebook, what is an alloy?

CONNECTION: Social Studies

The Bronze Age was a period of development between 3500 and 1200 B.C. The Bronze Age was named because of the widespread use of the alloy bronze during that time. Bronze is generally made by alloying copper with tin. It sometimes contains other elements, such as phosphorus, aluminum, or silicon. Tools, weapons, armor, and building materials made of bronze are harder and last longer than those made of stone or copper.

Extend It!

Research to learn about the following alloys: pewter, solder, nichrome, alnico, amalgam, cast iron, wrought iron, and chromoly. Identify the elements that make up each alloy and a common use for the alloy. Record your findings in table form in your Science Notebook.

● Teach

EXPLAIN that in this last section of the lesson, students will learn about alloys and their uses.

CONNECTION: Social Studies

The Bronze Age marks a period in history when the alloy of copper and tin called bronze was used to make tools and weapons. The Bronze Age occurred at different points in history in different parts of the world, and some regions and cultures skipped it entirely. In European history, the Bronze Age follows the Stone Age and precedes the Iron Age. Advancement in the sophistication of European civilization is marked by the use of these different materials for tools and weapons.

EXTEND Divide students into three groups. Assign each group one of the three ages. Have students research the types of tools and weapons that were made during each period. Ask each group to share its findings with the class.

Extend It!

In their pure forms, most metals are too soft to be useful in industry. A metal alloy is usually much harder than the base metal in its pure form. Alloys are made by melting the base metal and adding other substances to it.

● Assess

Use the After You Read questions and the Alternative Assessment to help you evaluate students' understanding of the lesson.

After You Read

1. A solute is dissolved in a solvent.
2. salt in water
3. An alloy is a solution of two or more metals.

Alternative Assessment

Provide each student with a list of the vocabulary terms from this lesson. Ask students to define each term and use each term in a sentence. Have students check their work against the definitions they wrote in their Science Notebooks.

Use the Visual: Figure 2.20

ANSWER Other metals are added to produce desirable properties, such as increased hardness or resistance to corrosion.

2.6 Introduce

ENGAGE students by asking: *How many of you used a colloid this morning or enjoyed one with your breakfast?* Explain to students that milk and gel toothpaste are both colloids. Tell them that a colloid is a special type of mixture that they will learn more about in this lesson.

Before You Read

Model an example of an outline on the board. Include a title, Roman numerals, capital letters, numbers, and lowercase letters. Ask students to look through the lesson and help you start the outline. Ask students to copy the outline into their Science Notebooks.

Teach

EXPLAIN to students that in this lesson they will learn to describe the properties of a colloid and to compare suspensions and colloids.

Emphasize the fact that classifying colloids is a type of taxonomy. All colloids are mixtures; however, the different properties of each type of colloid are used to distinguish among them and to classify them in an organized and orderly fashion. The large group is mixtures, then comes colloids (types of mixtures), and then comes emulsions, gels, and aerosols. Milk, for example, is a mixture (broad category), a colloid, and a specific colloid called an emulsion. Ask students to liken this to the classification of a human: vertebrate, mammal, human.

Vocabulary

colloid The prefix *coll-* in the word *colloid* comes from the Greek *kólla*, which means "glue." A colloid is a type of mixture in which the particles are "glued" together, rather than dissolved.

suspension Tell students that the root of the word *suspension* comes from the Latin *pendere*, which means "to hang." In a suspension, one material hangs in the other, and eventually the "hanging" particles settle to the bottom of the mixture.

Learning Goals

• Describe the properties of a colloid.

• Compare suspensions and colloids.

New Vocabulary

colloid
suspension

Figure 2.22
Although small, the particles in a colloid are larger than those in a solution. Mayonnaise, milk, and paints are examples of colloids.

Figure 2.23 A light beam is scattered by the colloid on the right, but it passes invisibly through the solution on the left. Light is scattered by fog because fog is a colloid.

2.6 Colloids and Suspensions

Before You Read

Create a lesson outline. Use the lesson title as the outline title. Label the headings with the Roman numerals I and II. Label the subheadings with the letters *A, B*, etc. Use numbers under each subheading to record information you want to remember.

When you pour yourself a glass of cold milk, you are pouring a mixture. Milk is a mixture of water, fats, and proteins. But what kind of mixture is it? You cannot clearly see the substances that make up milk. Yet milk is not a solution. There are two additional types of mixtures. They are known as colloids and suspensions.

Colloids

Milk is a type of mixture known as a colloid. A **colloid** (KAH loyd) is a heterogeneous mixture with particles that are larger than those in a solution, but not large enough to settle out. There are three basic types of colloids: gels, emulsions, and aerosols.

Gels Gelatin and jelly are types of gels. A gel is a colloid in which the particles are spread out in a solid.

Emulsions A colloid made of two liquids is an emulsion. Milk and mayonnaise are emulsions.

Aerosols An aerosol is a colloid formed when either solid or liquid particles are suspended in a gas. Fog and smoke are examples of aerosols.

It can be difficult to tell the difference between a solution and a colloid just by looking. One way to tell a colloid from a solution is by using light. The particles of a colloid scatter light. The scattering of light by the particles in a mixture is called the Tyndall effect. **Figure 2.23** shows how a beam of light passes straight through a solution but is scattered by a colloid.

Differentiate Instruction

Kinesthetic Provide students with flashlights and containers filled with several different colloids (such as milk, mayonnaise, grape jelly, and paint). Provide liquids that are not colloids, such as salt water or juice. Tell students to shine light through each of the containers and determine whether the substance it contains is a colloid or a solution. Have students describe their observations and predictions in their Science Notebooks.

Suspensions

If sand and water are mixed in a container and allowed to sit undisturbed, the particles of sand will settle to the bottom. A mixture of sand in water is a suspension. A **suspension** (suh SPEN shun) is a heterogeneous mixture containing a liquid in which visible particles settle. The particles in a suspension are larger than those in a colloid and those in a solution.

Salad dressing, another example of a suspension, is made by combining oil and vinegar, or oil and water. Shaking the oil and vinegar mixes them together temporarily. If left undisturbed, however, the two substances separate into layers.

The directions "shake well before using" appear on many medicine bottles. The reason is that many medicines are suspensions. Some of the ingredients settle out when the bottle is left untouched. The user must shake the medicine to mix the ingredients once again.

CONNECTION: Earth Science

Rivers can form suspensions as the moving water picks up soil and other particles. When the river slows down at its mouth, the suspended particles settle. In this way, they form a structure known as a river delta. Over time, a delta can become very deep. For example, the delta at the mouth of the Mississippi River is thousands of meters thick.

As You Read

Include definitions of the vocabulary terms in the outline in your Science Notebook.

How do the three types of colloids differ from one another?

Figure 2.24 A mixture of sand and water is called a suspension. Over time, the sand will settle out of the water.

Comparing Solutions, Colloids, and Suspensions

Description	Solutions	Colloids	Suspensions
Settle upon standing?	no	no	yes
Separate using filter paper?	no	no	yes
Particle size?	0.1–1 nm	1–100 nm	> 100 nm
Scatter light?	no	yes	yes

Figure 2.25 Solutions, colloids, and suspensions vary according to the size of the particles in them. A nanometer (nm) is 1.0×10^{-9} m.

Figure It Out

1. What are two ways in which colloids and solutions are similar?

2. The particles in a mixture are estimated to be about 65 nm. Which kind of mixture is it?

After You Read

1. What type of mixture is a colloid?

2. In terms of settling, how do suspensions compare to colloids and solutions?

3. Based on the lesson outline you made in your Science Notebook, describe how the particles in a suspension compare to the particles in a colloid.

ELL Strategy

Use Visual Information Have students study the table in **Figure 2.25.** Working in groups, tell students to design a matching game in which they describe different types of mixtures and then match them to their correct classifications. Groups can rotate and try each other's games.

Alternative Assessment

Provide each student with a lesson outline that is partially filled out in a variety of places. Ask students to fill in the empty portions of the outlines. Tell students to check their outlines against the ones in their Science Notebooks.

Teach

EXPLAIN to students that in this section of the lesson, they will learn the properties of a type of mixture called a suspension.

Figure It Out: Figure 2.25

ANSWER **1.** Neither colloids nor solutions settle upon standing, and neither can be separated using filter paper. **2.** colloid

As You Read

Check that students are creating their outlines properly. Have students work in small groups to compare outlines.
ANSWER Gels are solids, emulsions are liquids, and aerosols are gases.

CONNECTION: Earth Science

River deltas are named after the Greek letter delta, which is shaped like a triangle. A river delta often forms a triangular shape. Because the soil of most deltas is very fertile, deltas are used for growing many types of fruits, vegetables, and rice.

EXTEND Provide students with empty pans, sand, and pitchers of water. Have them work in groups to make a model of a delta. Tell students to describe their processes in their Science Notebooks.

Assess

Use the After You Read questions and the Alternative Assessment to help you evaluate students' understanding of the lesson.

After You Read

1. A colloid is a mixture with particles that are larger than those in a solution but smaller than those in a suspension.

2. The particles in a suspension settle over time, whereas the particles in solutions and colloids do not.

3. The particles in a suspension are larger and heavier than those in a colloid, and they therefore settle.

Chapter 2 Summary

MASTERING CONCEPTS

True or False

1. False, mass
2. False, atoms
3. False, pure substance
4. True
5. False, alloy
6. True

Short Answer

7. A pure substance, which can be an element or a compound, is made up of only one type of particle. An element is made up of identical atoms. A compound is made up of identical molecules. A mixture is made up of different types of particles.

8. The building blocks of elements are atoms, which are in turn made up of protons, neutrons, and electrons.

9. A compound is made up of different elements, as in carbon monoxide. O_2 is made up of only one type of element.

10. The solute is dissolved in the solvent. For example, salt is the solute dissolved in the solvent water.

11. According to the Tyndall effect, a colloid will scatter light so it can be seen, whereas a solution will not.

Chapter 2 Summary

KEY CONCEPTS

2.1 Classifying Matter

- Matter is anything that has mass and takes up space.
- Matter can be classified as a pure substance or a mixture.
- Pure substances include elements and compounds. Mixtures can be heterogeneous or homogeneous.

2.2 Elements

- Elements are defined as pure substances made up of only one type of atom.
- Elements are represented with chemical symbols.

2.3 Compounds

- A compound is a pure substance made up of a combination of two or more different elements that exist in specific ratios.
- Compounds are made of combinations of atoms called molecules.
- Chemical formulas made up of letters and subscripts are used to represent the ratio of atoms of combining elements in compounds.
- Compounds can be broken down into elements through chemical processes such as electrolysis.

2.4 Mixtures

- A mixture is a blend of substances that keep their individual identities and can exist in varying ratios.
- The substances in a heterogeneous mixture can be easily identified. The substances in a homogeneous mixture become so uniformly mixed that they cannot be recognized individually.
- Mixtures can be separated using processes such as filtration, distillation, paper chromatography, and evaporation.

2.5 Solutions

- A solution is a homogeneous mixture made up of a solute and a solvent. The solute is the substance dissolved, and the solvent is the substance doing the dissolving.
- Solutes and solvents can be solids, liquids, or gases.
- An alloy is a solid solution made of metals and other materials.

2.6 Colloids and Suspensions

- A colloid is a mixture with particles that are slightly larger than those of a solution.
- The particles in a suspension are larger than those in a colloid, and they settle.

VOCABULARY REVIEW

Write each term in a complete sentence or write a paragraph relating several terms.

2.1
matter, p. 21
molecule, p. 22
pure substance, p. 22
element, p. 22
compound, p. 22
mixture, p. 23
heterogeneous mixture, p. 23
homogeneous mixture, p. 23
solution, p. 23

2.2
chemical symbol, p. 25
atom, p. 26

2.3
chemical formula, p. 28
subscript, p. 28
electrolysis, p. 29

2.4
distillation, p. 32
filtering, p. 32
centrifuge, p. 32
paper chromatography, p. 32

2.5
dissolve, p. 33
solute, p. 34
solvent, p. 34
alloy, p. 35

2.6
colloid, p. 36
suspension, p. 37

PREPARE FOR CHAPTER TEST

To prepare for the chapter test, create a question from each Learning Goal. Answer each question. Then use these answers to write a well-developed essay about the chapter. Use the Key Concept on the first page of this chapter as your topic sentence.

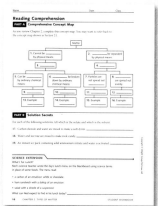

Reading Comprehension Workbook, p. 10

Vocabulary Review Workbook, p. 8

True or False
If the statement is true, write "true." If it is false, change the underlined word or words to make the statement true.

1. Matter is anything that has <u>length</u> and takes up space.

2. An element is made up of <u>molecules</u>.

3. A compound is a type of matter known as a(n) <u>mixture</u>.

4. A solution is an example of a(n) <u>homogeneous</u> mixture.

5. A(n) <u>colloid</u> is a solution of a metal mixed with a metal.

6. A(n) <u>suspension</u> is a mixture in which the particles settle over time.

Short Answer
Answer each of the following in a sentence or brief paragraph.

7. How is a pure substance different from a mixture?

8. What particles are the building blocks of elements? What is their structure?

9. Explain why a molecule of oxygen (O_2) is not a compound, whereas a molecule of carbon monoxide (CO) is a compound.

10. Compare the solute of a solution to the solvent. Give an example.

11. Explain how light can be used to distinguish between a solution and a colloid.

Critical Thinking
Use what you have learned in this chapter to answer each of the following.

12. **Classify** Label each of the following as *matter* or *not matter:* air, music, thoughts, clouds, hair, raindrops, heat.

13. **Compare and Contrast** Tell how a compound is similar to and different from a mixture.

14. **Design** Describe a method by which you can separate a mixture of white sand and salt.

15. **Apply** Explain why you think the packaging of some fruit juice, such as orange juice, directs the user to shake well before using.

Standardized Test Question
Choose the letter of the response that correctly answers the question.

16. The chemical formula for acetylene is C_2H_2. How many atoms are in each molecule of acetylene?

    A. 2

    B. 3

    C. 4

    D none of the above

Test-Taking Tip

If "none of the above" is one of the choices in a multiple-choice question, be sure that none of the choices are true.

Critical Thinking

12. Matter: air, clouds, hair, raindrops; Not matter: music, thoughts, heat

13. Both compounds and mixtures are made from combinations of different substances. However, in a compound, the substances combine in such a way that their properties change, and they cannot be separated by physical means. In a mixture, the substances retain their identities and properties, and they can be separated by physical means.

14. One way is to add water to the mixture. The salt will dissolve, but the sand will not. The mixture can then be poured through a filter to separate out the sand.

15. Fruit juices are suspensions, because the particles settle out.

Standardized Test Question

16. C

Reading Links

Iron and Steel: From Thor's Hammer to the Space Shuttle

Building on the chapter's introduction to metals and alloys, this book examines the historical use of iron and steel while presenting a scientific overview of the two substances, their properties, and their production. Informative sidebars, colorful visuals, discussion of modern relevance, and the inclusion of such resources as a map, time line, and glossary make the volume a good resource for student reports or individual enrichment.

Ruth Kassinger. Lerner Publishing Group. 80 pp. Illustrated. Library ISBN 978-0-7613-2111-8.

Chemistry for Every Kid: 101 Easy Experiments that Work

Packed with experiments that are quick, easy, and fun to perform for students of all levels, this book is a good addition to a classroom library and an ideal way for students to begin to acquaint themselves independently with unfamiliar topics in chemistry. Whether used in the classroom or at home, the activities memorably illustrate concepts that students will encounter as they learn more about matter and its properties in later chapters.

Janice Vancleave. John Wiley & Sons. 256 pp. Illustrated. Trade ISBN 978-0-471-62085-3.

Curriculum Connection
Workbook, p. 11

Science Challenge
Workbook, p. 12

2A Comparing Compounds

This prechapter introduction activity is designed to determine what students already know about compounds and how the ratio of the elements in a compound determines its properties.

Objectives

* observe the properties of compounds made from the same elements
* record data
* evaluate the relationship between the ratio of elements in chemical properties
* communicate conclusions

Planning

🕐 10 minutes plus 30 minutes waiting time

👥 groups of 3–4 students

Materials (per group)

* water
* 1 bottle hydrogen peroxide (5–6 % concentration)
* 2 clear plastic cups
* 2 small pieces of dark fabric
* medicine dropper

Advance Preparation

* Prepare the cups of water and hydrogen peroxide before class begins. Clearly label each cup.
* Make sure the dark fabric used is absorbent.

Engagement Guide

* Challenge students to think about how they can predict what will happen in the experiment by asking these questions:
* How do the formulas of the two compounds differ? (Hydrogen peroxide contains an extra oxygen atom.)
* Do water and hydrogen peroxide have any similar properties? If so, what are they? (Both are colorless and odorless liquids.)
* What properties do you think water and hydrogen peroxide will have that are different? (Accept all student responses. After completing the experiment, students should observe that the hydrogen peroxide contains more bubbles and bleaches dark fabric.)
* What types of test can be used to check for various physical and chemical properties? (Students should be able to list several chemical and/or physical properties and describe simple ways to determine them. Examples might include properties such as density, electrical conductivity, and specific heat.)
* Encourage students to communicate their conclusions in creative ways.

Going Further

Encourage students to explore the cleaning ability of hydrogen peroxide by having them soak dirty coins in hydrogen peroxide overnight. After 24 hours, have students make observations of the coins and present their conclusions to the class.

2B Paper Chromatography

Objectives

* separate a mixture using paper chromatography
* record observations about the composition of the ink mixture
* compare and contrast the composition of different ink mixtures
* communicate conclusions

Skill Set

observing, recording and analyzing data, comparing and contrasting, stating conclusions

Planning

🕐 30–35 minutes   👥 groups of 3–4 students

Materials

Materials for this activity are listed in the Student Laboratory Manual.

Advance Preparation

Cut the strips from coffee filters or filter paper in advance. Give students a variety of brands of water-soluble black markers. Test the different brands of markers ahead of time to ensure that several dyes are present in the black ink.

Answers to Observations

Sketches will vary but should show blurry but fairly well-defined areas for each dye. Descriptions will vary. If several varieties of markers are used, students should see differences in the colors and amounts of dyes used to make the black ink.

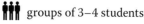

Answers to Analysis and Conclusions

1. The ink in the black line separated into several different colors and moved up the paper.

2. Answers will vary. Different varieties of markers contain different dyes and produce different results.

3. The process of mixing dyes to make ink is a physical change. Because the dyes do not chemically combine, they can be separated without changing their chemical makeup.

Going Further

Have students repeat this experiment using different colors of markers. Encourage students to share their results with the class.

2C Mixtures or Compounds?

Objectives

* observe the characteristics of salt and sand
* separate a mixture of sand and water into its different parts
* compare and contrast the properties of a compound and a mixture

Skill Set

observing, recording and analyzing data, comparing and contrasting, drawing conclusions

Planning

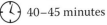 40–45 minutes　　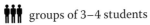 groups of 3–4 students

Materials

Materials for this activity are listed in the Student Laboratory Manual.

Advance Preparation

Obtain coarse sand, rock salt, and small, cone-shaped coffee filters for this activity. Only a small amount of sand and rock salt is needed for each lab station. The sand and rock salt can be placed in plastic cups with plastic spoons as scoops.

Answers to Observations: Drawings A and B

Drawing A should show the crystal structure of the rock salt. Although the crystals vary in size and shape, students will not see particles within the crystal. Drawing B should show the unique particles of sand with their different colors, shapes, and textures.

Answers to Observations: Characteristics of Sand and Water Before and After Filtering

When the sand and water are mixed, students should observe that the mixture has the properties of both sand and water. When the mixture is filtered, students should observe that the coffee filter separates the sand from the water. The sand stays in the coffee filter and the water passes through. The fact that the sand and water could be separated by physical means proves that it was a mixture—that its components were not chemically bonded together.

Answers to Analysis and Conclusions

1. The salt particles or crystals all have the same chemical composition (NaCl) and the same properties. The sand is made up of different tiny pieces of rock and other materials, all of which have unique characteristics. The composition and properties of sand are not uniform.

2. Sand is produced when parent rock material breaks into tiny grains. Depending on the location of the beach, the type of parent rock might differ. Different types of parent rock and other materials give different beaches their unique colors and textures.

3. The combination is a mixture. The fact that the sand and water can be separated by physical means (filtering) shows that that it is a mixture. Each component retains its properties.

4. Each component retains its properties.

5. The sand particles were too large to pass through the coffee filter. The smaller water molecules passed through the paper filter.

Going Further

Have students make a mixture of salt and water. Have them use a coffee filter to determine if they can separate the salt from the water, as they did with the sand and water mixture. After students observe that the salt is not separated from the water, ask them to design an experiment to separate the salt from the water. Have students communicate their ideas with other class members. If time permits, demonstrate how boiling away the water leaves behind a solid salt residue.

Introduce Chapter 3

As a starting activity, use Lab 3A on page 13 of the Laboratory Manual.

ENGAGE Ask students to look at the photograph of the cavern interior. Have students work in small groups to identify all of the substances they recognize. Then have the groups share their lists with the class. Ask students to think about different ways they can classify the substances written on the board. Suggest that one way would be by state of matter (solid, liquid, or gas).

Think About Classifying Changes to Matter

ENGAGE Discuss with students their experiences with cutting and cooking onions. Ask: *Have you cut and cooked an onion? What are the steps involved in cutting and cooking an onion?* Record and order students' responses on the board. For each step in the process, ask students how the onion has changed. Next to each step, record the type of change. For example, when you cut the onion, it changes in size and shape. Ask students to classify each change as a change in form or a change in composition. Write students' responses on the board next to each step. Have students summarize the changes to the onion in their Science Notebooks.

Chapter
3
Properties of Matter

KEY CONCEPT Matter can be described by its physical and chemical properties and by the changes in these properties.

Deep underground, far from the reaches of sunlight, a visitor can find some of the most spectacular sights in the world. Complex caverns have formed in rock below Earth's surface. Amazing structures have grown over time on the ceilings, floors, and walls.

These natural masterpieces are the products of changes in matter. This chapter will explore the properties of matter and the changes they undergo—changes that create caverns and many other products.

Think About Classifying Changes to Matter

You are responsible for many changes every day. When you write on a sheet of paper, tear it out of a notebook, and fold it up in your backpack, you are making changes to the paper. Think about changes that happen in the kitchen. For example, imagine someone cutting an onion and cooking it in a pan.

* In your Science Notebook, write a sentence that describes how the onion changes during each of the two steps.

* Label each step as a change in form or a change in composition. After you complete the chapter, go back and determine if you were correct.

NSTA

SCLINKS.
THE WORLD'S A CLICK AWAY

www.scilinks.org
Physical and Chemical Properties
of Matter **Code: WGPS03**

40

Chapter 3 Planning Guide

Instructional Periods	National Standards	Lab Manual	Workbook
3.1 2 Periods	B.1; B.2; UCP.1	**Lab 3A: p. 13** Properties of a Candle	Key Concept Review p. 13 Vocabulary Review p. 14
3.2 2 Periods	B.1; B.2; UCP.1	**Lab 3B: pp. 14–15** Physical Properties of Matter	Graphic Organizer p. 15 Reading Comprehension p. 16
3.3 2 Periods	B.1; B.2; UCP.1		Curriculum Connection p. 17
3.4 2 Periods	A.1, B.1, C.1; A.1, B.3, C.5; UCP.3	**Lab 3C: pp. 16–18** Chemical Changes	Science Challenge p. 18

Middle School Standard; High School Standard; **Unifying Concept and Principle**

Physical Properties

Before You Read
Reword the headings of this lesson so that they form questions. Write the questions in your Science Notebook. As you read, write answers to the questions.

Color, shape, and size are physical properties of matter. A **physical property** of matter is a characteristic that can be observed without changing the matter into a different substance. Each substance has a unique set of physical properties that distinguishes it from all other substances.

Figure 3.1 It is easy to identify the small spotted dog in the photo. It looks very different from the other dogs. Color and size are physical properties that differentiate the dogs. What are other physical properties of dogs?

It's a beautiful day at the beach. Dogs of all colors, shapes, and sizes are out playing in the sand and the water. Like all types of matter, dogs have many different properties. A **property** of matter is a characteristic that can be used to describe it. People use properties to identify how samples of matter are alike or different from one another. For example, the dogs in **Figure 3.1** can be grouped together according to their sizes or colors. The two dogs in the center are both large and yellow. The dog in the background is clearly different because it has a black coat. Imagine how difficult it would be to find a specific dog if all dogs had the same color and size.

Learning Goals
- Define a physical property of matter.
- List examples of physical properties of matter.

New Vocabulary
property
physical property
state of matter
melting point
boiling point
specific gravity
intensive property
extensive property

Recall Vocabulary
matter, p. 21
mass, p. 14
volume, p. 15
density, p. 16

Figure 3.2 The avocado has a rough, bumpy texture. The plum is smooth to the touch. What other properties can be used to describe these fruits?

CHAPTER 3   **41**

Introduce

ENGAGE Have students think about the ways in which they distinguish one dog from another. Ask: *What properties do you look for to distinguish among different dogs? Are some properties more important than others?* Have students work in pairs to list the different physical properties that they would use to identify dogs.

Vocabulary terms are listed on the first student page of each lesson. You may wish to preview the terms before introducing each lesson. Strategies for teaching the vocabulary appear on the pages where the terms are introduced.

Before You Read
Have students identify the headings in this lesson. Tell students to reword each heading into a question and write these questions in their Science Notebooks. Model this action by rewording and recording the following question: *What are observable properties?*

Teach

EXPLAIN to students that they will learn to define physical properties of matter and list examples of these properties.

Use the Visual:
Figure 3.1 ANSWER Sample answers include shape, mass, size of features, speed of movement, and sound quality of bark.
Figure 3.2 ANSWER color (red, purple), type of stem, type of pit, size

 Vocabulary

physical property Encourage students to think of common uses of the word *physical*. Discuss the meanings students provide, and encourage students to identify any relationships between those meanings and the definition provided in this lesson. *Physical* means "of the body," and a *physical property* is a property of the body of matter.

property Ask students if they are familiar with another meaning of the word *property*. Ask students to relate this definition to the scientific meaning (a characteristic that is used to identify matter). Explain to students that these identifying characteristics are "owned" by each sample of matter.

Teach

EXPLAIN to students that they will learn about the differences between observable and measurable properties.

Vocabulary

state of matter A state of matter refers to the condition of the matter at a certain time. Ask students to apply that meaning to the often-used term *state of mind.*

melting point Explain that the word *melting* comes from the old English word *mieltan,* meaning "to make liquid." Explain that the melting point is the point at which a substance changes from a solid to a liquid.

boiling point Explain that *boil* is derived from the Latin *bulla,* which means "to bubble." Ask students how this derivation relates to the definition of the term.

specific gravity Encourage students to think of common uses of the words *specific* and *gravity.* Discuss how the meaning changes when both words are put together. Remind students that the specific gravity of a substance sets it apart from all other substances.

intensive property Explain that the prefix *in-* comes from the Latin word meaning "within." An intensive property relates to the matter's "internal" condition.

extensive property Explain to students that the prefix *ex-* means "out." Tell students that an extensive property has to do with an "external" condition of the matter, such as the amount present. Discuss with students the fact that *extensive* and *intensive* are antonyms and have opposite meanings.

Figure It Out: Figure 3.3
[ANSWER] **1.** solid **2.** melting point

As You Read

Model a T-chart on the board. Ask students to brainstorm a list of objects. Record the objects on the board. Choose one object and fill in the T-chart with students. Tell students to choose another object from the list and draw and complete T-charts in their Science Notebooks. Students should label one side *Observable Properties* and the other side *Measurable Properties.*

[ANSWER] Density and specific gravity are physical properties that you can calculate if you know the mass and volume of an object.

---

1. In which state of matter are icicles and snow?
2. What physical property determines how warm it needs to be for ice to change into liquid water?

Figure 3.3 Matter exists in different states. The state of matter is a physical property.

As You Read

Draw and complete a T-chart in your Science Notebook. At the top of the chart, write the name of an object. On one side of the chart, list two observable physical properties of that object. On the other side, list two measurable physical properties of the object.

What physical properties can you calculate if you know an object's mass and volume?

Observable Properties

Learning about physical properties includes using the senses to gather information. Color and shape, for example, can be determined by looking at an object. Texture and hardness are physical properties that describe how an object feels. Matter can be smooth or rough. It can also be hard or soft.

Another physical property of matter is state. The **state of matter** tells whether a sample is a solid, a liquid, a gas, or plasma. The temperatures at which a sample of matter changes from one state to another are also physical properties. The **melting point** is the temperature at which a solid changes into a liquid. The **boiling point** is the temperature at which a liquid changes into a gas. These two properties vary with different substances.

Measurable Properties

Some physical properties are discovered by making measurements. For example, length and width can be measured with a ruler. Mass and volume are also physical properties of matter that can be measured. Recall that mass is the amount of matter in an object, and volume is the amount of space matter takes up.

The mass and volume of an object can be used to find another physical property—density. Density is the amount of mass in a given volume, and it is a unique property of matter that is useful in separating and identifying substances. The density of a sample can be used to find its specific gravity. **Specific gravity** is a physical property that is found by comparing the density of a material to the density of some standard material. The standard material is often water at a specific temperature or air at a standard temperature and pressure.

Figure 3.4 These liquids each have different densities, which make them float at different levels.

Differentiate Instruction

Kinesthetic, Logical, Artistic Create ten stations around the room. Place a substance at each station. Provide examples of solids, liquids, and gases. For the gas, use an "empty" jar. Divide students into pairs or small groups. Have students rotate to each station and record the observable and measurable properties of each object. If possible, provide triple-beam balances, graduated cylinders, and rulers at each station. Tell students to draw and describe each object in their Science Notebooks. Students should classify each property they record as observable or measurable.

Teacher Alert

Measurable properties are technically observable properties as well, but it is important that students are able to differentiate them from those that can be described without tools.

Figure 3.5 There are similarities and differences between the two samples of water shown in this figure. That's because some physical properties depend on the amount of water, and some do not.

Kinds of Properties

A maintenance worker fills a cup with pool water to test for proper chlorine amounts. The composition, or makeup, of the water in the pool is exactly the same as the composition of the water in the cup. Both samples are made up of water in liquid form. Thus both samples share certain properties related to this composition. However, there are some properties the samples do not share because the samples are present in different amounts. The properties used to describe a sample of matter fall into two categories: intensive properties and extensive properties.

Intensive Properties Physical properties such as density, melting point, boiling point, temperature, and color are all identical for the two samples. The fact that the samples are present in different amounts has no effect on these properties. A property that does not depend on the amount of matter present is known as an **intensive property**.

Extensive Properties Some physical properties of the cup of water and the pool of water are not the same, however. The most obvious of these properties is volume. Clearly the volume of the water in the pool is much greater than the volume of the water in the cup. The masses of the two samples are also different. A property that depends on the amount of matter present is known as an **extensive property**. Volume and mass are extensive properties.

After You Read

1. What is a physical property of matter?
2. Name one physical property that can be discovered with the senses alone and one that can be discovered through measurement.
3. Review the answers to the questions you have recorded in your Science Notebook. Then make a list of at least five physical properties of an orange.

Did You Know?

Water has some very interesting physical properties. For example, water is the only substance on Earth that exists naturally in three states—solid, liquid, and gas (water vapor).

Explore It!

Select an object in the classroom or elsewhere at your school. In your Science Notebook, write as many of the object's physical properties as you can. Read your list of properties to a classmate without identifying the object. Let your classmate try to guess the object. Challenge your classmate to add to your list.

Field Study

Take students outside with their Science Notebooks. Have each student choose a spot in which to sit away from their classmates. Ask students to observe the objects they see around them and choose one object to describe. Students should sketch their objects in their Science Notebooks and list all of the properties that they can identify about the objects. Encourage students to use all of their senses for this activity.-

Key Concept Review
Workbook, p. 13

Teach

EXPLAIN to students that they will learn about two different kinds of properties: intensive and extensive.

Explore It!

Place a variety of objects in a box or a bag. Divide students into pairs. Have each student reach into the bag and pull out an object. Tell students to conceal their objects from their partners. Allow students to return their objects to the bag and choose another in order to repeat the process. Discuss with the class the ways in which students were able to improve upon their lists after a second or third repetition.

Assess

Use the After You Read questions and the Alternative Assessment to help you evaluate students' understanding of the lesson.

After You Read

1. A physical property of matter is a characteristic that can be observed without changing the composition of the matter.
2. Sample answer: Texture can be felt and length can be measured.
3. Students' answers will vary but should include five of the following: color, smell, taste, texture, diameter, circumference, mass, volume.

Alternative Assessment

Provide each student with an object. Ask students to draw four-column charts in their Science Notebooks, labeling the columns *Observable, Measurable, Intensive,* and *Extensive*. Tell students to list at least two properties of the assigned object in each column.

3.2 Introduce

ENGAGE Direct students to look at **Figure 3.6.** Tell them to think about other things that they could do to the paper that would change its form or appearance but not its composition. Ask: *What could you do to the paper so that it would look different but still be paper? What could you do to the paper that would change what it is?* Encourage students to think about folding or crushing the paper. It would look different, but would still be paper. Explain to students that burning the paper would change its composition. After being burned, it would no longer be paper. Repeat this activity using the photo of a chef chopping vegetables.

Before You Read

Have students look through the lesson to identify the pictures. Ask students to share the page numbers for the pictures with the class. Record the page numbers on the board. Tell students that there are four figures in the lesson, some with multiple images, and encourage students to look at all of them before writing their questions.

● Teach

EXPLAIN to students that in this lesson, they will be learning to describe and identify examples of physical changes.

Vocabulary

physical change Encourage students to think of common uses of the word *change*. A change makes something different. A physical change makes the "body of matter" different; it changes what is observed while retaining the identity of the substance.

3.2 Physical Changes

Before You Read

Write the title of this lesson in your Science Notebook. Then look at the pictures in the lesson. Record any questions you have about physical changes.

On New Year's Eve around the globe, confetti fills the air. Confetti is produced by cutting larger sheets of paper into small shapes and strips. Is confetti still paper? Indeed it is. Cutting paper into small pieces does not change its composition. Instead, it changes only its form or appearance.

Any change that alters the form or appearance of matter without changing its composition is called a **physical change**. A substance that undergoes a physical change is still the same substance it was before it changed. Paper is still paper, even after it is cut into small pieces.

Paper is not the only example of matter that can be cut. Wood, food, hair, and string are other examples of matter that are commonly cut. Although each has a unique composition, that composition does not change when the matter is cut. The only thing that changes is the form or the appearance of the matter.

Changes in Appearance or Form

Like cutting, many physical changes alter the appearance or form of a substance. Bending a wire, blowing up a balloon, stretching a rubber band, and wrapping foil around a sandwich are all examples of these types of physical changes. They alter the appearance or form of a substance.

Figure 3.6 Cutting paper into small pieces to make confetti involves a physical change. So, too, does chopping vegetables into small pieces before cooking them. Whether the paper or the vegetables are whole or in small pieces, their compositions do not change.

ELL Strategy

Compare and Contrast Have students work in pairs to list what they could do to change a block of clay. Ask students to identify each action they list as a physical change or another type of change. Ask students to summarize what differentiates a physical change from another kind of change. Encourage students to think about cutting, mixing, wetting, and heating the clay. All but the last action would yield a physical change in the clay.

Graphic Organizer
Workbook, p. 15

Some types of physical changes occur when an object breaks. A glass jar shatters on the floor. A tree branch snaps under the weight of newly fallen snow. A plastic handle falls off of a toy. What do all these changes have in common? In each case, the matter definitely appears quite different after the change. However, the actual composition of the matter has not changed at all. The glass pieces are still glass, the broken tree branch is still wood, and the handle is still plastic.

Figure 3.7 The flag of the United States is customarily folded in thirteen steps. Each fold is a physical change that alters only the appearance of the flag.

Other types of physical changes occur when matter is formed into a new shape. A piece of wood can be sanded into a baseball bat. The bat is still made of wood even though it looks very different from its original form. In a similar way, clay can be sculpted into a work of art. The substances in the clay do not change as the clay is transformed from a shapeless lump into a molded pot.

A teacher accidentally steps on a piece of chalk and crushes it. Is this transition from a solid stick to a powder also a physical change? Yes, it is. The clue to recognizing any type of physical change is realizing that the composition of the matter did not change. All of the physical changes described here involve only a change in the form or appearance of some type of matter. The matter itself does not change.

Changes of State

On a warm day, ice cream melts quickly. What happens when ice cream melts? It changes from a solid to a liquid. Although they look different, both the solid ice cream and the melted liquid contain the same ingredients.

Figure 3.8 Sculpting, breaking, and sanding are three ways to cause physical changes in matter.

Explain It!

Some changes in matter are physical changes and some are not. In your Science Notebook, explain how cracking an egg is different from cooking an egg.

As You Read

With a partner, discuss the questions you both wrote in your Science Notebook. Then write answers to the questions you wrote about physical changes. Think about what all physical changes have in common.

How does matter change during a physical change?

● Teach

EXPLAIN to students that in this section of the lesson, they will learn about changes that alter the appearance or form of a substance.

Explain It!

Cooking involves a change in the composition of the egg. Cracking involves a physical change in the form of an egg. If possible, demonstrate both cracking and cooking an egg. Have students record their observations in their Science Notebooks.

As You Read

Ask students to share their questions and answers with the class. If students have the same questions, discuss the answers that they have found.

ANSWER During a physical change, matter changes in form or appearance but not in composition.

Differentiate Instruction

Artistic Have students turn a piece of blank paper sideways and fold it in half. On one side of the paper, have them draw an object before it has been physically changed; on the other side, have them draw the object after it has undergone a physical change. Tell students to label the object and identify the action that produced the change. For example, a student might choose to draw a picture of an apple before and after it has been sliced. He or she should label the apple and write *sliced* somewhere on the drawing. Encourage students to produce more than one drawing. Collect drawings for use in Lesson 3.4.

Teach

Tell students that in this section of the lesson, they will be learning about changes in state.

Figure It Out: Figure 3.9

ANSWER **1.** The formation of water droplets on the glass is the reverse of the process by which the puddle disappears. **2.** Matter changes form, but not composition.

Extend It!

Substances with a density less than the density of liquid water (1g/mL) will float in water. Substances denser than water will sink. Remind students that ice floats in water. Demonstrate this to the class. Discuss with students what Earth would be like if ice were denser than water. Remind students that the polar ice caps are floating ice and that they support important ecosystems. Also encourage students to think about what would happen to oceans and lakes if ice sank. Bodies of water would fill with ice and the water supply would be vastly depleted. Sea life would not be able to survive.

The boiling point of water is lower than 100°C at high elevations. This means that foods cooked in water will boil faster but require a longer cooking time.

Assess

Use the After You Read questions and Alternative Assessment to help you evaluate students' understanding of this lesson.

After You Read

1. The composition of the rock is not changed by the pounding of the waves.
2. solid to liquid (melting)
3. Students' answers will vary but might include cutting a sandwich, folding paper, or sharpening a pencil.

The only thing that changes during melting is the state of matter. Recall that the state describes whether matter is a solid, a liquid, or a gas. The particles in the solid are arranged somewhat differently from the way they are in the liquid, but the specific particles remain the same. Because the composition of the matter does not change, a change in the state of matter is a physical change.

What happens if the melted ice cream is returned to a freezer? It will change from a liquid back into a solid. This change of state, known as freezing, is also a physical change. Melting and freezing are not the only changes of state that can occur in matter. Other changes of state are summarized in **Figure 3.9**.

Figure It Out

1. Which photograph shows the change of state that is the reverse of the change that the puddle undergoes?
2. Why is each of these examples a physical change?

Extend It!

Some physical properties change with conditions, such as temperature and pressure. Conduct research to find out how the physical properties of water can change. In particular, find out how the boiling point of water changes at high elevations and how the density of liquid water is different from that of solid ice. Summarize your findings in your Science Notebook.

These droplets of water formed on the glass when water vapor (a gas) cooled and turned into liquid. This is the same change of state that produces clouds.

A puddle formed during a rainstorm disappears as sunlight shines on it. The liquid water in the puddle changes to water vapor (gas) in the air.

As it cools, this liquid metal will become solid gold.

Some types of matter can change from a solid directly to a gas. Dry ice changes into a gas at room temperature.

Figure 3.9 Matter can change from one state to another.

After You Read

1. A rough stone is made smooth by the repeated pounding of ocean waves. Why is this process an example of a physical change?
2. What change of state occurs when an ice cube melts?
3. Review the notes in your Science Notebook. Based on the descriptions you wrote, give an example of a physical change you encountered today.

Alternative Assessment

Have each student write two or three of the questions recorded in his or her Science Notebook on a sheet of paper. Redistribute the questions to other members of the class. Have those students answer the questions and then check back with the author of the questions to see if the answers are correct.

Background Information

At sea level, the air pressure is greatest because it has the weight of so much air pressing down from above. As altitude increases, air pressure decreases. Boiling occurs when the pressure created by the molecules of the liquid escaping into the atmosphere (vapor pressure) equals the pressure above the liquid (air pressure). The less pressure exerted above a liquid, the lower the temperature required for the liquid to reach its boiling point.

3.3 Chemical Properties

Learning Goals

- Define *chemical property.*
- Identify examples of chemical properties.
- Differentiate between physical and chemical properties.

New Vocabulary

chemical property
flammability
flammable

Before You Read

Create a working definition of the term *chemical property.* A working definition is one that develops as you read and think about an idea. Write what you know about the term before you begin reading. Then add to that definition as you read and discuss the lesson.

A shiny silver spoon will not stay shiny forever. Silver has the ability to tarnish when exposed to air. When something tarnishes, it becomes dull or dark. The ability to tarnish is a chemical property of some types of matter. A **chemical property** describes how the composition of a substance will change when the substance interacts with other substances or with some forms of energy. Energy is the ability to do work or cause change. Energy can exist in different forms, such as light, heat, and electricity.

Figure 3.10 Silver tarnishes over time. Silver tarnish is the compound silver sulfide. It forms when silver metal combines with sulfur compounds in the air. The ability to tarnish is what kind of property?

Like physical properties, chemical properties are used to classify substances. Unlike physical properties, however, chemical properties are observed only when the composition of a substance changes. They cannot be seen just by looking at the object or measuring it in some way.

Just as the ability of a substance to change into another substance is a chemical property, so too is the inability of a substance to change into another substance. For example, iron can form rust when it combines with air. This is a chemical property of iron. However, when iron is combined with nitrogen gas at room temperature, nothing happens. The iron does not change into another substance. This inability to change in the presence of nitrogen gas is another chemical property of iron.

Did You Know?

Scientists use the properties of matter to classify known substances and identify new ones. New substances are being discovered every day, and known substances are being discovered in new places. The American Chemical Society currently recognizes over 22 million substances! Each substance has a unique set of properties.

3.3 Introduce

ENGAGE students by discussing experiences they have had with objects that have tarnished. Ask: *Have you ever had a piece of jewelry that has tarnished? Have you ever seen a tarnished silver platter? Have you ever tried to polish silver that has been tarnished?* Explain to students that not all metals tarnish. Point out that an advantage of stainless steel silverware is that it doesn't tarnish. Tell students that the ability of a substance to tarnish is a chemical property. Ask students if they can think of another process similar to tarnishing (rusting, corroding).

Before You Read

Write the term *chemical property* on the board. Ask students to write a definition based on what they know about physical properties and the discussion they have had in class. Do this with students before they have read the text. As students continue through the lesson, encourage them to refine their definitions.

● Teach

EXPLAIN that in this lesson, students will be learning to define a chemical property and identify examples. They will also learn to differentiate between physical and chemical properties.

 Vocabulary

chemical property Explain to students that a chemical property describes how a substance will change when it interacts with other substances and/or with some form of energy. Tell students that the word *chemical* is related to the word *alchemy,* which refers to the belief that less desirable metals could be turned into silver or gold.

Use the Visual: Figure 3.10

ANSWER The ability to tarnish is a chemical property of matter.

Differentiate Instruction

Kinesthetic Divide students into small groups. Provide each group with a piece of tarnished metal and a number of different cleaning materials, such as water, alcohol, soap, and silver polish. Have students design an experiment to compare the effectiveness of the cleaners. Tell students to record the procedure, observations, and conclusions in their Science Notebooks.

Background Information

Energy is the ability to do work or cause change. It will be the subject of Chapters 15 and 16. When work is done on an object, a force is exerted on the object through a distance. The equation for work is *work = force × distance.*

Teach

Explain to students that in this lesson, they will learn about the chemical property of flammability.

 Vocabulary

flammability Explain to students that the root of the word *flammability* is *flame*, which refers to a burning gas or vapor. The chemical property of flammability indicates that a substance will burn.

flammable Discuss with students the precautions they should take when using flammable substances. Ask students to identify the part-of-speech relationship between the terms *flammability* and *flammable*.

As You Read

Have students work in pairs to refine their definitions of *chemical property*. When students are satisfied with their definitions, have them work with other pairs to reach a consensus on the definition. Continue to combine groups until the entire class has agreed upon a definition of the term.

ANSWER Chemical properties can be identified only by changing the substance into something different.

Figure It Out: Figure 3.12

ANSWER **1.** If a material is described as flammable, it means that it could easily burn. If something ignited the paint, it could burn. **2.** A spark from the lightning may have caused the paint to burst into flames.

Assess

Use the After You Read questions and the Alternative Assessment to help you evaluate students' understanding of the lesson.

After You Read

1. The ability to rust is a chemical property of an iron nail.
2. It describes the ability of a substance to burn.
3. A chemical property describes how the substance will change under certain conditions. It has the potential to change.

Figure 3.11 Plastic and paper will never rust, but metals containing iron can rust. The ability to rust is a chemical property.

As You Read

Add to the definition of *chemical property* that you wrote in your Science Notebook. Share your definition with a partner.

Why can't you identify a chemical property by observing a substance?

Have you ever seen a rusty old car, tractor, or set of tools? All of these objects may develop rust over time. Rust is a flaky, reddish-brown substance that can form on some metals when the metals are exposed to air. The ability to rust is a chemical property of iron and metals that contain iron.

Another chemical property is **flammability** (FLAM uh BIH leh tee), or the ability to burn. Paper and logs are examples of matter that have the ability to burn. Matter that can burn easily and quickly is described as **flammable**. Pure oxygen, gasoline, and many cleaning products are flammable. Warning labels appear on flammable materials instructing users to keep the materials away from flames.

Figure It Out

1. Explain what is meant by describing the paint as flammable.
2. What may have caused the flammable paint to burst into flames?

Figure 3.12 On May 6, 1937, the airship *Hindenburg* burst into flames as it attempted to land in Lakehurst, New Jersey. One explanation for the explosion is that a lightning strike ignited the highly flammable paint coating on the skin of the airship.

After You Read

1. Review your definition of the term *chemical property* in your Science Notebook. What chemical property can be used to describe an iron nail?
2. Why is flammability a chemical property instead of a physical property?
3. Explain why a chemical property is sometimes described as a "potential" of a substance.

ELL Strategy

Relate to Personal Experience Show students a picture of the image used to label products as flammable. Tell students to record the items that they find around their homes whose labels include this symbol. Also, encourage students to look for flammable products the next time they are in a supermarket or hardware store.

Over the course of a week, have students compile a list of flammable products in their Science Notebooks. Ask students to think about what these flammable products have in common and write about their conclusions in their Science Notebooks.

3.4 Chemical Changes

Before You Read

Make a T-chart in your Science Notebook. Label one column *Physical Changes*. Label the other column *Chemical Changes*. In the appropriate columns, write anything you already know about these kinds of changes.

Pure oxygen and hydrogen are flammable. This means that under the right conditions, they can burn rapidly. Having this chemical property, however, does not mean that they are always burning. It means that they have the potential, or the ability, to burn.

Under the right conditions, these two elements can be combined to produce a powerful explosion. It is this type of explosion that helps propel the Space Shuttle into orbit. When hydrogen burns in oxygen, both the hydrogen and the oxygen are chemically changed. A **chemical change** occurs when one type of matter changes into another type of matter. Unlike a physical change, a chemical change results in new substances with properties that are different from the original substances.

In a chemical change, the substances produced can not be easily changed back into the original substances. In the chemical change that launches the Space Shuttle, for example, hydrogen and oxygen change into water and energy. The water and energy cannot be easily turned back into hydrogen and oxygen.

Chemical Properties vs. Chemical Changes

Although they are closely related, a chemical property is different from a chemical change. A chemical property is the ability to undergo a chemical change. A chemical change is the actual transition that occurs when the substance is altered in some way. Flammability is a chemical property, and burning is a chemical change. Chemical properties include the ability to tarnish or the ability to rust. The actual processes of tarnishing and rusting are chemical changes.

Figure 3.13 Chemical changes produce new substances with different properties.

 CONNECTION: Art

Some of the most beautiful paintings in history are frescoes. A fresco is painted with natural pigments on plaster. The colors react with air and plaster to become permanent. Over time, however, moisture can cause chemical changes that damage fresco paintings. Fortunately, scientists have been able to use modern chemicals and even bacteria to restore some of the great works of art.

E L L Strategy

Compare and Contrast Have students refer back to the definitions of the terms *physical change* and *chemical change*. Ask students to draw a Venn diagram comparing and contrasting these two concepts.

Teacher Alert

It is important to stress the differences between chemical properties and chemical changes. Students are likely to confuse these two concepts. A chemical property refers to the potential of an object to change. A substance does not have to actually change in order to have a chemical property.

3.4 Introduce

ENGAGE Instruct students to carefully observe the following demonstration.

In a 500-mL beaker, mix one tablespoon of baking soda with one teaspoon of citric acid crystals. Fill another beaker halfway with water, and pour the mixture into the water.

Record students' observations on the board. Encourage one volunteer to draw and label the first step of the demonstration on the board, and ask another volunteer to draw and label the second step. (You may want to allow time for English language learners to work in pairs to create each step before volunteering to share the steps with the entire class.) Then have the class help two other volunteers identify and label the type of change that occurred in each beaker. (The mixing of baking soda and citric acid crystals is a physical change. The reaction of the solid mixture with water is a chemical change, as evidenced by the production of carbon dioxide bubbles.)

Before You Read

Model the T-chart on the board. Ask students to share with the class what they already know about physical and chemical changes. Record their answers on the board. Have students add to their lists.

Teach

EXPLAIN to students that in this lesson, they will learn to define a chemical change, identify examples, and compare physical and chemical changes.

Vocabulary

chemical change Review the definition of *chemical property*. When a chemical change occurs, the chemical properties of the substance change.

CONNECTION: Art

Water between the wall and the plaster of the fresco causes the paint to crack and peel.

EXTEND Allow students to look at art books with pictures of frescoes, or have them visit a virtual or actual museum to look at frescoes. Have students record their observations in their Science Notebooks.

Teach

EXPLAIN to students that in this section of the lesson, they will learn to identify the chemical changes around them.

As You Read

Encourage students to refer back to earlier sections of their Science Notebooks to help them to formulate their definitions. Have students turn to a partner and read and discuss each other's definitions. Allow students to refine their own definitions after having this conversation.

ANSWER The odor indicates that a chemical change occurred as the milk soured.

 CONNECTION: Biology

Explain to students that plants require sunlight to carry out photosynthesis. Tell them that the ability to convert carbon dioxide and water into sugar and oxygen is a chemical property. The process of photosynthesis is a chemical change.

EXTEND Bring in a house plant and use a paper clip to cover a portion of each leaf with a piece of aluminum foil or cardboard. Leave the plant in a location where it will get plenty of sunlight. After about four days, remove the aluminum foil or cardboard. Have students record their observations in their Science Notebooks.

As You Read

In the appropriate column of your T-chart, write a brief definition of each type of change. Compare your definitions with those of a partner. Rewrite your definitions if necessary.

Sour milk smells different from fresh milk. What does this tell you about the kind of change the milk has undergone?

Chemical Changes All Around

Chemical changes are occurring all the time. Some chemical changes occur quickly, such as a candle burning or food cooking. Others occur more slowly and cannot be noticed until they are almost complete. Fruit ripening, silver tarnishing, iron rusting, and copper forming a green coating called a patina are all slower chemical changes.

Recall the cavern described at the beginning of this chapter. Caverns and the structures within them form when rainwater seeps into cracks in rock. The water carries carbon dioxide from the air and soil. The carbon dioxide and water combine to form a substance called carbonic acid. This acid can break apart rock. Eventually, a large space in the rock— a cavern—is formed.

When water that contains the dissolved rock is exposed to the air in the cavern, it releases the carbon dioxide gas. This process is similar to the release of carbon dioxide bubbles, or fizz, when a carbonated drink is opened. As the carbon dioxide is released, the water deposits the dissolved rock on cavern walls, ceilings, and floors. Over time, the deposits of countless drops of water can form a cone called a stalactite on the ceiling. If the water that drops to the floor of the cave has dissolved rock in it, a structure called a stalagmite can form on the cave floor.

CONNECTION: Biology

Green plants carry out one of the most important chemical changes on Earth. During this chemical change, known as photosynthesis, plants convert carbon dioxide and water into sugar and oxygen. The energy that enables this chemical change to occur comes from the Sun.

The sugar produced during photosynthesis serves as food for most organisms in an environment. Organisms break down the sugar to release the energy they need to live.

Plants break down some of the sugars they produce to release energy for their own life processes. They store the remaining sugars in their tissues. An animal that feeds on a plant thus obtains the stored sugars. Some animals, such as cows and grasshoppers, feed directly on plants. Other animals feed on organisms that eat plants. For example, a hawk might obtain food by eating a mouse that fed on grass.

Sugars are not the only important product of photosynthesis. Living things need the oxygen produced during photosynthesis to use the food they obtain. Through another chemical change known as cellular respiration, living things use oxygen to break down sugars into usable energy.

Differentiate Instruction

Artistic Have students turn a piece of blank paper sideways and fold it in half. On one side of the paper, have them draw an object before it has been chemically changed; on the other side, have them draw the object after it has undergone a chemical change. Tell students to label the object and identify the action that produced the change. For example, a student might choose to draw a picture of wood before and after it has been burned. He or she should label the wood and write *burned* somewhere on the drawing. Encourage students to produce more than one drawing. Combine these drawings with those done in Lesson 3.2 illustrating physical changes. Create a classroom exhibit about physical and chemical changes.

Signs of Chemical Change

Not all chemical changes are as easy to identify. There are several clues that indicate a chemical change has occurred. One clue is often not enough to classify a change as either chemical or physical. A combination of two of these clues, though, provides a good idea of which type of change has occurred.

Change in Energy Energy can take many forms, including light, heat, electricity, or sound. Energy is either absorbed or released during a chemical change. Energy released in any of these forms is a sign that a chemical change has occurred.

Formation of a Gas An antacid tablet is dropped into a glass of water. Shortly afterward, bubbles of gas rise to the surface. The tablet has undergone a chemical change in the water. Whenever a gas is formed during a change, that change is likely to have been a chemical change.

Production of a Solid Sometimes when two liquids are mixed together, a solid material forms and settles to the bottom of the container. The solid is called a precipitate. The formation of a precipitate is a sign that a chemical change has occurred.

Color Change A half-eaten apple turns brown when left out on the counter. This color change is a sign that a chemical change has occurred.

Release of an Odor The smell of rotten eggs is hard to ignore. The odor is produced during a chemical change that occurs as eggs spoil. The release of an odor is another sign that a chemical change has taken place.

Conservation of Mass

The new substances formed during a chemical change have properties different from those of the original substances. Regardless of how different the original and newly formed substances are, however, it is important to know that during a chemical change, matter is neither created nor destroyed. Because matter has mass, this means that no mass is created or destroyed during a chemical change. The fact that mass is neither created nor destroyed has come to be known as the **law of conservation of mass**.

After You Read

1. How is matter altered during a chemical change?
2. Why is burning considered to be a chemical change?
3. Review the information you have recorded in the chart in your Science Notebook. Explain why bending gold into a ring is not considered a chemical change. Suggest a way to make gold undergo a chemical change.

Figure 3.14 Some chemical changes can have beautiful results.

Figure 3.15 The ashes left after a fire are different from the logs that burned. The mass of the ashes is less than the mass of the logs, but mass was not destroyed. Gases are released into the atmosphere during a fire. The mass of the gases plus the mass of the ashes is nearly identical to the mass of the logs that burned.

Chapter 3 Summary

VOCABULARY REVIEW

Check students' sentences or paragraphs to make sure they understand the meaning of each vocabulary term.

Evaluate students' essays using the following criteria:

1. The topic sentence, or main idea, should restate the Key Concept.

2. The supporting paragraphs should incorporate the answers to the Learning Goal questions students have written and include details, facts, and examples they have recorded in their Science Notebooks.

3. The concluding sentence should sum up the main idea of the chapter and restate the Key Concept.

MASTERING CONCEPTS

True or False

1. False, physical
2. False, extensive
3. False, physical
4. True
5. True
6. False, chemical

Short Answer

7. No two substances have exactly the same set of properties. Physical properties can be easily observed and do not require changing the composition of the matter.

8. Both the water vapor and the water droplets are made up of water molecules. The composition does not change during the change of state.

9. It is a chemical property because it describes how silver will change into a different substance under certain conditions.

10. Matter is neither created nor destroyed during chemical changes. Atoms that make up the original substances are rearranged during the chemical change to form new substances. Although there may be some conversion of matter into energy, the mass of the new substances (the products) is almost equal to the mass of the original substances (the reactants).

Chapter 3 Summary

KEY CONCEPTS

3.1 Physical Properties

- A physical property of matter can be observed without changing the composition of the substance.
- Some physical properties of matter can be directly observed, whereas others can be measured.
- Mass, volume, density, texture, and size are examples of physical properties of matter.

3.2 Physical Changes

- A physical change involves an alteration in the form, appearance, or state of matter.
- During physical changes, the composition of matter stays the same.
- Bending, folding, crushing, melting, and freezing are examples of physical changes in matter.

3.3 Chemical Properties

- A chemical property of matter is a characteristic that allows it to change into a different type of matter.
- The abilities to burn, rust, and tarnish are examples of chemical properties.
- Unlike physical properties, chemical properties are only observed when a substance's composition changes in some way.

3.4 Chemical Changes

- During a chemical change, one type of matter is changed into a new type of matter with different properties.
- Burning, rusting, and tarnishing are examples of chemical changes.
- Unlike physical changes, chemical changes result in new types of matter and cannot be easily reversed.
- The law of conservation of mass states that mass is neither created nor destroyed during a chemical change.

VOCABULARY REVIEW

Write each term in a complete sentence or write a paragraph relating several terms.

3.1
physical property, p. 41
property, p. 41
state of matter, p. 42
melting point, p. 42
boiling point, p. 42
specific gravity, p. 42
intensive property, p. 43
extensive property, p. 43

3.2
physical change, p. 44

3.3
chemical property, p. 47
flammability, p. 48
flammable, p. 48

3.4
chemical change, p. 49
law of conservation of mass, p. 51

PREPARE FOR CHAPTER TEST

To prepare for the chapter test, create a question from each Learning Goal. Use the information in your Science Notebook to answer each question. Then use these answers to write a well-developed essay about the chapter. Use the Key Concept on the first page of this chapter as your topic sentence.

Reading Comprehension Workbook, p. 16

Vocabulary Review Workbook, p. 14

MASTERING CONCEPTS

True or False
If the statement is true, write "true." If it is false, change the underlined word or words to make the statement true.

1. The density of water is one of water's <u>chemical</u> properties.

2. Mass and volume are <u>intensive</u> properties of matter.

3. Shaping metal into a wire is a <u>chemical</u> change.

4. During a <u>physical</u> change, the composition of matter does not change.

5. A substance is <u>flammable</u> if it burns easily and quickly.

6. Rusting is an example of a <u>physical</u> change.

Short Answer
Answer each of the following in a sentence or brief paragraph.

7. Why are physical properties important when separating samples of matter?

8. Water vapor in the air changes into liquid water droplets in clouds. Explain why this is a physical change in matter.

9. Which type of property describes silver's ability to tarnish? Explain your answer.

10. Describe the law of conservation of mass in your own words.

Critical Thinking
Use what you have learned in this chapter to answer each of the following.

11. **Identify** List several signs that indicate a chemical change has taken place.

12. **Design** Describe a method by which you can show that the law of conservation of mass is true when an ice cube melts.

13. **Compare and Contrast** Explain the difference between a chemical property and a chemical change.

14. **Classify** Label each of the following as a physical or a chemical change: (a) A copper statue turns green. (b) Batter is baked into a cake. (c) Water freezes into ice. (d) Sulfur shatters when hit.

Standardized Test Question
Choose the letter of the response that correctly answers the question.

15. Which figure clearly identifies a chemical change?

A.

B.

C.

D.

Test-Taking Tip
Don't get stuck on a difficult question. Instead, make a small mark next to the question. Remember to go back and answer the question later. Other parts of the test may give you a clue that will help you answer the question.

Critical Thinking

11. Change in color or odor, release of light or heat, change in energy, and production of a solid or gas are all signs that a chemical change has taken place.

12. Let the ice cube melt in a container on the pan of a mass balance and show that the balance does not move. Matter has neither been created nor destroyed during this physical change.

13. A chemical property of a substance is the potential, or ability, to change. A chemical change is the process through which the substance actually changes into a different substance.

14. a) chemical b) chemical c) physical d) physical

Standardized Test Question

15. D

Reading Links

Investigating Solids, Liquids, and Gases with Toys: States of Matter and Changes in State

The 24 hands-on experiments in this book illustrate the properties of matter in simple, effective ways. Each activity is clearly presented and accompanied by helpful visuals, scientific background information, and ideas for extensions and variations. The experiments are classroom-tested and developed with support from the National Science Foundation, and with titles like "Burping Bottle" and "Marshmallow in a Syringe," they are sure to engage a broad audience.

Jerry Sarquis, Lynn Hogue, Mickey Sarquis, and Linda Woodward. Terrific Science Press. 283 pp. Illustrated. Trade ISBN 978-1-883822-28-6.

Ceramics: From Magic Pots to Man-Made Bones

Pottery-making depends upon knowledge of physical and chemical properties and changes. This book presents the history, science, and modern development of ceramics in a comprehensive and accessible way, making it a great resource for students who are interested in extending their study of matter and its characteristics.

Ruth G. Kassinger. Lerner Publishing Group. 80 pp. Illustrated. Library ISBN 978-0-7613-2108-8.

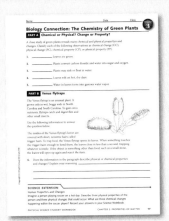

Curriculum Connection
Workbook, p. 17

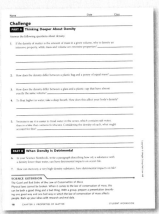

Science Challenge
Workbook, p. 18

3A Properties of a Candle

This prechapter introduction activity is designed to determine what students already know about the differences between physical and chemical properties of matter by engaging them in observing, examining, comparing, recording data, and making conclusions.

Objectives

• observe the physical properties of an unlighted candle
• observe the chemical properties of a lighted candle
• record data in a suitable way
• communicate conclusions

Planning

 15–20 minutes   groups of 3–4 students

Materials (per group)

• small candle
• matches
• metric ruler
• balance
• candleholder or foil-cupcake pan liner half-filled with sand

Advance Preparation

• Use small birthday cake candles. Have extra candles available in case some of them get broken.
• Remind students to keep hands, hair, and clothing away from the candle flames.

• Remind students of the locations of the fire extinguishers, as they will be working with open flames.
• Have students wear closed-toe shoes for this lab investigation.

Engagement Guide

• Challenge students to think about how they can predict what will happen in the experiment by asking these questions:
  • *Which type of property—physical or chemical—do you think will be easier to observe?* (Physical, because observing most physical properties only involves using your senses, not other materials.)
  • *What do you think will happen to the candle as it burns?* (Students should recognize that the candle will get smaller as it burns because the chemical reaction changes the candle wax into gases and vapors that escape into the air. They should also mention that the reaction produces heat and light.)
• Encourage students to communicate their conclusions in creative ways.

Going Further

Have students investigate the physical and chemical properties of sugar. Students can use a magnifying glass to help them observe the physical properties of sugar. Have students add sugar to water to demonstrate a physical change. The chemical properties of sugar can be observed by heating a small amount of sugar in a flameproof container.

3B Physical Properties of Matter

Objectives

• measure mass and volume and calculate density
• identify an unknown substance by comparing density values
• communicate conclusions

Skill Set

measuring, recording and analyzing data, comparing and contrasting, stating conclusions

Planning

 40–45 minutes   groups of 3–4 students

Materials

Materials for this activity are listed in the Student Laboratory Manual.

Advance Preparation

Make the saltwater mixture by adding and stirring salt into 1,000 mL of water until no more salt will dissolve. The unknown substance can be any of the three known substances. 100-mL graduated cylinders can be used if 50-mL cylinders are not available.

Answers to Observations: Data Table 1

Answers will vary. Student calculations should show correct substitution of known values into the density equation and values with units of g/mL. Students should obtain density values approximately as follows: water, 1.0 g/mL; rubbing alcohol, 0.76 g/mL; salt water, 1.2–1.3 g/mL. The density of the unknown liquid will depend on the substance used.

Answers to Analysis and Conclusions

1. Rubbing alcohol has the lowest density. Salt water has the highest density.

2. The density of the unknown substance can be compared to the densities of the three known substances to determine the identity of the unknown substance. Answers will vary depending on the unknown selected by the teacher.

3. Students should describe using the library or Internet to research the densities of pyrite and gold, measuring the mass and volume of the sample, calculating the density of the sample, and using the density to determine the identity of the substance.

Going Further

Pennies minted before 1982 were made mostly of copper, whereas those minted after 1982 were made mostly of zinc with a thin copper coating. Have students determine the densities of pre- and post-1982 pennies. They should calculate densities of about 8.85 g/mL and 7.14 g/mL for pre- and post-1982 pennies, respectively. Have students graph the three densities so they can visualize the difference between them. They should plot volume on the x-axis and mass on the y-axis.

3C Chemical Changes

Objectives

- measure the temperature change caused by a chemical change
- observe evidence of a chemical change
- record data
- communicate results

Skill Set

measuring, recording and analyzing data, classifying, drawing conclusions

Planning

 45–50 minutes   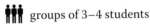 groups of 3–4 students

Materials

Materials for this activity are listed in the Student Laboratory Manual.

Advance Preparation

Use fresh, clean, steel wool, not steel wool scrubbing pads coated with soap. Steel wool pads are available in several coarsenesses, or grades, at home improvement and paint stores. The finest grades of steel wool, sold as 0000 and 000, work the best. Tear steel wool pads into quarters. 100-mL graduated cylinders can be used if 50-mL cylinders are not available.

Answers to Observations: Data Table 1

Answers will vary. Students should note that the reaction produces gas bubbles, an indicator of chemical change. Temperature recordings should show that the water temperature decreases after the effervescent tablet is added to the water.

Answers to Observations: Data Table 2

Answers will vary. The steel wool should initially look silver or gray and shiny. Temperature recordings should show that the temperature around the thermometer increases when the steel wool is wrapped around it. After five minutes have passed, the steel wool should appear darker and less shiny, an indication that a chemical change has taken place.

Answers to Analysis and Conclusions

1. The temperature decreased when the effervescent tablet was added to the water. The tablet disappeared and a gas was also given off.

2. The temperature increased when the steel wool was placed around the thermometer. Students should not conclude that a chemical change occurred just because the temperature increased.

3. Yes, chemical changes occurred in both cups, as evident by the production of a gas and a color change. The fact that a temperature change also occurred further supports the conclusion.

Going Further

Obtain an instant cold pack and/or hot pack. Cold packs and hot packs are often found at drug stores or stores that sell hiking and camping equipment. Allow students to feel the pack before you activate the chemicals in it. After you squeeze the pack, allow students to feel the pack again. Have students compare the chemical reaction in the pack to the activities they have completed in class. Ask students if they think the pack will continue to remain hot or cold for a long time. If time permits, allow students to feel the pack again after 30 minutes or more has passed to see if the temperature of the pack has changed. Students should observe that the chemical reaction will eventually stop, causing the pack to return to its original temperature.

Chapter 4 Lessons

Introduce Chapter 4

As a starting activity, use Lab 4A on page 19 of the Laboratory Manual.

ENGAGE Ask students to look at the photograph of the ice carving. Ask them if they have ever seen an ice carving. Have students share their experiences. Encourage them to work in pairs to brainstorm different uses for ice carvings. Discuss with students the temporary nature of most ice carvings due to the inevitable melting of the ice once the temperature rises. Ask students to consider places on Earth where ice carvings would last the longest.

Think About Comparing Forms of Matter

ENGAGE Discuss with students their experiences with ice and water. Ask: *How does it feel to put your hands in a bowl of water? How does it feel to hold an ice cube in your hand?* Record students' responses on the board. Encourage students to use all of their senses to describe the water and the ice. Have students record their observations in their Science Notebooks. After students have each written a short paragraph comparing ice to water, ask them to share their paragraphs aloud with partners.

Chapter 4 — States of Matter

KEY CONCEPT Matter exists in different states and can change from one state to another when it gains or releases energy.

Working many hours in freezing conditions, artists from around the world carve amazing castles out of ice like the one shown above. Visitors bundled in thick coats can enjoy the frozen details of the icy structure.

Once winter is over, the ice palace gradually turns into a huge puddle of water. This chapter will explore the differences between the solid castle, the liquid water, and the gaseous air around them. It will also explain how matter changes from one form to another.

Think About Comparing Forms of Matter

Different forms of matter surround you each day. The same type of matter can have different properties in different forms. Think about a sample of ice and a sample of liquid water. Observe a sample of each, if possible.

- In your Science Notebook, make a T-chart. Label one side *Ice* and the other side *Liquid Water*. In the chart, write several words or phrases describing water in each form.

- Use the information in your chart to write a well-developed paragraph comparing ice to liquid water. Mention how they might be alike or different.

www.scilinks.org
States of Matter **Code: WGPS04**

54

Chapter 4 Planning Guide			
Instructional Periods	**National Standards**	**Lab Manual**	**Workbook**
4.1 2 Periods	A.2, B.1, G.1, G.2; A.2, B.2, G.1, G.2; UCP.1	**Lab 4A: p. 19** Properties of Liquids **Lab 4B: pp. 20–22** It's a Gas! **Lab 4C: pp. 23–24** Making Ice Cream	Key Concept Review p. 19 Vocabulary Review p. 20 Interpreting Diagrams p. 21 Reading Comprehension p. 22 Curriculum Connection p. 23 Science Challenge p. 24
4.2 2 Periods	A.2, B.1; A.2, B.2; UCP.5		
4.3 2 Periods	B.1, G.1, G.2; B.2, G.1, G.2; UCP.2		
4.4 2 Periods	A.2, B.1, B.2, G.1, G.3; A.2, B.2, B.5, B.6, G.1, G.3; UCP.3		

Middle School Standard; High School Standard; Unifying Concept and Principle

4.1 Solids

Before You Read

Create a K-W-L-S-H chart in your Science Notebook. In the column labeled *K*, write a few notes describing what you already know about solids. In the column labeled *W*, write two questions you have about solids. Note some examples of solids with which you are familiar.

A solid planet, such as Earth, is very different from the gaseous air that surrounds it and the liquid water on its surface. Solids, liquids, and gases are three states of matter. Recall from Chapter 3 that a state of matter is the physical form in which a substance exists.

There is a fourth state of matter known as **plasma** (PLAZ muh). It is less abundant on Earth than solids, liquids, and gases are. However, plasma is common throughout the universe. In fact, scientists estimate that more than 99 percent of the known matter in the universe is in the plasma state. Matter exists in the plasma state only at extremely high temperatures. Under these conditions, the particles of matter break apart. Plasma is found naturally in lightning bolts, auroras, and stars. It is created artificially in fluorescent bulbs and neon lights.

Figure 4.1 Throughout a galaxy, matter exists in different states. What are four states of matter?

Learning Goals

- Identify four states of matter.
- Describe the characteristics of a solid.
- Differentiate between crystalline and amorphous solids.

New Vocabulary

plasma
solid
crystalline solid
amorphous solid

Recall Vocabulary

state of matter, p. 42

 **Extend It!**

Plasma televisions are a popular form of technology. Use resource materials or the Internet to find out what a plasma television is and how it works.

4.1 Introduce

ENGAGE Have students think about the different states of matter. Ask: *What are the four states of matter? Can you give an example of a type of matter that exists in each state? Do some types of matter exist in multiple states?* Draw four columns on the board and label them *Solid, Liquid, Gas,* and *Plasma*. Record students' examples in the proper columns.

Vocabulary terms are listed on the first student page of each lesson. You may wish to preview the terms before introducing each lesson. Strategies for teaching the vocabulary appear on the pages where the terms are introduced.

Before You Read

Ask students to share with the class what they already know about solids. Ask students to share with a partner one question they have about solids. Model a K-W-L-S-H chart on the board. Students should record their answers in the first two columns of the K-W-L-S-H charts in their Science Notebooks.

Teach

EXPLAIN to students that in this lesson, they will learn to identify four states of matter. They will also learn to describe the characteristics of a solid and to differentiate between crystalline and amorphous solids.

Use the Visual: Figure 4.1

ANSWER Solid, liquid, gas, and plasma are four states of matter.

 Extend It!

In a plasma TV, neon and xenon gases are sandwiched between two glass plates. As electricity passes from one glass plate to the other, the neon and xenon gases are ionized and form a plasma that emits ultraviolet light. The light reacts with a phosphor-coated screen to produce color.

ELL Strategy

Activate Background Knowledge Ask students to discuss in small groups what they already know about the different states of matter. Suggest that students refer to their Science Notebooks as a reference for the discussion. Students should also add to their K-W-L-S-H charts as they talk. For reference, provide each group with examples or pictures of matter in each of the four states.

Vocabulary

plasma Explain to students that the word *plasma* comes from the Greek *plásma*, which means "to form or mold." Ask students to think about examples of matter found in the plasma state that are "formed" or "molded," such as the particles of neon, which can be formed into letters and shapes within a glass container.

Teach

EXPLAIN to students that they will learn about the characteristics of solids.

Figure It Out: Figure 4.2

ANSWER **1.** A paintbrush is another solid, as are an easel, an apron, and a palette.
2. They resemble a cube.

PEOPLE IN SCIENCE

In 2001, three scientists—Eric Cornell and Carl Weiman from the University of Colorado and Wolfgang Ketterle from the Massachusetts Institute of Technology—won the Nobel Prize in Physics for "the achievement of Bose-Einstein condensation in dilute gases of alkali atoms, and for early fundamental studies of the properties of the condensates." They proved that Bose was right.

EXTEND Discuss with students how it must have felt for Bose to discover an error in the middle of his lecture. Have students write in their Science Notebooks about the benefits that can come from making mistakes. English language learners can share their own experiences of learning from mistakes with peers before writing their responses in their Science Notebooks.

As You Read

Have students work in pairs to discuss what they have learned thus far about solids. Ask students to record this information in their Science Notebooks.

ANSWER The particles do not move fast enough to overcome the forces of attraction between them.

As You Read

Add some information that you have learned about solids to the *L* column of the chart in your Science Notebook. Compare your chart with that of a partner. Make any necessary additions or corrections.

Why do the particles in a solid stay close together?

Solid

Figure 4.2 Artists apply paints to a solid canvas to create paintings such as this one, by Vincent van Gogh. The particles in a solid are packed together and vibrate in place.

Characteristics of a Solid

At a glance, the canvas painting in **Figure 4.2** looks like a perfectly smooth surface. Under high magnification, however, the tiny particles that make it up can be seen. Recall that matter is made up of smaller particles, such as atoms and molecules. These particles are in constant motion. As they move, they attract, or pull, other particles toward themselves. The state of matter is determined by how fast the particles move and how strongly they are attracted to one another.

The canvas painting is an example of a solid. Matter in the **solid** state has a definite volume and shape. Even if the painting is moved to a different wall in another museum, its shape and size will not change.

A solid maintains its volume and shape because the particles in it are packed tightly in relatively fixed positions. They are held together by strong attractive forces. This does not mean that the particles in a solid are completely still. They move, but they only vibrate about fixed points.

PEOPLE IN SCIENCE Satyendra Nath Bose (1894–1974)

Is there a fifth state of matter? Scientists say that there is, but it is rare and was extremely difficult to discover. Just ask Bengali Indian scientist Satyendra Nath Bose.

While working in the physics department at the University of Dhaka, Bose gave a lecture about light. His intention was to show his students how a theory predicted an outcome that was not supported by experimental results. However, Bose realized that his calculations showed that the data actually agreed with the prediction. After extensive analysis, he concluded that a basic behavior of particles was not true for microscopic particles.

Unfortunately, physics journals ignored his conclusions, arguing that he had made a mistake. Disappointed that his conclusions were rejected, Bose wrote to Albert Einstein to describe his findings. Einstein immediately recognized the importance of Bose's discovery, and Bose's ideas were finally accepted.

Einstein used Bose's discovery to predict the existence of a fifth state of matter. It is a dense collection of atom parts called bosons, and it exists at extremely low temperatures. Its existence was finally proven in experiment in 1995.

Differentiate Instruction

Artistic Have students refer back to the paragraphs they wrote in their Science Notebooks at the start of the chapter. Ask students to turn their paragraphs into poems that describe the different characteristics of a solid.

Field Study

Take students on a field trip to a local electronics store that sells plasma televisions. Have students record their observations of the plasma TVs and compare them to the other types of televisions sold in the store.

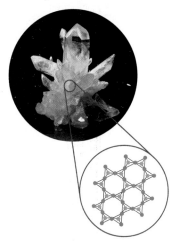
Crystalline (Quartz)

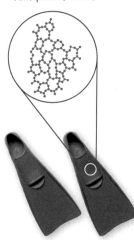
Amorphous (Rubber)

Figure 4.3 Rubber and quartz are different kinds of solids. Notice how the particles are arranged in each one. The particles in quartz are arranged in repeating rows, whereas the particles in rubber are not.

Types of Solids

Rubber flippers are not quite the same as quartz crystals, yet rubber and quartz are both solids. Rubber and quartz are different types of solids, however. Solids can be classified as crystalline solids or amorphous solids according to the arrangement of their particles.

Crystalline Solids   In quartz, the particles are arranged in an orderly three-dimensional arrangement called a crystal. **Figure 4.3** shows the arrangement of particles in a quartz crystal. Notice how the particles form a pattern. A solid in which the particles are arranged in a repeating pattern of rows is known as a **crystalline** (KRIHS tul lin) **solid**. Salt, sugar, sand, and ice are other examples of crystalline solids.

Amorphous Solids   In some solids, the particles are not arranged in any particular order. They often consist of large particles that are not arranged in a repeating pattern. A solid in which the particles are found in a random arrangement is known as an **amorphous** (uh MOR fus) **solid**. Rubber, glass, and wax are examples of amorphous solids.

After You Read

1. Which three states of matter are commonly found on Earth?
2. Describe a solid in terms of volume and shape.
3. Review the K-W-L-S-H chart you created in your Science Notebook. Use the information you have recorded in the chart to describe the difference between amorphous solids and crystalline solids.

Explore It!

Use a hand lens or microscope to look at a salt crystal. In your Science Notebook, describe what you see. Draw a diagram. Explain why salt is classified as a crystalline solid.

● Teach

EXPLAIN to students that they will learn about two different types of solids: crystalline solids and amorphous solids.

Vocabulary

solid   Ask students if they are familiar with any other meanings of the word *solid*. Examples might include someone who can be depended on, such as a "solid citizen." Ask students to relate this definition to matter in the solid state, which has a definite shape and volume.

crystalline solid   Tell students that the word *crystalline* comes from the Greek *krýstallos*, meaning "clear ice." Explain that ice is a crystalline solid because it has a definite shape and volume (solid) and its particles are arranged in a repeating pattern of rows (crystalline).

amorphous solid   Explain to students that the prefix *a-* in the word *amorphous* means "without," and the root *morph* means "shape." Ask students to relate these meanings to the term *amorphous solid*.

Explore It!

Provide students with spoons and plates to spread out the salt and hand lenses to examine the crystals more closely. If possible, obtain kosher salt or rock salt, both of which have large crystals that are easier to see.

● Assess

Use the After You Read questions and the Alternative Assessment to help you evaluate students' understanding of the lesson.

Background Information

Sir Nevill Mott was awarded the Nobel Prize in Physics in 1977 for his work with amorphous materials. His work helped other scientists understand the atomic composition of amorphous materials, which are disordered systems and are quite complex. Mott's work with amorphous materials also led to a better understanding of electric conductivity in disordered systems.

Alternative Assessment

Provide each student with a blank K-W-L-S-H chart and ask him or her to fill in as many of the columns as possible with accurate information about solids.

After You Read

1. Matter is commonly found on Earth in the solid, liquid, and gas states.
2. A solid has a definite volume and a definite shape.
3. The particles in a crystalline solid have a regular, repeating pattern, whereas the particles in an amorphous solid do not. The particles in an amorphous solid are found in a random arrangement.

4.2 Introduce

ENGAGE Bring in a measuring cup filled with a visibly measurable amount of milk. Place several transparent containers with different shapes on a table in front of students. Ask: *What will happen to the milk when I pour it into each container? Will the amount of milk change? How will the milk fill each container?* Ask students to write their predictions in their Science Notebooks. Pour the milk into and out of each container. Have students write their observations in their Science Notebooks. Ask students to share their observations with the class.

Before You Read

Have students work in pairs to turn each lesson heading into a question. Have students share their questions with the class.

Teach

EXPLAIN to students that in this lesson, they will learn to describe the characteristics of a liquid and to define *surface tension* and *viscosity.*

 Vocabulary

liquid Students are probably familiar with the word *liquid* as it relates to the liquids they drink, such as milk, water, or juice. Encourage students to see that all of these liquids have a definite volume (the amount doesn't change), but not a definite shape. If you pour milk into differently-shaped glasses, the amount in each will stay the same, but the milk will take the shape of the container it is in.

surface tension Explain to students that the prefix *sur-* in the word *surface* comes from the French word meaning "above." The word *tension* comes from the Latin *tendere,* which means "to stretch." When the particles of a liquid are stretched above the face or at the surface, it is called surface tension.

viscosity Tell students that the prefix *vis-* comes from the Latin word meaning "force." The prefix *co-* means "with." Explain that the more viscous a liquid is, the more "force" it will need to flow.

Learning Goals

- Describe the characteristics of a liquid.
- Define *surface tension* and *viscosity.*

New Vocabulary

liquid
surface tension
viscosity

Figure 4.4 Hot lava flows from an erupting volcano. Lava is formed from solid rock, but it is quite different from solid rock. Lava is an example of matter in the liquid state.

4.2 Liquids

Before You Read

Turn each heading in this lesson into a question before you read, and write these questions in your Science Notebook. After you read the lesson, answer all your questions. Try to use the vocabulary terms in your answers.

Fiery plumes of lava shoot into the air as a volcano erupts. The heated rock surges and streams onto Earth's surface. Lava is an example of another state in which matter can exist. Lava is rock in the liquid state. Matter in the liquid state is clearly different from matter in the solid state.

Characteristics of a Liquid

Matter in the **liquid** state has a definite volume, but not a definite shape. This means that the amount of liquid in a sample stays the same. If 200 mL of juice is poured from a carton into a tall bottle, the bottle will contain the same 200 mL of juice as the original carton did. Unlike a solid, however, a liquid takes the shape of its container. Juice from a carton will take the shape of a rounded bottle or a square cup.

Like with solids, the characteristics of liquids arise because of the particles within them. The particles in a liquid are close together, but they have enough energy to move past one another. In other words, liquids flow. **Figure 4.5** shows that the particles in a liquid move more rapidly than do those in a solid.

Figure 4.5 There is 200 mL of juice in all three containers, but the juice takes on the different shapes because the particles in a liquid can flow past one another.

ELL Strategy

Compare and Contrast Have students compare and contrast the characteristics of liquids and solids. Tell students to make two-column charts in their Science Notebooks, labeling one column *Similarities* and the other column *Differences.* Have students look through the textbook and their Science Notebooks to record the similarities and differences between solids and liquids. When they have completed their comparisons, have students share their responses with a partner and add any missing information to their charts.

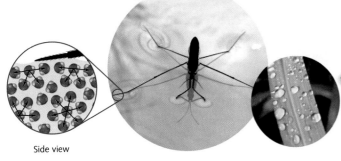

Side view

Figure 4.6 Surface tension enables a water strider to move gently across the surface of ponds, streams, and other quiet waters. Surface tension is also responsible for the formation of water drops.

Surface Tension

A stone thrown into a lake quickly sinks to the bottom. That is not the fate of the water strider shown in **Figure 4.6**. The water strider literally walks on water! How can it accomplish this amazing feat? The attractive forces that exist between the water particles make it possible.

The diagram in Figure 4.6 shows that particles below the surface of a liquid are pulled up, toward the sides, and toward the center. The particles on the surface of a liquid are also pulled toward one another. Since there are no liquid particles above those at the surface, the surface particles are pulled only toward the center and the sides. The effect of these uneven forces acting on the particles at the surface of a liquid is called **surface tension**.

Surface tension makes a liquid seem as if it has a thin film stretched across its surface. If only a small amount of a liquid is present, surface tension pulls the particles into a spherical shape. Raindrops and drops of dew form as a result of surface tension.

Viscosity

Honey drips slowly into a cup of tea. Different liquids flow at different rates. A liquid's resistance to flow is its **viscosity** (VIHS kos uh tee). Honey flows more slowly than water because it has a higher viscosity than water. A liquid's viscosity depends on the attractions between its particles. The stronger the attractions between the particles, the less the particles can flow past one another and the more viscous the liquid is.

After You Read

1. Describe a liquid in terms of its volume and shape.
2. What property of liquids enables water to form raindrops?
3. Review the questions you wrote in your Science Notebook. Give an example of a liquid with a high viscosity and a liquid with a low viscosity.

Figure It Out

1. Why does the water seem to have a thin film on it?
2. How are the forces acting on the particles at the surface of the water different from the forces acting on the particles beneath the surface?

As You Read

In your Science Notebook, write answers to your questions about liquids.

How is the movement of the particles in a liquid different from the movement of the particles in a solid?

Teach

EXPLAIN to students that in this section of the lesson, they will learn about surface tension and viscosity.

Figure It Out: Figure 4.6

ANSWER **1.** Surface tension pulls the water molecules together in such a way that they resist being pulled apart. **2.** The forces beneath the surface pull toward the center in all directions. The forces at the surface are unbalanced and pull into the liquid and toward the sides of the liquid.

As You Read

Ask students to share their questions and answers with the class. If students have the same questions, discuss the answers that they have found.

ANSWER The particles in a liquid can move past each other, whereas the particles in a solid are locked into place and can only vibrate.

Assess

Use the After You Read questions and Alternative Assessment to help you evaluate students' understanding of this lesson.

After You Read

1. A liquid has a definite volume, but it takes the shape of its container.
2. Surface tension enables water to form raindrops. Surface tension is the effect of the uneven forces acting on the particles at the surface of a liquid.
3. Honey has a high viscosity, as do molasses and ketchup; water, vinegar, and milk have low viscosities.

Alternative Assessment

Have each student write two or three of the questions recorded in his or her Science Notebook. Redistribute the questions to other members of the class. Have those students answer the questions and then check back with the author of the questions to see if the answers are correct.

Differentiate Instruction

Kinesthetic Provide groups of students with a container of small marbles and some additional containers of different sizes. Have each group count the number of marbles that it has and then pour the marbles into each of the different containers. Have students record their observations in their Science Notebooks. Ask each student to write a paragraph comparing the behavior of the marbles to the behavior of particles in a liquid.

Key Concept Review
Workbook, p. 19

4.3 Introduce

ENGAGE students by blowing up a balloon. Ask: *What am I putting into this balloon? What is happening to the balloon as I blow into it? What is happening inside the balloon?* Explain to students you are putting air into the balloon and that air is a gas. As you fill the balloon with air, it expands, and the gas particles spread out inside the balloon.

Before You Read

Write the word *gas* on the board. Ask students to write a definition based on what they know about gases and the discussion they have had in class. Do this with students before they read the lesson text. As students continue through the lesson, encourage them to refine their definitions.

● Teach

EXPLAIN that in this lesson, students will be learning to describe the properties of a gas. They will also learn to identify the relationship described by both Boyle's law and Charles's law.

Use the Visual: Figure 4.7

ANSWER Air is in the gas state.

Learning Goals

- Describe the properties of a gas.
- Identify the relationship described by Boyle's law.
- Identify the relationship described by Charles's law.

New Vocabulary

gas
diffusion
force
pressure
pascal
compressed
Boyle's law
Charles's law
absolute zero

Figure 4.7 Heated air spreads out to fill the spaces of giant balloons. In what state of matter is air?

4.3 Gases

Before You Read

In your Science Notebook, create a working definition of the word *gas*. A working definition is one that develops as you read and think about an idea. Write what you know about the term before you begin reading. Then add to that definition as you read and discuss the lesson. Make a drawing of something that contains a gas.

Every year in Albuquerque, New Mexico, some of the most spectacular balloons in the world fill the sky. They come in all shapes and sizes and a dazzling array of colors. What makes it possible for these balloons to leave the ground? The answer is matter in a form you often cannot even see. It is air, which is an example of a gas.

A **gas** is matter that does not have a definite volume or a definite shape. The particles in a gas move rapidly in all directions. Compared to the particles in solids and liquids, gas particles are at great distances from one another.

Because they are moving so quickly, gas particles overcome the attractive forces between them. If a gas is added to a container, the particles move as far apart as possible. As a result, the gas expands to fill its container. It takes on the volume and shape of the container. This is why air can fill balloons of so many different shapes.

As a gas spreads out, the particles become uniformly, or evenly, distributed throughout the container. The spreading of particles throughout a given volume until they become uniformly distributed is known as **diffusion**.

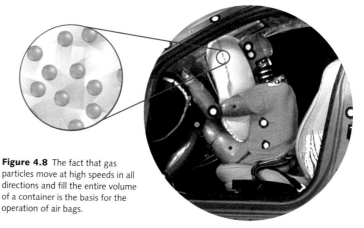

Figure 4.8 The fact that gas particles move at high speeds in all directions and fill the entire volume of a container is the basis for the operation of air bags.

ELL Strategy

Practice Using Vocabulary Throughout the lesson, have students make flashcards with vocabulary terms on one side and definitions on the other. Allow students to test themselves and others in the class on the vocabulary words in the lesson.

Gas Pressure

Imagine pumping air into a volleyball. Inside the ball, the air particles move rapidly in all directions. They collide with each other and the inside wall of the volleyball. As each particle collides with the inside wall of the ball, it exerts a small force. A **force** is a push or pull. The forces of all the individual particles that push on the ball add together to produce pressure. The **pressure** of a gas is the force exerted on a surface divided by the total area over which the force is exerted. The SI unit used to measure pressure is the **pascal** (Pa). One pascal is equal to a force of one newton (N) exerted over an area of one square meter (m^2), or one N/m^2. When discussing air pressure, a more useful unit called the kilopascal (kPa) is used. A kilopascal is 1,000 pascals.

When a small amount of air is pumped into the ball, the pressure is low. When more air is pumped into the ball, more particles collide with the inside wall. This causes the pressure to increase.

Boyle's Law

Unlike with solids and liquids, adding a little pressure to a gas can compress it. A gas is **compressed** when its particles are squeezed together. Breathing air for scuba divers, oxygen for patients in hospitals, and helium for balloons are examples of gases compressed into containers.

In the mid-1600s, the British scientist Robert Boyle recognized that the pressure and the volume of a gas are inversely related. *Inversely related* means that when one value goes up, the other goes down. When the pressure on a gas increases, the volume of the gas decreases. When the pressure on a gas decreases, the volume of the gas increases.

Boyle's law states that for a fixed amount of gas at a constant temperature, the volume of the gas increases as its pressure decreases. Conversely, the volume of a gas decreases as its pressure increases. The general relationship is represented by the graph in **Figure 4.10**.

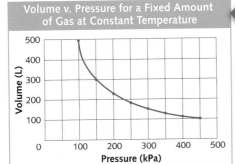

Figure 4.10 The downward curve of the graph shows that the volume of a gas decreases as pressure increases.

Figure 4.9 Without pressure, the volleyball would be soft and squishy. Filling it up with enough air gives the ball the pressure it needs to be used by the players.

Did You Know?

Water in the gas state is known as water vapor. A vapor is matter that exists in the gas state but is generally a liquid or solid at room temperature. Compounds such as carbon dioxide that are usually gases at room temperature are not described as vapors.

Figure It Out

1. What is the volume of the gas at 150 kPa?

2. What is the pressure of the gas when it is compressed to 100 L?

CHAPTER 4   **61**

Differentiate Instruction

Visual Have students draw a diagram that illustrates Boyle's law. Diagrams should show what the particles would look like when the pressure on the gas increases and decreases. Students should use color and labels to help explain their diagrams. Hang students' diagrams around the room.

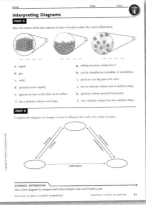

Interpreting Diagrams
Workbook, p. 21

● **Teach**

EXPLAIN to students that in this part of the lesson, they will learn about the relationship between pressure and volume as described by Boyle's law.

Vocabulary

gas Encourage students to think of the gases with which they are familiar, such as air, helium, oxygen, and carbon dioxide. Explain that a gas does not have a definite volume or shape. As you blow up a balloon with air or helium, the gas inside fills and takes the shape of the balloon.

diffusion Explain to students that the prefix *dif-* in the word *diffusion* means "not," and the root *fuse* means "together." When a gas *diffuses*, it spreads out; its particles are "not together."

force Ask students if they are familiar with any other meanings of the word *force*. Examples might include "forcing" someone to do something. Ask students to relate this definition to the scientific meaning of a push or pull on an object.

pressure Ask students to think about how it feels when they are under pressure. Encourage them to relate this to the feeling of being forced or pushed to do something that they might resist doing. Make sure students understand the meaning of the term *area* so that they can understand the definition of pressure as "force per unit area."

pascal Explain to students that a pascal is the SI unit of pressure, named in honor of the scientist Blaise Pascal. Direct students' attention to the fact that the unit is written with a lowercase *p* (pascal) but abbreviated with an uppercase *P* and lowercase *a (Pa)*.

compressed Tell students that the prefix *com-* in the word *compress* means "together." When a gas is *compressed*, its particles are "pressed together."

Boyle's law Explain to students that Boyle's law is named for Robert Boyle, who formulated it. Emphasize to students that Boyle's law is an inverse relationship.

Figure It Out: Figure 4.10

ANSWER **1.** 300 L **2.** 450 kPa

Teach

 EXPLAIN to students that in this part of the lesson, they will learn about the relationship between volume and temperature as described by Charles's law.

 Vocabulary

Charles's law Tell students that Charles's law is named for the scientist Jaques Charles. Emphasize to students that Charles's law is a direct relationship.

absolute zero Discuss with students the meaning of the word *absolute*. Encourage them to see that when something is absolute, it is whole or pure. At a temperature of absolute zero, matter would be purely nothing. It would cease to exist.

As You Read

When each pair has finished its definition of *gas*, have a class discussion. Try to come up with a common definition for the term *gas*.

[ANSWER] Gas particles move so fast they overcome attractive forces between them and expand as far as a container will allow.

 CONNECTION: Biology

Fish are the only vertebrates that live in the deep sea. These fish are small and have jelly-like skin to help them survive the extreme pressure of the deep sea. These fish also live in darkness, as light cannot penetrate the deep sea. As a result, many of these fish have very small eyes and are blind.

Assess

Use the After You Read questions and the Alternative Assessment to help you evaluate students' understanding of the lesson.

After You Read

1. Paragraphs should include the idea that a gas has no definite volume or shape.
2. For a fixed amount of gas at a constant temperature, the volume of the gas is inversely related to the pressure.
3. Volume and temperature are directly related. As one quantity changes, the other changes in the same way.

As You Read

Refine your definition of *gas*. Create a list of examples of objects that contain gases.

How is the motion of gas particles different from the motion of particles in liquids and solids?

CONNECTION: Biology

Fish that normally live deep in the sea die when they are brought to the surface. The reason is that water pressure increases with depth. As the fish are brought upward, the pressure on them decreases. The decrease in pressure results in an increase in the volume of gases in their bodies. This causes cells, bladders, and other parts of their bodies to burst.

Charles's Law

How can a balloon be popped? The obvious way is to poke it with something sharp. There is another way, however. Heating a balloon will make it pop, as well. Why? When a balloon is heated, the particles of air inside it start moving faster. As the particles move faster, they move farther apart. This increases the volume of the air. When the volume increases by more than the balloon can stretch, the balloon pops.

The relationship between the volume and temperature of a gas was identified by French scientist Jacques Charles in 1787. **Charles's law** states that for a fixed amount of gas, the volume of the gas increases as its temperature increases. Conversely, the volume of a gas decreases as its temperature decreases. In other words, volume and temperature are directly related.

Figure 4.11 shows the relationship identified by Charles's law. Note that this graph uses the Celsius temperature scale, which is described in Chapter 1. The graph shows solid, straight lines for each gas. As the temperature approaches −273° Celsius, or 0 K, the lines becomes dashed. The reason is that 0 K is called **absolute zero**. At this temperature, the particles of matter would come to a complete stop. There is no temperature lower than absolute zero.

Figure 4.11 The volume of a gas is directly related to temperature. As one quantity changes, the other changes in the same way.

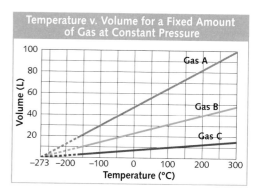

After You Read

1. Review the notes you wrote in your Science Notebook. Based on the information you recorded about the word *gas*, write a well-developed paragraph describing a gas in terms of volume and shape.
2. Explain Boyle's law.
3. Which quantities describing a gas are related by Charles's law? Is the relationship direct or inverse? Explain your answers.

Alternative Assessment

Ask students to define the term *gas* without referring to their Science Notebooks. When they are satisfied with their definitions, have each student turn to a partner and compare and discuss responses.

Differentiate Instruction

Visual Have each student draw a diagram that illustrates Charles's law. Diagrams should show what the particles would look like as the temperature of the gas increases and decreases. Students should use color and labels to help explain their diagrams. Hang students' diagrams around the room.

4.4 Changes of State

Before You Read

You can usually trace every effect back to its cause. In your Science Notebook, describe an everyday example of a cause and its effect. Look for examples of cause and effect as you complete this lesson.

How can a cook know a turkey is done? One way is to use a pop-up thermometer. A pop-up thermometer consists of a small stick on a spring attached to a soft metal. The metal is a solid when the turkey is cold. When it reaches the correct temperature, however, the metal changes into a liquid, and the stick pops up.

The change that the metal in this thermometer undergoes is a change of state. A **change of state** is the conversion of a substance from one physical form to another. Recall from Chapter 3 that a change of state is a physical change. The composition of a substance does not change as the substance is converted from one state to another.

Energy

All changes of state involve a change in energy. Recall that energy is the ability to do work or cause change. Energy exists in many different forms. The energy of motion is called kinetic energy. Any moving object, even a tiny particle of matter, has kinetic energy. The more kinetic energy a particle has, the faster and farther it moves. Particles with less kinetic energy move slower and stay closer together than do particles with more energy.

The total kinetic energy of all the particles in a sample is known as **thermal energy**. When matter changes from one state to another, thermal energy is absorbed or released. Thermal energy that is transferred from one substance to another is called heat. When matter is heated, it gains thermal energy. Matter releases thermal energy as it cools. Some particles in a sample of matter may have more energy than others. The average kinetic energy of all the particles is the sample's **temperature.**

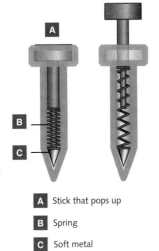

A Stick that pops up

B Spring

C Soft metal

Figure 4.12 Pop-up thermometers use a change of state to show when a turkey is cooked. A change of state is a physical change.

Learning Goals

- Define *change of state*.
- Describe how energy is related to changes of state.
- Compare different changes of state.
- Investigate the heating curve of water.

New Vocabulary

change of state
thermal energy
temperature
melting
freezing
freezing point
vaporization
boiling
evaporation
condensation
sublimation
endothermic process
exothermic process

Recall Vocabulary

melting point, p. 42
boiling point, p. 42

4.4 Introduce

ENGAGE Distribute an ice cube to each student. Ask: *What will happen to the ice cube as you hold it in your hand? How does it feel in your hand? How is the ice cube changing?* Tell students the ice cube starts as a solid. As heat from the hand warms the ice cube, the solid changes into a liquid. In both states, liquid and solid, the identity of the substance stays the same.

Before You Read

Draw a two-column chart on the board. Label one column *Cause* and the other column *Effect*. Ask students to think about the ice cube melting in their hands. Record students' responses on the board. Have students create cause-and-effect charts in their Science Notebooks and fill in the columns as they progress through the lesson.

Teach

EXPLAIN to students that in this lesson, they will learn to define a change of state. They will also learn how energy is related to changes of state. Students will be able to compare melting, freezing, vaporization, condensation, and sublimation. Finally, students will investigate the heating curve of water.

 Vocabulary

change of state Tell students that when a substance goes from a solid to a liquid and back or from a liquid to a gas and back, those are changes of state. Explain that plasma is not included in change of state because of the nature of the matter.

thermal energy Explain to students that the word *thermal* comes from the Greek *thérmē*, meaning "heat," and the word *energy* comes from the Greek word *énergos*, which means "active." Ask students to relate these meanings to the definition of the term.

temperature Discuss with students their understanding of the term *temperature*. Emphasize to students that temperature is not a measure of heat. It is a measure of the average kinetic energy of all the particles in a sample. Then ask students to relate temperature, heat, and thermal energy.

Differentiate Instruction

Kinesthetic Have a group of students model the change in movement of a particle of matter as its average kinetic energy, or temperature, increases. Ask about five students to stand close together and shift their weight back and forth. Point out that in a solid, the particles are close together and are moving slowly. Explain that as the substance gains thermal energy, the particles will move faster and farther apart. Have students move around more quickly without spreading too far apart. Point out that this is how the particles move in a liquid. Finally, tell students that the temperature has increased so that the particles are now a gas. Students should spread out and move around the room.

Teach

EXPLAIN to students that in this section of the lesson, they will learn about melting.

As You Read

Have students refer back to the two-column charts in their Science Notebooks for ideas. After students have written their sentences, ask them to share with a partner. Then ask for volunteers to share with the class.

ANSWER When matter is heated, it gains thermal energy. Matter releases thermal energy as it cools. A substance absorbs energy when it melts.

 CONNECTION: History

Today, mineral oils are used to make candles rather than animal fats. A wide variety of candles can be purchased for many different occasions. Since the discovery of electricity, candles have been mostly used for decorative and celebratory purposes.

As You Read

Think about the cause-and-effect relationship between energy and change of state. Write a sentence explaining this relationship. Then work with a partner to add more cause-and-effect relationships to the list in your Science Notebook.

How does the energy of a substance change when the substance melts?

Figure 4.14 Gallium is a metal that melts at around 30°C. Because normal body temperature is about 37°C, gallium can melt in a person's hand (*top*). Rather than changing into a liquid at a specific temperature, glass gradually softens. This makes it possible for glass blowers (*bottom*) to shape glass into ornaments and bowls.

Figure 4.13 Researchers have identified evidence of melting in ice sheets and glaciers. When ice melts, a solid absorbs energy and becomes a liquid.

Melting

Figure 4.13 shows massive shelves of ice falling from the Hubbard glacier. The shelves are falling because the glacier is melting. For a glacier to melt, it must be heated. A glacier is water in the solid state. When the particles in a solid absorb thermal energy, they begin to vibrate more vigorously. This faster motion means greater kinetic energy. The increase in the average kinetic energy causes the temperature of the solid to rise.

When the solid has acquired enough energy, the particles vibrate so intensely that the attractive forces between them are overcome. The temperature of the substance stops rising and the particles begin to move past one another. The solid changes into a liquid. The change from the solid state to the liquid state is called **melting**.

The temperature at which a substance changes from a solid to a liquid is the substance's melting point. Melting points vary widely among substances. The melting point of water is 0°C, whereas the melting point of table salt is 801°C. The melting point is a physical property that can be used to identify a substance. **Figure 4.14** shows how melting point can be used to identify the metal gallium.

Unlike crystalline solids, amorphous solids do not have a definite temperature at which they melt. Recall that the particles in an amorphous solid do not have a highly ordered structure. As it is heated, an amorphous solid gradually softens into a liquid over a range of temperatures. Glass, wax, and plastics melt in this way.

CONNECTION: History

Candles have been used for thousands of years as sources of light. Early candles were made from tallow, which is an animal fat. In the Roman Empire, people melted tallow until it became a liquid. They then poured it over the cotton or hemp that would become wicks. When the tallow cooled, it formed a solid candle. Over the years, many improvements have been made to candle-making. The production of modern candles, however, still depends on the melting of a substance onto a wick.

ELL Strategy

Practice Using Vocabulary Have students work in small groups to design vocabulary games using the vocabulary terms from this lesson. Encourage students to think about games that will help them remember the words and their meanings. Allow students to play each other's games.

Teacher Alert

Students often confuse the concepts of temperature, heat, and thermal energy. It might be helpful to create a three-column chart on the board to record the definition and unit of measurement for each concept.

Freezing

A liquid mixture of such ingredients as sugar, cream, and flavoring can be changed into a delicious treat—ice cream! To change a liquid into a solid, the liquid must be cooled.

When a liquid is cooled, it loses thermal energy. As a substance loses thermal energy, its temperature decreases and its particles slow down and come closer together. At some point, the attraction between the particles overcomes their motion. The temperature stops decreasing and the liquid becomes a solid. The change of state from a liquid to a solid is called **freezing**.

The temperature at which a substance freezes is called the **freezing point**. Freezing is the reverse of melting, so the freezing point is the same as the melting point. Therefore, the freezing point of water is 0°C.

Vaporization

On a hot day or while vigorously exercising, a person perspires, or sweats. Perspiring is the body's way of cooling off. Liquid perspiration changes into a gas. How does this help a person cool off?

When a liquid absorbs thermal energy, the motion of the particles increases and the temperature rises. When the liquid has enough energy to overcome the attractive forces between its particles, the particles become free to spread apart. At this point, the temperature stops rising and the liquid changes into a gas. The change of state from a liquid to a gas is called **vaporization** (vay per uh ZAY shun).

Perspiring cools a person because liquid perspiration removes thermal energy from the body as it changes into a gas. There are two different forms of vaporization: boiling and evaporation.

Boiling Vaporization that occurs throughout a liquid is called **boiling**. When a liquid boils, bubbles form within the liquid and rise to the surface. The temperature at which a substance boils is called the substance's boiling point. Like the melting point, the boiling point can be used to identify a substance. The boiling point of water is 100°C.

Boiling points are usually described at sea level. Like other gases, the atmosphere exerts pressure. Changes in atmospheric pressure alter the boiling point of a substance. Atmospheric pressure is lower at higher elevations than it is at sea level. Denver, Colorado, is 1.6 km above sea level. The boiling point of water in Denver is about 95°C.

Figure 4.15 Surrounding ice cream ingredients with ice can change the liquid into a sweet, solid treat. What is this change of state called?

Explore It!

Dip a cotton swab in a small amount of rubbing alcohol. Rub the cotton swab on the back of your hand. Observe the alcohol for several minutes. Then wash your hands.

In your Science Notebook, describe what happened to the alcohol. Tell how your hand felt. Propose an explanation for the sensation you felt.

Background Information

The stronger the bonds are between the particles in a substance, the higher the boiling point, and the harder it becomes to break those bonds to allow for boiling. The pressure of the atmosphere also affects the boiling point of a substance. The closer the substance is to sea level, the higher the atmospheric pressure. As the altitude increases, the atmospheric pressure decreases, as does the boiling point of a substance.

● Teach

 EXPLAIN to students that in this section of the lesson, they will learn about freezing, vaporization, and boiling.

Use the Visual: Figure 4.15

ANSWER This change of state is called freezing.

Vocabulary

melting Explain that the root of the word *melting* comes from the Old English word *mieltan*, meaning "make liquid." When a substance melts, it is made into a liquid.

freezing Discuss with students their experiences with freezing substances. Most students have probably seen and created frozen water. Ask students to identify the relationship between melting and freezing.

freezing point Tell students that the freezing point is the temperature at which a substance changes from a liquid to a solid. Explain that the word *point* comes from the Old French word *pointe*, meaning "a small measure of space or time."

vaporization Explain to students that *vapor* refers to a gas. Thus, vaporization is the process by which a liquid changes into a gas.

boiling Tell students that the word *boil* comes from the Latin word *bulla*, for "bubble." When a liquid boils, bubbles form within it and rise to the surface.

evaporation Explain that the prefix *e-* means "out." When something evaporates, the vapor comes "out" of the liquid. In other words, the liquid turns into a gas at temperatures below the boiling point.

Explore It!

Pour small amounts of rubbing alcohol into glass or plastic containers. Divide students into groups. Provide each group with a container of alcohol and each student with a cotton ball. Encourage students to close their eyes and concentrate of the sensation of the alcohol on their hands.

The alcohol evaporates by absorbing thermal energy from the body. As thermal energy leaves the skin, the skin cools. Evaporation is often called a cooling process.

Teach

EXPLAIN to students that in this section of the lesson, they will learn about condensation and sublimation.

Figure It Out: Figure 4.16

ANSWER **1.** The water in the pot is boiling. **2.** The water in each example vaporizes because it has absorbed thermal energy.

Use the Visual: Figure 4.17

ANSWER Clouds form through condensation.

 Vocabulary

condensation Tell students that the prefix *con-* means "together" and the root *dense* means "thick." When matter condenses, the particles come together and thicken. When a gas condenses to a liquid, the particles lose energy, cool down, and come together.

sublimation Tell students that the prefix *sub-* means "below," and the root *lim* comes from the Latin *līmen*, meaning "threshold." When matter sublimates, it goes from a solid to a gas below the threshold that it would take for it to pass through the liquid state of matter.

endothermic process Explain to students that the prefix *endo-* means "within." Remind students that the root *therm* comes from the Greek *thérmē*, meaning "heat." When matter goes through an endothermic process, it "takes in," or absorbs, thermal energy.

exothermic process Explain to students that the prefix *ex-* comes from the Greek word meaning "out." Remind students of the meaning of the root *therm*. When matter goes through an exothermic process, it "gives out," or releases, heat energy.

Figure 4.16 Bubbles of gas form at the bottom of the water boiling in a kettle. The bubbles rise to the surface and enter the air. In a related process, towels hang on a line to dry as water evaporates into the air.

Evaporation   Perspiring involves a form of vaporization called evaporation. **Evaporation** (ih va puh RAY shun) is vaporization that occurs at the surface of a liquid and at temperatures below the boiling point of a substance. Puddles of water on Earth's surface shrink and eventually disappear due to evaporation.

Condensation

When people look up at the sky, chances are they will see the result of another change of state of matter. White, fluffy clouds that look soft are actually made up of droplets of liquid water. The drops form when water vapor in the air changes from a gas to a liquid.

The change of state from a gas to a liquid is called **condensation** (kahn den SAY shun). Condensation occurs when a gas cools. As a gas releases thermal energy, its particles lose energy and the temperature of the gas drops. This causes the particles to slow down. When the particles reach the point where the forces of attraction pull them together, the temperature stops dropping. The gas changes into a liquid.

Figure 4.17 Clouds that form in the sky often indicate approaching weather patterns. Through which process do clouds form?

The condensation point of a substance is the temperature at which a gas condenses. Condensation is the reverse of boiling. Therefore, the condensation point is the same as the boiling point at a given pressure.

Sublimation

Recall from Chapter 3 that some substances can change directly from the solid state to the gas state. The change of state in which a solid changes directly to a gas is called **sublimation** (sub luh MAY shun). During sublimation, the particles of a solid absorb enough energy so that they change from being very tightly packed to being very spread apart. In addition to dry ice, snow is known to undergo sublimation at temperatures below the freezing point of water. Sublimation enables astronomers to observe comets, such as the comet in **Figure 4.18**.

Figure 4.18 As a comet approaches the Sun, some of the frozen, solid gases inside it change into gases through sublimation. This process results in the tail that is visible from Earth.

Teacher Alert

Reinforce the information presented in the Did You Know? feature, as students frequently confuse the concepts of water vapor and steam.

 **Strategy**

Model Ask students to work in groups to make models of the particles in a solid, a liquid, and a gas. Provide students with materials such as toothpicks and marshmallows to help them model the particle configurations. Then have students use their models to demonstrate the changes of state they have learned about: melting, freezing, vaporization, condensation, and sublimation.

Analyzing a Heating Curve

A change in energy is involved in every type of change of state. Some changes involve the absorption of energy. Melting, vaporization, and sublimation occur when matter absorbs energy. A process that absorbs energy is called an **endothermic** (en doh THUR mihk) **process**. Matter absorbs thermal energy when it is heated.

Other changes involve the release of energy. Freezing and condensation occur when matter releases energy. A process in which energy is given off or removed from a substance is called an **exothermic** (ek soh THUR mihk) **process**. Matter releases thermal energy when it is cooled.

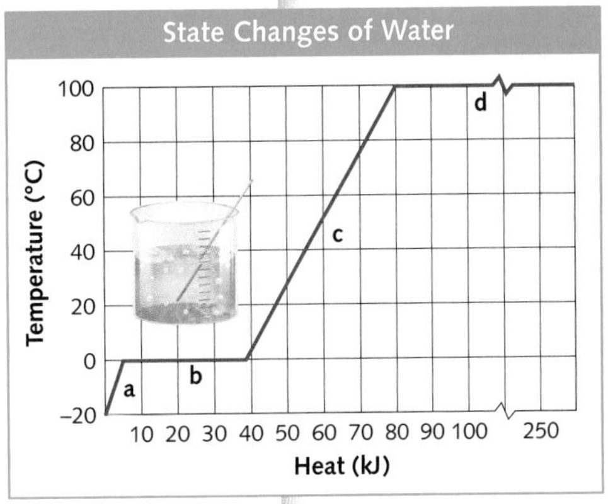

Figure 4.19 shows how the temperature of water changes as the water is heated. This type of graph is called a heating curve. Find −20°C on the graph. At this temperature, water is solid ice. As the ice is heated, the particles gain energy. This causes the temperature to rise. During the portion of the graph labeled *a*, the temperature of the ice is increasing.

When the ice reaches a temperature of 0°C, the melting point of water, it changes to a liquid. Notice from the flat section of the graph labeled *b* that the temperature does not change as the ice melts. All of the energy absorbed by the ice goes into overcoming the attractive forces between the particles. At that point, the water is a liquid.

Once the change of state is complete, heating the water causes its temperature to rise once again. The temperature of the water rises throughout the portion of the graph labeled *c*. When the temperature of the water reaches 100°C, the boiling point of water, the water changes to a gas. At this temperature, all of the energy absorbed by the liquid goes into overcoming the attractive forces between the particles. The portion of the graph labeled *d* represents vaporization. After the attractive forces are overcome, the water is a gas. Any additional energy then causes the temperature of the gas to increase.

State Changes of Water

Figure 4.19 The heating curve of water shows how the temperature of a sample changes as heat is added.

Explain It!

One important cycle on Earth is the water cycle. This cycle involves several changes in the state of matter. In your Science Notebook, describe at least two changes of state from the water cycle. If necessary, conduct research to learn more about the cycle.

After You Read

1. Explain what happens when matter changes from one state to another.
2. What change of state is the reverse of freezing?
3. Describe what the flat portions of the heating curve of water represent.
4. In your Science Notebook, review the causes and effects you have described. In a well-developed paragraph, identify the two changes of state that are exothermic processes and explain your answer.

Teach

EXPLAIN that in this last section of the lesson, students will learn to analyze a heating curve.

Use the Visual: Figure 4.19

The heating curve can also be used to analyze what happens to a sample of water that is cooled. Instead of reading the graph from left to right, the graph can be read from right to left, beginning at portion d of the graph. As heat is removed from water vapor, the water vapor condenses into a liquid. Then its temperature decreases until it reaches the freezing point. At the freezing point, the liquid changes into solid ice.

Explain It!

Students should mention evaporation of water from Earth's surface and oceans. They should also mention condensation of water vapor to form clouds. They might mention freezing, which results in snow and hail.

Assess

Use the After You Read questions and the Alternative Assessment to help you evaluate students' understanding of the lesson.

After You Read

1. When matter changes from one state to another, the arrangement of the particles changes, but the identity of the matter stays the same.
2. Melting is the reverse of freezing.
3. They represent changes of state, during which the temperature of a sample does not change.
4. Students' paragraphs should indicate that freezing and condensation are exothermic processes because heat released as a liquid becomes a solid (freezing) and as a gas becomes a liquid (condensation).

Alternative Assessment

Provide each student with a heating curve diagram and ask him or her to label each stage of the process using vocabulary terms.

Chapter Summary

VOCABULARY REVIEW

Check students' sentences or paragraphs to make sure they understand the meaning of each vocabulary term.

Evaluate students' essays using the following criteria:

1. The topic sentence, or main idea, should restate the Key Concept.
2. The supporting paragraphs should incorporate the answers to the Learning Goal questions students have written and include details, facts, and examples they have recorded in their Science Notebooks.
3. The concluding sentence should sum up the main idea of the chapter and restate the Key Concept.

MASTERING CONCEPTS

True or False

1. False, solid
2. False, surface tension
3. False, decreases
4. True
5. False, vaporization
6. True

Short Answer

7. Cotton candy is an amorphous solid.
8. Both evaporation and boiling are forms of vaporization through which a liquid changes into a gas. However, evaporation occurs at the surface of a liquid that is below the boiling point. Boiling occurs throughout a liquid that is at the boiling point.
9. As a substance melts, the particles absorb energy and move faster and farther apart. At the melting point, the particles gain enough energy to overcome the attractive forces holding them in fixed positions.
10. Energy is released during an exothermic process and absorbed during an endothermic process.

Summary

KEY CONCEPTS

4.1 Solids

- Matter can exist as a solid, liquid, gas, and as plasma.
- A solid is matter with a definite shape and a definite volume.
- The particles in a crystalline solid are arranged in an organized pattern of repeating rows, whereas the particles in an amorphous solid are not arranged in an organized pattern.

4.2 Liquids

- A liquid has a definite volume, but not a definite shape.
- Uneven forces on the surface particles of a liquid result in surface tension.
- A liquid's resistance to flow is its viscosity.

4.3 Gases

- A gas has neither a definite volume nor a definite shape.
- Boyle's law states that the pressure and volume of a gas are inversely related at a constant temperature.
- Charles's law states that the volume of a gas is directly related to its temperature.

4.4 Changes of State

- A change of state is a physical change in which matter changes from one state to another without changing its identity.
- Every change of state involves either the release or the absorption of energy.
- Melting, vaporization, and sublimation are endothermic changes of state. Freezing and condensation are exothermic changes of state.
- A heating curve shows the relationship between energy and temperature as a substance changes from one state to another.

VOCABULARY REVIEW

Write each term in a complete sentence or write a paragraph relating several terms.

4.1
plasma, p. 55
solid, p. 56
crystalline solid, p. 57
amorphous solid, p. 57

4.2
liquid, p. 58
surface tension, p. 59
viscosity, p. 59

4.3
gas, p. 60
diffusion, p. 60
force, p. 61
pressure, p. 61
pascal, p. 61
compressed, p. 61
Boyle's law, p. 61
Charles's law, p. 62
absolute zero, p. 62

4.4
change of state, p. 63
thermal energy, p. 63
temperature, p. 63
melting, p. 64
freezing, p. 65
freezing point, p. 65
vaporization, p. 65
boiling, p. 65
evaporation, p. 66
condensation, p. 66
sublimation, p. 66
endothermic process, p. 67
exothermic process, p. 67

PREPARE FOR CHAPTER TEST

Create a question from each Learning Goal. Use the information in your Science Notebook to answer each question. Use these answers to write an essay about the chapter. Use the Key Concept on the first page of this chapter as your topic sentence.

Reading Comprehension
Workbook, p. 22

Vocabulary Review
Workbook, p. 20

MASTERING CONCEPTS

True or False
If the statement is true, write "true." If it is false, change the underlined word or words to make the statement true.

1. A(n) <u>liquid</u> has a definite shape and a definite volume.

2. Water and other liquids can form drops as a result of <u>viscosity</u>.

3. According to Boyle's law, the volume of a gas will increase if the pressure <u>increases</u> at a constant temperature.

4. Absolute zero is the lowest temperature on the <u>Kelvin</u> scale.

5. A liquid changes to a gas during <u>condensation</u>.

6. A process that releases energy is <u>exothermic</u>.

Short Answer
Answer each of the following in a sentence or brief paragraph.

7. Cotton candy has a definite shape and volume. The particles in cotton candy are not arranged in any particular pattern. Describe the state of matter of cotton candy.

8. How are evaporation and boiling alike? How are they different?

9. How does the motion and arrangement of particles change as a substance melts?

10. How is an exothermic process different from an endothermic process?

Critical Thinking
Use what you have learned in this chapter to answer each of the following.

11. **Order** Arrange liquids, solids, and gases in order of increasing particle speed.

12. **Infer** A scientist adds 5 mL of a brown substance to a 10-mL container. The substance quickly fills the entire container. Decide if the substance is a solid, a liquid, or a gas.

13. **Explain** How can the temperature of a substance remain the same even if the substance is absorbing thermal energy?

14. **Classify** Describe each change as exothermic or endothermic: melting, freezing, boiling, evaporation, condensation, sublimation.

Standardized Test Question
Choose the letter of the response that correctly answers the question.

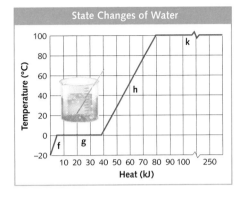

State Changes of Water

15. On which points of the graph is the added energy used to overcome the attractive forces between particles?
   A. F and G
   B. G and K
   C. F and H
   D. H and K

> **Test-Taking Tip**
>
> Circle key words in difficult questions to help you focus on what the question is asking. If you do not understand a key word and you are allowed, ask the teacher what it means.

Critical Thinking

11. solids, liquids, gases

12. It is a gas because it takes the volume and shape of the container.

13. The temperature can remain the same if the energy is overcoming the attractive forces between the particles of the substance. In other words, the substance is changing from one state to another.

14. exothermic: freezing and condensation; endothermic: melting, boiling, evaporation, and sublimation

Standardized Test Question

15. B

Reading Links

Great Inventions: The Steam Engine
This user-friendly book chronicles the invention and subsequent development and use of the steam engine, providing both relevant scientific background and interesting historical context. Readers will come away with a better appreciation for the relationship between societal change and scientific/technological innovation. Includes good visuals, index, bibliography, and a list of online resources.

James Lincoln Collier. Marshall Cavendish Corporation. 112 pp. Illustrated. Library ISBN 978-0-7614-1880-1.

Life Under Ice
Marine photographer Bill Curtsinger documents his investigation of life deep beneath antarctic ice, revealing the many ways in which organisms have adapted to their habitat's extreme conditions. While teaching about methodical scientific research, the book presents a variety of interesting facts in an accessible format that struggling readers will appreciate. Details about conditions and adaptations—such as "antifreeze" blood—draw upon this chapter's content in unusual ways.

Mary M. Cerullo. Tilbury House Publishers. 40 pp. Illustrated with photographs by Bill Curtsinger. Trade ISBN 978-0-88448-246-8.

Curriculum Connection
Workbook, p. 23

Science Challenge
Workbook, p. 24

4A Properties of Liquids

This prechapter introduction activity is designed to determine what students already know about the properties of liquids by having them observe the different flow rates of several liquids.

Objectives

• predict the effect of viscosity on the movement of a liquid
• record data in a suitable way
• communicate conclusions

Planning

 15–20 minutes   groups of 3–4 students

Materials (per group)

• 4 small plastic cups
• catsup
• honey
• milk
• corn syrup
• cardboard or poster board
• aluminum foil
• plastic plate
• several books, for use as a prop

Advance Preparation

• Cut poster board into planks that are 15 cm by 30 cm.
• Fill the different cups with catsup, honey, milk, and corn syrup before students arrive. Explain that the "liquids" used in the activity are actually solutions (solutes dissolved in solvents) and suspensions (particles suspended in a medium), but that they also exhibit viscosity.

Lab Tip

To integrate math skills in the activity, as well as encourage precision with measurement, require students to use a protractor to set the slope of the cardboard/foil strip and a stopwatch to measure the length of time used by each liquid to reach the base of the angled strip.

Engagement Guide

• Challenge students to think about how they can predict what will happen in the experiment by asking:
   • *Which substance do you think will be the first to get to the bottom of the cardboard? Which will be the last?* (Accept all answers. Most students will choose milk as the first substance to reach the bottom of the cardboard, but they may predict different substances to be the last to reach the bottom of the cardboard.)
   • *Why do you think substances have different viscosities?* (The solutions and suspension used have varying amounts of water in them. The more water each contains, the less its viscosity and the faster it flows. Differences in viscosity are due to differences in attraction between the particles in the substance.) Use positive nonverbals when accepting students' answers.
• Encourage students to communicate their conclusions in creative ways.

Going Further

Ask students determine how temperature affects viscosity. Have them test the same liquids after they have been heated in a hot water bath. Students should find that the viscosity decreases as the temperature increases.

4B It's a Gas!

Objectives

• collect carbon dioxide gas from a chemical reaction
• measure the amount of carbon dioxide produced
• compare data with other groups
• communicate conclusions

Skill Set

measuring, recording and analyzing data, comparing and contrasting, stating conclusions

Planning

 40–45 minutes   groups of 3–4 students

Materials

Materials for this activity are listed in the Student Laboratory Manual.

Advance Preparation

• Collect plastic beverage bottles in advance. Cut pieces of waxed paper into 8 cm × 8 cm squares. Clear plastic wrap can also be used instead of waxed paper.
• Discuss with students the nature of carbon dioxide gas and how to test for it. Carbon dioxide is heavier than air, and will extinguish a flaming splint. Also mention that carbon dioxide is part of each exhaled breath.

Answers to Observations: Data Table 1

Answers will vary. Students using equal-sized tablet pieces and proper and consistent experimental techniques should have consistent data.

Answers to Analysis and Conclusions

1. Answers will vary. The amount of gas produced by one tablet should be four times the average volume. The gas produced by 15 tablets should be 60 times the average volume.

2. Answers will vary. Students in different groups will take different amounts of time to place the tablet into the mouth of the bottle. A longer delay will cause less gas to be collected in the bottle. Also, the pieces of tablet will vary in size, producing different amounts of gas.

3. No, the volume of gas produced depends on the pressure. Because the pressure on the mountaintop is less, the volume of gas produced would be more. Gases are affected by pressure because their particles are far apart and can be compressed.

Going Further

Remind students that one characteristic of gases is that they take the shape of their container, no matter how large it is. Open a bottle of vinegar in the front of the classroom. Make sure all doors and windows are closed. Ask students to raise their hands as soon as they smell the vinegar. Ask students to explain why they were able to smell the vinegar. Ask students to explain why some students smelled the vinegar before others did. Students should observe that the vinegar fumes travel throughout the room, and those closest to the front of the room will smell the fumes first.

4C Making Ice Cream

Objectives

- describe property changes of a substance as it freezes or melts
- measure heat transfer between substances
- communicate conclusions

Skill Set

observing, measuring, recording and analyzing data, drawing conclusions

Planning

 40–45 minutes  groups of 3–4 students

Materials

Materials for this activity are listed in the Student Laboratory Manual.

Advance Preparation

Lab groups can share measuring cups, if necessary. If a freezer is not available, keep the ice in an ice chest. Ice cream salt is available at supermarkets. The large-size crystal of rock salt takes more time to dissolve in the water around the ice, allowing for even cooling of the ice cream.

Answers to Observations: Data Table 1

Answers will vary. Students should observe that the temperature of the ice and salt mixture at the end of the activity is lower than the temperature of the ice at the beginning of the activity.

Answers to Analysis and Conclusions

1. The ice cream ingredients began to freeze and the ice and salt mixture began to melt.

2. Answers will vary, but students should observe that the temperature of the ice and salt mixture is lower than the temperature of the ice alone.

3. The heat flows from the liquid ice cream ingredients to the ice and salt mixture. When the heat is removed from the ice cream ingredients, the mixture changed from a liquid to a solid. When the heat flowed into the ice, the ice began to melt.

4. Salt lowers the freezing point of water. As the ice melts, it dissolves the salt, forming a saltwater and ice mixture. The freezing point of this mixture is lower than that of ice alone. The salt also provides traction over the slippery ice.

Going Further

Expand on the study of heat flow by having groups of students design and build their own iceboxes, or coolers. Explain that coolers keep things cold by reducing the flow of heat into them. Test the coolers by placing a given mass of ice cubes into the cooler and timing how long it takes for the ice to melt.

Unit 1

Case Study 1: Melting Ice Caps

Gather More Information

Encourage students to use the library or the NSTA SciLinks Web site noted at the start of each chapter to learn more about these case study topics and conduct further research.

Have students use the following key terms to aid their searches:

- carbon dioxide pollution
- clean energy
- climate change
- Earth's water
- greenhouse gas
- polar ice
- sea level rise

Research the Big Picture

- Have students work in pairs to research the correlation between increasing greenhouse gases in the atmosphere and rising temperatures. Students can present their findings in a time line, graph, or data chart. Using the data they have gathered, have students predict global temperature rise in 10, 50, and 100 years.
- Have students work in groups to further research the shrinking of polar ice in Greenland, the arctic ice cap, and Antarctica. Ask students to describe the effects of ice melt in these areas on sea level rise. Encourage students to create a demonstration comparing ice melting on the surface of water with ice melting from a land mass. Students should conclude that a melting ice cap over the ocean does not raise the sea level, but ice melting on a land mass does.

Case Study 2: Restoring the Statue of Liberty

Gather More Information

Have students use the following key terms to aid their searches:

- copper
- galvanic corrosion
- oxidation
- restoration
- Statue of Liberty

Melting Ice Caps

Most of Earth's water is in the liquid state. In fact, only about two percent of Earth's water is solid ice. It is found in glaciers and in the thick ice caps that cover the polar regions. Unfortunately, the polar ice is melting, and scientists are worried about this change.

It is melting because the planet is getting warmer. Records show that Earth's average temperature rose during the 1900s. This increase is largely the result of an increase in carbon dioxide gas in the air. Much of the gas comes from the burning of fuels such as coal and oil to generate electricity and to run cars. Carbon dioxide is a greenhouse gas, which traps and holds in Earth's heat.

The arctic ice cap is shrinking at a rate of about nine percent each decade. Huge ice shelves at the edges of Antarctica have also crumbled into the sea.

The photo shows the arctic ice cap in 2003. The pink line shows where its boundary was in 1979.

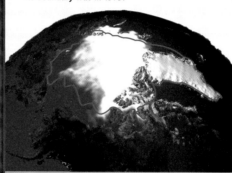

A warming Earth is also causing the sea level to rise. Warmer water expands, so the oceans have a greater volume. Water from melting ice caps spills into the oceans. Sea level rose between 15 and 23 centimeters in the 1900s. Scientists predict a rise of another 17 to 58 centimeters by the year 2100. This will change coastlines. Some lowland coastal areas and islands could disappear.

Scientists agree that reducing carbon dioxide pollution could help slow the melting. Cars that run on electric batteries or hydrogen would produce less carbon dioxide pollution—and less warming. Generating electricity from cleaner energy sources such as the Sun and wind could also help reduce pollution. Scientists hope these efforts will keep more of Earth's polar water in the solid state.

Research and Report

Much of the greenhouse gas carbon dioxide that is produced comes from the burning of fossil fuels. Fossil fuels are hydrocarbons.

Research to find out more about hydrocarbon fuels. Record your findings in your Science Notebook and create a report for your class.

CAREER CONNECTION MATERIALS SCIENTIST

The contributions of materials scientists are indeed impressive: they have developed plastics that stop bullets and tiles that shield spacecraft from heat as they re-enter Earth's atmosphere.

Materials scientists study the structure of every type of matter. They understand the properties of materials, so they know how the materials can be used and changed to make new things.

Materials scientists are problem-solvers. Perhaps an engineer needs a strong, flexible material for bridge cables. Medical researchers designing artificial organs would want a material that is light and strong,

but one that will not corrode when it comes in contact with body fluids. Materials scientists would find or make the materials to meet all these demands.

Most materials scientists have at least a bachelor's degree in chemistry, physics, or materials science. Many of them work in the chemical industry. They create and improve plastics, drugs, and other chemical products.

Others work with architects and engineers. They make materials used in airplanes and skyscrapers. Some materials scientists develop materials that can be used to build lighter, stronger cars. Materials scientists work in an important and creative field that is always changing.

70

CAREER CONNECTION: Materials Scientist

Have students read the feature and list in their Science Notebooks the types of substances that materials scientists have developed. When they have finished, ask students to think about the kinds of artificial materials they use in their own daily lives. Ask: *Which ones may have resulted from research by materials scientists?* Have each student write a paragraph describing what he or she thinks is the most important work of materials scientists. Ask students to speculate about the types of tasks these scientists might tackle in the future.

Restoring the Statue of Liberty

The Statue of Liberty has towered over the waters of New York Harbor since 1886. Over the years, exposure to rain, sea winds, sunlight, and polluted air has caused chemical changes to this special lady. Her inner frame corroded. Holes formed in her outer skin. The copper of her exterior, once bright and gleaming, turned a dull grey-green.

Engineers made plans to fix the damage. They knew that not all the chemical changes were bad for the statue. Oxidation had turned the outer layer of the statue's copper skin green. This thin film of corrosion protects the copper underneath, so Lady Liberty was allowed to keep her green coat. Other chemical changes were not as helpful, however. The statue's thin copper skin is attached to its inner iron frame with copper clips and bolts. This design caused problems because it put two unlike metals—iron and copper— in contact. A chemical reaction can occur when two unlike metals touch in a moist environment. The reaction causes a weak electric current to flow between the metals. This process, called galvanic corrosion, weakens the metals.

The statue's builders tried to prevent this problem from occurring. They put small asbestos pads between the copper clips and the iron frame to keep the two metals apart. The pads crumbled over time, however, and what was left of them absorbed moisture. Galvanic

corrosion began. The frame's iron bars became distorted from the buildup of corrosion. The swollen bars pulled out hundreds of the copper clips holding up the statue's copper skin.

The repairs in the 1980s fixed these problems. Workers replaced each iron bar with stainless steel— a material that resists corrosion. The old copper clips were replaced with a strong copper alloy. The Statue of Liberty is now protected against the chemical changes that harmed it in the past, thanks to the careful preservation efforts.

The statue's copper skin was attached to its iron frame by 1,500 U-shaped copper clips and 300,000 copper bolts.

The Newest Element—for Now

If you think all of the elements have been discovered, think again. Every so often, scientists find a new one. When Mendeleev created the first periodic table in 1869, he knew of about 60 elements. Since then, the number of known elements has nearly doubled.

Russian and American scientists discovered the newest element in 2006. Until tests confirm its existence, it does not have a name. For now, it is known simply as "element 118," based on the number of protons in its nucleus.

Element 118 isn't a natural element. The heaviest natural element, uranium, was discovered long ago.

That element has the atomic number 92. Elements beyond uranium were discovered in the lab.

Suppose you are a scientist looking for new elements. How do you go about it? You try to smash atomic nuclei together—and hope they stick. A group of scientists did just that to make element 118. The scientists shot calcium ions, which have 20 protons, at a target made of the element californium, which has 98 protons. For months, the ions zipped right through the target. Finally, however, the two known elements fused into a new one.

The scientists made just three atoms of element 118, and these lasted just a fraction of a second before they broke apart into other elements. Scientists will try to repeat their short-lived success again under the same conditions and create more atoms of element 118. This exciting research into the discovery of elements will continue and likely uncover even more elements.

Research the Big Picture

- Have students work in pairs to research in more detail the process and effects of oxidation. Tell students to create a poster or model that describes the chemical process and shows copper before and after oxidation. Some students might also be familiar with other examples of oxidation, such as tarnishing of silver and rusting of iron.

- Ask students if they know what pennies are made of. Many students will answer copper. Tell students to research the history of changes made in the composition of the penny. Have them write paragraphs or create time lines describing those changes and explaining why they were made.

Case Study 3: The Newest Element— for Now

Gather More Information

Have students use the following key terms to aid their searches:

- elements
- element 118
- Mendeleev
- periodic table
- transuranium elements

Research the Big Picture

- Have students work in pairs to research the origin and properties of other transuranium elements. Each pair should find out when, how, and by whom each element was discovered. Create a bulletin board display for the classroom.

- All transuranium elements are radioactive and have varying half-lives. As a class, discuss the potential risks and benefits associated with creating new radioactive elements. Talk about the consequences of the "escape" of transuranium elements into nature.

- After the discussion, have students write position papers about whether or not they believe that creating new elements is a positive scientific endeavor.

- Have students research the history of element 118. Several years ago, scientists reported the discovery of this new element, and then later retracted their report because they could not reproduce their results.

Unit 2

Introduce Unit 2

Explain to students that this unit is about the building blocks of matter.

Without referring to the periodic table, have each student make a list in his or her Science Notebook of familiar elements. Ask them to write down three questions about atoms and elements they would like to have answered. As they read the unit, have them answer the questions in their Science Notebooks.

Unit Projects

For each Unit Project, have students use the Presentation Builder on the Student CD-ROM to display their results.

Career Research Have each student choose a career related to atoms such as an atomic physicist or a welder. Have students identify local professionals or research people with their chosen careers. Have students write profiles describing what the person's job entails, how it relates to physical science, and what skills and education the person possesses. Students should share their completed profiles with their classmates in a binder or in a bulletin board display.

Hands-On Research Introduce and explain the idea of indirect evidence. Have students work in pairs. Each pair should create a black box model by covering both the top and bottom of a shoe box in black paper and then filling it with a variety of items. Then have pairs exchange their black boxes and try to determine the contents using as many of their senses and as many scientific tools as are available.

Technology Research Pose the question to students: *How do scientists study particles as tiny as atoms?* Help students understand that scientists first learned about the basic units of matter by watching how materials behaved. Now modern technologies, such as electron microscopes and particle accelerators, are used. Have students work in groups to research and report on one technology that scientists use to study atomic structure and properties.

Unit 2

Building Blocks of Matter

Chapter 5 — The Atom
How is the search for a description of the atom related to the current atomic model?

Chapter 6 — The Periodic Table
How does the arrangement of the elements in the periodic table account for the physical and chemical properties of the elements?

72

Software Summary

Student CD-ROM
—Interactive Student Book
—Vocabulary Review
—Key Concept Review
—Lab Report Template
—ELL Preview and Writing Activities
—Presentation Digital Library
—Graphic Organizing Software
—Spanish Cognate Dictionary

Interactive Labs
Chapter 5B—Atomic Structure
Chapter 5C—Modeling an Atom
Chapter 6B—Radioactive Isotopes

The Atom

5.1 Early Atomic Models

5.2 Improvements to the Atomic Model

5.3 Properties of Subatomic Particles

KEY CONCEPT Over thousands of years, scientists have developed and improved various models of the atom.

The model of a sports utility vehicle shown here is life-size. It shows realistic details such as color and vehicle parts.

If you look closely, you can see that the model is made out of many individual plastic blocks. Like this model, everything around you is made up of smaller particles. In this chapter, you will learn about the structures of the particles of matter. You will also find out how scientists use models to describe the particles of matter, much like this model shows the structure of a vehicle.

Think About Describing a Whole and Its Parts

The particles that make up matter are too small to be seen with the unaided eye. Many things around you, however, are made up of smaller parts you can see. Select an object that is made up of parts and observe its characteristics.

- In your Science Notebook, draw a diagram of the object. Label as many parts as you can.
- Write a few sentences describing the parts of the object you observed. Tell if any of the smaller parts are made up of even smaller parts.

NSTA

SCLINKS.
THE WORLD'S A CLICK AWAY

www.scilinks.org
Atomic Structure **Code: WGPS05**

73

Introduce Chapter 5

ENGAGE Have students work in pairs to list models they have seen or used. Provide a few examples to inspire students, such as a globe or a model airplane. Create a class list of models and keep the list visible during the study of this chapter. Discuss with students why and how models are used. Write their responses on the list and review these at the end of the chapter.

Think About Describing a Whole and Its Parts

ENGAGE Think aloud about an ordinary object in the classroom, such as a student desk or chair. Quickly sketch the item on the board and label its legs, seat, back, and other details, such as a pencil tray or screws and bolts. Describe the object's parts and write some of your observations on the board.

Have students complete the bulleted activities, using a different object as their model.

Chapter 5 Planning Guide			
Instructional Periods	National Standards	Lab Manual	Workbook
5.1 2 Periods	A2, B1, G1, G2, G3; A2, B1, B2, E2, G1, G2, G3; UCP1, UCP2, UCP5	**Lab 5A: p. 25** What's in an Atom? **Lab 5B: pp. 26–28** Atomic Structure	Key Concept Review p. 25 Vocabulary Review p. 26 Interpreting Diagrams p. 27 Reading Comprehension p. 28
5.2 2 Periods	A1, E2, G1, G2, G3; A1, B1, B2, E2, G1, G2, G3; UCP2, UCP5	**Lab 5C: pp. 29–30** Modeling an Atom	Curriculum Connection p. 29 Science Challenge pp. 30–31
5.3 2 Periods	B1; B1, B2; UCP3		

Middle School Standard; High School Standard; Unifying Concept and Principle

5.1 Introduce

ENGAGE Have available pictures of atomic models and/or three-dimensional models of atoms. Have students work with a partner to discuss the models and to hypothesize what the models represent. Explain to students that the models represent atoms of different elements. In this chapter, students will learn how scientists gained information about the structure and composition of atoms.

Vocabulary terms are listed on the first student page of each lesson. You may wish to preview the terms before introducing each lesson. Strategies for teaching the vocabulary appear on the pages where the terms are introduced.

Before You Read

Model the process of creating an outline as you preview the first pages of the lesson.

Teach

EXPLAIN to students that the model of the atom has changed a number of times over the past 2,000 years. In this chapter, they will learn about this evolution and the science that has informed the model's revision.

Encourage students to use the vocabulary section they created in their Science Notebooks. Remind them to record prefixes, suffixes, and root words to help them remember the meanings of vocabulary terms.

Vocabulary

model Encourage students to brainstorm common uses of the word *model*. Tell students that the word *model* is derived from Latin and means "a little measure." Ask students to describe how this derivation relates to the scientific definition.

theory Encourage students to think of common uses of the word *theory*. Explain that the word *theory* is derived from Greek and means "to view." Ask students to relate this meaning to the scientific definition.

atom Tell students that the word *atom* comes from a Greek word meaning "something that cannot be divided." Ask students to relate this derivation to the scientific definition.

Learning Goals

- Relate models to atomic theory.
- Describe the atomic models developed by Democritus, Dalton, Thomson, and Rutherford.

New Vocabulary

model
theory
atom
electron
proton
nucleus

Figure 5.1 This model railroad is a small version of an actual railroad town. Someone who has never seen the town can get a good idea of what it looks like by studying this model.

5.1 Early Atomic Models

Before You Read

Create a lesson outline. Use the lesson title as the outline title. Label the headings with the Roman numerals *I* through *IV* for the four models discussed in the lesson. Use the letters *A, B, C,* etc. for the subheadings. Record important facts and supporting details in the outline.

Onlookers can forget that they are looking at a model as the train zips around a miniature town, over highways and through tunnels. The railroad scene in **Figure 5.1** looks exactly like a real town, only smaller. Model railroad enthusiasts pay attention to even the tiniest details as they recreate a scene.

What Is a Model?

A toy railroad is a type of model. A **model** is a representation of an object or system. Models are not limited to use as toys and for hobbies. Scientists commonly use models to describe concepts and ideas about the natural world.

In science, a model may be built as a three-dimensional representation. These types of models are particularly helpful when representing objects that are too large or too small to be observed. A model may also be a description of a concept or understanding scientists have gained. Scientific models can often make it easier to describe topics that are difficult to comprehend or objects and events that have never been directly observed.

Scientific models are closely related to theories. A scientific **theory** is an explanation for a broad set of observations that is based upon proven hypotheses and is verified multiple times. Theories are generally broader and encompass more ideas and possibilities than do models.

One topic that is studied through models is the structure of the atom. Recall that an **atom** is the smallest particle into which an element can be divided and still be the same substance. For over 2,000 years, scientists have used models to explain the nature of matter and the properties and behaviors of atoms. Over the years, the models have changed as new information and technologies have developed, and as different scientists have investigated the topic.

ELL Strategy

Make a Model Have students work in groups to make a model of an atom. Each group should create a model based on that developed by Democritus, Dalton, Thomson, or Rutherford. Students should label the parts of the model and write a list of the ways that the model varies from those that historically preceded it.

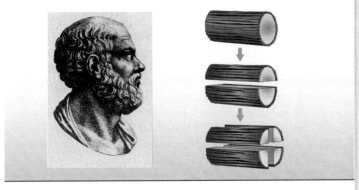

Figure 5.2 Democritus believed that a log could only be split a certain number of times before the pieces were no longer wood.

Early Greeks

The earliest atomic model was developed by the ancient Greeks. Around 440 B.C., a philosopher named Democritus proposed a theory of the atom built on the ideas of his teacher, Leucippus.

Democritus proposed the idea that all matter is composed of particles that are indivisible, which means they cannot be divided beyond a certain point and still be that same kind of matter. He reasoned that an object, such as a piece of wood, could be divided into two equal pieces. Those two pieces could then be divided again to form four pieces. Those four pieces could be divided to form eight, and then eight to form sixteen, and so on, as shown in **Figure 5.2.**

Democritus reasoned that eventually the wood would reach a point at which it could not be divided any further and still be wood. He described this point as the basic building block of all matter. The modern word *atom* comes from the Greek word *atomos*, which means "uncuttable."

According to Democritus's explanation, all matter is composed of atoms that cannot be further divided. Atoms are completely solid, and there is empty space between them. All changes, he reasoned, are the result of the movement of atoms. Atoms can differ from one another in size, shape, and weight.

Another Greek philosopher named Aristotle disagreed with Democritus. Aristotle proposed a theory suggesting that all matter is composed of four base elements—fire, water, earth, and air. He believed that no such indivisible particle could be reached. Aristotle had a strong influence on what people of the time believed. As a result, Democritus's ideas were generally ignored for centuries.

 CONNECTION: Literature

Primary sources are always preferred when studying history. A primary source is a firsthand account that is usually written by the person being studied. Unfortunately, almost all of the original writings of Leucippus and Democritus are lost. The only sources that remain to tell about their work are secondary sources in the form of quotations from other writers.

● Teach

EXPLAIN to students that Democritus was the first person to develop a model of the atom. His model described an atom as being solid and separated from other atoms with space.

Science Notebook EXTRA

Have students write in their Science Notebooks what they know about the history of your school. Then have students work in groups to learn more about the school's history. One or two groups should interview teachers and staff who have been at the school for a long time. Other groups can learn about the school by examining old photos, yearbooks, and school newspapers. Ask students to compare their new knowledge to their former understanding of the school. Ask them to discuss the advantages and disadvantages of learning from primary sources.

Differentiate Instruction

Linguistic Have students write about each model of the atom, being as descriptive as possible, without naming the scientist who developed it. They should then exchange descriptions with other students and try to name the scientists from the descriptions.

Background Information

The study of primary sources allows one to form one's own opinion. Many different things can be considered primary sources. Below is a list of different types and specific examples of primary sources.

Objects: artifacts, tools, weapons, inventions, uniforms, clothing, accessories

Images: photographs, film, video

Audio: oral histories, interviews, music, audio recordings

Statistics: census data, land surveys, maps, ordinances, blueprints, architectural drawings

Text: cookbooks, advertisements, journals, letters, diaries, documents in the original handwriting

The community: family photographs (of ancestors and their homes), memorabilia, souvenirs, recipes, ancestors' clothes, ancestors' papers, oral histories, local historical societies, genealogical information, and physical surroundings

● Teach

EXPLAIN to students that John Dalton proposed the next atomic model, and his model incorporated the work done by Boyle, Lavoisier, and Proust.

As You Read

Give students about five minutes to update their outlines. Have students share their outlines with partners and provide feedback on their partners' comprehension of the content as reflected in the outline. If students are struggling to organize their thinking, have them create new outlines, this time working with partners.

ANSWER Dalton used evidence from experimentation, whereas Democritus relied on logical reasoning only.

Science Notebook EXTRA

Have students examine the five statements proposed by John Dalton and trace the origin of each statement to its founding scientist. For instance, the third statement, "Atoms cannot be created nor destroyed," is related to the work of Lavoisier. He showed that mass is neither created nor destroyed (an idea known as the conservation of mass). For statements not traceable in this chapter, have students research other scientific texts and encyclopedias.

CONNECTION: History

John Dalton was not a chemist. He was a Quaker schoolteacher who also studied meteorology. He was interested in gases, air pressure, and the water cycle, and he kept a daily journal of the conditions of the atmosphere in Manchester, England, where he lived. To describe the nature of atoms, Dalton wrote, "We might as well attempt to introduce a new planet into the solar system, or to annihilate one already in existence, as to create or destroy a particle of hydrogen."

As You Read

Include each scientist named in this lesson as a heading in your outline. Include information about the scientists and their contributions to the development of the atomic model.

What did Dalton do in developing a model that Democritus did not do?

Dalton's Atomic Model

Although a few philosophers and scientists considered the atomic theory after Democritus, it wasn't until the early 1800s that the topic was seriously explored once again. By then, scientists had begun investigating scientific questions through experimentation, rather than through simply thinking about the questions. In particular, an English physicist named Robert Boyle had established the importance of using the scientific method to investigate questions about the natural world. Through experimentation, Boyle concluded that all gases are made up of smaller particles.

In 1789, a French chemist named Antoine Lavoisier carefully weighed substances before and after a chemical reaction. Lavoisier showed that mass is conserved. In other words, matter can change forms, but mass is neither created nor destroyed. This is known as the law of conservation of mass.

Then, in 1799, another French chemist named Joseph Louis Proust used experiments to show that a compound always contains the same elements in the same proportion by mass. Water, for example, always contains the same ratio of hydrogen to oxygen, no matter what amount of water there is or what its source. This discovery is known as the law of constant composition.

In 1803, a schoolteacher named John Dalton proposed a new atomic theory. Dalton used the discoveries of Lavoisier and Proust, as well as Democritus's ideas about atoms. His theory can be summarized by the following statements:

1. All matter is composed of tiny, indivisible particles called atoms.
2. Atoms of a given element are identical in their physical and chemical properties.
3. Atoms cannot be created or destroyed.
4. Atoms of different elements combine in simple whole-number ratios to form compounds.
5. A chemical reaction occurs when atoms are combined, separated, or rearranged.

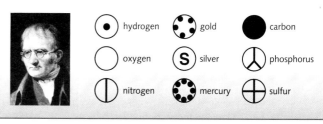

Figure 5.3 Dalton devised a system of symbols in which he represented atoms by circles. The contents of the circle distinguished atoms of different elements from one another.

Background Information

Scientists still consider three of John Dalton's statements to be accurate. Two statements have been disproved: the second and third. Since isotopes of an element may have varying numbers of neutrons in their nuclei, the second is not accurate. Nuclear fusion and fission have shown the third to be false.

Teacher Alert

The terms *superscript* and *subscript* can be easily confused. Remind students of the meanings of the prefixes *super-* (above, beyond, or over) and *sub-* (under or below), and provide other examples terms with these prefixes used in context. Examples might include *submarine*, *subconscious*, and *superhuman*.

Thomson's Atomic Model

The atomic model proposed by Dalton in the early 1800s was the accepted model until the end of that century. At that point, scientists began discovering characteristics about the atom that suggested a more complicated structure.

Cathode Ray Tubes   The first discovery that changed Dalton's model of the atom came from physics, not chemistry. Physicists had been working with cathode ray tubes. A cathode ray tube consists of a glass tube with a metal electrode on both ends. Most of the air is taken out of the tube. When electricity is applied to one end of the tube, a glowing ray appears between the two electrodes. The glowing ray, called a cathode ray, was believed to be some kind of light energy.

In the 1870s, a physicist named William Crookes observed that cathode rays could be attracted by a magnet. Because light would not be attracted in this way, Crookes and other scientists concluded that cathode rays consisted of particles. The direction in which the rays were deflected showed that they were made up of negatively charged particles, which were later called **electrons.**

Additional experiments with cathode ray tubes conducted by the scientist Eugene Goldstein suggested that cathode rays also consisted of positively charged particles, later named **protons.** The charge on protons is equal in magnitude, or size, to the charge on electrons.

While data had been gathered to support the existence of electrons and protons, other investigations cast doubt on these conclusions. Further experimentation was required. In 1897, the British scientist J. J. Thomson showed that cathode rays are deflected by electric charges as well as magnets. This final piece of evidence confirmed that cathode rays are charged particles. Then Thomson made a bold leap. He suggested not only that cathode rays are particles, but that they are the building blocks of the atom. For this, Thomson is given credit for the discovery of the electron.

Electron Properties   Thomson was able to calculate the ratio of the charge of an electron to its mass. However, because he was not able to measure its charge, he was unable to calculate the mass of an electron. This information was provided several years later by American physicist Robert Milliken. Milliken's experiments enabled Thomson to calculate the mass of both an electron and a proton. Thomson determined the mass of an electron to be 9.11×10^{-28} g and the mass of a proton to be 1.6726×10^{-24} g. This means the mass of a proton is almost 2,000 times the mass of an electron.

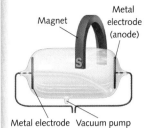

Magnet   Metal electrode (anode)

Metal electrode (cathode)   Vacuum pump

Figure 5.4 Because the magnet causes the cathode ray to bend, scientists knew the ray was not simply light.

Extend It!

J. J. Thomson was not only a brilliant scientist, but also a gifted teacher. Twenty-seven of his students went on to become fellows of the Royal Society, and seven of his students went on to earn Nobel Prizes. Aside from Rutherford and Bohr, find out who some of Thomson's students were and what they accomplished. Summarize your findings in your Science Notebook.

● Teach

EXPLAIN to students that John Dalton's model of the atom was accepted by scientists until results from experiments conducted with cathode ray tubes demonstrated the existence of electrons and protons. Then, J. J. Thomson used this new knowledge to modify the model and include electrons.

Vocabulary

electrons Explain to students that the prefix *electr-* means "electric"; an electron has a negative electric charge. The suffix *-on* as used here denotes an elementary particle.

protons Tell students that the prefix *prot-* is derived from Greek and means "first." Remind students of the meaning of the suffix *-on.*

Extend It!

Have students research other Nobel Prize winners in physics during and after the years that J. J. Thomson taught at Trinity College. Also suggest that students research fellows of the Royal Society during the same years. Have students work with partners to locate a scientist, note his or her accomplishments, and explain how J. J. Thomson might have influenced the scientist's work. Students should write this information in their Science Notebooks and then share their findings with their classmates in brief oral presentations.

Background Information

J. J. Thomson both attended and taught at Trinity College in Cambridge. He was responsible for making the Cavendish Laboratories at Cambridge a leading center for research in physics between 1894 and 1919. After his discovery of the electron, he started researching the positively charged channel rays in cathode ray tubes and found that electric and magnetic fields could separate a stream of channel rays into two or more parts. This information led to the discovery of isotopes by another of his students, Francis Aston.

Teach

EXPLAIN to students why Thomson's model of the atom was known as the "plum pudding" model. This model illustrated the atom as a sphere of positive charge that contained electrons. Encourage students to develop their own nicknames for this model based a dish familiar to them. Rutherford's later experiment with alpha particles and gold foil provided additional information about the location of electrons and protons.

 Vocabulary

nucleus Explain to students that the word *nucleus* is derived from Latin and means "kernel." Ask students to relate this meaning to the term's scientific definitions and explain why the term is appropriate for the part of the atom it describes.

Figure 5.5 Thomson's "plum pudding" model shows the atom as a ball of positive charge (the pudding) in which negatively charged electrons (the plums) are embedded.

Did You Know?

Plum pudding was an English dessert that was popular during Thomson's time. It consisted of a ball of breading with pieces of fruit stuck in it. In Thomson's model, the pieces of fruit represented the electrons and the bread was the positively charged matter.

Figure 5.6 In Rutherford's now-famous gold foil experiment, a beam of positively charged alpha particles was aimed at a sheet of gold foil. The locations where the particles struck the screen behind the foil could be used to determine how the foil affected the paths of the particles.

In 1903, Thomson revised Dalton's atomic model to account for these discoveries. Because he knew that atoms have no overall charge, he knew that there must be positive charges to balance the negative charges of electrons. He proposed a model that came to be known as the "plum pudding" model. Thompson's model featured the negatively charged electrons randomly stuck in a ball of positively charged matter.

Rutherford's Atomic Model

Between 1906 and 1908, a former student of Thomson's named Ernest Rutherford investigated the atom further. In the process, Rutherford and his associates performed one of the most famous experiments in chemistry: the gold foil experiment. Rutherford was studying the effects of bombarding thin gold foil with positively charged particles called alpha particles. Rutherford reasoned that the way alpha particles traveled through the gold foil would give him information about the structure of gold atoms in the foil.

Gold is a good metal for this use because it can be hammered into an extremely thin sheet and still hold together and retain all of its properties. The gold foil was placed in a chamber surrounded by a screen that was coated with a material called zinc sulfide. This substance glows when struck with alpha particles.

A New Discovery Rutherford's hypothesis at the beginning of the gold foil experiment was that the particles would pass directly through the foil. This was based on Thomson's plum pudding model, which suggested that the atom had mass and charge distributed evenly throughout. The majority of the observations supported the hypothesis. Most of the particles passed straight through the foil and struck the screen behind it.

Then Rutherford's group made a surprising discovery. A few of the particles were deflected to the right or left of center. Even more surprisingly, some particles were deflected directly back to the source.

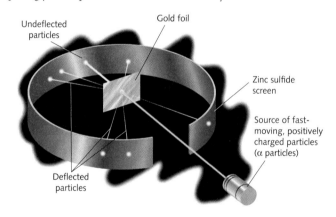

Background Information

Rutherford continued Becquerel's work and discovered alpha, beta, and gamma rays. He studied radioactive disintegration and believed that each radioactive element decayed into different intermediate elements, ultimately resulting in a stable element. He further observed that the decay happened at a fixed rate and that half of any quantity of a radioactive element disintegrated in a specific period of time (the half-life).

Rutherford compared this to shooting a cannon ball at a piece of tissue paper and having the ball bounce back to him. The unexpected behavior of the alpha particles meant an atom's mass and charge were not evenly distributed. Clearly, the plum pudding model was incorrect.

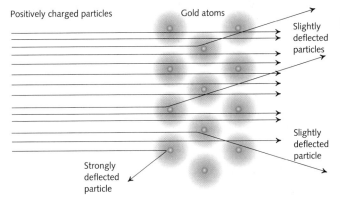

Figure 5.7 The circles represent the gold atoms in the foil. The arrows represent the paths of the alpha particles.

Another New Model In 1911, Rutherford and Danish scientist Niels Bohr proposed that since most of the alpha particles traveled right through the foil, an atom must consist of mostly empty space. Then they attempted to explain why some particles were deflected. Knowing that like charges repel each other, Rutherford and Bohr concluded that a dense region of positive charge deflected the alpha particles. Rutherford called this region in the center of the atom the **nucleus.**

Based on his experiments, Rutherford calculated the diameter of the nucleus to be about 100,000 times smaller than the diameter of a gold atom. This means that if an atom were the size of a professional football stadium, its nucleus would be about the size of a marble in the center of the field. This explains why most of the alpha particles passed through the foil without being deflected.

After You Read

1. Explain how a model is useful for describing an atomic theory.
2. Why did Thomson include positively charged matter in his model even though he had not observed it?
3. Review the outline you made in your Science Notebook. Using your notes, explain how Rutherford's model differs from Thomson's model.

Teach

EXPLAIN to students that in Rutherford's gold foil experiment, most particles passed through the foil, but some particles (1 in 8,000) were returned to the right, left, or straight back to the source. These results informed the new model created by Rutherford and Bohr.

Figure It Out: Figure 5.7

ANSWER **1.** Most alpha particles pass through the empty space surrounding the nucleus of a gold atom. **2.** Alpha particles are strongly deflected as they approach the positive center of each atom's nucleus.

Assess

Use the After You Read questions and the Alternative Assessment to help you evaluate students' understanding of the lesson.

After You Read

1. A model is a simpler way to represent a complex structure that cannot be directly observed, such as the atom.
2. He knew that atoms are electrically neutral, so there had to be positive charge to balance the negatively charged electrons.
3. Rather than embedding electrons in positive charge, Rutherford's model placed all of the positive charge in a dense region in the center of the atom.

Alternative Assessment

Have students use the outlines in their Science Notebooks to compare and contrast the atomic models developed by Democritus and Rutherford. Encourage them to describe how the work of other scientists contributed to Rutherford's model.

Background Information

Rutherford worked with Hans Geiger to investigate the scattering of alpha particles. People would count the flashes of light, but they could count accurately for only about a minute. (Geiger later developed the Geiger counter to count the pulses automatically in normal light.)

Geiger continued the work on alpha particle scattering with one of his research students, Ernest Marsden, and together they conducted the gold foil experiment. Geiger shared the results with Rutherford, knowing that Thomson's model of the atom had to be incorrect.

Write Robert Frost's poem "The Secret Sits" (1936) on the board:

We dance round in a ring and suppose,
But the Secret sits in the middle and
knows.

Tell students that Frost wrote this poem in reference to the Rutherford-Bohr model of the atom. Have students discuss the poem with a partner and interpret what the Secret is. If students require assistance, have them review the Rutherford-Bohr model. Discuss students' interpretations as a class, and explain that the Secret is the nucleus. "We" refers to scientists. Review with students the date Frost wrote the poem and what theories existed at that time about the atomic model.

Before You Read

Ask students to sketch in their Science Notebooks what they understand an atom to look like. Encourage students to label the nucleus, electrons, and protons.

● Teach

EXPLAIN to students that Niels Bohr, who worked with Rutherford, modified the atomic model; his model displayed electrons orbiting the nucleus and staying at specific energy levels throughout the orbit.

Learning Goals

- Describe Bohr's model of the atom.
- Discuss Chadwick's contribution to the atomic theory.
- Identify changes brought about by the modern theory of the atom.

New Vocabulary

emission line spectrum
neutron
electron cloud

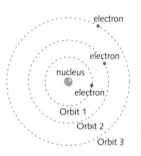

Figure 5.8 According to Bohr's model, the electron in a hydrogen atom is at a specific distance from the nucleus. The electron is found only in a specific energy level and nowhere in between.

5.2 Improvements to the Atomic Model

Before You Read

In your Science Notebook, draw a diagram that shows what you already know about the atom. As you read this lesson, add to and correct the information in the diagram.

Rutherford theorized that electrons traveled in orbits around the nucleus. However, he recognized that a better explanation was needed for the placement of electrons in his model. Remember that electrons are negatively charged and the nucleus is positively charged. Opposite charges attract each other. If electrons were stationary, they would be attracted to the nucleus and become part of it. If electrons were spinning around the nucleus, they would eventually lose energy and slow down. At some point, they would fall into the nucleus. There needed to be some better way to describe the position of electrons in an atom.

Bohr's Atomic Model

Rutherford's assistant, Niels Bohr, continued working to perfect the atomic model. Bohr speculated that electrons revolve around the nucleus in circular orbits. He went on to suggest that these orbits are at fixed distances from the nucleus. Because the distance is fixed, he argued, the amount of energy the electron possesses is also fixed. In this model, an electron was said to occupy a fixed energy level. Electrons could not exist between energy levels, and they did not lose energy while traveling in the energy level. The Bohr model of the atom is represented in **Figure 5.8.**

Bohr's model was based largely on the work of a German physics professor named Max Planck. In 1900, Planck proposed a theory stating that energy exists in tiny packets. Bohr reasoned that since energy existed in specific quantities, the electrons must exist in specific orbits around the nucleus. If an electron absorbs a certain amount of energy, it must move a specific distance to a different orbit.

ELL Strategy

Compare and Contrast Have each student use a compare-and-contrast chart to compare Bohr's first atomic model, Chadwick's model, and the modern model of the atom. Students should include the location of electrons, protons, and neutrons, as well as a discussion of mass.

Bohr's Evidence   At first, Bohr did not have experimental evidence to support his model. Coincidentally, Bohr received a research paper written by a physicist and mathematician named Johann Jakob Balmer at around the same time. The paper described an experiment in which hydrogen gas was sealed in a tube. An electric voltage was then used to excite the gas, or give it extra energy. The tube then released light that separated into a series of narrow lines when passed through a prism. The narrow slits of light made up what is known as an **emission line spectrum.** The individual slits of light are called spectral lines.

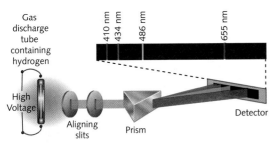

Figure 5.9 The emission line spectrum for hydrogen is produced when hydrogen gas is excited. As the emitted light is passed through a prism, four discrete lines can be seen.

Bohr immediately recognized that the spectrum of hydrogen was experimental evidence that supported his atomic model. Bohr reasoned that when the voltage was applied to hydrogen in the tube, the atoms became excited. In an excited hydrogen atom, the electron is forced to a higher energy level.

An excited atom is not stable. The electron quickly jumps back to a lower energy level. In the process, the electron loses a discrete, or distinct, amount of energy as light. The amount of energy determines the wavelength of light. For example, a red spectral line corresponds to an electron dropping from the third energy level to the second energy level. A violet line is produced when an electron drops from the fifth energy level to the second energy level.

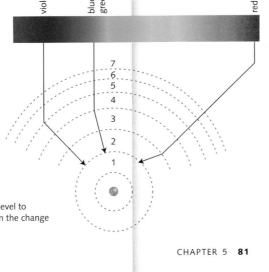

Figure 5.10 When an electron drops from one energy level to another, a spectral line is produced. The color depends on the change in energy levels.

● Teach

EXPLAIN to students that Bohr theorized that each specific energy level had sublevels, and the number of sublevels depended on the number of the principal energy level.

 Vocabulary

neutron Tell students that the root *neut-* is derived from Greek and means "neither." Remind students that the prefix *-on* denotes an elementary particle.

electron cloud Encourage students to list common uses of the word *cloud*. Examples might include clouds in the sky, a mass of dust in the air, or a feeling of gloom. Explain that an electron cloud is an area around a nucleus in which electrons could be located.

🖊 Explain It!

In your Science Notebook, create a time line that shows when each of the following people made a contribution to the atomic theory. Label the year with the name of the person, and write a sentence describing what that person concluded and why.

Dalton, Thomson, Rutherford, Bohr, Chadwick

Figure 5.12 This simplified diagram shows Bohr's model with a nucleus of protons and neutrons surrounded by electrons in discrete energy levels.

Principal Energy Levels and Sublevels Because the emission spectra for other elements had too many spectral lines to interpret, Bohr suggested that the principal energy levels may have sublevels. Those energy sublevels were labeled *s, p, d,* and *f.*

According to Bohr, the number of sublevels depends on the number of the principal energy level. The first principal energy level, energy level 1, has one sublevel, 1*s*. The second principal energy level, energy level 2, has two sublevels, 2*s* and 2*p*. The third principal energy level, energy level 3, has three sublevels, 3*s*, 3*p*, and 3*d*. The fourth principal energy level, energy level 4, has four sublevels, 4*s*, 4*p*, 4*d*, and 4*f*.

Figure 5.11 Bohr theorized that each principal energy level was separated into sublevels. This diagram shows a simplified version of how these levels might be organized.

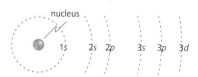

The number of electrons that can fit in a sublevel varies. An *s* sublevel can hold two electrons. A *p* sublevel can hold six electrons. A *d* sublevel can hold ten electrons. An *f* sublevel can hold up to 14 electrons. The total number of electrons a principal energy level can hold is the sum of the electrons in each sublevel. For example, the second principal energy level has two sublevels, 2*s* and 2*p*. The 2*s* level can hold two electrons, and the 2*p* level can hold six electrons. Therefore, the second principal energy level can hold a total of eight electrons.

Chadwick's Contributions

One final problem remained with the Bohr model of the atom. If an atom is electrically neutral, the number of positive charges must be equal to the number of negative charges. However, the total mass of the positive charges (protons) and negative charges (electrons) in an atom fell far short of the actual mass of an atom.

The solution to this problem was suggested by English physicist James Chadwick in 1932. Chadwick found that the nucleus of an atom contains a particle with no electric charge, which he called a **neutron.** The mass of the neutron is just slightly greater than the mass of a proton, at 1.6749×10^{-24} g.

Chadwick's discovery resulted in a revised model of the atom. In this model, the core of the atom is the atomic nucleus, which is made up of one or more protons and neutrons. Outside the nucleus are electrons traveling in discrete orbits.

Differentiate Instruction

Mathematical, Visual Have each student create a chart or model of an atom with four principal energy levels and corresponding sublevels. Students can also determine the maximum number of electrons that can fill each principal energy level based on the information provided about the number of electrons each sublevel can hold.

Key Concept Review
Workbook, p. 25

CONNECTION: Earth Science

Scientists cannot easily view the entire solar system, so they have used models to describe its structure and motion. The solar system consists of the Sun, eight planets, and a number of other objects, such as asteroids, comets, and meteors.

Like the atomic model, the modern model of the solar system has developed over a long period of time. In about 200 A.D., the Greek philosopher Ptolemy (TAWL uh mee) tried to explain why Earth had to be at the center of the solar system. This early model proposed that the Sun and planets orbited Earth.

In the sixteenth century, the astronomer Nicolai Copernicus (koh PER nih kus) proposed a model of the solar system that placed the Sun at the center. His model was opposed by many people on religious and scientific grounds. However, it was finally accepted, and it developed into the current understanding of the solar system.

Modern Atomic Theory

The next logical step in the development of the atomic model was to locate the electrons and measure their distances from the nucleus. Electrons are incredibly small, so locating them is no easy task. To locate an electron, scientists need to know its position and its velocity.

In 1927, the German scientist Werner Heisenberg reached an important conclusion. He recognized that it is impossible to know both the exact position and the exact velocity of an electron at the same time. The process of locating an electron changes the electron's velocity. If an electron's velocity could be measured, its position could not be known because it changes too quickly.

This uncertainty makes it impossible to describe electrons in terms of specific orbits. Instead, scientists can describe only a possible area where the electrons could be located at any specific time. This region is known as the **electron cloud.**

After You Read

1. How did Bohr describe the location of electrons in an atom?
2. What discovery did Chadwick make that slightly altered Bohr's model?
3. Refer to the diagram in your Science Notebook. In a well-developed paragraph, explain why scientists settled on an electron cloud rather than discrete orbits to describe electrons.

Nucleus

Electron cloud

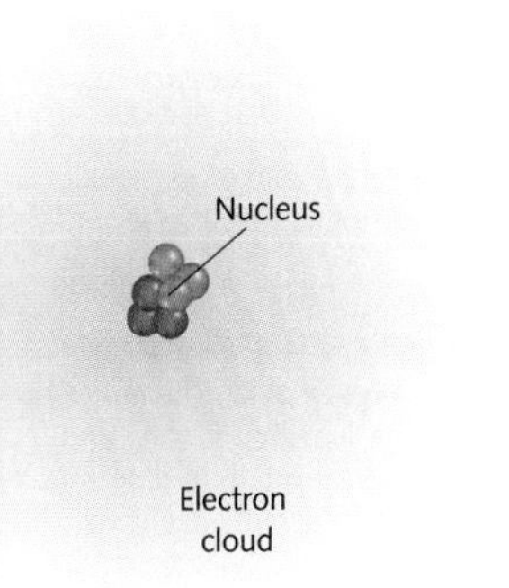

Figure 5.13 According to the modern theory of the atom, electrons move around in a region known as the electron cloud.

Background Information

Early astronomers thought that Earth did move; a Greek astronomer, Aristarchus, suggested that Earth and other planets orbited the Sun. Copernicus knew about those theories, and he thought that Ptolemy's theory was too complex. He postulated that the simplest explanation was that every planet orbited the Sun. Additionally, he believed that Earth rotated on its axis every 24 hours.

● Teach

EXPLAIN to students that the model of the atom was revised once more, by Werner Heisenberg; he determined that the exact locations of electrons could not be known. Electrons are described as being located in an area known as the electron cloud.

Science Notebook EXTRA

Have students work in groups of three or four to find out the names of the eight planets along with their sizes, locations, and distances from the Sun. Each group should then draw and label a model of the solar system using their new knowledge. Have students research the changes in the definition of a planet and the reasons why Pluto is no longer considered a planet. Each student should then write a persuasive letter to the International Astronomical Union in support or opposition of the decision not to classify Pluto as a planet.

● Assess

Use the After You Read questions and the Alternative Assessment to help you evaluate students' understanding of the lesson.

After You Read

1. Bohr described electrons as traveling in orbits at specific distances from the nucleus of an atom.
2. Chadwick discovered the neutron, which is an electrically neutral particle in the nucleus of an atom.
3. Heisenberg showed that the exact location of an electron could not be determined. Instead, scientists could identify only a region in which the electron is most likely to be located. This region is the electron cloud.

Alternative Assessment

Have students use the diagrams they created to explain the modern theory of the atomic model. Students should include details about the location and movement of electrons, protons, and neutrons.

5.3 Introduce

ENGAGE Draw examples of four or five different triangles on the board (include an equilateral, isosceles, and scalene). Have students work in pairs to list the characteristics that all the triangles share. Their lists might include the following: three sides, three angles, and the sum of interior angles is 180 degrees. Explain to students that the shared characteristics are also known as properties. They will be learning about the properties of electrons, protons, and neutrons in this lesson.

Before You Read

Model the process of creating a K-W-L-S-H chart on the board. Think aloud about what you and the class already know about subatomic particles, and write the facts on the board. It may be helpful to review the definition of *subatomic particle* as you think aloud. Have students create their K-W-L-S-H charts in their Science Notebooks, and encourage them to write additional facts in the *K* column.

Teach

EXPLAIN to students that electrons, protons, and neutrons are known as subatomic particles. Students will be learning more about these particles in this lesson.

Background Information

The scanning tunneling microscope is used for industrial and scientific research to study and view atoms on the surfaces of materials. The microscope works by tunneling electrons between the sharp tip of a probe and the surface of the material being studied. The tip of the microscope sweeps over the surface and is continuously adjusted to maintain a constant flow of electrons. The microscope creates a map of the surface by recording the height fluctuations of the tip.

Gerd Binnig and Heinrich Rohrer received a Nobel Prize in 1986 for inventing the scanning tunneling microscope. In addition to enabling scientists to form images of atoms, the STM also allows scientists to move individual atoms.

Learning Goals

- Compare and contrast the properties of subatomic particles.
- Determine the atomic number and mass number of an atom.
- Relate atomic mass to the isotopes of an element.

New Vocabulary

subatomic particle
atomic number
isotope
mass number
atomic notation
atomic mass unit
atomic mass

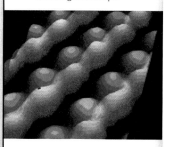

Figure 5.15 This image of gallium atoms *(blue)* and arsenic atoms *(red)* was formed with a scanning tunneling microscope.

Before You Read

In your Science Notebook, create a K-W-L-S-H chart. Think about the title of this lesson. In the column labeled *K*, write what you already know about subatomic particles. In the column labeled *W*, write what you want to learn about subatomic particles.

During the 2,000 or so years during which the modern atomic model has been developing, scientists have learned a tremendous amount about the structure of the atom. One of the fundamental concepts is that the atom consists of three particles, known as **subatomic particles.** The chart in **Figure 5.14** summarizes the properties of each particle.

Subatomic Particles

Particle	Symbol	Location	Charge
electron	e^-	outside nucleus	1–
proton	p^+	inside nucleus	1+
neutron	n^0	inside nucleus	0

Figure 5.14 The charge on the proton is exactly opposite the charge on an electron. Neutrons do not carry an electric charge.

Atomic Size

Despite centuries of research, scientists have never directly viewed a single atom or its structure. Why? Atoms are incredibly small. In fact, half the diameter of the period at the end of this sentence consists of more than one million atoms.

Atomic sizes are often described in units called nanometers (nm). *Nano-* is a prefix meaning 10^{-9} (0.000000001). An average atom is about 0.2 nm across. While the nucleus makes up most of the mass of an atom, the electron cloud makes up most of the atom's volume.

Because atoms are so small, they cannot be seen with optical microscopes. Instead, other techniques must be used to detect the positions of atoms on the surfaces of solids. Perhaps the best way to form images of atoms is with a device called a scanning tunneling microscope. This device uses an electric probe to scan a surface. While the microscope does not enable scientists to look directly at atoms or their internal structures, it makes it possible to form images of atoms and their arrangements.

ELL Strategy

Use a Concept Web Have each student create a concept web to organize the information about electrons, neutrons, and protons. The main idea should be *Properties of Subatomic Particles*, and the subtopics should be *Electrons, Neutrons,* and *Protons*. Students should add details to each subtopic about the location, charge, symbol, and relationship to atomic number and atomic mass.

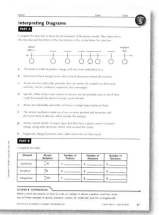

Interpreting Diagrams
Workbook, p. 27

Atomic Number

All atoms are made up of protons, electrons, and neutrons. All protons are the same, as are all electrons and all neutrons. Yet an atom of gold is very different from an atom of helium. What makes one element different from another? Atoms differ in the number of protons they have in their nuclei. The number of protons in the nucleus of an atom is known as the **atomic number.**

Every element has a unique atomic number. The atomic number of gold, for example, is 79. This means that every atom of gold has 79 protons in its nucleus. The atomic number of helium is 2. Every atom of helium has only two protons in its nucleus.

Recall that an atom is electrically neutral. This means that the number of protons in an atom is equal to the number of electrons. Therefore, the number of electrons in an atom is the same as the atomic number. An atom of gold has 79 electrons, and an atom of helium has two electrons.

Isotopes

Unlike the number of protons in an atom, the number of neutrons is not always fixed. For all but about 20 elements, the number of neutrons in the nucleus can vary. Atoms of the same element that have a different number of neutrons in their nuclei are called **isotopes** (I soh tohps).

For example, hydrogen atoms can exist in nature as two stable isotopes. One hydrogen isotope is called protium (PROH tee um). It does not have any neutrons in its nucleus. The other isotope, deuterium (dew TIH ree um), has one neutron in its nucleus. Both isotopes have one proton in their nucleus. That's what makes them hydrogen.

There is one more isotope of hydrogen, called tritium (TRIH tee um). It also has one proton in the nucleus, but it has two neutrons. Unlike the other two isotopes, tritium is unstable and breaks down. **Figure 5.17** lists the stable isotopes of the first several elements.

Figure 5.16 Both gold bars and helium gas are made up of atoms. The properties of gold and helium are different because their atoms are different. What property is unique to the atoms of each element?

Stable Isotopes

Atomic Number	Number of Protons	Number of Neutrons
1 hydrogen	1	0
1	1	1
2 helium	2	1
2	2	2
3 lithium	3	3
3	3	4
4 beryllium	4	5
5 boron	5	5
5	5	6
6 carbon	6	6
6	6	7
7 nitrogen	7	7
7	7	8

Figure It Out

1. What is the atomic number of the element in the chart that has no isotopes?

2. Give an example of isotopes of different elements that have the same number of neutrons.

Figure 5.17 This chart lists the number of protons and neutrons in the isotopes of the first seven elements.

● Teach

EXPLAIN to students that atoms are neutral. While the number of neutrons can vary for isotopes of elements, the numbers of protons and electrons remain consistent and are equal.

Vocabulary

subatomic particle Tell students that the prefix *sub-* means "under" or "below." Encourage students to think of common uses of the word *particle*. Students' responses may include a very small piece of something or a small amount of something. Explain to students that subatomic particles are pieces of the atom that are smaller than the atom itself.

atomic number Tell students that *atomic number* is also known as *proton number*. Ask students to explain why the two terms can be used interchangeably.

isotopes Explain to students that the prefix *iso-* denotes "the same" or "equal." The root *-tope* is derived from Greek and means "place."

Use the Visual: Figure 5.16

ANSWER Every element has a unique atomic number.

Figure It Out: Figure 5.17

ANSWER **1.** It has an atomic number of 4, which is beryllium. **2.** Sample answer: An isotope of carbon (atomic number 6) has 7 neutrons, as does an isotope of nitrogen (atomic number 7).

Background Information

Over 270 isotopes naturally occur. About 50 other isotopes are radioactive and are known as radioisotopes. Elements heavier than bismuth are radioactive and decay into isotopes of lighter-weight elements. These elements can be characterized into three radioactive decay series: U-238, U-235, and Th-232. These atoms further decay into other isotopes until they eventually become stable isotopes of lead. The length of time that is required for the decay is called half-life; each isotope has a specific half-life. These half-lives are used to identify elements present in matter.

● Teach

 EXPLAIN to students that scientists can represent the quantity of protons and neutrons in an atom by using atomic notation. Students will learn how to use atomic notation, as well.

Vocabulary

mass number Encourage students to think of common uses of the word *mass*. Examples might include weight, the greater part, a large collection of many items, or a body of indefinable shape. Review with students the meaning of *number* (represents quantity). Ask students to relate these meanings to the scientific definition of the term.

atomic notation Ask students to brainstorm common uses of the word *notation*. If needed, explain that the root is *note*. Students' examples might include writing something down or a set of symbols. Have students explain how this meaning relates to the scientific definition.

atomic mass unit Tell students that an atomic mass unit differs from a typical measurement of weight or mass because it is not an absolute measure but rather a comparison. The unit, also known as the dalton, is abbreviated amu.

atomic mass Have students postulate the literal meaning of the term *atomic mass* and then relate this to the scientific definition. Then have students explain the difference between atomic mass and mass number.

Use the Visual: Figure 5.18

(ANSWER) Protons and neutrons are located in the nucleus.

As You Read

Give students a few minutes to update their K-W-L-S-H charts in their Science Notebooks. Have students share their new facts with a partner.

(ANSWER) The mass number indicates the total number of particles in the nucleus of an atom (protons and neutrons).

As You Read

Add to the K-W-L-S-H chart you created in your Science Notebook. In the *L* column, list what you have learned about subatomic particles. Explain your chart to a partner and update your chart after your discussion.

What does the mass number indicate about an atom?

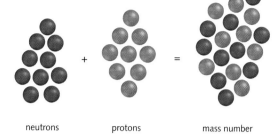

neutrons   protons   mass number

Figure 5.18 The mass number of an atom is the sum of its protons and neutrons. Where are these particles located in an atom?

Mass Number

The total number of protons and neutrons in the nucleus of an atom is called the **mass number.** Scientists use a shorthand method known as **atomic notation** to describe the numbers of protons and neutrons in an atom. The chemical symbol of the element is written with a superscript and a subscript before it. The superscript represents the mass number, and the subscript represents the atomic number. The protons and neutrons of a flourine atom are shown in **Figure 5.18.** The atomic notation for the fluorine atom is shown below. The notation shows that this fluorine atom has an atomic number of 9 and a mass number of 19.

$$^{19}_{9}\text{F}$$

If the atomic number and mass number of an atom are known, the number of neutrons can be determined. Look again at the atomic notation for fluorine. To find the number of neutrons in the nucleus, subtract the atomic number from the mass number. The atom has ten neutrons in its nucleus ($19 - 9 = 10$).

Here's another example. An atom of sodium is described by atomic notation as having a mass number of 23 and an atomic number of 11. The number of neutrons is the difference between the mass number and the atomic number. Thus the sodium atom has 12 neutrons in its nucleus ($23 - 11 = 12$).

A different way of describing atoms is to write the name of an element followed by its mass number. "Cobalt-60" represents an atom of cobalt with 27 protons and 33 neutrons in its nucleus.

Differentiate Instruction

Mathematical Have students write the atomic notations for all the elements and isotopes listed in **Figure 5.17** on page 85. Then have them check their atomic notations with a partner to ensure understanding.

Kinesthetic Have students draw models of the elements and isotopes listed in **Figure 5.17.** Encourage them to use one color to represent neutrons, a second color to represent protons, and a third to represent electrons. An alternative would be to provide three different colored papers and have students cut out circles or squares to represent neutrons, protons, and electrons. They could then paste the subatomic particles onto a model drawn on white paper. Remind students to create a key for their models and add labels.

Atomic Mass

Atomic masses are incredibly small. The mass of a carbon atom, for example, is 1.99×10^{-23} g. The atomic mass unit was developed to give scientists a more convenient way to describe atomic masses. This unit is not an absolute measure. Instead, it compares the mass of an atom to the mass of carbon-12. One **atomic mass unit** (amu) is equal to one-twelfth the mass of a carbon-12 atom.

When determining the mass of an atom of an element, scientists need to consider the isotopes of that element. Not all isotopes are as abundant as others. For example, carbon occurs naturally as two isotopes. One is carbon-12, and the other is carbon-13. Carbon-12 makes up 98.89 percent of all carbon. The remaining 1.11 percent is carbon-13.

If scientists determined the mass of carbon-12 and the mass of carbon-13 and averaged them, the result would not reflect the true value. Instead, scientists shift the calculation toward the mass that occurs in the greater abundance. This is known as a weighted average. The **atomic mass** of an element is the weighted average of all naturally occurring isotopes.

Returning to the carbon example, the mass of carbon-12 is 12.00000 amu, and the mass of carbon-13 is 13.00335 amu. To find the atomic mass of carbon, convert the abundance of each isotope to a decimal. Then multiply the decimals by the individual masses.

$$\text{carbon-12: } 12.00000 \text{ amu} \times 0.9889 = 11.87 \text{ amu}$$
$$+ \text{ carbon-13: } 13.00335 \text{ amu} \times 0.0111 = \underline{0.144 \text{ amu}}$$
$$12.01 \text{ amu}$$

Thus, the atomic mass of carbon is 12.01 amu. That does not mean that any single atom of carbon has a mass of 12.01 amu. It simply means that the weighted average of all naturally occurring isotopes of carbon is 12.01 amu.

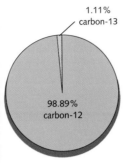

1.11%
carbon-13

98.89%
carbon-12

Figure 5.19 The two stable isotopes of carbon do not exist in the same abundance. The atomic mass reflects this fact by representing a weighted average of their masses.

After You Read

1. How do the charges and locations of the subatomic particles compare?
2. Explain how you can determine the number of neutrons in an atom if you know the atomic number and the mass number.
3. Why do scientists find a weighted average of the masses of the isotopes of an element?
4. Use the chart in your Science Notebook to write a well-developed paragraph about isotopes. Complete the chart by filling in the S column with questions you still have and the H column with ways you might find the answers.

Background Information

Today, scientists use mass spectrometry to identify unknown compounds, to quantify known compounds, and to investigate the makeup and chemical properties of molecules.

Alternative Assessment

Have students use the charts in their Science Notebooks to compare and contrast the properties of electrons, protons, and neutrons. They should include the locations and charges of the particles as well as how the particles differ in isotopes.

● Teach

EXPLAIN to students that the mass of an atom is amazingly small. An element's atomic mass is the average mass of its isotopes, adjusted for the mass that occurs most often. Thus the atomic mass is called a weighted average.

Tell students that in the first half of the twentieth century, a device called a mass spectrometer was developed to measure relative atomic masses. This device measures the amount by which atoms are deflected in a magnetic field. Lighter atoms are deflected more than heavier atoms are.

Science Notebook EXTRA

Obtain several shiny new pennies and several old, dirtier pennies. Do not use the same number of each type of penny. Each type of penny represents an isotope of an imaginary element.

Count and record the number of each type of penny. Then calculate the abundance of each "isotope." To do so, divide the number of each type of penny by the total number of pennies, and multiply by 100 (percent). Record your calculations.

Find the mass of each type of penny. Then multiply the mass by the abundance of that type of penny as a decimal. Add the masses together to find the atomic mass of the element.

● Assess

Use the After You Read questions and the Alternative Assessment to help you evaluate students' understanding of the lesson.

After You Read

1. Electrons and protons are electrically charged, whereas neutrons are electrically neutral. Protons and neutrons are found in the nucleus; electrons are found outside the nucleus.
2. You can subtract the atomic number (number of protons) from the mass number (number of protons and neutrons) to find the number of neutrons.
3. They do so because isotopes do not occur naturally in the same abundance.
4. Answers will vary.

Chapter 5 Summary

VOCABULARY REVIEW

Check students' sentences or paragraphs to make sure they understand the meaning of each vocabulary term.

Evaluate students' essays using the following criteria:

1. The topic sentence, or main idea, should restate the Key Concept.
2. The supporting paragraphs should incorporate the answers to the Learning Goal questions students have written and include details, facts, and examples they have recorded in their Science Notebooks.
3. The concluding sentence should sum up the main idea of the chapter and restate the Key Concept.

MASTERING CONCEPTS

True or False

1. False, Democritus
2. True
3. False, electron
4. False, positive
5. True
6. False, neutrons

Short Answer

7. J. J. Thomson discovered that electrons are subatomic particles by analyzing the results of studies using cathode ray tubes.

8. Bohr suggested that electrons orbit the nucleus in discrete energy levels, much like planets orbit the Sun.

9. An atomic mass unit is defined as one-twelfth the mass of a carbon-12 atom. It is not an absolute measure, but rather a comparison of the mass of an atom to the mass of carbon-12. Grams would be too big to measure the masses of atoms, which are incredibly small.

10. The atomic number is the number of protons, whereas the mass number is the number of protons plus the number of neutrons. The atomic number is always the same for an element, whereas the mass number changes with different isotopes.

Summary

KEY CONCEPTS

5.1 Early Atomic Models

- A model can be used to represent an object or process that is difficult to understand or impossible to observe, such as the structure of an atom.
- The earliest atomic model was proposed by Democritus, who suggested that all matter is made of indivisible particles called atoms.
- John Dalton used experimental data and observations to describe atoms as indivisible particles that cannot be created or destroyed, but can be combined, separated, and rearranged.
- J. J. Thomson identified the electron as the building block of the atom and proposed the plum pudding model, in which electrons are embedded in a mass of positive charge.
- Ernest Rutherford analyzed the results of the gold foil experiment to conclude that atoms consist of a dense center of positive charge surrounded by mostly empty space in which electrons exist.

5.2 Improvements to the Atomic Model

- Niels Bohr proposed a model of the atom that suggested that electrons orbit the nucleus in discrete energy levels.
- James Chadwick discovered the neutron, which is a subatomic particle that is electrically neutral.
- According to the modern theory of the atom, the specific location of electrons cannot be determined. Instead, a region in which they are likely to exist, called an electron cloud, can be described.

5.3 Properties of Subatomic Particles

- Protons, neutrons, and electrons are described as subatomic particles. Protons and neutrons make up the nucleus of an atom. Electrons are located outside the nucleus.
- The atomic number of an atom is the number of protons in its nucleus.
- The sum of the numbers of protons and neutrons in an atom's nucleus is the atom's mass number.
- Two atoms of the same element with different numbers of neutrons are known as isotopes. Each isotope exists naturally in a different abundance, so the atomic mass of an element is calculated as a weighted average.

VOCABULARY REVIEW

Write each term in a complete sentence or write a paragraph relating several terms.

5.1
model, p. 74
theory, p. 74
atom, p. 74
electron, p. 77
proton, p. 77
nucleus, p. 79

5.2
emission line spectrum, p. 81
neutron, p. 82
electron cloud, p. 83

5.3
subatomic particle, p. 84
atomic number, p. 85
isotope, p. 85
mass number, p. 86
atomic notation, p. 86
atomic mass unit, p. 87
atomic mass, p. 87

PREPARE FOR CHAPTER TEST

To prepare for the chapter test, create a question from each Learning Goal. Use the information in your Science Notebook to answer each question. Then use these answers to write a well-developed essay about the chapter. Use the Key Concept on the first page of this chapter as your topic sentence.

Reading Comprehension
Workbook, p. 28

Vocabulary Review
Workbook, p. 26

MASTERING CONCEPTS

True or False
If the statement is true, write "true." If it is false, change the underlined word or words to make the statement true.

1. <u>Aristotle</u> was a Greek philosopher who described an atom as indivisible.

2. <u>Dalton</u> recognized that atoms of different elements combine in simple whole-number ratios to form compounds.

3. J. J. Thomson is the scientist credited with discovering the <u>neutron</u>.

4. Rutherford's gold foil experiment showed that an atom has a dense region of <u>negative</u> charge known as the nucleus.

5. Bohr reasoned that emission spectra are produced when electrons jump to <u>lower</u> energy levels and lose energy.

6. Two atoms of the same element are isotopes if they have different numbers of <u>protons</u>.

Short Answer
Answer each of the following in a sentence or brief paragraph.

7. Describe the discovery that demonstrated for the first time that atoms are not the smallest particles of matter.

8. Explain why Bohr's model of the atom is sometimes known as the planetary model.

9. Define an atomic mass unit and explain why atomic masses are measured in amu rather than in grams.

10. Relate the atomic number and mass number of an atom.

Critical Thinking
Use what you have learned in this chapter to answer each of the following.

11. *Argue* A classmate says that an atom is a homogenous particle. Provide an argument to convince your classmate that he or she is not correct.

12. *Compare* How is the modern model of the atom similar to Bohr's model? How is it different?

13. *Sequence* Arrange the following scientists in the order in which they proposed changes to the existing atomic model: Bohr, Thomson, Dalton, Rutherford, Democritus.

14. *Calculate* An isotope of neon has 10 protons and 11 neutrons. What is its atomic number and its mass number?

Standardized Test Question
Choose the letter of the response that correctly answers the question.

15. Which statement is true, based on the diagram?

A   B

  A. A and B are the same atom.

  B. A is a carbon atom, whereas B is an oxygen atom.

  C. A and B are isotopes of carbon.

  D. A and B have the same mass number.

Test-Taking Tip

Read each question carefully. Think about what is asked. If you are not sure, read the question again. If you are still not sure, go on to the next question. Sometimes, a later question will help you remember information you need to answer a question you skipped. Remember to check all of your answers before turning in the test.

Critical Thinking

11. Most of the mass of an atom is in a dense nucleus in the center of the atom. The nucleus is tiny compared to the overall size of the atom. The remaining volume consists mostly of empty space, with electrons moving around the nucleus.

12. Both models describe a nucleus made up of protons and neutrons surrounded by electrons. However, Bohr placed electrons in discrete orbits around the nucleus, whereas the modern model describes regions, called electron clouds, in which electrons are likely to be found.

13. Democritus, Dalton, Thomson, Rutherford, Bohr

14. Its atomic number is 10 and its mass number is 21.

Standardized Test Question

15. C

Reading Links

Ernest Rutherford and the Explosion of Atoms

This biography's compelling narrative will provide students with a richer understanding of Rutherford's pioneering research and its impact on atomic theory. The book emphasizes social and scientific context alike while maintaining reader interest.

J. L. Heilbron. Oxford University Press. 144 pp. Illustrated. Trade ISBN 978-0-19-512378-4

J. J. Thomson and the Discovery of Electrons

A science-fiction novelist offers an interesting portrait of the life, work, and personality of Thomson in this short, entertaining book. The anecdotes and details it contains—stories of clumsy habits, broken test tubes, and classroom jokes—render one of the great figures in the history of science more human and accessible.

Josepha Sherman. Mitchell Lane Publishers. 48 pp. Illustrated. Library ISBN 978-1-58415-370-2.

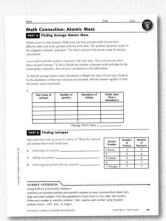

Curriculum Connection
Workbook, p. 29

Science Challenge
Workbook, pp. 30–31

5A What's in an Atom?

This prechapter introduction activity is designed to determine what students already know about gathering clues to describe something they cannot see by having them explore the behavior of an object inside a mystery box.

Objectives

- observe the behavior of the object(s) in the box
- predict how many objects are in the box
- record data in a suitable way
- communicate conclusions

Planning

 15–20 minutes   groups of 2–3 students

Materials (per group)

- mystery box
- pencil
- paper

Advance Preparation

- Ask students to suggest how they might organize a table to record their results.

- Use no more than three objects per box, such as marbles, dice, small batteries, paper clips, small metal bars, or coins.
- Use small jewelry gift boxes and glue or tape the lids on. Sophisticated kits are available from science supply houses.
- Keep a record of box numbers and contents. Students should not be told the contents; the focus should be on forming a mental image of the object.

Engagement Guide

- Challenge students to think about how they can predict what is in the box by asking these questions:
  - *How is a wrapped present or a gift like a mystery box?* (A gift is wrapped up and you cannot see what it is.)
  - *How can you determine what the gift is without opening the wrapped box?* (Students should explain how they might test the gift box by holding, shaking, or listening to it in order to visualize what is inside. They might also mention that knowing who the gift came from provides valuable information about what might be inside.)
- Encourage students to communicate their conclusions in creative ways.

Going Further

Encourage students to exchange boxes with other groups to see if their observations and results are similar.

5B Atomic Structure

Objectives

- make observations about a clay "atom" using probes
- predict the shape of the nucleus and model it with a sketch
- relate the activity to Rutherford's gold foil experiment

Skill Set

observing, predicting, comparing, illustrating, relating

Planning

 30–35 minutes   groups of 2–3 students

Materials

Materials for this activity are listed in the Student Laboratory Manual.

Advance Preparation

Use modeling clay to make balls that are 2–3 cm in diameter. Each ball should contain a small, hard object near its center. For the object, use a screw, bolt, or marble. For the probe,

use standard paper clips that have been straightened out except for one loop. Toothpicks may be used instead of paper clips. Remind students they can only use the probe 10 times and that they must plan how the probe will be placed before beginning. Tell students to carefully insert and pull out the probe; the clay ball "atoms" should not become mutilated.

Lab Tip

It may be easier for students to visualize the hidden object if they insert toothpicks into the clay lump, leaving each toothpick in place once it is inserted. To reduce the safety risk, students should use toothpicks that are blunt on one end.

Answers to Observations: Data Table 1

Students' Model sketches should show what they think the object looks like in an imaginary cut-away portion of the clay. The Actual sketch should show the position of the object inside the clay. Most students will be amazed at how accurate their descriptions are.

Answers to Analysis and Conclusions

1. Answers will vary. Students should first plan to use the probe to find the object and then use the probe to help identify the shape of the object.

2. Answers will vary. Students are usually very successful in determining what the object is. They may explain that the sketch gave them clues to what the object was and helped them identify it.

3. Answers will vary. Students should explain differences and similarities about the object's position, shape, and size when comparing the two sketches.

4. Students should explain that the clay ball represents the electron cloud of a gold atom and that the object in the middle represents the nucleus. The paper clip probe represents the alpha particles that were aimed at the gold foil. The process of gaining information about the object in the clay was similar to Rutherford's experiment; both relied on interactions that provided indirect information about the structure inside.

Going Further

In some ways, the atomic model is similar to the structure of the solar system. Encourage each student to write a paragraph or make a drawing comparing and contrasting the structure of the solar system and the structure of the atom.

 ## Modeling an Atom

Objectives

• calculate numbers of protons, neutrons, and electrons in an atom
• interpret data presented on the periodic table
• construct a Bohr model of an atom
• demonstrate an understanding of atomic structure
• identify the limitations of atomic models

Skill Set

analyzing, interpreting, modeling, comparing and contrasting, summarizing

Planning

30–45 minutes   groups of 2–3 students

Materials

Materials for this activity are listed in the Student Laboratory Manual.

Advance Preparation

Prepare a template page of 2-cm diameter circles to copy onto the red and blue paper. Other colors may be substituted, if available. If desired, have students use interactive online periodic tables to research atoms. Atoms of elements may be assigned to groups to ensure that all groups have a different atom.

Answers to Observations: Data Table 1

Answers will depend on the atom each group has been assigned. Students should round the atomic mass to the nearest whole number and subtract the number of protons to find the number of neutrons.

Answers to Analysis and Conclusions

1. the number of protons or atomic number

2. Because atoms are neutral, the number of protons and electrons must be equal. The total positive charge of the protons must balance the total negative charge of the electrons.

3. The atom is no loner neutral because it has an extra positive charge. The atom will form a 1+ ion.

4. The model shows the correct number and types of subatomic particles: protons and neutrons in the nucleus and electrons in energy levels outside the nucleus. The difference in the model is that these would be spinning and moving in the orbitals very fast. Scientists only understand a small amount about where electrons are in these orbitals.

5. In reality, protons and neutrons are more than 1,800 times larger than electrons. This activity also does not model the actual shape of the electron cloud; it simply models the groupings of electrons that occur within each energy level. Electrons follow three-dimensional paths, not circular ones as shown.

Going Further

Have students construct a three-dimensional model of an atom at school or at home. Use a wide variety of objects, such as rings, pipe cleaners, plastic foam balls, beads, wire, and modeling clay. Have students make mobiles of their creations and help them hang the mobiles from the classroom ceiling with fishing wire or string.

Example (Sodium)						
Symbol	Name	Atomic Number	Atomic Mass	Protons	Neutrons	Electron Configuration
Na	Sodium	11	22.990	11	12	2,8,1

6.1 Development of the Periodic Table

6.2 Types of Elements

6.3 Groups of Elements

Introduce Chapter 6

ENGAGE If possible, have available pictures or samples of the Fibonacci sequence in nature (such as a pineapple, daisy, or pinecone) and in art (such as da Vinci's *Mona Lisa* or *Vetruvian Man*).

Write the following line of numbers on the board: *0, 1, 1, 2, 3, 5, 8, 13 . . .* Ask students to write the list in their Science Notebooks, to analyze the pattern, and to calculate the next three numbers. Encourage students to calculate additional numbers if they are able. Discuss with students the pattern and how it progresses. Tell students that this is a well-known mathematical pattern called the Fibonacci sequence.

Explain that in this chapter, they will learn about natural patterns among elements, as organized in the periodic table.

Think About Patterns

Think aloud about the Fibonacci pattern or the pattern of seasons. Describe the pattern and draw a visual on the board to accompany the pattern. Then think aloud about how predicting the pattern is helpful to you. Have students complete the two bulleted items in their Science Notebooks. Encourage them to think of an example different from those listed in the text or discussed in class.

Chapter 6

The Periodic Table

KEY CONCEPT Chemical elements display periodic trends when arranged in order of increasing atomic number.

The shoreline of the Canadian province of Nova Scotia looks very different at low tide than it does at high tide. Just a few hours before this photo was taken, the fishing boats were floating at the dock, but they were left to sit in the mud when the tide rolled out.

All around Earth, high tides transition to low tides and back again in a continuous, repeating pattern. In this chapter, you will learn how chemists discovered a repeating pattern among chemical elements.

Think About Patterns

All around you, things occur in continuous, repeating patterns. Day becomes night and then day again, and the days of the week repeat themselves every seven days. All of these things happen in a predictable, repeating way. Think about something that changes in a pattern.

- In your Science Notebook, describe the pattern.
  Draw a picture to accompany the description, if you can.
- Write a few sentences telling how this pattern affects you.
  Why is it important for you to be able to predict the pattern?

www.scilinks.org
Periodic Table **Code: WGPS06**

90

Chapter 6 Planning Guide			
Instructional Periods	**National Standards**	**Lab Manual**	**Workbook**
6.1 2 Periods	A2, G1, G2, G3; A2, B2, G1, G2, G3; UCP1, UCP5	**Lab 6A: p. 31** Organizing the Elements **Lab 6B: pp. 32–33** Radioactive Isotopes	Key Concept Review p. 32 Vocabulary Review p. 33 Interpreting Diagrams p. 34 Reading Comprehension p. 35
6.2 2 Periods	B1; B2; UCP5	**Lab 6C: pp. 34–36** Comparing Metals, Nonmetals, and Metalloids	Curriculum Connection p. 36 Science Challenge pp. 37–38
6.3 2 Periods	A1, E1, F1, F3, F4; A1, E1, F1, F5; UCP3, UCP5		

Middle School Standard; High School Standard; Unifying Concept and Principle

6.1 Development of the Periodic Table

Before You Read

In your Science Notebook, draw a horizontal time line. Label the left end *1700* and the right end *2000*. Mark intervals of 25 years. Preview the lesson for important years and record these years on the time line.

Learning Goals

- Compare Mendeleev's periodic table with those of his predecessors.
- Identify Moseley's contribution to the periodic table.
- Describe the organization of the modern periodic table.

New Vocabulary

periodic law
periodic table
period
group

Recall Vocabulary

atomic mass, p. 87

A quick visit to a garden store can be a lengthy adventure if the plants are not properly organized into groups. Chemists of the nineteenth century faced a similar challenge in organizing the elements. Elements were being discovered at a rapid pace. In 1700, only 12 elements were known; by 1869, 63 elements had been discovered. Scientists began to search for methods of classifying and organizing the elements.

Triads and Octaves

In 1829, German chemist Johann Döbereiner noticed that the atomic mass of strontium was midway between the masses of calcium and barium. Calcium and barium have similar chemical properties. Döbereiner proposed the idea that elements could be grouped into triads, or threes, in which the middle element had properties that were an average of the other two elements when ordered by atomic mass. This concept became known as the law of triads.

In 1865, the English chemist J.A.R. Newlands separated the elements into groups of seven, as shown in **Figure 6.1.** According to this arrangement, the first element in each group shared similar properties with the first elements in the other groups. All of the second elements in each group also shared similar properties, as did the third elements, fourth elements, and so on. This became known as the law of octaves because properties repeated every eighth element.

Triads

Li	Li	Na	K
Ca	Ca	Sr	Ba
S	S	Se	Te
Cl	Cl	Br	I
Cr	Cr	Mn	Fe

Octaves

1	2	3	4	5	6	7	8
H	F	Cl	Co, Ni	Br	Pd	I	Pt, Ir
Li	Na	K	Cu	Rb	Ag	Cs	Tl
Be	Mg	Ca	Zh	Sr	Cd	Ba, V	Pb
B	Al	Cr	Y	Ce, La	U	Ta	Th
C	Si	Ti	In	Zr	Sn	W	Hg
N	P	Mn	As	Di, Mo	Sb	Nb	Bi
O	S	Fe	Se	Ru, Rh	Te	Au	Os

Figure 6.1 The elements in each of Döbereiner's triads showed remarkably similar properties. Newlands's octaves consisted of groups of seven elements. The properties of the first element of one octave were very similar to those of the element that appeared eight places later.

ELL Strategy

Model Have students (or pairs of students) make sets of flashcards for the first 36 elements. Students should label an index card with each element's symbol, atomic mass, and atomic number. Students should then arrange the cards in ways similar to the various methods used by the scientists they encounter as they read this lesson.

6.1 Introduce

ENGAGE List a variety of element symbols on the board. Include some more familiar elements, such as oxygen (O), carbon (C), calcium (Ca), and hydrogen (H), and some lesser-known elements, such as strontium (Sr), osmium (Os), tantalum (Ta), and tellurium (Te). Have students work in pairs to name the elements from the given symbols. Then ask students to brainstorm all the element names and symbols that they know. Create a class list and discuss what students already know. Tell students that they will be learning about the organization of elements in the periodic table and about their characteristics.

Vocabulary terms are listed on the first student page of each lesson. You may wish to preview the terms before introducing each lesson. Strategies for teaching the vocabulary appear on the pages where the terms are introduced.

Before You Read

Model the time line on the board and the process of calculating space for the intervals. Preview this page and note the dates 1700, 1829, and 1869 on the time line. Have students create their own time lines. Encourage them to use rulers or other straight edges to draw the lines and to allow space to write the dates and people.

Teach

EXPLAIN to students that they will learn about the history of the periodic table and its organization. In the table's early stages, two scientists, Döbereiner and Newlands, helped make sense of the organization of the elements.

● Teach

EXPLAIN to students that Dmitri Mendeleev analyzed the properties of elements and arranged the elements in order of increasing atomic mass.

Have each student use letters, shapes, or numbers (or any combination of the three) to create a pattern. Then have students swap patterns with classmates and try to predict the next item in the partner's sequence.

 Vocabulary

periodic law Encourage students to brainstorm common uses of the word *law.* Examples might include rules or procedures, an act passed by a legislature or government, the legal professional field, or the system of rules that can be enforced. Explain to students that the word *periodic* is derived from the Greek word *peri,* meaning "round," and *hodos,* meaning "way." The suffix *-ic* denotes "belonging or relating to." *Periodic* means "a way around" or "cyclic." The periodic law states that periodic or patterned traits can be observed when elements are arranged in a specific way.

periodic table Ask students to think of common uses of the word *table.* Students' responses might include a piece of furniture, a chart, or the act of postponing. Review with students the meaning of the word *periodic.* Ask students to relate the scientific definition to the common meanings of the term.

Mendeleev's Organization of the Elements

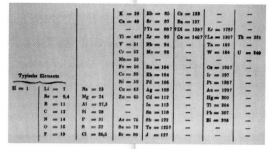

Figure 6.2 Mendeleev is considered one of the first modern scientists because he did not rely on his work alone. Instead, he corresponded with scientists around the world and considered their data along with his own.

In 1869, the Russian chemist Dmitri Mendeleev (DMEE tree • men duh LAY uf) compared various properties of individual elements, including color, atomic mass, density, melting point, and boiling point. Mendeleev concluded that the elements should be arranged in order of increasing atomic mass.

Mendeleev's original table, shown in **Figure 6.2,** arranged the elements in vertical columns in order of increasing atomic mass. In a brilliant and daring move, Mendeleev left blank positions that did not fit any of the known elements. In this way, Mendeleev predicted the existence and properties of elements before their discoveries.

Although many scientists were skeptical of Mendeleev's table at first, they were convinced when his predictions came true. Three of the five elements whose existence he predicted were soon discovered. These elements were gallium (in 1875), scandium (in 1879), and germanium (in 1886). Most important, each element displayed the physical and chemical properties that Mendeleev predicted it would have.

PEOPLE IN SCIENCE Dmitri Ivanovich Mendeleev (1834–1907)

Dmitri Ivanovich Mendeleev was born in Siberia, the youngest of at least 14 children. His father was a teacher of Russian literature and philosophy. As a student, Mendeleev excelled at science and mathematics.

Mendeleev attended the University of St. Petersburg's science teacher training program in 1850. By 1863, he had become a professor of chemistry there. Unable to find an acceptable chemistry textbook, Mendeleev began writing his own. It was in the process of writing *The Principles of Chemistry* that Mendeleev first created a table of elements.

In 1900, Mendeleev resigned his post at the university. He was appointed Director of the Bureau of Weights and Measures in 1903, where he remained until his death from pneumonia. Mendeleev fell one vote short of receiving the Nobel Prize in Chemistry, but many believe the award was rightly his. He is generally remembered as the "father" of the periodic table.

Background Information

Mendeleev had strong political beliefs as well as scientific beliefs. He resigned from his university post after speaking out against repression in Russia. He had carried a student petition to the Minister of Education that the Minister refused to acknowledge. Mendeleev's final lecture was stopped by police, who were afraid it might encourage political uproar among students.

Moseley's Contribution to the Periodic Table

Despite its success, Mendeleev's periodic system was not without flaws. Mendeleev himself corrected for some of them. In 1871, he revised his table to consist of horizontal rows rather than vertical columns. In addition, he found that when arranged strictly according to atomic mass, not all elements fell into their proper groups. Some elements fit into the proper group only if their positions were switched with their neighbors'.

At that time, it was difficult to calculate the atomic mass of an element. Mendeleev assumed that flaws in his table were primarily the result of inexact values. It was the insight of a physicist named Henry Moseley that changed the logic behind the table.

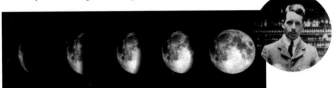

Figure 6.3 A periodic event is one that repeats itself after some amount of time—like the different phases of the Moon. Henry Moseley identified the atomic numbers of chemical elements and discovered periodic trends that occur when elements are organized according to atomic number.

Recall from Chapter 5 that in the early 1900s, Ernest Rutherford's group discovered the atomic nucleus. Moseley was one of Rutherford's students. Moseley was able to show that the atomic number is the number of protons in the atomic nucleus. Before Moseley's work, the atomic number of an element was based on the element's atomic mass. Moseley gave the atomic number a measurable basis.

In 1913, Moseley arranged the elements according to increasing atomic number instead of atomic mass. Immediately, some of the inconsistencies associated with Mendeleev's table were eliminated.

The patterns identified by Mendeelev, Moseley, and others serve as the foundation of the periodic law. The modern **periodic law** states that the properties of elements have a regular, repeating pattern when elements are arranged in order of increasing atomic number. The resulting arrangement of elements has come to be known as the **periodic table.** The modern periodic table is shown on the next pages.

The last major changes to the periodic table were made in the mid-twentieth century as a result of the work of Glen Seaborg. Seaborg discovered the elements with atomic numbers 94 to 102. In 1951, he was awarded the Nobel Prize in Chemistry, and element 106 was later named seaborgium in his honor.

Extend It!

Some elements are named for the country of origin of the scientist who discovered them. Other elements are named in honor of people. Research the discovery of elements named after people or places. Record your findings in a chart. Tell what you would name a new element if you were to discover it.

As You Read

On your time line, add the names of scientists discussed in this lesson. Describe how they contributed to the periodic table.

How did Henry Moseley improve upon Mendeleev's table of elements?

● Teach

 EXPLAIN to students that Mendeelev continued to refine the organization of the periodic table. With the discovery of the atomic number, the organization became easier and more apparent.

Extend It!

Model the process for students using the element bohrium (Bh), named after Niels Bohr. Provide students with science reference books and internet access. Have students work in pairs and choose three to four elements to research. Each pair should create a chart on large paper with three columns, titled *Name of element, Element symbol,* and *Derivation of name.* Students should post their charts around the room.

As You Read

Give students a few minutes to update their time lines. Have students compare their work with that of a partner to receive feedback. Check students' work for accuracy and understanding.

ANSWER Moseley arranged the elements according to increasing atomic number instead of atomic mass. By analyzing X-ray patterns of elements, he identified the elements' atomic numbers. The inconsistencies associated with Mendeleev's table were eliminated.

Differentiate Instruction

Musical, Linguistic Have each student write a poem about the elements, including the names or symbols. Students could set the poems to music from well-known songs or just describe the organization of the periodic table. Students could also write an acrostic poem for one or two specific elements.

Teach

Have students work with a partner to preview the periodic table. Ask them to discuss the following questions:

What do you notice on the table? Do you see any patterns on the table? What do the letters in the boxes represent? What do the numbers in the boxes represent?

Then discuss students' responses as a class. Record their answers and add to them throughout the chapter as students learn more about the periodic table.

Figure 6.4 The modern periodic table includes over 100 elements. The properties of an element can be predicted based on that element's position in the table.

PERIODIC TABLE OF THE ELEMENTS

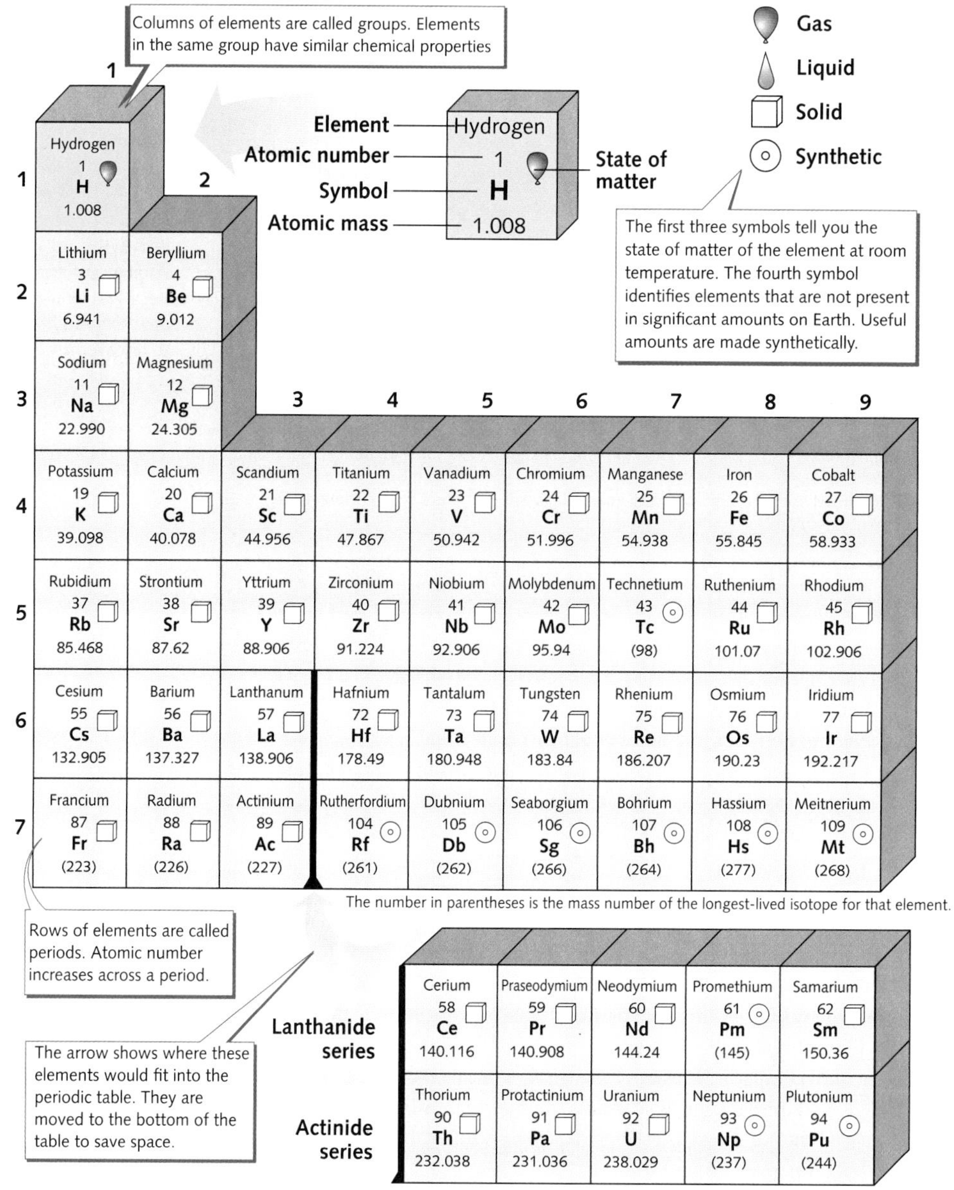

Columns of elements are called groups. Elements in the same group have similar chemical properties
Gas
Liquid
Solid
Synthetic
Element
Atomic number
Symbol
Atomic mass
Hydrogen 1 H 1.008
State of matter
The first three symbols tell you the state of matter of the element at room temperature. The fourth symbol identifies elements that are not present in significant amounts on Earth. Useful amounts are made synthetically.
1 2 3 4 5 6 7 8 9
1 2 3 4 5 6 7
Hydrogen 1 H 1.008
Lithium 3 Li 6.941
Beryllium 4 Be 9.012
Sodium 11 Na 22.990
Magnesium 12 Mg 24.305
Potassium 19 K 39.098
Calcium 20 Ca 40.078
Scandium 21 Sc 44.956
Titanium 22 Ti 47.867
Vanadium 23 V 50.942
Chromium 24 Cr 51.996
Manganese 25 Mn 54.938
Iron 26 Fe 55.845
Cobalt 27 Co 58.933
Rubidium 37 Rb 85.468
Strontium 38 Sr 87.62
Yttrium 39 Y 88.906
Zirconium 40 Zr 91.224
Niobium 41 Nb 92.906
Molybdenum 42 Mo 95.94
Technetium 43 Tc (98)
Ruthenium 44 Ru 101.07
Rhodium 45 Rh 102.906
Cesium 55 Cs 132.905
Barium 56 Ba 137.327
Lanthanum 57 La 138.906
Hafnium 72 Hf 178.49
Tantalum 73 Ta 180.948
Tungsten 74 W 183.84
Rhenium 75 Re 186.207
Osmium 76 Os 190.23
Iridium 77 Ir 192.217
Francium 87 Fr (223)
Radium 88 Ra (226)
Actinium 89 Ac (227)
Rutherfordium 104 Rf (261)
Dubnium 105 Db (262)
Seaborgium 106 Sg (266)
Bohrium 107 Bh (264)
Hassium 108 Hs (277)
Meitnerium 109 Mt (268)
The number in parentheses is the mass number of the longest-lived isotope for that element.
Rows of elements are called periods. Atomic number increases across a period.
The arrow shows where these elements would fit into the periodic table. They are moved to the bottom of the table to save space.
Lanthanide series
Cerium 58 Ce 140.116
Praseodymium 59 Pr 140.908
Neodymium 60 Nd 144.24
Promethium 61 Pm (145)
Samarium 62 Sm 150.36
Actinide series
Thorium 90 Th 232.038
Protactinium 91 Pa 231.036
Uranium 92 U 238.029
Neptunium 93 Np (237)
Plutonium 94 Pu (244)

ELL Strategy

Make a Model Have each student choose an element from the first 18 and construct a model of one of its atoms. Provide for student use a variety of materials, such as plastic foam balls, beads, pins, pipe cleaners, markers, and paint. Have students label the element name, electrons, neutrons, and protons. Display the element models around the room. English language learners should be given an opportunity to explain their model to peers or the class, using the vocabulary from the lesson and previous chapter.

Teacher Alert

When using the periodic table, students might confuse atomic number with number of valence electrons. Review the definitions of *valence electron* and *atomic number* in Chapter 5. Select several elements and have students practice determining atomic number and number of valence electrons for reinforcement of this distinction.

Periodic Table (Figure 6.4)

Metal
Metalloid
Nonmetal

The color of an element's block tells you if the element is a metal, nonmetal, or metalloid.

			13	14	15	16	17	18
								Helium 2 He 4.003
			Boron 5 B 10.811	Carbon 6 C 12.011	Nitrogen 7 N 14.007	Oxygen 8 O 15.999	Fluorine 9 F 18.998	Neon 10 Ne 20.180
10	11	12	Aluminum 13 Al 26.982	Silicon 14 Si 28.086	Phosphorus 15 P 30.974	Sulfur 16 S 32.065	Chlorine 17 Cl 35.453	Argon 18 Ar 39.948
Nickel 28 Ni 58.693	Copper 29 Cu 63.546	Zinc 30 Zn 65.409	Gallium 31 Ga 69.723	Germanium 32 Ge 72.64	Arsenic 33 As 74.922	Selenium 34 Se 78.96	Bromine 35 Br 79.904	Krypton 36 Kr 83.798
Palladium 46 Pd 106.42	Silver 47 Ag 107.868	Cadmium 48 Cd 112.411	Indium 49 In 114.818	Tin 50 Sn 118.710	Antimony 51 Sb 121.760	Tellurium 52 Te 127.60	Iodine 53 I 126.904	Xenon 54 Xe 131.293
Platinum 78 Pt 195.078	Gold 79 Au 196.967	Mercury 80 Hg 200.59	Thallium 81 Tl 204.383	Lead 82 Pb 207.2	Bismuth 83 Bi 208.980	Polonium 84 Po (209)	Astatine 85 At (210)	Radon 86 Rn (222)
Darmstadtium 110 Ds (281)	Unununium * 111 Uuu (272)	Ununbium * 112 Uub (285)		Ununquadium * 114 Uuq (289)		**116		**118

* The names and symbols for elements 111–114 are temporary. Final names will be selected when the elements' discoveries are verified.
** Elements 116 and 118 were thought to have been created. The claim was retracted because the experimental results could not be repeated.

Europium 63 Eu 151.964	Gadolinium 64 Gd 157.25	Terbium 65 Tb 158.925	Dysprosium 66 Dy 162.500	Holmium 67 Ho 164.930	Erbium 68 Er 167.259	Thulium 69 Tm 168.934	Ytterbium 70 Yb 173.04	Lutetium 71 Lu 174.967
Americium 95 Am (243)	Curium 96 Cm (247)	Berkelium 97 Bk (247)	Californium 98 Cf (251)	Einsteinium 99 Es (252)	Fermium 100 Fm (257)	Mendelevium 101 Md (258)	Nobelium 102 No (259)	Lawrencium 103 Lr (262)

Teach

As students study the periodic table, reinforce the significant fact that the table is an organizational tool. Incredible amounts of information about the elements, as well as important trends in physical and chemical properties, are organized and summarized in this scientific tool. It might be helpful to review the concept of physical and chemical properties before getting into the specifics of the table.

Use the Visual: Figure 6.4

Have students review the periodic table and identify three to five elements with which they are familiar. Ask students to make a three-column chart in their Science Notebooks listing information about what they believe to be the most common elements. The column headings should be *Element Name, Symbol,* and *Use.* Students should create a row for each of the familiar elements selected.

Encourage students to peruse images from magazines or from the Internet and identify additional examples of uses of the elements. Each student should then create a collage of words and images for a chosen element.

Differentiate Instruction

Mathematical Students should add atomic numbers to their index cards. Working in groups of two or three, they can use the cards to quiz each other. Encourage them to ask the following:

How many electrons does an atom of the element have?

How many protons does an atom of the element have?

How many neutrons does an atom of the element have?

Field Study

Students should explore their own classroom and one additional room in the school to identify objects made of elements in the periodic table. Students should add the information to their charts from the Use the Visual activity above.

Teach

EXPLAIN to students that the periodic table is arranged in periods (rows) and groups (columns) and that important trends in physical and chemical properties can be observed as a result of this arrangement. The trends have to do with numbers of protons and electrons, atomic radius, and ionization energy.

 Vocabulary

period Review with students the meanings of the word *period*. On the periodic table, a period refers to a horizontal row.

group Ask students to brainstorm common uses of the word *group*. Students' responses might include a set of people or things that belong together, people who share something in common, or a small number of musicians who play together. Elements in a group on the periodic table share characteristics.

Figure It Out: **Figure 6.5**

ANSWER **1.** The Group 16 element has a smaller atomic radius because there is a greater attraction between the positive nucleus and the electrons. **2.** Strontium has a greater atomic radius and therefore holds onto its outer electrons less tightly than magnesium does.

Assess

Use the After You Read questions and the Alternative Assessment to help you evaluate students' understanding of the lesson.

After You Read

1. Mendeleev organized all of the known elements in order of increasing atomic mass. Döbereiner organized elements into groups of three, in which the atomic mass of one element was between those of the other two. Newlands organized the elements into groups of seven, for which the first elements of each group exhibited similar properties.

2. The periodic law states that the properties of elements have a regular, repeating pattern when elements are arranged in order of increasing atomic number.

3. Almost 50 years after Mendeelev's table was introduced, Moseley presented a revised version.

---

1. Two elements are in the same period. One element is in Group 2, and the other is in Group 16. Which element should have a smaller atomic radius?

2. Why does strontium (Sr) have a lower ionization energy than magnesium (Mg) does?

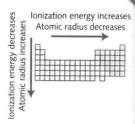

Figure 6.5 Periodic trends can be used to predict the properties of elements.

CONNECTION: Art

Some periodic tables are also works of art. Conduct research on the Internet to find artistic displays of the periodic table. Then select a period or group from the table and create a poster showing the elements in your own artistic way.

The Modern Periodic Table and Periodic Trends

Each element in the periodic table has its own square. The square includes the element's name, chemical symbol, atomic number, atomic mass, and natural state. The key for the periodic table in **Figure 6.4** illustrates how to find this information for each element.

Each horizontal row of the periodic table is called a **period.** For example, the row from sodium (Na) to argon (Ar) is Period 3. Each of the 18 vertical columns of the periodic table is called a **group.** The elements in a group generally have similar chemical and physical properties. A group is sometimes called a family.

The changing patterns of the periodic table are referred to as periodic trends. Certain periodic trends can be identified from left to right across periods and down groups.

Numbers of Protons and Electrons Elements are arranged in order of increasing atomic number. Because the number of electrons is equal to the number of protons, both the number of protons and the number of electrons increase across a period and down a group.

Atomic Radius The atomic radius is essentially the distance from the nucleus to the outermost electrons of an atom. Moving across a period, one electron and one proton are added to each element. The increased attraction between positively charged protons in the nucleus and negatively charged electrons in the energy levels pulls the electrons closer to the nucleus. Thus atomic radius decreases across a period.

Moving down a group, new energy levels in the electron clouds of the elements are added to accommodate additional electrons. Thus atomic radius increases down a group.

Ionization Energy The energy required to completely remove an electron from a neutral atom in the gaseous state is known as ionization (I uh nuh ZAY shun) energy. The closer an electron is to the nucleus, the more tightly held it is—and therefore the more difficult it is to remove. Ionization energy increases from left to right across a period because electrons are held closer to the nucleus. Ionization energy decreases moving down a group because atomic radius increases.

After You Read

1. How did Mendeleev's table compare to Döbereiner's and Newlands's tables?

2. State the periodic law in your own words.

3. According to the time line in your Science Notebook, about how many years separated Mendeleev's table from Moseley's table?

CONNECTION: Art

Give students the option of working individually or with a partner, and encourage them to be creative. Provide the following suggestions:

• Show real-life uses of the element.
• Create abstract representations.
• Use patterns.
• Include subatomic particles.

Background Information

The Royal Society of Chemistry has created *A Visual Interpretation of the Table of Elements*, which is available online. Each of the elements is displayed in symbolic and creative ways. Another group, HYLE (International Journal for Philosophy of Chemistry), displays a virtual art exhibition of which the periodic table is a focus.

Before You Read

Select a metal and a nonmetal. In your Science Notebook, create a chart to compare and contrast the two elements by writing the properties of each.

Elements fall into three general classes—metals, nonmetals, and metalloids. Look at the periodic table in Figure 6.4 again. Notice the zigzag line toward the right side of the table. This line serves to identify metals, nonmetals, and metalloids. Refer to this line as each type of element is described.

Metals

Most elements in the periodic table are **metals**. They are found to the left of the zigzag line in the periodic table. Some of these properties of metals are summarized in **Figure 6.6**.

Metals, such as chromium, are shiny. When light bounces off the shiny surface, it can produce a reflection.

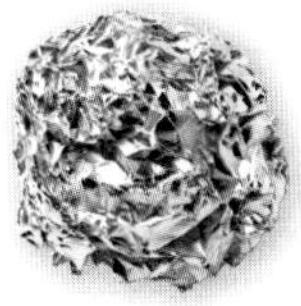

With the exception of mercury, metals are solids at room temperature. Metals generally melt only at high temperatures.

Most metals are **ductile** (DUKT tul). This means that they can be drawn into thin wires.

Most metals are **malleable** (MAL yuh bul). They can be folded and reshaped without shattering.

Metals are generally good conductors of heat and electricity. This means that they allow heat or electric charges to pass through easily. A metal pot transfers heat from a stovetop to the food in the pot.

Figure 6.6 The chemical and physical properties of metals make them very useful for a variety of applications.

- Describe the properties of metals and nonmetals.
- Relate metalloids to metals and nonmetals.

New Vocabulary

metal
malleable
ductile
nonmetal
metalloid
semiconductor

6.2 **Introduce**

ENGAGE Have available a variety of examples of metals for students to view and/or handle. Examples might include pennies, nickels, silver dollars, silver spoons, pots or pans, aluminum foil, copper wiring or tubing, a desk chair (if appropriate), soda cans, and washers.

Students should work with partners to identify common characteristics among the items. With the class, discuss students' responses. Identify the characteristics of metals in the responses.

Before You Read

Model a compare-and-contrast chart on the board using two items familiar to students, such as a school day and a weekend day. Ask students to list qualities that the two types of days share. Their responses might include eating meals, seeing friends, taking showers, and doing chores. Then ask students to list differences between the two days. Reponses might include the amount of free time, types of activities, and amount of stress. Place their responses in the appropriate locations. Ask students to create their own charts in their Science Notebooks and to begin entering information about a metal and nonmetal.

● Teach

EXPLAIN to students that elements can be classified as metals, nonmetals, and metalloids. They will learn about the properties of each class of elements in this lesson.

Vocabulary

metal Tell students that the word *metal* is derived from the Greek word for "mine." Have students analyze the metallic elements on the periodic table and then relate the derivation to the scientific definition.

malleable Explain to students that the word *malleable* comes from the Latin word meaning "hammer." Ask students to relate the scientific definition to the derivation.

ductile Tell students that the word *ductile* comes from the Latin word meaning "flexible." Ask students to relate the scientific definition to the derivation.

ELL Strategy

Use a Concept Map Have each student make a concept map to organize his or her understanding of the types of elements. The main idea should be *Types of Elements*, and the subtopics should be *Metals, Nonmetals,* and *Metalloids*. Students should add details to their maps as they read the lesson.

Differentiate Instruction

Visual, Kinesthetic Students should code their element cards as metals, nonmetals, and metalloids. Students could use a different color or shape to identify each type.

Teach

EXPLAIN to students that nonmetals have properties different from metals. Metalloids share properties of metals and nonmetals.

As You Read

Give students a few minutes to add the metalloid information to their charts. Place students in groups of three, and have each student list the properties for a metal, nonmetal, or metalloid group. The others in the group should check that student's chart.

ANSWER A semiconductor is a substance that conducts electricity under certain conditions but not others.

Figure It Out: Figure 6.7

ANSWER **1.** It should be dull, brittle, and a poor conductor. **2.** Nonmetals are insulators that prevent the flow of electricity from passing beyond the wires.

Explore It!

Using some of the items from the *Engage* activity, make models for this activity as a class. Include on the poster the element's name, chemical symbol, atomic number, atomic mass, and natural state. Review with students the properties of the element and write them on the back of the square.

Have students bring in items (with permission) to display on their posters.

Assess

Use the After You Read questions and the Alternative Assessment to help you evaluate students' understanding of the lesson.

After You Read

1. It can be hammered into sheets without shattering, and it can be drawn into wires.
2. Nonmetals are dull, brittle, and poor conductors of heat and electricity.
3. Metalloids have properties of metals and nonmetals. Elements become less metallic from left to right across a period.

As You Read

Add one column to the chart in your Science Notebook for the properties of metalloids.

What is a semiconductor?

Figure It Out

1. What properties would you expect the nonmetal phosphorus to have?
2. Why are compounds of nonmetals used to wrap metal wires that carry electricity?

Explore It!

Collect samples of elements such as copper, iron, carbon, aluminum, and nickel. Attach each sample to a large square of poster board. Make each square represent the element's square in the periodic table by providing the necessary information. On the reverse side of the square, identify the element as a metal, nonmetal, or metalloid, and list its properties.

Nonmetals

With the exception of hydrogen, the **nonmetals** are found to the right of the zigzag line on the periodic table. More than half of the nonmetals are gases at room temperature. The properties of nonmetals are essentially the opposite of the properties of metals. These properties are summarized in **Figure 6.7.**

Nonmetals, such as this lump of coal (made mostly of carbon), are not shiny. They are said to be dull.

Nonmetals are brittle. If they are hit with a hammer, they will shatter instead of flattening as a metal would.

Nonmetals are poor conductors of heat and electricity. Air is used to prevent the flow of heat into or out of a thermos bottle.

Figure 6.7 Nonmetals display a wider variety of properties than metals do. However, nonmetals share certain basic properties and applications.

Metalloids

Between the metals and the nonmetals are seven elements known as metalloids. They are located on either side of the zigzag line in the periodic table. A **metalloid** (ME tul oyd) is an element that has properties of both a metal and a nonmetal. There are seven metalloids.

All metalloids are solids at room temperature. They can be shiny or dull, malleable or brittle. Metalloids typically conduct heat and electricity better than nonmetals do, but not as well as metals do. Whether or not a metalloid acts as a conductor depends on conditions such as temperature, light, and exposure to other elements. A substance that can conduct electricity under certain conditions but not others is known as a **semiconductor** (se mih kun DUK tor).

After You Read

1. What does it mean to describe a metal as malleable and ductile?
2. List three properties of nonmetals.
3. Review the chart you created in your Science Notebook. Based on your notes, why are metalloids located between metals and nonmetals on the periodic table?

Vocabulary

nonmetal Tell students that the prefix *non-* means "not" or "the opposite of." Review with students the meaning of the word *metal*. Ask students to compare the literal definition of *nonmetal*, the opposite of a metal, to its scientific definition.

metalloid Tell students that the suffix *-oid* means something similar to, or with the form of, the specified thing (the root word).

semiconductor Explain to students that the prefix *semi-* means "partly." Review with students the meaning of the word *conductor*. The literal definition of *semiconductor* is "something that partly conducts."

6.3 Groups of Elements

Before You Read

Create a three-column, nine-row chart in your Science Notebook. As you read the lesson, use the chart to summarize the properties of the groups of elements, identify examples, and indicate uses.

All of the elements in a group of the periodic table share certain properties because they have the same number of valence electrons, or electrons in the outermost energy level. An atom will bond with another atom to gain a complete set of valence electrons by either transferring or sharing electrons. An element that is likely to transfer or share electrons with other elements is described as being reactive. Because all of the elements in a group have the same number of valence electrons, they are likely to behave in similar ways to obtain a complete set of valence electrons.

Group 1: Alkali Metals

Group 1, known as the **alkali** (AL kuh li) **metals,** consists of the elements lithium, sodium, potassium, rubidium, cesium, and francium. Alkali metals are soft enough to be cut with a knife. They are usually silver in color, shiny, and have low densities.

Each of the alkali metals has one valence electron and reacts with other elements by losing that one electron. These metals are so reactive that they are never found uncombined in nature, and they sometimes react violently. To prevent them from reacting, alkali metals in a laboratory must be stored under oil in sealed containers.

The alkali metals and the compounds they form have many common uses. Sodium chloride is table salt that is used to flavor food. Lithium is used to produce long-life batteries. Cesium is used to produce highly precise clocks. Potassium can be found in fireworks, liquid detergents, fertilizers, and dietary supplements. Rubidium is often used in photocells, such as those found in some motion detectors.

3
Li
Lithium
11
Na
Sodium
19
K
Potassium
37
Rb
Rubidium
55
Cs
Cesium
87
Fr
Francium

Figure 6.8 The element sodium can be cut with a knife. Place the element in water and flames will soon rise from the container. Each alkali metal is more reactive than the one above it in the periodic table. Which alkali metal is the most reactive?

6.3 Introduce

ENGAGE Divide the class into nine groups and assign each a number corresponding to a group from the periodic table (1, 2, 3–12, etc.). Then assign each group two to three elements from that periodic group, and tell students to determine the number of valence electrons in an atom of each element. Model an example before students begin; it may be necessary to review the principal energy levels and sublevels. Have students share their findings with the class.

Ask students to predict how the number of valence electrons affects an element's position in the periodic table and its chemical reactivity. Have students write their predictions in their Science Notebooks.

Before You Read

Model the chart on the board. Label the three columns *Properties*, *Examples*, and *Uses*. Preview with the students the headings in the lesson to identify the nine groups of elements. Have students draw and appropriately label the charts in their Science Notebooks.

● Teach

EXPLAIN to students that they will learn about the groups of elements. Group 1 is the alkali metals. Alkali metals have one valence electron and are the most reactive.

 Vocabulary

alkali metal Show students Group 1 on the periodic table, and explain that these elements are alkali metals. Tell students that these metals dissolve in water to produce an alkaline, or basic, solution, and they neutralize acids to form salts.

ELL Strategy

Think, Pair, Share Have students answer the following questions individually in their Science Notebooks for each element group:

What are two properties for the group?

How are the elements used in real life?

Name two example elements for this group.

After students have answered the questions, have them discuss their responses with partners. If any pairs have difficulty with a question, have them consult another group.

● Teach

EXPLAIN to students that Group 2 elements have two valence electrons and are reactive; however, they are not as reactive as alkali metals.

Explain It!

Have students work with partners to research the concept of Recommended Dietary Allowance (RDA) for guidance about healthful diets. Provide current resources for students to research, including Web sites and scientific or medical journals. Students should identify five elements and corresponding reference foods that contain those elements.

Have each student keep a food diary in his or her Science Notebook for two days. Students should evaluate their food choices to determine whether they contain the recommended elements and compare their daily intake to the RDAs.

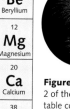

Figure 6.9 Group 2 of the periodic table consists of the very reactive alkaline earth metals. Magnesium and strontium are used to manufacture fireworks.

Explain It!

Some Group 1 and Group 2 metals, such as calcium, are essential to human health. Research other elements that are a necessary part of a healthful diet. Prepare a poster describing your findings and providing pictures of foods that contain these elements.

Group 2: Alkaline Earth Metals

The elements in Group 2—beryllium, magnesium, calcium, strontium, barium, and radium—are the **alkaline** (AL kuh lun) **earth metals.** These elements are generally hard, gray-white, and good conductors of electricity.

Alkaline earth metals have two valance electrons. These metals react by losing the two electrons. Although they are not as reactive as the alkali metals, alkaline earth metals are more reactive than most other metals. Like the alkali metals, they are never found uncombined in nature.

The alkaline earth metals have a variety of applications. Beryllium is applied to high-speed aircraft, missiles, spacecraft, and communication satellites. Magnesium is often combined with other metals to form alloys used in the manufacture of aircraft as well as other products that need both strength and light weight. It is also used to manufacture medicines, flares, and fireworks.

Calcium is very abundant in Earth's crust. Limestone, marble, and many other rocks are made of calcium compounds. Calcium is essential to strong human teeth and bones.

Strontium is used to give fireworks their red color. Barium can be found in compounds that are used to manufacture ceramics and some types of glass.

Radium is a radioactive element. In a **radioactive element,** there are either too many protons or too few neutrons in the nucleus. The result is an imbalance between the forces that hold the nucleus together and the forces that pull it apart. Particles and energy are emitted from the nucleus. Through this process, the unstable nucleus decays, or breaks down, into a stable nucleus. The particles and energy released as a radioactive element decays can be harmful to living cells. However, radium is commonly used in the treatment of cancer.

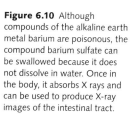
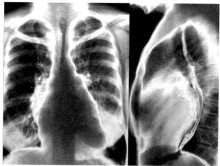

Figure 6.10 Although compounds of the alkaline earth metal barium are poisonous, the compound barium sulfate can be swallowed because it does not dissolve in water. Once in the body, it absorbs X rays and can be used to produce X-ray images of the intestinal tract.

Background Information

Elements that are necessary for a healthful diet include arsenic, boron, calcium, chromium, copper, fluorine, iodine, iron, magnesium, manganese, molybdenum, nickel, phosphorus, selenium, silicon, vanadium, and zinc.

Many items that glow in the dark contain phosphors, a substance that produces visible light after being energized.

Television screens, fluorescent lights, and computer monitors also contain phosphors. In items such as watches, a phosphor is mixed with a radioactive element, and the radioactive emissions energize the phosphor. Tritium (a radioactive isotope of hydrogen) and promethium (a radioactive element) are currently used most often in watches.

21	22	23	24	25	26	27	28	29	30
Sc	Ti	V	Cr	Mn	Fe	Co	Ni	Cu	Zn
39	40	41	42	43	44	45	46	47	48
Y	Zr	Nb	Mo	Tc	Ru	Rh	Pd	Ag	Cd
57	72	73	74	75	76	77	78	79	80
La	Hf	Ta	W	Re	Os	Ir	Pt	Au	Hg
89	104	105	106	107	108	109	110	111	112
Ac	Rf	Db	Sg	Bh	Hs	Mt	Ds	Rg	Uub

Figure 6.11 The transition metal tungsten forms the filament in an incandescent lightbulb. Compounds of transition elements are used to color paints.

Groups 3–12: Transition Elements

The periodic table can be divided into representative elements and transition elements. Groups 1 and 2, along with Groups 13 through 18, are known as the **representative elements,** or main group elements. The behavior of representative elements is generally predictable. For example, sodium always reacts with chlorine to form sodium chloride.

The elements in Groups 3 through 12 are known as **transition elements,** or transition metals. The behavior of transition elements is less predictable. For example, iron might react with oxygen to form FeO or Fe_2O_3, depending on the amount of oxygen available. Transition elements can lose different numbers of electrons during reactions.

Despite the differences and unpredictability, transition elements share some general properties. Most of these metals are hard, shiny, and are good conductors of electricity. They form colored compounds, and they can be used to speed up chemical reactions. Transition metals are less reactive than the metals in Groups 1 and 2. This makes them particularly useful for products that need to last a long time, such as coins.

Lanthanides Some transition metals are placed in two rows below the main table to keep the table from becoming too wide. The elements in the first row are known as the lanthanides (LAN thuh nides). Lanthanides are soft, malleable, shiny metals that are highly conductive. They are often mixed with other metals to form alloys.

Actinides The elements in the second row are called the actinides (AK tuh nides). Only four of these elements—actinium (Ac), thorium (Th), protactinium (Pa), and uranium (U)—occur naturally. Elements with atomic numbers greater than 92 are made in a laboratory by forcing nuclear particles to crash into each other. The nuclei of these elements are extremely unstable and quickly decay into smaller nuclei. Some last only fractions of a second after they are formed.

58	59	60	61	62	63	64	65	66	67	68	69	70	71
Ce	Pr	Nd	Pm	Sm	Eu	Gd	Tb	Dy	Ho	Er	Tm	Yb	Lu
90	91	92	93	94	95	96	97	98	99	100	101	102	103
Th	Pa	U	Np	Pu	Am	Cm	Bk	Cf	Es	Fm	Md	No	Lr

Figure 6.12 The lanthanides and actinides are placed below the main body of the periodic table.

As You Read

Work with a partner to add the number of valence electrons for each group in the chart in your Science Notebook.

Which group is least reactive as a result of its valence electrons?

Figure It Out

1. Why are the lanthanides and actinides placed below the main periodic table?

2. How are the elements with atomic numbers greater than 92 different from the other transition metals?

● Teach

EXPLAIN to students that another way to classify elements in the periodic table is as representative elements and transition elements.

Have students note in their Science Notebooks how the classification of metals, nonmetals, and metalloids compares to the classification of representative and transition elements.

Vocabulary

alkaline earth metal Show students Group 2 on the periodic table and explain that these elements are alkaline earth metals. These elements also dissolve in water to produce an alkaline (basic) solution, conduct electricity well, burn in air, and are powerful reducing agents.

radioactive element Tell students that a radioactive element is one that emits energy in the form of particles as the element decays.

representative element Ask students to list common uses of the word *representative*. (If students struggle with *representative*, use its root, *represent*.) Students' examples might include a sample or type of something, an agent for a company, or someone who speaks or votes on behalf of someone. Ask students to relate the common definition to the term's scientific definition.

transition element Explain to students that the word *transition* is derived from the Latin word *transitio* and means "going across." Ask students to view the periodic table and to relate the scientific definition to the term's derivation.

As You Read

Give students about five minutes to update their charts. Encourage them to include the valence electron information in the *Properties* column. Have each student review his or her chart with a partner.

ANSWER Group 18 is least reactive because its elements' atoms do not lose or gain electrons to become stable.

Figure It Out: Figure 6.12

ANSWER **1.** This prevents the table from becoming too wide and difficult to manage. **2.** They do not occur naturally.

Differentiate Instruction

Visual Have students label their element cards with group categorizations. Again, students should use a color or shape to differentiate among groups.

Kinesthetic Assign each student an element that he or she will represent. Have students sit in element order and arrange themselves in the shape of the periodic table. Have students stand when you call out a property of an element or group that applies to the assigned element.

Background Information

Three of the transition elements have a special property. Iron, cobalt, and nickel are the only elements known to produce a magnetic field.

Teach

EXPLAIN to students that they will learn about Groups 13 and 14. These groups are comprised of metals, nonmetals, and metalloids. Review with students the location of the groups on the periodic table and the classifications of metals, nonmetals, and metalloids.

Science Notebook EXTRA

Have students research and then compare the prices paid for scrap aluminum and gold. Before doing the research, have students predict the amount of money (per pound) that they think each metal is worth. Students should then compare their predictions to the actual costs. Have students also note which other metals have scrap value.

Encourage students to recycle used aluminum beverage cans. Have students plan and create collection sites around the school. Students can take the cans to a recycling center and use the proceeds to fund an activity or to support a local charitable organization. Have students record their plans and results in their Science Notebooks.

5 **B** Boron
13 **Al** Aluminum
31 **Ga** Gallium
49 **In** Indium
81 **Tl** Thallium

Figure 6.13 All elements in the boron family are solids with three valence electrons. Boron is a metalloid.

Group 13: Boron Family

The group of elements that begins with boron is also known as the boron family. This family consists of one metalloid (boron) and four metals (aluminum, gallium, indium, and thallium).

Boron is a hard, black solid that is also very brittle. At room temperature, boron is a poor conductor. At high temperatures, however, boron becomes a good conductor. This is why it is a metalloid.

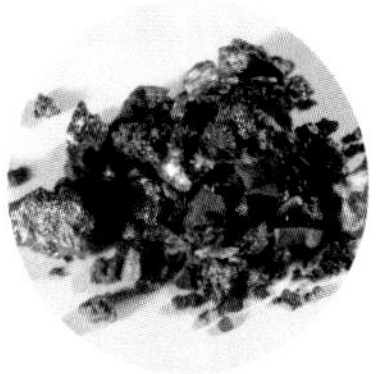

Aluminum is the third most abundant element in Earth's crust. As an excellent conductor of heat and electricity, aluminum is used in some wiring as well as in pots and pans and in foil that holds foods. Adding small amounts of silicon and iron to aluminum makes it significantly harder. Because it is lightweight, aluminum is commonly used to make parts for beverage cans, airplanes, cars, and trucks.

At room temperature, gallium is soft and can be cut with a knife. However, it has an abnormally low melting point and will begin to melt in the palm of a person's hand. Gallium is used in electronic devices.

Group 14: Carbon Family

The carbon family consists of one nonmetal (carbon), two metals (tin and lead), and two metalloids (silicon and germanium). Each element in the carbon family can gain, lose, or share four electrons.

Carbon is the fourth most abundant element in the universe. It exists in different forms, two of which are diamond and graphite. A rare carbon isotope is used to find the ages of ancient objects and fossils.

Silicon is second only to oxygen in abundance in Earth's crust. It is the main component of sand and an essential element in semiconductor technology, as is germanium. Germanium is rather rare.

People have known of tin since ancient times. The discovery that tin could be combined with copper to make bronze marked the beginning of the Bronze Age.

Lead is a blue-gray metal that resists corrosion, making it useful in building materials, ceramics, plumbing, and glassmaking. Lead can cause damage to human tissues when absorbed in large amounts.

Did You Know?

The chemical symbol for lead is derived from the Latin word *plumbum*. The modern words *plumbing* and *plumber* have the same origin because plumbing was originally done with lead pipes.

Figure 6.14 Group 14 of the periodic table is the carbon family. There are close to ten million known carbon compounds, many of which are vital to living things like this lion.

6 **C** Carbon
14 **Si** Silicon
32 **Ge** Germanium
50 **Sn** Tin
82 **Pb** Lead

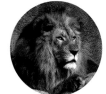

Background Information

Until the 1880s, aluminum was considered a precious metal because the process used to produce pure aluminum was very costly. In fact, for many years aluminum was actually more expensive than gold. Today, the price of aluminum is drastically reduced from its nineteenth century value.

In 1886, Charles Martin Hall discovered an economical method of releasing aluminum from its ore. He passed an electric current through a solution of aluminum oxide in molten cryolite. This invention marked the foundation of the aluminum industry in North America. One ton of aluminum produces 60,000 beverage cans or seven space frames for full-size cars.

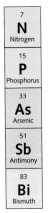

Figure 6.15 Group 15 is the nitrogen family of the periodic table. Among its other uses, liquid nitrogen is used to preserve samples by keeping them at extremely low temperatures.

Group 15: Nitrogen Family

The nitrogen family consists of two nonmetals (nitrogen and phosphorus), two metalloids (arsenic and antimony), and one metal (bismuth). Although all of these elements have five electrons in their outermost energy level, they show a range of properties and behaviors.

Nitrogen, which is the most abundant gas in the atmosphere, is an example of an element that exists as a diatomic molecule, N_2. A **diatomic** (di uh TAHM ihk) **molecule** is made of two atoms. Nitrogen is essential to living things, where it is used to build protein molecules, cell parts, and genetic information.

Phosphorus occurs in at least ten forms. It is extremely reactive and is always found combined in nature. One common form of phosphorus is a component of the striking surface of a match.

Group 16: Oxygen Family

The oxygen family consists of three nonmetals (oxygen, sulfur, and selenium) and two metalloids (tellurium and polonium). These elements all have six electrons in their outermost energy level.

Oxygen is a colorless, odorless, and tasteless gas at room temperature. It is the most abundant element in Earth's crust and makes up about one-fifth of Earth's atmosphere.

Oxygen forms a diatomic molecule (O_2) in air. It can also form a triatomic molecule (O_3) called ozone. Ozone occurs naturally in the upper atmosphere, where it acts as a shield to prevent some of the Sun's ultraviolet radiation from reaching Earth's surface. Near Earth's surface, ozone acts as a dangerous pollutant because it is very reactive.

Sulfur is a tasteless and odorless solid with a light-yellow color. However, a compound of sulfur (H_2S) smells like rotten eggs. Sulfur compounds are used as preservatives in food, in the manufacturing of rubber products, and in bleaching and refrigeration.

Polonium is a rare radioactive element. It was discovered by Marie and Pierre Curie in 1898 and named for their native country, Poland.

CONNECTION: Literature

The element arsenic is in the nitrogen family. Arsenic is perhaps best known for being toxic. It is often the weapon of choice in murder mysteries and other forms of literature, such as the play *Arsenic and Old Lace*, written by Joseph Kesselring in 1939.

Figure 6.16 Oxygen is the first element in Group 16 of the periodic table. Animals depend on oxygen to survive. Much of the oxygen in the atmosphere is produced by plants during photosynthesis.

● Teach

EXPLAIN to students that they will learn about Groups 15 and 16. The nitrogen family elements have five valence electrons; the oxygen family elements have six valence electrons.

Science Notebook EXTRA

Tell students that a minute amount of arsenic is present in groundwater and is of natural origin. Have students investigate the standard of allowable arsenic concentration in their local groundwater source. Then have them research how arsenic can be removed from drinking water and read about the symptoms of arsenic poisoning.

Vocabulary

diatomic molecule Tell students that the prefix *di-* means "two." Literally, *diatomic* means "two atoms." Have students describe the literal translation of *diatomic molecule*.

Background Information

The World Health Organization's standard of arsenic concentration is ten parts per billion. Primary symptoms of arsenic poisoning are a metallic taste in the mouth, excessive saliva production, and difficulty swallowing. This is followed by vomiting and diarrhea, stomach cramping, and excessive sweating. The patient will experience seizures and then go into shock; he or she will likely die within a few hours or days, when kidney failure occurs.

If historic documents such as the Declaration of Independence are exposed to air, they will react with oxygen. In time, they will decay and fall apart. To protect them, such documents are encased in airtight containers filled with nitrogen gas.

Teach

 EXPLAIN to students that elements in Group 17, the halogen family, are extremely reactive (like Group 1 elements). Group 17 elements have seven valence electrons and achieve stability (having a complete valence set of eight electrons) by gaining or sharing an electron with another element. Review with students the properties of nonmetals.

Vocabulary

halogen Explain to students that the word *halogen* is derived from Greek and means "salt." A halogen forms a salt when combined with a metal.

noble gas Ask students to brainstorm common uses of the word *noble*. Their examples might include being an aristocrat, having high ideals or moral character, or being impressive in quality. Ask students to relate these common meanings to the term's scientific definition.

Science Notebook EXTRA

Have students check their understanding of the periodic table by developing a game in which they have a partner guess an element's identity from clues. Have students write their clues and the answers in their Science Notebooks and then question their partners. Suggest that students write clues such as:

This element is in Group X, Period Y.

This element has X valence electrons and an atomic mass of Y.

This element is a metal found in Group X, Period Y.

This is an element with an atomic number of X.

This element is very reactive and is used to help prevent tooth decay.

Students could also create four or five questions (and answers) each and play the game in small groups.

Group 17: Halogen Family

The halogen family is made up of five nonmetals (fluorine, chlorine, bromine, iodine, and astatine). All **halogens** have seven valence electrons and generally gain or share one electron with other elements. This makes them very reactive. In their uncombined forms, all of the halogens are dangerous to humans. Many of their compounds, however, are extremely useful. Like nitrogen and oxygen, the halogens exist as diatomic molecules: F_2, Cl_2, Br_2, I_2, and At_2.

Figure 6.17 The halogens make up Group 17 of the periodic table. The halogens are the only group in which elements exist in three states of matter at room temperature. Chlorine *(left)* is a gas, bromine *(center)* is a liquid, and iodine *(right)* is a solid.

Fluorine is a greenish-yellow gas that is never found uncombined in nature. It is the most reactive element. Compounds of fluorine are used in fluoridated toothpaste and public water systems to help prevent tooth decay. Other fluorine compounds are used to make such products as nonstick coating on cookware.

Chlorine is also a greenish-yellow gas at room temperature that is never found uncombined in nature. Its name comes from the Greek word *chloros*, meaning "greenish-yellow." The best-known compound of chlorine is probably sodium chloride (NaCl), which is common table salt. Chlorine is commonly used to make drinking water safe and to treat swimming pools. Large amounts of chlorine are used in industrial processes such as the production of paper products, plastics, dyes, and antiseptics.

At room temperature, bromine is a reddish-brown liquid with a strong odor. Its name comes from the Greek word *bromos*, which means "stench." It is the only nonmetal that is a liquid under normal conditions. Bromine causes painful burns that heal slowly. It is currently used in dyes, disinfectants, and photographic chemicals.

Elemental iodine is a dark-gray solid with a slig ht metallic luster. Iodine is an essential part of the human diet—in small amounts—for the proper function of the thyroid gland. For this reason, iodine is added to table salt. Astatine is a radioactive halogen that is very unstable and decays quickly.

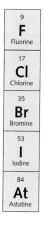

Did You Know?

In high concentrations, chlorine is quite toxic. As a liquid, chlorine burns the skin, and as a gas, it irritates the lining of the respiratory system. It was used in World War I as a poison gas.

Background Information

Scientists in Japan have developed a chlorinated air filtration system that suppresses more than 99 percent of airborne avian influenza viruses. The system holds electrolyzed water containing a 10-mg/L concentration of free residual chlorine, and it can quickly clean the air in a large room. Scientists in the U.S. have created a hand sanitizer that kills more than 98 percent of the bird flu virus H5N1 on skin for up to four hours.

Key Concept Review
Workbook, p. 32

Group 18: Noble Gases

As the name suggests, all of the elements in this group are gases at room temperature. The **noble gases** include helium, neon, argon, krypton, xenon, and radon. These elements are generally not reactive because they have a complete set of valence electrons. For helium, two electrons make a complete set. All of the other noble gases have eight valence electrons.

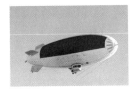 

This group was originally called the inert gases because chemists thought they did not form any compounds at all. In the 1960s, chemists discovered that krypton and xenon do form some compounds.

All of the noble gases are present in the atmosphere. Helium is the second most abundant gas in the universe. It must be extracted from the atmosphere or separated from deposits of natural gas.

Neon is also extracted from the atmosphere, where it is more common than helium. Neon is best known for its use in lights that bear its name. However, most "neon" lights actually contain other noble gases.

Hydrogen

Hydrogen is the only element that does not fit into any other group of the periodic table. It is placed alone in the upper-left corner of the table. Made up of just one proton and one electron, hydrogen is the most abundant element in the universe. Stars use hydrogen to produce energy.

Hydrogen is a colorless, odorless gas that is very flammable. It combines with other elements to form compounds, including water (H_2O), table sugar ($C_{12}H_{22}O_{11}$), and ammonia (NH_3). When combined with oxygen, liquid hydrogen is used as fuel to lift rockets into space.

2
He
Helium
10
Ne
Neon
18
Ar
Argon
36
Kr
Krypton
54
Xe
Xenon
86
Rn
Radon

Figure 6.18 Group 18, the noble gases, is made up of the most stable elements in the periodic table. Helium is used to make a balloon float in air, to lift modern airships, and to dilute the oxygen that a scuba diver breathes. Neon and other noble gases are used to make decorative lights.

Did You Know?

Forms of the noble gas radon that can cause cell damage are produced when some heavy metals, such as uranium, decay in the ground. Radon can build up in homes and other buildings. Soil and homes are usually checked for radon before they are sold. In addition, people can install radon detectors to identify radon buildup.

After You Read

1. How do valence electrons determine the properties of the Group 1 and 2 metals?
2. How are the transition metals different from the representative metals?
3. How do the valence electrons change from Group 13 to Group 18?
4. Hydrogen does not fit into any groups of the periodic table. In the chart in your Science Notebook, add information about hydrogen, such as its atomic structure and examples of where it is found and how it is used.

Background Information

Car companies are predicting that hydrogen cars will be available by 2012 to 2015. Hydrogen cars are powered by a fuel cell stack that converts hydrogen and oxygen into electrons and water. The fuel cell is estimated to be 50 to 60 percent efficient; gasoline cars are only 14 percent efficient. Some challenges include creating filling stations, lowering the cost of manufacture, and a more cost-effective manner of production.

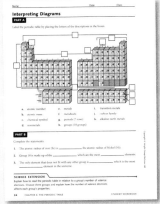

Interpreting Diagrams
Workbook, p. 34

● Teach

EXPLAIN to students that the noble gases have a complete set of valence electrons and thus are not reactive most of the time. Hydrogen is a unique element and is placed alone on the table.

● Assess

Use the After You Read questions and the Alternative Assessment to help you evaluate students' understanding of the lesson.

After You Read

1. They become stable by giving up one or two electrons, respectively. As a result, they are very reactive and are never found uncombined in nature.
2. Their behavior is less predictable because the number of electrons involved in reactions can vary depending on the conditions.
3. The Group 13 elements have three valence electrons. They increase one at a time to Group 18, in which the elements have a complete set of valence electrons.
4. Hydrogen is a gas that has one proton and one electron. On Earth, it is commonly found in water. It is the most abundant element in the universe, existing in stars and planets. People use hydrogen as a fuel, in foods, and to form ammonia.

Alternative Assessment

Have students use their charts to compare two element groups of their choice. They should include in their comparison the properties and uses of elements in each group. Encourage students to also explain how the valence electrons describe the position of each group on the periodic table.

Chapter 6 Summary

MASTERING CONCEPTS

True or False

1. False, mass

2. False, Moseley

3. False, period

4. True

5. False, ductile

6. True

7. True

8. False, noble gases

Short Answer

9. Some elements were placed out of order to fit with the other elements in terms of properties. Mendeleev assumed that the atomic masses were incorrect, so he rearranged elements accordingly. It turned out that the calculation of atomic masses was not the problem.

10. Each square contains an element's name, chemical symbol, atomic number, atomic mass, and natural state.

11. Metals are generally good conductors of electricity; nonmetals are insulators. Metalloids are semiconductors, which means that they conduct electricity under specific conditions.

12. The halogens have seven valence electrons, which means they need one electron to become stable. They react with most other elements to obtain this one electron. Noble gases already have a filled outer level of electrons, so they do not need to react to become stable.

Chapter 6

Summary

KEY CONCEPTS

6.1 Development of the Periodic Table

- Mendeleev developed the first working model of the periodic table by arranging chemical elements in order of increasing atomic mass.

- Moseley improved upon Mendeleev's table by arranging elements in order of atomic number rather than atomic mass.

- The modern periodic table is arranged in horizontal rows called periods and vertical columns called groups or families.

- According to the periodic law, chemical elements display a repeating pattern of properties when arranged in order of increasing atomic number.

6.2 Types of Elements

- Metal elements are generally shiny, malleable, ductile, and good conductors of heat and electricity.

- Nonmetal elements are usually dull, brittle, and poor conductors of heat and electricity.

- Metalloids exhibit some properties of metals and some properties of nonmetals.

6.3 Groups of Elements

- The alkali metals, or Group 1 elements, have one valence electron to give up and are very reactive as a result.

- The alkaline earth metals, or Group 2 elements, have two valence electrons to give up.

- The transition metals in Groups 3 through 12 are less predictable than the representative elements because the number of electrons involved in a reaction can depend on the conditions of the reaction.

- The elements in Groups 13 through 18 have different numbers of valence electrons that determine their reactivity. Halogens are the most reactive nonmetals because they need only one electron to become stable. The noble gases are the least reactive elements because they have complete valance levels of electrons.

VOCABULARY REVIEW

Write each term in a complete sentence or write a paragraph relating several terms.

6.1
periodic law, p. 93
periodic table, p. 93
period, p. 96
group, p. 96

6.2
metal, p. 97
malleable, p. 97
ductile, p. 97
nonmetal, p. 98
metalloid, p. 98
semiconductor, p. 98

6.3
alkali metal, p. 99
alkaline earth metal, p. 100
radioactive element, p. 100
representative element, p. 101
transition element, p. 101
diatomic molecule, p. 103
halogen, p. 104
noble gas, p. 105

PREPARE FOR CHAPTER TEST

To prepare for the chapter test, create a question from each Learning Goal. Use the information in your Science Notebook to answer each question. Then use these answers to write a well-developed essay about the chapter. Use the Key Concept on the first page of this chapter as your topic sentence.

**Vocabulary Review
Workbook, p. 33**

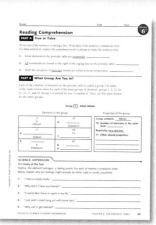

**Reading Comprehension
Workbook, p. 35**

MASTERING CONCEPTS

True or False
If the statement is true, write "true." If it is false, change the underlined word or words to make the statement true.

1. Mendeleev organized the elements in order of increasing atomic <u>number</u>.

2. <u>Rutherford</u> identified the atomic numbers of elements by observing patterns of X rays.

3. A horizontal row in the periodic table is also called a(n) <u>family</u>.

4. Atomic radius <u>decreases</u> from left to right across a period.

5. Metals are <u>malleable</u>, which means they can be drawn into wires.

6. An alkali metal <u>gives up</u> one valence electron during a chemical reaction.

7. Actinides and lanthanides are examples of <u>transition</u> elements.

8. The <u>halogens</u> are not very reactive because they do not need to gain or lose electrons to become stable.

Short Answer
Answer each of the following in a sentence or brief paragraph.

9. How did Mendeleev account for discrepancies in the ordering of elements by atomic mass in his table? Was he correct?

10. Summarize the information that is presented in an element's square in the periodic table.

11. Compare metals, nonmetals, and metalloids in terms of how they conduct electricity.

12. The halogens are right next to the noble gases in the periodic table, yet the halogens are highly reactive and the noble gases are almost nonreactive. How can you account for this difference?

Critical Thinking
Use what you have learned in this chapter to answer each of the following.

13. **Relate** Tell how Mendeleev built on the work of his predecessors and what made his organization of the elements useful.

14. **Compare** How was Moseley's evaluation of an element's atomic number different from Mendeleev's assignment of atomic numbers?

15. **Arrange** Describe the general locations of metals, nonmetals, and metalloids in the periodic table.

16. **Summarize** Explain how the number of protons and electrons, the atomic radius, and the ionization energy change across a period and down a group in the periodic table.

Standardized Test Question
Choose the letter of the response that correctly answers the question.

17. According to chlorine's square in the periodic table, how many electrons does each neutral atom of chlorine have?

Chlorine
17
Cl
35.453

A. 17
B. 18
C. 35
D. 36

Test-Taking Tip

Use scrap paper to write notes. Sometimes making a sketch, such as a diagram or table, can help you organize your ideas.

Critical Thinking

13. Scientists had been trying to find ways to organize the elements. In particular, Johann Döbereiner organized elements in triads, and J. A. R. Newlands organized them in octaves. Both had arranged elements according to atomic mass, as did Mendeleev. Mendeleev went on to organize all of the known elements in such a way that he could predict the existence of elements that had not yet been discovered.

14. Before Moseley's work, an element's atomic number was a random assignment based on its order when the elements were arranged according to atomic mass. Moseley gave the atomic number a measurable basis by using X rays to determine the nuclear charge, or number of protons in an atom of an element.

15. Metals, which take up most of the table, are located in the left and center. Nonmetals are located toward the right side of the table. Metalloids are located along a zigzag line that separates the metals from the nonmetals.

16. The number of protons and electrons increases across a period and down a group. Atomic radius decreases across a period, but increases down a group. Ionization energy increases across a period, but decreases down a group.

Standardized Test Question

17. A

Reading Links

The Elements: What You Really Want to Know

Packed with information about the elements and the periodic table, this book is a useful resource for projects and student research. The text provides a thorough overview of specific elements and emphasizes historical background and the discovery process.

Ron Miller. Lerner Publishing Group. 136 pp. Illustrated. Library ISBN 978-0-7613-2794-3.

Gold: From Greek Myth to Computer Chips

This engaging study of gold provides readers with a rich and memorable portrait of one chemical element.

Ruth Kassinger. Lerner Publishing Group. 80 pp. Illustrated. Library ISBN 978-0-7613-2110-1.

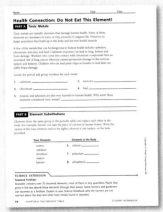

Curriculum Connection
Workbook, p. 36

Science Challenge
Workbook, pp. 37–38

6A Organizing the Elements

This prechapter introduction activity is designed to engage students and determine what they already know about the periodic table's organization by having them to design their own shape-based tables.

Objectives

- observe similar properties of shapes
- determine an organizational system to use for a periodic table
- communicate conclusions

Planning

 15–20 minutes   groups of 2–3 students

Materials (per group)

- bag of shapes
- pencil
- paper
- colored pencils
- ruler

Advance Preparation

- Prepare a set of five shapes in five colors for each group. Cut cardstock or laminated tag board into different shapes, such as circles, triangles, squares, ovals, and hexagons. As an alternative, plastic or wooden shapes can be purchased from a math supply house or educational store.

- Remind students that they can have as many families (columns) and periods (rows) in their tables as necessary. Suggest that they choose a single property to classify the shapes.

- Ask students to draw their tables on paper using a ruler and colored pencils.

Engagement Guide

- Challenge students to think about how they can organize the shapes into groups by asking:
  - *What are some different types of organizational systems?* (clothes closets, grocery stores, fishing tackle boxes, libraries, refrigerators, etc.)
  - *How often do you use organizational systems, and why do you use them?* (Students should recognize that they use organizational systems all the time to help them find things more quickly.)
- Encourage students to communicate their conclusions in creative ways.

Going Further

Remove one or two shapes from each bag of shapes and encourage students to repeat the activity. Point out to students that gaps will occur in their tables because some shapes are missing. Relate this to how difficult it was for scientists to develop the periodic table at a time when some of the elements had yet to be discovered.

6B Radioactive Isotopes

Objectives

- model radioactive half-life using pennies
- record and analyze data
- communicate conclusions with a graph

Skill Set

modeling, recording and analyzing data, graphing, predicting, drawing conclusions

Planning

 30–45 minutes   groups of 3–4 students

Materials

Materials for this activity are listed in the Student Laboratory Manual.

Advance Preparation

Two-sided candies with printing on one side can be used instead of pennies. Plastic containers with lids can be used

instead of shoe boxes. Make sure students shake the box up and down and not side-to-side.

Answers to Observations: Data Table 1

Students' answers will vary, but probability suggests that about half of the heads-up pennies will remain after each trial until no pennies remain. Students' data tables should reflect these numbers. Students may need to add more rows to their tables.

Answers to Observations: Graph

Students should plot a graph using two different colored pencils. The curve showing number of heads-up pennies remaining after each trial should slope downward and the slope should flatten out as the number of trials increases. The curve showing the total number of pennies that decayed should slope upward and the slope should flatten out as the number of trials increases. The graph shows that the number radioactive isotopes decreases and the number of stable atoms increases over time.

Answers to Analysis and Conclusions

1. Answers will vary.

2. Each trial represents a half-life. With each trial of five shakes, about half of the tails-up pennies were removed. A half-life is the time it takes for half the radioactive nuclei to decay.

3. after 1 half-life: 300 nuclei; after 2 half-lives:150 nuclei; and after 3 half-lives: 75 nuclei

4. A half-life corresponds to the time needed for half of a sample to decay. Find the point on the graph at which half of the radioisotopes remain. Trace this data point downward to the x-axis and determine the time. The time value is the half-life of the element.

Going Further

Have students pool the class data by adding the number of heads-up pennies of all class groups for each toss. Using the pooled data, have students prepare a graph by plotting the number of heads-up pennies on the y-axis and the number of trials (half-lives) on the x-axis. Have students compare their group graphs with the class data graph and share their results. Have students research how radioactive decay is used in the real world.

6C Comparing Metals, Nonmetals, and Metalloids

Objectives

- describe and compare properties of various elements
- classify elements as metals, nonmetals, or metalloids
- arrange elements based on their properties

Skill Set

observing, comparing and contrasting, classifying, recording and analyzing data, drawing conclusions

Planning

45–60 minutes   groups of 3–4 students

Materials

Materials for this activity are listed in the Student Laboratory Manual.

Advance Preparation

Prepare sets of six vials for each group. Number the vials 1 through 6. Fill each vial with a sample as follows: (1) carbon, (2) iron filings, (3) mossy tin, (4) sulfur, (5) mossy zinc, and (6) silicon. Prepare a 6M solution of hydrochloric acid and fill one dropper bottle of acid for each group. Make a conductivity apparatus available to each group. Prepare the conductivity apparatus using a 9-volt battery, a small appliance light bulb, and pieces of insulated copper wire. Construct an open circuit and use it to test each sample's conductivity. Adapting this lab so that you perform the conductivity and acid tests as cemonstrations while students record observations speeds up the lab and reduces safety hazards.

Lab Tip

Students should not handle hydrochloric acid with a concentration greater than 2M. Please do not use the powdered form of any of the test chemicals, including graphite, sulfur, and silicon. The powdered form is flammable and a potential irritant if inhaled.

Answers to Observations: Data Table 1

The metals are in vials 2 (iron), 3 (tin), and 5 (zinc). Students' answers should reflect the properties of metals.

The nonmetals are in vials 1 (carbon) and 4 (sulfur). Students' answers should reflect the properties of nonmetals.

The metalloid is in vial 6 (silicon). Students' answers should reflect the properties of metalloids.

Answers to Analysis and Conclusions

1. Metals have a shiny luster, are malleable (can flatten without shattering), conduct heat and electricity, and react with acids. Nonmetals are dull, not shiny, and brittle, are nonconductors of heat and electricity, and do not react with acids. Metalloids have properties of both metals and nonmetals.

2. Vials 2, 3, and 5 contain metals. Vials 1 and 4 contain nonmetals. Vial 6 contains a metalloid.

3. Students should realize that the metalloids are toward the right side of the periodic table between the metals and nonmetals. Students may realize that metalloids are all those elements that touch the "staircase" between metals and nonmetals.

4. Other tests that could be performed are tests for density, thermal conductivity, and ductility.

Going Further

Have each student imagine that he or she has discovered a new element and write a description of the element, including the results of tests used to determine its properties. Students could also make posters or brochures to advertise their elements.

Unit 2

Case Study 1: Nuclear Energy: Is Now the Time?

Gather More Information

Have students use the following key terms to aid their searches:

- Chernobyl
- nuclear energy
- nuclear fission
- Three Mile Island
- radioactive waste
- uranium

Research the Big Picture

- Have students work in pairs to research the distribution of electric power generation in the United States. From the feature, students should know that nuclear plants provide 20 percent of U.S. electric power. What percentages are provided by other energy sources? Have each pair create a circle graph presenting this information. Then, ask each pair to study its graph and decide if the long-term maintenance of this distribution is feasible. If they believe it is, have pairs defend their positions in a paragraph. If not, ask each pair to develop a second circle graph showing its recommendation for the future of electric power generation. Have students write paragraphs explaining why they chose this new distribution.

- Have students choose one of the nuclear accidents, Three Mile Island or Chernobyl, to research further and write a short article about. Ask them to determine the source of the problem, the negative effects, how the danger was contained, and what precautions, if any, were subsequently taken. Have them compare the features at these nuclear plants with plants operating in the U.S. today.

- As a class, hold a debate on the merits of nuclear energy. Tell students that some European countries depend far more heavily on nuclear power than the United States does. Should the U.S. move in that direction? Divide the class into two groups, pro and con, to debate the expansion of nuclear energy use in the U.S. Stress that students should base their arguments on scientific information and historical data as much as possible, rather than emotions and speculation.

Nuclear Energy: Is Now the Time?

The first nuclear power plant opened in the United States in the late 1950s. By the 1970s, there were dozens of nuclear plants producing electric power. Then came the accidents at Three Mile Island in Pennsylvania (1979) and Chernobyl in Russia (1986). After the Chernobyl explosion and fire, millions of people were exposed to radiation.

Public fear of nuclear power plants grew. No nuclear plants have been built in the United States for many years. Nuclear power can, however, provide a lot of the energy we need. Does it make sense to increase our use of this form of energy?

It takes a lot of electricity to keep all the lights, computers, and air conditioners in the United States running. Most of the power people need is produced by burning fossil fuels. About 20 million barrels of oil and 2 million tons of coal keep power flowing to American homes, offices, and schools each day.

Unfortunately, there are problems associated with the use of fossil fuels. Fossil fuels like oil produce a great deal of pollution—pollution that contributes to acid rain and global warming. Fossil fuels are also nonrenewable, which means that their supplies will eventually run out.

Today, nuclear plants provide about 20 percent of the electric power used in the United States. There are about 100 nuclear power plants currently in operation, but more will be needed to generate a greater percentage of electricity.

Nuclear power plants do not produce a lot of air pollution, so they do not contribute to unhealthful atmospheric conditions and global warming. They use uranium, atoms of which are split to release huge amounts of energy in a process called nuclear fission.

Although nuclear power plants do not produce a lot of carbon dioxide, they do produce dangerous radioactive waste. This waste remains radioactive for many years. The U.S. government is working on establishing a safe site to store waste permanently.

Nuclear plants use huge quantities of water to cool their reactors. The heated water is released into lakes and streams, raising water temperature and harming fish and other forms of life.

The need for new sources of clean energy is undeniable. Many people think that nuclear power will have to play a significant role. What do you think?

Research and Report

After you read about the advantages and disadvantages of nuclear power, find out more about the topic. Form your own opinion about whether the United States should increase its use of nuclear power. Then write a well-developed essay in which you support your point of view.

It's Elemental

Earth's elements make up everything around you. But how much do you know about them—even those that sound very familiar?

Gold Gold is a shiny, soft, yellow metal. You see gold mostly in jewelry, but it has many other uses. Gold conducts electricity better than many other metals do, so it's used for electrical connectors and printed circuit boards in computers. Gold also reflects heat better than any other metal, so it's useful in space. Gold film is used to shield spacecraft from the Sun's infrared (heat) rays. Visors on astronauts' helmets also contain gold film.

Hydrogen Hydrogen gas is the most abundant element in the universe. Stars, including the Sun, are made of it. Nuclear reactions in the Sun fuse hydrogen atoms together, producing helium and enormous amounts of heat and light. Hydrogen could someday be used on Earth in powerful ways. Today, cars are actually running on hydrogen fuel.

Carbon Carbon exists naturally in many forms. A black, sooty substance called lampblack is a form of carbon used in inks and paints. A dark, soft form of carbon called graphite is the "lead" in many pencils. If carbon atoms are subjected to very high temperature and pressure, another form results: diamond, Earth's hardest natural substance.

Helium Helium is a common element in the universe, but it's not that common on Earth. There is a bit of helium in Earth's crust, produced by the decay of certain radioactive substances. Because it's lighter than air, however, the helium rises into the atmosphere through cracks in the crust and leaks into space. The lightness of helium makes the gas useful for filling balloons, blimps, and inflated floats for parades.

Neon You normally cannot see neon. It's a colorless gas. Put it into a tube and shoot electricity through it, however, and the gas glows bright red. This discovery led to the creation of neon lights. Although they're all called "neon" lights, various gases other than neon produce the other bright colors in these light displays.

Nitrogen What's the most common gas in the air humans breathe? Most people would say oxygen, but it's actually nitrogen. Almost 80 percent of the air is nitrogen. This makes Earth unique. No other planet in the solar system has an atmosphere of mostly nitrogen and oxygen.

CAREER CONNECTION SCIENCE WRITER

Suppose you read an article about astronauts in a magazine. You might watch a television report about global warming. You might use the Internet to find information about dinosaurs. What does the information you read or hear from these different sources have in common? It was written by a science writer.

Science writers do not work as scientists, but they often talk to scientists and describe their work. Some science writers travel all over the world. A science writer might go on a journey to Antarctica to write about a lake discovered under the polar ice, or to describe life at a station at the South Pole. He or she might follow an astronaut around for a day to see what it's like to train for space travel. Or the writer might visit a wildlife preserve in India to write about endangered tigers.

Science writers have to understand the science they write about. They must make sure it's correct. They spend a lot of time interviewing people, checking facts, and writing and editing their articles.

A science writer usually has a college degree in English, journalism, or communication. They work as "print" writers for newspapers, magazines, and books. They write the copy that science reporters on TV or the radio read, or they might report stories themselves. They write science books. They also write the science articles that appear on the Internet. Although science writers are not scientists, they help make the world of science understandable for everyone.

CAREER CONNECTION: Science Writer

Have students read the feature and consider recent books, articles, films, or news stories they have read that have been prepared by science writers. Call on volunteers to share some of these stories, and make a list of responses on the board. Ask: *Have you ever wished you could learn firsthand about a science topic that interests you?* Have students write personal essays telling whether they think a science writing career might be right for them. Students should describe what they would find most enjoyable about this career, as well as what they would find most challenging or difficult.

Case Study 2: It's Elemental

Gather More Information

Encourage students to use the library or the NSTA SciLinks Web site noted at the start of each chapter to learn more about these case study topics and to conduct further research.

Have students use the following key terms to aid their searches:

- carbon
- element
- gold
- helium
- hydrogen
- neon
- nitrogen

Research the Big Picture

- Have students work in pairs to further research one of the common elements presented in the feature. Each pair should create a poster of its chosen element that presents its chemical formula, structure, and other information from the periodic table. Posters should also present where and in what form the element occurs on Earth, and how it is useful to living things, including people.

- Have students research neon lights and describe their findings in their Science Notebooks. Have them find out what gases in "neon" lights are responsible for various colors and how and where neon lights are popularly used.

- As a class project, create an element display or exhibit. Assign or have students choose elements or groups of elements other than the six noted in the feature. Students should draw from information in the unit as well as conducting additional research. Encourage students to be creative in presenting information about their element(s). Posters, brochures, models, or hands-on demonstrations are just a few project possibilities.

Unit 3

Introduce Unit 3

Explain to students that the topic of this unit is interactions of matter. Ask: *What do you think of when you hear the word* interaction? *What does it mean when two people interact?* Help students understand that in this unit they will read about how matter interacts through the bonding of atoms and molecules, and how chemical reactions form new substances. They will learn about the properties and chemistry of solutions, carbon compounds, and unstable molecules.

Have students write the five chapter titles in their Science Notebooks. Ask them to write a definition for each term to the best of their abilities. As they read the unit, have them revise their definitions.

Unit Projects

For each Unit Project, have students use the Presentation Builder on the Student CD-ROM to display their results.

Career Research Have each student choose a career related to interactions of matter such as baker, chemist, or pharmacist. Have students imagine that they are interviewing for their chosen jobs. Have them research thoroughly and make a list of experience and skill requirements. Then have them prepare resumés for people who are well-suited for these careers.

Hands-On Research Provide each student group with separate containers of vegetable oil, vinegar, water, salt, and a crushed antacid tablet. Also provide three beakers for mixing. Have them mix together the oil and vinegar, the water and salt, and the water and crushed antacid tablet. For each mixing sample, ask students to record what they observe in their Science Notebooks.

Technology Research Help students understand that scientists use sophisticated equipment in the laboratory. Have students research and report on tools used by nuclear scientists, such as particle accelerators, cyclotrons, and containment technologies.

Unit 3

Interactions of Matter

Chapter 7 **Bonding**
How are atoms held together in compounds?

Chapter 8 **Chemical Reactions**
What is a chemical reaction?

Chapter 9 **Solutions**
What are the properties and classifications of solutions?

Chapter 10 **Carbon Chemistry**
What are the properties, forms, and uses of carbon compounds?

Chapter 11 **Nuclear Chemistry**
What happens when unstable nuclei change to become more stable?

110

Software Summary

Student CD-ROM
—Interactive Student Book
—Vocabulary Review
—Key Concept Review
—Lab Report Template
—ELL Preview and Writing Activities
—Presentation Digital Library
—Graphic Organizing Software
—Spanish Cognate Dictionary

Interactive Labs
Chapter 11B—Simulating Radioactive Decay
Chapter 11C—Radiation and Genetic Damage

Bonding

7.1 What Is Bonding?

7.2 Types of Bonds

7.3 Predicting Types of Bonding

KEY CONCEPT When atoms interact, they can form chemical bonds to become new substances called compounds.

Atoms are the basic building blocks of matter. Atoms interact in a variety of ways to form the millions of substances that fill the world around you—the atmosphere, the oceans, lakes, and streams, the rocks and soil, and all the diverse forms of life. The interaction of atoms is also responsible for the cells of your body.

Atoms combine and recombine over and over through time. If atoms could not interact, there would be no Sun and no Earth. There would be no plants, animals, water, or air. Life as you know it would not exist.

Think About Bonding

Think about the items around you. Which items are pure elements?

- Make a T-chart in your Science Notebook. On one side of the chart, list things that are made from just one element. Aluminum foil is an example. On the other side of the chart, list things that are made of more than one element.

- Which side of the chart contains more items? What hypothesis might explain this? Think about the term *bonding*. Write what this word means to you. What might bonding have to do with atoms?

NSTA
SCI LINKS.
THE WORLD'S A CLICK AWAY

www.scilinks.org
Chemical Bonding **Code: WGPS07**

111

Introduce Chapter 7

As a starting activity, use Lab 7A on page 37 of the Laboratory Manual.

ENGAGE Tell students that they will be learning how atoms bond. Have them read this page with partners and then talk about what is meant when atoms are described as the basic building blocks of matter. Ask students what they know about building blocks from when they were younger from watching a child play with them. How are they used? What can they make? Have pairs share their discussions with the class.

Provide several easy-level books about atoms for the class to browse. English language learners can use these books to compile a list of facts about atoms. Ask students to note several interesting facts in their Science Notebooks. When students have finished browsing, have them share their information in small groups.

Think About Bonding

ENGAGE Remind students what elements are (pure substances made up of only one kind of atom that cannot be broken down into simpler substances that retain the properties of the element). Draw a T-chart on the board with the headings *Pure Elements* and *Not Pure Elements*. Fill in one or two examples of each type and solicit more examples from students. Have students copy the T-chart into their Science Notebooks.

Ask students to discuss with partners what the term *bonding* means.

Chapter 7 Planning Guide

Instructional Periods	National Standards	Lab Manual	Workbook
7.1 2 Periods	A2, B1, G2; A2, B1, B2, G2; UCP1, UCP2	**Lab 7A: p. 37** Bonding Atoms	Key Concept Review p. 39 Vocabulary Review p. 40
7.2 2 Periods	A2, B1, G1, G3; A2, B1, B2, G1, G3; UCP2, UCP3, UCP5	**Lab 7B: pp. 38–39** Chemical Bonding **Lab 7C: pp. 40–42** Ionic Bonding	Interpreting Diagrams p. 41 Reading Comprehension p. 42 Curriculum Connection p. 43 Science Challenge pp. 44–45
7.3 2 Periods	A1, B1, G2; A1, B2, G2; UCP2		

Middle School Standard; High School Standard; Unifying Concept and Principle

ENGAGE Have students brainstorm what they already know about atoms, protons, neutrons, and electrons.

Vocabulary terms are listed on the first student page of each lesson. You may wish to preview the terms before introducing each lesson. Strategies for teaching the vocabulary appear on the pages where the terms are introduced.

Before You Read

Preview the first page or two of the lesson by doing a think-aloud that includes predictions. Invite students to continue previewing the rest of the lesson with partners, and tell them to record all of their predictions in their Science Notebooks.

Students' predictions should suggest that they will learn about bonding and the relationship between the arrangement of electrons around an atom's nucleus and its ability to form bonds.

Teach

EXPLAIN to students that in this lesson, they will learn about chemical bonds and how compounds are formed.

Learning Goals

- Explain how compounds are formed.
- Describe a chemical bond.
- Relate the arrangement of electrons around an atom's nucleus to the ability of the atom to form chemical bonds.

New Vocabulary

chemical bond
electron cloud
energy level
valence electron
electron-dot diagram

7.1 What Is Bonding?

Before You Read

Read the lesson title, the headings and subheadings, and the Learning Goals. Look at the photos and illustrations. Predict what you think you will learn in this lesson. Write your predictions in two or three sentences in your Science Notebook.

At present, there are 117 known elements, each with its own unique properties. However, there are many more than 117 kinds of substances on Earth. In fact, there are probably more pure substances on Earth than any one person can count! Water is a pure substance, but it is not an element. Table salt, sugar, and vinegar are pure substances, but none of these are elements, either. Where do all of the millions of substances come from? How do they form from only 117 elements?

Combined Elements

Recall from Chapter 2 that atoms of different elements can join together. When they do, they form new substances called compounds. Water and table salt are examples of familiar compounds. Each compound forms when certain atoms join together in a specific way. Water forms when two hydrogen atoms chemically combine with one oxygen atom. Table salt forms when sodium atoms chemically combine with chlorine atoms.

Atoms of the same elements can combine in different ratios to form new substances that are different from the combining elements. In this way, just a few elements are able to make the millions of different substances on Earth. Vinegar and rubbing alcohol, for example, are very different from one another. Yet both compounds are made up of carbon, oxygen, and hydrogen atoms. However, each compound contains different numbers of these atoms. **Figure 7.1** shows additional examples of compounds made from these elements.

Figure 7.1 Sugar, olive oil, and acetone are each made up of carbon, oxygen, and hydrogen atoms joined together in different ratios. Those ratios can be seen in the chemical formula for each compound. Each substance is very different from the carbon, oxygen, and hydrogen from which it is made.

(sugar) $C_{12}H_{22}O_{11}$ (olive oil) $C_{17}H_{35}COOH$ (acetone) C_3H_6O

Teacher Alert

Remind students of the role subscripts play in a chemical formula. Point out that in formulas such as those for vinegar, rubbing alcohol, and olive oil, the numbers of the same element are not combined. This is because the $-COOH$ and $-OH$ endings are functional groups, which students will learn about in Chapter 10.

ELL Strategy

Use Visual Information Have students read and examine the photographs in **Figure 7.1** and then talk with partners or in small groups about why they think that the same elements are able to combine in different ways to make different compounds.

The Atom

What does it mean for an atom to chemically combine with another atom? It means the atoms form a bond, or link together. The bonds that atoms form are called **chemical bonds.** Chemical bonds hold atoms together. A chemical bond is like atomic glue. It causes two or more atoms to "stick" together.

Recall from Chapter 5 that atoms are made up of smaller particles called electrons, protons, and neutrons. Positively charged protons and neutral neutrons are held tightly together in an atom's nucleus. Negatively charged electrons are found outside the nucleus, spinning around in an area known as the **electron cloud.** Electrons are organized in distinct layers in the electron cloud. Each layer is called an **energy level.** Imagine cupping your hands around a floating marble. If the marble were an atom's nucleus, your hands would form the atom's first energy level. If a friend cupped her hands around yours, her hands would form the second energy level. Each energy level surrounds the previous one in a series of spheres. Relatively huge amounts of empty space lie between each energy level. **Figure 7.2** shows a model of how these energy levels may look.

As shown in **Figure 7.3,** the first energy level can hold up to two electrons. The second energy level can hold eight electrons; the third can hold 18. The farther an energy level is from the nucleus, the more electrons it can hold. The farther electrons are from the nucleus, the more energy they have and the less attracted they are by the nucleus.

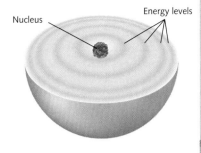
Nucleus · Energy levels

Figure 7.2 Scientists use energy levels to predict where in the electron cloud an electron is likely to be. Each energy level represents a different amount of energy.

CONNECTION: Math

Energy level *n* can hold a maximum of $2n^2$ electrons. To use the formula, plug in the energy level number for *n*. For example, energy level 2 can hold $2(2)^2 = 8$ electrons.

Figure It Out

1. Which energy level shown can hold the most electrons?

2. Which electrons have more energy—the electrons in energy level 2 or the electrons in energy level 3? Put the energy levels shown in order from most energy to least.

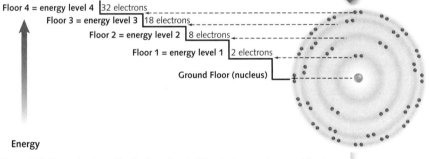

Floor 4 = energy level 4 | 32 electrons
Floor 3 = energy level 3 | 18 electrons
Floor 2 = energy level 2 | 8 electrons
Floor 1 = energy level 1 | 2 electrons
Ground Floor (nucleus)

Energy

Figure 7.3 Energy levels are like the floors in a building. Just as people cannot float between floors, electrons cannot float between energy levels.

● Teach

EXPLAIN to students that they will learn about the arrangement of electrons in atoms and how this arrangement affects bonding.

Vocabulary

chemical bond Tell students that the term *chemical* is an adjective that means "relating to or used in chemistry," and that the term *bond,* as it is used in this context, is a noun meaning "something used for tying, binding, or holding."

electron cloud Tell students that an electron is a subatomic particle that has a negative electric charge and carries electricity in solids. Ask students what they know about clouds, and what the term could mean.

energy level Ask students what they remember about energy from previous chapters (that it refers to the ability to do work). Ask what they know about the term *level,* and give examples of how it is used. Tell them that it is a noun meaning "a specific position or degree." Have students put the two terms together and suggest a meaning for the term.

CONNECTION: Math

Using the formula, students should calculate that the fifth energy level can hold 50 electrons and the sixth energy level can hold 72 electrons. The sixth energy level can therefore hold 22 more electrons than the fifth energy level.

Figure It Out: Figure 7.3

[ANSWER] **1.** Energy level 4 can hold the most electrons. **2.** The electrons in energy level 3 have more energy than the electrons in energy level 2. The energy levels in order from most energy to least energy are energy level 4, energy level 3, energy level 2, and energy level 1.

Differentiate Instruction

Visual Have each student draw a chemical bond, an electron cloud, and an energy level. Drawings can be either realistic or an artistic representation (such as an elevator representing energy levels).

Field Study

Have each student take his or her Science Notebook and a pencil outside to observe the environment. Have students add to their lists of elements and compounds by noting substances that they see. If necessary, point out things such as soil, water, rocks, cement, air, tree bark, and car parts.

Teach

 EXPLAIN to students that they will learn how electrons are arranged in energy levels, or electron configuration. Students may need some help with the term *configuration,* so tell them that it means "a certain arrangement of parts."

Vocabulary

valence electron Tell students that the word *valence* comes from the Latin word *valentia,* meaning "strength" or "capacity."

electron-dot diagram Tell students that a diagram is a sketch or drawing that shows the most important features of a structure and is often labeled. Have students tell what they know about dots.

Use the Visual: Figure 7.4

ANSWER 2, 5

As You Read

Have students share their predictions, confirmations, and revisions with partners and discuss why they confirmed or revised each prediction.

ANSWER Electrons are arranged in the electron cloud around an atom's nucleus in energy levels. Energy levels fill up in order (2, 8, 18, 32), with the attainment of a complete valence shell resulting in a stable atom.

Explain It!

Guide students to notice patterns in the periodic table regarding electron configuration. All the elements in Group 1 have one valence electron, all the elements in Group 2 have two valence electrons, all the elements in Group 7 have seven valence electrons, and so on. The number of valence electrons the atoms in each period have increases by one going across the period. Provide students with opportunities to discuss their ideas about patterns they see.

As You Read

Confirm or revise the predictions you made in your Science Notebook.

How are electrons arranged around an atom's nucleus?

Explain It!

Work in groups to study the atomic models shown in Figure 7.4. What do you notice about the number of valence electrons the atoms in each period have? What about in each group? In your Science Notebook, write about patterns you see and what you think they illustrate.

Electron Configuration

As electrons arrange themselves around the nucleus of an atom, they tend to fill energy level 1 first. Once the first energy level is filled, electrons begin to fill energy level 2. Electrons continue filling the energy levels in such a way that the most stable atom is formed. The most stable atom is one that is least likely to chemically combine with another atom.

The portion of the periodic table on this page shows how electrons are arranged in atoms with atomic numbers 1 through 18. Recall that the atomic number is the number of protons in an atom's nucleus. In a neutral atom, the number of protons is equal to the number of electrons.

On the periodic table, each element has one more electron than the element before it does. For example, hydrogen has one electron, helium has two, lithium has three, and so on. Because energy level 1 can hold a maximum of two electrons and is filled first, hydrogen's one electron and helium's two electrons are in the first energy level. Two of lithium's three electrons fill energy level 1, and the remaining one is in energy level 2. The arrangement of electrons in an atom of an element is known as the electron configuration of the element.

The outermost energy level that contains electrons is called the valence shell. The electrons in this energy level are called **valence electrons.** In general, an atom is stable when it has eight valence electrons in its valence shell. Helium is an exception. It is stable with two electrons in its valence shell. According to **Figure 7.4,** in addition to helium, neon and argon are stable elements.

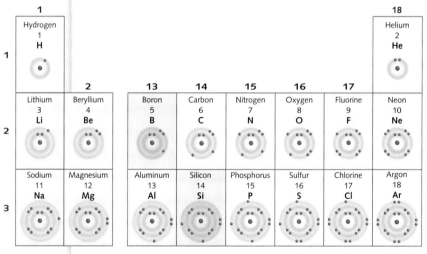

Figure 7.4 This table shows how electrons are arranged in the atoms of the elements with atomic numbers 1 through 18. What is the electron configuration for nitrogen?

Background Information

The most stable configuration for an atom is the one that requires the least energy. Using an analogy may help students understand this concept. Walking requires less energy than running. It is easier to walk for several hours than it is to run for several hours. In the same way, it is easier for atoms to maintain a low-energy configuration than a high-energy configuration.

Formation of Bonds

There is an important relationship between the number of valence electrons in an atom and the bonding ability of that atom. Atoms form a chemical bond in order to become more stable, or have complete valence shells. A chemical bond is the sharing or exchanging of valence electrons between two atoms.

As **Figure 7.4** shows, the atoms of most of the elements shown do not have eight electrons in their valence shells. In other words, they do not have complete outermost energy levels. Therefore, the atoms must form bonds with other atoms in order to obtain eight valence electrons. By gaining, losing, or sharing electrons, atoms can achieve the eight valence electrons needed for maximum stability. Most atoms form bonds with another atom in such a way that each atom achieves a complete outermost energy level and becomes more stable as a result of the bond.

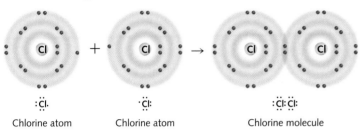

| Chlorine atom | Chlorine atom | Chlorine molecule |

Figure 7.5 Count the number of valence electrons around the bonded atoms. How does each atom become more stable by sharing electrons in a bond?

Noble gases (elements in the last column of the periodic table) have eight valence electrons and are the most stable elements. Their valence shells are full, so they tend not to form bonds with other elements.

Electron-Dot Diagrams The number of valence electrons determines many of an atom's chemical properties, such as whether it can form bonds. It also helps determine which other atoms it may bond with. An **electron-dot diagram** shows an atom's valence electrons. The symbol in the center of each drawing is the chemical symbol. Each dot around the chemical symbol is one valence electron.

After You Read

1. How do compounds form?

2. Describe what a chemical bond is, and explain why atoms form bonds.

3. Review the predictions you made in your Science Notebook. Were your predictions correct? How did they change as you read? Write a summary of the lesson in your Science Notebook. Include new things you learned.

Nitrogen contains five electrons in its outermost energy level.

Iodine contains seven electrons in its outermost energy level.

Figure 7.6 Electron-dot diagrams show an atom's valence electrons only.

● Teach

EXPLAIN to students that in this section, they will learn how atoms form chemical bonds and about drawings that show an atom's valence electrons.

Use the Visual: Figure 7.5

ANSWER By sharing electrons, the hydrogen atoms achieve a complete outermost energy level containing two electrons. The chlorine atoms have eight electrons in their outermost energy levels as a result of sharing electrons.

● Assess

Use the After You Read questions and Alternative Assessment to help you evaluate students' understanding of this lesson.

After You Read

1. Compounds form when two or more atoms chemically combine.

2. A chemical bond is what ties atoms together. Atoms form bonds to achieve complete outermost energy levels and thus become more stable.

3. Students' summaries should include information involving the Learning Goals.

Background Information

Neon, a rare gas discovered in 1898, is colorless, odorless, nontoxic, and nonflammable. Georges Claude created the first neon lamp in France around 1902.

Alternative Assessment

Have students finish sharing their predictions, confirmations, and revisions with a partner. Then have each student review what he or she learned in this lesson by reviewing all notes taken about the lesson. Have each student write the important information from the lesson in the form of a bulleted list in his or her Science Notebook.

7.2 Introduce

ENGAGE Have students read the first two paragraphs on this page. When they are finished reading, ask them to think of something that they gave to a friend, something that a friend gave to them, and something that they shared. Students should discuss these ideas in small groups. Tell students that in the same way they lend, borrow, and share items, atoms lend, borrow, and share electrons.

Before You Read

Draw and label a three-column chart on the board. Have students read the first two paragraphs of this page and discuss their understanding of how atoms behave. Then have them look at **Figure 7.9** and explain why this is an ionic bond. Note relevant information in the first column of the chart. Tell students to do the same, and to continue to note characteristics of each type of bond as they read the chapter.

Teach

EXPLAIN to students that they will learn about an ionic bond, one of the three main types of bonds that atoms form. Have students look at the chart on page 122 (**Figure 7.16**) to preview the three types of bonds.

Use the Visual: Figure 7.7

[ANSWER] The outermost energy level in sodium has one valence electron. The outermost energy level in chlorine has seven valence electrons. Neither atom has a complete valence shell.

Before You Read

In your Science Notebook, create a chart with three columns. Label the first column *Ionic Bonds*, the second column *Covalent Bonds*, and the third column *Metallic Bonds*. As you learn about these three kinds of bonds, add information to your chart that describes their characteristics.

Imagine you and your friend are looking through your video game collection. There's a video game that is not one of your favorites, but it is one your friend really likes. You happily give the game to her. Now imagine that the video game she finds among your collection is one that you play a lot. You agree to share the game if she'll share one of hers.

Atoms behave in a manner somewhat similar to this, except that atoms exchange electrons. Atoms can gain or lose electrons, share electrons, or pool their electrons in order to become more stable. In each instance, a different kind of bond forms between them. Atoms tend to form three main types of bonds: ionic, covalent, and metallic bonds.

Ionic Bonds

When one atom loses one or more electrons and another atom gains one or more electrons, an **ionic bond** forms. Ionic bonds tend to form between metals and nonmetals.

Sodium and chlorine atoms form an ionic bond when they interact. The compound formed is called sodium chloride. Sodium is a highly reactive, silvery metal. Chlorine is a greenish, poisonous gas. Sodium chloride is table salt. **Figure 7.7** shows the atomic structure of an atom of sodium and an atom of chlorine.

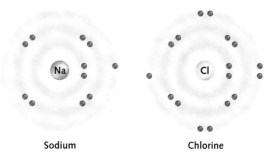

Sodium   Chlorine

Figure 7.7 The electron configurations of sodium and chlorine explain why atoms of these elements react when combined. How would you describe the outermost energy level in each atom?

ELL Strategy

Read Aloud and Discuss Have students take turns reading aloud and discussing this lesson in small groups. Have them make a group list of the characteristics of the three types of bonds. Also suggest that they compile a list of questions they have about the information. At the conclusion of the lesson, groups can exchange lists, comparing facts and trying to answer questions.

As **Figure 7.7** shows, a chlorine atom has seven valence electrons. It needs to gain one more electron to have eight in its valence shell. Recall that having eight valence electrons, or a complete outermost energy level, is the most stable configuration.

If a sodium atom loses the only electron in its valence shell, the energy level below will become the new valence shell. That energy level already has eight electrons, which means that it is complete.

Sodium needs to lose one electron and chlorine needs to gain one electron to become more stable. When chlorine accepts an electron from sodium, both atoms have complete outermost energy levels—eight electrons in their valence shells—and greater stability.

How does this transfer of electrons actually occur? Recall that atoms are electrically neutral; they have an equal number of protons and electrons and thus no overall charge. When an atom loses or gains electrons, the number of protons in the atom is no longer equal to the number of electrons. The atom is no longer electrically neutral. An atom that is no longer neutral because it has lost or gained electrons is called an **ion.** In the sodium chloride example, sodium lost an electron, so it has one more proton than it has electrons. It becomes a positively charged sodium ion. Chlorine gained an electron and has one more electron than it has protons in its nucleus. It becomes a negatively charged chloride ion. **Figure 7.8** illustrates this idea.

The positively charged sodium ion and the negatively charged chloride ion are strongly attracted to each other. An ionic bond forms between them. An ionic bond is the attractive force that holds oppositely charged ions together. **Figure 7.9** summarizes this process.

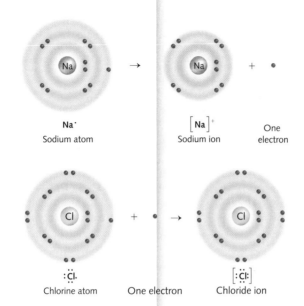

Na˙
Sodium atom

[Na]⁺
Sodium ion

One electron

Cl

:Cl˙
Chlorine atom

One electron

[:Cl:]
Chloride ion

Figure 7.8 Chlorine gains an electron from sodium when chlorine and sodium combine. Ions form as a result. The plus sign with the symbol for sodium indicates that sodium has become a positive sodium ion with a charge of 1+. The minus sign with the symbol for chlorine indicates that chlorine has become a negative chloride ion with a charge of 1–.

$$Na^{˙} \quad + \quad ˙\overset{..}{\underset{..}{Cl}}: \quad \rightarrow \quad [Na]^{+}[:\overset{..}{\underset{..}{Cl}}:]^{-}$$

Figure 7.9 Just as the attractive force between protons and electrons causes them to be held together in atoms, the attractive force between oppositely charged ions causes the ions to be held together in compounds.

● **Teach**

 EXPLAIN to students that they will continue to learn about ionic bonds and the formation of ions.

Vocabulary

ionic bond Tell students that the word *ionic* is the adjective that comes from the word *ion*. Have students combine *ionic* with *bond* and suggest what the term means.

ion Tell students that *ion* is a Greek word meaning "going."

Science Notebook EXTRA

Have students select several elements from the periodic table on pages 94 and 95 to create ions for. Have them first determine the number of electrons in an atom of each element and then the number of valence electrons. Have them draw electron-dot diagrams for the atoms and use the electron configuration to determine if the atom will become a positively or negatively charged ion. Finally, have students refer to **Figure 7.8** to represent each ion.

E L L **Strategy**

Activate Background Knowledge Review with students the photos in Chapter 2 of sodium, chlorine, and salt. Remind students how a compound's properties are very different from those of the combining elements.

Teach

EXPLAIN to students that atoms of elements form positive or negative ions according to how easily they lose or gain electrons. A measure of an element's ability to attract electrons in a chemical bond is called *electronegativity.* The energy required to remove an electron from an atom is called *ionization energy.* Students will learn about these terms in this section of the lesson.

As You Read

Have students review pages 117 and 118 to find important information to record in their charts. Remind them that only facts should be included, not examples. Demonstrate this strategy by reading aloud the first few paragraphs on page 117 and recording the information in the chart on the board.

English language learners should use their notes to create questions about the lesson. They can exchange their questions with partners, who would then use their own notes to answer their peers' questions. In this way, the pairs can determine that they have included the important facts and that they comprehend the information.

(ANSWER) The key feature of ionic bonds is that they form when one atom gains electrons and one atom loses electrons. With the gain or loss of electrons, the atoms become ions and are held together by electrostatic attraction.

Figure It Out: Figure 7.11

(ANSWER) **1.** Iodine is more electronegative than magnesium because it can attract the one electron it needs to complete its valence shell easily. This can be determined by noting that iodine is much farther to the right on the periodic table than magnesium. **2.** It would require more energy to pull an electron from oxygen because oxygen has six valence electrons, compared with lithium's one. Oxygen's electrons are held more tightly and require more energy to be removed.

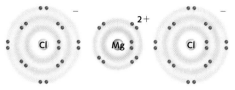

Magnesium chloride   Magnesium oxide

Figure 7.10 Magnesium has two valence electrons. If it loses one of these electrons to each of two chlorine atoms, the compound magnesium chloride forms. If it loses both of its valence electrons to one atom of oxygen, the compound magnesium oxide forms.

As You Read

With a partner, review the notes you have written in your Science Notebook. Add to or revise your notes. Then record information about ionic bonds.

What key feature describes an ionic bond?

Figure It Out

1. How can you determine which element is more electronegative, iodine or magnesium?
2. Why would it require more energy to pull an electron from oxygen than to pull an electron from lithium?

Ion Formation

Why does sodium lose one electron instead of gaining seven, when gaining seven electrons would also make the atom stable? Likewise, chlorine could lose seven electrons instead of gaining one. Why doesn't this happen? What controls how ions form? The answers have to do with forces and energy.

Attracting Electrons Some elements can attract electrons more easily than other elements can. They exert a greater attractive force on the electrons. This property of elements is called electronegativity. **Electronegativity** (ih lek troh neg uh TIH vuh tee) describes an element's ability to attract electrons in a chemical bond. The more electronegative an element is, the more able it is to attract electrons.

Elements with six or seven valence electrons, such as the Group 16 and Group 17 nonmetals, are very electronegative. They attract electrons easily. When they gain electrons, they release energy and become more stable. Because chlorine and elements like it are highly electronegative, they readily attract electrons and form negative ions.

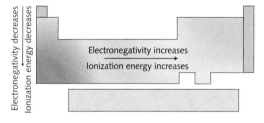

Figure 7.11 Electronegativity decreases from top to bottom down a group. It increases from left to right across a period. Fluorine is the most electronegative element. Ionization energy also decreases from top to bottom down a group. It generally increases from left to right across a period.

Background Information

There are seven systems, or groupings, of crystals that are used to describe their shapes. The simplest is the cubic system. The other systems are hexagonal, tetragonal, rhombohedral, orthorhombic, monoclinic, and triclinic.

Elements with one or two valence electrons, such as those in Group 1 and Group 2 of the periodic table, have low electronegativities. They do not attract electrons easily. Rather, they tend to give up electrons. Because sodium and elements like it are not highly electronegative, they do not readily attract electrons. Thus they tend to form positive ions rather than negative ions.

Removing Electrons Atoms cannot lose electrons on their own. It takes energy to pull electrons from atoms. The energy required to remove an electron from an atom is called **ionization** (I uh nuh ZAY shun) **energy.** The amount of energy needed differs from element to element. Elements that have just one or two valence electrons, such as the Group 1 and Group 2 metals, have low ionization energies. Little energy is required to remove an electron from an atom of one of these elements because the electrons are not held very tightly. Metals easily give up electrons, so they tend to form positive ions.

Elements that have atoms with six or seven valence electrons, such as those in Group 16 and Group 17, have high ionization energies. It requires a great deal of energy to remove electrons from atoms of these elements because the electrons are held very tightly. Nonmetals do not easily give up electrons, so they do not tend to form positive ions.

Ionic Compounds

Compounds that form as a result of ionic bonds are called ionic compounds. Ionic compounds share certain properties. They tend to be solids at room temperature and form structures called crystals. A **crystal** is a solid in which atoms or ions are arranged in a regularly repeating pattern. They tend to dissolve easily in water and conduct electricity when they are dissolved. They generally have high melting and boiling points. Although ionic compounds form from charged ions, they are electrically neutral. The charges of their individual ions cancel each other out.

Figure 7.12 Ionic compounds tend to form crystals, of which there are many different shapes. Cubes and rectangular prisms are two examples. In the compound table salt, each sodium ion is surrounded by six chloride ions. Each chloride ion is, in turn, surrounded by six sodium ions. A cube-like crystal forms as a result. Even the smallest visible grain of salt contains several quintillion sodium and chloride ions!

● **Teach**

EXPLAIN to students that they will learn about ionization energy and ionic compounds in this section.

Vocabulary

electronegativity Have students identify the word parts in the term *electronegativity* and relate their meanings to the definition of the term (*electro-* denotes electricity; *negative* denotes the charge on an electron; and *-ity* is a suffix that means "a state or quality").

ionization energy Tell students that *ionization* has two parts: *ionize*, a verb meaning "to produce or make something produce ions," and the suffix *-ation*, meaning "an action or result." Have students use those meanings to define the term *ionization energy*.

crystal Tell students that the word *crystal* comes from the Greek word *krystallos*, meaning "ice." Ask them why they think crystals were so named.

Explore It!

Each pair or small group will need a microscope, microscope slides, a spoon, water, oil, and several ionic compounds (including table salt, baking powder, magnesium sulphate/Epsom salt, and potassium iodide). Guide students to observe the preserved crystalline shape of each compound—each grain of table salt has a cubic shape, as does each grain of potassium iodide. Discuss the fact that the crystalline shapes are not random formations, but are instead determined by the ions that make up the compound. Encourage students to investigate and determine on their own the general properties of ionic compounds. By tapping the compounds with a spoon, students should recognize that ionic compounds are brittle and break apart easily. (This can be compared to metals, which tend not to be brittle.) Students should also recognize that all ionic compounds dissolve easily in water but do not dissolve well in solvents such as oil.

Background Information

You might wish to demonstrate the electrolytic properties of ionic compounds, as well, with the following activity: Set up a circuit by attaching one wire to each end of a battery. Attach the free end of one of these wires to a bulb arranged in a socket. Attach a third wire to the opposite side of the bulb. Put deionized water into a small petri dish. Place the free end of the wire attached to the bulb and the free end of the wire attached to the battery into the petri dish. The battery should not light. Remove the wires from the water and add some salt to the water. Again place the wires in the dish. This time, the bulb should light. Discuss with students the fact that ionic compounds conduct electricity when dissolved in water. Under your supervision, have students test this property using the other ionic compounds.

● Teach

 EXPLAIN to students that they will learn about the second type of bond that atoms form: a covalent bond.

🔘 Vocabulary

covalent bond Tell students that in the term *covalent,* the prefix *co-* means "with" or "together." Have students use this meaning and their understanding of valence electrons and bonding to define this term.

Use the Visual:

Figure 7.13 [ANSWER] By sharing, each atom achieves a complete outermost energy level, which makes the atom stable.

Figure 7.14 [ANSWER] Carbon forms a double bond with each oxygen atom in a carbon dioxide molecule. Two nitrogen atoms form a triple bond with each other in the formation of a molecule of nitrogen.

Partial negative charge

Partial positive charge

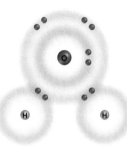

Figure 7.13 Two hydrogen atoms share electrons with one oxygen atom to form a molecule of water. How has sharing electrons made these three atoms more stable?

Did You Know?

Electrons are not always shared equally in a covalent bond. Although oxygen is not electronegative enough to completely pull electrons away from hydrogen, it is more electronegative than hydrogen. This means it pulls on the shared electrons a little more than hydrogen does. The electrons spend more time around the oxygen atom than they do around the hydrogen atoms.

Covalent Bonds

Some atoms do not easily gain or lose electrons. Instead, they share electrons to gain a more stable structure. When two atoms share electrons, a **covalent bond** forms between the atoms. A covalent bond is different from an ionic bond in that neither atom in the bond entirely loses or gains an electron. The atoms in a covalent bond do not become ions and do not become electrically charged.

Covalent bonds form when two relatively electronegative atoms interact. Since both atoms are similar in their ability to attract electrons in a chemical bond, neither one can completely pull electrons away from the other. For example, when hydrogen and oxygen atoms interact, they form a covalent bond. An oxygen atom has six valence electrons. It needs two more electrons for maximum stability. Hydrogen has one valence electron and needs a total of two for maximum stability. Oxygen is not electronegative enough to pull an electron away from hydrogen. Likewise, hydrogen is not electronegative enough to pull an electron away from oxygen.

As a "compromise," the atoms share electrons. The shared electrons move back and forth between the two atoms. They spend some time around the hydrogen atom and some time around the oxygen atom. This enables both atoms to have complete valence shells some of the time. Because oxygen needs two electrons, it forms covalent bonds with two hydrogen atoms, as shown in **Figure 7.13.** Other examples of covalent bonds are shown in **Figure 7.14.**

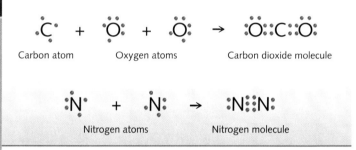

Carbon atom   Oxygen atoms   Carbon dioxide molecule

Nitrogen atoms   Nitrogen molecule

Figure 7.14 Atoms can share more than one electron each. When they share two electrons each, a double bond forms. When they share three electrons each, a triple bond forms. What kind of bond forms between carbon and each oxygen atom in a molecule of carbon dioxide? What kind of bond forms between two nitrogen atoms?

🄴🄻🄻 Strategy

Paraphrase Encourage students to meet in small groups to put the concepts of ionic bonds and covalent bonds into their own words. After students discuss the meanings of these terms, suggest that they create group definitions for each type of bond. Groups can then display their definitions for the class and see if classmates can identify each bond based on the definition.

Differentiate Instruction

Visual Provide library books and/or internet resources to illustrate and describe the seven types of crystal systems. Have students draw and label each system.

Molecular Compounds

Compounds that form as a result of covalent bonds are called molecular compounds. One unit of a molecular compound is a molecule. One molecule of carbon dioxide consists of a single carbon atom bonded to two oxygen atoms.

Molecules tend to be gases, liquids, or low-melting-point solids at room temperature. They do not generally conduct electricity and do not generally dissolve well in water. Molecules can range in size from just two atoms to hundreds of atoms. No matter how many atoms they are made of, molecules are electrically neutral.

Polyatomic Ions   Some molecules can easily gain or lose electrons to become ions. Such ions are called polyatomic ions. *Polyatomic* means the ions contain many atoms. The formation of a polyatomic ion often involves the transfer of a hydrogen atom from one molecule to another. Some examples of polyatomic ions are shown in **Figure 7.15**. Polyatomic ions can form ionic bonds with other ions.

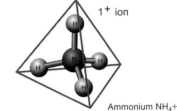

1$^+$ ion

Hydroxide OH$^-$

Ammonium NH$_4$$^+$

Figure 7.15 The charge on a polyatomic ion is shared by all the atoms in the ion. The polyatomic ions shown here formed when hydrogen atoms were transferred from one molecule to another.

PEOPLE IN SCIENCE: Gilbert Newton Lewis (1875–1946)

Gilbert Newton Lewis was born in Massachusetts and received much of his early schooling at home. He entered college at the age of 14 and completed his doctorate degree from Harvard University in 1899 at the age of 24.

Lewis began his career as a chemistry professor, spending time both teaching and doing research. By 1912, he had become the dean of the chemistry department at University of California, Berkeley. He remained at Berkeley for the rest of his career.

Lewis researched the electron-pair bonding theory of atoms and molecules and was the first to suggest that electrons may be partially transferred from one atom to another. Lewis believed that atoms could bond by sharing one electron from each of two atoms. His description of shared electrons was the first description of a covalent bond. Lewis also helped develop the "octet rule"—the rule stating that atoms bond to attain eight valence electrons. He developed electron-dot diagrams, also called Lewis diagrams in his honor, as a means of showing atoms' valence electrons.

● Teach

EXPLAIN to students that in this part of the lesson, they will learn about molecular compounds, polyatomic ions, and the noted scientist Gilbert Newton Lewis.

PEOPLE IN SCIENCE

Gilbert Newton Lewis is considered to be among the greatest American chemists of the twentieth century. His four main areas of research were thermodynamics and applying its laws to chemical systems; isotopes; the interaction of light and matter; and the theory of electron pairs bonding in atoms and molecules. In 1930, he was awarded the Society of Arts and Sciences Medal for being "the outstanding chemist in America." He was never awarded the Nobel Prize in Chemistry, although he was nominated for it over 30 times!

EXTEND Have students research what the Nobel Prize in Chemistry is. How is a person nominated for it? What are the requirements? Then have students research several chemists who received the award in the 1930s, noting their accomplishments. Finally, have them compare the winners' work to Lewis's work and express an opinion as to whether Lewis deserved a Nobel Prize.

Background Information

What is the difference between baking soda and baking powder? Both are used as leavening agents to make foods rise. Baking soda is pure sodium bicarbonate (NaHCO$_3$). When it is combined with moisture in a batter and an acidic ingredient is added, such as buttermilk or yogurt, the chemical reaction produces bubbles of carbon dioxide, which grow larger in the oven. Baking soda is about four times stronger than baking powder.

Baking powder is made up of sodium bicarbonate, cream of tartar and/or sodium aluminum sulfate (acidifying agents), and cornstarch (a drying agent). Because it already contains an acidifying agent, it does not need an acidic ingredient to cause a chemical reaction. Double-acting baking powder, commonly used in recipes today, first reacts to the moisture in a batter, and then reacts to the heat of an oven.

Teach

EXPLAIN to students that they will learn about metallic bonds, the third type of bond, in this last section of the lesson.

 Vocabulary

metallic bond Tell students that the word *metallic* is an adjective that means "made of metal."

🔍 **Explore It!**

Provide each group of students with a spoon, water, and a few metal samples. Encourage students to explore the properties of the metals. As they are observing and recording information in their Science Notebooks, encourage them to discuss their observations with group members.

Assess

Use the After You Read questions and Alternative Assessment to help you evaluate students' understanding of this lesson.

After You Read

1. The three main types of chemical bonds are ionic bonds, covalent bonds, and metallic bonds.

2. Students' answers will vary. Students should recognize that ionic bonds form when electrons are gained or lost, whereas covalent bonds form when electrons are shared. Metallic bonds form when pooled valence electrons are shared among a group of atoms. Bonds are similar in that they involve valence electrons, increase the stability of atoms, and hold atoms together.

3. Ionic compounds tend to be solids at room temperature, form crystals, dissolve well in water, and conduct electricity when they are dissolved. They generally have high melting and boiling points. Molecular compounds tend to be liquids, gases, or low-melting-point solids at room temperature. They do not tend to dissolve well in water or conduct electricity.

4. Students' summaries should include key characteristics of each type of bond as well as the compounds they form.

🔍 **Explore It!**

Examine a few metals. What can you observe about them? Draw a picture in your Science Notebook of how they look, and make a chart to describe the properties of each. Do the metals break apart easily? Can you bend or fold the metals? Do they dissolve in water? Compare the properties of these metals to the properties of the ionic compounds you observed.

Metallic Bonds

As discussed earlier, metal atoms form ionic bonds with nonmetal atoms because the valence electrons in metal atoms are not tightly held. For this same reason, metal atoms can also form bonds with other like metal atoms. The loosely held valence electrons move freely among the metal ions, forming a sea of electrons. The bond that results is called a metallic bond. A **metallic bond** forms when metal ions share their pooled valence electrons.

A metallic bond is somewhat like a cross between an ionic bond and a covalent bond. As with an ionic bond, the atoms in a metallic bond form ions. Like a covalent bond, the electrons are shared among multiple atoms rather than being associated with just one atom. Unlike ionic and covalent bonds, however, a metallic bond usually does not form between two specific atoms. Instead, metallic bonds tend to form in groups among many atoms of the same element.

Metallic bonds are responsible for many of the physical properties of metals. They make metals malleable, or able to be pounded or rolled into thin sheets, and ductile, or able to be drawn into a wire. Metallic bonds cause metals to conduct electricity and heat. They also account for the high melting and boiling points of metals.

The Three Types of Chemical Bonds	
Type of Bond	**Characteristics**
ionic	• forms when one atom gains electrons and another atom loses electrons • involves the formation of ions
covalent	• forms when two atoms each share one or more electrons • does not involve the formation of ions
metallic	• forms when metals share their pooled valence electrons • involves the formation of ions

Figure 7.16 This table summarizes the three main types of chemical bonds.

After You Read

1. What are the three main types of chemical bonds?

2. Compare the three main types of chemical bonds. How are they alike? How do they differ?

3. Describe the key features of ionic compounds and molecular compounds.

4. Review the information you recorded in your Science Notebook about chemical bonds. Use your notes to write a summary of this lesson.

Alternative Assessment

Give students time to finish the three-column charts of different types of chemical bonds. Have them review their work and complete any missing information. Each student should explain his or her chart to a partner and make any necessary changes that result from the explanation.

 **Strategy**

Use Visual Information English language learners can use **Figure 7.16** as a means of review. The chart can be reproduced and split into nine strips: three for the types of bonds and six for the each of the characteristics. Students can then match the two characteristics with the three types of bonds.

7.3 Predicting Types of Bonding

Before You Read

Create a K-W-L-S-H chart in your Science Notebook. Think about the title of this lesson. In the column labeled *K*, write what you already know about bonding. In the column labeled *W*, write what you want to learn about predicting types of bonds.

What controls the type of bond that forms between atoms? Why do sodium and chlorine atoms form ionic bonds, while oxygen and hydrogen atoms form covalent bonds? Is there a way to predict what kind of bond two atoms will form when they interact?

Rules for Predicting Bonding Types

The kind of bond that forms between atoms is governed by each atom's atomic number, or the number of protons in the atom's nucleus. It is also governed by the number of valence electrons each atom has and by the distance of those electrons from the atom's nucleus. A few simple rules can help predict what kind of bond two atoms will form.

The Periodic Table   The periodic table of elements contains a great deal of useful data. Recall that the periodic table is arranged in order of increasing atomic number and that each element falls into a particular period and group. The elements in a period have the same number of energy levels. The elements in a group have the same number of valence electrons and tend to form similar bonds. Follow these rules when using the periodic table to predict bond formation.

- When a metal in Group 1 or 2 interacts with a nonmetal in Group 16 or 17, an ionic bond tends to form.
- When two nonmetals interact, a covalent bond tends to form.
- When two metals interact, a metallic bond tends to form.

Valence Electrons   Valence electrons are the electrons in the outermost energy level. They are the electrons that are usually involved in bond formation. They are gained, lost, shared, or pooled. Follow these rules to use the number of valence electrons to predict bond formation.

- Atoms with just one or two valence electrons generally lose those electrons, become positive ions, and form ionic bonds.
- Atoms with six or seven valence electrons generally gain electrons, become negative ions, and form ionic bonds.
- Atoms with three, four, or five valence electrons generally cannot lose or gain electrons. Instead, they must form covalent bonds.

Learning Goals

- Recognize that atoms interact with one another in predictable ways.
- Predict the type of bond two atoms will form.
- Identify the information provided by a chemical formula.

New Vocabulary

chemical formula
subscript
oxidation number

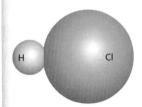

Figure 7.17 The two nonmetals hydrogen and chlorine combine to produce hydrogen chloride. What kind of bond is formed between the hydrogen and chlorine atoms?

7.3 Introduce

ENGAGE students by having them discuss in small groups what they know about predicting and/or predictions. Have them answer several questions, such as: *When do we predict? For what do we use predictions? Why are they helpful?*

Before You Read

Model a K-W-L-S-H chart on the board. Have students tell what they already know about bonding, and record their answers in the *K* column of the chart on the board. Have students tell what they want to know about predicting types of bonds, and record these responses in the column labeled *W*. Have students copy the chart into their Science Notebooks and fill in the first two columns.

● Teach

EXPLAIN to students that this lesson is called *Predicting Types of Bonding*. Have them preview the headings and figures in the lesson to determine what they will learn.

Use the Visual: Figure 7.17

ANSWER   A covalent bond forms between hydrogen and chlorine.

Science Notebook EXTRA

Have students provide examples for the rules regarding use of the periodic table to predict bond formation. They should provide two to three examples for each rule. Have them record their examples in their Science Notebooks, and then share the information with partners. After the discussion, they may need to revise their examples.

ELL Strategy

Ask and Answer Questions In small groups, have students ask and answer questions about predicting bond formation. Suggest that groups make lists of questions that they cannot answer easily and share the lists with the class. Other groups may have appropriate answers to such questions.

Key Concept Review
Workbook, p. 39

● Teach

EXPLAIN to students that they will learn about chemical formulas: what they are, what they represent, and what information can be derived from them.

 Vocabulary

chemical formula Ask students to remember what the word *chemical* means ("relating to chemistry"). Tell them that the common meaning of the word *formula* is "the combination of ingredients used in a product." Ask students for examples (baby formula, cough formula, cleaning agent formula). Have students apply the word meanings to provide a definition of the term.

subscript Tell students that *sub-* is a prefix meaning "below" or "under," and *script* comes from the Latin word *scribere,* meaning "to write." Ask students how these meanings can be used to remember the definition of *subscript.*

oxidation number Point out to students that the word *oxidation* can be broken down into *oxide,* a noun referring to any compound of oxygen and another element, and *-ation,* a suffix meaning "an action or result." Tell students that in chemistry, the word *oxidation* refers to a loss of electrons during a chemical reaction, whether the chemical reaction involves oxygen or not.

As You Read

In pairs, have students fill in the *L* column of their charts. Then have the pairs share what they learned with the class. Give students a few minutes to add to their charts after the class discussion.

[ANSWER] Students should be able to predict that two bromine atoms will form a covalent bond when they interact.

Figure It Out: **Figure 7.18**

[ANSWER] **1.** The ratio of C:H:O atoms is 6:12:6, or 1:2:1. There are six oxygen atoms. **2.** Both hydrogen peroxide and water are made up of hydrogen and oxygen atoms. Hydrogen peroxide has one more oxygen atom than water does and a total of four atoms in each molecule.

As You Read

In the column labeled *L* of your K-W-L-S-H chart, fill in information you have learned about predicting bonding. Add any new questions you have to the column labeled *W*.

Predict what kind of bond will form when two bromine atoms interact.

Figure It Out

1. What is the ratio of carbon to hydrogen to oxygen atoms in one molecule of glucose? How many oxygen atoms are there?

2. The chemical formula for hydrogen peroxide is H_2O_2. How does this compare with water?

Chemical Formulas

Scientists represent the atoms that form a compound by writing a chemical formula. A **chemical formula** is a combination of chemical symbols and numbers that indicates which elements and how many atoms of each element are present in one unit of a compound. A few chemical formulas are shown in **Figure 7.18.** As the figure shows, a chemical formula is made up of the chemical symbols of the elements in the compound. The *H* and *O* in the chemical formula for water, H_2O, indicate that water is made up of hydrogen and oxygen atoms. The *Na* and *Cl* in the chemical formula for salt, *NaCl*, indicate that salt is made up of sodium and chloride ions.

A chemical formula often includes a small number written after the symbol for an element. The number, called a **subscript,** indicates the number of atoms of that element that are in the compound. The subscript *2* after the *H* in H_2O indicates that there are two hydrogen atoms in one molecule of the compound water. When there is no subscript after an element's chemical symbol, it is understood that there is only one atom of that element in the compound.

Oxidation Numbers An **oxidation number** is the charge an atom would have if it formed an ionic bond. It indicates the number of electrons an atom gains, loses, or shares when the atom bonds. The oxidation number is related to the number of valence electrons.

For elements in an ionic compound, the oxidation number is the same as the charge on the ions. A sodium ion has a charge of 1+, so its oxidation number is 1+. A chloride ion has a charge of 1−, so its oxidation number is 1−.

Chemical Formulas for Common Compounds

Compound	Chemical Formula	Combining Elements	Number of Atoms of Each Element	Total Number of Atoms
water	H_2O	hydrogen and oxygen	hydrogen: 2 oxygen: 1	3
sodium chloride (table salt)	NaCl	sodium and chlorine	sodium: 1 chlorine: 1	2
glucose (simple sugar)	$C_6H_{12}O_6$	carbon, hydrogen, and oxygen	carbon: 6 hydrogen: 12 oxygen: 6	24
acetic acid (vinegar)	$C_2H_4O_2$	carbon, hydrogen, and oxygen	carbon: 2 hydrogen: 4 oxygen: 2	9

Figure 7.18 Chemical formulas show the number of atoms of each element that make up a compound. They can be used to quickly determine the chemical composition of a compound.

Differentiate Instruction

Logical/Mathematical In pairs, have students research the chemical formulas of five more compounds and create a chart similar to that in **Figure 7.18.** Provide library resources and copies of the periodic table to aid students in finding compounds.

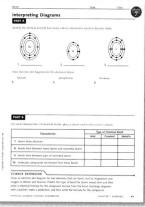

Interpreting Diagrams Workbook, p. 41

Periodic Table (Figure 7.19)

1+										0
Hydrogen 1 H	2+		3+	4+	3−	2−	1−			Helium 2 He
Lithium 3 Li	Beryllium 4 Be			Boron 5 B	Carbon 6 C	Nitrogen 7 N	Oxygen 8 O	Fluorine 9 F		Neon 10 Ne
Sodium 11 Na	Magnesium 12 Mg			Aluminum 13 Al	Silicon 14 Si	Phosphorus 15 P	Sulfur 16 S	Chlorine 17 Cl		Argon 18 Ar
Potassium 19 K	Calcium 20 Ca			Gallium 31 Ga	Germanium 32 Ge	Arsenic 33 As	Selenium 34 Se	Bromine 35 Br		Krypton 36 Kr
Rubidium 37 Rb	Strontium 38 Sr			Indium 49 In	Tin 50 Sn	Antimony 51 Sb	Tellurium 52 Te	Iodine 53 I		Xenon 54 Xe
Cesium 55 Cs	Barium 56 Ba			Thallium 81 Tl	Lead 82 Pb	Bismuth 83 Bi	Polonium 84 Po	Astatine 85 At		Radon 86 Rn
Francium 87 Fr	Radium 88 Ra									

Figure 7.19 The number at the top of each group is the most common oxidation number.

For elements in a molecular compound, the oxidation number is the number of valence electrons each element shares. In a molecule of water, oxygen shares two of its valence electrons, so its oxidation number is 2. Hydrogen has one valence electron to share, so its oxidation number is 1. Oxygen is more electronegative than hydrogen. To indicate this, a minus sign is placed after oxygen's oxidation number (2−) and a plus sign is placed after hydrogen's oxidation number (1+).

Figure 7.19 shows the oxidation numbers of eight groups of the periodic table. The elements in the middle can have several oxidation numbers. The atoms of all elements have an oxidation number of 0 when they are not bonded to another atom.

Writing Chemical Formulas   To write a chemical formula for a compound that contains two elements, first record the chemical symbols for the elements. Determine the oxidation number of each element and write it to the upper right of the chemical symbol. Then "criss-cross" the oxidation numbers (without the signs), so that the number of one ion becomes the subscript of the other ion.

Li^{1+} N^{3-}

means

Li_3N_1 or Li_3N

Figure 7.20 In a molecule of lithium nitride, nitrogen's oxidation number (3−) is lithium's subscript. Lithium's oxidation number (1+) is nitrogen's subscript.

After You Read

1. Identify three rules for predicting the kind of bond two atoms will form.

2. Predict what kind of bond will form between atoms of the following elements: potassium and iodine; sodium metal; carbon and oxygen.

3. Use your completed K-W-L columns to write a summary of this lesson. In the *S* column, write what you would still like to know about bonding. In the *H* column, write how you can find this information.

Extend It!

Practice writing chemical formulas for the compounds formed when the pairs of elements listed below interact.

hydrogen + chlorine
magnesium + bromine
carbon + hydrogen

How many atoms make up each compound?

Teach

EXPLAIN to students that in this section, they will learn about oxidation numbers and how to write chemical formulas. Ask students to preview the figures to get an idea of what they will learn and discuss their ideas with partners.

Extend It!

Show students how to figure out the first formula, hydrogen + chlorine, using the information provided. If necessary, say: *To write a chemical formula, first write the chemical symbols for the elements that make up the compound. Then, "criss-cross" their oxidation numbers.* Write the formula on the board, and then explain how to count the number of atoms in it. Explain that once they know how to write a chemical formula, students can do this for any compound.

ANSWER The atoms that make up each compound are as follows: HCl (2 atoms), $MgBr_2$ (3 atoms), CH_4 (5 atoms), NH_3 (4 atoms), K_3N (4 atoms).

Assess

Use the After You Read questions and Alternative Assessment to help you evaluate students' understanding of this lesson.

After You Read

1. Students' answers will vary. Answers should be based on the rules outlined on page 124.

2. potassium and iodine—ionic bond; sodium metal—metallic bond; carbon and oxygen—covalent bond

3. Students' answers will vary. Encourage students to think about questions they still have. Check students' summaries to make sure that they reflect an understanding of the lesson's main points.

Alternative Assessment

On the board, write one or two examples of *S*- and *H*-column entries, and then guide students to complete their charts and discuss them in small groups.

Background Information

Russian scientist Dmitri Mendeleev is known as the father of the periodic table of elements. He discovered that by arranging elements in order of increasing atomic mass, a pattern emerged that showed the elements' chemical properties. He published the first periodic table in 1869, leaving empty spaces for three undiscovered elements, which he predicted would fit there. When they were discovered, he was found to be correct.

Chapter 7 Summary

MASTERING CONCEPTS

True or False

1. False, Ionic bonds
2. False, eight
3. True
4. True
5. True
6. False, more

Short Answer

7. Atoms can form ionic, covalent, or metallic bonds.

8. Two nonmetals will likely form a covalent bond when they interact.

9. A metal and nonmetal will likely form an ionic bond when they interact.

10. A valence electron is an electron that is in an atom's outermost energy level.

11. An electron-dot diagram is a simple diagram that shows an atom's chemical symbol and its valence electrons.

KEY CONCEPTS

7.1 What Is Bonding?

- Atoms combine with one another to form new substances called compounds.

- Electrons are arranged around an atom's nucleus in energy levels. The electrons in the outermost energy level are called valence electrons. Atoms are most stable when they have eight valence electrons.

- A chemical bond is a force that holds atoms together. Chemical bonds form when atoms exchange or share valence electrons. Atoms form bonds to become more stable.

7.2 Types of Bonds

- Ionic, covalent, and metallic bonds are the three main types of bonds that atoms can form.

- Bonds differ in the way electrons are exchanged or shared between atoms.

- Ionic bonds form when one atom loses electrons and another atom gains electrons. Covalent bonds form when atoms share one or more of their valence electrons. Metallic bonds form when metals pool together and share their electrons.

7.3 Predicting Types of Bonding

- Atoms interact with one another in predictable ways.

- By using the periodic table or the numbers of valence electrons the atoms have, it is possible to predict the type of bond two atoms will form.

- Chemical formulas show at a glance the elements and number of atoms that make up a compound.

VOCABULARY REVIEW

Write each term in a complete sentence or write a paragraph relating several terms.

7.1
chemical bond, p. 113
electron cloud, p.113
energy level, p. 113
valence electron, p. 114
electron-dot diagram, p. 115

7.2
ionic bond, p. 116
ion, p. 117
electronegativity, p. 118
ionization energy, p. 119
crystal, p. 119
covalent bond, p. 120
metallic bond, p. 122

7.3
chemical formula, p. 124
subscript, p. 124
oxidation number, p. 124

PREPARE FOR CHAPTER TEST

To prepare for the chapter test, create a question from each Learning Goal. Use the information in your Science Notebook to answer each question. Then use these answers to write a well-developed essay about the chapter. Use the Key Concept on the first page of this chapter as your topic sentence.

Vocabulary Review Workbook, p. 40

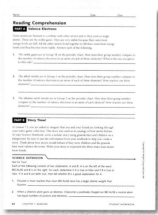

Reading Comprehension Workbook, p. 42

MASTERING CONCEPTS

True or False
If the statement is true, write "true." If it is false, change the underlined word or words to make the statement true.

1. <u>Covalent bonds</u> involve the gain or loss of electrons.

2. Atoms with <u>five</u> valence electrons are the most stable atoms.

3. <u>Chemical formulas</u> include both chemical symbols and numbers.

4. <u>Metallic bonds</u> form when metals share their pooled electrons.

5. The <u>periodic table</u> can be used to predict the type of bond two atoms will form.

6. When atoms form bonds, they become <u>less</u> stable.

Short Answer
Answer each of the following in a sentence or brief paragraph.

7. What are three ways atoms can bond?

8. Predict what type of bond two nonmetals will form when they interact.

9. Predict what type of bond will form when a metal interacts with a nonmetal.

10. What is a valence electron?

11. What is an electron-dot diagram?

Critical Thinking
Use what you have learned in this chapter to answer each of the following.

12. **Compare and Contrast** How are ionic compounds different from molecular compounds?

13. **Explain** What is the relationship between an atom's valence electrons and the atom's ability to form bonds?

14. **Infer** Why do scientists draw electron-dot diagrams?

Standardized Test Question
Choose the letter of the response that correctly answers the question.

15. Covalent bonds typically form between which of the following?

   A. two metals
   B. two nonmetals
   C. a metal and a nonmetal
   D. all of the above

> **Test-Taking Tip**
>
> If "all of the above" is one of the choices in a multiple-choice question, be sure that none of the choices are false.

Critical Thinking

12. Ionic compounds form as a result of ionic bonds, whereas molecular compounds form as a result of covalent bonds. Ionic compounds tend to be solids at room temperature, form crystals, dissolve well in water, and conduct electricity when they dissolve. They tend to be brittle and have high melting and boiling points. Molecular compounds, in contrast, tend to be liquids, gases, or low-melting-point solids at room temperature. They generally do not dissolve well in water and do not conduct electricity.

13. An atom's ability to form bonds is closely related to the number of valence electrons the atom has. Atoms with fewer than eight valence electrons form bonds to attain a complete outermost energy level (eight valence electrons). Atoms with eight valence electrons—the noble gases—tend not to form bonds.

14. Scientists draw electron-dot diagrams to see at a glance the number of valence electrons an atom has. Because valence electrons are important to understanding bonding, these drawings help scientists think about the way an atom will bond or behave.

Standardized Test Question

15. B

Reading Links

Antoine Lavoisier: Father of Chemistry

This accessible biography tells of Lavoisier's life, methodical approach to scientific inquiry, and contribution to chemistry. The reading level and interesting visuals make it a good text for independent student projects.

Marylou Morano Kjelle. Mitchell Lane Publishers. 48 pp. Illustrated. Library ISBN 978-1-58415-309-2.

Atoms and Molecules

With engaging illustrations and easy-to-read text, this book presents information about atoms and molecules in a clear way that struggling readers will find rewarding.

Phil Roxbee-Cox. EDC Publishing. 32 pp. Illustrated. Trade ISBN 978-0-7460-0988-8.

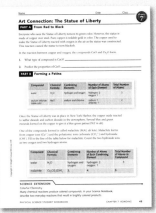

Curriculum Connection
Workbook, p. 43

Science Challenge
Workbook, pp. 44-45

7A **Bonding Atoms**

 This prechapter introduction activity is designed to determine what students already know about atomic structure and introduce them to the role of electrons in bonding by having them model atoms, analyze structures, and identify valence electrons.

- Students can help prepare cut-out circles the day before doing the activity. Once the circles are cut out, these materials can be saved to use year after year with just replacements added as circles go missing or are damaged. Note that the electrons should be smaller than the protons and neutrons.

Objectives

- model atomic structure and electron energy levels
- identify valence electrons
- evaluate the role of electrons in the bonding of atoms

Planning

 25–35 minutes   groups of 3–4 students

Materials (per group)

- red, green, and yellow paper circles
- 5 atomic modeling sheets

Advance Preparation

- The atomic modeling sheets can be made by students ahead of time. For each sheet, draw a circle about 5 cm in diameter in the center of the sheet, and then draw three larger-diameter concentric circles around the nucleus. Explain that the central circle represents the nucleus and the ring-like regions are the energy levels in an atom.

Engagement Guide

- Challenge students to think about atomic structure and the role of outer-shell electrons in bonding by asking:
  - *Why do you think electrons fill the energy levels closest to the nucleus before they fill the higher energy levels?* (The lower energy levels are more greatly attracted by the positive charge of the nucleus; thus, electrons fill these levels first.)
  - *Why do you think the outermost electrons are the ones involved in chemical bonding?* (The outermost electrons are farther from the nucleus and not as tightly held as those closer in.)
  - *How do you think the number of electrons in the outermost energy level of an atom is related to its position in the periodic table?* (Discuss this key point in terms of the representative elements only. For example, lithium and sodium each have one valence electron; they are found in Group 1A (1). Chlorine has seven valence electrons and is found in Group 7A (17). Discuss also that atoms are stable when their outer energy level is full, and that this—except for He—corresponds to having eight valence electrons.)

 7B **Chemical Bonding**

Objectives

- model the valence electrons of sodium and chlorine
- apply the octet rule in chemical bonding formation
- model bonding between two elements

Skill Set

observing, comparing and contrasting, recording and analyzing data, stating conclusions

Planning

 20 minutes   groups of 3–4 students

Materials

Materials for this activity are listed in the Student Laboratory Manual.

Advance Preparation

Reuse the colored paper circles and atomic modeling sheets from Lab 7A for this activity. Each group needs enough of the colored circles to model sodium (11 protons, 11 electrons, and 12 neutrons) and chlorine (17 protons, 17 electrons, and 18 neutrons). You might want to let students pick out the correct numbers of each to help with their understanding of atomic number and mass.

Answers to Observations: Sketches of NaCl and Cl_2

(NaCl) Students' sketches should show 2, 8, and 1 electron in the energy levels for sodium. The sketch for chlorine should show 2, 8, and 7 electrons in the energy levels. Note: These sketches can be used to introduce ionic bonding.

(Cl_2) Each sketch for chlorine should show 2, 8, and 7 electrons in the energy levels. Note: These sketches can be used to introduce covalent bonding.

Answers to Analysis and Conclusions

1. Sodium will lose one electron, obtaining the electron configuration of neon. Chlorine will gain one valence electron, obtaining the electron configuration of argon. Atoms tend to gain or lose the fewest number of electrons needed in order to obtain the configuration of the nearest noble gas on the periodic table.

2. Sodium forms Na+, and chlorine forms Cl–.

3. Students should suggest that sodium gives its electron to chlorine so that each has a filled valence shell. Students will likely have a harder time seeing how the electrons are shared in the covalent bond in a chlorine molecule; accept all reasonable explanations. Be sure to explain to students how each atom shares one electron, resulting in a filled valence shell around each chlorine atom.

Going Further

Have students research and learn about Lewis structures, also called electron-dot diagrams. Have them draw the Lewis structures for sodium and chlorine and to use the diagrams to explain the bonds in NaCl and Cl_2.

 # 7C Ionic Bonding

Objectives

• determine relationships among elements on the periodic table
• explore ionic bonding
• build models of ionic compounds

Skill Set

observing, recording and analyzing data, classifying, inferring, drawing conclusions

Planning

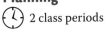 2 class periods   groups of 3–4 students

Advanced Preparation

• Element squares can be made by students ahead of time. To make the element grid sheet, mark off 1-inch or 2-cm squares on a sheet of paper. Make copies as needed.

• When writing the ion charges, students may find writing out plus and minus signs more helpful; that is, + + + instead of 3+. This will make it easier for some students to keep track of the total charge on the compound formed.

Answers to Observations

Data Table 1						
Element 1	Element 2	Ion Formed by Element 1	Ion Formed by Element 2	Atoms of Element 1 in Compound	Atoms of Element 2 in Compound	Chemical Formula of Compound
Lithium	Chlorine	1+	1–	1	1	LiCl
Calcium	Bromine	2+	2–	1	1	CaBr
Magnesium	Fluorine	2+	1–	1	2	MgF_2
Beryllium	Oxygen	2+	2–	1	1	BeO
Sodium	Sulfur	1+	2–	2	1	Na_2S
Hydrogen	Iodine	1+	1–	1	1	HI
Aluminum	Oxygen	3+	2–	2	3	Al_2O_3

Data Table 2	
Compound Formula	Compound Name
LiCl	Lithium chloride
CaBr	Calcium bromide
MgF_2	Magnesium fluoride
BeO	Beryllium oxide
Na_2S	Sodium sulfide
HI	Hydrogen iodide
Al_2O_3	Aluminum oxide

Answers to Analysis and Conclusions

1. Elements with the same number of valence electrons are found in the same group, or column, on the table. Group 1, 2, 13, 14, 15, 16, 17, and 18 elements have 1, 2, 3, 4, 5, 6, 7, and 8 electrons, respectively.

2. Group 13 elements have three valence electrons. These atoms lose three electrons to become more stable, forming 3+ ions. Group 16 elements have six valence electrons. These atoms gain two electrons to become more stable, forming 2- ions.

Going Further

Ask students to research common prefixes used to modify the chemical names they wrote in Part B. The prefixes are used to identify the number of atoms of each element present in the compound. Have students write the names of the compounds in Data Table 2 using prefixes.

Chapter 8 Lessons

8.1 Nature of a Chemical Reaction

8.2 Types of Chemical Reactions

8.3 Energy and Reaction Rates

Introduce Chapter 8

As a starting activity, use Lab 8A on page 43 of the Laboratory Manual.
ENGAGE Tell students that they will be learning about chemical reactions. To demonstrate a large-scale chemical reaction, have students visit NASA's Web site to view a space-shuttle launch. Then encourage them to discuss what they viewed and how it is related to a chemical reaction.

Think About Changes in Matter

ENGAGE On the board, write the examples of changes in matter that are listed in the text. With students, label each change as physical or chemical and have students give reasons why. Ask students for two or three more examples and record them on the board. Instruct students to list and label in their Science Notebooks at least five more examples of changes in matter.

Chapter 8 — Chemical Reactions

KEY CONCEPT A chemical reaction is the process by which a chemical change takes place.

A spacecraft launches into the air with a thunderous roar. Smoke and flames shoot out from behind. It shakes violently as it hurtles upward. Just eight minutes after liftoff, the craft is in orbit hundreds of kilometers above Earth.

A spacecraft can travel at speeds of more than 27,000 kilometers per hour. At such speeds, a spacecraft can complete an entire trip around Earth in less than an hour and a half! What provides the craft with so much energy? The answers involve a simple chemical change.

Think About Changes in Matter

The various forms of matter that surround you change in many ways. Think about the ways in which matter in your school changes. Classroom boards get marked up and erased every day. Students eat their lunches. Cars and buses transport students and teachers. How else does matter change around you?

- In your Science Notebook, list at least five ways that matter changes.

- Classify each change as a physical change or a chemical change. What evidence did you use to make your classifications?

SCI LINKS.
THE WORLD'S A CLICK AWAY

www.scilinks.org
Chemical Reactions **Code: WGPS08**

128

Chapter 8 Planning Guide			
Instructional Periods	National Standards	Lab Manual	Workbook
8.1 2 Periods	A1, B1, B3, G1, G2, G3; A1, B2, B3, B6, G1, G2, G3; UCP1, UCP3	**Lab 8A: p. 43** Observing Chemical Change **Lab 8B: pp. 44–46** Chemical Reactions **Lab 8C: pp. 47–48** Conservation of Mass	Key Concept Review p. 46 Vocabulary Review p. 47 Interpreting Diagrams p. 48 Reading Comprehension p. 49 Curriculum Connection p. 50 Science Challenge pp. 51–52
8.2 2 Periods	A2, B1, C1; A2, B3; UCP1, UCP3, UCP4		
8.3 2 Periods	A2, B1, B3, C1; A2, B3, B6; UCP2, UCP3		

Middle School Standard; High School Standard; Unifying Concept and Principle

8.1 Nature of a Chemical Reaction

Before You Read
Read the lesson title, Learning Goals, headings, and subheadings and look at the photos and diagrams. Predict what you think you will learn in this lesson. Write three sentences in your Science Notebook explaining your predictions.

Cars are piled one on top of the other at a car junkyard. Some cars were in accidents and are beyond repair. Others are just old and unwanted. Most are covered with dents and scratches. Many are turning brown with rust. The strong metal they were made from is beginning to crumble and flake away.

Car junkyards can be interesting places to visit. Abandoned and left out in the open, the cars are lessons in history and change. Each scratch, dent, and particle of rust is evidence of the changes matter undergoes.

Changes in Matter
Recall that matter can undergo both physical and chemical changes. A physical change occurs when the physical properties of matter change. Physical properties include shape, mass, volume, density, and state. An example of a physical change is boiling. When water boils, it changes from a liquid to a gas. Although it looks different and its physical properties have changed, the water is still made up of H_2O molecules. As liquid water or gaseous water vapor, it is still the same substance. Its identity does not change, thus its chemical properties do not change.

A chemical change occurs when the chemical properties of matter change. Unlike physical changes, chemical changes cause new substances to form. Rusting is an example of a chemical change. When iron rusts, a substance made up of iron and oxygen atoms forms. The chemical properties of this substance are different from those of iron. The physical properties of rust, such as its color and hardness, are also different from those of iron. When matter changes chemically, both its physical properties and its chemical properties change.

Figure 8.1 What examples of changes in matter can you identify in this car junkyard? Which changes are physical changes? Which changes are chemical changes?

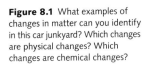
Learning Goals
- Explain what a chemical reaction is.
- Recognize that mass is conserved during a chemical reaction.
- Describe the components of a balanced chemical equation.

New Vocabulary
chemical reaction
reactant
product
law of conservation of mass
chemical equation
coefficient
balanced chemical equation

Recall Vocabulary
chemical bond, p. 113
chemical formula, p. 124
subscript, p. 124

8.1 Introduce

ENGAGE Have students share examples of chemical reactions that they have seen or read about on television or the Internet, and in movies and books. Ask: *How do you know these examples are chemical reactions?* Elicit from students the idea that the chemical properties of the reacting substances change during a chemical reaction. If necessary, review physical properties/changes and chemical properties/changes using a Venn diagram.

Vocabulary terms are listed on the first student page of each lesson. You may wish to preview the terms before introducing each lesson. Strategies for teaching the vocabulary appear on the pages where the terms are introduced.

Before You Read
Read aloud the lesson title, Learning Goals, headings, and subheadings for this lesson. As you do so, share one or two predictions about what you think you will learn in this lesson. Record them on the board. Ask students to work with a partner and do the same with the rest of the first lesson and record their predictions in their Science Notebooks.
Students' predictions should reflect that they will learn about the nature and characteristics of chemical changes.

Teach
EXPLAIN to students that in this lesson, they will learn about chemical reactions.

Use the Visual: Figure 8.1
ANSWER Students' answers will vary but should include dents, scratches, and broken glass (physical changes), as well as rust (chemical change).

Teach

EXPLAIN to students that they will learn how chemical reactions are described.

 Vocabulary

chemical reaction Ask students to remember what they already learned about the word *chemical*. Ask what they know about the word *reaction*. Tell them that it is a noun and that the common meaning is "a response that shows how someone feels or thinks about something." Ask for examples.

reactant Tell students that the word *react* is a verb meaning "to act in response to something," and *-ant* signifies someone or something that performs a specific action. Have students put the meanings together to form a definition for the term.

product Ask students what they know about the word *product* and have them give examples. Tell them that it is a noun meaning "something that is produced or made."

law of conservation of mass Tell students that the word *conservation* is a noun that comes from the verb *conserve,* which means "to protect from damage or undesirable change."

Figure It Out Figure 8.3

(ANSWER) **1.** Hydrogen and oxygen are the reactants. Water is the product. **2.** The number of atoms of each element stays the same over the course of the reaction, though they are arranged differently as products than they were as reactants.

 Explore It!

For each group of students, provide the following materials: a few pieces of steel wool, small pieces of aluminum foil or another aluminum product (such as a frozen dinner tray or other food storage container), copper wire or piping, several cups, water, putty or clay, and a pie pan or other shallow dish.

(ANSWER) Students should recognize that only items containing iron will rust. This is because rust is made partly of iron atoms. Students should also recognize that rust only forms in the presence of oxygen and water.

 Explore It!

Gather a few pieces of steel wool (which is made mostly of iron), a few pieces of aluminum foil, and a few pieces of copper wire. Leave one sample of each metal on a table. Place another sample of each metal in its own cup filled with water. Finally, use putty or clay to stick a third sample of each metal in the bottom of its own cup. Place these cups upside down in a pie pan filled with water. Observe the metals over the next few days. Record your observations and explanations in your Science Notebook.

Figure It Out

1. Which substances are the reactants? Which are the products?

2. Compare the number of oxygen and hydrogen atoms on the left of the arrow to the number of hydrogen and oxygen atoms on the right of the arrow. What happens to the number of atoms of each element?

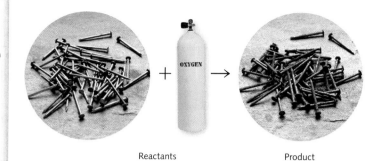

Reactants   Product

Figure 8.2 When iron and oxygen combine under the right conditions, the product rust forms. The arrow shown between the reactants and the products indicates that a change has taken place.

Chemical Reactions

The process by which a chemical change takes place is called a **chemical reaction.** In a chemical reaction, two or more substances interact with one another and one or more new substances are formed. The substances that interact in a chemical reaction are called **reactants** (ree AK tunts). These are the original substances. The new substances that form from a chemical reaction are called **products**. In **Figure 8.2**, iron and oxygen are the reactants. Rust is the product.

When a chemical reaction takes place, atoms are rearranged. The chemical bonds between some atoms are broken and new chemical bonds are formed. This rearrangement of atoms is what causes new substances to form. **Figure 8.3** illustrates this idea. When hydrogen interacts with oxygen, the bonds holding the hydrogen atoms together are broken. The bond holding the oxygen atoms together is broken, too. A new bond forms between each of the hydrogen atoms and one of the oxygen atoms. The new substance, water, forms as a result.

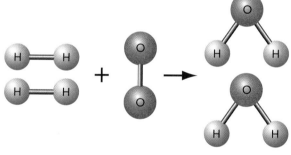

Figure 8.3 In a chemical reaction, new elements are not formed. Instead, the atoms or ions of the elements are rearranged. Some chemical bonds are broken and new chemical bonds are formed.

Background Information

Copper is used in construction in a variety of ways, including in roofing and gutters. Although it is more expensive than other roofing materials, copper is often chosen because of its appearance: as it ages, a chemical reaction causes it to have a patina (a grayish-green coating, like on the Statue of Liberty). Copper is also very durable; it lasts several hundred years, which is longer than other materials used for roofing. The problem with this metal is that as it ages, rain water washes away some of the copper and damages the soil and water supply.

Conservation of Mass Atoms cannot disappear during a chemical reaction. All of the atoms that make up the reactants must be found among the products. At the same time, new atoms cannot appear. Only atoms found in the reactants will be found in the products. Atoms are neither created nor destroyed during chemical reactions. They are simply rearranged.

This idea is expressed in one of the most important laws of chemistry. The **law of conservation of mass** states that in a chemical reaction, the combined mass of the reactants is equal to the combined mass of the products. Matter is conserved; it is neither created nor destroyed.

Energy In addition to changes in matter, chemical reactions involve changes in energy. Some reactions involve the absorption of energy. Others involve the release of energy. When liquid hydrogen reacts with liquid oxygen, a great deal of energy is given off. This energy is used to power a spacecraft such as the space shuttle.

$HC_2H_3O_2 + NaHCO_3$
Reactants

$NaC_2H_3O_2 + H_2O + CO_2$
Products

Figure 8.4
According to the law of conservation of mass, the number and type of atoms must be the same for reactants and products.

Teach

PEOPLE IN SCIENCE: Antoine Lavoisier (1743–1794)

Antoine Lavoisier was expected to follow in his father's footsteps and become a lawyer. Among the broad range of subjects he studied, science was his favorite. Though he received his license to practice law in 1764, he chose to pursue a career in science instead.

During Lavoisier's time, chemistry was just becoming a true science. People did not yet understand the nature of matter or changes in matter. Lavoisier was particularly interested in learning more about exactly what happens when substances change form.

In one experiment, Lavoisier heated a carefully measured mass of mercury oxide in a sealed tube. He observed that the red powder changed into a silver liquid and a gas. Lavoisier recognized the liquid as the metal mercury. When he measured the mass of the sealed tube again, he discovered that the new substances had exactly the same mass as the mercury oxide he had started with. This experiment led him to suggest the law of conservation of mass.

With this discovery and many other accomplishments, Antoine Lavoisier helped make chemistry a more rigorous science. Lavoisier is recognized today as the father of modern chemistry. Unfortunately, Lavoisier was beheaded for political reasons during the French Revolution.

Background Information

Some examples of chemical reactions that occur in our everyday lives are an iron bar rusting (iron and oxygen in the air make rust), sugar in grapes fermenting with yeast to make alcohol and carbon dioxide (gas bubbles in champagne and beer), and an antacid (calcium hydroxide) neutralizing stomach acid (hydrochloric acid).

The experiment Lavoisier performed with mercury oxide is a dangerous reaction, as the decomposition of the reactant yields mercury vapor, which is extremely toxic. The reaction should not be performed unless the required provisions for ventilation are present.

● Teach

EXPLAIN to students that in this section, they will learn about chemical equations and how they are related to chemical reactions.

 Vocabulary

chemical equation Ask students what they already know about the word *equation*, and ask them to give examples. Tell them that the word *equation* refers to the state of being equal, and ask them to identify the equality in a chemical reaction.

coefficient Ask students to remember what the prefix *co-* means ("together"). Tell them that the common meaning of the word *efficient* is "competent" or "economical." Have students put the meanings together to form a definition.

balanced chemical equation Tell students that the word *balanced*, as it is used in this term, is an adjective that means "equalized" or "equivalent." Have them define the new term based on what they already know about the term *chemical equation*.

As You Read

Read aloud the predictions you previously wrote on the board. Record your revisions and/or confirmations. Ask students to do the same. Model how to determine and record important information. Have students record important information in their Science Notebooks as they read the lesson.

(ANSWER) A chemical equation describes a chemical reaction. It shows with words or formulas and symbols the reactants and products of a chemical reaction.

As You Read

Review the predictions you made in your Science Notebook. Explain your predictions to a partner. Then let your partner explain his or her predictions to you. Confirm or revise your predictions as you gain new information.

What is a chemical equation?

Symbols in Chemical Equations

Symbol	Meaning
→	produces or forms
+	plus
(s)	solid
(l)	liquid
(g)	gas
(aq)	aqueous—a substance is dissolved in water
heat→	the reactants are heated
light→	the reactants are exposed to light
elec.→	an electric current is passed through the reactants
0°C→	the reaction is carried out at 0°C

Figure 8.5 The symbols shown here are a few of those commonly used in chemical equations.

Chemical Equations

Scientists use chemical equations to describe chemical reactions. A **chemical equation** shows at a glance the reactants and products involved in a chemical reaction.

A chemical equation is like a math equation. The reactants are shown on the left and the products are shown on the right.

$$\text{reactants} \rightarrow \text{products}$$

The two sides of the equation are separated by an arrow. The arrow indicates that something is produced or formed. Words above the arrow can describe the conditions under which the reaction takes place. They can show, for example, if the reaction requires heat to occur. Each reactant is separated in the equation by a plus sign (+), as shown in the equations below. Each product is also separated by a plus sign.

Using Words Chemical equations can be written in words, using each substance's chemical or common name. The word equation for the reaction that takes place when hydrogen reacts with oxygen looks like this. The symbols in parentheses indicate whether each substance is a liquid (l), a solid (s), or a gas (g).

$$\text{hydrogen (g)} + \text{oxygen (g)} \rightarrow \text{water (l)}$$

According to the word equation, hydrogen gas combines with oxygen gas to produce liquid water.

Using Formulas A more convenient way is to write chemical equations using chemical formulas. The equation shown above looks like this when formulas are used instead of words:

$$2H_2 \text{ (g)} + O_2 \text{ (g)} \rightarrow 2H_2O \text{ (l)}$$

Notice that in this equation, a number appears in front of some of the chemical formulas. These numbers are called coefficients. In a chemical equation, **coefficients** (koh uh FIH shunts) indicate how many molecules of each substance are involved in the reaction. Recall from Chapter 2 that a molecule is a particle formed when two or more atoms combine. Coefficients indicate exactly how the reaction takes place. If there is no coefficient in front of a formula, the coefficient is assumed to be one.

Balancing Equations Look at the following chemical equation written without coefficients.

$$H_2 \text{ (g)} + O_2 \text{ (g)} \rightarrow H_2O \text{ (l)}$$

Count the number of atoms on each side of the equation. Recall that the subscripts indicate the number of atoms in one molecule of a compound. There are two hydrogen atoms and two oxygen atoms on the reactant side of the equation.

Differentiate Instruction

Mathematical/Logical Provide students with a few simple, unsolved chemical equations written in words. Have them solve the equations and convert them into formulas. Then have students create several more equations with a partner. Refer students to **Figure 8.5** for guidance.

There are two hydrogen atoms but only one oxygen atom on the product side of the equation. The number of atoms on each side of the equation is not the same. This means that the reaction as written cannot take place because it violates the law of conservation of mass.

Coefficients are used to write a **balanced chemical equation,** or an equation in which the number of atoms of each element is the same on both sides of the equation. Adding coefficients to a chemical equation does not change the reactants or products. It simply shows the ratios of substances involved in the reaction.

Balancing a chemical equation is often a trial-and-error process. To balance the equation on page 132, place the coefficient 2 in front of the formula for water. This signifies that two molecules of water are produced for every one molecule of oxygen that reacts.

$$H_2\ (g) + O_2\ (g) \rightarrow 2H_2O\ (l)$$

Notice that oxygen is now balanced in the equation. There are two oxygen atoms on the left side of the equation and two on the right. Hydrogen, however, is now unbalanced. To balance hydrogen, place the coefficient 2 in front of hydrogen on the reactant side of the equation.

$$2H_2\ (g) + O_2\ (g) \rightarrow 2H_2O\ (l)$$

The number of atoms of each element on the left is now equal to the number of atoms of that element on the right. The equation is balanced. **Figure 8.6** provides some simple steps for balancing chemical equations.

Step 1	Identify reactants and products and write their chemical formulas on the appropriate sides of the equation.
Step 2	Count the number of atoms of each element on each side of the equation. If you need to, use a table to keep track of the numbers.
Step 3	Try coefficients that will balance the equation. Start with elements that appear only once on each side of the equation. Never change the subscripts in a chemical formula to balance an equation. That changes the identity of the substances.
Step 4	Check to be sure you have the same number of atoms of each element on both sides of the equation.

Figure 8.6 Here are some simple steps to follow to balance chemical equations.

After You Read

1. What is a chemical reaction? What happens during a chemical reaction?
2. What information about a reaction is represented in a chemical equation?
3. Review the information you recorded in your Science Notebook. Then write a well-developed paragraph that summarizes the nature of chemical reactions.

Explain It!

Copy the following chemical equations in your Science Notebook:

$H_2 + Br_2 \rightarrow HBr$

$Al + O_2 \rightarrow Al_2O_3$

$KClO_3 \rightarrow KCl + O_2$

$NH_4NO_3 \rightarrow N_2O + H_2O$

Work in pairs to balance each equation. Make sure you have the same number of atoms of each element on both sides of the equation. Then compare your results with those of other groups. Write a paragraph summarizing how you balanced the equations.

Teach

EXPLAIN to students that they will learn how to balance a chemical equation.

Explain It!

Refer to **Figure 8.6** as you balance a sample chemical equation on the board. Check for students' understanding of the process, and then have pairs work together to balance the given equations.

ANSWER Correctly balanced equations should look like this:

$H_2 + Br_2 \rightarrow 2HBr$

$4Al + 3O_2 \rightarrow 2Al_2O_3$

$2KClO_3 \rightarrow 2KCl + 3O_2$

$NH_4NO_3 \rightarrow N_2O + 2H_2O$

Assess

Use the After You Read questions and the Alternative Assessment to help you evaluate students' understanding of the lesson.

After You Read

1. A chemical reaction is the process by which a chemical change takes place. Bonds between atoms break and new bonds form during a chemical reaction. The atoms making up the reactants are rearranged. New atoms are not created, and existing atoms are not destroyed.
2. A chemical equation shows the reactants and products of a reaction. It can show what state each substance is in when it reacts and what special conditions are required for the reaction to occur. It shows the ratios of each substance in the reaction.
3. Students' answers will vary but should include the definition of a chemical change, a chemical reaction, a chemical equation, and the law of conservation of mass.

Field Study

Bring students to the school cafeteria or a nearby restaurant kitchen when people are working. Each student should have a clipboard and pencil. Have them observe and record the cooking, baking, washing, and other activities being performed. When they return to the classroom, have students work in small groups to determine (and research, if necessary) the chemical and physical reactions they saw. They should also include a reason for each answer. Possible examples of chemical reactions include dough rising, eggs cooking, batter baking, and meat roasting. Possible examples of physical reactions include water boiling or freezing and vegetables changing color as they are cooked.

8.2 Introduce

ENGAGE Divide students into small groups. Give each group several photographs of chemical reactions that occur in nature, such as forest fires, decaying trees or leaves, and fermenting grapes. Have each group look at the pictures and discuss why they show chemical reactions. Groups should then share their discussions with the class.

Before You Read

Begin the outline for this lesson on the board with students' help. Write *Types of Chemical Reactions,* followed by *Synthesis Reactions.* Instruct students to do the same in their Science Notebooks, reminding them to leave space between each heading and subheading so that they can add notes as they read the lesson.

Have students discuss with a partner what they may already know about the outline categories (for example, the definition of *synthesis* or *decomposition*).

● Teach

EXPLAIN to students that in this lesson, they will learn about the five main types of chemical reactions.

Use the Visual: Figure 8.7

ANSWER Students might identify the cooking of foods on a grill and the burning of fuel in a grill or fire.

8.2 Types of Chemical Reactions

Before You Read

Create a lesson outline in your Science Notebook using the title, headings, and subheadings of this lesson. Use the outline to think about what you will learn in this lesson.

As you read this sentence, billions of chemical reactions are happening all around you. For many people, the term *chemical reaction* brings to mind a scientist standing over bubbling test tubes in a laboratory. Chemical reactions, however, are a part of nature. The billions of different chemical reactions include those in which elements combine to form compounds, those in which compounds break down into elements, and those in which one element replaces another.

Classification of Reactions

In order to study the billions of chemical reactions that occur, scientists have classified reactions into five main types. These main types are synthesis reactions, decomposition reactions, combustion reactions, single-displacement reactions, and double-displacement reactions. In each type of reaction, atoms are rearranged and substances are changed in a specific way. In all the reactions, the law of conservation of mass is observed: matter is neither created nor destroyed.

Figure 8.7 Every second of every day, billions of chemical reactions take place, both around you and inside your body, keeping you alive and healthy. Can you identify some of the chemical reactions taking place in this photo?

ELL Strategy

Model Divide students into five small groups and assign each a different type of chemical reaction that is described in this lesson. Using poster board, have each group generate a diagram, artwork, and/or text that describes the assigned chemical reaction. Upon completion of the lesson, have each group present its model to the class.

Synthesis Reactions

Green plants are among the most important organisms on Earth. Taking place inside the cells of green plants is a chemical reaction—photosynthesis—that almost all living things depend on for survival. During photosynthesis, green plants absorb energy from the Sun and use it to change carbon dioxide and water into food and oxygen. This food in turn supports the entire food chain by providing organisms with energy.

Photosynthesis is an example of a synthesis reaction. In a **synthesis** (SIHN thuh sus) **reaction,** two or more substances combine to form a new substance. Synthesis reactions are among the most common reactions. They are also among the easiest to recognize. The general formula for a synthesis reaction is

$$A + B \rightarrow AB$$

A few examples of synthesis reactions are shown in **Figure 8.8**. Notice that the products tend to be larger, more complex substances than the reactants.

Examples of Synthesis Reactions

Reaction	Chemical Equation
photosynthesis (production of food in green plants)	$6CO_2$ (g) + $6H_2O$ (l) $\xrightarrow{\text{sunlight}}$ $C_6H_{12}O_6$ (s) + $6O_2$ (g) (carbon dioxide + water → glucose + oxygen)
formation of rust	$4Fe$ (s) + $3O_2$ (aq) → $2Fe_2O_3$ (s) (iron + oxygen → rust)
formation of water	$2H_2$ (g) + O_2 (g) → $2H_2O$ (l) (hydrogen + oxygen → water)
formation of table salt	$2Na$ (s) + Cl_2 (g) → $2NaCl$ (s) (sodium + chlorine → sodium chloride)

Figure 8.8 Although some synthesis reactions produce two or more products, most produce only one product.

Decomposition Reactions

In a **decomposition reaction,** one substance breaks down into two or more simpler substances. This can be thought of as the opposite of a synthesis reaction. The general formula for a decomposition reaction is

$$AB \rightarrow A + B$$

One of the most recognizable forms of decomposition happens in nature when organisms break down dead plant and animal material into simpler substances. The electrolysis of water to produce hydrogen and oxygen gas is another common example of a decomposition reaction.

As You Read

Use your lesson outline to record information about the types of reactions you read about. Write unanswered questions you have about each reaction, as well.

How is a synthesis reaction different from a decomposition reaction?

Figure 8.9 When an electric current is passed through it, water decomposes into hydrogen and oxygen gas. Most decomposition reactions require the addition of light, heat, or electricity. This is because the products of decomposition tend to be less stable than the reactants.

Teach

EXPLAIN to students that they will learn about two types of chemical reactions, synthesis and decomposition.

As You Read

Have students work with a partner to record information about each type of reaction in this lesson. Demonstrate recording information under the appropriate sections of the outline. Students should also record any lingering questions they have about the lesson content in the correct sections of their outlines.

ANSWER A synthesis reaction involves two or more substances combining to form a new substance. A decomposition reaction involves one substance breaking down into two or more simpler substances. The two reactions can be thought of as opposites.

Vocabulary

synthesis reaction Tell students that the word *synthesis* refers to the process of putting together separate parts to form a complex whole. Tell them that the word *reaction*, as it is used in chemistry, refers to a process of change.

decomposition reaction Ask students to break down the word *decomposition* into its parts. *De-* is a prefix meaning "removal" or "reversal," *compose* is a verb meaning "to make up something," and *-tion* is a suffix signifying a result or state.

Background Information

Decomposition, the breaking down of organic materials, takes place constantly in nature. When animals die or leaves fall from a tree in a forest, other organisms known as decomposers break them down into chemical parts and eat them. These decomposers, such as bacteria, fungi, maggots, and worms, then produce waste that other living organisms use for nutrition. This process is known as aerobic ("with oxygen") decomposition.

● Teach

EXPLAIN to students that on this page, they will learn about combustion and displacement reactions.

🌀 Extend It!

Provide students access to books and articles about global warming, fuel combustion, and combustion reactions to use as resources. Guide students to find the chemical equation for the combustion of a variety of fuels. Help them recognize that the products of combustion can contribute to air pollution and global warming. Encourage them to brainstorm ways in which further global warming can be prevented by reducing the use of fossil fuels.

Teaching students about how to protect the environment early in their lives allows them to make informed decisions and behave more responsibly in the future.

🔗 CONNECTION: Biology

A person's basal metabolic rate (BMR) refers to the amount of energy a person produces through the burning of Calories while at rest. A person's BMR is determined by several factors, including genetics, exercise, muscle mass, and certain health conditions. This rate affects a person's weight, as it is easier for a person with a higher BMR to burn more Calories.

Science Notebook EXTRA

In their Science Notebooks, have students record ways in which they could increase their BMR. If desired, have each student calculate and record his or her BMR using an online BMR calculator. For a given period of time (a week or several weeks), have students record steps that they take to increase their BMR. At the end of this time, have students calculate their BMR again to see if it has changed.

🌀 Extend It!

Because it releases a great amount of energy, the combustion of fuel is used to power cars, trains, and many machines. Some of the products of these combustion reactions, however, contribute to global warming. Research global warming and the reactions involved in the combustion of gasoline and other fuels. What is global warming? What causes it? How might its increase be prevented? Write a well-developed paragraph in your Science Notebook explaining your findings.

🔗 CONNECTION: Biology

People, like all living things, have combustion reactions occurring inside their bodies. The metabolism of food is an example of a combustion reaction. Glucose, a simple sugar, reacts with oxygen inside the cells. Energy that the person can use to move, power other body functions, and grow is produced as a result.

Combustion Reactions

With a boom, pop, or sizzle, fireworks explode in the air. Their bright colors and shapes are dazzling. First invented nearly 2,000 years ago, fireworks have long been used to celebrate special occasions. Each display is the result of a combustion reaction.

Combustion is more commonly known as burning. A **combustion reaction** is a type of chemical reaction in which a substance combines with elemental oxygen. Combustion reactions always produce energy. This energy is usually given off as light in the form of flames or a glow, and as heat. In addition to energy, combustion reactions also produce one or more products that contain the elements in the reactants. For example, the reaction between carbon and oxygen produces carbon dioxide.

Many combustion reactions are examples of other types of reactions. The burning of carbon in air, during which carbon combines with oxygen, is also a synthesis reaction.

People use combustion reactions in many ways. The burning of wood or fossil fuels, such as gas and coal, provides people with light and heat. The burning of gasoline powers cars and machines.

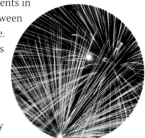

Figure 8.10 Fireworks are the result of a combustion reaction involving a metal burning in oxygen.

Displacement Reactions

Fireworks are made primarily with metals. Many metals exist in nature as compounds, bonded with other elements. The metals are separated from the other elements and made available for use as a result of displacement reactions. There are two types of displacement reactions: single-displacement reactions and double-displacement reactions.

Single Displacement In a **single-displacement reaction,** an ion or atom in a compound is replaced by an ion or atom of a different element. The general equation for a single-displacement reaction is

$$A + BC \rightarrow AC + B$$

According to this equation, element A replaces element B in the compound BC. The new compound AC forms as a result.

Single-displacement reactions are useful for separating a particular element from a compound. These reactions have widespread uses in industry for this reason. A few examples of single-displacement reactions are shown in **Figure 8.11** on the next page.

Background Information

What is the difference between an internal and an external combustion engine? Internal combustion engines are found in most cars today. Gasoline burns inside this engine and results in the car being put into motion. External combustion engines were used in the past for steamboats and trains. Fuel burns outside the engine, resulting in the production of steam, which then creates motion inside the engine. Internal combustion engines are prevalent today because they are more efficient and smaller than their external predecessors.

Examples of Displacement Reactions

Type of Displacement	Reaction	Chemical Equation
metal displacement	displacement of silver from silver nitrate	$Cu\ (s) + 2\ AgNO_3\ (aq) \rightarrow Cu(NO_3)_2\ (aq) + 2\ Ag\ (s)$
metal displacement	displacement of titanium from titanium chloride	$2Mg\ (l) + TiCl_4\ (g) \rightarrow Ti\ (s) + 2MgCl_2\ (l)$
halogen displacement	displacement of bromine from potassium bromide	$Cl_2\ (g) + 2KBr\ (aq) \rightarrow 2KCl\ (aq) + 2Br_2\ (l)$
hydrogen displacement	displacement of hydrogen from cold water	$2Na\ (s) + 2H_2O\ (l) \rightarrow 2NaOH\ (aq) + H_2\ (g)$

Figure 8.11 Because copper is more active, it replaces silver in silver nitrate. The resulting compound, copper nitrate, turns the solution blue. Silver builds up on the coil of wire *(top)*. The displacement of hydrogen from water by sodium is a violent reaction *(bottom)*.

Single-displacement reactions can be further classified into three smaller groups. These are hydrogen displacement, metal displacement, and halogen displacement. In hydrogen displacement, the hydrogen in water or an acid is replaced by a metal. In metal displacement, a metal is replaced by another more reactive metal. In halogen displacement, a halogen is replaced by another more reactive halogen.

Single-displacement reactions occur only when element A is more reactive than element B. To predict whether a single-displacement reaction will occur, chemists often use an activity series such as the one shown in **Figure 8.12.** An activity series rates elements by how reactive they are. An element can replace any of the elements below it in the series. It cannot replace the elements above it.

Double Displacement In a **double-displacement reaction,** atoms or ions are exchanged between two compounds. The general equation for a double-displacement reaction is

$$AX + CY \rightarrow AY + CX$$

According to this equation, element X replaces element Y in the compound CY, and element Y replaces element X in compound AX. Two new compounds form as a result.

Activity Series of Metals

Name	Symbol
lithium	Li
potassium	K
calcium	Ca
sodium	Na
magnesium	Mg
aluminum	Al
zinc	Zn
iron	Fe
lead	Pb
hydrogen	H
copper	Cu
mercury	Hg
silver	Ag

decreasing activity ↓

Figure 8.12 Each element can replace the elements below it in the activity series, but not the elements above it.

Figure It Out

1. Can magnesium replace mercury? Explain your answer.
2. Predict what will happen when zinc reacts with copper sulfate.

Teach

EXPLAIN to students that they will learn about single- and double-displacement reactions in this section.

Vocabulary

combustion reaction Tell students that combustion is the process of burning, which involves a chemical combination with oxygen.

single-displacement reaction Tell students that the word *single* means "individual." Have them break down the word *displacement* into *dis-*, a prefix that forms the opposite of the base word, and explain that the verb *place* means "to put or position," and *-ment* is a suffix that refers to a process or result.

double-displacement reaction Tell students that *double* means "twice as many." Have them combine this meaning with the term *displacement reaction*.

Figure It Out: Figure 8.12

ANSWER **1.** Yes, because it is above mercury in the activity series. **2.** When zinc reacts with copper sulfate, it will replace copper, and the new compound zinc sulfate will form.

Differentiate Instruction

Visual With a partner, have students look in books or on the Internet for photographs, illustrations, or diagrams of each of the five types of chemical reactions. Each student pair should then share its findings with another pair.

EXPLAIN to students that they will learn about the fifth type of chemical reaction, oxidation-reduction (also called redox reactions).

Vocabulary

oxidation-reduction reaction Remind students that the word *oxidation* can be broken down into *oxide,* a noun referring to any compound of oxygen and another element, and *-ation,* a suffix referring to an action or result.

oxidation Ask students to remember what they learned about oxidation. In a redox reaction, *oxidation* refers specifically to the loss of electrons.

reduction Tell students that the term *reduction,* as used in chemistry, refers to the gain of electrons. It might be helpful associate the terms by remembering the *o* in *oxidation* corresponds to the *o* in *loss.*

Use the Visual: Figure 8.13

(ANSWER) A combustion reaction involves the combining of a substance with elemental oxygen. When it combines with another element, it becomes a negatively charged ion. Thus, it has gained electrons, and a redox reaction has occurred.

Assess

Use the After You Read questions and the Alternative Assessment to help you evaluate students' understanding of the lesson.

After You Read

1. In a synthesis reaction, two simpler substances combine to form a complex substance. In decomposition, one substance breaks down into two or more simpler substances.

2. An activity series shows the relative reactivity of metals. An activity series can be used to predict whether a particular element will displace another.

3. a) single-displacement and redox reaction
   b) decomposition and redox reaction
   c) combustion and redox reaction

4. Students should be able to correctly describe synthesis, decomposition, combustion, single-displacement, and double-displacement reactions.

Oxidation-Reduction Reactions

Many chemical reactions known as **oxidation-reduction reactions** involve the transfer of electrons from one element or compound to another. Oxidation-reduction reactions are known as "redox reactions" for short.

A redox reaction can be thought of as two reactions in one. In the first part of the reaction, electrons are lost by one substance. The substance becomes more positively charged. Its oxidation number changes to a more positive number. This part of the reaction is called oxidation. **Oxidation** describes the loss of electrons.

The electrons that are lost by one substance are then gained by another substance in the second part of the redox reaction. The substance that gains electrons becomes more negatively charged. Its oxidation number changes to a more negative number. This part of the reaction is called reduction. **Reduction** describes the gain of electrons. Although it is convenient to think of oxidation and reduction as two separate steps, oxidation and reduction always happen together. One cannot occur without the other.

Some of the chemical reactions already discussed can also be classified as redox reactions. The reaction of sodium with chlorine to produce salt is an example. The electrolysis of water is, too. Most reactions that involve a pure element can be classified as redox reactions.

Figure 8.13 All combustion reactions are redox reactions. Can you explain why?

After You Read

1. Compare and contrast a synthesis reaction and a decomposition reaction.
2. What is an activity series? How is it used?
3. Classify the following reactions.

   Zn (s) + CuSO$_4$ (aq) → ZnSO$_4$ (aq) + Cu (s)

   2HgO (s) $\xrightarrow{\text{heat}}$ 2Hg (l) + O$_2$ (g)

   C$_6$H$_{12}$O$_6$ + 6O$_2$ → 6CO$_2$ + 6H$_2$O

4. Review the lesson outline in your Science Notebook. Use the outline to identify and describe the five types of chemical reactions.

Alternative Assessment

Have each student create and complete a compare-and-contrast chart in his or her Science Notebook describing combustion, displacement, and oxidation-reduction reactions. When students have finished, ask them to write a few paragraphs comparing the five types of reactions.

Background Information

Redox reactions are often discussed in terms of half-reactions. In the equation for a half-reaction, electron gain or loss is explicitly shown. Using the formation of table salt as an example, the reaction can be described using half-reactions as follows:

2Na + Cl$_2$ + 2NaCl

oxidation: 2Na + 2Na$^+$ + 2e$^-$

reduction: Cl$_2$ + 2e$^-$ + 2Cl$^-$

8.3 Energy and Reaction Rates

Before You Read
Create a K-W-L-S-H chart in your Science Notebook. Think about the title of this lesson. In the column labeled *K*, write what you already know about energy and reaction rates. In the column labeled *W*, write what you want to learn about the topic.

Considered by many to be Earth's final frontier, the deep ocean is a vast and mysterious place. It stretches from 800 m below the water's surface down to the deepest trenches on the seafloor. Sunlight never reaches these depths, keeping the deep ocean extremely cold and dark.

Though most organisms could not survive in this inhospitable environment, it is home to some fascinating creatures. Jellyfish, squid, bacteria, and a variety of fish live there. Rather than relying on the Sun for light, many of these organisms make their own light! Their bodies glow like lamps, providing the only source of light in the deep ocean.

Energy Changes

The phenomenon just described is called bioluminescence (bi oh lew muh NE sunts). Bioluminescence is an adaptation in which an organism produces light as a result of a chemical reaction. Bioluminescence works on the principle that chemical reactions involve a change in energy.

Some chemical reactions release energy. These kinds of reactions are involved in bioluminescence. Other chemical reactions absorb energy. Whether energy is released or absorbed, nearly all chemical reactions involve a change in energy.

Figure 8.14 The anglerfish is a deep-ocean organism. The growth on the top of its head lights up as a result of a chemical reaction. The light attracts other animals, which the anglerfish attacks when they come near.

Learning Goals
- Define *activation energy* and describe its importance to chemical reactions.
- Compare and contrast exothermic and endothermic reactions.
- Relate collision theory to the factors that affect the rate of a reaction.

New Vocabulary
activation energy
exothermic reaction
endothermic reaction
collision theory
catalyst

8.3 Introduce

ENGAGE Have students look at the photographs in this lesson and discuss what they think the items shown have in common.

Before You Read
Draw a K-W-L-S-H chart on the board. Ask students to brainstorm what they think this chapter will be about. Ask what they know about energy and reaction rates, and record their answers on the board. Have students draw a similar chart in their Science Notebooks and complete the *K* column. Then have them talk with partners about what they want to know about this topic and record their questions in their Science Notebooks. Have pairs share their questions with the class, and record these in the *W* column on the board. Give students time to add questions to their charts.

Teach

EXPLAIN to students that in this lesson, they will learn about the concept of activation energy, exothermic and endothermic reactions, and the collision theory.

ELL Strategy

Reinforce Vocabulary Have students write each vocabulary term from this lesson on one side of an index card and its definition on the other side. Students should then practice quizzing each other on the word parts, their meanings, and the full definitions. As an extension of this activity, students can compete to create the longest list of words derived from the same root—for example, *reduce, reducing, reduced,* etc.

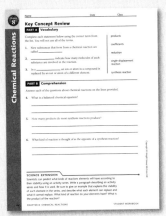

Key Concept Review
Workbook, p. 46

● Teach

EXPLAIN to students that they will now learn about the energy changes that occur during chemical reactions, and how reactions are classified based on those energy changes.

💿 Vocabulary

activation energy Ask students to break down the word *activation* into its parts. Tell them that the verb *activate* means "to make something start to work." Remind them that the suffix *-ation* refers to an action or result. Ask them to remember what energy is (the capacity to do work). Have them apply these word meanings to a definition of the term *activation energy.*

exothermic reaction Tell students that the prefix *exo-* means "out" or "outside," and that *thermic* is an adjective meaning "relating to or producing heat." Ask students to use these meanings to provide their own definitions of the term.

endothermic reaction Tell students that the prefix *endo-* is the opposite of *exo-*. Ask them to determine what this prefix means ("inside"). Then have them use the word parts to provide their own definitions of the term.

collision theory Tell students that a collision is a crash. Have them provide examples of objects that collide. Have students identify what is colliding in the collision theory and how the word meanings apply to the phenomenon.

catalyst Tell students that synonyms for this noun are *trigger, stimulus,* and *activator.* Have students explain why these are appropriate synonyms.

As You Read

Ask students what they learned about energy changes that occur during chemical reactions. Record information in the *L* column of the chart on the board, and then have students record learned information in their own charts. Remind them to add any questions that arise as they read to the *W* column of their charts.

ANSWER An endothermic reaction is a reaction in which heat is absorbed. An exothermic reaction is a reaction in which heat is released.

As You Read

In the column labeled *L* of your K-W-L-S-H chart, record information about chemical reactions and energy. Add to the column labeled *W* any new questions you have. Share your questions with at least three other students.

What is an endothermic reaction? How does it differ from an exothermic reaction?

Did You Know?

Glow sticks contain an ester (a type of organic compound), a dye, and hydrogen peroxide (H_2O_2). The ester and dye are found in the outer part of the stick, and the hydrogen peroxide is in the center in a glass tube. When the stick is bent, the glass tube breaks and the three different chemicals react.

Starting Energy Recall from Chapter 7 that it takes energy to remove electrons from atoms. In a similar way, it takes energy to break the chemical bonds between atoms or ions in a compound. This means that all chemical reactions require some energy to get started. The minimum amount of energy required for a chemical reaction to occur is called **activation energy.**

Different reactions require different amounts of activation energy. Some reactions need only a little energy to get started. Others need a great deal of energy to get started. Light, heat, electricity, and motion are some common sources of activation energy.

Releasing Energy Although all reactions require activation energy, some reactions give off energy once they are underway. Overall, they release more energy than they absorb. Think of logs burning in a campfire or fireplace. Logs do not start burning spontaneously. It takes energy to get them to start burning. Once burning, however, they give off a great deal of energy in the form of light and heat. All combustion reactions involve a release of energy.

Energy can be released in the form of light, motion, or electricity. In most reactions, however, energy is released in the form of heat. Reactions that release heat are called **exothermic** (ek soh THUR mihk) **reactions.** The term *exothermic* means "release of heat."

The energy given off in a chemical reaction comes from the original bonds that are broken (the reactant bonds) and the new bonds that are formed (the product bonds) during the reaction. If the products of a reaction are more stable than the reactants, energy will be released as the products are formed. Recall that "more stable" means the bonds require less energy.

Absorbing Energy Some chemical reactions require not only activation energy, but also a continuous supply of energy in order for the reaction to move forward. Such reactions stop when that energy source is removed. The reactants no longer react, and the products no longer form. Overall, these reactions absorb more energy than they give off. Reactions that absorb heat are described as **endothermic** (en doh THUR mihk) **reactions.** The term *endothermic* means "taking in heat." Reactions absorb energy when the products formed are less stable—their bonds require more energy—than the reactants.

Figure 8.15 When magnesium burns in oxygen, energy is released in the form of a bright light. This reaction is often used in emergency flares.

Background Information

An exergonic reaction releases energy. The products of this type of chemical reaction have less energy than the initial materials. An example of an exergonic reaction is a match burning.

The opposite type of chemical reaction is endergonic, which uses energy. The products of an endergonic reaction have more energy than the initial materials. An example is photosynthesis.

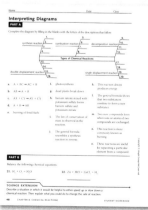

Interpreting Diagrams
Workbook, p. 48

Reaction Rates

Some reactions happen very quickly, in just fractions of a second. Others take hours or even years to complete. A reaction's rate depends on the nature of the substances involved. It also depends on how often the particles of those substances collide with one another. The more the particles collide, the more likely the substances are to react and the faster the reaction will be. The idea that reaction rates are related to particle collisions is called **collision theory.**

Collision theory is based on the principle that substances cannot react unless their particles come in contact with one another. Four factors can affect reaction rates: concentration, temperature, surface area, and catalysts.

Concentration Concentration describes how much of a substance is in a given unit of volume. A high concentration of reactants means that there are a great many particles per unit volume. There are more reactant particles available for collisions. More collisions occur and more product is formed in a certain amount of time.

A low concentration of reactants means that there are fewer particles per unit volume. With fewer reactant particles available, there will be fewer collisions. Less product will form in a certain amount of time.

Temperature Heating a substance increases the speed at which the particles move. The faster the particles move, the more frequently they will collide with the particles of other substances. Adding heat to most reactions will cause the reactions to occur more quickly. Cooling reactions tends to cause them to occur more slowly.

Surface Area The greater a solid's surface area is, the more chances there are for a liquid or gas to come in contact with the solid. Increasing the surface area usually increases the number of collisions that can occur, and thus increases the rate of a reaction.

Catalysts A **catalyst** (KA tuh list) is a substance that increases the rate of a reaction but does not itself change as a result of the reaction. Catalysts work by providing a lower the activation energy for a reaction. Because less energy is required to get started, the reaction rate increases.

Figure It Out

1. In which solution are reactions likely to happen more quickly?
2. How could you increase the reaction rate of the solution on the bottom?

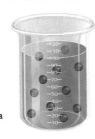

a

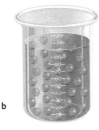

b

Figure 8.16 Increasing the concentration of reactants increases the likelihood that the particles will collide. A greater number of collisions means that the reaction will go quickly and more product will form.

After You Read

1. What is activation energy?
2. How are exothermic and endothermic reactions alike? How do they differ?
3. How is collision theory related to the rate of a reaction?
4. Use your completed K-W-L columns to write a well-developed summary of this lesson. In the *S* column, write what you would still like to know about reactions. In the *H* column, write how you can find this information.

Teach

EXPLAIN to students that they will learn about the factors that affect the rate of a chemical reaction: concentration, temperature, surface area, and catalysts.

Figure It Out: Figure 8.16

ANSWER **1.** Reactions are likely to happen more quickly in the solution that is more concentrated. **2.** You could increase the reaction rate by adding more reactants.

Assess

Use the After You Read questions and the Alternative Assessment to help you evaluate students' understanding of the lesson.

After You Read

1. Activation energy is the minimum amount of energy required for a reaction to occur.
2. Both involve heat. Endothermic reactions absorb heat, while exothermic reactions release heat.
3. The particles of reacting substances must collide for a reaction to take place. The more the particles collide, the more likely the substances are to react and the faster the reaction will be. The idea that reaction rates are related to particle collisions is called collision theory.
4. Students' answers will vary. Encourage students to select at least one question to research and answer.

Alternative Assessment

Have students review and complete the first three columns of their K-W-L-S-H charts. Then have them share any lingering questions with the class. Record these in the *S* column of the chart on the board. Ask how students could find the answers to their questions, and record responses in the *H* column of the class chart. Then answer one or two of the questions. Have students finish their own charts, and check these for completion.

Differentiate Instruction

Kinesthetic Have students touch and smell decaying and nondecaying fruits and vegetables. Students should wear gloves when they touch the rotting fruit. They could also do the same with other foods, such as cheeses and meats. Discuss with students the fact that food spoils as a result of chemical reactions. Because temperature affects the rate at which reactions take place, people cool food to help slow down the chemical reactions involved with spoiling. Cooling helps keep food fresh and helps it last longer. Foods such as milk and lunchmeats should always be kept in the refrigerator.

Teacher Alert

Alert students to the dangers of eating decaying foods. Many foodborne illnesses result from eating spoiled foods, especially meats. Spoilage can often be discovered by noticing how the food smells, feels, and looks.

Chapter 8 Summary

VOCABULARY REVIEW

Check students' sentences or paragraphs to make sure they understand the meaning of each vocabulary term.

Evaluate students' essays using the following criteria:

1. The topic sentence, or main idea, should restate the Key Concept.

2. The supporting paragraphs should incorporate the answers to the Learning Goal questions students have written and include details, facts, and examples they have recorded in their Science Notebooks.

3. The concluding sentence should sum up the main idea of the chapter and restate the Key Concept.

MASTERING CONCEPTS

True or False

1. True
2. True
3. False, decomposition reaction
4. False, chemical equation
5. False, coefficient
6. True

Short Answer

7. The five main types of chemical reactions are synthesis (A + B → AB), decomposition (AB → A + B), combustion, single-displacement (A + BC → AC + B), and double-displacement (AX + CY → AY + CX).

8. Catalysts work by providing an alternative route for a reaction that often has a lower activation energy.

9. Concentration, surface area, temperature, and catalysts can affect the rate of a reaction. The chemical properties of the substances involved in a chemical reaction also affect the reaction rate.

10. An activity series shows the relative reactivity of different elements. The relative reactivity determines what elements can displace others in single-displacement reactions.

11. The law of conservation of mass says the total mass of the starting materials equals the total mass of the products.

142 CHEMICAL REACTIONS

KEY CONCEPTS

8.1 Nature of a Chemical Reaction

- A chemical reaction is the process by which a chemical change takes place.

- Mass is conserved during a chemical reaction. The number of atoms of each element present in the reactants must be equal to the number of atoms of those elements present in the products. Atoms cannot be created or destroyed during a chemical reaction.

- A balanced chemical equation includes the reactants and products of a chemical reaction and coefficients to show the ratio of each substance in the reaction.

- A balanced chemical equation shows the law of conservation of mass.

8.2 Types of Chemical Reactions

- The five main types of chemical reactions are synthesis reactions, decomposition reactions, combustion reactions, single-displacement reactions, and double-displacement reactions. Oxidation-reduction reactions, or redox reactions, are reactions that involve a transfer of electrons.

- Oxidation is the loss of electrons. Reduction is the gain of electrons.

8.3 Energy and Reaction Rates

- All reactions require energy to get started. This energy is called activation energy.

- In an exothermic reaction, energy is released in the form of heat. In an endothermic reaction, heat is absorbed.

- A reaction's rate depends on the nature of the substances involved and on how often the particles of those substances collide with one another.

- The rate of a reaction can be affected by concentration, temperature, surface area, and catalysts.

142 CHEMICAL REACTIONS

VOCABULARY REVIEW

Write each term in a complete sentence or write a paragraph relating several terms.

8.1
chemical reaction, p. 130
reactant, p. 130
product, p. 130
law of conservation of mass, p. 131
chemical equation, p. 132
coefficient, p. 132
balanced chemical equation, p. 133

8.2
synthesis reaction, p. 135
decomposition reaction, p. 135
combustion reaction, p. 136
single-displacement reaction, p. 136
double-displacement reaction, p. 137
oxidation-reduction reaction, p. 138
oxidation, p. 138
reduction, p. 138

8.3
activation energy, p. 140
exothermic reaction, p. 140
endothermic reaction, p. 140
collision theory, p. 141
catalyst, p. 141

PREPARE FOR CHAPTER TEST

To prepare for the chapter test, create a question from each Learning Goal. Use the information in your Science Notebook to answer each question. Then use these answers to write a well-developed essay about the chapter. Use the Key Concept on the first page of this chapter as your topic sentence.

Vocabulary Review
Workbook, p. 47

Reading Comprehension
Workbook, p. 49

MASTERING CONCEPTS

True or False
If the statement is true, write "true." If it is false, change the underlined word or words to make the statement true.

1. All reactions require <u>activation energy</u>.

2. A(n) <u>combustion reaction</u> is a reaction in which a substance burns in oxygen.

3. A(n) <u>synthesis reaction</u> is characterized by the breakdown of a substance into simpler substances.

4. A(n) <u>chemical formula</u> shows the reactants and products of a chemical reaction.

5. A(n) <u>subscript</u> is the number that precedes a chemical formula in a chemical equation.

6. The rate of a reaction can be affected by <u>heat</u>.

Short Answer
Answer each of the following in a sentence or brief paragraph.

7. What are the five main types of chemical reactions? Include general equations in your answer.

8. Describe the relationship between activation energy and catalysts.

9. What factors can affect the rate of a reaction?

10. Why is the information in an activity series important?

11. Explain the law of conservation of mass.

Critical Thinking
Use what you have learned in this chapter to answer each of the following.

12. **Explain** Why do scientists use chemical equations? What do chemical equations show?

13. **Apply Concepts** Why can a sugar cube be used in hot coffee while granulated sugar (in small crystals) is preferred in iced coffee?

14. **Predict** An inhibitor is the opposite of a catalyst. Many cereals contain an inhibitor known as BHT. What do you think is the function of this inhibitor? Explain your answer.

Standardized Test Question
Choose the letter of the response that correctly answers the question.

15. All of the following can increase the rate of a chemical reaction except _____.

   A. decreasing concentration

   B. increasing temperature

   C. increasing surface area

   D. adding a catalyst

> **Test-Taking Tip**
>
> Be careful of words such as *except*. This word often means that all the answers are correct *except* for one.

Critical Thinking

12. Scientists use chemical equations to show at a glance the substances involved in a chemical reaction. A chemical equation shows the reactants and products of a chemical reaction. It can show the state of each substance and the conditions under which the reaction takes place. It can also show the substances' ratios.

13. The temperature of hot coffee helps dissolve the sugar cube, providing more surface area for particle collisions. This is not the case for the iced coffee, and so smaller crystals, which provide increased surface area, are preferred because they dissolve faster.

14. A catalyst speeds up a chemical reaction, so an inhibitor slows down a chemical reaction. BHT is added to cereals to slow the spoiling of the cereal and increase its shelf life.

Standardized Test Question

15. A

Reading Links

How to Read a French Fry: And Other Stories of Intriguing Kitchen Science
This book's entertaining, easy-to-read prose and appealing subject matter make it an entertaining enrichment option for motivated students, as its author—an acclaimed food journalist—examines the basic science behind familiar cooking processes and brings chemistry to bear on the everyday for a lay audience. Over one hundred recipes are included.

Russ Parsons. Houghton Mifflin. 320 pp. Trade ISBN 978-0-618-37943-9.

Fireworks

Part of a series aimed at engaging struggling or reluctant readers with interesting applications of science, this brief book discusses the chemical reactions involved in pyrotechnics. The content nicely reinforces this chapter's discussion of combustion and other key topics.

Vicki Cobb. Lerner Publishing Group. 48 pp. Illustrated. Trade ISBN 978-0-7613-2771-4.

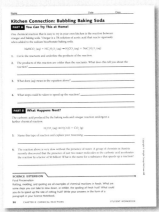

Curriculum Connection
Workbook, p. 50

Science Challenge
Workbook, pp. 51-52

8A Observing Chemical Change

This prechapter introduction activity is designed to determine what students already know about chemical change by having them observe a simple chemical reaction and draw conclusions about what happened.

Objectives

* create a chemical reaction
* observe a change reaction
* communicate conclusions

Planning

 15–20 minutes   groups of 3–4 students

Materials (per group)

* plastic zip-type bag containing 5 g of baking soda
* cup containing 10 mL of red cabbage juice
* cup containing 50 mL of vinegar

Advance Preparation

* Ask students to suggest how they might organize a table to record their results. Have them create a chart ahead of time so everyone will have the same boxes to record observations.
* Pre-measure materials for the lab. Seal the baking soda in each bag.
* A chemical reaction will cause the indicator (the cabbage juice) to change color. The reaction between the baking soda and the vinegar will cause a gas to form (bubbles will be visible) and also cause a decrease in temperature.

Engagement Guide

* Challenge students to think about physical and chemical changes by asking:
  * *What are several examples of physical change? What characterizes this type of change?* (Accept all reasonable answers; physical change examples might include cutting, grinding, bending, dissolving, melting, etc. A change that does not alter a material's composition is a physical change.)
  * *What are several examples of chemical change?* (Accept all reasonable answers; chemical change examples might include rusting, combustion, decomposition, acid-base reactions, etc.)
  * *What are the characteristics of a chemical change? What is evidence that a reaction has occurred?* (A chemical reaction is characterized by one or more substances changing into new substances. Evidence includes formation of a precipitate, formation of a gas, and a color change. A temperature change is often associated with a reaction, but a temperature change alone does not guarantee that a reaction has occurred.)
* Encourage students to compare and contrast physical and chemical changes.

Going Further

Ask student groups to create a table of chemical reactions they observe throughout the day. The table should describe the initial substances, identify the new substances formed, and list the evidence for a reaction. Have the groups post their tables in the class and present one of their reactions to the class.

8B Chemical Reactions

Objectives

* observe chemical reactions
* identify reactants and products
* develop an operational definition of a chemical reaction

Skill Set

observing, comparing and contrasting, recording and analyzing data, stating conclusions

Planning

 30–35 minutes   groups of 3–4 students

Materials

Materials for this activity are listed in the Student Laboratory Manual.

Advance Preparation

* On the day of the lab put each experiment on a different table and have students rotate through each one. Doing this avoids having to make sets of materials for each group.
* The potato slices can be cut ahead of time and stored under water in a container to prevent them from turning brown.
* Glow sticks can be purchased from camping supply sellers or from military surplus stores. The reactions involving glow sticks and the hot and cold packs can be done as a class to save money. If you have time, model this for your students as the first station. This will give them an opportunity to see how the lab is supposed to be run.
* Warn students not to smell the ammonia vapors. If possible, do this portion of the experiment in a fume hood.
* Epsom salts are magnesium sulfate.

Answers to Observations: Data Table 1

Note: Temperature change alone is not sufficient evidence for a chemical change.

Reaction 1: Epsom salts are large, clear-whitish crystals. Ammonia is a clear liquid. When mixed, a cloudy precipitate (solid) forms. The formation of a precipitate is evidence of a chemical reaction.

Reaction 2: The potato is a somewhat porous, light-colored solid. Hydrogen peroxide is a clear liquid. Catalase, an enzyme in the potato, causes the hydrogen peroxide to quickly decompose into water and oxygen gas. The bubbles seen are oxygen gas. The formation of a gas is evidence of a chemical reaction.

Reaction 3: Baking soda (sodium bicarbonate) and calcium chloride are both white solids. When mixed together with cabbage juice, a double replacement reaction takes place and a precipitate forms and the cabbage indicator changes color. The color change occurs because an acid is formed during the reaction. The formation of a precipitate and a color change are evidence of a chemical reaction.

Reaction 4: Observations will vary depending on the light stick used. When activated, the light stick emits light. The emission of light is evidence of a chemical change.

Reaction 5: Observations will vary depending on the hot packs and cold packs used. When activated, packs heat up or cool down. Although the packs do create a chemical reaction, the temperature change alone is not sufficient evidence for a chemical change.

Answers to Analysis and Conclusions

1. Answers will vary. Students should mention formation of a gas, formation of a solid (a precipitate), a change in color, and the emission of light as ways to tell if a chemical change has taken place. Students will likely mention a temperature change as being an indicator of a chemical change; accept this answer but explain that a temperature change alone does not ensure that the change is a chemical change. Explain the phase changes of water are physical and involve a temperature change.

2. Answers will vary. Accept examples that illustrate each form of evidence for a chemical change.

3. Answers will vary. Students will likely describe a chemical change as one in which the formation of new substances with new properties is accompanied by one or more of the following: a change in color or temperature, the emission of light, the formation of a solid, or the formation of a gas.

Going Further

Ask students to describe the reactions in the lab using chemical formulas. Have them research the reactions and write the chemical equation for each. Ask students to present their findings to the class by writing the equations on the board and then explaining them out loud.

8C Conservation of Mass

Objectives
- develop a testable hypothesis
- design an experiment
- collect and analyze data
- draw conclusions

Skill Set

hypothesizing, designing an experiment, observing, identifying, recording and analyzing data, classifying, drawing conclusions

Planning
 60 minutes   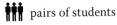 pairs of students

Materials

Materials for this activity are listed in the Student Laboratory Manual.

Advance Preparation
- Students are designing their own experiment to verify that the conservation of mass applies to a chemical reaction.

Answers to Observations: Hypothesis

Mass is conserved in a chemical reaction.

Answers to Observations: Data Table 1

Student data tables will vary, but should support their procedures.

Answers to Analysis and Conclusions

1. Student presentations will vary. The basic procedure should be similar to the following: Measure the mass of the tablet and record it. Add a small amount of water to the bag, measure the combined volume of the bag and the water, and record it. Calculate the mass before the reaction by adding the masses of the water, the bag, and the tablet. Record the starting mass.

   Drop the tablet in the bag and seal the bag. The bag will inflate as the tablet reacts with the water. Let the reaction finish. Measure the mass of the bag and its contents again. Record the final mass after the reaction. Subtract the final mass from the initial mass. The calculation should show that mass is conserved.

2. Possible error sources may include measurement errors associated with the balance, mass lost when handling the tablet, calculation errors, allowing gas to escape from the bag before it is sealed, and using plastic bags (gas will leak out of the corners).

Going Further

Challenge groups to come up with alternative methods for verifying the conservation of mass using different materials. Approve plans and have students conduct the experiment.

Chapter 9 Lessons

9.1 How Solutions Form

9.2 Solubility

9.3 Acids, Bases, and Salts

Introduce Chapter 9

As a starting activity, use Lab 9A on page 49 of the Laboratory Manual.

EXPLORE Have students make (or observe the making of) chocolate milk, coffee, and iced tea. The substances should be combined in various quantities to make them into solutions. For example, strong or weak chocolate milk could be made, depending on the amount of chocolate used. Explain that these are solutions made from individual substances.

Think About Solutions

ENGAGE Have students work in small groups to answer the questions and come up with a definition of the term *solution*. Have them record the information their Science Notebooks and share their answers with the class. The class should come to an agreement on the definition of *solution*.

Chapter 9 Solutions

KEY CONCEPT A solution, which forms when one or more pure substances dissolve in another pure substance, has properties that are determined by the interaction of solutes and solvents.

It's a warm, sunny day at the beach. You take a deep breath and then dive into the cool water. You may encounter a variety of living things that make the ocean their home, including jellyfish, crabs, and seaweed. As you emerge from the water, the taste of salt stings your lips.

Air and seawater are two of the most abundant materials on Earth. Both are natural resources that humans depend on for life. Both are examples of solutions.

Think About Solutions

Many of the items around you are formed from solutions. What does the term *solution* mean to you? What are some examples of solutions? How do solutions differ from other forms of matter?

* In your Science Notebook, write a definition for the term *solution*. Then brainstorm a list of examples of solutions. Write the list under your definition.

* Discuss with classmates how solutions are different from elements or compounds. If necessary, revise your definition as you hear others' ideas.

NSTA
SCi LINKS.
THE WORLD'S A CLICK AWAY

www.scilinks.org
Solutions **Code:** WGPS09

144

Chapter 9 Planning Guide			
Instructional Periods	**National Standards**	**Lab Manual**	**Workbook**
9.1 2 Periods	A2, B1, B2; A2, B2, B5; UCP1, UCP2, UCP4	**Lab 9A: p. 49** A Stirring Experiment **Lab 9B: pp. 50–52** Acids, Bases, and pH **Lab 9C: pp. 53–54** Solubility of Gases	Key Concept Review p. 53 Vocabulary Review p. 54 Interpreting Diagrams p. 55 Reading Comprehension p. 56 Curriculum Connection p. 57 Science Challenge p. 58
9.2 2 Periods	A1, B1, C1, C3, E1; A2, B2; UCP3, UCP5		
9.3 2 Periods	A1, B1, C1, C3, F1; B2, B3, F1; UCP1, UCP4, UCP5		

Middle School Standard; High School Standard; Unifying Concept and Principle

9.1 How Solutions Form

Before You Read
In your Science Notebook, write three facts that you already know about solutions. As you read the lesson, add at least three more facts.

What does a teardrop have in common with a steel bridge? Although they seem quite different from each other, they have more in common than one might think. Both are types of matter. Both are produced by humans. The similarities go beyond that, however. Both are examples of solutions. A tear is a solution of water, salt, and other compounds. Steel is a solution of iron, carbon, and other elements.

Nature of Solutions
Recall from Chapter 2 that a **solution** is a homogeneous mixture of two or more pure substances. A solution forms when one substance uniformly spreads out in another substance. The substances are evenly distributed in the mixture so that every drop or granule of the mixture is exactly the same as the others. Shampoo, tea, apple juice, liquid soap, air, brass, and steel are common examples of solutions. Each is formed when one or more substances dissolve, or break apart, in another substance.

In contrast to a heterogeneous mixture, such as a mixture of cinnamon and sugar, the individual substances that make up a solution cannot be seen—not even with a microscope! Solutions are uniform, or the same throughout. They do not settle into layers. Solutions are usually transparent or are evenly colored. They often look like single, pure substances, a characteristic that makes them difficult to recognize.

Types of Solutions Solutions can exist as solids, liquids, or gases. They can form from different combinations of the states of matter. Club soda is a liquid solution that is made from a mixture of a gas and a liquid. Air is a gaseous solution made up of 78 percent nitrogen, 21 percent oxygen, and 1 percent other trace gases. Brass is a solid solution. It is made from a mixture of copper and zinc.

Learning Goals
- Describe the characteristics of a solution.
- Explain why water is a good solvent, and describe how substances dissolve in water.
- Identify factors that affect the rate of dissolving.

New Vocabulary
solution
solute
solvent
aqueous solution
polar
dissociation

Recall Vocabulary
covalent bond, p. 120
ionic bond, p. 116

Figure 9.1 Although many common solutions are liquids, solutions can exist as all three states of matter. The steel used to build the Golden Gate Bridge in San Francisco, California, is a solution of iron, carbon, and other elements. What other solutions are present in this photograph?

ELL Strategy
Read Aloud, Paraphrase As students continue through this lesson, have them work in small groups to take turns reading the text aloud. After each paragraph, the students should collaborate to paraphrase the text.

9.1 Introduce

ENGAGE In small groups, have students observe some of the solutions mentioned in this page's introduction (shampoo, tea, apple juice, etc.), as well as heterogeneous mixtures such as cinnamon and sugar and salt and pepper. Ask students to divide the substances into two groups and describe the categorizations.

Vocabulary terms are listed on the first student page of each lesson. You may wish to preview the terms before introducing each lesson. Strategies for teaching the vocabulary appear on the pages where the terms are introduced.

Before You Read
As a class, brainstorm information that students already know about solutions. Record responses on the board. Instruct students to record the information in their Science Notebooks, leaving space between each item.

Teach
EXPLAIN to students that in this section, they will learn about the characteristics of solutions.

Vocabulary
solution Explain to students that the common use of the term *solution* refers to an answer to a problem or puzzle. Ask students for examples of this usage. Then have students contrast this meaning with the scientific definition (a homogeneous mixture of two or more pure substances).

Use the Visual: Figure 9.1
ANSWER San Francisco Bay, air, steel

Teach

EXPLAIN to students that they will learn about the various types of solutions and their makeups.

Vocabulary

solute Tell students that the word *solute* comes from the Latin word *solutum,* meaning "to loosen."

solvent Tell students that the word *solvent* comes from the Latin word *solvens,* meaning "to dissolve" or "to pay." Have students use this meaning and the meaning of the word *solute* to develop their own definitions of the two terms.

aqueous solution Tell students that the word *aqueous* is an adjective that comes from the Latin word *aqua,* meaning "water."

polar Tell students that the word *polar* is an adjective that relates to the north or south pole, or the regions near them and their characteristics. It comes from the Latin word *polus,* meaning "pole." Explain to students that the word is used in science to denote regions of electric charge or magnetic force.

dissociation Explain to students that the word *dissociation* is a noun that comes from the verb *dissociate,* meaning "to separate or disconnect."

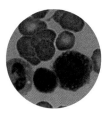

Figure 9.3 The cells of most organisms, like these human red blood cells, are made up of about 80 percent water. Nutrients dissolve in this water and can thus be transported throughout an organism's body.

146 SOLUTIONS

compressed air

bronze

sugar water

Different States of Solutions			
	Compressed air	**Bronze**	**Sugar Water**
Solvent (state)	nitrogen (gas)	copper (solid)	water (liquid)
Solute (state)	oxygen (gas)	tin (solid)	sugar (solid)
State of Solution	gas	solid	liquid

Figure 9.2 Solutions form when solute particles separate and mix evenly among solvent particles. A solution's state is usually determined by the state of the solvent.

Solutes and Solvents All solutions consist of two parts. The substance that makes up the smaller amount of a solution is called the **solute** (SAHL yewt). The solute is the substance that dissolves. The substance that makes up the larger amount of a solution is called the **solvent** (SAHL vunt). The solvent is the substance that dissolves the solute. The solvent breaks apart the particles of the solute and surrounds them. In a solution of air, nitrogen is the solvent and oxygen is the solute. In a solution of seawater, water is the solvent and salt is the solute. In a solution of chocolate milk, the solvent is milk and the solute is chocolate syrup or powder. In brass, the solvent is copper and the solute is zinc. To determine what the solute or solvent is in a solution, think about which substance is present in the greater amount.

Solutions form as a result of the interactions between the particles of a solvent and the particles of a solute. In order for a solution to form, solute particles must separate from one another, and the solute and solvent particles must mix.

Aqueous Solutions When the solvent in a solution is water, the solution is called an **aqueous** (AY kwee us) **solution**. The word *aqueous* means "related to water." Fruit punch, tea, contact lens solution, liquid soap, and vinegar are examples of aqueous solutions. If you read the ingredients in these products, water will be listed first because water makes up most of the solution.

Recall from Chapter 2 that many different kinds of substances can dissolve in water. Because so many substances dissolve in water, water is often called the universal solvent.

Background Information

For a solution to form, solute particles must separate from one another, and the solute and solvent particles must mix. This happens when the attractive force between the solute and solvent particles is greater than the attractive force holding the solute particles together. If the attractive force between the solute and solvent particles is great enough, the solvent will dissolve the solute. That is, it will pull apart the solute particles and surround them. If the attractive force between the solute and solvent particles is much weaker than the attractive force holding the solute particles together, however, the solvent will not easily pull apart the solute particles. The solute will not readily dissolve, and a solution will not readily form.

The Solution Process

Water is the universal solvent; it can dissolve many substances. To understand why, one must examine atoms and bonds. Recall from Chapter 7 that atoms can form ionic, covalent, or metallic bonds. In a covalent bond, electrons are shared between atoms. This sharing of electrons is not always equal. When electrons spend more time around a certain atom, that atom gains a slight negative charge. The other atom gains a slight positive charge. In such a case, the bond between the atoms is described as a polar covalent bond. The molecule is a polar molecule. **Polar** means having two sides that are opposite in nature or charge.

Water is a polar molecule. The oxygen atom in a water molecule pulls on the shared electrons slightly more than do the hydrogen atoms. This gives the oxygen atom a partial negative charge and the hydrogen atoms partial positive charges. This enables water to dissolve many substances.

Dissolving Ionic Compounds   Because water molecules are polar, they can attract charged particles. This means that when an ionic compound is added to water, the positively charged ions are attracted to the partially negative oxygen atoms of the water molecules. The negatively charged ions are attracted to the partially positive hydrogen atoms of the water molecules. The force keeping the ions of the ionic compound together weakens as the ions are pulled toward the oppositely charged ends of the water molecules. The compound dissociates, or splits into its individual ions. **Dissociation** (dih soh see AY shun) is the process in which an ionic compound separates into its positive and negative ions. Each ion becomes surrounded by water molecules, as shown in **Figure 9.5**. This process happens at the surface of the compound. Over time, layer after layer of the compound dissolves.

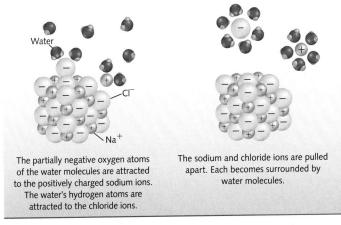

The partially negative oxygen atoms of the water molecules are attracted to the positively charged sodium ions. The water's hydrogen atoms are attracted to the chloride ions.

The sodium and chloride ions are pulled apart. Each becomes surrounded by water molecules.

Figure 9.5 Sodium chloride, or table salt, dissolves in water as a result of dissociation.

Partial negative charge

Partial positive charge

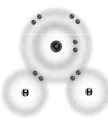

Figure 9.4 Water is a polar molecule. Electrons spend more time around the oxygen atom than around the hydrogen atoms.

Extend It!

The formation of a solution can be an exothermic or an endothermic process. Recall that an exothermic process releases heat and an endothermic process absorbs heat. The heat released or absorbed during the formation of a solution is known as the heat of solution. Do research to find out about the heat of solution for a variety of solutions. How is the heat of solution measured? Write a well-developed paragraph in your Science Notebook explaining your findings.

CHAPTER 9   **147**

● Teach

EXPLAIN to students that they will learn why water is a good solvent and how substances dissolve in water.

 Extend It!

Ask students to research heat of solution in class or at home. Encourage them to share their findings with one another. Ask them to think about some practical uses for this phenomenon.

Science Notebook EXTRA

Have students study the diagrams in **Figure 9.5.** Then have each student draw a series of diagrams illustrating the solution process similar to those in the figure, including a callout for each diagram.

Differentiate Instruction

Kinesthetic Have students mix salt with cold, warm, and hot water and observe what happens in each case. Have them combine their observations with the information found in **Figure 9.5.** In their Science Notebooks, have students record what they observed and learned from the figure and the activity.

Teach

EXPLAIN to students that in this section, they will learn about two factors that determine how quickly solutes dissolve: the type of solvent and stirring.

Figure It Out: Figure 9.6

ANSWER **1.** Students should recognize that in both processes, solute particles are split apart and are surrounded by water molecules due to attractive forces between the solute particles and water. They should also recognize that the processes differ in that the dissolving of an ionic compound involves the separation of the compound into ions, while the dissolving of a molecular compound involves the separation of molecules and does not involve the formation of ions or the breakdown of the individual molecules. **2.** Students' answers will vary but should reflect that the sugar molecules are separated from one another due to attractive forces with water, but the molecules do not dissociate.

As You Read

Have students share with partners new facts that they learned about solutions and make any changes or revisions necessary based on the discussion. Students should then record the facts in their Science Notebooks.

ANSWER An aqueous solution is a solution in which the solvent is water.

Use the Visual: Figure 9.7

ANSWER Water cannot be used to clean oil-based paint from brushes because oil-based paint, a nonpolar compound, will not dissolve in water, a polar compound.

Figure It Out

1. Compare the illustrations shown in Figure 9.5 to the illustration shown here. Describe how the processes are similar. How do they differ?

2. Explain what happens to sugar as it dissolves in water.

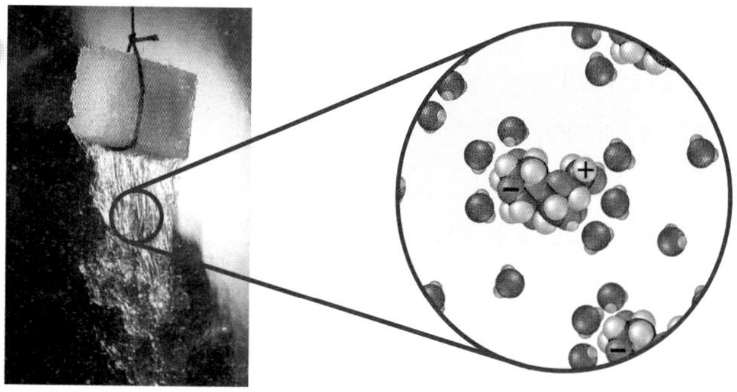

As You Read

Compare the facts you recorded in your Science Notebook before and during your reading. Make necessary changes to your original facts.

What is an aqueous solution?

Dissolving Molecular Compounds   Water can dissolve other polar covalent compounds, or compounds like itself, in addition to ionic compounds. When water dissolves covalent compounds, however, the compounds generally do not dissociate, as do ionic compounds. The molecules simply become separated from one another. Each molecule becomes surrounded by a group of water molecules.

Figure 9.6 When polar molecules such as sugar dissolve in water, they do not dissociate. Instead, the molecules are pulled from one another, surrounded by water molecules, and evenly distributed in the water.

Rate of Dissolving

Different solutes dissolve in different solvents at different rates. Some solutes may dissolve quickly in a particular solvent. Others may dissolve more slowly in that solvent. Rate of dissolving is a measurement that describes how quickly a solute dissolves in a given solvent.

The rate at which a solute dissolves is affected by several factors. It depends on the type of solvent involved. It also depends on stirring, surface area, and temperature.

Type of Solvent   Polar solutes and ionic solutes dissolve in polar solvents. Nonpolar solutes dissolve in nonpolar solvents. This general rule can be summarized as "like dissolves like."

Stirring   The rate of dissolving can be increased with stirring or agitation, which usually means shaking up. This helps bring fresh solvent in contact with a solute and helps the solute dissolve more quickly.

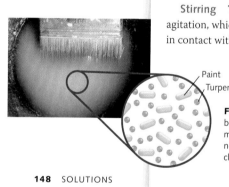

Paint
Turpentine

Figure 9.7 Turpentine can be used to clean oil-based paint from brushes because both turpentine and oil-based paint are nonpolar molecules. The nonpolar paint from this brush quickly dissolves in the nonpolar turpentine, leaving the brush clean. Can water be used to clean oil-based paint from brushes? Explain your answer.

148   SOLUTIONS

Background Information

Organic solvents, defined as those containing carbon, can be harmful to one's health. Possible problems from overexposure to organic solvents include headache, nausea, and tiredness; dermatitis; lung, nose, and throat irritation; and eye irritation. Some common organic solvents are certain types of spray paint, paint strippers, glue, and dry-cleaning solvents. If an organic solvent is swallowed, it could be lethal.

Teacher Alert

For the Explore It! activity on page 149, review with students the concept of variables and the importance of controlling variables during an experiment. Remind students that only one variable at a time should be changed because if more than one variable is changed, they will not be able to determine which variable caused their results.

Surface Area Breaking a solid into smaller pieces will increase the solid's rate of dissolving in the same way that it increases its rate of reaction. Dissolving occurs at the surface of a solid. Breaking up a solid increases the solid's surface area. Increasing the surface area increases the amount of solute that comes in contact with the solvent. This causes the solute to dissolve more quickly.

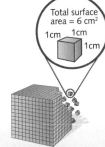
Total surface area = 6 cm²
1cm 1cm
1cm

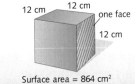
12 cm
12 cm
one face
12 cm

Surface area = 864 cm²

A face of a cube is the outer surface that has four edges. A cube has six faces.

6cm
6cm
6cm

Surface area = 1,728 cm²

The cube can be pulled apart into smaller cubes of equal size. Here there are eight cubes and 48 faces.

Surface area = 10, 368 cm²

If the cube is divided into smaller cubes that are 1 cm on a side, there will be 1,728 cubes and 10,368 faces.

Figure 9.8 Breaking up a solid into smaller pieces increases the surface area that is exposed to the solvent. Because dissolving happens at the surface of a solid, this increases the rate of dissolving.

Temperature When the solute is a liquid or a solid, the rate of dissolving can be increased by increasing the temperature of the solvent. Increasing the temperature causes solute and solvent particles to come in contact with one another more quickly and more frequently. The particles move around and interact with one another at a faster rate. This helps bring fresh solvent in contact with the solute.

Stirring a solution, increasing the surface area of a solute, and increasing the temperature of a solvent can each increase the rate of dissolving. However, dissolving can happen even faster when two or more of these techniques are combined. For example, think about a cube of sugar placed in a glass of cold water. The sugar will dissolve, but heating the water will make it dissolve faster. Crushing the cube and stirring the heated water will result in the fastest rate of dissolving.

After You Read

1. What are the parts of a solution?

2. How does water dissolve substances?

3. Name four factors that can affect the rate at which a solute dissolves in a solvent.

4. Review the new facts you recorded about solutions in your Science Notebook. Use your notes to write a well-developed paragraph summarizing this lesson.

Explore It!

Choose one factor that affects rate of dissolving. Working with a group, design an experiment to observe and measure how this factor affects the dissolving rate of sugar. If you choose the type of solvent, for example, you can try dissolving sugar in several polar and nonpolar solvents to determine the dissolving rate. With your teacher's permission, perform the experiment and record your observations. Draw conclusions about how the rate at which sugar dissolves can be changed. Present your findings to the class.

Teach

EXPLAIN to students that they will learn about two other factors that affect the rate at which solutes dissolve: surface area and temperature.

Explore It!

Divide the class into groups and have each group experiment with a different factor that affects rate of dissolving. Provide students with materials such as water, thermometers, graduated cylinders, pan balances, stopwatches, granulated sugar, powdered sugar, and sugar cubes for experimenting with the effects of surface area. Substitute heaters and ice baths for the powdered sugar and sugar cubes so that students can experiment with the effects of temperature. Substitute spoons for heaters and ice baths so that students can measure the effects of stirring. Substitute a variety of solvents, such as alcohol (has both polar and nonpolar ends), turpentine (nonpolar), oil (nonpolar), vinegar (polar), and nail polish remover (polar), for spoons so that students can experiment with the effects of solvent type. Students should write procedures before they begin experimenting. Review each group's procedure before students begin.

Assess

Use the After You Read questions and the Alternative Assessment to help you evaluate students' understanding of the lesson.

After You Read

1. A solution is made up of a solute and a solvent.

2. Because water is a polar molecule, it can attract the oppositely charged ions that make up an ionic compound and cause the ions to dissociate; it can also attract and separate other polar molecules.

3. Four factors that can affect the rate at which a solute dissolves in a solvent are: type of solvent, stirring, surface area, and temperature.

4. Students' summaries will vary. Make sure that students have incorporated the key ideas from each section of the lesson.

ELL Strategy

Ask and Answer Questions Have students work with partners or in small groups to ask and answer questions about this lesson. Students should create questions on index cards (one for each lesson segment), placing the answer on the reverse side. Pairs may then exchange cards with another group, who will be able to check their answers to the questions.

Alternative Assessment

In their Science Notebooks, ask students to complete their lists of facts about solutions. Then have them review the initial three facts that they recorded before reading this lesson. Ask them to revise or change any information as needed. After they have each written a paragraph summarizing the lesson, students should read their work aloud to partners.

9.2 Introduce

ENGAGE In front of the class, combine oil and vinegar in a glass or clear plastic container. Ask students what they see. Have one student assist by mixing the substances with a spoon and then shaking the closed container. Ask what students notice about the two substances. (They do not combine.) Explain that some solutes do not dissolve in a solvent. Ask for other examples of non-dissolving (insoluble) substances.

Before You Read

Show students how to reword a statement into a question. Have students suggest how to change the first heading into a question, and record responses on the board. Have students work with partners to rewrite the remaining headings as questions.

● Teach

EXPLAIN to students that in this lesson, they will learn about soluble and insoluble substances.

Vocabulary

insoluble Tell students that the word *insoluble* is an adjective that comes from the Latin word *insolubilis,* from the prefix *in-,* meaning "not," and *solvere,* meaning "to free" or "to dissolve."

soluble Ask students to figure out the meaning of this word based on the definition given for *insoluble.*

solubility Tell students that *solubility* is the noun form of the adjective *soluble.* Ask students to use the word in a sentence.

solubility curve Ask students what they already know about the word *curve* from previous chapters or from math classes. If necessary, tell them that a curve is any smoothly arched line or shape. Ask them to put together this meaning with the definition of *solubility* and come up with a definition of the term *solubility curve.*

Learning Goals

• Relate solubility, solubility curves, and factors that affect solubility.

• Identify ways in which solutions can be described.

• Compare and contrast freezing-point depression and boiling-point elevation.

• Describe ways in which solutions can be separated.

New Vocabulary

insoluble
soluble
solubility
solubility curve
concentration
saturated
unsaturated
supersaturated
freezing-point depression
boiling-point elevation

Figure 9.9 Vinegar and oil do not mix. The nonpolar oil molecules are not attracted to the polar water molecules that make up the vinegar solution.

9.2 Solubility

Before You Read

Reword this lesson's headings so that they all form questions. Write the questions in your Science Notebook. Answer the questions as you read.

Suppose you decide to eat a salad for lunch. You want to add a little oil and vinegar to the salad, so you mix the ingredients together in a container. You stir the oil and vinegar and then shake the container, but no matter what you do, the two liquids do not form a solution. Although they will mix at first, they will not stay mixed. Why is this so?

What Will Dissolve?

Some substances will not form a solution no matter how much they are stirred, shaken, heated, or ground up. Vinegar will not dissolve in oil. Oil will not dissolve in water. When a substance does not easily dissolve in a solvent, the substance is said to be **insoluble** (ihn SAHL yuh bul) in that solvent. Vinegar is insoluble in oil. Oil is insoluble in water.

Although oil will not form a solution with water, it will dissolve in detergents. When a substance is capable of dissolving in a solvent, the substance is said to be **soluble** (SAHL yuh bul) in that solvent. Sugar, salt, vitamins, and minerals are all soluble in water.

Recall the rule "like dissolves like." Polar substances will dissolve in polar solvents, but nonpolar substances will not. Conversely, nonpolar substances will dissolve in nonpolar solvents, but polar substances will not. Whether a substance is soluble or insoluble depends on both the substance and the solvent involved.

How Much Will Dissolve?

A solute's ability to dissolve in a solvent can be described by a measurement called solubility. **Solubility** (sahl yuh BIH luh tee) is the maximum amount of a solute that can dissolve in a given amount of a solvent under a given set of conditions. If a solute has a high solubility, a large amount of the solute can dissolve in the solvent under the given conditions. The solute is highly soluble. If a solute has a low solubility, only a small amount of the solute can dissolve in the solvent under the given conditions. The solute is not highly soluble. When a solute has an extremely low solubility, it is considered insoluble. Solubility is usually expressed in grams of solute per 100 g of solvent.

E L L Strategy

Practice Using Vocabulary In pairs, have students orally practice using the vocabulary words in this lesson. For each word, students should provide a definition and use the word in a sentence. One student can also give the definition of a word, allowing the partner to provide the vocabulary word and use the word in a sentence.

Solubility of Substances in Water at 20°C	
Substance	**Solubility in g/100 g of Water**
Solid Substances	
salt (sodium chloride)	35.9
baking soda (sodium bicarbonate)	9.6
washing soda (sodium carbonate)	21.4
lye (sodium hydroxide)	109.0
sugar (sucrose)	203.9
Gaseous Substances*	
hydrogen	0.00017
oxygen	0.0005
carbon dioxide	0.16

*at normal atmospheric pressure

Temperature and Solubility The solubility of liquids and solids generally increases as temperature increases. The solubility of gases in liquid solvents, by contrast, generally decreases as temperature increases.

Scientists use graphs called **solubility curves** to show how temperature affects a substance's solubility. Each point on a solubility curve shows the maximum amount of solute that can dissolve in an amount of solvent at a given temperature.

Pressure and Solubility
Pressure has no effect on liquid and solid solutes, but it can affect the solubility of gaseous solutes in liquid solvents. Increasing pressure causes the solubility of gases in liquid solvents to increase. Decreasing pressure causes the solubility of gases in liquid solvents to decrease. Soda is bottled under pressure to keep carbon dioxide gas in solution. When the bottle is opened, the pressure is released. The gas bubbles out of solution, making the soda taste flat over time.

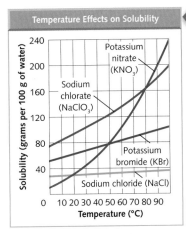

Figure 9.11 A solubility curve can be used to determine how much solute will dissolve in a given amount of water at a certain temperature.

Figure 9.10 Compare the solubility of these common substances. Which is most soluble in water? Which is least?

Explain It!

In a group of four, discuss what you know about the particles in solids, liquids, and gases. Then work with a partner to develop an explanation for why the solubility of liquids and solids increases as temperature increases, but the solubility of gases decreases as temperature increases. Record your ideas in your Science Notebook. Share your ideas with the class.

Figure It Out

1. Calculate the solubility of sodium chlorate at 20°C. What is its solubility at 100°C?

2. How does the solubility of potassium nitrate change as temperature increases? How does the solubility of sodium chloride change as temperature increases?

Teach

EXPLAIN to students that they will learn about the solubility of substances.

Use the Visual: Figure 9.10

ANSWER Sugar is most soluble. Of the solid substances, baking soda is the least soluble. Of the gaseous substances, hydrogen is the least soluble.

Explain It!

Remind students that temperature is a measure of the average kinetic energy that particles of matter have. When particles of matter move quickly, they have a high temperature. When particles of matter move more slowly, they have a lower temperature. Guide students to recognize that the molecules of most substances spread out as temperature increases. The molecules are held together less tightly, providing more space between the particles in which solutes and solvents can interact.

This idea can be modeled by having ten students move around one another in a tight cluster and having ten other students try to "dissolve" in the cluster. Then "turn up the temperature" by having the students in the cluster spread out a little bit and move more quickly around one another. Have the other ten students try to dissolve again. Because the particles are in faster motion and have more space between them, more should be able to dissolve.

Figure It Out: Figure 9.11

ANSWER **1.** The solubility of sodium chlorate is about 95 g/100 g of water at 20°C and about 200 g/100 g of water at 100°C.
2. Potassium nitrate's solubility increases as temperature increases. The solubility of sodium chloride also increases as temperature does, but only by a small amount.

Background Information

Gas particles have more energy and move about more quickly at higher temperatures. They escape from solutions at higher temperatures rather than staying dissolved. This can be observed with a can of soda. When you open a can of soda that has been kept cold in a refrigerator, little gas escapes from the solution. The gas stays dissolved. When you open a can of soda that has been heated or kept at room temperature, however, gas quickly bubbles

out of the solution. The gas is less soluble, so it does not stay dissolved.

Fish and most other animals that live in water depend on dissolved oxygen to survive. As the temperature of the water increases, the solubility of oxygen decreases. For this reason, during summer and warm months, fish and other water animals are often found deeper in the water where the water stays cooler and more oxygen is present.

● Teach

EXPLAIN to students that on this page, they will learn that solutions can be more precisely described using either concentration or solubility.

Vocabulary

concentration Explain that in chemistry, *concentration* refers to the amount of solute that is dissolved in a given amount of solute. Concentration is abbreviated with brackets that contain the formula for the solute or solvent, such as [NaCl] or [H_2O].

saturated Tell students that *saturated* is an adjective, from the verb *saturate*. Tell them that the common meaning of *saturated* is "soaked." Ask for examples of items that could be saturated (clothes, hair, soil).

unsaturated Tell students that the prefix *un-* refers to the opposite of the base word. Ask them to put the word parts together to derive a definition for *unsaturated*.

supersaturated Tell students that the prefix *super-* means "great" or "extreme in size or degree." Ask for examples of words that use this prefix (*supermarket, supernatural*).

freezing-point depression Remind students that freezing point is the temperature at which the liquid form of a substance turns into a solid. Tell students that as used in this term, the noun *depression* is made up of the verb *depress*, meaning "to make lower," and the suffix *-tion,* signifying action or state. Have students put the meanings together to define *depression.*

boiling-point elevation Remind students that boiling point is the temperature at which a particular substance changes from a liquid to a vapor. Tell students that the noun *elevation* comes from the verb *elevate,* meaning "to raise or lift," and the suffix *-tion,* signifying an action or state.

As You Read

Have students share answers to the heading question with the class and then answer the second question in their Science Notebooks. Remind students to look for answers to the remaining questions as they read.

(ANSWER) Concentration describes the amount of solute that is dissolved in a quantity of solvent.

Figure 9.12 Concentration can be described in percent by mass or percent by volume.

As You Read

Look for information that can help you answer the questions you wrote in your Science Notebook. Try to answer each question as you gain new information.

What is concentration?

Describing Solutions

A solution can contain different proportions of solute and solvent. A cup of coffee may be strong or weak. A glass of lemonade may be sweet or sour. For this reason, it is useful to describe solutions more precisely.

Using Concentration Scientists often use concentration to describe solutions. **Concentration** is the amount of solute that is dissolved in a quantity of solvent. If there is only a little solute in a solution, the solution is called dilute. If there is a lot of solute in a solution, the solution is said to be concentrated.

Concentration can be described more precisely by providing the proportions of the substances in a solution. A solution of cranberry juice, for example, might have 100 percent juice or only ten percent juice. A solution of steel could contain 2 g of carbon to every 98 g of iron.

Using Solubility Scientists use solubility to describe how much solute is in a solution. When a solution contains the maximum amount of dissolved solute it can hold at a given temperature, the solution is **saturated** (SA chuh ray ted). If more solute is added to a saturated solution under the existing conditions, the solute will not dissolve. When a solution contains less than the maximum amount of solute it can hold at a given temperature, the solution is **unsaturated** (un SA chuh ray ted). More solute will dissolve if it is added to the solution under the existing conditions. A solution is **supersaturated** when it contains more dissolved solute than a saturated solution under the same conditions. *Supersaturated* means the solution is "more than saturated."

A solution can become supersaturated if it is saturated at a high temperature and then cooled very slowly. The slow cooling allows all of the solute to remain dissolved, although the solution is holding more solute than it normally could hold at the lower temperature. Supersaturated solutions are unstable. If they are disturbed, the excess solute comes out of the solution. Rock candy is produced by making a supersaturated sugar solution to which seed crystals are added. The seed crystals cause the sugar to crystallize onto a string so they can be eaten.

A reaction starts moments after a seed crystal is added to a supersaturated solution of sodium acetate.

The crystallization continues to pull solute from the solution.

Figure 9.13 When a supersaturated solution is disturbed in some way, the excess solute quickly is drawn out of the solution.

Differentiate Instruction

Linguistic Remind students that *un-* and *super-* are prefixes. Have them work in small groups to create a chart of at least ten prefixes, their meanings, and two or three examples of words that use each one.

Background Information

Solvents can typically hold more solute at higher temperatures than at lower temperatures. If a solution is saturated at 100°C and then cools quickly, the excess solute will come out of solution as the solubility of the solute. This can be demonstrated with a sugar-water solution. If the solution is cooled slowly, the excess solute may not come out, causing the solution to become supersaturated.

Properties of Solutions

In states across the U.S., halite, or rock salt, is sprinkled over sidewalks and roads to help melt snow and ice. It works by causing water to freeze at a lower temperature. This means that the roads on which halite is sprinkled are ice-free at 0°C, water's normal freezing point, instead of being frozen and slippery.

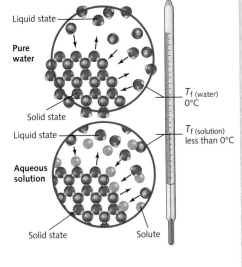

Liquid state
Pure water
Solid state
Liquid state
Aqueous solution
Solid state
Solute

$T_{f \text{ (water)}}$ 0°C
$T_{f \text{ (solution)}}$ less than 0°C

The freezing point of a solution is always lower than the freezing point of the pure solvent. When a liquid freezes, its particles become arranged in an orderly pattern and are held together more tightly. The particles of a solute interfere with the attractive forces between the particles of the solvent. They prevent the solvent from entering the solid state at its normal freezing point. The difference between the normal freezing point of the solvent and the freezing point of the solution is called the solution's **freezing-point depression.**

The boiling point of most solutions is higher than the boiling point of the pure solvent. The particles of the solute interfere with the evaporation of the solvent's particles. The difference between the normal boiling point of the solvent and the boiling point of the solution is called the solution's **boiling-point elevation.**

Freezing-point depression and boiling-point elevation depend on how much solute is in solution. The more solute, the greater the effect will be on the solvent's properties.

Freezing-point depression and boiling-point elevation have important practical uses. Adding antifreeze to the radiator fluid in a car, for example, helps prevent the radiator fluid from freezing in cold weather. It also helps keep the fluid from boiling over. Certain proteins in the bodies of some fish and arctic animals keep the animals from freezing in cold conditions.

Figure 9.14 The particles of a solute in an aqueous solution interfere with the freezing process by blocking molecules of water as they try to join the developing ice crystals.

 Explore It!

How many grams of sugar does it take to increase the boiling point of water one degree? Does it take more, less, or the same amount of salt to increase the boiling point of water by one degree? Design an experiment to find the answers. With your teacher's approval, perform the experiment and record your observations. What can you conclude about boiling-point elevation?

Figure 9.15 Fish that swim in waters around Antarctica have "built-in antifreeze." A protein they produce keeps them from freezing in their icy environment.

● **Teach**

EXPLAIN to students that they will learn that the greater the amount of solute in a solution, the greater the effect on the solvent's properties.

 Explore It!

Suggest that students perform this Explore It! activity with partners or in groups of three or four. Carefully review students' experimental designs. Perhaps even discuss each design as a class. In doing so, point out all appropriate safety precautions, as students will be boiling water. If students' designs meet with your approval, allow pairs or groups to perform the experiment and observe and analyze their results. Guide students to recognize that boiling point elevation is determined by the amount of dissolved solute and not by the properties of the solute. Freezing-point depression and boiling-point elevation are known as colligative properties for this reason.

Field Study

On their own or with the class, have students observe arctic animals at a nearby aquarium or zoo. Instruct students to list the animals that they see. When they return to the classroom, students should work in small groups to research one or more animals they observed, determining the temperature range of the organism's environment, proteins that keep the animal from freezing, and other features that protect it from freezing.

Background Information

The freezing point of a solution is not a true freezing point. Nor is the boiling point of a solution a true boiling point. As the solvent in a solution freezes or boils, the remaining solution becomes more and more concentrated. With more solute particles per solvent particles in the solution, the freezing point is further lowered and the boiling point is further elevated.

Teach

EXPLAIN to students that they will learn about the three ways that solutions can be separated: evaporation, condensation, and distillation.

CONNECTION: Social Studies

The most common method of desalination is reverse osmosis. In this process, water is forced through permeable membranes, which separates the salt from it. Reverse osmosis is usually used with seawater, but brackish groundwater (underground water) can also be treated. More than half of all desalination plants are in the Middle East. About 12 percent are in the United States (mostly along the coasts).

Assess

Use the After You Read questions and the Alternative Assessment to help you evaluate students' understanding of the lesson.

After You Read

1. Solubility is a measure of the maximum amount of a solute that can dissolve in a quantity of solvent under certain conditions. Temperature and pressure affect the solubility of a solute in a solvent.

2. An unsaturated solution contains less than the maximum amount of solute it can hold at a given temperature. A saturated solution contains the maximum amount of solute it can hold at a given temperature. A supersaturated solution contains more dissolved solute than a saturated solution does under the same conditions.

3. Solutes can lower the freezing point and elevate the boiling point of a solution.

4. Solutions can be separated by condensation, evaporation, and distillation. Students should explain each method in their answers to this question.

CONNECTION: Social Studies

Although 75 percent of Earth is covered by water, freshwater is considered a limited resource. Most of Earth's water is salt water and is not suitable for drinking, cooking, cleaning, and other uses. Saltwater contains seven times more salt than the human body can tolerate. For centuries, people have tried to find effective ways of removing salt from seawater.

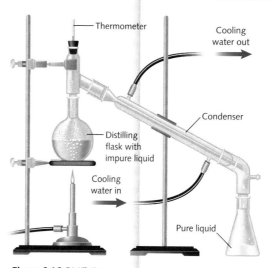

Figure 9.16 Distillation can be repeated for each substance in the solution.

After You Read

1. What is solubility? What factors affect it?
2. Compare unsaturated, saturated, and supersaturated solutions.
3. How does a solute affect the freezing point and boiling point of a solution?
4. Review the answers to the Learning Goal questions you wrote in your Science Notebook. Use your notes to discuss three ways of separating solutions.

Separating Solutions

Most of the rainwater that falls to Earth comes from Earth's oceans. Water evaporates from the oceans. It condenses in the atmosphere and forms clouds. Then it falls back to Earth as precipitation. However, unlike ocean water, rainwater is not salty.

Evaporation When a solvent evaporates from a solution, the solute does not evaporate with it. The evaporated solvent is pure. Evaporation is one way to separate a solvent from a solution. When water evaporates from the salty ocean and rises into the atmosphere as water vapor, the salt stays behind. The water vapor is pure water.

Condensation Condensation is another method for separating the components of a solution. Condensation can be used to separate a solution of gases when one gas has a much lower boiling point than the others. The gas with the lowest boiling point condenses first and can be collected as the solution is cooled.

Distillation Distillation is a third method for separating solutions. Like condensation and evaporation, distillation works when the components of a solution have different boiling points. During distillation, a solution is heated in a special apparatus similar to the one shown in **Figure 9.16.** The component with the lowest boiling point vaporizes first and travels up the column and into the condenser. As the vapor comes in contact with the water-cooled surfaces of the condenser, it becomes a liquid again. The purified liquid is collected in a clean container. When all of the low-boiling-point substance has vaporized, condensed, and been collected, the container can be removed and replaced with a clean one.

Alternative Assessment

In pairs, have students review their answers to the questions they wrote in their Science Notebooks and make any necessary revisions. Have each student choose one answer on which to elaborate in a well-developed paragraph.

Background Information

Crude oil—the thick, black oil that is dug from the ground—is not useful in its natural state. It must be separated into its individual components in a process known as oil refining. Oil refining is distillation. Because the substances in crude oil boil at different temperatures, they can be easily separated into purer fractions that can then be used in a variety of ways.

9.3 Acids, Bases, and Salts

Before You Read

Draw a three-column chart in your Science Notebook for comparing and contrasting acids, bases, and salts. As you complete the lesson, think about the ways in which acids, bases, and salts are alike and different.

You take a bite of a sandwich, chew, and then swallow. The food travels down your esophagus and into your stomach. Within an hour or so, that tasty bite of sandwich is changed into an unappetizing, pasty mixture. This chemical change is accomplished in the stomach with the help of a compound called an acid. An **acid** is a type of compound that releases positively charged hydrogen ions, H^+, when it dissolves in water. The hydrogen ions interact with water molecules to form **hydronium** (hi DROH nee um) **ions**, H_3O^+, as shown in **Figure 9.17.**

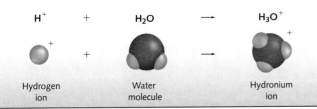

Figure 9.17 Hydrogen ions can combine with water molecules to produce hydronium ions.

Acids

Vinegar, orange juice, lemon juice, batteries, and the body's digestive fluids all contain acids. Acids share some common properties. They tend to taste sour. They are highly reactive and can corrode metals. They can cause a burning or stinging sensation when they touch the skin. They also react with indicators to produce a color change. An **indicator** is a compound that changes color when it is mixed with an acid or a base. Blue litmus paper is an example of an indicator. It turns red in acids.

Because an acid releases positively charged hydrogen ions, H^+, and a positively charged hydrogen ion has only one proton and no electrons or neutrons, an acid is often referred to as a "proton donor." It donates, or gives up, a proton when it dissolves in water.

Figure 9.18 Acids turn blue litmus paper red.

Learning Goals

- Identify the nature and properties of acids and bases.
- Define *pH* and explain how the pH of a solution can be measured.
- Describe a neutralization reaction.

New Vocabulary

acid
hydronium ion
indicator
electrolyte
nonelectrolyte
base
pH
neutral
salt
neutralization reaction

9.3 Introduce

ENGAGE Provide library books or access to Web sites containing information about acids, bases, and salts. Working in small groups, have students read and record new information. Each group should share what it has learned with the class when students have finished researching.

Before You Read

Draw a three-column chart on the board and label the columns *Acids*, *Bases*, and *Salts*. Have students do the same in their Science Notebooks. Ask them to read the first paragraph of the lesson and write the definition of *acid* in the appropriate column. Have a student share his or her definition, and record it on the board in the *Acids* column. Tell students to continue recording facts about acids as they read this lesson.

Teach

EXPLAIN to students that in this section, they will begin to learn about acids.

Vocabulary

acid Tell students that use of the word *acid* is as a noun referring to any sour substance. It can also be used as an adjective meaning "sour" or "tart." Ask for examples of the word used as a noun and as an adjective.

hydronium ion Tell students that the word *hydronium* can be broken down into *hydr-*, meaning "water" or "liquid," and *-onium*, a suffix referring to an ion with a positive charge. Ask students to recall the meaning of *ion* from previous chapters.

indicator Tell students that the word *indicator* is commonly used to refer to an instrument or gauge that shows a measurment such as temperature, fuel level, etc. Ask students for examples, such as indicator lights in cars.

ELL Strategy

Relate to Personal Experience As students read, have them connect the information to experiences that they have had with examples of acids, bases, and salts (i.e., foods that fit into each category or road salt). They may investigate products in their home and create a list of items, classifying them into groups. Encourage them to look at **Figures 9.20** and **9.22** as points of reference, but to look at product labels to expand their search.

Teach

EXPLAIN to students that on this page, they will learn how acids break apart when they dissolve in water and how an acid's strength is related to dissociation.

Figure It Out: Figure 9.19

ANSWER **1.** When hydrogen chloride dissolves in water, a hydronium ion and a chloride ion form. **2.** A hydrogen atom is made up of only one proton and one electron. When it loses its electron and becomes a positively charged ion, it is essentially a proton. An acid dissociates in water to form a positively charged hydrogen ion, or proton, and a negatively charged ion. The hydrogen ion combines with a water molecule to form a hydronium ion. Thus, an acid can be considered a proton donor.

Science Notebook EXTRA

Have students study **Figure 9.20** and then record in their Science Notebooks personal experiences with some or all of the acids listed in the table.

Figure It Out

1. What ions form when hydrogen chloride dissolves in water?

2. Explain why an acid can be thought of as a proton donor.

Figure 9.20 Acids have different strengths. Some acids are weak and safe to drink. Other acids are so strong that they require the use of protective equipment to handle.

Dissolving Unlike most molecular compounds, acids dissociate when they dissolve in water. This means that they break apart and form ions. One of the ions formed is a positively charged hydronium ion. The other is a negatively charged ion. Hydrogen chloride forms hydronium ions (H_3O^+) and chloride ions (Cl^-) in water. Acetic acid forms hydronium ions (H_3O^+) and acetate ions (CH_3COO^-) in water.

The strength of an acid is determined by the degree to which the acid dissociates in solution. An acid is considered strong if nearly all the molecules are converted into ions in water. An acid is considered weak if only a small fraction of the molecules dissociate in water.

Whether strong or weak, all acids are electrolytes. **Electrolytes** (ih LEK truh lytes) are substances that form ions in water and can conduct an electric current. Compounds that do not form ions in water and cannot conduct an electric current are called **nonelectrolytes.** Sugar, gasoline, and most other molecular compounds are nonelectrolytes.

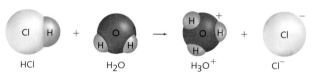

HCl H_2O H_3O^+ Cl^-

Figure 9.19 An acid dissociates in water to produce a positively charged hydronium ion and a negatively charged ion.

Strengths of Different Acids

Strength	Name and Formula	Found in	Uses
Weak	acetic acid, CH_3COOH	vinegar	• flavoring of food • preservation of food
	citric acid, $C_6H_8O_7$	citrus fruits—oranges, lemons, grapefruits, limes	• flavoring of food • preservation of food • environmental cleaning agent
	salicylic acid, $C_7H_6O_3$	aspirin	• pain relief • treatment of acne • treatment of dandruff
Strong	hydrochloric acid, HCl	digestive fluids	• breakdown of food • removal of rust from iron • production of PVC and other plastics • processing of food • oil recovery
	sulfuric acid, H_2SO_4	battery acid, acid rain	• production of many manufactured goods • removal of rust from iron • processing of wastewater • as electrolyte in lead batteries
	nitric acid, HNO_3	fertilizers	• production of fertilizers • production of explosives

---

Background Information

Acid rain is a combination of air pollutants (mostly nitric and sulfuric acids), oxygen, and water in the atmosphere. Car and power plant emissions are its major causes. Acid rain damages lakes, streams, soil, and high-elevation trees.

Key Concept Review
Workbook, p. 53

Bases

Ammonia vapors can be so strong that they can cause a person to tear up or even get a bloody nose. Ammonia is a base. A **base** is a type of compound that produces negatively charged hydroxide ions, OH⁻, when it dissolves in water. Because the hydroxide ions produced by bases can combine with hydrogen ions, bases are often referred to as "proton acceptors." They are able to receive protons. Ammonia water, milk of magnesia, human tears, and most soap products contain bases. Like acids, bases share some common properties. They tend to taste bitter. They are highly reactive and can break down living tissue. They feel slimy or slippery to the touch. They are electrolytes. They produce a color change. Bases turn red litmus paper blue.

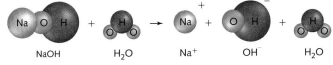

Figure 9.21 A base dissociates in water to produce a negatively charged hydroxide ion and a positively charged ion. When sodium hydroxide dissolves in water, a positively charged sodium ion and a negatively charged hydroxide ion are produced.

Dissolving Like acids, bases dissociate when they dissolve in water. They form negatively charged hydroxide ions and positively charged ions. Sodium hydroxide forms sodium ions (Na^+) and hydroxide ions (OH^-) when it dissolves in water. Ammonia forms ammonium ions (NH_4^+) and hydroxide ions (OH^-) when it dissolves in water.

Bases are considered strong if they dissociate completely when added to a solvent and weak if they dissociate to a limited degree. Strong bases are electrolytes; weak bases are nonelectrolytes.

Strengths of Different Bases

Strength	Name and Formula	Found in	Uses
Weak	ammonia, NH_3	ammonia water	• cleanser and disinfectant • production of nitric acid • fertilizer
Strong	calcium hydroxide, $Ca(OH)_2$	cement, industrial cleaning products	• leather-tanning and hair removal • production of mortar and plaster
	sodium hydroxide, $NaOH$	lye	• drain cleaner • preparation of food • production of soap
	magnesium hydroxide, $Mg(OH)_2$	milk of magnesia	• for relief of indigestion and stomach cramps • as a laxative

Did You Know?

Many natural products are indicators. Beet juice changes from red to purple in very basic solutions. Hydrangeas, which are flowering plants, are blue in acidic soil but pink in basic soil. Some natural indicators can even show how acidic or basic a solution is. Add a strong base to red cabbage juice, for example, and the juice will turn bright yellow. Add a weaker base instead and the juice will turn green.

Figure 9.22 Bases are often used as cleaning agents. According to the information in this table, would it be safe to use sodium hydroxide as a cleanser? Explain your answer.

Teach

EXPLAIN to students that on this page, they will learn about bases.

Vocabulary

electrolyte Explain to students that *electrolyte* can be broken down into *electro-*, which means "electricity," and the Greek word *lytos*, meaning "released."

nonelectrolyte Have students combine the meaning of the prefix *non-*, "not," with the definition of *electrolyte* to come up with a definition for this term.

base Tell students that as used in chemistry, the word *base* refers to any compound that produces negatively charged hydroxide ions, OH⁻, when it dissolves in water.

Use the Visual: Figure 9.22

ANSWER No, it would not be safe to use sodium hydroxide as a cleanser. Sodium hydroxide, or lye, is a strong acid, which means it is highly reactive and can cause damage to human tissue.

Science Notebook EXTRA

Have students study **Figure 9.22** and then record in their Science Notebooks personal experiences with some or all of the bases listed in the table.

Background Information

Many household cleaners contain toxic ingredients that can harm plants, animals, and people. Natural cleaners, such as baking soda, lemon juice, cornstarch, vinegar, and isopropyl alcohol, are safer, effective alternatives. There are also many natural, environmentally friendly products available in stores today.

Interpreting Diagrams
Workbook, p. 55

Teach

EXPLAIN to students that on this page, they will learn about pH, a measurement used to determine how acidic or basic a solution is.

Vocabulary

pH Tell students that this term is German, and comes from *potenz*, meaning "power," and *H*, the symbol for hydrogen. Ask students to relate these meanings to the definition of the term.

neutral Tell students that one common use of *neutral* refers to not taking sides in a quarrel or war. Ask students to explain how this meaning relates to the chemical definition.

salt Explain to students that salt is commonly thought of as sodium chloride, a chemical used to season and preserve food. Point out, however, that the scientific use of the word refers to an ionic compound formed from the negative ions of an acid and the positive ions of a base. A salt need not contain either the sodium ion or the chloride ion.

neutralization reaction Tell students that the word *neutralization* can be broken down into the verb *neutralize*, which refers to canceling out the effect of something or to making it useless, and the suffix *-ation*. Ask students to combine the word parts and the meaning of *reaction* to come up with a definition for the term *neutralization reaction*.

As You Read

Give students time to record information about acids and bases in their charts. Then have partners share information with one another and revise, change, or add information as necessary.

(ANSWER) A neutral solution is a solution that is neither acidic nor basic. It has an equal number of hydronium and hydroxide ions. It has a pH of 7.

Use the Visual: Figure 9.23

(ANSWER) Drain cleaner is more basic than milk of magnesia.

As You Read

Use the chart in your Science Notebook to record information about the pH of solutions of acids and bases. Include an explanation of how the strength of an acid or a base affects its pH.

What is a neutral solution?

---

pH of a Solution

Acids and bases vary in strength. So, too, do solutions containing acids and bases. Some might have a high concentration of hydronium ions and thus be very acidic. Others might have only a small concentration of hydronium ions and thus be much less acidic.

To determine how acidic or basic a solution is, scientists use a measurement called pH. The **pH** of a solution is a measure of the concentration of hydronium ions in the solution. The greater the hydronium ion concentration, the more acidic the solution is and the lower the pH. The lower the hydronium ion concentration, the more basic the solution is and the higher the pH. To indicate pH, a pH scale is used.

A pH scale ranges from 0 to 14. If a solution has a pH lower than 7, it is considered acidic. If a solution has a pH higher than 7, it is considered basic. If a solution has a pH of exactly 7, it is considered neutral. **Neutral** means the solution is neither acidic nor basic. It has an equal number of hydronium and hydroxide ions. Pure water is neutral.

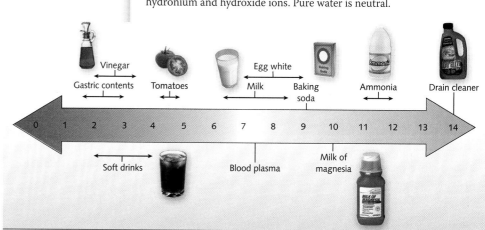

Figure 9.23 The lower the pH of a solution, the more acidic the solution is. The higher the pH of a solution, the more basic the solution is. Which is more basic, milk of magnesia or drain cleaner?

Determining pH The pH of a solution can be determined by using an indicator called pH paper. A strip of pH paper changes color according to the exact pH of a solution. By dipping the paper into a solution and then matching its color to a key, the pH of the solution can be determined.

Another way to determine the pH of a solution is with a pH meter. A pH meter is an electronic device that can measure the hydronium ion concentration of a solution.

Figure 9.24 A piece of pH paper can be used to measure the acidity of soil or water, which helps people determine if these substances are safe for living things.

Background Information

A neutralization reaction is a double-displacement reaction. The negative ion in the acid combines with the positive ion in the base to form a salt. The hydrogen ion in the acid combines with the hydroxide ion in the base to form water. If necessary, review with students this type of chemical reaction, which is covered in Chapter 8.

Teacher Alert

Explain to students that the words *acidic* and *basic* are the adjective forms of the nouns *acid* and *base*. Share other examples of nouns and adjective forms, such as *citrus* and *citric*, *sulfur* and *sulfuric*, and *nitrogen* and *nitric*.

CONNECTION: Biology

All higher life forms require a balance of electrolytes to survive. The major electrolytes for humans are sodium (Na^+), potassium (K^+), calcium (Ca^{2+}), and bicarbonate (HCO_3^-). Sodium, potassium, and calcium enable the brain and other organs to communicate with one another. They regulate the transmission of electrical signals from the brain to the body's muscles and vice versa. They are also involved in maintaining the body's

heart rate. Bicarbonate helps control the amount of acid in the body.

Electrolytes can be obtained from grains, fruits, vegetables, dairy products, and meats, as well as from some sports drinks. Because the body loses electrolytes in sweat, athletes often use sports drinks to replenish their supply. A person can experience muscle weakness, irregular heartbeats, or seizures if the body's electrolytes are not in proper balance.

Acid-Base Reactions

Acids and bases can also react with each other. When an acid is added to a base in solution, the hydroxide ions and hydrogen ions combine to form molecules of water. The other ions combine to form a salt. A **salt** is an ionic compound formed from the negative ions of an acid and the positive ions of a base.

The reaction of an acid with a base is called a **neutralization** (new truh luh ZAY shun) **reaction.** This is because the products formed are neutral—they are neither acids nor bases. The general formula for an acid-base reaction is

acid + base → salt + water

Here is an example.

HCl (aq) + NaOH → NaCl (aq) + H$_2$O (l)

Although people often think only of table salt when they hear the term *salt,* there are hundreds of different salts. A salt is usually made from a positively charged metal ion and a negatively charged monatomic ion such as Cl^- or Br^-, or a polyatomic ion such as NO_3^- or HCO_3^-.

Figure 9.25 A salt forms when an acid reacts with a base.

After You Read

1. Review the information you recorded in your Science Notebook chart. Then write a well-developed paragraph comparing acids and bases.
2. What determines the strength of an acid or a base? How is that related to whether the acid or base is an electrolyte or a nonelectrolyte?
3. What is the pH of a solution? Describe the pH scale and how it is used.
4. What is a neutralization reaction?

● Teach

EXPLAIN to students that in this section, they will learn about electrolytes and salts.

CONNECTION: Biology

Infants, children, and the elderly are especially susceptible to low electrolyte levels because they have less body water than adults do. Vomiting, diarrhea, fever, and insufficient fluid intake are likely causes.

EXTEND Have students research and list specific foods and drinks that are high in electrolytes.

● Assess

Use the After You Read questions and the Alternative Assessment to help you evaluate students' understanding of the lesson.

After You Read

1. Acid: produces hydrogen ions when it dissolves in water, tends to taste sour, is highly reactive, can corrode metals, can cause a burning or stinging sensation when it touches the skin, turns blue litmus paper red.
   Base: produces hydroxide ions when it dissolves in water, tastes bitter, is highly reactive and can break down living tissue, feels slippery to the touch, is an electrolyte, turns red litmus paper blue.
2. The strength of an acid or a base is determined by the degree to which it dissociates in water. Strong acids and bases dissociate (ionize) to a great degree, so they are electrolytes. Weak acids and bases do not dissociate to a great degree, so there are fewer ions in solution and an electric current cannot be conducted.
3. The pH of a solution is a measure of the concentration of hydronium ions in the solution. The pH of a solution describes how acidic or basic the solution is. The pH scale is a scale ranging from 0 to 14. The greater the hydronium ion concentration, the more acidic the solution is and the lower the pH.
4. A neutralization reaction is a chemical reaction between an acid and a base. The products are salt and water.

Differentiate Instruction

Kinesthetic and Visual Divide students into small groups and provide each with several acidic and basic materials, such as different amounts of water and ammonia, cleaning products, milk of magnesia, orange juice, vinegar, and water. Have students dip pH paper into each solution to determine the pH. Each group should record the results in a chart to share with the class.

Alternative Assessment

Give students time to complete their three-column charts. Have them share the information they recorded with the class, and make note of responses on the board. Then allow students to add to or revise their individual charts.

Chapter Summary

MASTERING CONCEPTS

True or False

1. False, hydronium, hydroxide
2. False, polar
3. False, solvent
4. False, salt
5. True
6. False, base

Short Answer

7. Solubility is the maximum amount of a solute that can dissolve in a given amount of a solvent under certain conditions.

8. The amount of solute that is dissolved in a solvent can be described in terms of concentration and solubility. A solution can be dilute or concentrated. It can also be saturated, unsaturated, or supersaturated.

9. Type of solvent, stirring, surface area, and temperature can affect the dissolving rate of a solute.

10. The particles of the solute interfere with the freezing process (formation of ice crystals). The boiling point of most solutions is higher than the boiling point of the pure solvent. The particles of the solute interfere with the evaporation of the solvent's particles.

11. The pH of a solution describes how acidic or basic a solution is. Indicators such as pH paper or instruments such as a pH meter are used to measure pH.

Chapter **9**

Summary

KEY CONCEPTS

9.1 How Solutions Form

- A solution is a homogeneous mixture that can be described by its solute and solvent.
- The solute is the substance that dissolves. The solvent is the substance that dissolves the solute. The solvent makes up the larger amount of the solution.
- Many substances can dissolve in water because water is a polar molecule. Water is often called the universal solvent.
- Dissociation is the process in which an ionic compound separates into its positive and negative ions when dissolved.
- Factors that affect the rate of dissolving are the type of solvent, stirring, surface area, and temperature.

9.2 Solubility

- Solubility describes the amount of a solute that can dissolve in a quantity of solvent under certain conditions. Using solubility, solutions can be described as unsaturated, saturated, or supersaturated.
- The solubility of liquids and solids tends to increase as temperature increases, while the solubility of gases tends to decrease as temperature increases.
- Increasing pressure causes the solubility of gases in liquid solvents to increase. Decreasing pressure causes the solubility of gases in liquid solvents to decrease.
- Concentration describes the amount of solute that is dissolved in a given quantity of solvent.
- The freezing point of a solution is lower than the freezing point of the pure solvent. The boiling point of a solution tends to be higher than the boiling point of the pure solvent.
- Solutions can be separated by evaporation, condensation, and distillation.

9.3 Acids, Bases, and Salts

- An acid is a substance that produces hydronium ions when it dissolves in water. Acids taste sour, can corrode metals, cause a burning or stinging sensation when they touch the skin, and turn blue litmus paper red.
- A base is a substance that produces hydroxide ions when it dissolves in water. Bases taste bitter, can break down living tissue, feel slimy or slippery to the touch, and turn red litmus paper blue.
- A solution's pH describes how acidic or basic the solution is.
- The reaction that takes place between an acid and a base is called a neutralization reaction. When acids and bases react, they produce water and a salt.

VOCABULARY REVIEW

Write each term in a complete sentence or write a paragraph relating several terms.

9.1
solution, p. 145
solute, p. 146
solvent, p. 146
aqueous solution, p. 146
polar, p. 147
dissociation, p. 147

9.2
insoluble, p. 150
soluble, p. 150
solubility, p. 150
solubility curve, p. 151
concentration, p. 152
saturated, p. 152
unsaturated, p. 152
supersaturated, p. 152
freezing-point depression, p. 153
boiling-point elevation, p. 153

9.3
acid, p. 155
hydronium ion, p. 155
indicator, p. 155
electrolyte, p.156
nonelectrolyte, p. 156
base, p. 157
pH, p. 158
neutral, p. 158
salt, p. 159
neutralization reaction, p. 159

PREPARE FOR CHAPTER TEST

To prepare for the chapter test, create a question from each Learning Goal. Use the information in your Science Notebook to answer each question. Then use these answers to write a well-developed essay about the chapter. Use the Key Concept on the first page of this chapter as your topic sentence.

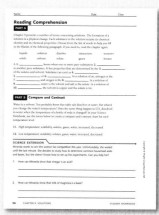

Vocabulary Review
Workbook, p. 54

Reading Comprehension
Workbook, p. 56

True or False

If the statement is true, write "true." If it is false, change the underlined word or words to make the statement true.

1. In solution, an acid produces <u>hydroxide ions</u> and a base produces <u>hydronium ions</u>.

2. Water is the universal solvent in part because it is a(n) <u>nonpolar</u> molecule.

3. A(n) <u>solute</u> is the substance present in the greater amount in a solution.

4. Sodium chloride is an example of a(n) <u>base</u>.

5. A solubility curve shows how the solubility of a substance in a solvent changes with <u>temperature</u>.

6. The pH of a strong <u>acid</u> would be close to 14.

Short Answer

Answer each of the following in a sentence or brief paragraph.

7. What is solubility?

8. In what two ways can the amount of solute that is dissolved in a solvent be described?

9. What factors can affect the dissolving rate of a solute?

10. How does the addition of solute particles affect the freezing point and boiling point of a solution?

11. What is the pH of a solution? How is it measured?

Critical Thinking

Use what you have learned in this chapter to answer each of the following.

12. **Explain** How can a solution become supersaturated? Why are supersaturated solutions unstable?

13. **Apply Concepts** A medical condition known as decompression sickness, or "the bends," sometimes occurs in deep-sea divers as they rise toward the surface quickly. It is caused by nitrogen gas gushing out of the diver's organs in a manner similar to the way gas gushes out of a soda can that has been shaken. Based on what you know about solubility, explain why this condition might occur.

14. **Predict** Is it possible to have a concentrated weak acid? Explain your answer.

Standardized Test Question

Choose the letter of the response that correctly answers the question.

15. Which of the following statements is not true of a neutralization reaction?

   A. An acid and a base are the reactants.

   B. A salt and water are the products.

   C. The pH of the resulting solution is 12.

   D. The salt is an ionic compound formed from the negative ions of an acid and the positive ions of a base.

Test-Taking Tip

Remember that terms such as *most likely* and *not* may change the meaning of a question. Be sure to read the question carefully before examining all the answer choices.

Critical Thinking

12. A solution can become supersaturated if it is saturated at a high temperature and then cooled very slowly. Supersaturated solutions are unstable because they contain more dissolved solute than a saturated solution does under the same conditions.

13. The solubility of a gas generally increases as pressure increases and decreases as pressure decreases. As a diver descends in the water, the pressure acting on his or her body increases as a result of the weight of the water above. With this increased pressure, the solubility of nitrogen gas increases. More nitrogen inhaled from the diver's gas tank dissolves in the diver's organs. The body cannot use nitrogen in the way that it uses oxygen, so this nitrogen builds up in the organs. As the diver ascends to the surface of the water, the pressure on the diver's body decreases and the solubility of nitrogen decreases. The dissolved nitrogen in the diver's body becomes less soluble.

14. Yes, because the acid dissolves well but ionizes poorly.

Standardized Test Question

15. C

Reading Links

Acid Rain (Earth at Risk)

Presenting a strong, scientifically sound, and uncontroversial examination of the causes, effects, and potential solutions associated with acid rain, this book connects the chapter's lessons in chemistry to important environmental concerns in terms that struggling readers can understand.

Peter Tyson. Facts on File, Inc. (Chelsea House). 128 pp. Illustrated. Library ISBN 978-0-7910-1577-3.

Chemistry Science Fair Projects: Using Acids, Bases, Metals, Salts, and Inorganic Stuff

Students seeking inspiration for projects will find this book clear, informative, and helpful. The experiments emphasize the scientific method while underscoring topics students have studied and encouraging creative investigation.

Robert Gardner. Enslow Publishers, Inc. 128 pp. Illustrated. Library ISBN 978-0-7660-2210-2.

Curriculum Connection
Workbook, p. 57

Science Challenge
Workbook, p. 58

9A A Stirring Experiment

This prechapter introduction activity is designed to determine what students already know about solutions by engaging them in experimenting, observing, and drawing conclusions about several factors affecting the rate at which a substance dissolves in water.

Objectives

* observe solution formation
* compare rates of solution formation
* draw conclusions about factors affecting dissolving rates

Planning

🕐 20–30 minutes   👤👤👤 groups of 3–4 students

Materials (per group)

* 2 beakers
* samples of confectioners' sugar and granulated sugar
* decanters of ice water and hot water
* plastic spoon

Advance Preparation

* Use insulated decanter thermoses to hold the ice water and hot water. The hot water should be hot, but not boiling; do not use water hot enough to cause burns. Clearly label each decanter thermos as *ice water* and *hot water*.

* Confectioners' sugar and granulated sugar are available at grocery stores. If rock sugar cannot be found, any sugar product having crystals larger than granulated will do.

Engagement Guide

* Challenge students to think about rates of dissolving by asking:
  * *How is the temperature of water related to the energy of its particles?* (The higher the temperature of the water, the higher the average kinetic energy of the water molecules.)
  * *How might the energy of the water molecules affect the number of interactions the water molecules have with the solid that is to be dissolved?* (More interactions per unit of time will occur with higher temperature water.)
  * *What other factors might affect the number of interactions between water molecules and solid particles that occur per unit of time?* (Students should realize that stirring the mixture increases interactions, as does decreasing the size of the substance to be dissolved.)
* Encourage students to compare and contrast physical and chemical changes.

Going Further

Ask groups to design an experiment to investigate the maximum amount of sugar (measured by mass) that can dissolve in hot and cold water.

9B Acid, Bases, and pH

Objectives

* develop a useable pH scale
* observe properties of acids and bases
* apply the pH scale to identify unknown substances
* draw conclusions

Skill Set

observing, comparing and contrasting, recording and analyzing data, illustrating, stating conclusions

Planning

 45–60 minutes   groups of 3–4 students

Materials

Materials for this activity are listed in the Student Laboratory Manual.

Advance Preparation

* If you do not have access to 96-well reaction plates, you can use a sheet of paper inserted into a heavy-duty plastic sheet protector. Have students draw 36 equal-sized circular spaces on the sheet of paper before slipping it into the sheet protector. Students can then use the circular test areas as needed in the activity. Sheets should be flat during use.

* To simplify lab preparation and cleanup, place all of the solutions in beakers at one location in the room. Make sure each beaker is clearly labeled and contains its own dropper pipette. This cannot be done if students are using plastic sheet protector reaction surfaces.

* Prepare the needed solutions beforehand. Make all solutions with distilled water (instead of tap water) to avoid pH changes. Any of the available antibacterial soap products should work fine. Steep the green tea in hot water and allow it to cool. Red cabbage juice can be made by juicing or pureeing red (purple) cabbage. Use a coffee filter to drain the cabbage pieces from the juice. Dissolve a piece of bar soap in water to form its solution. Stir baking soda into water to make its solution. Some of the "solutions" will

settle out and will need to be stirred before they are used. Dilute the ammonia by half with water.

- The mystery substances should be an acid and a base of your choosing, perhaps food samples that are pureed so they are unrecognizable to students. Make sure the mystery substances are clearly acidic and clearly basic.

Answers to Observations: Data Table 1

1. lemon juice: dark red; red; red (acid); 2
2. vinegar: red; red; red (acid); 3
3. soda water: light red; red; red (acid); 4
4. red cabbage juice: light red; light red; no change (approximately neutral); 6.5
5. baking soda: light blue; blue (base); blue; 8.5
6. bar soap: blue; blue (base); blue; 10
7. ammonia: dark blue; blue (base); blue; 11
8. green tea: light red; red; red (acid); 5
9. antibacterial soap: blue; blue (base); blue; 9
10. apple juice: light red; red; red (acid); 6
11. solution A: answers will vary depending on substance used
12. solution B: answers will vary depending on substance used

Answers to Analysis and Conclusions

1. The red cabbage juice and red and blue litmus paper were indicators. An indicator tells where a substance falls in the pH range whether neutral, acidic, or basic.
2. red litmus tests for bases, blue litmus tests for acids, cabbage juice can test for acids and bases (red, purple, violet are acids: blue, blue green and greenish yellow are bases)
3. As acidity increases, H^+ ion concentration increases, and pH decreases.
4. As basicity increases, OH^- ion concentration increases, and pH increases.
5. Answers will vary depending on the unknowns used.

Going Further

There are many applications for pH indicators in consumer products, business, and industry. Have each group research one of these applications and prepare a written report of their findings.

9C Solubility of Gases

Objectives

- observe affects of pressure and temperature on gas solubility
- draw conclusions

Skill Set

observing, recording and analyzing data, drawing conclusions

Planning

 30 minutes   groups of 3–4 students

Materials

Materials for this activity are listed in the Student Laboratory Manual.

Advance Preparation

- Heat and store the water in a thermos or coffee pot.
- The vacuum stopper and pump can be found at many grocery stores and wine specialty stores. This portion of the lab is probably best set up as a station so student groups can pass through one at a time. It could also be performed as a demo if desired.

Answers to Observations:

Unopened soda bottle: contents are clear; no bubbles visible

Opened soda bottle: Bubbles come out of solution and move to the surface of the soda water.

After pumping: Additional bubbles form and move to the surface of the soda.

Answers to Observations: Data Table 1

Control cup: After soda rests in cup, some bubbles cling to side and some move to surface. Least amount of bubbling in comparison to other cups.

Stirred cup: After soda rests in cup, some bubbles cling to side and some move to surface. When stirred, additional bubbles come out of solution and to the surface. More bubbling than control cup.

Heated cup: As the cup is heated, additional bubbles form and move to the surface. More bubbling than control cup.

Answers to Analysis and Conclusions

1. The contents of the bottle are under pressure; opening the bottle decreases the pressure in the air about the soda water.
2. Heating the soda water and stirring the soda water both caused more bubbles to form.
3. Increased temperature and decreased pressure decrease the solubility of gases in a liquid.

Going Further

Have student groups research the dangerous diving complication known as "the bends." Students should prepare a small poster that describes the condition, what causes it, and how it is treated. Posters can be displayed around the classroom.

Introduce Chapter 10

As a starting activity, use Lab 10A on page 55 of the Laboratory Manual.

ENGAGE Have students read the first two paragraphs aloud to each other in small groups and then look at the photograph below. Have group members discuss the similarities and differences in the items and note their common factor: carbon.

Think About Carbon

ENGAGE Have students use the periodic table on pages 94–95 of Chapter 6 to answer the questions. Review the concepts of chemical symbols, atomic number, and atomic mass. Students should be able to identify carbon's symbol as C, its atomic number as 6, and its mass as 12.011. They should know that the electron arrangement is 2, 4. Thus, carbon has four valence electrons, which makes covalent bonding the predominant type.

Some students may recognize that each carbon atom can form four covalent bonds with atoms of carbon or with atoms of other elements, thus producing the large number of carbon compounds. Some students may also know that the covalent bonds carbon forms can be single, double, or triple— another reason why there are so many carbon compounds.

Chapter 10

Carbon Chemistry

KEY CONCEPT Carbon compounds, which exist in many forms and have many uses, are the largest group of compounds.

Carbon compounds are the most abundant and useful substances on Earth. They are the building blocks of all living things. Almost everything in the picture—the flowers, the plastic pots, and even the greenhouse—is made from carbon compounds. Gasoline, plastic wrap, and many other items you use every day contain carbon compounds.

Carbon compounds can be solids, liquids, or gases at room temperature. They can be brittle, flexible, or soft. They can be natural or artificial. In this chapter, you will learn about the properties, types, and uses of carbon compounds.

Think About Carbon

Think about the element carbon and its characteristics.

- Find carbon on the periodic table. In your Science Notebook, record carbon's chemical symbol, atomic number, and atomic mass.

- Predict the bonding properties of carbon. How many valence electrons does it have? What kinds of bonds do you think it forms? Record your predictions and hypothesize about why carbon can form so many compounds.

NSTA

SCI**LINKS**.
THE WORLD'S A CLICK AWAY

www.scilinks.org
Carbon Compounds **Code: WGPS10**

162

Chapter 10 Planning Guide			
Instructional Periods	**National Standards**	**Lab Manual**	**Workbook**
10.1 2 Periods	A2, B1, G1, G2; A2, B2, G1, G2; UCP1, UCP2	**Lab 10A: p. 55** Chemical Indicators	Key Concept Review p. 59 Vocabulary Review p. 60
10.2 2 Periods	A1, B1, E1, E2, F5, G1, G2, G3; B2, B3, E1, E2, F6, G1, G2, G3; UCP3, UCP5	**Lab 10B: pp. 56–57** Testing Starches **Lab 10C: pp. 58–60** Carbohydrates	Graphic Organizer p. 61 Reading Comprehension p. 62 Curriculum Connection p. 63 Science Challenge pp. 64–65
10.3 2 Periods	B1, F1; B2, B3, C2, F1; UCP1, UCP4, UCP5		

Middle School Standard; High School Standard; Unifying Concept and Principle

10.1 Nature of Carbon Compounds

Before You Read

Create a lesson outline in your Science Notebook using the title, headings, and subheadings of this lesson. Use the outline to formulate questions that you can answer as you read this lesson.

All living things are composed of chemical compounds. Chemical compounds form the cells of living things. This includes all the cell structures and DNA, the "blueprint" for life. They allow organisms to sense their environments and respond to stimuli.

Although unique in size and arrangement, many of the compounds in a living thing contain the element carbon. Carbon is often thought of as the "element of life." It forms a huge group of compounds known as organic compounds.

Organic Compounds

Of the millions of compounds in the world, the vast majority—more than 90 percent—are classified as organic compounds. **Organic compounds** are compounds that contain the element carbon. Rubbing alcohol, sugar, and vitamin C are organic compounds. Each of these substances contains one or more carbon atoms.

The term **inorganic compound** is applied to any compound that is not an organic compound. Compounds that contain metals or metalloids are generally considered inorganic. A few compounds containing carbon atoms are also considered inorganic. Carbon dioxide and carbon monoxide are two examples. While there are millions of known organic compounds, there are little more than 100,000 known inorganic compounds. Among these are Earth's minerals and salts.

The study of organic compounds is a special branch of chemistry called **organic chemistry.** Organic chemistry deals with the structure, properties, reactions, and synthesis of organic compounds.

Sugar
$C_{12}H_{22}O_{12}$

Rubbing alcohol
C_3H_8O

Vitamin C
$C_6H_8O_6$

Learning Goals

- Distinguish between organic and inorganic compounds.
- Explain why carbon is able to form different compounds.
- Recognize the properties of organic compounds and some common functional groups of organic compounds.

New Vocabulary

organic compound
inorganic compound
organic chemistry
structural formula
space-filling model
isomer
hydrocarbon
substituted hydrocarbon
functional group

Recall Vocabulary

valence electron, p. 114
nonelectrolyte, p. 156

Figure 10.1 Compare the chemical formulas for the organic compounds shown here. What property of organic compounds is apparent from these formulas?

CHAPTER 10 **163**

10.1 Introduce

ENGAGE Have students work in small groups to research examples of organic and inorganic items. Each group should create a list of each type and explain what the categories mean.

Vocabulary terms are listed on the first student page of each lesson. You may wish to preview the terms before introducing each lesson. Strategies for teaching the vocabulary appear on the pages where the terms are introduced.

Before You Read

Create an outline of this lesson on the board with students' input. Have them brainstorm a few questions that they have about the lesson content and record responses on the board underneath the outline.

Teach

EXPLAIN to students that in this lesson, they will learn about carbon compounds.

Vocabulary

organic compound Tell students that the meaning of the word *organic* is "from life." Scientists in the nineteenth century used the term to describe compounds produced by living things. Ask for examples of organic items. Explain that the common meaning of the word *compound* is "something made up of two or more parts." Have students provide the definition they learned for this word ("a substance in which the atoms of two or more elements combine").

inorganic compound Tell students that the prefix *-in* means "not" or "lacking." Have them combine the prefix with the definition of the term *organic compound* to derive a definition.

organic chemistry Ask students to use the meanings of the words *organic* and *chemistry* (the study of the composition, properties, and reactions of chemical elements and their compounds) to form the meaning of the term *organic chemistry.*

Use the Visual: **Figure 10.1**

ANSWER All organic compounds contain carbon.

Teach

EXPLAIN to students that on this page, they will learn about carbon's valence electrons and its ability to form covalent bonds.

 Vocabulary

structural formula Tell students that the word *structural* comes from the noun *structure,* which comes from the Latin word *structura,* meaning "to build." The suffix *-al* makes the word an adjective and means "of, relating to, or characterized by." Ask students to remember what a formula is in chemistry (a combination of chemical symbols that represents the chemical composition of a particular substance).

space-filling model Tell students that the word *space-filling* in this term is an adjective describing the word *model.* The common meaning of *space* is "a limited extent of distance, area, and/or volume." *Filling* is the act of putting as much as can be held into something. Explain to students that a model is a small-scale representation of something. Ask for examples (cars, planes, houses).

isomer Tell students that the prefix *iso-* means "same," and *-mer* comes from the Greek word *meros,* meaning "part." Have students relate these word meanings to the definition of the term.

As You Read

Review with students the way important information should be recorded in an outline. Discuss with students the difference between the main idea and supporting details, and explain how an outline enables them to record both. Have students give examples of each from this lesson.

[ANSWER] An organic compound is a compound that contains carbon atoms.

Figure 10.2 With its four valence electrons, each carbon atom can form four covalent bonds with other atoms.

As You Read

Use your lesson outline to record important information as you read. With a partner, write a summary of the information you have recorded in your Science Notebook.

What is an organic compound?

Did You Know?

The term *organic* was originally used by scientists to describe compounds produced by living things. *Organic* means "from life." Organic compounds were thought to be produced only by living things. Over time, scientists discovered that organic compounds contained the element carbon and could be synthesized from compounds obtained from nonliving things.

Bonding of Carbon

Carbon can form more compounds than any other element because of the structure of a carbon atom. Each carbon atom has four valence electrons in its outermost energy level, as the electron-dot diagram in **Figure 10.2** illustrates. Valence electrons are the electrons involved in bonding. Carbon's four valence electrons determine many of the element's chemical properties.

Like most other atoms, carbon atoms need eight valence electrons for maximum stability. This means that each carbon atom needs four more valence electrons. Carbon atoms obtain these electrons by forming covalent bonds with other atoms. A covalent bond is a bond in which two atoms share a pair of electrons. Each carbon atom can form four covalent bonds with atoms of carbon or with atoms of other elements.

This large number of bonds that each carbon atom can form is one reason why so many carbon compounds exist. These compounds range from small compounds used as fuel to large, complex compounds found in dyes, medicines, and plastics.

Another reason why so many carbon compounds exist is that carbon atoms can form single, double, or triple covalent bonds with other carbon atoms. Carbon atoms can also link together in straight chains, branched chains, and rings. **Figure 10.3** shows examples of these arrangements.

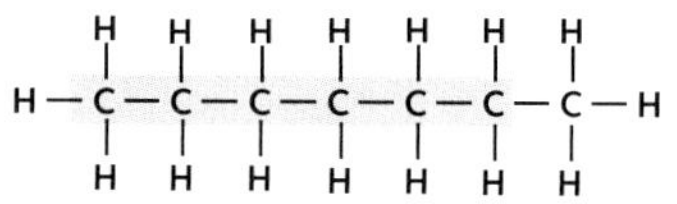

Heptane is found in gasoline.

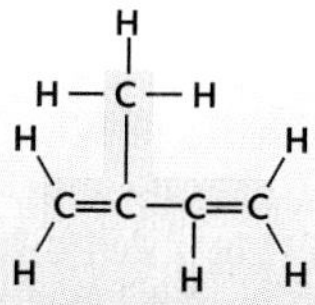

Isoprene exists in natural rubber.

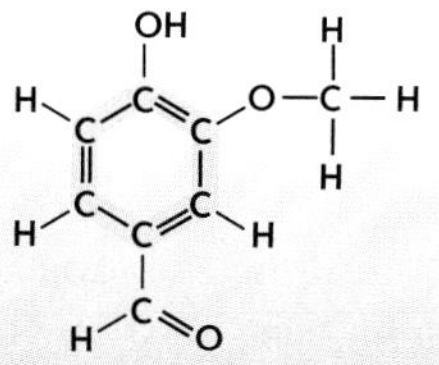

Vanillin is found in vanilla flavoring.

Figure 10.3 Carbon atoms form covalent bonds with other carbon atoms in straight chains, branched chains, and rings.

In addition to forming bonds with one another, carbon atoms often form single covalent bonds with hydrogen atoms. Carbon atoms can also form covalent bonds with atoms of elements located near carbon on the periodic table. These elements include oxygen, nitrogen, sulfur, and the halogens.

Differentiate Instruction

Visual, Kinesthetic Have students use the information and visuals relating to the different ways in which carbon bonds to make models of the structures of straight-chain, branched, and ring compounds. Provide ball-and-stick kits, if available, or common materials such as pipe cleaners, plastic foam balls, and markers.

Representing Organic Compounds Scientists often represent organic compounds with structural formulas rather than with chemical formulas alone. **Structural formulas** show the arrangement, number, and types of atoms in a compound. Structural formulas for butane and isobutane are shown in **Figure 10.4.** Each line between atoms represents a single covalent bond.

Organic compounds can also be shown with space-filling models. **Space-filling models** show the geometry of a compound. They show how the atoms are arranged in space.

As you can see from the structural formulas, both butane and isobutane have the same formula (C_4H_{10}). However, the arrangement of the four carbon atoms is different. In a molecule of butane, the carbon atoms form a straight chain. In a molecule of isobutane, the atoms form a branched chain. The arrangement of carbon atoms in each compound changes the shape of the molecule and can affect the compound's physical properties. Compounds that have the same chemical formula but different molecular structures and shapes are **isomers** (I suh murz).

Properties of Organic Compounds Because the covalent bonds between carbon atoms are particularly stable and nonpolar, organic compounds tend to be less reactive and less soluble in water than inorganic compounds are. They also tend to be nonelectrolytes.

Most organic compounds have melting and boiling points below 300°C. Some organic compounds form solid crystals.

Figure It Out

1. Compare the structural formula and the space-filling model for butane. What does each show?
2. Explain why butane and isobutane are isomers.

Butane
C_4H_{10}

Isobutane
C_4H_{10}

Figure 10.4 Structural formulas and space-filling models help scientists describe and study organic compounds. In the space-filling models, carbon atoms are gray and hydrogen atoms are blue.

PEOPLE IN SCIENCE Percy Julian (1899–1975)

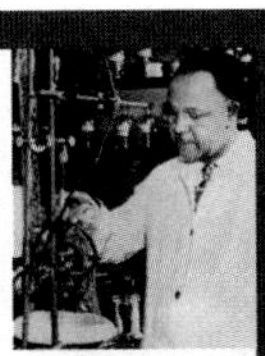

Percy Lavon Julian was born in Birmingham, Alabama, and grew up during a time when African Americans experienced discrimination throughout the United States. Because public education beyond eighth grade was not offered to blacks in Birmingham at that time, Julian received his high school diploma from the State Normal School for Negroes in Montgomery, Alabama.

Despite the prejudice that he faced, Julian graduated at the top of his DePauw University class in 1920. He completed a master's degree at Harvard University and then obtained a PhD in organic chemistry from the University of Vienna in 1931.

Upon his return to the United States, Julian worked on synthesizing organic compounds derived from living things. He is probably best known for his work in developing synthetic cortisone.

Julian's other accomplishments include the synthesis of an organic compound used to treat glaucoma, the development of a compound used by the military in World War II to put out oil and gasoline fires, and the production of compounds used in making water-based paints and coating paper.

Teach

EXPLAIN to students that they will learn about two ways scientists represent organic compounds: by using structural formulas and space-filling models.

Figure It Out: Figure 10.4

ANSWER **1.** The structural formula of butane shows all the atoms that make up a butane molecule as well as their general arrangement. The space-filling model shows the shape of a butane molecule. **2.** Butane and isobutane have the same chemical formula but different molecular structures. Butane is a straight-chain molecule; isobutane is a branched-chain molecule.

PEOPLE IN SCIENCE

Percy Julian was the second African American to become a member of the National Academy of Sciences. He also received 18 honorary degrees. He was an active civil-rights advocate, mentoring many young black chemists, giving civil rights speeches, and leading a national fundraising campaign for the NAACP Legal Defense and Education Fund.

EXTEND Have students visit educational Web sites to find more information about Percy Julian. The Public Broadcasting Service aired a NOVA episode about Julian entitled "Forgotten Genius" that students might find helpful and informative. Excerpts from the video are available on the PBS Web site.

Background Information

There are three types of isomers. Structural isomers differ in the arrangement of the atoms' covalent bonds. Geometric isomers share the same covalent partners, but differ in spatial arrangements. Enantiomers are mirror images of each other.

CHAPTER 10 165

Teach

 EXPLAIN to students that they will learn about hydrocarbons and substituted hydrocarbons in this section.

Vocabulary

hydrocarbon Tell students that in this word, *hydro-* refers to hydrogen. Ask students to use this meaning to develop a definition of the word *hydrocarbon.*

substituted hydrocarbon Tell students that *substituted* means "put or used in the place of another." Have them combine this definition with the meaning of the word *hydrocarbon* to form a new definition.

functional group Explain that *functional* is an adjective meaning "in working order" or "operational." Ask students what a group is (a number of people or things gathered or placed together).

Extend It!

Provide reference materials from the library and a list of useful Web sites to help students learn more about substituted hydrocarbons.

Have students work in pairs. Encourage them to choose different substituted hydrocarbons so that every hydrocarbon listed is researched by at least one pair. Invite students to share their findings as oral presentations.

Assess

Use the After You Read questions and the Alternative Assessment to help you evaluate students' understanding of the lesson.

After You Read

1. Organic compounds are most compounds that contain carbon. Hydrocarbons and alcohols are two examples.

2. Carbon is able to form many different compounds because each carbon atom has four valence electrons in its outermost energy level and can form four covalent bonds with other atoms.

3. Isomers are compounds that have the same chemical formula but different molecular structures and shapes.

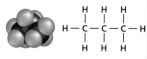

Propane
C_3H_8

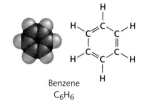

Benzene
C_6H_6

Figure 10.5 Propane and benzene are hydrocarbons because they contain only hydrogen and carbon atoms.

Extend It!

A chlorofluorocarbon (CFC) is a specific kind of substituted hydrocarbon. Working with a partner, research CFCs. Prepare a report about the general properties and uses of them and share your findings with the class.

Groups of Carbon Compounds

Although there are millions of organic compounds, most can be classified into a few large groups, some of which are discussed here.

Hydrocarbons The simplest organic compounds are called hydrocarbons. A **hydrocarbon** is a compound made up of hydrogen and carbon atoms only. Natural hydrocarbons are often used as fuels, as well as in industry to produce other organic compounds.

Propane and benzene are examples of hydrocarbons. Their structural formulas and space-filling models are shown in **Figure 10.5.** Propane is used to heat homes, as well as to fuel gas grills. Benzene is a sweet-smelling hydrocarbon that is used in industry.

Straight-chain hydrocarbons, such as propane, and branched-chain hydrocarbons are called aliphatic (al uh FAH tihk) hydrocarbons. Hydrocarbons that contain one or more rings, such as benzene, are called aromatic hydrocarbons. Aromatic hydrocarbons are named as such for the strong aroma, or odor, these compounds tend to have.

Substituted Hydrocarbons One or more of the hydrogen atoms in a hydrocarbon can be replaced by another atom or group of atoms. A **substituted hydrocarbon** is a hydrocarbon that contains atoms other than hydrogen and carbon.

The atoms or groups of atoms that replace hydrogen are called **functional groups.** A functional group determines the compound's chemical properties.

| Methane | Fluoromethane (Methyl fluoride) | Difluoromethane (Methylene fluoride) | Trifluoromethane (Fluoroform) |

Figure 10.6 Substituted hydrocarbons are created when one or more hydrogen atoms in the hydrocarbon methane are replaced with fluorine atoms.

After You Read

1. Review the lesson outline in your Science Notebook. What is an organic compound? Provide two examples based on the information in your outline.

2. Why is carbon able to form many different compounds?

3. What are isomers?

Alternative Assessment

Have each student write a paragraph that includes information from at least two of his or her outline topic headings. Have pairs of students exchange their paragraphs for evaluation and discussion. Students should then make necessary changes/additions.

Background Information

The simplest hydrocarbons are the alkanes, which are saturated hydrocarbons. The general formula for the alkane series is C_nH_{2n+2}. The alkenes are unsaturated hydrocarbons in which at least one pair of carbon atoms is joined by a double covalent bond. The alkene series formula is C_nH_{2n}. The alkynes, also unsaturated, contain at least one pair of carbon atoms joined by a triple covalent bond. The series formula is C_nH_{2n-2}.

10.2 Polymers

Before You Read

Create a concept map in your Science Notebook for the term *Polymers*. Preview the pictures and subheadings in this lesson. What do you predict you will include in your concept map?

Look around your school or home. How many items can you find that are made from plastic? Stereos, sneakers, pens, tables, chairs, sporting equipment, microwave ovens, telephones, refrigerators, and thousands of other common products all contain plastic. Indeed, it is difficult to find items today that do not contain plastic. First invented in the early 1900s, plastics have proved to be durable, multi-purpose materials.

Monomers and Polymers

Plastics are part of a group of organic compounds called polymers. A **polymer** (PAH luh mur) is a large molecule that consists of many small molecules linked together by covalent bonds. The small molecules that form a polymer are called **monomers** (MAH nuh murz). Two common polymers are shown in **Figure 10.8.**

Polymers are usually long carbon chains that contain repeating units of a single monomer. Although many polymers, including plastics, are synthetic polymers, some are produced in nature by living things. Such polymers are called natural polymers.

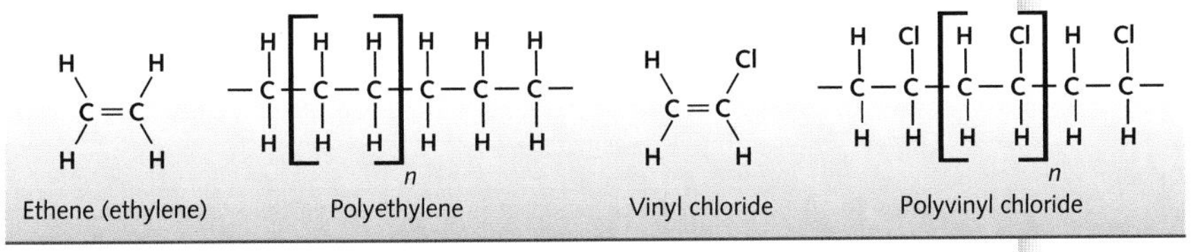

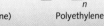

Ethene (ethylene)   Polyethylene   Vinyl chloride   Polyvinyl chloride

Figure 10.8 Polyethylene (PE) is the simplest polymer. It is made of repeating ethylene monomers and is used to produce such things as plastic bags, food containers, and children's toys. Polyvinyl chloride (PVC) is a polymer of repeating vinyl chloride monomers. It is used to make piping and flooring materials.

Learning Goals

- Describe a polymer.
- Distinguish between natural and synthetic polymers, and provide examples of each.
- Explain how polymers form.

New Vocabulary

polymer
monomer
polymerization

Figure 10.7 From medical devices, adhesives, and common household objects to high-strength industrial fibers, plastics have a range of uses that exceeds that of any other material.

10.2 Introduce

ENGAGE Have students work in small groups to identify plastic items found in the classroom, other areas of the school, or outdoors. Ask groups to record the information and share the lists with the class.

Before You Read

Discuss with students their predictions about the chapter. Draw a concept map for this lesson on the board and ask students what it should include. Tell them to draw similar concept maps in their Science Notebooks. As they read the lesson, have them revise, change, or add to their maps.

● Teach

EXPLAIN to students that they will learn about polymers and monomers in this section.

 Vocabulary

polymer Tell students that the prefix *poly-* means "many." Ask students to remember the meaning of *-mer* ("part").

monomer Tell students that the prefix *mono-* means "one." Ask students to remember the meaning of *-mer* ("part").

Background Information

While most polymers are organic compounds, they can also be inorganic. Polymers made up of mostly silicon, for example, are used in computers.

● Teach

EXPLAIN to students that they will learn about natural polymers—those made in nature.

As You Read

Have students provide terms that describe or are examples of polymers (*monomers, natural, rubber, cellulose, starch*). Add one or two of these terms to the concept map on the board, and then have students do the same in their Science Notebooks and continue working independently.

ANSWER Natural polymers are polymers found in nature.

Figure 10.9 Rubber trees are the major source of natural rubber. Paper products are made mostly of the natural polymer cellulose.

As You Read

Fill in your concept map with terms that describe polymers. Use lines to connect terms and identify relationships. Include key concepts and supporting details. Then explain your map to a partner. Make any necessary corrections or additions.

What are natural polymers?

Natural Polymers

Natural rubber, silk, wool, cotton, and cellulose are natural polymers that have long been used as natural resources. Protein is one of many natural polymers that play vital roles in the biological processes of all living things.

Natural rubber is a waterproof material obtained from rubber trees. Unlike most materials, rubber returns to its original shape after being stretched. It also bounces when it hits solid objects. Natural rubber is made up of repeating isoprene units. Its scientific name is polyisoprene.

The main component of wood and cotton is the natural polymer cellulose. Cellulose is a strong, insoluble substance made up of glucose monomers. Cellulose molecules are nearly straight chains that line up with other cellulose molecules to form fibers. These fibers can be spun into threads and used to make fabrics and other textiles. The cellulose in wood is used to make paper products. The cellulose in cotton is used to make clothing, carpets, bedding, toys, and many other products.

Starch is another natural polymer. It is found in foods such as potatoes, corn, and rice. Like cellulose, starch is also made from glucose monomers. Unlike cellulose, however, starch is a soluble molecule that humans can digest. Starches provide the body with sugars needed for energy.

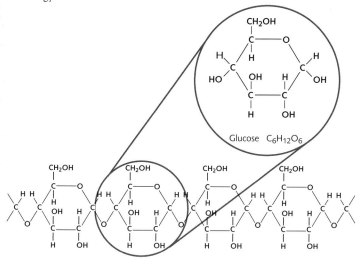

Figure 10.10 Starch is made up of repeating glucose monomers. Water is produced when the glucose monomers link up. Notice that each glucose monomer in the chain is missing two hydrogen atoms and one oxygen atom.

ELL Strategy

Activate Background Knowledge
Have students form small groups to discuss what they already know about natural polymers. Students should brainstorm a list of natural polymers. Allow students to make posters illustrating as many polymers as they have come up with, including any additional information.

about those polymers. This information might include where they are found and how they are used. Have students report back on their groups' discussions. Encourage students to supplement their posters with samples of the natural polymers, if easily obtained.

Synthetic Polymers

Vinyl, nylon, and nonstick coating are synthetic polymers. Synthetic polymers were first developed to replace natural polymers, which were sometimes difficult or expensive to obtain. Synthetic polymers are often referred to as plastics.

The properties of a polymer depend on the polymer's shape and the monomers from which the polymer is made. Thus scientists can design synthetic polymers for different uses. Some synthetic polymers are designed to be clear, stretchable solids that can be used in food packaging. Others are designed to be durable, high-melting-point solids that can be used in car manufacturing. Some common synthetic polymers are described in the table in **Figure 10.11**.

Common Synthetic Polymers

Common Name	Properties	Uses
polyvinyl chloride (PVC)	strong, rigid solid	pipes, raingear, siding, flooring
polypropylene (PP)	soft, elastic solid	drink containers, ropes, netting, carpeting, upholstery
polytetrafluoroethylene (PTFE, Teflon)	smooth, nonstick solid	nonstick coatings, electrical insulation, lubricants
polyvinyl acetate (PVac)	sticky, soft solid	latex paints, adhesives
polyurethane (spandex)	soft, smooth, stain-resistant elastic fiber	clothing
polyethylene terephthalate (PET, Dacron, Mylar, polyester)	semi-rigid to rigid transparent solid	drink containers, clothing, insulation on International Space Station

Figure 10.11 Synthetic polymers tend to be easy and inexpensive to produce.

Figure It Out

1. What properties of spandex make it useful for clothing?

2. Compare the properties of polyvinyl chloride and polypropylene. How are they similar? How do they differ?

 CONNECTION: **Economics**

Nylon was developed as the first synthetic fiber in the 1930s and introduced at the New York World's Fair in 1939. It was unveiled as a substitute for silk, a natural polymer. Silk is a lightweight, stretchable fiber produced by silkworms, the larvae of Asian moths. Because it is harvested from their cocoons, it is expensive to obtain. Nylon is both cheaper and easier to obtain. It is also stronger, more flexible, and more durable than silk.

Teach

EXPLAIN to students that they will learn about synthetic (human-made) polymers: their origins , properties, uses, and some common examples.

Figure It Out: **Figure 10.11**

ANSWER **1.** Spandex is useful for clothing because it is stain-resistant, elastic, and can be drawn into fibers. **2.** Polypropylene (PP) and polyvinylchloride (PVC) are both polymers consisting of long chains of carbon atoms. They differ in that PVC is a strong, rigid solid and PP is a soft, elastic solid.

CONNECTION: **Economics**

Other synthetic fibers and the time of their development include:

rayon, 1910 (based on cotton or tree pulp cellulose)

acetate, 1924 (also based on cotton or tree pulp cellulose)

acrylic, 1950

polyester, 1953

olefin, 1959

spandex, 1959

Science Notebook EXTRA

Have students check the tags in their shirts for the presence of the synthetic materials listed in the Connection feature above. Have students create a class graph of the shirts' contents and analyze the results for synthetic versus natural materials. Note that this activity may not be a good choice if students relate fabric contents and cost of clothing.

Differentiate Instruction

Linguistic Have students research the names of the synthetic polymers listed in the table in **Figure 10.11** and identify the meanings of prefixes, suffixes, and other word parts.

Field Study

Have students view or tour a local recycling center with an employee. Encourage them to learn about the classification of plastics.

Teacher Alert

Students often think that all polymers are plastics, and thus synthetic. While synthetic polymers are often called plastics, many natural polymers exist. Take time to discuss the distinctions, and use a graphic organizer to visually represent them.

Teach

 EXPLAIN that on this page, students will learn about addition and condensation polymerization.

Vocabulary

polymerization Explain that the suffix *-ization* creates a noun when added to a word. Have students combine this meaning with what they know about the word *polymer.*

Explain It!

Different types of polymers take varying amounts of time to decompose. A plastic milk jug takes approximately one million years, a disposable diaper about 550 years, a plastic soda bottle about 450 years, and a plastic bag 10 to 20 years.

Discuss with students the benefits and environmental risks associated with synthetic polymers. Encourage students to form opinions about synthetic polymers and to defend their opinions in well-developed essays.

Assess

Use the After You Read questions and the Alternative Assessment to help you evaluate students' understanding of the lesson.

After You Read

1. Students' answers will vary but should include a definition of the term *polymer*, a comparison of synthetic and natural polymers, and a discussion of polymerization reactions.

2. Polymers form through a process known as polymerization, in which monomers link together.

Alternative Assessment

Have students review and edit their concept maps. Then, have them construct two Venn diagrams: one for comparing and contrasting natural and synthetic polymers and the other for comparing and contrasting monomers and polymers.

Explain It!

Synthetic polymers are inexpensive, easy to produce, and stronger and more durable than natural fibers. However, many synthetic polymers do not easily decompose. They can build up in dumps and landfills and can pollute Earth. Synthetic polymers are also often produced from fossil fuels, a nonrenewable resource. In a well-developed paragraph, express your opinion about the production, use, and disposal of synthetic polymers.

Polymerization

The process by which a polymer is formed from smaller individual monomers is called **polymerization** (pah lih muh ruh ZAY shun). Polymerization is similar to a synthesis reaction. It involves the combining of many small molecules to form one large, more complex molecule.

In the polymerization reaction shown in **Figure 10.12,** the polymer polyethylene is formed from ethylene monomers. The double bond in each ethylene molecule breaks, and the two carbon atoms then form new bonds with carbon atoms in other ethylene molecules. The ethylene molecules add to one another until the larger polyethylene molecule is formed. Polymerization reactions such as this are called addition polymerization. Addition polymerization is used to form molecules such as PVC, polystyrene, and natural rubber.

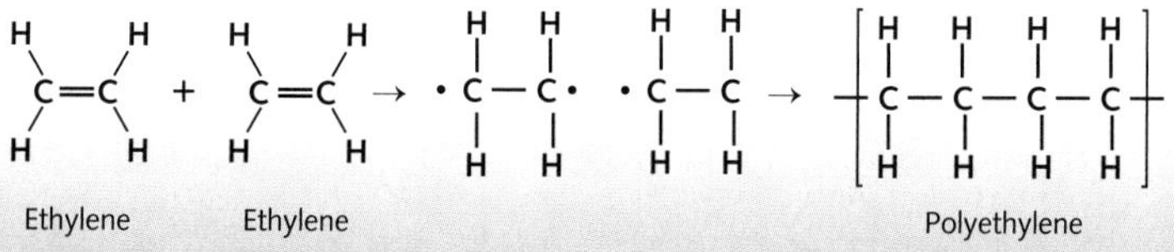

Ethylene   Ethylene   Polyethylene

Figure 10.12 Polymers that form as a result of addition polymerization are called addition polymers. Addition polymerization can result in molecules containing more than 10,000 monomers.

Other polymerization reactions involve the release of small molecules such as water. The reaction shown in **Figure 10.13** involves the combination of the amino acids glycine and alanine and the loss of a molecule of water. Polymerization reactions such as this are called condensation polymerization. Condensation polymerization is used to form molecules such as polyesters, nylon, and spandex.

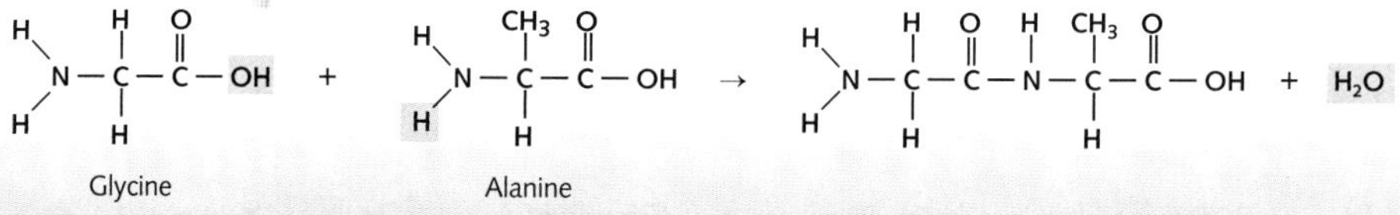

Glycine   Alanine

Figure 10.13 Polymers that form as a result of condensation polymerization are called condensation polymers. *Condensation* refers to the formation of water.

After You Read

1. Review the concept map in your Science Notebook. Use the information you recorded to write a well-developed paragraph that describes polymers.

2. How do polymers form?

Background Information

Recycled plastic lumber has been produced since the early 1980s. Some materials that it is made from include plastic milk jugs, plastic and bubble wrap, grocery bags, detergent bottles, and water bottles. Decks and docks are made from recycled plastic lumber, as it is resistant to decay caused by salt water, freshwater, or soil. The initial cost of recycled plastic lumber is more than that of wood, but because of its longer life and lack of required maintenance, recycled plastic lumber is more cost-effective over time.

Before You Read

Create a K-W-L-S-H chart in your Science Notebook. Think about the title of this lesson. In the column labeled *K*, write what you already know about proteins, lipids, carbohydrates, and nucleic acids. In the column labeled *W*, write what you would like to learn about these substances.

You are probably familiar with the terms *proteins, fats,* and *carbohydrates*—organic compounds that are important to the proper functioning of the human body.

Proteins, Lipids, and Carbohydrates

Proteins, lipids, and carbohydrates are types of organic compounds that make up most of the foods people eat. Each plays an important role in maintaining good health. Each is responsible for different functions in the body.

Proteins A **protein** is an organic polymer. Proteins are made up of amino acids linked together in a specific way. Proteins make up much of the body's cells. They are involved in nearly all the chemical reactions that take place in living things.

Proteins control all cellular processes. They provide structural support and help a cell maintain its shape. They act as enzymes, or biological catalysts, to speed up the rates of chemical reactions inside the body. They help cells communicate with one another. They help the body fight disease and infection.

Twenty amino acids are commonly found in the proteins of living things. Humans can synthesize ten of these. They must obtain the other ten from the foods they eat. Failure to obtain these amino acids can lead to health problems. Eating a well-balanced diet including fruits, vegetables, meat, and dairy products can help people ensure that they get all the amino acids they need.

Glycine   Cysteine   Peptide
                              Glycyl cysteinate   Water forms

Figure 10.14 An amino acid is a small organic compound that has both an amino group and a carboxyl group. When amino acids combine to form proteins, the amino group of one amino acid bonds to the carboxyl group of another amino acid. The bond is called a peptide bond. Proteins are often referred to as polypeptides.

10.3 Introduce

ENGAGE Initiate a class discussion of the six main categories of nutrients: carbohydrates, proteins, fats, vitamins, minerals, and water. Identify the properties and common sources of each.

Then have students work in small groups to identify the role of proteins, lipids, and carbohydrates in the functioning of the human body.

Before You Read

Discuss with students what they already know about proteins, lipids, and carbohydrates. Create a K-W-L-S-H chart on the board and record students' prior knowledge.

● Teach

EXPLAIN to students that they will learn about proteins, a type of organic polymer that makes up much of the human body's cells.

💿 Vocabulary

protein Explain that *protein* comes from the Greek word *proteios*, which means "primary."

ELL Strategy

Compare and Contrast Have students work in pairs to create charts in their Science Notebooks comparing and contrasting proteins, carbohydrates, and lipids. They should include specific examples of each substance, possibly including examples from their dietary intake for the week.

Key Concept Review Workbook, p. 59

Teach

 EXPLAIN to students that they will learn about lipids and carbohydrates in this section.

Vocabulary

lipid Explain that *lip-* or *lipo-* comes from the Greek word *lipos*, meaning "fat" or "fatty," and the suffix *-id* refers to a member of a particular group or family.

fatty acid Explain that fatty acids are obtained from animal and vegetable fats. They are used in soaps and detergents as lubricants.

carbohydrate Explain that the word *carbohydrate* is made up of the words *carbon* and *hydrate*. Tell students that a hydrate is a compound containing hydrogen and oxygen in the same ratio as found in water (2:1).

saccharide Tell students that the word *saccharide* comes from the Latin word *saccharum*, meaning "sugar."

nucleic acid Tell students that the term *nucleic acid* was derived from the molecule's occurrence in cell nuclei.

nucleotide Explain that the word *nucleotide* comes from *nucleo*, denoting "nucleus," and *-ide*, which refers to a compound of an element and some other element.

Use the Visual: Figure 10.15

(ANSWER) Stearic acid is a saturated fatty acid; oleic acid is an unsaturated fatty acid.

Explore It!

Provide library and internet resources containing nutritional information and guidelines.

Science Notebook EXTRA

Have students record recommended daily servings of each category of organic compound in their Science Notebooks.

Stearic acid   Oleic acid

Figure 10.15 Fatty acids that contain only single bonds between carbon atoms are called saturated fatty acids. Fatty acids that contain one or more double or triple bonds between carbon atoms are called unsaturated fatty acids. Which type of fatty acid is stearic acid? Oleic acid?

Explore It!

Make a list of 15 types of food you eat. Classify the foods as sources of primarily proteins, lipids, or carbohydrates according to what you have learned about these organic compounds. Use internet or library resources for nutritional information and guidelines.

Lipids Fats and oils are lipids. A **lipid** is a large, nonpolar organic compound. Lipids serve two main functions in the body. They help the body store energy, and they make up a large part of the structure of cell membranes. They also help cushion some of the body's internal organs and help provide the body with insulation.

Lipids are made up of carbon, hydrogen, and oxygen atoms. They are insoluble in water. They usually contain a building block called a fatty acid. A **fatty acid** is a carboxylic acid that has a long carbon chain. Examples of fatty acids are shown in **Figure 10.15.** Fatty acids are often found in the body bonded to glycerol. Glycerol is a molecule made up of three carbon atoms that are each bonded to a hydroxyl group. When three fatty acids are bonded to a glycerol molecule, the lipid is called a triglyceride. Fats and oils are triglycerides. At room temperature, fats are usually solids, and oils are usually liquids.

Lipids are an essential part of a healthful diet. They can be obtained from meats and dairy products, as well as from fats and oils such as butter and olive oil. Although including lipids in one's daily diet is important, people should consume them in limited amounts.

Carbohydrates A **carbohydrate** is an organic compound made up of carbon, hydrogen, and oxygen atoms, usually in a ratio of two hydrogen atoms to one oxygen atom. An example of a carbohydrate is shown in **Figure 10.16.**

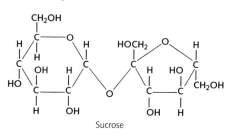

Figure 10.16 Sucrose, or table sugar, is a disaccharide.

Sucrose

Carbohydrates range in size from single monomers to huge polymers. The basic unit of a carbohydrate is a **saccharide** (SA kuh ride), or simple sugar. Monosaccharides, the simplest carbohydrates, are made up of a single saccharide molecule. Glucose and fructose are examples. Disaccharides such as sucrose are made up of two saccharide molecules bonded together. Polysaccharides, such as starch and cellulose, are polymers made up of many saccharide molecules bonded together. Polysaccharides are often called complex carbohydrates.

Because many carbohydrates are soluble in water, they can be quickly used by the body. They serve as the body's main source of energy. Carbohydrates can be obtained from fruits, vegetables, breads, cereals, and milk. They are an essential part of a healthful diet.

Background Information

Dietary fats are divided into two categories: saturated and unsaturated. Saturated fats come from animal products, including beef, veal, lamb, pork, and full-fat dairy products. They are also found in palm oil, palm kernel oil, coconut, and coconut oil. Saturated fats increase LDL ("bad" cholesterol).

Unsaturated fats are divided into two categories: polyunsaturated and monounsaturated. Polyunsaturated fats are found in fish, nuts, seeds, and plant oils. Monounsaturated fats include olive and canola oils. Unsaturated fats help lower LDL and increase HDL ("good" cholesterol).

An increased LDL level is a major contributor to heart disease. Eating foods that contain too much of either type of fat could lead to obesity, which is a risk factor for heart disease and some cancers.

Nucleic Acids

Nucleic acids are biological molecules found in the nuclei of cells that store and transmit genetic information. Nucleic acids are made up of long chains of nucleotides. A **nucleotide** (NEW klee uh tide) is the monomer that makes up a nucleic acid. A nucleotide has three distinct parts. It has a phosphate group, a five-carbon monosaccharide, and a nitrogen-containing structure called a nitrogen base. The monosaccharide and the nitrogen base vary from one nucleotide to another. The phosphate group is the same in all nucleotides.

DNA is one of two kinds of nucleic acids found in the human body. DNA stands for deoxyribonucleic acid. DNA is composed of two chains of nucleic acids wound together like a spiraling ladder, as shown in **Figure 10.17**. DNA is the genetic code of life. It stores instructions for building all of the body's proteins.

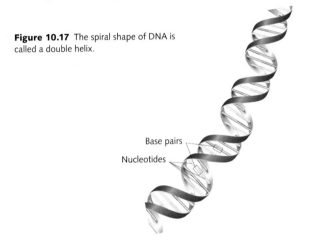

Figure 10.17 The spiral shape of DNA is called a double helix.

Base pairs

Nucleotides

The other kind of nucleic acid found in the human body is called RNA. RNA stands for ribonucleic acid. It is composed of a single chain of nucleic acids. RNA enables cells to use the information coded in DNA to build the body's proteins.

After You Read

1. What three organic compounds make up most of the foods you eat?
2. What is a nucleic acid? Describe the functions of nucleic acids.
3. In the S column of your K-W-L-S-H chart, indicate what you would still like to know about biological compounds. Complete the chart by writing in the H column how you could find this information.

As You Read

In the column labeled *L* in your K-W-L-S-H chart, write what you have learned about the organic compounds that make up living things.

What are lipids?

Figure It Out

1. How many different kinds of nucleotides make up a DNA molecule?
2. Do the nucleotides form base pairs in any particular way? Explain your answer.

● Teach

EXPLAIN to students that they will learn about the two types of nucleic acids in the human body: DNA and RNA.

As You Read

Have students discuss with a partner what they have learned about DNA and RNA in this lesson. Then have them record this information in the appropriate column of their charts.

ANSWER Lipids are organic compounds made up of carbon, hydrogen, and oxygen atoms. Many lipids found in the body are triglycerides.

Figure It Out: Figure 10.17

ANSWER **1.** Four different nucleotides make up a DNA molecule. **2.** Base-pairing occurs in a definite way. In this diagram, blue nucleotides pair only with orange nucleotides; yellow nucleotides pair only with green nucleotides.

● Assess

Use the After You Read questions and the Alternative Assessment to help you evaluate students' understanding of the lesson.

After You Read

1. proteins, lipids, and carbohydrates
2. A nucleic acid is an organic polymer made up of nucleotide monomers. Nucleic acids store and transmit genetic information.
3. Students' answers will vary. Encourage students to include at least two new questions.

Differentiate Instruction

Kinetic Using a student DNA kit that is available for purchase at an educational store or online, have students extract, view, and map the DNA of vegetables.

Graphic Organizer
Workbook, p. 61

Alternative Assessment

Give students time to review their K-W-L-S-H charts. Have them work with a partner to develop alternative questions based on the *K* and *L* columns of their charts and then answer those questions.

Chapter 10 Summary

VOCABULARY REVIEW

Check students' sentences or paragraphs to make sure they understand the meaning of each vocabulary term.

Evaluate students' essays using the following criteria:

1. The topic sentence, or main idea, should restate the Key Concept.

2. The supporting paragraphs should incorporate the answers to the Learning Goal questions students have written and include details, facts, and examples they have recorded in their Science Notebooks.

3. The concluding sentence should sum up the main idea of the chapter and restate the Key Concept.

MASTERING CONCEPTS

True or False

1. False, amino acids
2. True
3. False, Organic compounds
4. True
5. True
6. False, Isomers

Short Answer

7. A carbohydrate is an organic compound made up of carbon, hydrogen, and oxygen atoms.

8. Polymers are formed through a process known as polymerization. Polymerization involves the combining of many small molecules to form one large, more complex molecule. There are two types of polymerization: addition and condensation.

9. Proteins, lipids, carbohydrates, and nucleic acids are organic compounds that are essential for living things.

10. Organic compounds contain one or more carbon atoms that are covalently bonded. Covalent bonds between carbon atoms are stable and nonpolar. This makes organic compounds less reactive and less soluble in water than inorganic compounds are.

11. An alcohol is a substituted hydrocarbon that contains the hydroxyl (–OH) functional group. Ethanol and isopropyl alcohol are two examples.

Chapter 10 Summary

KEY CONCEPTS

10.1 Nature of Carbon Compounds

- Most compounds that contain carbon are organic compounds.
- Carbon is able to form many different compounds because each carbon atom has four valence electrons and is able to form four covalent bonds with other atoms.
- Carbon molecules can be straight chains, branched chains, and rings. They can contain single, double, or triple bonds.
- Compounds that have the same chemical formula but different molecular structures and shapes are called isomers.
- The simplest organic compounds, hydrocarbons, are made up of hydrogen and carbon only.
- Hydrocarbons with one or more hydrogen atoms replaced by other atoms or groups of atoms are called substituted hydrocarbons.

10.2 Polymers

- A polymer is a large molecule made up of many small molecules linked together by covalent bonds.
- The small molecules that form a polymer are called monomers.
- Natural polymers are polymers made in nature. Rubber, cellulose, and starch are examples.
- Synthetic polymers are polymers made in laboratories. Polyester, nylon, and nonstick coating are examples.
- Polymers form through a process known as polymerization.

10.3 Living Things and Organic Compounds

- Living things need proteins, lipids, carbohydrates, and nucleic acids.
- Proteins are polymers made up of chains of amino acids. They control and are involved in many biological functions.
- Lipids are organic compounds made up of carbon, hydrogen, and oxygen. Most lipids in the body exist as fatty acids. Lipids form the structure of cell membranes and provide the body with energy.
- Carbohydrates are organic compounds made up of sugars; they are the body's main source of energy.
- Nucleic acids are organic polymers made of nucleotides. They are found in the nuclei of cells. Nucleic acids store and transmit genetic information.

VOCABULARY REVIEW

Write each term in a complete sentence or write a paragraph relating several terms.

10.1
organic compound, p. 163
inorganic compound, p. 163
organic chemistry, p. 163
structural formula, p. 165
space-filling model, p. 165
isomer, p. 165
hydrocarbon, p. 166
substituted hydrocarbon, p. 166
functional group, p. 166

10.2
polymer, p. 167
monomer, p. 167
polymerization, p. 169

10.3
protein, p. 171
lipid, p. 172
fatty acid, p. 172
carbohydrate, p. 172
saccharide, p. 172
nucleic acid, p. 173
nucleotide, p. 173

PREPARE FOR CHAPTER TEST

To prepare for the chapter test, create a question from each Learning Goal. Use the information in your Science Notebook to answer each question. Then use these answers to write a well-developed essay about the chapter. Use the Key Concept on the first page of this chapter as your topic sentence.

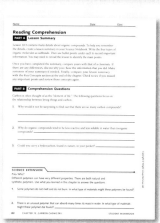

Vocabulary Review
Workbook, p. 60

Reading Comprehension
Workbook, p. 62

True or False

If the statement is true, write "true." If it is false, change the underlined word or words to make the statement true.

1. A protein is a polymer made up of <u>nucleotides</u>.

2. A fatty acid is a component of many <u>lipids</u>.

3. <u>Inorganic compounds</u> are compounds that contain carbon.

4. A polymer is made up of many small molecules called <u>monomers</u>.

5. Plastics are <u>synthetic</u> polymers.

6. <u>Isotopes</u> are compounds that have the same chemical formulas but different molecular structures and shapes.

Short Answer

Answer each of the following in a sentence or brief paragraph.

7. What is a carbohydrate?

8. Describe the process through which polymers are formed.

9. What are some types of organic compounds that are essential for living things?

10. What are some properties of organic compounds?

11. What is an alcohol? Name two alcohols.

Critical Thinking

Use what you have learned in this chapter to answer each of the following.

12. **Explain** What is a substituted hydrocarbon?

13. **Compare and Contrast** How are carbohydrates and lipids alike? How do they differ?

14. **Predict** What kind of compound will form when hundreds of ethylene molecules bond together?

Standardized Test Question

Choose the letter of the response that correctly answers the question.

15. The basic unit of a nucleic acid is a(n) _____.

   A. nucleotide
   B. amino acid
   C. carbohydrate
   D. polymer

Test-Taking Tip

If more than one choice for a multiple-choice question seems correct, ask yourself if each choice completely answers the question. If a choice is only partially true, it is probably not the correct answer.

Curriculum Connection
Workbook, p. 63

Science Challenge
Workbook, pp. 64-65

Critical Thinking

12. A substituted hydrocarbon is a hydrocarbon in which one or more of the hydrogen atoms bonded to a carbon atom is substituted with another atom or group of atoms. Substituted hydrocarbons have different chemical properties from their parent hydrocarbons.

13. Carbohydrates and lipids are both made up of carbon, hydrogen, and oxygen atoms. Carbohydrates are made up of saccharides; most lipids are made up of fatty acids. Carbohydrates are more soluble in water than lipids are. Carbohydrates are used by the body for energy; lipids help the body store energy and make up most of the structure of cell membranes. Carbohydrates can be obtained from fruits, vegetables, breads, cereals, and milk; lipids can be obtained from meats and dairy products, as well as from fats and oils.

14. When hundreds of ethylene molecules bond together, they form the polymer polyethylene.

Standardized Test Question

15. A

Reading Links

Polymers All Around You!

This concise collection of activities includes a variety of ways for students at different ability levels to explore the makeup, properties, and uses of polymers. The experiments and demonstrations range in complexity and succeed at bringing the relevant chemistry topics from this chapter to bear on everyday life.

Linda Woodward. Terrific Science Press. 31 pp. Trade ISBN 978-1-883822-26-2.

Food and Nutrition (Science News for Kids)

To build on students' study of organic polymers, this introduction to food science provides useful information about nutrients and situates facts in an everyday context. The engaging topic, short articles, approachable text, colorful visuals, and accessible presentation of current scientific research make this volume a good choice for independent reading.

Emily Sohn. Facts on File, Inc. (Chelsea Clubhouse). 64 pp. Illustrated. Trade ISBN 978-0-7910-9121-0.

10A Chemical Indicators

This prechapter introduction activity is designed to determine what students already know about carbon dioxide's role in the body by engaging them in conducting an experiment using a chemical indicator and making observations and predictions.

Objectives

◆ make predictions

◆ observe a chemical change

◆ draw conclusions

Planning

 20 minutes   pairs of students

Materials (per group)

3 test tubes

test-tube rack

tape

marker

graduated cylinder

water

bromothymol blue solution

dropper

2 straws

Advance Preparation

◆ Be sure students use caution while blowing into the test tube. Warn students not to suck the water-bromothymol into their mouths. Students may want to cover the test tube with plastic wrap to prevent bubbles from spilling out of the test tube.

◆ Bromothymol blue can stain clothing, so be sure students clean up any spills immediately.

◆ Students should wash their hands after completing the experiment.

◆ Have containers available for students to discard their samples.

Engagement Guide

◆ Challenge students to think about the movement of carbon dioxide from humans to plants and back again by asking:

  ◆ *What do you take into your lungs when you breathe?* (Students may give any of the following answers: air, oxygen, carbon dioxide, atmosphere)

  ◆ *How do plants move carbon dioxide?* (Plants take in carbon dioxide and release oxygen)

  ◆ *What happens to your breathing when you exercise?* (you breathe harder and faster as your body tries to take in more oxygen and release more carbon dioxide)

◆ Encourage students to draw a diagram of the two test tubes with their differences labeled.

Going Further

◆ Remind students that plants take in carbon dioxide and release oxygen. Encourage students to design an experiment using a straw, a plant, and a beaker of water and bromothymol blue to show how plants and humans use and exchange carbon dioxide. Have students present their experimental procedure to the class.

◆ Have students do another experiment in addition to the plant experiment. Inside a test tube put bromothymol blue, a small piece of plastic (to support the insect), and an insect (mealworms work well). The indicator should change colors as the mealworm breathes. Make sure the test tube is sealed shut with a cork or stopper.

10B Testing Starches

Objectives

◆ predict whether or not a certain food contains starch

◆ conclude from testing if predictions were correct

Skill Set

predicting, observing, recording and analyzing data, drawing conclusions

Planning

 45 minutes   groups of 2–3 students

Materials

Materials for this activity are listed in the Student Laboratory Manual.

Advance Preparation

◆ Suggested food samples include brown sugar, peanut butter, rice, baked potato, kidney bean, apple juice, cooked bacon, and butter. Cook the foods that contain starch (such as potatoes, rice, beans) so the iodine penetrates them more easily.

◆ Be sure to include foods that contain starch and those that do not.

- Remind students that they may mash the softer foods before adding the iodine. Liquids may be tested as is. Water should be added to powdered substances before adding iodine.
- Remind students that iodine can stain your clothes and skin. Spills should be reported immediately.

Answers to Observations: Data Table 1

Answers will vary based on the foods used. For example, cornstarch, potato, rice, beans, and peanut butter all contain starches and will turn dark blue or black with iodine. Apple juice, cooked bacon, sugar, and butter do not contain starches.

Answers to Analysis and Conclusion

1. Answers will vary based on the samples students are given.
2. Answers will vary based on the samples students are given. A color change to blue or black indicates the presence of starch.
3. Students might recognize that foods derived from plants are likely to contain starch. Accuracy of predictions will vary.

Going Further

Remind students that other materials they use in their everyday lives are made of plant material as well. Have students conduct a similar experiment to determine what common substances contain starch. Have students create wall charts of their results.

10C Carbohydrates

Objectives
- identify types of carbohydrates
- make and record observations
- draw conclusions based on data

Skill Set

observing, comparing and contrasting, recording and analyzing data, drawing conclusions

Planning

 45–60 minutes groups of 3–4 students

Materials

Materials for this activity are listed in the Student Laboratory Manual.

Advance Preparation

- Prepare the known carbohydrate solutions as follows: apple juice for the monosaccharide; powdered sugar dissolved in water for the disaccharide; oats dissolved in water for the polysaccharide.
- Prepare the following solutions: table sugar dissolved in water, white rice dissolved in water, pure corn syrup dissolved in water.
- Warn students of the potential dangers of using the hot plate. Ensure that they are using it safely.
- Warn students that to report spills immediately. Benedict's solution can burn skin, and iodine can stain clothes and skin.
- You may want to make the oat solution and the sugar solutions before the lab starts.
- Provide a receptacle disposal of waste materials.

Answers to Observations: Data Table 1

Monosaccharide will turn green, yellow, orange, or red in Benedict's solution and rust-colored or white in iodine.

Disaccharides will remain unchanged (blue) in Benedict's solution and rust-colored or white in iodine.

Polysaccharides will remain unchanged (blue) in Benedict's solution and turn deep blue in iodine.

Answers to Observations: Data Table 2

Honey: green, yellow, orange, or red in Benedict's solution, rust-color and white visible in iodine—is a monosaccharide.

Rice solution: blue in Benedict's solution, blue in iodine—is a polysaccharide.

Table sugar solution: blue in Benedict's solution, rust-color and white in iodine—is a disaccharide.

White grape juice: green, yellow, orange, or red in Benedict's solution, rust-color and white visible in iodine—is a monosaccharide.

Corn syrup solution: blue in Benedict's solution, rust-color and white in iodine—is a disaccharide.

Answers to Analysis and Conclusions

1. When Benedict's solution is added to a monosaccharide and then heated, the solution turns green, yellow, orange, or red. If it is added to a disaccharide or a polysaccharide, the color remains unchanged, or blue.
2. The iodine does not change color with monosaccharides or disaccharides. Iodine will turn deep blue or black when a polysaccharide is present.
3. You must test with both solutions because it is not possible to get a definitive classification by just using one. You know whether a sample is a monosaccharide if you use Benedict's alone, but you are unable to distinguish a disaccharide from a polysaccharide using Benedict's. A similar situation exists with iodine, as well. You can tell a substance is a polysaccharide with iodine, but iodine does not help determine whether a substance is a disaccharide or a monosaccharide.
4. No, you do not know which specific type it is. You only know that it is not a monosaccharide; it could be a disaccharide or a polysaccharide.

Going Further

How does the carbohydrate content of sports drinks compare to that of water, soda, and fruit juices? Have students conduct an experiment that looks at the carbohydrate content of different beverages. Have students write up lab reports of their results.

Introduce Chapter 11

As a starting activity, use Lab 11A on page 61 of the Laboratory Manual.

ENGAGE Remind students that observation is one of the key skills scientists use to learn information. In small groups, have students discuss what they've learned by observing, and create a list of their responses and observations. Tell them that scientists learn about nuclear energy by observing its effects.

Think About Nuclear Chemistry

ENGAGE Students might mention that the following can be inferred about the airplane: direction, altitude (relative to other vapor trails), speed (a very rough estimate), and how long ago the plane passed (a very rough estimate).

Observations might include things such as animal tracks in snow, tire tracks in mud, skid marks on a road, etc.

Chapter 11

Nuclear Chemistry

KEY CONCEPT Nuclear reactions release huge amounts of energy when unstable nuclei change to become more stable.

Have you ever seen long, thin, white streaks criss-crossing a clear blue sky? The cloudlike streaks get narrower as they stretch into the distance. However, the streaks are not strangely-shaped clouds. The vapor trails were made by high-flying airplanes. Even though the airplanes have moved on, these tracks of condensed water vapor and ice crystals record their paths. As you will learn in this chapter, some scientists study nuclear reactions in much the same way—by observing tracks.

Think About Nuclear Chemistry

An atom is extremely small, and the nucleus of an atom is smaller still. Particles smaller than the nucleus are often ejected during nuclear reactions. How do scientists study the motions and interactions of things so small?

- By observing vapor trails, you can infer things about the motion of an airplane. What information can you gather by looking at an airplane's vapor trail? Record your ideas in your Science Notebook.

- In your Science Notebook, describe one or two other observations you can make about an object without observing the object itself.

NSTA

SCLINKS
THE WORLD'S A CLICK AWAY

www.scilinks.org
Radioactivity **Code: WGPS11**

Chapter 11 Planning Guide

Instructional Periods	National Standards	Lab Manual	Workbook
11.1 2 Periods	A1, B3, G1, G2; A1, A2, B1, B2, B4, G1, G2, G3; UCP2, UCP3	**Lab 11A: p. 61** Chain Reactions **Lab 11B: pp. 62–63** Simulating Radioactive Decay	Key Concept Review p. 66 Vocabulary Review p. 67 Graphic Organizer p. 68 Reading Comprehension p. 69 Curriculum Connection p. 70 Science Challenge pp. 71–72
11.2 2 Periods	B2, B3, E2, F3; A1, B1, B2, B4, B6, D1, E2, F5; UCP1, UCP4		
11.3 2 Periods	A1, B3, E2, F3; A1, B1, B2, B4, B5, B6, C5, E2, F5, F6; UCP5	**Lab 11C: pp. 64–66** Radiation and Genetic Damage	

Middle School Standard; High School Standard; **Unifying Concept and Principle**

11.1 Radioactivity

Before You Read

Create a K-W-L-S-H chart in your Science Notebook. Think about the title of this lesson. In the column labeled *K*, write what you already know about radioactivity. In the column labeled *W*, write what you want to learn about radioactivity.

One day in 1896, French chemist Henri Becquerel stored photographic film in a drawer along with uranium salts. The next day, he observed that the film had unexpectedly turned foggy despite being in the dark. Becquerel hypothesized that invisible rays emitted by uranium might be the cause. Several years later, Marie and Pierre Curie proved Becquerel to be correct. The Curies showed that rays given off by uranium cause the film to become cloudy. By accident, Becquerel had discovered **radioactivity,** a process in which materials emit, or give off, particles and energy.

The Nucleus

Understanding radioactivity requires looking inside the atom to the nucleus. Recall that electrons move around the nucleus, and that the nucleus is made up of positively charged protons and neutral neutrons that are tightly packed in a very small space.

Because like charges repel each other, there must be a reason why the positively charged protons can be packed into the nucleus. This reason is the strong force. The **strong force** acts to pull the neutrons and protons together. Its strength rapidly decreases as the distance between protons and neutrons increases. The electrostatic force pushing like-charged protons apart is much weaker than the strong force, but it acts over much greater distances. The effect of distance on the forces acting within the nucleus is shown in **Figure 11.1.**

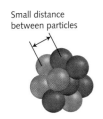

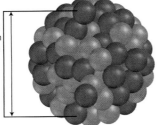

Small distance between particles

Large distance between particles

Small Nucleus

Large Nucleus

Learning Goals

- Identify the two primary forces acting within the nucleus.
- Predict what will happen to an unstable nucleus.
- Explain why large nuclei are more likely to decay than small nuclei.
- Define the two numbers used to describe a nucleus.

New Vocabulary

radioactivity
strong force
radioactive decay
transuranium element
isotope
radioisotope
atomic number
mass number

Figure 11.1 The distance between particles in a nucleus depends on the size of the nucleus. When the distance between particles is small *(left)*, the strong force is very strong. As distance increases *(right),* the strength of the strong force becomes insignificant.

CHAPTER 11 **177**

11.1 Introduce

ENGAGE In pairs, have students read and discuss the lesson's photographs and captions. Then have them discuss what they think they will learn about radioactivity.

Vocabulary terms are listed on the first student page of each lesson. You may wish to preview the terms before introducing each lesson. Strategies for teaching the vocabulary appear on the pages where the terms are introduced.

Before You Read

Draw a K-W-L-S-H chart on the board. Have students brainstorm what they know about radioactivity. Record the information in the first column (*K*). Repeat this procedure for the *W* column, recording what students want to know.

Teach

EXPLAIN to students that in this lesson, they will learn about radioactivity, a process in which materials give off particles and energy.

Vocabulary

radioactivity Tell students that this compound word is made up of *radio*, from the Latin word *radius*, meaning "spoke" or "ray," and *activity*, meaning "the state of being busy or active."

strong force Ask students what they know about the words *strong* (an adjective meaning "powerful," "muscular," etc.) and *force* (a noun referring to power, energy, strength, a push or pull, etc.).

ELL Strategy

<u>Ask and Answer Questions</u> Have students work in pairs to create at least five questions about the content of this lesson, writing out the answers on a separate sheet of paper. Students may use the lesson divisions or vocabulary words as ways of focusing their questions. Have pairs exchange questions and quiz one another on the content of the lesson. Any questions about answer validity should be settled by an exploration of the text.

Teach

EXPLAIN to students that on this page, they will learn about the factors that contribute to the stability or instability of nuclei.

Figure It Out: Figure 11.2

ANSWER **1.** from approximately 1:1 to 1.5:1
2. unstable because its neutron-to-proton ratio is 1.65:1

Explain It!

Students will need graph paper and a copy of the periodic table. Explain by example how to create and plot results on a graph.

Atom	Neutrons	Protons	Neutron-to-Proton Ratio
Ne	10	10	1:1
Ca	20	20	1:1
Zr	51	40	1.275:1
Cs	78	55	1.418:1
Pb	125	82	1.524:1

Students' graphs should reflect the data shown in the table above.

Vocabulary

radioactive decay Tell students that the word *radioactive* is the adjective form of the noun *radioactivity*. Explain that one of the meanings of the word *decay* is "to decrease in quantity" and another is "to decompose or disintegrate." Have students define the term in their own words.

transuranium element Tell students that *trans-* is a prefix meaning "across," and *uranium* is a dense, silvery-white, radioactive metallic element. Ask them to remember what an *element* is. Have students use the periodic table in Chapter 6 to identify the transuranium elements based on this definition.

isotope Tell students that *iso-* denotes same or equal, and *tope* comes from the Greek word *topos,* meaning "place." Take the opportunity to work with students to differentiate between *isotope* and *isomer.*

Figure It Out

1. Identify the range of the neutron-to-proton ratio for stable nuclei.

2. Imagine that an element with 165 neutrons and 100 protons is formed in a laboratory. Is the element stable?

Explain It!

Use the periodic table and other sources to determine the number of neutrons, the number of protons, and the neutron-to-proton ratio for Ne, Ca, Zr, Cs, and Pb atoms. Create a graph similar to the one in Figure 11.2. Plot your results, and label each atom's neutron-to-proton ratio. Explain how your results are related to the forces acting within the nucleus.

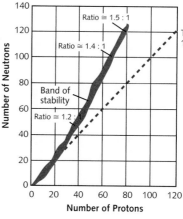

The dashed line represents a 1:1 neutron-to-proton ratio.

Figure 11.2 This graph shows the number of neutrons versus the number of protons for all known stable nuclei. Notice how the neutron-to-proton ratio of stable nuclei changes as the nuclei become larger (as the number of protons increases).

Forces and Stability

As shown in **Figure 11.1** on page 177, many of the particles in a large nucleus are far from one another. This decreases the strength of the strong force. To offset this decrease, large nuclei contain additional neutrons. These additional neutrons act as glue, adding to the strong force without increasing the repulsive electrostatic force. As shown in **Figure 11.2,** there exists an ideal, most-stable neutron-to-proton ratio for atoms depending on their size. The region of stable nuclei shown on the graph is known as the band of stability. Nuclei outside the band of stability are unstable.

What does it mean to be unstable? Unstable things undergo change. Imagine trying to stand on one leg on a very windy day. Your position is unstable and will likely undergo change—you will fall over. In a similar way, unstable nuclei change in order to become more stable. An unstable nucleus will spontaneously emit matter and energy in a process known as **radioactive decay.**

Radioactive Decay

Large nuclei are much more likely to be unstable and to decay than are small nuclei. In fact, all elements having 84 or more protons decay. These elements are all radioactive. The elements with 93 or more protons, however, rarely exist in nature. These elements, known as **transuranium elements,** have been made in laboratories. Transuranium elements decay almost immediately after they are formed.

It is important to realize, however, that many nuclei with less than 84 protons are radioactive. Even nuclei with one or two protons can be radioactive. The key is the ratio of neutrons to protons in the nucleus. Nuclei with too few neutrons or too many neutrons are radioactive.

---

radioisotope Ask students what the common meaning of *radio* is. Then ask them to remember what *isotope* means. Have them combine the words and come up with a meaning.

atomic number Tell students that *atomic* is an adjective that means relating to atoms. Have them figure out the meaning of the term.

mass number Tell students to develop a definition of this term by remembering the definition of *mass* they learned earlier.

Differentiate Instruction

Linguistic Have pairs of students look for prefixes and suffixes in the vocabulary words found in this lesson. They should create two lists: one containing the prefixes with their meanings and one containing the suffixes with their meanings. Have students add to the lists as they read the chapter. As an extension of this activity, students can recall other words that have the same prefix or suffix and write the definitions of those words.

Isotopes and Radioisotopes

The number of protons in the nucleus of an atom determines the identity of the atom. The number of protons also determines the number of electrons in an atom. However, the number of protons does not determine the number of neutrons in an atom. Nuclei that have the same number of protons but different numbers of neutrons are called **isotopes** (I suh tohps). If an isotope is unstable and undergoes radioactive decay, it is known as a **radioisotope.** All elements have isotopes, and some of these are radioisotopes.

Two isotopes of helium are shown in **Figure 11.3.** Each nucleus contains two protons. Note that one isotope contains one neutron, while the other contains two neutrons. The number of neutrons in the various isotopes of an atom does not change the way the atoms react chemically. All isotopes of an element have the same chemical properties.

Describing Nuclei

Nuclei are usually described in terms of protons and neutrons. The number of protons in a nucleus is the atom's **atomic number.** The periodic table is arranged in order of increasing atomic number.

The mass of an atom is almost the same as the mass of its protons and neutrons combined. Because of this, the total number of protons and neutrons in a nucleus is called the atom's **mass number.** In **Figure 11.3,** the mass number is used to identify the isotopes helium-3 and helium-4.

Chemical symbols, mass numbers, and atomic numbers are used to identify nuclei and the changes they undergo. The stable carbon-12 isotope is represented below.

$$\text{mass number} \rightarrow \quad ^{12}_{6}C \leftarrow \text{chemical symbol}$$
$$\text{atomic number} \rightarrow$$

The symbol for carbon is C. Carbon's atomic number is 6. The mass number of carbon is 12. Because mass number equals the total number of protons and neutrons in the nucleus, and there are 6 protons, the number of neutrons is $12 - 6$, or 6.

As You Read

In the column labeled *L* in your K-W-L-S-H chart, write three or four facts about radioactivity. Work with a partner to add to your list.

Describe the opposing forces acting within the nucleus.

Helium-3   Helium-4

Figure 11.3 These two isotopes of helium have different numbers of neutrons. What is the neutron-to-proton ratio in each isotope?

After You Read

1. Describe how neutrons help hold a nucleus together.

2. Compare and contrast the isotopes of an element.

3. Using the K-W-L columns of your chart, describe why some nuclei are stable, whereas others decay. Indicate what you would still like to know in the *S* column, and, in the *H* column, how you can find this information.

Background Information

The atomic mass of an element is usually not a whole number because it is the weighted average of the naturally occurring isotopes of the element. For example, carbon has three isotopes, the greatest abundance of which is C-12. There are few C-13 atoms and few C-14 atoms. Carbon's atomic mass (weighted average) is 12.011, which indicates that C-12 atoms are the most abundant.

Alternative Assessment

Have students use index cards to write the vocabulary terms in this lesson (one term per card). On the reverse side of each card, have students write the correct definition. Working in pairs, have students test their partners by holding up each card and evaluating the response.

● Teach

EXPLAIN to students that they will learn that the number of protons in an atom can be used to determine the atomic number of the atom, the identity of the atom, the number of electrons in the atom, and, by subtracting it from the atomic mass, the number of neutrons in the atom. They will also learn about isotopes and radioisotopes.

As You Read

Ask students what the *L* on the chart means. Solicit student input and record one or two responses in the class chart on the board. Discuss what opposing forces are and have students give examples.

ANSWER An electrostatic force of repulsion acting between the positively charged protons acts to break the nucleus apart.

Use the Visual: Figure 11.3

ANSWER Helium-3 has one neutron and two protons, so its neutron-to-proton ratio is 1:2. Helium-4 has two neutrons and two protons, so its neutron-to-proton ratio is 2:2, or 1:1.

● Assess

Use the After You Read questions and the Alternative Assessment to help you evaluate students' understanding of the lesson.

After You Read

1. Neutrons increase the magnitude of the strong force inside the nucleus without increasing the electrostatic force of repulsion.

2. Isotopes of an element have the same number of protons and electrons, but different numbers of neutrons. The chemical properties of the isotopes of an element are identical.

3. There exists a range of stable neutron-to-proton configurations of the nucleus. Isotopes with ratios outside this range are unstable, and they decay.

ENGAGE Provide copies of the Greek alphabet to small groups of students. Have students read the names of the letters and discuss similarities and differences between the English and Greek alphabets.

Before You Read

Have students discuss why they think the three types of radiation contain letters of the Greek alphabet and why those three letters were chosen. Draw the three-column chart on the board and have students do the same in their Science Notebooks.

● Teach

EXPLAIN to students that they will learn about one type of radiation: alpha particles.

 Vocabulary

nuclear reaction Tell students that *nuclear* is an adjective that means "having the nature of, or like, a nucleus." Ask if anyone can give an example or definition of the word *reaction*. Remind students that they learned about chemical reactions in Chapter 8. This should help them define the term *nuclear reaction*.

alpha particle Tell students that alpha is the first letter of the Greek alphabet, and a particle is a tiny piece of matter.

beta particle Explain that beta is the second letter of the Greek alphabet.

gamma ray Tell students that gamma is the third letter of the Greek alphabet, and the common meaning of the word *ray* is "any of a set of lines fanning out from a central point."

Use the Visual: Figure 11.4

[ANSWER] The atom's atomic number decreases by two, and the mass number decreases by four.

 CONNECTION: Health

Have students research the health risks of radon gas in your area. Instruct them to summarize their findings in their Science Notebooks. Encourage students to report on how radon is detected and what is done to minimize its level inside buildings.

- Identify the three types of radiation.
- Compare the penetration ability of the three types of radiation.
- Relate transmutation to changes in position on the periodic table.
- Define *half-life* and relate the amount of a radioisotope remaining to the number of half-lives passed.

New Vocabulary

nuclear reaction
alpha particle
beta particle
gamma ray
transmutation
artificial transmutation
half-life

Recall Vocabulary

chemical reaction, p. 130

 **CONNECTION: Health**

Radon gas is a radioactive decay product of uranium. Because uranium naturally occurs in soil, radon gas is naturally present in the air. There are serious health risks related to breathing radon gas. Once inhaled, radon emits damaging radiation inside the body.

11.2 Nuclear Decay and Radiation

Before You Read

In your Science Notebook, divide a page into three columns. Label the first column *Alpha Radiation*, the second column *Beta Radiation*, and the third column *Gamma Radiation*. As you learn about radiation, add information to your chart that describes the characteristics of each.

No two chemical or nuclear reactions are the same. Chemical reactions involve changes in electrons. **Nuclear** (NEW klee ur) **reactions** involve changes in nuclei. Both types of reactions can be represented by equations. Recall from Chapter 8 that an equation shows the reactants on the left side and the products on the right side.

Mass is conserved in chemical reactions. However, nuclear reactions do not obey the law of conservation of mass. In fact, radioactive decay only occurs if the products of the reaction have less mass than the reactants. This loss of mass explains why nuclear reactions release much more energy than do chemical reactions. Some of the mass in a nuclear reaction is converted into energy.

Nuclear Radiation

During radioactive decay, atoms can emit three types of radiation: alpha particles, beta particles, and gamma rays. These different types of radiation are identified by using the first three letters of the Greek alphabet: α (alpha), β (beta), and γ (gamma).

Alpha Particles Like a helium atom, an **alpha** (AL fuh) **particle** is made up of two protons and two neutrons. Because an alpha particle contains two protons, it has a 2+ charge. Alpha particles are represented in nuclear equations as α or $_2^4$He. The alpha decay, or emission of alpha particles by the decaying nucleus, of a uranium-238 radioisotope is shown in **Figure 11.4**.

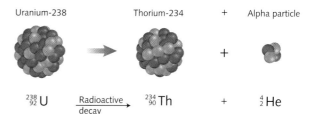

$$_{92}^{238}\text{U} \xrightarrow{\text{Radioactive decay}} \,_{90}^{234}\text{Th} + \,_2^4\text{He}$$

Figure 11.4 When a U-238 isotope decays by emitting an alpha particle, a new type of isotope is formed, Th-234. How does an atom's nucleus change during alpha decay?

E L L **Strategy**

Discuss Have students discuss information in this lesson or chapter. Students may choose to do this either in English or in their native language(s). Using main ideas and supporting details, have students report on their discussions.

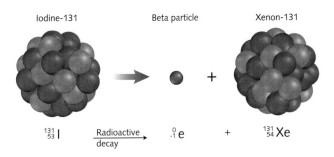

Iodine-131   Beta particle   Xenon-131

$$^{131}_{53}\text{I} \xrightarrow{\text{Radioactive decay}} ^{0}_{-1}\text{e} + ^{131}_{54}\text{Xe}$$

Beta Particles   A **beta** (BAY tuh) **particle** is simply an electron. The charge of an electron is 1–. In nuclear reaction equations, beta particles appear as β or $^{0}_{-1}\text{e}$.

The beta particle forms when a neutron changes into a proton. The fast-moving particles are ejected from unstable nuclei during beta decay. The beta decay of iodine-131 is shown in **Figure 11.5.**

Gamma Rays   The third type of radiation emitted during nuclear decay is not a particle, but rather a ray. A **gamma** (GAM uh) **ray** is high-energy electromagnetic radiation. Gamma rays are often emitted along with alpha and beta particles during nuclear decay.

Gamma rays and visible light are both part of the electromagnetic spectrum. Neither has mass or electric charge. The main difference between the two is that gamma rays have much greater energy than do light rays. The electromagnetic spectrum is discussed in Chapter 21.

In equations, gamma rays are represented by γ. An example of gamma radiation is seen in the alpha decay of thorium-230.

$$^{230}_{90}\text{Th} \rightarrow ^{226}_{88}\text{Ra} + ^{4}_{2}\text{He} + \gamma$$

Thorium-230   Radon-226   Alpha particle   Gamma ray

Penetrating Power

If you have ever had an X ray taken at a hospital, you may recall having to wear a heavy vest during the procedure. The lead-lined vest is worn to stop unwanted radiation from penetrating your body and causing harm. Alpha, beta, and gamma radiation vary greatly in their abilities to penetrate objects. As shown in **Figure 11.6,** alpha particles are the most easily stopped. Gamma rays are the most difficult to stop.

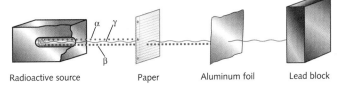

Radioactive source   Paper   Aluminum foil   Lead block

Figure 11.5 Iodine-131 decays by emitting a beta particle. Note that the atomic number of the atom produced increases by one. How does the mass number of the product compare to the original nucleus?

As You Read

Review the information you have recorded in each column of the chart in your Science Notebook. Share your chart with a partner. Add to or adjust the information in your chart as needed.

What type of radiation results in the formation of a proton?

Figure 11.6 Because of their 2+ charge and relatively slow speed, alpha particles can be stopped by a sheet of paper. The faster-moving and less-charged beta particles are stopped by a sheet of aluminum foil. High-energy gamma rays have no charge and are difficult to stop, requiring a thick layer of lead.

Teach

EXPLAIN to students that they will learn about two other types of radiation: beta particles and gamma rays.

Use the Visual: Figure 11.5

ANSWER The mass number is unchanged.

As You Read

Additional materials containing basic information about the three types of radiation should be made available to students to use for further research, if necessary. Have students share the information in their charts with the class. Record the information in the class chart.

ANSWER Beta decay results in the formation of a proton.

Science Notebook EXTRA

Have students summarize the three types of radioactive decay by creating charts in their Science Notebooks in which they record the important information associated with each type. Leave it up to students to determine the format of their charts. Have students share their completed charts with the class, and then select the chart that is most usable and complete.

Teach

EXPLAIN to students that on this page, they will learn about transmutation, the process in which one element changes into another through nuclear decay.

Vocabulary

transmutation Tell students that *trans-* is a prefix that means "across" or "beyond," and that a mutation is a change.

artificial transmutation Ask what students know about the word *artificial* (which means "not occurring naturally"), and have them give examples of items that are artificial.

half-life Ask what students know about the words *half* (it refers to one of two equal parts that form a whole) and *life* (the duration for which something exists). Have students use these word meanings to develop their own definitions of the term.

Figure It Out: Figure 11.7

ANSWER **1.** There is more than one possible decay reaction for the polonium radioisotope. **2.** The arrows that slant downward and to the left represent alpha decay. The arrows that point to the right represent beta decay.

Differentiate Instruction

Mathematical/Logical Have small groups of students research other sources and amounts of radiation exposure. Have each group use that information as well as the data in the Background Information feature to create a circle graph and present it to the other groups.

Figure It Out

1. What can you infer from the fact that two arrows are shown leaving polonium (Po) in the diagram?
2. Which arrows on the diagram represent alpha decay? Which represent beta decay?

Transmutation

Look again at **Figures 11.4** and **11.5** on the previous pages. Notice that a new kind of element is formed in both alpha decay and beta decay. The original atom decayed into an atom of a different element. The process in which one element changes into another through nuclear decay is known as **transmutation** (trans myoo TAY shun).

During alpha decay, two protons are lost from a decaying atom. Thus, the new atom has an atomic number that is two less than the original atom's. The periodic table is organized by increasing atomic number, so the new atom is an element located two places back on the table.

During beta decay, an electron is ejected and a neutron changes into a proton. A proton is formed, so the atomic number of the product atom is one greater than the atomic number of the original atom. The new atom will be an element located one place forward on the periodic table.

Radioisotopes decay both forward and backward on the periodic table. Often, the product of a decay reaction is not stable. This unstable atom will eventually decay, forming an atom that might or might not be stable. Thus, radioisotopes can go through a series of decay reactions, both forward and backward on the periodic table. This can be seen in the decay reactions of uranium-238 shown in **Figure 11.7**.

Transmutation can be forced to occur. In **artificial transmutation**, scientists slam high-energy particles into nuclei, forming new elements. The transuranium elements, those above uranium in the periodic table, have all been created through artificial transmutation.

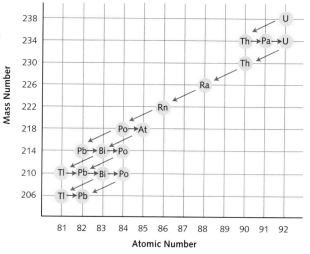

Figure 11.7 Uranium-238 decays to form lead-206 through a complicated series of reactions. Notice that there are several possible paths through the decay series.

Background Information

Some sources of common radiation exposure are listed in the chart to the right in terms of annual dose (units called millirems). The average annual exposure of a person living in the U.S. is about 360 millirems.

Common Radiation in Terms of Annual Dose (in millirems)

Cosmic radiation		Ground radiation, depending on the area of the U.S.		Other radiation	
at sea level	26	Atlantic coast	23	in body from food and water	40
Additional cosmic radiation, depending on local elevation		Gulf coast	23	radon (from air)	200
up to 1000 feet above sea level	2	Colorado plateau	90	X-ray luggage machine at airport	0.002
1000 to 2000 feet above sea level	5	other areas	46	television	1
2000 to 3000 feet above sea level	9			computer terminal	0.1
				medical X rays (each)	40

Half-Life

The **half-life** of a radioisotope is the time needed for one-half of the atoms to decay. Highly unstable atoms decay quickly. For example, the half-life of polonium-214 is about 0.000164 second. Other radioisotopes decay much more slowly. The half-life of uranium-238 is more than 4 billion years.

Carbon-14, which is used to determine the age of ancient artifacts, has a half-life of 5,730 years. **Figure 11.8** shows how much of a 1-kg carbon-14 sample remains after one, two, and three half-lives pass. To calculate the mass of the radioisotope remaining, multiply the original mass (1 kg) by $\frac{1}{2}$ for each half-life that passes.

Amount remaining after 1 half-life: $\qquad 1 \text{ kg} \times \frac{1}{2} = \frac{1}{2} \text{ kg}$

Amount remaining after 2 half-lives: $\qquad 1 \text{ kg} \times \frac{1}{2} \times \frac{1}{2} = \frac{1}{4} \text{ kg}$

Amount remaining after 3 half-lives: $\qquad 1 \text{kg} \times \frac{1}{2} \times \frac{1}{2} \times \frac{1}{2} = \frac{1}{8} \text{ kg}$

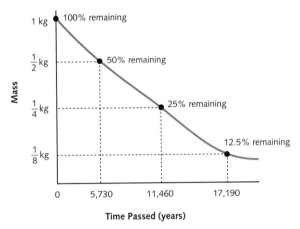

Figure 11.8 The half-life of carbon-14 is 5,730 years. The amount remaining decreases by half with the passing of each half-life period of time.

After You Read

1. Summarize how the nucleus is changed by alpha, beta, and gamma radiation.
2. How many half-lives have passed when one-sixteenth of the original sample remains?
3. Review the information in the chart in your Science Notebook about the types of radiation. Compare and contrast alpha, beta, and gamma radiation using a three-circle Venn diagram. Then write a well-developed paragraph explaining each type of radiation.

Explore It!

Obtain ten dice. Imagine that each die represents an atom of a specific radioisotope of a radioactive element. Roll all of the dice at once and remove those that show the number 1. Record this roll as Number 1, and also record the number of dice remaining after this roll. Continue rolling and recording your results until only half the original number of dice remains. The number of rolls required to reach this point represents the "half-life" of the dice, or the half-life of the specific radioisotope. Graph the number of dice remaining versus the number of rolls.

Repeat the activity, removing dice that show the number 1 or the number 2. What do you think this represents? How do the results compare?

● Teach

EXPLAIN that on this page, students will learn about the half-life of a radioisotope.

Explore It!

Each group of students will need ten dice and graph paper. More consistent results are obtained by increasing the number of dice used. Each roll of the dice represents the passing of a fixed amount of time.

ANSWER Both curves have similar shapes, but the curve representing the removal of ones and twos indicates a faster rate of decay than does the curve that represents the removal of only ones.

Science Notebook EXTRA

Using library books and other resources, have students research several biological artifacts and their ages. Have them list the artifacts and their ages in their Science Notebooks and explain how carbon-dating was used.

● Assess

Use the After You Read questions and the Alternative Assessment to help you evaluate students' understanding of the lesson.

After You Read

1. Alpha and beta decay change the composition of the nucleus; gamma radiation does not. Alpha decay decreases the atomic number by two and the mass number by four. Beta decay increases the atomic number by one but does not alter the mass number.
2. four half-lives; $\frac{1}{2} \times \frac{1}{2} \times \frac{1}{2} \times \frac{1}{2} = \frac{1}{16}$
3. Venn diagrams will vary.

Background Information

Carbon-14 dating, developed in 1949, is used to determine the age of biological artifacts up to about 50,000 years old. Living things take in carbon-12 and carbon-14 from the atmosphere. When an organism dies, the carbon-14 decays. The carbon-12 does not decay. Figuring out the ratio of carbon-12 to carbon-14, and then comparing this ratio to the ratio in a living organism, can determine the age of the dead organism.

Alternative Assessment

Have each student review and complete the radiation chart in his or her Science Notebooks and then write a paragraph comparing and contrasting the three types of radiation.

On the board, demonstrate how to calculate half-lives for one or two radioisotopes (phosphorus-32: 14.3 days; sodium-24: 15 hours; chlorine-36: 400,000 years). Then have students solve several similar problems.

11.3 Introduce

ENGAGE Provide photographs of the atomic bombs dropped on Hiroshima and Nagasaki during World War II. Small groups or pairs of students should look at them and discuss what they see and their reactions to the photographs.

Before You Read
On the board, demonstrate how to outline the first page or two of this lesson by creating a sample outline with Roman numerals and letters.

Teach
EXPLAIN to students that they will learn about nuclear fission.

Vocabulary
nuclear fission Ask students to remember the definition of the word *nuclear* (it is an adjective that refers to having the nature of or being like a nucleus). Tell them that fission is a splitting or breaking.

Use the Visual: Figure 11.9
ANSWER The products are Kr-91, Ba-142, and three neutrons. Note that the energy released is largely associated with the kinetic energy of the fission fragments.

Learning Goals
- Describe nuclear fission and fusion reactions.
- Relate mass and energy in fission and fusion reactions.
- Identify the risks and benefits of nuclear power plants.
- Describe beneficial uses of radioisotopes.

New Vocabulary
nuclear fission
nuclear fusion
tracer

Did You Know?
Albert Einstein proposed the relationship between mass and energy in his special theory of relativity. According to the theory, mass can be converted to energy according to the equation

$$E = mc^2$$

where E is the energy released, m is the mass, and c is the speed of light. Because the quantity c^2 is a huge value, a very small mass can be converted into a huge amount of energy.

11.3 Nuclear Reactions and Their Uses

Before You Read
Create a lesson outline in your Science Notebook. Use the lesson title as the outline title. Label the headings with Roman numerals I through IV. Use letters A, B, C, etc. to label each subheading. Under each subheading, record important information.

There are currently more than 100 nuclear power plants operating in the United States. These power plants supply electricity to about one-fifth of the homes and businesses in this country. Nuclear reactions have many uses, but they also have serious risks.

Nuclear Fission
The word *fission* means "to split or break into parts." The splitting of a nucleus into several smaller nuclei is called **nuclear fission** (NEW klee ur • FIH zhun). Nuclear fission occurs in large nuclei, such as in uranium and plutonium. Recall that a large uranium nucleus is barely stable. When the nucleus is disturbed, the forces within are thrown out of balance. If the disturbance is large enough, the out-of-balance forces will split the nucleus apart. The first fission reaction occurred in 1938 when scientists split a uranium-235 nucleus into smaller nuclei by striking it with a neutron. **Figure 11.9** shows this nuclear fission reaction.

Mass and Energy Mass is not conserved in nuclear fission. The fission products have slightly less mass than do the original nucleus and the colliding neutron. The missing mass is converted into energy. The conversion of mass to energy explains why nuclear reactions are so much more powerful than chemical reactions.

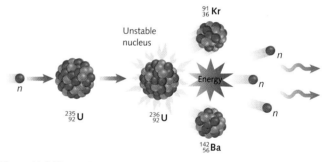

Figure 11.9 The uranium-235 nucleus becomes unstable after it absorbs the incoming neutron. The unstable nucleus splits, releasing a tremendous amount of energy. What are the products of the reaction?

ELL Strategy
Read Aloud and Paraphrase Have students form small groups and take turns reading aloud a section of the lesson. Each student should paraphrase the section he or she has just read. Then, the group should discuss the information and identify the main ideas and supporting details. Have each group designate a recorder to record the elements of the discussion.

Teacher Alert
Before showing students photographs of the atomic bombs dropped in Japan during World War II, explain what they are about to view and tell them that the photographs may be upsetting. If students are not comfortable viewing the photographs, excuse them from the activity.

Chain Reactions   Some people like to arrange dominoes so they will fall one after the other once the first domino is knocked over. This can be described as a chain reaction, one in which the first event is linked to the next. Nuclear fission reactions can occur in much the same way. Look back at **Figure 11.9**. Note that the incoming neutron produces two additional neutrons when fission occurs. If each of these neutrons strikes another nucleus, the fission reaction continues. This is a nuclear chain reaction. **Figure 11.10** illustrates a nuclear chain reaction.

When an uncontrolled chain reaction occurs in a large mass of material, a nuclear explosion is the result. The atomic bomb is an example of an uncontrolled nuclear chain reaction. When a nuclear chain reaction is controlled, it can be used to generate power. Nuclear power plants use fission reactions to produce electricity.

Nuclear Power Plants   The Three Mile Island nuclear power plant shown in **Figure 11.11** uses the heat produced from nuclear fission to produce steam. The steam is then used to power steam turbines that generate electricity. Nuclear power plants produce large amounts of electricity without polluting air or water. However, several important issues have limited the number of nuclear power plants built.

Nuclear reactors produce waste products that remain dangerously radioactive for thousands of years. The safe transport and storage of these wastes is a significant problem. Another problem is the potential for a dangerous plant malfunction. Two major nuclear plant accidents have occurred since 1979: at the Three Mile Island plant in the United States and the Chernobyl plant in the former Soviet Union. Both of these accidents released harmful radiation into the environment.

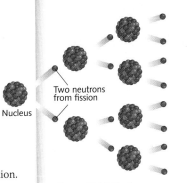

Neutron   Nucleus   Two neutrons from fission

Figure 11.10 Neutrons emitted by the first fission reaction trigger other fission reactions to occur.

Figure 11.11 Nuclear power plants are often located near a river or an ocean. Large volumes of water are used to cool the reactor. Cool water is taken in from the water source, and warmer water is discharged back into it.

As You Read

Look at the information about nuclear power plants in the outline in your Science Notebook. Make any necessary additions or corrections to your outline. With a partner, write a bulleted list of the problems associated with nuclear power plants.

CONNECTION: History

Nuclear weapons are a grim reality of nuclear chemistry research. Only two nuclear weapons have been used in a time of war. In World War II, the United States dropped two atomic bombs, devastating the Japanese cities of Hiroshima and Nagasaki.

● **Teach**

EXPLAIN to students that they will learn about nuclear chain reactions as well as the benefits and drawbacks of nuclear power plants.

As You Read

To assist in the analysis, have students create a T-chart titled *Nuclear Power Plants* in their Science Notebooks. Have them label one side *Benefits* and the other side *Drawbacks*.

ANSWER   Problems include transportation and storage of radioactive waste, possible release of radiation into the environment, and damage to the local water ecosystem due to the discharge of warm water.

CONNECTION: History

Have students conduct research to find out which countries now have nuclear weapons. In their Science Notebooks, have them record their findings and write a short paragraph describing how they feel about nuclear weapons. Check for the most up-to-date information on which countries have nuclear capabilities. Students' responses about their feelings will likely vary widely.

Differentiate Instruction

Illustrate/Presentation   For this lesson, English language learners can create posters demonstrating the uses of nuclear reactions. They should research industrial, medical, and other uses of nuclear energy in creating their illustrations. On their posters, they should include both beneficial uses and the potential drawbacks of nuclear energy. Students can use images from magazines and the internet or create their own drawings.

Interpersonal   In small groups, have students find information about families or individuals who were victims of the Three Mile Island nuclear power plant accident. Suggest that students look for information in magazines and newspapers from the time and location of the accident or that they explore Web sites. Next, have students take the victims' point of view and discuss how they feel about nuclear power.

● Teach

EXPLAIN to students that they will learn about nuclear fusion, the combining (fusing) of two nuclei to make a higher-mass nucleus.

Vocabulary

nuclear fusion Ask students to remember the definition of the word *nuclear* ("having the nature of, or like, a nucleus"). Tell them that fusion is the act of joining together. Then ask students to compare and contrast the terms *nuclear fission* and *nuclear fusion*.

tracer Tell students that a tracer is someone or something that traces, or follows step by step.

Figure It Out: **Figure 11.12**

ANSWER **1.** A proton (hydrogen-1) is combining with a hydrogen-2 isotope to form helium-3. A huge amount of energy is released in the reaction. **2.** Fusion requires temperatures of millions of degrees. The center of the Sun is hot enough to sustain fusion reactions.

Extend It!

Research the current work being done by scientists to make nuclear fusion a power source that can be used. Assess the progress that has been made. Predict if and when fusion power will become a practical source of electrical power.

Did You Know?

One of the obstacles to producing nuclear fusion reactions is achieving the high temperatures needed to start the reaction. Those high temperatures have been reached by using an atomic bomb. The atomic bomb sets off a hydrogen bomb, which is an example of an uncontrolled nuclear fusion reaction. In other words, fission is used to produce fusion.

Figure It Out

1. Describe what is happening in this step of the fusion reaction that occurs in the Sun.

2. Why are solar fusion reactions possible?

Nuclear Fusion

You now know that huge amounts of energy are released when nuclei are split apart. Interestingly, even more energy is released when nuclei combine. The word *fusion* means "to combine." Thus, **nuclear fusion** (NEW klee ur • FYEW zhun) occurs when two low-mass nuclei combine to form a single higher-mass nucleus. The products of a fusion reaction have less mass than do the original isotopes because some of the mass is converted into energy.

Temperature and Fusion It is difficult to get positively charged nuclei to combine. Strong forces of repulsion act to keep the nuclei apart. To overcome the repulsion, the nuclei must travel at very high speeds. Such high speeds occur only at temperatures of millions of degrees. The center of the Sun and other stars are the only places in nature hot enough to sustain fusion reactions.

Solar Fusion The Sun is a huge nuclear fusion reactor. Most of the Sun's radiant energy comes from the fusion of hydrogen atoms. Each second, the Sun fuses 600 million tons of hydrogen into 596 million tons of helium. The missing 4 million tons of matter is converted into energy.

The fusion reactions in the Sun occur in several steps. One of these steps is shown in **Figure 11.12.** In this reaction, a proton (hydrogen-1) combines with a hydrogen-2 isotope to form helium-3. A huge amount of energy is released in the reaction. The net result of the series of steps in the fusion reaction is the formation of one helium nucleus from four hydrogen nuclei and the production of a huge amount of energy.

Fusion Reactions on Earth Fusion reactions are a nearly ideal power source. They do not pollute the air, the radioactive by-products are minimal, and, unlike fission reactions, fusion reactions cannot easily become uncontrollable. Unfortunately, scientists have so far produced only short-lived fusion reactions in the laboratory. However, fusion research is ongoing.

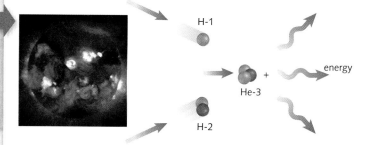

Figure 11.12 Nuclear fusion reactions occur in the Sun's extremely hot core. The temperature of the Sun's core is estimated to be 15,000,000°C.

Background Information

The Sun is made up of about 75 percent hydrogen, 25 percent helium, and a small amount of several heavier elements. The middle of the Sun contains an ionized, hot gas. A nuclear reaction occurs as hydrogen is fused and helium is created. This reaction causes extra energy to be released as visible and ultraviolet light, infrared radiation, X rays, and gamma rays.

Key Concept Review
Workbook, p. 66

Detecting Radiation

You cannot see, hear, smell, or feel radiation. For these reasons, devices to detect, study, and monitor nuclear reactions have been developed. Film badges that detect radiation are worn by people working near radioactive sources. Geiger counters measure beta radiation levels. **Figure 11.13** shows how bubble chambers were once used to study nuclear reactions. Electronic sensors are now used to detect radiation.

Nuclear Medicine

Medicine has benefited greatly from nuclear reactions. For example, cancer cells are often directly exposed to damaging radiation. The exposure kills many of the cells and weakens tumors. Because radioisotopes emit radiation that can be detected with the proper monitoring device, they are used as **tracers** to study chemical reactions and molecular structures. Radioisotopes are used to detect disorders of the thyroid gland, brain, and skin. As shown in **Figure 11.14**, a procedure called positron emission tomography, or PET, is used to diagnose brain disorders.

Figure 11.13 As charged particles move through the pressurized superheated liquid in the bubble chamber, they change atoms in the liquid to ions. The ions cause the liquid to boil, forming visible tracks of bubbles.

CONNECTION: **Particle Physics**

Nuclear reactions are a major area of research for many physicists. Particle physicists study the fundamental components and interactions of matter and radiation. Many of the particles studied do not exist in nature. Extremely energetic collisions made inside powerful particle accelerators are used to create the particles.

Because the research involves highly energetic particles, particle physics is also known as high-energy physics. High-energy physics experiments require large, expensive labs like the Stanford Linear Accelerator Center (SLAC), located in Northern California. The accelerator is 3 km long. Using its length and high-energy electromagnetic waves, the accelerator is capable of producing very high-energy collisions. The collisions create numerous subatomic particles that pass through detectors.

Figure 11.14 This PET scan image shows levels of brain activity.

After You Read

1. Explain why nuclear reactions release more energy than chemical reactions.
2. Describe nuclear fission and nuclear fusion. Draw a diagram showing what happens to the nuclei involved in each reaction.
3. Review your outline. Use the information you have recorded to describe two ways in which nuclear chemistry is used in medicine.

Background Information

A PET scan uses a radioactive tracer that combines with the body's glucose to show abnormally functioning organs and tissues. In addition to detecting thyroid, brain, gland, and skin disorders, the scan can detect cancer, how the body is responding to cancer treatment, and whether cancer has recurred. A PET scan is also used to detect heart disease, as it can show decreased blood flow to the heart, early coronary artery disease, and damaged heart muscle.

Graphic Organizer
Workbook, p. 68

● Teach

EXPLAIN to students that they will learn about the detection and medical uses of nuclear radiation.

CONNECTION: **Particle Physics**

Physicists created the accelerator to study the nucleus and the interactions of neutrons and protons that form it. Accelerators allow artificial, high-energy particles to collide with one another.

EXTEND Have students conduct research to learn more about other laboratories where particle accelerators are used.

● Assess

Use the After You Read questions and the Alternative Assessment to help you evaluate students' understanding of the lesson.

After You Read

1. Unlike chemical reactions, where mass is conserved, some of the mass in a nuclear reaction is converted to energy.
2. In fission, a large nucleus splits into smaller nuclei, releasing several neutrons in the process. Fusion reactions involve smaller nuclei combining to form a larger nucleus and the emission of large amounts of radiant energy. Students' diagrams should reflect this information.
3. Examples of nuclear chemistry in medicine will vary but might include the use of radiation to kill cancer cells, the use of radioisotopes as tracers, and the use of PET imaging.

Alternative Assessment

Give students time to review their outlines. Have them add more information to one or two subheadings that could be improved. Then have each student use the outlines to write a well-developed paragraph summarizing the lesson.

Chapter 11 Summary

MASTERING CONCEPTS

True or False

1. True
2. False, mass, neutrons
3. False, Nuclear
4. True
5. False, fourth
6. False, fission
7. True
8. True

Short Answer

9. The strong force is a very attractive force for nearby protons. The strong force is almost zero for far-away protons.
10. The neutron-to-proton ratio for light atoms is about 1:1, and for heavy atoms, it is about 1.5:1.
11. Transmutation is the process in which one element changes into another through nuclear decay.
12. The three radiation types are alpha, represented as α or $^4_2$He; beta, represented as β or $^0_{-1}$e; and gamma, represented as γ.
13. The neutrons from a nuclear fission reaction trigger additional fission reactions within a large fissionable mass.
14. Nuclei that combine in a fusion reaction must travel at high speeds to overcome the electrostatic force of repulsion from the protons. These speeds occur at extremely high temperatures.

KEY CONCEPTS

11.1 Radioactivity

- Radioactive materials emit particles and energy.
- The strong force acts within the nucleus to hold it together.
- The neutron-to-proton ratio of a nucleus determines whether it is stable.
- Radioisotopes of unstable nuclei undergo radioactive decay.

11.2 Nuclear Decay and Radiation

- The three types of radiation are alpha (α), beta (β), and gamma (γ).
- Transmutation occurs when an atom of a new element is formed through radioactive decay.
- Gamma rays are the most penetrating type of radiation.
- Half-life is a measure of the decay rate of a radioisotope.

11.3 Nuclear Reactions and Their Uses

- Nuclear reactions convert small amounts of mass into huge amounts of energy.
- Nuclear fission is the splitting of a nucleus; nuclear fusion is the combining of nuclei.
- Nuclear power plants produce electricity but pose serious environmental concerns.
- Radioisotopes are used extensively in medicine.

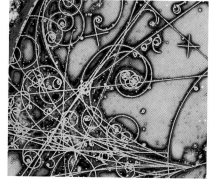

VOCABULARY REVIEW

Write each term in a complete sentence or write a paragraph relating several terms.

11.1
radioactivity, p. 177
strong force, p. 177
radioactive decay, p. 178
transuranium element, p. 178
isotope, p. 179
radioisotope, p. 179
atomic number, p. 179
mass number, p. 179

11.2
nuclear reaction, p. 180
alpha particle, p. 180
beta particle, p. 181
gamma ray, p. 181
transmutation, p. 182
artificial transmutation, p. 182
half-life, p. 183

11.3
nuclear fission, p. 184
nuclear fusion, p. 186
tracer, p. 187

PREPARE FOR CHAPTER TEST

To prepare for the chapter test, create a question from each Learning Goal. Use the information in your Science Notebook to answer each question. Then use these answers to write a well-developed essay about the chapter. Use the Key Concept on the first page of this chapter as your topic sentence.

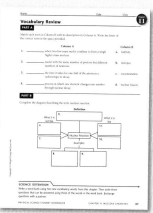

Vocabulary Review
Workbook, p. 67

Reading Comprehension
Workbook, p. 69

MASTERING CONCEPTS

True or False
If the statement is true, write "true." If it is false, change the underlined word or words to make the statement true.

1. The <u>strong</u> force acts to hold the nucleus together.

2. The <u>atomic</u> number is the total number of <u>electrons</u> and protons in an atom.

3. <u>Chemical</u> reactions involve changes in nuclei.

4. <u>Alpha</u> decay and <u>beta</u> decay cause <u>transmutation</u>.

5. One-<u>eighth</u> of a radioisotope remains after two half-lives pass.

6. Nuclei split in nuclear <u>fusion</u> reactions.

7. <u>Nuclear</u> reactions convert mass to energy.

8. <u>Fusion</u> reactions require high temperatures.

Short Answer
Answer each of the following in a sentence or brief paragraph.

9. Describe how the strong force affects nearby and far-away protons in a nucleus.

10. Identify the neutron-to-proton ratio for stable light atoms and for stable heavy atoms.

11. Explain what transmutation is.

12. Name the three types of radiation, indicate how they are represented in nuclear reaction equations, and describe their penetrating abilities.

13. Describe how a nuclear fission chain reaction occurs.

14. Explain why fusion occurs only at high temperatures.

Critical Thinking
Use what you have learned in this chapter to answer each of the following.

15. **Compare and Contrast** How are nuclear fission and nuclear fusion similar? How are they different?

16. **Apply Concepts** An unknown nuclear decay reaction occurs in a laboratory. It is known that the product isotope has a greater atomic number than the original radioisotope does. Identify the type of decay that has occurred.

17. **Calculate** A 20.0-g sample of a radioisotope exists in a lab. If the half-life of the radioisotope is five days, what mass remains after 25 days?

Standardized Test Question
Choose the letter of the response that correctly answers the question.

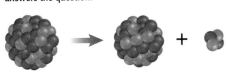

18. Which of the following best describes the nuclear reaction shown?

  A. An artificial transmutation reaction has occurred.

  B. Transmutation by gamma decay has occurred.

  C. A fission reaction has occurred.

  D. Transmutation by alpha decay has occurred.

Test-Taking Tip

If you finish before time is up, check your answers. Make sure you answered each part of every question and didn't skip any parts.

Critical Thinking

15. Both reactions release tremendous amounts of energy when mass is converted to energy. Both produce radioactive products (though fusion creates much less). Fission involves splitting nuclei, while fusion involves combining nuclei. Fusion requires extreme temperatures, whereas fission does not.

16. Atomic number increases by 1 during beta decay.

17. $25 \text{ days} \times \dfrac{1 \text{ half-life}}{5 \text{ days}} = 5 \text{ half-lives}$

$20.0 \text{ g} \times \frac{1}{2} \times \frac{1}{2} \times \frac{1}{2} \times \frac{1}{2} \times \frac{1}{2} = 0.625 \text{ g}$

Standardized Test Question

18. D

Reading Links

Three Mile Island: Nuclear Disasater

This book examines the accident at Three Mile Island in 1979 in a thoughtful and accessible way, detailing the causes and repercussions of an incident that had a lasting impact on public perceptions of nuclear technology. The well-researched volume includes information about other nuclear disasters and is ideal for student reports.

Michael D. Cole. Enslow Publishers. 48 pp. Illustrated. Library ISBN 978-0-7660-1556-2.

Lise Meitner: Pioneer of Nuclear Fission

The life of an often unrecognized but influential female scientist, a fission researcher who fled Nazi Germany in 1938 while her collaborator remained and later won a Nobel Prize, receives sensitive treatment in this book. The study acknowledges the historical context of the research and concludes with simple electron-movement experiments that students can conduct to reinforce the concepts presented.

Janet Hamilton. Enslow Publishers. 128 pp. Illustrated. Library ISBN 978-0-7660-1756-6.

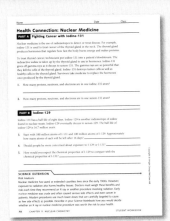

Curriculum Connection
Workbook, p. 70

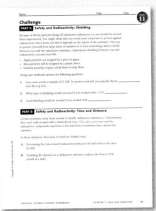

Science Challenge
Workbook, pp. 71–72

Labs

11A Chain Reactions

This prechapter introduction activity is designed to determine what students already know about chain reactions by engaging them in predicting and observing a model chain reaction.

Objectives
- model a chain reaction
- observe the nature of a chain reaction
- draw conclusions

Planning

 15 minutes   4 students per group, could also be done as a class demonstration

Materials (per group)
9 mousetraps
10 table-tennis balls
cardboard viewing box

Advance Preparation
- This activity would work well as a demonstration for the whole class. If done as a demo, try to use more traps and balls. The greater number of traps set, the more dramatic the resulting chain reaction is.
- If a large clear plastic box or fish aquarium can be found, that can be used in place of the cardboard viewing box. To make the cardboard viewing box, remove the top flaps from the box, and cut out two large side panel areas, leaving a cardboard border about 2 inches wide all around. Cover the side openings with clear plastic wrap and tape the plastic wrap down to the cardboard border. Cut a small hole in the bottom of the box, slightly larger than the size of a table-tennis ball.
- Caution students about the danger associated with mousetraps. You may want to set the traps yourself.
- Make sure students are separated from the snapping traps by the plastic box.

Engagement Guide
- Challenge students to think about chain reactions by asking:
  - *What will happen to a mousetrap when it tripped, or set off?* (Students should recognize that the mousetrap will move quite a bit when it is tripped, possibly flipping over and tripping another trap)
  - *If you place table-tennis balls on the mousetraps, what will happen to the table-tennis balls when one of the traps is tripped?* (The balls will begin to bounce all over the place.)
  - *How does this activity model nuclear fission?* (The traps represent large nuclei. The dropped ball represents an incoming neutron. The traps will trip (the nucleus will split), sending off the balls (neutrons), which will then in turn set off another trap (split another nucleus), releasing more balls (neutrons), and so on.)
- Encourage students to create diagrams of what they observe.

Going Further
Encourage students to think about the random nature of nuclear fission. Challenge students to think of alternative ways of setting up this demonstration to see how distance between the traps or number of traps may affect the chain reaction. Ask students to share their findings with the class.

11B Simulating Radioactive Decay

Objectives
- model radioactive decay
- predict outcomes
- interpret data collected from the models
- draw conclusions

Skill Set
observing, modeling, predicting, drawing conclusions, interpreting

Planning

 45–55 minutes   groups of 2–3 students

Materials
Materials for this activity are listed in the Student Laboratory Manual.

Advance Preparation
- You may want to count out the peas before the lab begins to speed up the activity, or have students count them out before they begin.
- Students may need help setting up their graphs.

Lab Tip
Remind students to use different symbols on their graphs to distinguish the white rice data points from those for the split peas.

It would help to point out that the split pea/white rice activity is not completely analogous to radioactive decay. If radioactive decay was a random event, then it would not be a reliable measurement of age.

Answers to Observations: Data Table 1

Answers will vary but students should find that with each observation, the number of split peas decreases and the number of grains of rice increases.

Answers to Analysis and Conclusions

1. The half-life of the peas is slightly greater than one observation or trial. The half-life in minutes is about 5.1 minutes. Accept responses close to these values.

2. Students should recognize that half of the nuclei decay each half-life, thus 50 peas remain after two half-lives, and 25 remain after three.

Going Further

Tell students that some elements have very long half-lives. For example, Uranium-238 has a half-life of about 4.5 billion years. Other elements have short half-lives. For example, Carbon-14 has a half-life of 5,730 years. Challenge students to graphically represent the decay of Carbon-14 and Uranium-238.

11C Radiation and Genetic Damage

Objectives

- compare plants grown from irradiated and non-irradiated seeds
- observe and measure physical differences in plants
- make and record observations
- draw conclusions

Skill Set

comparing, measuring, recording observations, drawing conclusions

Planning

 30–35 minutes (Day 1); 15–20 minutes (per day after first sprout appears)

 groups of 3–4 students

Materials

Materials for this activity are listed in the Student Laboratory Manual.

Advance Preparation

- You may purchase irradiated seeds from laboratory supply sources. You might be able to find a local dentist or doctor that will irradiate the seeds using an X-ray machine. Note the radiation dosage received by the seeds so students can enter the data in their data table.
- Use fast-growing plant seeds, such as grass seeds or the seeds of some flowers. You want to see the results as soon as possible. Wisconsin fast plants of the *Brasicacae* family are quick-growing, work well, and do not need much room to grow.

Lab Tip

Whether irradiated locally or purchased commercially, avoid using seeds/plants that would trigger an allergic reaction.

Answers to Observations: Data Table 1

Data will vary depending on seeds tested.

Answers to Observations: Data Table 2

Data will vary depending on seeds tested and growing conditions. Students should keep careful notes of what they observe, even if they do not have any changes to report.

Answers to Observations: Data Table 3

Sketches will vary depending on seeds tested and growing conditions. Plants from irradiated seeds are likely to have some abnormalities.

Answers to Analysis and Conclusions

1. The control in the experiment was the seeds that received no radiation. The control allows for comparison between the irradiated and non-irradiated seeds.
2. If the conditions are consistent, then the observed differences are likely to be the result of the radiation exposure and not due to soil conditions.
3. Answers will vary depending on particular observations. Students should recognize that there is less germination in the radiated seeds.

Going Further

Have student groups investigate how the amount of radiation a plant receives damages its genetic material. Provide students with seeds that have been exposed to X rays for varying lengths of time and allow them to conduct a new experiment. Have groups share their results with the class.

Unit 3

Case Study 1: Unhealthful Bond: Living with Mercury

Gather More Information

Have students use the following key terms to aid their searches:

- mercury
- mercury waste
- methylmercury
- Minamata Bay
- shellfish contamination

Research the Big Picture

- Have students research the levels of mercury and other contaminants in fish and shellfish from different areas. Encourage students to draw conclusions about why some species might be more contaminated than others (position on food chain, proximity to pollutants, etc.).

- Have students work in groups to investigate the effects of contamination from other potentially hazardous elements, such as arsenic or lead. Have each group choose one element and prepare a report describing its toxic effects and where and how contamination and exposure are likely to occur. Reports should also include procedures and laws created to prevent future hazards.

Case Study 2: Fusion Power?

Gather More Information

Have students use the following key terms to aid their searches:

- electricity
- nonpolluting energy
- nuclear fission
- nuclear fusion
- solar energy

Research the Big Picture

- Have students work in pairs to compare and contrast the processes of nuclear fission and nuclear fusion. They should present their work in the form of a research paper or poster. Their finished products should identify and explain the advantages and disadvantages of fusion. Encourage students to use diagrams or other visuals to enhance their work.

- Have students investigate the history of nuclear energy research and prepare time lines of significant discoveries.

Unhealthful Bond: Living with Mercury

In 1956, strange things started to happen in Minamata, Japan. First, animals began to get sick. Then many people got sick, too. Their symptoms included uncontrollable shaking and convulsions. About 1,000 people eventually died.

At first, no one understood why people were getting sick and dying. Finally, scientists traced the problem to the fishing village of Minamata Bay. There was a factory in Minamata that had dumped tons of mercury waste into the bay. When scientists tested the bay's water, they found high levels of mercury. The mercury was also in the tissues of fish in the bay. The people of Minamata got sick after eating fish loaded with mercury.

Mercury is an element—a shiny, silvery-white liquid metal. Since ancient times, people have known that mercury can cause sickness. However, the metal has always been useful. For example, coal, which is burned to produce electricity, contains mercury. Burning coal sends mercury into the air. Much of that mercury washes out of the air and into water and soil. Then it can get into living things.

When mercury combines with carbon, the two elements form methylmercury, an organic compound that is highly toxic. Living organisms, such as bacteria, make methylmercury from mercury that gets into water and soil. In lakes or streams, the mercury is absorbed by small plants that are then eaten by animals. The mercury passes up the food chain as one contaminated animal eats another.

People are most often exposed to mercury by eating contaminated fish or shellfish, which is what happened to the residents of Minamata Bay. High levels of methylmercury can cause brain damage, paralysis, and blindness. When pregnant women are exposed, their babies can have serious health problems.

Today, government agencies in the United States track the amount of mercury in bodies of water. The government then warns people not to eat fish in areas with high mercury levels. People must also throw away products containing mercury—such as batteries, thermometers, and fluorescent lightbulbs—at special waste sites. This prevents mercury from entering the environment and causing more harm.

CAREER CONNECTION FOOD SCIENTIST

During your last trip to the grocery store, you might have seen many of the following food items: breakfast cereals, juices, cookies, cake mixes, frozen dinners, and canned soups. Did you know that each one of them came from the laboratory of a food scientist?

Food scientists create the components of packaged foods sold at a grocery store. That means everything from the barbecue flavor on potato chips to the chocolate powder that can be stirred into milk. Food scientists work on ways to make boxed powders turn into cakes. They figure out how to make bread stay fresh for a long time on store shelves. They make ice cream creamy, and they make peanut butter thick and smooth. Some food scientists specialize as flavor chemists. They are responsible for the taste of fruit drinks and the smell of ketchup. To do all this, food scientists must know the chemistry of food.

Most food scientists first get a bachelor's degree in chemistry. Then they earn a master's degree in food science. Most food scientists work for food companies. Some work for the government, doing research on nutrition and food safety, and some also teach.

 CAREER CONNECTION: **Food Scientist**

After students read the feature, have them list in their Science Notebooks all the different things that food scientists do. Then ask them to think about packaged foods they have at home and see if they can add to their lists.

Students should recognize that some of the foods food scientists prepare must have long shelf lives, and others must be able to be prepared or eaten quickly. Ask students why they would or would not enjoy food science as a career field.

Fusion Power?

What would the perfect energy source be like? It would create unlimited energy with no pollution. It would also be cheap and plentiful. Scientists know of such an energy source. It's called nuclear fusion. The problem is that they haven't been able to make it work well enough to produce electricity—yet.

Hundreds of power plants around the world already use nuclear reactions to generate electricity, but they do this using nuclear fission, not fusion. A fission reaction splits atoms, releasing lots of heat energy. That heat is used in power plants to make electricity. Nuclear fusion is the opposite reaction. Fusion smashes atoms together to release energy.

The Sun provides a good example of nuclear fusion at work. The Sun is a huge nuclear fusion power plant. Under conditions of extreme heat and pressure, hydrogen nuclei on the Sun fuse to form helium. Solar fusion reactions release enormous amounts of energy. That energy is the heat and light that make life on Earth possible.

Making fusion work on Earth is harder. Atoms must be heated to millions of degrees for the reaction to take place. A special device is also needed to contain the reaction. Although scientists have been able to create fusion reactions, those reactions have been short-lived. For generating electricity, fusion reactions must be self-sustaining. They must also release more energy than they absorb in getting started. So far, such reactions haven't been achieved, and it could be another 20 years or more before scientists are successful in using fusion to generate electricity. However, the development of a nonpolluting power source that does not contribute to global warming seems well worth the wait.

Research and Report

Research some common chemical reactions and choose one. Write the chemical equation that describes the reaction on a large piece of cardboard. Label the elements or compounds that react with each other. Then label the products of the reaction. Identify the type of chemical reaction you have chosen, as well.

Storing Carbon

Fossil fuels produce most of the world's electricity and run most of our cars, trucks, trains, and planes. However, burning fossil fuels has significant drawbacks. For example, it sends billions of tons of carbon dioxide into the air each year—a major cause of global warming.

There are many ways to fight global warming. Most involve producing less carbon dioxide. A recent alternative solution, however, suggests that it is not necessarily a matter of producing less carbon dioxide: we just have to get rid of what we produce before it goes into the air. This process is called carbon sequestration.

How would carbon sequestration work? One idea is to use the oceans, where there is a lot of space for carbon dioxide deep in the water. However, some scientists say the process is too risky. They fear that the gas could eventually rise to the surface, harming sea life.

Another idea is to find a way to combine carbon dioxide with another compound in order to turn it into rock. That could trap the carbon dioxide for millions of years with no harm to the environment. Only time will tell if these ideas can become real solutions. Until that happens, producing less carbon dioxide is still the best option.

Carbon dioxide from this natural gas plant doesn't rise into the atmosphere. It's stored underground.

- Have students work in small groups to write mock proposals asking a government agency for funding to continue research in nuclear fusion. If some students do not believe fusion is a good alternative energy source, ask them to write counter-proposals explaining why a different technology would be more deserving of funding.

Case Study 3: Storing Carbon

Gather More Information

Have students use the following key terms to aid their searches:
- carbon dioxide
- carbon sequestration
- fossil fuel
- global warming
- trapping carbon dioxide

Research the Big Picture

- Have students work in pairs to produce promotional brochures for their own hypothetical undersea carbon sequestration companies. The brochures should explain why industries or nations that release greenhouse gases should invest in their services. They should also summarize how the technology works. Encourage students to be creative in coming up with company names, logos, and slogans.
- Another form of carbon sequestration is planting trees, which take up excess carbon dioxide. Have students compare the relative merits of three strategies of carbon sequestration: pumping carbon dioxide into undersea sediments, planting trees to absorb carbon dioxide, and trapping carbon dioxide in rock.

191

Introduce Unit 4

Explain that the topic of this unit is motion and forces. Have students create two to three related questions for each chapter topic. For instance, for Chapter 12, students might write: *How does the size of an object affect its velocity?* Create a class list of questions for each chapter and review and answer the questions during the unit.

Unit Projects

For each Unit Project, have students use the Presentation Builder on the Student CD-ROM to display their results.

Career Research Have each student research a career that is related to motion and forces such as aerospace engineer, bulldozer operator, or pilot.

Ask each student to describe what the job entails, and identify the skills or experience needed to prepare for the job. Have students record this information in their Science Notebooks.

Have each student prepare a three- to five-minute presentation of their information and share this within a small group of classmates.

Hands-On Research In small groups, have students design their own ideal roller coasters. Students in each group should draw a model of the ride and then describe the scientific principles responsible for both the ride's safety and its thrill.

Provide resource materials (books, magazine articles, and/or internet sites) for students' use. Students should include a three- to four-paragraph writeup describing the group's decisions as well as the mathematical calculations involved in the design process.

Technology Research Have students consider the calculations they performed for the Hands-On Research project. Then, in small groups, have students investigate what types of technology roller coaster designers (and other design engineers, such as automobile designers) use to simulate the effects of changing factors such as mass, velocity, and design.

Unit 4
Motion and Forces

Chapter 12 **What Is Motion?**

How do speed, velocity, acceleration, and momentum describe the movement of objects relative to a reference point?

Chapter 13 **Nature of Forces**

What is a force and what is its effect?

Chapter 14 **Forces in Fluids**

How do the physical properties of fluids make fluids essential to life on Earth?

Chapter 15 **Work, Power, and Simple Machines**

What are the relationships among work, power, and simple machines?

192

Software Summary

Student CD-ROM
—Interactive Student Book
—Vocabulary Review
—Key Concept Review
—Lab Report Template
—ELL Preview and Writing Activities
—Presentation Digital Library
—Graphic Organizing Software
—Spanish Cognate Dictionary

Interactive Labs
Chapter 12 B—Graphing Motion
Chapter 13 B—Observing Projectile Motion
Chapter 14 C—Flying with Bernoulli

What Is Motion?

KEY CONCEPT Objects can move relative to some reference point in ways that can be described by speed, velocity, acceleration, and momentum.

Gliding gracefully through the water and leaping through the air, dolphins travel in search of food. Changing speed as they wish, they swim miles and miles, only to return to familiar territory.

Like these dolphins, people, animals, and objects are constantly moving from one place to another. This chapter explains how to describe and measure different types of motion.

Think About Moving Objects

Some objects move quickly. Others move slowly. Many can vary how they move according to the situation. Think of something that can move fast or slowly.

- In your Science Notebook, describe the object. Does it move by itself, or does something move it? A snail, for example, moves on its own, whereas a soccer ball moves only when it is kicked.

- Compare a situation in which the object moves slowly to one in which it moves quickly. For example, a car might move quickly when it is traveling on the highway, but slowly while it is being parked in a garage.

NSTA

SCiLINKS.
THE WORLD'S A CLICK AWAY
www.scilinks.org
Measuring Motion **Code: WGPS12**

193

Introduce Chapter 12

As a starting activity, use Lab 12A on page 67 of the Laboratory Manual.

ENGAGE Bring a variety of balls to the classroom. Throw a ball to several different students. Have students toss the balls to each other for a few minutes. Collect the balls. Ask students to think about the motion of the different balls. Have students discuss how they might measure the motion of the balls. Ask what they might measure. Encourage students to think about more than just the speed of the balls. Record students' ideas on the board.

Think About Moving Objects

Discuss with students their experiences with moving objects. Ask: *Can you name some objects that move quickly? Can you name some objects that move slowly?* Record students' responses on the board. Have students record the objects in their Science Notebooks. For each object, ask students to provide a description and tell if it moves by itself or with help. Ask students to think about situations in which objects move slowly and quickly. Have students share their descriptions with the class.

Chapter 12 Planning Guide			
Instructional Periods	**National Standards**	**Lab Manual**	**Workbook**
12.1 2 Periods	A1, A2, B2, C3, C5, D3, G2; A2, B4, C6, G2; UCP2, UCP4	**Lab 12A: p. 67** Measuring Speed **Lab 12B: pp. 68–69** Graphing Motion **Lab 12C: pp. 70–72** Acceleration and Marbles	Key Concept Review p. 73 Vocabulary Review p. 74 Interpreting Diagrams p.75 Reading Comprehension p. 76 Curriculum Connection pp. 77–78 Science Challenge p. 79
12.2 2 Periods	A1, B1, C1, C3, C5; A2, B4, B6, C5, C6; UCP1, UCP5		
12.3 2 Periods	A2, B2, B3; A2, B4, B5, B6; UCP1, UCP3		

Middle School Standard; High School Standard; Unifying Concept and Principle

12.1 Introduce

ENGAGE Ask one student to walk from one side of the room to the other side. Ask: *Who was in motion? How do you know? How could you measure the student's rate of motion?* Encourage students to recognize that when they observe an object's motion and measure its rate of motion, they are using objects that are not moving as reference points.

Vocabulary terms are listed on the first student page of each lesson. You may wish to preview the terms before introducing each lesson. Strategies for teaching the vocabulary appear on the pages where the terms are introduced.

Before You Read

Ask students to preview the lesson and identify the vocabulary terms. Record the terms on the board. Choose one of the terms and ask several different students to use it in a sentence. Have students record the term and one of the sentences in their Science Notebooks.

Teach

EXPLAIN to students that in this lesson, they will learn to define motion relative to different reference points. They will also learn to compare distance and displacement, relate average and instantaneous speed, and interpret distance-time graphs of motion.

 Vocabulary

motion Explain to students that the word *motion* comes from the Latin word *mōtiō*, meaning "to move." An object in motion "moves" from one location to another.

reference point Tell students that the prefix *re-* in the word *reference* means "back," and the root *ferre* comes from the Latin word meaning "to take or bring." A reference point is a stationary object used to judge the motion of other objects.

displacement Explain to students that the prefix *dis-* means "out." When something is displaced, it is "placed out." Displacement, as used to define motion, measures the distance "out of place" from where an object starts to where it finishes.

- Define *motion* relative to different reference points.
- Compare distance and displacement.
- Relate average and instantaneous speed.
- Interpret distance-time graphs of motion.

New Vocabulary

motion
reference point
displacement
speed
average speed
instantaneous speed

12.1 Measuring Motion

Before You Read

Write the vocabulary terms for this lesson in your Science Notebook. As you read their definitions, write a sentence for each term that includes its meaning.

Look around the classroom. Are people holding onto their seats? Are they attached to their chairs by seatbelts? Probably not. More likely, they are sitting comfortably in their seats without having to hold on. Nonetheless, they are moving extremely fast. In fact, everyone on Earth is moving almost 30 kilometers every second! To understand how this can be true, it is first necessary to define *motion*.

Figure 12.1 Moving objects are all around. A bird in flight, children in a race, and dogs pulling a sled are just a few examples of motion.

Motion and Position

An object is in **motion** when it changes position. An object's position is its location. When an object moves from one location to another, it is changing position. The eagle in **Figure 12.1** is in motion as it flies from one tree to another. The children are in motion as they move away from the starting line toward the finish line of the wheelbarrow race. The dogsled is in motion as its place along the racecourse changes.

Reference Point In the description above, each of the examples of motion in Figure 12.1 was compared with an object or group of objects that were considered to be stationary, or still. The eagle was compared with nearby trees. The children were compared with the ground. The dogsled was compared with the racecourse.

An object or group of objects that is considered to be stationary is known as a **reference point.** An object changes position if it moves in relation to some reference point. Earth's surface and everything attached to it are common reference points.

Relative Motion In addition to Earth, other objects in the universe—such as the Sun, other stars, and the planets—can be used as reference points. When the Sun is used as a reference point, Earth is moving.

E L L Strategy

Model Have groups of students use clay or other materials to make a model of Earth revolving around the Sun. Students should use string or wire to rotate Earth on its axis and revolve it around the Sun. Then they should do the same thing with the Moon, rotating it on its axis and revolving it around Earth. Ask students to think about using Earth as a reference point for the Moon and using the Sun as a reference point for Earth. Have each group present its model to the class and describe the relative movements of the objects in its Sun-Earth-Moon system.

It takes one year for Earth to orbit, or travel around, the Sun. Earth can move this great distance in a relatively short amount of time because the planet travels very quickly—over 100,000 kilometers an hour. Everything on Earth moves with Earth and is therefore moving relative to the Sun. This explains how students in a classroom can be moving even when they are sitting in their seats.

Motion is described as *relative* because it depends on the reference point with which an object is being compared. Objects that are moving when compared with one reference point may not be moving when compared with another. A student who is not moving relative to a desk is moving relative to the Sun. The jets in **Figure 12.2** are moving very fast relative to the ground, but they are not moving at all relative to one another. This makes it possible for them to perform dangerous maneuvers in midair.

Displacement

A honeybee travels away from its nest in search of food. To let other bees from its hive know that it has located nectar, the bee does what is known as a "waggle dance." The nature of the dance provides information about the distance, direction, and amount of nectar. The bee moves in a pattern similar to the one shown in **Figure 12.3.**

The motion of the bee can be described in terms of distance and displacement. The distance the bee moves is the actual length the bee travels. The **displacement** is the distance and direction from the starting point to the ending point. In the case of the waggle dance, the bee ends up where it started, so although it traveled some distance, it does not have any overall displacement.

Both distance and displacement are lengths, so they are measured in units of length, such as meters or kilometers. **Figure 12.4** shows how distance and displacement can vary when walking around the block.

Figure 12.2 The jets of the Blue Angels move relative to Earth and the Sun, but not relative to one another.

Waggle Dance

Figure 12.3 A honeybee travels a large distance, but its overall displacement can be quite small.

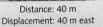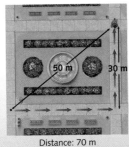

Distance: 40 m	Distance: 70 m	Distance: 140 m
Displacement: 40 m east	Displacement: 50 m northeast	Displacement: 0 m

Figure 12.4 How does the distance walked differ from the displacement in these examples?

Teach

Teach

EXPLAIN to students that they will learn about two different measures of speed: average speed and instantaneous speed.

 Explore It!

Choose medium to small balls made of lightweight or soft materials (foam balls work best). Go outside for this activity, or spread groups of students around the room.

Students' throwing techniques will vary but might include bouncing off the ground, bouncing off a wall, and lobbing at three different heights. Check students' diagrams for accuracy in comparing distance and displacement.

As You Read

Have students share their sentences with partners. Encourage students to make changes to their sentences as they discuss the meaning of the vocabulary terms in pairs.

ANSWER Because the bus stops and starts many times, it does not travel at the same speed throughout the trip. Its average speed is the total distance it travels divided by the total time it takes. Its instantaneous speed changes throughout the entire trip.

Use the Visual: Figure 12.5

ANSWER instantaneous speed

 Vocabulary

speed Students are probably familiar with the word *speed* as it relates to how fast a vehicle or person is moving. Explain to students that the speed of an object is calculated by dividing distance by time. Point out to students that speed is directly proportional to distance and inversely proportional to time.

average speed Remind students of the meaning of the word *average* and the method of calculating averages in math. Then have students combine this meaning with the meaning of the word *speed* to develop a definition of the term.

  Explore It!

Stand about 3 m from a partner. Throw a ball to your partner at least three different ways so that the distance the ball travels is different from its displacement.

In your Science Notebook, draw a diagram showing the three different paths of the ball. Estimate to compare the distance with the displacement of the ball each time.

As You Read

Review the sentences you have recorded in your Science Notebook for *speed, average speed*, and *instantaneous speed*. Revise facts or supporting details as needed.

Why is the average speed of a school bus different from its instantaneous speed as the bus runs its morning route?

Speed

How fast or slow an object moves is its speed. Speed is a rate, which means it compares two measurements. Speed compares the change in an object's position with time. An object's **speed** is the distance it travels divided by the time it takes to travel that distance. Speed can be calculated using the following equation:

$$\text{speed} = \frac{\text{distance}}{\text{time}}$$

Distance is measured in units of length, such as meters or kilometers. Common units of time are seconds or hours. Speed, therefore, is measured in a unit of length divided by a unit of time. The SI unit of speed is meters per second (m/s). Kilometers per hour (km/h) is another common unit of speed.

Average Speed Some objects travel at a constant speed, which is speed that does not change. Most often, however, an object's speed changes as it moves. Think about traveling in a car that is speeding up to enter a highway, slowing down to make a turn, or coming to a stop at a red light. Overall, the car travels a 5-km trip in 0.25 hour. Should the car's speed be described as its fastest speed, slowest speed, or something in between? The speed of an object that changes speed can be described by an average. **Average speed** is the total distance divided by the total time. The car's average speed was

$$\text{average speed} = \frac{5 \text{ km}}{0.25 \text{ h}} = 20 \text{ km/h}$$

Instantaneous Speed Even though the speed of an object changes, the speed at a given point in the trip can be calculated. The speed of an object at one instant in time is its **instantaneous** (ihn stan TAY nee uhs) **speed.** To compare average speed and instantaneous speed, consider a student walking to the library. The student might travel 2 km in 0.5 h, for an average speed of 4 km/h. The instantaneous speed might have been 3 km/h while walking on a sidewalk, 6 km/h while running across the street, and 0 km/h while waiting at a crosswalk.

Figure 12.5 Throughout a trip, a car changes speed many times. The speedometer shows how fast the car is moving at any given instant. What type of speed is this?

instantaneous speed Explain to students that the word *instantaneous* means "occurring or present at a particular instant." Have students combine this meaning with the meaning of the word *speed* to develop a definition of the term. Then have students compare and contrast average speed and instantaneous speed using their definitions.

Field Study

Divide students into groups and have them brainstorm lists of various types of motions they can observe at school and outside of school. Instruct groups to monitor these areas and check off motions they can observe within a class period. Tell students to complete the activity by describing the speed of the motion they observed as constant, average, or instantaneous.

Graphing Motion

One way to represent an object's speed is to use a distance-time graph, on which time is plotted on the horizontal axis and distance is plotted on the vertical axis. Each axis must cover the range of numbers to be plotted. Then each axis can be divided into equal intervals.

The graph in **Figure 12.6** represents the motion of three swimmers during a 30-minute workout. Mary's motion is represented by the red line. Kathy's motion is represented by the blue line. Both of these lines are straight because both girls swam at a constant speed. Note, however, that the red line is steeper than the blue line. A line's steepness, or slant, on a graph is known as its slope. Mary's line has a steeper slope because she swam faster than Kathy did. The green line on the graph represents Julie's motion. Julie did not swim at a constant speed.

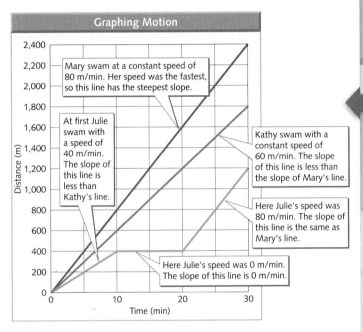

Figure 12.6 A line's slope on a distance-time graph is the speed of a moving object.

After You Read

1. Give an example in which the distance you travel is different from your displacement.
2. Review the sentence you wrote in your Science Notebook about a distance-time graph. Explain how a line's slope is related to an object's speed.

Musical pieces can be described by their speed, which is known as tempo. Tempo is a steady pulse, much like the ticking of a clock. The tempo can be fast, slow, or something in between. It can also change at different parts of the piece. The tempo of a piece affects how the music sounds and the mood it creates. Usually written at the beginning of a musical piece, tempo is measured in beats per minute (BPM).

Figure It Out

1. Determine Mary's instantaneous speed at five minutes.
2. What is Julie's average speed over the 30-minute period?

 Extend It!

Look through magazines and newspapers to find photos that show motion. Make a collage on poster board showing the different examples of motion you collected.

Teach

EXPLAIN to students that they will learn how to graph the speed of an object.

 CONNECTION: **Music**

Play students several different music selections with different BPM values. Ask students to estimate the beats per minute. Discuss with students the way in which the number of beats per minute affects the experience of listening to the song.

Have students write about their music preferences. Ask students to look up the BPM for their favorite songs and see if any patterns emerge.

Figure It Out: Figure 12.6
ANSWER **1.** 80 m/min **2.** 40 m/min

Extend It!

Ask students to bring in old copies of newspapers and magazines. As students look for pictures, encourage them to also look for patterns in the types of pictures they find.

Assess

Use the After You Read questions and the Alternative Assessment to help you evaluate students' understanding of the lesson.

After You Read

1. Sample answer: The student might walk from store to store in a mall and return to the starting point, so there is no overall displacement.
2. The steeper the slope of a line on the graph, the greater the speed of the object. A horizontal line indicates that the object is not moving.

Teacher Alert

Students often mistake a flat line on a distance-time graph as an indication that the object is moving at a constant speed. It is important to reinforce the idea that a flat line indicates that the object is not moving. If there is no change in distance, there is no motion. You may wish to draw a speed-distance graph and describe how a flat line on this graph indicates constant speed.

ELL Strategy

Act Out Divide students into groups of three. Have each group study the distance-time graph in **Figure 12.6,** which represents the motion of three different swimmers. Have students each act out the speed of one of the objects. The student representing the object with the steepest slope should be the student who travels at the fastest speed.

Alternative Assessment

Provide students with a list of the vocabulary terms from the lesson. Ask students to write a definition for each term in their own words and use it in a sentence.

12.2 Introduce

ENGAGE Have four student volunteers stand in the front of the room. Divide them into two pairs. Have one member of each pair stand on the left side of the room, and the other on the right. Each pair should be given a ball: for one pair it should be the student on the left side of the room, and for the other, the student on the right side of the room. Ask each pair to pass the ball back and forth in opposite directions. Encourage the pairs to time their passes so the balls are moving simultaneously across the room in opposite directions. Ask: *How do the speeds of the balls compare? How do the velocities compare?* Encourage students to see that while the balls are moving at the same or similar speeds, their velocities are different because they are moving in different directions.

Ask students to draw a diagram of the two balls in motion in their Science Notebooks. Then, have them write an explanation of how the speed and velocity of the balls differ.

Before You Read

Ask students to preview the lesson and find the titles, headings, and subheadings. Have students work with partners to record the lesson outline in their Science Notebooks. Encourage students to check each other's work for completeness.

● Teach

EXPLAIN to students that in this lesson, they will learn to distinguish between velocity and speed. Tell students that they will also learn to relate velocity to acceleration, to calculate acceleration, and to interpret speed-time graphs.

Use the Visual: Figure 12.7

[ANSWER] Speed describes the distance traveled by an object in a given amount of time. Velocity describes both the speed of an object and the direction of its motion.

Figure 12.7 While the speed of a chair on the ski lift might be 2 km/h, the velocity might be 2 km/h northward or 2 km/h southward. How is velocity different from speed?

Figure 12.8 Velocities can be added together if they are in the same direction or subtracted from each other if they are in opposite directions.

12.2 Velocity and Acceleration

Before You Read

Create a lesson outline in your Science Notebook using the title, headings, and subheadings of this lesson. Use the outline to think about what you will learn.

A tourist wants to climb to the top of a snow-covered mountain. A baseball player wants to catch a shallow fly ball. In each case, both the speed and direction of motion must be considered. The tourist needs to move up. The baseball player needs to move toward home plate.

Velocity

The chairs of the ski lift in **Figure 12.7** are rising up the mountain at the same speed as the chairs that are coming down. The difference in their motion is their direction. **Velocity** (vuh LAH suh tee) describes both the speed of an object and the direction of its motion.

Like all properties of motion, velocity is measured relative to some reference point. Again, Earth is the most commonly used reference point. If an object moves relative to another object that is considered to be moving relative to Earth, the velocities of the objects combine. The velocities can combine either by adding together or subtracting from each other. The overall velocity is known as the resultant velocity.

Adding Velocities Suppose a train is moving eastward at 100 km/h relative to an observer on the ground. A passenger walks toward the front of the train at 8 km/h relative to the people seated on the train. The observer on the ground would then measure that passenger's overall velocity as 108 km/h eastward (100 km/h eastward + 8 km/h eastward).

Subtracting Velocities Now suppose the same passenger walks at 8 km/h toward the back of the train. In this case, an observer on the ground would then measure the passenger's overall velocity as 92 km/h eastward (100 km/h eastward − 8 km/h westward).

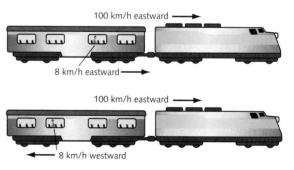

100 km/h eastward

8 km/h eastward

100 km/h eastward

8 km/h westward

ELL Strategy

Illustrate Direct students' attention to **Figure 12.8.** Explain that this visual illustrates the concept of velocity and how velocities combine. Tell students to draw their own examples of combining velocities by addition and subtraction. Have each student present his or her drawing to the class and explain how the velocities are combined.

CONNECTION: Life Science

An echo is produced when a sound reflects off a distant object. The amount of time that passes between the production of the sound and the perception of the echo can be used to calculate the distance to the object. This method of measuring distance and creating a map of a region is known as echolocation.

Echolocation is essential to some animals that are blind or live in darkness, such as bats. Bats use echolocation to navigate and to hunt. A bat sends short bursts of sound out in different directions. The sound reflects off nearby objects and returns to the bat. The bat can then determine both the distance to and direction of the object. Both the speed of the sound and the direction in which it travels, and therefore the velocity, are essential to using echolocation.

Acceleration

The velocity of an object is constant only if the object's speed and direction remain the same. If the speed or direction of an object changes, the velocity of the object changes. The rate of change in velocity is called **acceleration** (ak sel uh RAY shun). An object accelerates when it speeds up, slows down, or changes direction.

Speeding Up   The runners in **Figure 12.9** are at the starting blocks. When the gun sounds, the runners will start moving and continue to move faster and faster. They are accelerating because their speed is increasing, which means their velocity is changing.

Slowing Down   The Space Shuttle in Figure 12.9 is slowing down upon its return to Earth. Its velocity is changing because its speed is decreasing. A change in velocity that results from slowing down is known as negative acceleration, or deceleration.

Changing Direction   The people on the swing carousel in Figure 12.9 are traveling at constant speed, neither speeding up nor slowing down. However, their direction is changing as they move in a circle. Therefore, their velocity is changing and they are accelerating.

Figure 12.9   Acceleration is a change in velocity. An object's velocity changes when the object speeds up, slows down, or changes direction.

● Teach

EXPLAIN to students that in this section of the lesson, they will learn about acceleration.

CONNECTION: Life Science

Echolocation is also used in ultrasound technologies to produce two-dimensional images of organs inside the body. One of the most common uses of ultrasound is to see an image of a human fetus inside a woman's uterus.

EXTEND Give students an opportunity to experiment with the concept of echolocation by providing the following problem for calculation:

Suppose an echo is heard 2.2 seconds after the sound is produced. If the speed of sound in air is 345 m/s, how far away is the reflecting object? If it took 2.2 seconds to hear the echo, then it took half that time, or 1.1 seconds, for the sound to reach the reflecting object and 1.1 seconds to travel back from the reflecting object. Rearranging the speed equation shows that the distance to the reflecting object is 345 m/s $\times$ 1.1 s = 379.5 m.

Vocabulary

velocity   Tell students that the word *velocity* comes from the Latin word *vēlōcitās*, meaning "swift." Velocity is a description of the "swiftness" of an object and the direction of its motion.

acceleration   Explain to students that the word *acceleration* comes from the Latin word *accelerāre*, which means "to quicken." Acceleration measures a change in velocity when an object "quickens," slows down, or changes direction.

Teach

 EXPLAIN to students that in this section of the lesson, they will learn how to calculate acceleration and understand the difference between positive and negative acceleration.

Use the Visual: Figure 12.10

ANSWER Acceleration is calculated by dividing the change in velocity by the time during which the change occurred. To determine the change in velocity, the initial velocity is subtracted from the final velocity. The equation is acceleration = (final velocity − initial velocity)/time.

CONNECTION: Math

Draw a number line on the board using positive and negative numbers. Have a student stand at the zero mark on the number line. Ask the student to move to a number on the line. As the student moves, record the addition and subtraction on the board. Use this example to model adding and subtracting positive and negative numbers.

Discuss with students the following concept: Positive numbers are greater than zero. For every positive number, there is a negative number that is its opposite. Negative numbers are written with a minus sign in front. Subtracting a greater number from a smaller one results in a negative number.

Did You Know?

The change in velocity of an object moving in a circle is known as centripetal acceleration. The word *centripetal* comes from the Latin words *centrum*, meaning "center," and *petere*, meaning "tending toward." The amount of centripetal acceleration depends on the radius of the circle and the speed of the object.

CONNECTION: Math

In science, positive and negative numbers can represent objects that are speeding up or slowing down, respectively. They can also be used to indicate direction.

Figure 12.10 An object that is speeding up has positive acceleration, whereas an object that is slowing down has negative acceleration. How is acceleration calculated?

Calculating Acceleration

For an object moving in a straight line, acceleration is the rate of change in velocity. To determine the acceleration of an object, first calculate the change in velocity by subtracting the initial velocity from the final velocity. Then divide the change in velocity by the amount of time over which the change occurred.

$$\text{acceleration} = \frac{\text{(final velocity − initial velocity)}}{\text{time}}$$

If the direction of motion does not change, the change in velocity is the same as the change in speed. The change in velocity is then the final speed minus the initial speed. The change in velocity is a unit of speed, such as m/s. Therefore, the unit of acceleration is a unit of speed divided by a unit of time. Time is commonly measured in seconds. In SI units, acceleration is measured in meters per second per second, or m/s^2.

Positive Acceleration An object that speeds up has positive acceleration. Its final velocity is greater than its initial velocity. Consider a boat at rest at a dock. The boat then travels in a straight line and speeds up to 50 m/s in 25 s. Because it started from rest, its initial speed was zero. Its acceleration can be calculated as follows:

$$\text{acceleration} = \frac{\text{(50 m/s − 0 m/s)}}{25 \text{ s}} = 2 \text{ m/s}^2$$

Notice that the calculated acceleration is a positive value.

Negative Acceleration An object that slows down has negative acceleration. Now consider a person on rollerblades moving in a straight line. She slows down from 3 m/s and comes to a stop in 2 s. Her acceleration can be calculated as follows:

$$\text{acceleration} = \frac{\text{(0 m/s − 3 m/s)}}{2 \text{ s}} = -1.5 \text{ m/s}^2$$

In this case, the calculated acceleration is a negative value.

Differentiate Instruction

Logical and Mathematical Provide students with graphs that show the velocity of several different objects over time. Have students use the data from the graphs to calculate the acceleration for each of the objects. Students should perform their calculations individually and then compare their results with their peers. If their calculations differ, have students recalculate the acceleration together.

Key Concept Review
Workbook, p. 73

Graphing Acceleration

Like speed, the acceleration of an object can be represented using a graph. For this graph, speed is plotted on the vertical axis and time is plotted on the horizontal axis. The resulting graph is known as a speed-time graph. In this graph, the slope of the line provides information about the rate of acceleration.

Examine the graph in **Figure 12.11**. In section A, speed increases from 0 m/s to 10 m/s in 2 s. The acceleration during this section is therefore 5 m/s². The line in section A slopes upward, and the acceleration is positive. An object that is speeding up is represented by a line with a positive, or upward, slope on a speed-time graph.

In section B of the graph, the line is flat, so the slope of the line is zero. The speed is not zero. The object is moving at a constant speed of 10 m/s. However, the acceleration is zero because the speed is not changing.

An object that is slowing down is represented by a line with a negative, or downward, slope on a speed-time graph. In section C, the object is slowing down from a speed of 10 m/s to 4 m/s in 2 s. Its acceleration is therefore −3 m/s².

Figure 12.11 Acceleration is represented by a speed-time graph. When the line slants upward, the object is speeding up. When the line slants downward, the object is slowing down.

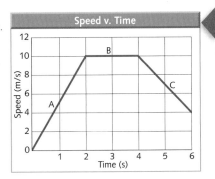

 CONNECTION: Life Science

Reaching top speeds of up to 120 km/h, the cheetah is the fastest animal on land. It is also capable of amazing acceleration: from rest to 80 km/h in just 3 s. Moving so fast uses a great deal of energy. Cheetahs can maintain these speeds for only short periods of time, after which they must stop to rest and cool down.

Figure It Out

1. What is the speed of the object during section B?

2. What is the acceleration of the object during section B?

After You Read

1. Explain how speed and velocity are alike and how they are different.

2. How is velocity related to acceleration?

3. Calculate the acceleration of a person riding a bicycle in a straight line who speeds up from 4 m/s to 6 m/s in 5 s.

4. In the outline you have developed in your Science Notebook, add a sketch of a speed-time graph below the heading for *Graphing Acceleration*. Show positive, negative, and zero acceleration on the graph.

Background Information

The cheetah stands out from other wild cats in several ways. It is the world's fastest land animal. The cheetah is not an aggressive animal, using its speed to avoid rather than confront predators. It has many physical adaptations that increase its speed and acceleration. The cheetah has a long, narrow, lightweight body; a strong heart; and specialized muscles that allow for fast turns and prevent rollover.

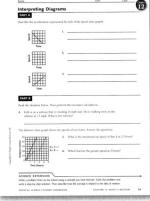

Interpreting Diagrams
Workbook, p. 75

● Teach

EXPLAIN to students that in this section of the lesson, they will learn how to read and interpret a graph of acceleration.

CONNECTION: Life Science

The cheetah population has declined rapidly since the 1900s due to hunting and the disappearance of its natural habitat.

Have students work in pairs to research some other animals that are capable of achieving great speeds. Also, have them identify animals at the other extreme. Suggest that student pairs present their findings to the class in the form of creative displays. After English language learners research their chosen animal, they should collaborate with one or two other pairs to compare the results of this research. The larger group can create a graphic illustrating the range of speeds among the animals, labeling the illustration fully. They can present their individual pair findings, as well as the larger group findings, to the entire class.

Figure It Out: Figure 12.11
ANSWER **1.** 10 m/s **2.** 0 m/s²

● Assess

Use the After You Read questions and Alternative Assessment to help you evaluate students' understanding of this lesson.

After You Read

1. Both speed and velocity measure the change in distance relative to a change in time. However, velocity includes the direction of motion, whereas speed does not.

2. Acceleration is the rate of change in velocity.

3. 0.4 m/s²

4. Sketches will vary.

Alternative Assessment

Provide students with a list of the headings from the lesson. Ask students to write examples for each of the headings without referring to their Science Notebooks.

12.3 Introduce

ENGAGE Hang two balls from two strings. Hold the two strings in one hand, and with the other hand, pull one of the balls away and then let it swing back to hit the other ball. Ask: *What happens to the balls when they hit each other? How does the direction of each ball change when they come in contact with each other? What would it look like if I used larger or heavier balls for this demonstration?* Explain to students that the momentum of the ball causes the other ball to move. Tell students that they will learn more about momentum in this lesson.

Before You Read

Write the word *momentum* on the board. Ask students to work in pairs to write definitions of the word. Have pairs share their definitions with the class. Encourage students to refine their definitions as they learn more about momentum in this lesson.

Teach

EXPLAIN that in this lesson, students will learn to calculate the momentum of an object and to recognize that momentum is conserved.

Use the Visual: Figure 12.12

ANSWER Momentum is mass times velocity.

 Vocabulary

momentum Tell students that the word *momentum* comes from the Latin word *mōmentum*, meaning "moving power." Momentum measures the "movement" (velocity) and the "power" (mass) of an object. The greater the mass and/or the velocity of an object, the greater its momentum.

law of conservation of momentum
Explain to students that the prefix *con-* in the word *conservation* means "with," and the root *servāre* means "to preserve." Tell students that the law of conservation of momentum states that when objects collide, no momentum is created or lost. It is "preserved with" the objects.

Learning Goals

- Calculate the momentum of an object.
- Recognize that momentum is conserved.

New Vocabulary

momentum
law of conservation of momentum

12.3 Momentum

Before You Read

Make predictions about what you think *momentum* is. Write your predictions in your Science Notebook using descriptive words and examples.

In a popular desktop toy known as Newton's cradle, one ball is pulled back and allowed to swing into a row of suspended balls. The impact of the ball causes the ball at the other end to swing upward. When this ball swings back into the row, the first ball is sent swinging once again. What causes the balls to behave in this way? One major cause of the motion is momentum.

Calculating Momentum

Momentum is a property of a moving object that is equal to the mass of the object multiplied by the velocity of the object. Because velocity includes direction, momentum has a direction associated with it. An object's momentum is in the direction of its velocity.

Momentum can be calculated as follows:

$$\text{momentum} = \text{mass} \times \text{velocity}$$

If mass is measured in kilograms and velocity in meters per second, momentum has units of kilogram-meters per second, or $kg \cdot m/s$.

Momentum and Velocity The greater the velocity of an object is, the greater the object's momentum is. Consider, for example, a 12-kg bicycle. The calculations below show how the bicycle's momentum increases as its velocity increases.

At 2 m/s southward:
momentum = 12 kg × 2 m/s
= 24 kg • m/s southward

At 3 m/s southward:
momentum = 12 kg × 3 m/s
= 36 kg • m/s southward

Momentum and Mass The greater the mass of an object is, the greater the object's momentum is. This time, consider a cart moving at a velocity of 2 m/s westward. Bricks can be added to the cart to change its mass. The calculations below show how the cart's momentum increases as its mass increases.

At 2 kg:
momentum = 2 kg × 2 m/s
= 4 kg • m/s westward

At 5 kg:
momentum = 5 kg × 2 m/s
= 10 kg • m/s westward

Figure 12.12 This is an example of Newton's cradle. The momentum of one ball can cause a different ball to move. What is momentum?

Differentiate Instruction

Kinesthetic Provide students with marbles of different sizes. Have students find the mass of each marble and record the data in their Science Notebooks. Set up a marble "track" and measure the distance from the start to the finish. Use a stopwatch to record the time it takes for each marble to travel the distance. Have students calculate the momentum of each marble using the data they have collected. Ask students to compare the momentum of each marble. Ask students how the mass of an object affects its momentum.

Conservation of Momentum

When two objects collide, one object's momentum can be transferred to the other object. No momentum is created or lost in the process. The **law of conservation of momentum** states that if no other forces act on the objects, their total momentum remains the same after they interact.

The law of conservation of momentum explains the Newton's cradle shown in **Figure 12.12.** The ball that is pulled back has a certain amount of momentum. When it collides with the next ball in line, its momentum is transferred to that ball. That ball has nowhere to move, so its momentum is transferred to the next ball. These transfers continue until the last ball in line is reached, where the ball is free to swing away.

Collisions Between Objects

The amount of momentum that is transferred when two objects collide depends on the objects' initial motion. In the photo on the left in **Figure 12.13,** both pucks are moving toward the right. They have the same mass, but the puck on the left is moving faster. Its momentum is greater than the momentum of the puck on the right.

After they collide, both pucks will continue to move in the same direction. The puck on the right will speed up, and the puck on the left will slow down. The momentum of each puck will change, but the total momentum of both pucks will be the same as it was before the collision.

In the photo on the right, the pucks are moving at the same speed toward each other. As a result, their momentum is equal in magnitude but opposite in direction. After they collide, each reverses direction. They again travel at the same speed, but in opposite directions. Thus their total momentum is the same before and after the collision.

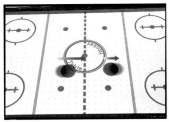 

Figure 12.13 Momentum is conserved when two objects collide.

After You Read

1. What is the momentum of a 50-kg dolphin swimming 10.4 m/s?
2. Use the notes in your Science Notebook to compare the momentum of two billiard balls before and after they collide.

CHAPTER 12 **203**

Teach

EXPLAIN to students that in this part of the lesson, they will learn about conservation of momentum.

As You Read

Have students work with partners to compare and refine their definitions of *momentum.* When each pair is satisfied with its definition, have those students join with another pair and continue to compare and refine the definitions. Record the final definitions on the board.

ANSWER The equation is:
momentum = mass × velocity

Figure It Out: Figure 12.13

ANSWER **1.** Multiply the mass of one puck by its velocity, and add the product to the product of the mass of the other puck and its velocity. **2.** The total momentum is zero.

Assess

Use the After You Read questions and Alternative Assessment to help you evaluate students' understanding of this lesson.

After You Read

1. 520 kg · m/s
2. The momentum is the same due to the law of conservation of momentum, which states that if no other forces act on the objects, the total momentum of the objects remains the same after the objects interact.

Alternative Assessment

Ask students to write their own definitions of *momentum* without referring to their Science Notebooks.

ELL Strategy

Illustrate Divide students into small groups or pairs. Provide each group with four marbles and the lid of a shoe box. Have students roll the marbles so that they collide with each other. Ask students to illustrate the path of the marbles.

Have students describe in their Science Notebooks the momentum of the marbles as illustrated by their drawings. Their descriptions should include observations about any differences that relate to mass, as well as a description of the momentum.

Chapter 12 Summary

VOCABULARY REVIEW

Check students' sentences or paragraphs to make sure they understand the meaning of each vocabulary term.

Evaluate students' essays using the following criteria:

1. The topic sentence, or main idea, should restate the Key Concept.
2. The supporting paragraphs should incorporate the answers to the Learning Goal questions students have written and include details, facts, and examples they have recorded in their Science Notebooks.
3. The concluding sentence should sum up the main idea of the chapter and restate the Key Concept.

MASTERING CONCEPTS

True or False

1. False, stationary or still
2. False, position
3. True
4. False, divided
5. False, slope
6. True
7. False, negative
8. False, mass
9. False, conserved

Short Answer

10. His average speed is 4 km/h. His instantaneous speed cannot be determined because he might not have walked at a constant speed.
11. The velocity is greater relative to the other car because the other car is also moving and the velocities combine in this case.
12. The object is not accelerating.
13. The racehorse will have greater momentum because it has more mass than the pony does.

Chapter 12 Summary

KEY CONCEPTS

12.1 Measuring Motion

- Motion is a change in an object's position relative to some reference point that is considered to be stationary.
- Distance is the actual length an object moves, whereas displacement is the distance between the starting and ending points.
- An object's average speed is the total distance it travels divided by the total amount of time it takes to travel that distance.
- Instantaneous speed is an object's speed at a specific instant in time.
- The speed of an object can be represented on a distance-time graph, in which the slope of the line is determined by the object's speed.

12.2 Velocity and Acceleration

- Velocity describes an object's motion in terms of speed and direction.
- The rate of change in an object's velocity is called acceleration.
- Acceleration is equal to the change in an object's velocity divided by the time during which the change occurred.
- A speed-time graph can be used to represent an object's acceleration. The slope of the line is determined by the object's acceleration.

12.3 Momentum

- The momentum of an object is equal to the product of its mass and velocity.
- According to the law of conservation of momentum, the total momentum of a system does not change if outside forces do not act on the system.

VOCABULARY REVIEW

Write each term in a complete sentence or write a paragraph relating several terms.

12.1
motion, p. 194
reference point, p. 194
displacement, p. 195
speed, p. 196
average speed, p. 196
instantaneous speed, p. 196

12.2
velocity, p. 198
acceleration, p. 199

12.3
momentum, p. 202
law of conservation of momentum, p. 203

PREPARE FOR CHAPTER TEST

To prepare for the chapter test, create a question from each Learning Goal. Use the information in your Science Notebook to answer each question. Then use these answers to write a well-developed essay about the chapter. Use the Key Concept on the first page of this chapter as your topic sentence.

Vocabulary Review
Workbook, p. 74

Reading Comprehension
Workbook, p. 76

True or False
If the statement is true, write "true." If it is false, change the underlined word or words to make the statement true.

1. A reference point is considered to be <u>moving</u>.
2. An object is in motion when its <u>mass</u> changes.
3. The <u>displacement</u> of an object is the distance between the starting position and the ending position.
4. Speed is equal to distance <u>multiplied</u> by time.
5. The <u>length</u> of a line on a distance-time graph is determined by an object's speed.
6. The rate of change in <u>velocity</u> is acceleration.
7. An object that slows down has <u>positive</u> acceleration.
8. The momentum of an object is equal to its velocity multiplied by <u>distance</u>.
9. Momentum is <u>destroyed</u> when two objects collide.

Short Answer
Answer each of the following in a sentence or brief paragraph.

10. A boy leaves school at 3:00 P.M. and walks 2 km to his house. If he gets home at 3:30 P.M., what was his average speed? Are you able to determine his instantaneous speed? Explain.
11. Two cars are approaching each other. How does the velocity of one car relative to the other compare with the velocity relative to the ground?
12. What does a horizontal line on a speed-time graph indicate about the motion of an object traveling in a straight line?
13. Compare the momentum of a small pony and a large racehorse trotting with the same velocity.

Critical Thinking
Use what you have learned in this chapter to answer each of the following.

14. **Predict** A girl walks 2 km north, then 2 km east, then 2 km south, then 2 km west. What is the total distance she walks? What is her total displacement?
15. **Describe** How might an object with an acceleration of 0 m/s² be moving?
16. **Infer** The stopping distance is the length traveled by a car after the driver applies the brakes. Suggest why the stopping distance increases with the mass of the car for cars traveling at the same velocity.
17. **Use an Analogy** Conservation of momentum can be compared with the use of money to buy and sell things. Use an example to describe how the two concepts can be likened to each other.

Standardized Test Question
Choose the letter of the response that correctly answers the question.

Runner	Distance Covered (km)	Time (min)
Daisy	12.5	42
Jane	7.8	38
Bill	10.5	32
Joe	8.9	30

18. The table shows the distance traveled by four runners and the time it took each runner to travel that distance. Which runner has the fastest average speed?
    - **A.** Daisy
    - **B.** Jane
    - **C.** Bill
    - **D.** Joe

Test-Taking Tip
If you don't understand the directions, you can usually ask the teacher to explain them better. When the directions are clear enough for you to understand the question completely, you are less likely to pick the wrong answer.

Critical Thinking
14. The distance she traveled is 8 km. Her displacement is zero because she ends up back at her starting point.
15. It would move in a straight line at constant speed.
16. The greater the mass, the greater the momentum. Momentum describes how difficult it is to change, or stop, an object's motion.
17. Assume the total amount of money in circulation is constant. People exchange money with each other. The amount one person has might decrease, whereas the amount another person has might increase. The total amount, however, remains the same.

Standardized Test Question
18. C

Reading Links

An Invisible Force: The Quest to Define the Laws of Motion (Science Quest)
Tracing the evolution of ideas from Copernicus and Galileo to Newton and the modern age, this highly readable book will equip readers with a better understanding of the concepts of motion and gravity and help them apply that knowledge.

Glen Phelan. National Geographic Society. 64 pp. Illustrated. Trade ISBN 978-0-7922-5540-6.

Objects in Motion: Principles of Classical Mechanics
This simple but comprehensive survey of the principles of motion, acceleration, momentum, and gravitation makes for a useful supplement to this chapter's introduction to the material. The book includes biographies of relevant scientists, suggested experiments, and guidance for additional research, among other valuable information.

Paul Fleisher. Lerner Publishing Group. 80 pp. Library ISBN 978-0-8225-2985-9.

Curriculum Connection
Workbook, pp. 77–78

Science Challenge
Workbook, p. 79

12A Measuring Speed

This prechapter introduction activity is designed to determine what students already know about speed by engaging them in measuring the speed of a running person and inferring the effect of stride length on a runner's speed.

Objectives

- predict the effect of stride length on speed
- measure the speed of runners with varying strides
- record data in a suitable way
- communicate conclusions

Planning

 15–20 minutes   groups of 3–4 students

Materials (per group)

- tape measure
- stopwatch
- masking tape or chalk

Advance Preparation

- Find an outdoor area or an indoor area such as a gym where students can run. You will likely need about 30 m; 10 m for students to accelerate, 10 m for data recording, and 10 m to slow down and stop. Have students clearly mark with tape or chalk the starting line and the 10-m and 20-m marks. Explain that they are to time the portion of the run between the 10-m and 20-m marks only.
- Suggest that students discuss the reasons for their predictions in their groups.

- Remind students that the same person must do the running.
- Keep in mind that some runners may get tired easily. An alternative is to do the experiment with multiple runners to see if their speeds decrease as the runs are repeated.

Engagement Guide

- Challenge students to think about measuring speed and the effect of varying a runner's stride by asking these questions:
  - *To determine the speed of a runner, what quantities must be measured?* (distance and time)
  - *Knowing what must be measured, what can you do to ensure the most accurate results?* (Responses will vary but should mention accurately measuring the distance and starting and stopping the stopwatch at the correct times.)
  - *How do you think decreasing the stride length will affect the speed of a runner?* (Many students will predict that taking shorter strides will decrease the average speed of a runner.)
- Encourage students to discuss the factors that affect a runner's speed.

Going Further

Have students investigates a runner's acceleration. A series of students with stopwatches can time a runner in 10-m increments. Comparing interval times will show that the runner is accelerating. If possible, have students determine how much distance is needed for the runner to reach full speed. Have students present their conclusions to the class.

12B Graphing Motion

Objectives

- measure and record distance and time data
- graph distance and time data
- analyze a speed v. time graph
- communicate conclusions

Skill Set

measuring, recording and analyzing data, comparing and contrasting, inferring, stating conclusions

Planning

 40–45 minutes   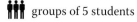 groups of 5 students

Materials

Materials for this activity are listed in the Student Laboratory Manual.

Advance Preparation

- Use an empty three-ring binder as a ramp for the marble. You might want to use a carpeted area, as it is important for the marble to slow down fairly quickly.
- Test how far the marble rolls when released from the top of the incline formed by the binder. Ideally, the marble should roll several meters and come to a stop within two seconds or so. Adjust as needed before the lab begins. Instruct students to mark off 0.5-m intervals on the floor based on the expected maximum distance. Depending on the actual conditions used, you might want to instruct student timers to use intervals other than those used in the procedure.

Answers to Observations: Data Table 1

Data will vary, but should show that the time required to travel each additional 0.5-m interval increases. This is an indication that the marble's speed is slowing.

Answers to Observations: Speed v. Time Graph

Graphs will vary, but should show a definite curved shape; the slope should decrease with increasing time.

Answers to Analysis and Conclusions

1. Yes, the marble slows down. The time required to cover each successive 0.5-m interval increases, indicating decreased speed. The flattening distance v. time curve also indicates slowing speed.

2. The slope of the curve is the distance/time, or speed. The curve represents the speed of the marble at various times.

Going Further

Extend the lab to introduce the topic of instantaneous speed. Tell students that the slope of the curve at any point gives the instantaneous speed of the marble. Calculate instantaneous speed at several points. Another example of time v. speed can be repeated outdoors with a runner and a student on a bike. Have students mark off 70 m, with a set of students at each 10-m mark. One student should keep track of time, and the other should be a recorder. Four students should be at each 10-m mark (one for the runner and one for the biker). Have all timers start their stopwatches when the runner and biker begin. Each timer should stop his or her stopwatch when the biker or runner passes the meter mark at which he or she is standing. Have the students plot the times on a time v. speed graph.

12C Acceleration and Marbles

Objectives

- measure the deceleration of a marble as it moves across a surface
- record data in a suitable way
- infer why the marble decelerates as it travels
- communicate conclusions

Skill Set

measuring, recording and analyzing data, inferring, drawing conclusions

Planning

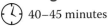 40–45 minutes 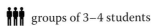 groups of 3–4 students

Materials

Materials for this activity are listed in the Student Laboratory Manual.

Advance Preparation

- Use wooden ramps that are about 15 cm wide and 60 cm long. (Ask your school's shop teacher or art teacher for scraps of wood or leftover wood that may be cut to these dimensions.)
- Perform this lab ahead of time to verify the proper height of books to use.
- For this activity, use an uncarpeted area, if possible, to reduce friction.
- Calculators may be provided to groups for faster calculation of the speeds and their averages.

Answers to Observations: Data Table 1

Answers will vary, but students should observe that the marble's average speed decreases the farther it rolls; that is, the marble decelerates.

Answers to Analysis and Conclusions

1. Answers will vary. Students' data should show that the marble traveled more slowly in each successive distance interval. Answers will vary for the amount of speed lost between the first and last intervals.

2. The marble accelerated positively as it moved down the ramp. Gravity caused the acceleration.

3. The marble decelerated from 0 m to 3 m. Friction between the marble and the rolling surface caused the marble to decelerate.

4. The deceleration would be much less on the gymnasium floor and much greater on the sand. The gym floor is very hard and smooth and offers little friction, whereas the friction between the marble and sand is very high.

Going Further

Have students collect photographs that depict motion from newspapers and magazines. Students should then make collages of their pictures on construction paper. Ask students to go through the pictures in their collages to determine whether each picture shows acceleration or deceleration. Encourage students to explain to the class how they categorized each picture.

Introduce Chapter 13

As a starting activity, use Lab 13A on page 73 of the Laboratory Manual.

ENGAGE Give small groups of students a variety of children's toys, such as toy cars, trains, cranes, balls, and yo-yos, to experiment with. They should figure out what actions each toy can perform (pushing, pulling, lifting, lowering) and keep a list of what they discover.

Think About Forces

Students' answers will vary but might include a rake, shovel, garbage pail, chair, pen, gate, door, wagon, blanket, computer mouse, or eating utensil. Have students volunteer some of the entries they have made and describe each with an appropriate verb. Record responses in a class chart.

Chapter
13 Nature of Forces

KEY CONCEPT A force is a push or pull on an object that can change the motion of the object.

Powerful thunderstorms roll through a region on a summer afternoon. Suddenly, a dark, funnel-shaped cloud appears in the sky. This violent storm, known as a tornado, is made up of swirling winds that reach speeds of up to 300 kilometers per hour. In only a few minutes, the storm pulls trees out of the ground, lifts cars into the air, and sends loose objects flying like missiles.

The destructive pushing and pulling actions of a tornado represent examples of the forces of nature. There are many types of forces in the universe. This chapter is about forces: their characteristics, measurement, and uses.

NSTA
SCiLINKS
THE WORLD'S A CLICK AWAY
www.scilinks.org
Forces **Code: WGPS13**

206

Think About Forces

You push and pull on other objects all the time. You might lift your books, throw a ball, or pedal a bicycle.

- In your Science Notebook, list five examples of objects that you move.
- Write a word that describes each example of motion you listed. Consider words such as *push, pull, lift,* and *lower.*

Chapter 13 Planning Guide

Instructional Periods	National Standards	Lab Manual	Workbook
13.1 2 Periods	A2, B2, D3; A2, B4, D1; UCP1, UCP5	**Lab 13A: p. 73** Falling Objects	Key Concept Review p. 80 Vocabulary Review p. 81
13.2 2 Periods	B3, E1; B4, B6, D1, E2, G2; UCP2, UCP4	**Lab 13B: pp. 74–76** Observing Projectile Motion	Interpreting Diagrams p. 82 Reading Comprehension p. 83 Curriculum Connection p. 84
13.3 2 Periods	A1, B2, B3, D1, D3, E2, F5, G3; A2, B4, B5, B6, D1	**Lab 13C: pp. 77–78** Friction and Forces	Science Challenge p. 85
13.4 2 Periods	A1, B2, B3, C1, E1, E2, F5, G3; A1, B4, B5, B6, C6, D1, E2		

Middle School Standard; High School Standard; **Unifying Concept and Principle**

13.1 What Is Force?

Before You Read

Preview the lesson by looking at the pictures and reading the headings and subheadings. In your Science Notebook, summarize what you already know about forces.

Amazingly, an African elephant's trunk is both strong and agile. It is able to push down an entire tree, but it can also pull a single piece of straw from a large pile. The push on the tree and pull on the straw by an elephant's trunk are examples of forces. A **force** is defined as a push or a pull.

A force is exerted between two objects that are interacting in some way. The elephant interacts with the tree when it pushes the tree down. A teacher interacts with a door when he or she pulls it open. A softball player interacts with a ball when he or she throws it.

Types of Forces

Not all forces are exactly the same. Some forces are known as contact forces. Other forces are described as action-at-a-distance forces.

Contact Forces   Forces in which the two interacting objects are physically touching each other are called contact forces. A child throwing a snowball is touching the snowball. A horse pulling a wagon is touching the wagon. Additional contact forces, such as friction, will be discussed in detail later in this chapter.

Action-at-a-Distance Forces   Forces in which the two interacting objects are not physically touching each other are known as action-at-a-distance forces. When a magnet is brought near a paper clip, the magnet exerts a force on the paper clip without having to touch it. The Moon exerts a gravitational pull on Earth's oceans even though the Moon is hundreds of thousands of kilometers away from Earth. Magnetism and gravity are two action-at-a-distance forces. They will be discussed in detail later in this chapter, as well as in later chapters.

Combining Forces

Often there is more than one force acting on an object at a particular time. Different forces acting on the same object combine. The combination of all the forces acting on an object is the **net force.**

Learning Goals

- Recognize that a force is a push or pull.
- Combine forces by addition and subtraction.
- Differentiate between balanced and unbalanced forces.

New Vocabulary

force
net force
balanced force
unbalanced force

Figure 13.1 This African elephant exerts a strong force to knock down the tree. What is a force?

As You Read

Correct or add to the sentences in your Science Notebook describing forces.

What is an example of a contact force?

ELL Strategy

Compare and Contrast and Illustrate

Have students use a compare-and-contrast chart to describe contact and action-at-a-distance forces. Additionally, they should collaborate on an additional example not discussed in the lesson. Then, they can illustrate as many examples of both types of forces as they could name.

13.1 Introduce

ENGAGE Have students read the first paragraph of the lesson to a partner, and then discuss the ability of an elephant to exert force on different objects.

Vocabulary terms are listed on the first student page of each lesson. You may wish to preview the terms before introducing each lesson. Strategies for teaching the vocabulary appear on the pages where the terms are introduced.

Before You Read

Have students create an outline in their Science Notebooks using the lesson's headings and subheadings. Have them record what they already know about forces in the appropriate parts of the outline. Ask students to volunteer some of their outline entries.

Encourage students to return to their outlines as they read the lesson and make necessary corrections and additions.

Teach

EXPLAIN to students that they will learn about two types of forces—contact forces and action-at-a-distance forces— and the combining of forces.

Vocabulary

force Tell students that the common meaning of the word *force* is "power" or "strength." Ask students to use the word in a sentence and explain how this meaning is related to the scientific definition.

net force Tell students that one meaning of the word *net* refers to what is left after additions or deductions. Ask students how this meaning applies to the term *net force*.

Use the Visual: Figure 13.1

ANSWER A force is a push or a pull.

As You Read

Have students add information from the lesson to their outlines.

ANSWER Examples will vary. A contact force is any force that involves physical contact.

Teach

EXPLAIN to students that on this page, they will learn about balanced and unbalanced forces.

Vocabulary

balanced force Explain to students that *balance* comes from the Latin word *bilanx,* meaning "having two scales." Ask for suggestions of what the term *balanced force* means.

unbalanced force Ask students to remember what the prefix *un-* means ("not" or "the opposite") and to use this to determine the meaning of the term *unbalanced force.*

Figure It Out: Figure 13.3

ANSWER **1.** Equal and opposite forces cancel out, resulting in a net force of zero. Balanced forces do not change the motion of an object. **2.** The forces exerted on the rope must be unbalanced, resulting in a net force. A net force changes the motion of the rope.

Assess

Use the After You Read questions and the Alternative Assessment to help you evaluate students' understanding of the lesson.

After You Read

1. The net force is 18 N northward.
2. Balanced forces are equal and opposite forces that cancel out. They do not change the motion of an object. Unbalanced forces do not cancel out and result in a net force on an object. They do change the motion of an object.

Alternative Assessment

Give students time to complete their outlines and then share them with partners for feedback. Have student pairs develop questions based on their outlines to pose to other student pairs.

Did You Know?

A lack of motion does not necessarily mean there are no forces acting on an object. There may be balanced forces acting on the object.

Figure It Out

1. Explain why the rope doesn't move when the forces on it are balanced.
2. What must be true of the forces on the rope if the rope moves toward one of the teams?

Figure 13.3 People playing tug-of-war are exerting forces on the rope.

Look at the people in **Figure 13.2**. Each person is exerting a force on the box. If forces are exerted in the same direction, they add together. The direction of the net force is in the direction of the individual forces. If two forces are exerted in opposite directions, the net force is the difference between them. The net force is in the direction of the larger force. The length of the arrows represents the magnitudes of the forces.

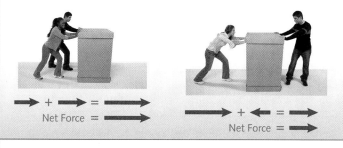

Figure 13.2 When forces are exerted in the same direction *(left)*, they combine to form a larger force. When forces are exerted in different directions *(right)*, the smaller force subtracts from the larger one. The box moves in the direction of the larger force.

Balanced Forces Two or more forces exerted on an object are **balanced forces** if they cancel each other when they are combined. The forces exerted on the rope in **Figure 13.3** are equal in magnitude, but opposite in direction. When they are combined, the net force is zero.

Balanced forces do not change the motion of an object. Although they are exerted on an object, they do not cause the object to accelerate in any way. Recall from Chapter 12 that acceleration occurs when an object speeds up, slows down, or changes direction.

Unbalanced Forces If multiple forces result in a net force on an object, the forces are said to be **unbalanced forces.** Unbalanced forces do not cancel out. An unbalanced force causes an object to accelerate.

The metric unit used to measure force is the newton (N). One newton is the amount of force required to give a 1-kg mass an acceleration of 1 m/s^2.

$$1 \text{ Newton} = 1 \text{ kg} \times \frac{m}{s^2}$$

After You Read

1. A force of 10 N is exerted to push an object northward. A second force of 8 N is exerted to pull the same object northward. What is the net force on the object?
2. Review the sentences in your Science Notebook about forces. Write a well-developed paragraph that compares balanced and unbalanced forces.

Differentiate Instruction

Kinesthetic Weather permitting, divide the class in half and have them play tug-of-war. Afterward, have pairs of students summarize what happened during the game, including answering which side won, why, and what forces were being exerted.

At the completion, students can evaluate each competition; first, the two recording groups could compare their assessment of movement and forces, while the playing teams summarize their struggle. Then, the teams will switch their roles in assessing.

This activity will allow students to assure they understand the concepts and promote language use with the vocabulary terms.

13.2 Friction

Before You Read
In your Science Notebook, write each of the vocabulary terms in this lesson. Leave some space below each term. Using your own words, write a definition for each term as you come across it in the lesson.

A person runs easily on a sandy beach but slides dangerously on an icy path. What is the difference between the two surfaces? The answer is friction. **Friction** is the force that resists the motion of an object. Friction is greater when walking on sand than when walking on ice.

Friction is produced because most surfaces are not perfectly smooth. Even a marble floor that appears smooth has little bumps and ridges in it when observed under a microscope. When two surfaces move past each other, their microscopic peaks and valleys catch on one another and form a mechanical type of bond, or glue.

Factors Affecting Friction

The friction produced when a cloth is rubbed across a piece of wood is much less than it is when sandpaper is used. This is because the friction between two surfaces depends on the types of surfaces involved and how hard the surfaces are pressed together.

Rougher surfaces have more bumps and larger bumps than do smooth surfaces. When rougher surfaces are rubbed together, they catch on one another more easily. Therefore, rougher surfaces have more friction than do smooth surfaces. This explains why sand creates more friction than ice does.

When a larger force is pushing two objects together, bumps that normally do not come into contact with one another are made to. More bumps catching on one another means that there is more friction between the objects.

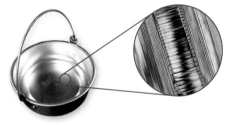

Figure 13.4 Metal feels quite smooth to the touch. Under a microscope, however, its surface is covered with bumps and ridges. Friction is produced when these bumps get caught on the microscopic bumps of other surfaces.

Learning Goals
- Define *friction* and identify its cause.
- Compare different types of friction.
- Identify ways in which friction is helpful and ways in which it is harmful.

New Vocabulary
friction
static friction
sliding friction
fluid friction
rolling friction

Explain It!
Why do delivery people often place heavy items on carts with wheels rather than sliding them?

ELL Strategy

Vocabulary Practice For vocabulary in this lesson, English language learners can create flashcards with the word on one side and an illustration on the reverse side. Students can quiz each other by showing the illustration to a partner. The partner should give the word and its definition.

13.2 Introduce

ENGAGE In small groups, have students look at illustrations or photos of the four types of friction. They should try to identify what is happening in each photo.

Before You Read
For the definitions of the various types of friction, encourage students to provide meanings for both words in the term and put the meanings together to develop their definitions. Most students should have some knowledge of the words *static, sliding, fluid,* and *rolling.* Tell students that they can use diagrams in their definitions.

● Teach

EXPLAIN to students that they will learn about friction and factors affecting friction.

Vocabulary

friction Explain to students that the common meaning of *friction* is the rubbing of one thing against another. Have students think of examples, such as a shoe that does not fit causing a blister by rubbing on the foot, or the more common example of rubbing two sticks together to start a fire.

Explain It!

Have students work in small groups to answer the question. Suggest that groups slide an object such as a carton, chair, or stack of books along the floor and describe the degree of difficulty doing so. Then have them move the same object using a skateboard. Have groups decide which is the easiest method and explain their answers.

ANSWER Rolling friction is less than sliding friction, so using a cart makes the task easier.

Teach

 EXPLAIN to students that they will learn about four types of friction.

 Vocabulary

static friction Tell students that the word *static* comes from the Greek word *statikos*, meaning "causing to stand."

sliding friction Explain to students that the verb *slide* means "to move or cause to move" or "to run smoothly along a surface." Have students give examples of things that slide, such as feet on ice or a person sledding down a snow-covered hill.

fluid friction Tell students that the word *fluid* comes from the Latin word *fluidus*, meaning "flowing."

rolling friction Tell students that the word *rolling* comes from the verb *roll* and means "to move or make something move by turning over and over." Ask students for examples, such as rolling wheels or marbles.

As You Read

Have students add two or three examples of each type of friction to their definitions.

ANSWER Sliding friction is less than static friction, and rolling friction is less than sliding friction.

Figure It Out: Figure 13.5

ANSWER **1.** Friction always acts in the opposite direction. **2.** It would increase, because the crate would be pressed more strongly against the ramp.

Use the Visual: Figure 13.6

ANSWER The kite experiences fluid friction.

As You Read

Review the definitions you wrote in your Science Notebook for the different types of friction.

How do the strengths of static friction, sliding friction, and rolling friction compare?

Figure It Out

1. Describe the direction of static friction relative to the direction of an object's motion.

2. How would the static friction between the crate and the ramp change if another heavy box were placed on the crate?

Figure 13.6 What type of friction does the kite experience as it moves through the air?

 210 NATURE OF FORCES

Types of Friction

There are several different types of friction. They depend on the nature of the surfaces and the type of motion involved.

Static Friction Push on a table and it may not move at first. Use a little extra force and the table might seem to almost break free from its position. The friction that acts on unmoving objects is called **static friction.** The word *static* describes an object that is fixed or stationary.

Once the force exerted on the object becomes greater than the static friction, the object moves. Static friction is no longer exerted on an object once it is moving.

Sliding Friction Once the wooden crate in **Figure 13.5** starts moving, it experiences sliding friction, or kinetic friction. **Sliding friction** occurs because two surfaces are sliding past each other. Sliding friction slows an object down.

Sliding friction is produced when the bumps on the surfaces stick together, break apart, and reform in different places. To overcome sliding friction, a force must be constantly exerted. Sliding friction is less than static friction, so it is easier to move an object once it gets going.

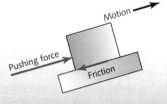

Figure 13.5 Even when a force is exerted on the crate, the crate might not move. Increasing the force eventually makes the crate move.

Fluid Friction The force that resists motion when a fluid is involved is called **fluid friction.** A fluid is a liquid or a gas. The frictional force can be exerted either on the fluid or on the object through which the fluid moves. Water flowing through a hose and a kite flying through air both experience fluid friction.

Rolling Friction The frictional force between a rolling object and its surface is called **rolling friction.** This type of friction acts over the area where the wheel is in contact with the surface.

Rolling friction is much less than sliding friction. It depends on the material of the wheel and the type of surface the wheel is rolling across. A rubber tire will produce more rolling friction than a steel wheel will. For this reason, a car with rubber tires will gradually slow down due to rolling friction, whereas a train with steel wheels will roll much farther.

210 NATURE OF FORCES

Differentiate Instruction

Mathematical/Logical Have students create a crossword puzzle using the vocabulary terms and concepts in this lesson. When they are finished, copy the puzzles and ask students to hand them out to classmates to solve.

Using Friction

Friction is often a very helpful force. Sometimes, actions are taken to increase friction because it is so useful.

People could not walk without friction between their feet and the ground. Treads on the bottoms of shoes increase friction.

Cars could not move without friction between tires and the ground. Tire chains increase friction to allow cars to move on icy roads.

Friction between nails and beams prevents nails from slipping out of place. This helps hold buildings together.

Figure 13.7 These images show examples of how friction can be helpful.

Reducing Friction

Sometimes, friction can be a problem. It causes kinetic energy to be converted into heat that is usually wasted. It can also cause surfaces to be worn away over time. In these situations, people try to reduce friction.

 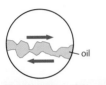 

One way to reduce friction is by lubricating, or adding oil to, a surface. The oil fills in some of the bumps and ridges on a surface so the surfaces slide past each other more easily.

Another way to reduce friction is to use ball bearings, which are small metal balls. Ball bearings allow two surfaces to roll past each other.

Air can sometimes be used to reduce friction. An air hockey table blows air through small holes. The puck can move a long distance without stopping because there is so little friction.

Figure 13.8 Friction can often be a nuisance. These examples to show how friction might be reduced.

After You Read

1. What is friction, and how does it affect motion?
2. Explain why is it easier to move a couch once it starts moving.
3. Use the definitions in your Science Notebook to make a T-chart that lists at least two examples of how friction is helpful and how it is not helpful.

 CONNECTION:
Meteorology

Friction causes wind speeds to decrease near Earth's surface. At higher altitudes, wind is not affected by friction. Near Earth's surface, however, mountains, valleys, and buildings change the speed and direction of wind. Wind speeds are changed more by rough land terrain than by the surface of a calm ocean.

Background Information

The amount of rolling friction that a tire generates has to do with several factors. One is the amount of inflation. Low tire pressure results in higher rolling friction because of the surface area of the tire that is in contact with the road. The thickness of tread is another factor. Less tread results in lower friction.

● Teach

EXPLAIN to students that they will learn about how friction can be helpful and not helpful.

CONNECTION: Meteorology

Provide students with a topographic map of the United States and have them identify areas where they think friction would have the greatest effect on wind speeds. Ask students to explain their reasoning.

● Assess

Use the After You Read questions and the Alternative Assessment to help you evaluate students' understanding of the lesson.

After You Read

1. Friction is a force that opposes the motion of an object.
2. It is easier because sliding friction is less than static friction.
3. Lists will vary. Examples of helpfulness include that friction prevents people from slipping when walking or sitting, makes it possible for cars to move and to stop, and keeps objects such as nails from slipping out of place. Examples of unhelpfulness include causing parts to wear out and wasting energy as heat.

Alternative Assessment

Draw a T-chart on the board for the students to use as a model. Label one side *Helpful* and the other side *Unhelpful*. Ask students for a few examples of items to include on each side.

13.3 Introduce

ENGAGE Have students drop several classroom objects from their desks, such as a paper clip, a piece of paper, a pencil, and an eraser. They should observe whether some objects fall more quickly than others and hypothesize why this occurs. Students should then repeat the activity from a higher and lower height and observe whether the objects drop more or less quickly than from the desk height. Again, they should discuss why they think this occurs.

Before You Read

In small groups, have students brainstorm what they know about gravity. Then have the groups share the information with the rest of the class. Record the information on the board, and then have students record three of the facts in their Science Notebooks.

Teach

EXPLAIN to students that they will learn about famous people in history who studied and developed theories about gravity.

Learning Goals

- Describe the nature of the gravitational force.
- Relate the force of gravity to mass and distance.
- Differentiate between weight and mass.
- Discuss free fall and terminal velocity.

New Vocabulary

gravity
law of universal gravitation
free fall
weight
air resistance
terminal velocity

Newton's Orbital Cannon

Figure 13.9 Isaac Newton was the first person to consider that gravity extended beyond Earth's surface. He imagined launching a cannon ball at a high enough velocity that it would actually fall around Earth.

13.3 Gravity

Before You Read

In your Science Notebook, write three facts that you already know about gravity. Leave six lines of space below each fact. As you read the lesson, add at least two more facts to each fact you already know.

Clip the stem of an apple on a tree and the apple will fall to the ground. If an unbalanced force is required to change the motion of an object, what force changes the apple's motion? The force is known as gravity. **Gravity** is a force of attraction between two objects. In this case, gravity is exerted between Earth and the apple.

The Study of Gravity

Over 2,000 years ago, Aristotle suggested that lighter objects fall more slowly than heavier objects. According to Aristotle, a cannon ball that is twice as heavy as another cannon ball should fall twice as fast.

Aristotle's explanation was considered to be correct until the seventeenth century, when Galileo performed his studies of gravity. He determined that all objects, regardless of mass, fall at the same rate.

In 1687, Sir Isaac Newton proposed a theory explaining gravity. According to popular legend, an apple fell on Newton's head while he was sitting under an apple tree. Newton reasoned that the force causing the apple to accelerate was gravity. He then reasoned that since apples can fall from higher parts of the tree, the force must extend to the top of the tallest apple tree. Newton went on to imagine that if the force of gravity reached to the top of the tallest tree, it might reach even farther. He thought it might reach all the way to the Moon. If so, the orbits of the Moon and planets might be a result of the gravitational force.

Newton theorized that if a cannon were fired horizontally from a high mountain, as shown in **Figure 13.9,** the cannon ball would eventually fall to the ground due to Earth's gravitational pull. If the velocity of the cannon ball were increased, the ball would travel farther and farther before landing. Newton reasoned that if the right velocity were achieved, the cannon ball would travel completely around Earth. It would always be falling toward Earth due to the gravitational force, but it would never reach Earth because Earth curves away from it at the same rate as the cannon ball falls.

Newton concluded that the Moon is in orbit around Earth in the same way. It too falls toward the planet at a rate that keeps it traveling around Earth without ever reaching Earth.

212 NATURE OF FORCES

ELL Strategy

Illustrate Have students draw or find illustrations of gravity and present them in small groups.

Act Out English language learners could choose either Aristotle, Galileo, or Newton, learning more of the legends surrounding that man's explorations in gravity. In small groups, they should write a script for the investigations and then perform for the class.

Law of Universal Gravitation

According to Newton's **law of universal gravitation,** the force of gravity is exerted between any two objects that have mass. Earth exerts a gravitational force on everything on its surface. Everything on Earth's surface exerts a gravitational force on Earth. The planets, their moons, and stars exert a gravitational force on one another.

If every object exerts a gravitational force, why aren't all objects pulled together? Newton determined that the force of gravity depends on the masses of the objects and the distance between them. Newton developed an equation to identify this relationship.

$$F = \frac{Gm_1m_2}{r^2}$$

In this equation, F represents the gravitational force, m_1 is the mass of one object, m_2 is the mass of the other object, and r is the distance between their centers. The letter G is the universal gravitational constant. This is a value that is the same for objects everywhere in the universe. Its value was first determined experimentally by Henry Cavendish in 1797. Its accepted value is $G = 6.67 \times 10^{-11}$ N·m^2/kg^2.

Look again at the equation. It shows that the strength of the gravitational force is directly proportional to the product of two objects' masses. This means that the attraction between two objects gets stronger as mass increases. The force gets weaker as mass decreases.

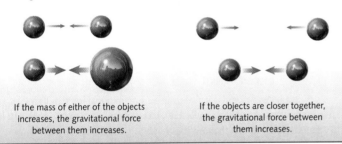

If the mass of either of the objects increases, the gravitational force between them increases.

If the objects are closer together, the gravitational force between them increases.

Figure 13.10 The gravitational force between two objects depends on the objects' masses and the distance between them.

The equation shows that the force of gravity is inversely proportional to the square of the distance between objects. A number's square is the number multiplied by itself. The square of one is one (1 × 1), the square of two is four (2 × 2), the square of three is nine (3 × 3), and so on. This means that if the distance between two objects is doubled, the attraction will become one-fourth its original strength. If the distance is tripled, it will become one-ninth its original strength. This is an inverse square law.

Did You Know?

Scientists know how gravity behaves and how objects in the universe are affected by it. However, no one knows for sure what gravity actually is. Some scientists speculate that gravity is made up of particles called gravitons. However, after many investigations, scientists are still unable to uncover any such particles.

Extend It!

By the beginning of the 1900s, scientists had discovered a small flaw in Newton's theory. In 1915, Albert Einstein corrected Newton's error in a theory called general relativity. Einstein's new theory completely changed scientists' understanding of the structure of the universe. Research how Einstein improved upon Newton's theory.

● Teach

EXPLAIN to students that they will lea[r]... about Newton's law of universal gravitatic...

Vocabulary

gravity Explain to students that the word *gravity* comes from the Latin word *gravitas,* meaning "heaviness" or "seriousness."

law of universal gravitation Ask students to remember what a law is (a rule or principle). Tell them that the word *universal* is the adjective derived from *universe,* meaning "entire" or "whole." Tell them that *gravitational* comes from the word *gravity* combined with *-ation,* the suffix denoting a process or an action. Have students put the meanings together to arrive at a meaning for the term.

Extend It!

Supply resources from the library and the NSTA SciLinks Web site about Einstein's theory of general relativity. Have students work in pairs to research information on the theory and write two or three paragraphs about what they learned.

EXPLAIN to students that science is an ever-changing area of study. Theories and ideas that scientists hold today could change as a result of new experiments and discoveries.

Background Information

The circumstances surrounding many discoveries are not always clear from historical documents. Over time, legends have developed to tell the stories of the discoveries. It may be that some aspects of the legends are true, but most of the details have been embellished as the stories were passed down. This is probably true for the stories of Galileo's use of the Tower of Pisa and Newton's experience with the apple tree.

Teacher Alert

Students may need more of an explanation of the equation for gravitational force. Explaining what the universal gravitational constant is, for example, will help students understand the equation. Tell students that they should be able to explain the relationship between the force of gravity and the two objects' masses and the force of gravity and the distance between the two objects.

that they will learn
 ects the acceleration of
ey will learn about Sir

...ry

free fall Ask students for a definition of
the word *free* ("not fastened or shut in," "not
restricted," "costs nothing"). Tell students
that the word *fall* in this term is a noun
meaning "a drop or descent." Have students
come up with a meaning of the term *free fall*.

weight Tell students that the common use
of the noun *weight* refers to the heaviness of
something, or how much it weighs.

Figure It Out Figure 13.11
(ANSWER) **1.** It is a constant 9.8 m/s². **2.** It
increases each second the object falls.

⬤ CONNECTION: Geography

Have students work in pairs to hypothesize
which of Earth's locations has the strongest,
weakest, and intermediate gravitational pull,
and why.

Figure It Out

1. Is the acceleration due to
gravity constant as the
object falls, or does it
change?

2. How is the velocity of a
falling object related to
the length of time the
object falls?

⬤ CONNECTION: Geography

The acceleration due
to gravity varies with
latitude. For example, the
acceleration due to gravity
in New York is generally
9.80 m/s², but it is 9.78
m/s² at the equator and
9.83 m/s² at the north
pole. This means a person
weighs less on the equator
than in New York!

Falling Objects

An object is said to be in **free fall** when the only force acting on the
object is gravity. When the force of gravity is unbalanced, it causes the
velocity of an object to change and the object to accelerate. This change
in velocity is known as the acceleration due to gravity, which is
represented by *g*. For objects falling in a straight line near Earth's surface,
the acceleration due to gravity is 9.8 m/s². That means that the speed of a
falling object increases by 9.8 m/s each second that the object falls, as
shown in **Figure 13.11.** However, the acceleration due to gravity is
different on other planets because they have different masses and sizes.

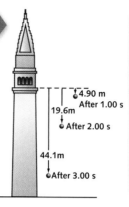

Acceleration Due To Gravity			
Planet	Radius (m)	Mass (kg)	g (m/s²)
Mercury	2.43 x 10⁶	3.2 x 10²³	3.61
Venus	6.073 x 10⁶	4.88 x10²⁴	8.83
Mars	3.38 x 10⁶	6.42 x 10²³	3.75
Jupiter	6.98 x 10⁷	1.901 x 10²⁷	26.0
Saturn	5.82 x 10⁷	5.68 x 10²⁶	11.2
Uranus	2.35 x 10⁷	8.68 x 10²⁵	10.5
Neptune	2.27 x 10⁷	1.03 x 10²⁶	13.3

Figure 13.11 In the illustration, a falling object is pulled downward by the force of
gravity. The chart shows that the acceleration due to gravity depends on a planet's
mass and size.

Weight Versus Mass

When a person steps on a scale, Earth's gravitational force pulls the
person downward onto the scale. The scale measures the person's weight.
Weight is a measure of the force of gravity at the surface of a planet.

Weight and mass are often confused with each other. Although
weight depends on mass, they are not the same quantity. Mass (*m*) is the
amount of matter in an object. Weight (*W*) is a force that is equal to the
mass of an object multiplied by the acceleration due to gravity (*g*).

weight = mass × acceleration due to gravity   W = mg

Weight is a force, so it is measured in newtons. To find the weight of
an object on Earth's surface, multiply the mass in kilograms by 9.8 m/s².
For example, a person who has a mass of 60 kg will weigh 588 N.

$$W = 60 \text{ kg} \times 9.8 \text{ m/s}^2$$
$$= 588 \text{ kg} \cdot \text{m/s}^2 = 588 \text{ N}$$

214 NATURE OF FORCES

Differentiate Instruction

Mathematical/Logical Have students
work in pairs to analyze the table in
Figure 13.11 and create a list that orders
the planets from least gravity to most
gravity. Then, have them write short
explanations of how and why they ordered
their lists.

Like other forces, weight can be measured using a spring scale such as the one shown in **Figure 13.12**. A spring scale is a device that has a hook onto which an object can be placed. As gravity pulls down on the object, the spring scale measures the force of gravity, which is the weight of the object. Mass, however, is measured with a balance. A balance is a device that has a pan onto which an object can be placed. Many balances use measured objects that are placed on another pan until the pans are balanced. The sum of the masses of the measured objects is the mass of the object being measured.

An acceleration of 9.8 m/s² can be used when calculating weight on Earth. Remember that the acceleration due to gravity, however, varies from one planet to another. Therefore, a person's weight would change on different planets. **Figure 13.13** shows a person's weight on other planets.

What happens to a person's mass as the person travels to other planets? Nothing! Unlike weight, the amount of matter in an object does not change as the object moves from one place to another. Therefore, the mass of an object remains the same unless the object is physically changed in some way.

Figure 13.12
A spring scale is used to measure force, whereas mass is measured with a balance.

As You Read

Write a fact about Newton's law of universal gravitation in your Science Notebook.

Why isn't Earth pulled to objects just above its surface, such as an airplane?

Weights of a 60-kg Person on Different Planets	
Planet	Weight (N)
Mercury	222
Venus	533
Earth	588
Mars	222
Jupiter	1,390
Saturn	539
Uranus	523
Neptune	662

Figure 13.13 A person's weight would change from one planet to the next. On which planet would the person weigh the most?

PEOPLE IN SCIENCE Sir Isaac Newton (1643–1727)

Sir Isaac Newton made major contributions to the study of light, the understanding of how objects move, the exploration of the universe, and the development of calculus. Newton entered Trinity College in Cambridge in 1661. Four years later, when the university closed for two years due to a plague epidemic, Newton returned home and pursued his scientific studies in isolation. It was during those two years that he made many of his discoveries in both science and math.

In 1667, Newton returned to Cambridge, where he soon became a professor of mathematics. In 1668, Newton developed a reflecting telescope. In 1684, he published a paper on the movement of planets. In 1687, Newton published the *Principia*, in which he showed how gravity is a universal force. In *Opticks*, he described his experiments into the nature of light and his discovery that white light is composed of all the colors of the rainbow.

In 1705, Newton was knighted. Upon his death, he was buried in Westminster Abbey, becoming the first scientist to be given this honor.

CHAPTER 13 **215**

Teach

EXPLAIN to students that in this section they will learn about weight, mass, and the difference between them.

As You Read

Have students work with a partner to review the section on Newton's law of universal gravitation. Then have them discuss what they learned about it and record a few facts in their Science Notebooks.

ANSWER The gravitational force depends on both force and distance. The mass of the airplane is small compared to the huge mass of Earth.

Use the Visual: Figure 13.13

ANSWER The person would have the greatest weight on Jupiter.

Science Notebook EXTRA

Have each student draw a T-chart in his or her Science Notebook with the headings *Weight* and *Mass* and write several facts about each quantity.

PEOPLE IN SCIENCE

Isaac Newton overcame several hardships in his childhood. His father died three months before he was born, and his birth was so premature that doctors did not expect him to live. His mother remarried when he was three, leaving him to be raised by his grandmother for the next five years. Newton did not like his stepfather. His mother returned to Newton and his grandmother with three younger children to care for when her second husband died. Newton went away to school at age ten and returned at 17 because he was expected to take care of the family farm. He failed at farming and instead went to Cambridge University.

Background Information

The human ear, the sense organ of sound, is also responsible for enabling a person to maintain balance. It does this because special structures called otoliths located in the inner ear determine whether the body is speeding up, slowing down, or changing direction. Otoliths do this by comparing the body's movement with the downward force of gravity. As otoliths move in response to the body's movement, they pull on tiny hair cells that send nerve impulses to the brain. The brain interprets these impulses and sends signals to the body to respond, if necessary.

Teach

EXPLAIN to students that they will learn about the way air acts on a falling object.

Vocabulary

air resistance Ask students what air is (a mixture of gases surrounding Earth). Tell them that *resistance* is the act of resisting or opposing. Have students develop a definition for the term *air resistance*.

terminal velocity Tell students that *terminal* is an adjective that comes from the Latin word *terminus,* meaning "boundary, limit, or border." Velocity describes both the speed of an object and its direction.

Explore It!

For each small group of students, provide toothpicks, napkins, tissue paper, writing paper, string, yarn, masking tape, cellophane tape, and glue.

Have students relate the choice of materials to the way the parachute falls. Each group should create a poster or diagram explaining how their experiment was conducted and what they learned about gravity.

Use the Visual: Figure 13.15

ANSWER Terminal velocity is the velocity at which the upward force of air resistance is equal to the downward force of gravity.

Assess

After You Read

1. Gravity is a force of attraction between two objects. The law of universal gravitation states that the force of gravity is exerted between any two objects that have mass. This force can be calculated according to the equation $F = Gm_1m_2/r^2$.

2. The force of gravity decreases by one-fourth, because the gravitational force is inversely related to the square of the distance between the masses.

3. Answers will vary. Terminal velocity is reached when the downward force of gravity is balanced by the upward force of air resistance.

Figure 13.14
All objects fall at the same rate regardless of mass. This is only true in a vacuum. Air resistance slows the motion of some objects, making them fall at different rates.

Explore It!

Parachutes are designed to slow a person falling through the air. Use a variety of materials to create several different parachutes that can be used on a small object such as a plastic toy or a metal washer. Observe how the size and shape of the parachute design affect how the object falls.

Air Resistance

All objects should fall at the same rate. Yet when Galileo investigated the rate at which objects fell, he discovered slight differences among the times different objects landed because they were falling through air.

As an object falls, it collides with the particles of matter that make up air. Each collision produces a force on the falling object. Millions of collisions add up to produce a sizeable force. The force produced as an object moves through air is a type of friction called **air resistance.** For a falling object, air resistance acts in the upward direction. Air resistance explains why objects do not fall at the same exact rate.

The faster an object is moving, the more collisions it experiences with particles in air. As a result, air resistance increases with velocity. Recall that the velocity of a falling object increases as the object falls. Therefore, the air resistance on the object also increases as the object falls.

Eventually, the upward air resistance becomes equal to the downward force of gravity. The velocity at which the gravitational force on a falling object equals the air resistance on the object is called **terminal velocity.** The terminal velocity is the highest velocity a falling object will reach.

The terminal velocity of an object depends on the size and shape of the object. The graph in **Figure 13.15** shows how opening a parachute decreases the terminal velocity of a skydiver. The decrease enables the skydiver to make a safe landing.

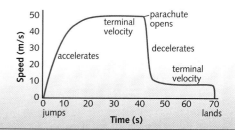

Figure 13.15 For a skydiver with a closed parachute, the terminal velocity is about 50 m/s. Opening the parachute reduces the terminal velocity to less than 10 m/s. What is terminal velocity?

After You Read

1. What is gravity? Explain the law of universal gravitation.

2. How does the force of gravity between two objects change as the distance between the objects is doubled?

3. Add one fact that you learned about terminal velocity to the list of facts in your Science Notebook.

Alternative Assessment

Have students review the list of facts regarding gravity that they recorded for this lesson. Have them change any facts that they found to be incorrect, expand on facts that they learned more about, and add more relevant facts.

Differentiate Instruction

Musical Have small groups of students research songs that contain terms from this lesson. Possibilities include *gravity, Galileo, Isaac Newton,* and *velocity.* Each group should choose one term, print out or copy the lyrics of all songs found, and discuss what was learned from the songs. Finally, students should share the lyrics and songs with other groups.

Before You Read

In your Science Notebook, create a chart with three columns. Label the first column *Law of Motion*, the second column *Description*, and the third column *Examples*. As you learn about the laws of motion, add facts to your chart.

In the seventeenth century, Sir Isaac Newton published three laws that explain the motion of objects. These rules have come to be known as Newton's three laws of motion.

Newton's First Law of Motion

According to Newton's **first law of motion,** an object at rest tends to stay at rest, and an object in motion tends to stay in motion with the same speed and in the same direction, unless an unbalanced force acts on it. Thus, an object tends to resist any change in its motion.

If the ball in **Figure 13.16** is at rest, it will stay at rest until an unbalanced force is exerted on it. For example, it might be hit with a pool stick. If the train is in motion with a constant velocity, it will continue moving at this velocity until an unbalanced force acts on it.

The tendency of an object to resist any change in its motion is called **inertia** (ih NUR shuh). Newton's first law of motion is also known as the law of inertia. The more mass an object has, the greater its inertia.

The results of Newton's first law of motion are experienced all the time. Consider a group of people riding in a car. When the driver steps on the brakes, an unbalanced force is exerted to stop the car. There is no unbalanced force to change the motion of the passengers in the car. They continue to move forward at the same speed and in the same direction until they are acted upon by an unbalanced force, the seat belt.

For nearly 2,000 years, people believed that the natural tendency of all objects was to return to a rest position. It was Newton who explained that an object in motion comes to a stop not because of the absence of force, but because of the presence of force—friction!

Figure 13.16 Objects resist changes in their motion. They tend to keep doing what they're doing. An unbalanced force is required to change an object's motion.

Figure 13.17 Passengers in a car continue moving until an unbalanced force causes them to stop, even if the car has already stopped moving. Fortunately, this force can be provided by their seat belts. The unbalanced force that will stop this biker, however, is the ground.

CHAPTER 13 **217**

13.4 Introduce

ENGAGE Have students
that they already know
partner or small group
record the information to sha
discussion after this exchange.

Before You Read

Ask students what they think motion is. Record their responses on the board. Have them guess what Newton's laws of motion might be. Draw a three-column chart on board with the titles *Law of Motion*, *Description*, and *Examples*. Have students do the same in their Science Notebooks.

Teach

EXPLAIN to students that they will learn about the first of Newton's three laws of motion.

 Vocabulary

first law of motion Ask students what *first* means (when counting, the initial or original), then what a *law* is (a rule or principle). Tell them that *motion* is the act of moving. Ask what the term could mean when put together.

inertia Explain that the word *inertia* comes from the Latin word *iners,* meaning "unskilled" or "idle." Ask students to relate the meaning "idle" to the definition of the word.

ELL Strategy

Model Have students work in small groups to make posters or diagrams that represent Newton's first law of motion. Afterward, each group should present its work to another group. Students should leave room on their poster to add diagrams of Newton's second and third laws as they study those concepts.

Key Concept Review
Workbook, p. 80

...ch

XPLAIN to students that they will learn
about Newton's second law of motion and
begin to learn about Newton's third law of
motion.

Vocabulary

second law of motion Ask students what
second means (when counting, the next
after the first), and then have them describe
the term.

third law of motion Ask students what
third means (when counting, the next after
the second), and then have them describe
the term.

As You Read

Review with the class the information in their
charts. Record their answers on the board
chart. Then have students work with a
partner to review their recorded information
and make any necessary corrections or
additions.

ANSWER Newton's first law can be used
because the probe's inertia causes it to move
until an unbalanced force acts on it.

Figure It Out Figure 13.18

ANSWER **1.** The acceleration is halved
because the acceleration of an object
produced by a net force is directly
proportional to the magnitude of the
net force. **2.** There is no change in the
acceleration of the cart. The increase in force
is cancelled out by the increase in mass.

Explore It!

Each pair of students will need two spring
scales, paper, and a pencil. Have students
create a chart and record the readings on
both scales each time they pull on one or the
other. Then have them write an explanation
of how the scale readings demonstrate
Newton's third law of motion.

In every case, the forces of the scales pulling
on each other were equal and opposite.

As You Read

Check that you have
completed the first two rows
of the chart in your Science
Notebook. Work with a
partner to add to or correct
the recorded information.

Which law explains why a
space probe continues to
move through space when
no forces are acting on it?

Figure It Out

1. Is the acceleration of the
   cart doubled or halved if
   the mass of the cart is
   constant and the force
   exerted is halved? Explain.

2. Suppose the woman
   doubles the mass on the
   cart and doubles the force
   exerted. What is the net
   effect on the acceleration
   of the cart? Explain.

Explore It!

Working with a partner,
use two spring scales to
demonstrate Newton's
third law of motion.

Newton's Second Law of Motion

According to Newton's **second law of motion,** an object acted upon
by a force will accelerate in the direction of the force. Acceleration can
be determined by the following equation:

$$\text{acceleration} = \frac{\text{net force}}{\text{mass}} \qquad a = \frac{F_{net}}{m}$$

Acceleration is measured in m/s^2, net force is measured in N, and
mass is measured in kg. According to the equation, the acceleration of an
object produced by a net force is directly proportional to the magnitude
of the net force, in the same direction as the net force, and inversely
proportional to the mass of the object.

Suppose a person is pushing a cart, as in **Figure 13.18.** The person
exerts some force on the cart to accelerate it. If the person doubles the
force he or she exerts on the cart without changing its mass, the
acceleration will also double. If the person pushes with half the original
force, the cart will experience half the acceleration.

Figure 13.18 The woman
exerts a force to accelerate the
cart. The acceleration is related to
the mass of the cart and the net
force exerted on it.

Now suppose the person exerts a constant force on the cart. How will
acceleration change if the mass of the cart is doubled? Because mass is
inversely related to acceleration, the acceleration of the cart will be half
its original value. If enough objects are taken off the cart to make the
cart half its original mass, the acceleration of the cart will be doubled.

Newton's Third Law of Motion

According to Newton's **third law of motion,** forces always act in
equal but opposite pairs. These two forces are called action and reaction
forces. Both forces are exerted at the same time. Either force can be
considered the action force or the reaction force.

Differentiate Instruction

Interpersonal Invite a local mechanical
engineer, inventor, or scientist into the
classroom to discuss how he or she uses
Newton's laws of motion in his or her
work.

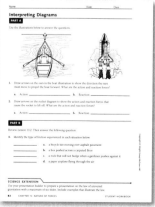

Interpreting Diagrams
Workbook, p. 82

According to this law, whenever two objects interact with each other, they exert forces on each other. When you sit in a chair, your body exerts a downward force on the chair and the chair exerts an upward force on your body. The action and reaction forces resulting from this interaction are the force on the chair and the force on your body.

The magnitude of the force on the first object equals the magnitude of the force on the second object. The direction of the force on the first object is the opposite of the direction of the force on the second object. Look at the man exercising in **Figure 13.19.** As he pushes off the ground with his hands, he exerts a force on the ground. The ground exerts an equal and opposite force on the man.

If equal and opposite forces on an object cancel out, why don't action and reaction forces cancel out? Action and reaction forces do not act on the same object. Forces can cancel out only if they act on the same object. The golf club in **Figure 13.20** exerts a force on the golf ball. The ball exerts an equal and opposite force on the golf club. The action force acts on the ball, whereas the reaction force acts on the club.

Third Law in Action When a person takes a step, the person's foot exerts a backward action force on the ground. The ground, which is Earth, exerts a reaction force that pushes the person forward. Because Earth has so much mass, it does not move noticeably. A fish also takes advantage of the third law of motion. It uses its fins to push water backward. The water exerts a reaction force on the fish, propelling it forward.

One of the most spectacular examples of Newton's third law of motion is the launch of a rocket. When rocket fuel is ignited, a gas is produced. The hot exhaust gas is allowed to flow through a nozzle at the rear of the rocket. This release produces a downward force. An equal and opposite force is exerted on the rocket, causing it to move upward.

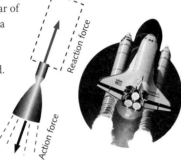

Figure 13.21 A rocket launch is a very dramatic event that is explained by Newton's third law of motion.

After You Read

1. Use the notes in the chart in your Science Notebook to explain why Newton's first law of motion is also known as the law of inertia.

2. Describe Newton's second and third laws of motion.

3. Why don't action and reaction forces cancel out?

Figure 13.19 This man exerts a force as he does a push-up. The ground exerts a force back on the man.

Figure 13.20 A golf club and a golf ball exert equal and opposite forces on each other. One force is on the club and the other is on the ball. As a result, the forces do not cancel out.

Extend It!

The Chinese were the first to launch rockets. Use research materials to learn about the history of rocketry. Obtain pictures that show how rockets have changed over time. Present the pictures to your class along with an explanation of how rockets work and how they depend on Newton's third law of motion.

Teach

EXPLAIN to students that they will learn more about Newton's third law of motion.

Extend It!

Provide library resources and Web sites about rocketry. Have students work in small groups to research and prepare a visual demonstration (poster, collage, etc.) of what they learn.

Assess

Use the After You Read questions and the Alternative Assessment to help you evaluate students' understanding of the lesson.

After You Read

1. An object's inertia is its resistance to any change in its motion. The first law states that an object at rests stays at rest, and an object in motion stays in motion unless an unbalanced force acts on it. In other words, objects resist changes in their motion.

2. Newton's second law of motion states that an object acted upon by a force will accelerate in the direction of the force. The third law of motion states that forces always act in equal but opposite pairs. These two forces are called action and reaction forces.

3. They do not cancel out because they do not act on the same object.

Alternative Assessment

Give students time to complete and review their charts. Have them work with a partner to review and include additional information, if necessary. Then have each partner write two questions based on the information in his or her chart to pose to the other partner.

ELL Strategy

Model Give groups of students the following materials and instruct them to use the materials to model Newton's third law of motion: a rigid cardboard strip about 15 cm × 75 cm, a skateboard, and a motorized or wind-up toy car. The cardboard strip is the road for the car. Students should position the skateboard upside-down in order and place the road over the wheels to observe the action-reaction of the car moving along the road. After students have designed and performed their activity, test their understanding by asking: *Why is it you do not see the road moving away from you when you are in an actual car?* (The road's mass is so large that its motion is unobservable.)

Chapter 13 Summary

Check students' sentences or paragraphs to make sure they understand the meaning of each vocabulary term.

Evaluate students' essays using the following criteria:

1. The topic sentence, or main idea, should restate the Key Concept.
2. The supporting paragraphs should incorporate the answers to the Learning Goal questions students have written and include details, facts, and examples they have recorded in their Science Notebooks.
3. The concluding sentence should sum up the main idea of the chapter and restate the Key Concept.

MASTERING CONCEPTS

True or False

1. True
2. False, Unbalanced
3. False, Static
4. False, fluid
5. False, reduce/decrease
6. False, decreases
7. False, weight
8. True
9. False, acceleration

Short Answer

10. Yes, a force must be acting on the flag because the flag is moving. The force is exerted by the wind.
11. It comes to a stop because an unbalanced force acts on it to change its motion. The force is friction.
12. Air resistance is friction produced as an object collides with particles of air. For a falling object, air resistance is a force in the upward direction. As the velocity of an object increases, the air resistance on it also increases. When it increases to the point at which it is equal and opposite to the downward force of gravity, the two forces become balanced. The object no longer accelerates; it continues to fall at its terminal velocity.
13. It is also 5 N, but it is in the opposite direction.

Chapter 13 — Summary

KEY CONCEPTS

13.1 What Is Force?

- A force is a push or a pull exerted in a specific direction.
- The net force is the combination of all the forces acting on an object.
- Forces exerted in the same direction combine by addition, whereas forces exerted in opposite directions combine by subtraction.
- Balanced forces are equal and opposite forces that cancel out, whereas unbalanced forces do not cancel out.

13.2 Friction

- Friction is a force that opposes the motion of an object.
- Static friction is friction that exists between surfaces that are not moving.
- Sliding friction exists between two surfaces that are sliding past each other.
- An object moving through a fluid or a fluid moving through some object produces fluid friction.
- Rolling friction exists between a rolling object and the surface over which it rolls.
- Friction can be helpful in that it makes some types of motion possible. It can be unhelpful in that it wastes energy as heat and wears out objects over time.

13.3 Gravity

- The gravitational force is an attractive force that exists between every pair of objects in the universe.
- The force of gravity is directly related to the product of the masses of two objects and inversely related to the square of the distance between the two objects.
- Weight is a measure of the force of gravity on the surface of a planet, whereas mass is the amount of matter in an object.
- An object in free fall is acted upon by the force of gravity. It speeds up until it reaches terminal velocity, at which point the downward force of gravity is balanced by the upward force of air resistance.

13.4 Newton's Laws of Motion

- Newton's first law of motion explains that an object will resist any change in its motion.
- According to Newton's second law of motion, the acceleration of an object depends on the net force exerted on the object and the mass of the object.
- Newton's third law of motion states that for every action force, an equal reaction force is exerted in the opposite direction.

VOCABULARY REVIEW

Write each term in a complete sentence or write a paragraph relating several terms.

13.1
force, p. 207
net force, p. 207
balanced force, p. 208
unbalanced force, p. 208

13.2
friction, p. 209
static friction, p. 210
sliding friction, p. 210
fluid friction, p. 210
rolling friction, p. 210

13.3
gravity, p. 212
law of universal gravitation, p. 213
free fall, p. 214
weight, p. 214
air resistance, p. 216
terminal velocity, p. 216

13.4
first law of motion, p. 217
inertia, p. 217
second law of motion, p. 218
third law of motion, p. 218

PREPARE FOR CHAPTER TEST

To prepare for the chapter test, create a question from each Learning Goal. Use the information in your Science Notebook to answer each question. Then use these answers to write a well-developed essay about the chapter. Use the Key Concept on the first page of this chapter as your topic sentence.

Vocabulary Review
Workbook, p. 81

Reading Comprehension
Workbook, p. 83

MASTERING CONCEPTS

True or False
If the statement is true, write "true." If it is false, change the underlined word or words to make the statement true.

1. The <u>net force</u> is the combination of all the forces acting on an object.
2. <u>Balanced</u> forces cause an object to accelerate.
3. <u>Kinetic</u> friction exists between two surfaces that are not moving.
4. A bird flying through air experiences <u>rolling</u> friction.
5. Machine parts are often lubricated to <u>increase</u> friction.
6. The gravitational force between two objects increases if the distance between the objects <u>increases</u>.
7. An object's <u>mass</u> is a measure of the gravitational force on it.
8. The terminal velocity of an object is the <u>greatest</u> velocity a falling object reaches.
9. When the net force on an object is increased, the object's <u>mass</u> increases.

Short Answer
Answer each of the following in a sentence or brief paragraph.

10. A flag on a pole is blowing back and forth. Is a force being exerted on the flag? If so, what is the source of the force?
11. The tendency of an object in motion is to stay in motion. Why, then, does a ball kicked on a field come to a stop?
12. Relate air resistance to the terminal velocity of a falling object.
13. You push on a wall with a force of 5 N. What is the force the wall exerts on your hands?

Critical Thinking
Use what you have learned in this chapter to answer each of the following.

14. **Interpret an Illustration** What is the net force on the box?

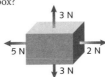

15. **Analyze** Is it possible for an object at rest to have forces acting on it?
16. **Predict** A gravitational force is exerted between two objects. How does the gravitational force between them change if the mass of each object is doubled?
17. **Calculate** A 0.4-kg object accelerates at 2 m/s². Find the net force on the object.
18. **Compare** A canoe has a mass of 45 kg and a person has a mass of 75 kg. If the person jumps out of the back end of the canoe into the water, which will have a greater acceleration, the person or the canoe?

Standardized Test Question
Choose the letter of the response that correctly answers the question.

19. The figure shows the horizontal forces that act on a box that is pushed from the side with a force of 12 N. What is the box's acceleration?

A. 27 m/s²
B. 4.8 m/s²
C. 4.3 m/s²
D. 0.48 m/s²

> **Test-Taking Tip**
>
> Make a small mark next to a difficult question. Remember to go back and answer it later. Another part of the test may give you a clue to help you answer the question.

Critical Thinking

14. 3 N to the left
15. Yes. The forces on the object can be balanced. Therefore, the motion of the object does not change.
16. The gravitational force is multiplied by four.
17. $F_{net} = 0.4 \text{ kg} \times 2 \text{ m/s}^2 = 0.8 \text{ N}$
18. The canoe has a greater acceleration because the forces on the person and the canoe are the same, but the canoe has less mass, so it will have greater acceleration.

Standardized Test Question

19. C

Reading Links

The Isaac Newton School of Driving: Physics and Your Car

Topics explored in this chapter—friction, forces, and the laws of motion—are among the many aspects of physics illustrated by the operation of cars, as this book describes. This lighthearted application of abstract principles will draw readers in and reinforce what they have learned in the classroom.

Barry Parker. Johns Hopkins University Press. 264 pp. Illustrated. Trade ISBN 978-0-8018-7417-8.

Project Mercury (Out of This World)

This approachable history of the first leg of the U.S. manned space program describes the early race to achieve and master space flight. From rocketry to the training of astronauts in zero-gravity conditions, this story is one of physics at work.

Ray Spangenburg and Kit Moser. Scholastic Library Publishing. 112 pp. Illustrated. Trade ISBN 978-0-531-13974-5.

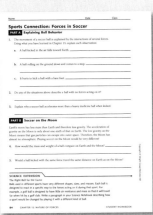

Curriculum Connection
Workbook, p. 84

Science Challenge
Workbook, p. 85

13A Falling Objects

This prechapter introduction activity is designed to determine what students already know about the effect of gravity on the pull of objects toward Earth by engaging them in predicting, recording data, evaluating, and communicating conclusions about the effect of mass on the speed at which an object is pulled to Earth.

Objectives

- predict the effect of mass on free-falling objects
- record data in a suitable way
- compare the accuracy of different testing techniques
- communicate conclusions

Planning

 15–20 minutes   groups of 3–4 students

Materials (per group)

- metric ruler
- marbles of different masses

Advance Preparation

- Obtain marbles of different masses.
- Remind students that they should do more than one trial in an activity to make certain their observations are accurate.

Engagement Guide

- Challenge students to think about testing falling objects and forces that act on them by asking:
  - *Which marble do you think will hit the ground first?* (Some students will think that the two marbles will hit at the same time. Other students may think that the larger marble will hit the ground first.)
  - *What force pulls the marbles to the ground?* (gravity)
  - *Do any other forces act on the marbles as they fall to the ground?* (Air resistance also acts; air resistance is negligible in this lab.)
  - *Are numerical values always helpful in analyzing the results of an experiment?* (Students will likely answer yes.)

Encourage students to explain reasons why they think the outcome will be as they predict.

Going Further

Give students two sheets of notebook paper. Have students crumple one sheet of paper into a ball. Have students drop the sheet of paper and ball of paper from the same height at the same time and observe which paper hits the ground first. Have students crumple the sheet of paper into another ball. Have students drop both balls of paper from the same height at the same time. Ask students to compare their observations from both parts of the activity and explain why the results were different.

13B Observing Projectile Motion

Objectives

- observe projectile motion
- record and analyze data
- illustrate projectile motion
- communicate conclusions

Skill Set

observing, predicting, recording and analyzing data, evaluating, illustrating, stating conclusions

Planning

 30–35 minutes   groups of 3–4 students

Materials

Materials for this activity are listed in the Student Laboratory Manual.

Advance Preparation

- For safety reasons, you will perform the dropping of the tennis balls while students observe and record data.

- This activity requires a lot of room. Locate an area either inside or outside that allows you to drop objects from a height of several meters. Bleacher seating areas are one possible location. The area should allow for a free fall of the balls to the ground and provide clear sight lines for students. Make sure no students are in the area below where the balls are dropped.
- Use a long board at a steep angle to give the ball a projectile motion. This can also be accomplished by rolling the ball along the board with the board laid flat.

Answers to Observations: Data Table 1

Answers will vary. Students should observe that the dropped ball and the projected ball take the same amount of time to strike the ground. Results that are contrary to this are due to timing errors.

Answers to Observations: Illustrations

Students' illustrations should show that the dropped ball travels vertically downward; the projected ball follows a downward-arcing, curved path.

Answers to Analysis and Conclusions

1. It makes a downward-arcing path.
2. The downward-arcing path is caused by downward acceleration.
3. Taking experimental error into account, the times are the same.
4. Projectile motion has no effect on the speed at which an object is pulled to Earth. Falling objects and objects in projectile motion will hit the ground at the same time.

Going Further

Have students measure the vertical distance the balls fell through in the experiment. Have them research the equations of motion that govern a freely falling object. Guide students on selecting the correct equations to use to calculate the acceleration due to gravity acting on the balls. Have groups draw up a large-size poster of the experiment showing the paths of each ball and the accompanying equations. (Students should obtain acceleration values of approximately 10 m/s^2.)

13C Friction and Forces

Objectives

- measure forces of sliding and rolling friction
- compare and contrast static and sliding friction
- communicate conclusions

Skill Set

measuring, recording and analyzing data, comparing and contrasting, drawing conclusions

Planning

40–45 minutes   groups of 3–4 students

Materials

Materials for this activity are listed in the Student Laboratory Manual.

Advance Preparation

- Screw a small eye hook into each of the wood blocks. The wood blocks should be about 3 cm thick × 10 cm wide × 15 cm long.
- Adding weights on top of the wood block might yield more consistent results; if needed, explore this option.
- Wood dowels can be substituted for pencils in this activity.

Answers to Observations: Data Table 1

Answers will vary. Students should observe that the average value for rolling friction is much less than the value for sliding friction.

Answers to Analysis and Conclusions

1. Answers will vary. Students should observe that the average value for rolling friction is much less than the value for sliding friction.
2. Pulling upward or downward on the spring scale changes the force acting vertically on the block. Because sliding friction varies with the vertical force acting on the block, altering the angle alters the amount of sliding friction.
3. The force of rolling friction would increase for the licorice and decrease for the steel cylinders. Rolling friction is affected in relation to the friction between the two surfaces in contact; harder surfaces generally produce less friction.

Going Further

Ask students to design an experiment to determine the effect of weight on the forces of sliding and rolling friction. Review their proposed procedure and have them conduct the experiment. How do the results compare with the previously conducted lab? Students should write up their test procedure and results for review.

Chapter 14 Lessons

14.1 Fluids and Pressure

14.2 Depth and Pressure

14.3 Buoyancy

14.4 Bernoulli's Principle

Introduce Chapter 14

As a starting activity, use Lab 14A on page 79 of the Laboratory Manual.

ENGAGE List the following on the board: *lemonade, air, soda, tomato sauce, oil*
Ask students to list with partners the characteristics that the items have in common. Talk as a class about classification methods, and emphasize that the items all flow and can change shape. Students might classify them as liquids. Explain that you will be using the term *fluids* to describe substances that may be liquid or gas and that share the characteristics just discussed.

Think About Air and Water

ENGAGE Model the T-chart on the board. Have students brainstorm two to three items for each column and discuss how the items are used in their everyday lives. Then have students create their own T-charts in their Science Notebooks.

Chapter 14 Forces in Fluids

KEY CONCEPT The physical properties of fluids—they flow and take the shape of their containers—make fluids essential to life on Earth.

Windsurfers ride the waves and sail through the air. Although they might not realize it, windsurfers are able to enjoy their sport because of the forces exerted by fluids. Air and water are fluids. They are very different from one another; for example, water is denser than air. But air and water still move and react to external forces in much the same way.

All fluids, whether they are air, water, molasses, or molten asphalt, exhibit the same basic behaviors. This chapter examines the physical behavior of fluids.

Think About Air and Water

Everything that we do happens inside a fluid. Both air and water are fluids.

- In your Science Notebook, make a T-chart with *Air* in one column and *Water* in the other. In the appropriate columns, list things from your everyday life that you think use air or water pressure.

- Think about animals that live on land and animals that live in water. In your T-chart, write your observations about the shapes and lives of these animals.

NSTA

SCI LINKS.
THE WORLD'S A CLICK AWAY

www.scilinks.org
Buoyancy **Code: WGPS14**

222

Chapter 14 Planning Guide

Instructional Periods	National Standards	Lab Manual	Workbook
14.1 2 Periods	A1, A2, B1, B2, C1, E1, F5, G2; A1, A2, B2, B4, B6, E2, G2	**Lab 14A: p. 79** Applying Air Pressure **Lab 14B: pp. 80–81**	Key Concept Review p. 86 Vocabulary Review p. 87 Interpreting Diagrams p. 88
14.2 2 Periods	A1, B2, B3, D1, E1; A1, A2, B4, B6, E1; UCP1	A Cartesian Diver **Lab 14C: pp. 82–84**	Reading Comprehension p. 89 Curriculum Connection p. 90
14.3 2 Periods	A2, B2, E1; A2, B4, E1; UCP2, UCP5	Flying With Bernoulli	Science Challenge p. 91
14.4 2 Periods	A2, B2, C1, E1, E2, F2; A2, B4, C5, C6, E1, E2, F6; UCP2		

Middle School Standard; High School Standard; Unifying Concept and Principle

14.1 Fluids and Pressure

Before You Read

Create a K-W-L-S-H chart in your Science Notebook. Title the chart *Facts About Fluids*. In the *K* column of the chart, write what you already know about fluids. In the *W* column, write what you would like to learn about fluids.

Air is a gas. Water is a liquid. What makes them both fluids? A **fluid** is any substance that lacks a definite shape and has the ability to flow. A solid is not a fluid because a solid has a definite shape and does not have the ability to flow.

Attractive Forces in Fluids

The particles in a fluid are attracted to one another. Therefore, a fluid tends to stick together. However, some fluids stick together more strongly than others do. The "stickiness" of a fluid, or its resistance to flow, is called its **viscosity.** Honey has a higher viscosity than water does. Water has a higher viscosity than air does. A fluid's viscosity depends on the attractions between its particles. The stronger the attractions between the particles, the less freely the particles flow past one another and the more viscous the fluid is.

What Is Pressure?

Step out onto a new snowdrift in hiking boots and you will sink down to your knees. If you strap on a pair of snowshoes, however, you can climb easily over the top of the drift. The difference is due to the amount of pressure your body exerts on the snow. **Pressure** is the force per unit area that is applied on the surface of an object. A force that is applied over a small area produces a larger pressure than does the same force applied over a large area. In this example, the force applied to the snow is your weight. Your weight does not change when you strap on the snowshoes, but the snowshoes spread your weight over a larger area and reduce the pressure you exert on the snow.

Learning Goals

- Describe the properties of a fluid.
- Define and calculate pressure.
- Explain Pascal's principle.
- Relate pressure differences to the movement of fluids.

New Vocabulary

fluid
viscosity
pressure
pascal
Pascal's principle
hydraulic device

Figure 14.1 Fluids behave differently from solids. When a solid object is placed in a container *(left),* the object retains its shape. When a fluid is poured into a container *(right),* it takes the container's shape. This is true whether the fluid is a liquid or a gas.

Background Information

Some fluids behave like solids when a force is applied quickly and like liquids when a force is applied slowly. This property is what makes snail mucus slippery when the snail is moving forward and sticky when a bird tries to pull it off the ground.

14.1 Introduce

ENGAGE Have available in beakers fluids of different viscosities (honey, water, vegetable oil, motor oil, ketchup, hand lotion, milk, etc.). Pass the beakers around to students and ask them to describe what they observe. Suggest that students swirl the beakers carefully and also tilt them carefully to make detailed observations about the fluids. Discuss with students which fluids will flow the fastest and the slowest. Record their answers on the board. Then construct an apparatus to test their predictions.

Vocabulary terms are listed on the first student page of each lesson. You may wish to preview the terms before introducing each lesson. Strategies for teaching the vocabulary appear on the pages where the terms are introduced.

Before You Read

Model the K-W-L-S-H chart on the board. In the *K* column, write: *A fluid can be a liquid or gas.* In the *W* column, write: *How does pressure affect fluids?* Have students draw their K-W-L-S-H charts in their Science Notebooks. Encourage them to write three to five items in each of the two columns.

● Teach

Explain to students that they will learn about the forces in fluids, the way pressure affects fluids, and the movement of fluids.

 Vocabulary

fluid Explain to students that the word *fluid* is derived from the Latin word *fluidus,* meaning "flowing." Ask students how this derivation relates to the definition of the term.

viscosity Tell students that the root *viscous* is Latin and means "sticky." The suffix, *-ity,* means "a state or quality" or "an instance." Ask students how these meanings might help them remember the meaning of *viscosity.*

pressure Explain to students that this word is derived from Latin and means "to press." Ask students how this derivation relates to the scientific meaning of the word.

● Teach

Explain to students that pressure can be calculated using an equation in which force is divided by area. The pressure of fluids is a result of their weight.

 Vocabulary

pascal Explain to students that the pascal is the unit of pressure in the SI system and is named after the scientist Blaise Pascal. Point out to students that the unit name (pascal) is not capitalized, but the first letter of the unit abbreviation is (Pa). Ask students if they can recall another unit that follows this style (newton, N).

Pascal's principle Review with students the work of Blaise Pascal. Ask students to describe how Pascal's inventions illustrate Pascal's principle.

hydraulic device Explain to students that *hydraulic* a compound word. *Hydr-* is from the Greek word *hydor* and means "water," and *aulos* is also derived from Greek and means "pipe." Tell students that a device is a tool or instrument. Have students put the meanings together and compare the literal definition to the scientific definition.

As You Read

Give students a few minutes to update the K-W-L-S-H charts in their Science Notebooks.

Have partners write two questions that they still have about Pascal's principle. Ask volunteers to share questions with the class, and record these on the board. Use the opportunity to re-teach information that seems to be confusing students.

ANSWER Pascal's principle states that when a force is applied to a fluid in a closed container, an increase in pressure is transmitted equally to all parts of the fluid. In other words, the pressure in every part of the fluid increases by the same amount. Pascal's principle can be observed when an inflated balloon is squeezed at one end and the other end expands.

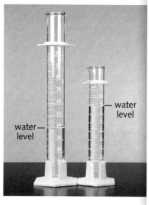

Figure 14.2 Although both graduated cylinders contain the same amount of water, the water in the narrower cylinder rests on a smaller area of glass, so it exerts more pressure on the table.

As You Read

In the *L* column of your K-W-L-S-H chart, list the new things you have learned about fluids. Then discuss Pascal's principle with a partner. Finally, write a few well-developed sentences describing Pascal's principle.

Calculating Pressure

Pressure is calculated using the following formula:

$$\text{pressure} = \frac{\text{force}}{\text{area}} \quad \text{or} \quad P = \frac{F}{A}$$

The unit for pressure in the SI system is the **pascal,** abbreviated Pa. One pascal is equal to the force of one newton exerted over an area of one square meter. In other words, $1\ \text{Pa} = 1\ \text{N/m}^2$.

As the formula indicates, the pressure increases when the applied force increases or the area of contact decreases. The pressure decreases when the applied force decreases or the area of contact increases.

Pressure in Fluids

Fluids exert pressure as a result of their weight. The pressure is the weight of the fluid divided by the area it rests on. Water in a narrow glass exerts more pressure on a table than does the same amount of water poured into a wide bowl. This is because the area that the water in the narrow glass is resting on is less than the area that the water in the bowl is resting on, even though the weight of the water is the same in both containers.

The pressure of a fluid can be changed. Think about what happens when a stopper is pushed into a bottle completely filled with water. Some water squirts out the top. This happens because the stopper exerts a force on the water in the bottle. The increase in force over the same area results in an increase in pressure. The water transmits the increase in pressure equally in all directions—including up! It is this pressure that causes the water to squirt out the top.

Figure 14.3 When the force on the water in a confined space such as a bottle is increased, the pressure of the water increases. This pressure is transmitted equally in all directions, causing the water to squirt out the top.

The behavior of the water is an example of Pascal's principle. **Pascal's principle** states that when a force is applied to a fluid in a closed container, an increase in pressure is transmitted equally to all parts of the fluid. In other words, the pressure in every part of the fluid increases by the same amount.

Differentiate Instruction

Mathematical Have students create real-life problems for other students to solve using the equation for calculating pressure. Students should provide the solutions separately and then exchange problems with a partner. Encourage students to sketch the problems to help them find the solutions.

Hydraulic Devices

Although gases and liquids are both fluids, gases can be compressed and liquids cannot. People have used this property along with Pascal's principle to build hydraulic devices. **Hydraulic devices** use a liquid or compressed gas to transmit and amplify, or increase, forces. These hydraulic devices include the hydraulic lifts in auto repair shops, the automatic transmission and hydraulic brakes in cars, and the lifting mechanism in large construction machines such as cranes and forklifts.

A simple hydraulic device contains two pistons on opposite sides of a liquid. One piston is larger than the other, as in the hydraulic lift in **Figure 14.4.** When a force is applied to the small piston, it increases the pressure inside the liquid. This force is known as the input force. As a result of the input force, the pressure increases by the same amount throughout the liquid. Because the liquid cannot be compressed, the input force acts on the larger piston. Because the area of the larger piston is greater than the area of the smaller piston, the larger piston exerts a force that is larger than the input force. The force exerted by the larger piston is known as the output force. In this way, a hydraulic device can turn a small input force into a much larger output force.

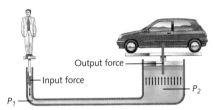

Figure 14.4 The design of hydraulic devices takes advantage of Pascal's principle—because the pressure at all points of the fluid is the same, changing the area to which the pressure is applied can also change the force it produces.

The change in forces can be calculated because it is known that pressure is the same throughout the fluid and that $P = F/A$.

$$P_1 = P_2 \quad \text{or} \quad \frac{F_1}{A_1} = \frac{F_2}{A_2}$$

Solving the equation for the output force F_2 gives the expression

$$F_2 = A_2\left(\frac{F_1}{A_1}\right)$$

Here is an example. If a smaller piston has an area of 1 m² and a larger piston has an area of 5 m², when a force of 100 N is applied to the smaller piston, the larger piston will push up with a force of 500 N.

$$F_2 = 5\ m^2\left(\frac{100\ N}{1\ m^2}\right) = 500\ N$$

The larger piston multiplies the force applied to the smaller piston.

CHAPTER 14   225

Explain It!

The typical chair in a barbershop or hair salon is an example of a hydraulic device. In your Science Notebook, write a few sentences explaining how you think such a chair operates. Be sure to include the terms *input force, output force, pressure, fluid,* and *Pascal's principle.*

Figure It Out

1. Which force is larger in this system, the input force or the output force?

2. Calculate the magnitude of the output force if the input force is 4 N, the input piston has an area of 1 m², and the output piston has an area of 25 m².

● Teach

Explain to students that Pascal's principle is responsible for hydraulic machines such as a jack, which is used to lift a car so that a tire can be changed or repairs can be made.

Explain It!

Review with students how a barbershop chair works (provide a picture or diagram if the concept is unfamiliar). It may be useful for students to sketch their responses before writing their sentences.

Students' explanations should include the following information: The chair is a hydraulic device, and like all hydraulic devices, it operates according to Pascal's principle. When the operator steps on the pedal (piston) of the chair, an input force is applied over a small area. This increases the pressure in the fluid inside the chair's mechanism. According to Pascal's principle, this pressure is transmitted equally throughout the fluid and pushes on the larger piston. Because the area of the larger piston is greater than the area of the smaller piston, the output force is larger than the input force. The output force is great enough to raise the chair and the person sitting in it.

Figure It Out: Figure 14.4
ANSWER **1.** The output force is larger.
2. The output force is 100 N.

Field Study

Have students walk with a partner throughout the school and note any examples of hydraulics they can find. Students should write their observations in their Science Notebooks and then compare their findings with those of their classmates. Display the class results on the board. Then suggest that students continue their search at home and in their neighborhoods, recording their observations.

ELL Strategy

Personal Experience Illustrate English language learners can expand this field study activity by researching on the internet the structure and function of the devices they have discovered. They may also explore other types of hydraulic devices and their uses within different industries or jobs (e.g., hydraulic lifts used by window washers). In their Science Notebook, they can draw those devices, labeling the *input force* and *output force.*

● Teach

Explain to students that fluids move from high-pressure areas to low-pressure areas.

● Assess

Use the After You Read questions and the Alternative Assessment to help you evaluate students' understanding of the lesson.

After You Read

1. Answers will vary, but students should provide appropriate comparisons. For example, fluids take the shape of a container, while solids retain their shape. Fluids also have viscosity, while solids do not.

2. Applying a force over a larger area decreases the pressure.

3. The lowest fluid pressure is found in the capillaries. Students should recall that fluids move from areas of high pressure to areas of lower pressure.

4. Pascal's principle states that if you change the pressure of a fluid on one end of a closed container, the same pressure is exerted everywhere in the fluid simultaneously. A syringe is a closed container with a plunger at one end and a small hole at the other. When the plunger is pressed down, the pressure increases inside the entire syringe. Fluid moves out the small hole toward the region of lower pressure.

Alternative Assessment

Have students use their K-W-L-S-H charts to explain what pressure is, how to calculate pressure, Pascal's principle, and how fluid pressure is responsible for the operation of hydraulic devices. Students should use real-life examples and numbers to illustrate their explanations.

Moving Fluids

When fluids flow, they tend to move from areas of higher pressure to areas of lower pressure. For example, an air-filled balloon contains air that is at a higher pressure than the air outside the balloon. The air stays inside the balloon as long as someone holds the opening shut. If the person lets go of the balloon, however, the pressurized air inside quickly flows toward the nearest area at lower pressure—outside the balloon.

Figure 14.5 The air inside an inflated balloon is at a higher pressure than the air outside the balloon. If the balloon is opened, the higher-pressure air flows into the lower-pressure air outside the balloon.

There are many situations in which a difference in pressure makes fluids flow. People move air into their lungs partly by expanding their ribs. Making the chest cavity larger during inhalation lowers the pressure inside the lungs, allowing air from the outside environment to enter. Similarly, a person drinking through a straw lowers the pressure inside the mouth (by expanding the lungs) to make fluid flow up the straw from the glass.

After You Read

1. In the S column of the K-W-L-S-H chart in your Science Notebook, add information about what you would still like to know about fluids. In the H column, explain ways in which you can find answers to your questions. Underneath the chart, list two ways in which a fluid is different from a solid.

2. If a force is applied over a larger area, does the pressure increase or decrease?

3. Blood in the circulatory system travels from the aorta to the arteries and into the capillaries. Which of these vessels will have the lowest fluid pressure? Explain your answer.

4. Use Pascal's principle to explain how a syringe works.

Teacher Alert

Students might confuse the effect of a larger surface area on the calculation of pressure ($P = F/A$) and its effect in a hydraulic device. In the former, in which the pressure exerted by a fluid on a given area is being calculated, increasing the area will decrease the pressure. In the latter, in which input and output forces are being calculated, increasing the area of the output piston will increase the pressure.

Depth and Pressure

Before You Read

Create a concept map in your Science Notebook by writing and circling the word *Pressure*. Draw a larger circle outside the smaller circle. In the outside circle, write or draw any information that you already know about pressure.

If you have ever driven up a mountain or flown on an airplane, you know that your ears can feel blocked and uncomfortable as you climb higher and higher. Swallowing, yawning, or wiggling your jaw eventually makes your ears "pop," and the discomfort goes away. Why does this happen? Ear discomfort is caused by the change in air pressure as you move higher in the atmosphere.

Pressure Inside a Fluid

Remember that a fluid's weight exerts pressure on solid surfaces and on other fluids. A taller column of fluid exerts more pressure on the surface underneath it than a shorter column of fluid does. But what if an object is suspended in the fluid? In this case, the fluid exerts pressure on every side of the object, not just on its top.

The amount of pressure on the object depends on the object's depth. The pressure comes from the weight of the fluid that is above the object. If the object moves deeper in the fluid, there is more fluid above it and the pressure increases. If the object moves higher up in the fluid, there is less fluid above it and the pressure decreases.

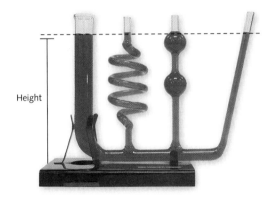

Height

Figure 14.7 The pressure in a fluid depends on the fluid's height above a surface. The shape of the container has no effect on the pressure in the fluid at any depth.

Learning Goals
• Explain how a fluid's depth affects its pressure.
• Describe air pressure and how it is measured.

New Vocabulary

air pressure
barometer

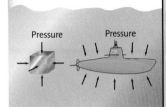

Pressure   Pressure

Figure 14.6 A fluid exerts pressure on objects inside of it. The pressure is exerted perpendicular to every surface of the object, whether it is a regular shape like a cube or an irregular shape like a submarine.

As You Read

As you read this lesson, add circles to your concept map. Include facts about how pressure changes with depth.

Compare the pressure a tall column of fluid exerts on the surface underneath it with the pressure a short column of fluid exerts on the surface underneath it.

ENGAGE Have students talk with partners to identify how scuba diving and fluid depth are related. Students might know that one can dive at different water depths and that at greater depths, the pressure on one's lungs increases. Write *14.7 PSI, 33 feet, 66 feet,* and *99 feet* on the board. Explain to students that that air around us, at sea level, has a pressure of 14.7 pounds per square inch. When a person dives to 33 feet, his or her lungs feel twice the pressure as on land. At 66 feet, the pressure is three times as great, and at 99 feet it is four times as great. Suggest that students calculate the actual pressures for these three depths.

Before You Read

Model the process of creating the concept map on the board. In the larger circle, write *Fluids move from areas of higher pressure to areas of lower pressure.* Have students complete the task, and encourage them to include information learned from the first lesson of the chapter.

Teach

Explain to students that both air pressure and water pressure increase with depth. In this section, students will learn more about how pressure changes.

As You Read

Give students a few minutes to update their concept maps. Students should add to their maps the idea that the height of a fluid is directly related to the pressure the fluid exerts.

ANSWER A tall column of fluid exerts more pressure on the surface underneath it than a short column of fluid does.

ELL Strategy

Paraphrase Have students work in groups of three. Each student should paraphrase one of the three topics in the lesson: *Pressure Inside a Fluid, Air Pressure,* or *Water Pressure.* Each student should then write an overview of the topic complete with a diagram and share it with the other group members.

Teach

Explain to students that air pressure decreases as one moves higher in the atmosphere. On this page, students will learn about changes in air pressure and how air pressure is measured.

Use the Visual: Figure 14.8

Have students make a graph of the data in this figure. Students could represent the data using a side-by-side bar graph.

 Vocabulary

air pressure Encourage students to brainstorm common uses of the word *air*. Examples might include a light breeze, an appearance or look, the mixture of gases surrounding Earth, or a usage related to airplanes or aircraft.

barometer Tell students that *barometer* is a compound word. *Baro-* is derived from the Greek word *baros* and means "weight," and *-meter* refers to an instrument for measuring. The literal definition of *barometer* is "a tool for measuring weight." Ask students to relate this to the scientific definition.

Science Notebook EXTRA

Have students find out about different types of barometers, including aneroid barometers. Provide resource materials for research. Instruct students to write descriptions and draw diagrams in their Science Notebooks for each barometer.

 Extend It!

Review the local newspaper's weather page and highlight where the barometric pressure and weather conditions are located. Some resources will also show whether the pressure is increasing or decreasing. Suggest that students note their observations each day at the same time. Encourage students to also note the barometric pressure when weather changes occur.

ANSWER Students should be able to correlate rainy weather with lower barometer readings.

 CONNECTION: Chemistry

People who live high in the mountains have to change the way they cook their food. At altitudes higher than 900 m above sea level, the lower atmospheric pressure also lowers the temperature at which water boils. Because the food is cooking at a lower temperature, it has to be cooked longer.

 Extend It!

Draw a chart in your Science Notebook with three columns: *Day, Barometric Pressure,* and *Weather Conditions.* For two weeks, record the barometric pressure and the weather conditions (sunny, cloudy, rainy, and so forth). You can get barometric pressure data from a real barometer or the newspaper, television, radio, or Internet.

After two weeks, look at your weather data. Is there a connection between the barometric pressure and the weather conditions? Write your conclusions in your Science Notebook.

Air Pressure

The atmosphere is a layer of air that surrounds Earth. When objects move up and down in the atmosphere, the pressure changes can have noticeable effects. Ear discomfort on airplanes or at the top of mountains illustrates this phenomenon. The ear canal and the middle ear are separated by a thin piece of skin called the eardrum. As an airplane climbs, it moves to a higher point in the atmosphere. Because there is less air above the plane, the air pressure is lower. **Air pressure** is the pressure caused by the weight of Earth's atmosphere. Air pressure is also referred to as atmosphereic pressure.

The air pressure inside the ear canal quickly changes with the outside air pressure, but the air inside the middle ear stays at a higher pressure. The higher-pressure air in the middle ear pushes against the eardrum. Swallowing and yawning equalize the pressure between the middle ear and the ear canal, removing the discomfort.

Air Pressure at Different Altitudes	
Distance Above Sea Level (m)	Air Pressure (kPa)
0	101 (sea level)
1,609	83.4 (altitude of Denver, Colorado)
8,848	31.5 (top of Mt. Everest)
12,192	18 (747 maximum flight altitude)
18,000	10.1 (top of the troposphere)

Figure 14.8 Atmospheric pressure gets lower as one moves closer to outer space because the layer of air pressing down toward Earth gets thinner.

Air puts pressure on your body all of the time, but the amount of pressure it exerts depends on the amount of air above you. At sea level, the weight of the atmosphere exerts a pressure of approximately 100 kPa, or 100,000 Pa. At the top of Mount Everest, the air pressure drops to only 31.5 kPa. Air around an airplane cruising at 12 km is exerting only 18 kPa of pressure. Thicker layers of air produce higher atmospheric pressures.

Background Information

Cooking is affected by higher elevations in three ways: the boiling point of water decreases; liquids evaporate more quickly; and leavening gases expand more quickly. Each 500-foot increase in altitude lowers the boiling point of water by about one degree. Baked goods may rise too fast if leavening gases expand too quickly.

Differentiate Instruction

Visual Have students draw a diagram of the ear and how it changes with lower air pressure. Students will illustrate the changes in the middle ear.

Air pressure can be measured with an instrument called a **barometer** (bah RAH meh tur). A barometer is an upright glass column that is closed at the top and filled with a dense fluid, usually mercury. The bottom of the barometer is open to the atmosphere. When air presses down on the fluid, the pressure it exerts pushes the fluid up into the tube. The fluid stops rising when its weight against the bottom of the barometer is the same as the pressure of the atmosphere. Higher atmospheric pressures push the fluid higher in the tube. Lower atmospheric pressures make the fluid column shorter.

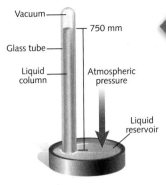

Figure 14.9 The height of the liquid in this barometer rises as the atmospheric pressure increases.

Water Pressure

Like air, water also exerts pressure on the objects in it. However, because water is heavier than air, a column of water exerts more pressure than an identical column of air does. Water pressure also increases much faster as the water gets deeper. In water, pressure increases by about 100 kPa every ten meters. At the surface of the water, a scuba diver is under 100 kPa of pressure from the atmosphere. At 20 m, the diver feels 300 kPa of pressure: the 100 kPa from the atmosphere plus an additional 200 kPa from the water. The animals that live at the bottom of the ocean are under tremendous pressure. The pressure at the bottom of the Mariana Trench in the Pacific Ocean—the lowest point on Earth—is more than 100,000 kPa!

After You Read

1. Hypothesize what happens to the air in a person's lungs when he or she dives to the bottom of a swimming pool that is 6 m deep.

2. Review the concept map in your Science Notebook. Then draw a picture of an object that is underwater. Add arrows to show how the water exerts pressure on the object.

3. Why does water pressure increase faster than air pressure does with increasing depth?

Figure It Out

1. According to this barometer, what is the current atmospheric pressure in millimeters (mm) of mercury (Hg)?

2. If 1 mm of Hg equals 0.133 kPa, calculate the current atmospheric pressure in kPa.

Water Pressure at Different Depths

Depth (m)	Pressure (kPa)
0 (surface)	100 (atmospheric pressure only)
20	300
50	600
100	1,100
1,000	10,100

Figure 14.10 The pressure exerted by the water increases as one moves deeper and deeper.

Teach

Explain to students that similarly to fluid pressure, water pressure increases as the depth of the object increases.

Figure It Out: Figure 14.9

ANSWER **1.** This barometer reads 750 mm of Hg. **2.** After calculating the conversion from mm Hg to kPa, students should find that the current atmospheric pressure is approximately 100 kPa.

Assess

Use the After You Read questions and the Alternative Assessment to help you evaluate students' understanding of the lesson.

After You Read

1. When the person dives into a deep pool, his or her lungs are compressed by the higher water pressure. Because the pressure increases by about 100 kPa every 10 m, the increase at 6 m would be slightly more than 50 kPa.

2. Students' drawings should show arrows on every side of the object, because water exerts pressure equally on every side of a submerged object.

3. Water pressure increases faster than air pressure with increasing depth because water is heavier than air.

Alternative Assessment

Have each student use his or her concept map to write a paragraph discussing how the pressure on an object changes as it is submersed deeper in water, and then how the pressure changes when the same object moves higher into the atmosphere.

Background Information

The Italian physicist Evangelista Torricelli invented the barometer. His original device was a long glass tube filled with mercury that was inverted in a cup of mercury. The column of mercury in the tube settled about 76 cm (30 in.) above the surface of mercury in the cup; thus the pressure of the air on the surface of the mercury in the cup supported the mercury in the tube. Consequently, Torricelli proved that atmospheric pressure was the same as the weight of a 30-inch column of mercury.

14.3 Introduce

ENGAGE Provide pairs of students with the following items: two tall clear glass containers, water, a measuring cup, ½ cup salt, an egg, a spoon, and a pencil. Have them fill both glass containers halfway with water and stir the salt into one of the containers. Using the spoon, have them lower the egg into the glass with the plain water. Ask students to notice whether the egg sinks or floats. Then have them remove the egg and gently lower it into the glass with salt water. Again, have students note whether the egg sinks or floats. Then ask them to gently pour the plain water down the side of the container with the egg and salt water. Again, ask students to note the position of the egg. Ask students to explain their observations. If this is difficult, tell them they will be able to explain them after learning about buoyancy.

Before You Read

Have students work with partners to brainstorm everything they know about buoyancy. Suggest that they organize their ideas and then write a few sentences to define the term in their Science Notebooks. Explain that they will refine their definitions as they learn more throughout the lesson.

● Teach

Explain to students that they will learn why some items float (the egg in salt water) and others do not (the egg in plain water).

Vocabulary

buoyancy Explain to students that the root *buoyant* means "able to float in or on the surface of a liquid." The suffix *-y* signifies a quality or state.

buoyant force Review with students the meaning of *buoyant*. Tell students that the word *force* is derived from the Latin word *fortia*, meaning "strength."

neutral buoyancy Explain to students that *neutral* is derived from the Latin word *neuter*, meaning "neither." Review with students the meaning of *buoyancy*. Ask students how these word meanings relate to the definition of the term.

- Describe the forces that produce buoyancy.
- Explain Archimedes' principle.
- Relate an object's shape to its buoyancy.

New Vocabulary

buoyancy
buoyant force
neutral buoyancy
displacement
Archimedes' principle
density

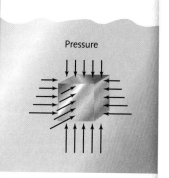

Figure 14.11 The pressure exerted on the bottom of this cube is larger than the pressure exerted on its top. The pressure difference produces a net force pointing up called the buoyant force.

14.3 Buoyancy

Before You Read

Create a working definition of the term *buoyancy* in your Science Notebook. Then add to the definition as you read the lesson.

If you drop a steel bar into a pond, it sinks. If you mold the same amount of steel into a toy boat, however, it floats. Both objects are made of the same material, but the shape of the material affects the buoyancy of each object. **Buoyancy** (BOY un see) is a measure of an object's ability to float in another substance.

The Buoyant Force

When an object is in a fluid, it experiences pressure in all directions. Because pressure varies with depth, the pressure pushing down on the top of the object is less than the pressure pushing up on the bottom of the object. The difference in pressure results in a net upward force on the object called the **buoyant** (BOY unt) **force.** This concept is illustrated in **Figure 14.11**.

The buoyant force pushes up on the object while the force of gravity pulls down on the object. If the buoyant force is smaller than the force of gravity on the object (which is the object's weight), the object sinks. If the buoyant force is either equal to or larger than the force of gravity on the object, the object floats. When the two forces are perfectly balanced, the object floats without either rising or sinking. This condition is called **neutral buoyancy.**

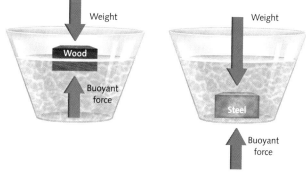

Figure 14.12 An object floats if its buoyant force is the same or larger than its weight. An object sinks if its weight is larger than its buoyant force.

ELL Strategy

Model Challenge students to make a boat from aluminum foil that holds the most pennies possible. Provide the option for students to work independently or with a partner. Encourage groups to try to meet or beat the highest number of pennies held by the class boats.

Background Information

An average egg weighs 0.071 kg and has a volume of about 0.0006 cubic meters. Water weighs 1,000 kg per cubic meter, and salt water weights about 1,300 kg per cubic meter.

Increasing the surface area of an object increases the buoyant force on the object. A larger area will give the upward pressure of the fluid more surface to act upon.

Figure 14.13 The buoyant force on an object increases when the object's surface area increases.

Archimedes' Principle

In the third century B.C., a mathematician named Archimedes discovered that the buoyant force on an object is always the same as the weight of the fluid that the object displaces, or pushes aside. The process of pushing liquid aside is called **displacement.** If you fill a bowl to its rim with water and place a block of wood in it, the buoyant force on the wood will be the same as the weight of the water that spills out of the bowl. This observation is called **Archimedes' principle.**

Archimedes' principle shows that there is a relationship between an object's mass and the volume of space the object fills. This relationship is called **density.** It is calculated using the formula

$$\text{density} = \frac{\text{mass}}{\text{volume}} \qquad D = \frac{m}{V}$$

Imagine a pair of identically shaped cubes, one made of wood and the other of steel. The cubes have the same volume, but the steel cube has much more mass than the wood cube. The steel is denser than the wood because it has more mass packed into the same volume.

Figure It Out

1. What forces cause an object to either float or swim?
2. Why does one shape float and the other shape sink?

As You Read

Relate your working definition of *buoyancy* to the definition of the term *density* on this page. Write your ideas in your Science Notebook.

What is density? How is it calculated?

PEOPLE IN SCIENCE Archimedes (287 B.C.–212 B.C.)

Archimedes was born in Sicily. He studied in Alexandria before returning home to spend the his life solving mathematical and engineering problems. His inventions included a simple machine to move water from low areas to higher areas, called the Archimedes screw, as well as a number of weapons to defend his city.

Archimedes is said to have worked out the principles of buoyancy when King Hiero asked him to determine whether a crown was solid gold or a mix of other metals. When Archimedes took a bath, he realized that there was a relationship between his weight and the water that he displaced as he got in. If the crown were made of lighter metals, it would displace more water than would an equal weight of gold, because it would have to have a larger volume to weigh the same as the gold. According to legend, Archimedes was so excited that he leaped from his bath and ran, completely naked, to the palace, shouting, "Eureka!" ("I have found it!").

● Teach

Explain to students that density and buoyancy are related. Density refers to how closely packed molecules are.

 Vocabulary

displacement Tell students that the prefix *dis-* refers to the opposite of the base word. Encourage students to brainstorm common uses of the word *place*. The suffix *-ment* refers to a quality or condition. The literal definition of the term is "the condition of being moved from a typical location."

Archimedes' principle Discuss with students the difference between the words *principle* and *principal*. Encourage students to note that *principal* ends with *pal*, a familiar word. A principle is a scientific law that explains a natural phenomenon or the way a machine works.

density Ask students to list common meanings of the root word *dense*. Examples might include "closely packed," "thick," or "slow to understand."

Figure It Out: Figure 14.13

[ANSWER] **1.** Buoyant force and weight determine if an object floats. **2.** The flat foil has a greater buoyant force due to its larger surface area.

As You Read

Give students a few minutes to refine their definitions of *buoyancy* and to find a relationship between density and buoyancy.

[ANSWER] Density is the relationship between mass and volume. It is calculated by using the formula density = mass/volume ($D=m/v$).

PEOPLE IN SCIENCE

Archimedes' original writings were lost, but many were copied first. One copy containing seven of Archimedes' works was later reused to make part of a medieval prayer book. This book is now being studied with ultraviolet and X-ray imaging to recover some of Archimedes' mathematical work.

Differentiate Instruction

Mathematical, Visual Have students investigate the densities of different solids, liquids, and gases and make graphs that note each item and its density. Display the graphs around the room and have the class note which items have the highest densities and which have the lowest densities.

Science Notebook EXTRA

Have students assume the role of Archimedes and write a letter in their Science Notebooks to King Hiero explaining how they knew the crown was not solid gold. Students should include the terms *density* and *buoyancy* in their explanations.

● Teach

Explain to students that displacement depends on an object's shape; this explains why boats are able to float.

🔍 Explore It!

Direct students to pour the fluids slowly down the side of the beaker. Have them predict how the fluids will be layered, and ask them to draw and label their predictions in their Science Notebooks.

The fluids will layer themselves with the densest fluid at the bottom and the least dense at the top. Given corn syrup (liquid glucose), water, and corn oil, students will see the oil on top, the water in the center, and the corn syrup at the bottom.

CONNECTION: Biology

Have students investigate types of fish that do not have a swim bladder and the anatomical conditions that enable such fish to maintain buoyancy.

● Assess

Use the After You Read questions and the Alternative Assessment to help you evaluate students' understanding of the lesson.

After You Read

1. Gravity and the buoyant force act on an object in a fluid.

2. Students can explain that ships decrease the pressure they exert on water because of their large surface areas or that their overall density is reduced by enclosing a large volume of low-density materials.

3. It sloshes because the body displaces an amount of water equal to its weight.

4. The positively buoyant object will have a large arrow (buoyant force) pointing up and a small arrow (gravity) pointing down. The negatively buoyant object will have a large arrow pointing down (gravity) and a small arrow pointing up (buoyant force). The neutrally buoyant object will have arrows of equal size.

🔍 Explore It!

Fluids can have different densities. To explore this idea, get 10 mL of corn syrup, 10 mL of vegetable oil, and 10 mL of water. Add several drops of food coloring to the water, and pour all of the fluids into a 50-mL beaker. Wait ten minutes, and then observe how the fluids are layered.

In your Science Notebook, draw a picture of the beaker and the positions of the fluids. Which fluid has the highest density? Which one has the lowest density?

CONNECTION: Biology

Many species of fishes control their buoyancy with their swim bladder, an organ filled with enough air to make the fish neutrally buoyant. When the fish dives, the air in the swim bladder compresses, making the fish sink faster. When the fish swims upward, the air expands, making the fish rise faster.

Density and Displacement

If a cube of steel with a volume of 1 cm³ is placed in a deep bowl of water, it sinks to the bottom. The cube is then completely underwater, so it displaces exactly 1 cm³ of water. The weight of this 1 cm³ of water is equal to the buoyant force acting on the steel cube. Since the cube sinks, the weight of the 1-cm³ cube must be greater than the weight of the 1 cm³ of water. This means the steel must have more mass in the same amount of volume than water does. In other words, the sinking steel is more dense than water. Any object that is more dense than water will also sink. In general, if an object is more dense than the fluid in which it is placed, then the object will sink. If the object is less dense than the fluid, then the object will float. If the object has the same density as the fluid, then the object will be neutrally buoyant.

The amount of fluid an object displaces depends on the object's shape. Figure 14.13 on page 231 shows that giving an object greater surface area increases the buoyant force.

Also, an object's volume can be increased by changing its shape. This decreases the object's overall density, but does not change the densities of the individual materials making up the object. The steel that goes into a ship has the same density as a solid steel bar does. The hollow ship, however, includes both the dense metal in its hull and all of the less-dense air inside of it. The air makes the overall density of the ship lower than the density of the water, so the ship floats. Balloons use the same principle to float in air. The balloon is made of nylon, which is much denser than air. The balloon is filled with a gas such as helium or with hot air that is less dense than the cold air outside the balloon. When enough fills the balloon, it becomes buoyant and rises.

Figure 14.14 Heating the gas inside a hot-air balloon reduces the gas's density. When the total density of the balloon and the gas inside of it is less than the density of the outside air, the balloon will rise.

After You Read

1. Name the two forces that act on an object in a fluid.

2. Explain why large ships can float even though they are built of materials that are denser than water.

3. Why would water slosh onto the floor if a person got in a bathtub that was completely filled with water?

4. Objects that float upward are called positively buoyant. Objects that sink are called negatively buoyant. Objects that float without rising or sinking are called neutrally buoyant. Draw diagrams of each type of object in your Science Notebook. Use arrows to show the forces acting on the objects. Use your working definition of *buoyancy* to help you draw the diagrams.

Alternative Assessment

Students should use their working definitions of *buoyancy* to explain the results of the egg experiment from the Engage activity on page 230. Students' explanations should include why the egg sank in plain water, floated in salt water, and was suspended in the middle of the mixture of plain and salt water. Instruct students to use as many of the lesson's vocabulary terms in their explanations as possible.

14.4 Bernoulli's Principle

Before You Read

You can usually trace back every effect you observe to something that caused it. In your Science Notebook, describe an example of a cause and its effect from your everyday life. Then look for examples of cause and effect in this lesson.

Try this activity: hold a single sheet of paper at both corners of one side as shown in **Figure 14.15**. Now blow across the top surface of the paper. What do you observe? Do you see that the paper rises? Blow harder, and the paper rises even farther. The paper moves because the pressure in the air moving next to it has changed.

Moving Fluids

Daniel Bernoulli (1700–1782) discovered a relationship between the speed of a moving fluid and its pressure. This relationship is now called Bernoulli's principle. **Bernoulli's principle** states that as the velocity of a fluid increases, the pressure the fluid exerts decreases.

When you blew across the top of the sheet of paper, you made the air on one side move faster than the air on the other side. When the air sped up, its pressure decreased. There was a different air pressure on each side of the paper: the underside had a higher pressure than the upper side. The high-pressure air pushed the sheet of paper up into the low-pressure area. The harder you blew, the larger the pressure difference became.

The relationship between pressure and velocity on each side of the sheet of paper can be calculated with the following equation:

$$\text{pressure}_1 - \text{pressure}_2 = \frac{(\text{density of fluid})(\text{velocity}_2{}^2 - \text{velocity}_1{}^2)}{2}$$

$$P_1 - P_2 = \frac{D(V_2{}^2 - V_1{}^2)}{2}$$

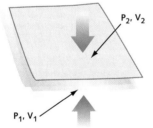

Figure 14.16 Bernoulli's principle states that a fluid's pressure will drop when the fluid moves faster.

P_2, V_2

P_1, V_1

Low Pressure

High Pressure

Figure 14.15 The air moves faster over the top of the sheet of paper, lowering the pressure. The higher-pressure air underneath the sheet of paper pushes the paper up.

ENGAGE Working in pairs, ask students to compare the flights of an airplane, rocket, hang glider, and paper airplane. Ask them to note how the flights are similar and how they are different. Have students share their observations with the class, and record these on the board. Then write the words *thrust, lift, gravity,* and *drag* on the board. Have students infer which words are related to initiating flights and which are related to ending flights. Tell students that they will learn more about lift in this lesson.

Before You Read

Talk aloud about an example of a cause and effect in your life, such as using the snooze button an extra time in the morning. Getting up late might cause you to miss breakfast, encounter extra traffic, arrive late to school, and feel rushed all morning. Encourage students to think of a different example and to write about it in their Science Notebooks. Have students share some of their examples with the class.

Teach

Explain to students that they will learn about lift and other factors that influence flight.

Vocabulary

Bernoulli's principle Review with students the meaning of the word *principle* and then the details of Bernoulli's discovery. Explain that energy is conserved in a moving fluid. If a fluid moves in a horizontal direction, the pressure decreases as the speed of the fluid increases.

Learning Goals

- Describe Bernoulli's principle.
- Explain how wing shape produces lift.

New Vocabulary

Bernoulli's principle
lift

ELL Strategy

Activate Background Knowledge Have students talk with partners about what they already know about thrust, lift, and gravity. Encourage students to refer to sports, hobbies, or traveling experiences in the discussion.

Key Concept Review
Workbook, p. 86

● Teach

Explain to students that Bernoulli's principle describes the movement of curveballs in baseball as well as the effect of a large truck passing a car on the highway.

As You Read

Give students a few minutes to review and revise their cause-and-effect statements in their Science Notebooks.

ANSWER The cause is any event that speeds up a fluid. The effect is the pressure drop in the moving fluid, and the movement of fluid from high-pressure areas to low-pressure areas.

⊙ CONNECTION: Meteorology

Have students research tornado safety and then create tornado safety posters with tips about where one should take shelter during a tornado. Students could illustrate the posters to show where the safest locations are.

In their Science Notebooks, students should summarize the safety information and relate the shelter tips to Bernoulli's principle.

As You Read

Review the examples of cause-and-effect relationships you wrote in your Science Notebook. Discuss them in a small group. Then write a sentence that explains the cause and effect described by Bernoulli's principle.

Figure 14.17 Smoke moves up a chimney faster when the wind is blowing than when the air is still. The wind lowers the pressure of the air at the top of the chimney.

⊙ CONNECTION: Meteorology

Tornadoes are rapidly spinning weather systems with intense winds. The wind on the inside of the tornado moves faster than the air on the outside does, creating a central area with very low pressure.

Applications of Bernoulli's Principle

If you've ever flown a paper airplane, watched smoke rise up a chimney, or been "attacked" by a shower curtain, you've had firsthand experience with Bernoulli's principle.

The chimney of a fireplace lets smoke rise up out of the house. The hot air from around the fire rises up the chimney because the hot air is lighter than the colder air in the room, but it rises faster when it's windy outside. As the wind blows by the house, it lowers the air pressure at the top of the chimney. The air at the bottom of the chimney is now at a higher pressure than the air at the top. The pressure difference forces air up the chimney.

Prairie dogs are burrowing rodents that live on the windy Great Plains in the central United States. Their burrows are usually about 3 m deep and have two openings spaced about 15 m apart. The burrows are deep enough that fresh air cannot move to the bottom of the burrow by diffusion. The burrow has to be ventilated, or the prairie dogs will suffocate. Bernoulli's principle provides the moving air. A prairie dog makes one opening of its burrow slightly higher than the other. When wind blows across the openings, it produces a pressure difference between them that forces fresh air through the burrow.

Figure 14.18 Prairie dogs build one entrance to a burrow higher than the other, creating a pressure difference that draws fresh air through the tunnel. Air enters through the lower mound and moves toward the higher one.

A thin shower curtain will often billow into the shower stall after the water is turned on. It doesn't matter whether the water is hot or cold. As long as the shower spray is on, the air inside the shower stall is moving. While the air moves, the air pressure outside the shower stall is higher than the pressure inside the shower stall, and the curtain gets pushed in.

Differentiate Instruction

Kinesthetic, Visual Have students experiment with different shapes of paper airplanes to determine which shape produces the most lift, as identified by the length of the flight. Provide students with a variety of papers to construct planes and stopwatches to measure the lengths of flights.

Background Information

During very windy and violent storms, the high speeds of the winds blowing over houses cause a pressure difference great enough to lift house roofs unless they are very firmly anchored. Once the roof is airborne, the wind blowing under the roof equalizes the pressure below and above. The lifting force then is gone, and the roof crashes down. During the time that the roof is suspended, winds can enter the house and blow the walls outward.

Flight

Bernoulli's principle is what explains how airplanes fly. The shape of a wing takes advantage of Bernoulli's principle to push an airplane off the ground. Wings are not flat plates. The top of a wing is curved, and the bottom of a wing is somewhat flat. When a wing is pushed through the air at an angle, the air that moves over the top of the wing moves faster than the air that moves over the bottom of the wing. This makes the pressure drop over the top of the wing. The pressure difference causes a net upward force on the wing that pushes the wing upward. This force is called **lift.**

Figure 14.19 The fluid moving over the top of a wing moves faster than the fluid moving over its bottom. The difference in speed produces a low pressure on top of the wing and a high pressure below it. The net force pushing up on the wing is called lift.

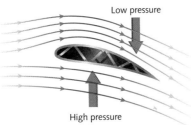

Low pressure

High pressure

◄ **Figure It Out**

Figure It Out

1. Which force on the wing is the larger force, gravity or lift?

2. Hypothesize what will happen to the lift on the wing if the wing moves through the fluid faster.

Any wing moving through a fluid can produce lift. The wing can be pulled through the air as part of a glider, such as a paper airplane or a flying squirrel. Or a wing can be actively pushed through the air. Birds, bats, and insects use their muscles to pull their wings through the air, while airplanes are pushed forward by engines. A wing moving through a denser fluid like water can also produce lift. Sea lions, penguins, and sea turtles all swim by using wing-shaped flippers to "fly" through the water.

Figure 14.20 Gliders and powered fliers both use wing-shaped structures to produce lift.

After You Read

1. Describe Bernoulli's principle.

2. Select one real-world example of Bernoulli's principle. In your Science Notebook, describe its cause and its effect.

3. In a well-developed paragraph, define *lift* and identify three things that move by generating lift.

Background Information

Scientists conducted wind tunnel tests on scale-model humpback whale flippers and found that the scalloped, bumpy flippers have a more efficient wing design than the design used by airplanes. The bumpy flippers do not stall as quickly and produce more lift and less drag than similarly sized sleek flippers. These findings could help engineers design airplane wings and underwater vehicles.

Interpreting Diagrams
Workbook, p. 88

● Teach

Explain to students that Bernoulli's principle explains how airplanes are able to fly.

 Vocabulary

lift Ask students to list common uses of the word *lift*. Students' examples of its use as a verb might include carrying or raising something, transporting something in an aircraft, revoking something, or making someone happier. Examples of noun usage might include a rise in spirits or mood, a free ride as a passenger, an elevator, or the placing of someone in a higher position.

Figure It Out: Figure 14.19

ANSWER **1.** Lift is the larger force on the wing. **2.** If the wing is moved forward faster, the pressure at the top of the wing will decrease further and lift will increase.

● Assess

Use the After You Read questions and the Alternative Assessment to help you evaluate students' understanding of the lesson.

After You Read

1. Bernoulli's principle states that as the velocity of a fluid increases, the pressure it exerts decreases.

2. Answers will vary but should contain an example in which an increase in fluid speed produces a localized pressure gradient.

3. Lift is an upward force caused by a pressure difference above and below a wing. Examples will vary but can include airplanes, helicopters, gliders, paper airplanes, bats, birds, insects, sea turtles, penguins, sea lions, stingrays, and maple seeds.

Alternative Assessment

Have students use their cause-and-effect statements to illustrate the concept of lift. Each student should draw a diagram of an item that moves by lift and use arrows to identify the forces of lift.

Chapter 14 Summary

MASTERING CONCEPTS

True or False

1. True
2. False, increases
3. True
4. False, viscosity
5. True
6. False, decreases

Short Answer

7. The mercury level in the barometer will drop as the barometer is carried up the mountain because atmospheric pressure decreases.

8. Snowshoes increase the surface area where the person's feet touch the ground and reduce the pressure the person exerts on the snow.

9. The force is lift, and it results when the air is forced to move faster over the top of the curved hand than it moves over the bottom.

10. Water and air both flow when they are pushed on and take the shape of the containers they are poured into.

11. As the leaking boat fills with water, its total density increases.

KEY CONCEPTS

14.1 Fluids and Pressure

- A fluid is a material that flows and takes the shape of its container.
- Pressure is force acting over an area and can be calculated using the formula $P = \frac{F}{A}$.
- A fluid in a closed container has the same pressure at all of its points.
- Pascal's principle, which is the basis for the operation of hydraulic devices, states that when a force is applied to a fluid in a closed container, an increase in pressure is transmitted equally to all parts of the fluid.
- Fluids move from areas of high pressure to areas of low pressure.
- Hydraulic devices use Pascal's principle to amplify small input forces into large output forces.

14.2 Depth and Pressure

- The pressure in a fluid depends on the fluid's depth.
- Air pressure is the pressure caused by the force Earth's atmosphere exerts. Air pressure is also referred to as atmospheric pressure. It is measured with a barometer.

14.3 Buoyancy

- An object in a fluid feels both the force of gravity and the buoyant force.
- According to Archimedes' principle, the buoyant force on an object equals the weight of the fluid the object displaces.
- Increasing the surface area of a given weight of material increases the material's buoyancy.

14.4 Bernoulli's Principle

- As the velocity of a fluid increases, the pressure the fluid exerts decreases.
- When fluid moves over a wing, the difference in pressure on the upper side of the wing and the underside of the wing creates lift.

VOCABULARY REVIEW

Write each term in a complete sentence or write a paragraph relating several terms.

14.1
fluid, p. 223
viscosity, p. 223
pressure, p. 223
pascal, p. 224
Pascal's principle, p. 224
hydraulic device, p. 225

14.2
air pressure, p. 228
barometer, p. 229

14.3
buoyancy, p. 230
buoyant force, p. 230
neutral buoyancy, p. 230
displacement, p. 231
Archimedes' principle, p. 231
density, p. 231

14.4
Bernoulli's principle, p. 233
lift, p. 235

PREPARE FOR CHAPTER TEST

To prepare for the chapter test, create a question from each Learning Goal. Use the information in your Science Notebook to answer each question. Then use these answers to write a well-developed essay about the chapter. Use the Key Concept on the first page of this chapter as your topic sentence.

Vocabulary Review
Workbook, p. 87

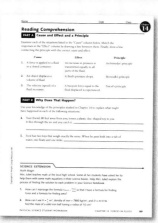

Reading Comprehension
Workbook, p. 89

MASTERING CONCEPTS

True or False
If the statement is true, write "true." If it is false, change the underlined word or words to make the statement true.

1. <u>Pressure</u> is a force exerted over an area.
2. As an object moves deeper into a fluid, the pressure on it <u>decreases</u>.
3. The shape of a wing creates <u>lift</u> when air moves over it.
4. The resistance of a fluid to flow is called the fluid's <u>density</u>.
5. The <u>buoyant force</u> is produced by the net upward pressure of a fluid on an object.
6. As the velocity of a fluid <u>increases</u>, the fluid's pressure increases.

Short Answer
Answer each of the following in a sentence or brief paragraph.

7. Describe what will happen to the mercury level in a barometer when the barometer is carried up a mountain. Explain your answer.
8. Explain why snowshoes keep a person from sinking through the snow.
9. When you put your hand outside the window of a moving car, you can feel a force pushing your hand upward. Name this force, and explain what causes it.
10. Explain why water and air are both fluids.
11. Why does a leaking boat sink?

Critical Thinking
Use what you have learned in this chapter to answer each of the following.

12. **Predict** You feel a pull on your car when an 18-wheel truck speeds past it on the highway. Predict which way your car will be pulled, and explain why.
13. **Infer** Two identical-looking objects are placed in a tub of water. One floats, and the other sinks. What can you infer about the density of each object?
14. **Compare** You are looking at two columns of water. One is 3 m high and 5 cm² at its base, the other is 1 m high and 8 cm² at its base. Compare the pressure exerted by the fluid columns at their bases.

Standardized Test Question
Choose the letter of the response that correctly answers the question.

15. Which of the following statements is true?

A. The pressure is larger in the small column than in the large column.
B. The pressure is larger in the large column than in the small column.
C. The pressure is the same in both columns.
D. There is no pressure in either column.

Test-Taking Tip

Avoid changing your answer unless you have read the question incorrectly. Usually, your first choice is the correct choice.

Critical Thinking

12. Your car will be pulled toward the truck, because the air around the truck is moving faster than the air around your car is moving. This makes the air pressure near the truck lower than the air pressure around your car. The high-pressure air pushes the car toward the low-pressure air.
13. The floating object is less dense than the water. The sinking object is denser than the water.
14. The 3-m-tall column exerts the larger pressure at its base. In this problem, only height matters; the taller column has the higher pressure.

Standardized Test Question

15. C

Reading Links

Liquids and Gases: Principles of Fluid Mechanics (Secrets of the Universe)

This clear, concise volume presents a sound overview of Archimedes', Pascal's, and Bernoulli's principles, Boyle's and Charles's laws, and other relevant concepts and scientific contributions. The format and level of coverage make this an accessible resource for struggling readers.

Paul Fleisher. Lerner Publishing Group. 80 pp. Illustrated. Library ISBN 978-0-8225-2988-0.

The Airplane (Great Inventions)

The history and development of the airplane draws on important concepts in physics. This application of the principles behind flight—pressure in fluids, lift, and more—is sure to interest students and serves as an interesting chapter supplement.

Harold Faber. Benchmark Books. 128 pp. Illustrated. Library ISBN 978-0-7614-1876-4.

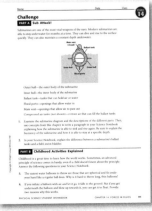

Curriculum Connection
Workbook, p. 90

Science Challenge
Workbook, p. 91

14A Applying Air Pressure

This prechapter introduction activity is designed to determine what students already know about air pressure by having them make predictions, evaluate, and draw conclusions about how differences in air pressure can cause an aluminum can to change its shape.

Objectives

- predict the strength of air pressure exerted on an object
- observe as air pressure differences act on an object
- communicate conclusions

Planning

 15–20 minutes   groups of 3–4 students

Materials

- 12-oz. aluminum beverage cans
- hot plate
- large plastic bucket
- water
- tongs
- protective gloves
- ice

Advance Preparation

- Be careful of the hot can and the steam produced in the can. Wear safety goggles and protective gloves during this demonstration. Make sure the water boils long enough to fill the can with water vapor. Fill your bucket half-full with water and ice. The water must be cold for this experiment to work properly.

- Practice this demonstration before showing it to students. The noise and water splash may surprise you the first time you perform this demonstration. The plastic bucket should be about half full. The key to this activity is dunking the can in the water so that the opening of the can is sealed off as quickly as possible. Dunking the can seals the vapor in the can, which then cools rapidly, thus exerting less pressure. The pressure difference crushes the can.

- Students may ask you to repeat this demonstration, so have extra empty aluminum cans.
- After hitting the water in the bucket, the can should immediately be crushed, making a loud noise and sending water splashing out of the bucket.

Engagement Guide

- Challenge students to think about the force exerted by air by asking these questions:
  - *Air pressure is exerted on your body at this moment. Why don't you feel it?* (You do not feel the pressure because there is no difference between the air pressure exerted inside and outside your body.)
  - *How does the space between vapor particles inside the can when the water is boiling compare with the spacing between particles outside the can in the air?* (Because the vapor particles inside the can are at a higher temperature, they have more energy and motions and are spaced farther apart.)
  - *How is the pressure inside and outside the can related while the water is boiling inside the can?* (Pressures are roughly equal.)
- Encourage students to think of creative examples of air pressure and its effects.

Going Further

Ask students if the results would be the same if a heated metal container were sealed and then allowed to slowly cool. Perform this demonstration and show that the effect is the same; the rate at which the fluid inside the container cools does not affect the pressure difference that is exerted. A good way to show this is to use an Erlenmeyer flask with a small balloon attached to the top. Heat a small amount of water inside of the flask with the balloon secured to the top. Wait for the balloon to expand. Take the flask off the heat and allow cooling. In most cases, the balloon will be sucked backwards into the container. This can be shown quickly, by placing the flask in cold ice water, or slowly, by allowing it to sit out and cool.

14B A Cartesian Diver

Objectives

- investigate relationships among fluid pressure, volume, and buoyancy
- record data in a suitable way
- communicate conclusions

Skill Set

investigating, recording and analyzing data, stating conclusions

Planning

 40–45 minutes   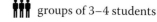 groups of 3–4 students

Materials

Materials for this activity are listed in the Student Laboratory Manual.

Advance Preparation

- You may wish to cut 10-cm pieces of copper wire before students begin this activity.
- The key to a successful diver is that it should float with about 95 percent of its volume submerged in the water. Guide students in adjusting the water in the dropper and changing the amount of wire around the dropper to obtain the proper buoyancy.
- The lab calls for glass medicine droppers. If plastic droppers are used, you will need to adjust the amount of water inside the dropper to have it operate properly.
- It is important for students to test their diver in a small cup of water before putting it in the bottle. This will cut down on a lot of frustration on the students' and teachers' parts. Make sure the cups are large enough to fit the whole diver in without it touching the bottom.

Answers to Observations: Data Table 1

Students should observe that the dropper sinks when the sides of the bottle are pushed and rises when the sides are released.

Answers to Analysis and Conclusions

1. The dropper sinks when the sides of the bottle are pushed, and it rises when the sides of the bottle are released.
2. a. The fluid pressure inside the bottle increases.
   b. The volume of air inside the dropper is compressed; the volume decreases.
   c. As the volume of the dropper decreases, its density increases and its buoyancy in water decreases.

Going Further

Leave one experimental setup in a place where students can observe it over the course of several days. Ask students to explain why this device can be used to observe air pressure.

Flying With Bernoulli

Objectives

- create a flying object
- observe the motion of the object after it is thrown
- illustrate the motion of air as it travels around the object
- communicate conclusions

Skill Set

creating, observing, illustrating, drawing conclusions

Planning

 35–40 minutes   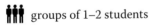 groups of 1–2 students

Materials

Materials for this activity are listed in the Student Laboratory Manual.

Advance Preparation

- Provide pieces of copier paper for this activity. Recycled paper from your classroom or school would work best and would model recycling for your students.
- You may wish to demonstrate how to build the flying cylinder before having students build their own.

Answers to Observations: Illustrations

Illustrations will vary depending on the speed of the cylinder and the throwing technique of the student. In the second illustration, students should show air moving above, below, and through the cylinder.

Answers to Analysis and Conclusions

1. Differences in thickness at different parts of the cylinder roughly model the shape of an airplane wing, helping to lift the cylinder.
2. Answers might include the force of the throw, wind speed and direction, the technique used by the thrower, and construction differences between the cylinders.
3. The hollow bones decrease the bird's weight, thus requiring less effort to fly.

Going Further

Have students perform the same experiment with other designs of flying paper objects. Students may wish to experiment with traditional paper airplane designs or make a flying object with a different design. Ask students to sketch their designs and show how Bernoulli's principle applies. Have students share the airplanes, sketches, and explanations with the class.

Chapter 15 Lessons

15.1 Work and Power

15.2 Machines

15.3 Types of Machines

Introduce Chapter 15

As a starting activity, use Lab 15A on page 85 of the Laboratory Manual.

ENGAGE Arrange students in small groups and ask them to list as many machines as they can in two minutes. (Tell them not to include electronic devices.) Then have the groups review the lists to determine how the machines are similar. Students should note that machines make work easier. If time permits, have students organize their lists by common purpose or mechanics. Explain to students that they will review their lists at the end of the chapter.

Think About Work

ENGAGE Demonstrate work, such as the examples noted or moving a book, passing out papers, or writing on the board. Sketch the action and note the direction of your force and the direction in which the object moves, thinking aloud as you do so. Have students think of three different examples and complete the bulleted tasks.

Chapter 15

Work, Power, and Simple Machines

KEY CONCEPT Work, which is done when a force moves an object some distance, can often be made easier by machines that change force, distance, or direction.

These people-movers deliver passengers to and from airplane gates. The people-movers, operating much like horizontal escalators, make it easier for people to travel from one area of the terminal to another. Gliding smoothly along the floor, they save passengers time and effort.

A people-mover is a machine. You use different types of machines every day. In fact, you have machines right inside your body. Machines make work easier to do. This chapter discusses the scientific meaning of work and the role of machines in doing work.

Think About Work

Push a door open or pull a window shut, and you are doing work. Think of three situations in which you exert a force on an object that causes it to move.

- In your Science Notebook, list the three examples you have selected.
- Draw a diagram that shows the direction of each force and the direction in which the object moves. Refer back to the diagrams once you learn the scientific definition of *work*.

NSTA

SCiLINKS.
THE WORLD'S A CLICK AWAY

www.scilinks.org
Simple Machines **Code: WGPS15**

238

Chapter 15 Planning Guide

Instructional Periods	National Standards	Lab Manual	Workbook
15.1 2 Periods	A2, B2, B3, G1, G2, G3; A1, B4, B6, G1, G2, G3; UCP3	**Lab 15A: p. 85** That's Hard Work! **Lab 15B: pp. 86–87** Inclined Planes	Key Concept Review p. 92 Vocabulary Review p. 93 Interpreting Diagrams p. 94 Reading Comprehension p. 95
15.2 2 Periods	B2, B3, E1; B4, E2; UCP1, UCP2, UCP4	**Lab 15C: pp. 88–90** Pulleys and Forces	Curriculum Connection p. 96 Science Challenge pp. 97–98
15.3 2 Periods	A1, B2, B3, E1, F6, G3; A2, B4, B5, B6, E2, F6, G3; UCP5		

Middle School Standard; High School Standard; Unifying Concept and Principle

15.1 Work and Power

Before You Read

Before you read, turn each heading in this lesson into a question in your Science Notebook. Answer your questions as you read. Use the vocabulary terms in your answers.

It has been a long night of studying for a difficult test. Hours of reading, memorizing, and thinking can be exhausting. Yet in the scientific sense, homework is not work at all! In science, **work** is done when a force moves an object in the same direction as the force is exerted. Work is done when a teacher lifts a chair, a horse pulls a wagon, and a dancer leaps into the air.

Not all forces result in work. In order for work to be done, two conditions must be met. First, a force must be exerted on an object that causes that object to move. Second, the force must be exerted in the same direction that the object moves.

Force and Motion

Imagine a group of people pushing with great force against a car that has broken down. No matter how great the force, the car just will not budge. Even though a force has been exerted on an object, no work is done because the force did not cause the object to move.

Figure 15.1 Despite the effort it takes to study, this student is not doing work in the scientific sense. Work is done when a force moves an object some distance.

Figure 15.2 A force exerted on an object does not do work if the object does not move.

CHAPTER 15 **239**

Learning Goals

- Identify the conditions required for work to be done.
- Relate power to work.
- Calculate work and power.

New Vocabulary

work
power

ELL Strategy

Make a Concept Map Have each student create a concept map to organize his or her thoughts about work. The main topic should be *Work*; subtopics should include *Force, Direction, Energy,* and *Power.* Students should describe the relationship of each topic to work. In addition to writing definitions or explanations, students can create a diagram under the concept map that demonstrates the relationship between the words. As the chapter study proceeds, they can correct or refine this diagram.

15.1 Introduce

ENGAGE Write the following phrases on the board: *study and pass the SAT exam; open a bottle of soda;* and *carry a load of bricks across a driveway.* Ask students to rate the tasks from the most work to the least work. Have students share their ratings and reasons for the ratings. Write the most popular responses on the board. Explain to students that they will learn about the scientific definition of work in this lesson and will rate the tasks again at the end of the lesson.

Vocabulary terms are listed on the first student page of each lesson. You may wish to preview the terms before introducing each lesson. Strategies for teaching the vocabulary appear on the pages where the terms are introduced.

Before You Read

Thinking aloud, talk about the first heading in the lesson. Tell students that you could change the heading into two or three different questions, such as: *What are work and power? How are work and power related? How are work and power different?* Write the questions on the board. Tell students to review the lesson and to write questions for each heading in their Science Notebooks, leaving space between questions for answers.

Teach

EXPLAIN to students that every type of work requires an input force to be exerted over a distance.

 Vocabulary

work Ask students to brainstorm common uses of the word *work*. Their responses might include a place where one is employed; a literary, musical, or artistic composition; tasks to be done; or physical or mental effort to achieve or make something. Have students relate the common meanings to the scientific definition.

Teach

EXPLAIN to students that work is done only when the object moves in the same direction as the force is applied.

Figure It Out: **Figure 15.3**

ANSWER **1.** A force must be exerted on the basket, and the basket must move in the same direction as the force. **2.** The motion is not in the same direction in which the force is exerted.

As You Read

Give students about five minutes to answer the questions in their Science Notebooks. Review students' answers for accuracy and understanding.

ANSWER Examples will vary. Possible answers include exerting a force to lift a heavy suitcase, pushing a large bookcase, or pulling on a refrigerator without causing it to move.

Force and Direction

One student lifts a book from the floor to a shelf one meter above the ground. A second student lifts the same book to the same height and then carries it to a shelf across the room. Which student does more work on the book? The answer might surprise you, because the answer is neither student. Both students do the same amount of work on the book.

Figure It Out

1. Identify the two conditions that are met when work is done on the laundry basket.
2. Why isn't any work done on the basket when it is carried across the room?

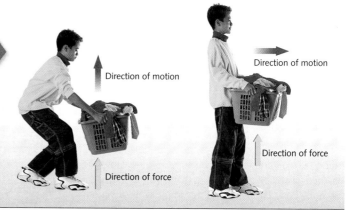

Figure 15.3 Work is done on the laundry basket when the basket is lifted, but not when the basket is carried across the room.

As You Read

Review the questions you have written in your Science Notebook. Answer any questions that you can.

Give an example of a situation in which you exerted a force but did not do work.

Work is done only when a force causes an object to move in the same direction as the force is applied. Therefore, work is done when an upward force is exerted to lift the laundry basket. If the force is exerted in a direction that is different from the direction in which the object moves, no work is done. This means that no additional work is done when the basket is carried across the room. The force on the basket is upward, whereas the direction of motion is horizontal.

Sometimes, only part of a force causes an object to move. Think about someone pushing a lawn mower, as shown in **Figure 15.4.** The person exerts a force at an angle to the ground. Part of the force is forward, and part of the force is downward. Only the part of the force that is in the same direction as the motion of the mower—forward—does work.

Total force
Forward force
Downward force

Figure 15.4 When a force is exerted at an angle, only part of the force does work—the part that is in the same direction as the motion of the object.

Differentiate Instruction

Interpersonal Have students interview someone in a profession involved with work, power, and force. Possibilities include an employee from a moving or delivery company, a personal trainer, a weightlifter, and a strength and conditioning coach. Students should prepare questions in advance, interview the person, and then share the results in small groups. English language learners can work in pairs to create their questions, conduct interviews, and write summaries of their interviews before sharing the results in small groups.

Calculating Work

Work is done when a force moves an object some distance. The amount of work done is equal to the force that makes the object move times the distance the object moves, as shown by the following equation:

$$\text{work} = \text{force} \times \text{distance} \qquad W = Fd$$

When force is measured in newtons and distance is measured in meters, the SI unit of work becomes the newton·meter (N·m). The newton·meter is named a joule (J) in honor of James Prescott Joule.

The work done can be determined if the force and the distance are known. For example, suppose a weightlifter lifts a dumbbell weighing 70 N a distance of 1 m. How much work does he do? The force required to lift an object near Earth's surface is equal and opposite to the weight of the object. The weightlifter must exert an upward force of 70 N to lift the dumbbell. The force moves the dumbbell a distance of 1 m.

$$W = 70\ N \times 1\ m = 70\ N{\cdot}m = 70\ J$$

The equation shows that the amount of work done increases if the force exerted on an object or the distance the object moves is increased. **Figure 15. 5** shows how the amount of work the weightlifter does depends on the force he exerts and the distance over which he exerts it.

$W = 70\ N \times 1\ m = 70\ J$ $\qquad$ $W = 70\ N \times 2\ m = 140\ J$ $\qquad$ $W = 140\ N \times 2\ m = 280\ J$

Figure 15.5 Increasing the force or the distance increases the amount of work done.

Work and Energy

Energy is the ability to do work. When work is done on an object, energy is transferred to the object. When a force causes the velocity of an object to increase, its kinetic energy increases. An object has gravitational potential energy because of its position above the ground. This type of energy increases when work is done to lift an object.

CONNECTION: History

James Prescott Joule (1818–1889) was a physicist who experimentally verified the law of conservation of energy. He went on to show that one form of energy can be converted into another.

Explore It!

Hook a spring scale to a 1-kg mass. Use the spring scale to slowly raise the mass 1 m. Read the spring scale and calculate the amount of work you have done.

● Teach

EXPLAIN to students that work can be quantified and calculated by multiplying the amount of force used by the distance the object moves.

CONNECTION: History

Demonstrate the actions of a Newton's cradle or another similar apparatus. Have students work with partners to sketch the parts and movements of the apparatus and write a brief paragraph about how the actions support the theory of the conservation of energy.

Explore It!

Provide pairs of students with a spring scale, metersticks, and a one-kilogram mass. (Alternatively, make a mark on the wall at one meter at various places around the room for students to use.) Show students how to slowly raise the spring scale so that it is not accelerating. Remind students that work is the product of multiplying force and distance. As follow-up, English language learners should write a description of the process they followed, explaining the results of their Explore It! activity. Their description should make use of the lesson's vocabulary words.

ANSWER The amount of work should be 1 J.

Background Information

The law of conservation of energy states that energy is neither created nor destroyed when it changes from one form to another. James Joule conducted experiments demonstrating that energy seemingly lost is actually converted into heat. This work supported the theories of Hermann von Helmholtz, Julius Robert van Mayer, and Lord Kelvin. Joule went on to discover a mathematical relationship between the energy of an electric current and the amount of heat produced by that current. Subsequently, he noticed a similar relationship between mechanical energy and heat.

Differentiate Instruction

Kinesthetic, Mathematical Have students use different masses (1.5 kg, 2 kg) and distances (.5 m and 1.5 m) to calculate the work done to move an object.

Teach

Demonstrate driving a screw into a board using a screwdriver and then using a drill or battery-powered screwdriver, and ask students to identify which example used more power. Have students explain their responses. Explain that power increases as the amount of time to complete work decreases.

Pair students, and have them share examples of work being done with more power and with less power. Then have pairs share their examples with the class. Write a list of their comparisons on the board.

Vocabulary

power Have students list common uses of the word *power*. Responses might include control over others, strength or force, or the physical skill or authority to do something. Ask students how the common meanings help them remember the scientific definition.

Use the Visual: Figure 15.6

ANSWER Power measures the rate at which work is done.

 Explore It!

Pair students and provide each pair with a stopwatch and a meterstick or measuring tape.

Some students might need help calculating their weight in newtons; demonstrate the calculation using 50 pounds (50 lbs × 4.5 = 225 newtons).

ANSWER The work was the same walking and running because it is independent of speed. More power is used when running than walking, because the same amount of work is done in less time.

 Explore It!

1. Find a set of stairs that you can safely walk and run up. Measure the vertical height of the set of stairs in meters.

2. Record how many seconds it takes you to first walk up the stairs and then run up the stairs.

3. Calculate the work you did in walking and running up the stairs. (For force, multiply your weight in pounds by 4.5 to find your weight in newtons.)

4. Calculate the power you needed to walk and run up the stairs.

How does the work you did in each situation compare? How does the power needed in each situation compare?

Power

A rock climber takes a relatively long period of time to lift herself just a few meters up a steep cliff. She can rise the same distance in a much shorter period of time if she hikes on a mountain trail. In both situations she can do the same amount of work, yet she can do it in different amounts of time. The quantity that measures the rate at which work is done is called **power.**

Figure 15.6 The same amount of work can be done at different rates. What quantity measures the rate at which work is done?

Calculating Power Power is the work done divided by the time during which it is done. It can be calculated using the following equation:

$$\text{power} = \frac{\text{work}}{\text{time}} \qquad p = \frac{W}{t}$$

When work is measured in joules and time in seconds, the unit of power is the joule per second. This unit is named the watt (W) in honor of James Watt, the inventor of the steam engine. Power can be calculated if the work and time are known. For example, what is the power when a person does 140 J of work in 20 s?

$$p = \frac{140 \text{ J}}{20 \text{ s}} = 7 \text{ W}$$

How does the power change if the time is decreased to 10 s? It would double to 14 W (p = 140 J/10 s = 14 W). Thus, power increases as work is done faster.

Figure 15.7 A common unit of power used to describe car engines is horsepower. This unit was named by James Watt, who needed a way to describe the power of his steam engines. He calculated the average power of a horse. One horsepower is equivalent to 746 watts.

Background Information

The watt measures both electrical and mechanical power. A machine requires a power of 1 watt if it uses 1 joule of energy in 1 second. Current engineers suggest that a more reasonable estimation of horsepower, for a horse working an eight-hour day, is about 500 watts. Lance Armstrong, a Tour de France winner, could maintain about 0.25 horsepower when riding a bike.

Power and Velocity Look again at the equation for power. Recall that work equals force multiplied by distance. Another way to write the power equation is:

$$\text{power} = \frac{\text{work}}{\text{time}}$$
$$= \frac{(\text{force} \times \text{distance})}{\text{time}}$$
$$= \text{force} \times \frac{\text{distance}}{\text{time}}$$
$$= \text{force} \times \text{velocity}$$

Distance divided by time equals velocity. When the equation is written in this form, it becomes easier to see that a powerful machine or person is both strong (as a result of force) and fast (as a result of velocity).

Power and Energy Another way to consider power is in terms of energy. Recall that work is the transfer of energy. Therefore, power is the rate at which energy is transferred. When energy is transferred, the power involved can be calculated by dividing the energy transferred by the time during which the transfer occurs.

$$\text{power} = \frac{\text{energy transferred}}{\text{time}}$$

For example, when the lightbulb in **Figure 15.9** is lit, energy is transferred from the electric circuit to the filament in the bulb. The power of the lightbulb is the amount of electric energy transferred to the lightbulb each second.

Figure 15.8 These football players are powerful because they exert a strong force at a high velocity.

Figure 15.9 This 100-watt lightbulb converts 100 joules of electric energy into light and heat each second.

After You Read

1. Why doesn't a waiter do work on a tray when he exerts an upward force on it as he carries it across a dining room?
2. Explain how power is related to work.
3. A person exerts a force of 75 N to move a couch 5 m. If all of the force results in the motion of the couch, how much work does the person do?
4. A motor does 10,000 J of work in 20 s. What is the power of the motor?
5. In your Science Notebook, write and answer a question that relates work, power, and energy.

Teach

EXPLAIN to students that velocity and power are directly related; as velocity increases, so does power.

Science Notebook EXTRA

Have students review the Engage activity on page 239 and rate the tasks from most work to least work again based on what they have learned. Have them write their ratings and reasons in their Science Notebooks. Discuss how their rating of work has changed because of their new understanding of the scientific definition of work. Challenge students to provide additional examples, and rate these together as a class.

Assess

Use the After You Read questions and the Alternative Assessment to help you evaluate students' understanding of the lesson.

After You Read

1. For work to be done, the force must be exerted in the same direction as the object's direction of motion.
2. Power is the rate at which work is done.
3. $W = 75 \text{ N} \times 5 \text{ m} = 375 \text{ J}$
4. $P = 10,000 \text{ J}/20 \text{ s} = 500 \text{ W}$
5. Questions will vary. Sample question: *How are work and power related to energy?* (Work is the transfer of energy, and power is the rate at which energy is transferred.)

Alternative Assessment

Students should use the questions in their Science Notebooks to describe how work is done, using the terms *force* and *distance* in their descriptions.

Background Information

The efficiency of a machine is measured by how much energy is transferred from the source to the machine, and then by how much is transferred to do the job. Some energy is lost during the transfer as heat; thus, machines are not 100 percent efficient. The human body is only about 25 percent efficient for doing mechanical jobs. That means that 75 percent of the energy stored in muscles is converted into heat.

15.2 Introduce

ENGAGE Write the following words on the board: *screwdriver, wheelbarrow, scissors, sewing machine, car,* and *saw.* Ask students to think about the list and to identify what the words have in common. If students need support, have photos of the objects and suggest that students think about what the items do. Talk with the class about the common characteristics of the items and emphasize that they are all machines. Have students work in pairs to brainstorm a list of machines they use or know. If time permits, have students organize their lists of machines by how the machines make work easier.

Before You Read

Write *machine* on the board, and then write the phrase *a device that makes doing work easier.* Have students work with a partner to use *machine* in a sentence that includes the meaning of the word. Have pairs share their sentences. Then highlight the best sentences on the board, identifying the meaning included in each sentence. Have students write the vocabulary terms in their Science Notebooks, leaving space after the words for their sentences.

● Teach

EXPLAIN Point out to students that a machine is not necessarily a large or complicated device. It does not have to be electronic or modern. Explain that a machine is a device that does work when work is done on it.

Use the Visual: Figure 15.11

ANSWER A machine is any device that makes it easier to do work.

Learning Goals

- Identify ways in which machines make work easier.
- Define and calculate mechanical advantage.
- Compare the efficiency of ideal and real machines.

New Vocabulary

machine
input work
output work
input force
output force
mechanical advantage
efficiency

Figure 15.11 A device does not have to be complicated to be a machine. How is a machine defined in science?

15.2 Machines

Before You Read

Write the vocabulary terms for this lesson in your Science Notebook. As you read the lesson, use each term in a sentence of your own. Make sure that your sentences show the meaning of each term.

The word *machine* often brings to mind images of complex devices with intricate parts. While some machines fit this description, others are very simple. A **machine** is any device that makes doing work easier.

For any type of machine, work is done on the machine and by the machine. The work that is done on the machine is the **input work.** The work that the machine does is the **output work.**

Work is a force exerted over some distance. Therefore, two forces are involved when a machine is used. The force exerted on a machine is called the **input force.** The input work is equal to the input force times the distance over which the input force is exerted. The force exerted by the machine is called the **output force.** The output work is equal to the output force times the distance over which the output force is exerted.

Input work
(input force × distance)

Machine

Output work
(output force × distance)

Figure 15.10 Input work is done on a machine and output work is done by a machine.

Making Work Easier

Work is the transfer of energy. Recall that energy is neither created nor destroyed—it is conserved. Therefore, the output work cannot be greater than the input work for any machine. If a machine does not multiply work, how is it useful? A machine makes work easier by multiplying force or distance or changing the input force's direction.

Multiplying Force Trying to insert a screw into a piece of wood using fingers alone can be impossible. A screwdriver, however, can make the task simple. A screwdriver makes work easier by decreasing the amount of force that must be exerted. Because work is the product of force and distance, the distance over which the force is exerted must increase in order for the amount of work to stay the same. The handle of a screwdriver is turned over a longer distance than the screw is turned.

244 WORK, POWER, AND SIMPLE MACHINES

ELL Strategy

Model Throughout the lesson, have students sketch diagrams of the machines mentioned and label the following parts of each: where the input work is done, where the output work is done, input force, and output force. Have students post the diagrams around the room and note how the machines are similar and different.

In a similar way, imagine trying to lift the back of a car to change a tire. Doing this work would be extremely difficult. To make this work easier, a person might use a car jack similar to the one shown in **Figure 15.12.** The person pushes down on the jack, which lifts the car up. The output force of the jack is much greater than the input force of the person. However, the distance the person pushes down on the handle is longer than the distance the jack lifts the car. Therefore, the car jack increases the force applied to it, but not the amount of work done.

Multiplying Distance Some machines make work easier by decreasing the distance over which the input force must be exerted. A pile of sand can be placed in a wheelbarrow so that it is easier to lift. The input force is greater than the output force. However, it can be exerted over a shorter distance by using the wheelbarrow.

In a similar way, the handle of a rake can be moved a short distance across a pile of leaves. The other end of the rake then moves over a greater distance. For work to remain the same, the input force must be greater than the output force.

Changing Direction A worker needs to lift a water pail to the top of a well. She can try pushing or pulling the pail upward. However, it would be easier to pull downward. That way she can use her weight as part of the input force. The pulley in **Figure 15.14** enables the worker to lift the pail by pulling downward. She must exert the same amount of force over the same distance. A pulley is a machine that makes work easier by changing the direction of the input force.

Some machines can both multiply force and change direction. Look back at the car jack in Figure 15.12. It not only multiplied force, it changed the direction of the input force, as well.

Figure 15.14 It is easier to pull downward to raise the pail upward. A machine that changes the direction of the input force makes this work easier.

Figure 15.12 Some machines, like car jacks, increase the force exerted on them.

Figure 15.13 Machines such as wheelbarrows and rakes exert the output force over a longer distance than the input force.

As You Read

Review the sentences you have recorded in your Science Notebook.

What is the relationship among the following terms: *machine, input work, output work, input force,* and *output force*?

CHAPTER 15 **245**

Teach

Review with students the three factors of work that machines can change: force, distance, or direction.

Figure It Out: **Figure 15.15**

ANSWER **1.** They can multiply distance or they can change the direction of the force. **2.** Examples will vary. A crowbar used to pry open a lid multiplies force and changes direction.

Use the Visual: **Figure 15.15**

Have students work in pairs to analyze each machine in the figure and determine which factor (force, distance, or direction) the machine is changing.

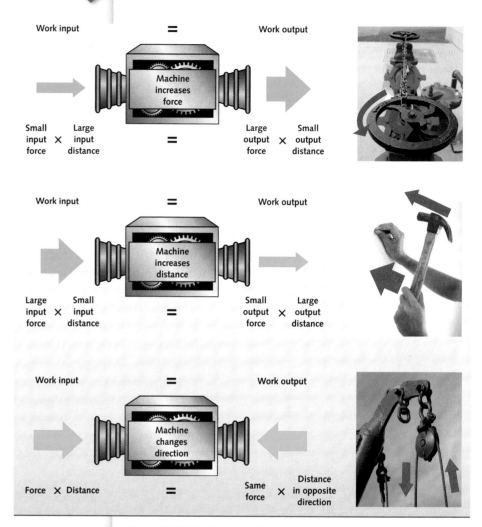

Figure 15.15 Machines do not change the amount of work that needs to be done. Instead, they change force, distance, or direction.

ELL Strategy

Act Out Arrange students in small groups. Assign each group a different type of machine, such as a sewing machine, rake, bicycle, skateboard, or mixer, and have the students act out the machines. The other groups should watch each presentation and identify the machine, the machine's input and output forces, and how it makes work easier.

Mechanical Advantage

The number of times a machine increases the input force is the **mechanical advantage** (MA) of the machine. The mechanical advantage of a machine is the ratio of the output force to the input force. It can be calculated using the following equation:

$$\text{mechanical advantage} = \frac{\text{output force}}{\text{input force}} \qquad MA = \frac{F_{out}}{F_{in}}$$

Both the input force and the output force are measured in newtons. As a result, the units cancel out. Mechanical advantage does not have any units associated with it.

Multiplying Force   For a machine that multiplies force, the output force is greater than the input force. The mechanical advantage of this type of machine is greater than 1. Suppose a person applies a force of 50 N to a nutcracker. The nutcracker then applies a force of 750 N to crack a walnut. What is the mechanical advantage of the nutcracker?

The input force of the person is 50 N. The output force of the nutcracker is 750 N.

$$\text{mechanical advantage} = \frac{750\ N}{50\ N} = 15$$

Multiplying Distance   For a machine that multiplies distance, the output force is less than the input force. The mechanical advantage of this type of machine is less than 1. Consider a machine for which the input force is 60 N and the output force is 30 N. What is the mechanical advantage of this machine?

$$\text{mechanical advantage} = \frac{30\ N}{60\ N} = 0.5$$

Changing Direction   If a machine changes only the direction of the input force, then the input force is equal to the output force. Dividing a number by itself equals 1. So the mechanical advantage of a machine that changes only the direction of the force is 1.

 Explain It!

A friend argues that a machine cannot be useful if it does not decrease the amount of work you must do. Write an explanation for your friend identifying the error in his or her logic.

Figure 15.16 The mechanical advantage of a machine that multiplies force, such as this nutcracker, is greater than 1. The mechanical advantage of a machine that multiplies distance, such as this fishing pole, is less than 1. What is the mechanical advantage of a machine that changes neither force nor distance, but reverses the direction of the input force?

EXPLAIN to students that the ratio of the input force to the output force of a machine can be calculated mathematically. Mechanical advantage can be greater than one, less than one, or equal to one.

 **Vocabulary**

mechanical advantage   Ask students to list common uses of the word *advantage*. Responses might include a benefit, a point scored in tennis, or a favorable position. Tell students that the word *mechanical* is derived from the Greek word meaning "work." Ask students to relate these common meanings to the term's scientific definition.

Explain It!

Encourage each student to create a graphic organizer with information about work and about machines. Students should then add details about the two topics that are directly relevant to the explanations they are composing. Have students write their explanations in the form of a letter to the friend, complete with introductory and concluding statements. English language learners should work in pairs to evaluate the argument and create an explanation. They should be encouraged to illustrate their response to their friend, using the vocabulary terms. They should refer to the diagrams they completed earlier to build a strong explanation.

Use the Visual: Figure 15.16
ANSWER   The mechanical advantage is 1.

Differentiate Instruction

Mathematical   Have students create story problems involving multiplying force and multiplying distance for other students to solve. Students must provide the mathematical solution and an explanation with each problem. Students should then trade and solve the problems. English language learners can work in pairs to write their story problems. After trading problems, groups should be encouraged to explain how they arrived at their answers.

Teach

 EXPLAIN to students that the output work of a real machine is always less than the input work. This difference is usually the result of friction and determines the machine's efficiency.

 Vocabulary

efficiency Explain to students that the root *efficient* is derived from Latin and means "to accomplish." The prefix *-y* refers to having a quality or characteristic. Have students relate the derivation to the scientific definition of the term.

CONNECTION: Math

Write the following math problems on the board: 2 × 1; 2 × 10; 2 × 100; 2 × 1,000; and 2 × 10,000. Have students calculate the answers and then look for the pattern. If students need further assistance, have them calculate the answers using 0.2 and 0.02. Highlight the results of multiplying by various powers of ten.

Use the Visual: Figure 15.17

ANSWER Decreasing friction increases the efficiency of a machine.

Assess

Use the After You Read questions and the Alternative Assessment to help you evaluate students' understanding of the lesson.

After You Read

1. Work is the transfer of energy. Energy is neither created nor destroyed. Therefore, the amount of work cannot change. Instead, force, distance, or direction can change to make work easier.
2. It might change the direction of the input force.
3. An ideal machine is 100 percent efficient because there is no friction. An ideal machine does not exist. The efficiency of a real machine must always be less than 100 percent due to friction.

 **CONNECTION: Math**

To multiply a number by 100%, move the decimal point two places to the right. A decimal such as 0.45, for example, becomes 45%.

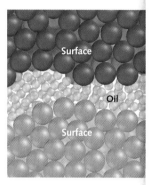

Figure 15.17 Lubricants decrease the friction between two surfaces. How does this affect the efficiency of the machine to which they belong?

Efficiency

In an ideal situation, the input work of a machine is equal to the output work. For real machines, however, this is not exactly true. Some of the work done is to overcome friction. Recall that friction is the force that opposes the motion of an object.

Due to friction, the output work of a machine is always less than the input work. A measure of how much of the input work is changed into useful output work by a machine is called **efficiency** (ih FIH shun see).

Calculating Efficiency Efficiency is equal to the output work divided by the input work. It can be calculated using the following equation:

$$\text{efficiency} = \frac{\text{output work}}{\text{input work}} \times 100\%$$

Efficiency is expressed as a percentage that describes what portion of the work input is converted into work output. As an example, consider the efficiency of a machine that does 720 J of work if the input work is 2,400 J.

$$\text{efficiency} = \frac{720\text{ J}}{2,400\text{ J}} \times 100\% = 30\%$$

Increasing Efficiency No machine has an efficiency of 100 percent. A machine with such an efficiency is known as an ideal machine because it does not exist. The efficiency of a real machine is always less than 100 percent. The mechanical advantage that is calculated using the equation *output force/input force* is for an ideal machine. For this reason, the calculated mechanical advantage is also known as the ideal mechanical advantage (IMA). The actual mechanical advantage of a real machine must be measured.

Machines can be made more efficient by reducing friction. Lubricants such as oil and grease can be added to surfaces that rub together. **Figure 15.17** shows how the lubricant fills the gaps between the surfaces, enabling them to move past each other more easily.

After You Read

1. Explain why machines can't decrease the amount of work required to complete a task.
2. Why might a machine be useful if its mechanical advantage is 1?
3. Refer to the sentences in your Science Notebook to explain how the efficiency of a real machine compares to that of an ideal machine.

Alternative Assessment

Students should use the following vocabulary terms to describe how digging a hole is easier with the use of a shovel: *machine, input work, output work, input force,* and *output force.* Students should also explain whether the shovel changes force, distance, or direction. Have students write their responses as several sentences in their Science Notebooks.

Background Information

In 2005, the U.S. Department of Energy set a goal of improving automobile engine efficiency for passenger vehicles from 30 percent (the 2004 baseline) to 45 percent by 2012. The goal for commercial vehicles was an increase from the 2002 baseline of 40 percent to 55 percent by 2013. These increases in efficiency would reduce engine fuel consumption by 10 to 15 percent.

15.3 Types of Machines

Before You Read

Create a four-column chart in your Science Notebook. Label the first column *Type of Simple Machine*, the second column *Diagram*, the third column *Example*, and the fourth column *Advantage*. After previewing the lesson, fill in any information you already know. As you read the lesson, complete the chart.

Machines are not recent inventions. During the time of Leonardo da Vinci (1452–1519), water wheels were used to grind grain, and Archimedes' screw lifted water from streams for drinking and washing.

The basic machines used hundreds of years ago are still used today. The most basic machines are called simple machines. A **simple machine** is a machine that does work with only one movement of the machine. There are six basic types of simple machines.

Inclined Plane

Lombard Street in San Francisco, California, is known for being very crooked. The street zigzags up a long hill. Walking or driving straight up the steep incline would be much more difficult than traveling along the winding, sloped path. A gentler slope reduces the amount of force that is needed to move an object. The simple machine that takes advantage of this principle is the inclined plane. An **inclined plane** is a flat surface set at an angle to a horizontal surface.

Advantage of an Inclined Plane   A ramp is an example of an inclined plane. The ramp in **Figure 15.18** shows that the same amount of work is done to lift a box as to push it up an inclined plane.

To lift the box, the amount of work done is equal to the force of 1,500 N times the distance of 1 m, or $W = 1,500 \text{ N} \times 1 \text{ m} = 1,500 \text{ J}$. To push the box along the ramp, the amount of work done is equal to the force of 300 N times the distance of 5 m, or $W = 300 \text{ N} \times 5 \text{ m} = 1,500 \text{ J}$. The same amount of work is done to lift the box as to push it up the ramp.

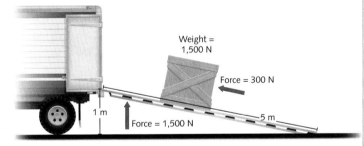

Weight = 1,500 N

 Force = 300 N

1 m

5 m

Force = 1,500 N

Figure 15.18 Using an inclined plane to move a box into a truck does not change the amount of work required. What is the advantage of using an inclined plane?

ELL Strategy

Prepare Presentations Arrange students into six small groups. Each group should choose one of the six simple machines to research. Have each group present a lesson about its simple machine, including three examples of uses, a model of the machine, a brief history of its invention, and a poster describing its mechanical advantage.

15.3 Introduce

ENGAGE Create a Rube Goldberg-type of invention for the class to observe or provide images of such a machine. Have students work with partners to identify and list all the steps involved in the machine. Then ask students to identify any real machines that require a chain reaction of other machines to complete a task. Explain that many of the single steps use simple machines; a machine that involves a combination of machines is known as a compound machine.

Before You Read

Draw the four-column chart on the board. Review the page aloud, and then write *Inclined Plane* in the first column. Sketch an inclined plane in the second column, and then write *sidewalk cuts* and *wheelchair ramps* in the third column. Talk aloud about the advantages. Have students create their own charts in their Science Notebooks and list the types of simple machines after previewing the lesson.

Teach

EXPLAIN to students that in this lesson, they will learn about the six types of simple machines, which work with only one movement of the machine. Simple machines may be combined to create a complex machine.

Vocabulary

simple machine Ask students to list common uses of the word *simple*. Examples might include being easy to do, having few parts, or having little importance. Review with students the meaning of the word *machine*. Ask them to give the literal definition of *simple machine* and then compare it to the scientific definition.

inclined plane Explain to students that *inclined* is derived from Latin and means "to bend toward." *Plane* also comes from Latin and means "a level surface." Ask students to relate these derivations to the scientific definition of the term.

Use the Visual: Figure 15.18

(ANSWER) It allows the mover to do the same amount of work with a smaller force.

● Teach

Pass large screws around to students and ask them to observe the structure. Have students share their observations aloud, and write several of their ideas on the board. Explain that a screw is an inclined plane wrapped around a core.

 Vocabulary

screw Explain to students that the word *screw* is derived from the Latin word for sow (female hog) because the shape of a pig's tail resembles the thread of a screw.

wedge Explain to students that the word *wedge* describes a shape, often for a piece of cheese or pie. The simple machine has the same shape.

 Extend It!

Provide students with resources such as encyclopedias, science reference books, internet access, and biographies about Leonardo da Vinci. Encourage students to skim three different resources to obtain varied information, and tell them to keep bibliographical details. Each student should take notes during this preview and then create an outline from which he or she will write the report.

 **Extend It!**

Leonardo da Vinci could be described as a scientist, mathematician, engineer, inventor, painter, sculptor, architect, musician, and writer. Conduct research to learn about the life and work of da Vinci. Prepare a brief report describing your findings. Then identify an aspect of his life that you consider particularly interesting.

The advantage of the inclined plane is that it enables the mover to use a smaller force. The trade-off is that the force must be exerted over a longer distance.

IMA of an Inclined Plane   The IMA of an inclined plane depends on the height to which the object is being lifted (the height of the slope) and the length of the inclined plane. It can be calculated from the following equation:

$$\text{IMA (inclined plane)} = \frac{\text{length of inclined plane}}{\text{height of slope}}$$

According to the equation, the IMA for a given height increases as the inclined plane becomes longer. The IMA for the inclined plane in Figure 15.18 on page 249 is shown below.

$$\text{IMA (inclined plane)} = \frac{5 \text{ m}}{1 \text{ m}} = 5$$

The mechanical advantage of the ramp is 5. Using the ramp, the mover can exert a force that is five times less than would be needed to lift the box without the ramp.

Figure 15.19 The shorter inclined plane has a mechanical advantage of 2, whereas the longer inclined plane has a mechanical advantage of 3. Notice how the mechanical advantage increases as the inclined plane becomes longer and the slope decreases.

Screw

Some simple machines are modified versions of other simple machines. A **screw** is an inclined plane wrapped in a spiral around a central cylinder. Look closely at the screws in **Figure 15.20.** The spirals, or threads, of the screws form small ramps that run upward from the tips. Unlike a ramp over which a person might push a box, the inclined plane of a screw moves through an object or material. Screws are found in many common devices, such as jar lids, lightbulbs, and bolts.

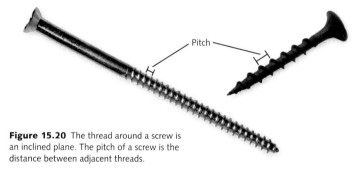

Figure 15.20 The thread around a screw is an inclined plane. The pitch of a screw is the distance between adjacent threads.

Background Information

The Archimedes' screw is a machine that has been used throughout history to raise water from a low-lying body of water to a higher irrigation ditch. This machine consists of a large screw, usually inside a hollow pipe. When the screw is turned, the bottom end scoops up water. This water is then transferred up the tube until it finally pours out the top. Versions of the Archimedes' screw continue to be used in sewage treatment plants, snowblowers, and grain elevators.

Advantage of a Screw When a person twists a screw into an object, such as a piece of wood, an input force is exerted on the screw. Like an inclined plane, the threads of the screw increase the distance over which the force is exerted. The threads, then, exert a greater output force on the wood. This force pulls the screw into the wood.

IMA of a Screw The IMA of a screw depends on the spacing of the threads. The distance between two adjacent threads of a screw is called the pitch of the screw. Each time the screw is turned one full turn, it moves a distance equal to the pitch. The IMA of a screw is the distance around the screw, or its circumference, divided by its pitch. Therefore, a screw in which the threads are closer together has a greater IMA than a screw in which the threads are farther apart.

Wedge

Like the screw, a wedge is a simple machine in which an inclined plane moves through an object or material. A **wedge** is an inclined plane with one or two sloping sides. It is thick at one end and tapers to a thin edge. Wedges are generally used for separating objects or holding them in place. Knives, axes, and shovels are common examples of wedges.

Advantage of a Wedge Like an inclined plane, a wedge makes work easier by decreasing the input force that is required. In turn, the input force must be exerted over a longer distance. A wedge also changes the direction of the input force. Look at the carving tool in **Figure 15.21.** As the tool is moved through the wood, the downward input force is changed into a horizontal force that pushes the wood apart.

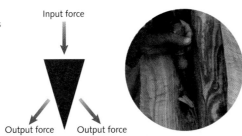

Figure 15.21 A knife is a wedge that changes both the force and its direction.

Input force

Output force   Output force

IMA of a Wedge The IMA of a wedge can be calculated by dividing the length of its slope by its thickness at the big end. Suppose, for example, a wedge has a slope that is 10 cm long and a thickness of 5 cm. The IMA of the wedge is 10 cm ÷ 5 cm, which is 2.

For a given thickness, the IMA increases as a wedge becomes longer and thinner. This is why a sharp knife cuts more easily than a dull knife.

As You Read

Some simple machines are closely related. Use the notes and diagrams in your Science Notebook to write a well-developed paragraph explaining how screws and wedges are related to inclined planes.

● Teach

EXPLAIN to students that the third type of simple machine presented in this lesson is a wedge: a triangular-shaped machine used to separate or secure objects.

As You Read

Give students five to ten minutes to add information to the charts in their Science Notebooks. Then have students use concept maps to organize their ideas about screws, wedges, and inclined planes.

ANSWER Screws and wedges are modified inclined planes. A screw is an inclined plane wrapped around a cylinder. A wedge is an inclined plane that moves through a material. The IMA of all three machines increases as the length of the inclined plane increases.

Differentiate Instruction

Kinesthetic, Mathematical Have available a wide variety of each of the six simple machines, including those that students might have used for the ELL Strategy on page 249. Encourage students to explore the machines and their different uses. Then have students calculate the IMA for each of the machines.

Teach

EXPLAIN to students that the fourth type of simple machine presented, the lever, can be divided into three classes.

 Vocabulary

lever Tell students that the derivation of the word *lever* is the Latin word *levare,* meaning "to raise." Ask students to relate this derivation to the scientific meaning.

 Explore It!

The edge of the table is the fulcrum. The book is the load. It is easier to move an object, such as the book, when the fulcrum is closer to the load.

Figure It Out: **Figure 15.22**

ANSWER **1.** If the mechanical advantage is greater than 1, it multiplies force. If the mechanical advantage is less than 1, it multiplies distance. If the mechanical advantage is equal to 1, it changes the direction of the input force. **2.** It decreases the mechanical advantage.

Explore It!

1. Place a ruler on your desk so that part of it hangs over the edge. Place a book on the other end of the ruler.

2. Try to lift the book by pressing down on the part of the ruler sticking out.

3. Repeat step 2, moving the book to the edge of the desk by pulling on the ruler.

You used the ruler as a lever. What was the fulcrum? The load? How did the position of the load relative to the fulcrum affect the IMA?

Figure It Out

1. What does the IMA of a first-class lever indicate about how the lever makes work easier?

2. How does moving the fulcrum closer to the input force affect the IMA?

Lever

A **lever** is a rigid bar that is free to rotate about a fixed point to lift something, known as the load. The fixed point the lever rotates about is called the fulcrum. The part of the lever between the input force and the fulcrum is known as the input arm. The part between the fulcrum and the output force is the output arm of the lever.

The mechanical advantage of a lever depends on the lengths of the input and output arms. The longer the input arm is relative to the output arm, the greater the IMA of the lever. The IMA can be calculated using the following equation:

$$\text{IMA (lever)} = \frac{\text{length of input arm}}{\text{length of output arm}}$$

There are three classes of levers. The differences among them depend on the positions of the input force, output force, and fulcrum.

First-Class Lever A crowbar, a see-saw, and a boat oar are examples of first-class levers. In a first-class lever, the fulcrum is located between the input and output forces. The fulcrum's position determines how easy it is to lift the load. When the fulcrum is closer to the load than to the input force, the mechanical advantage is greater than 1. The input force is multiplied because it is exerted over a longer distance. Thus, when a crowbar is used to pry open a can, the input force is multiplied.

When the fulcrum is in the center of the lever, the mechanical advantage is 1. Neither force nor distance is multiplied, but the input force's direction is changed. A see-saw is an example of this type of lever.

In some first-class levers, the fulcrum is closer to the input force than to the load. When this happens, the mechanical advantage is less than 1. Although the input force is not multiplied, a gain in distance is produced. A boat oar takes advantage of this principle.

  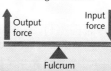

Mechanical advantage > 1   Mechanical advantage = 1   Mechanical advantage < 1
Multiplies force   Changes direction   Multiplies distance

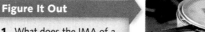
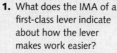
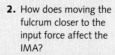

Figure 15.22 The mechanical advantage of a first-class lever depends on the position of the fulcrum.

Background Information

While kayaking, thirteen-year-old Mary Lou Hedberg noticed that her paddle produced swirls in the water. This made her wonder if the swirls resulted from lost energy, and if so, how the paddle's efficiency could be improved. She experimented in a self-made flume with different paddles made from plastic spoons that she reshaped. After making over 300 measurements, Hedberg concluded that a spoon-shaped blade with a bent shaft delivered the most force. She consequently filed a provisional patent application for the improved kayak paddle shape.

Second-Class Lever A wheelbarrow and a bottle opener are examples of second-class levers. In this type of lever, the output force is located between the input force and the fulcrum. The mechanical advantage of a second-class lever is always greater than 1. This means that this type of lever multiplies force. As in a first-class lever, the closer the output force is to the fulcrum, the greater the mechanical advantage of the lever. Unlike a first-class lever, however, the input force and the output force in a second-class lever move in the same direction.

Figure 15.23 In a second-class lever, the output force is between the input force and the fulcrum. This type of lever always multiplies the input force, but does not change its direction. Bottle openers and wheelbarrows are second-class levers.

Third-Class Lever A fishing rod and a baseball bat are examples of third-class levers. A third-class lever's fulcrum is at the end of the lever. The input force is exerted between the fulcrum and the output force.

The mechanical advantage of a third-class lever is less than 1. The input force is always greater than the output force. In addition, a third-class lever does not change the direction of the input force. It makes work easier by increasing the distance over which the force is applied.

CONNECTION: Biology

Levers are not only used to lift dirt or catch fish. People use levers to perform many basic, everyday functions. The human body itself is composed of numerous levers.

Muscles in the body are attached to bones by tendons. When muscles contract, or tighten, they pull on bones. In doing so, they make bones act like levers. The point where two bones connect is known as a joint. Most of the joints of the human body act as fulcrums to different types of levers.

The base of the neck, for example, is the fulcrum of a first-class lever for which the neck muscles provide the input force. The output force lifts the weight of the head. The feet become second-class levers when a person stands on his or her toes. There is a third-class lever for which the elbow can act as the fulcrum. The biceps muscle provides the input force, while the forearm provides an output force to lift some object.

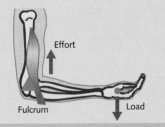

Figure 15.24 In a third-class lever, the input force is between the output force and the fulcrum. A third-class lever multiplies the distance over which a force is exerted. A hammer and a baseball bat are examples of third-class levers.

Teach

EXPLAIN to students that in both second- and third-class levers, the fulcrum is at one end of the lever. Second-class levers have the output force between the input force and the fulcrum. Third-class levers have the input force between the output force and fulcrum.

CONNECTION: Biology

Have students work in pairs to analyze different joints and identify them as first-, second-, or third-class levers. Provide students with references such as anatomy posters and books. Ask them to name five different joints, and, for each, to note the class of lever and identify the fulcrum, input force, and output force. Pairs should sketch the five joints and then share these sketches with the class.

EXTEND Have students research a common joint injury, such as tennis elbow, runner's knee, or ankle sprain. Students should note the common causes of the injury and relate the causes to the input output forces. Students should then write short reports on their findings.

Background Information

The knee is an example of a third-class lever; hamstrings (input force) contract to flex the lower leg (output force). The knee is the largest joint in the body, allowing a person to stand, walk, climb, and kick. The knee's ligaments and tendons stabilize it and hold the joint together. The most common knee injuries are sprains, tendonitis, iliotibial band syndrome, torn cartilage, arthritis, and runner's knee.

Key Concept Review
Workbook, p. 92

● Teach

 EXPLAIN to students that the fifth type of simple machine presented is a pulley, which can be fixed or movable.

🔘 Vocabulary

pulley Explain to students that the word *pulley* is derived from the Greek word meaning "to revolve."

fixed pulley Review with students the meaning of *pulley*. Tell students that *fixed* means "stationary" or "not movable."

movable pulley Review with students the meaning of *pulley*. Explain that *fixed* and *movable* are antonyms, or opposites. The root of movable is *move;* thus, movable pulleys move with the object.

wheel and axle Have students list common examples of the word *wheel*. Examples could include a wheel on a bicycle or car or a steering wheel. Tell students that the word *axle* comes from the word for "crossbar."

compound machine Explain to students that *compound* is derived from the Latin prefix *com-*, meaning "together," and the root *pōnere*, meaning "to put." The literal definition is "to put together a machine."

 Extend It!

Provide students with resources such as encyclopedias, access to science museums' online material, and biographies. Preview one or two pictures of Rube Goldberg-type devices with students and talk aloud about the different steps involved. Each student should then choose one example and explain the task and the simple machines used to complete the task.

 Extend It!

Rube Goldberg (1883–1970) was a cartoonist famous for developing "Rube Goldberg machines." These machines performed very simple tasks in indirect and convoluted ways. Find out more about Rube Goldberg. Select one of his machines and find out what task it performed and how it did so. Locate a drawing of the machine and present it to the class. Identify the simple machines included in the device.

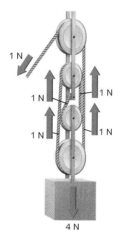

Figure 15.26 The block and tackle multiplies the input force by 4. Therefore, a force of just 1 N can be exerted to lift a load that has a weight of 4 N.

Pulley

A **pulley** is a grooved wheel with a rope, chain, or cable running along the groove. Pulleys can be fixed or movable.

Fixed Pulleys A **fixed pulley** is attached to something that does not move, such as a ceiling or a wall. The distance the rope is pulled down equals the distance the load moves upward. For the input work to equal the output work, the input force on the rope must equal the output force on the load. Therefore, a fixed pulley does not change either force or distance. A fixed pulley changes the direction of the input force. The IMA of a fixed pulley is 1. Using the fixed pulley in **Figure 15.25**, a person needs to exert a force of 4 N to lift the 4-N weight. However, the person is able to pull downward instead of upward, which is usually an easier way to do work.

Movable Pulleys A pulley that is attached to the object being moved is called a **movable pulley.** Unlike a fixed pulley, a movable pulley multiplies force. Therefore, the input force must be exerted over a greater distance. The mechanical advantage of a movable pulley is greater than 1. It is equal to the number of rope segments holding up the load. Using the movable pulley in Figure 15.25, force is multiplied because the input force is exerted over twice the distance of the output force. A force of 2 N can be exerted to lift a load that weighs twice as much, or 4 N.

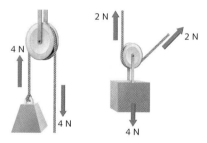

Figure 15.25 A fixed pulley changes only the direction of the input force *(left)*. Its IMA is 1. A movable pulley multiplies force *(right)*. The IMA of this movable pulley is 2 because there are two rope segments supporting the load.

Pulley Systems When fixed and movable pulleys are combined, a system of pulleys is formed. **Figure 15.26** shows a pulley system. A pulley system that consists of both fixed and movable pulleys is known as a block and tackle. The IMA of a pulley system is equal to the number of rope segments that support the load.

Count the ropes supporting the load in Figure 15.26. Do not count the rope segment on which the input force is exerted, because it is not supporting the load. There are four rope segments supporting the load, so the block and tackle has an IMA of 4. The IMA can be increased by increasing the number of pulleys in the system.

Background Information

Rube Goldberg was a cartoonist, author, and sculptor. After earning a college degree in engineering, he worked for San Francisco's Water and Sewers Department. He continued to pursue drawing. He quit his job as engineer, and after working as an office boy in the sports department of a small newspaper, worked his way to drawing daily cartoons. He won a Pulitzer Prize in 1948 for his political cartooning.

Field Study

Have students walk through the school building with a partner and find examples of simple machines in use. Students should note in their Science Notebooks at least five examples of simple machines. For each, they should identify the object, the object's use, and the simple machine at work. Encourage students to look in a variety of locations. Alert school staff members and explain the assignment to them before the tour.

Wheel and Axle

A **wheel and axle** is a simple machine consisting of two circular objects of different sizes. The axle, which is the smaller of the two circular objects, is attached to the center of a larger wheel. The wheel and axle rotate together.

The input force can be applied to either the wheel or the axle. The IMA of a wheel and axle depends on the sizes of the wheel and the axle. It can be calculated from this equation:

$$\text{IMA (wheel and axle)} = \frac{\text{radius of wheel}}{\text{radius of axle}}$$

In many devices, a small input force is exerted on the wheel. The force is then multiplied, but it is exerted over a shorter distance by the axle. Doorknobs, screwdrivers, and faucet handles are examples of wheel and axles. The IMA can be increased by increasing the radius of the wheel relative to the radius of the axle.

Figure 15.27 The hands of the clock turn thanks to a wheel and axle. A small force exerted on the wheel results in a large force exerted by the axle.

Compound Machines

Many machines are compound machines. A **compound machine** is made up of two or more simple machines that can operate together. Bicycles and can openers are examples of compound machines.

A car is another example of a compound machine. Burning fuel in the cylinders of the engine causes the pistons to move up and down. This up-and-down motion makes the crankshaft rotate. The force exerted by the rotating crankshaft is transmitted to other parts of the car, such as the transmission and the differential. Both of these parts contain gears, which are wheel and axles. Cars also contain levers and pulleys.

After You Read

1. Scissors are which type of simple machine?
2. Using the notes in your Science Notebook, identify the class of lever for which the output force is always greater than the input force.
3. What is the IMA of a steering wheel that has a radius of 20 cm and is attached to an axle of 2 cm?

Figure 15.28 A bicycle is just one of many compound machines. What simple machines make up a bicycle?

● Teach

EXPLAIN to students that the sixth type of simple machine presented is the wheel and axle.

Use the Visual: Figure 15.28

ANSWER A bicycle contains wheel and axles (wheels), levers (brakes), and pulleys (chain).

● Assess

Use the After You Read questions and the Alternative Assessment to help you evaluate students' understanding of the lesson.

After You Read

1. Scissors are an example of both two wedges and a machine made from two levers put together.
2. This is true for a second-class lever.
3. IMA = 10

Alternative Assessment

Students should use the charts in their Science Notebooks to identify the simple machines in one of the following compound machines: shovel, pencil sharpener, or nail clippers. Students should list each of the simple machines involved and describe its function in the compound machine.

Teacher Alert

The wheel and axle is a first-class lever. The cylinder acts as the fulcrum; the radius of the axle is the output force. The radius of the wheel is the input force. The simplest wheel and axle has a large wheel and a cylinder, which turn on the same axis and are attached.

Interpreting Diagrams
Workbook, p. 94

Chapter 15 Summary

MASTERING CONCEPTS

True or False

1. False, distance
2. False, power
3. True
4. False, greater
5. False, friction
6. False, inclined plane
7. False, narrower
8. False, third
9. True

Short Answer

10. The scientific definition requires that a force act on an object and that the object move in the direction of the force. The everyday meaning might refer to a job or to the exertion of effort.

11. A machine's mechanical advantage indicates whether it multiplies force or distance, or whether it changes the direction of the input force.

12. In a real machine, some of the input work is converted into heat by friction.

13. In a first-class lever, the fulcrum is located between the input and output forces. In a second-class lever, the output force is located between the input force and the fulcrum. In a third-class lever, the input force is exerted between the fulcrum and the output force.

Chapter **15** Summary

KEY CONCEPTS

15.1 Work and Power

- Work is done when a force is exerted on an object that moves the object some distance in the direction of the force.
- Power is the rate at which work is done.
- Work is the product of force and distance, and it is measured in joules.
- Power, which is measured in watts, is the work done divided by the time during which it is done.

15.2 Machines

- Machines do not change the amount of work that is done.
- Machines make work easier by multiplying force, multiplying distance, or changing the direction of the input force.
- The mechanical advantage (MA) of a machine is the output force divided by the input force.
- The efficiency of a machine is the output work divided by the input work.
- Efficiency is 100 percent for an ideal machine only, whereas it is always lower for a real machine.

15.3 Types of Machines

- The six types of simple machines are the inclined plane, wedge, screw, lever, pulley, and wheel and axle.
- The ideal mechanical advantage (IMA) of an inclined plane is the length of the inclined plane divided by the height.
- For a screw, the IMA increases as the spacing between the threads decreases.
- The IMA of a wedge is the length divided by the thickness.
- For each type of lever, the IMA is the length of the input arm divided by the length of the output arm.
- The IMA of a pulley is equal to the number of ropes supporting the load.
- The IMA of a wheel and axle is the radius of the wheel divided by the radius of the axle.

VOCABULARY REVIEW

Write each term in a complete sentence or write a paragraph relating several terms.

15.1
work, p. 239
power, p. 242

15.2
machine, p. 244
input work, p. 244
output work, p. 244
input force, p. 244
output force, p. 244
mechanical advantage, p. 247
efficiency, p. 248

15.3
simple machine, p. 249
inclined plane, p. 249
screw, p. 250
wedge, p. 251
lever, p. 252
pulley, p. 254
fixed pulley, p. 254
movable pulley, p. 254
wheel and axle, p. 255
compound machine, p. 255

PREPARE FOR CHAPTER TEST

To prepare for the chapter test, create a question from each Learning Goal. Use the information in your Science Notebook to answer each question. Then use these answers to write a well-developed essay about the chapter. Use the Key Concept on the first page of this chapter as your topic sentence.

Vocabulary Review
Workbook, p. 93

Reading Comprehension
Workbook, p. 95

MASTERING CONCEPTS

True or False
If the statement is true, write "true." If it is false, change the underlined word or words to make the statement true.

1. The work done on an object is equal to force times <u>mass</u>.
2. The rate at which work is done is <u>energy</u>.
3. A machine is useful because it makes work <u>easier</u>.
4. A machine that multiplies force has a mechanical advantage that is <u>less</u> than 1.
5. The efficiency of a real machine is less than 100 percent due to <u>gravity</u>.
6. A ramp over which a wheelchair might travel is an example of a(n) <u>pulley</u>.
7. The IMA of a wedge increases as the wedge becomes <u>thicker</u>.
8. A baseball bat is an example of a(n) <u>first</u>-class lever.
9. The IMA of a wheel and axle equals the radius of the wheel <u>divided</u> by the radius of the axle.

Short Answer
Answer each of the following in a sentence or brief paragraph.

10. How is the scientific definition of *work* different from the word's everyday meaning?
11. What does the mechanical advantage of a machine indicate?
12. Why is the output work less than the input work for a real machine?
13. How do the three types of levers differ from one another?

Critical Thinking
Use what you have learned in this chapter to answer each of the following.

14. **Calculate** What is the force a person exerts in pulling a wagon 20 m if 1,500 J of work are done?
15. **Evaluate** Two students are asked to unload identical boxes of books. One student completes the job in ten minutes, whereas the other takes 20 minutes. Compare the work and power of the two students.
16. **Calculate** Find the force needed to lift a 1,950-N weight using a machine with a mechanical advantage of 15.
17. **Relate** How are fixed and movable pulleys modified levers?

Standardized Test Question
Choose the letter of the response that correctly answers the question.

18. If the distance between the lever's input force and fulcrum is 6 cm, and the distance between the fulcrum and the output force is 24 cm, what is the ideal mechanical advantage of the lever?

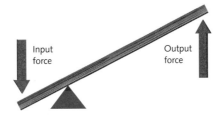

Input force

Output force

A. 0.25
B. 0.75
C. 1
D. 4

Test-Taking Tip
Remember that qualifying words such as *usually*, *sometimes*, and *generally* mean that the statement can be considered both true and false depending on the specific circumstances.

Critical Thinking
14. $F = 1,500 \text{ J}/20 \text{ m} = 75 \text{ N}$
15. They do the same amount of work. However, the student who did the work faster had greater power.
16. input force $= 1,950 \text{ N}/15 = 130 \text{ N}$
17. A fixed pulley is a modified first-class lever. The fulcrum is between the input force and the output force. A movable pulley is a modified second-class lever. The point where the rope is attached to the ceiling is the fulcrum. The output force is between the fulcrum and the input force.

Standardized Test Question
18. A

Reading Links

Simple Machines (Hands-On Science)
This comprehensive guide will deepen readers' understanding of the topics introduced in this chapter, further familiarizing them with the types of simple machines, the applications of these devices, and the principles involved.
Steven Souza and Joseph Shortell. Walch Publishing. 104 pp. Trade ISBN 978-0-8251-4263-5

Leonardo Da Vinci (Giants of Science)
Full of the sorts of well-researched anecdotes and details that bring a historic figure to life, this spirited biography of Da Vinci is sure to capture readers' imaginations, instill in them a greater appreciation for the scientific endeavor, and, in the process, memorably impart information about work, power, and simple machines that will reinforce the chapter's coverage.
Kathleen Krull. Penguin Group. 128 pp. Illustrated by Boris Kulikov. Trade ISBN 978-0-670-05920-1.

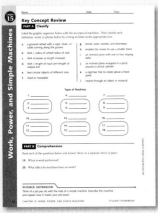

Curriculum Connection
Workbook, p. 96

Science Challenge
Workbook, pp. 97–98

15A That's Hard Work!

This prechapter introduction activity is designed to determine what students already know about forces, work, and power by engaging them in observing, measuring, calculating, and drawing.

Objectives

* measure force, distance, and time
* record data in a suitable way
* calculate work done
* communicate conclusions

Planning

 15–20 minutes   groups of 3–4 students

Materials (per group)

* spring scale (newtons)
* string
* textbooks
* stopwatch
* meterstick
* masking tape

Advance Preparation

* Cut 1-m long pieces of string in advance.
* Provide textbooks or other books for student groups to use.
* If students work at small desks, you may wish to complete the activity on the floor.
* Use spring scales that measure in newtons. Instruct students to keep the spring scales perfectly horizontal as

they pull the books through the 1-m long zone. As a way to minimize error, have students repeat the activity until they record two trials with similar times and force values. When the second book is added, the force required will increase. Make sure students pull the book at the same speed in all trials; the time required to cover the 1-m zone should be the same in each trial.

Engagement Guide

* Challenge students to think about force and motion and work by asking:
  * *What quantities must be measured in order to determine the work done?* (Students should mention force and distance. They might also mention time, but time as measured in this lab is used as a way to keep trial results consistent and is not needed to calculate work. Power, which is closely related to work, does involve time.)
  * *How do you think the mass or weight of an object is related to the amount of force and work needed to move it?* (Heavier or more massive objects will require more force to move; therefore, they require more work.)
  * *What units would you expect to be associated with work?* (Answers may vary, but should mention a unit of distance, such as a meter, and a unit of force, such as a newton.)
* Encourage students to communicate their ideas about work in creative ways.

Going Further

Have students repeat the activity by pulling the books over different type of surfaces with different coefficients of friction. Have them determine the effect of increased friction on the work done. Students can present their results in the form of a table.

15B Inclined Planes

Objectives

* construct a model
* measure forces
* record and analyze data
* calculate mechanical advantage
* draw conclusions

Skill Set

constructing a model, measuring, recording and analyzing data, calculating, drawing conclusions

Planning

 45–50 minutes   groups of 3–4 students

Materials

Materials for this activity are listed in the Student Laboratory Manual.

Advance Preparation

* The wood boards should be about 10 cm wide and at least 50–60 cm long. The wood blocks should be about 3 cm thick × 10 cm wide × 15 cm long. Screw a small eye hook into each of the wood blocks.
* Provide textbooks or other books for student groups to use.
* Students may wish to complete this activity on the floor if tables or desks are not long enough.

Answer to Observations: Weight of Wood Block

Answers will vary.

Answers to Observations: Data Table 1

Answers will vary. Students should observe that the force required to move the wood block up the ramp with one to two books is less than the weight of the block. The mechanical advantage of the ramp with one to two books should be greater than the mechanical advantage of the ramp made using additional books.

Answers to Analysis and Conclusions

1. Answers will vary. Students should observe that the amount of force needed to move the wood block up the inclined plane lying on one book is less than the force needed to move the wood block up the inclined plane lying on two books.

2. The steeper the inclined plane, the lower the mechanical advantage.

3. The length of the inclined plane increases with increasing mechanical advantage.

Going Further

Explain to students that the ideal mechanical advantage of an inclined plane can be calculated by dividing the length of the inclined plane by the height of the inclined plane. Have students calculate the ideal mechanical advantage of a wheelchair-access ramp at school by having them measure the length and height of the ramp. Students should present their findings in a one-page report showing a sketch of the ramp with dimensions and the supporting calculations.

15C Pulleys and Forces

Objectives

• observe pulleys
• measure forces
• record data
• compare and contrast fixed and movable pulley
• draw conclusions about pulleys

Skill Set

observing, measuring, recording data, comparing and contrasting, drawing conclusions

Planning

 30–35 minutes   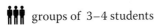 groups of 3–4 students

Materials

Materials for this activity are listed in the Student Laboratory Manual.

Advance Preparation

• You may wish to cut a 50-cm long piece of string for each group before the activity begins.
• If the metal weights do not have hooks on them, you can tie metal wire around them to create a hook or loop. Groups of metal washers work well for this activity.
• Have students use the scissors to cut the piece of string from the ring when they finish the activity.

Answers to Observations: Weight of Metal Weight

Answers will vary.

Answers to Observations: Data Table 1

Answers will vary. Students should observe that the amount of force needed to move a weight with a fixed pulley is about the same as the weight of the metal weight. Students should observe that the amount of force need to move a weight with a movable pulley is about half the weight of the metal weight.

Answers to Observations: Force Sketches

Answers will vary. The fixed pulley sketch should show one upward force arrow representing the force applied by the string. The movable pulley sketch should show two upward pointing arrows, one for each of the two strings.

Answers to Analysis and Conclusions

1. A fixed pulley changes the direction of a force. A movable pulley does not change the direction of a force.

2. A fixed pulley helps a person do work by allowing the person to pull down to move the object up. A movable pulley helps a person do work by decreasing the amount of force need to move an object.

3. A pulley system could be created that contains both a fixed and movable pulley.

Going Further

Have students repeat this activity measuring the distance the string moves in relation to the distance the weight moves when fixed and movable pulleys are used. Students should observe that the string on the fixed pulley moves the same distance as the weight. The string on the movable pulley moves twice as far as the weight moves. Have students share their results with the class. Have students create a compound set of pulleys and show what the mechanical advantage would be.

Unit 4

Case Study 1: Riding the Vomit Comet

Gather More Information

Have students use the following key terms to aid their searches:

zero gravity

G (gravitational constant)

astronaut training

weightlessness

free-fall

Research the Big Picture

- Have students work with a partner to draw the probable path that the airplane takes. On the path, students should note at what point free-fall occurs. It may be helpful to provide grid paper on which students can draw the path.

- Have students work in pairs to hypothesize about how NASA discovered the means of simulating the weightless environment of space. Then have pairs research NASA's process and present findings to the class.

- Have students research how the simulation compares to a real weightless environment. Students should determine how the two environments are similar and different and make a Venn diagram to present their information.

Riding the Vomit Comet

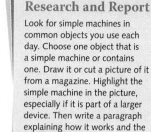

Research and Report

Look for simple machines in common objects you use each day. Choose one object that is a simple machine or contains one. Draw it or cut a picture of it from a magazine. Highlight the simple machine in the picture, especially if it is part of a larger device. Then write a paragraph explaining how it works and the job it does.

The National Aeronautics and Space Administration (NASA) sends astronauts into space, where they become weightless. These astronauts need to be trained in a weightless environment, but gravity makes that impossible on Earth. NASA has a special solution to this problem. It's a regular passenger airplane with padded walls inside. Depending on how it moves, the plane can simulate the weightless environment of space.

How can zero-gravity conditions be created on an airplane? First,

the plane takes off and flies at an altitude between 7.6 and 11.8 km. Then it performs a series of steep climbs and dives. It shoots up steeply at about a 45-degree angle. Then it quickly turns and dives just as steeply. The plane does 30 to 40 of these steep climbs and dives. It's like a huge roller coaster ride in the air. At the top of each arc, the plane's upward acceleration cancels the downward acceleration due to Earth's gravity. This creates 20 to 30 seconds of weightlessness, where everything in the plane that isn't tied down

floats freely. As the plane then dives, passengers feel an increase in the forces pressing on them. At the bottom of the arc, the force of gravity they feel is about 2 Gs—twice the normal amount.

Bouncing up and down during a several-hour flight is too much for some people. About one-third of the passengers who ride NASA's special plane become extremely nauseous, which accounts for the plane's nickname—the Vomit Comet. Still, most passengers agree that being in the zero-gravity environment is an exciting and useful experience.

 CAREER CONNECTION AMUSEMENT-PARK RIDE DESIGNER

Think about the many rides at an amusement park—the water slide, the Ferris wheel, and the roller coaster. Have you ever wondered who thinks of and creates these rides? That person is the amusement-park ride designer.

Each amusement park ride obeys the laws of physics, so ride designers must know about forces, gravity, and the laws of motion. For example, they have to know the speed a roller coaster will reach under various conditions of track length and track slope. They have to know how to design a ride so that everyone will be safe when it whips around a curve or flips upside-down.

Many ride designers earn college degrees in mechanical, structural, or electrical engineering. It takes imagination and creativity to make rides exciting and enjoyable, but it takes engineering knowledge to make rides function properly and safely. Because much of the planning and design is done on computers, ride engineers also have to be familiar with a variety of computer design programs. For many ride designers, the biggest thrill is seeing their ideas transformed from the computer screen to the amusement park.

258

CAREER CONNECTION: Amusement-Park Ride Designer

Have students work with a partner to read the article and then identify the skills necessary to be successful as an amusement-park ride designer. Students should then compare the knowledge they gained in this unit to add to the skill list and determine what they would still need to learn to perform the job.

The Science of Curveballs

The pitcher straightens up on the pitcher's mound. Then he rocks back and forth, quickly stretching his pitching arm back and whipping it forward. The baseball speeds toward the batter, curving sharply downward. The batter, with just a split second to see the ball, swings hard—but the bat and ball do not connect. Strike three!

For baseball pitchers who can throw one, a curveball is a great "out" pitch. Several things help a pitcher throw a good curveball, including a strong arm and great pitching technique—but there is something else at work, too. A curveball relies on a principle of physics called the Magnus effect.

In the mid-1800s, Gustav Magnus discovered that when a spinning object moves through a fluid—air or water—it creates a force that pulls or pushes the object away from a straight path. In other words, the object moves to the side or down. When a pitcher throws a curveball, he or she releases it with a snap of the wrist that makes the ball spin downward. Gravity will move the ball down anyway, but the topspin on the ball makes it dip down more sharply. This is because the ball splits the air in front of it as it flies forward.

The ball's movement creates a low-pressure area behind it. The unequal pressure between the front and back of the ball slows the ball's forward movement, so it curves more sharply downward than it would with no spin.

In the case described here, the pitched ball curves straight down. Pitchers, however, can release a ball in slightly different ways to produce curveballs that move a bit differently. For example, sidespin can make the ball curve down and to the left or the right.

Because of the way a good curveball moves, it's hard to hit. Baseball batters might prefer a fastball—although, moving at almost 160 kilometers per hour, a good fastball isn't easy to hit either!

Building the Pyramids

The Great Pyramid of Giza is made of 2.3 million blocks, each of which weighs more than 2 tons. Building a structure such as this would be an amazing feat today, with power tools to cut the blocks and cranes to move them into place. The Great Pyramid, however, was built about 4,500 years ago. Its builders had only hand tools and the power of their own muscles. How did they do it?

No one really knows. The designers and builders didn't leave records describing what they did and how. However, historians and archeologists know the types of tools the ancient Egyptians had and how these tools were probably used. Some of the tools used were simple machines: the wedge, the lever, and the inclined plane.

The Great Pyramid is constructed of several types of stone, including limestone and granite. Workers used copper chisels (wedges) to cut out limestone blocks. They used quartz, the hardest of several minerals in granite, to slowly scrape cuts in the granite. Workers forced the blade of a saw down onto quartz particles on the rock's surface. The quartz slowly cut into the rock.

Workers used ramps (inclined planes) to push the blocks into place. The ramps were extended as the pyramid rose higher. Each block was put onto a wooden platform. Workers secured the block and platform onto a track of wooden rollers, which were placed on the ramps. As the block was pushed and pulled, it rolled along on top of the track of rollers.

Hundreds of workers dragged the heavy blocks up the ramps. Then workers used poles (levers) and ropes to get each block into its correct place. It took thousands of people many years to build the Great Pyramid. Today, it's one of the wonders of the world.

Case Study 2: The Science of Curveballs

Gather More Information

Have students use the following key terms to aid their searches:

Magnus effect

Gustav Magnus

curveball

pitching techniques

Research the Big Picture

- Have students work in small groups to brainstorm questions to ask a baseball pitcher or coach about the technique required to throw a curveball. As a class, choose five to seven questions to use in an actual interview. Then have two or three students from the class interview the school's baseball coach or pitcher and share the responses with the class.

- Students should research the Magnus effect and find other examples of it. Have students work in pairs to identify at least one example and compare that example to the use in baseball pitching. Pairs should then present findings to the class.

Case Study 3: Building the Pyramids

Gather More Information

Have students use the following key terms to aid their searches:

Great Pyramid

Giza

Seven Wonders of the World

ancient Egypt

Research the Big Picture

- Have students compare moving five cement bricks up steps to the method described. Students should estimate the amount of effort on a scale of 1 (low) to 10 (high) for each method.

- Have students work in small groups to guess the approximate dimensions of individual blocks in the Great Pyramid (and explain their reasoning). Students should then research the actual sizes and compare this information to their predictions.

- Have students compare the building methods of ancient Egyptians to those used in the construction of modern skyscrapers. Students should identify the tools and machinery used to construct skyscrapers and explain the benefits of modern technology.

Unit 5

Introduce Unit 5

Explain that the topic of this unit is energy. Have students work with a partner to define *energy*. Their definitions could include common uses as well as scientific uses. Have pairs share their definitions of energy with the class and create a class definition. Students should write the class definition in their Science Notebooks and revise it as necessary throughout the unit.

Unit Projects

For each Unit Project, have students use the Presentation Builder on the Student CD-ROM to display their results.

Career Research Have each student research a career that is related to energy such as electrical engineer, dietician, or automotive mechanic. Ask each student describe the responsibilities of the job and identify the skills, education, or experience needed to prepare for the job. Have students record this information in their Science Notebooks.

Have each student then create an advertisement recruiting others to the profession. The advertisement could be in the form of a poster or oral presentation.

Hands-On Research Challenge students to create an efficient solar cooker. First, have students work in small groups to research solar cooking devices. Groups should then devise their own solar cookers as inexpensively as possible. Efficiency may be measured by the amount of time needed to heat water to boiling.

Groups should showcase their cookers at the end of the two weeks and give presentations about the related cost, efficiency, and scientific principles.

Technology Research Have groups conduct further research on solar technologies, such as photovoltaics, passive solar energy, solar hot water, and a solar electric system. Each student should then choose one technology and present the benefits and challenges of using it.

Unit 5

Energy: Its Forms and Changes

Chapter 16 — **Nature of Energy**
What is energy, and in what forms does it exist?

Chapter 17 — **Thermal Energy and Heat**
How does thermal energy flow, and what physical changes does it produce?

Chapter 18 — **Heat Technology**
What are some important applications of thermal energy?

260

Software Summary

Student CD-ROM
—Interactive Student Book
—Vocabulary Review
—Key Concept Review
—Lab Report Template
—ELL Preview and Writing Activities
—Presentation Digital Library
—Graphic Organizing Software
—Spanish Cognate Dictionary

Interactive Labs
Chapter 17 C—Observing Kinetic Energy
Chapter 18C—Home Solar Heat
Chapter 19B—Properties of Waves
Chapter 19C—Sunscreen and Ultraviolet Waves

Nature of Energy

KEY CONCEPT Energy, in its many forms, makes everything happen in the universe.

Can you sense the energy in this scene? Running uses energy of movement. Leaping into the air involves energy of position. The sound of clashing bodies is a form of energy. All of this energy has a source.

Football players' bodies convert food into movement, heat, and sound. All around you, plants, animals, and machines are converting energy from one form to another. Almost all of this energy can be traced back to the Sun. Scientists from every branch of science study the pathways taken by energy as it travels through the world. Scientists hope to find new sources of energy. Engineers work to develop uses of energy that support human activities without damaging the natural world.

Think About Analyzing Energy Needs

When you analyze, you try to identify each factor that influences a result.

- Think of a time when you felt very tired in the middle of the day. How did you spend your energy? What did you eat to provide energy to your body?

- Write one or two sentences in your Science Notebook describing how analyzing can help you solve problems.

NSTA

SCiLINKS
THE WORLD'S A CLICK AWAY

www.scilinks.org
Energy **Code: WGPS16**

261

Introduce Chapter 16

As a starting activity, use Lab 16A on page 91 of the Laboratory Manual.

ENGAGE Have students think about what they do during one school day. Ask them to talk with a partner about all of the activities and whether or not each requires energy. Have students share some of their activities and engage the class in a discussion about energy. Help students understand that everything they mentioned involves energy.

Think About Analyzing Energy Needs

ENGAGE Ask students to provide more examples of analysis. If necessary, suggest being in an uncomfortable social situation and analyzing who is there, what is happening, and how you will act as a result. Have students discuss in pairs a time when they were tired in the middle of the day and the factors that influenced that feeling. Then have students write about it in their Science Notebooks. Have them conclude by discussing in pairs how analysis can help to solve problems, and then encourage them to write about it in their Science Notebooks.

Chapter 16 Planning Guide

Instructional Periods	National Standards	Lab Manual	Workbook
16.1 2 Periods	A2, B3, G2; A2, B3, B6, G2; UCP1, UCP3	**Lab 16A: p. 91** Making a Pickle Battery	Key Concept Review p. 99 Vocabulary Review p. 100
16.2 2 Periods	A1, B3, C1, C3, E1, E2, G1, G2, G3; A1, B6, C5, E1, E2, G1, G2, G3; UCP3, UCP4, UCP5	**Lab 16B: pp. 92–93** The Effect of Friction **Lab 16C: pp. 94–96** Follow the Bouncing Balls	Interpreting Diagrams p. 101 Reading Comprehension p. 102 Curriculum Connection p. 103
16.3 2 Periods	A2, B1, B3, E1, E2, F2, F4, F5, G1, G2; A2, B1, B2, B5, B6, D1, E1, E2, F3, F4, F5, F6, G1, G2; UCP1, UCP2, UCP4		Science Challenge pp. 104–105
16.4 2 Periods	A2, B1, B3, E1, F1, F2, F4, F5; A2, B2, B3, B5, B6, D1, E1, F1, F3, F4, F5, F6; UCP2, UCP5		

Middle School Standard; High School Standard; **Unifying Concept and Principle**

16.1 Introduce

ENGAGE Ask students to brainstorm what they know about the Sun. Record their answers on the board. Ask them to speculate about how the Sun provides most of the energy in the solar system. Record their speculations.

Vocabulary terms are listed on the first student page of each lesson. You may wish to preview the terms before introducing each lesson. Strategies for teaching the vocabulary appear on the pages where the terms are introduced.

Before You Read

Talk with students about what it means for two factors to be correlated. Ask them to share other examples with the class.

Show students how you would preview the lesson to look for factors that are correlated with each form of energy. Think aloud as you do so. On the board, draw a T-chart with the headings *Energy* and *Correlated Factors*. Tell students that they will be completing the chart as they read the lesson.

● Teach

EXPLAIN to students that they will learn about energy and its relationship to everything in the universe.

Encourage students to use the vocabulary section they created in their Science Notebooks. Remind them to record prefixes, suffixes, and root words to help them remember the meanings of vocabulary terms.

Vocabulary

energy Explain to students that the word *energy* comes from the Greek word *energeia*, from the words meaning "in" and "work."

joule Tell students that this unit is named after James Prescott Joule, a British physicist who lived from 1818 to 1889.

kinetic energy Tell students that the word *kinetic* comes from the Greek word *kineein*, meaning "to move."

Learning Goals

- Explain the concept of energy.
- Describe kinetic energy and potential energy.
- Distinguish among the various forms of energy.

New Vocabulary

energy
joule
kinetic energy
potential energy
thermal energy
chemical energy
electrical energy
radiant energy
nuclear energy

16.1 What Is Energy?

Before You Read

Two factors that change together are said to be correlated. For example, a person's weight generally increases as he or she grows taller. Height and weight are correlated. Describe two more examples of correlations in your Science Notebook.

Energy Makes Everything Happen

A car races by. A light switches on. Sounds filter out from the music room at school. Motion, light, and sound are all forms of energy. Every action is connected to energy in one form or another. **Energy** is the ability to do work or make things happen.

Most of the energy on Earth comes from the Sun. Some of this energy is used directly to warm and light the planet. A portion of this energy heats the atmosphere. Winds are formed when parts of the atmosphere are heated unevenly. Energy from the Sun is also responsible for powering the water cycle. As water absorbs and loses heat, it changes from one state to another. In the process, clouds and rain are produced. Sunlight also provides the energy that plants use to make food—food that humans and other animals eat. In fact, energy stored by ancient plants millions of years ago is being used as the fossil fuels of today.

Energy Units Scientists measure energy in **joules** (JEWLZ). The joule (J) is a very small unit in terms of most human uses of energy. It takes about one joule of energy to lift an apple one meter off the ground. Eating the apple provides the body with about 250,000 J of energy. Every form of energy, including movement, stored energy, heat, light, and nuclear energy, can be measured in joules.

Figure 16.1 Everything on Earth is connected to energy in one form or another. Even rocks perched on a peak possess energy. The Sun provides most of the energy on Earth. Plants store the Sun's energy in a form that humans can eat, feed to livestock, or burn for fuel. Powerful winds of a tornado are caused by the uneven heating of Earth's atmosphere.

Background Information

James Prescott Joule is considered one of the great experimental scientists of the nineteenth century. His research dealt with heat, electricity, and thermodynamics. He determined the relationship between heat energy and mechanical work, which formed the basis of the law of conservation of energy and led to the first law of thermodynamics.

Kinetic Energy

Objects can have energy due to either their movement or their position. Energy of movement is called **kinetic energy.** An object with kinetic energy can do work on another object. For example, a moving baseball bat can cause a baseball to change direction and fly through the air. Rubbing your hands together can generate heat and sound. Moving air molecules of a tornado can lift the roof off a house.

The amount of kinetic energy of an object depends on two things: the object's mass and how fast the object is moving. In mathematical terms, the amount of kinetic energy (*KE*) an object has is given by the equation

$$KE = \frac{1}{2}mv^2$$

where *m* equals the mass of an object and *v* equals its velocity.

This equation says that if two objects are moving at the same velocity, the object with more mass will have more kinetic energy. So if a 135-kg football player and a 68-kg science teacher were racing at the same speed, the football player would have more kinetic energy.

Figure 16.2 Imagine that all of these horses are running at the same velocity. Which horses have the most kinetic energy?

The equation also says that if two objects have equal mass, the one moving faster will have more kinetic energy. For example, a 1,000-kg car will have more kinetic energy when it travels at 50 m per second than it will if it goes 25 m per second. Not only will the car have more kinetic energy at higher speeds, but the equation says that an increase in an object's velocity equals a much larger increase in its kinetic energy. If a car doubles its speed, its kinetic energy beomes four times greater.

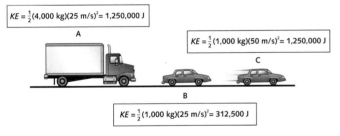

$$KE = \frac{1}{2}(4,000 \text{ kg})(25 \text{ m/s})^2 = 1,250,000 \text{ J}$$

$$KE = \frac{1}{2}(1,000 \text{ kg})(50 \text{ m/s})^2 = 1,250,000 \text{ J}$$

$$KE = \frac{1}{2}(1,000 \text{ kg})(25 \text{ m/s})^2 = 312,500 \text{ J}$$

Figure 16.3 A small change in velocity can equal a big change in kinetic energy. The fast car has the same kinetic energy as the slow truck even though the truck has four times the mass of the car.

As You Read

In your Science Notebook, record the factors correlated with each form of energy. Work with a partner to record several examples.

How is kinetic energy related to the velocity of an object?

Explore It!

Fill three small plastic bowls with cold water. Add one marble to each bowl and allow the water to settle. Add one drop of food coloring to each bowl.

Observe the first bowl without touching the marble or the water. Gently push the marble in the second bowl with your finger and observe. For the third bowl, push the marble harder so that it moves faster.

Describe the relationship between the energy you gave the marble and the kinetic energy of the water.

Teach

EXPLAIN to students that kinetic energy is energy of movement, whereas potential energy is stored energy. Tell them that they will first learn about kinetic energy.

Use the Visual: Figure 16.2

ANSWER The larger, more massive horses have more kinetic energy than the smaller horses.

As You Read

Discuss with students what they have learned so far about kinetic energy and the factors related to it. Give them time to record the information in the T-charts in their Science Notebooks.

ANSWER Kinetic energy is related to the square of the velocity of an object.

Explore It!

For each small group, provide three plastic bowls, one bottle of food coloring, three marbles, and a pitcher of water or access to a faucet.

This activity can be extended by using balls of various densities. Students can compare the swirling caused by a rubber ball, a glass marble, and a steel ball bearing.

ANSWER Moving the marbles faster gives them more kinetic energy. As the kinetic energy is transferred to the water in the bowl, the food coloring mixes and swirls in the water. Dropping a marble converts the marble's gravitational potential energy into kinetic energy, which is then transferred to the water in the bowl. Dropping from a greater height results in more swirling of the coloring in the water.

As English language learners perform this task, they should create diagrams of the activity and label them, indicating the kinetic energy states, in addition to recording their observations. This will allow them more opportunities to work with the concept and the terms.

● Teach

EXPLAIN to students that they will learn about potential, or stored, energy.

Use the Visual: Figure 16.4

ANSWER The archery photo shows elastic potential energy.

 Explore It!

Have students work with a partner during this activity. Each pair will need several rubber bands of the same length and width. Discuss safety issues with students. Make sure they wear safety goggles and do not shoot rubber bands in the direction of other students.

Demonstrate what to do with the rubber bands to explore potential energy. Explain that the distance the rubber band travels is related to the energy it has. Students should observe more energy as they stretch the rubber bands farther.

Remind students to be careful when jumping from different heights. Students might jump from a stool, a chair, and a bench. Make sure the item is supported as the student jumps. Help students conclude that they have more energy at greater heights.

 Explore It!

To explore elastic potential energy, stretch identical rubber bands different distances and carefully determine how far they fly when released. Identify the relationship between distance stretched and distance flown.

To explore gravitational potential energy, jump from different safe heights and feel the energy absorbed by your feet when you land. Identify the relationship between height and energy absorbed.

Potential Energy

Imagine stretching a rubber band. Your hands are pulling the rubber, and the rubber is exerting a force against you. When the rubber band is stretched, it has energy. The rubber band can fly across the room when you release it. Energy stored when something moves against a force is **potential energy.** Stretching gives an object elastic potential energy.

An object's position in space can also give it energy. For example, a roller coaster car at the top of a hill can do work by sliding down the hill. Energy was stored in the car when the car was hauled up the hill against gravity. Raising an object above the ground gives it gravitational potential energy. Gravitational potential energy (*GPE*) is related to the mass of the object raised, gravity, and the height the object is raised off the ground. This can be expressed mathematically as

$$GPE = mgh$$

where *m* equals the mass of the object, *g* equals the acceleration due to gravity, and *h* equals the height to which the object is raised.

Potential energy can take other forms. Chemical potential energy can be stored in the bonds between atoms and is released in chemical reactions such as digestion or burning. Electrical potential energy is stored when like charges are forced together. Static electricity is an example of electrical potential energy.

Figure 16.4 Each of these scenes shows a different form of potential energy. Which picture shows elastic potential energy?

E L L Strategy

Practice Using Vocabulary Have students practice using vocabulary from this lesson in small groups. Each student should choose a term and use it in context.

Visual English language learners can create a grid that has three columns labeled *Type of Energy, Definition,* and *Example & Diagram* at the top. Then, as they read the lessons, they can fill the grid with the appropriate terms, allowing them to create the context for the use of the words.

Forms of Energy

Energy is always the to do work or cause change. However, there are several forms of energy.

Thermal Energy   The atoms and molecules that make up matter are never still. They are always moving. Particles of a liquid or gas flow from place to place. Even the molecules of a solid vibrate. **Thermal energy** is associated with the particles that make up matter. Part of that energy is the kinetic energy of these vibrations and movements of particles. The human body senses thermal energy when it flows as heat. Faster-moving particles have more energy and feel hotter to the skin.

Chemical Energy   When a match is struck, it emits light, sound, and thermal energy. All of this energy had been stored in the match in the form of chemical energy. **Chemical energy** is the potential energy stored in the bonds between the atoms of a substance. This energy can be released in a chemical reaction. Plants store chemical energy in sugars formed during photosynthesis. People use chemical energy from plants when they digest food or burn wood.

Electrical Energy   Electrons are negatively charged atomic particles that naturally repel each other. Electrical potential energy is generated when electrons are forced together. The friction of shuffling feet on a carpet rubs electrons from the carpet onto the feet. This buildup of charge generates electrical potential energy. Potential energy becomes kinetic energy when a static shock carries the charges into a doorknob. **Electrical energy** is energy that arises from the movement of electric charges. Electric energy powers many machines, including lights, toasters, computers, and televisions.

Figure 16.5 Lightning is electrical energy moving between the atmosphere and the ground. When lightning strikes a tree, it increases the thermal energy of the wood. The wood may become hot enough to start burning. Fire is a chemical reaction that releases the stored chemical energy of the wood.

● Teach

EXPLAIN to students that they will learn about forms of energy. Have them read the subheadings on these pages to preview what they will be learning.

   Vocabulary

potential energy Ask students to give examples of uses of the word *potential*. Tell them that the common usages refer to possibility or likelihood, such as a potential customer or living up to one's potential.

thermal energy Tell students that the word *thermal* comes from the Greek word *therme*, meaning "heat."

chemical energy Explain to students that the word *chemical* comes from *chemic*, meaning "relating to alchemy or chemistry."

electrical energy Ask students what *electric* means. Tell them that *electrical* is the adjective derived from *electricity*. Tell them that *electricity* commonly refers to energy that results from the movement of charged particles.

Background Information

Thermal energy is transferred from one sample of matter to another as heat. Many natural processes, such as chemical reactions, are either endothermic or exothermic depending on the flow of heat. An endothermic process is one that absorbs energy in the form of heat. The Greek prefix *endo-* means "inside," and the Greek suffix *-thermic* means "to heat." Cooking food and melting ice are two examples of endothermic processes. An exothermic process is one that releases energy in the form of heat. The Greek prefix *exo-* means "outside." Examples include water freezing and respiration. These are opposite processes.

Teach

EXPLAIN to students that they will continue learning about forms of energy.

Figure It Out: Figure 16.6
ANSWER **1.** violet light **2.** ultraviolet waves

Assess

Use the After You Read questions and the Alternative Assessment to help you evaluate students' understanding of the lesson.

After You Read

1. Answers will vary. Possible answers include lights shining, people moving, sounds of voices, a heater warming air, sunlight through windows, moving air (wind), potential energy of raised objects, etc.
2. Nuclear energy is stored in the nucleus of an atom. When atoms are split apart or fused together, the energy is released. It is converted to forms of radiant energy, such as gamma rays.
3. Gravitational potential energy is correlated with mass, the force of gravity, and height.

Alternative Assessment

Give students time to complete their T-charts. When they are finished, have each student write a paragraph comparing two types of energy and correlated factors.

 Vocabulary

radiant energy Tell students that the word *radiant* is Latin and comes from *radiare*, meaning "to radiate or emit rays."

nuclear energy Tell students that *nuclear* is the adjective derived from the word *nucleus*. Ask if anyone recalls what a nucleus is. Explain that it is the central part of an atom or cell.

Radiant Energy   Heat on a sunny day, microwaves that cook food, and X rays that reveal bones have a lot in common. Each is a type of energy that is carried by electromagnetic waves. Energy that radiates out in waves from its source is called **radiant energy.** The many forms of radiant energy are shown in **Figure 16.6.**

Figure It Out

1. Which color of light has the shortest wavelength?
2. Which carries the most energy, infrared or ultraviolet waves?

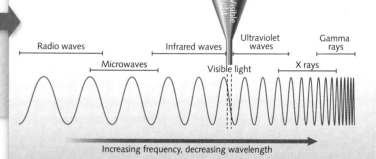

Figure 16.6 Microwaves, X rays, visible light, and gamma rays are all forms of radiant energy. Radiant energy is carried by waves. Shorter waves carry more energy.

Nuclear Energy   The nuclei of atoms contain a tremendous amount of potential energy. Energy stored in the nucleus of an atom is **nuclear energy.** It holds the particles of the nucleus together. Nuclear energy can be released when nuclei are combined, as in reactions in the Sun. Nuclear energy can also be released when nuclei are split apart, as is nuclear reactors on Earth.

The nuclei of some elements are unstable. As a result, they undergo radioactive decay. During this process, the unstable nuclei emit particles and energy in the form of electromagnetic waves.

Figure 16.7 Naturally radioactive elements are useful for glow-in-the-dark watch dials. Radiation is also used to improve the color of gemstones, treat cancer, and kill bacteria on food.

After You Read

1. Describe five examples of energy around you.
2. Explain how radiant energy and nuclear energy are related.
3. According to the notes in your Science Notebook, which factors are correlated with gravitational potential energy?

266 NATURE OF ENERGY

Background Information

Radiation is the transfer of energy as particles or waves. Sunlight is one of the most familiar forms of radiation. Without ample sunlight, no life would exist on Earth. Visible light is just one form of radiation from the Sun. The Sun emits radiation in wavelengths from long-wave infrared to short-wave ultraviolet.

Other types of radiation include background radiation (which occurs naturally in the environment), terrestrial radiation (which occurs in populated areas where granite or mineralized sands are present), cosmic radiation (which occurs in high-altitude areas), and radiation from radon (a gas present in Earth's crust).

Before You Read

An important way to explain or understand a new idea is through examples. In your Science Notebook, draw three boxes. Leave enough space to write a few sentences inside each box. As you preview the lesson, look for examples of energy conversions.

Energy can change forms in many different ways. Potential energy can change into kinetic energy when objects speed up. Energy conversions often happen in living things. Plants convert radiant energy into chemical energy. Electric eels convert chemical energy into electrical energy. Running deer convert chemical energy into kinetic energy.

Kinetic and Potential Energy Conversions

Kinetic and potential energy can be converted back and forth. Imagine a roller coaster sitting at the top of a tall roller coaster hill. The coaster has a lot of potential energy, but no kinetic energy. As the cars begin to roll down the hill, they pick up velocity, and potential energy is converted to kinetic energy. Kinetic energy is converted back to potential energy as the cars climb up the next hill. The sum of an object's kinetic energy and its potential energy of position is its **mechanical energy.** Not counting friction, the mechanical energy of the roller coaster remains the same as the coaster travels along its track.

No energy conversion is 100 percent efficient. Some thermal energy is generated every time that energy changes form. Power stations convert about 35 percent of their fuel into electrical energy. A typical car engine converts only about 15 percent of the chemical potential energy in gasoline into the car's kinetic energy. The human body loses more than 95 percent of its food energy as waste heat!

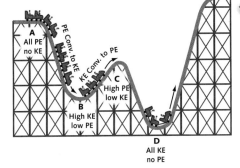

Figure 16.8 Energy is converted between potential and kinetic forms as a roller coaster travels down its track. Ignoring friction, the total mechanical energy remains the same throughout the ride.

Learning Goals

- Describe the relationship between mechanical energy, kinetic energy, and potential energy.
- Explain how the law of conservation of energy applies to energy conversions.
- Trace the path of energy through a number of conversions.

New Vocabulary

mechanical energy
law of conservation of energy

Figure It Out

1. Describe where the roller coaster has the most kinetic energy.

2. In terms of kinetic and potential energy, explain what will happen when the coaster travels up the tallest hill.

ENGAGE Ask students if they know what the word *convert* means. One definition, which they will learn about in this lesson, refers to changing from one form or function to another. Have students preview this lesson's subheadings with a partner.

Before You Read

Draw three boxes on the board and tell students that they should do the same in their Science Notebooks. Have students read the first paragraph of this page to learn about a few examples of energy conversions. Ask a volunteer to provide one example, and record this in a box on the board. Tell students that they should do the same in their Science Notebooks as they read the lesson.

● Teach

EXPLAIN to students that they will learn about kinetic and potential energy conversions.

 Vocabulary

mechanical energy Tell students that the word *mechanical* means "having to do with machines or mechanics." Ask for examples or definitions of machines and mechanics. If necessary, tell students that a mechanic is a skilled worker who repairs or constructs machinery.

Figure It Out: **Figure 16.8**

ANSWER **1.** The roller coaster has the most kinetic energy at Point D, just as it reaches the bottom of the hill. **2.** The coaster will not make it to the top of the tallest hill. At a height slightly greater than Point A, the coaster will have no more kinetic energy and will come to a stop. Next, the car will roll back toward Point D.

ELL Strategy

Read Aloud and Discuss In small groups, have students read aloud and discuss the lesson either in their native language or in English.

Teach

EXPLAIN to students that on this page they will learn about an important physics concept: the law of conservation of energy. Ask what they already know about Albert Einstein. Tell them that they will also learn about Einstein and his contribution to science.

Explain It!

Provide print resources or internet sites about energy conversions for students to use during this assignment.

(ANSWER) Answers will vary according to the topics chosen.

As You Read

Ask for an example of a chemical energy conversion and record it in a box on the board. Ask students to look for two additional examples. Make sure that students are giving a brief explanation with each example.

(ANSWER) Examples of chemical energy conversions include the stomach digesting food, muscles converting chemical energy to kinetic energy, and electric eels converting chemical energy to electricity.

 ### Vocabulary

law of conservation of energy Ask students to define the word *law* ("one in a collection of rules that people live by"). Tell students that *conservation* comes from the Latin word *conservare,* meaning "to save." Ask them to think about what the full term means.

 ### Explain It!

Many processes require that energy go through several transformations. Choose a finished product and trace the energy conversions that made the product possible. Describe all of the energy changes, including energy lost as heat. Some ideas include:

- how a bee makes honey
- how a lightbulb works

As You Read

Add examples of each type of energy conversion in the lesson to the chart in your Science Notebook. Share your chart with a partner. Add or correct information as necessary. Then describe two examples of chemical energy conversions to another form of energy.

Conversions Among Energy Forms

Each of the forms of energy can be converted into the others. An energy conversion takes place almost every time something happens.

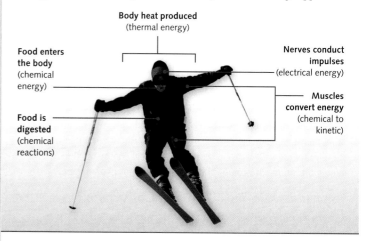

Figure 16.9 Many energy transformations occur within the human body.

The human body provides many examples of energy conversions. First, the body takes in chemical potential energy in the form of food. The food is converted into other chemicals in the digestive system. Sugars provide chemical energy for bodily functions, and fats store potential energy for later use. Second, the heart and other muscles convert chemical energy to kinetic energy as blood circulates and the body moves. Third, some of the body's energy is converted to sound. Sounds are vibrations in the air that carry kinetic energy. Fourth, the body releases thermal energy in the form of heat, or infrared (IN fruh red) energy. Finally, nerves use electrical energy to communicate within the body.

 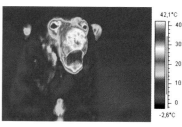

Figure 16.10 Animals produce heat as they convert chemical potential energy into other forms. Some heat produced by this polar bear is radiated out as infrared energy.

Background Information

The number of Calories burned by running at a rate of 14 kilometers per hour for 30 minutes depends on a person's mass. A 57-kilogram (125-pound) person burns approximately 398 Calories, a 68-kilogram (150-pound) person burns 477 Calories, and a 91-kilogram (200-pound) person burns 636 Calories, for example.

Conservation of Energy

People often speak about energy as if it were used up or lost during an activity. In fact, the energy still exists, but in a form that is not useful to people. The **law of conservation of energy** states that energy can be changed in form, but not created or destroyed.

It can take some detective work to follow the path of the energy as it changes forms. For example, it takes a lot of energy to run a race. After the race, the runner's body has less energy than it had before. The energy used to power muscles has been converted into heat. However, the total amount of energy in the universe is just the same after the race as it was before. No energy is ever truly destroyed.

Figure 16.11 After a race, a person's body has less energy than it had before.

PEOPLE IN SCIENCE Albert Einstein (1879–1955)

Most people connect the name Einstein with high intelligence. Albert Einstein was a Jewish scientist born in Germany in 1879. Einstein struggled in school as a teen. However, he went on to develop theories that solved several important problems in physics.

Einstein is best known for his mass-energy equation. According to Einstein, energy has mass, and mass is a form of energy. Mass and energy are related in a special way: energy equals mass times the speed of light squared. Einstein described this relationship in a famous equation:

$$E = mc^2$$

Lifting an object increases its potential energy. According to this equation, that means its mass has increased, too. However, the change in mass is so tiny that it normally goes unnoticed. For example, a person who walks up a 15-m hill gains about 10^{-9} g, or one billionth of a gram. Nuclear weapons provide a more obvious example of the energy released by the conversion of matter. A tremendous amount of energy can be released from the conversion of a small amount of mass.

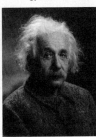

In 1933, Adolf Hitler took power in Germany and fired all Jewish university professors. Einstein chose to spend the rest of his career working in the United States. At first, he urged the U.S. government to develop nuclear weapons before Hitler could. Then, Einstein was shocked by the effects of the atomic bombs dropped on Japanese cities. He regretted that his work had helped lead to the development of nuclear weapons. Einstein worked for peace until his death in 1955.

● Teach

EXPLAIN to students that they will learn about energy conversions in humans and animals. Ask if they can think of any examples before reading the page.

PEOPLE IN SCIENCE

People have wondered whether Einstein's brain was different from the "average" person's brain. Several studies have been conducted to answer the question. In 1999, for example, Sandra F. Witelson and her colleagues inspected samples of Einstein's preserved brain tissue and discovered that it lacked a particular small wrinkle called the parietal operculum. Likely as a result of this lacking feature, Einstein's brain was 15 percent wider than the average brain. The area of additional width is connected with visual imagery and mathematical thinking, so Witelson speculated that Einstein was better able to think in these ways. Because this research was done on Einstein's brain only and did not include other brains in a comparison group, however, the findings are not conclusive.

EXTEND Using the Internet or library resources, have students research Einstein's childhood and teen years.

Differentiate Instruction

Mathematical/Logical Give students several problems to solve using Einstein's equation, $E = mc^2$. If students are interested, they may also research more of Einstein's physics theories.

● Teach

EXPLAIN to students that they will learn about how machines convert energy.

Figure It Out: Figure 16.12

[ANSWER] **1.** In Step D, the cannonball's gravitational potential energy is converted to kinetic energy as it falls. The golf ball (I) is also released from the ice tongs to fall onto the tee. **2.** In each step, some energy will be lost as heat. Energy could be lost as friction between the tee and the gun, as friction between the cannonball and the board, from inefficient use of energy by the groundhog, etc.

Use the Visual: Figure 16.13

[ANSWER] The scene violates the law of conservation of energy. It appears that energy is being created out of nothing to lift the water back up above the waterfall.

● Assess

Use the After You Read questions and the Alternative Assessment to help you evaluate students' understanding of the lesson.

After You Read

1. The law of conservation of energy states that energy cannot be created or destroyed.

2. At every step, some of the energy put into a machine is converted into waste heat.

3. Plants convert radiant energy from the Sun into the chemical energy of sugars during photosynthesis.

Alternative Assessment

Have each student write a paragraph describing energy conversion based on the information that he or she wrote in the three-box graphic organizer.

Machines as Energy Converters

Chapter 15 described machines as devices that make work easier to do. A machine can also modify energy and transmit it in a new form. Radios, for example, take electrical energy and convert it into sound waves. Winding a toy transforms kinetic energy into the elastic potential energy of a spring. Potential energy is converted back to kinetic energy as the toy moves.

Figure It Out

1. Name a step where gravitational potential energy is converted to kinetic energy.

2. Describe how energy could be lost as heat as the machine operates.

Figure 16.12 Rube Goldberg, an American cartoonist best known for his drawings of complicated machines meant to do simple jobs, designed this machine to tee up a golf ball without bending over.

No machine is perfectly efficient. Some energy is lost as heat every time a machine makes an energy conversion. For this reason, no machine can run forever without occasional additions of energy.

Inventors have been trying to develop a perpetual motion machine for over 1,300 years. A perpetual motion machine is a device that puts out more energy than it takes in. M. C. Escher's "Waterfall" shows this type of machine. Unfortunately, such machines violate the law of conservation of energy. No successful perpetual motion machine has ever been built. The attempts have either failed to work or actually relied on sources of energy hidden from viewers.

Figure 16.13 M. C. Escher designed the lithograph "Waterfall" in 1961. What principle of physics is violated in this scene?

After You Read

1. What is wrong with saying that energy is "used up" by a machine?

2. Explain why no mechanical system is 100 percent efficient.

3. Using the information you recorded in your Science Notebook, describe an example of the conversion of radiant energy into chemical energy.

Differentiate Instruction

Visual Share more examples of Rube Goldberg's cartoons with students. In small groups, ask students to create their own cartoons that show complicated machines designed to do simple jobs. Students should draw the cartoons on poster board and share them with the class. You may wish to refer back to any examples you described or created in Chapter 15 when discussing simple machines.

16.3 Energy Resources

Before You Read

Every action affects its surroundings. In your Science Notebook, describe an action you took that had both positive and negative effects on your surroundings. Preview the lesson and write the lesson headings in your Science Notebook. Leave a few lines blank after each heading to record the effects of using each energy resource.

Energy resources are energy sources that are used to meet the needs of human society. Early humans warmed themselves in the sunlight and ate plants and animals to meet their chemical energy needs. Perhaps 500,000 years ago, they learned to control fire. More recently, humans harnessed, or learned how to control and use, the energy of wind and running water to grind grain. In the last century, people turned to fossil fuels and electricity for energy. Today, there are many energy resources to choose from. Each resource offers advantages, but also comes with costs and limitations.

Making Electricity

Electricity is a convenient form of energy. It is easy to transport electricity and to convert it into many other forms of energy. Electricity is typically generated in a power plant, such as the one illustrated in **Figure 16.14.** The potential or kinetic energy of a resource is converted into electricity in several steps. At each step, some energy is lost as thermal energy. Power plants typically convert about 35 percent of a fuel's energy into electricity.

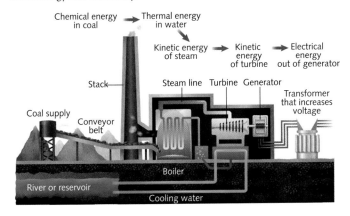

Figure 16.14 Most electricity is generated in power plants. Water, steam, or wind turns the blades of a turbine. The turbine rotates a shaft in the generator to produce electricity. The power plant in this diagram uses coal as a fuel. The energy to turn the turbine could also come from biomass, natural gas, flowing water, nuclear energy, or geothermal heat.

CHAPTER 16 **271**

Learning Goals

- Explain the importance of energy resources.
- Describe the source of each energy resource.
- Compare the characteristics of each energy resource.
- Contrast renewable and nonrenewable resources.

New Vocabulary

energy resource
renewable resource
solar energy
hydroelectric power
biomass fuel
fossil fuel
nonrenewable resource
fusion
fission
geothermal power

16.3 Introduce

ENGAGE Ask students to think about their school. How is it warmed or cooled? How are the lights kept on? How are the computers kept working? Have students brainstorm a list of all the possible energy sources used at the school. Record students' ideas on the board.

Before You Read

Explain to students what positive and negative effects are. They might be more familiar with the terms *pros* and *cons*. Give them an example from your own experience. Ask students to talk in small groups about examples of positive and negative effects in their own lives.

● Teach

EXPLAIN to students that in this lesson, they will learn about the various types of energy resources used around the world.

💿 Vocabulary

energy resource Explain to students that a resource is someone or something that provides a source of help or support when needed. Ask for examples of resources.

E L L Strategy

Use a Concept Map Have each student draw a concept map in his or her Science Notebook with *Energy Resources* in the center. As they read the lesson, instruct students to add the resources they learn about to their maps. Their concept maps should include examples, source of each form, and potential or actual uses of each energy resource.

Teach

EXPLAIN to students that they will learn about three energy resources generated from the Sun: solar, wind, and hydroelectric power.

Figure It Out: Figure 16.15

ANSWER **1.** petroleum **2.** Chemical potential energy is contained in petroleum, natural gas, and coal. Biomass also contains chemical potential energy (included in the "other" category in the pie chart).

As You Read

On the board, write the headings *Positive Effects* and *Negative Effects,* leaving space underneath each category. Ask a student volunteer to supply one energy resource and its positive and negative effects. Record the information on the board. Instruct students to do the same with other energy resources and record the information in their Science Notebooks.

ANSWER Hydroelectric power disrupts fish breeding cycles and floods areas upstream from the dam.

Figure It Out

1. Which resource is used the most in the United States?
2. Which resources contain chemical potential energy?

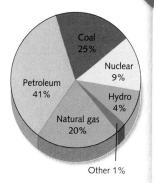

Figure 16.15 Alternative energy sources produce about 14 percent of the energy used in the U.S.

As You Read

In the space provided under the headings you wrote in your Science Notebook, list positive and negative effects of using each energy resource.

What are some negative effects of using hydroelectric power?

Energy Resources from the Sun

The Sun is the source of nearly all of the energy on Earth. Sunlight warms the air and Earth's surface. The Sun causes the wind to blow, rain to fall, and plants to grow. All of these effects can be harnessed to provide energy for human tasks. The Sun's energy is a **renewable resource** because it cannot be used up by humans.

Solar Power Energy that comes directly from the Sun is **solar energy.** Solar energy can be used to warm houses and provide hot water. It can also be collected in solar cells to produce electricity. Solar energy is free, but solar cells are expensive and inefficient. An investment in solar power can take many years to pay for itself in energy savings. This payoff time will likely decrease as energy prices rise and solar technology improves. Solar power is very useful in remote locations. For example, space satellites and wireless internet stations can be powered by solar energy.

Wind Power Wind can be collected by large turbines, or windmills, that generate electricity. No power plant is necessary, and no pollution is produced. Wind turbines are effective only in cleared areas where the wind is fairly constant. However, advances in technology are improving the price and efficiency of wind power every year.

Hydroelectric Power The energy of flowing water can be harnessed to produce **hydroelectric power.** Water passing through holes in a dam spins turbines, which generate electricity. Hydroelectric power is very efficient and creates no pollution. However, water power is limited by the number of rivers present. Dams also disrupt fish breeding cycles and flood the land behind the dam.

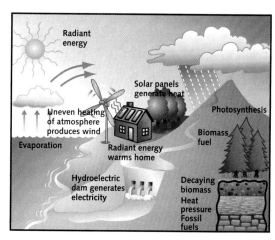

Figure 16.16 Most energy resources are produced by the Sun's energy.

Background Information

Solar power supplies less than one percent of United States' power needs. A major reason for this small percentage is that harnessing solar power is very expensive, even though costs have fallen about 90 percent since the 1970s. To be cheaper than power from fossil fuels, the price will have to be cut in half again. In the past several years, at least 38 states have passed laws that require utility companies to integrate residential solar panels into the power grid and to compensate owners for their energy output. Twenty-four states give rebates to people who purchase solar panels.

Biomass Plants convert the Sun's energy into sugar through photosynthesis. Humans harvest plants for food, building materials, and fuel. Plant tissues used for fuel are called **biomass fuels.** Biomass can be burned to heat homes, converted into fuels such as soy biodiesel, or used to generate electricity. Biomass fuels are inexpensive, but they can create pollution when they are burned. Biomass is also the origin of fossil fuels.

Fossil Fuels The biomass of dead organisms may be buried and preserved. Over millions of years, it is converted to carbon compounds that burn easily. Energy sources made from ancient biomass remains are called **fossil fuels.** For example, petroleum develops from sea creatures.

Fossil fuels are very useful sources of energy. Coal and natural gas are used to generate most of the electricity used in the United States. Petroleum is converted to gasoline in refineries. In fact, 86 percent of the energy used in the U.S. comes from burning fossil fuels. However, the use of fossil fuels produces much of the air and water pollution on Earth. Also, because fossil fuels take so long to develop, humans are using them faster than they are forming. Resources like fossil fuels that can be used up are called **nonrenewable resources.** If current trends in energy usage continue, fossil fuels will become scarce in the next century.

Figure 16.17 The fossil fuel petroleum is a thick, gooey black liquid used to make gasoline.

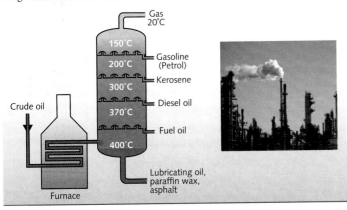

Figure 16.18 Crude oil is petroleum out of the ground. Crude oil is a mixture of chemical substances that are separated in a refinery. Refineries produce gasoline, asphalt, and other substances by heating petroleum to different temperatures.

Energy from Atoms

The protons and neutrons in an atom's nucleus are held together by extremely strong forces. An immense amount of energy is released when two atoms fuse together or when an atom breaks apart. Nuclear energy (energy from the nuclei of atoms) is produced in the Sun when small atoms join in **fusion** reactions. Inside Earth, heavy elements such as uranium spontaneously break into lighter elements in **fission** reactions.

Did You Know?

About ten percent of petroleum is used for products other than fuel. Plastic, rubber, glue, wax, and petroleum jelly are all typically made from petroleum.

CHAPTER 16 **273**

● Teach

EXPLAIN to students that they will learn about two more energy resources related to the Sun: biomass fuels and fossil fuels.

 Vocabulary

renewable resource Ask students to define the prefix *re-* ("again") and the suffix *-able* ("must" or "may be"). Then ask students to put the word parts together and come up with a definition for *renewable*.

solar energy Tell students that the word *solar* comes from the Latin word *sol*, meaning "sun."

hydroelectric power Tell students that *hydro-* refers to water. Ask what *hydroelectric* means.

biomass fuel Tell students that the word *biomass* refers to the total mass of living organisms in an area at a particular time. Ask for an example of a fuel, and then tell students that it refers to a material that releases energy when burned.

fossil fuel Tell students that a fossil is the petrified remains, impression, or cast of an animal or plant that is preserved within a rock. Ask students what they already know about fossils.

nonrenewable resource Tell students that the prefix *non-* means "not." Ask them to define the word *nonrenewable*.

fusion Tell students that the word *fusion* means "to join together."

fission Tell students that the word *fission* comes from the Latin word *fissio*, meaning "splitting." Tell them that *fission* and *fusion* are antonyms (opposites).

Background Information

Clusters of wind machines called wind farms are used to produce electricity. U.S. wind machines generate enough electricity to power 1.6 million homes, about 0.4 percent of the country's need. Some drawbacks of wind farms are that wild birds are sometimes killed by the machines, the natural look of the landscape is affected, and a substantial amount of noise can be produced.

Teacher Alert

Make sure that students understand that these energy resources are derived from the Sun. Solar power results from nuclear reactions in the Sun. Wind is produced when the Sun heats the atmosphere unevenly. Hydroelectric power depends on the water cycle, which results when heat from the Sun is absorbed or released by water. Biomass fuels and fossil fuels contain chemical energy stored as a result of photosynthesis.

EXPLAIN to students that they will learn about two more types of energy: energy from atoms and energy from Earth.

💿 **Vocabulary**

geothermal power Explain to students that *geo-* signifies "Earth." Have them figure out what the term *geothermal power* means.

● **Assess**

Use the After You Read questions and the Alternative Assessment to help you evaluate students' understanding of the lesson.

After You Read

1. Much of the energy in fuel is lost as heat during the generation of electricity.

2. Fossil fuels are nonrenewable. People are burning them at a rate that will make them scarce in the next century. Renewable energy sources will last forever.

3. biomass and fossil fuels: petroleum, coal, and natural gas

4. Wind is free and does not cause pollution. On the other hand, wind can be used to generate electricity only where the land is clear and the wind is strong and constant. Fossil fuels must be extracted from the ground, and they cause pollution when burned. However, fossil fuels are easily transported wherever they are needed and can be burned at any time.

Alternative Assessment

Have each student choose one type of energy described in this lesson and write a persuasive paragraph explaining why he or she agrees or disagrees with its use.

Figure 16.19 Uranium ore (*top*) is processed to make fuel for nuclear power plants. The nuclear core (*middle*) is the part of a nuclear power plant (*bottom*) that produces energy.

Humans have learned to control fission reactions and use them to power electrical generators. Nuclear fuel is a nonrenewable resource. However, there is enough of it on Earth to last for thousands of years. No pollution is released into the air from a nuclear reactor, but used nuclear products can produce dangerous radiation for thousands of years. People worry that something will go wrong and a nuclear reactor will release radiation into the atmosphere. Fusion reactions take place at such high temperatures that scientists have not yet learned to control them.

Energy from Earth

In its early stages, Earth was a violent place. Falling meteors transferred kinetic energy to the planet's surface. Fission inside Earth released radiation. The new planet's gravity squeezed it smaller. All of these factors increased the temperature inside Earth. Rocks trap the heat below Earth's crust. For the last few billion years, this heat has slowly seeped to the surface in the form of volcanoes, geysers (GI zurz), and hot springs.

Electricity generated using Earth's heat is **geothermal power.** A geothermal power plant is located where hot rocks lie just below Earth's surface. The hot rocks turn water into steam, and the steam powers a generator. Geothermal energy is not renewable, but there is a practically limitless supply within Earth. No pollution is produced by geothermal power plants, and the electricity they make is inexpensive. The major limit on geothermal power is the number of locations where hot rocks are close to the surface.

After You Read

1. Why is electricity an inefficient use of energy resources?

2. Explain why it is important to develop renewable sources of energy.

3. Name the energy resources that are formed from living organisms.

4. Review the notes in your Science Notebook. Compare your notes with those of a partner. Make any necessary additions or corrections. Then compare the effects of using wind power and the effects of using fossil fuels. Write your comparison as a well-developed paragraph in your Science Notebook.

Differentiate Instruction

Kinesthetic Have students design simple machines that generate wind. Provide them with such materials as straws, foil, paper clips, and toy construction materials.

Field Study

Bring students on a walking tour of the school's areas where energy is produced. These might include the heating, ventilation, and air-conditioning (HVAC) room and the electrical room.

16.4 Energy Choices

Before You Read

Relating the content of a science lesson to your own life can make the material easier to understand. Make three boxes in your Science Notebook, and leave enough space in each to write two to three sentences. Look through the lesson for ideas that are relevant to your own life.

Daily life in the United States has changed a great deal in the last century. People now drive to work and school, take hot showers, and turn on electric lights in every room. People buy plastic items made and shipped from across the world. Inexpensive energy has allowed for all of these advances. As the world's population increases in size and wealth, more and more energy is needed to support it.

Fossil Fuel Problems

Fossil fuels provided most of the world's energy in the twentieth century. Fossil fuels powered our factories and changed our lifestyles. Cars, electric lighting, and plastic were all made possible by fossil fuels. However, the use of fossil fuels has led to a number of problems.

First, fossil fuels are nonrenewable resources. The supply of fossil fuels in the world is shrinking. The remaining fossil fuels are becoming harder to find and more expensive to extract. Second, the burning of fossil fuels causes pollution. Pollution harms the environment and contributes to global climate change. Scientists now think that many thousands of people die each year from breathing pollution caused by burning fossil fuels. Finally, fossil fuels must be extracted from the ground. The mining, drilling, and transportation of fossil fuels are processes that damage the natural world. They also put coal miners at risk. Each year, mining accidents kill thousands of coal miners around the world.

Figure 16.20 Fossil fuel extraction can cause environmental damage. For example, oil spills kill wildlife and ruin beaches (left). Roads and pipelines have to be built in order to drill for oil. People must balance the need for more petroleum with the risk of damaging a beautiful place like the Arctic National Wildlife Refuge (right).

Learning Goals

- Explain why energy conservation and alternative energy sources will be necessary in the future.
- Compare and contrast the costs and benefits of different energy resources.
- Describe actions that conserve energy.

New Vocabulary

energy conservation

 CONNECTION: Economics

Would you pay more for your favorite collectibles if they were hard to find? Economists predict that you would. Economists study the connections among people's buying behavior, price, and the amount of goods available. Economists predict that the prices for fuel and electricity will rise as fossil fuels become scarce.

16.4 Introduce

ENGAGE Ask students to think about living without cars or electricity. Have students discuss what a 24-hour period in their lives would be like under such circumstances. Help students to recognize how much they rely on energy resources. Explain that the human population will need to rely more heavily on alternative forms of energy in the future and find ways to cut down on energy use.

Before You Read

Tell students that they should continue thinking about the ways in which energy affects their lives as they read this lesson. After drawing three boxes on the board, demonstrate previewing the lesson to look for ideas that relate to your own life. Tell students that they should do the same.

Teach

EXPLAIN to students that they will learn about problems associated with the use of fossil fuels.

 CONNECTION: Economics

In small groups, have students think about items that were popular among high school students during the past year or two. Ask them to think about what happened when the items became unavailable or more difficult to obtain.

Differentiate Instruction

Mathematical/Logical Using print resources or the Internet, have students research world energy use for the period from 2000 to the present. Challenge students to identify any trends in the data they obtain.

Key Concept Review
Workbook, p. 99

Teach

EXPLAIN to students that they will learn about alternative sources of energy.

As You Read

Ask students to take a few minutes to record the ways in which the lesson relates to their lives. Tell them to think about their homes. Make a connection to your own life and write the information in one of the boxes on the board. Ask students to think about their homes and make a connection to fossil fuels, biomass fuels, or solar energy. They should record the information in their Science Notebooks.

(ANSWER) Answers will vary according to the use of energy in students' homes. Homes may burn natural gas, fuel oil (fossil fuel), or wood for heat and hot water. Solar energy may be used to warm houses through windows, to heat water, or to generate electricity in solar panels. If students' homes use electricity only, talk about how electricity is generated in your area.

Science Notebook EXTRA

Have students choose two energy sources found in the chart in **Figure 16.21** to compare and contrast. Which is less expensive? Better? Safer? More plentiful? Students should write their answers in their Science Notebooks.

As You Read

Think about how you use energy in your life. In the boxes you drew in your Science Notebook, describe how your actions relate to the content of the lesson. How does your home use fossil fuels, biomass, and solar energy?

Energy Alternatives

Fossil fuels alone cannot support the energy needs of the world for long. At the same time, there is no single alternative energy resource that can take the place of fossil fuels. Every energy resource has costs and benefits. **Figure 16.21** summarizes the features of each energy resource. People will use a combination of different resources to meet energy needs in the next century and beyond.

Conservation Options

One way to reduce energy costs is to find clean, renewable energy sources. People can also practice **energy conservation,** or reduce the energy they use to perform work. Conserving energy prevents pollution, preserves energy resources for future use, and saves consumers money.

Advantages and Disadvantages of Energy Resources

Energy Resource	Benefits and Advantages	Costs and Limitations
Fossil Fuels: Petroleum, Coal, and Natural Gas	• easily transported • inexpensive while supply lasts • available for use at all times	• nonrenewable • price of fuel is unpredictable • release CO_2 and pollutants into the air • extraction and transportation result in health problems and environmental damage
Wind Power	• renewable • doesn't create pollution • free supply	• efficient only in locations with open land and steady winds • may kill migrating birds
Solar Power	• renewable • doesn't create pollution • free supply	• solar cells are expensive • generates electricity only on sunny days
Hydroelectric Power	• renewable • doesn't create pollution • efficient source of power	• limited number of streams to dam • disrupts fish breeding cycles • requires flooding of land behind the dam
Biomass Fuels	• renewable • free if trash or agricultural waste is used • easily used in vehicles • easily transported	• release CO_2 and pollutants into the air • corn and other grains require fertilizer and other petroleum products
Geothermal Power	• enough supply to last thousands of years • doesn't create pollution • free supply	• limited to areas with hot rock just below the surface
Nuclear Power	• enough supply to last thousands of years • doesn't create air pollution • inexpensive after power plant is built	• creates hazardous radioactive wastes • slight risk of radiation leak

Figure 16.21 Each energy resource has advantages and disadvantages.

E L L Strategy

Use Visual Information Ask students to work with a partner and use the chart in Figure 16.21 to draw some conclusions about the features of the listed energy resources. Students should record their findings and share them with the class.

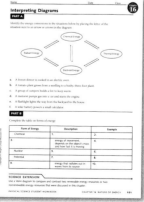

Interpreting Diagrams
Workbook, p. 101

Figure 16.22 shows some ways to reduce energy use. You can also use the "three Rs" to conserve energy: reduce, reuse, and recycle.

Reduce Buy only what you need. The average American throws away 500 kg of trash each year. Purchasing goods in larger units reduces packaging waste and the energy needed to produce it.

Reuse Buy products that can be used repeatedly. Using an item more than once saves the energy needed to make it. A canvas shopping bag can replace hundreds of plastic bags.

Recycle Make an effort to recycle all of the materials you can. Recycled materials reduce the energy needed in manufacturing. For example, recycling aluminum cans requires only five percent of the energy needed to make aluminum from bauxite ore.

Home Conservation Tips

Area of Energy Use	How Energy is Lost	Ways to Conserve Energy
Heating and Cooling	Heat escapes outside and hot outside air comes in	• improve house insulation • open windows on cool evenings • use south-facing windows to provide solar heating in winter • circulate water underground to use geothermal heating and cooling
Lighting	Incandescent lightbulbs lose most of their energy as heat	• use efficient fluorescent lightbulbs and LEDs (light-emitting diodes) • turn off lights when not in use
Appliances	Energy is lost as heat	• purchase energy-efficient models with good insulation • keep freezers full • use rooftop solar water heater

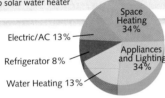

Figure 16.22 Homes consume a lot of energy. There are many steps consumers can take to reduce their energy use and save money.

Electric/AC 13%
Refrigerator 8%
Water Heating 13%
Space Heating 34%
Appliances and Lighting 34%

After You Read

1. Explain why the world's energy use continues to increase.
2. According to Figure 16.21, which energy resource creates dangerous wastes but no air pollution?
3. Using the information recorded in your Science Notebook, write five steps you could take to conserve energy. Create a chart to present your answers.

Figure It Out

1. Describe the household functions that use the most energy.
2. What is the total percentage of energy use that goes to providing space heating and air-conditioning (AC)?

Extend It!

Research the energy that could be saved by a simple change in your behavior. Report on your findings, and include answers to the following questions: How much effort is needed to make the change? How much energy is saved per year? What would happen if every person in your community took the same action?

Background Information

In addition to reducing, reusing, and recycling, people can also practice composting in their backyards. Less space is needed in landfills when home and yard waste is put to local use instead of being thrown away. Composting is the decomposition of organic matter (that with plant and animal origins). The proper mix of carbon, nitrogen, oxygen, and water is needed to allow the organisms that decompose to thrive and create the rich soil that enhances plant growth.

Teach

EXPLAIN to students that they will learn about ways to conserve energy.

 Vocabulary

energy conservation Ask students to recall the meanings of both words and come up with the meaning of the term.

Figure It Out: Figure 16.22

ANSWER **1.** space heating, appliances, and lighting **2.** 47 percent

Extend It!

Make print and internet resources available to give students ideas for possible changes. After students have settled on an energy conservation measure, they should put it into action. Local utilities and online calculators can help students determine their energy and money savings. Energy savings presentations can show the rest of the class that conservation can be accomplished by anyone.

Assess

Use the After You Read questions and the Alternative Assessment to help you evaluate students' understanding of the lesson.

After You Read

1. The energy needs of the world are increasing because the world's population is growing and its people expect a higher standard of living.
2. nuclear power
3. Answers will vary. If students have difficulty answering the question, suggest that they use reference books and Web sites that give lists of ideas.

Alternative Assessment

Ask students to think about ways that they can conserve energy in their everyday lives. After students share their ideas with the class, they should write about the topic in their Science Notebooks.

Chapter 16 Summary

VOCABULARY REVIEW

Check students' sentences or paragraphs to make sure they understand the meaning of each vocabulary term.

Evaluate students' essays using the following criteria:

1. The topic sentence, or main idea, should restate the Key Concept.

2. The supporting paragraphs should incorporate the answers to the Learning Goal questions students have written and include details, facts, and examples they have recorded in their Science Notebooks.

3. The concluding sentence should sum up the main idea of the chapter and restate the Key Concept.

MASTERING CONCEPTS

True or False

1. False, Energy conservation
2. True
3. False, Mechanical energy
4. False, mass and velocity
5. True
6. True

Short Answer

7. Chemical energy in muscles is converted into other forms, such as kinetic energy.

8. Kinetic energy is related to the square of an object's velocity. This energy is transferred to the vehicle's occupants.

9. Each of these energy resources has its limitations. Solar energy cells are expensive, inefficient, and useful only in sunny locations. Wind turbines can be located only in clear areas with strong, steady wind. Hydroelectric power depends on fast-moving water and disrupts the area's ecosystems.

10. Possible examples of energy conversions in a car include: chemical energy in fuel burned to make thermal energy, thermal energy changed to kinetic energy in pistons, and chemical energy in battery changed to electrical energy, which is converted to sound in radio.

11. Thermal energy is associated with the motion of the atoms and molecules that make up a substance.

KEY CONCEPTS

16.1 What Is Energy?

- Energy is the ability to do work or make things happen.
- Energy of movement is kinetic energy, and stored energy is potential energy.
- The equation for calculating kinetic energy is $KE = \frac{1}{2}mv^2$.
- Gravitational potential energy can be calculated using the equation $GPE = mgh$.
- Potential and kinetic energy can exist in many forms, including thermal, chemical, electrical, radiant, and nuclear.

16.2 Energy Conversions

- Energy can be converted from one form to another, but it cannot be created or destroyed.
- In any conversion, some useful energy is lost as heat.

16.3 Energy Resources

- Energy resources are energy sources that are used to meet the demands of human society.
- The Sun is the origin of most energy resources, including solar energy, hydroelectric power, wind, biomass fuel, and fossil fuels.
- Atomic energy comes from the nuclei of atoms, and geothermal energy comes from deep inside Earth.
- Renewable energy resources will last forever, but nonrenewable resources can be used up.

16.4 Energy Choices

- Fossil fuels alone cannot meet human needs.
- Every energy resource has advantages and limitations.
- Energy conservation can reduce energy needs and save money.

278 NATURE OF ENERGY

VOCABULARY REVIEW

16.1
energy, p. 262
joule, p. 262
kinetic energy, p. 263
potential energy, p. 264
thermal energy, p. 265
chemical energy, p. 265
electrical energy, p. 265
radiant energy, p. 266
nuclear energy, p. 266

16.2
mechanical energy, p. 267
law of conservation of energy, p. 269

16.3
energy resource, p. 271
renewable resource, p. 272
solar energy, p. 272
hydroelectric power, p. 272
biomass fuel, p. 273
fossil fuel, p. 273
nonrenewable resource, p. 273
fusion, p. 273
fission, p. 273
geothermal power, p. 274

16.4
energy conservation, p. 276

PREPARE FOR CHAPTER TEST

To prepare for the chapter test, create a question from each Learning Goal. Use the information in your Science Notebook to answer each question. Then use these answers to write a well-developed essay about the chapter. Use the Key Concept on the first page of this chapter as your topic sentence.

Vocabulary Review
Workbook, p. 100

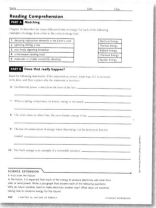

Reading Comprehension
Workbook, p. 102

True or False

If the statement is true, write "true." If it is false, change the underlined word or words to make the statement true.

1. The law of conservation of energy means reducing the energy used to perform work.

2. Solar power, biomass, and wind energy are all renewable resources.

3. Chemical energy is the sum of the kinetic energy and potential energy of position in a system.

4. Kinetic energy depends on mass and gravity.

5. Some energy is lost as heat in every energy conversion.

6. The Sun is the source of most of Earth's energy resources.

Short Answer

Answer each of the following in a sentence or brief paragraph.

7. What happens to the energy that you "use up" when you do an activity?

8. Explain why high-speed car crashes are much more destructive than low-speed crashes.

9. Why aren't solar, wind, and hydroelectric power used to generate most of the electricity in the United States?

10. Give five examples of energy conversions that take place in a car.

11. Why is thermal energy considered a form of kinetic energy?

12. Which form of potential energy is represented by each of the following: gasoline, a skateboard at the top of a ramp, a stretched spring, a charged battery?

13. Why can't a machine run forever without the addition of energy?

Critical Thinking

Use what you have learned in this chapter to answer each of the following.

14. Predict Reserves of fossil fuels are shrinking around the world. Predict what will happen in the future if people do not conserve energy or develop renewable sources of energy.

15. Design A Rube Goldberg device is a machine that takes many steps to accomplish a simple task. Design a machine that takes at least five steps to open a refrigerator door. Explain the energy conversions that take place in each step.

16. Evaluate Imagine that a new power plant is needed in your area. Evaluate the resources of your area and recommend an energy resource to be used.

Standardized Test Question

Choose the letter of the response that correctly answers the question.

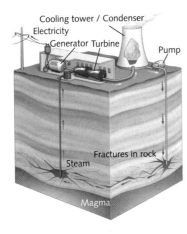

17. The energy used to generate electricity in the power plant below comes from _____.

   A. geothermal heat
   B. wind energy
   C. solar energy
   D. fossil fuels

Test-Taking Tip

For multiple-choice questions, use the process of elimination. First eliminate answers you know are incorrect. Then compare your remaining choices to solve the problem or make an educated guess.

12. gasoline: chemical potential energy; a skateboard at the top of a ramp: gravitational potential energy; a stretched spring: elastic potential energy; a charged battery: electrical potential energy

13. Machines are not 100 percent efficient. Every step creates some waste heat. Therefore, machines require the input of energy to keep functioning.

Critical Thinking

14. Fossil fuels will become scarce and expensive. People will not be able to afford as much energy usage; they will be forced to conserve. Materials made from petroleum, such as plastic and rubber, will also rise in price.

15. Answers will vary. Students could draw diagrams or describe the invention in words.

16. Answers will vary. Students should take into account the wind, water, geothermal, and sunlight resources of the area. The density of the population, pollution level, types of agricultural production, and transportation networks should also influence their recommendations.

Standardized Test Question

17. A

Reading Links

Energy Projects for Young Scientists

The fundamentals of power, work, and energy are illustrated and reinforced in the simple activities presented in this collection.

Robert Gardner and Richard C. Adams. Tandem Library Books. 160 pp. Illustrated. Library ISBN 978-0-613-59469-1.

Renewable Energy

This book explores the modern global energy crisis from a variety of angles, ultimately looking forward to a sustainable future of alternative energy use and offering valuable information about developing technologies and practices.

Nigel Saunders and Steven Chapman. Raintree (Steck-Vaughn). 48 pp. Illustrated. Trade ISBN 978-1-4109-1701-0.

Curriculum Connection
Workbook, p. 103

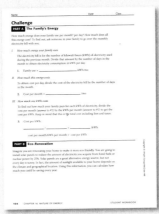

Science Challenge
Workbook, pp. 104–105

16A Making a Pickle Battery

This prechapter introduction activity is designed to determine what students already know about the conversion of chemical energy into electrical energy by having them experiment and draw conclusions about using a pickle to generate electricity.

Objectives

♦ predict how a pickle can generate electricity

♦ evaluate data from successive trials

♦ compare and contrast the potential of a variety of foods to produce electricity

♦ communicate conclusions

Planning

 15–20 minutes   groups of 3–4 students

Materials (per group)

♦ dill pickle

♦ a variety of fruits or vegetables, such as a lemon or a potato

♦ strip of galvanized sheet metal, 1 cm × 5 cm

♦ strip of copper sheet metal, 1 cm × 5 cm

♦ 2 bell wires with alligator clips

♦ LED lamp with wire leads

♦ paper towel

Advance Preparation

♦ A piezo buzzer or a small incandescent lamp can be used in place of the LED.

♦ Explain to students that the batteries used in many electronic devices use copper and zinc to create an electric current. Suggest that foods can act like the paste that carries electrons inside a battery.

Engagement Guide

♦ Challenge students to think about how they can predict what will happen in the experiment by asking:

  ♦ *Why do you think a battery made from one type of food might produce more electricity than another?* (Students should recognize that foods differ in their ability to conduct electricity.)

  ♦ *Why do you think two different types of metals must be used in a battery?* (Electrons must be exchanged between the two metals. For this to occur, the electrons must be more attracted to one of the metals. Thus, different metals must be used.)

  ♦ *How can the amount of electricity produced by the battery be measured in this activity?* (The brightness of the lamp will depend on the amount of electricity produced.)

♦ Encourage students to predict the kinds of foods that will work best in a battery.

Going Further

Encourage students to create a more powerful electrical current by connecting several food batteries in a series. Have students predict how to connect the batteries to produce the most current.

16B The Effect of Friction

Objectives

♦ observe how friction affects motion

♦ compare and contrast the effects of different surfaces on friction

♦ draw conclusions about the qualities that affect friction

Skill Set

observing, comparing and contrasting, recording and analyzing data, predicting, stating conclusions

Planning

 30–35 minutes   groups of 3–4 students

Materials

Materials for this activity are listed in the Student Laboratory Manual.

Advance Preparation

Choose a toy car that rolls at least one meter across the cotton cloth when it is rolled down the incline made by a three-ring binder. Make as many such sets of materials as there are student groups. Instruct students to carefully tape down the various surfaces so they do not slide or bunch up under the toy car and affect the results.

Answers to Observations: Data Table 1

Students should find that the car rolled the farthest across the bare floor. For the cloth surfaces, the smoother surfaces produced less friction and thus allowed the car to roll for a greater distance.

Answers to Analysis and Conclusions

1. Students should find that the car traveled the greatest distance on a hard floor, less on the polyester cloth, even less on the cotton cloth, and least on the corduroy cloth.

2. Some surfaces produce more friction than others; the greater friction slows the car more quickly and shortens the distance it travels.

3. Students should recognize that the harder and smoother surfaces produce less friction, whereas soft and fuzzy surfaces produce more friction.

Going Further

Bring in a long piece of stiff cardboard and use it as an incline, varying the height with books. Have students conduct trials, rolling the car down the cardboard onto different surfaces. Have students plot their results to determine how the height of the incline affects the distance the car travels on different surfaces.

16C Follow the Bouncing Balls

Objectives

- observe how different surfaces affect the rebound height of a dropped ball
- predict which materials will absorb the most energy
- predict which materials will reflect the most energy
- draw conclusions based on experimental results

Skill Set

observing, recording and analyzing data, classifying, predicting, drawing conclusions

Planning

 45–60 minutes   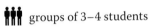 groups of 3–4 students

Materials

Materials for this activity are listed in the Student Laboratory Manual.

Advance Preparation

Provide a set of the materials for each group. Make sure that the balls are new enough to bounce high when dropped. Instruct students to carefully tape down the surface materials so that movement of the surface beneath the ball does not affect their results. Stress the importance of dropping the ball from exactly the same height for each trial.

Answers to Observations: Data Table 1

Students should observe the balls bounce, highest to lowest, on the surfaces as follows: bare floor, paper towel, felt sheet, and cotton towel. The height the balls bounce depends on the type of ball and the type of surface.

Answers to Analysis and Conclusions

1. Students will rank the surfaces based on their own experiences.

2. Students should observe the balls bounce, from highest to lowest, as follows: bare floor, paper towel, felt sheet, and cotton towel.

3. Students should recognize that the greater the energy stored at impact, the higher the bounce. The potential energy is converted back into kinetic energy during the rebound. Harder surfaces produce greater compression in the ball, producing higher bounces. Students should also note that the material the ball is made from affects the height of the bounce.

4. Students should note that the surfaces affected the bounce of both balls, but absorbed more of the energy of the table-tennis ball. This occurred because of the ball's smaller mass. Because most of its energy was absorbed, the table-tennis ball did not compress as much, and therefore did not bounce as high.

Going Further

Have students perform the same experiment after placing the balls in a bowl of ice water to reduce their temperatures. Ask them to predict how the change in temperature will affect the elastic properties of the balls and how high they will bounce. Ask the students to predict which type of ball will be most affected by the change in temperature.

Introduce Chapter 17

As a starting activity, use Lab 17A on page 97 of the Laboratory Manual.

ENGAGE Tell students that they will be learning about thermal energy, and explain that erupting volcanoes illustrate many aspects of this concept. Provide several books on volcanoes for the class to browse through. Ask students to note several interesting facts on index cards and then share the facts with each other.

Think About Heat Flow

ENGAGE Ask students what they know about diagrams. Ask: *What are some examples? What is the definition?* On the board, draw a diagram of the heat flow through all or part of your home. Think aloud as you explain the flow of heat. Ask students to diagram their home's heat flow in their Science Notebooks.

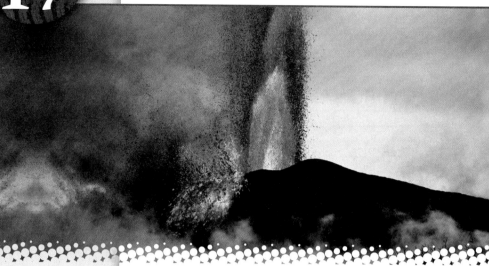

Chapter 17

Thermal Energy and Heat

KEY CONCEPT Thermal energy flows as heat from warmer to cooler objects, causing physical changes such as melting and expansion.

Volcanoes are dramatic examples of the power of thermal energy. Red-hot lava flows down the sides of mountains. Glowing rocks are thrown into the air from deep inside Earth. Hot ash and gases form clouds that travel thousands of kilometers and affect world temperatures.

All of this heat comes from the tremendously hot rock that lies beneath Earth's surface. The hot rock expands and puts pressure on the rocky crust of the planet. Volcanoes erupt where the rocky crust is weak enough to allow lava and hot gases to escape. Thermal energy is the difference between solid rock and flowing lava.

Think About Heat Flow

In your Science Notebook, draw a simple diagram of the way heat flows through your home. Where is the heat created? How does the heat move from place to place inside your home? Does heat escape outside through doors, windows, and walls? Then write one or two sentences in your Science Notebook explaining how diagramming can help you understand a difficult concept.

NSTA
SC/**LINKS**
THE WORLD'S A CLICK AWAY

www.scilinks.org
Heat and Temperature **Code: WGPS17**

280

Chapter 17 Planning Guide			
Instructional Periods	**National Standards**	**Lab Manual**	**Workbook**
17.1 1 Period	A1, B1, B2, G2; A2, B2, B4, B6, G2; UCP1, UCP3	**Lab 17A: p. 97** Thermal Expansion of a Balloon	Key Concept Review p. 106 Vocabulary Review p. 107
17.2 2 Periods	A2, B1, B3, E1; A1, B2, B5, B6, E2; UCP1, UCP4, UCP5	**Lab 17B: pp. 98–100**	Interpreting Diagrams p. 108 Reading Comprehension p. 109
17.3 2 Periods	A1, B3, E1, E2, F1; A1, B5, B6, E1, E2; UCP1, UCP3	Thermal Energy and Temperature	Curriculum Connection p. 110 Science Challenge p. 111
17.4 2 Periods	A1, B3, C3; A2, B6, C6; UCP2, UCP3	**Lab 17C: pp. 101–102** Observing Kinetic Energy	
17.5 2 Periods	A1, B3, E1, E2, F5; A1, B6, E1, E2, F6; UCP1, UCP2		

Middle School Standard; High School Standard; Unifying Concept and Principle

17.1 What Is Thermal Energy?

Before You Read

In your Science Notebook, write the headings in this lesson. Leave several blank lines under each heading. Write what you already know about each subject under its title.

A table, a sandwich, and a sidewalk may appear to be perfectly still. However, the molecules, or particles of matter, that make up all three objects are in constant, random motion. In fact, the molecules of any form of matter are always moving randomly. The energy of these random movements of molecules is called thermal energy. As described in Chapter 16, thermal energy is associated with kinetic energy. Thermal energy can warm a substance, melt it, or do work on it. For example, thermal energy is what lifts a hot-air balloon into the air.

Laws of Thermodynamics

Thermal energy behaves and moves in predictable ways. Scientists have observed thermal energy for centuries and established a number of rules that explain its behavior. The **laws of thermodynamics** describe how thermal energy moves and how it is associated with the movement of matter. **Figure 17.2** summarizes the laws of thermodynamics.

The first law of thermodynamics states that in any process, the total energy of the universe remains constant. Thus the first law of thermodynamics is equivalent to the law of conservation of energy. The other laws of thermodynamics describe the movement of thermal energy and particles of matter.

Solid

Liquid

Gas

Figure 17.1 The thermal energy of molecules is associated with their constant motion. The molecules of solids vibrate in place. The molecules of liquids and gases bounce around inside their containers.

First Law of Thermodynamics (Law of Conservation of Energy)	In any process, the total energy of the universe remains constant.
Second Law of Thermodynamics	Heat flows naturally from hotter to colder objects.
Third Law of Thermodynamics	Molecules would have no thermal energy at the temperature of absolute zero (-273°C).

Figure 17.2 Thermodynamics is the study of how energy flows. The laws of thermodynamics predict the behavior of many processes in the universe.

17.1 Introduce

ENGAGE Place a glass of ice water on your desk. Ask students to predict how the thermal energy of the ice water will change. Challenge them to explain their predictions. Set the glass aside and allow students to observe it again at the end of class. Discuss the changes in terms of the laws of thermodynamics once you review them. Vocabulary terms are listed on the first student page of each lesson. You may wish to preview the terms before introducing each lesson. Strategies for teaching the vocabulary appear on the pages where the terms are introduced.

Before You Read

Have students preview the lesson along with you. Write the lesson's headings on the board, leaving space between each one, as you encounter them in the text. Ask students to do the same in their Science Notebooks. Think aloud about facts that you already know about one or two topics and record them in the appropriate place on the board. Have students do the same in their Science Notebooks.

Teach

EXPLAIN to students that in this lesson, they will learn about temperature, thermal energy, heat, and the relationships of these concepts to one another.

Vocabulary

laws of thermodynamics Ask students what they already know about the laws of thermodynamics from the previous chapter. If necessary, tell them that a law is a set of rules that people live by, *thermo-* is a prefix signifying "heat," and *dynamics* comes from the Greek word *dynamis*, meaning "power."

Background Information

The first law of thermodynamics states that energy can be neither created nor destroyed. However, during an energy conversion, not all of the original energy is converted into a useful form. For example, the heat produced by the lightbulb goes unused, so even though energy is not destroyed, it is considered wasted energy.

Teacher Alert

Although they are related, there is a distinct difference between heat and thermal energy. Thermal energy is the total energy of the particles in a sample. An object can gain or lose thermal energy. Thermal energy that flows from one sample to another is called heat. In other words, heat is the flow of thermal energy.

Teach

EXPLAIN to students that they will learn about heat and temperature on this page.

Vocabulary

heat Tell students that the word *heat* has several definitions. Ask what they already know about heat. Tell students that in this lesson, they will be using heat as a noun, not a verb, and that a synonym is *warmth*.

temperature Explain to students that temperature is the degree of hotness or coldness of an object, body, or medium (such as air or water), as measured by a thermometer.

Celsius temperature scale Tell students that the Celsius temperature scale, also called the Celsius thermometer, is named after its inventor, a Swedish astronomer named Anders Celsius. Tell them that a scale is a measuring device with markings at regular intervals.

Fahrenheit temperature scale Explain to students that the Fahrenheit temperature scale, or thermometer, is named after G. D. Fahrenheit, a German physicist.

absolute zero Tell students that *absolute* means "complete" or "total." Ask what they know about the word *zero*. If necessary, tell them that *zero* means "nothing."

Kelvin temperature scale Tell students that the Kelvin temperature scale is named after Sir William Thomson, a British physicist also known as Lord Kelvin.

As You Read

Think aloud about the scientific explanation of thermal energy and write it on the board. Have students do the same, and then continue with laws of thermodynamics and heat (writing each term as a heading and the explanation beneath).

[ANSWER] Heat flows from warmer to colder objects.

CONNECTION: Language

Have students think of other words or terms that are relative (*happy, sad, pain, dark, bright*) and absolute (*yes, no, on, off*).

As You Read

As you read, fill in the scientific explanation of each lesson topic in your Science Notebook. Compare your notes with a partner. Make adjustments to your list as needed.

According to the laws of thermodynamics, in which direction does heat flow between objects?

CONNECTION: Language

Words used to describe heat and energy can be relative or absolute. Relative terms depend on the viewpoint of the observer. *Warm* and *cold* are relative terms. The same pool of water may feel warm to one person and cold to another. Absolute terms are measured against an unchanging standard. Water molecules at 23°C have the same average kinetic energy no matter who feels them. Scientists use absolute measurements to make their meanings clear to all.

ELL Strategy

Think, Pair, Share Have students write relative and absolute words in their native language. Then, if possible, have them share with a partner who speaks the same language.

Heat

Molecules not only possess thermal energy, they also transmit energy to their surroundings. A person who stands in the sunlight or takes a warm shower can feel the thermal energy coming from the Sun or water. This movement of energy is heat. **Heat** is the flow of thermal energy between objects at different temperatures. The direction of heat flow is from hotter to colder objects. This is the second law of thermodynamics. The hotter object tends to cool as it warms the cooler object. Heating continues until both objects are at the same temperature. Heat can also cause a solid to melt or a liquid to change to a gas.

Early scientists and philosophers thought that heat was a substance that flowed from one object to another. They named this hot substance "caloric." Later observations and experiments showed that heat results from the motions of molecules. Scientists observed that the source of heat does not determine the effects heat has on the surroundings. Whether from chemical reactions, friction, nuclear reactions, or electricity, heat has the same effect. The joule (J) is the SI unit for heat and all other forms of energy.

Figure 17.3 Nuclear reactions in the Sun, electricity passing through a stove burner, and friction from a meteorite falling through the atmosphere are all sources of heat.

Temperature

Temperature is a familiar concept. People refer to temperature when they describe the weather as hot or ice cream as cold. However, weather that feels hot to one person may seem cool to another. This is why scientists use temperature scales to communicate in a clear way.

Temperature is a measure of the average kinetic energy of the molecules in a substance. As molecules gain kinetic energy, their temperature increases. The **Celsius temperature scale** was designed with 0°C as the freezing point of water and 100°C as the boiling point of water at one atmosphere of pressure. Each degree on the Celsius scale represents 1/100th of the interval between the freezing point and boiling point of water.

The Fahrenheit temperature scale is commonly used in the United States. Water boils at 212°F and freezes at 32°F on the **Fahrenheit temperature scale.** Each degree on the Fahrenheit scale represents 1/180th of the distance between the freezing point and boiling point of water. Fahrenheit and Celsius temperatures can be converted by using the following formulas:

$$°C = (°F - 32) \times \frac{5}{9}$$

$$°F = (°C \times \frac{9}{5}) + 32$$

1. Which temperature scale has water's boiling point at 212°?
2. Is there a temperature for which the Celsius and Kelvin scales give the same measurement?

Figure 17.4 The Celsius and Kelvin temperature scales are commonly used by scientists. People in the United States also use the Fahrenheit scale to describe temperatures.

Absolute Zero   As an object loses thermal energy, its temperature generally decreases. The molecules in the substance move at a slower and slower rate. The third law of thermodynamics predicts that all molecular motion will stop at a temperature of −273.15°C. This temperature is called **absolute zero.** Absolute zero is the base of the **Kelvin temperature scale.** Kelvin degrees (K) are the same size as Celsius degrees, but 0 K is set at absolute zero, −273.15°C. For most uses, the value of absolute zero is rounded off to −273. Celsius temperatures can be converted to the Kelvin scale by adding 273. The freezing point of water is 273 K, and the boiling point of water is 373 K.

After You Read

1. Explain in terms of thermal energy what happens to food when you put it in the refrigerator.
2. Review the notes you took in your Science Notebook. Use the information you have recorded to explain the differences between thermal energy, heat, and temperature.
3. Convert 77°F to Celsius and Kelvin measurements. Check to make sure your answers make sense using Figure 17.4.

Explore It!

Fill one bowl with ice water, one bowl with room-temperature water, and one bowl with very warm water. Put a hand in the ice water for five seconds. Then move the hand to the room-temperature water. Describe your observations. Repeat this step with your other hand, first putting it in the very warm water for five seconds.

In your Science Notebook, explain why it is important to use measurements to indicate temperatures.

Background Information

The Metric Conversion Act of 1975 stated that the U.S. would voluntarily change from the use of standard to the use of metric measurements. The U.S. Metric Board was set up to implement the act, but the public largely ignored it. In 1982, the Metric Board was disbanded. Today, most Americans still use standard measurements, but the metric system is used for technology, electricity, energy, and, to some extent, in education.

Alternative Assessment

Give students time to complete the scientific definitions of the terms in this lesson's headings. They should write this information in their Science Notebooks and then check their work for accuracy with a partner.

Teach

EXPLAIN to students that they will continue to learn about temperature in this section.

Figure It Out: **Figure 17.4**

ANSWER **1.** Fahrenheit **2.** No, Kelvin scale measurements are always equal to degrees Celsius plus 273.

Explore It!

Each pair of students will need three bowls, a cup of ice cubes, a small pitcher of room-temperature water, and access to very warm tap water (or a burner on which to heat the water, with supervision).

ANSWER Numerical measurements are important for clear communication. If a scientist described weather or water as *warm,* a reader would have to guess at the temperature. Three readers might interpret *warm* in three very different ways.

Assess

Use the After You Read questions and the Alternative Assessment to help you evaluate students' understanding of the lesson.

After You Read

1. Thermal energy, or heat, flows from the warm food into the refrigerator air and shelves until these all reach the same temperature.
2. Thermal energy is the energy of the random movements of molecules. Heat is the transfer of thermal energy from a hotter object to a cooler object. Temperature is a measure of the average kinetic energy of the molecules in a substance.
3. $°C = (°F - 32) \times 5/9$, $K = °C + 273$
   $77°F = 25°C = 298\ K$

17.2 Introduce

ENGAGE Ask students to touch a wooden surface, such as a desk. Ask them what they feel. They should notice that the wood felt cooler than their hands. Tell them that this observation results from the transfer of heat. If the wood feels cool, it is because heat is being transferred from their hands to the wood. Next, ask students to touch a metal object, such as the leg of a desk. Does the metal feel colder than the wood? Help students realize that heat flows more easily through the metal than the wood. This makes the metal feel colder than the wood.

Before You Read

Discuss the concept of heat transfer with students and provide one or two examples (holding hands under warm water, sitting next to a fire). Ask students to think of additional examples and share them with a small group. Then ask them to list five examples in their Science Notebooks.

● Teach

EXPLAIN to students that in this lesson, they will learn how heat is transferred from one object to another. Tell them this occurs in three ways: conduction, convection, and radiation.

 Vocabulary

conduction Explain to students that this noun contains the root word *conduct,* which comes from the Latin word *conductus,* meaning "guide."

conductor Tell students that this noun also contains the root word *conduct.* The suffix *-or* denotes a person or thing that performs an action or function. Ask students for examples of other words that end with *-or* (*elevator, actor*). The common meaning of *conductor* is "a person who leads a choir or orchestra."

insulator Tell students that this noun contains the root word *insulate,* a verb meaning "to surround with a material that prevents or slows down the flow of heat, electricity, or sound."

convection Explain to students that the word *convection* comes from the Latin word *convectio,* meaning "together" (*con-*) and "to carry" (*vectum*).

284 THERMAL ENERGY AND HEAT

Learning Goals

- Compare and contrast the transfer of thermal energy by conduction, convection, and radiation.
- Compare and contrast thermal insulators and conductors.

New Vocabulary

conduction
conductor
insulator
convection
radiation

Recall Vocabulary

radiant energy, p. 266

Figure 17.5 Animals huddle together in cold weather to conserve heat. Thermal energy travels by conduction from one monkey to its neighbor. How do these monkeys use insulation to retain their thermal energy?

284 THERMAL ENERGY AND HEAT

17.2 Heat Transfer

Before You Read

Being able to relate what you read to your own observations and experiences can help you understand new concepts. You have seen heat transferred through space or from object to object many times. With a partner, make a list in your Science Notebook of five examples of heat transfer.

When heat is transferred, thermal energy moves from hotter objects to colder objects. This process can occur in three ways: by conduction, by convection, and by radiation.

Conduction

Conduction is the transfer of thermal energy between particles that collide with each other. In a collision, the particle with more thermal energy passes some energy to the lower-energy particle. For example, electric stove burners transfer thermal energy by conduction to the bottom of a pan of water. The hot pan's molecules transfer their energy to the cooler water in the pan. Heat is also conducted from your hand to a cold snowball. In scientific terms, cold is not transferred to your hand. Instead, your hand warms the snow. In all cases of heat transfer by conduction, thermal energy is transferred by the collisions between particles.

Conductors and Insulators A **conductor** is a material that allows heat to travel through it. When you apply heat to one end of a good conductor, the other end quickly reaches the same temperature. Metals and other dense solids are excellent conductors. Metal feels colder than wood because the metal conducts heat from your hand faster.

An **insulator** is a material that slows the flow of heat. Substances such as gases and nonmetals tend to be good insulators. Insulators have spaces between their molecules, and this makes collisions between molecules less frequent. Many types of insulation depend on tiny pockets of air to prevent conduction.

Figure 17.6 Fiberglass makes a good insulator. Tiny air pockets in the fiberglass slow the conduction of heat through the material. What would happen to the insulating power of fiberglass if it got wet?

284 THERMAL ENERGY AND HEAT

Use the Visual:

Figure 17.5 ANSWER The monkeys huddle together to use each others' fur for added insulation.

Figure 17.6 ANSWER Water would fill the tiny air spaces in the fiberglass and lower its ability to insulate.

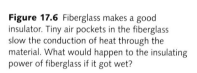 **Strategy**

Use a Concept Map Have each student create a concept map in his or her Science Notebook with *Heat Transfer* in the middle circle and *Conduction, Convection,* and *Radiation* in the outer circles. Have students write the definitions of the terms in the appropriate circles as they read the lesson. Students should also give an example or diagram each process under its definition.

Convection

Unlike molecules in solids, molecules in liquids and gases can mix and flow past one another. This allows heat to be transferred through space as molecules with more thermal energy move and mix with molecules with less thermal energy. The transfer of thermal energy by the movement and mixing of molecules is called **convection.** Convection occurs in fluids, which include liquids and gases. Convection can be forced by a fan or an animal's breathing. Gravity and random motions of molecules also cause convection.

Molecules with more thermal energy move faster and tend to spread apart. When thermal energy moves into a fluid, the fluid expands. This means the volume of the heated fluid increases but its mass remains the same. This increase in volume causes the density of the fluid to decrease. Recall that density is how much mass is packed in a certain volume of material. The density of the warmer fluid is less than the density of the cooler fluid that surrounds it.

Recall how an electric stove burner conducts heat to a pan of water. The water being warmed at the bottom of the pan becomes less dense than the cooler water above it. The cool, dense water sinks, pushing the warm water upward. As it rises, the heated water transfers its heat to the colder water by conduction. By the time the heated water reaches the top of the pan, it is cooler and denser. It then sinks to the bottom of the pan, and the process begins again. The rising-and-sinking action of the water molecules is a convection current. Convection currents transfer thermal energy from warmer to cooler parts of a fluid.

An ice cube in a cup of water is another example of convection. Cold water melting from the ice cube sinks because it is more dense. The cold water mixes with the warmer water below. As it does so, it gains thermal energy from the warmer water by conduction. The increase in thermal energy causes its temperature to increase, its volume to increase, and its density to decrease. The water rises, and a convection current is created.

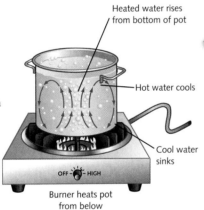

Figure 17.7 The cool, denser water sinks and pushes the warm water to the top. This forms a convection current.

Heated water rises from bottom of pot

Hot water cools

Cool water sinks

OFF — HIGH

Burner heats pot from below

Explore It!

Make two colored ice cubes by adding two drops of food coloring to the water in two compartments of an ice cube tray and freezing.

Fill a tall, clear container with room-temperature water. After the water has settled for two minutes, add one colored ice cube.

Observe the convection currents in the container by looking at it from the side. Record your observations, including a diagram, in your Science Notebook.

Figure It Out

1. Why does the warm water rise to the top?
2. What makes the water at the top of the pot cool?

● Teach

EXPLAIN to students that they will learn about convection heat transfer.

Explore It!

Each small group of students will need one bottle of food coloring, an ice cube tray, a tall plastic or glass container filled with room-temperature water, and access to a freezer.

Students should see tendrils of colored water sinking slowly to form a colored pool at the bottom of the container. All of the water will gradually take on the coloring of the dye as it mixes through convection. If students do not allow time for the water to settle, the tendrils of color will spin around and quickly mix into the water of the container.

Science Notebook EXTRA

In their Science Notebooks, have students write the procedures for the Explore It! activity above. Encourage them to use diagrams, labels, and vocabulary from this lesson to strengthen their work.

Figure It Out: Figure 17.7

ANSWER **1.** Heated water rises because the denser cold water sinks and pushes it to the top. **2.** The water is farther away from the heat source and is heated less by convection. It can also radiate thermal energy to the air.

Background Information

Another example of convection heat is the operation of a convection oven, which has a fan inside that keeps air circulating around the food. The benefits of a convection oven include the fact that heat is evenly distributed, so food is cooked more consistently; the cooking process is faster; and food has a layer of heat around it, preventing flavor from other foods from entering it when multiple items are being cooked simultaneously.

Field Study

Visit the school's cafeteria or home economics room to view the heating appliances. Have students list these and identify which type of heat transfer each uses.

● Teach

 EXPLAIN to students that they will learn about the third type of heat transfer, radiation.

Vocabulary

radiation Tell students that this noun comes from the Latin word *radiare,* meaning "to shine or emit rays."

As You Read

Ask students to review the five examples of heat transfer that they wrote in their Science Notebooks. With a partner, have them label each as conduction, convection, or radiation.

ANSWER When you breathe out on a cold day, heat from your body is transferred to the air by convection.

Extend It!

Provide Internet access to the NASA Web site and reference materials on the Space Shuttle for students' use. Working in small groups, students should find information about the various temperatures to which the Space Shuttle is exposed during a mission.

● Assess

Use the After You Read questions and the Alternative Assessment to help you evaluate students' understanding of the lesson.

After You Read

1. Conduction and convection must be transmitted through matter.

2. An animal might huddle with other animals to increase the group's insulation, prevent convective heat loss by finding shelter in a cave, or reduce its surface area by crouching into a compact size.

3. Light reflected from the Moon travels through empty space by radiation, which does not require matter. Steam rises into the sky by the convection of moving air molecules. A cold penny is warmed by conduction as heat moves from the hand molecules to the the penny molecules.

As You Read

Review the list of examples of heat transfer you wrote in your Science Notebook. As you read the lesson, label each of the examples *conduction, convection,* or *radiation.* Then work with a partner to explain why you labeled each example as you did.

Which type of heat transfer are you making when you breathe out warm air on a cold day?

Extend It!

Space vehicles such as the Space Shuttle pass through a wide range of temperatures during a mission. In outer space, the temperature of a thermometer can fall to −270°C. The surface of the Shuttle reaches 1,427°C as the spacecraft descends through the atmosphere. Research the design of the Space Shuttle. In your Science Notebook, describe how the inside of the spacecraft is kept at a comfortable temperature throughout its mission.

Radiation

Radiation is thermal energy transferred as electromagnetic waves. There are many kinds of electromagnetic waves, and these are discussed more in Chapter 21. Unlike conduction and convection, radiation can travel through empty space. For example, the Sun's energy radiates nearly 150 million kilometers through space to Earth.

Every object above 0 K radiates heat in some form. Most objects on Earth emit infrared radiation. This type of radiation is not visible to the human eye, but can be detected with special equipment to form images such as **Figure 17.8.** As the temperature of an object increases, the radiation emitted takes the form of visible light. The color changes from dull red through yellow-orange to white as the object is heated more and more.

When radiation emitted from one object reaches another object, it can be absorbed or reflected. For example, shiny objects reflect visible light, while transparent objects allow it to pass through. Black materials absorb most visible light. To keep cool in a hot climate, people generally wear light-colored clothes to reflect as much radiant energy as possible.

Figure 17.8
Most objects on Earth give off infrared radiation.

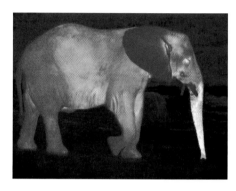

After You Read

1. Explain why heat from the Sun does not reach Earth by conduction or convection.

2. Describe three ways in which an animal in a cold climate could prevent heat loss from conduction and convection.

3. Using the information you have recorded in your Science Notebook, explain how each of the following examples shows conduction, convection, or radiation: light reflected from the Moon reaches Earth, steam from a factory rises into the sky, holding a cold penny warms the penny.

Alternative Assessment

Have students finish labeling their examples of heat transfer. Using the information they have learned in this lesson, have students illustrate heat transfer. They should include at least two examples in their illustrations.

Differentiate Instruction

Kinesthetic Have students identify all of the places through which heat can enter or leave the classroom, such as through windows and from radiators. Have them get close to and/or touch each one to see if they can feel heat being transferred.

17.3 Measuring Heat

Before You Read

Construct a concept map for this lesson in your Science Notebook. Start by writing the title of the lesson in the middle of an empty page. Write the headings and subheadings in circles around the title. As you read, record important information in the appropriate place on the map.

Learning Goals

- Explain the concept of specific heat and its applications.
- Describe how heat is measured.

New Vocabulary

calorie
specific heat
calorimeter

Heat is the flow of thermal energy from one place to another. The only way to measure heat is to observe the effects it has on its surroundings. Heat is often measured by tracking the temperature changes it causes in surrounding materials. Heat can also be measured when it causes a change in physical state.

Calories

Warm-blooded animals produce most of their body heat by digesting and burning food. In the United States, food energy is measured in calories. One **calorie** is the amount of heat needed to raise the temperature of one gram of water by one degree Celsius.

Most foods contain thousands of calories per serving. For this reason, food energy content is listed in kilocalories, or Calories. Each Calorie is 1,000 calories, or 4,180 joules. **Figure 17.9** shows the energy values of some foods and the energy used to perform activities. The average adult needs about 2,000 Calories, or 8,360,000 joules, for one day's energy needs.

TABLE A: Energy from Food

Food	Energy Value (Calories/100 g)	Energy Value (kJ/100 g)
sugar	389	1,627
white bread	266	1,112
margarine	620	2,590
potato, baked	89	372
hamburger (no cheese)	275	1,150
oranges, raw	47	196
carrots, raw	41	171
eggs, fried	201	840
cheese pizza	257	1,075
chocolate-chip cookies, low-fat	453	1,895
carbonated cola drink	37	154
corn flakes, breakfast cereal	360	1,506

TABLE B: Human Energy Demands

Activity	Energy Needed (Calories/minute)	Energy Needed (kJ/minute)
resting in bed, watching TV	0.9	3.9
washing, dressing	3.3	13.8
walking	4.9	20.5
standing	1.8	7.5
cycling	6.6	27.6

Figure 17.9 The energy value of food is described as the heat that would be produced by burning it. How long could a person walk using the energy provided by a 100-g baked potato?

17.3 Introduce

ENGAGE Ask students to think about what happens to matter when it absorbs heat energy. Describe examples, such as heating a pot of water on a stove. Lead students to realize that the sample becomes warmer. Ask students what instrument they might use to measure this change. (Students should suggest a thermometer.)

Before You Read

Remind students of the purpose of a concept map (to organize information so that it can be better understood). Write the lesson heading in the middle of the board and ask students to do the same in their Science Notebooks. Ask them to go through the lesson and write headings and subheadings around the title to indicate topics covered in this lesson. Ask them to fill in important information about each topic as they read.

Teach

EXPLAIN to students that on this page, they will learn about calories. Ask what they already know about this word.

Vocabulary

calorie Tell students that the word *calorie* comes from the Latin word *calor,* meaning "heat."

Use the Visual: Figure 17.9

ANSWER about 18 minutes

ELL Strategy

Use Visual Information Pair students and ask them to use the tables in **Figure 17.9** to generate several questions about energy value in comparison to energy need. Pairs should then exchange and solve each other's questions. For example, how many carrots would provide enough energy for a student to run for 30 minutes?

Teach

EXPLAIN to students that they will learn about specific heat, which is the energy needed to raise the temperature of one gram of a substance by one degree Celsius. Have students look at **Figure 17.10** for examples.

Vocabulary

specific heat Explain that the adjective *specific* means "particular" or "exact."

calorimeter Tell students that the word *calorimeter* is a combination of the words *calorie* and *meter*. The suffix *-meter* denotes an instrument for measuring.

As You Read

Give students a few minutes to work on their concept maps. Explain how to draw arrows and write explanations to indicate the relationships among terms.

ANSWER Specific heat describes the amount of energy needed to raise the temperature of a substance by one degree Celsius. Energy can be measured in joules or calories. The specific heat of liquid water is 4.18 J/g°C. This amount of energy, 4.18 J, is equal to one calorie.

As You Read

Draw arrows between the terms in your concept map as you read about the ways in which the terms are connected. Write a brief description next to each arrow explaining how the ideas are related.

What is the connection between the calorie and specific heat?

Specific Heat

Adding heat to any substance causes the molecules of that substance to gain kinetic energy. Some materials rise in temperature quickly as they gain kinetic energy. Other materials must be heated much longer to make them hot. The energy required to raise one gram of a substance by one degree Celsius is that substance's **specific heat.** The unit for specific heat is J/g°C and is read as "joule per gram per degree Celsius." The specific heat of liquid water is one calorie, or 4.18 J/g°C. Imagine a trip to the beach on a sunny day. The sand would feel hot while the water is still cool. Sand heats up faster than water because sand's specific heat is much lower than water's. Sand requires only one-eighth as much heat as water to raise its temperature.

Water has a higher specific heat than most other substances. Water can absorb or transmit a lot of thermal energy without much change in temperature. This property makes water a good coolant for car engines. The temperature inside the engine needs to be cooled from 300°C down to 90°C for proper engine function. Water and antifreeze absorb this heat and transfer it to the radiator. This heat is transferred to the air by radiation. A fan speeds the process of cooling by causing convection.

Water's high specific heat has important consequences for life on Earth. Most living organisms function well within a narrow range of body temperatures. At high temperatures, proteins are destroyed. At low temperatures, chemical reactions proceed too slowly to sustain life. People, plants, and other organisms are made mostly of water. The high specific heat of water allows these living things to absorb or lose a lot of heat without a large change in body temperature.

Specific Heat

Material (25°C)	Specific Heat (J/g°C)
water	4.18
air	1.16
sand	0.84
aluminum	0.24

Figure 17.10 Specific heat describes the amount of heat energy needed to raise the temperature of one gram of a substance by one degree Celsius or Kelvin.

Figure 17.11 Cars use a mixture of water and antifreeze to cool their engines. The high specific heat of the coolant allows it to take in a lot of heat without a large temperature change. Coolant heated by the engine loses heat to the air in the radiator by radiation and convection.

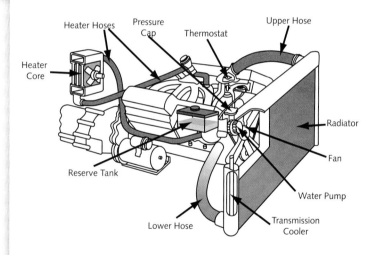

Differentiate Instruction

Mathematical/Logical, Visual In small groups, have students research the specific heat of several other substances. Then have them work in groups to create charts that display the information. Groups should share their information with the class.

Measuring the Heat of a Chemical Reaction

Chemical reactions generally result in a gain or loss of heat. The energy of a reaction is transferred between the reactants and their surroundings. Scientists use a device called a **calorimeter** (kal uh RIH meh tur) to measure the heat change during a reaction. **Figure 17.12** shows a diagram of a calorimeter and how it works.

Heat from a chemical reaction affects the temperature of the water in the calorimeter. Using the known specific heat of water, the experimenter can calculate the energy change caused by the reaction. The formula used is

heat gained or lost =
mass of water × temperature change × specific heat of water

For example, a reaction may raise the temperature of 1,000 g of water by 10°C. The energy given off is

1,000 g × 10°C × 4.18 J/g°C = 41,800 J

Food scientists use calorimeters to determine the energy released by foods when they are digested. The energy value of a food is listed in Calories on its package.

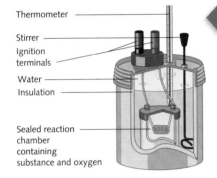

Figure 17.12 Scientists use a bomb calorimeter to measure the energy content of foods. First, a sample of dried food is weighed and placed in the reaction chamber. The temperature of the water in the calorimeter is recorded. Next, the sample is burned inside the chamber. The temperature of the water in the calorimeter is recorded after burning the food. The change in water temperature shows how much energy was released by burning the food.

Thermometer

Stirrer
Ignition terminals

Water
Insulation

Sealed reaction chamber containing substance and oxygen

Figure It Out

1. Explain the purpose of the stirrer in the calorimeter.
2. Why is good insulation around the calorimeter important to making an accurate measurement of the energy in the food?

After You Read

1. Using information you have recorded on your concept map, hypothesize about what would happen to a living creature made of a substance with a very low specific heat.

2. Review your concept map. Use the information you have recorded to explain why it is important to understand the concept of specific heat and know the specific heat of the fluid when using a calorimeter.

3. A calorimeter containing 2,000 g of water is used to measure heat given off by a chemical reaction. The water's temperature increases from 23°C to 28°C. Calculate the thermal energy produced by the reaction.

Teach

to students that they will learn about an instrument called a calorimeter, which measures heat change during a chemical reaction.

Figure It Out: Figure 17.12

ANSWER **1.** The stirrer causes mixing, or convection, to bring all of the water in the calorimeter to the same temperature. **2.** The insulation around the calorimeter prevents loss or gain of thermal energy from outside. The calorimeter would not provide accurate measurements of the heat of a reaction without the insulation.

Assess

Use the After You Read questions and the Alternative Assessment to help you evaluate students' understanding of the lesson.

After You Read

1. The body temperature of a living creature made of a substance with a very low specific heat would rise and fall rapidly. If the creature created heat by digesting food or exercising, its body temperature would rise. If the outside temperature changed, the creature's temperature would also change.

2. The specific heat of the fluid in the calorimeter determines how quickly its temperature will rise or fall. If you did not know the specific heat of the fluid in a calorimeter, you could not use it to measure the heat of a reaction.

3. 41,800 J

Alternative Assessment

Have students complete their concept maps with important information from the lesson. When students are finished, have them each write a paragraph about what they learned based on one part of the map.

Background Information

Teenagers between the ages of 14 and 18 have different caloric and nutritional needs than adults. Girls who are moderately active (one hour of activity per day) require 2,000 Calories per day, and moderately active boys require 2,200 to 2,400. Teens' diets should also be examined to ensure that they are getting adequate amounts of vitamins A and C, fiber, iron, and calcium. Teenage girls are especially prone to having low iron and calcium levels. Fat intake should not exceed 25 to 35 percent of a teen's total daily caloric intake.

ENGAGE Arrange students in small groups and ask them to brainstorm examples of solids, liquids, and gases. Have each group keep a written list and compare it with other groups' lists when complete.

Before You Read

Ask students what an application is (a use or purpose). Give examples, such as applying prior knowledge to understand a new concept or idea. Ask students to provide more examples.

● Teach

EXPLAIN to students that in this lesson, they will learn about changes in the state of matter (solid, liquid, gas) for several substances.

Figure It Out: Figure 17.13

[ANSWER] **1.** conduction **2.** Gloves act as insulators. Little heat would be transferred from hands wearing gloves to the icicle. The icicle would melt slowly, if at all.

 CONNECTION: Food Science

Provide more uses of freeze-dried foods, such as the ready-to-eat military meals (MREs), emergency kits, earthquake preparedness kits, and supplies for outdoor activities such as boating or hiking.

Buy several packets of freeze-dried food for students to sample. Have students decide whether or not these taste like fresh food.

Learning Goals

- Describe how heat can cause changes in the physical state of matter.
- Explain how heat of fusion and heat of vaporization affect changes in state.
- Provide examples of the effects of heat of fusion and heat of vaporization.

New Vocabulary

heat of fusion
heat of vaporization

Figure It Out

1. Is heat transferred from the hand to the ice by conduction, convection, or radiation?
2. Describe how this scene would change if the person in the photo were wearing gloves.

17.4 Heat and Changes in State

Before You Read

Many scientific ideas make more sense when you know of a real-life application. Write each heading from this lesson in your Science Notebook. Leave several blank lines between the headings for applications.

Water has many unusual qualities. It has one of the highest specific heats of any substance and is found in nature in all three states of matter.

The state of a substance depends in part on the thermal energy possessed by its particles. Air or gas pressure also plays a role in determining physical state. Heating and cooling can cause materials to change from one state to another.

Changes in State

A piece of ice held in a bare hand will begin to drip. Heat is transferred from the hand to the ice by conduction. The added heat raises the temperature of the ice to its melting point of 0°C. The ice changes from a solid to a liquid. At the same time, the molecules in the hand lose thermal energy. Skin that is allowed to fall to its freezing point will freeze.

Water droplets landing in a fire absorb heat and rise in temperature. When the droplets reach the boiling point of water, 100°C, they change into gaseous water vapor. The vapor rises into the air and cools as it transfers its thermal energy to the air. The temperature of the vapor decreases to its condensation point. The vapor condenses into liquid droplets of water.

Figure 17.13 A bare hand transfers heat to a piece of ice. The temperature of the ice rises to its melting point while the hand cools toward its freezing point.

CONNECTION: Food Science

Instant coffee, astronaut ice cream, and dried camping food all have something in common. These products are freeze-dried. Freeze-drying uses the process of sublimation to vaporize ice without melting it. Sublimation is the process by which a solid becomes a gas without passing through the liquid state. Freeze-dried foods last for many years without special care. When hot water is added, freeze-dried foods taste remarkably like they did when fresh.

ELL Strategy

Read Aloud and Discuss Set aside time for students to read the lesson aloud and discuss it in small groups. Students should be in groups of three or four. After one student reads a paragraph, a second student can summarize what the first student read. Then, another student can write a question about an important feature of that paragraph. For example, what do we call the extra heat that changes a boiling liquid to gas? The remaining students will answer the question. After each paragraph, roles will rotate among the students.

Heat of Fusion and Vaporization

Melting does not happen instantly when a substance reaches its melting point. For example, ice remains floating in 0°C water. More heat must be applied to overcome the attractions between the molecules of the solid ice. The **heat of fusion** is the energy needed to change a solid at its melting point to a liquid. Heat of fusion does not raise the temperature of the substance. The liquid formed is still at the melting point of the substance.

Extra heat must be added again at the boiling point to cause a change from a liquid to a gas. The **heat of vaporization** is the energy needed to change a liquid at its boiling point to a gas. The heat of vaporization is absorbed by the molecules as they change from a liquid to a gas.

When a substance condenses from a gas to a liquid, the heat of vaporization is given off to its surroundings. Gaseous steam condensing back to water releases a lot of heat. Steam burns cause much worse damage than hot water burns do because water's heat of vaporization is transferred to the skin as the steam condenses. A liquid freezing to a solid gives off its heat of fusion in the same way.

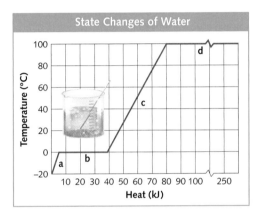

Figure 17.14 Heating water from ice to its boiling point does not result in a steady rise in temperature. Ice molecules at the melting point must absorb the heat of fusion before they melt into a liquid. At the boiling point, water molecules absorb the heat of vaporization before vaporizing into a gas.

● Teach

Teach

EXPLAIN to students that they will continue to learn about the heat of fusion and vaporization. Ask students what they know about evaporation, and ask them to give examples. Have them read the first paragraph if they do not have any examples.

Assess

Use the After You Read questions and the Alternative Assessment to help you evaluate students' understanding of the lesson.

After You Read

1. thermal energy and pressure
2. the ice cube, because it would absorb the heat of fusion before it started to warm to the temperature of the drink
3. Water evaporated from your wet body, removing its heat of vaporization and leaving your body colder.

Alternative Assessment

Instruct students to complete their lists of applications and examples in their Science Notebooks. Ask them to share their ideas with a partner and make any necessary changes.

Did You Know?

Not all liquids can be safely heated to their boiling points. Many cooking oils, for example, begin to smoke below 200°C. About one in seven house fires is started by overheated fat or grease. The most important ways to prevent oil fires are to use a fryer with a thermostat and to pay close attention while cooking.

Figure 17.16 Water's high heat of fusion causes ice and snow to melt slowly. These photographs were taken in Yellowstone National Park in June. The air temperature was far above 0°C.

Figure 17.15 Panting helps lower a dog's temperature. The dog breathes very quick, shallow breaths that speed evaporation from its mouth, throat, and lungs. Evaporating water carries heat away from the dog's body. Evaporation is a cooling process.

Cooling by Evaporation A liquid will turn to a gas if it is heated to its boiling point. But a liquid can also slowly turn to a gas at lower temperatures. This is called evaporation. Evaporation causes puddles to dry up and wet swimmers to dry on the beach.

Evaporating molecules carry away their heat of vaporization in the same way as boiling molecules do. Evaporation is used by humans and animals to keep them cool. For example, people sweat when their bodies are too hot. As the sweat evaporates, it carries its heat of vaporization into the air with it. The remaining molecules of the body become cooler.

Animals use evaporation to cool themselves in several ways. Dogs pant to speed up the vaporization of water from their mouths and throats. On hot days, wasps bring water to their nest. The wasps fan their wings over the water to make it evaporate. The evaporating water carries heat away from the nest. Other animals make themselves wet by licking and are cooled by evaporation from their skin.

Using the Heat of Fusion Picnic coolers take advantage of the heat of fusion to keep food cold for several hours. Ice is added to the cooler. As the ice melts, it absorbs the heat of fusion from the food surrounding it. Strawberry farmers also use the heat of fusion. Farmers spray their strawberry plants with water to save them from freezing weather. As the water on the plants freezes, it releases its heat of fusion. The heat warms the plants and prevents them from freezing.

After You Read

1. What factors determine the physical state of a substance?
2. Which would do more to cool a drink: a 50-g ice cube at 0°C, or 50 g of liquid water at the same temperature? Explain your answer.
3. Review the real-life applications you wrote in your Science Notebook. Explain why you feel cold after stepping out of a swimming pool or shower.

Background Information

Farmers are not always able to save their crops during a freeze. In late December of 2006 and early January of 2007, record cold temperatures destroyed up to 70 percent of California's orange crop. Farmers pumped fields with heated water and used wind machines to circulate warm air, but they were not able to combat several nights of below-freezing temperatures. Many vegetables and other citrus fruits were also destroyed.

Before You Read

Not all scientific principles are absolute laws. Think of an exception to the principle, "What goes up must come down." Draw four boxes on top of each other in your Science Notebook. Leave enough space to write a few sentences in each box. Preview the lesson to get a sense of the main ideas.

Thermal Expansion

Thermal expansion is the tendency of matter to increase in volume or pressure when it is heated. Adding heat to molecules gives the molecules more thermal energy. The more-energetic molecules move more and spread out from each other. Substances expand as their temperatures increase. On the other hand, matter typically fills less space as it loses heat. It is important to note that the spaces between the molecules expand and contract, not the molecules themselves. **Figure 17.17** illustrates this idea.

Nearly all solids, liquids, and gases expand as they gain thermal energy. Thermal expansion impacts many aspects of everyday life. The solid lid on a jar can be loosened by running it under hot water. Heating causes the jar lid to expand so that it can be easily unscrewed. Water in pipes also expands when it gets hot. Water supplies can be dirtied by toilet water that expands and flows backward into pipes.

Adding thermal energy causes gases to expand if they are in a stretchy container. Balloons shrink in the freezer and expand when they are removed. However, gases cannot expand in a container that cannot stretch. The pressure of a gas in a stiff container increases as the gas's temperature rises. For example, tire pressures rise with the temperature.

  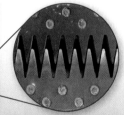

Figure 17.18 Nearly all substances expand as their thermal energy increases. Engineers must consider thermal expansion in their designs. Bridges are often built with expansion spacers to allow the bridge to expand without damage. Pipelines can be buried underground to decrease temperature changes. Pipelines are also designed to expand and contract without leaking.

Learning Goals

- Explain thermal expansion and its effects.
- Describe the behavior of water when it freezes.

New Vocabulary

thermal expansion
thermometer
thermostat

Figure 17.17 Heating causes the molecules of a solid to gain thermal energy. The molecules vibrate faster and spread out from each other. The size of the solid object expands as the object's temperature increases.

Figure It Out

1. Which of these structures can expand without changing shape? Explain your answer.

2. How will the bridge spacers look on a very cold day? On a very hot day?

CHAPTER 17 **293**

ENGAGE Ask students if they have ever noticed the gaps that cut across a sidewalk at regular intervals. Explain that the gaps are intentionally added to the concrete when the sidewalk is formed. Tell students that they will discover the reason for the gaps as they read this lesson.

Before You Read

Tell students that a scientific principle is a law that explains something in nature or the way a machine works. Write the phrase *What goes up must come down* on the board and tell students that this is an example of a scientific principle. Ask them to think about what it means and whether they've heard it before. Explain that this means that gravity causes objects to be drawn to its surface.

Teach

EXPLAIN to students that they will learn about thermal expansion. Tell them that matter can expand or contract as a result of changes in thermal energy.

 Vocabulary
thermal expansion Ask students to remember what the word *thermal* means "pertaining to heat." Tell them that the word *expansion* contains the root word *expand*, meaning "to become greater in size."

Figure It Out: Figure 17.18

ANSWER **1.** When the bridge expands, it fills the expansion spacers but does not change shape. **2.** On a very cold day, the bridge spacers will have a large gap. On a very hot day, the spacers will be closed.

ELL Strategy

Relate to Personal Experience Have students talk in small groups about experiences they have had with thermal expansion. Ask them to think about being on the beach on a hot day or in a warm room. Tell them to think about what happens to objects and to themselves.

Key Concept Review
Workbook, p. 106

Teach

EXPLAIN to students that they will learn about exceptions to the general trend of thermal expansion on this page.

 Vocabulary

thermometer Ask students to break down the word *thermometer* into two familiar parts (*thermo-* and *meter*) and to remember what each part means. (*Thermo-* is a prefix meaning "heat," and *meter* denotes an instrument for measuring).

thermostat Tell students that the suffix *-stat* denotes a device that maintains a stationary or constant condition.

As You Read

Ask students to review the lesson to find the scientific principle and write it in the first box in their Science Notebooks. Discuss with students what the principle is, and ask them why it is generally true. Students should write their own explanations in the second box. Ask what an exception is. Tell them to be looking for an exception to the principle as they read, and to record it in the third box.

[ANSWER] Potholes fill with water. When the water freezes, it expands, making the holes larger.

CONNECTION: Biology

Penguins' internal body temperature is between 37.8°C and 38.9°C. Their feathers provide a waterproof layer that allows them to survive in water as cold as 2.2°C. They are insulated by down on their feathers and a layer of fat. Still, to generate body heat in the water, they must stay active. Some species spend up to 75 percent of their time in water, only coming on land to breed and molt.

Have students convert the Celsius temperatures in the Connection feature to Fahrenheit. Supply the necessary equation.

As You Read

Record the major principle of this lesson in the first box you drew in your Science Notebook. In the second box, explain why this principle is generally true. As you read, look for the major exception to the principle and record it in the third box. Finally, record an explanation for the exception in the fourth box.

Why do potholes get larger during a cold winter?

Exceptions to Thermal Expansion

Water near its freezing point is an important exception to the rule that substances expand as they gain thermal energy. Ice, or solid water, forms a crystal structure with spaces between the molecules. The structure of ice makes water expand as it approaches freezing and begins to crystallize. The expansion of freezing water worsens potholes and bursts pipes in the winter. It also makes ice float.

Scientists have recently developed a substance that contracts as it gains thermal energy. Zirconium tungstate (ZrW_2O_8) could solve many engineering problems. For example, dental fillings expand and can cause headaches when people consume hot drinks. Including some zirconium tungstate could result in fillings that do not expand at any temperature.

Figure 17.19 Water expands as it cools below 4°C and freezes. Freezing water molecules form hollow structures. The expansion of ice makes a bottle of water bulge when it is frozen.

CONNECTION: Biology

Water is one of the only substances that expands as it freezes. That simple fact makes life as we know it possible on Earth.

Water below 4°C expands as it cools. Water below 4°C floats on warmer water and does not mix. As a result, ice forms on the top of a body of water. Under the ice, the liquid water is insulated from cold air. Water under the ice stays around 4°C no matter how cold the outside air gets. Penguins, fish, and sea lions can swim under the ice of Antarctica even when the surface temperature is –70°C!

Imagine a world where water contracted upon freezing. Ice would sink to the bottom of lakes and oceans. More and more ice would form each winter. Eventually, most of the water on Earth would be locked up in great ice blocks near the poles. Little sea life would survive. The land surface of Earth would turn into cold or hot deserts with almost no rain. The special properties of water make it a necessary ingredient for life on Earth.

Differentiate Instruction

Interpersonal Invite an engineer into the classroom to share his or her knowledge of and experiences with thermal expansion. Students should prepare questions to ask ahead of time relating to this topic.

Interpreting Diagrams
Workbook, p. 108

Applications of Thermal Expansion

Thermal expansion affects every natural process and every manufactured object. Many products take advantage of thermal expansion. For example, glass canning jars are packed with hot food and covered with a lid. Next, the jar is heated to kill bacteria and heat the air in the jar. Hot air expands, rises, and escapes past the lid of the jar. When the food cools, it contracts. This creates a vacuum that seals all microorganisms out of the jar. Sealed glass jars have a dent in the lid caused by the thermal contraction of the cooling food. When the jar is opened, air enters and the dent pops up.

Thermometers   A **thermometer** is a device that measures temperature. Many thermometers contain colored alcohol in a thin tube. Rising temperature causes the alcohol in the thermometer to expand and move higher in the tube. Markings along the tube show the height that the alcohol will reach at each temperature.

Thermostats   A **thermostat** (THUR muh stat) is a device that turns a heating or cooling system on and off to maintain a fairly steady temperature. **Figure 17.20** shows the metal coil of a thermostat. Thermal expansion of the coil turns on the heat or air conditioning only when it is needed. Thermostats also control the fans and coolant that cool car engines.

Figure 17.20 This thermometer (*left*) contains colored alcohol. The liquid expands and fills more of the tube inside as the temperature rises. Some thermostats include a coil of metal (*right*). The coil contracts or expands as the metal loses or gains thermal energy. The movement of the coil activates the heating or cooling system when it is needed.

After You Read

1. Hypothesize what happens to a balloon when it is heated from room temperature.

2. Review the notes you wrote in your Science Notebook. Use your notes to answer the following question: Why does water contract as it melts?

3. Apply what you have learned in this lesson to describe how a plumber could use heat to loosen a tight joint in a pipe.

4. Explain the difference between a thermometer and a thermostat.

Did You Know?

Another effect of rising temperature is increased resistance to electrical flow. Digital thermometers and thermostats measure electrical resistance to tell the temperature of a body or house.

Explain It!

Thermal expansion can help people or can damage their property. In your Science Notebook, explain one way in which thermal expansion is beneficial and one way in which thermal expansion can be damaging.

Teach

EXPLAIN to students that they will learn about applications of thermal expansion. Bring in a few jars of food and show students the dent in the lid. Explain that this is an example of thermal expansion. Have students read the first paragraph aloud with a partner for an explanation.

Explain It!

Discuss with students examples of a beneficial effect and a damaging effect of thermal expansion. Because metal expands more than glass, a stuck metal lid on a glass jar can be loosened by running hot water over the joint between the lid and the container. Thermal expansion can cause damage to objects, such as water heaters and concrete structures, if they are not designed to account for changes in size.

Assess

Use the After You Read questions and the Alternative Assessment to help you evaluate students' understanding of the lesson.

After You Read

1. The air inside the balloon expands as its temperature rises. A rubber balloon is stretchy, so its volume increases. If the balloon is heated enough, it will pop.

2. Ice crystals take up more space than liquid water because of their hollow structure. When water melts, the crystals disappear and the water contracts.

3. The plumber could heat the tight nut to make it expand. As the hole in the nut expanded, the joint would become looser.

4. A thermometer measures the average kinetic energy of a substance. A thermostat uses the thermal expansion of a metal to control the heating or air-conditioning unit in a building.

Background Information

The Galileo thermometer is a sealed glass cylinder filled with water and floating, colored, water-filled glass balls and an attached metal marker, which indicates a temperature. The weights are calibrated according to the balls' density. The water either expands or contracts as a result of the surrounding air's temperature—a change in density. The ball that sinks the most indicates the current temperature.

Alternative Assessment

Give students a few minutes to complete the boxes in their Science Notebooks. Have students share their answers, and record a few answers on the board. After the discussion, give students a few more minutes to add more information.

Chapter 17 Summary

MASTERING CONCEPTS

True or False

1. False, joule
2. True
3. True
4. False, calorimeter
5. True

Short Answer

6. The scientist could use a calorimeter. The sample would be burned and the temperature change of the water in the calorimeter would be noted. Using the formula *heat = mass of water × temperature change × specific heat of water,* the scientist could calculate the energy given off by the food.

7. Very hot objects emit radiation in the form of visible light.

8. First: energy can be transferred but not created or destroyed. Second: heat will flow from the oven to the potato.

9. °F = (°C × 9/5) + 32 = (185°C × 9/5) + 32 = 365°F; K = °C + 273 = 185°C + 273 = 458 K

10. Radiant heat will heat the air inside. The bottle of soda will absorb heat, and the temperature of the air and soda in the bottle will rise. The air and soda will expand, increasing the pressure inside the bottle.

11. As water water vaporizes, it carries away its heat of vaporization, leaving the person cooler.

Summary

KEY CONCEPTS

17.1 What Is Thermal Energy?

- Thermal energy is the energy of the random movements of molecules.
- The laws of thermodynamics describe the behavior of thermal energy.
- Heat is the flow of thermal energy from warmer to cooler objects.
- Temperature describes the average kinetic energy of molecules and is measured using Celsius, Fahrenheit, and Kelvin scales.

17.2 Heat Transfer

- Heat can be transferred by conduction, convection, and radiation.
- Conductors and insulators can be used to control heat flow.

17.3 Measuring Heat

- Heat can only be measured by observing its effects on its surroundings.
- The amount of heat needed to raise the temperature of one gram of a substance by one degree Celsius is that substance's specific heat.
- The heat of a reaction can be measured using a calorimeter.

17.4 Heat and Changes in State

- The physical state of a substance is determined by its temperature and pressure.
- Materials do not change state as soon as they reach their melting or boiling points; the heat of fusion or vaporization must be absorbed or released first.

17.5 Thermal Expansion

- Most substances expand when heated.
- Thermometers and thermostats are among the many products that rely on thermal expansion.
- The crystal structure of water causes it to expand as it approaches its freezing point.

VOCABULARY REVIEW

Write each term in a complete sentence or write a paragraph relating several terms.

17.1
laws of thermodynamics, p. 281
heat, p. 282
temperature, p. 282
Celsius temperature scale, p. 282
Fahrenheit temperature scale, p. 283
absolute zero, p. 283
Kelvin temperature scale, p. 283

17.2
conduction, p. 284
conductor, p. 284
insulator, p. 284
convection, p. 285
radiation, p. 286

17.3
calorie, p. 287
specific heat, p. 288
calorimeter, p. 289

17.4
heat of fusion, p. 291
heat of vaporization, p. 291

17.5
thermal expansion, p. 293
thermometer, p. 295
thermostat, p. 295

PREPARE FOR CHAPTER TEST

To prepare for the chapter test, create a question from each Learning Goal. Use the information in your Science Notebook to answer each question. Then use these answers to write a well-developed essay about the chapter. Use the Key Concept on the first page of this chapter as your topic sentence.

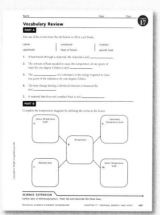

Vocabulary Review
Workbook, p. 107

Reading Comprehension
Workbook, p. 109

MASTERING CONCEPTS

True or False
If the statement is true, write "true." If it is false, change the underlined word or words to make the statement true.

1. The <u>calorie</u> is the SI unit for heat and thermal energy.

2. The energy needed to change a solid to a liquid at its melting point is its <u>heat of fusion</u>.

3. Most objects on Earth radiate <u>infrared energy</u>.

4. A <u>thermostat</u> is an instrument used to measure the heat of a chemical reaction.

5. <u>Thermal expansion</u> is the tendency of matter to increase in volume when it is heated.

Short Answer
Answer each of the following in a sentence or brief paragraph.

6. A new food product claims to provide 100 Calories per serving. Explain how a food scientist could double-check that number.

7. Why does an electric stove burner turn red when it gets very hot?

8. A cold potato is put into a hot oven. How do the first and second laws of thermodynamics apply to the flow of heat that follows?

9. A French recipe calls for a cake to be baked at 185°C. What is this temperature on the Fahrenheit scale? On the Kelvin scale?

10. Describe what will happen to a two-liter bottle of soda left in a car on a sunny day.

11. How does a fan cool a person on a hot day?

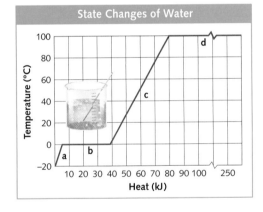

State Changes of Water

Critical Thinking
Use what you have learned in this chapter to answer each of the following.

12. **Evaluate** Is the following statement true or false? Explain your answer. *If the thermal energy of an object increases, its temperature must also increase.*

13. **Design** Deserts can be very hot during the day and below freezing at night. Design a desert animal that could maintain a steady body temperature through both hot and cold temperature extremes. What behaviors and body structures would help this animal survive?

14. **Analyze** How do the reflective surface and the vacuum between the layers of a thermos bottle help keep the temperature of the liquid inside constant?

Outer case

Reflective surface

Vacuum

Standardized Test Question
Choose the letter of the response that correctly answers the question.

15. The graph to the left shows how the temperature of water rises as it is heated. What explains the level section at 100°C?

   A. Gaseous water must lose its specific heat before it condenses.

   B. Gaseous water must absorb its heat of vaporization before it can become a liquid.

   C. Liquid water must absorb its heat of vaporization before it can become a gas.

   D. Solid water must absorb its heat of fusion before it melts.

Test-Taking Tip
After you read a multiple-choice question, answer it in your head before reading the choices provided. This way, the choices will be less confusing.

Critical Thinking

12. The statement is not true. At the melting point or boiling point of a substance, heat can be absorbed or released without causing a change in state. The heat of fusion or vaporization changes the arrangement of the particles in the substance but does not change the temperature of the substance.

13. Answers will vary. Possible features include sweating, panting, and licking itself to use evaporative cooling; having light colors to reflect radiant energy and/or dark colors to absorb energy; having fur or fat as insulation from heat loss; eating high-energy food to gain energy; resting in water when possible to avoid extreme temperatures; having a compact body shape to conserve energy or a long, thin body to radiate out energy; and engaging in huddling behavior with other animals.

14. The reflective surface of the thermos bottle reduces heat loss from radiation. The vacuum between the layers of the bottle reduces conductive and convective heat transfer.

Standardized Test Question

15. C

Reading Links

The Snowflake: Winter's Secret Beauty

For a closer look at the intricacy and beauty that results when water vapor condenses into ice, students can explore this compelling, highly visual treatment of snowflakes.

Kenneth Libbrecht. Whitecap Books. 112 pp. Illustrated with photographs by Patricia Rasmussen. Trade ISBN 978-1-55285-557-7.

Probing Volcanoes

Among the most dramatic applications of the concept of thermal energy are volcanoes, which this book explores in thrilling depth by profiling scientists who work in close proximity to the dangerous sources of the data they collect.

Laurie Lindop. Lerner Publishing Group. 80 pp. Illustrated. Library ISBN 978-0-7613-2700-4.

Curriculum Connection
Workbook, p. 110

Science Challenge
Workbook, p. 111

17A Thermal Expansion of A Balloon

This prechapter introduction activity is designed to determine what students already know about thermal energy and heat by engaging them in observing and drawing conclusions about the effect of heat on the confined air in a balloon.

Objectives

* predict the effect of temperature change on the volume of a confined gas
* observe the effect of temperature change on a gas
* compare and contrast the observed results
* draw conclusions about the effect of temperature change on gas

Planning

 about 20 minutes   groups of 3–4 students

Materials (per group)

* 3 balloons
* felt-tip marking pen
* cloth tape measure
* string
* scissors

Advance Preparation

* Make sure that all the balloons are of the same type.

* Perform the experiment on a sunny day or heat balloon A gently with a hair dryer.
* Remind students to measure the circumference of each balloon at its widest part.

Engagement Guide

* Challenge students to think about what will happen in the experiment by asking:
  * *How do you think the different temperature of each location will affect the air molecules inside the balloons?* (Students should suggest that increased temperatures will make the air molecules move faster and decreased temperatures will make the molecules move slower.)
  * *What do you think will happen to the size of the balloons as the kinetic energy of air inside increases or decreases? What will cause this change?* (Students should recognize that the balloons will expand or contract as the kinetic energy changes. The changes in size of the balloon are due to changes in the pressure exerted by the gas particles.)
* Encourage students to predict whether the balloons will change size and why.

Going Further

Encourage students to repeat the experiment with a sealed solid container fitted with a pressure gauge. Have students predict how the difference in temperature will affect the pressure of the air.

17B Thermal Energy and Temperature

Objectives

* predict the affect of thermal energy on melting ice
* compare and contrast the effects of temperature and thermal energy
* draw conclusions from observations of melting ice

Skill Set

observing, comparing and contrasting, recording and analyzing data, predicting, stating conclusions

Planning

 30–35 minutes   groups of 3–4 students

Materials

Materials for this activity are listed in the Student Laboratory Manual.

Advance Preparation

Warn the students to be careful handling the hot plate and hot water. Make sure that the ice cubes are about the same size and that the carafe and mug do not have such different insulating properties that it will affect the results of the experiment.

Answers to Observations: Data Table 1

Students' data should show that the temperature decreases more quickly in the mug.

Answers to Observations: Data Table 2

Students observations should describe how the ice melted much more quickly in the carafe.

Answers to Analysis and Conclusions

1. The ice melts faster in the carafe because the water in the carafe has much more thermal energy to transfer to the ice.

2. The water temperature changes faster in the mug because it has less thermal energy. As the energy is transferred to the ice, the temperature of the water decreases quickly.

3. Thermal energy and temperature are both related to the kinetic energy of the particles that make up matter. Thermal energy is the total energy of a substance, whereas temperature is a measurement of the average kinetic energy of a substance.

4. Students should predict that the water in the carafe would still melt the ice faster because of its much greater thermal energy.

Going Further

Have students measure the temperature of a beaker of ice as it melts. Take temperature measurements throughout the class period. Have them note how the temperature remains at the freezing point of water as the ice continues to gradually melt. Use this activity to discuss the energy of fusion.

17C Observing Kinetic Energy

Objectives

- observe how dye diffuses in water at different temperatures
- compare and contrast rates of diffusion
- draw conclusions based on experimental results

Skill Set

observing, recording and analyzing data, drawing conclusions

Planning

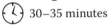 30–35 minutes   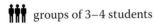 groups of 3–4 students

Materials

Materials for this activity are listed in the Student Laboratory Manual.

Advance Preparation

- Prepare a container of water with ice to provide the ice water for each group.
- Demonstrate the proper technique for heating the test tube over the flame of a Bunsen burner. Warn students to be careful when handling the Bunsen burner and hot water. Direct students to only handle the hot test tube with a test-tube holder.

Answers to Observations: Data Table 1

Students should observe that the dye diffuses more quickly in the hot water than in the room-temperature water, and the dye may mix completely in the hot water.

Answers to Observations: Data Table 2

Students should observe that the dye diffuses more slowly in the ice water than in the room-temperature water, and the dye may settle on the bottom of the test tube in the ice water.

Answers to Analysis and Conclusions

1. The dye diffuses fastest in the hot water, because the higher kinetic energy speeds up the mixing of molecules. The dye diffuses the slowest in the ice water, because the slower kinetic energy slows down the mixing of molecules.

2. Students should recognize that the molecules were moving the fastest in the hot water and the slowest in the ice water. Students should also recognize that these factors determined how rapidly the food color molecules were able to spread throughout the water.

Going Further

Have students extend the activity by adding a solid substance such as salt or sugar to each test tube. Ask students to observe the rates at which the substances dissolve in each test tube. The rates are directly related to the temperature of the water in each test tube.

Introduce Chapter 18

As a starting activity, use Lab 18A on page 103 of the Laboratory Manual.

ENGAGE Take students on a mini field trip in and around the school to identify different thermal energy applications (the furnace, generator, refrigerators, snack and soda machines, drinking fountains, cars, lawn mowers, other lawn machines, etc.). When students return to the classroom, have small groups list the machines and discuss what each does.

Think About Tracing Pathways

ENGAGE Have students brainstorm ideas about the fuel that provides energy for the vehicle. Encourage them with questions about how the fuel was formed, how it is obtained, how it is converted into a usable form, and how it is burned. Record their responses on the board. Have students guide you in drawing a fuel pathway diagram. Have students describe the diagram in their Science Notebooks.

Chapter
18 Heat Technology

KEY CONCEPT Thermal energy has many applications, including use in heating, refrigeration, and engines.

In the early 1900s, cars had top speeds of 45 miles per hour. Today, hot-rod racing cars can blast to over 300 miles per hour in less than five seconds. Over the past 100 years, automobiles have changed greatly in almost every way. However, one thing remains the same: heat from the burning of fuels powers the engines. Other vehicles, such as airplanes and trains, work on the same principle.

Thermal energy can do much more than run engines. The mastery of heat technology allows humans to control their environments and live in comfort.

Think About Tracing Pathways

Thermal energy follows a pathway from its generation until it is released into the environment. Think about the energy that powers your car or school bus.

- What fuel provides the energy for this vehicle?
- What pathway does the fuel follow from its formation to its end as waste heat? Describe the steps in a paragraph or a diagram in your Science Notebook.

NSTA
SCiLINKS.
THE WORLD'S A CLICK AWAY
www.scilinks.org
Heating and Cooling Systems
Code: WGPS18

298

Middle School Standard; High School Standard; Unifying Concept and Principle

18.1 Heating Systems

Before You Read

Make a T-chart in your Science Notebook. Label one side *Heating System* and the other side *Characteristics*. In the chart, write anything you already know about heating systems.

Heat is the flow of thermal energy from one object to another. People use heat in countless ways. Furnaces warm homes, stoves cook food, and blow-dryers dry hair. Surprisingly, air conditioners and refrigerators also use heat technology to create cool areas. Most cars and other vehicles run on the heat created by burning fuels.

One of the most important applications of heat technology is the home heating system. Almost every region of the United States gets cold enough during some part of the year to require a heat source.

Figure 18.1 In addition to the uses of heat technology shown here, what other uses can you think of?

Early Heating Systems

The earliest humans relied on sunlight and shared body heat for warmth. The discovery of ways to start and control fire led to a great improvement in their quality of life. With fire, people could live in colder climates, cook food, provide light after sunset, and fend off wild animals. Early people kept fire in a fire pit and huddled close to keep warm.

The building of homes allowed people to move their fire indoors, where it could create a warm living space. Fireplaces and stoves burned wood, coal, or other fuels. Heat spread through the room by conduction, convection, and radiation. There was no system to circulate the heat evenly through several rooms. Early stoves created many problems, including house fires, inefficient use of fuel, and smoky rooms. Engineers worked to develop new heating systems to address these problems.

Learning Goals

- Describe the different home heating systems.
- Explain the advantages and disadvantages of each heating system.

New Vocabulary

central heating system

Recall Vocabulary

heat, p. 282
conduction, p. 284
convection, p. 285
radiation, p. 286
thermostat, p. 295
solar energy, p. 272

Figure 18.2 Early American homes used an open hearth for heating, cooking, and heating water for washing and bathing.

18.1 Introduce

ENGAGE Show students photographs and illustrations of ways in which people have heated their homes in the past. Have them arrange these images chronologically and then find information about one heat source in library books or on the Internet.

Vocabulary terms are listed on the first student page of each lesson. You may wish to preview the terms before introducing each lesson. Strategies for teaching the vocabulary appear on the pages where the terms are introduced.

Before You Read

Discuss with students what a heating system is and what it does. Have students share their background knowledge about heating systems in small groups or with the class.

Teach

EXPLAIN to students that in this lesson, they will learn about home heating systems used in the past.

Use the Visual: Figure 18.1

(ANSWER) Students' answers will vary. Students might mention toasters, ovens, heating pads, heating blankets, and similar devices. They might also mention applications such as using heat to shape glass or metal.

ELL Strategy

Activate Background Knowledge Have pairs of students review the recall vocabulary listed on page 299. If they are uncertain about a word or term, have them refer to the page on which it was introduced and reread it. In pairs, English language learners could review these terms by creating crossword puzzles. Pairs could then exchange their puzzles to complete them.

Teach

EXPLAIN to students that they will learn about several types of heating systems currently in use.

Vocabulary

central heating system Tell students that *central* is an adjective that comes from the noun *center*. *Central* means "middle," "interior," or "primary." Have students put the meaning together with *heating system* and come up with a definition for the full term.

As You Read

On the board, create a T-chart with *Heating Systems* and *Characteristics* as headings. Write *Central heating systems, Radiant hot-water systems,* and *Forced-air systems* in the first column. Have students do the same in their Science Notebooks and then brainstorm information about each system with a partner.

[ANSWER] Radiators and forced-air heating separate the fire from the living space of the home. Smoke travels directly outside through a pipe, and flames cannot escape the furnace. Heat is distributed efficiently by radiators or ducts.

Use the Visual: Figure 18.4

[ANSWER] No. The fire in the furnace is enclosed in a metal box. Air in the duct circulates around the hot box. Heat moves by radiation and conduction from the box to the air in the ducts.

Science Notebook EXTRA

For homework or in class, have students list in their Science Notebooks the forms of heating, cooling, and heat engines they use in their daily lives. They should then share the information with the class.

Figure 18.3 Older water heating systems used radiators (*top*) to warm rooms. Some newer systems use plastic tubing under the floors to provide heat (*bottom*). The pipes are covered with concrete and tiles.

As You Read

In your Science Notebook, record information about the various heating systems. Be sure to include key facts and supporting details. Share your chart with a partner and add information as needed.

How do radiators and forced-air heating solve the problems of earlier heating systems?

Central Heating Systems

The next great advance in the heating of homes enabled heat to be spread to every room. A **central heating system** produces thermal energy that is piped or blown throughout a building. A thermostat controls the temperature throughout the house. Heat is created in a furnace by electricity or burning fuel. Early fuels included wood and coal. Natural gas and heating oil are fuels commonly used today.

Radiant Hot-Water System Heat from a central furnace can warm a tank of water. A system of pipes carries hot liquid water or steam around the house. The hot water radiates heat to each room it passes through. Gradually, the hot water cools. The cooler water returns to the furnace to be heated again. In the earlier radiant hot-water systems, pipes traveled through a device called a radiator, like the one shown in **Figure 18.3.** A radiator contains many loops of hot-water piping. Some newer systems pump hot water through pipes under the floors of rooms. The warm floors create a comfortable feeling, and the warm air rises by convection to fill the room.

Forced-Air System Warm air is another way to carry heat around a house. A furnace heats air, which is pumped around the house in large pipes called ducts. Ducts open into vents in each room. Cool air returns to the furnace through additional vents, where it is reheated. Forced-air systems are the most common type of heating system in the United States today.

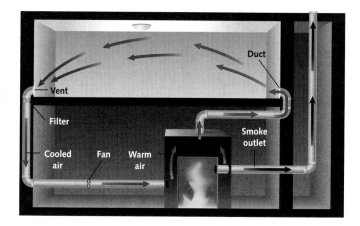

Figure 18.4 In a forced-air heating system, air heated by the furnace is delivered to all the rooms through ducts. Does the air in the duct directly contact the furnace fire?

Differentiate Instruction

Visual, Mathematical/Logical Have students interview each other to find out the types of heating and cooling systems used at home. Have students work in groups to present the information that they collect in the form of a chart, graph, or other visual.

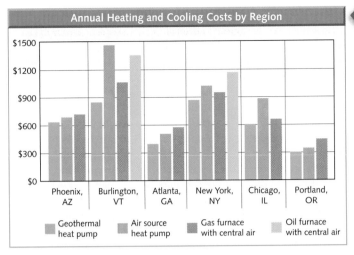

Annual Heating and Cooling Costs by Region

	Geothermal heat pump	Air source heat pump	Gas furnace with central air	Oil furnace with central air

Figure 18.5 Annual heating and cooling costs vary by geographic location. This graph shows the energy costs for heating systems by region.

Geothermal System Geothermal heating systems take advantage of the heat stored within Earth. The temperature two meters underground stays at 10°C to 20°C all year. Geothermal systems extract heat from the ground and circulate it around a home. The heat can be distributed by radiators, forced air, or radiant floor systems.

Geothermal heating systems are more expensive to install than a typical furnaces. However, fuel costs can be 25 to 70 percent lower for geothermal heat than for other heating systems. Homeowners save so much in energy costs that geothermal systems are cheaper in the long-term. Homes in areas with cold winters can save the most energy.

Active Solar System An active solar heating system is another way to make use of energy provided by nature. Sunlight heats a liquid or air in solar collectors. Heat from the collectors is transferred to a tank and pumped around the house. Solar heating systems are usually designed to provide 40 to 80 percent of a home's heating needs. Additional heat is generated by an electrical heating system or furnace.

Active solar systems can also be used as low-cost water heaters during the summer. In this case, the heat from the solar collectors warms water to be used in the home. Solar heating systems can be expensive to install, but the savings in fuel costs over the years will make up for the initial high price of the system. Solar heating is more practical in areas that have many sunny days.

Figure It Out

1. Explain which heating and cooling system is least expensive in each region.

2. How much money could a homeowner in Burlington, VT save each year by replacing an oil furnace with a geothermal heat pump?

 CONNECTION: Economics

The economic resources of each family, the price of fuel, and environmental concerns all influence decisions about home heating. State and federal governments may also offer money to convince consumers to purchase energy-efficient models.

Figure 18.6 Solar collectors mounted on the roof absorb the Sun's energy. The absorbed energy heats water in pipes above the plate. A pump circulates the hot water to radiators in rooms of the house. What is the purpose of the black metal plate?

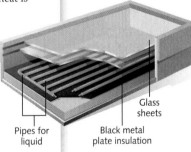

Pipes for liquid

Glass sheets

Black metal plate insulation

● **Teach**

EXPLAIN to students that they will learn about two less-common heating systems: geothermal and active solar.

Figure It Out: **Figure 18.5**

ANSWER **1.** Geothermal heat pumps are least expensive in every region. **2.** about $450 to $500

 **CONNECTION: Economics**

Geothermal heat systems not only make sense from an economic point of view; they also are friendly to the environment. Many heat systems burn fossil fuels that cause air pollution and harm the atmosphere. Geothermal heat is natural; it is generated within Earth and produces no harmful emissions. Have students find out whether the state in which they live offers incentives to purchase energy-efficient home heating systems. If so, have them identify specifics about these incentives.

Use the Visual: **Figure 18.6**

ANSWER It absorbs solar energy.

Background Information

Another heating system used today is hydro-air, which combines forced-air and hot-water systems. The heated air is moister, and therefore more comfortable, than forced-air heat. The water that is heated in the boiler can also be used domestically. Hydro-air can be used for cooling air during warmer months.

● Teach

to students that they will learn about several other heating systems.

Explain It!

Provide library books and Web sites with information on electric heaters and lightbulbs. Have students organize their notes by filling out an index card for each item with information about its purpose, efficiency, location, and waste products. Using the notes as a guide, each student should then to write a compare-and-contrast paragraph in his or her Science Notebook.

Use the Visual:

Figure 18.7 ANSWER Homes need an additional heat source for cloudy or very cold days.

Figure 18.8 ANSWER Regions farther from the equator get less sunlight each day and are colder.

 CONNECTION: Math

Have students look through home improvement store advertisements or Web sites to find heating and cooling systems that have power listed in Btus. Also have them find out how price relates to power.

● Assess

Use the After You Read questions and the Alternative Assessment to help you evaluate students' understanding of the lesson.

After You Read

1. Hearths and stoves were smoky, inefficient fire hazards that could not distribute heat evenly throughout a home.

2. Geothermal heating systems require less fuel than many other systems do because they use heat stored within Earth. Geothermal heating produces little pollution or carbon dioxide. However, these systems are more expensive and can be difficult to add to existing homes.

3. A wood stove would work well in a cabin that is small and not used very often.

Explain It!

Electric heaters and lightbulbs both produce heat from electricity. Compare and contrast the two in a paragraph in your Science Notebook. Consider the purpose, efficiency, location, and waste products of each.

Figure 18.7 Sunlight falling on the U.S. contains 600 times more energy than the country needs. Why can't passive solar heating provide all of the country's home-heating energy needs?

 **CONNECTION: Math**

Consumers in the U.S. might see the power of heating and cooling systems expressed in British thermal units (Btu). One Btu is the energy needed to raise the temperature of one pound of water by one degree Fahrenheit. One Btu equals 1,055 joules.

Other Heating Systems

In some cases, heating an individual room makes more sense than a central heating system. For example, a workshop or cabin might need heat only a few weeks out of the year. Installing ducts in a room addition to a house might be too expensive. An older home might have cold rooms due to a poor heating system design.

Room Heaters Single electric heaters can be installed near the floor, or baseboard, of a room. Heating coils similar to those on an electric stove generate thermal energy from electricity. Heat radiates out from the coils, warming the air nearby. Warm air travels around the room by convection. Electric baseboard heaters have individual thermostats that control the temperature in each room separately.

A wood or corn pellet stove can also warm a room. Wood may be available for low or no cost if there is a woodlot nearby. The price of corn pellets depends on the current price of corn. Stoves and fireplaces are generally less fuel-efficient than furnaces.

Passive Solar System A passive solar heating system uses radiant energy from the Sun to heat a home. Walls facing the Sun contain many windows to allow sunlight into the home. Materials inside the house absorb solar energy and heat up during the day. Thick walls absorb and hold a lot of thermal energy. During cool nights, heat radiates from the wall back into the room. Passive solar systems cost little and help reduce the energy costs of a house. Another heating system is usually needed to provide additional heat on the coldest days, however.

Figure 18.8 In a passive solar heating system, solar energy is transferred through the windows into a room. In what regions of the United States would passive solar heating systems be impractical?

After You Read

1. Explain why people switched from using hearths and stoves to using central heating systems.

2. In a well-developed paragraph, describe the advantages and disadvantages of geothermal heating systems. Use the characteristics you have recorded in your Science Notebook.

3. Which type of heating system makes sense for a small cabin in the woods that is used three weeks out of the year? Explain your answer.

Alternative Assessment

After completing the T-chart in his or her Science Notebook, have each student write a compare-and-contrast paragraph about two types of home heating systems. Have students list positive and negative aspects of each, along with any other relevant information from this lesson.

18.2 Cooling Systems

Before You Read

Look at the photographs and diagrams in this lesson. In your Science Notebook, write two questions that this lesson might answer. Your questions should relate to something you would like to know about refrigeration and air-conditioning.

Heating is the transfer of thermal energy to a room or substance. Cooling is the opposite: the movement of heat from a room or substance to another place. The second law of thermodynamics states that heat naturally flows from high-temperature objects to low-temperature objects. Work is needed to make heat flow from a cooler object to a warmer one.

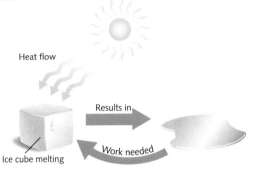

Figure 18.9 Heat flows naturally from high-temperature objects to lower-temperature objects. Work is required to make heat flow from cold objects to hot objects. This diagram shows heat flow on a warm day.

Early Cooling Systems

The earliest human need for cooling was to keep food from spoiling. At first, food was simply placed in a stream to keep it cool. People began to use ice and snow for refrigeration thousands of years ago. Blocks of ice were cut during the winter and moved to a cave or hole in the ground. Straw or another insulator kept the ice from melting well into the summer. Meat placed in an ice house stayed fresh for months.

Early cooling systems relied on nature to provide the energy needed for cooling. Gradually, humans learned to use mechanical work to remove heat from one object and transfer it to a new location. Modern cooling systems are **heat movers** that absorb heat from one place, carry it to another, and transfer it to the surrounding air or water.

Figure 18.10 People have collected ice for refrigeration for thousands of years. Iceboxes kept food cold in American homes well into the twentieth century.

CHAPTER 18 **303**

18.2 Introduce

ENGAGE Have students work in small groups to hypothesize about how they could keep ice frozen on a hot summer day without access to a freezer. Each group should then share its ideas with the class.

Before You Read

Demonstrate by thinking aloud how to look through the photographs and diagrams in this lesson and come up with questions that relate to the content. Have students do the same and record their questions in their Science Notebooks.

● Teach

EXPLAIN to students that they will learn how people used to keep food cold before refrigerators were invented.

Vocabulary

heat mover Ask students to recall the definition of *heat* from previous chapters. Tell them that a mover is something or someone that moves, or transfers, something else. Ask them to put the word meanings together and come up with a definition for the term *heat mover*.

Differentiate Instruction

Interpersonal For a homework assignment, have students research cooling systems used during the first part of the twentieth century. If possible, have students interview someone who remembers that time. Working with partners, have students create a list of interview questions beforehand.

Questions might include: *How did you keep foods cool? How did you keep cool on hot days?* If no one is available for the interview, challenge pairs to exchange questions and try to answer the questions based on their research as if they had lived during that time.

Teach

EXPLAIN to students that they will learn about how a refrigerator keeps food cold.

Vocabulary

heat pump Tell students that a pump is a device that forces liquids or gases into or out of something. Have them recall the meaning of *heat* and put the two word meanings together to define the term.

As You Read

Have students record additional questions as they read the lesson. They should answer as many of the questions as they can by the end of the lesson. Explain that not all questions will be answered and they will have to go to other sources to locate this information.

ANSWER Refrigerator coils contain coolant that has passed through the compressor. Compression causes gases to increase in temperature. The hot coils radiate heat from the refrigerator into the room or hand.

Explore It!

For each pair of students, provide an eyedropper and a small quantity of rubbing alcohol. Demonstrate how to carefully place a drop or two of alcohol on your arm and fan it dry with the opposite hand.

The student's arm will feel cold as the alcohol evaporates. Vaporizing the coolant in a refrigerator makes the coolant drop in temperature. Cold coolant can absorb heat from the contents of the refrigerator.

Figure It Out: Figure 18.11

ANSWER **1.** The coolant, just after it leaves the compressor, is at the highest temperature. **2.** No. The heat removed from the food compartment is radiated out into the room. More heat is produced by the compressor. Leaving the refrigerator open would heat up the room.

As You Read

As you read the lesson, identify and record answers to the questions you wrote in your Science Notebook.

Why are refrigerator coils warm to the touch?

Explore It!

Put a drop or two of alcohol on your arm and fan the spot with your other hand. What sensation do you feel as the alcohol evaporates? In your Science Notebook, explain the purpose of vaporizing the liquid coolant in a refrigerator.

Figure It Out

1. Which part of the refrigerator is at the highest temperature?
2. Would this refrigerator cool the kitchen if the door were left open?

Refrigerators

A refrigerator is a heat mover that absorbs thermal energy from food and other materials inside it. Refrigerators work on two basic principles. First, heat moves from warmer to cooler substances. Second, gases get hotter when they are compressed and colder as they expand. Heat is carried away from food to the room outside the refrigerator. Air surrounding the refrigerator absorbs the heat.

Absorbing Heat The refrigerator contains a long tube filled with coolant. Liquid coolant is pushed by a pump through an expansion valve, where it becomes a cold gas. The cold gaseous coolant travels in its tube to an evaporator coil. A fan blows the air in the freezer across the evaporator coil. This is where heat from the warmer food and air is transferred to the cold coil. The coolant warms as it absorbs the heat.

Releasing Heat The coolant is still colder than room temperature after it travels through the evaporator coil. Coolant can only transfer heat to the air in the room when it is warmer than the room air. Because of this, the coolant passes through a compressor that compresses it and makes it hotter. The hot gas can now release its heat into the surrounding air. The coolant cools and condenses back into a liquid in the condenser coils. The liquid coolant is pumped back to the expansion valve, where it begins the cycle again.

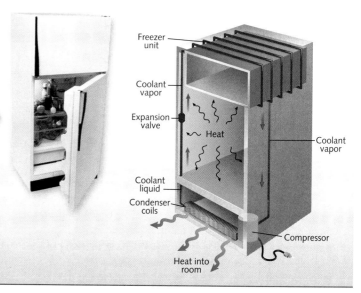

Figure 18.11 A refrigerator uses a liquid coolant to move thermal energy from inside the compartment to outside the compartment. Electricity provides the energy necessary to move heat from the cooler contents of the refrigerator to the warm room.

ELL Strategy

Think, Pair, Share After students read this page, have them work with partners to diagram or outline the cooling system used in a refrigerator.

Key Concept Review
Workbook, p. 112

Air Conditioners Like a refrigerator, an air conditioner is a heat mover. It refrigerates the space inside a building and transfers heat outside. A room air conditioner rests in a window and blows cooled air into a single room.

Central air conditioners cool entire buildings. The ducts, radiators, or under-floor tubing used by a central heating system are shared by the cooling system. Cool air, water, or coolant is piped throughout a building to maintain an even temperature in every room, as shown in **Figure 18.12**.

Heat Pumps

A **heat pump** is a heat mover that transfers heat from a cooler location to a warmer location. Refrigerators and air conditioners are both heat pumps. Other examples of heat pumps include water coolers and refrigerated water fountains. Geothermal heat pumps can provide cooling as well as heating of homes.

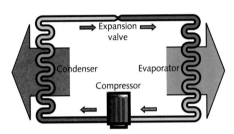

Figure 18.13 A heat pump carries heat from a cooler location to a warmer one. The direction of coolant flow determines whether a heat pump functions as a cooler or a heater.

One special property of heat pumps is their ability to switch between heating and cooling. Coolant flowing through the heat pump in one direction produces air-conditioning in a home. Heat is moved from the air in the room and transferred to the outdoor air. Reversing the flow of coolant extracts heat from outdoor air and transfers it to the home. Heat pumps range in size from personal units that heat and cool cars or tents to large systems that keep hospitals comfortable.

After You Read

1. Would a refrigerator work more efficiently in a hot kitchen or a cold kitchen? Explain what would happen in a very hot kitchen.
2. Use the information you recorded in your Science Notebook to explain how an air conditioner is like a refrigerator.
3. What is a major difference between early cooling systems and heat pumps?

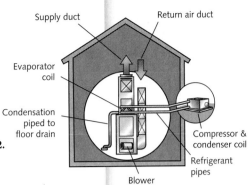

Central Air Conditioner on a Forced Air System

Supply duct
Return air duct
Evaporator coil
Condensation piped to floor drain
Compressor & condenser coil
Refrigerant pipes
Blower

Figure 18.12 An air conditioner transfers heat from a home to the outside. The blower, under-floor tubing, or radiators of a central heating system are used to create even cooling throughout the home.

Did You Know?

Waste heat from an air conditioner can warm the water in a water heater. Using waste heat costs no money and improves the efficiency of the air conditioner. Waste heat can provide all of the water heating needed in warm climates.

● Teach

EXPLAIN to students that they will learn about air conditioners and heat pumps.

● Assess

Use the After You Read questions and the Alternative Assessment to help you evaluate students' understanding of the lesson.

After You Read

1. A refrigerator would be more efficient in a cold kitchen. Heat from the condenser coils would radiate out faster into the cool air. In a very hot kitchen, heat would travel into the coils from the room. The refrigerator would not be able to move heat away from the food inside.
2. An air conditioner transfers heat from a home to the outside air. A refrigerator uses liquid coolant to move thermal energy from inside the compartment to outside the compartment. Electricity provides the energy necessary to move heat from the cooler contents of the refrigerator to the warm room. In an air conditioner, cool air, water, or coolant is piped throughout the building to maintain an even temperature in every room.
3. Early cooling systems relied on natural processes to remove heat. Heat traveled from warm food or air to cold ice or water without any work. Heat pumps use work to reverse the natural direction of heat flow. They can move heat from a cool substance to a warmer one.

Alternative Assessment

Give students time to review the questions and answers they recorded in their Science Notebooks. For unanswered questions, give them time to locate information using other sources.

Background Information

Air-conditioning is among the most expensive home energy uses. To avoid running it inefficiently or more than is necessary, there are several steps that a homeowner can take. Ceiling fans can be installed and used with or without the air-conditioning system. Shade trees can be planted, window awnings installed, and curtains closed on the sunny side of the house. Lights and computer equipment can be turned off when not in use. Outdoor grills and crock pots can be used more instead of the oven and stove. The house can be checked for air leaks and the attic for proper ventilation.

ENGAGE Working in small groups, have students review the lesson's photos, diagrams, and captions. Have them discuss what they already know about the content and what they predict the lesson is about.

Before You Read

Ask students for an example of a word that they have learned recently. Ask how they first learned it and what they have learned about it subsequently. Tell them that they are most likely gaining a deeper understanding of the word each time they read or hear it.

● Teach

EXPLAIN to students that they will learn about heat engines and one particular type of heat engine, the steam engine.

Learning Goals

- Describe the purpose of a heat engine.
- Compare and contrast internal and external combustion engines.
- Explain the causes and results of engine inefficiency.

New Vocabulary

heat engine
external combustion engine
internal combustion engine
thermal pollution

Recall Vocabulary

mechanical energy, p. 267
potential energy, p. 264
fission, p. 273
chemical energy, p. 265
nonrenewable resource, p. 273

18.3 Heat Engines

Before You Read

Create a working definition of the term *engine*. Create a concept map to record what you know about the term before you begin reading. Then add to that definition as you read and discuss the lesson.

It is easy to produce thermal energy by doing work. For example, the friction of rubbing your hands together makes them warm. However, it is more difficult to get work from thermal energy. Machines that use heat to move objects are relatively new inventions.

Heat Engines

A device that converts thermal energy into mechanical energy that can perform useful work is called a **heat engine.** For example, a car burns fuel. The heat produced is converted to mechanical energy as the car accelerates (kinetic energy) or moves uphill (potential energy).

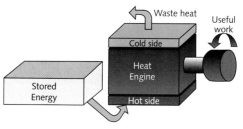

Figure 18.14 Heat engines convert thermal energy into useful mechanical work and waste heat.

A heat engine can use any source of heat to do work. Electricity, sunlight, nuclear fission, and chemical energy from burning fuels are all possible heat sources. Cars with hybrid engines use both chemical fuel and electricity to power their engines. Heat engines must follow the law of conservation of energy: no heat engine can create or destroy energy. Instead, heat engines transform some of their thermal energy into mechanical work. Every heat engine also produces waste heat that is released into its surroundings.

Steam Engines The steam engine, invented around the year 1700, was the first practical heat engine. Steam engines use heated steam to press against a moving part such as a turbine fan. The turbine turns a shaft that does work. Early steam engines pumped water and powered the first tractors and train locomotives. Steam still powers many electrical generators today.

ELL Strategy

Use a Concept Map Have each student draw a concept map in his or her Science Notebook. They should label the center circle *Heat Engine* and one outer circle *Steam Engine*. Have students work in pairs to come up with a definition for each term and write it in the appropriate circle on the map.

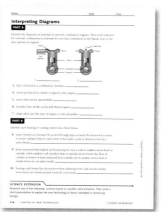

Interpreting Diagrams
Workbook, p. 114

External Combustion Engines

A heat engine in which fuel is burned outside the engine is called an **external combustion engine.** Combustion is a type of chemical reaction in which a substance, the fuel, combines with oxygen to produce carbon dioxide, water, and energy. Steam engines, for example, burn fuel to generate heat. The heat changes water to steam in a boiler. Pipes carry the high-temperature, high-pressure steam to the engine. In the engine is a turbine, or a fan with many blades attached to a driveshaft. The steam expands as it rushes through the turbine and pushes on the fan blades. The blades force the shaft to spin around and do useful work. Ship engines often use external combustion engines to drive their propellers.

The hot steam cools as it expands and leaves the turbine. It is no longer hot enough to do useful work in the engine. It may become the exhaust often seen billowing from stacks incorrectly named "smokestacks." In other cases, the cooled steam condenses and returns in pipes to the boiler to be used again.

Internal Combustion Engines

Internal combustion engines use heat to produce work, just like external combustion engines do. However, the **internal combustion engine** burns fuel in a combustion chamber inside the engine. The burning fuel creates heat that causes the gases in the combustion chamber to expand. Expanding gas pushes on the moving parts that do work in the engine. Cars, airplanes, buses, boats, trucks, tractors, and chainsaws are all machines that use internal combustion engines.

Figure 18.16 Internal combustion engines power many of the vehicles and machines people use every day.

Figure 18.15 The white clouds seen billowing from smokestacks may well be steam from the turbines of external combustion engines.

As You Read

As you read the lesson, add to your definition of the term *engine* to make it more complete. Be sure to record important facts, supporting details, and specific examples.

What is produced by every engine?

Teach

EXPLAIN to students that they will learn about different kinds of internal combustion engines used in vehicles.

 Vocabulary

thermal pollution Tell students that the word *pollution* can be broken down into the verb *pollute*, meaning "to contaminate something with harmful substances or impurities," and *-tion*, a suffix signifying action, result, or state. Ask students to remember what *thermal* means ("relating to heat") and then combine the meanings to define the term *thermal pollution*.

Extend It!

The first stroke of the engine cycle is the intake stroke, the second is the compression stroke, the third is the power stroke, and the fourth is the exhaust stroke. A detailed description and diagrams of the engine cycle are available through NASA's Web site.

Explain to students that this information will probably be useful to them in the future. Knowledge about how an automobile engine functions can be very helpful when purchasing a new automobile or having a used one repaired.

Figure It Out: Figure 18.17

(ANSWER) **1.** four **2.** The engine would continue to run unchanged. However, the wheels would not turn because they would not be connected to the engine.

Use the Visual: Figure 18.18

(ANSWER) The chainsaw has a two-stroke engine; the car has a four-stroke, or Otto-cycle, engine; and the construction equipment has a diesel engine.

Extend It!

Research the four-stroke engine to identify the four different strokes. Write a brief explanation of each stroke in your Science Notebook. Then draw a diagram of each stroke and label the following parts: intake valve, cylinder, piston, fuel-air mixture, spark plug, crankshaft, exhaust valve, and exhaust gases.

Figure It Out

1. How many cylinders are in this engine?
2. Describe what would happen if the crankshaft broke between the transmission and the differential.

Figure 18.18 Which type of engine would you expect to find in each of these machines?

Car Engines Most cars have engines with four or more combustion chambers, or cylinders. The cylinder is where the power for the engine is produced. More cylinders make cars more powerful. Every cylinder contains a piston that can move up and down. A mixture of fuel and air is pushed into the cylinder. This mixture is ignited, which causes an explosive combustion reaction. The energy from this reaction pushes the piston down. The up-and-down movement of the piston turns a crankshaft, which moves the wheels of the car. **Figure 18.17** shows how a car engine converts thermal energy from burning fuel into the work of rotating wheels.

Engine Cycles The first internal combustion engines created work with each stroke of the engine. However, this design wasted a lot of energy and burned extra fuel. Nikolaus Otto and his coworkers designed a more efficient engine cycle in which only one out of each four strokes provides power to the engine. This four-stroke cycle, or Otto cycle, is still used by most car engines today.

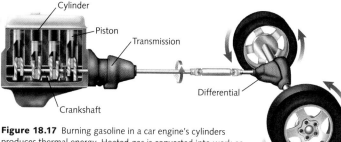

Figure 18.17 Burning gasoline in a car engine's cylinders produces thermal energy. Heated gas is converted into work as the pistons move up and down. The crankshaft, transmission, and differential convert the motion of the pistons into rotation of the wheels.

Other types of internal combustion engines are also popular. Dirt bikes, chainsaws, and jet skis use a two-stroke engine cycle. Two-stroke engines have the advantage of greater power and lighter weight than Otto cycle engines. However, two-stroke engines burn a lot of oil, create more pollution, and wear out faster. Engineers are working to develop lighter, more powerful four-stroke engines to replace the two-stroke engine.

Heavy trucks and earthmovers typically use diesel engines. The diesel cycle is similar to the Otto cycle, but it uses diesel fuel in place of gasoline. Diesel engines run more efficiently and last longer than Otto-cycle engines do. However, they are usually heavier, smokier, and more expensive. Newer models of diesel engines will likely overcome these problems.

Background Information

With recent public concern about the environment, dependence on foreign oil, and higher gasoline prices, many people are interested in purchasing hybrid cars. Hybrids use a gasoline engine, an electric engine, and an electric battery. The gasoline engines are smaller and more efficient than conventional cars, allowing for lighter, smaller vehicles that take less energy to operate.

Teacher Alert

Alert students not to touch any parts of the car that are under the hood when a car is running or has been running recently. This could result in serious burns.

Engine Efficiency

A perfectly efficient engine would convert all of the energy of its fuel into work. No waste heat would be generated. Unfortunately, real car engines are typically about 20 percent efficient. Four-fifths of their fuel's energy becomes waste heat. Energy is lost through the cooling system and hot exhaust. The large number of moving parts in an engine also creates a great deal of friction.

Waste heat from factories and power plants can damage the environment. **Thermal pollution** results when the temperature of a body of water is raised by waste heat. Oxygen is less soluble in warm water than in cold water. Warm water may not hold enough oxygen for fish and other organisms to survive.

Inefficient engines can be a big problem. First, consumers pay a lot of money in extra fuel. Second, higher fuel use increases the nation's dependence on foreign oil. The petroleum used to make gasoline and diesel fuel is also a nonrenewable resource. Finally, inefficient engines can lead to pollution. Poorly-running engines fail to completely burn fuel. The unburned fuel is sent out the exhaust pipe and into the air. Many scientists and engineers are working to improve the efficiency of all types of engines.

Figure 18.19 Heat engines can cause environmental damage through their exhaust and waste heat.

PEOPLE IN SCIENCE Nikolaus Otto (1832–1891)

Nikolaus Otto was born in Germany. Although he did well in school, he did not attend college, but instead worked as a clerk and a salesman. As he traveled, Otto learned about the invention of the internal combustion engine. This engine was noisy, hot, and inefficient. Expensive gaseous fuel was needed to power it.

In his spare time, Otto experimented with engine designs, always trying to make engines more powerful and efficient. In 1876, he developed the four-stroke Otto engine. The first cars of the 1880s contained an Otto engine set into a stagecoach. A version of the Otto engine is still used in cars on the road today.

After You Read

1. What features do all heat engines have in common? Base your answer on the working definition of *engine* in your Science Notebook.

2. Explain the major difference between external and internal combustion engines.

3. List several advantages of fuel-efficient engines.

Teach

EXPLAIN to students that they will learn about engine efficiency and about Nikolaus Otto.

PEOPLE IN SCIENCE

In 1864, Otto paired with an investor who provided financial support to create engines. Their first invention, the atmospheric gas power machine, was manufactured in their new company. In 1867, they entered this energy-efficient engine in the Paris Exhibition and won the gold medal. As a result, there was more public demand for the engine than the company could meet. They found more investors over time and continued manufacturing. Otto invented the four-stroke Otto engine in 1876. Between 1876 and 1889, the company sold about 8,300 Otto engines.

EXTEND Tell students that engineers have been working toward making automobile engines more fuel-efficient. Direct students to research the fuel efficiency of modern cars. Ask pairs of students to make a chart listing five cars and their fuel-efficiency ratings. Compare charts throughout the class to look for a relationship between vehicle size and fuel efficiency. Then challenge students to list at least five ways to improve on the fuel efficiency of any car. For example, students might suggest removing unnecessary loads from the vehicle and keeping tires properly inflated.

Assess

Use the After You Read questions and the Alternative Assessment to help you evaluate students' understanding of the lesson.

After You Read

1. All heat engines transform heat into useful work and waste heat.

2. External combustion engines burn fuel to make steam, which is piped into the engine. Fuel is burned in a cylinder inside an internal combustion engine.

3. Fuel-efficient engines cost less money in fuel and produce less air pollution. Using less fuel can reduce the nation's dependence on foreign oil.

ELL Strategy

Use a Concept Map Give students time to complete their concept maps. *Engine Efficiency* should be added as a topic branching off the center circle, and *Car Engines* and *Engine Cycles* should be added around *Internal Combustion Engine*.

Alternative Assessment

Give students time to complete their definitions of the term *engine*. Then have them compare their definitions with the information in their concept maps and add to, reorganize, or change their definitions if necessary. Suggest that they refer to the concept maps as they think about how they might more logically organize the information in their definitions.

Chapter 18 Summary

VOCABULARY REVIEW

Check students' sentences or paragraphs to make sure they understand the meaning of each vocabulary term.

Evaluate students' essays using the following criteria:

1. The topic sentence, or main idea, should restate the Key Concept.

2. The supporting paragraphs should incorporate the answers to the Learning Goal questions students have written and include details, facts, and examples they have recorded in their Science Notebooks.

3. The concluding sentence should sum up the main idea of the chapter and restate the Key Concept.

MASTERING CONCEPTS

True or False

1. True
2. True
3. False, forced-air
4. False, refrigerator
5. True
6. False, Heat engines

Short Answer

7. The waste heat is released into the surrounding air or water.

8. Radiant hot-water heating and forced-air heating systems are both forms of central heating. Both systems require a source of heat. Hot-water heating systems pump liquid water or steam through pipes in radiators or under floors. Forced-air heating systems blow warm air through ducts into rooms.

9. Answers will vary. Encourage students to describe the fuel, delivery system, and thermostat(s) used in their heating systems.

10. Cooling systems cannot make the heat in a home or refrigerator disappear. Instead, they heat one place while cooling another. Heat engines produce heat by converting chemical or another form of energy to thermal energy. Some of the thermal energy is transformed into mechanical energy that can do work on the engine parts.

Chapter 18 Summary

KEY CONCEPTS

18.1 Heating Systems

- Open fires and stoves were early heating systems with many disadvantages.
- Central heating systems create or collect heat that is piped or blown throughout a building.
- Types of central heating systems include radiant hot-water systems, forced-air systems, geothermal systems, and active solar systems.
- In many cases, it makes sense to heat rooms separately or collect sunlight in a passive solar heating system.

18.2 Cooling Systems

- Early people used ice and flowing water for cooling food.
- Modern cooling systems are heat movers that absorb heat from one place and transfer it to another location.
- Refrigerators and air conditioners are heat movers that use expansion and compression of coolants to move heat away from food or homes.
- A heat pump transfers heat from a cooler to a warmer location. Heat pumps can be reversed to perform as either a heating unit or a cooling unit.

18.3 Heat Engines

- A heat engine converts thermal energy into mechanical energy that can perform useful work.
- External combustion and internal combustion engines burn fuel to produce heat and useful work.
- Popular types of internal combustion engines include four-stroke (Otto), diesel, and two-stroke engines.
- Today's engines are mostly inefficient machines that produce waste heat and pollution.

VOCABULARY REVIEW

Write each term in a complete sentence or write a paragraph relating several terms.

18.1
central heating system, p. 300

18.2
heat mover, p. 303
heat pump, p. 305

18.3
heat engine, p. 306
external combustion engine, p. 307
internal combustion engine, p. 307
thermal pollution, p. 309

PREPARE FOR CHAPTER TEST

To prepare for the chapter test, create a question from each Learning Goal. Use the information in your Science Notebook to answer each question. Then use these answers to write a well-developed essay about the chapter. Use the Key Concept on the first page of this chapter as your topic sentence.

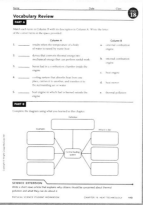

Vocabulary Review
Workbook, p. 113

Reading Comprehension
Workbook, p. 115

True or False
If the statement is true, write "true." If it is false, change the underlined word or words to make the statement true.

1. A(n) <u>active solar</u> heating system uses solar collectors to warm a liquid or air.

2. The first practical heat engine was the <u>steam engine</u>.

3. Warm air is blown into each room of a house in a(n) <u>geothermal</u> heating system.

4. A(n) <u>air conditioner</u> transfers heat from food to the air in a room.

5. Pistons, cylinders, and strokes are all features of <u>internal combustion</u> engines.

6. <u>Heat pumps</u> convert thermal energy into useful work and waste heat.

Short Answer
Answer each of the following in a sentence or brief paragraph.

7. Where does the waste heat from heat engines go? Provide two examples.

8. Compare and contrast radiant hot-water heating and forced-air heating systems.

9. Describe the heating system in your home. If room heating is used, explain how and why.

10. How does the law of conservation of energy apply to cooling systems and heat engines?

11. Four-stroke, two-stroke, and diesel engines are all popular types of engines. Explain why more than one type of engine is needed.

12. Explain why geothermal and solar heating systems are more efficient than fuel-burning heating systems.

13. Diagram the temperature changes of coolant as it travels through a refrigerator.

Critical Thinking
Use what you have learned in this chapter to answer each of the following.

14. Hypothesize Diesel-powered generators use internal combustion engines to produce electricity. Why are these generators not used for home heating systems?

15. Infer Why do heating systems use fuel more efficiently than cooling systems and heat engines do?

16. Evaluate Heat engines are used for many different applications. How would your life be different without the invention of heat engines?

Standardized Test Question
Choose the letter of the response that correctly answers the question.

17. What is the purpose of the compressor in a refrigerator?

   A. to raise coolant temperature so that it can absorb heat from food

   B. to lower coolant temperature so that it can absorb heat from food

   C. to raise coolant temperature so that it can release heat to the room

   D. to lower coolant temperature so that it can release heat to the room

Test-Taking Tip
Use scrap paper to write notes. Sometimes making a sketch, such as a diagram or table, can help you organize your ideas.

11. Each has advantages and disadvantages. For example, two-stroke engines are light and powerful, but they are also inefficient, polluting, and short-lived.

12. Geothermal and solar heating systems use heat provided by nature. Therefore, they do not require as much fuel to heat a home and do not create air pollution.

13. Sample answer: coolant from expansion valve: cold; absorbing heat from refrigerator compartment: warmer; after compressor: hot; passing through condenser coils: cooler

Critical Thinking

14. Internal combustion engines are not efficient. Most of the fuel becomes waste heat; diesel is an expensive fuel; and generators produce polluting exhaust.

15. Heating systems are efficient because their fuel is converted almost entirely into the desired product: heat. Cooling systems require mechanical work to move heat from a cool place to a warmer one. The heat produced by cooling systems represents wasted energy. Heat engines are inefficient because they can only produce work with hot steam or air.

16. Answers will vary. Without heat engines, there would be no cars, trucks, buses, or other mechanized transportation.

Standardized Test Question

17. C

Reading Links

Solar Power
This comprehensive overview of solar power will increase students' awareness as energy consumers.

Clay Farris Naff, ed. Greenhaven Press. 244 pp. Illustrated. Trade ISBN 978-0-7377-3565-9.

The Automobile (Great Inventions)
Readers of this engaging study of automobiles will learn more about the internal combustion engine and its relation to thermal energy.

James Lincoln Collier. Benchmark Books. 112 pp. Illustrated. Library ISBN 978-0-7614-1877-1.

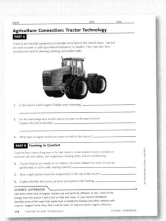

Curriculum Connection
Workbook, p. 116

Science Challenge
Workbook, pp. 117–118

18A How Effective Is Insulation?

This prechapter introduction activity is designed to determine what students already know about heat technology by engaging them in observing, examining, comparing, recording data, and making conclusions about insulating materials.

Objectives

• predict insulator effectiveness
• observe and evaluate the effectiveness of insulators
• compare and contrast the insulating properties
• communicate conclusions

Planning

 15–20 minutes, and 5 minutes every hour for one day

 groups of 3–4 students

Materials (per group)

• 5 cardboard boxes, approximately 30-cm square
• enough of each of the following to fill a box:
  foam packing popcorn
  bubble wrap
  crumpled newspaper
  cotton rags
• 5 half-liter water bottles filled three-quarters full with ice

Advance Preparation

• Prepare a set of materials for each group.
• Fill the bottles three-quarters full with water, recap them, and place in a freezer until frozen solid. Ensure each bottle contains the same amount of water before freezing it.

• Remind students to place the water bottles in the center of the boxes. The bottles should not touch any of the six sides except for the box without insulation. Stress the importance of doing the hourly check quickly and making sure the insulation materials are back in place before the boxes are resealed.

• Since this experiment can take a few hours, it may be a good idea to have your first class of the day set it up, and then have the following classes take down their own predictions. On the second day, you can have each class look at the results from the previous day.

Engagement Guide

• Challenge students to think about heat flow and the effectiveness of insulation by asking these questions:
  • *What types of clothing keep you warm?* (Clothes with thick tight weaves or puffy insulated liners are especially warm.)
  • *What physical structure or property might make one insulator more effective than another?* (Insulators having low thermal conductivities and that trap pockets of air are usually good insulators.)
  • *Why is limiting the movement of air in an insulating material important for its effectiveness?* (Moving air transfers heat by convection.)
• Encourage students to predict the kinds of insulators that will work best in keeping the ice frozen.

Going Further

Encourage students to perform the same experiment with a heat pack and a thermometer with remote sensor. Have students predict which insulators will retain the heat best.

18B Heat Transfer in Water

Objectives

• predict final temperatures
• observe the effects of temperature and volume on heat transfer
• analyze the accuracy of your predictions
• draw conclusions from experimental results

Skill Set

predicting, measuring, comparing and contrasting, recording and analyzing data, stating conclusions

Planning

 30–35 minutes   groups of 3–4 students

Materials

Materials for this activity are listed in the Student Laboratory Manual.

Advance Preparation

• Prepare a set of materials for each group.
• Heat the water to a hot but safe temperature. Choose safe, heat-resistant containers that will maintain the temperature of the water.
• Provide heat-resistant mittens or potholders for the students, if necessary.
• Explain to the students that if the two thermometers they use to measure the mixed water give different readings, then they should record an average of the readings.

Answers to Observations: Data Table 1

Accuracy of students' predictions will vary. Students should find that the change in temperature is related to the initial volumes and temperatures.

Answers to Analysis and Conclusions

1. Students should cite that heat always flows from hot to cold, that the final temperature must be between the two sources, and that the relative volume determines the final temperature.

2. Students should explain that the final temperature depends on the ratio of hot water to cold water. The greater the ratio of hot to cold, the greater the final temperature.

Going Further

To extend this activity, students could repeat it using other liquids in place of or in addition to water. Liquids such as vegetable oil or corn syrup could be used. Mixing different liquids brings in another factor that affects the final temperature—the specific heat of each substance.

18C Home Solar Heat

Objectives

- observe how different materials affect the heating and cooling of a simulated house
- compare and contrast the reaction of different materials to solar heat
- analyze why certain materials affect the heating and cooling of a house differently
- draw conclusions based on experimental results.

Skill Set

observing, recording and analyzing data, drawing conclusions

Planning

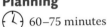 60–75 minutes

groups of 3–4 students

Materials

Materials for this activity are listed in the Student Laboratory Manual.

Advance Preparation

- Provide a set of the materials for each group. Warn the students to be careful with the infrared lamp and to always keep it a safe distance from objects that may burn or get hot.
- Remind students to insert the thermometer near the top of the boxes they make so it does not receive direct heat from the lamp. The thermometer must be placed in the same spot inside each box and it must be readable from outside the box.
- If a shorter lab is desired, heat and cool the box for 15 minutes instead of 20.

Lab Tip

The infrared lamp used should have a wattage no higher than 250 W. The bulb should be shatter-resistant and safety coated. The acrylic plastic and the corrugated cardboard should be fire resistant.

Answers to Observations: Data Tables 1 and 2

Results will vary according to how the boxes are constructed. Students should observe that the acrylic-faced box rises in temperature more quickly than the white-faced box. The difference in cooling between the two boxes should be less pronounced.

Answers to Analysis and Conclusions

1. Students should observe that the box with the acrylic plastic sheet heated much more rapidly because it allowed more of the infrared heat to enter. The white box reflected more of the infrared heat.

2. Results will vary depending on how the boxes are constructed. Students should observe that the box with the acrylic plastic sheet cools faster because it is not as efficient an insulator as the cardboard.

3. Students should recognize that houses in cooler climates can be designed to allow more of the Sun's heat to enter the house, and houses in hotter climates can be designed to reflect more of the Sun's heat.

Going Further

Have students study houses in their community with regard to how they are designed to make use of or limit the impact of solar energy. Ask students to develop a presentation showing different methods used to control solar heat gain and loss.

Unit 5

Case Study 1: On a Roll!

Gather More Information

Have students use the following key terms to aid their searches:

- roller coaster
- potential energy
- energy conversion
- kinetic energy
- coaster mechanics
- track design

Research the Big Picture

- Have students work with partners to research one roller coaster and determine the number of hills, the height of each hill, the maximum speed attained and when, and any other factors related to energy and energy conversions, such as twists and turns. Students should share their findings with the class in a brief presentation.

- Students should then compare the energy requirements of all researched roller coasters and determine a way to present their comparisons. For instance, presentations could be in the form of graphs, tables, or pictograms.

Case Study 2: Keeping Warm

Gather More Information

Have students use the following key terms to aid their searches:

- mammal
- fur
- blubber
- warm-blooded
- contour feathers
- cold-blooded
- reptiles

Research the Big Picture

- Have students work in small groups to identify the ways in which animals regulate body heat. Then have students research one animal that lives in an extreme region (hot or cold) and describe the region and the specific adaptations the animal has to survive in that environment. Students should present their findings in a group composed of other students researching animals in a similar environment.

SCIENCE JOURNAL

On a Roll!

You're buckled into a roller coaster car that is moving slowly up the first steep hill. At the top of the hill, the car seems to stop for a second. Then, suddenly, you and the car are plunging down, down, down. Roller coasters are a great source of fun, and they also illustrate how energy in a system can constantly change from one form to another.

Many roller coasters speed around their tracks at almost 160 kilometers per hour. But even the fastest coasters don't have engines pushing them along. A motor pulls the coaster to the top of its first hill, and gravity does the rest, sending the coaster downhill at impressive speeds. That energy pushes the coaster for the rest of the ride.

In order to use the kinetic energy that comes from a falling object, the coaster has to start high up. The first hill is always the coaster's tallest one. The energy the cars acquire from plunging down that first hill is enough to get the coaster over the slightly smaller second hill. The energy it builds up on the second hill is enough to push it over the slightly smaller third hill, and so on.

As the coaster rolls up and down, potential energy is constantly converted to kinetic energy and back again. As the coaster is pulled slowly up the first hill against the force of gravity, its potential energy increases. At the top of that first hill, the coaster has its maximum amount of potential energy. As the coaster races downhill, potential energy becomes the kinetic energy of motion. The coaster loses potential energy as it falls, but it gains kinetic energy as it speeds up. At the bottom of the hill, its potential energy is zero, but its speed and kinetic energy are at their maximum. Then the coaster rolls up the next hill, and the process repeats.

Luckily, you don't have to think about all the energy conversions taking place while you're on a roller coaster. You can just sit back and enjoy the ride.

Research and Report

Choose one type of energy resource listed below. Research its current use in your state. Also research its potential for future use. Like a science writer, write an article for your local newspaper detailing your findings. Work with a partner to research and write your article.

coal	oil
natural gas	wind
solar	geothermal
hydroelectric	nuclear
biomass	

CAREER CONNECTION PLUMBER

Plumbers fix and install the pipes that bring clean drinking water to sinks in homes, schools, and offices. They also install the systems that take dirty water from tubs or toilets to septic tanks or sewage systems. Plumbers do a lot more than that, however.

Plumbers install heating and air-conditioning systems in homes, factories, skyscrapers, boats, and shopping centers. Pipe layers lay the huge pipes that carry water, gas, or sewage across cities. Pipe fitters install pipes that carry water through places such as hydroelectric dams and nuclear power stations. They also install sprinkler systems in buildings to prevent fires.

Many plumbers learn the trade by enrolling in apprenticeship programs. The apprentice takes courses in math, blueprint reading, plumbing regulations, safety, and building codes. He or she also learns by working with plumbers in the field. In most places, plumbers must pass a test to get certified, showing that they are qualified as plumbers. Some plumbers work for large companies, but many plumbers enjoy owning their own businesses.

CAREER CONNECTION: Plumber

Have students read the article and list the different responsibilities that plumbers can have. Then have students compare their list with a partner's to check for understanding. Finally, have pairs look around the classroom and identify the places where a plumber might be needed to make a repair. Students should sketch the room and note the locations in the sketch. Have pairs share their ideas with the class, and create a class list.

Keeping Warm

Animal coverings, such as fur, feathers, and scales, serve many purposes. They can provide protection and help some animals blend in with their surroundings. One of the most important functions, however, is to regulate body heat. Animals live in every environment on Earth—from the hottest deserts to the coldest polar regions. No matter where they live, animals must have enough body heat so that they can survive.

Polar bears, caribou, and arctic foxes are mammals that live in extremely cold environments. Mammals are warm-blooded, which means that they produce their own body heat. They also have adaptations that allow them to retain most of this heat. One such adaptation is thick fur that covers their bodies. Some polar mammals also have a layer of fat, or blubber, under their skin or fur. This fatty layer helps animals such as whales and walruses retain their body heat even in cold waters.

Bird feathers also help regulate body temperature. Like mammals, birds are warm-blooded. Most birds

have two layers of feathers. Down feathers make up a soft inner layer that holds heat close to a bird's skin. Contour feathers grow over the down feathers and help insulate them. By moving their contour feathers, birds can adjust heat flow near their bodies. They can fluff the feathers up to trap warm air when the weather is cold. They can also move the feathers to release air near their bodies and cool themselves.

Reptiles, such as alligators and lizards, are cold-blooded. Unlike mammals and birds, they cannot regulate their body temperatures. They rely on external heat sources. A lizard might sit in the sunlight to warm itself after a cold night, for example. Dark scales on a reptile's body also help absorb heat from the Sun.

In the Gas Tank

Not all gasoline is the same. If you look at a gas pump, you will see that there are labels for different types of gas—regular, plus, and premium. The labels indicate the gasoline's octane rating, which is a measure of how easily the gasoline burns. The lower the octane number, the easier the gas ignites and burns in the car's engine. The higher the octane number, the more the gas resists burning. Each car works best with gas of a certain octane rating. The engine gets the best mileage and burns most efficiently at that rating.

Many people used to think that the higher the octane rating, the better the gasoline. They would buy premium gas because it reduced an engine noise called knock. What is knock? Like any fuel, gasoline needs oxygen to burn. In older cars, a carburetor mixed air and gasoline together as the fuel entered the engine. If the carburetor wasn't adjusted correctly, too much gas would be mixed in, and the gas would not burn completely. Some of that extra gas got soaked up by carbon deposits in the engine. In the high heat of the engine, the gas would sometimes ignite. This caused a loud noise in the engine called knock. Drivers could

usually stop knock by using a gasoline of a higher octane, because the gas didn't burn as easily.

Which gas is best to use—high-octane premium or lower-octane regular? Engines are different today, and knock isn't usually a problem. Most of today's cars run just fine on regular gasoline—unless the car manual recommends a higher grade. It's advisable to follow the manufacturer's recommendation in order to keep the car running well.

- Have students work with partners to compare the adaptations and behaviors of cold-blooded and warm-blooded animals. Ask: *What are the advantages of each type? What are the disadvantages? How does each type of animal survive in the winter? In the summer?*

Case Study 3: In the Gas Tank

Gather More Information

Have students use the following key terms to aid their searches:

octane

gasoline

carburetor

compression ratio

high-performance engine

premium gasoline

Research the Big Picture

- Have students calculate the price difference between the use of regular gas and the use of premium gas in a car for one year. Students should use the current price of gas and estimate use at a rate of one 18-gallon tank of gas per week.

- Have students work with partners to research the manufacturing processes for different types of gasoline. Students should identify the chemical composition of each type.

- Have students work in small groups to research the effects of carbon dioxide, a product of the combustion of gasoline, on the environment and on people. Students should present their findings in a poster format.

Unit 6

Introduce Unit 6

Present sound and light to students. Have students read the questions under each chapter heading. Then ask: *What do sound and light have in common?* Help students understand that sound and light travel in energy units called waves. Elicit from students some examples of visible waves. Explain to students that they will learn about waves, the production of sound, the electromagnetic spectrum, and visible light.

Ask students to write in their Science Notebooks about the importance of sound and light in their daily lives and to describe objects that produce sound and light.

Unit Projects

For Unit Project, have students use the Presentation Builder on the Student CD-ROM to display their results.

Career Research Have each student research a career related to sound and light such as audiologist or optician.

Have students imagine that they are recruiting employees for their chosen career. Ask each student to prepare a three- to five-minute presentation about the career aimed at persuading fellow students to consider it for the future.

Hands-On Research Have students work in groups to investigate wave movement. Provide each group with a basin of water and a water dropper. First, have students take turns blowing gently across the surface of the water. Ask them to draw and describe what they see in their Science Notebooks. Then ask them to try releasing water drops into the basin using the dropper. Have them record their observations.

Technology Research Help students understand that sound and light waves cannot be observed without specialized equipment. As a class, brainstorm ways to investigate the presence and properties of these types of waves. Have each student research a sound- or light-measuring technology and report his or her findings.

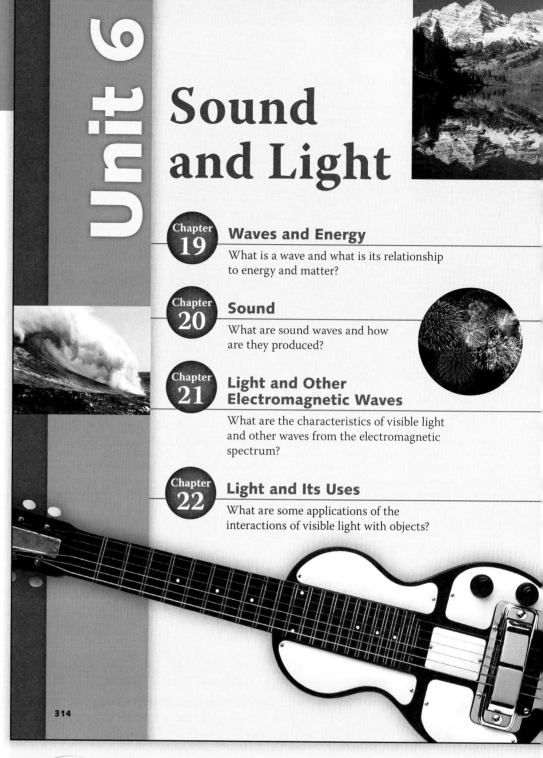

Unit 6

Sound and Light

314

Software Summary

Student CD-ROM
—Interactive Student Book
—Vocabulary Review
—Key Concept Review
—Lab Report Template
—ELL Preview and Writing Activities
—Presentation Digital Library
—Graphic Organizing Software
—Spanish Cognate Dictionary

Interactive Labs
Chapter 21 B—Electromagnetic Spectrum

Waves and Energy

KEY CONCEPT Vibrations produce waves that carry energy.

Imagine you are sitting outside on a warm summer day. Although you might think you are alone, you soon discover otherwise. A nearby honey bee senses you and moves in. A faint buzzing sound alerts you to the bee's approach. You jump up and move away from the bee, trying to avoid it. How exactly is the buzzing sound related to the honey bee?

Think About Waves and Energy

All moving objects have kinetic energy. Thus, the back-and-forth beating of a honey bee's wings indicates that the wings have kinetic energy. Is this kinetic energy related to the buzzing sound produced? If so, how does the sound travel through the air to your ears?

- A bee flaps its wings in a back-and-forth motion. This type of motion can be described as rhythmic or as periodic. In your Science Notebook, list several other examples of this type of motion that you have observed.

- Write a description in your own words explaining how you think motion, energy, and sound are related. Review and revise your explanation after completing this chapter.

NSTA
SCiLINKS.
THE WORLD'S A CLICK AWAY

www.scilinks.org
Waves **Code**: WGPS19

315

Chapter 19 Lessons

19.1 The Nature of Waves

19.2 Types of Waves

19.3 Properties of Waves

19.4 The Behavior of Waves

Introduce Chapter 19

As a starting activity, use Lab 19A on page 109 of the Laboratory Manual.

ENGAGE Pair students and ask: *If a tree falls in the forest, does it make a sound?* Have student pairs agree upon a response and provide three reasons for the answer. Encourage students to include scientific reasoning in their responses. Hold a brief class debate between the "yes" and "no" groups. Tell students that at the end of this chapter, they will better understand how to respond to that question.

Think About Waves and Energy

ENGAGE Think aloud about driving to work in the morning and the rhythmic sounds that you hear, such as noises from the wheels or windshield wipers. Direct students to complete the bulleted items in their Science Notebooks.

- Observations might include such things as the swinging motion of a pendulum clock or a park swing, a spinning airplane propeller or helicopter rotor, a ringing bell, etc. Accept all reasonable answers.

- Students' explanations will vary. The kinetic energy of a vibrating object creates sound waves that propagate through the air and reach the ears.

Chapter 19 Planning Guide			
Instructional Periods	**National Standards**	**Lab Manual**	**Workbook**
19.1 2 Periods	B2, B3, E2, F5; B4, B6, E2, F6; UCP2	**Lab 19A: p. 109** How Waves Travel	Key Concept Review p. 119 Vocabulary Review p. 120 Interpreting Diagrams p. 121
19.2 2 Periods	A2, B2, B3, C1; A2, B4, B6, C6; UCP3, UCP5	**Lab 19B: pp. 110–112** Properties of Waves	Reading Comprehension p. 122
19.3 2 Periods	A2, B2, B3; A2, B4, B6; UCP1, UCP4	**Lab 19C: pp. 113–114** Sunscreen and Ultraviolet Rays	Curriculum Connection p. 123
19.4 2 Periods	B2, B3, E2, F5, G1; B4, B5, B6, E2, F5, F6, G1; UCP2, UCP3		Science Challenge p. 124

Middle School Standard; High School Standard; **Unifying Concept and Principle**

19.1 Introduce

ENGAGE Provide small groups of students with a basin, water to fill the basin about one-third full, and a wooden spoon or spatula. Have students experiment with making various types of waves in the basin by moving the spoon in different ways. Encourage students to pay close attention to how the wave reacts when it hits a barrier (such as the edge of the basin). Discuss students' observations as a class and explain that they created waves when they made vibrations in the water.

Vocabulary terms are listed on the first student page of each lesson. You may wish to preview the terms before introducing each lesson. Strategies for teaching the vocabulary appear on the pages where the terms are introduced.

Before You Read

Model the process of writing a fact about waves. An example of a fact you could share is *Sound and light travel in waves*. Write the fact on the board, and then ask students to write three of their own facts in their Science Notebooks. Remind them to leave space between each fact.

Teach

EXPLAIN to students that in this chapter, they will be learning about different types of waves, wave properties, and how waves behave. Reinforce the idea that their experiment with the water involved just one type of wave, and that there are others.

Encourage students to use the vocabulary section they created in their Science Notebooks. Remind them to record prefixes, suffixes, and root words to help them remember the meanings of vocabulary terms.

Vocabulary

wave Ask students to brainstorm common uses of the word *wave*. Reponses may include hand-waving, waves in hair, and ocean waves. Explain that these examples all involve a repeated motion. The scientific definition includes the fact that a wave is a disturbance that travels through matter or space.

Learning Goals

- Identify the source of all waves.
- Explain how waves, energy, and matter are related.
- Compare and contrast mechanical waves and electromagnetic waves.

New Vocabulary

wave
mechanical wave
medium
electromagnetic wave

19.1 The Nature of Waves

Before You Read

In your Science Notebook, write three facts you already know about waves. Leave six lines of space below each fact. As you read the lesson, add at least two more details to each fact you already know. If you find that one of your original facts is incorrect, replace it.

Picture a bowl of chicken soup resting on your lunch food tray. The surface of the soup is still and flat. Now imagine tapping your spoon on the surface. The tap sends a ripple, or disturbance, spreading across the surface. Tapping the surface once every second would send a series of ripples across the surface. These ripples are waves. A **wave** is a repeating disturbance that travels through matter or space.

Sound waves, ocean waves, shock waves, and radio waves are familiar types of waves. The world around you is a world of waves. In fact, the senses of sight and sound rely on waves. What causes waves, and what is the nature of waves?

Waves and Vibration

When something vibrates, it moves back and forth. The swinging motion of a giant pendulum is a vibration. So too are the flapping of a bird's wings and the up-and-down jumping motion of someone on a pogo stick.

Vibrations cause waves. Every wave is formed by something that is vibrating. How an object vibrates, or the properties of a vibration, are directly related to the properties of the wave that forms.

Figure 19.1 Back-and-forth and up-and-down motion can be described as vibration.

E L L Strategy

Activate Prior Knowledge Have students share the facts from their Science Notebooks in groups of three. Encourage students to further explain what they know about those facts and to share how they know the facts (by relating personal experiences or discussing books that they have read, for example).

Waves and Energy

Waves carry energy from place to place. The energy of a wave generally spreads out into space as the wave travels. This can be illustrated by tossing a pebble into a pond. As shown in **Figure 19.2,** waves carry energy away from the splash in all directions across the surface. In a similar way, radio waves broadcast from a radio tower spread in all directions through space. This explains why a car radio can tune in to a nearby radio station regardless of the car's location.

A wave's movement continues as long as the wave has energy to carry. This energy, as discussed in Chapter 16, has the ability to do work. When a wave encounters an object along its path, it does work on the object. For example, a resting boat will be set into motion by a passing wave. As work is done on the boat, the wave loses energy. Waves lose energy as they do work. Sea cliffs are formed because energy-carrying waves erode the rock below them.

Waves and Matter

An important property of waves is that they transfer energy, but not matter, from place to place. **Figure 19.3** illustrates this concept. A quick flick of the wrist sends a wave from left to right along the rope. The wave does not transport matter (the rope) along with it. Although the wave moves the rope up off the table, there is no additional rope on the left after the wave passes. The same is true for the water waves shown in Figure 19.2. The disturbance moves away from the source, but the water does not. Waves do not move matter from place to place.

Figure 19.2 The water waves carry energy away from the source (the splash).

As You Read

Review the information you have recorded in your Science Notebook. Share your facts with a partner and add any information that is needed.

Identify what is transferred from place to place by a wave.

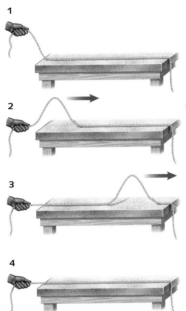

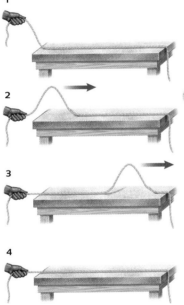

Figure 19.3 The wave passes through the rope without moving the rope in the direction of the wave. Energy, but not matter (the rope), is transferred from left to right.

Figure It Out

1. Identify the source of the disturbance.

2. Imagine a point located at the middle of the rope in the top image. Describe the motion of this point as the wave moves through the rope in the next three images.

● Teach

EXPLAIN to students that one of the most important properties of waves is that they only transfer energy from place to place; waves do not transfer matter. Remind students that since waves originate with vibrations or disturbances, the energy from the vibration is carried by the wave.

As You Read

Give students a few minutes to review and revise the facts in their Science Notebooks. Encourage them to refer to section titles and illustrations if they need help remembering facts they have learned.

ANSWER Energy is transferred from place to place by a wave.

Figure It Out: Figure 19.3

ANSWER **1.** The source of the disturbance is the movement of the hand. **2.** The point moves up and then down, but it does not move in the direction of the wave.

Differentiate Instruction

Kinesthetic Provide pairs of students with a piece of fairly heavy rope. Have students experiment with transferring energy along the rope by moving the rope in different ways. Suggest that students create vibrations by moving the rope side-to-side and then up-and-down and comparing the transfer of energy in each case. Students should also try having only one person hold one end of the rope as well as having one person hold each end.

● Teach

EXPLAIN to students that mechanical waves require matter; electromagnetic waves can move through empty space as well as through matter.

Explain It!

Students' paragraphs should discuss electromagnetic waves, light waves, and sound waves and how they travel. The data from the probe were transmitted through space by electromagnetic waves. The displayed images travel through the air to the eyes in the form of light waves, another type of electromagnetic wave. The speaker's voice is created by vibrating vocal cords. These vibrations travel through the air as sound waves. When the sound waves reach the ears, they cause the eardrums to vibrate. These vibrations are sensed by the brain as sound.

● Assess

Use the After You Read questions and the Alternative Assessment to help you evaluate students' understanding of the lesson.

After You Read

1. Sound is a mechanical wave that requires a medium through which to travel.

2. Both are disturbances that carry energy, but not matter, from place to place. Mechanical waves require a medium, while electromagnetic waves do not.

3. Answers will vary. Accept any answer that describes a wave applying a force and causing movement. The energy of a wave decreases when the wave does work.

Alternative Assessment

Have each student use the facts from his or her Science Notebook to write a paragraph describing the nature of waves. The paragraph should include information about vibration, energy, and matter.

Figure 19.4 A space probe sends data back to Earth using electromagnetic waves.

Explain It!

Imagine you are attending a presentation in which a NASA engineer is showing and discussing live images transmitted to Earth by a space probe orbiting Mars. Write a paragraph explaining how the words and the images you see reach your ears and eyes.

Mechanical Waves

Some waves can travel only through matter. For example, sound waves reach your ears by traveling through the air. Ocean waves transmit energy through water. Sound waves and ocean waves are examples of mechanical waves. **Mechanical** (mih KA nih kul) **waves** are waves that are only able to travel through matter. The matter through which a wave travels is called the **medium** (MEE dee um). Solids, liquids, and gases can be mediums for waves.

Why would the loudest stereo speakers on Earth be useless in space? Mechanical waves cannot exist without matter to travel through. Space is a vacuum, meaning that it contains no matter. Thus, the vibrations from the speakers have nowhere to go. Space is completely silent.

Electromagnetic Waves

Some waves can travel through the vacuum of space. As shown in **Figure 19.4,** NASA engineers can receive communication signals from space probes that are hundreds of millions of kilometers away. Waves that can travel through a vacuum are called **electromagnetic** (ih lek troh mag NEH tik) **waves**. Electromagnetic waves can also travel through solids, liquids, and gases.

There is a wide range of electromagnetic waves. The range of waves makes up what is known as the electromagnetic spectrum. Radio waves, microwaves, infrared waves, light waves, and X rays are some of the electromagnetic waves that make up the electromagnetic spectrum.

You sense electromagnetic waves every day. The Sun radiates energy that travels through space to reach Earth. The light you see and the warmth you feel are radiant energy in the form of light waves and infrared waves, respectively. Electromagnetic waves are discussed in Chapter 21.

After You Read

1. Explain why sound cannot travel from Mars to Earth.

2. How are mechanical waves and electromagnetic waves similar? How are they different?

3. Review the notes you took in your Science Notebook. Use the facts you recorded to describe a situation in which a wave does work. Describe how the energy of the wave is related to the work that is done.

Vocabulary

mechanical wave Explain to students that the word *mechanical* is derived from the Greek word *mechane,* meaning "a contrivance or machine." A machine does work to move an object, much as a mechanical wave moves matter.

medium Tell students that the word *medium* comes from the Latin word *medius,* meaning "middle." The medium is between the origin and the source.

electromagnetic wave Explain to students that *electro-* denotes electricity; *magnetic* denotes operation by a magnet or magnetism. *Electromagnetic,* then, suggests a combination of electricity and magnetism.

19.2 Types of Waves

Before You Read

In your Science Notebook, divide a page into two columns. Label the first column *Transverse Waves* and the second column *Compressional Waves*. As you read about these waves, add information to your chart that describes the characteristics of each.

Waves can be grouped into two major categories based on whether or not they need a medium in order to travel. Electromagnetic waves do not require a medium. Mechanical waves are those that require a medium. Waves can also be categorized into two types, based on the direction of the vibration relative to the wave's direction.

Transverse Waves

One type of wave is a transverse wave. In a **transverse** (tranz VURS) **wave**, the vibration is at right angles to the direction in which the wave travels. Electromagnetic waves are transverse waves, and some mechanical waves are also transverse waves.

Note that the rope in **Figure 19.5** moves up and down, whereas the wave moves to the right. The two motions are at right angles, or perpendicular, to each other. The peaks and valleys in the rope match the up-and-down vibration of the source—the moving hand. If the hand moves up and down at a constant rate, then the peaks and valleys will be evenly spaced. The peaks in a transverse wave are called **crests** (KRESTZ), and the valleys are called **troughs** (TRAWFS).

The medium of the wave in Figure 19.5 is the rope. Transverse waves also form in water. The motion of water causes the up-and-down motion in a buoy. Like the wave in the rope, the direction of the water wave is at a right angle to the movement of the water.

Did You Know?

The word *transverse*, which means "being across" or "set crosswise," comes from the Latin word *transversus*, which means "to turn across."

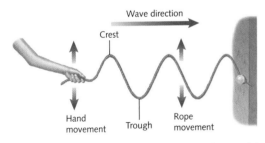

Figure 19.5 A transverse wave moves through the rope. The up-and-down motion of the hand creates a similar up-and-down motion in the rope.

Figure It Out

1. What will happen to the waves in the rope if the hand stops moving?

2. In what direction will the trough move?

ELL Strategy

<u>Model</u> Provide students with a variety of materials, such as paint, markers, yarn, string, and glue. Have students illustrate both transverse and compressional waves and identify the crest and trough for each.

19.2 Introduce

ENGAGE Place students in groups of three and provide each group with a metal or plastic spring toy. Briefly allow students to play with the springs. Have students sit and face one another with one person holding each end of the toy on a table or the floor. One student should stretch the spring toward himself or herself and then release it. The other student should hold the end still. Students should observe the type of wave generated by the spring and note their observations in their Science Notebooks. Discuss students' observations of the springs. Explain that the activity generated a type of compressional wave.

Before You Read

Model the two-column chart on the board. Briefly review the section about transverse waves with students, and include the definition of *transverse wave* in the appropriate column on the board. Have students create their two-column charts in their Science Notebooks.

● Teach

EXPLAIN that mechanical waves, those that travel through a medium, move in one of two ways in relation to the medium. The wave can move parallel to the motion of the medium or perpendicular to it.

 Vocabulary

transverse wave Tell students that the prefix *trans-* means "across." The root *verse* is from the Latin word *versus* and means "line" or "row." Transverse waves travel across (at right angles to) the medium.

crest Explain to students that *crest* is derived from the Latin word *crista*, meaning "plume." *Crest* or *plume* can refer to a tuft of feathers or fur on the top of the head of some birds or animals, or to the topmost part of a mountain or hill.

trough Tell students that *trough* can refer to any low point; it is used to describe low atmospheric pressure and a gully or ditch.

Figure It Out: Figure 19.5

ANSWER **1.** New waves will not form, and the existing waves will fade out. **2.** upward

● Teach

EXPLAIN to students that compressional waves move parallel to the direction in which the medium vibrates. Review the meaning of *longitudinal* ("relating to length") and ask students to discuss in pairs which word is easier for them to remember when describing wave movement.

 Vocabulary

compressional wave Explain to students that the prefix *com-* means "with" or "together." Ask students to brainstorm common uses of the word *press*. Their responses might include the act of pushing, publicity, newspapers, or the act of compelling someone. A compressional wave has parts that are pushed together.

compression Review with students the meaning of the word *compress* ("to push together"). The suffix *-ion* denotes a process, state, or result. Have students combine these word parts to define *compression*.

rarefaction Explain to students that *rarefaction* is derived from the Latin word *rarefacere,* from words meaning "rare" and "to make." In an area of rarefaction, molecules are farther away (more rare) than in an area of compression.

seismic wave Tell students that the word *seismic* is from the Greek word *seismos,* meaning "a shaking." Review with students the meaning of the word *wave*. Literally, a seismic wave results from a shaking of the land, or an earthquake.

As You Read

Give students about five minutes to update their two-column charts. Pair students and have them quickly review one another's work and provide suggestive feedback.

(ANSWER) A transverse wave can be modeled by shaking a rope back and forth.

Figure It Out: **Figure 19.6**

(ANSWER) **1.** The disturbance comes from the fingers holding the coils together.
2. The point moves back and forth as the coils compress and then returns to rest when the wave passes. The direction of the vibrating movement of the point is parallel to the movement of the wave.

As You Read

With a partner, review the characteristics you have recorded for transverse waves and compressional waves in the chart in your Science Notebook. Add information to your chart as needed.

Name the type of wave that can be modeled by shaking a rope back and forth.

 **Figure It Out**

1. Identify the source of the disturbance.
2. Imagine a point in the middle of the spring in the first image. Describe the motion of this point as the wave moves through the spring.

CONNECTION: Biology

Dolphins use echolocation, or locating underwater objects by sending out clicking sounds. When sound waves strike an object, part of the waves' energy bounces back, or echoes. Dolphins can accurately locate even distant objects by noting the time it takes for an echo to return and the echo's energy.

Compressional Waves

The second type of mechanical wave is a compressional wave. In a **compressional** (kum PRESH uh nal) **wave,** the medium moves back and forth parallel to the direction in which the wave travels. Compressional waves are also called longitudinal waves.

Something that is compressed is pushed or squeezed together. You can make a compressional wave by squeezing together several coils of a stretched-out spring and releasing them, as shown in **Figure 19.6.** Notice that the vibration of the medium is parallel to the wave's motion. Like a transverse wave, a compressional wave transports energy, but not matter.

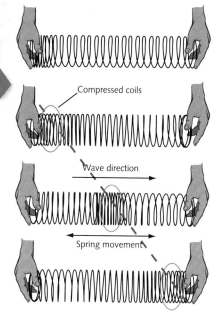

Figure 19.6 The compression of the coils travels to the right through the coiled spring. The medium, the spring, moves back and forth parallel to the direction in which the compressional wave travels.

Compressed coils

Wave direction

Spring movement

Sound Waves

Every sound that you hear is a compressional wave. When an object vibrates, sound waves are formed. The waves then travel through the air.

Figure 19.7 shows the formation of a sound wave by a drum. When the drumhead is struck, it begins vibrating. As the drumhead moves upward, it squeezes the nearby air molecules together and creates a region of **compression.** Molecules in the compressed region collide with and transfer energy to nearby molecules in uncompressed regions. These collisions transfer energy away from the vibrating drumhead.

Differentiate Instruction

Kinesthetic Arrange students in groups of four and have them create a skit or movement to describe either compressional or transverse waves. Have groups present their skits to the class, and have the class identify the wave movement each skit depicts.

As the vibrating drumhead moves downward, nearby air molecules expand into the space. These molecules, which are now more spread-out, form a region of **rarefaction** (rair uh FAK shun). As the drum continues to vibrate, regions of compression and rarefaction spread through the air.

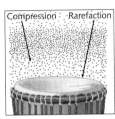

Figure 19.7 The vibrating drumhead creates regions of compression and rarefaction.

Seismic Waves

Earthquakes are dramatic displays of the energy-carrying nature of waves. Buildings can be destroyed during earthquakes as huge areas of land shake. Earthquakes occur when plates in Earth's crust temporarily break free from each other and move abruptly. Vibrations from the breaking crust create energy-carrying **seismic** (SIZE mihk) **waves.**

Seismic waves are a combination of transverse waves and compressional waves. Seismic waves travel through Earth and along its surface. Structures shake as seismic waves do damaging work on them.

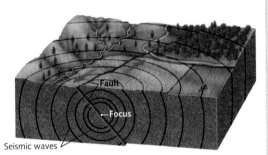

Figure 19.8 Earth's crust is made up of plates that push against one another. Forces can move two plates, causing an earthquake. Seismic waves carry energy away from the break.

After You Read

1. A student shakes a rope back and forth to form waves. Compare the rate of the rope's vibration with the rate at which crests and troughs are formed.

2. Summarize wave types by correctly grouping these terms: *transverse wave, rarefaction, crest, compression, trough,* and *compressional wave.*

3. Review the chart in your Science Notebook about wave types. Compare and contrast transverse waves and compressional waves.

 Explore It!

Move a pencil back and forth across a sheet of paper at a constant speed. What does this motion model? Now have a classmate pull the paper in a direction perpendicular to your motion at a constant speed while you continue the back-and-forth motion of the pencil. Describe the shape drawn by the pencil. Explain which type of wave the drawing represents. Repeat the process while pulling the paper at a faster speed. How does the shape change? Identify any crests or troughs, or areas of compression or rarefaction.

Teacher Alert

Explain to students that unlike the speed of light, which is constant, the speed of sound varies based on the type of medium and the temperature of the medium through which the waves are traveling.

EXPLAIN to students that sound waves are a specific example of compressional waves.

 Explore It!

Be sure to explain and demonstrate the concept of constant speed. The motion of the pencil at a constant speed models a vibration. The wave drawn when the paper is pulled should resemble a transverse wave. When the paper is pulled at a faster speed, the distance between consecutive crests increases. Crests and troughs correspond to points of maximum positive and negative displacement from the rest position.

● **Assess**

Use the After You Read questions and the Alternative Assessment to help you evaluate students' understanding of the lesson.

After You Read

1. The rate at which the rope vibrates equals the rate at which crests and troughs are formed in the rope.

2. transverse wave, crest, trough; compressional wave, rarefaction, compression

3. Both carry energy, but not matter, from place to place, and both require a medium. In a transverse wave, the medium vibrates at a right angle to the wave direction, whereas in a compressional wave, the medium vibrates back and forth in the same direction as the wave's motion.

Alternative Assessment

Have each student use his or her two-column chart to write a summary sentence describing the terms *transverse wave* and *compressional wave*. Then have students name two examples for each type of wave.

19.3 Introduce

ENGAGE Have a variety of numbered rocks on display for students to observe. Ask students to list their observations about the physical appearance of one or two rocks. Model this process once before asking students to do the activity. Encourage them to include details about the color, texture, size, and shape of the rocks. As a class, discuss the physical characteristics for two rocks. Point out that these characteristics are properties, and explain that students will be studying the properties of waves in this lesson.

Before You Read

Write the words *crest* and *trough* on the board. Then draw a picture of a wave and label both the crest and trough. Explain to students that they should write the terms in their Science Notebooks and illustrate each with a quick sketch.

Teach

EXPLAIN Briefly review with students the two types of mechanical waves and their properties. Explain that each type has a specific shape and pattern.

Use the Visual: Figure 19.9

ANSWER a compressional wave

Learning Goals

- Define *wavelength, frequency, period,* and *amplitude.*
- Identify the relationship among a wave's speed, frequency, and wavelength.
- Relate a wave's amplitude to its energy.

New Vocabulary

wavelength
frequency
period
amplitude

19.3 Properties of Waves

Before You Read

In your Science Notebook, write each of the vocabulary terms in this lesson along with the terms *crest, trough, compression,* and *rarefaction.* Leave some space below each term. Write the definition for each term and draw a simple sketch that illustrates each definition.

What would you say if you were given a rock sample and asked to describe it? You would likely describe the rock's appearance, its color and texture, and perhaps whether it is dull or shiny. You might also measure the rock's mass and volume, or determine what elements it is made of. All of these things describe properties of the rock. Just like a rock, waves also have properties that can be used to describe them.

The Parts of a Wave

Waves have distinct shapes and patterns. Two distinct wave shapes are shown in **Figure 19.9.** A transverse wave is formed when a hand shakes a rope back and forth. This forms a repeating pattern of crests and troughs. The rest position, which is shown by the dotted line, represents the medium when a wave is not traveling through it.

A different pattern exists in the compressional wave in the spring. In this wave, there is a repeating pattern of squeezed-together and spread-apart coils. The squeezed coils are areas of compression, and the spread-apart coils are areas of rarefaction. The rest position, which is not shown, describes the spacing of the coils when the spring is at rest (not stretched or compressed).

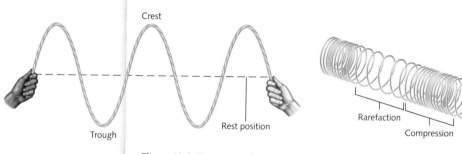

Figure 19.9 Transverse and compressional waves have distinct characteristics. In which of the waves are the direction of the wave and the movement of the medium parallel?

322 WAVES AND ENERGY

ELL Strategy

Paraphrase Arrange students in groups of three and have them divide the lesson by topic (such as the parts of a wave, wavelength, frequency, etc.). Each student should then choose three topics and write two or three sentences paraphrasing the information about each one to share with the group. Students could provide diagrams to share with their peers as they read their paraphrase. They should be encouraged to use and define vocabulary words from this lesson as they paraphrase their sections.

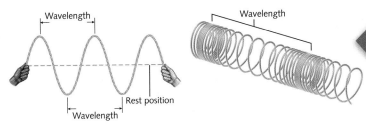

Figure 19.10 The length of a wave can be measured between any two successive identical points. Note that in terms of wavelength, the areas of compression and rarefaction in the spring correspond to the crests and troughs in the rope.

Wavelength

Waves are often described by wavelength. **Wavelength** is the distance between a point on a wave and the next identical point. For a transverse wave, this means from the top of one crest to the top of the next, or from the bottom of one trough to the bottom of the next. For a compressional wave, wavelength can be measured from the center of one compression to the center of the next, or from the center of one rarefaction to the center of the next. **Figure 19.10** shows the wavelengths of two waves.

Waves have a wide range of wavelengths. For example, ocean waves have wavelengths measured in meters (m), whereas light waves have wavelengths measured in billionths of a meter (0.000000001 m). For sound waves that humans can hear, wavelengths range from a few centimeters to about 15 m.

Frequency

A passenger on a boat anchored in the ocean might keep busy by counting the number of waves that pass by the boat each minute. In other words, the passenger could measure how frequently the waves pass. The **frequency** (FREE kwen see) of a wave is the number of wavelengths that pass a given point in one second (1 s).

Frequency is measured in units of hertz (Hz). One hertz is equal to one complete cycle, or wavelength, per second. Thus, if five wavelengths pass each second, the wave has a frequency of 5 cycles/second, or 5 Hz.

Just as waves have a wide range of wavelengths, they also have a wide range of frequencies. The frequency of ocean waves is less than 1 Hz, whereas the frequency of visible light is about 1,000,000,000,000,000 Hz (10^{15} Hz).

Did You Know?

The unit of hertz is also used as a measure of processing speed in the computer industry. The "clock speed" is the speed with which a computer's central processing unit, or CPU, processes information. A computer with a CPU rated at five gigahertz (5 GHz) can perform five billion operations each second.

● Teach

EXPLAIN to students that two properties of waves are wavelength and frequency. Light waves, which are visible to the human eye, correspond to a very narrow wavelength range of 400 to 700 nanometers (nm). Light waves vary from 10^{-6} nm for gamma rays to 100 km for radio waves. Drawing this scale on the board would help demonstrate the wide range of light wavelengths. The electromagnetic spectrum is presented in Chapter 21.

 Vocabulary

wavelength Explain to students that *wavelength* is a compound word. Review the meaning of *wave* and then ask students to brainstorm common uses of the word *length*. Their responses might include the distance between two points, a quality of being long, and a stretch or extent. The wavelength is the distance between two consecutive identical points on a wave.

frequency Tell students that the word *frequency* is derived from the Latin word *frequens,* meaning "happening often." Ask students how this derivation relates to the term's definition.

Figure It Out: Figure 19.10

ANSWER **1.** 2.5 **2.** In the rest position, the coils would be closer together than the areas of rarefaction and farther apart than the areas of compression.

Differentiate Instruction

Kinesthetic In the classroom, have students make a wave similar to the kind sometimes formed by spectators at a ballpark. Have one student stand up and sit down to start the wave. Students immediately to the right should then stand up and sit down, and so on. This may be easier to do with students seated in a circle. Experiment with different speeds of sitting and standing to demonstrate frequency.

Background Information

Gamma rays have wavelengths from 10^{-6} nm to 10^{-2} nm. X rays range from 10^{-2} nm to 10 nm. Ultraviolet radiation can be 10 nm to 100 nm. Infrared radiation has a longer wavelength than visible red light (ranging from 780 nm to 1 mm). Microwaves operate in 1-mm to 10-cm wavelengths, and radio wavelengths range from 10 cm to 100 km.

● Teach

EXPLAIN that both period and frequency are related to wavelength. Period and frequency can be easily confused; tell students that period is the amount of time that it takes for one wavelength to pass. Frequency is a measure of how many wavelengths pass a point during a given amount of time.

 Vocabulary

period Explain to students that *period* is derived from the Greek word *periodos*, meaning "circuit" or "going round," and that the prefix *peri-* means "round" and the root *hodos* means "way." A period is a complete cycle.

As You Read

Give students a few minutes to update their definitions and sketches. Review students' work for accuracy and then, if time permits, have each student create a drawing illustrating one of the terms to display in the classroom.

[ANSWER] Frequency and period are inversely related, as described by the formula frequency = 1/period.

 CONNECTION: Music

Arrange students in small groups and provide each group with pre-cut pieces of PVC pipe, modeling clay, rubber bands, and sandpaper. (Prepare the pipe segments in advance by cutting the a one-meter segment into several pieces of different lengths for each group.) Have students seal one end of each pipe piece with modeling clay and arrange the pieces in order from shortest to longest. They should use a rubber band to secure the pipes together. Have students blow across the tops of the pipes and write in their Science Notebooks which pipe produces the longest and the highest frequency, and why.

Alternatively, students could explore frequencies with musical instruments such as xylophones or a pipe organ.

Use the Visual: Figure 19.11

[ANSWER] an inverse relationship

As You Read

Review the definitions and sketches in your Science Notebook. In a small group, decide on one definition for each term. Then, as a class, develop a final definition for each vocabulary term.

How is the frequency of a wave related to its period?

CONNECTION: Music

The frequency and wavelength of sound waves determine how the waves are perceived by human ears. The pitch of a sound is how high or low it is perceived to be. As the frequency of a sound wave increases, its pitch also increases. Thus, high-pitched sounds have higher frequencies (and shorter wavelengths) than do lower-pitched sounds.

Frequency and Period

Closely related to the frequency of a wave is the period of a wave. The **period** of a wave is the amount of time needed for one wavelength to pass a given point. Consider a wave with a frequency of 2 Hz. This frequency means that two wavelengths pass a given point each second. If two wavelengths pass each second, then one wavelength must pass each half-second. The period of the wave is 0.5 s.

In mathematical terms, frequency and period are inverses of each other. The following equations show this inverse relationship.

$$\text{frequency} = \frac{1}{\text{period}} \qquad \text{period} = \frac{1}{\text{frequency}}$$

Thus, if you know the frequency, you can calculate the period, and vice versa.

Frequency and Wavelength

Wavelength and frequency are related for waves traveling in the same medium. This relationship can easily be modeled using a rope. Imagine shaking a rope back and forth, creating a transverse wave. If the rope is shaken faster, more crests and troughs form each second. In other words, shaking the rope faster increases the frequency of the waves.

However, as shown in **Figure 19.11,** increasing the frequency of the waves decreases their wavelengths. Thus, the frequency and wavelength of a wave are also inversely related. If the frequency in the rope doubles, as shown in Figure 19.11, the wavelength will be halved. If the frequency triples, the wavelength will decrease by a factor of three. This relationship is always true—as frequency increases, wavelength decreases.

Something else that is always true is that the frequency of a wave is equal to the frequency of the vibrating source that creates it. When the frequency of the vibrating source (the hand) doubles, the frequency of the wave formed doubles.

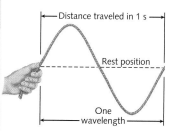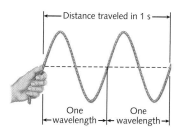

Figure 19.11 As the frequency of a wave increases, the wavelength decreases. What mathematical term describes this type of relationship?

Background Information

Sound frequency is measured in hertz (Hz). The human ear hears sounds ranging from about 20 hertz to 17,000 hertz. Notes such as middle C, B flat, and F sharp have specific frequencies. For instance, the A note below middle C is at 220 Hz. Middle C is at about 262 Hz.

Wave Speed

You have likely experienced a severe storm with thunder and lightning similar to that shown in **Figure 19.12.** You probably know that the flash of the lightning reaches your eyes before the sound of the thunder reaches your ears. This happens because sound waves and light waves travel at different speeds.

The speed of a wave depends on the medium through which it travels. Sound waves, for instance, travel at about 340 m/s through air, at more than 1,400 m/s in water, and at about 5,100 m/s in steel. The speed of sound in air is also affected by temperature; sound travels faster at higher temperatures. In general, sound waves travel faster in liquids and solids than they do in gases.

Light waves are also affected by the medium through which they travel. The speed of light is 3.0×10^8 m/s in the vacuum of space. The speed slows in gases, and it slows more in liquids and solids.

Because the speed of a wave is determined by the wave's medium, waves of the same type that are in the same medium must travel at the same speed. This means that the two waves in the rope shown in Figure 19.11 have the same speed, even though their frequencies and wavelengths differ.

Calculating Wave Speed If a wave's frequency and wavelength are known, the wave's speed can be calculated using the following equation:

$$\text{speed} = \text{frequency} \times \text{wavelength}$$

This equation can be written using the symbol v for speed, the symbol f for frequency, and the Greek letter lambda (λ) for wavelength.

$$v = f \times \lambda$$

For a frequency that is in hertz and a wavelength that is in meters, the speed calculated will be in meters per second (m/s). Consider a sound wave with frequency of 160 Hz and a wavelength of 2.13 m. What is the speed of the sound wave?

$$
\begin{aligned}
v &= f \times \lambda \\
&= 160\ \text{Hz} \times 2.13\ \text{m} \\
&= \tfrac{160}{s} \times 2.13\ \text{m} \\
&= 341\ \tfrac{m}{s}
\end{aligned}
$$

Figure 19.12 Light waves travel much faster through the air than do sound waves.

Explore It!

Obtain a selection of mediums (three or four types of string, twine, and rope of equal lengths). Choose one medium. With a partner, stretch out a medium and hold each end on the ground. Send a wave through the medium by making a single quick back-and-forth movement of one end of the medium. Observe the wave's speed. Repeat using a faster back-and-forth motion. How do the wave speeds compare? Repeat this procedure with each medium and compare your results. Is wave speed affected by the medium or by the speed of the back-and-forth movement?

● Teach

EXPLAIN to students that wave speed can be calculated by multiplying the frequency by the wavelength. The calculation is the same for any type of wave.

Explore It!

Pair students and make available scissors and different types of string, twine, and rope. Have students make charts in their Science Notebooks to document the experiment. The mediums should be listed in the left column; speeds, such as normal and fast, should be listed in the second and third columns.

ANSWER The wave speed does not change; the medium determines wave speed. Wave speeds vary in different mediums, but the speed of the back-and-forth movement in a given medium has no effect.

Science Notebook EXTRA

Have students research the relationship between storm distance and the lapse between the time that lightning is viewed and thunder is heard. Students should find that by counting the seconds between a viewed lightning strike and a heard thunderclap and dividing by five, they can determine the distance to the lightning's origin in miles.

Differentiate Instruction

Logical/Mathematical Have students calculate how long it would take for a sound wave traveling 340 m/s to travel the length of the classroom, the gym, and the school, and then to travel to their home. Remind students that the wave will travel in a straight line.

Background Information

Light travels from the lightning bolt to one's eye almost instantaneously; the sound waves from thunder travel at about 340 m/s. Therefore, it takes about three seconds for sound to travel a kilometer.

Teach

EXPLAIN to students that for both compressional and transverse waves, the amplitude is directly related to the amount of energy the wave is carrying. Demonstrate a transverse wave with a rope: make small waves by moving your wrist up and down and then by moving your whole arm up and down. Ask students to compare the amount of energy you exerted for those moves. As the rope went higher and lower while you moved your whole arm, you also transferred a great deal more energy than when you created smaller waves with your wrist.

 Vocabulary

amplitude Tell students that this word is of Latin origin and means "abundance." Ask students how this word meaning might help them remember the meaning of *amplitude* in relation to waves.

Use the Visual: Figure 19.14

(ANSWER) Moving the hand a greater distance will increase the wave's amplitude.

Assess

Use the After You Read questions and the Alternative Assessment to help you evaluate students' understanding of the lesson.

After You Read

1. All sound waves travel at the same speed in air.

2. The distance between the rest point and a crest or trough (amplitude) will be greater in the higher-energy wave than it is in the lower-energy wave.

3. Transverse and compressional waves have the following properties: wavelength, frequency, period, amplitude, and speed. Students' answers should correctly define each property and then explain how frequency and period are related; how frequency and wavelength are related; how speed, frequency, and wavelength are related; and how amplitude is related to energy and to crests and troughs/ compressions and rarefactions.

Figure 19.13
The amplitude, or energy, of a compressional wave depends on the compression of the medium.

Amplitude

Throughout the year, hundreds of earthquakes occur along the Ring of Fire, a very active seismic and volcanic region of Earth's crust. Most of these earthquakes cause little damage. Occasionally, however, an earthquake does cause major damage. Clearly, some earthquakes carry greater energy than others do. The **amplitude** (AM pluh tewd) of a wave is related to the amount of energy it carries. The greater the energy of a wave, the greater its amplitude. The amplitude of an earthquake is measured using the Richter scale.

Amplitude of Compressional Waves The amplitude of a compressional wave depends on how tightly the medium is squeezed together in its regions of compression. As shown in **Figure 19.13,** the coils are more tightly squeezed in the higher-amplitude wave. These more tightly squeezed coils carry more energy than the less tightly squeezed coils.

Amplitude of Transverse Waves The amplitude of any transverse wave is the distance from the rest position to either a crest or a trough, as shown in **Figure 19.14.** As the energy of a transverse wave increases, the distance between the wave's rest position and its crests and troughs increases.

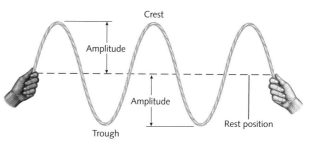

Figure 19.14 The amplitude of a transverse wave is the distance from the rest position to a crest or a trough. How could the amplitude of this wave be increased?

After You Read

1. Two sound waves travel through the air. If the frequency of one wave is twice that of the other, which wave travels at a higher speed?

2. Compare the appearance of a higher-energy transverse wave to that of a lower-energy transverse wave.

3. Review the definitions and sketches in your Science Notebook. Identify and relate the properties of transverse waves and compressional waves.

Alternative Assessment

Students can use the definitions and sketches in their Science Notebooks to identify the relationship among speed, frequency, and wavelength for a wave.

Background Information

The Richter scale measures the magnitude of an earthquake as the logarithm of the amplitude of waves recorded by seismographs. Earthquakes with magnitudes of 2.0 or less are labeled microearthquakes and are not usually noticed. Earthquakes with magnitudes of 4.5 or stronger can be measured by sensitive seismographs all over the world. About one great earthquake occurs each year with a magnitude of 8.0 or higher.

19.4 The Behavior of Waves

Before You Read

Create a lesson outline in your Science Notebook using the title, headings, and subheadings of this lesson. Use the outline to think about what you will learn in this lesson. Record any knowledge you already have about the content of the lesson in the appropriate place in your outline.

Waves are constantly passing through and bouncing off you and the things around you. These waves interact with each other and with matter in many different ways. What happens depends on the type of wave, the type of matter, and a variety of other conditions. The result is a wide range of interesting phenomena.

Reflection

Bounce a basketball in an empty gymnasium and you may be surprised by what you hear. Instead of hearing the sound of each bounce once, you might hear it twice. If the floor of the gymnasium has been recently polished, you might also be able to see your own image there. Both of these occurrences have to do with the reflection of waves. A **reflection** (reh FLEK shun) occurs when a wave hits a surface and bounces off. All types of waves can be reflected.

Echoes An echo is a reflected sound wave. Sound waves reflect off all surfaces. If a ball is bounced in an empty gym, some of the sound waves travel directly to the listener's ears. Other waves, however, reflect off the floor, ceiling, and walls before traveling to the listener's ears. Because these waves travel farther, they arrive later and create the echo.

Law of Reflection Light reflects when it hits a surface. The image seen in a shiny gymnasium floor is from light waves that reflect off the viewer's face, then reflect off the floor and pass into the viewer's eyes. Similar reflections allow a person to see his or her image in a mirror.

In the reflection shown in **Figure 19.15,** a beam of light from a flashlight strikes and reflects off a mirror. In order to discuss the behavior of a light ray as it is reflected off a mirror, an imaginary line called the **normal** is drawn perpendicular to the surface. Note how the incident, or incoming, light and the reflected light make equal angles with the normal. The **law of reflection** states that the angle of the incident light is equal to the angle of the reflected light. All reflected waves obey the law of reflection.

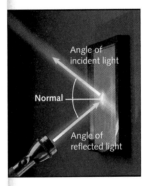

Angle of incident light

Normal

Angle of reflected light

Figure 19.15 The light from the flashlight's beam bounces off the mirror at the same angle at which it strikes the mirror.

19.4 Introduce

ENGAGE Pair students and provide each pair with two pieces of window screen (about 6" square). Have students place one piece on top of the other and look through both layers toward a bright light, such as the overhead light. (Avoid letting students look directly at the Sun.) Have them observe the patterns created by sliding one layer from side to side or rotating one layer. Explain to students that these patterns are called Moiré patterns and are caused by a pattern in the image formed by one's eye. These patterns illustrate wave interference, which students will learn about in this lesson.

Before You Read

Review aloud this page's contents and model the process of creating an outline. Write the following on the board:

I. The Behavior of Waves

  A. Reflection

    a. Echoes

    b. Law of Reflection

Explain to students that *Echoes* and *Law of Reflection* are subtopics of *Reflection*. Have students write their own outlines in their Science Notebooks.

● Teach

EXPLAIN to students that in this lesson, they will learn how waves behave when they hit a surface, encounter a new medium, and overlap a different wave.

💿 Vocabulary

reflection Explain to students that *reflect* is derived from the Latin word *reflectere,* meaning "to bend back."

normal Ask students to define the word *normal* based on everyday usage. Point out that the word has very different meanings in math and science. In the context of reflection, normal means *perpendicular*.

law of reflection Encourage students to think of common uses of the word *law*. Responses might include a rule, the legal profession, or a principle. The law of reflection is a principle explaining how light acts during reflection.

🅴🅻🅻 Strategy

Illustrate Have students illustrate the terms *reflection, normal, law of reflection, refraction, diffraction,* and *interference* in their Science Notebooks. Encourage them to refer to the figures for guidance.

Field Study

Have students walk around the school campus and look for examples of Moiré patterns and the law of reflection. Students should sketch what they observe in their Science Notebooks and identify the principle responsible for their observations. Chain-link fences and bird feathers are two real-life Moiré examples.

● Teach

EXPLAIN to students that waves refract, or bend, when moving from one medium to another at an angle.

 Vocabulary

refraction Tell students that the root of the word *refraction, refract,* is derived from the Latin word *refringere,* meaning "to break." A wave breaks or bends as it enters a new medium.

diffraction Explain to students that the origin of *diffract* is the Latin word *diffringere,* meaning "to shatter." A wave bends or shatters as it passes around an object or through an opening.

As You Read

Have students update and revise their outlines as necessary. Review students' work for accuracy.

(ANSWER) Reflection and refraction cause waves to change direction.

EXPLORE Pair students partners and provide each pair with a wide, clear glass jar filled almost to the top with water, a flashlight, a hand mirror, and white paper. Have students place the mirror into the water, tilted slightly upward. Darken the room and have students shine the flashlight into the water toward the mirror and hold the white paper opposite the mirror. A rainbow should appear on the paper.

Explain to students that the spectrum they created is similar to a natural rainbow they might see in the sky; the water in the jar replaces the raindrops. The light has bent, or refracted.

Use the Visual: Figure 19.15, Figure 19.17

Have students analyze the images in these two figures and compare and contrast reflection and refraction in their Science Notebooks. If students have difficulty with the two concepts, encourage them to explore the principles with a flashlight, a mirror, and a jar of water. Use the activity described above to guide their investigation.

Figure 19.16 Changes in the speed of light waves as they pass through air, water, and glass cause the broken appearance of the straw.

As You Read

Several types of wave behavior are responsible for waves changing direction. Using the information you have recorded in the lesson outline in your Science Notebook, identify two wave behaviors that cause a wave to change direction.

Refraction

Have you ever noticed that a straw in a glass of water appears to be broken into two separate pieces? This odd-looking occurrence is shown in **Figure 19.16.** Perhaps you have noticed that objects submerged in water are not located where they appear to be. Both of these phenomena are caused by refraction.

Refraction and Wave Speed The bending of a wave as it passes from one medium into another at an angle is **refraction** (rih FRAK shun). Refraction is caused by a change in the speed of the wave as it enters the new medium. Because the medium determines a wave's speed, a change in medium changes a wave's speed. The greater the speed change in the new medium, the more the wave bends.

Refraction and Apparent Position When a light wave bends, it alters the apparent position of an object. That is, the bending changes where the object seems to be located. The bending of the waves fools the human brain. The brain interprets the light rays reflected from the object as if they had traveled in straight-line paths from the object to the eyes. **Figure 19.17** shows how light waves bend when entering and leaving water, and how this causes a change in apparent position. Light waves travel faster in air than they do in water. Thus, light waves slow down when entering the water and bend toward the normal. When light waves speed up upon entering the air from the water, they bend away from the normal. This relationship between speed change and direction is true for all refracted waves.

Refraction and Color Sunlight is made up of many different colors of light. If sunlight passes through a piece of angled glass known as a prism, it refracts and breaks into its component colors. Something similar occurs when sunlight passes through water droplets in the air. The result is a rainbow.

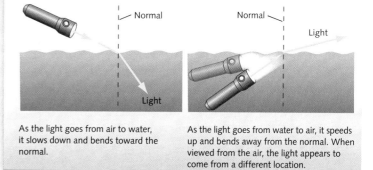

As the light goes from air to water, it slows down and bends toward the normal.

As the light goes from water to air, it speeds up and bends away from the normal. When viewed from the air, the light appears to come from a different location.

Figure 19.17 As the light waves change speed upon entering a new medium, they bend. Note that the normal is drawn perpendicular to the air-water surface.

Differentiate Instruction

Musical Play for the class recordings of songs about rainbows, such as "Somewhere Over the Rainbow" or "The Rainbow Connection." Have students write their own verses for the songs using as many vocabulary terms as they can.

Diffraction

Waves can bounce off surfaces and bend as they pass through materials. Waves can also bend around objects and through openings. The bending of a wave around a barrier or object or through an opening is called **diffraction** (dih FRAK shun). Note that refraction and diffraction are similar, as both cause waves to bend. The difference is that refraction occurs when waves pass through objects, whereas diffraction occurs when waves pass around objects.

All waves can diffract, and diffraction can occur with very large objects or very small ones. An example of diffraction on a large scale is shown in **Figure 19.18**. Here, ocean waves bend as they pass between and around a group of islands. Diffraction on a much smaller scale is shown in **Figure 19.19**. The water waves are shown diffracting through a small opening in a wall-like barrier. Note how the waves bend and spread out after passing through the opening.

Diffraction and Wavelength For any wave, the amount of diffraction that occurs depends on the size of the opening or object compared to the wavelength of the wave. In general, diffraction is most noticeable when the wavelength of the wave is approximately the same as the size of the object or opening.

Everyday Diffraction Diffraction is easily observed on most days at school. Imagine walking down a hallway toward a side hall door that is open. Voices from inside the room can be heard as you near the room. This occurs because the sound waves are about the same size as the door opening, and the waves diffract into the hallway. Note, however, that you cannot see into the room before reaching the door. Because the wavelengths of the light waves are very small compared to the size of the door opening, the light waves undergo almost no diffraction.

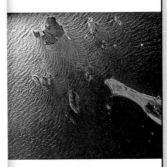

Figure 19.18 Ocean waves diffract as they pass between the islands.

Figure 19.19
Water waves bend after passing through a small opening.

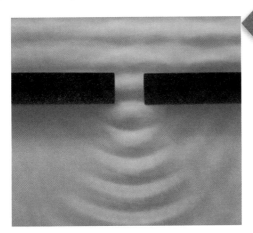

Figure It Out

1. If the photo shown is actual size, what is the wavelength of the water waves?

2. Describe the wavelength of the water waves relative to the size of the opening through which they diffract.

CHAPTER 19 **329**

● Teach

 EXPLAIN to students that another behavior of waves is interference. There can be both constructive and destructive interference. Remind students that the prefix *con-* means "with" and the prefix *de-* relates to removal or reversal. These prefixes help explain the events involved in each behavior.

Vocabulary

interference Tell students that the root *interfere* is derived from the French word *s'entreferir,* meaning "to strike each other." Interference occurs when two waves strike one another.

resonance Explain to students that the suffix *-ance* denotes a state or condition. The root *resonate* means "to resound or echo."

Use the Visual: Figure 19.20

ANSWER The amplitude of the new wave is equal to sum of the amplitudes of the original two waves.

Interference

When two people push an object in the same direction, the individual forces add together. If the people push in opposite directions, the forces interfere with each other and subtract from each other. If the forces are equal in size but opposite in direction, they cancel each other and no change occurs. Waves can behave in a similar way. **Interference** (ihn tur FEER uhns) occurs when two or more waves overlap and combine to either form a new wave or cancel each other.

Constructive Interference The interference of two waves in a rope is shown in **Figure 19.20.** Two separate waves travel toward each other. Constructive interference occurs as the waves pass through each other and their amplitudes add together. This creates a larger-amplitude wave. Although the amplitudes temporarily add, the energy possessed by each wave is not affected. After the waves pass, they continue on as if they had never met.

Destructive Interference Waves can also cancel each other. Destructive interference occurs when waves pass through each other and their amplitudes subtract. Imagine that the two waves in Figure 19.20 have equal but opposite amplitudes (one up, one down). As the waves pass through each other, they destructively interfere—that is, their amplitudes subtract and cancel. Although the amplitudes temporarily cancel, the energy possessed by each wave is not affected. After passing, the waves continue on as if they had never met.

Figure 19.20 As the two waves overlap, they interfere. How would you describe the amplitude of the new wave in diagram b?

a

Two waves travel toward each other.

b

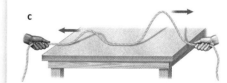

As the waves overlap, they constructively interfere. The wave amplitudes add.

c

The waves are not affected after passing through each other.

Background Information

The principle of superposition defines what the new wave looks like when it is produced during interference. When two or more waves interfere, the resulting displacement of the medium at any location is the sum of the individual wave displacements. For instance, if two waves overlap that each have an amplitude of 1 and the shape of a sine wave, the resulting shape of the medium would have an amplitude of 2 units and be a sine wave.

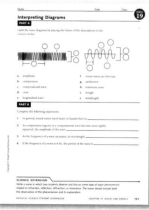

Interpreting Diagrams
Workbook, p. 121

Resonance

When you ring a bell, it vibrates at a particular frequency. A larger-sized bell vibrates at a different frequency. A fork also vibrates at a particular frequency when it is dropped and strikes the ground. In fact, all objects have a natural frequency at which they vibrate. The frequency depends on many factors, including size, shape, mass, and material.

Resonance (REZ uh nuhns) occurs when the frequency of the forced vibration applied to an object matches that object's natural frequency. When resonance occurs, small applied forces can produce large-amplitude vibrations. An example of resonance is shown in **Figure 19.21.**

Figure 19.21 When one tuning fork is struck, its vibrations cause a second identical tuning fork to begin vibrating.

⬤⬤⬤ CONNECTION: Structural Engineering

Structural engineers model, analyze, and design structures. They work on small consumer products as well as on buildings and bridges. An important part of an engineer's analysis is the determination of the structure's natural frequencies. Most structures vibrate at several frequencies. Once the frequencies are known, the engineer works to make sure resonance will not become a problem. Natural sources of vibrations that engineers design for include winds and earthquakes.

When an applied forced vibration matches a structure's natural frequency, large amplitudes can build within the structure. These large-amplitude motions can have catastrophic results. Several such events have happened throughout history. In 1850, a column of several hundred French soldiers marching in step began crossing a suspension bridge near Angers, France. The rhythmic marching evidently matched the natural frequency of the bridge. Resonance occurred and the bridge collapsed. Since that event, soldiers and other large groups often break out of marching formation when crossing bridges.

⟳ Extend It!

Research earthquakes and their effect on modern building design. Describe earthquake waves and explain at least one way in which buildings are designed to withstand earthquakes.

After You Read

1. A light wave strikes at wall at an angle of 30 degrees. At what angle will the light reflect? Explain your answer.

2. You see two waves approaching each other on a rope. For a moment, the waves disappear. Explain what is happening.

3. Use the information from the outline in your Science Notebook to write a well-developed paragraph that summarizes the five wave behaviors. Be sure to include a familiar example of each behavior in your paragraph.

⬤ Teach

EXPLAIN to students that one additional behavior of waves is that of resonance. Another example of sound waves creating resonance is a singer singing a high note and a glass shattering. Realistically, that sound would have to be amplified loud enough to require hearing protection for those involved.

⟳ Extend It!

Answers will vary. Earthquake waves are a combination of transverse and compressional waves, and they include S-waves, P-waves, Love waves, and Rayleigh waves. Buildings are designed to withstand the anticipated shaking caused by earthquakes. Some modern buildings use isolators to absorb the motion of an earthquake.

EXPLORE Pair students and provide them with dry spaghetti, white glue, and clear tape. Challenge pairs to build the strongest bridge that they can using only the available materials. Have each pair sketch the design for the bridge before beginning construction. Show pictures of different types of bridges, such as beam, arch, cantilever, and suspension, to demonstrate possible approaches. When all bridges are built, hold a contest to see which bridge can hold the most weight.

⬤ Assess

Use the After You Read questions and the Alternative Assessment to help you evaluate students' understanding of the lesson.

Background Information

An estimated 226 people died when the Bridge of Angers completely collapsed. In 1940, the Tacoma Narrows Bridge also was partially destroyed due to resonance. It too was a suspension bridge. Since that event, all new bridges have been modeled in wind tunnels.

Alternative Assessment

Have students use the outlines in their Science Notebooks to compare and contrast refraction and diffraction.

After You Read

1. The light will reflect at 30 degrees. According to the law of reflection, the angle of the incident light is equal to the angle of the reflected light.

2. Destructive interference of two equal but opposite waves has occurred.

3. Students' paragraphs will vary but should include a definition and example for each of the following: reflection, refraction, diffraction, interference, and resonance.

Chapter 19 Summary

VOCABULARY REVIEW

Check students' sentences or paragraphs to make sure they understand the meaning of each vocabulary term.

Evaluate students' essays using the following criteria:

1. The topic sentence, or main idea, should restate the Key Concept.

2. The supporting paragraphs should incorporate the answers to the Learning Goal questions students have written and include details, facts, and examples they have recorded in their Science Notebooks.

3. The concluding sentence should sum up the main idea of the chapter and restate the Key Concept.

MASTERING CONCEPTS

True or False

1. False, vibration
2. False, energy
3. False, Electromagnetic
4. False, compressional
5. False, compression
6. True
7. True
8. False, approximately equal to

Short Answer

9. The buoy moves up and down, and slightly forward and back, as the wave moves past. The buoy does not move in the direction of the wave.

10. The bending of a wave around an object is called diffraction.

11. Particles in an area of compression are closer together than those in an area of rarefaction.

12. The medium determines a wave's speed; all sound waves in air travel at the same speed.

13. Light reflects off the viewer's face and then strikes and reflects off the mirror. The light reflected from the mirror passes into the viewer's eyes.

14. When the push is applied at the natural frequency of the swing, the swing's amplitude builds quickly. Each push adds energy to the swinging person.

Chapter **19** Summary

KEY CONCEPTS

19.1 The Nature of Waves

- A wave is a disturbance that travels through matter or space.
- All waves are caused by vibrations.
- Waves transfer energy, but not matter, from place to place.
- Mechanical waves require a medium through which to travel, whereas electromagnetic waves do not.

19.2 Types of Waves

- In a transverse wave, the motion of the medium is at right angles to the wave's direction.
- Transverse waves have crests and troughs.
- In a compressional wave, the medium moves back and forth parallel to the direction in which the wave travels.
- Compressional waves have areas of compression and rarefaction.

19.3 Properties of Waves

- Waves can be described by the properties of wavelength, frequency, period, and amplitude.
- The medium determines the speed of a wave traveling through it.
- The speed of a wave can be calculated using the equation speed = frequency × wavelength, or $v = f \times \lambda$.
- The amplitude of a wave is a measure of the energy it carries.

19.4 The Behavior of Waves

- The law of reflection states that the angle of incident light equals the angle of reflected light.
- Refraction causes the direction of a wave to change. It occurs as waves change speed when entering a new medium at an angle.
- Waves can bend, or diffract, around objects and through openings.
- Wave amplitudes add or subtract when waves interfere with each other. The increase or decrease in wave amplitude is temporary, however, because the energy possessed by each wave is not affected.
- Resonance occurs when the frequency of a forced vibration applied to an object matches the object's natural frequency. When resonance occurs, small applied forces can produce large-amplitude vibrations.

VOCABULARY REVIEW

Write each term in a complete sentence or write a paragraph relating several terms.

19.1
wave, p. 316
mechanical wave, p. 318
medium, p. 318
electromagnetic wave, p. 318

19.2
transverse wave, p. 319
crest, p. 319
trough, p. 319
compressional wave, p. 320
compression, p. 320
rarefaction, p. 321
seismic wave, p. 321

19.3
wavelength, p. 323
frequency, p. 323
period, p. 324
amplitude, p. 326

19.4
reflection, p. 327
normal, p. 327
law of reflection, p. 327
refraction, p. 328
diffraction, p. 329
interference, p. 330
resonance, p. 331

PREPARE FOR CHAPTER TEST

To prepare for the chapter test, create a question from each Learning Goal. Use the information in your Science Notebook to answer each question. Then use these answers to write a well-developed essay about the chapter. Use the Key Concept on the first page of this chapter as your topic sentence.

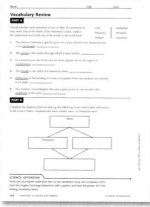

Vocabulary Review
Workbook, p. 120

Reading Comprehension
Workbook, p. 122

MASTERING CONCEPTS

True or False
If the statement is true, write "true." If it is false, change the underlined word or words to make the statement true.

1. Any back-and-forth motion can be described as a(n) <u>force</u>.
2. Waves carry <u>matter</u> from place to place.
3. <u>Transverse</u> waves can travel through the vacuum of space.
4. Sound waves are <u>transverse</u> waves.
5. Particles of matter in a region of <u>rarefaction</u> are tightly squeezed together.
6. The <u>frequency</u> and <u>wavelength</u> of a sound wave in air are related.
7. A wave bends <u>toward</u> the normal when it enters a new medium and slows down.
8. Diffraction is maximized when a wave's wavelength is <u>much larger than</u> the object or opening.

Short Answer
Answer each of the following in a sentence or brief paragraph.

9. Describe the motion of an ocean buoy as an ocean wave moves past.
10. Identify the wave behavior related to waves bending around an object.
11. Compare the spacing of particles in an area of compression with the spacing of particles in an area of rarefaction.
12. Explain why sound waves with different frequencies travel at the same speed in air.
13. Describe how a person is able to see his or her reflection in a mirror.
14. Explain how resonance can be used to push someone high into the air on a swing.

Critical Thinking
Use what you have learned in this chapter to answer each of the following.

15. **Compare and Contrast** How are diffraction and refraction similar? How are they different?
16. **Calculate** A wave has a wavelength of 3.25 m and a frequency of 2.30 Hz. What is the speed of the wave?
17. **Apply Concepts** Two long hallways cross at right angles. At the end of one of the hallways, a light is turned on and a bell is rung. Describe what can be seen and heard from the end of the other hallway. Explain your reasoning.

Standardized Test Question
Choose the letter of the response that correctly answers the question.

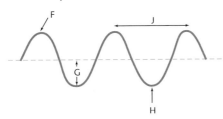

18. **What wave property is shown at the area labeled *J*?**
   A. frequency
   B. amplitude
   C. wave speed
   D. wavelength

> **Test-Taking Tip**
>
> If you don't know an answer and you won't be penalized for guessing, make an educated guess. Use context clues if you don't understand the question.

Critical Thinking

15. Both refraction and diffraction cause waves to change direction. The change of direction by refraction is due to changes in speed, whereas diffraction does not involve a speed change. Also, refraction occurs when waves pass through an object, whereas diffraction occurs when waves pass around an object.
16. speed = 2.30 Hz × 3.25 m = 7.48 m/s
17. The sound waves have wavelengths that are approximately equal to the hallway opening, and thus they are able to diffract into the other hallway. Light waves, because they are much shorter, do not readily diffract. The sound of a bell will be heard, but a light will not be seen.

Standardized Test Question

18. D

Reading Links

Rubber-Band Banjos and a Java Jive Bass: Projects and Activities on the Science of Music and Sound

Students who make use of this quirky collection of activities will create their own musical instruments, learn how various instruments work, be introduced to musical notation and its relation to science, read about prominent scientists with musical proclivities, and in other ways gain a better understanding of the scientific principles and concepts related to sound and music.

Alex Sabbeth. John Wiley & Sons. 112 pp. Illustrated. Trade ISBN 978-0-471-15675-8.

Waves: From Surfing to Tsunami

This interesting study of ocean waves, written by the former editor of a surfing magazine and well-supplemented with photographs and illustrations, offers readers a closer look at perhaps the most familiar type of wave. In doing so, it underscores ideas that apply more generally to waves and the topics covered in this chapter.

Drew Kampion. Gibbs Smith. 80 pp. Illustrated. Trade ISBN 978-1-58685-212-2.

Curriculum Connection
Workbook, p. 123

Science Challenge
Workbook, p. 124

Labs

19A How Waves Travel

This prechapter introduction activity is designed to determine what students already know about waves by having them create and observe waves in water.

Objectives

- form waves in water and observe their movement
- describe the pattern the waves make
- communicate results using a diagram

Planning

 10–15 minutes   groups of 3–4 students

Materials (per group)

- pan of water
- medicine dropper
- a cork
- paper towels
- pencil and paper

Advance Preparation

- Use shallow pans that are at least 20 cm across.
- Students should draw the pattern of waves (ripples) coming out from the center of the pan and the end of the pan. Use the same paper to diagram the water moving horizontally as the cork moves vertically up and down.

Engagement Guide

- Challenge students to think about the patterns the waves will make in the experiment by asking these questions:
  - *What kind of waves have you seen and how were the waves created?* (Students are likely to mention gentle ripples in a pond and crashing waves at the beach. Causes include wind and objects hitting the water.)
  - *What did the waves look like? How did they move?* (Students might describe waves as a disturbance on the water surface. They should mention that the waves move horizontally whereas the water moves up and down.)
- Encourage students to communicate their observations in creative ways.

Going Further

Encourage students to design an experiment to test how the speed of the air blowing across the surface of water affects the waves formed. Have students conduct these experiments and present their conclusions to the class.

19B Properties of Waves

Objectives

- observe particle movement in a medium
- compare and contrast transverse and compressional waves
- illustrate waves accurately
- draw conclusions

Skill Set

observing, comparing and contrasting, identifying, illustrating, drawing conclusions

Planning

 30–35 minutes   groups of 3–4 students

Materials

Materials for this activity are listed in the Student Laboratory Manual.

Advance Preparation

Cut pieces of colored ribbon 15–20 cm long. Coiled springs that can be stretched to a length of about 3 meters work better than shorter lengths. Two plastic toy springs joined end-to-end with PVC cement can also be used. Some students may be able to see the waves more clearly when a brightly colored plastic coil spring is used. Remind students not to overstretch the spring, as it may lose its shape. Caution students to firmly hold on to the ends of the spring—a stretched spring that is suddenly released might cause injury.

Answers to Observations: Data Table 1

Steps 2–3: Students should observe the ribbon move from its resting position, to one side, to the other side, and then back to the resting position. The direction of this motion is perpendicular to the direction the wave travels. Students' drawings should show a transverse wave.

Step 4: Students will see the ribbon move back and forth, parallel to the direction that the wave travels. Student drawings should show a compressional or longitudinal wave. The compressed coils move together as a unit through the spring.

Answers to Analysis and Conclusions

1. Both motions are back-and-forth in nature. In steps 2–3 the ribbon moves side-to-side, perpendicular to the wave direction. In step 4, the ribbon moves back-and-forth, parallel to the wave direction.

2. The waves in steps 2–3 are transverse because the movement of the medium is at right angles to the direction the wave is traveling. The wave in step 4 is compressional because the movement of the medium is in the same direction as the wave is traveling.

3. As the rate increases, frequency increases and wavelength decreases.

4. Moving the end of the spring a greater distance increased the amplitude of the wave.

5. It requires energy to make the spring move. This energy came from the motion (vibration) of the hand holding the spring.

Going Further

On a drawing of a transverse wave, have students label the crest, trough, wavelength, and amplitude. Have students share their drawings with the class.

19C Sunscreen and Ultraviolet Rays

Objectives

- perform a controlled experiment to test sunscreens
- compare and rate SPF strengths of sunscreens
- record data in a suitable way

Skill Set

- observing, comparing, rating, recording and
- analyzing data, drawing conclusions

Planning

 45–60 minutes   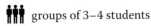 groups of 3–4 students

Materials

Materials for this activity are listed in the Student Laboratory Manual.

Advance Preparation

UV beads can be purchased through a science supply house or online. Prepare four resealable plastic bags containing a handful of beads for each group. Collect various strengths of sunscreens—SPFs of 4, 15, and 30 are suggested, but other values are fine to use also. This activity works best on a sunny day.

Answers to Observations: Data Table 1

Observations assume students used SPFs of 4, 15, and 30. Student observations should describe the UV beads in the lowest SPF labeled bag as having the most color. The UV beads in the highest SPF labeled bag will have the least color. The SPF ratings should be as follows: control (no sunscreen): 5; SPF 4: 4 or 5, indicating the least effective; SPF 15: 2 or 3; SPF 30: 1, indicating the most effective.

Answers to Analysis and Conclusions

1. The SPF 30 sunscreen was the most effective sunblock and received the best rating of 1. The beads had the least color.

2. Answers will vary depending on the original hypothesis.

3. Ultraviolet rays are invisible electromagnetic waves. They have more energy than visible light waves and can damage the skin and cause cancer. Sunscreens contain substances that can block some or all of the UV rays, preventing the rays from penetrating and damaging your skin.

Going Further

Have students test the beads with different types of lights such as fluorescent, mercury vapor (gymnasium lights), and a black light. Determine which lights give off the most UV rays. Have students create a data table to record their observations and then share their conclusions with the rest of the class.

Chapter 20 Lessons

Introduce Chapter 20

As a starting activity, use Lab 20A on page 115 of the Laboratory Manual.

ENGAGE Pair students and provide each pair with a blindfold and a quiet noisemaker, such as a ticking clock. Have one student sit and cover one ear, and have the other student make noise at various distances and angles from the first student. The second student should also make note of where he or she is when the partner can hear the noise, recording estimates of the distance and angle. Have students analyze their data and note their observations. As a class, discuss their observations and any hypotheses students might have about sound, how it travels, and how humans hear.

Think About Sound

Review with students how particles of matter are arranged in solids, liquids, and gases. It might be helpful to have a display of dominoes modeling sound. Allow students to play with the model if they are unfamiliar with the play space described.

Direct students to complete the bulleted items in their Science Notebooks. Students' explanations will vary but should describe how the energy of motion of a source causes particles to collide. These collisions cause other collisions and result in a pulse being sent through the medium.

Chapter 20

Sound

KEY CONCEPT Sound waves are compressional waves produced when matter vibrates.

Have you ever watched an elaborate set of dominos put into motion? Once the first domino is knocked over, it starts a chain reaciton that causes each domino in the set to be knocked over. Every movement causes the dominos to collide and sends energy-carrying "pulses" through the rest of the domino set. An object in motion in air behaves in a similar way—sending energy-carrying pulses away from the source. These pulses are what produce sound, the subject of this chapter.

Think About Sound

Sound waves transmit energy of motion away from the source. They also require a medium in which to travel.

- The medium a sound wave travels through is a form of matter. Recall how particles of matter are arranged in solids, liquids, and gases. In your Science Notebook, explain which form of matter is best modeled by the dominos.

- Then write an explanation of how a domino setup can be used as a model of sound waves moving through a medium.

NSTA
SCiLINKS.
THE WORLD'S A CLICK AWAY

www.scilinks.org
Sound Code: WGPS20

334

20.1 The Nature of Sound

Before You Read

In your Science Notebook, rewrite this lesson's headings and subheadings so that they form questions. As you read, write the answers to the questions.

Chapter 19 introduced the concepts of vibrations, waves, and wave characteristics. As discussed in that chapter, there are different kinds of waves. One kind is a wave you are quite familiar with because it is part of your daily life—the sound wave. In this lesson, the formation of sound waves and the factors that affect the speed of sound will be explored.

Sound Waves

Vibrations cause sound waves, and sound waves carry energy. Sound waves are compressional waves. This means the medium vibrates back and forth parallel to the direction in which the wave moves.

How Sound Waves Form Vibrating objects have kinetic energy. If an object vibrates in air, kinetic energy is transferred to the air as sound waves. When the tuning fork in **Figure 20.1** is struck, the *U*-shaped ends of the tuning fork vibrate side-to-side. Much like a child in a ball-filled play area, the tuning fork is completely surrounded by particles. The moving ends of the tuning fork interact with these particles.

As the ends of the tuning fork move outward, they push nearby molecules in the air together. This region of tightly-packed molecules is known as a compression. As the ends of the tuning fork move inward, the molecules in the air expand into the space. This loosely packed region is called a rarefaction.

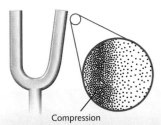

Compression

When the tuning fork vibrates outward, it forces molecules in the air next to it closer together, creating a region of compression.

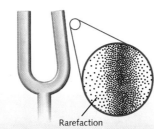

Rarefaction

When the tuning fork moves back, the molecules in the air next to it spread farther apart, creating a region of rarefaction.

Figure 20.1 The vibrating tuning fork transfers energy to the air. A compressional wave moves away from the tuning fork.

CONNECTION: Music

A tuning fork is a *U*-shaped steel device with a handle. When a tuning fork is struck, it produces a relatively pure tone of a specific frequency. Tuning forks are often used to tune musical instruments. The most commonly used tuning fork vibrates at 440 Hz, a frequency known as concert pitch. Concert pitch has long been used as the standard tuning note for orchestra musicians.

ELL Strategy

Use a Concept Map Have each student create a concept map to organize the information they learn about sound. The main idea should be *Sound,* and the first subtopic should be *Sound Waves.* Students should add information about how sound waves form to the *Sound Waves* circle. Students can use this concept map for the first two lessons of this chapter.

Background Information

Tuning forks are useful because they are unaffected by moisture and other conditions that affect many other musical instruments, though temperature does slightly affect the tone. The most commonly used tuning forks are for the notes of A, B flat, or the C above middle C (440 Hz). Pitch pipes and electronic devices are also used to tune musical instruments.

20.1 Introduce

ENGAGE Depending on the quantity of tuning forks available, you might do the following activity as a class demonstration, with small groups, or with pairs of students. Provide each group with a tuning fork and a wide-lipped bowl of water. Ask students to strike the tuning forks and to write in their Science Notebooks their observations about what they see and hear. Then have students strike the forks again and then quickly place the tuning forks in the water. Have them write their observations in their Science Notebooks. English language learners could also draw what they observe.

Discuss students' observations and ask them to explain why the tuning fork caused movement in the water. Tell students they will learn the cause of the movement in this lesson.

Vocabulary terms are listed on the first student page of each lesson. You may wish to preview the terms before introducing each lesson. Strategies for teaching the vocabulary appear on the pages where the terms are introduced.

Before You Read

Model the process of rewriting a heading as a question. Have students repeat the process for the next heading and write both questions in their Science Notebooks. Remind students to leave space between questions for their responses.

Teach

EXPLAIN to students that they will be learning about sound waves. In the last chapter, they learned about different kinds of waves; this chapter focuses on how one particular type of wave—a sound wave—is formed and travels, and how people hear sounds.

Teach

Review with students the meanings of the terms *wavelength, frequency, compression,* and *rarefaction.* Explain that sound waves travel from the source in an outward direction, similar to the pattern formed when a pebble is dropped into still water. Remind students that sound waves do not travel in outer space, but do travel through solids, liquids, and gases.

Figure It Out: **Figure 20.2**

ANSWER **1.** 2 wavelengths **2.** The density of the particles in a compression is much greater than the density of the particles in a rarefaction.

As You Read

Give students a few minutes to review and respond to the questions they wrote in their Science Notebooks. If students are struggling, have them work with a partner to answer the questions. Check students' responses for accuracy.

ANSWER Sound waves form when a vibrating object interacts with the surrounding medium, creating a series of compressions and rarefactions that move away from the source. The wavelength of a sound wave is the distance from one compression to another or from one rarefaction to another.

 Explore It!

ANSWER The tapping sound should be louder when heard underwater.

Figure It Out

1. Identify the number of complete wavelengths shown.

2. Compare the densities of the particles in a compression and in a rarefaction.

As You Read

Use the information you have learned to answer the heading and subheading questions recorded in your Science Notebook. Share your answers with a partner and make any necessary changes.

What is the wavelength of a sound wave?

 Explore It!

Compare sound traveling through different mediums next time you take a bath. First, make the room as quiet as possible. Then, with your head above the water, tap lightly on the tub and listen to the sound. Repeat the tapping with your head submerged under the water. How do the two sounds compare?

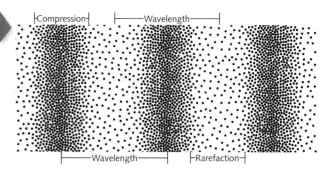

Figure 20.2 The wavelength of a compressional wave is the distance from one compression to another, or from one rarefaction to another.

How Sound Waves Travel Particles in a compression collide with other nearby particles. These collisions transfer energy from particle to particle away from the source. As an object continues to vibrate, it sends a series of compressions and rarefactions through the surrounding medium. **Figure 20.2** shows the sound waves produced by a vibrating tuning fork. Like all waves, sound waves can be described in terms of wavelength and frequency. The wavelength of the sound waves is shown in Figure 20.2.

When the bell in your classroom rings, sound waves travel away from the bell in all directions. The sound waves reflect off of the walls, the ceiling, and the floor. They also diffract, or bend, around corners and through openings. As a result, you can hear the bell in all parts of the room.

Sound Waves in Different Mediums

Sound waves make compressions and rarefactions in any solid, liquid, or gas. Most sounds travel through the air. However, you may have heard sounds underwater. If so, you might have noticed that faint sounds are easily heard through water. Water is a good conductor of sound. The performers in **Figure 20.3** rely on hearing sound through water.

Sound travels easily through solids such as steel. To discover this yourself, position your ear near a metal railing while a friend taps on it. The sound should be easy to hear even if the tapping is faint and fairly far away. It is important to remember that sound waves are mechanical waves. This means sound requires a medium. Sound waves cannot form when matter is not present. Because of this, sound does not travel through the vacuum of space.

Figure 20.3 An underwater speaker allows synchronized swimmers to hear the music to which they are performing.

Background Information

To clarify, the speed of sound refers to the speed of transmission of a small disturbance through a medium. Sound is the sensation created in the brain in response to sensory inputs from the inner ear. The speed of sound (A) is equal to the square root of the ratio of specific heat (g) multiplied by the gas constant (R) multiplied by the temperature (T).

The Speed of Sound

The speed of sound depends on the medium it travels through. In general, sound travels fastest in solids, somewhat more slowly in liquids, and more slowly still in gases. Sound travels through all mediums in the same way: by transferring energy through a series of collisions. The speed of sound in several different mediums is given in the table in **Figure 20.4.** Several factors, including a medium's elasticity and its temperature, affect the speed of sound.

Speed and Elasticity   Sound generally travels faster through elastic materials. Something that stretches or distorts and returns to shape is **elastic** (i LAS tik). A rubber band is elastic. So are many other materials. Although it may not be obvious, steel is a very elastic material. The speed of sound through steel can be over 5,000 m/s, which is very fast!

Elasticity affects the speed of sound because sound waves spread through collisions. Particles in elastic mediums are tightly packed together. The tightly packed particles react quickly to an applied force. In other words, the collisions occur more quickly. Thus, the speed of sound is usually faster through more elastic mediums. Elastic mediums also transfer energy with little loss.

As you might recall, particles are tightly packed in solids, somewhat less tightly packed in liquids, and loosely packed in gases. As a result, solids are generally more elastic than liquids, and liquids are more elastic than gases. Not surprisingly, the speed of sound through each state of matter generally corresponds to the packing of the particles of matter.

Speed and Temperature   The speed of sound generally increases as the temperature of the medium increases. This means sound travels faster through the air on a hot day. The increased speed is due to the motion of the particles in the medium. As temperature increases, the particles in a medium move more quickly. These faster-moving particles collide more quickly. The result is an increase in the speed of sound.

Speed of Sound in Different Mediums

Medium	Physical State	Speed of Sound (m/s)
air (at 20°C)	mixture of gases	343
helium (at 0°C)	gas	972
water	liquid	1,482
glass	solid	5,640
steel	solid	5,960

Figure 20.4 The speed of sound varies greatly in different mediums.

Did You Know?

For each 1°C increase in air temperature, the speed of sound increases by about 0.6 m/s. The equation for this relationship is

speed = $(331.4 + 0.6T_C)$ m/s

where T_C is the air temperature in °C. Use the equation to verify the speed of sound at 20°C given in Figure 20.4.

After You Read

1. Identify the types of mediums that sound waves can travel through.
2. If the speed of sound in a medium is 5,200 m/s, is the medium most likely a solid, liquid, or gas? Use Figure 20.4 to help you answer this question.
3. Review the answers to the heading and subheading questions in your Science Notebook. Use the answers to explain why the temperature and the elasticity of a medium affect the speed of sound.

Differentiate Instruction

Logical and Mathematical   Have each student create a graph to visually represent the information in **Figure 20.4.** Have students calculate how long it would take for sound to travel (unassisted by electronic devices) to your classroom from different locations in the school building or yard.

● Teach

EXPLAIN to students that the speed of sound varies with the elasticity and temperature of the medium through which it is traveling. Before reading the lesson, ask students to hypothesize how each factor affects the speed.

 Vocabulary

elastic   Encourage students to brainstorm common uses of the word *elastic*. Examples might include stretchy pieces of clothing or a rubber band. Explain that these examples involve the quality of stretching and returning to the original shape. Materials with a greater amount of elasticity transfer sound more easily.

● Assess

Use the After You Read questions and the Alternative Assessment to help you evaluate students' understanding of the lesson.

After You Read

1. Sound waves can travel through any medium.
2. The medium is most likely a solid.
3. Sound travels faster at higher temperatures because the particles of the medium are moving at higher speeds. These higher-speed particles collide and transfer energy more quickly. Sound travels faster in elastic materials because the tightly-packed particles in elastic materials respond more quickly to an applied force.

Alternative Assessment

Have students use the questions they wrote in their Science Notebooks to explain how sound waves form and travel from tuning forks. Students should explain what happens to the sound waves when they encounter a solid, liquid, and gas.

As an extension, have students research the relationship between density and the speed of sound.

20.2 Introduce

ENGAGE Tell students that you will be experimenting with sound pitch by making sounds with a xylophone. Discuss the meaning of the term *pitch* (how high or low a sound is). Ask students to hypothesize whether low or high sounds are easier for humans to hear and to write their hypotheses in their Science Notebooks. Then have them close their eyes and sit as far from you as possible. Play a variety of notes on the xylophone and have students raise their hands when they can hear you. Write on the board the number of hands raised for each note. Experiment with playing louder and softer sounds.

Share the results of the experiment with students and ask them to review their hypotheses for accuracy.

Before You Read

Model on the board a working definition of a term that is familiar to students. Write what you know about the term, and then ask students to tell you more about the definition and add the new information. After hearing from four to five students, create a new working definition of the term. Give students a few minutes to define *loudness* in their Science Notebooks.

● Teach

EXPLAIN to students that in this lesson, they will learn about the properties of sound: pitch, frequency, amplitude, energy, intensity, and loudness. They will also learn how some of the properties are related.

Use the Visual: Figure 20.5

[ANSWER] The higher C (524 Hz) has twice the frequency of the lower C (262 Hz).

Learning Goals

- Relate the pitch and frequency of a sound wave.
- Relate the amplitude, energy, intensity, and loudness of a sound wave.
- Describe how loudness is measured, and identify sound levels that can cause hearing damage.
- Describe the Doppler effect.

New Vocabulary

pitch
intensity
loudness
decibel
Doppler effect
echo
beat

Recall Vocabulary

frequency, p. 323
amplitude, p. 326

Figure 20.6 Both sound waves travel at the same speed in air.

20.2 Properties of Sound

Before You Read

Create a working definition of the term *loudness*. A working definition is one that develops as you read and think about an idea. Write what you know about the word *loudness* before you begin reading. Then add to that definition as you read and discuss the lesson.

In the wild, hearing is a key to survival. Animals constantly listen for sounds of danger. Predators are aware of this, and they often avoid making excessive noise when stalking prey. Although your world is very different from the wild, sound still provides valuable information about your surroundings. Much of the information carried by sound is due to sound's properties.

Frequency and Pitch

Try singing the *do–re–mi–fa–so–la–ti* musical scale shown in **Figure 20.5.** Your voice starts with a low tone and becomes higher with each note. The pitch is different for each note.

Figure 20.5 Each note has a unique frequency and a distinct pitch. How is the frequency of the higher C related to that of the lower C?

C	D	E	F	G	A	B	C
do	re	mi	fa	so	la	ti	do
262 Hz	294 Hz	330 Hz	349 Hz	393 Hz	440 Hz	494 Hz	524 Hz

The **pitch** of a sound is how high or low the sound seems to be. The pitch of a sound is related to the sound wave's frequency. Frequency is a measure of how many wavelengths pass a given point each second. Look at the two waves shown in **Figure 20.6.** Because both waves travel at the same speed in air, their wavelengths and frequencies are related. The wave with the shorter wavelength has a higher frequency.

As the frequency of a sound increases, so does the sound's pitch. Thus, a 400-Hz note has a higher pitch than a 200-Hz note does. A healthy human ear can detect sounds ranging from 20 Hz to 20,000 Hz.

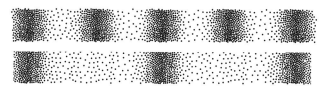

338 SOUND

ELL Strategy

Activate Prior Knowledge Have students work in pairs to write what they know about each vocabulary term from the lesson in their Science Notebooks. Students' responses may take the form of complete sentences or word maps. Have students update their responses as their understanding of the terms improve.

Updates should include relationships that exist between the terms (for example, loudness & intensity) and examples (decibel level variation as shown in **Figure 20.9** or from personal experiences).

Energy, Intensity, and Loudness

People often turn up the volume of a radio when they hear a song they like. Although the frequencies of the sound remain the same, something about the higher-volume sound is different. The difference is that louder sound waves carry more energy.

Energy The amount of energy carried by a wave is related to the wave's amplitude. For a sound wave, the density of the particles in the compressions and the rarefactions determines amplitude. Compare the compressions and rarefactions of the two sound waves in **Figure 20.7**. High-energy vibrations produced the high-amplitude sound wave. This wave has densely packed compression particles and widely spaced rarefaction particles. The areas of compression and rarefaction in a high-amplitude wave are easy to identify. Low-energy vibrations produced the low-amplitude sound wave. Because the particles are more evenly distributed throughout the low-amplitude wave, the compressions and rarefactions in a low-amplitude wave are harder to identify.

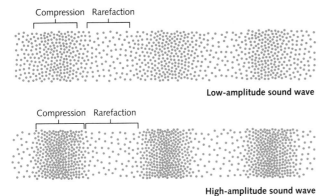

Compression Rarefaction

Low-amplitude sound wave

Compression Rarefaction

High-amplitude sound wave

Figure 20.7 eCpatic sCinCtCo -amp t eCo n C a eCaeCáir Cœn C istri te CInCcoratst,C eC i -amp it eCson C a eC aC e - efine CompressionsC an Craefactions Co C oCteCa e n t sCofCteC o C a esCcompare

Intensity The **intensity** (in TEN si tee) of a sound wave is the rate at which energy passes through a specific area. Higher-energy sound waves have higher intensities. Sound intensity determines how far away a sound is heard. Shouting produces high-energy, high-intensity sound waves that can be heard across a large distance. In contrast, you must be very close to hear the low-intensity sound of a whisper.

Sound travels through a series of collisions. With each collision, some of the wave's energy is lost. As a result, a wave loses energy and intensity as it travels. This explains why a shout is reduced to a whisper after traveling a long distance.

Figure It Out

1. Use a centimeter ruler to measure the wavelength of each wave. Assume each wave is shown in its true size.

2. What is the frequency of each wave? Assume each wave passes by a given point in one second.

● Teach

EXPLAIN to students that three properties of sound—energy, intensity, and loudness—are related. Ask students to close their eyes and imagine that they are at a loud music concert. Ask them to think about what they hear and what they feel. Ask several students to share some of their mental images and feelings with the class. Some students will mention hearing loud music and being able to feel the beat. Tell students that the ability to feel the beat is a result of the increased energy that louder sound waves carry.

Vocabulary

pitch Ask students if they are familiar with any other meanings of the word *pitch*. Discuss the meanings and encourage students to identify any relationships between these and the definition provided. (*Pitch* as a noun could mean "throw," "level," "slope," "the plunging and rising motion of a ship," or "the distance between teeth on a saw.")

intensity Explain to students that this word comes from the Latin word *intensum*, meaning "to stretch toward." Ask students how this derivation relates to the definition of the term.

Figure It Out: **Figure 20.7**

ANSWER **1.** Both wavelengths are about 4 cm. **2.** The frequencies of both waves are slightly greater than 3 Hz.

Differentiate Instruction

Intrapersonal Have students interview the instrumental or vocal music teacher(s) about how that teacher's knowledge of sound affects his or her work. Students can work with partners to prepare questions. Examples of questions might include: *What properties of sound do you consider during preparations for a concert? How do you tune your instruments? What principles of sound should musicians know about?*

Teach

EXPLAIN to students that their perception of sound is the result of the brain interpreting nerve impulses from the ears. Until sound waves cause those impulses in the human ear, sound is actually only vibrations. Sound is measured in decibels.

As You Read

Have students review and revise their definitions of *loudness*. Then have them briefly outline or map their paragraphs. Pair students if they are having difficulty relating *loudness* to the given terms.

Students' final paragraphs should include the following information: Loudness is the human perception of sound intensity. That means that loudness is related to sound intensity. Sound intensity is the rate at which energy passes through a specific area. Higher-energy sound waves have higher intensities. The amount of energy carried by a wave is related to the wave's amplitude. For a sound wave, the density of the particles in the compressions and the rarefactions determines amplitude. As the energy of a sound wave increases, so do the amplitude, intensity, and loudness.

Figure It Out: Figure 20.8

ANSWER **1.** power mower, chain saw, jet plane taking off; any sound louder than 85 dB can cause damage **2.** The airplane is 40 dB louder; 40 dB louder = (10)(10)(10)(10) = 10,000 times louder.

As You Read

Review the updated definition of *loudness* in your Science Notebook. Using that definition, write a well-developed paragraph explaining how loudness is related to amplitude, energy, and intensity.

Figure It Out

1. Identify the sounds that can cause hearing damage.
2. Compare the loudness of a jet airplane taking off and the loudness of a power mower. How many times louder is the airplane?

Loudness The brain interprets nerve impulses from the ears as sound. **Loudness** is the human perception of sound intensity. Although each person's sense of loudness varies, loudness is related to sound intensity. As the intensity of a sound wave increases, so does the loudness of the sound that is heard.

A Scale for Loudness The intensity of a sound can be measured. The unit of sound intensity is the **decibel** (DES uh buhl), abbreviated dB. The decibel is named for Alexander Graham Bell, the inventor of the telephone. The faintest sound a healthy human ear can detect is defined as 0 dB. This sound level is also called the threshold of hearing. Sounds with intensities less than 0 dB cannot be heard by the human ear.

The decibel scale is based on powers of ten. Each 10-dB increase represents an increase in intensity of ten times. This means a 10-dB sound is ten times louder than a 0-dB sound. Likewise, a 20-dB sound is ten times louder than a 10-dB sound, and 100 times louder than a 0-dB sound. The average speaking voice is about 60 dB.

Very loud sounds cause hearing damage. Once hearing damage has occurred, there is no treatment, medicine, surgery, or device that can completely restore it. Damage occurs at sound levels of approximately 85 dB and higher. Examine the sound intensities listed in **Figure 20.8**. Many sounds are loud enough to cause hearing damage. The amount of damage caused depends on the sound's frequency, loudness, and duration. Loud music concerts, with sound levels of 115–120 dB, cause hearing damage.

Loudness in Decibels

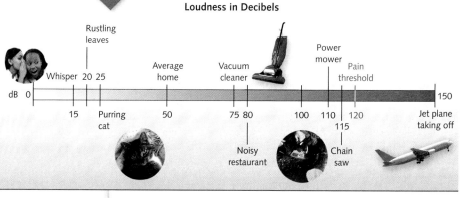

Figure 20.8 Sound intensity is measured in decibels (dB). The faintest sound that can be heard has an intensity of 0 dB.

Background Information

Hearing loss is increasing in children and teenagers; loud music and headphone use with portable radios and mp3 players may be responsible for this trend. Overall, ten percent of Americans have a level of hearing loss that impacts their ability to understand normal speech. When noise is too loud, cells in the inner ears are killed; as more exposure to the noise occurs, more hair cells die. The damage is irreversible.

The Doppler Effect

Have you ever watched an auto race? If so, you probably noticed that the sound of the cars changes as the cars drive past. As each car passes, the pitch, or frequency, of the sound decreases. The change in frequency that occurs when a sound-emitting object moves relative to the listener is known as the **Doppler effect**.

The Doppler effect occurs whenever there is movement—a change in distance—between the sound source and the listener. A moving source or a moving listener produces the Doppler effect.

Examine the sound waves produced by the race car in **Figure 20.9.** The sound source (the car) moves toward a nonmoving listener (the person with the checkered flag). Note how the waves in front of the car become compressed. The compression is caused by the movement of the car. The flagger hears these compressed waves as the car approaches. Because the waves are closer together, more compressions pass the flagger each second than if the car were at rest. As a result, the flagger hears the higher pitch of these sound waves. The motion of the car also causes the waves trailing behind it to spread apart, or elongate. The trailing waves have a greater wavelength and lower frequency, or pitch, than do the waves in front of the car. The flagger hears the lower pitch of these sound waves as the car passes by.

All waves are subject to the Doppler effect, including electromagnetic waves. Sports teams and law enforcement officers often use radar guns. A radar gun sends out radio waves. The waves reflect from moving objects and return to the gun. Electronic circuitry converts the frequency change of the radio waves into a speed; this is the speed of the moving object.

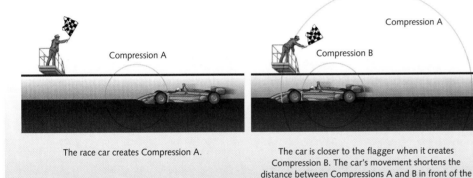

The race car creates Compression A.

The car is closer to the flagger when it creates Compression B. The car's movement shortens the distance between Compressions A and B in front of the car and lengthens the distance between the compressions in back of the car. The flagger hears a sudden decrease in the pitch, or frequency, of the sound as the car passes by.

Figure 20.9 The Doppler effect occurs because the sound-emitting car moves toward the listener. The Doppler effect changes a wave's wavelength and frequency.

CHAPTER 20 **341**

● Teach

EXPLAIN to students that the Doppler effect describes why the pitch of a moving object changes. One example to share with students is the sound from the siren of an ambulance or police car. As the source of the sound approaches a listener, the pitch of the siren seems to rise. It then drops as the source passes the listener and moves away. The actual frequency of the sound produced by the siren does not change. However, the sound waves become bunched together as the source approaches the listener and spread apart as the source moves away from the listener. Ask students to share other examples of the Doppler effect that involve light or sound waves. They may need to conduct additional research to find examples.

Vocabulary

loudness Encourage students to think of common uses of the word *loud*. Examples might include making great sound or something tasteless, bright, or garish. Explain to students that the suffix -*ness* denotes a state, degree, or condition of something.

decibel Explain to students that the prefix *deci-* means "one-tenth." Ask students how the decibel scale is based on tenths.

Doppler effect Encourage students to think of common uses of the word *effect*. Examples might include a result or the act of making something happen. Tell students that Christian Doppler was a physicist who discovered that the frequency and wavelength of a wave change when the listener moves relative to the source of a sound.

Background Information

The Doppler effect is used in meteorological science. Weather radars transmit radio waves, and objects in the air, such as snow, rain, and hail, reflect the waves back to the antenna. The reflected radio waves are converted into pictures to show the amount and location of precipitation. In accordance with the Doppler effect, waves reflected from something moving away from the antenna change to a lower frequency; objects moving toward the antenna change to a higher frequency. These pictures provide information about wind motions and are used to forecast weather.

Teach

EXPLAIN to students that two additional properties of sound are echoes and beats. Echoes are the result of sound waves reflecting; beats result from sound waves with similar frequencies interfering.

 Vocabulary

echo Explain to students that this word is derived from the Greek word meaning "sound." Ask students how this derivation relates to the definition of the term.

beat Encourage students to brainstorm common uses of the word *beat*. Examples might include a pulse, a regular course or journey, mixing ingredients together, or striking something repeatedly. Explain that a beat is often a regularly occurring sound that results from interfering sound waves.

Explain It!

The frequency of the humming is slightly different from the frequency of sound from the rotating ventilation fan. The two sounds interfere and create beats.

Assess

Use the After You Read questions and the Alternative Assessment to help you evaluate students' understanding of the lesson.

After You Read

1. As the frequency of a sound wave increases, so does the sound's pitch.
2. There must be relative movement between the sound source and the listener.
3. The unit of sound intensity is the decibel, dB. Each 10-dB increase in intensity represents a tenfold increase in loudness.

Alternative Assessment

Have students use their definitions of *loudness* to write a paragraph comparing what they used to think about loudness to what they know after reading the lesson. You could provide prompts such as *I used to think . . . Now I know . . .*

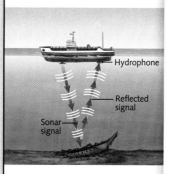

Figure 20.10 By continually measuring depth, objects can be located and the features of the ocean floor can be mapped.

Explain It!

In a well-developed paragraph, explain why beats can be heard when you hum at a constant pitch in a shower while a ventilation fan runs.

Echoes

Sound waves reflect, or bounce, off surfaces they strike. An **echo** (EK oh) is a reflected sound wave. If the distance is large enough, you may hear an echo when you shout into a canyon or toward a distant mountain. Sonar, which stands for "sound navigation and ranging," is a technology that makes use of echoes. As **Figure 20.10** shows, sonar uses reflected sound waves to measure distances. The time required for the sound to reflect and return is used to calculate distance.

Beats

All waves, including sound waves, can interfere with each other. When two tones with slightly different frequencies occur at the same time, they produce a variation in loudness known as **beats.** The sound is soft, then loud, then soft, and so on.

As shown in **Figure 20.11,** beats form when 440-Hz and 442-Hz tuning forks are sounded at the same time. Each vibrating fork produces compressional waves. Because the frequencies are different, a pattern of constructive and destructive interference develops. Times of increased loudness correspond to periods of constructive interference. For the 440-Hz and 442-Hz tuning forks, the loudness peaks twice per second.

$$442 \text{ Hz} - 440 \text{ Hz} = 2 \text{ Hz}$$

A beat frequency of 2 Hz is heard.

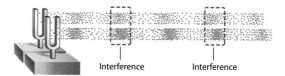

Figure 20.11 Interfering sound waves cause beats.

Beats are used to tune pianos. Each note is tuned in relation to a pitch—usually that of a 440-Hz tuning fork. Beats form when an out-of-tune 440-Hz A-note is played while the tuning fork is struck. The piano's A-note is brought into tune by adjusting the piano string's tension. When the note is in tune, the beating disappears.

After You Read

1. Explain how the pitch of a sound wave is related to the sound's frequency.
2. Identify what must happen in order for the Doppler effect to occur.
3. Review the working definition of *loudness* in your Science Notebook. Identify the unit used to measure sound intensity. Use your working definition to describe how the unit relates sounds of different loudness.

Background Information

Many animal species use echolocation, such as porpoises, dolphins, toothed whales, whippoorwills, swifts, and most species of bats. Animals use it to navigate, to avoid predators, to detect prey, and to communicate.

20.3 Music and Sound Quality

Before You Read

Create a lesson outline in your Science Notebook. Use the lesson title as the outline title. Label the headings with the Roman numerals *I* through *IV*. Use the letters *A*, *B*, *C*, etc. under each heading to record information that you want to remember.

Do you enjoy listening to the sound of static from a radio that is not tuned to a station? How do you react to the sound of chalk squeaking across a chalkboard? Why are some sounds pleasing and others irritating? The answers lie in the nature of music and sound quality.

What Is Music?

People have a wide range of musical tastes. Some people like classical music performed by an orchestra. Others prefer country, hip-hop, or rock. What is the difference between these forms of music and the static noise heard on a radio? **Music** is a group of sounds that have been deliberately used to make a regular, or repeating, pattern. Noise, in contrast, is a random group of sounds having no pattern.

Natural Frequencies   Elastic materials vibrate at one or more **natural frequencies.** Musical instruments make use of natural frequencies. A guitar string vibrates at its natural frequency when plucked. At the same tension, the string produces the same pitch. The length, thickness, and tension of each string allow a guitar to produce a wide range of sounds. Other instruments use reeds, membranes, or columns of air vibrating at natural frequencies to produce sound.

Resonance   Musical instruments make use of resonance. Resonance occurs when something is made to vibrate by absorbing energy at its natural frequency. When a clarinet player blows into the instrument, a thin reed in the mouthpiece vibrates. An air column inside the clarinet absorbs energy from the vibrating reed and begins to resonate. Resonance amplifies, or makes louder, the sound produced by many instruments.

Noise has no specific or regular sound wave pattern.

Music is organized sound. Music has regular sound wave patterns and structures.

Figure 20.12 Music has a definite pattern. Noise does not.

ELL Strategy

Compare and Contrast Have students compare the types of instruments and compare their ability to create music or noise: string, brass and woodwind, and percussion instruments. Working with a partner, students should compare each set of concepts in a chart.

Learning Goals

- Distinguish between noise and music.
- Describe how different musical instruments produce sound.
- Explain why different musical instruments have different sound qualities.

New Vocabulary

music
natural frequency
sound quality
timbre
fundamental frequency
overtone
resonator

Recall Vocabulary

resonance, p. 331

20.3 Introduce

ENGAGE Have students work with a partner to discuss the following questions: *What is good music? What is bad music?* Students may respond with a list of bulleted items or a concept map for each question. As a class, try to reach a consensus as to the characteristics of good music and bad music. Tell students that taste in music can be based on personal preferences; however, sound quality can be quantified.

Before You Read

Model the process of creating an outline. Write the following information on the board, reviewing the lesson and talking aloud about the process as you write.

Music and Sound Quality
I. What Is Music?
   A. Natural Frequencies
   B. Resonance
II. Sound Quality

Give students about ten minutes to create their outlines in their Science Notebooks.

Teach

EXPLAIN to students that in this lesson, they will learn about the different qualities of musical instruments, how they produce sound, and why instruments sound different.

 Vocabulary

music Explain to students that the word *music* is derived from the Greek word *mousike*, which relates to muses. Muses were goddesses who embodied the arts. Ask students to think about how muses are related to the definition of *music* and its difference from noise.

natural frequency Ask students to list common meanings of the word *nature*. Responses might include "a sort or type," "the outdoors," "animals and plants," or "what something consists of." Review with them the meaning of *frequency*. After providing the definition of the term from the lesson, ask students to describe how the common meaning of *natural* relates to its scientific definition.

Teach

EXPLAIN to students that sound quality describes why a note, played by two different instruments, sounds different on each instrument. Sound quality includes fundamental frequency and overtones.

Figure It Out: Figure 20.13

(ANSWER) **1.** 524 Hz/262 Hz = 2; 786 Hz/262 Hz = 3; 1048 Hz/262 Hz = 4 **2.** 5(262 Hz) = 1,310 Hz

 Vocabulary

sound quality Encourage students to think of common uses of the word *quality*. Examples might include a characteristic, a high standard, or the general standard or grade of something. Review with students the meaning of *sound*. Discuss the meanings of *quality* that students provided, and encourage students to identify the relationship between those meanings and the definition provided in this lesson.

timbre Explain to students that this word is derived from the Greek word *tympanon*, meaning "drum." *Timbre* is defined as the distinctive quality of a tone. Ask students how the derivation relates to the definition of the term.

fundamental frequency Explain to students that the word *fundamental* is derived from the Latin word *fundamentum*, meaning "foundation." Review with students the meaning of *frequency*. Ask students to relate the derivation to the meaning provided in this lesson.

overtone Tell students that *overtone* is a compound word; *over* means "above." A tone is a musical sound. An overtone is a sound with frequencies "above," or higher.

resonator Explain to students that the root is derived from *sonare*, meaning "to sound." The prefix *re-* means "to do again," and the suffix *-or* signifies a thing that performs a function. Have students discuss the literal meaning formed by putting these word parts together.

Use the Visual: Figure 20.14

(ANSWER) The higher C (523.2 Hz) has twice the frequency of the lower C (261.6 Hz).

Figure It Out

1. Calculate each overtone's multiple of the fundamental frequency.
2. If the guitar produced a fourth overtone, at what frequency would it occur?

Figure 20.14 A piano can produce this series of notes known as a musical scale. How are the frequencies of the two C-notes on the scale related?

Sound Quality

Imagine that a flute and a piano play the same musical note at the same loudness. Though the pitch of the notes is the same, each tone sounds unique. The character of a sound that distinguishes it from another sound of the same pitch and loudness is called **sound quality.** An instrument's sound quality is due to the combination of a number of distinct frequencies. Sound quality is also known as **timbre** (TAM ber).

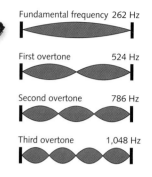

Figure 20.13 The guitar string vibrates at a fundamental frequency and at several higher-frequency overtones. Note that the overtones are multiples of the fundamental frequency of 262 Hz.

Fundamental frequency	262 Hz
First overtone	524 Hz
Second overtone	786 Hz
Third overtone	1,048 Hz

Overtones When a guitar string is plucked, the pitch that is heard is the lowest frequency of the vibrating string. The lowest frequency of a vibrating object is called the object's **fundamental frequency.** However, most objects that produce sounds vibrate at several different frequencies at the same time. These higher frequencies are called **overtones.** As shown in **Figure 20.13,** overtones have frequencies that are whole-number multiples of the fundamental frequency. The intensity of the overtones is almost always less than that of the fundamental frequency. The combination of the fundamental and overtone frequencies gives each instrument its unique sound quality.

Musical Scales

Musical instruments can usually make a sequence of sounds known as a musical scale. Each sound in the scale has a specific frequency. The eight notes of the C musical scale produced on a piano are shown in **Figure 20.14.** A series of eight musical notes is called an octave. Other musical scales are made up of different sets of frequencies.

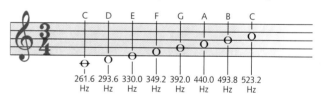

C 261.6 Hz D 293.6 Hz E 330.0 Hz F 349.2 Hz G 392.0 Hz A 440.0 Hz B 493.8 Hz C 523.2 Hz

---

Differentiate Instruction

Musical, Kinesthetic Borrow simple musical instruments from the music department and have students experiment with comparing sound qualities. Instruments such as the harmonica, piano, xylophone, and recorder create sound fairly easily.

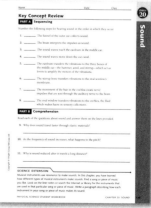

Key Concept Review Workbook, p. 125

Musical Instruments

The members of a school band play a variety of musical instruments. A musical instrument is any device used to produce a musical sound. Most instruments can be categorized into a few main groups.

Strings   String instruments make sounds when their strings are made to vibrate. Common string instruments include the piano, guitar, and violin. Different methods are used to make strings vibrate. As shown in **Figure 20.15,** violin strings vibrate when a bow is drawn across them. Piano strings vibrate when hammers strike them. Guitar strings are plucked or strummed.

Because the sound produced by a vibrating string is not loud, most string instruments have a resonator. A **resonator** is a hollow air-filled chamber. Air in the chamber resonates with the vibrating strings. The vibrating air also causes the body of the instrument to vibrate. These additional vibrations greatly amplify the sound of the instrument.

Brass and Woodwinds   Trumpets, clarinets, and tubas are examples of brass or woodwind instruments. Each uses a vibrating air column to produce sound. Brass instruments are wind instruments that are usually made of brass and have cup-shaped mouthpieces. Wind instruments that are not brass are known as woodwinds.

The vibration used to make the air column resonate occurs at the mouthpiece. For brass instruments, the player blows into a cup-shaped mouthpiece, as shown in **Figure 20.16.** When the player's lips vibrate against the mouthpiece, the air column resonates. To play a flute, the player blows air across the mouthpiece. This causes the air inside the flute to resonate. Other woodwinds use a reed to cause vibrations. A reed is a thin piece of wood or plastic that is held in the mouthpiece. As the player blows, the reed vibrates, causing the air column to resonate.

The length of the resonating air column determines the pitch of the sound produced. As shown in **Figure 20.17,** valves are used to change the length of the air column in a saxophone. Most brass and woodwind instruments use valves. An exception is the trombone. A sliding tube is moved in and out to change the air column length in a trombone.

Sound waves

Figure 20.15 When the bow is drawn across the strings, the strings vibrate. Air inside the violin resonates with the vibrating strings and amplifies the sound.

As You Read

Review the information about sound quality in your outline. Compare your outline with those of other students in the class. Discuss any differences in your outlines and make adjustments as needed.

Explain how the fundamental frequency and overtones are related to sound quality.

Figure 20.16 When a tubist makes the mouthpiece vibrate, air inside the tuba resonates and amplifies the sound.

Figure 20.17 The opening and closing of valves alters the length of the resonating air column in a saxophone. Changing the length of the air column changes the pitch of the sound produced.

● Teach

EXPLAIN to students that musical instruments can be categorized into three main groups: strings, brass and woodwinds, and percussion. Instruments from each of the different categories have different ways of producing sound.

As You Read

Give students a few minutes to review and update their outlines. Check students' outlines for accuracy.

ANSWER An instrument vibrates at its fundamental frequency and at several overtone frequencies. The combination of all these frequencies determines the sound quality of the instrument.

Background Information

Instruments can also be classified into the following categories: strings, brass, woodwinds, percussion, keyboard, and electronic. Instruments generate sound in the following ways:

Strings: Strings are plucked, picked, strummed, and/or slapped. Sound depends on the thickness, tension, density, and length of the string.

Brass: Sounds result from a vibrating column of air inside the tube of the instrument. The volume of air and the speed at which a player's lips vibrate affect the pitch.

Woodwinds: Sounds come from the vibrating column of air inside the tube. Vibrations occur from air blowing across an edge, between a reed and the instrument, or between two reeds.

Percussion: Sounds are made from a vibrating membrane or piece of solid material. Most percussion instruments do not have definite pitch; exceptions include xylophones, marimbas, handbells, and chimes.

Keyboard: Sounds are produced in a variety of ways; harpsichords, clavichords, and pianos use strings; pipe organs have pipes; and accordions use metal reeds.

Electronic: Sounds are created through electrical signals that are converted into vibrations by a speaker.

Teach

EXPLAIN to students that the last type of instrument, percussion, includes drums, blocks, cymbals, and xylophones. These instruments are often easy to distinguish in a musical ensemble because of their distinct sounds.

Explore It!

The sound is formed as molecules in the air vibrate and the air column in each bottle resonates with the vibrations. Students should discover that the bottle with the highest level of water has the sound with the highest pitch. This is not a function of the water, however. It is a function of the length of the resonating air column. The higher the height of the water, the shorter the air column, which produces a sound of higher pitch.

Assess

Use the After You Read questions and the Alternative Assessment to help you evaluate students' understanding of the lesson.

After You Read

1. Both are produced by vibrations. Music has a repeating pattern, whereas noise does not.

2. The player blows into a cup-shaped mouthpiece, and his or her lips vibrate against the mouthpiece. These vibrations cause the air column inside the instrument to resonate. The player changes pitch by moving a sliding tube in or out.

3. A vibrating guitar string causes the air within the guitar's hollow air-filled chamber to resonate, amplifying the sound. The air column within a membrane-covered drum resonates with the vibrating drumhead and amplifies the sound. A vibrating air column resonates inside a flute and amplifies the sound.

Figure 20.18 The vibrating membrane causes the air within the drum to resonate.

Explore It!

Even a plastic soda bottle can be a musical instrument. Obtain three or four clean, empty, 2-L plastic soda bottles. Fill the bottles with water to different heights and put them on a flat surface. From the side, blow air across the top of each bottle and listen for a tone. Explain how the sound is formed. Describe how the height of the water in the bottle affects the pitch of the sound produced.

Percussion People have always been drawn to the deep thumping sound of a drum. Throughout human history, drums have been used to send signals, to intimidate enemies, and to entertain friends. Drums and other percussion instruments were likely the first musical devices created. Percussion instruments are usually struck, shaken, brushed, rubbed, or scraped in order to cause the vibrations that produce sound.

A membrane-covered drum is shown in **Figure 20.18.** The tightly stretched membrane, or drumhead, creates a resonating air chamber within the drum. When the membrane is struck, it begins to vibrate. These vibrations cause the air within the drum to resonate, greatly increasing the loudness of the drum. The pitch of a membrane-covered drum can often be adjusted by altering the tension of the membrane.

A Caribbean style of drum known as a steel drum is shown in **Figure 20.19.** Because steel is very elastic, the steel drum surface produces high-intensity sounds without needing a resonating air chamber. Instead, the steel sides of the drum act as a resonator. A steel drum produces different notes in a musical scale when different portions of the drum's surface are struck.

Not all percussion instruments are drums. Wooden blocks, cymbals, washboards, and rattles all produce sounds when they are made to vibrate. An unusual percussion instrument is the xylophone. The xylophone is made up of wooden bars of varying length that are struck with small mallets. Below each wooden bar is a suspended tube resonator. The vibrating wooden bar causes the air column in each tube to resonate.

Figure 20.19 The sound of a drum is greatly affected by the type of medium that vibrates. Steel drums have an interesting and unique sound.

After You Read

1. Compare noise and music.

2. Explain how a trombone creates sound and changes pitch.

3. Review the outline you created in your Science Notebook. Use it to describe how resonance plays a role in the sounds formed by a guitar, a drum, and a flute.

Alternative Assessment

Have students use their outlines to compare the sound qualities of two musical instruments of their choice. They should include discussion of the natural frequency, fundamental frequency, overtones, and sound quality of each instrument.

Field Study

Have students attend a school band or orchestra practice. Ask them to listen to the practice and to observe an instrument from each of the groups: strings, brass and woodwinds, and percussion. Have students note where the resonator is on each instrument. Encourage students to try to hear the instrument's sound quality within the context of the whole musical ensemble.

20.4 How You Hear

Before You Read

It can be helpful to diagram a complicated step-by-step process. In your Science Notebook, draw a horizontal line. Place marks at the left end, center, and right end of the line. Label the first mark *Outer Ear*, the second *Middle Ear*, and the third *Inner Ear*. Now imagine a sound wave entering the ear. As you read the lesson, record the name of each structure the sound wave encounters in order and in the proper location on the diagram.

Make a mental list of the sounds you have heard today. A brief version of the list might include screeching tires, singing birds, ticking clocks, rustling leaves, purring cats, crying babies, and people's voices. These sounds are very different. Each has a unique frequency, pitch, sound quality, and loudness. In spite of this, you can detect and make sense of each sound. The ears and the brain work together to provide one of the body's important senses—the sense of hearing.

The Ear

Making sense of sound waves is a multi-step process that begins with the ears. The human ear is a complicated sensory organ. It is able to detect sounds with frequencies from 20 to 20,000 Hz. Waves with frequencies above 20,000 Hz, known as **ultrasonic** (uhl truh SON ik) **waves,** cannot be heard. Likewise, **infrasonic** (in fruh SON ik) **waves,** with frequencies below 20 Hz, also cannot be heard.

The ear detects a wide range of sound intensities, and it is especially sensitive to sounds between 1,000 Hz and 5,000 Hz. Because of this, faint sounds between 1,000 Hz and 5,000 Hz are more easily heard than sounds outside this range. Most human speech falls within a frequency range of 200 Hz to 8,000 Hz.

Some animals have much larger hearing ranges than humans. Dogs, for example, can hear sounds with frequencies up to 45,000 Hz. That is much higher than humans can hear. The whistle in **Figure 20.20** is barely audible to people but is easily heard by dogs. Bats are thought to be able to sense frequencies as high as 120,000 Hz.

Figure 20.20 This dog whistle produces sound frequencies to which dogs are most sensitive. Dogs can hear the whistle from up to 3.2 km away.

- Identify the three parts of the ear.
- Describe how structures in the ear function to detect sound.
- Explain the role of the brain in hearing.

New Vocabulary

ultrasonic wave
infrasonic wave
eardrum
cochlea

20.4 Introduce

ENGAGE Pair students and provide each pair with a blindfold and a rope. Have one student cover his or her eyes with the blindfold and the other student serve as the guide. The guide should ensure that his or her partner is safe and walk slowly and carefully. Pairs should hold opposite ends of the rope and maintain tension so that the follower can use it to move and turn when necessary. Discourage students from talking. If time permits, have students switch roles. After the walk, discuss the following questions with students: *How did not being able to see affect your listening? What types of sounds do you remember? Did something startle or surprise you? Would you be able to repeat the walk using the sounds as a guide?*

Before You Read

Model the process of creating the line on the board and adding the labels *Outer Ear*, *Middle Ear*, and *Inner Ear*. Drawing a picture of an ear superimposed on the line might help students better understand the diagram. Have students draw similar diagrams in their Science Notebooks.

● Teach

EXPLAIN to students that the ears are part of the process of interpreting sound waves. The process begins as sound waves reach the outer ear, continues as they move through the middle ear to the inner ear, and ends in the brain.

 Vocabulary

ultrasonic wave Explain to students that the prefix *ultra-* means "beyond a place or limit," and the root *sonic* means "related to sound or sound waves." Waves with frequencies above the range heard by the human ear are ultrasonic.

infrasonic wave Tell students that the prefix *infra-* means "below." Converse to ultrasonic waves, infrasonic waves have frequencies below the range heard by the human ear.

ELL Strategy

Read Aloud Have students work in small groups to read the lesson aloud. Each student should read one or two paragraphs, and then the next student should continue. If possible, place students with the same native languages together. Encourage students to write a short summary of the information at the end of each topic. Students should also repeat any vocabulary words and their definitions from context.

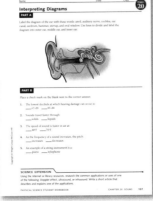

**Interpreting Diagrams
Workbook, p. 127**

Teach

EXPLAIN to students that the three parts of the ear—the outer, middle, and inner ear—process physical sound waves or vibrations. The outer ear collects the waves and funnels them to the middle ear. The bones in the middle ear act as levers to amplify the vibrations and pass them to the inner ear. In the inner ear, hair-tipped cells in the cochlea send impulses from the auditory nerve to the brain.

 Vocabulary

eardrum Explain to students that *eardrum* is a compound word, consisting of *ear* and *drum*. Review the definition of *ear,* and then remind students that a drum is a percussion instrument consisting of a hollow frame with a skin or membrane stretched tightly across its opening. Ask students why this is an appropriate name for this ear structure.

cochlea Explain to students that this word is derived from Greek and means "snail with a spiral shell." Ask students why this is an appropriate name for the structure of the inner ear.

Figure It Out: Figure 20.21

ANSWER **1.** Sound waves in air stop when they strike the eardrum. **2.** A musical drum uses a resonating air column to amplify sound, whereas the middle ear uses the lever-like action of interconnected bones.

As You Read

Give students a few minutes to review and revise the diagrams in their Science Notebooks. Have students share their diagrams with a partner to check their understanding.

ANSWER The three parts of the ear are the outer ear, the middle ear, and the inner ear. The order is hammer, anvil, stirrup.

Figure It Out

1. How far into the ear do sound waves in air travel?

2. Contrast how a musical drum and the middle ear amplify sound.

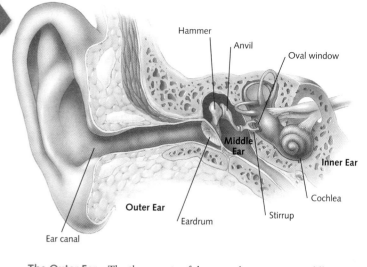

Figure 20.21 The human ear is made up of the outer ear, the middle ear, and the inner ear.

As You Read

Review the information you have recorded in the line diagram in your Science Notebook. What are the three parts of the ear? Identify the order in which each of the three bones in the middle ear moves in response to a sound wave.

348 SOUND

The Outer Ear The three parts of the ear—the outer ear, middle ear, and inner ear—are shown in **Figure 20.21**. The outer ear is made up of the visible part of the ear and the ear canal. Note that the visible part of the ear is shaped somewhat like a funnel. The funnel shape helps the outer ear collect sound waves and direct them into the ear canal. The ear canal is a narrow passage that leads to the eardrum of the middle ear.

The Middle Ear The purpose of the middle ear is to amplify sound. The process begins when sound waves strike a thin membrane called the **eardrum.** The eardrum transfers the vibrations to three small connected bones. These bones—the hammer, anvil, and stirrup—act as levers to amplify the motion of the vibrations. The stirrup bone connects to a membrane on the oval window. As the stirrup bone vibrates, so does the oval window's membrane.

The Inner Ear The inner ear converts vibrating motion into nerve impulses. Vibrations are transferred by the oval window into a fluid-filled structure called the **cochlea** (KOH klee uh). **Figure 20.22** shows that the cochlea is lined with tiny hair-tipped sensory cells. The vibrational energy of the fluid makes the hairs move. When the hairs move, nerve impulses are sent through the auditory nerve to the brain. The brain interprets the impulses as sound.

Figure 20.22 Tiny hair-tipped sensory cells line the inside of the cochlea.

Teacher Alert

Be sensitive when discussing deaf and hard-of-hearing people. The National Association of the Deaf prefers those terms to "hearing-impaired." Students might have deaf or hard-of-hearing friends or relatives.

Differentiate Instruction

Kinesthetic Provide students with a variety of craft materials, such as cardboard tubes, cardboard, heavy paper, and yarn. Have small groups of students work to create a model of one of the three parts of the ear. Students should label the structures within the chosen part.

Hearing Loss

Many people cannot hear the full range of sound. In the United States, it is estimated that one in three people between the ages of 65 and 75 has hearing loss. Disease, age, and exposure to loud noises can damage the hair-tipped sensory cells in the cochlea. When sensory cells in the ear die, they are not replaced. The gradual loss of sensory cells over time is the cause of poor hearing in many older people.

One of the first noticeable effects of age-related hearing loss is difficulty hearing high-pitched sounds. The *s* and *th* sounds in speech are higher in pitch than other speech sounds are, and people with hearing loss often have a hard time telling the sounds apart. A hearing aid can improve the hearing of some people who suffer from hearing loss. Hearing aids work by amplifying the incoming sound. Some hearing aids amplify only high-frequency sounds, which are the sounds most commonly associated with age-related hearing loss.

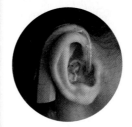

Figure 20.23 Hearing loss is often treated with the use of a hearing aid.

 CONNECTION: **Medicine**

Although ultrasonic waves cannot be heard, they have a wide range of important uses. Ultrasound has proven to be especially useful in the medical field. Like X rays, ultrasonic waves can be used to form images of the internal body. Unlike X rays, however, ultrasound does not pose a radiation risk. Ultrasound is used to diagnose a variety of medical problems.

An image formed with ultrasound is called a sonogram. Obtaining a sonogram is a simple procedure. A medical technician directs the ultrasound at the desired area. Ultrasound reflects from body tissues and organs. The reflected sound pattern is converted into an image. Sonograms like the one shown are often used to monitor a fetus's development during pregnancy.

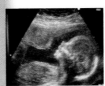

High-frequency ultrasound waves are also used to treat medical problems, such as kidney stones. A kidney stone is a hard, calcium-based deposit that can form in the kidneys. Ultrasound gives doctors a nonsurgical method of removing the stones. Bursts of ultrasound literally vibrate the stones apart. The fragments then pass out of the body through the urine.

After You Read

1. Summarize the function of the ear by correctly pairing each ear part with its function (amplifying, collecting, interpreting).

2. Describe how the ear amplifies sound.

3. Use the information from the line diagram in your Science Notebook as a guide to describe the sequence of events that occur in the inner ear in a well-developed paragraph. What is the brain's role in the process?

 Extend It!

Many unwanted, undesirable, and harmful sounds are produced every day. Research noise pollution sources in your area and report on any local laws designed to limit it.

Background Information

In 1915, Paul Langevin invented a device that used piezoelectricity to produce sounds. These sounds became known as sonar. Ultrasound devices were first used in the 1930s to examine metals for flaws and to heat-damaged tissues. In the 1950s, ultrasound started being used to detect, examine, and analyze tumors, kidneys, and the gallbladder.

Alternative Assessment

Have students use their line diagrams to describe how sound travels and is processed from the outer ear to the inner ear.

Teach

EXPLAIN to students that most hearing loss is irreversible. Some problems can be improved by the use of hearing aids, which amplify sound.

 CONNECTION: **Medicine**

One of the most familiar applications of ultrasound technology in medicine is its use in creating images of unborn babies. Other exams include advanced ultrasound, which targets specific locations, and Doppler ultrasound, which detects slight changes in the frequency of sound waves as they reflect off of moving objects such as blood cells. Ultrasounds provide doctors with important information about abnormalities and conditions that may need to be treated before or upon the baby's birth.

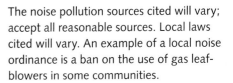 **Extend It!**

The noise pollution sources cited will vary; accept all reasonable sources. Local laws cited will vary. An example of a local noise ordinance is a ban on the use of gas leaf-blowers in some communities.

Assess

Use the After You Read questions and the Alternative Assessment to help you evaluate students' understanding of the lesson.

After You Read

1. outer ear: collecting; middle ear: amplifying; inner ear: interpreting

2. The vibrating motion of the eardrum is magnified as it acts through the lever-like action of the hammer, anvil, and stirrup bones.

3. The vibrating oval window transfers vibrations to the fluid-filled cochlea. Sensory hairs in the cochlea move in response to the waves in the fluid. The sensory cells send nerve impulses to the brain. The brain interprets the signals as sound.

Chapter 20 Summary

VOCABULARY REVIEW

Check students' sentences or paragraphs to make sure they understand the meaning of each vocabulary term.

Evaluate students' essays using the following criteria:

1. The topic sentence, or main idea, should restate the Key Concept.

2. The supporting paragraphs should incorporate the answers to the Learning Goal questions students have written and include details, facts, and examples they have recorded in their Science Notebooks.

3. The concluding sentence should sum up the main idea of the chapter and restate the Key Concept.

MASTERING CONCEPTS

True or False

1. True
2. False, energy/loudness/intensity
3. False, elastic materials, solids
4. True
5. False, Beats
6. False, whole-number multiple
7. True
8. False, amplify

Short Answer

9. In general, the greater the elasticity of the material, the greater the speed of sound through the material will be.

10. Higher-temperature air molecules move faster and collide more quickly than do lower-temperature molecules. Because the collisions occur at a faster rate, the sound waves spread through the air at a higher speed.

11. The overtone has the higher frequency because it must be a whole-number multiple of the fundamental frequency.

12. Sounds that are quieter than the threshold of hearing cannot be heard. The threshold of hearing is 0 dB.

13. If the sound source moves toward the listener, the frequency of the sound increases. If the sound source moves away from the listener, the frequency of the sound decreases.

KEY CONCEPTS

20.1 The Nature of Sound

- Vibrating objects surrounded by a medium create compressional sound waves that move away from the source.
- Sound waves move and transfer energy through a series of collisions.
- The speed of sound in room-temperature air is about 343 m/s.
- In general, sound travels fastest in solids, somewhat more slowly in liquids, and much more slowly in gases.

20.2 Properties of Sound

- Pitch is how high or low a sound seems to be. As the frequency of a sound wave increases, so does the sound's pitch.
- High-energy waves have tightly packed compression particles and widely spaced rarefaction particles.
- The more intense a sound is, the louder it sounds. Intensity is measured in decibels (dB). A 10-dB increase in intensity corresponds to a sound that is ten times louder.
- Sounds less than 0 dB cannot be heard. Sounds 85 dB and louder can cause hearing damage.
- The Doppler effect is the change in the pitch, or frequency, of a sound due to the movement of the source or the listener.

20.3 Music and Sound Quality

- Music is sound with a regular pattern. Noise is sound that has no pattern.
- All elastic materials vibrate at one or more natural frequencies. A material resonates when it is made to vibrate by absorbing energy at its natural frequency.
- Objects vibrate at a fundamental frequency and several overtone frequencies. Overtone frequencies are multiples of the natural frequency. An instrument's sound quality is due to the combination of its fundamental and overtone frequencies.
- Musical instruments can be string, percussion, brass, or woodwind. Most rely on a resonator to amplify sound.

20.4 How You Hear

- The three parts of the ear are the outer ear, the middle ear, and the inner ear. The outer ear collects sound, the middle ear amplifies sound, and the inner ear interprets sound.
- Hair-tipped sensory cells in the cochlea of the inner ear generate nerve impulses when they move. The brain interprets the impulses as sound.
- The ear can detect sounds from 20 Hz to 20,000 Hz. Ultrasonic waves are above the human hearing range. Infrasonic waves are below the human hearing range.

VOCABULARY REVIEW

Write each term in a complete sentence or write a paragraph relating several terms.

20.1
elastic, p. 337

20.2
pitch, p. 338
intensity, p. 339
loudness, p. 340
decibel, p. 340
Doppler effect, p. 341
echo, p. 342
beat, p. 342

20.3
music, p. 343
natural frequency, p. 343
sound quality, p. 344
timbre, p. 344
fundamental frequency, p. 344
overtone, p. 344
resonator, p. 345

20.4
ultrasonic wave, p. 347
infrasonic wave, p. 347
eardrum, p. 348
cochlea, p. 348

PREPARE FOR CHAPTER TEST

To prepare for the chapter test, create a question from each Learning Goal. Use the information in your Science Notebook to answer each question. Then use these answers to write a well-developed essay about the chapter. Use the Key Concept on the first page of this chapter as your topic sentence.

**Vocabulary Review
Workbook, page 126**

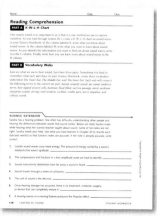

**Reading Comprehension
Workbook, page 128**

True or False

If the statement is true, write "true." If it is false, change the underlined word or words to make the statement true.

1. The speed of sound in air <u>increases</u> as the temperature of the air increases.

2. The <u>pitch</u> of a sound wave is related to how tightly the particles are packed in the compressions and rarefactions.

3. Sound travels fastest through <u>inelastic</u> materials such as <u>gases</u>.

4. High-pitched sounds have <u>high</u> frequencies.

5. <u>Echoes</u> occur when two waves with slightly different frequencies interfere.

6. The frequency of an overtone is a <u>fraction</u> of the fundamental frequency.

7. A(n) <u>woodwind</u> instrument makes use of a resonating air column to amplify sound.

8. The bones of the inner ear <u>interpret</u> sound waves.

Short Answer

Answer each of the following in a sentence or brief paragraph.

9. Relate the elasticity of a material to the speed of sound through the material.

10. Explain why the speed of sound in air increases as the temperature of the air increases.

11. Explain which has the higher frequency, the fundamental frequency of a guitar string or its third overtone.

12. Explain what the threshold of hearing is.

13. Relate the change in frequency of a sound wave to the direction the source moves relative to the listener.

14. Describe how a resonator amplifies the sound of a violin.

Critical Thinking

Use what you have learned in this chapter to answer each of the following.

15. **Hypothesize** It is observed that the speed of sound is slower in air at high altitude than it is at low altitude. Form a hypothesis to explain this observation.

16. **Apply Concepts** A 260-Hz tuning fork and a 263-Hz tuning fork are struck at the same time. Describe listening to the resulting sound and determine its beat frequency.

17. **Contrast** How is the way the pitch is changed in a trombone different from the way it is changed in a saxophone?

Standardized Test Question

Choose the letter of the response that correctly answers the question.

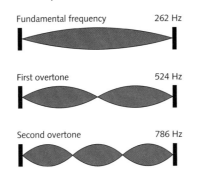

Fundamental frequency	262 Hz
First overtone	524 Hz
Second overtone	786 Hz

18. What is the frequency of the third overtone?

A. 1,572 Hz

B. 1,048 Hz

C. 786 Hz

D. none of the above

Test-Taking Tip

If "none of the above" is one of the choices in a multiple-choice question, be sure that none of the choices are true.

14. The air-filled chamber in the violin begins to resonate with the vibrations from the strings. This also causes the body of the violin to vibrate. These additional vibrations amplify the sound.

Critical Thinking

15. The particles in the less-dense, high-altitude air are farther apart. As a result, the speed of sound at high altitudes is lower. Also accept hypotheses based on the high-altitude air having a lower temperature.

16. The loudness of the sound will fluctuate at a regular rate. The beat frequency is 263 Hz – 260 Hz = 3 Hz.

17. The trombone uses a sliding tube to change the length of the resonating air column, whereas the saxophone uses valves.

Standardized Test Question

18. B

Reading Links

Deafness (Diseases and Disorders)

This well-organized and thorough treatment of deafness, good for struggling readers, will reinforce and extend the chapter's introduction to the hearing process. The book treats both the medical and social aspects of hearing loss with accessible text and visuals.

Barbara Sheen. Lucent Books. 112 pp. Illustrated. Library ISBN 978-1-59018-408-0.

The Science of Sound: Projects and Experiments with Music and Sound Waves

The hands-on activities in this collection can be conducted in the classroom or by students and their families for individual enrichment. As clear demonstrations of important sound principles, these tasks will strengthen students' understanding of the concepts involved while engaging them in the material in unexpected ways.

Steve Parker. Heinemann Library. 32 pp. Illustrated. Library ISBN 978-1-4034-7281-6.

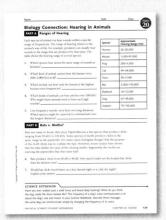

Curriculum Connection
Workbook, p. 129

Science Challenge
Workbook, p. 130

20A Sound and Pitch

This prechapter introduction activity is designed to determine what students already know about sound and pitch by engaging them in predicting, observing, listening, comparing, contrasting, and experimenting with a vibrating source of varying frequency.

Objectives

- compare sounds produced by a vibrating piece of metal or plastic
- relate the pitch of sound to the length of a vibrating object
- record data in a suitable way
- communicate conclusions

Planning

 15–20 minutes   groups of 2–3 students

Materials (per group)

- metal or plastic ruler
- pencil
- paper

Advance Preparation

- Ask students to suggest how they might organize a table to record their results. Display their ideas as examples to follow.
- Suggest that students discuss the reasons for their predictions in their groups.

Engagement Guide

- Challenge students to think about what types of sound the ruler will make by asking these questions:
  - *What are different kinds of musical instruments you have seen and heard?* (Students should describe musical instruments such as a trumpet, flute, drum, and guitar. They may also describe them as wind, string, and percussion.)
  - *What are the differences between the unique sounds each instrument has?* (Each instrument has a unique sound quality. Most also have a range of pitch. Sound quality, or timbre, describes the differences between sounds of the same pitch and loudness.)
- Encourage students to communicate their observations and descriptions of sounds in creative ways.

Going Further

Have students make a straw kazoo and experiment with the sound by changing the length of the straw. Students should compare the ruler experiment with that of the kazoo and then present their conclusions to the class.

20B Measuring the Speed of Sound

Objectives

- measure a large distance
- predict how long it will take sound to travel 100 m
- measure and record the time it takes sound to travel 100 m
- calculate the speed of sound

Skill Set

observing, measuring, predicting, calculating, comparing, recording and analyzing data

Planning

 30–35 minutes   groups of 3–4 students

Materials

Materials for this activity are listed in the Student Laboratory Manual.

Advance Preparation

Choose an appropriate outdoor location. Obtain drums or use an alternate noisemaker. Any instrument that makes a short, loud noise such as an empty coffee can and metal spoon, or two boards that can be slapped together, can be used in place of drums. Have students read the procedure before going outdoors. Put students into groups and assign roles of drummer (noise maker), watcher, and listener. Groups can take turns until all groups have done the activity. Measure distance in meters and time in seconds so that speed will be expressed in meters/second. If a metric tape measure is not available, use a conversion factor and work through the conversion of 100 meters to yards or feet with the class. (1 m = 3.281 feet: 100 m 5 3.281 feet/1 m = 328.1 feet, or about 328 feet $1\frac{1}{4}$ inches; 1 m = 1.0936 yards: 100 m 5 1.0936 yards/1 m = 109.36 yards, or about 109 yards 13 inches)

Answers to Analysis and Conclusions

1. Students' answers will vary according to their data. Inconsistent data is likely due to errors in starting and stopping the stopwatch.

2. The sound traveled 100 meters. Students' data should show times of approximately 0.3 second. Answers about comparing the actual time with the predicted time will vary.

3. Students should recognize that the speed of sound increases as the air temperature increases.

4. Accept answers between 200 m/s and 500 m/s. Because the time is so short, about 0.3 second, the error in measuring the time is relatively large. This error results in a relatively large error in the calculation for the speed of sound.

Going Further

Have students repeat the procedure once a week for a month to see how temperature affects the speed of sound in air. Have students record their data in a table and write a conclusion.

20C Are Two Ears Better Than One?

Objectives

* measure distance in meters
* observe the effectiveness of a single ear for determining the distance to a sound source
* recording and analyzing data
* drawing conclusions

Skill Set

 measuring, observing, recording and analyzing data, drawing conclusions

Planning

⏱ 45–60 minutes   👥 groups of 3–4 students

Materials

Materials for this activity are listed in the Student Laboratory Manual.

Advance Preparation

Reserve time in the gymnasium or find a quiet place outside to do this activity. Caution students to keep background noise to a minimum because it can affect their results. Mark an "X" on the ground where the activity will be carried out or let each group measure out their distances as described in the procedure. Use the masking tape for indoors and the chalk for outside. Divide the class into groups of three and have students read through the procedure before going outside or to the gym.

If you have groups of three, most classes will have six to eight groups of students. In a gymnasium, each group ringing a bell will cause extra background noise. It may be a good idea to suggest different types of noisemakers so each group has a distinct sound to listen for. An alternative would be to have Group One make its first ring (or noise), then Group Two, and so on. This would allow each group to hear its ring without other interference.

Answers to Observations: Data Table 1

Data should reflect that a person using both ears is more likely to guess the correct distance of the sound.

Answers to Analysis and Conclusions

1. Students' answers will vary according to data.

2. Both ears should have been, in general, better at determining distances.

3. Students may have been aware of other noises and that the noises may have affected their results.

4. With two hearing aids they would have a better chance of hearing where the sound was coming from.

5. Each ear picks up the sound in a slightly different way. The brain interprets the different signals from the same source to determine position and distance to the source.

Going Further

Have each student choose a topic on a hearing issue such as hearing loss, hearing protection, or hearing aids. Have students research their topics and make posters or write reports to share with the class.

Introduce Chapter 21

As a starting activity, use Lab 21A on page 121 of the Laboratory Manual.

ENGAGE Divide students into small groups and provide each group with a prism and a small flashlight. Darken the room and ask students to shine the flashlight at an angle to the edge of the prism. Ask students to write their observations in their Science Notebooks. Discuss with students the colors of the spectrum: red, orange, yellow, green, blue, and violet. Introduce the mnemonic "Roy G. Bv" as a way of remembering the spectrum. Explain that students are seeing visible light; there is also light that they cannot see. In this chapter, they will learn about light and how it travels.

Think About Light

ENGAGE Model the process of thinking aloud about things you see as you walk around your classroom. Then turn off the lights. Again, describe aloud what you see, or ask students to share what they can see. Compare a few of your observations aloud.

• Answers will vary, but students should mention that they can see fewer details at night because of the darkness.

• Answers will vary, but students might note that objects can only be seen if they emit light or if light from another source shines on them. Night vision is enhanced by the use of light sources such as flashlights.

Chapter
21

Light and Other Electromagnetic Waves

KEY CONCEPT Visible light waves make up a very small portion of the electromagnetic spectrum.

A city can look very different in the day than it does in the night. Many things that are visible during the daylight hours cannot be seen at night. Other objects, such as stars in the night sky, were not visible during the day but can be seen clearly at night. This chapter is about the waves that allow most people to see. It is also about many other similar waves that cannot be seen.

Think About Light

Describe the things that you might see as you walk along the road during the day. Then describe the things that might be seen along the road at night.

• Compare your two sets of observations. How are they alike? How are they different?

• Identify what it is that allows you to see any object, during the day or at night. Write one or two sentences in your Science Notebook describing how your ability to see things at night can be improved.

NSTA
SCiLINKS®
THE WORLD'S A CLICK AWAY
www.scilinks.org
Producing Light **Code: WGPS21**

352

Chapter 21 Planning Guide

Instructional Periods	National Standards	Lab Manual	Workbook
21.1 2 Periods	A2, B3, E2, G2; A2, B6, E2, G2; UCP2, UCP3	**Lab 21A: p. 121** Reflecting Rainbows **Lab 21B: pp. 122–124** Looking at the Electromagnetic Spectrum **Lab 21C: pp. 125–126** The Lightbulb Challenge	Key Concept Review p. 131 Vocabulary Review p. 132 Interpreting Diagrams p. 133 Reading Comprehension p. 134 Curriculum Connection p. 135 Science Challenge pp. 136–137
21.2 2 Periods	A2, B3, E1, E2, F1, F3, F4, F5, G1, G3; A2, B6, E1, E2, F1, F5, F6, G1, G3; UCP1, UCP5		
21.3 2 Periods	B3, E1, E2, F5; B5, B6, E1, E2, F6; UCP3		

Middle School Standard; High School Standard; Unifying Concept and Principle

21.1 What Is an Electromagnetic Wave?

Before You Read

As you read about waves, compare and contrast electromagnetic waves and mechanical waves. Draw a Venn diagram in your Science Notebook and use that to organize your facts. Label one circle *Mechanical Waves* and the other circle *Electromagnetic Waves*. Write one example of each kind of wave in the appropriate circle. Add anything you already know about these types of waves. Use the area where the circles overlap to record ways in which the two types of waves are alike.

It may seem that a sunburn and a radio have very little in common. However, each involves electromagnetic waves. As discussed in Chapter 19, electromagnetic waves are very different from mechanical waves such as sound waves and water waves. The formation of electromagnetic waves and their unique properties are explored in this lesson.

Describing Electromagnetic Waves

Electromagnetic waves are waves that can travel through a vacuum. Most can also travel through solids, liquids, and gases. Like all waves, electromagnetic waves transfer energy. The light you see and the warmth you feel from the Sun are different forms of electromagnetic waves.

Vibrating Source   Electromagnetic waves form when electrically charged particles vibrate. Recall that electrons are subatomic particles that carry an electric charge. The frequency of a vibration is usually equal to the frequency of the wave it produces. A 100-trillion-hertz (10^{14}-Hz) light wave is formed by an electron vibrating at this same rate.

Waves in Space   Because vibrating electrons in matter are virtually everywhere, so too are electromagnetic waves. Some of these waves, such as light waves, can be sensed. You see light. However, most electromagnetic waves cannot be detected by people. Although you cannot sense them, electromagnetic waves are passing through your body right now! **Figure 21.1** shows two important uses of invisible electromagnetic waves.

Learning Goals

- Explain how electromagnetic waves are produced.
- Describe the properties of electromagnetic waves.
- Identify wave properties and particle properties of light.

New Vocabulary

photoelectric effect
photon

Recall Vocabulary

electromagnetic wave, p. 318
mechanical wave, p. 318
transverse wave, p. 319
interference, p. 330

Figure 21.1 Unseen electromagnetic waves include microwaves used by mobile phones and radio waves used by radar speed guns.

ELL Strategy

Use a Concept Map Have each student create a concept map in his or her Science Notebook with *Electromagnetic Waves* as the main topic. Subtopics should include *How Waves Form, Energy Transfer, Properties,* and *Particles and Waves.* Students should add details to the topics as they read the lesson.

21.1 Introduce

ENGAGE Write the following on the board: the terms *microwave, laser beam, X ray,* and the names of a local AM radio and television station. Alternatively, have pictures of a microwave oven, laser pen, radio, television, and X ray on display for the class. Ask students to work in small groups to hypothesize what characteristic(s) the items share. Have groups share responses. If no groups suggest that all items use electromagnetic waves, tell students this information. Explain that in this lesson, they will learn about the properties of electromagnetic waves and how those items work.

Vocabulary terms are listed on the first student page of each lesson. You may wish to preview the terms before introducing each lesson. Strategies for teaching the vocabulary appear on the pages where the terms are introduced.

Before You Read

Model the process of creating a Venn diagram on the board, labeling each circle as directed. Remind students that characteristics specific to mechanical waves and electromagnetic waves should be written in the appropriate circles. Characteristics that are shared should be written in the overlapping area.

Teach

EXPLAIN to students that electromagnetic waves are classified by wavelength and frequency. Every type of electromagnetic wave travels at the same speed: the speed of light, or 300,000 km/s. Humans are able to see only a small portion of the spectrum: visible light.

● Teach

EXPLAIN to students that light waves have both electric and magnetic fields. A magnetic field generally attracts or repels metallic objects, and an electric field acts on any other point charge (positive or negative). Similarly, a gravitational field acts on any mass.

Use the Visual:

Figure 21.2 [ANSWER] A compass can be used to detect a magnetic field.

Figure 21.3 [ANSWER] The magnetic field is crosswise, or perpendicular, to the direction in which the electrons move.

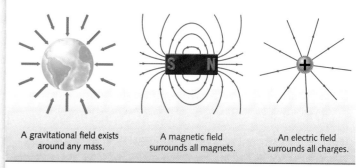

A gravitational field exists around any mass.

A magnetic field surrounds all magnets.

An electric field surrounds all charges.

Figure 21.2 Force fields extend into space around every mass, magnet, and electric charge. Identify a device that can be used to detect a magnetic field.

How Electromagnetic Waves Form

A light wave is partly electric and partly magnetic—hence the name *electromagnetic wave.* All electromagnetic waves consist of electric and magnetic fields. To understand electromagnetic waves, it is important to first understand electric and magnetic force fields.

Force Fields Sometimes a force can be exerted on an object without touching it. For example, a metal paper clip can be moved by a nearby magnet. Likewise, Earth can pull a nearby asteroid into its atmosphere. In both cases, forces are exerted on objects that are not touching each other. These forces are arranged in a force field. The paper clip is acted on by a magnetic force field; the asteroid is acted on by a gravitational force field. Similarly, an electric force field surrounds an electric charge. **Figure 21.2** illustrates gravitational, magnetic, and electric force fields. The force fields extend out into space and exist whether matter is present or not.

Electric and Magnetic Fields An interesting thing happens when an electric charge moves: it creates a magnetic field. As shown in **Figure 21.3,** the motion of the electrons causes a magnetic field to form around the wire. A changing magnetic field creates a changing electric field. Changing electric and magnetic fields form electromagnetic waves.

Figure 21.3
An electric current consists of moving electrons. The motion of the electric charges causes a magnetic field to form around the wire. How is the magnetic field oriented relative to the direction in which the electrons move?

Magnetic field lines

Differentiate Instruction

Kinesthetic, Visual Provide students with both strong and weak magnets and a variety of magnetic items. Have students experiment in pairs, comparing the strength of the fields of the different magnets. Students should sketch each magnet and its force field in their Science Notebooks.

Background Information

Black holes are thought to result from stars that were ten to fifteen times as massive as the Sun. When a star that massive experiences a supernova explosion, a stellar remnant may be produced that collapses inward, creating zero volume and infinite density (known as a singularity). All photons are trapped into an orbit by the immense gravitational field.

Electromagnetic Wave Formation

An electromagnetic wave develops when an electric charge vibrates. This vibration creates both a changing electric field and a changing magnetic field. The changing electric field generates a changing magnetic field, and the changing magnetic field generates a changing electric field. That is, each type of changing field generates the other, over and over again. The process continually repeats as the electromagnetic wave moves through space. The wave moves away from the vibrating charge in all directions. **Figure 21.4** shows the formation of an electromagnetic wave.

Properties of Electromagnetic Waves

Any piece of matter, no matter how small, contains charged particles. Because the charges are in constant motion, they emit, or give off, electromagnetic waves. Thus, all matter emits electromagnetic waves. The frequencies and wavelengths of the emitted waves vary greatly.

Frequency and Wavelength   When a rope is shaken up and down, the frequency of the wave formed equals the rate at which the hand shakes. The situation is similar for a vibrating electric charge. Each back-and-forth motion of the charge produces one wavelength of an electromagnetic wave. A comparison of the wavelength of a mechanical wave in a rope and an electromagnetic wave is shown in **Figure 21.4**. Note that the wavelength from peak-to-peak or trough-to-trough is the same for both the electric field and the magnetic field.

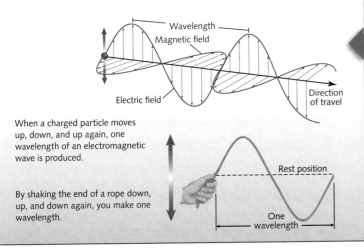

When a charged particle moves up, down, and up again, one wavelength of an electromagnetic wave is produced.

By shaking the end of a rope down, up, and down again, you make one wavelength.

Figure 21.4 A vibrating electric charge creates an electromagnetic wave that travels away from the source in all directions. For simplicity, only one wave direction is shown.

As You Read

As you read the lesson, record any new facts you learn about mechanical and electromagnetic waves in the Venn diagram in your Science Notebook. In a group of four students, discuss your Venn diagram. Then work with a partner to record a few key points of the discussion. Finally, add to or modify your Venn diagram as necessary.

Describe how each type of wave forms.

Figure It Out

1. What two types of fields radiate from a vibrating charge?
2. Determine how the electric and magnetic fields vibrate relative to the direction in which the wave travels. Identify an electromagnetic wave as a transverse wave or a compressional wave.

● Teach

EXPLAIN to students that all matter is made up of charged particles—protons and electrons—and that these particles are constantly moving.

As You Read

Give students about fives minutes to update their Venn diagrams in their Science Notebooks. Check students' diagrams for accuracy.

ANSWER A mechanical wave forms when a vibrating object disturbs the particles in a medium, causing them to vibrate as well. An electromagnetic wave forms when an electric charge vibrates, setting up vibrating electric and magnetic fields. An electromagnetic wave does not require a medium through which to travel, whereas a mechanical wave does.

Figure It Out: Figure 21.4

ANSWER **1.** electric and magnetic fields
2. The electric and magnetic fields vibrate perpendicular to the direction in which the wave travels. Thus, an electromagnetic wave is a transverse wave.

Background Information

In 1905, Albert Einstein published a paper in which he demonstrated that light was a stream of particles, or photons. He won a Nobel Prize for this explanation of the photoelectric effect. When light is shined on certain metals, a stream of electrons is emitted. The properties of the emission contradict the theory that light is a wave. If light were a wave, both the energy and the quantity of electrons emitted should increase with a more intense light. However, Einstein's experiments showed that only the number of the electrons, not the energy, increased with the increase in light intensity. The photoelectric effect observed could only be explained if individual particles of light were penetrating the metal and knocking electrons loose from the atoms.

● Teach

EXPLAIN to students that light has a dual nature: it acts as both a wave and a collection of particles. Einstein postulated that light can be described as particles, also known as photons. The behavior of the particles supports the photoelectric effect.

Use the Visual: Figure 21.5

ANSWER Light travels fastest in a vacuum, slightly slower in gases, slower still in liquids, and slowest in solids.

Vocabulary

photoelectric effect Explain to students that *photoelectric* is a compound word. The root *photo-* is derived from Greek and means "light." *Electric* means "relating to, produced by, or generating electricity."

photon Review with students the meaning of *photo-* ("light"). Tell students that as used in physics, the suffix *-on* denotes an elementary or basic particle. Literally, *photon* means "the basic particle of light."

 Explore It!

Explain to students that distance can be calculated by multiplying speed and time.

distance = 9.5 × 10¹² km

● Assess

Use the After You Read questions and the Alternative Assessment to help you evaluate students' understanding of the lesson.

After You Read

1. A moving electric charge creates changing electric and magnetic fields.

2. The photoelectric effect can be explained by the particle model of light.

3. Mechanical and electromagnetic waves are formed by vibrations and transfer energy. Both types can be transverse waves. Electromagnetic waves do not need a medium through which to travel, whereas mechanical waves do. Only a mechanical wave can be compressional.

Speed of Light	
Medium	Speed (km/s)
vacuum	300,000
air	< 300,000
liquid water	226,000
glass	200,000
diamond	124,000

Figure 21.5 The speed of light in a vacuum is an incredibly fast 3.00 × 10⁸ m/s, or 300,000 km/s. How is the speed of light affected by solid, liquid, and gas mediums?

Figure 21.6 Electrons that pass through very narrow slits behave like a wave.

 Explore It!

Work with a partner to calculate the distance a beam of light travels through space in one year. Begin with the speed of light in space, 300,000 km/s. Present your step-by-step calculation to the class on a small poster.

Wave Speed The speed of light in the vacuum of space is 300,000 km/s. The phrase "speed of light" is a little misleading because this is the speed of *all* electromagnetic waves in a vacuum. An electromagnetic wave's speed in a medium, however, depends on the wave's frequency and the medium. **Figure 21.5** shows the speed of light in different mediums.

The Dual Nature of Waves and Particles

In this lesson, light has been treated as a wave and matter has been treated as a collection of particles. At times, though, waves act like particles and particles act like waves. Scientific knowledge of light waves and matter requires two models: a wave model and a particle model.

Waves Acting Like Particles The **photoelectric effect** is the ejection of electrons from the surface of a metal when light shines on it. Only certain colors, or frequencies, of light cause the photoelectric effect. Increasing the light's amplitude has no effect. Albert Einstein explained the results by treating light as tiny particles, now known as **photons.** He theorized that only high-frequency, high-energy photons could cause the photoelectric effect.

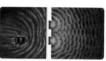

Spray paint particles sprayed through two slits only hit the area directly behind the slits.

Electrons fired at two closely-spaced slits form a wave-like interference pattern.

Water waves produce a pattern after moving through two openings.

Particles Acting Like Waves Just as waves can behave like particles, particles can behave like waves. If a beam of electrons is aimed at a barrier with two narrow slits in it, it seems logical to expect the electrons to pass directly through the slits and not spread out. Instead, the particles form an interference pattern similar to that formed by water waves. It is now known that all particles can behave like waves.

After You Read

1. Describe how the electric and magnetic fields of an electromagnetic wave are related.

2. Describe a phenomenon that supports the particle model of light.

3. Review the Venn diagram in your Science Notebook. Write a well-developed paragraph comparing and contrasting mechanical and electromagnetic waves.

Alternative Assessment

Have students use their Venn diagrams to compare the following characteristics of mechanical waves and electromagnetic waves: how they are formed, and how mediums affect their speed, wavelengths, frequency, and type (compressional or transverse).

21.2 The Electromagnetic Spectrum

Before You Read

In your Science Notebook, draw a horizontal arrow from left to right. Below the arrow, write the label *Increasing Frequency*. As you read the lesson, record on this line diagram the name and description of each type of electromagnetic wave discussed. Place the waves in order of increasing frequency.

Look around. What colors do you see? Your observations might include red backpacks, green leaves, and countless colors in between. Each color you see has its own frequency. This seems like a lot, but it is in fact a very small portion of the electromagnetic waves in the universe.

Classifying Waves

The complete range of electromagnetic waves makes up the **electromagnetic spectrum** (SPEK truhm). **Figure 21.7** shows that the spectrum is continuous, or contains no gaps. The continuous range of waves is arranged left-to-right by increasing frequency. High-frequency waves have greater energy. Names are used to classify waves within certain ranges of the spectrum. Notice that the names and frequency ranges are not exact and that they overlap in places. Human eyes are sensitive to light in the visible portion of the electromagnetic spectrum.

Speed, Wavelength, and Frequency A wave's speed is the product of its frequency and wavelength. The equation for this relationship is

$$\text{speed} = \text{frequency} \times \text{wavelength}$$

Electromagnetic waves travel at the speed of light in a vacuum. This means that in space, the product of frequency and wavelength always equals the speed of light. Thus, as an electromagnetic wave's frequency increases, its wavelength decreases. Frequency and wavelength are inversely related. This inverse relationship can be seen in **Figure 21.7.**

Learning Goals

- Identify, describe, and compare waves from different regions of the electromagnetic spectrum.
- Identify uses for different kinds of electromagnetic waves.
- Relate an electromagnetic wave's frequency to its energy.

New Vocabulary

electromagnetic spectrum
radio wave
microwave
infrared wave
visible light
ultraviolet wave
X ray
gamma ray

Recall Vocabulary

Doppler effect, p. 341

Figure 21.7
Electromagnetic waves are described by different names depending on their frequencies and wavelengths. Which waves have the highest frequencies?

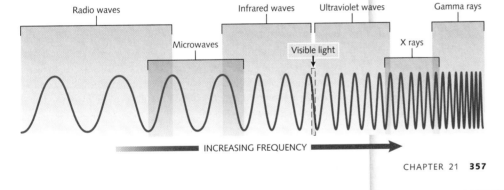

Radio waves • Infrared waves • Ultraviolet waves • Gamma rays • Microwaves • Visible light • X rays

INCREASING FREQUENCY

ELL Strategy

Paraphrase Have students choose two different types of electromagnetic waves to read about, and then have them paraphrase the material. Have each student share his or her paraphrased information so that other students benefit from the paraphrased work. Students who struggle with the reading can work with a partner.

21.2 Introduce

ENGAGE Write the word *inverse* on the board and have students work in pairs to define it. Provide support and examples as necessary. After pairs can define *inverse*, have them brainstorm as many examples of inverse relationships as they can. Examples might include addition and subtraction, multiplication and division, pressure and volume of gases, and the amount of time spent at the mall and the amount of money in one's pocket. Discuss students' examples. Explain that on the electromagnetic spectrum, frequency and wavelength are inversely related. As a wave's frequency increases, its wavelength decreases.

Before You Read

Draw the horizontal arrow on the board and label it as directed. Model the process of reading the first section of the lesson and labeling the arrow *Electromagnetic Spectrum*. Have students draw and label their own arrows in their Science Notebooks. Suggest to students that they use a different color for each type of wave and its description.

● Teach

EXPLAIN to students that they will learn about the different kinds of waves in the electromagnetic spectrum. Visible light comprises only a small part of the spectrum.

💿 Vocabulary

electromagnetic spectrum Explain to students that *electromagnetic* is a compound word that refers to something with both electrical and magnetic properties. Tell students that *spectrum* is Latin and means "appearance." Ask students to explain how these meanings relate to the scientific definition of the term.

Use the Visual: Figure 21.7

ANSWER Gamma rays have the highest frequencies.

Teach

 EXPLAIN to students that they will learn about radio waves and microwaves. These types of waves are located on the farthest left part of the spectrum—that is, radio waves have the lowest frequency and microwaves have the next lowest frequency.

Vocabulary

radio wave Encourage students to think of common uses of the word *radio*. Examples might include a radio station, a portable radio, or a car radio. Explain to students that radios use radio waves to receive and transmit information.

microwave Explain to students that the prefix *micro-* means "very small." Review with students the meaning of *wave* ("a repeating disturbance that travels through time and space"). Microwaves have shorter wavelengths than television and radio waves.

infrared wave Tell students that the prefix *infra-* means "below." Literally, *infrared* means "below red." The frequencies of infrared waves are lower than those of visible light near the red end of the visible portion of the spectrum.

As You Read

Have students update the line diagrams in their Science Notebooks. Students should work in pairs to discuss their questions and review their diagrams for errors.

(ANSWER) Radio waves have the longest wavelengths.

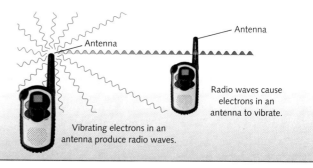

Figure 21.8 The antennae of these walkie-talkies are used to send and receive radio signals. Vibrating electrons within the sending antenna cause similar vibrations to form in the receiving antenna.

Radio Waves

The longest waves in the electromagnetic spectrum are **radio waves.** The wavelengths of radio waves range from the length of a football to longer than a football field. Radio waves have the lowest frequencies and carry the least energy of all electromagnetic waves. Low-energy radio waves are used by televisions, radios, and cellular phones.

Sending and Detecting Radio Waves Like all electromagnetic waves, radio waves are produced when electric charges vibrate. Radio waves can be broadcast, or sent, by making electrons in a piece of metal vibrate. **Figure 21.8** illustrates this process. The metal rod or element that sends the signal is called an antenna. Voice, music, or other data is coded into waves by electronic circuitry. The circuitry alters the amplitude and frequency of the broadcast waves.

An antenna also detects, or receives, radio signals. A radio wave causes electrons in a receiving antenna to vibrate. The back-and-forth vibrations produce an alternating current in the antenna. Electronic circuitry in the receiving TV, radio, or phone converts the current into audio or video.

Microwaves Radio waves that have wavelengths between 1 mm and 30 cm are **microwaves.** These higher-frequency radio waves are used by microwave ovens, portable phones, and cellular phones. Microwave ovens heat food by passing microwaves through the food. The waves cause water molecules within the food to vibrate quickly and generate heat. Similar microwaves are used by cellular phones. In fact, a cellular phone could accurately be described as a microwave phone. **Figure 21.9** shows a microwave sending and receiving tower used by cellular phone networks.

As You Read

Review the information you have recorded on the line diagram in your Science Notebook. Use it to write three questions. Exchange questions with a partner, and answer your partner's questions. Then discuss your questions and answers.

Identify the type of electromagnetic wave with the longest wavelengths.

Figure 21.9 Microwave transmitters and receivers are mounted on towers to limit the interference of their signals from buildings, trees, and landforms.

Differentiate Instruction

Musical, Linguistic Have students write lyrics to a song or poem describing the electromagnetic spectrum. Encourage students to either include all the different waves or to focus on one type. Students could work with partners to compose the lyrics using a familiar tune for the music, if they have chosen to create a song. Have students share their songs or poems with the class.

Visual, Mathematical Have students identify the range of wavelengths for radio waves, microwaves, and infrared waves and then identify a real-world object that has a comparable length. Students should sketch the object and the related electromagnetic wave.

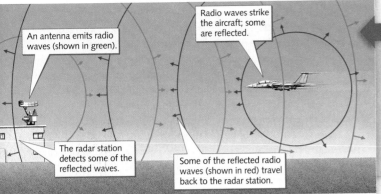

An antenna emits radio waves (shown in green).

Radio waves strike the aircraft; some are reflected.

The radar station detects some of the reflected waves.

Some of the reflected radio waves (shown in red) travel back to the radar station.

Figure 21.10 Radio waves detect an aircraft's location, direction, and speed.

Radar During flight, bats locate objects using echolocation, or the broadcast and reception of sounds. A technology called radar uses radio waves in a similar way. The term *radar* stands for *ra*dio *d*etecting *a*nd *r*anging. Radar is used to track aircraft in flight and the movement of weather fronts. **Figure 21.10** shows radar in use at an airport.

The radar station broadcasts radio waves. The waves reflect off objects in the air and return to the station. The time it takes the waves to return determines the distance to the objects. Changes in the frequency of the returned wave due to the Doppler effect can be used to determine the object's direction and speed. Because radio waves travel at nearly 300,000 km/s through air, the process takes only a fraction of a second.

Infrared Waves

The warmth of sunlight on the skin is from **infrared waves.** The wavelengths of infrared waves are shorter than those of radio waves but longer than those of light that you can see. Infrared, or IR, waves are approximately 0.00075 mm to 1 mm in length.

Infrared Subgroups Infrared waves are divided into three groups: near-infrared, mid-infrared, and far-infrared. Far-infrared waves are close to microwaves in the electromagnetic spectrum. Infrared waves that feel warm on the skin are far-infrared waves. Near-infrared waves are close to the visible portion of the spectrum. Television remote controls use near-infrared wavelengths.

Detecting Infrared Waves The image in **Figure 21.11** shows the infrared energy emitted by a person's hand. The bands of color indicate different levels of infrared energy. The image was formed by an electromagnetic sensor. Orbiting satellites use infrared imagery to analyze Earth's surface. Some animals can also detect infrared waves.

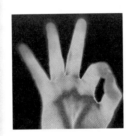

Figure 21.11 People with normal body temperature emit primarily infrared waves with wavelengths of about 0.00001 mm. Which color in this photo of a person's hand represents the highest temperatures?

Teach

EXPLAIN to students that visible light is located toward the center of the electromagnetic spectrum. Visible light carries amounts of energy that are greater than radio, microwave, and infrared waves and lower than ultraviolet waves, X rays, and gamma rays. Ultraviolet (UV) waves are classified into UVA, UVB, and UVC waves.

EXPLORE Before class, obtain a large sheet of white poster board. Using a green marker, write a short message in large letters. Then color over the message with red and yellow markers. Present students with red and green filters and ask them to decipher your message by looking at the poster through one or both of the filters. Once students are able to read the message, ask them to discuss with partners what scientific principle was at work. Ask students to share their thoughts with the class. If students are unsure, tell them that they will learn more about that concept in this lesson.

Use the Visual: Figure 21.13

Recall that a wave's intensity is the rate at which energy passes through a certain area.
(ANSWER) Visible light waves have the greatest intensity.

 CONNECTION: Food Science

Have students work together to write a letter to the food services department of your school explaining why it should or should not purchase and serve irradiated food. Have students first work in pairs to brainstorm points to include in the letter, and encourage students to relate their reasons to the scientific principles of the electromagnetic spectrum and how waves travel.

Figure 21.12 The color of a glowing object depends on its temperature. Molten metal is hot enough to glow bright yellow.

 CONNECTION: Food Science

Electromagnetic waves can be used to make our food and water safer. For example, water can be purified by using ultraviolet rays to kill harmful bacteria in the water.

Higher-energy Xrays and gamma rays are used in treating some foods in a method called irradiation. This method reduces the risk from harmful organisms. The U. S. Food and Drug Administration has approved the irradiation of meat, poultry, fresh fruits, vegetables, and spices.

Visible Light

As an object gets warmer, its particles—including its charged particles—move more quickly. The faster-moving charges produce higher-frequency electromagnetic waves. An object that is hot enough begins to glow. The glowing object gives off electromagnetic waves that the human eye can detect, known as **visible light.** Visible light has wavelengths of approximately 0.0004 mm to 0.0007 mm.

The different colors of visible light have different frequencies. When all of the colors of the visible spectrum are present, the light appears white. The Sun emits white light. Few objects, however, emit light. Most things are visible because they reflect light given off by the Sun or another source, such as a lightbulb.

Visible light is extremely important to Earth's organisms. Plants use the red and blue bands of the spectrum to create food in a process called photosynthesis. Almost all living things on Earth depend on this process.

Ultraviolet Waves

Ultraviolet waves have higher frequencies and energies than do visible light waves. Ultraviolet, or UV, waves are between ten-billionths and 400-billionths of a meter long. The waves carry enough energy to damage living cells and cause sunburn. Too much exposure to UV waves can lead to skin cancer. As shown in **Figure 21.13,** the Sun emits infrared, visible, and ultraviolet waves.

Beneficial Uses Short exposures to ultraviolet waves are beneficial. The human body uses the ultraviolet energy to produce vitamin D, a necessary nutrient. Most people's daily activities give them enough exposure to UV waves. Hospitals use UV waves to disinfect surgical equipment. Some materials fluoresce (floor ES), or emit visible light, when struck by ultraviolet waves. Police detectives sometimes use fluorescent powder and an ultraviolet light source to look for fingerprints.

Figure 21.13
The Sun emits mainly infrared and visible light. Which type of electromagnetic wave emitted by the Sun has the greatest intensity?

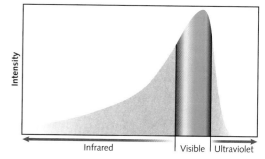

Electromagnetic Waves from the Sun

Intensity

Infrared | Visible | Ultraviolet

Background Information

All UVC and some UVA and UVB waves are blocked by the ozone layer. Both UVA and UVB waves impact human skin. The waves damage the DNA in skin cells, and those damaged cells die or are repaired by the body. If the damage is very extensive, the damaged cells can turn into skin cancer. UVB causes tans and is the main factor in sunburn and skin cancer; however, more UVA waves penetrate the ozone layer, and they penetrate deeper into skin than UVB waves.

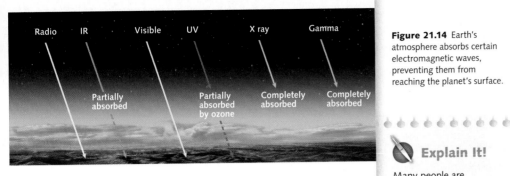

Radio   IR   Visible   UV   X ray   Gamma

Partially absorbed   Partially absorbed by ozone   Completely absorbed   Completely absorbed

Figure 21.14 Earth's atmosphere absorbs certain electromagnetic waves, preventing them from reaching the planet's surface.

The Ozone Layer

Ozone (O_3) is a molecule made up of three oxygen atoms. Ozone is vital to life on Earth because it absorbs harmful ultraviolet waves emitted by the Sun. Most of the ozone in the atmosphere is concentrated in a layer about 15 km above Earth's surface. Here, ozone molecules are constantly being formed and destroyed by ultraviolet waves.

Several decades ago, scientists discovered that the ozone layer was diminishing. Chlorofluorocarbons, or CFCs, used in cleaning fluids and refrigeration systems were determined to be the source of the problem. **Figure 21.15** shows how a CFC molecule can react with and destroy an ozone molecule. With many countries now reducing or eliminating use of CFCs, it is hoped that the ozone layer can recover.

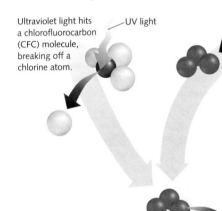

Ultraviolet light hits a chlorofluorocarbon (CFC) molecule, breaking off a chlorine atom.

UV light

Once free, the chlorine atom reacts with another ozone molecule.

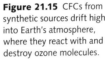

A free oxygen atom pulls the oxygen atom off the chlorine monoxide molecule.

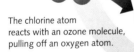

The chlorine atom reacts with an ozone molecule, pulling off an oxygen atom.

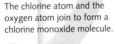

The chlorine atom and the oxygen atom join to form a chlorine monoxide molecule.

Figure 21.15 CFCs from synthetic sources drift high into Earth's atmosphere, where they react with and destroy ozone molecules.

Explain It!

Many people are surprised when they get a sunburn on a cloudy day. Write a paragraph explaining why it is possible to get sunburned on a cloudy day when the Sun cannot be seen.

Teach

EXPLAIN to students that the ozone layer is part of Earth's atmosphere and prevents some ultraviolet waves from reaching Earth's surface.

Vocabulary

visible light Explain to students that *visible* means "capable of being seen." The visible light spectrum includes red, orange, yellow, green, blue, and violet.

ultraviolet wave Tell students that the prefix *ultra-* means "far beyond the norm." Ask students to list common words with this prefix and define each word. Then relate the prefix to the scientific definition of *ultraviolet wave*.

Explain It!

Have students organize their knowledge by making diagrams that show how ultraviolet waves travel from the Sun to Earth. Remind students to include clouds and the ozone layer in their diagrams. Check students' work for understanding.

ANSWER Students' paragraphs should mention that clouds only partially absorb ultraviolet waves from the Sun. Even on a cloudy day when the Sun is not visible, UV waves still reach Earth and cause sunburn.

Differentiate Instruction

Kinesthetic Have students work in small groups to make models that show a CFC molecule interacting with an ozone molecule. Provide materials such as plastic foam balls, markers, cardboard, toothpicks, and pipe cleaners. Ask students to model and label each step of the process as shown in **Figure 21.15.**

Key Concept Review
Workbook, p. 131

Light and Other Electromagnetic Waves

Teach

EXPLAIN to students that the electromagnetic waves with the highest energy are gamma rays, and that X rays have the next highest amount of energy. Both types of waves can be potentially harmful to the human body.

Vocabulary

X ray Tell students that this type of electromagnetic wave was named by its discoverer, W. C. Roentgen. He named them with an *X* because they were an unknown quantity.

gamma ray Explain to students that gamma rays were named by Ernest Rutherford, who had already been using *alpha* and *beta* to refer to unidentified rays he was studying. He needed to name a third type of ray, and the Greek word for "third" is *gamma*.

PEOPLE IN SCIENCE

Provide written and online resources about Hubble so that students can learn more about his discovery and the nature of galaxies.

Assess

Use the After You Read questions and the Alternative Assessment to help you evaluate students' understanding of the lesson.

After You Read

1. The Sun emits infrared, visible, and ultraviolet waves. Ultraviolet waves are damaging to the skin.

2. As the frequency of an electromagnetic wave increases, so does its energy.

3. In order from low to high energy: radio waves, microwaves, infrared waves, visible light, ultraviolet waves, X rays, gamma rays.

Alternative Assessment

Have students use the line diagrams in their Science Notebooks to list and describe three types of electromagnetic waves. Descriptions should include the wave's location on the spectrum, examples of the wave, comparison of its frequency and energy to another wave, and its uses.

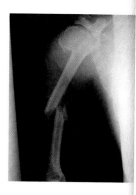

Figure 21.16 X-ray images are used to diagnose medical and dental conditions. This image of a broken bone will aid the doctor in resetting the bone so that it can heal properly. The image forms because dense tissues such as bone absorb more X rays than do the softer surrounding tissues. A shadow forms as X rays pass through the softer tissue.

X Rays, Gamma Rays, and Their Uses

X rays are high-energy electromagnetic waves with shorter wavelengths than those of ultraviolet waves. Whereas ultraviolet waves can penetrate the top layer of a person's skin, X rays have enough energy to pass through skin and muscle. The shortest-wavelength, highest-energy electromagnetic waves are **gamma rays.**

X rays and gamma rays have important uses in medicine. Images like the one shown in **Figure 21.16** are formed when X rays are beamed through a person's body. The rays then strike a film plate or an electronic sensor, creating an image of the internal structures. Gamma rays are used to treat some cancers. Exposing a cancerous tumor to a highly focused beam of gamma rays can kill the cancerous cells.

PEOPLE IN SCIENCE Edwin Hubble (1889–1953)

Edwin Hubble was born in 1889. His childhood interest in science led him to become a famous astronomer. Hubble earned college degrees in mathematics and astronomy and went on to study law before deciding on being an astronomer. His first job as an astronomer was at the Mount Wilson Observatory in California. There, he discovered the existence of several galaxies—including our own Milky Way galaxy.

Hubble developed a classification system for the galaxies he observed. From his observations, he noticed that the frequencies of visible light emitted by distant galaxies were shifted toward the red end of the spectrum. He went on to show that the red shift was caused by the galaxies moving away from each other. The photo shows NASA's Hubble Space Telescope, which is named in honor of Edwin Hubble.

After You Read

1. List the types of electromagnetic waves emitted by the Sun. Identify the type of emitted wave that is damaging to the skin.

2. Review the information from the line diagram in your Science Notebook. Identify how an electromagnetic wave's frequency is related to its energy.

3. List the types of electromagnetic waves in order of increasing energy.

Background Information

U.S. government scientists and other researchers reviewed several hundred studies on the effects of food irradiation before judging it to be safe for human consumption. Independent scientific committees in Denmark, Sweden, the U.K., and Canada have reaffirmed the safety of food irradiation. Irradiation has been approved for more than 40 different food products in 37 countries.

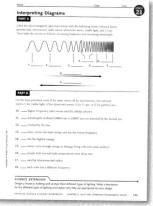

Interpreting Diagrams
Workbook, p. 133

21.3 Producing Light

Before You Read

Look at the subheadings in this lesson to find the types of lighting discussed. In your Science Notebook, draw a T-chart. Label one side *Type of Lighting* and the other side *How Produced*. Write anything you already know about each type of lighting in the appropriate columns.

Candles, oil lanterns, and gas lights were used in the past to provide light. Lighting technology has progressed greatly since those times. Modern lighting devices use glowing metals, energized solids, liquids and gases, and semiconducting materials to produce light. This lesson explores the technologies used in modern lighting devices.

Types of Lighting

Objects that do not emit light must reflect light in order to be seen. An **illuminated** (ih LOO muh nayt ed) **object** reflects light that strikes it. The Moon is an illuminated object in the night sky; it reflects light from the Sun. Objects that emit light are **luminous** (LEW mih nus) **objects.** Few objects are luminous. The Sun, a burning piece of wood, and lightbulbs are luminous objects.

Incandescent Lights   An **incandescent** (ihn kan DEH sunt) **light** produces light by heating a thin metal wire until it glows. **Figure 21.17** shows an example of an incandescent light. The thin wire, called a filament, heats up as electricity flows through it. The heat generated by an incandescent bulb is the bulb's biggest disadvantage. Most of the energy used by an incandescent bulb is wasted as heat. Only about 10 percent of the energy is used to produce light. Most of the lights in your home likely use incandescent lightbulbs. The use of incandescent lightbulbs is declining because they are so inefficient. In many cases, incandescent lightbulbs are being replaced with energy-efficient lamps.

Figure 21.17 The filament of an incandescent bulb is usually made of the metal tungsten. The electric resistance of the metal causes the filament to heat up and give off light. Unfortunately, 90 percent of the energy given off is in the form of thermal energy.

ELL Strategy

Practice Using Vocabulary
The vocabulary terms in this lesson are commonplace words that students will encounter in other areas of life. Have students learn the terms by illustrating their meanings and by writing a definition of each in their own words. Provide time for students to explore the school grounds to identify and discuss the types of lighting in different areas. Encourage them to go to rooms such as the auditorium, gym, and offices to encounter the types of lights discussed in this lesson.

21.3 Introduce

ENGAGE Have students brainstorm all the different types of lights they have used in the past 24 hours. Encourage them to think about different places they have been, vehicles in which they have ridden, and the various types of lighting used in various locations. Then have students work in small groups to classify the lights. Encourage them to create their own categories, and then ask student groups to share these and their reasons for the classifications.

Before You Read

Draw the T-chart on the board. Think aloud about one or two types of lights, such as a fluorescent lightbulb from a light in the classroom and a halogen light in a car's headlight. Discuss how fluorescent lights work: phosphors produce light when they are exposed to light. Describe how fluorescent lights become brighter as they warm up, and write the information on the T-chart on the board. Have students draw and complete their T-charts in their Science Notebooks.

● Teach

EXPLAIN to students that they will learn about different types of lighting, how each produces light, and what the advantages and disadvantages of the various devices are.

 Vocabulary

illuminated object Tell students that the prefix *il-* is similar to *in-*, denoting the opposite of the root word. The root *lumen* is Latin and means "light." The literal meaning of the word *illuminated* is "not having light." An object is an item or a thing. An illuminated object does not have light, but rather reflects it.

luminous object Remind students that the root *lumen* means "light." The prefix *-ous* denotes a quality. A luminous object has the quality of light.

incandescent light Tell students that the word *incandescent* is Latin for "to glow or become white." Encourage students to think of common uses of the word *light*. Explain to students that an incandescent light becomes bright as heat flows through it.

Teach

EXPLAIN to students that fluorescent and neon lights depend on gases and electrodes to produce lights. In fluorescent lights, electrodes emit electrons that collide with gas atoms and release ultraviolet radiation. The phosphor-coated tube absorbs the UV waves and emits the energy as visible light. In neon lights, the electrodes energize the neon or other gas, and collisions between electrons and gas molecules release visible light.

Figure It Out: Figure 21.18

ANSWER **1.** The electrons flow through a mixture of mercury vapor and argon or neon gas. **2.** The phosphors absorb the ultraviolet radiation and reemit it as visible light.

As You Read

Give students about five minutes to update their T-charts. Have students work with partners to compare T-charts and correct misunderstandings or errors. Check students' charts for accuracy.

Figure It Out

1. Through what medium do the electrons flow within the lightbulb?
2. Why are phosphors used to coat the inside of the fluorescent lightbulb?

As You Read

As you read the lesson, complete the column in your T-chart titled *How Produced* for each type of lighting. Also, record any advantages or disadvantages of each type of lighting device.

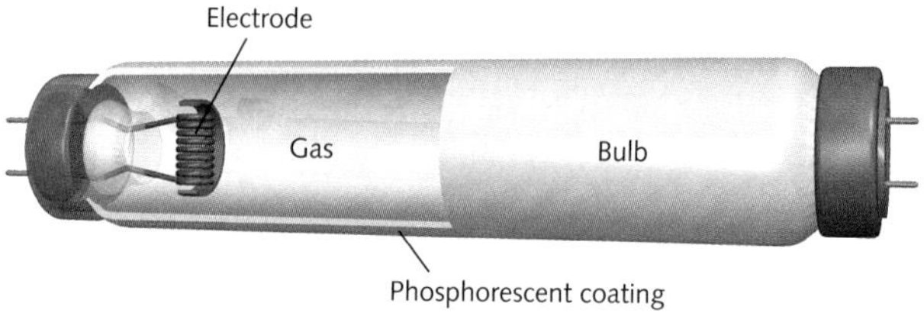

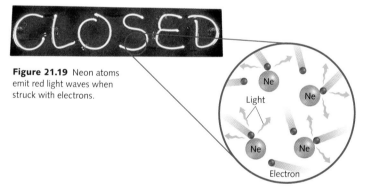

Figure 21.18 A fluorescent lightbulb contains mercury vapor and argon or neon gas.

Fluorescent Lights Schools and most business and office buildings are illuminated with fluorescent lights. A **fluorescent** (floo REH sunt) **light** consists of a low-pressure gas contained in a phosphor-coated glass tube. As shown in **Figure 21.18**, each end of the tube contains an electrode. When electricity flows to the tube, the electrodes emit negatively charged electrons. The electrons collide with the gas atoms, causing ultraviolet radiation to be emitted. The phosphor coating absorbs the UV waves and then reemits the energy as visible light.

Fluorescent lightbulbs are very energy-efficient. They require only about one-fourth to one-fifth the energy used by an incandescent lightbulb to produce the same amount of light. The small amount of mercury contained in fluorescent lightbulbs, however, poses environmental dangers and health risks. Because mercury is a toxic metal, fluorescent lightbulbs cannot be thrown in the trash. Fluorescent lightbulbs must be returned to special handling facilities to avoid breakage.

Neon Lights Neon lights produce the vivid, glowing colors shown in **Figure 21.19**. Neon lights contain a gas, usually neon, in a clear glass tube. Electrodes energize the gas, and collisions between electrons and gas molecules release visible light. Neon gas produces red light. Other colors are obtained using a mixture of other gases.

Figure 21.19 Neon atoms emit red light waves when struck with electrons.

Differentiate Instruction

Mathematical, Kinesthetic Have students attach strip thermometers to an incandescent light and a fluorescent light before they are turned on. Tell students to record the temperature of each bulb and predict what the temperature will be at the end of class. Later, have students read the temperature of both lights again. Warn students not to touch the bulbs. Compare the temperature readings of each type of light.

Field Study

Have students walk around and note what types of lightbulbs are in the building, and then count the number of each. After students complete the Extend It! activity on page 365, have them calculate how much money could be saved if all or most of the incandescent lights could be changed to fluorescent.

Tungsten-Halogen Lights Tungsten-halogen lights are used when extremely bright light is required. The light is produced by a very hot tungsten filament inside a halogen-gas-filled quartz tube. The halogen gas used is either fluorine or chlorine. Tungsten-halogen lights are used on movie sets, in underwater photography, and to light airport runways.

LEDs An LED is a light-emitting diode. Unlike incandescent bulbs, LEDs do not have filaments to burn out and they do not get hot. They can be designed to emit infrared, visible, and near-ultraviolet waves. LEDs are energy-efficient, rugged, and long-lasting devices. Applications of tungsten-halogen lights and LEDs are shown in **Figure 21.20.**

Lasers A **laser** is a device that produces a narrow beam of coherent light. As shown in **Figure 21.21, coherent** (koh HEER ehnt) **light** waves all have the same frequency and travel with their crests and troughs aligned. Because coherent light does not spread significantly as it travels, its energy remains concentrated in a small-diameter beam. This allows lasers to apply large amounts of energy to very small areas. All other visible light sources produce **incoherent light** waves with various frequencies whose crests and troughs are not aligned. Incoherent waves spread apart as they travel.

The unique qualities of laser light make lasers extremely useful. Industrial uses of lasers include cutting and welding materials. Surveyors and builders use lasers for measuring and leveling. Rapidly switching the beam off and on allows lasers to be used for communication and data transmission. Lasers are also commonly used in corrective eye surgery.

These waves are coherent because they have the same frequency and travel with their crests and troughs aligned.

Incoherent waves such as these can contain more than one frequency and do not travel with their crests and troughs aligned.

Figure 21.21 Lasers emit coherent light. All of the other light sources described in this lesson emit incoherent light.

After You Read

1. Contrast light production in incandescent and fluorescent lightbulbs.
2. Describe the characteristics of laser light that make lasers useful in many situations.
3. Review the T-chart in your Science Notebook. Summarize which lighting devices use light emitted by energized gases or vapors to produce light.

Figure 21.20 Each type of light has certain advantages. Tungsten-halogen lights, such as those shown here on an airport runway, are extremely bright. LED lights, such as the one in this flashlight, are rugged, efficient, and long-lasting.

 Extend It!

Research the cost of incandescent and fluorescent lightbulbs with the same light output. Light output (in lumens) will be listed on the package. Using the cost of electricity in your area (check a household electric bill), determine how long it takes for the fluorescent lightbulb to make up for its greater cost. Summarize your research in your Science Notebook. Then present your summary to the class.

Chapter 21 Summary

Check students' sentences or paragraphs to make sure they understand the meaning of each vocabulary term.

Evaluate students' essays using the following criteria:

1. The topic sentence, or main idea, should restate the Key Concept.

2. The supporting paragraphs should incorporate the answers to the Learning Goal questions students have written and include details, facts, and examples they have recorded in their Science Notebooks.

3. The concluding sentence should sum up the main idea of the chapter and restate the Key Concept.

MASTERING CONCEPTS

True or False

1. False, the vacuum of space
2. True
3. False, electric charge
4. True
5. True
6. False, Ultraviolet
7. False, Lasers
8. False, Incandescent

Short Answer

9. All electromagnetic waves travel at the speed of light in a vacuum. The higher-frequency wave carries more energy than the lower-frequency wave does.

10. The rate at which the electric charge vibrates determines the frequency of the electromagnetic wave produced. The frequency of the oscillating electric and magnetic fields also equals the rate at which the charge vibrates.

11. The UV waves have higher frequencies and thus carry more energy. These higher-energy waves damage cells.

12. They are absorbed by the atmosphere.

13. As the wavelength increases, its frequency and energy decreases.

Chapter 21

Summary

KEY CONCEPTS

21.1 What Is an Electromagnetic Wave?

- Vibrating electric charges produce electromagnetic waves. An electromagnetic wave is made up of electric and magnetic fields that regenerate each other as the wave travels.

- In a vacuum, all electromagnetic waves travel at the speed of light, 300,000 km/s. They travel at almost the speed of light in gases, more slowly in liquids, and even more slowly in solids.

- The photoelectric effect supports the dual nature of light: light can act as both a wave and a particle. Particles of light are called photons. Matter can also act as a wave.

21.2 The Electromagnetic Spectrum

- The electromagnetic spectrum is made up of the entire range of electromagnetic waves. The spectrum is divided into ranges of waves, including radio waves, microwaves, infrared waves, visible light, ultraviolet waves, X rays, and gamma rays. Visible light waves are the only waves that can be seen.

- As the frequency of an electromagnetic wave increases, so does its energy.

- Electromagnetic waves can be broadcast and received by an antenna. Ultraviolet waves, X rays, and gamma rays can damage living cells.

- Earth's atmosphere partially absorbs infrared and ultraviolet waves from the Sun. Most of the ultraviolet energy emitted by the Sun is absorbed by Earth's ozone layer.

- Electromagnetic waves have many uses in science, industry, and consumer products.

21.3 Producing Light

- Luminous objects such as the Sun emit light. Most objects are illuminated by light from other light sources.

- Many lighting technologies exist, including incandescent, fluorescent, neon, tungsten-halogen, LED, and laser.

- There are advantages and disadvantages associated with each type of lighting device.

- Incandescent lightbulbs are much more efficient than fluorescent lightbulbs.

- Lasers produce concentrated beams of coherent light that do not spread as they travel.

366 LIGHT AND OTHER ELECTROMAGNETIC WAVES

VOCABULARY REVIEW

Write each term in a complete sentence or write a paragraph relating several terms.

21.1
photoelectric effect, p. 356
photon, p. 356

21.2
electromagnetic spectrum, p. 357
radio wave, p. 358
microwave, p. 358
infrared wave, p. 359
visible light, p. 360
ultraviolet wave, p. 360
X ray, p. 362
gamma ray, p. 362

21.3
illuminated object, p. 363
luminous object, p. 363
incandescent light, p. 363
fluorescent light, p. 364
laser, p. 365
coherent light, p. 365
incoherent light, p. 365

PREPARE FOR CHAPTER TEST

To prepare for the chapter test, create a question from each Learning Goal. Use the information in your Science Notebook to answer each question. Then use these answers to write a well-developed essay about the chapter. Use the Key Concept on the first page of this chapter as your topic sentence.

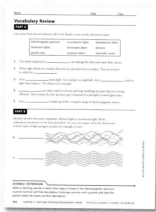

Vocabulary Review
Workbook, page 132

Reading Comprehension
Workbook, page 134

366 LIGHT AND OTHER ELECTROMAGNETIC WAVES

MASTERING CONCEPTS

True or False
If the statement is true, write "true." If it is false, change the underlined word or words to make the statement true.

1. The speed of light is fastest in a(n) <u>solid</u> <u>material</u>.
2. Electromagnetic waves are partly <u>electric</u> and partly <u>magnetic</u>.
3. A vibrating <u>neutron</u> creates an electromagnetic wave.
4. <u>Infrared</u> waves from the <u>Sun</u> feel warm on the skin.
5. <u>Visible light</u> is a very small portion of the electromagnetic spectrum.
6. <u>Visible light</u> waves cause sunburn.
7. <u>Incandescent lightbulbs</u> emit coherent light.
8. <u>Fluorescent</u> lightbulbs use a hot glowing filament to produce light.

Short Answer
Answer each of the following in a sentence or brief paragraph.

9. Compare high-frequency and low-frequency electromagnetic waves in terms of their speed in a vacuum and the energy they carry.
10. Identify what determines the frequency of an electromagnetic wave.
11. Explain why ultraviolet waves from the Sun are more damaging to living cells than infrared waves from the Sun are.
12. Explain why X rays and gamma rays coming from space do not reach Earth's surface.
13. Explain how the wavelength of an electromagnetic wave is related to the energy the wave carries.
14. Describe the differences between coherent and incoherent light.

Critical Thinking
Use what you have learned in this chapter to answer each of the following.

15. **Appraise** A classmate explains that sound cannot be heard in space because waves are not able to travel where there is no matter. Correct this explanation and give evidence supporting the fact that waves can travel in space.
16. **Apply Concepts** Which type of lighting device would you select for each of the following uses: an eye-catching sign for a restaurant, an outdoor soccer stadium, and a storage warehouse? Explain your answers.
17. **Propose** Describe situations in which an electric charge is surrounded only by an electric field and when it is surrounded by both an electric field and a magnetic field.

Standardized Test Question
Choose the letter of the response that correctly answers the question.

18. Which best describes the light waves shown?
    - A. ultraviolet
    - B. coherent
    - C. incoherent
    - D. high-intensity

> **Test-Taking Tip**
>
> If more than one choice for a multiple-choice question seems correct, ask yourself if each choice completely answers the question. If a choice is only partially true, it is probably not the correct answer.

---

14. The crests and troughs of coherent light waves are aligned as they travel, and all of the waves have the same frequency. A beam of coherent light does not spread out because all the waves travel in the same direction. A beam of coherent light is concentrated over a small area, so the light is intense. Incoherent waves have different frequencies and are not aligned with one another. A beam of incoherent light spreads out because the waves are traveling in different directions, so it is much less intense than a beam of coherent light.

Critical Thinking

15. Some waves cannot travel without a medium, but other waves, such as electromagnetic waves, can. Visible light and infrared waves have traveled to Earth through the vacuum of space.
16. A colorful neon sign would be a good choice for the restaurant. Extremely bright tungsten-halogen lights are the best choice for an outdoor soccer stadium. Economical fluorescent bulbs are a good choice for the warehouse. Accept other answers if the explanations are reasonable.
17. An electric charge is always surrounded by an electric field. When an electric charge moves, it produces a magnetic field in addition to the electric field.

Standardized Test Question

18. B

Reading Links

Waves: Principles of Light, Electricity, and Magnetism

Readers will come away with a firmer grasp of the many interconnected concepts presented in the unit and be pointed in the right direction to conduct further research.

Paul Fleisher. Lerner Publishing Group. 80 pp. Illustrated. Library ISBN 978-0-8225-2987-3.

Electricity and the Lightbulb

This book examines the history of the lightbulb and the scientific advances that led to its development.

James Lincoln Collier. Benchmark Books. 112 pp. Illustrated. Library ISBN 978-0-7614-1878-8.

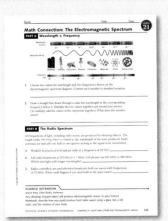

Curriculum Connection
Workbook, p. 135

Science Challenge
Workbook, pp. 136–137

21A Reflecting Rainbows

This prechapter introduction activity is designed to determine what students already know about reflection and refraction of light by engaging them in observing, examining, comparing, illustrating, and making conclusions.

Objectives

- observe light reflected and refracted from a prism and a CD
- relate the colors to a spectrum or rainbow
- explain the bending of light to produce colors

Planning

 15–20 minutes   groups of 3–4 students

Materials (per group)

- prism
- compact disc (CD)
- flashlight
- magnifying glass
- white paper
- colored pencils

Advance Preparation

- Find a suitable place outside. Caution students not to look directly at the Sun. If it is cloudy, you might consider only performing the flashlight portion of the activity.
- Students may need some help positioning the prism so they can see the colors. Prisms may be purchased at a science-supply house.
- The color patterns formed by the CD and the prism are created by different phenomena. The prism refracts light; changes in speed and direction separate the colors. The surface of a CD creates an interference color pattern; light

waves reflecting off different surfaces interfere and create a pattern of colors.

Engagement Guide

- Challenge students to think about how white light is broken into a spectrum of its component colors by asking:
  - *What occurs when a light wave passes from one material to another, such as from air to water?* (At any angle other than a right angle, the light wave changes speed and bends in the new medium. This is called refraction.)
  - *What exists in the air following a rainstorm? How might this cause light rays to refract?* (Many tiny water droplets exist in the air following a rainstorm. These droplets can act as prisms and refract light.)
  - *Where do the colors of a rainbow come from?* (The colors are the component colors that make up white light.)
  - *Do you think all light sources are made up of the same color components?* (No, each type of light source has a unique set of frequencies and intensities.)
- Encourage students to communicate their conclusions in creative ways.
- Warn students to be careful when shining any light directly at their eyes.

Going Further

Encourage students to observe how light waves are refracted when they pass from air to water by putting a spoon in a beaker of water. Have students describe how the spoon looks, and then ask them to explain what is happening. Students should present their conclusions to the class.

21B Looking at the Electromagnetic Spectrum

Objectives

- compare wavelength across the electromagnetic spectrum
- identify the visible portion of the electromagnetic spectrum
- convert between units
- model the electromagnetic spectrum to scale

Skill Set

comparing and contrasting, relating, measuring, modeling

Planning

 30–35 minutes   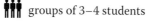 groups of 3–4 students

Materials

Materials for this activity are listed in the Student Laboratory Manual.

Advance Preparation

- Purchase paper in each color or use construction paper.
- Calculations for actual wavelengths in nanometers are provided in Data Table 1 (column three), but can be omitted. Explain to students that one nanometer (1 nm) is 10^{-9} m (one-billionth of a meter). For comparison, tell students that the diameter of a penny is 19 billion nanometers. These following conversion factors were used to convert wavelengths to nanometers: 10^{-6} m = 1,000 nm; 10^{-7} m = 100 nm; 10^{-8} m = 10 nm; 10^{-9} m = 1 nm. The scale for the model is 1 nanometer = 1 millimeter. You might want to provide these conversions to your students.

Answers to Observations

Data Table 1		
Actual wavelength (nm)	Scale wavelength (mm)	Actual frequency (Hz)
1000 nm	1000 mm	3.0×10^{14}
750 nm	750 mm	4.0×10^{14}
625 nm	625 mm	4.8×10^{14}
575 nm	575 mm	5.2×10^{14}
525 nm	525 mm	5.7×10^{14}
450 nm	450 mm	6.6×10^{14}
400 nm	400 mm	7.5×10^{14}
30 nm	30 mm	1.0×10^{16}

Answers to Analysis and Conclusions

1. red, orange, yellow, green, blue, and violet

2. The range of visible wavelengths is from 400 nm (violet) to 750 nm (red). The range of visible frequencies is from 4.0×10^{14} Hz (red) to 7.5×10^{14} Hz (violet). The infrared wave is 33.3 times longer than the ultraviolet wave.

3. The speed of all electromagnetic waves is 3.0×10^8 m/s.

4. Three meters is equal to 3,000 mm.

5. Students should recognize that some of the other electromagnetic waves are significantly longer than the scale model of infrared, visible light, and ultraviolet waves. The model shows the small portion the visible spectrum represents on the electromagnetic spectrum.

Going Further

Working in groups, have students make a list of the seven electromagnetic waves and identify some useful and harmful properties of each wave. Students may use books or computers to help them find information. Call on each group to share their information about one of the electromagnetic waves.

21C The Lightbulb Challenge

Objectives

* design experiments to compare light outputs of lightbulbs
* conduct an experiment and control variables
* measure the light output of lightbulbs
* draw conclusions

Skill Set

designing experiments, controlling variables, measuring, predicting outcomes, drawing conclusions

Planning

 45–60 minutes   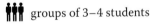 groups of 3–4 students

Materials

Materials for this activity are listed in the Student Laboratory Manual

Advance Preparation

* Choose incandescent and fluorescent bulbs with approximately the same light output—see the light output rating on the box. Label the bulbs with numbers and record the data specific to each bulb for later use. Make sure to record the power rating, cost, light output, and expected lifetime (in hours) for each bulb. Make sure students change the lightbulbs only after their lamps are switched off and unplugged. Allow time for the bulbs to cool.
* Provide cardboard boxes.
* The same student should do the viewing for each bulb. Remind them to wait for their pupils to stop dilating before making observations. Tell students not to look directly at the light.

Lab Tip

The lightbulb wattage should be limited to 60 watts or less.

Answers to Observations: Data Table 1

Sample Data Table

Data Table 1						
Bulb #	Type of Bulb	Power (Watts)	Light Output (lumens)	Life (hrs)	Cost ($)	Distance from Bulb to Light Box (cm)
1	fluorescent	18	1,100	6,000	$3.29	43 cm
2	incandescent	75	1,125	1,125	$0.89	42 cm

Answers to Analysis and Conclusions

1. Answers will vary, but should be supported by student data. The bulb that allowed the secret letter to be read from a greater distance is the brighter bulb.

2. Answers will vary, but the brighter bulb will likely have a higher lumens rating.

3. Answers will vary, but in general, the fluorescent bulb is much more efficient in terms of light produced per watt of power.

4. Answers will vary.

5. Answers will vary, but should show the fluorescent bulb has a lower overall cost.

Going Further

Have students research environmental issues related to electrical energy use and lightbulb use. Tell them to investigate pollution from electricity production and from dangerous substances (such as mercury) contained in CFLs. Have student groups present their findings to the class in the form of a poster or verbal presentation.

Introduce Chapter 22

As a starting activity, use Lab 22A on page 127 of the Laboratory Manual.

ENGAGE Ask students to close their eyes and imagine they are in their favorite places. Ask them to imagine what they see in those places. Have each student write a paragraph in his or her Science Notebook about his or her favorite place. Tell students that a number of scientific principles explain how they see, including the interaction of light and objects and how their eyes work.

Think About Light and Its Uses

ENGAGE Think aloud about driving in a car at night and watching a car pass in the opposite direction. Tell students that they should think of two examples and answer the questions.

• Answers will vary, but students might mention the use of flashlights, car headlights, etc. The descriptions should mention that the beams traveled in straight lines. Some students might mention that the beams spread slightly as they traveled. Differences might include how the beam interacted with objects.

• Answers will vary, but might mention the light beam being reflected, absorbed, or transmitted.

Chapter
22   Light and Its Uses

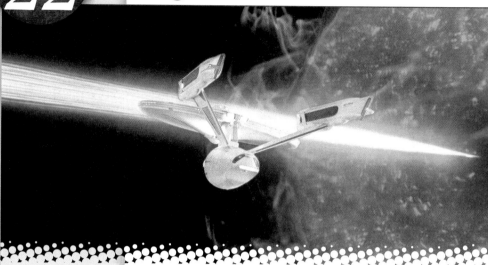

KEY CONCEPT Visible light interacts with objects in a variety of ways, allowing color images, distant objects, and very small objects to be seen.

The characters in science fiction shows commonly have ray guns as weapons. Although such ray guns used to be considered strictly science fiction, laser technology of today gives us much more than ray guns, and this could not happen without understanding how light behaves as a ray. This chapter explores the uses of light, including the application of mirrors and lenses for practical purposes, and the process by which humans see.

Think About Light and Its Uses

Think of two situations in which you have seen light travel as a ray or beam. What was the source of the beam? Did the beam pass through objects or was it stopped by them? How far did the beam travel?

• Describe the two situations in your Science Notebook. How are they alike? How are they different?

• Light interacts with the things it strikes. Write one or two sentences describing what happened when the light beams struck various objects.

NSTA
SCILINKS.
THE WORLD'S A CLICK AWAY

www.scilinks.org
Light **Code:** WGPS22

368

22.1 Shadows and Reflections

Before You Read

In your Science Notebook, create a chart with three columns. Label the first column *Plane Mirrors*, the second column *Concave Mirrors*, and the third column *Convex Mirrors*. Record any information you already know about these types of mirrors. As you read the lesson, add information to your chart that describes the characteristics of each type of mirror.

Light is an electromagnetic wave. Sometimes, however, it is easier to think of light waves as thin beams of light called rays. For example, the beam from a car's headlight can be thought of as a group of light rays traveling together; so can the beam of a flashlight. These light rays travel in straight lines until they strike something.

Shadows

When light shines on an object, some of the rays are absorbed and others are reflected. The rays that do not strike the object continue on their path in a straight line. A **shadow** (SHAD oh) forms in the area where the light rays cannot reach.

Shadows usually have a dark central region and a blurry-looking outer edge. The dark region, called the umbra, occurs where no light rays strike. The blurry region, called the penumbra, is a partial shadow. It occurs where rays from other light sources or from a wide beam begin to fill in the shadow. **Figure 22.1** shows the different kinds of shadows that can form, depending on lighting conditions.

Where there is light, there are usually shadows. Some shadows, like that from the cone, are small. A huge shadow occurs when the Moon passes directly between the Sun and Earth. This event, called a solar eclipse, casts a shadow over large areas of Earth's surface.

Learning Goals

- Contrast regular and diffuse reflection.
- Relate the characteristics of an image to the type of mirror that formed it.
- Explain the difference between real and virtual images.

New Vocabulary

shadow
plane mirror
regular reflection
diffuse reflection
convex mirror
virtual image
concave mirror
focal point
real image

Recall Vocabulary

law of reflection, p. 327

Figure 22.1 Shadows can be soft and blurry or dark, sharp, and clearly defined, depending on lighting conditions.

CHAPTER 22   **369**

⏹⏹⏹ Strategy

Model In small groups, have students illustrate and compare regular and diffuse reflections and plane, convex, and concave mirrors. All illustrations should include the path of light rays. Drawings of mirrors should include the image.

22.1 Introduce

ENGAGE Arrange students in small groups and provide each group with a flashlight and hand mirror. Ask students to experiment with shadows and reflections and then write a definition for each. Have groups share their definitions of each term with the class. Create working definitions as a class based on these discussions. Post the definitions on a bulletin board and revise them throughout the chapter.

Vocabulary terms are listed on the first student page of each lesson. You may wish to preview the terms before introducing each lesson. Strategies for teaching the vocabulary appear on the pages where the terms are introduced.

Before You Read

Draw the three-column chart on the board and label it as directed. Show students an example of a plane mirror as you think aloud about it, stating that this type of mirror is often used for hand mirrors, in dressing rooms, and in bathrooms, and it reflects a true or accurate image. Write your facts in the *Plane Mirror* column. Ask students to draw their charts in their Science Notebooks and to write what they know about each type of mirror.

● Teach

EXPLAIN to students that they will learn about different types of shadows and reflections in this lesson. Ask students to think about times when they might have seen a shadow that was not dark and clear. Have students share their responses with partners.

Vocabulary

shadow Explain to students that the word *shadow* is derived from *shade*. Encourage students to think of common uses of the word *shadow*. Examples might include someone who follows closely, a darker area of a picture, a very small amount, or a dark shape cast on a surface when an object is between the surface and the light source.

CHAPTER 22   **369**

● Teach

Review with students the class definition of *reflection*. Demonstrate both regular and diffuse reflections. Highlight the differences in the reflections, and then create a class definition for *diffuse reflection*.

Explore It!

Have students work in groups of three. Encourage them to observe the shadows and to draw their observations in their Science Notebooks. Sharp shadows are more easily formed by smaller light sources, such as a narrow flashlight beam. Large sources, such as a long fluorescent tube, tend to produce softer-edged shadows because more rays are able to fill in behind the object. Distance from the wall also affects the sharpness of the shadow.

Use the Visual:

Figure 22.2 [ANSWER] For each ray, the angles are equal.

Figure 22.3 [ANSWER] Yes, the law of reflection still applies. The difference is that the angle of the incident ray varies with the shape of the surface.

 **Vocabulary**

plane mirror Tell students that the word *plane* is derived from Latin and means "level surface." A plane mirror is a flat surface that reflects the image in front of it.

regular reflection Ask students if they are familiar with other meanings of the word *regular*. Discuss those meanings.

diffuse reflection Tell students that *diffuse* is derived from Latin and means "to pour out in various directions."

convex mirror Explain to students that *convex* is derived from Latin and means "arched." Review with students the meaning of *mirror*. Ask students how the derivations relate to the scientific definition of the term.

virtual image Ask students to think of common uses of the word *virtual*. Examples might include "nearly," virtual computer memory, or being so in effect (as in virtual reality). Tell students that the word *image* is derived from Latin and means "a likeness." A virtual image is nearly an image; that is, it can only be seen in a mirror.

 **Explore It!**

Obtain several light sources, such as a flashlight, an incandescent lamp, and a fluorescent tube lamp. Experiment by shining light on an object placed in front of a wall. Describe the lighting conditions that produce sharp-edged and blurry shadows. Determine if the distance of the object from the wall has any effect on the shadow produced.

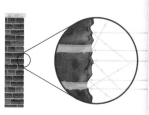

Figure 22.3 The brick wall's rough surface scatters the incident light rays in many directions. Rough surfaces cause diffuse reflections. Does the law of reflection apply to the light rays striking the wall?

Differentiate Instruction

Linguistic Have students write poems describing how they see their own reflections or shadows. The poems could be literal or figurative. If students are willing, post the untitled poems on the wall and have others guess who authored each poem.

Reflection of Light

Shadows form where light rays cannot reach. Often, the rays cannot reach an area because they are absorbed or reflected by an object in their path. Chapter 19 described how reflections occur when waves bounce off a surface. As shown in **Figure 22.2,** light waves obey the law of reflection. The law states that the angle of the incident light is equal to the angle of the reflected light. The mirror shown in Figure 22.2 is similar to one you likely looked into this morning before coming to school. This type of mirror—one that is flat and smooth—is called a **plane mirror.**

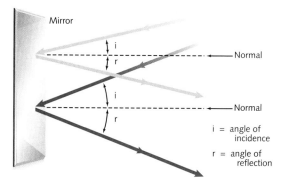

Figure 22.2 Light rays striking this plane mirror obey the law of reflection. How is the angle of incidence related to the angle of reflection for each of the rays shown?

Regular and Diffuse Reflection Sometimes a plate glass window or a motionless lake surface can act like a plane mirror. In fact, any smooth reflective surface can produce an image-like reflection. The reflections are crisp and detailed because the smooth surfaces reflect the incident rays uniformly. The reflection of light rays from a smooth surface is known as **regular reflection.** A rough surface, such as the brick wall in **Figure 22.3,** reflects rays in many directions and produces a **diffuse** (di FYOOS) **reflection.** Diffuse reflections do not form clear images. Like bright sunlight bouncing off a white wall, a diffuse reflection is seen as simply a certain amount of brightness.

Convex Mirrors

A mirror whose reflecting surface curves outward is called a **convex** (kahn VEKS) **mirror. Figure 22.4** shows that the back of a spoon is a convex mirror. The curved surface reflects light rays and forms an image.

Light rays that reflect from a convex mirror diverge, or spread apart, as shown in **Figure 22.5.** The imaginary line running through the center of the mirror is called the optical axis. It is drawn perpendicular to the surface of the mirror at the mirror's center. The optical axis is the symmetry line of the mirror. The diverging rays cause the image to *appear* as if it comes from a location in back of the mirror. The location of the image formed by a convex mirror is found by tracing the reflected rays backward until they meet. An image that is formed by diverging light rays is called a **virtual** (VUR chuh wul) **image.** Convex mirrors and plane mirrors always form virtual images. Although a virtual image can be seen in a mirror, the image cannot be projected onto a screen. Images formed by convex mirrors are never upside-down; they are always upright. The mirrors also allow very large areas to be viewed.

Figure 22.4 The image formed by the convex-shaped back of a spoon cannot be projected onto a surface—it is a virtual image.

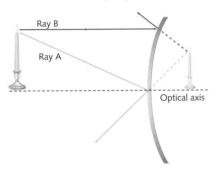

Ray B

Ray A

Optical axis

Figure 22.5 A convex mirror forms a reduced-size, upright virtual image. Note that the reflected rays diverge, or spread apart.

These traits make convex mirrors useful for security and safety purposes. Convex mirrors placed in the corners of buildings allow store employees to observe customers. Convex mirrors are often placed at dangerous road intersections so that drivers and pedestrians can see what is coming. They are also used in automobile rearview and side-view mirrors to widen the field of view. However, because the image created by a convex mirror is smaller than the actual object, distance perception can be distorted. Objects look like they are farther away than they truly are, which is why side mirrors carry the warning "Objects in mirror are closer than they appear."

Figure 22.6 The wide field of view of this convex mirror allows motorists to see if there is an oncoming vehicle.

Figure It Out

1. What law do the reflected rays A and B obey?
2. How does the size of the image formed compare to the size of the object?

As You Read

Record the characteristics of images formed by convex mirrors in the chart in your Science Notebook. Compare your chart with a partner's chart. Make any necessary corrections or additions.

What kind of light rays form a virtual image in a convex mirror?

● Teach

EXPLAIN that a second type of mirror is a convex mirror. Review **Figure 22.4** with students and discuss the virtual image of a convex mirror.

Tell students that convex mirrors also have focal points, just as concave mirrors do, and ask students to hypothesize about the location of the focal point. Explain that the point is located behind the mirror. All reflected rays from a convex mirror are traced back through the focal point.

Figure It Out: **Figure 22.5**

ANSWER **1.** the law of reflection **2.** The size of the image is reduced.

As You Read

Give students a few minutes to update the *Convex Mirror* column notes in their Science Notebooks. Have students share their notes with partners to check for understanding.
ANSWER Diverging light rays form virtual images.

Science Notebook EXTRA

For homework, ask students to notice uses of round and rectangular convex mirrors in public locations. Have students list the locations and uses of the mirrors. Create a class list of responses. Then ask students to think of locations in the school where a convex mirror might be useful.

Background Information

Round convex and rectangular convex mirrors are often used to improve visibility in difficult-to-maneuver areas such as parking garages, blind alleys, curving roads, corners in heavily-trafficked areas in hospitals, and loading docks in warehouses.

Teach

EXPLAIN to students that another kind of mirror is a concave mirror. The reflection of a concave mirror can be real or virtual.

 Vocabulary

concave mirror Tell students that *concave* is derived from Latin and means "hollow." Note the shape of a concave mirror, and ask students how light rays will reflect in a mirror with a hollow shape.

focal point Ask students to think of common uses of the word *focus*. Examples might include tan area of concern or the quality of being sharply defined.

real image Encourage students to brainstorm common uses of the word *real*. Examples might include genuine, sincere, factual, or having actual physical existence.

CONNECTION: Environmental Science

Have students work in small groups to explore why concave mirrors, and not plane or convex mirrors, are used to collect solar power. Students should create a list of reasons and draw illustrations of how they believe the solar power plant works. Encourage students to use the concept of focal point in their explanations.

Use the Visual: Figure 22.8

[ANSWER] The bulb is located at the focal point.

Assess

Use the After You Read questions and the Alternative Assessment to help you evaluate students' understanding of the lesson.

After You Read

1. Rough reflecting surfaces produce diffuse reflections. Smooth reflecting surfaces produce regular reflections and are required to form a sharp image.

2. Real images, which can be projected onto a screen, form where light rays converge, or come together. Virtual images are formed by diverging rays and cannot be projected onto a screen.

3. Plane, concave, and convex mirrors can form virtual images. Only concave mirrors can form real images.

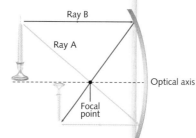

Figure 22.7 Ray A passes through the focal point, strikes the mirror, and is reflected parallel to the optical axis. Ray B travels parallel to the optical axis, strikes the mirror, and is reflected through the focal point. A reduced-size, inverted image of the object forms where the rays intersect.

CONNECTION: Environmental Science

Several experimental solar power plants use concave mirrors. The mirrors focus parallel light rays from the Sun onto small energy-collecting tubes. Each tube is located at the focal point of its mirror.

Concave Mirrors

A mirror with a reflecting surface that curves in on itself is called a **concave** (KAHN kayv) **mirror.** Light rays that reflect from a concave mirror converge, or come together. **Figure 22.7** shows one way in which a concave mirror forms an image. The optical axis of the mirror forms a line that is perpendicular to the center of the mirror. Any ray that travels parallel to the optical axis and strikes the concave mirror will be reflected through the **focal point.** Reversing the path, any ray that passes through the focal point and then strikes the concave mirror will be reflected parallel to the optical axis.

Trace the paths of Rays A and B shown in Figure 22.7. Both rays strike the mirror, are reflected, and then intersect. At the point where the rays intersect, they form an image of the flame. Tracing two similar rays from each point on the candle results in the formation of a reduced-size, upside-down image of the candle, as shown. Unlike the virtual images formed by plane mirrors and convex mirrors, the image forms where light rays intersect. An image formed by intersecting light rays is called a **real image.** A real image can be projected onto a screen.

Depending on an object's position relative to a concave mirror, the image formed may be larger or smaller than the object, upright or inverted, and real or virtual.

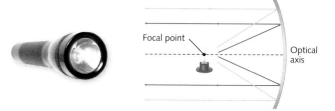

Figure 22.8 The flashlight uses a concave mirror to form a beam of parallel light rays. At what point is the bulb located?

After You Read

1. Relate the smoothness of a reflecting surface to the type of reflection it produces. What type of surface is required to form a sharp, detailed image?

2. Explain the differences between real and virtual images.

3. Review the chart in your Science Notebook. Use the information you wrote to identify the types of mirrors that can form virtual images. Which mirrors form real images?

Alternative Assessment

Have each student use the charts in his or her Science Notebook to write a paragraph comparing two types of mirrors. Students should include the shape of each mirror, the type of image that is formed, and real-life examples of the mirror.

Background Information

Concentrated solar power systems are being developed to collect direct solar radiation. The radiation is focused through optical devices onto a receiver, and the radiation is then transformed into heat. A solar furnace utilizes a heliostat to reflect sunlight onto the concave mirrors; from the mirror, the light is focused on a furnace located at the focal point of the mirror.

22.2 Refraction—The Bending of Light

Before You Read

Draw a T-chart in your Science Notebook. Label one side *Convex Lenses* and the other side *Concave Lenses*. Write anything you already know about each type of lens in the appropriate column. As you read the lesson, add information to your chart.

Waves refract, or bend, when passing into a new material at any angle other than a right angle. The bending is due to a change in speed of the wave in the new material. The amount of bending depends on how great the change in speed is.

The Index of Refraction

Recall that light travels at a speed of 3.00×10^8 m/s in a vacuum. When light moves through any material, its speed decreases. The **index of refraction** is a property of a material that indicates how much the speed of light in the material is reduced.

The larger a material's index of refraction, the slower light will travel through it. For example, light travels much more slowly through diamond (with an index of refraction of 2.42) than it does through water (with an index of refraction of 1.33). Many natural phenomena can be explained by the refraction of light.

Prisms and Rainbows   Rainbow-like colors can be seen when sunlight strikes a wedge-shaped piece of glass known as a prism. White light from the Sun is made up of many colors, and each color corresponds to a particular wavelength. When white light passes at an angle into the glass, it travels at a different speed through the glass. The light is refracted, and each wavelength is refracted by a different amount. Although the variation is small, it is enough to cause the colors to separate, as shown in **Figure 22.9**. The longer the wavelength, the less bending there will be. Red, with the longest wavelength, is refracted the least. When a rainbow is formed, the raindrop acts like a prism.

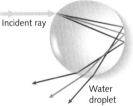

Sunlight

Incident ray

Water droplet

Learning Goals

- Relate the index of refraction of a material to the speed of light through the material.
- Describe the shapes of convex and concave lenses.
- Relate the characteristics of an image to the type of lens that formed the image.

New Vocabulary

index of refraction
mirage
convex lens
concave lens
critical angle

Recall Vocabulary

refraction, p. 328

Did You Know?

People often use the made-up name "Roy G. Biv" to remember the colors of the rainbow (*red, orange, yellow, green, blue, indigo,* and *violet*).

Figure 22.9 Refraction in the glass prism and the raindrop separates white light into its component colors. Each color has a different wavelength and is refracted a different amount. Which color is refracted the most?

CHAPTER 22   **373**

22.2 Introduce

ENGAGE Place students in small groups and provide each group with a pencil and a clear container filled at least halfway with water. Have students place the pencil at various angles in the water (upright, leaned across the glass, and angles between those positions). Have students write their observations in their Science Notebooks. Students should notice that the pencil appears bent when it leans in the glass. This distortion is the result of refraction. Discuss with students the results of their observations and ask them to hypothesize about why the pencil looks bent. Explain that they will learn more about refraction in this lesson.

Before You Read

Draw the T-chart on the board and think aloud about concave lenses. Explain to students that you remember the shape of these lenses by the word *cave* (the shape curves inward, similar to a real cave). Sketch an example of a concave lens. Have students draw their T-charts in their Science Notebooks and add information that they already know about the topics.

Teach

EXPLAIN Review with students the idea that the speed of light decreases when it enters any medium from space. Explain that the index of refraction is a measure of the decrease in the speed of light.

Vocabulary

index of refraction Encourage students to think of common uses of the word *index*. Examples might include a reference to the pointer finger, a list of names or topics included in a book, or a catalog in a library that contains information about each book. Explain to students that the word *refract* is derived from Latin and means "to break." Tell students that the index of refraction is a measure of how much bending or breaking light will do when it enters a new medium.

Use the Visual: Figure 22.9

ANSWER violet

Teach

EXPLAIN to students that refraction causes mirages. In movies, people sometimes see a mirage of a body of water when they are trapped in a desert.

Vocabulary

mirage Explain to students that the word *mirage* is derived from the French verb *mirer,* meaning "to reflect." Ask students how this derivation relates to the definition of the term.

convex lens Remind students that the word *convex* is derived from Latin and means "arched." A convex lens is arched.

As You Read

Give students about five minutes to update their T-charts. Review their charts for accuracy and remind students to focus on the lenses' characteristics.

ANSWER A convex lens causes light rays to converge.

As You Read

As you read about convex and concave lenses, add information to your chart that describes their characteristics.

Which type of lens causes light rays to converge?

Figure 22.10 Light travels faster through the hot air near the surface, causing it to bend. A mirage is the additional image of an object caused by the refraction.

Mirages A **mirage** (mi RAHZH) is an out-of-place image of an object caused by refraction. A mirage is an example of refraction of light caused by Earth's atmosphere. The index of refraction of air depends on the temperature of the air. When light passes from air at one temperature to air at another temperature, the light bends. The greater the difference in temperature, the more the light will bend.

The wet-looking road shown in **Figure 22.10** is a mirage. The road is actually dry. The refraction is caused by a layer of hot, less-dense air near the surface of the road. Similarly, downward-traveling light rays from the car in Figure 22.10 enter warm air near the road, and their speed increases. Because of the increase in speed, the rays are bent upward. The bent rays form the upside-down mirage seen beneath the car.

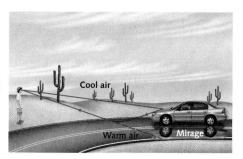

Cool air

Warm air   Mirage

Convex Lenses

Lenses are optical devices that bend light. As light passes through a lens, it bends and then forms an image. Lenses affect light in completely different ways than do mirrors. However, just as mirrors can have concave and convex shapes, so too can lenses. A **convex lens** is thicker at its center than at its edges. Rays passing through the center of the lens are not bent. As a ray's distance from the center increases, the amount the ray is refracted increases. The convex shape causes all rays traveling parallel to the optical axis to converge, or come together, at the focal point of the lens. A convex lens is shown in **Figure 22.11.** The amount of refraction a convex lens produces is determined by the degree to which the lens is curved. A very curved lens will refract light more than a lens whose surface is only slightly curved.

Focal length

Focal point

Figure 22.11 Convex lenses cause light rays to converge. The distance from the center of the lens to the focal point is the focal length of the lens.

Differentiate Instruction

Mathematical Have students research the index of refraction for a variety of materials and create posters to display their results. Students can arrange the materials from the lowest index of refraction (vacuum) to the highest index (gallium phosphide). Have students note how the density of a material relates to its index of refraction.

Teacher Alert

Terminology for convex and concave lenses can differ. A double convex lens has a convex shape on both sides; a double concave lens has a concave shape on each side of the lens. Double convex lenses may also be converging or positive lenses, and double concave lenses are known as diverging or negative lenses.

How Convex Lenses Form Images A convex lens forms images that are enlarged or reduced, upright or inverted, and virtual or real, depending on the position of the object relative to the lens. **Figure 22.12** shows how a convex lens can be used to magnify, or enlarge, the image of an object. The different images that can be formed by a convex lens are shown in **Figure 22.13**. In each diagram in the figure, note that Ray B, which is not parallel to the optical axis and passes through the center of the lens, is not refracted.

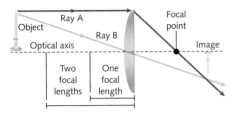

a When the candle is more than two focal lengths away from the lens, its image is real, reduced, and upside-down.

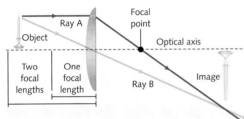

b When the candle is between one and two focal lengths from the lens, its image is real, enlarged, and upside-down.

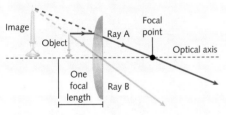

c When the candle is less than one focal length from the lens, its image is virtual, enlarged, and upright.

Figure 22.13 The image formed by a convex lens depends on the position of the object relative to the lens.

Figure 22.12 This handheld magnifying lens uses a convex lens. By placing the lens very close to the object, an upright, enlarged image is formed. Which diagram in Figure 22.13 corresponds to this photo?

Figure It Out

1. Describe the position of the object relative to the lens in order to form an image that is inverted, smaller, and real.

2. Describe the position of the object relative to the lens that causes the refracted rays to diverge. Identify the type of image formed by the diverging rays.

● Teach

EXPLAIN to students that convex lenses cause light rays to converge; the images that are produced vary depending on the placement of the object.

Use the Visual: Figure 22.12

ANSWER Diagram C

Figure It Out: Figure 22.13

ANSWER **1.** The object must be located more than two focal lengths away from the lens. **2.** The object must be less than one focal length away from the lens. Virtual images are formed by diverging rays.

Science Notebook EXTRA

Have students summarize their understanding of **Figure 22.13** in their Science Notebooks. Students should illustrate each concept using an example different from the candle. They should draw this simple object as seen by the unaided eye and then again when viewed by a convex lens more than two focal lengths away, between one and two focal lengths away, and less than one focal length from the lens away. Allow English language learners to work in pairs to explain the image in relationship to the chapter's concepts and to use vocabulary terms before completing this task.

Background Information

Modern optical telescopes are either refracting telescopes or reflecting telescopes. The Hubble Space Telescope is a large reflecting telescope that was designed by NASA and launched into orbit in 1990 with a life expectancy of 15 years. Reflecting telescopes use mirrors to gather and focus light. Light enters the open tube of the telescope and goes to the primary parabolic mirror. This mirror reflects the light rays to a second plane mirror, which then reflects the light to the eyepiece of the telescope. In a refracting telescope, light enters through a large convex lens. The lens bends light toward the eyepiece, and the image is produced.

Teach

EXPLAIN to students that a concave lens is shallower at the center of the lens. The lens diverges, or spreads, light rays, which makes images look smaller and farther away. Nearsighted people usually have concave lenses in their eyeglasses.

 Vocabulary

concave lens Remind students that the word *concave* is derived from Latin and means "hollow." A concave lens is hollow.

critical angle Have students brainstorm common uses of the word *critical*. Examples might include the quality of being urgent or absolutely necessary or the act of finding fault, analyzing, or judging something. Ask students to relate the common uses to the scientific meaning of the term *critical angle*.

 Explore It!

Have available appropriate flashlights (or pictures of flashlights) for students to view. It might be helpful to demonstrate how to hold the flashlight using a large sink.

[ANSWER] The critical angle is 48.6 degrees.

Assess

Use the After You Read questions and the Alternative Assessment to help you evaluate students' understanding of the lesson.

After You Read

1. The speed decreases, but not as much as in a medium with a higher index of refraction.

2. A convex lens is thicker at its center than at its edges. A concave lens is thicker at its edges than at its center. A convex lens can produce converging and diverging light rays.

3. The point at which light rays parallel to the optical axis converge is the focal point. The focal length is the distance from the center of the lens to the focal point.

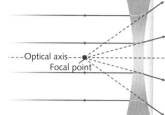

Figure 22.14 A concave lens causes light rays to diverge.

Explore It!

Obtain a waterproof, battery-powered flashlight. Fill a bathtub with water. Turn the room's lights off and turn the flashlight on. **CAUTION:** *Do not use any light source that plugs into an electrical outlet.* Hold the flashlight under the water with its beam aimed upward at the surface. Change the angle of the flashlight and observe the results. Estimate the critical angle for the flashlight's beam.

Concave Lenses

A **concave lens** is thicker at its edges than at its center. As shown in **Figure 22.14,** light rays parallel to the optical axis refract and spread apart. Because the refracted rays diverge, they cannot form a real image. If you trace the refracted rays backward in a straight line along the directions they travel, you will find that they converge at a focal point located in front of the lens. The image formed by a concave lens is always virtual, upright, smaller than the object, and located between the object and the lens. Corrective eyeglasses and telescopes make use of concave lenses.

Total Internal Reflection

Usually, light is both reflected and refracted when it enters a new material. Some of the light is reflected back, and the rest is refracted into the new material. This can be seen in **Figure 22.15.** In the figure, a flashlight beam held beneath the water is aimed at the surface at an angle. As the beam makes a larger and larger angle with the normal, the amount of light that refracts decreases.

At the **critical angle,** the refracted beam skims the surface. At any angle greater than the critical angle, all of the light is reflected; no light is refracted. This is known as total internal reflection. Later in this chapter, you will learn how total internal reflection is used in optical devices and fiber optics.

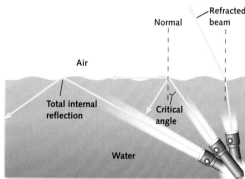

Figure 22.15 As the beam makes with the normal increases, less light is refracted. Beyond the critical angle, total internal reflection occurs.

After You Read

1. Identify how the speed of light changes when light enters a material with a low index of refraction.

2. Describe the shapes of convex and concave lenses. Which shape can produce both converging and diverging light rays?

3. Review the chart in your Science Notebook. Use the information to define the focal point and focal length of a lens.

Alternative Assessment

Have each student write a paragraph comparing and contrasting concave and convex lenses. The paragraph should include the shapes of the lenses, what type of light rays are produced (converging or diverging), and what type of image is produced.

Background Information

For total internal reflection (TIR) to occur, light rays must be moving from a more optically dense medium toward a less optically dense medium, and the angle of incidence must be greater than the critical angle. TIR will occur when light moves from water to air, but not vice versa. TIR happens because the angle of refraction reaches a 90-degree angle before the angle of reflection does; thus, light will bend away from the normal.

22.3 Color

Before You Read

In your Science Notebook, write three facts you already know about color. Leave several lines below each of your facts. As you read the lesson, add at least two facts to each fact you already recorded.

Learning Goals

- Differentiate among opaque, translucent, and transparent objects.
- Explain why objects appear the colors they do.
- Contrast the result of mixing the three primary colors of light and the three primary colors of pigment.

New Vocabulary

opaque
transparent
translucent
pigment

Recall Vocabulary

visible light, p. 360

When light strikes an object, part of the light is usually absorbed and part is reflected. Sometimes, a portion of the light can pass through the object. What happens to the light depends on the material.

Opaque, Transparent, and Translucent Objects

Every object reflects and absorbs light waves. An **opaque** (oh PAYK) material only reflects and absorbs light. Nothing can be seen through an opaque material because no light passes through it. A sheet of aluminum foil is opaque. **Transparent** (trans PE runt) materials such as glass let almost all the light that strikes them pass through. **Translucent** (trans LEW sunt) materials such as wax paper let some light pass through them. Objects viewed through translucent materials are visible, but not clear.

Color

White light is made up of all the colors of the visible spectrum. When all the wavelengths of white light are present at the same time, human eyes see white. Why don't all objects look white, then, when sunlight or another source of white light strikes them? The answer is illustrated in **Figure 22.16.** White light shines on the leaf. The leaf absorbs all of the wavelengths except those that correspond to green light. In other words, the leaf reflects green light. The eyes detect the reflected green light and see the leaf as green. Something that reflects all wavelengths of the visible spectrum appears white, whereas something that absorbs all wavelengths appears black.

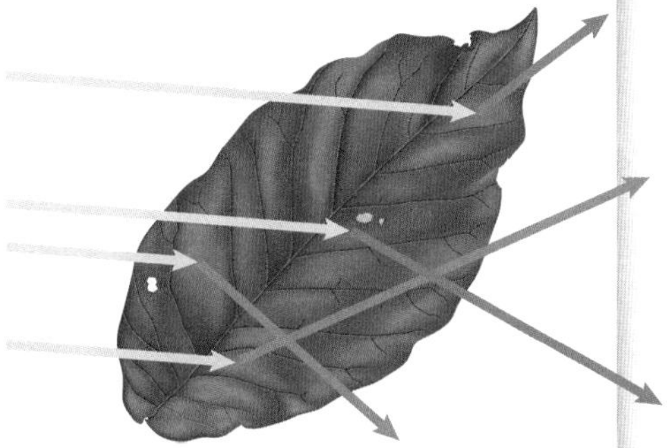

Figure 22.16 The leaf appears green because it reflects the green wavelengths of light from the Sun. Is the leaf opaque, translucent, or transparent?

ELL Strategy

Use a Venn Diagram Have each student make a Venn diagram in his or her Science Notebook that compares the primary colors of light and the primary colors of pigment. Encourage students to use colored pens for the diagram and to note why all pigment colors are not in the visible spectrum of light (such as pink).

22.3 Introduce

ENGAGE Arrange students in small groups and provide each group with either three flashlights and red, blue, and green filters or with white paper and cyan, magenta, and yellow crayons, paints, or markers. Ask students to experiment with their colors to make as many new colors as possible. Have students record the results of color combinations in a table. Encourage students with flashlights to combine all three colors. Tell students that they will learn more about the differences between pigments and light in this lesson.

Before You Read

Model the process of writing facts that you already know on the board. Thinking aloud, tell students that white light, when viewed through a prism, is comprised of all the colors; write this as a fact on the board. Continue this modeling process, noting that some colors can be mixed to make a new color (such as blue and red making purple). Direct students to each write three facts in their Science Notebooks.

Teach

EXPLAIN to students that every object reflects and absorbs light waves. Objects can be opaque, transparent, or translucent. Explain that most objects in the room are opaque, and point out examples to students.

Vocabulary

opaque Tell students that the word *opaque* is derived from Latin and means "dark" or "shaded." Ask students how this derivation is related to the scientific meaning.

transparent Tell students that the prefix *trans-* means "across," and the root *parere* is Latin and means "to appear." Ask students to relate the literal definition to the scientific definition.

translucent Review with students the meaning of the prefix *trans-*. Explain that the root *lucere* is Latin and means "to shine." Translucent materials allow some light to shine through.

Use the Visual: Figure 22.16

ANSWER opaque

CHAPTER 22 377

• Teach

EXPLAIN to students that the primary colors of light are different from the primary colors that they have learned about in art class. Tell them that white light is produced when all three primary light colors are combined.

🖊 Explain It!

The white light given off by fluorescent lights is not the same as sunlight. Fluorescent lights do not give off the complete spectrum of visible light. Thus, the light reflected from your face does not contain the same colors as a similar reflection from sunlight. The result is a different, odd-looking skin tone.

Figure It Out: **Figure 22.17**

ANSWER **1.** red and green **2.** Yellow light formed from mixing red and green light consists of a mixture of wavelengths (corresponding to red and green light), whereas yellow light from the visible spectrum is of a single wavelength.

As You Read

Give students a few minutes to review and revise the color facts in their Science Notebooks. Have students share new facts with a partner.

ANSWER When red, blue, and green light mix, white light forms.

🖊 Explain It!

Have you ever looked at your face in the mirror in a bathroom illuminated with bright fluorescent lights? The lights make the color of your skin look odd. Write a paragraph explaining why this occurs.

Figure It Out

1. What colors overlap to produce yellow light?
2. How is the yellow light produced by combining colors of light different from the yellow light formed when sunlight passes through a prism?

As You Read

Review the facts you recorded in your Science Notebook before beginning this lesson. If needed, revise the facts so that they are correct.

What color is formed when red, blue, and green light mix?

Primary Light Colors

Red, blue, and green are known as the primary colors of light. Virtually all of the colors you see can be formed by mixing these three colors. Creating new colors by mixing the primary colors of light, a process shown in **Figure 22.17,** is known as color addition. White light is produced when all three of the primary light colors are mixed.

Mixing pairs of the primary light colors creates colors known as secondary colors. The secondary colors yellow, magenta, and cyan can also be seen in Figure 22.17. Yellow, magenta (a bluish-red color), and cyan (a greenish-blue color) are formed by combining red and green, red and blue, and green and blue, respectively.

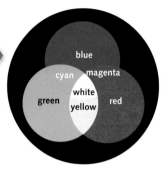

Figure 22.17 The three primary colors of light are red, blue, and green. When two or more of the primary colors overlap, other colors are formed.

Some colors you see are not present in the visible spectrum of light—the wavelengths that make up the colors of the rainbow. Pink is one example. Pink does not exist in the visible light spectrum, and it does not have a related wavelength. The brain sees pink when red and violet wavelengths of visible light are viewed at the same time. Other colors, such as yellow, can be sensed in two ways. A prism will separate sunlight into its components, one of which is yellow. Each shade of yellow from the visible spectrum that is seen has a unique wavelength. Yellow, however, is also sensed by the brain when red and green light waves are viewed at the same time.

Primary Pigment Colors

Inks and paints that are used to change the color of objects are called **pigments** (PIG muntz). The three primary pigments are different from the three primary light colors. Cyan, magenta, and yellow are the primary pigments. The color of a pigment is determined by the wavelengths the pigment reflects. Mixing two or more pigments results in a very different color than does mixing the same colors of light. **Figure 22.18** shows some of the results of mixing primary pigments.

Differentiate Instruction

Visual Provide students with colored pencils, crayons, or paints. Working with a partner, have students make color wheels for primary light colors and primary pigment colors. Students should label primary and secondary colors. They may need to conduct research to learn about color wheels. Colors are arranged in a specific way. For example, if any two colors exactly opposite each other on the color wheel are mixed, the result is white.

Black forms when the three primary pigments are mixed. The mixture is black because it absorbs all of the primary colors of light. Mixing pigments together gradually removes, or subtracts, wavelengths of reflected light. Forming colors by mixing pigments is called color subtraction. It is possible to make virtually any color pigment by mixing different amounts of the primary pigment colors.

Figure 22.18 Black is the result of mixing the three primary pigments: cyan, magenta, and yellow.

PEOPLE IN SCIENCE Garret Morgan (1877–1963)

Garret Morgan was born in Kentucky, the seventh of eleven children. At age fourteen, Morgan moved to Ohio to get a better education. He soon learned about sewing machines and opened a shop that sold new machines and repaired old ones. His first invention came in 1909. While trying to develop a friction-reducing liquid to help sewing machines perform better, he ended up producing the first hair-straightener.

In 1912, Morgan developed a device called a "safety hood" and patented it as a breathing device. Garret Morgan himself would end up wearing the invention during a heroic rescue effort that saved the lives of several workers trapped underground by a tunnel explosion. Morgan became a successful and respected businessman. He is thought to be one of the first African Americans to purchase an automobile. After witnessing a traffic accident, Morgan decided to develop a mechanical way to direct traffic. He went on to patent a traffic signal. Although Morgan did not invent the first traffic signal, he was awarded a citation for his signal by the U.S. government shortly before his death in 1963.

After You Read

1. What colors are reflected and what colors are absorbed when white light shines on a pair of red shoes?

2. Explain how it is possible for the human eye to see pink even though pink is not part of the visible light that comes from the Sun.

3. Use the facts and details you listed in your Science Notebook to write a well-developed paragraph explaining why mixing all the primary light colors produces white, whereas mixing all the primary pigments produces black.

Did You Know?

The color photographs in this book are printed using four inks: the primary pigments plus black. Printers have found that adding black ink is needed to get a true, deep black on the page.

Alternative Assessment

Have students use the notes in their Science Notebooks to summarize their knowledge of color. As prompts, they could write statements starting with *I used to think...* and *Now I know...* Have students include at least five new facts in their summaries and write in complete sentences.

● Teach

EXPLAIN to students that the color of a mixture of two primary pigments is determined by the primary light colors reflected by both pigments.

 **Vocabulary**

pigment Explain to students that *pigment* is derived from Latin and means "paint." Pigments can be any matter used in water, oil, or other liquids to give color to paint or paper.

PEOPLE IN SCIENCE

The Morgan traffic signal was a hand-cranked, *T*-shaped pole unit that had three positions: *Stop, Go,* and an all-directional stop position. The stop position allowed pedestrians to cross streets more safely. This signal was used throughout North America until automatic red, yellow, and green light traffic signals replaced them.

EXTEND Have students work with a partner to redesign Morgan's original traffic signal so that the result is different from familiar signals used today. Encourage students to experiment with different shapes, colors, and movements. Have pairs sketch their designs and explain their variations, describing how the new signal would be an improvement on those currently in use.

● Assess

Use the After You Read questions and the Alternative Assessment to help you evaluate students' understanding of the lesson.

After You Read

1. All wavelengths except red are absorbed; red is reflected.

2. When certain wavelengths of light are viewed at the same time, the brain interprets them as a new color. This occurs with the color pink. Pink is seen when red and violet light are viewed at the same time.

3. Colors of light add together, eventually forming white. Pigments subtract visible colors of light when mixed, eventually producing black.

22.4 Introduce

ENGAGE Write the following words on the board: *cornea, pupil, lens, retina.*

Ask students to quickly sketch a human eye and to use the words on the board to label as many parts as they can. Explain to students that they have been learning about how light interacts with objects; now they will learn how their eyes interpret light. Tell students that they will learn about the different parts of the eye, and they will return to their drawings to review and revise them as needed.

Before You Read

Model the process of reviewing aloud the first few headings and subheadings. Create a table on the board and write the first two headings from the lesson. Then write a sentence about *The Eye and Vision,* such as *The eye has different structures to allow it to view and interpret images.* Have students draw their tables in their Science Notebooks.

● Teach

Vocabulary

cornea Tell students that the cornea is the clear front window of the eye. It is comprised of five layers.

pupil Tell students that the pupil is the dark circular opening in the center of the iris that controls the amount of light that enters the retina.

lens Tell students that the literal meaning of *lens* in Latin is "lentil." Ask students to compare the shape of a lentil to the shape of the lens in the eye, and ask them how this might help them remember the definition of the term *lens.*

retina Explain to students that the word *retina* is derived from Latin and means "a net." The retina could be described as the net that catches the light rays from the lens.

- Describe the structures of the eye and the process of vision.
- Explain how lenses are used to correct vision problems.

New Vocabulary

cornea
pupil
lens
retina

22.4 Vision—How You See

Before You Read

Look at the main headings and subheadings in this lesson. Divide a sheet of paper in your Science Notebook into six sections. Write one lesson heading in each section. Then write a sentence summarizing what you know about each topic.

You have likely heard the phrase, "A picture is worth a thousand words." The phrase is accurate in the sense that people obtain a tremendous amount of information and details about their surroundings through sight.

The Eye and Vision

Good vision depends on the proper structure and function of the eyes. **Figure 22.19** shows the structures that make up the human eye. Light enters the eye by passing through a tough, transparent layer of cells known as the **cornea** (KOR nee uh). The convex shape of the cornea causes the incoming light rays to bend and begin converging. The light then passes through an opening called the **pupil.** Muscles control the amount of light entering the eye by changing the size of the pupil.

After passing through the pupil, the light strikes a flexible, convex lens. The **lens** bends the light so that it converges at a focal point on the back of the eye. Muscles change the shape of the lens so the eye can focus on nearby or faraway objects. Light rays come to a focus on the **retina** (RET nuh), the inner lining of the eye. Groups of light-sensitive cells lining the retina convert the light into nerve impulses. These impulses travel through the optic nerve to the brain. The brain interprets the impulses as vision.

Figure 22.19
Light bends as it passes through the eyes. The bending primarily occurs as light passes through the cornea and the lens. The incoming light rays come to a focus on the retina at the back of the eye.

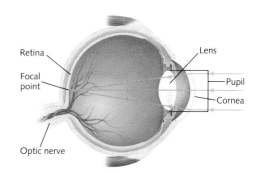

E L L Strategy

Discuss Arrange students in small groups and have them read the lesson aloud, taking turns for each section. Ask students to work with partners to discuss and summarize each section in a few sentences. Students should then write their summaries in their Science Notebooks. Students should include diagrams with their summaries.

Key Concept Review
Workbook, p. 138

Vision Problems

Properly shaped corneas and lenses are needed for good vision. So, too, are a flexible lens, good muscle control, and sensitive sensory cells. A problem in one or more of these areas causes reduced or poor vision. The most common vision problems—farsightedness, astigmatism, and nearsightedness—are easily fixed.

Farsightedness   Someone who is farsighted can see faraway objects clearly but cannot focus on nearby objects. The image is focused behind the retina instead of on the retina. As shown in **Figure 22.20,** the problem might be due to a lens that is not curved enough or an eyeball that is not long enough. Another cause of farsightedness is age. The lenses in the eyes become less flexible with age. The less-flexible lenses are not able to bend into the shape required to focus light on the retina. Fortunately, farsightedness is easy to correct. Placing a properly shaped convex lens in front of the eye will make the incoming light rays converge more quickly and come to a focus on the retina.

Figure It Out

1. Is the lens used to correct farsightedness a concave lens or a convex lens?
2. Why are the incoming light rays from the nearby object not parallel?

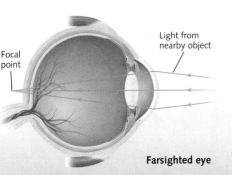

Farsighted eye

In a farsighted eye, the focal length of the eye is too long to form a sharp image of nearby objects on the retina.

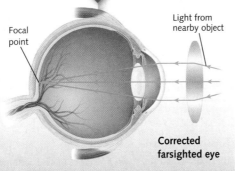

Corrected farsighted eye

A convex lens in front of a farsighted eye enables a sharp image to be focused on the retina.

Figure 22.20 Nearby objects are not brought into focus on the retina by people who are farsighted. A convex lens corrects the problem.

Astigmatism   When the cornea has an uneven curve, astigmatism (uh STIGH muh tih zum) results. Astigmatism commonly occurs when a cornea is oval in shape rather than round. Astigmatism results in blurry vision at all distances. The problem is corrected by wearing unevenly curved corrective lenses that cancel out the effects of the astigmatism.

As You Read

As you read the lesson, add facts to each section in the table in your Science Notebook. Be sure to include both main ideas and supporting details.

How does farsightedness affect a person's vision?

Teach

EXPLAIN to students that vision problems in humans occur when one of the eye structures does not function properly. Vision problems are often corrected with eyeglasses that have concave or convex lenses or another type of corrective lens.

Figure It Out: **Figure 22.20**

(ANSWER) **1.** convex lens **2.** Reflected light rays travel away from an object in all directions. When the viewer is close to an object, more of these diverging rays pass into the eye. By contrast, the rays from distant objects are nearly parallel.

As You Read

Have students update the facts in their Science Notebooks. Review students' work for accuracy.

(ANSWER) Farsightedness prevents a person from focusing clearly on nearby objects.

Differentiate Instruction

Kinesthetic Provide students with modeling clay and have them create three-dimensional models of the human eye. Suggest that students use a different color of clay for each part of the eye, and then have them provide a key to the colors and parts.

Background Information

One type of corrective eye surgery is refractive photokeratectomy (PKR). This surgery reshapes the cornea by removing microscopic amounts of tissue from the outer surface with a cool, computer-controlled ultraviolet beam of light.

A second type of surgery, LASIK, uses an excimer laser to change the cornea's shape. A flap is cut in the cornea, and pulses from a computer-controlled laser remove a portion of the stroma.

Teach

EXPLAIN to students that color blindness, unlike nearsightedness, farsightedness, and astigmatism, cannot be corrected with lenses. People with color blindness are born with the trait, like curly hair or brown eyes.

Use the Visual: Figure 22.22

ANSWER the number 8

Assess

Use the After You Read questions and the Alternative Assessment to help you evaluate students' understanding of the lesson.

After You Read

1. a lens that is not curved enough, an eyeball that is not long enough, a less-flexible lens caused by age

2. farsightedness: convex lens; nearsightedness: concave lens; astigmatism: lens with an uneven curvature to compensate for the effects of astigmatism

3. light passes through the cornea and is bent; light passes through the pupil and enters the lens; the lens bends the light and brings it to a focus on the retina; sensory cells on the retina convert the light into nerve impulses; the nerve impulses travel through the optic nerve to the brain; the brain interprets the impulses as vision

Alternative Assessment

Have students use the facts in their Science Notebooks to describe three types of vision problems. They should include the cause of each problem and how the problem can be resolved.

Nearsightedness In some ways, nearsightedness is the opposite of farsightedness. People who are nearsighted can see nearby objects clearly but cannot focus on distant objects. As shown in **Figure 22.21,** the problem occurs when light rays come to a focus before reaching the retina. An overly curved lens or an eyeball that is too long can cause nearsightedness. Placing a concave lens in front of the eye causes the light rays to diverge and increases the distance the light rays travel before coming into focus. A concave lens is used to correct nearsightedness.

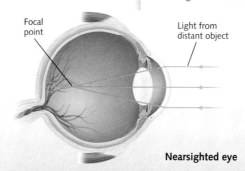

Nearsighted eye

When a nearsighted person looks at distant objects, the light rays from the objects are focused in front of the retina.

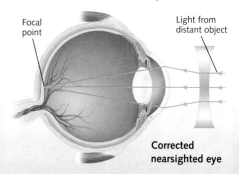

Corrected nearsighted eye

A concave lens in front of a nearsighted eye will diverge the light rays so they are focused on the retina.

Figure 22.21 Distant objects are not brought into focus on the retina by people who are nearsighted. A concave lens placed in front of the eye corrects nearsightedness.

Color Blindness Recall that the retina is lined with light-sensitive cells. Some of these sensory cells, called cones, allow a person to see color. There are three types of cones, each sensitive to wavelengths in a certain range of the visible spectrum. When one or more of the types of cones is missing or not functioning properly, color blindness occurs. Most people with color blindness do see colors, but they cannot see all of the colors that people with normal vision can. The number of people with some form of color blindness varies within groups of people. In general, however, about eight percent of men and somewhat less than one percent of women are color-blind. **Figure 22.22** shows a typical test used to diagnose color blindness.

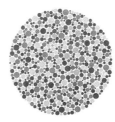

Figure 22.22 Color blindness is an inherited genetic trait. Tests that hide a number or letter in a field of colored dots are used to diagnose the problem. What number do you see in the figure?

After You Read

1. List several causes of farsightedness.

2. Identify the type of lenses needed to correct farsightedness, nearsightedness, and astigmatism.

3. Use the information in the table in your Science Notebook to create a flowchart that explains the process of vision.

Background Information

People with normal cones and light-sensitive pigment (trichromasy) can see all the different colors by using the cones sensitive to red, blue, and green. A mild form of color blindness occurs when one or more of the three cones are mildly affected. A more severe form of color blindness exists when the cones' light-sensitive pigments are strongly affected. About five to eight percent of males and 0.5 percent of females are born colorblind. Color blindness can be red-weakness or green-weakness; the inability to differentiate among red, orange, yellow, and green; or the dimming of red, orange, and yellow.

22.5 Using Light

Before You Read

Write the vocabulary terms for this lesson in your Science Notebook. As you read the lesson, use each term in a sentence of your own. Make sure that each of your sentences shows the meaning of the term.

Images produced by visible light contain a lot of information about one's surroundings. Because of this, many devices have been developed to collect and analyze light. Other devices use light to accomplish a task, such as transmitting data.

Polarized Light

Light is a transverse wave. Recall that transverse waves can be made in a rope by shaking the rope back and forth in any direction. Light waves emitted by the Sun are similar to those in a set of randomly shaken ropes—that is, the waves vibrate in all directions. Light waves that vibrate in all directions are said to be unpolarized. The waves of **polarized** (POH luh rizd) **light,** however, vibrate in a single direction only.

The lenses in some sunglasses have polarizing filters. Only sunlight that is polarized in a specific direction is able to pass through the lenses. When worn, polarizing lenses greatly reduce glare and make it easier to see on a sunny day. As shown in **Figure 22.23,** the polarizing lenses act like a group of parallel slits. Only transverse light waves with vibrations that align with the slits can pass through. If a second filter were positioned at a right angle to the first, all the light would be blocked.

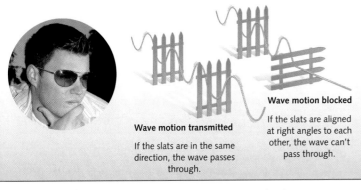

Wave motion transmitted

If the slats are in the same direction, the wave passes through.

Wave motion blocked

If the slats are aligned at right angles to each other, the wave can't pass through.

Figure 22.23 Polarizing sunglasses reduce glare from horizontal surfaces. The polarizing filters in the lenses are like slats in a fence.

Interpreting Diagrams
Workbook, p. 140

22.5 Introduce

ENGAGE Write the following phrases on the board: *making glass, accessing the Internet, drilling for oil, examining the liver.* Pair students and ask them to hypothesize about what these activities have in common. You might need to remind them that the lesson is about light, and the shared quality is related to light. Encourage students to discuss the processes involved in each phrase. Tell them that all of the processes involve fiber optics. Explain that fiber optic technology is one use of light that they will learn about in this lesson.

Before You Read

Write *polarized light* on the board. Have students work with partners to read the paragraphs about polarized light and then write a sentence that correctly uses the term. Ask students to share their sentences with the class, and provide support to students who did not define the term clearly.

Have students write the remaining vocabulary terms in their Science Notebooks, leaving space to write a sentence after each.

Teach

EXPLAIN to students that they will learn about using light to do work, such as in fiber optic technology, and to collect information about an environment.

Vocabulary

polarized light Explain to students that *pole* is the root of *polarize.* Ask students to brainstorm common uses of the word *pole.* Examples might include opposite ends of a magnet, the north or south poles, a long, straight piece of wood or metal, or two oppositional positions. Tell students that polarized light vibrates in one direction, similar to traveling the length of a pole.

Learning Goals

- Distinguish between polarized light and unpolarized light.
- Describe the uses of optical fibers.
- Relate telescopes and microscopes to the location and size of the objects they are used to observe.

New Vocabulary

polarized light
optical fiber
telescope
microscope

Recall Vocabulary

laser, p. 365

● Teach

EXPLAIN to students that light travels through optical fibers; the light travels within the fiber through total internal reflection. That is, the light reflects at an angle greater than the critical angle.

As You Read

Have students define *optical fiber* in a sentence in their Science Notebooks.
[ANSWER] Polarized light waves vibrate in a single direction (plane), whereas unpolarized light waves vibrate in random directions.

Figure It Out: **Figure 22.24**

[ANSWER] **1.** glass **2.** The light strikes the inside of the cable at an angle greater than the critical angle for the material, and the light undergoes total internal reflection. Even without the plastic sheathing, light would not escape from the fiber.

As You Read

Review what you have written in your Science Notebook about polarized light. Explain polarized light to a partner. Add to your notes if necessary.

How is unpolarized light different from polarized light?

Figure It Out

1. What material does the light travel through in the optical fiber?
2. Explain why the plastic coating shown covering the fiber is not required to keep the light from escaping.

Optical Fibers

Some laser applications require the laser light to be sent into hard-to-reach places. As shown in **Figure 22.24,** this is accomplished using optical fibers. **Optical fibers** are small "wires" made of transparent glass or plastic that use total internal reflection to transmit light. Total internal reflection occurs when light strikes a boundary at an angle greater than the critical angle. Regardless of the curving path the laser light follows within the optical fiber, total internal reflection occurs inside the fiber, and the light is trapped within the fiber—skipping off the interior glass layer. This allows nearly all of the laser energy to be transmitted to the end of the fiber.

Optical fibers are used frequently in communications. Telephone conversations, video data, and computer data can be converted into pulsing laser light. The laser signal is then transmitted along optical fibers. At the end of the fiber, a device converts the pulsing light data back into a signal that can be used. Optical fibers are also used by doctors to explore the inside of the body. Light is provided by one bundle of fibers, and images are carried back by another bundle of fibers.

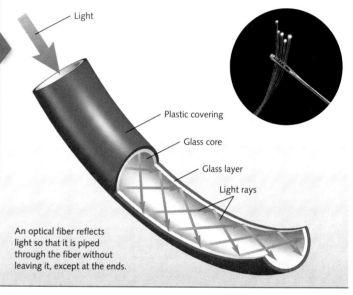

Light

Plastic covering

Glass core

Glass layer

Light rays

An optical fiber reflects light so that it is piped through the fiber without leaving it, except at the ends.

Figure 22.24 Optical fibers make use of total internal reflection to transmit light along curving paths.

Differentiate Instruction

Kinesthetic, Visual Have available a variety of optical fibers, telescopes, microscopes, binoculars, and cameras for students to examine. You might be able to obtain samples of optical fibers from your school computer department, science laboratory, or local telephone company. Allow students to observe the devices and identify the types of lenses in each.

Field Study

Have students walk around the school grounds and compare their vision with and without the use of optical devices. Have students note what they are able to observe with binoculars and telescopes and the level of visual detail available to them. English language learners should make notes of their observations while doing their field studies. Then, they should summarize their observations in their Science Notebooks.

Telescopes, Microscopes, and Cameras

Many optical devices use a series of lenses and mirrors to collect and magnify light. Common optical devices include the telescope, microscope, and camera.

Telescopes   A **telescope** (TEL uh skohp) uses a set of lenses and mirrors to collect light from very distant objects. A refracting telescope uses only lenses, whereas a reflecting telescope uses primarily mirrors. Because large lenses are extremely heavy and are difficult and expensive to manufacture, most larger-sized telescopes are reflecting telescopes. NASA's Hubble Space Telescope is a type of reflecting telescope.

Microscopes   The **microscope** (MI kruh skohp) uses two convex lenses to magnify small objects. The objective lens forms a magnified real image of the object. This real image is magnified again by the convex eyepiece lens, forming a larger virtual image for viewing. Magnifications of several hundred times are possible.

Cameras   The most popular consumer optical device is the camera. Most modern cameras use an optical sensor to record the image. When a person takes a photo, a shutter opens for a specific amount of time. Light reflected from the object passes through the lens, through the open shutter, and is focused on the surface of the optical sensor. The focused image is real, inverted, and smaller than the actual object. The optical sensor records the image as a pattern of pixels, or dots.

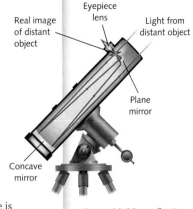

Eyepiece lens — Real image of distant object — Light from distant object — Plane mirror — Concave mirror

Figure 22.25 A reflecting telescope uses two mirrors to form a real image. The real image is then magnified for viewing by a convex eyepiece lens.

Eyepiece lens
Magnified real image
Objective lens
Object
Light source
Mirror

Figure 22.26 When the object to be viewed is one or two focal lengths away from the objective lens, a greatly magnified image is formed.

After You Read

1. Explain why optical fibers are used in communications and in medicine.
2. Explain why there are few large refracting telescopes.
3. Use the information about the vocabulary terms in your Science Notebook to explain which optical device is most similar to the human eye.

 Extend It!

Research the use of fiber optics in industry and medicine. Find out why optical fibers are useful for a particular application and why their use has advantages over other techniques. Summarize your findings in a short, well-developed paragraph.

● Teach

EXPLAIN to students that telescopes, microscopes, and cameras use both mirrors and lenses to collect light and form an image.

Vocabulary

optical fiber   Tell students that the root *optic* is derived from Greek and means "seen" or "visible." Ask students to list common uses of the word *fiber*. Responses might include plant cell walls, thread, cloth or material, or the fundamental character or quality of something. An optical fiber transmits light in a very thin filament.

telescope   Explain to students that the prefix *-tele* is Greek and means "far." The root *scope* is derived from Greek and means "to watch or view." Ask students how these derivations relate to the definition.

microscope   Tell students that the prefix *micro-* is derived from Greek and means "little." Remind students of the meaning of *scope*. The literal meaning of *microscope* is "to see little."

Extend It!

Accept any well-presented summary of why optical fibers are a useful technology for a particular application.

● Assess

Use the After You Read questions and the Alternative Assessment to help you evaluate students' understanding of the lesson.

After You Read

1. Optical fibers allow light data to be transmitted along curving paths to hard-to-reach places.
2. Large lenses required by a large refracting telescope are very heavy and expensive to manufacture. The large lenses also begin to distort under their own weight.
3. A camera is most similar to the human eye. Both adjust focus for nearby and distant objects, control the amount of light that enters, form real and inverted images, and focus the image on a light-sensitive surface.

Background Information

In 1590, a Dutch eyeglass maker named Zaccharias Janssen and his son, Hans, noticed that objects viewed through a tube appeared much larger. This was the beginning of both the compound microscope and telescope. In 1674, Anton van Leeuwenhoek built a simple microscope with one lens. He also created new methods to grind and polish lenses to increase their curvatures and improve magnification.

Alternative Assessment

Students should use the sentences in their Science Notebooks to compare and contrast telescopes and microscopes.

Chapter 22 Summary

MASTERING CONCEPTS

True or False

1. False, Regular
2. True
3. False, refract
4. True
5. False, Translucent
6. False, white
7. False, far-away
8. False, concave

Short Answer

9. A smooth surface allows a reflection to form a clear image. A pond's surface is not smooth when it is windy.

10. The light rays will be reflected and converge at the focal point of the mirror.

11. Sunlight strikes a spherical water droplet in the air and refracts. The different wavelengths refract different amounts inside the drop, so the white light separates into a band of colors.

12. Sodium vapor lamps primarily emit yellow-orange light of a single wavelength. Thus, objects that normally reflect wavelengths other than this yellow-orange wavelength look odd.

13. Light inside the eye mainly refracts as it passes through the cornea and the lens.

14. A polarizing filter acts like a group of parallel slits. Only transverse light waves with vibrations that align with the slits can pass through.

KEY CONCEPTS

22.1 Shadows and Reflections

- Shadows form where light rays cannot reach.
- Regular reflection occurs when light reflects evenly from a surface. Diffuse reflection scatters rays in many directions.
- Diverging light rays form virtual images. Virtual images cannot be projected onto a screen. Converging light rays form real images that can be projected onto a screen.
- Common mirror shapes are plane, convex, and concave. Plane and convex mirrors produce virtual images. Concave mirrors can form virtual and real images.

22.2 Refraction—The Bending of Light

- The index of refraction is a measure of the change in the speed of light as it enters a material.
- A prism breaks white light into components because each wavelength refracts a different amount through the prism.
- A mirage occurs when a low layer of hot air bends light rays.
- Convex lenses can form images that are upright or inverted, enlarged or reduced, and real or virtual. Concave lenses can form reduced-size virtual images.
- Total internal reflection occurs when light strikes a new material at an angle greater than the critical angle.

22.3 Color

- Nothing can be seen through an opaque material. Light, but not clear images, can be seen through translucent materials. Clear images can be seen through transparent materials.
- Objects appear the color of the visible light waves they reflect.
- The primary light colors form white light when mixed. The primary pigments mix to form black.

22.4 Vision—How You See

- The eye's main structures are the cornea, pupil, lens, retina, and optic nerve. The brain receives nerve impulses from the retina.
- Common vision problems include farsightedness, astigmatism, and nearsightedness, which can be corrected with lenses.
- The inability to see certain colors is known as color blindness.

22.5 Using Light

- Polarized light waves all vibrate in the same direction.
- Fiber optics use total internal reflection to transmit light energy.
- Telescopes magnify light from distant objects. Microscopes magnify small objects. Cameras use lenses and an optical sensor to record the image of an object.

VOCABULARY REVIEW

Write each term in a complete sentence or write a paragraph relating several terms.

22.1
shadow, p. 369
plane mirror, p. 370
regular reflection, p. 370
diffuse reflection, p. 370
convex mirror, p. 370
virtual image, p. 371
concave mirror, p. 372
focal point, p. 372
real image, p. 372

22.2
index of refraction, p. 373
mirage, p. 374
convex lens, p. 374
concave lens, p. 376
critical angle, p. 376

22.3
opaque, p. 377
transparent, p. 377
translucent, p. 377
pigment, p. 378

22.4
cornea, p. 380
pupil, p. 380
lens, p. 380
retina, p. 380

22.5
polarized light, p. 383
optical fiber, p. 384
telescope, p. 385
microscope, p. 385

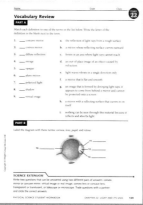

Vocabulary Review
Workbook, p. 139

Reading Comprehension
Workbook, p. 141

MASTERING CONCEPTS

True or False

If the statement is true, write "true." If it is false, change the underlined word or words to make the statement true.

1. <u>Diffuse</u> reflection forms clear images.

2. Diverging light rays form <u>virtual</u> images.

3. A mirage forms when a hot air layer causes light waves to <u>interfere</u>.

4. When total internal reflection occurs, there is no <u>refraction</u>.

5. <u>Opaque</u> materials allow some light to pass though them.

6. Mixing red, blue, and green light creates <u>black</u> light.

7. Someone with nearsightedness cannot see objects that are <u>nearby</u>.

8. A <u>convex</u> lens causes light rays to diverge.

Short Answer

Answer each of the following in a sentence or brief paragraph.

9. Explain why you can often see your reflection in a pond on a still morning but cannot on a windy morning.

10. Describe what will happen when light rays travel toward a concave mirror parallel to its optical axis.

11. Explain how a rainbow forms.

12. Explain why objects look odd when viewed at night under the bright yellow light from an outdoor lamp.

13. Identify the two main locations where light rays refract inside the eye.

14. Explain how a polarizing filter works.

Critical Thinking

Use what you have learned in this chapter to answer each of the following.

15. **Infer** Why can't a convex mirror or a concave lens form a real image?

16. **Select** Which type of mirror would you select for each of the following uses: to monitor the aisles of a small store, to see how your clothes look before school, and to see an enlarged image of your face? Explain your answers.

17. **Apply Concepts** A shoe appears red in sunlight. How will the shoe look if all wavelengths of visible light except red shine on it? Explain your answer.

Standardized Test Question

Choose the letter of the response that correctly answers the question.

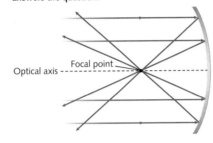

18. Which describes a light ray that passes through the focal point and then strikes the mirror?

   A. It travels parallel to the optical axis.

   B. It forms a real image.

   C. It is reflected back through the focal point.

   D. It forms a virtual image.

> **Test-Taking Tip**
>
> Don't get stuck on a difficult question. Instead, make a small mark next to the question. Remember to go back and answer the question later. Other parts of the test may give you a clue that will help you answer the question.

Critical Thinking

15. Each causes light rays to diverge. Real images only form when light rays converge.

16. A convex mirror should be used for the store because it offers a wide field of view and produces an upright image. A plane mirror forms clear life-sized images and would work well for checking one's appearance before leaving for school. The upright and magnified image formed by a concave mirror is ideal for examining the face up-close.

17. The shoe will appear black because it does not reflect any visible light.

Standardized Test Question

18. A

Reading Links

Highlights from the Hubble Telescope: Postcards from Space

With a stunning array of color images captured by the Hubble and engaging, manageable text, this book will appeal to students with a range of interests and ability levels. Readers will discover more about the telescope and its capacity to document such remarkable objects in the universe.

Melanie Chrismer. Enslow Publishers. 48 pp. Illustrated. Library ISBN 978-0-7660-2135-8.

Louis Daguerre and the Story of the Daguerreotype

Readers of this simple and informative biography will learn how one pioneer's scientific curiosity, careful experimentation, understanding and manipulation of light, and artistry led to important developments in photography at a critical juncture.

John Bankston. Mitchell Lane Publishers. 48 pp. Illustrated. Library ISBN 978-1-58415-247-7.

Curriculum Connection
Workbook, p. 142

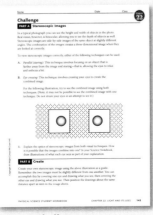

Science Challenge
Workbook, p. 143

22A Mirror Images

This prechapter introduction activity is designed to determine what students already know about mirrors and the reflection of light by having them make observations, compare, relate, and draw conclusions about how images are formed.

Objectives

- observe images
- describe image properties
- relate shapes to convex and concave mirrors
- record observations

Planning

 15–20 minutes   groups of 3–4 students

Materials (per group)

- shiny metal spoon
- pencil
- paper
- meterstick

Advance Preparation

- Ask students to make a table to record their observations.
- Purchase or bring large, shiny serving spoons from home. This activity also works with smaller spoons, but the effects are less dramatic.
- Encourage all students in the group to produce images using the spoon.

Engagement Guide

- Challenge students to think about what kind of images will be formed by the spoon by asking:
  - *What kinds of mirrors have you used or seen that were curved outward?* (Students should recognize that mirrors that curve outward—convex—provide wide angle views, so they are used in rearview or side-view mirrors of cars. They are also used in security mirrors in banks and stores.)
  - *Where have you seen mirrors that were curved inward?* (Students should recognize that mirrors that curve in—concave—are in shaving mirrors and makeup mirrors. They form an enlarged, upright image of a person's face.)
  - *Will the curved mirror surfaces send the reflected rays away from one another or make them converge?* (Students should recognize that a convex mirror can only cause the rays to diverge; concave mirrors can cause light rays to converge or diverge, depending on the location of the object.)
- Encourage students to communicate their conclusions in creative ways.

Going Further

Encourage students to make a list of all the mirrors they see during an average day. Have students describe what each is used for and try to identify each one as flat, concave, or convex. Have students share their lists with the rest of the class.

22B Mixing Colored Lights

Objectives

- observe the mixing of colored light
- relate color components to the resulting color formed
- illustrate color mixing that yields white light

Skill Set

observing, predicting, illustrating, inferring, drawing conclusions

Planning

 45–60 minutes   groups of 3–4 students

Materials

Materials for this activity are listed in the Student Laboratory Manual.

Advance Preparation

- Colored cellophane may be purchased at craft stores or florists. Supply each group with enough colored cellophane to cover the end of the flashlight.
- Rubber bands or tape may be used to secure cellophane to the flashlight.
- Small flashlights, such as those on the ends of keychains, can be used.
- A white wall may be used instead of making a screen.
- Find out if any students are color-blind, and pair them up with students who are not.

Answers to Observations: Data Table 1

Data Table 1		
Color Light Combination	Color Formed From Mixing	Drawing of Color Combinations
Red + Green	Yellow	Drawing shows overlapped red and green light with yellow in the center between them.
Green + Blue	Cyan	Drawing shows overlapped green and blue light with cyan in the center between them.
Red + Blue	Magenta	Drawing shows overlapped red and blue light with magenta in the center between them.
Red + Green + Blue	White	Drawing shows overlapped red, green, and blue light with white in the center.

Answers to Analysis and Conclusions

1. The three secondary colors are yellow, cyan, and magenta.
2. White is formed because all of the primary light colors are reflected. Because you do not see any of the colors, white light is not considered a true color.
3. Pairs of secondary colors mix to form the primary color; yellow, cyan, and magenta will combine in pairs to create red, green, and blue.
4. You would not get white paint because you would not have the same result as you would mixing primary colors of light. All of the colors would be absorbed, and you would end up with a nearly black can of paint. Black is not a color, but a lack of color.
5. Red, green, and blue lights are called primary color lights because you can get all the colors you see by mixing these three colors in different proportions.

Going Further

Have students repeat the activity using yellow, cyan, and magenta cellophane. Students can use combinations of these colors to see if they can create the red, green, and blue primary colors. Ask students to produce white light by combining the three colors of light. Have them present their findings in a colored chart.

22C Reflection of Light

Objectives

- observe light rays
- identify and measure angles of incidence and reflection
- relate angles of incidence and reflection

Skill Set

observing, comparing and contrasting, recording and analyzing data, illustrating, stating conclusions

Planning

 30–35 minutes   groups of 3–4 students

Materials

Materials for this activity are listed in the Student Laboratory Manual.

Advance Preparation

- Prepare corrugated cardboard for each group by cutting the cardboard into 23-cm × 30-cm pieces.
- Small mirrors, 4" × 6", can be purchased at a science supply house or discount store.
- Supply each group with two pieces of clay to support the mirror.

Answers to Observations: Data Table 1

Students' answers for Data Table 1 should reflect that the angle of incidence is equal to the angle of reflection.

Students' drawings from the activity should be turned in. Students' drawings should have the incident light ray labeled *I*; the reflected light ray labeled *R*; the dotted line at a right angle to the mirror labeled *normal*; the angle between the incident light ray and the normal line labeled *angle of incidence*; and the angle between the normal line and the reflected light ray labeled *angle of reflection*.

Answers to Analysis and Conclusions

1. Students' answers should reflect that the angle of incidence is equal to the angle of reflection.
2. Students' results should verify the law of reflection. Results should be consistent throughout the class.
3. The image appears to be located as far behind of the mirror as the object is located in front of the mirror.
4. All reflected waves obey the law of reflection. Regular reflection occurs when light rays reflect from a smooth surface at the same angle. This produces a clear image. The surface of a brick wall is rough and reflects the incident rays in many directions. These waves still obey the law of reflection, they just don't reflect uniformly or form an image.

Going Further

Draw a diagram of a plane mirror on the board along with three incident rays approaching it at different angles. Have student volunteers draw the normal line for each ray and then determine its path of reflection.

Unit 6

Case Study 1: Wave Power

Gather More Information

Have students use the following key terms to aid their searches:

- clean energy
- Islay power station
- New Jersey wave power plant
- ocean waves
- wave power

Research the Big Picture

- Have students work in groups to explore wave power designs in more detail. Groups should find out more about how the technology works and create a labeled diagram or model, which they can present to the class. They should also find information about the amount of electricity the plant can produce, where it can be sited, and any potential problems and precautions that engineers must consider.

- Have students work in pairs to research another clean, renewable energy source that could help reduce reliance on oil and other fossil fuels. Some possibilities are wind power, solar power, geothermal energy, and bioenergy. Pairs should find out how the technology works, how much energy it can generate, and how widespread its use is today. Ask pairs to develop a poster or visual presentation.

Case Study 2: New Eye in Space

Have students use the following key terms to aid their searches:

- infrared sensors
- James Webb Space Telescope
- Hubble Space Telescope
- light-gathering mirror
- reflecting telescope
- spectrometer

Research the Big Picture

- Have students work in pairs to compare and contrast the new James Webb Telescope and the Hubble Telescope. In their research, students should focus on how the new telescope's technologies, such as infrared sensors and a light-gathering mirror, can expand on the Hubble's past discoveries. The finished projects can take the form of a poster, illustration, or pair of models.

Wave Power

The search is on for new ways to produce electricity. Today, most power plants burn coal, oil, and natural gas to generate electric power. Those fossil fuels create pollution, however—especially gases such as carbon dioxide that increase global warming. Scientists looking for cleaner, cheaper energy sources may have found one in ocean waves.

How do you produce electricity from ocean waves? In one process, the power plant stands where waves crash on the shore with great force. The waves enter a chamber, and as they rush in, they compress a column of air inside the chamber. The air is forced through a hole to turn the blades of a turbine. The turbine then spins a generator that produces an electric current. As the water then rushes out, it sucks air out with it, creating additional

pressure. This pressure also forces the turbine to turn. A small wave power station on the coast of a Scottish island named Islay works this way. It supplies power for a few hundred homes.

There are several other wave power designs. One funnels waves into an enclosure on the shore. The rushing water turns a turbine as it spills over the walls of the enclosure and flows back out to sea.

Several small projects testing ways to harness wave power are currently underway. One such test plant sits off the coast of New Jersey. Another might soon be placed in New York City's East River. Planners in San Francisco hope to use waves in San Francisco Bay to produce power for the city. There is also a group of wave generators in use off the coast of Portugal.

Wave power plants do present some problems. For example, engineers must make sure they do not harm sea life. However, wave power is clean and inexpensive. Once the power plants are built, the fuel is free and plentiful.

Wave power will never provide most of the electric power countries need, but it could help human populations depend less on coal and oil. Energy from the ocean could be the wave of the future.

CAREER CONNECTION SIGN LANGUAGE INTERPRETER

You've probably seen something like this many times: An official is giving an important speech. To the side, a person is gesturing with his or her hands. That person is a sign language interpreter. He or she is translating the speech into signs that the deaf can read.

A sign language interpreter's job is to help deaf people and people who can hear communicate with each other. Sign language interpreters in the U.S. must know American Sign Language (ASL) and English. ASL is made up of hand gestures, facial expressions, and body movements.

There is a great need for sign language interpreters. They work at town meetings, in school classrooms, in hospitals, and in courtrooms. In fact, you can find them

anywhere the deaf and the hearing need to communicate with each other.

Many sign language interpreters have college degrees, but not all of them do. They must take college-level courses in ASL. They typically take other courses, such as public speaking and linguistics. They also take courses on deaf culture and must practice sign language interpretation under the guidance of a teacher. When interpreters finish training, they take a test to earn a certificate.

Standards for sign language interpreters are high. They do an important job: they are a bridge between the deaf and people who can hear.

CAREER CONNECTION: Sign Language Interpreter

As students read the feature, have them list in their Science Notebooks all the different places that sign language interpreters work. If they can think of any additional places, have them add those to the list, as well. Then have each student write a brief essay about the importance of sign language

interpreters in our society and some of the interesting aspects of their work. Ask them to consider and describe some of the challenges of translating spoken language into visible symbols. Ask: *What types of things might be relatively easy to translate? What might be more difficult?*

New Eye in Space

The Hubble Space Telescope went into orbit around Earth in 1990. Without Earth's atmosphere in the way, the Hubble telescope allowed astronomers to see objects in space better than ever. However, the Hubble telescope is getting old. Scientists are now gaining a new eye in the sky—the James Webb Space Telescope.

The Webb telescope will be more than just a newer Hubble telescope. It will be a more powerful telescope with the ability to see wavelengths of light that the Hubble telescope could not see. Like the Hubble telescope, the Webb telescope will be a reflecting telescope. However, the Webb telescope will pick up mostly infrared radiation from space rather than visible light. The only way to see the most distant objects in the universe is to pick up the infrared light they emit. With the Webb telescope, astronomers will see many of these objects for the first time.

Its infrared sensors will see through the gas and dust that blocks light telescopes. Astronomers hope to find new galaxies and solar systems, and they expect to see the birth of new stars. The Webb telescope will also carry a spectrometer. This tool can analyze radiation from an object in space to find its chemical composition, temperature, and motion.

The Webb telescope will have a light-gathering mirror that measures 6.5 meters in diameter, which will be six times the diameter of the Hubble telescope's mirror. In 2013, a rocket will take the telescope into orbit. Its orbit will be much farther from Earth than the Hubble's. It will be almost 1.5 million kilometers from Earth—beyond the orbit of the Moon. It will be this far because the telescope must stay icy cold. If not, its own heat would interfere with its infrared sensors, and at this distance it will stay at a temperature of about –233°C. A sunshield will also fold out to protect the telescope from direct sunlight and sunlight reflected from Earth or the Moon.

Named in honor of the man who led NASA during the time of the Apollo program, the James Webb Space Telescope will be a powerful new eye in space.

Blocking the Sun

People used to think that suntans were healthy. Now we know that a suntan means that the Sun has damaged the skin. To protect itself, the skin's cells produce a dark pigment called melanin, which is what produces the tan.

Sunlight is energy of many wavelengths. It is ultraviolet (UV) radiation, however, that does the damage. Most UV is a type called UVA, which has the longest wavelengths and penetrates deep into the skin. Over time, too much UVA causes skin to get tough and wrinkled. UVA is also linked to skin cancer. Another UV type, called UVB, doesn't

penetrate as deeply into skin as UVA does, but it is more intense. UVB is the part of UV that tans and burns the skin. It is strongly linked to skin cancer. A third type of UV, called UVC, is blocked by ozone in the atmosphere.

Sunscreens help people avoid some of the damage that ultraviolet radiation can cause. Sunscreens contain chemicals that help block UV from reaching the skin. However, many sunscreens block only UVB. In fact, the SPF (Sun Protection Factor) numbers displayed on sunscreen labels refer only to UVB protection. They indicate the degree of protection by comparing the time it takes for the skin to get red and burn with and without the sunscreen. For example, if a person's skin normally burns in 20 minutes, an SPF-15 sunscreen will protect the skin for about five hours. Dermatologists recommend the use of sunscreens that block both types of UV, so reading labels is important.

389

- Have students research the history of the Hubble Space Telescope and create an illustrated time line of its development, use, and scientific contributions.

Case Study 3: Blocking the Sun

Have students use the following key terms to aid their searches:

melanin

skin cancer

solar energy

sunscreen

ultraviolet radiation

UVA

UVB

UVC

Research the Big Picture

- Have students work in groups to research commercially available Sun protection. They can visit local supermarkets and drug stores to survey products and protection potential. Then they should augment their research with any product information they can find in news publications, on the Internet, or from consumer advocacy organizations. Have students create charts or spreadsheets listing their top ten recommendations, and have them each write a paragraph explaining the choices.

- Have students work in pairs to research ultraviolet radiation and other kinds of solar energy in more detail. Students should be able to identify the wavelengths of different types of solar energy, including those of UVA, UVB, and UVC. Have pairs create diagrams or charts displaying these wavelengths, identifying which ones are blocked by the ozone layer, which are harmful, and which are necessary to people and other life forms.

Unit 7

Introduce Unit 7

Introduce the topic of the final unit, electricity and magnetism. Ask: *How many ways do you use magnets and electric charges and currents in your own homes?* Help students understand that they will learn how electric charges and currents are created and how they behave. They will also learn about magnetic poles and fields, and how electricity can produce magnetism and vice versa. Finally, they will explore the nature of electronic devices.

Ask students to write five facts they already know about electricity and magnetism in their Science Notebooks. Then have them write five things they want to learn.

Unit Projects

For each Unit Project, have students use the Presentation Builder on the Student CD-ROM to display their results.

Career Research Have each student choose a career related to electricity and magnetism such as electrician or computer systems engineer.

Have students research the chosen career. Each student should be able to provide a detailed job description, including any skills and education requirements. Encourage students to be creative in presenting their careers.

Hands-On Research Have students experiment with static electricity by providing small groups with at least some of the following materials: a glass; swatches of nylon, wool, fur, silk, cotton, and polyester; a rubber comb; an inflated balloon. Have students experiment by rubbing different combinations of materials together and observing what happens.

Technology Research Have students research navigational, medical, and communications technologies that utilize magnets. Explain that MRI machines create detailed images of organs and structures inside the human body by using the magnetic properties of atoms.

Unit 7

Electricity and Magnetism

Chapter 23 Electric Charges and Currents
What is electricity?

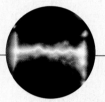

Chapter 24 Magnetism
What kind of forces do magnets produce?

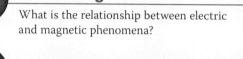

Chapter 25 Electromagnetism
What is the relationship between electric and magnetic phenomena?

Chapter 26 Electronic Technology
What is the relationship between electricity and electronic devices?

390

Software Summary

Student CD-ROM
—Interactive Student Book
—Vocabulary Review
—Key Concept Review
—Lab Report Template
—ELL Preview and Writing Activities
—Presentation Digital Library
—Graphic Organizing Software
—Spanish Cognate Dictionary

Interactive Labs
Chapter 26B—Telegraphing Messages

Electric Charges and Currents

KEY CONCEPT Electricity is the movement of charged subatomic particles called electrons.

One hot August day in northeast Ohio, a high-voltage power line started to sag, brushing against a few overgrown tree branches. Instantly, electric current surged through the tree and headed for the ground. A computer system quickly detected the line's short circuit and shut it down. Other lines soon overloaded and shut down as well. Over the next two hours, over 100 power plants were shut down, and 50 million people in the northeast United States and Canada were left in the dark.

Electricity is the movement of charged particles from one place to another. These movements can light up cities, produce lightning bolts, and cause massive blackouts.

Think About Electricity

People use electric energy by converting it into other kinds of energy, such as heat, motion, sound, or light.

- In your Science Notebook, list some things you use electricity for every day.
- For each item on your list, write the form of energy into which the electric energy is converted.

NSTA
SCLINKS.
THE WORLD'S A CLICK AWAY
www.scilinks.org
Electricity **Code: WGPS23**

391

Introduce Chapter 23

As a starting activity, use Lab 23A on page 133 of the Laboratory Manual.

ENGAGE Have students read the introductory paragraph. Then either supply them with or have them locate additional sources that relate to the blackout, such as articles from newspapers in northeastern U.S. cities. Have pairs of students read different articles and share the information with other pairs.

Think About Electricity

ENGAGE Write the word *electricity* in the center of the board, and write *heat, motion, sound,* and *light* underneath it. Ask students to think about activities that they took part in yesterday and today that required electricity. Ask which kind of energy it was converted into: heat, motion, sound, light, or something else. Record a few responses on the board.

Chapter 23 Planning Guide

Instructional Periods	National Standards	Lab Manual	Workbook
23.1 2 Periods	B.2; B.4; UCP.2, UCP.3;	**Lab 23A: p. 133** Static Electricity	Key Concept Review p. 144
23.2 1 Period	A.1, B.1, B.2, F.1, F.3; A.1, B.2, B.4, F.1, F.5; UCP.1, UCP.4	**Lab 23B :**	Vocabulary Review p. 145
23.3 2 Periods	A.2, B.1, B.2, C.1, E.2, G.2; A.2, B.2, B.4, B.6, C.1, E.2, G.2; UCP.1, UCP.5	**pp. 134–135** Conductors and Insulators	Interpreting Diagrams p. 146 Reading Comprehension p. 147 Curriculum Connection p. 148 Science Challenge pp. 149–150
23.4 3 Periods	A.1, B.2, B.3, E.1, F.5; A.1, B.4, B.6, E.1, F.5, F.6; UCP.1, UCP.3	**Lab 23C:** **pp. 136–137** Series and Parallel	
23.5 1 Period	A.1, B.3, E.2, F.5; A.2, B.6, E.2, F.6; UCP.3	Circuits	

Middle School Standard; High School Standard; Unifying Concept and Principle

ENGAGE Have students look at the photographs and read the captions in this lesson. Then have them predict what they will learn.

Vocabulary terms are listed on the first student page of each lesson. You may wish to preview the terms before introducing each lesson. Strategies for teaching the vocabulary appear on the pages where the terms are introduced.

Before You Read

Ask students how to create a lesson outline. Ask what the purpose of an outline is and why they think they will be creating one for this lesson. Have a volunteer provide information from the first page of the lesson that belongs in the outline. Tell students to complete the outline in their Science Notebooks for this lesson.

● Teach

EXPLAIN to students that in this lesson, they will learn about positively charged protons, electrically neutral neutrons, and negatively charged electrons.

Encourage students to use the vocabulary section they created in their Science Notebooks. Remind them to record prefixes, suffixes, and root words to help them remember the vocabulary terms.

◯ Vocabulary

atom Tell students that the word *atom* is from the Greek word *atomos,* meaning "something that cannot be divided."

nucleus Tell students that the word *nucleus* comes from the Latin word for "kernel."

proton Tell students that *proton* comes from the Greek word *protos,* meaning "first."

neutron Explain to students that the word *neutron* comes from the Latin word *neuter,* meaning "neither," and the suffix *-on,* which is used in physics to indicate an elementary particle.

electron Explain to students that *electron* is a noun that comes from *electro,* which denotes electricity, and the suffix *-on.*

ion Tell students that *ion* is a Greek word meaning "going."

Learning Goals

- Identify which parts of an atom carry charge.
- Explain how charged particles interact with one another.
- Describe the behavior of an electric field.

New Vocabulary

atom
nucleus
proton
neutron
electron
ion
electric field

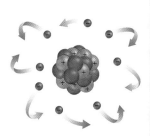

Figure 23.2 Every atom is made up of positively charged protons (orange), uncharged neutrons (blue), and negatively charged electrons (red). What must be true of the numbers of protons and electrons in an electrically neutral atom?

Use the Visual: Figure 23.2

ANSWER In an electrically neutral atom, the number of protons must be equal to the number of electrons.

23.1 What Is Electric Charge?

Before You Read

Create a lesson outline in your Science Notebook using the title and headings of this lesson. Use the outline to think about what you will learn in this lesson.

Have you ever rubbed an inflated balloon against your hair and then placed it on the wall? If so, you know that the balloon sticks to the wall. What seems like magic is actually the result of electric charge. There are two types of electric charge: positive and negative. Rubbing the balloon against your hair gives the balloon a negative charge. The charged balloon sticks to things with a positive charge, like the wall. The charge itself is invisible. It comes from the tiny particles that are inside atoms.

Figure 23.1 When a balloon is rubbed against hair, the balloon becomes negatively charged and the hair becomes positively charged. The hair is attracted to the charged balloon.

Atoms and Electric Charge

Everything around you is made up of atoms. **Atoms** are the basic building blocks of matter. An atom is made up of three kinds of subatomic particles. Some of the particles are electrically charged. The **nucleus** (NEW klee us), or center, of an atom contains positively charged **protons** (PROH tahnz) and neutral, or uncharged, **neutrons** (NEW trahnz). Tiny, negatively charged **electrons** (ih LEK trahnz) move around the nucleus in the electron cloud. An electron has exactly the same amount of negative charge as a proton has positive charge. If an atom has the same number of protons and electrons, the charges cancel out and the atom is said to be electrically neutral.

Electrons can move from one atom to another. If electrons are stripped off an atom, the atom will have more protons than electrons and become positively charged. If an atom attracts extra electrons, it will have more electrons than protons and become negatively charged. A positively or negatively charged atom is called an **ion** (I ahn).

ⒺⓁⓁ Strategy

Practice Using Vocabulary, Paraphrase Have students work in pairs to practice using the vocabulary terms in this lesson. Encourage students to use the terms in sentences, give examples, and put the definitions in their own words.

Electric Forces

It is not possible to look at an object and tell whether it is positively or negatively charged. However, charged particles exert forces on one another. These forces can affect matter. They make your hair stand up when you take off a wool hat. They make socks just out of the clothes dryer stick together. They can produce small sparks and large lightning bolts. When charged particles move, they produce the electrical current that runs equipment like MP3 players and toasters.

Charged particles behave in predictable ways. Objects with the same type of charge always repel one another. If you move two positively charged objects close to each other, they will try to push apart. The same thing happens for two negatively charged objects. Objects with opposite charges, however, always attract one another. A negatively charged object will move toward a positively charged object. You can observe this by moving a comb near your head after running it through your hair. The comb strips electrons from hair, so the comb becomes negatively charged and the hair becomes positively charged. When the comb is placed near the charged hair, the hair moves toward the comb.

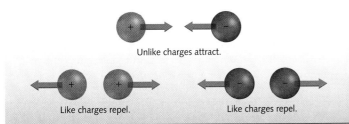

Unlike charges attract.

Like charges repel.   Like charges repel.

Figure 23.3 An object with a positive charge and an object with a negative charge are attracted to each other. Objects with the same charge—either two positives or two negatives—repel each other.

Recall that a force is a push or pull between objects. The electric force is the attraction between opposite charges and the repulsion between like charges. The strength of the electric force between a pair of charged objects depends on the magnitude of the charge on each object and the distance between the objects. The electric force is directly related to the magnitude of the charges of the objects. The charge is inversely related to the distance between the objects. In other words, the electric force between a pair of charged objects increases as the charge on those objects increases, and the electric force decreases as the distance between the objects increases.

CHAPTER 23 **393**

As You Read

Using the information in your outline, draw a diagram of a carbon atom in your Science Notebook. A carbon atom has six protons and six neutrons in its nucleus. Label the protons, neutrons, and electrons with their charges. Write a sentence explaining why the overall charge on the atom is zero.

What is an ion?

 **CONNECTION: Technology**

Photocopiers use charged particles to make identical copies of original documents. Each machine contains a negatively charged material that is sensitive to light, as well as ink with a positive charge. When a document is placed inside a photocopier, the dark areas on the paper remain negatively charged and attract droplets of the positively charged ink. When the ink soaks into the paper, it makes an exact copy of the original document.

Differentiate Instruction

Kinesthetic Have students experiment with their hair, combs, balloons, clothes, and other objects to demonstrate positive and negative electric charges. Students should rub different combinations of objects together and then place them near other objects, such as bits of tissue paper or a thin stream of water from a faucet, to observe any changes.

● Teach

EXPLAIN to students that they will learn about charged particles. Explain that a particle is a tiny piece of matter.

As You Read

Give students time to fill in their outlines and draw and label their atom diagrams. Then have each student write a paragraph explaining his or her diagram.

ANSWER The overall charge on the atom is zero, because the atom has the same number of electrons and protons (six). The positive and negative charges cancel each other out. An ion is an atom with an unequal number of protons and electrons.

Science Notebook EXTRA

Have students record in their Science Notebooks what they discovered about positive and negative charges from the Differentiate Instruction activity below.

 CONNECTION: Technology

Explain to students that before photocopiers, carbon copies were used. When a person needed to copy something, he or she placed a piece of carbon paper between sheets of paper and then either used a typewriter or wrote by hand on the top sheet. What the person typed or wrote was copied onto the sheets below.

Give each student a piece of photocopied paper and ask him or her to label the negatively and positively charged parts of the page.

● Teach

 EXPLAIN that students will learn about electric fields, which describe the forces exerted by charged particles.

Vocabulary

electric field Tell students that *electric* is an adjective meaning "relating to or produced by electricity," and that *field* is a noun that commonly means "an area of open grassland."

Figure It Out: Figure 23.4

[ANSWER] **1.** The positive charge would move away from the positively charged particle. **2.** The negatively charged particle would move toward the positive one.

● Assess

Use the After You Read questions and the Alternative Assessment to help you evaluate students' understanding of the lesson.

After You Read

1. The new diagram shows a positively charged ion that has six protons, six neutrons, and five electrons.
2. An atom has an equal number of protons (positively charged particles) and electrons (negatively charged particles). An ion is a charged atom. It has either lost or gained one or more electrons.
3. The objects will repel each other.
4. The electric fields created by the particles extend into the space around the particles. The force can be felt throughout the fields.

Alternative Assessment

Give students time to finish their outlines. Then have each student write a paragraph explaining what he or she learned about atoms, electric charges, or electric fields.

Electric Fields

In the experiment with the hair and comb, the hair is attracted to the charged comb even when the two objects are not touching. The charges exert force on one another through an electric field. An **electric field** consists of electric forces exerted in the area around an electric charge.

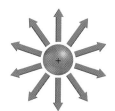 

Figure 23.4 These diagrams show the electric fields around charged particles as a set of arrows. The arrows point in the direction that a positive charge would move if it were placed inside the field.

Every charged particle produces an electric field that is perpendicular to the particle's surface. The strength of the field depends on the distance from the particle. Closer to the charged particle, the electric field is stronger. Farther away from the particle, it is weaker. Any charged particle that is placed inside an electric field will get pushed away or pulled closer, depending on that particle's charge. Stronger electric fields attract and repel other charged particles with greater force than do weaker fields.

After You Read

1. Imagine that one electron has been removed from the diagram you drew in your Science Notebook. Based on the information you have recorded in your outline, draw a second diagram that shows the newly formed ion.
2. What is the relationship between an atom and an ion?
3. Explain how two positively charged objects behave if they are brought close together.
4. Explain why charged particles react to one another even when they are not touching.

Background Information

Benjamin Franklin is credited with developing the naming convention of positive (plus) and negative (minus) charges for particles. The names themselves are arbitrary. There is nothing inherent in a charge that makes one positive and the other negative. Franklin simply wanted to identify them as opposites. He could have chosen the charge on an electron to be positive and the charge on a proton to be negative. Such a reversal would not have had any affect on the understanding of the concept. Just as easily, Franklin could have also named the charges A and B. The convenient thing about positive and negative, however, is that mathematically they add to zero, or a neutral quantity.

23.2 Static Electricity

Before You Read

In your Science Notebook, start a concept map with the term *Static Electricity* in the center. Record information you already know about this term. As you read, record the facts about static electricity that you want to remember.

You're sitting down and quietly watching television when you hear a soft scuffing noise behind you. When you turn to look—SNAP! Your younger brother gives you a shock and runs away laughing. Your brother isn't plugged into the wall, so where did the electricity come from?

What Is Static Electricity?

The electrons in an atom are normally attracted to the protons in the atom's nucleus. Some atoms, however, hold onto their electrons more tightly than do others. Other atoms hold onto their electrons less tightly. Loosely held electrons can get stripped away from these atoms. When one atom loses electrons, another atom gains them. This creates an unbalanced set of charges in which one object has more electrons than the other. The unbalanced charges are called static charges, and the buildup of excess electric charge on an object is called **static electricity** (STA tik • ih lek TRIH suh tee).

For example, when a person drags his or her feet across a carpet, the person's shoes strip electrons off the carpet fibers. The carpet loses electrons and becomes positively charged. The shoes pick up extra electrons and become negatively charged. The person is now carrying a buildup of static electricity. When he or she touches another object, the extra electrons on his or her body will flow to the new object and create a spark. The rapid movement of electrons from one place to another is called an **electric discharge.**

Figure 23.6 You might get a shock if you touch a metal object after you walk across a rug. As you walk, your feet strip electrons off the rug. The electrons stay on your body until you touch the doorknob. Then the extra electrons flow from your hand to the doorknob, and you see and feel a spark.

Learning Goals

- Define *static electricity*.
- Identify three ways to produce a static charge.
- Describe what happens during an electric discharge.

New Vocabulary

static electricity
electric discharge
friction
conduction
conductor
insulator
induction

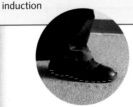

Figure 23.5 Normally, a carpet and the soles of a person's shoes are electrically neutral. When the shoes are scuffed across the carpet, however, electrons move from the carpet onto the surface of the shoes. The carpet becomes positively charged, and the shoes become negatively charged.

As You Read

Add the terms *friction*, *conduction*, and *induction* to your concept map. As you continue reading, write what you learn about each term.

What is an electric discharge?

Teacher Alert

To ensure that students understand **Figure 23.5,** have them read the caption and explain what they think it means. Ask someone to demonstrate what *scuffing* means, as this word could be unfamiliar to English language learners.

23.2 Introduce

ENGAGE Have students read the first paragraph of the lesson. Then have them describe in their own words what is happening in the scenario. Ask them if or when they have felt a shock like this, and have them share what happened to cause it and what it felt like.

Before You Read

Write *Static Electricity* on the board. Tell students that this term is the beginning of a concept map for this lesson. Have them write the term in their Science Notebooks. As a class, brainstorm one or two facts that students already know about static electricity. Have students talk with partners about what else they know about static electricity and add the information to their concept maps.

Teach

EXPLAIN to students that they will learn about static electricity in this lesson.

Vocabulary

static electricity Tell students that *static* comes from the Greek word *statikos*, meaning causing "to stand," and that *electricity* is a noun that means "an electric charge or current" as used in this term. Have students combine the two meanings to arrive at a definition.

electric discharge Ask students to remember what *electric* means ("relating to or produced by electricity"), and then tell them that *discharge*, as it is used in this term, is a noun made up of the prefix *dis-*, meaning "the opposite or reverse," and the verb *charge*, meaning "to give an excess or shortage of charged particles."

As You Read

On the board, show students what their maps should look like after they add the three new terms. Tell them to include information that they learn about each term in the corresponding circle.

ANSWER An electric discharge is the rapid movement of electrons from one place to another.

Teach

EXPLAIN to students that they will learn how electrons move through objects and how they are transferred from one object to another.

 Vocabulary

friction Explain to students that the word *friction* comes from the Latin word *frictio,* meaning "to rub."

conduction Tell students that *conduction* comes from the verb *conduct,* meaning "to lead or guide." Ask students to remember what the suffix *-tion* indicates (action, result, or condition).

conductor Ask students to remember what the word *conduct* means ("to lead or guide"). Tell them that the suffix *-or* denotes a person or thing that performs an action or task. Ask for examples of other words that contain this suffix (*actor, director, elevator*) and what they mean.

insulator Ask students to identify the word parts of *insulator* (*insulate* and *-or*). Tell them that *insulate* is a verb that comes from the Latin word *insula,* meaning "island." Ask them to remember what the suffix *-or* means (it relates the word to a person or thing that performs an action or task).

induction Ask students to identify the word parts of *induction* (*induct* and *-tion*). Tell them that *induct* comes from the Latin word *inducere,* meaning "to lead in." Ask students to remember what the suffix *-tion* indicates (action, result, or condition).

 Explore It!

Divide students into small groups. Each group will need a piece of wool from a blanket, sweater, sock, etc.; a hard rubber comb; several small sheets of tissue paper; and a balloon.

ANSWER The pieces of tissue paper will be attracted to the charged comb, as will the uncharged balloon. When the balloon is rubbed with wool, however, it will also pick up a negative charge. When the charged comb is brought near the charged balloon, the negative charges will repel one another.

Figure 23.7 A Van de Graff generator makes static electricity by rubbing a rubber belt against a piece of silicon at high speeds.

 Explore It!

Give a hard rubber comb a negative charge by rubbing it with a piece of wool. Move the comb over some small pieces of tissue paper. Next, move the charged comb near an inflated balloon. Move the comb away and rub the balloon with the wool. Then move the comb back toward the balloon. Describe what happens in each step. Explain your observations in terms of static charge.

Charging Objects

Rubbing two materials together can transfer electrons from one material to the other. This process charges the materials by **friction** (FRIHK shun). That is, the process physically moves electrons from one place to another. Friction is often described as the force that separates charges into groups of positive and negative charges.

Electrons can also move along the surface of an object and onto other objects that are touching it in a process called **conduction** (kun DUK shun). A material that allows electrons to move through it easily is called a **conductor** (kun DUK tor). Good conductors include water and metals such as copper and aluminum. A material that holds its electrons tightly and keeps them from moving easily is called an **insulator** (IHN suh lay tor). Good insulators include materials such as glass, air, plastic, rubber, and wood.

Figure 23.8 Electrons flow easily through conductors like these copper wires *(left).* The rubber on these clamps *(right)* is an insulator that keeps electricity from flowing into the user.

Because charged objects produce electric fields, an object with a static charge can rearrange the electrons on a nearby neutral object. This process of charging a neutral object by bringing a charged object near it is called **induction** (in DUK shun). For example, if you rub a balloon on your hair, the balloon will become negatively charged. If you hold the charged balloon near a neutral wall, the extra electrons on the balloon will repel the electrons on the surface of the wall. As the electrons move away, they leave behind a positively charged area on the wall that attracts the balloon. The charged balloon will stick to the wall, held there by an electric force.

Figure 23.9 The balloon sticking to this girl's sweater is negatively charged. It repelled electrons on the sweater, producing a positively charged area by induction.

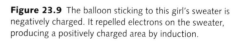

ELL Strategy

Read Aloud, Paraphrase Have pairs of students read aloud sections of the lesson and stop to discuss the content in their own words. As they read aloud and discuss, English language learners can illustrate or diagram the concepts in their Science Notebooks.

Background Information

Inside a clothes dryer, clothes rub against one another and build up a large static charge. Fabric-softener sheets reduce the static buildup. The sheets are made of materials that release positively charged ions when they get warm. The ions bond to any clothes that have picked up a negative charge. The process gives all the clothes in the dryer similar charges, so they won't stick together.

Electric Discharges

Electric discharges occur when electrons jump from a negatively charged object to a neutral or positively charged object. Discharges can be small, like the shock you get when you touch metal after walking across a carpet. They can also be giant, releasing 100 million volts of electric energy in seconds. A lightning bolt is a natural static discharge.

Lightning is produced when air currents separate charges inside a storm cloud. The top of the cloud becomes positively charged, while the bottom becomes negatively charged. The negative charge on the underside of the cloud then induces a positive charge on the ground or in nearby clouds. When the charge difference grows large enough, the induced positive charge attracts electrons from the cloud, then rises to meet them when they get close enough to the ground. This surge of charges becomes a lightning bolt that can move from the cloud to the ground, from the ground to the cloud, or from the cloud to another cloud.

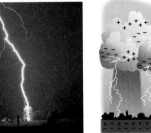

Figure 23.10 Lightning is a giant natural static discharge.

A lightning rod is a metal pole attached to a wire that is anchored to a metal grid in the ground. The rod does not attract lightning. Rather, the rod provides a way for the electricity from the lightning to reach the ground through the wire instead of through the house or the people inside it.

You can protect yourself from lightning by staying away from high places, open areas, trees, and conductors such as metal fences and large bodies of water. The safest place to be during a thunderstorm is inside a building or a hard-topped car, because both are made of conducting metals that can redirect electricity away from you.

After You Read

1. If a brush becomes negatively charged when you comb your hair, do you become charged? Explain.
2. Describe how a lightning bolt forms.
3. Use your concept map to write a well-developed paragraph explaining how a static charge is created by friction, by conduction, and by induction.
4. Compare how a conductor and an insulator hold onto electrons.

Figure It Out

1. In what three directions can a lightning bolt move?
2. Hypothesize why seeking shelter under a tree during a thunderstorm is not safe.

Did You Know?

Although getting struck by lightning is rare, it is very dangerous. The large electric energies in lightning can disrupt the human nervous system, producing cardiac arrest or brain damage.

Differentiate Instruction

Musical Using the Internet or library books, have students find and list songs that contain the word *lightning* in the lyrics or title. They should share the songs, titles, and/or lyrics with one another.

23.3 Introduce

ENGAGE Ask students to think about objects in their homes or in the classroom that are plugged into outlets. Have small groups of students work together to list the objects. Then have them discuss why they think the objects are plugged in.

Before You Read

Instruct students to write a definition of each vocabulary term before writing their own sentences. As an example, find and define the first vocabulary term with the class.

● Teach

EXPLAIN to students that they will learn about electric currents in this lesson.

 Vocabulary

electric current Ask students to remember the definition of the word *electric*. Tell them that *current* refers to the flow of something in a particular direction.

ampere Tell students that the ampere is named after the French physicist André Marie Ampère.

circuit Tell students that the word *circuit* comes from the Latin word *circuitus,* meaning "a complete course" or "round trip." Ask students what a race course and a driving course have in common. Help them recognize that these courses both form a complete path and that they both start and finish at the same point.

voltage Tell students that the word *voltage* is made up of the noun *volt* and the suffix *-age,* meaning "collection" or "group."

volt Tell students that the volt is named after Italian physicist Alessandro Volta, who lived from 1745 to 1827.

battery Ask students for examples of different types and brands of batteries with which they are familiar. Show them several examples.

electrode Tell students that the word *electrode* is a noun made up of the root *electro* and the suffix *-ode,* meaning "path." Ask them to remember what *electro-* means (it relates to electricity).

Learning Goals

- Define *current, voltage,* and *resistance.*
- Identify the variables that affect the resistance of a circuit.
- Describe the relationship represented by Ohm's law and solve problems using Ohm's law.
- Explain the difference between direct current and alternating current.

New Vocabulary

electric current
ampere
circuit
voltage
volt
battery
electrode
electrolyte
photocell
resistance
ohm
Ohm's law
direct current
alternating current

Figure 23.11 Like a water system, an electric current only continues to flow when it moves through a closed loop.

23.3 Making Electrons Flow

Before You Read

Write the vocabulary terms for this lesson in your Science Notebook. As you read the lesson, use each term in a sentence of your own. Make sure that your sentences show the meaning of each term.

Sparks of energy from an electric discharge are too irregular to power common appliances. Electric devices need an **electric current,** a flow of charge created when electrons or ions move through a conductor. Current is measured in **amperes** (AM pihrz) (A). An ampere represents about six billion-billion electrons moving past a point per second.

Creating a Current

Unlike static electricity, in which charges do not move until they discharge, an electric current involves charges that flow. Like water that flows in a pipe, charges need a path through which to move. An electric **circuit** (SUR kut) is a closed path of conductors through which current can flow. If there is any break in the curcuit, current will not flow.

The water in **Figure 23.11** will not rise into the tank on its own. Instead, a pump is needed to push the water up. The gravitational potential energy of the water increases because the water gains height. Now if the water is allowed to flow, it will naturally move downward from a position of higher energy to a position of lower energy. Similarly, electrons need a push to start flowing through a circuit. A circuit must have a difference in the electric potential energy. This difference, known as the potential difference, is called **voltage** (VOHL tihj). Voltage is what causes current to flow. The voltage of a circuit is measured in **volts** (V).

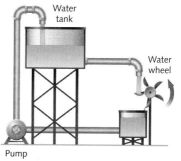

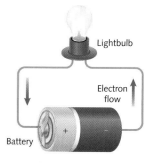

In a closed water system, the pump provides the pressure difference that makes the water flow.

In an electrical system, the battery provides the voltage difference that makes the current flow.

electrolyte Remind students that the root *electro-* relates to electricity. Tell them that *-lyte* comes from the Greek word *lytos,* meaning "released."

photocell Tell students that the word *photocell* is a noun made up of the prefix *photo-,* meaning "light," and the root *cell.* In this use, *cell* refers to a device that generates electricity. Ask students to define this term on their own.

ELL Strategy

Illustrate Provide books that contain photographs and illustrations of analogies for electric currents that students can use as references. In small groups, have students illustrate and label an electric current. Allow them to come up with their own analogies if they prefer.

Power Sources

Devices that establish voltage are known as power sources. One common source is a generator, which converts mechanical energy into electric energy. Generators will be discussed in Chapter 25.

A **battery** contains chemicals that can convert stored chemical energy into electric energy. All batteries contain two **electrodes** (il LEK trohdz), or electron conductors, made of different materials. The electrodes are surrounded by an electrolyte. An **electrolyte** is a material containing free ions. When the outside ends of the electrodes, called the battery's terminals, are attached to a circuit, the chemical reaction inside the battery produces a positive charge at one terminal and a negative charge at the other. Electrons at the negative terminal are pushed through the circuit toward the positive terminal.

In dry-cell batteries, one electrode is the container and the other is the carbon rod. The electrolyte is a paste of chemicals. In wet-cell batteries, the electrodes are metal plates, and the electrolyte is a liquid.

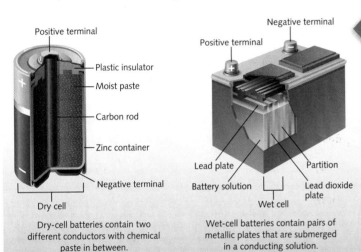

Positive terminal
— Plastic insulator
— Moist paste
— Carbon rod
— Zinc container
— Negative terminal
Dry cell

Dry-cell batteries contain two different conductors with chemical paste in between.

Negative terminal
Positive terminal
Lead plate
Battery solution
Partition
Lead dioxide plate
Wet cell

Wet-cell batteries contain pairs of metallic plates that are submerged in a conducting solution.

Figure 23.12 Chemical reactions inside batteries produce voltage differences between their positive and negative terminals. When the batteries are hooked into a circuit, electric current flows.

Photocells turn light into electricity. They are built of two kinds of silicon, one with a positive charge and one with a negative charge. When light hits the photocell, it frees electrons from some of the silicon atoms. The electrons are pulled into the positively charged silicon layer, starting a chain reaction as new electrons move to replace them in the negatively charged silicon layer. The moving electrons produce an electric current.

As You Read

Review the vocabulary meanings you have recorded in your Science Notebook. Work with a partner to describe a battery.

What are the functions of electrodes?

Figure It Out

1. What are the two electrodes in the dry-cell battery?
2. What is another name for the battery solution in the wet-cell battery?

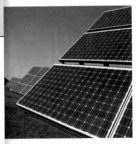

Figure 23.13 Photocells in a solar panel produce electric current from sunlight.

● Teach

EXPLAIN to students that they will learn about batteries and photocells.

As You Read

Give students time to record vocabulary definitions and accompanying sentences. Ask students to reread the section about power sources to identify the vocabulary terms related to *battery*. Ask them to describe a battery, making sure to include the related terms.

(ANSWER) All batteries contain two electrodes made of different materials. The electrodes are surrounded by an electrolyte, which is a material containing free ions. It reacts chemically with the electrodes to produce electric current.

Figure It Out: Figure 23.12

(ANSWER) **1.** The positive electrode is the carbon rod. The negative electrode is the zinc container. **2.** The battery solution is the electrolyte.

Background Information

A photocell collects sunlight and turns it into electrical energy. This is called the photoelectric effect. Solar panels and outdoor lighting are two devices that use photocells. There must be enough sunlight to power the devices so that there is always more energy stored in the photocells than is used for energy. This can be challenging in certain geographical areas and during certain times of the year. The initial cost of installation for devices using photocells is high, but this is somewhat offset by later savings.

● Teach

Tell students that they will learn about variables that affect the resistance of an electrical current.

 Vocabulary

resistance Tell students that the common meaning of *resistance* is "opposition" or "defiance." Ask how this relates to the scientific definition.

ohm Tell students that the ohm is named after the German physicist and mathematician Georg Simon Ohm, who lived from 1787 to 1854.

Ohm's law Tell students that this law, which describes the relationship among voltage, current, and resistance in a circuit, was discovered by Ohm and is named after him.

direct current Tell students that the common meaning of the adjective *direct* is "straight" or "uninterrupted." Ask them to remember what *current* refers to (the flow of something in a particular direction). Have them put the words together to form a definition for the term.

alternating current Tell students that *alternating* comes from the Latin word *alternare,* meaning "to do one thing after another." Remind them what *current* means, and have them put the words together to form a definition.

 CONNECTION: **Materials Science**

Examples of metals that are superconductors are zinc, aluminum, tin, and mercury. Certain ceramics were also recently classified as superconductors.

Have students find information on the Internet or in the library about uses of superconductors, including magnetically levitated (maglev) trains and/or small magnets used for magnetic resonance imaging (MRI).

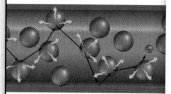

Figure 23.14 Electrons bump into atoms and ions as they move through a conductor, turning some of their energy into heat and light.

 CONNECTION: **Materials Science**

Superconductors are metals and metallic compounds that have no resistance when they are chilled to very low temperatures. Many of these materials only become superconductors at temperatures near absolute zero. The warmest superconductor works at about -140°C.

Resistance

As electrons move through a circuit, they collide with the atoms and ions inside the wires. These collisions oppose the movement of the electrons and turn some of their electric energy into heat and light. The tendency of a material to oppose a current is called its **resistance** (rih ZIHS tunts). Resistance is measured in **ohms** (OHMZ). The symbol for ohm is the Greek letter omega (Ω).

Most materials resist current, although conductors have lower resistance than insulators do. Household wire is often made of copper, which has a low resistance and does not become hot when a current passes through it. The tungsten filament inside an incandescent lightbulb has a high resistance, so it becomes hot and glows when a current moves through it.

The resistance of a wire is also affected by the wire's diameter and length. A narrow wire has a higher resistance than a wide wire does, because there is less room for the electrons to move and they encounter more opposition. A long wire has a higher resistance than a short one does, because electrons have to travel farther through a long wire. They lose more energy along the way.

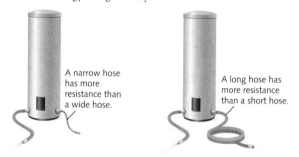

A narrow hose has more resistance than a wide hose.

A long hose has more resistance than a short hose.

Figure 23.15 The resistance of a wire is like the resistance of a hose. A narrow hose has more resistance than a wide hose because the thick hose lets more water through in a given amount of time. A long hose has more resistance than a short hose because the water has to travel farther to get out of it.

The temperature of a material also affects the material's resistance. For some materials, resistance increases as the material gets warmer. This is true of most metals. For materials such as carbon and silicon, however, resistance decreases when the material gets warmer.

Ohm's Law

The relationship among the voltage (V), current (I), and resistance (R) in a circuit is described by **Ohm's law.** According to this law, in every circuit, the voltage is equal to the current multiplied by the resistance.

Background Information

Besides copper, other materials that have low resistance include silver, gold, and aluminum. Materials that have high resistance include tin, platinum, and iron.

Ohm's law can be written as the following equation.

$$\text{voltage} = \text{current} \times \text{resistance} \qquad V = IR$$

This means that if the voltage difference from one end of the circuit to the other stays the same, reducing the resistance in the circuit will increase the current. Electrons will flow faster through the circuit.

Direct and Alternating Current

There are two ways to produce current in a circuit. In **direct current** (DC), electrons flow in only one direction. They move from the negative terminal of the power source to its positive terminal. Batteries produce direct current.

In **alternating current** (AC), the direction of the current changes over time. The electrons move back and forth in the wire 60 times a second. This means that the terminals of the power source are constantly changing from positive to negative and back again. The current in your house is alternating current.

CONNECTION: Biology

Nerves are specialized cells that transmit electric impulses by controlling the movement of ions in the cells. In a resting nerve cell, positively charged sodium ions are pumped to the outside of the cell membrane. The ions cannot diffuse back through the membrane, so the outside of the cell becomes positively charged and the inside of the cell becomes negatively charged.

When a signal reaches one end of the nerve cell, it triggers changes in the cell membrane that result in the sodium ions flowing back into the cell. The inside of the cell becomes positively charged, and a wave of positive charge moves along the length of the nerve. When the impulse reaches the end of the nerve, chemicals are released that create an electric impulse in the next nerve cell.

Human nerves send millions of these electrical signals each day.

After You Read

1. Name two devices that can provide voltage to a circuit.
2. A narrow wire in a circuit is replaced with a wider wire. What will happen to the current in the circuit if the voltage remains constant?
3. Use the sentences you have recorded in your Science Notebook to explain the difference between direct current and alternating current.

Differentiate Instruction

Logical/Mathematical Review how to solve one or two problems that require using Ohm's law. Give students several more problems to solve, and encourage them to write short explanations of how they solved each problem.

Alternative Assessment

Have each student write an explanation of how material, diameter and length, and temperature affect the resistance of a current. Demonstrate the process of rereading the text to find answers and highlighting or noting main points.

● Teach

Tell students that they will learn about the equation for Ohm's law, two types of currents, and nerves in the body.

CONNECTION: Biology

A recent study shows that the amygdala, the part of the brain connected to emotion and memory, contains fewer neurons (nerve cells) in males with autism than in the general population. More research related to other areas of the brain in autistic and nonautistic people is required to determine if there are other differences in the number of neurons.

EXTEND Ask students to conduct research to find out how the shape of a nerve cell is related to the movement of nerve impulses. Have students draw or copy a diagram of a nerve cell. Students should label the parts and describe how the form of each is related to its function. Challenge students to find the speed at which a nerve impulse is transferred throughout the body.

● Assess

Use the After You Read questions and the Alternative Assessment to help you evaluate students' understanding of the lesson.

After You Read

1. Answers will vary, but any power source that produces a voltage difference can provide voltage to a circuit. Answers might include generators, batteries, or photocells.
2. The wider wire has lower resistance than the narrow one. According to Ohm's law, $V = IR$, reducing the resistance will increase the current.
3. Direct current travels in only one direction. The current produced by batteries is DC. Alternating current changes direction over time. The current supplied to the electrical outlets in homes is AC.

23.4 Introduce

ENGAGE students by having someone turn a classroom light switch on and off. Have students discuss their thinking about how the switch controls the electric current in the lights.

Before You Read

Model the Venn diagram on the board, labeling one circle *Series Circuits* and the other *Parallel Circuits*. Instruct students to do the same in their Science Notebooks. Tell them to complete the diagram as they read the lesson.

Teach

EXPLAIN to students that they will learn about open and closed circuits.

 Vocabulary

open circuit Ask students what *open* means and have them give examples (an open door, window, or box). Ask what they remember about the word *circuit* (it refers to a complete course or round trip). Have them define the term based on these two word meanings.

closed circuit Tell students that as it is used in this term, *closed* is an adjective that means "shut" or "blocked." Ask what they think the term means.

series circuit Tell students that a series is a number of similar things arranged or produced in succession. Ask for examples (television, book, concert). Ask for the definition of *circuit*. Then have students define the term based on the two word meanings.

Learning Goals

- Differentiate between open circuits and closed circuits.
- Compare and contrast a series circuit and a parallel circuit.
- Describe the function of fuses and circuit breakers.

New Vocabulary

open circuit
closed circuit
series circuit
parallel circuit
fuse
circuit breaker

23.4 Electric Circuits

Before You Read

Draw a Venn diagram in your Science Notebook. Label one circle *Series Circuits* and the other circle *Parallel Circuits*. As you read the lesson, complete the diagram so that it indicates how these two types of circuits are alike and different.

Flip on a light switch and the lightbulb turns on. Flip it off and the bulb goes dark. A lightbulb glows when a current of electrons moves through it. How does the switch start and stop the current?

Figure 23.16 Millions of electric circuits light up cities at night.

Open and Closed Circuits

The switch is a part of the circuit that opens or closes the path through which current flows. Remember that a circuit is a closed path of conductors. Charges flow through the circuit from one side of the power source to the other. Electrons will not flow unless they can return to their power source. The position of the switch determines whether electrons will flow in the circuit.

Figure 23.17 on the next page shows a simple circuit that powers a lightbulb. When the switch is open, there is a break in the circuit. Electrons cannot travel back to the power source. They have to stop at the open switch. Because the electrons stop moving, there is no current in the circuit. A circuit in which there is no current flowing is called an **open circuit.**

When the switch is closed, it connects the two free ends of the circuit and lets electrons start flowing in the loop. A circuit in which there is current flowing is called a **closed circuit.**

ELL Strategy

Compare and Contrast With partners, have students compare and contrast open and closed circuits, series and parallel circuits, and circuit breakers and fuses. Have students record the information in paragraph or diagram form in their Science Notebooks.

Circuits in Series

Every circuit contains three things. It has a power source (a battery or a generator) to create the voltage difference that runs the circuit. It has a loop of connected conductors (wires) to move charges through the circuit. It has one or more devices that turn electric energy into heat or motion. A circuit can also contain switches to open and close parts of the circuit. There are two distinct ways to arrange these materials to form a circuit.

A **series circuit** has only one path for the current to follow. If any part of the path breaks, it becomes an open circuit. The current stops flowing and all of the devices hooked up to it stop working. Have you ever tried to hang a strand of decorative bulbs that will not light up? You have to search through the strand to find the one bulb that is burned out. The lights are wired in series. If one burns out, it breaks the circuit and stops the current from reaching all of the other lights.

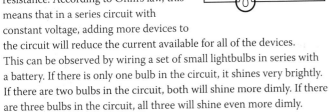

Figure 23.17 The current follows only one path in a series circuit.

The current in a series circuit is the same at all parts of its path. Each device added to the circuit, however, has some resistance. According to Ohm's law, this means that in a series circuit with constant voltage, adding more devices to the circuit will reduce the current available for all of the devices. This can be observed by wiring a set of small lightbulbs in series with a battery. If there is only one bulb in the circuit, it shines very brightly. If there are two bulbs in the circuit, both will shine more dimly. If there are three bulbs in the circuit, all three will shine even more dimly.

Figure It Out

1. How does a current flow through this circuit? Use the last photo to sketch a series of arrows showing the direction in which the current travels.

2. Predict what will happen if one of the bulbs in the circuit burns out. Explain your prediction.

Figure 23.18 As bulbs are added to a circuit in series, they become dimmer and dimmer.

● Teach

EXPLAIN to students that they will learn about series circuits on this page.

Figure It Out: Figure 23.18

ANSWER **1.** The sketch should show current moving from the negative terminal of the battery through each bulb in turn and back to the positive terminal of the battery. **2.** If one bulb in the circuit burns out, all the bulbs will go dark.

Differentiate Instruction

Kinesthetic Give small groups of students two types of electric lightbulb strings: an older series-circuit string and a newer parallel-circuit string. If both kinds of light strings are not available, set up simple versions of each type of circuit using bulbs, wires, and batteries. Instruct students to take one bulb out of each string and note the result of plugging in the strings. Have them identify and describe which is series and which is parallel. Students should record their findings in their Science Notebooks.

Teach

EXPLAIN to students that they will learn about parallel circuits on this page.

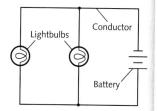

Vocabulary

parallel circuit Ask students to define the word *parallel* and give examples of its use ("the same distance apart everywhere"). Ask for the definition of the word *circuit*. Have students then define the term based on the two word meanings.

fuse Tell students that *fuse* comes from the Latin word *fusum,* meaning "to melt."

circuit breaker Tell students that a breaker is someone or something that breaks, splits, or becomes damaged. Have them put this definition together with the definition of *circuit* to come up with a meaning for the term.

As You Read

Read the observation aloud to the class. Have students share their ideas with partners and then record their ideas on the Venn diagram.

ANSWER Students' explanations will vary but should include the definitions of the terms and the similarities and differences between a series circuit and a parallel circuit.

Figure 23.19 The current has more than one path to follow in a parallel circuit.

As You Read

Use the Venn diagram in your Science Notebook to explain the following observation: When one bulb in a circuit containing three bulbs burned out, the other two bulbs remained lighted. Use the following terms in your explanation: *series circuit, parallel circuit, current, path, open circuit, closed circuit.*

Circuits in Parallel

Think about all of the electric devices in a typical home. Can one or more be used at the same time? Several lights and a television can be on at the same time. None of the lights get dimmer when the television is on, and the TV can be turned off without the lights shutting off. This is because buildings are wired using parallel circuits.

A **parallel circuit** has branching wires that let the current follow more than one path. If one part of the circuit is opened, electrons can still flow through other parts of the circuit. Thus a burned-out bulb in the living room does not turn off the refrigerator.

In a parallel circuit, each electric device resists current without affecting the devices on other branches of the circuit. The voltage remains the same in each branch of the circuit. According to Ohm's law, this means that more current will run through the devices that have lower resistance.

Household Circuits

A typical kitchen can contain many electric devices. These might include a refrigerator, a stove, a toaster, a microwave oven, a blender, a hand mixer, a dishwasher, and electric lights. Because buildings are wired with parallel circuits, a cook can use many of these devices at once. If he or she uses too many of the cooking appliances at the same time, however, the power to the room will go out. This happens because the parallel circuits are designed to fail before they get dangerously hot.

Ohm's law shows that if more and more machines are run at the same time in a parallel circuit, the current in the circuit will increase. If too much current runs through the wires, the wires can get hot enough to melt their insulation and start an electrical fire in the walls.

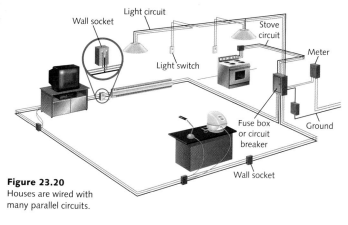

Figure 23.20 Houses are wired with many parallel circuits.

Background Information

Circuit breakers and fuses are usually found in the garage or basement of a home. They are in a metal or plastic rectangular box attached to the wall. Inside the box, circuit breakers look like large, horizontal light switches with *On* and *Off* printed on either side of each one. Fuses are usually screws with round, bottle cap-like tops. Older houses usually are equipped with fuse boxes.

Fuses and Circuit Breakers

Fuses and circuit breakers are devices that keep circuits from getting dangerously hot. Both of them limit the amount of current that is running through the circuit. If the current gets larger than 15 A or 20 A, one of these devices opens the circuit. When the circuit is opened, the current stops.

A **fuse** contains a small piece of metal that melts at a lower temperature than the rest of the wiring in a building does. When the current gets too high, the metal in the fuse melts and stops the flow of current in the circuit. This is often called "blowing a fuse." Blown fuses have to be replaced before the circuit will work again.

Metal

Figure 23.21 A fuse is a device that keeps wires from overheating. It contains a piece of metal that melts when the wires get too hot. What is true of the melting point of the metal fuse as compared to the melting point of the wires?

Circuit breakers are a more recent invention. A **circuit breaker** contains a piece of metal that bends when it gets warm. When the current gets too high, the metal bends and flips a switch that opens the circuit. Breakers can be reset by flipping them back to the "on" position. However, if the electrical problem is not solved first, the breaker will just flip off again.

After You Read

1. Compare an open circuit and a closed circuit.
2. Using the Venn diagram in your Science Notebook, explain why houses are wired in parallel instead of in series.
3. Name the devices that are used to protect household wiring.

Explain It!

People sometimes replace a blown fuse with a coin instead of a new fuse. In your Science Notebook, explain why the coin can close the circuit. Then explain why doing this is not a good idea.

Figure 23.22 Newer buildings are protected with a set of circuit breakers.

● Teach

EXPLAIN to students that they will learn about devices that keep circuits from overheating and causing a fire.

Explain It!

Suggest that students illustrate and label a coin in a fuse box and write an accompanying explanation of its function.

ANSWER The coin is a conductor. Because electrons can move through it, it forms part of a closed circuit. Replacing a fuse with a coin is dangerous, however, because the coin does not melt when the wires get overloaded. An electrical fire can start as a result of the overloaded wires.

Use the Visual: Figure 23.21

ANSWER The melting point of the metal is lower than that of the wires.

● Assess

Use the After You Read questions and the Alternative Assessment to help you evaluate students' understanding of the lesson.

After You Read

1. Current does not flow through an open circuit because the circuit does not contain a closed loop of conductors. A closed circuit contains a closed loop of conductors.
2. Wiring a building in parallel lets people use many different electric devices at the same time without the devices affecting one another.
3. fuses and circuit breakers

Alternative Assessment

Have students add *homes* to their Venn diagrams in the correct circle (*Parallel Circuits*) along with an explanation of why these are used. Then ask them to add any other relevant information from the lesson to their diagrams. Each student should write a paragraph explaining the information in his or her diagram.

Field Study

For a homework assignment, have each student find out if his or her home contains circuit breakers or fuses. Each student should write a paragraph that explains his or her findings.

Teacher Alert

Tell students not to touch any of the fuses or circuits. Doing so could disrupt the building's flow of electricity and endanger the student.

ENGAGE Ask students to think about and record what they will do today when they get home from school. Have each student share his or her list with a partner to identify which activities require electric power. Have pairs share their lists and decisions with other class members when they are finished.

Before You Read

Review with students how to preview the lesson by demonstrating with the first page or two. Remind them to look at pictures and read captions and headings. Ask students to continue previewing the rest of the lesson on their own and to write a paragraph describing what they think the lesson will be about.

Teach

EXPLAIN Tell students that they will learn about electric power and how it is measured.

 Vocabulary

electric power Ask students to remember the definition of *electric* ("relating to or produced by electricity"). Ask what power is (in physics, the rate of doing work or converting energy from one form into another). Then ask what the term means.

Learning Goals

- Define and calculate electric power.
- Calculate the electric energy used by an appliance.
- Describe how to use electricity safely.

New Vocabulary

electric power
electric energy

23.5 Electric Power

Before You Read

Preview the lesson by looking at the pictures and reading the headings. Discuss the lesson with a partner. In your Science Notebook, write a paragraph describing what you think the lesson is about. As you read, add more information to your description or correct any misinformation you included.

Often when students get home from school, they go to the refrigerator for a snack. Maybe you put a taco or some popcorn in the microwave, turn on some music, and switch on the computer to write an essay. All of these actions involve devices that use electric power.

Figure 23.23 Home appliances convert electricity into other forms of energy.

Power

Electricity is converted into other kinds of energy for a variety of uses. A toaster oven converts an electric current into heat, a fan converts it into motion, a stereo speaker converts it into sound vibrations, and a television set converts it into light. The rate at which an electric current is converted into other forms is called **electric power.**

Electric power is measured in watts (W). A watt is a fairly small unit of power, so the electricity people use in their homes is measured in kilowatts (kW). One kilowatt is 1,000 watts. Electric power is calculated by multiplying the voltage provided to a device by the current that flows through the device.

$$\text{electric power} = \text{current} \times \text{voltage difference} \qquad P = IV$$

ELL Strategy

Relate to Personal Experience As students are reading this lesson, have them discuss in small groups how the information connects to their personal experiences.

For example, consider a typical table lamp. The lamp contains at least one lightbulb. A lightbulb converts electricity into heat and light. How much power does it take to turn on a lightbulb?

The answer depends on the kind of lightbulb inside the lamp. Some electrical outlets in the United States supply 120 V to circuits. A typical incandescent bulb uses 0.50 A of current. Power is calculated by multiplying current times voltage, so the incandescent bulb uses 60 W of power.

$$P = (0.50 \text{ A})(120 \text{ V}) = 60 \text{ W}$$

A compact fluorescent bulb that produces the same amount of light will use 0.125 A of current. This bulb uses only 15 W of power.

$$P = (0.125 \text{ A})(120 \text{ V}) = 15 \text{ W}$$

Incandescent bulb   Compact fluorescent bulb

Figure 23.24 Lightbulbs can be designed to use different amounts of power to provide the same amount of light.

Other appliances also use different amounts of power, depending on what they are designed to do. Most home appliances use about 100 W of power. Some, however, use a lot more—particularly devices that turn electricity into heat. Appliances that are designed to run on batteries, such as portable CD players, cell phones, and flashlights, use much less.

Figure 23.25 Every appliance has a power rating that shows how much power it uses.

Power Ratings

Appliance	Power (kW)
CD player	0.02
incandescent bulb	0.06
color TV	0.07
refrigerator	0.12
desktop computer	0.15
air conditioner	0.62
microwave	1.10
waffle iron	1.20
toaster	1.45
hair dryer	1.90

Figure It Out

1. Which has the larger power rating, an air conditioner or a waffle iron?

2. Calculate how much current the waffle iron will draw when it is plugged into a 110-V socket.

EXPLAIN to students that they will continue learning how electric power is measured and will identify the power rating of various household appliances.

Figure It Out: Figure 23.25

ANSWER **1.** the waffle iron, with a power rating of 1.2 kW **2.** current = power/voltage = 1200 W/110 V = 10.9 A

Differentiate Instruction

Mathematical/Logical Have students research the power rating of several models of a household appliance, find the estimated annual operating cost of each model, and list the information in a chart. They should also include which models are EnergyStar-rated and what the criteria are for this rating system.

Key Concept Review
Workbook, p. 144

Teach

EXPLAIN to students that they will learn about electric energy, which is the amount of power an electrical appliance uses over time.

Vocabulary

electric energy Ask students to recall the definition of the word *electric*. Ask them what they remember about energy (in physics, it refers to the capacity to do work). Then ask what the term means.

As You Read

Give students time to record information that they learned in this lesson in their Science Notebooks. In addition, have them correct any misinformation that they wrote before reading the lesson.

(ANSWER) Electric power measures how quickly current can be converted into other forms of energy, and electric energy is the amount of power that is used over a period of time.

Use the Visual: Figure 23.26

(ANSWER) Electric energy is the amount of power an electric device uses over time.

Extend It!

Tell students that they can find the electric meter on the outside of the house. Explain how to read it before assigning them this activity, which will help them better understand the cost of home energy use. Students could see a difference in energy used (and potential savings) when an effort is made to conserve.

As You Read

Share the paragraph in your Science Notebook with a partner and make corrections or additions as needed. Then write a sentence that compares electric power and electric energy.

Extend It!

Find the electric meter in your house or school. Record the meter value in your Science Notebook. Read the meter again after one day and after one week. Calculate the average amount of energy (in kWh) used each day during the week, and compare it to the reading from the first day.

Use the price of electricity per hour charged by your electric company to calculate the week's cost.

Electric Energy

People can run appliances for long periods of time. Watching a movie runs a DVD player for about two hours. A load of laundry runs the washing machine for 30 minutes. Making toast runs the toaster for about five minutes. The amount of power an electric device uses over time is called **electric energy.** Electric energy is measured in kilowatt-hours (kWh). One kilowatt-hour is enough energy to light up ten 100-W lightbulbs for one hour.

Figure 23.26 Power companies use meters that measure the amount of electric energy a home uses over time. What is electric energy?

When people buy electricity, the power company charges them for the amount of electric energy they used. Energy use depends on the amount of power the electric appliances use over time.

electric energy = electric power × time $E = Pt$

The amount of power an appliance uses can be misleading. An appliance that uses a small amount of power for a long period of time can use much more electric energy than an appliance that uses a large amount of power for a short time.

For example, a refrigerator uses 0.12 kW of power. This is much smaller than the 1.45 kW it takes to run a toaster. However, a toaster is used for only about five minutes a day, while the refrigerator may run for 14 hours during the same period. The electric energy used by each appliance is calculated by multiplying its power by the amount of time it uses electricity.

E of toaster = (1.45 kW)(0.08 h) = 0.12 kWh

E of refrigerator = (0.12 kW)(14 h) = 1.68 kWh

Even though the refrigerator uses less power than the toaster, it uses more than ten times more electric energy in a typical day.

Background Information

Electric companies bill customers by the kilowatt-hour (1,000 watts used in one hour). The electric power meter outside a house shows the amount of electric current being drawn at a given time. When electric current is taken from the power lines into the home, the meter gears rotate. When more power is being drawn, the gears move faster. The meter is read from the right dial to the left dial.

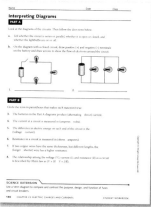

Interpreting Diagrams
Workbook, p. 146

Electric Safety

Electricity is one of the most useful forms of energy. Just imagine what life would be like without it! However, electricity can be dangerous if it is not used carefully. About 400 people die from electrocution each year. Electrical fires cause about 400 deaths, 4,000 injuries, and 1.6 billion dollars in property damage each year. Electric shocks from damaged or incorrectly used electrical equipment can cause injuries ranging from mild burns to cardiac arrest. Electrical accidents can be avoided by following a few simple rules.

- Keep electric appliances away from water. Never touch electric devices with wet hands.
- Always unplug appliances before repairing them.
- Never put anything inside an electric outlet.
- Never use appliances with frayed or damaged electric cords. Frayed cords can cause short circuits and start fires. A short circuit is an unintended connection that allows current to take a shorter path around a circuit. Because a shorter path has less resistance, it also has higher current.
- Never plug too many devices into one outlet or extension cord. This can make the wires in the walls too hot and cause a fire.
- Never touch power lines, even with an object. Don't let ladders and kite strings touch raised power lines, and never touch a downed power line.

Local and national government agencies provide information and enforce regulations regarding electric safety. Established national standards as well as local housing, building, and wiring codes help ensure the safe use of electricity in homes and industries.

Figure 23.27 Plugging too many devices into an outlet can cause the wires to overheat and start on fire.

After You Read

1. Calculate how much energy a television using 0.9 A of current will use in three hours in a house that supplies 110 V to circuits.
2. Power companies charge for electricity by the kilowatt-hour. In your Science Notebook, make a list of ways in which you can reduce the amount of energy your household uses in a month.
3. Review the information you recorded in your Science Notebook. Explain why you should keep electric devices away from water.

● Teach

EXPLAIN to students that they will learn about using electricity safely.

● Assess

Use the After You Read questions and the Alternative Assessment to help you evaluate students' understanding of the lesson.

After You Read

1. The television has a power rating of 99 W = 0.099 kW. Over three hours, it uses (0.099 kW) (3 h) = 0.297 kWh of energy.
2. Answers will vary but should all be ways to reduce energy use. Acceptable answers include turning off lights and appliances when they are not in use, using devices that have lower power ratings, and using devices for shorter periods of time.
3. Water is a good conductor, and electric charges can use it to move outside the normal circuit.

Alternative Assessment

Have students finish recording information that they learned in this lesson. Ask them to make up several word problems (with answers) that require calculating electric energy. Each answer should be accompanied by an explanation of the solution process.

Background Information

Electricity is one of the most inefficient types of energy people consume. Two-thirds of energy generated at electric power plants is wasted as heat loss. The production of electricity from fossil fuels emits 21 percent more carbon dioxide than does burning fuel for transportation. One of the easiest and least expensive ways to reduce electricity in the home is to change incandescent lightbulbs to fluorescent bulbs. Another way is to replace older kitchen appliances with newer, more efficient models. The refrigerator uses the most electricity in a kitchen, especially if it is more than ten years old.

Chapter 23 Summary

VOCABULARY REVIEW

Check students' sentences or paragraphs to make sure they understand the meaning of each vocabulary term.

Evaluate students' essays using the following criteria:

1. The topic sentence, or main idea, should restate the Key Concept.

2. The supporting paragraphs should incorporate the answers to the Learning Goal questions students have written and include details, facts, and examples they have recorded in their Science Notebooks.

3. The concluding sentence should sum up the main idea of the chapter and restate the Key Concept.

MASTERING CONCEPTS

True or False

1. False, Electrons
2. True
3. True
4. False, watts
5. False, closed
6. True

Short Answer

7. $I = (10 \text{ V})/(100 \text{ } \Omega) = 0.10$ A;
   $V = (220 \text{ A})(0.5 \text{ A}) = 110$ V

8. energy $= Pt = (0.06 \text{ kW}) (5 \text{ h}) = 0.3$ kWh

9. Replacing a short wire with a longer wire will increase the resistance in the circuit.

10. A metal is a good conductor because it contains many electrons that are loosely held by their atoms.

11. The battery provides the potential difference that moves electrons in a circuit.

KEY CONCEPTS

23.1 What Is Electric Charge?

- Atoms contain electrically charged particles.
- Protons are positively charged, and electrons are negatively charged.
- Like charges repel one another, but opposite charges attract.
- Charged particles exert forces on one another through electric fields.

23.2 Static Electricity

- Static electricity is the buildup of charge on an object.
- A static charge can be produced by friction, conduction, or induction.
- An electric discharge occurs when electrons move quickly from one object to another.

23.3 Making Electrons Flow

- The movement of charge in a circuit produces electric current.
- Current is powered by a difference in electric potential.
- Electrons meet with resistance as they move through a circuit.
- Ohm's law describes the relationship among voltage, current, and resistance.
- Buildings are powered by alternating current.

23.4 Electric Circuits

- Current can only flow through a closed circuit.
- A series circuit has only one path for current to follow.
- A parallel circuit has multiple paths for current to follow.
- Buildings are wired in parallel.

23.5 Electric Power

- Electric power is the rate at which current is changed into other forms of energy.
- Electric energy is the amount of power used over time.
- Caution is needed when using electricity.

VOCABULARY REVIEW

Write each term in a complete sentence or write a paragraph relating several terms.

23.1
atom, p. 392
nucleus, p. 392
proton, p. 392
neutron, p. 392
electron, p. 392
ion, p. 392
electric field, p. 394

23.2
static electricity, p. 395
electric discharge, p. 395
friction, p. 396
conduction, p. 396
conductor, p. 396
insulator, p. 396
induction, p. 396

23.3
electric current, p. 398
ampere, p. 398
circuit, p. 398
voltage, p. 398
volt, p. 398
battery, p. 399
electrode, p. 399
electrolyte, p. 399
photocell, p. 399
resistance, p. 400
ohm, p. 400
Ohm's law, p. 400
direct current, p. 401
alternating current, p. 401

23.4
open circuit, p. 402
closed circuit, p. 402
series circuit, p. 403
parallel circuit, p. 404
fuse, p. 405
circuit breaker, p. 405

23.5
electric power, p. 406
electric energy, p. 408

Vocabulary Review
Workbook, p. 145

Reading Comprehension
Workbook, p. 147

MASTERING CONCEPTS

True or False
If the statement is true, write "true." If it is false, change the underlined word or words to make the statement true.

1. <u>Neutrons</u> have a negative charge.
2. A negative charge is attracted to a(n) <u>positive</u> charge.
3. A current can take more than one path through a(n) <u>parallel</u> circuit.
4. Electric energy is measured in <u>amperes</u>.
5. A current flows through a(n) <u>open</u> circuit.
6. As the resistance in a circuit increases, the current in the circuit <u>decreases</u>.

Short Answer
Answer each of the following in a sentence or brief paragraph.

7. What is the current in a circuit when it is attached to a 10-V battery and a bulb with a resistance of 100 Ω? What is the voltage provided by an outlet if a lightbulb with a resistance of 220 Ω produces a current of 0.5 A?
8. How much energy would a personal computer with a power rating of 0.06 kW use if it were on for five hours?
9. A short wire inside a circuit is replaced with a longer wire. What happens to the resistance in the circuit?
10. Explain why a metal is a good conductor.
11. What is the function of a battery in a circuit?

Critical Thinking
Use what you have learned in this chapter to answer each of the following.

12. **Infer** When you scuff your feet along a carpet and touch a doorknob, you get a shock. But you feel nothing if you touch a wall before you reach for the knob. Infer what happens to the extra electrons on your body when you touch the wall.
13. **Hypothesize** You are cooking Thanksgiving dinner for your family, but your kitchen only has one outlet. You are using an extension strip to run a blender, a bread machine, and a convection oven. When you plug in the hand mixer, all of the appliances turn off. Hypothesize what has made the machines stop working.
14. **Predict** You can often see birds perching on a single high-voltage power line. Predict what would happen if a bird touched two wires instead of one.

Standardized Test Question
Choose the letter of the response that correctly answers the question.

15. Which of the following statements is true?
    A. This device channels the electricity from lightning into the ground.
    B. This device converts sunlight into electricity.
    C. This device opens circuits that are getting too hot.
    D. This device generates light from electricity.

> **Test-Taking Tip**
>
> Resist the urge to rush, and don't worry if others finish before you. Use all the time you have. If you are able, clear your mind by closing your eyes and counting to five or taking another type of short break. Extra points are not awarded for being the first person to finish.

Critical Thinking

12. When you touch the wall, the extra electrons flow to the ground.
13. Running the mixer overloaded the outlet. Too much current was flowing through the circuit, and it either blew the fuse or tripped the breaker to keep the wires from getting too hot.
14. The bird would be electrocuted. When the bird touches two wires, it becomes a conductor in the circuit.

Standardized Test Question

15. B

Reading Links

Electric Mischief: Battery-Powered Gadgets Kids Can Build

This book presents clear, well-diagrammed instructions for the completion of six projects that demonstrate the operation of electric circuits in memorable, hands-on ways, including the construction of such devices as electric dice, an illuminated fork, a bumper car, and a robotic hand.

Alan Bartholomew. Kids Can Press, Ltd. 48 pp. Illustrated. Trade ISBN 978-1-55074-923-6.

Awesome Experiments in Electricity and Magnetism

Through a collection of over 70 activities and demonstrations that range from standard (using a static-charged comb) to unusual (constructing a Morse code transmission station), this book provides a comprehensive classroom resource that is valuable for teacher and independent student use alike.

Michael DiSpezio. Sterling Publishing Co. 160 pp. Illustrated. Trade ISBN 978-1-4027-2370-4.

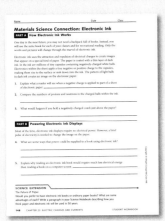

Curriculum Connection
Workbook, p. 148

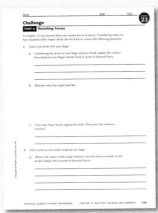

Science Challenge
Workbook, pp. 149-150

23A Static Electricity

This prechapter introduction activity is designed to determine what students already know about static electricity and how it is produced by engaging them in making predictions, evaluating, and drawing conclusions about the effect of friction on electron movement.

Objectives

* model static electricity
* observe the effects of static electricity
* record data in a suitable way
* communicate conclusions

Planning

 15–20 minutes   groups of 3–4 students

Materials (per group)

* sheet of tissue paper
* piece of silk cloth
* felt-tip marker
* plastic pen
* cardboard circle
* scissors

Advance Preparation

* Use a compass to make cardboard circles that are about 20 cm across.
* Doing this activity on a dry day will yield better results.

* You may wish to create a tissue-paper spiral in advance so students have an example to follow as they make their own spirals.
* Note that the static electric attraction gradually diminishes as the net charge leaks away.

Engagement Guide

* Challenge students to think about the nature of electric charge by asking:
    * *Why is the pen rubbed with the silk cloth before it is brought close to the tissue paper?* (Friction causes electrons to move from the silk to the pen, causing the pen to acquire a negative charge.)
    * *What do you think will happen when you bring the pen toward the tissue paper after the pen has been rubbed with the silk cloth?* (The positive charges in the tissue paper are attracted to the negative static electric charge of the pen, causing the tissue paper to rise as the pen is lifted away.)
    * *What does it mean to say something is static? What does* static electricity *mean?* (*Static* means stationary. Static electricity is the buildup of nonmoving charges.)
* Encourage students to communicate their conclusions in creative ways.

Going Further

Have students blow up a balloon and tie it off. Ask them to rub the balloon against the piece of silk cloth and place the balloon against a wall in the classroom. Let students observe what happens. Ask students to explain what occurred and why. (charging by friction; opposite charges attract)

23B Conductors and Insulators

Objectives

* model an electric circuit
* observe current flow through materials
* record and analyze data
* draw conclusions based on data

Skill Set

constructing a model, observing, recording and analyzing data, drawing conclusions

Planning

 35–40 minutes   groups of 3–4 students

Materials

Materials for this activity are listed in the Student Laboratory Manual.

Advance Preparation

* Use wire cutters to cut five pieces of insulated copper wire about 12 cm long for each group. Strip away about 1 cm of plastic from each end of the wires.
* Make sure the students do not connect a piece of wire between the positive and negative terminals of the battery, as this could create a short circuit.
* Have students wear safety goggles for this activity.

Answers to Observations: Data Table 1

Answers will vary for students' predictions. Students should observe that the coin, paper clip, pencil point, metal part of the pencil, and iron nail are conductors of electricity. Students should observe that the plastic spoon, wood part of the pencil, pencil eraser, glass beaker, and paper towel are insulators.

Answers to Analysis and Conclusions

1. All of the conductors except for the pencil point are made of metal.
2. The plastic acts as an insulator of electricity, so a person holding a wire with electricity flowing through it will not get shocked.
3. Since aluminum foil is a metal, it will be a conductor of electricity.
4. Metals have a unique atomic structure that allows their electrons to move freely. These freely moving electrons make metals excellent conductors.

Going Further

Have students perform the same experiment using other classroom objects such as a plastic pen, stapler, tape, computer paper, scissor blades, and metric ruler. Have student groups share their results with other groups in the class.

23C Series and Parallel Circuits

Objectives

- construct series and parallel circuits
- compare and contrast a series circuit and a parallel circuit by observation
- draw conclusions about series and parallel circuits based on descriptions

Skill Set

constructing models, observing, comparing and contrasting, recording and analyzing observations, stating conclusions

Planning

30–35 minutes   groups of 3–4 students

Materials

Materials for this activity are listed in the Student Laboratory Manual.

Advance Preparation

- Use wire cutters to cut five pieces of insulated copper wire about 12 cm long for each group. Strip away about 1 cm of the insulation from each end of the wires.
- Make sure the students do not connect a piece of wire between the positive and negative terminals of the battery, as this could create a short circuit.
- Have students wear safety goggles for this activity.

Answers to Observations: Data Table 1

In the series circuit, the bulbs become less bright as another bulb is added to the circuit. When one bulb is removed from the series circuit, the other two bulbs go out. In the parallel circuit, the brightness of the bulbs is not affected by adding another bulb. When one bulb is removed from the parallel circuit, the other bulbs remain lit.

Answers to Analysis and Conclusions

1. In a series circuit, all bulbs go out when one bulb is removed from the circuit. In a parallel circuit, the other bulbs stay lighted when one bulb goes out.
2. If too many lights are connected in a series circuit, each lightbulb might not get enough electricity to fully light up.
3. The resistance in the series circuit decreases as evidenced by the dimming of the lightbulbs when the third bulb was added. Resistance in the parallel circuit actually decreases with each additional bulb, or added branch.
4. If holiday lights were connected in a series circuit, the entire string of lights would go out if one lightbulb burned out. When the lights are connected in parallel circuits, the other lights can stay lighted if one or more bulbs burn out.

Going Further

Have student groups use a voltmeter to measure the voltage across the bulbs in each type of circuit. Groups should observe that the voltages around the bulbs in the parallel circuit are larger than the voltages around the bulbs in the series circuit. Have each group summarize its results and write an explanation as to why the voltages are different.

Introduce Chapter 24

As a starting activity, use Lab 24A on page 138 of the Laboratory Manual.

ENGAGE Write the following pairs of words on the board:

fire, water

north, south

yin, yang

Have students talk with a partner about how the pairs are alike (all are examples of opposites). Then have students brainstorm other examples of opposites, and encourage them to be creative. Create a class list of opposites to post in the classroom. Explain to students that the concept of opposites is important in the behavior of magnets, and ask for predictions about how the topics are related.

Think About Magnets

ENGAGE Think aloud about an object that contains a magnet, such as a credit card or bank card. Tell students that ATMs and credit-card machines also have magnets to read the cards. Have students complete the bulleted items and write their responses in their Science Notebooks. Encourage students to consider a variety of examples, including refrigerator doors and toys they might have seen or used.

Chapter 24 Magnetism

KEY CONCEPT Magnets produce invisible attractive and repulsive forces.

July 11, 2020: The doors slide shut on the Tokyo-to-Osaka express. Silently, the train begins to move, picking up speed until it moves as fast as a jet plane. At 500 km/h, the 390-km journey takes less than one hour. An old wheeled bullet train used to make the trip in three hours, but the maglev train is much faster. By using powerful magnets to levitate the train above the track, the train moves at nearly half the speed of sound.

The Tokyo-Osaka maglev is still science fiction. One of the only working maglev trains in the world today makes a short 30-km run between the outskirts of Shanghai, China, and the city's airport. However, it uses the same principles of magnetism that let you use a compass or pick up spilled paper clips with a magnet.

www.scilinks.org
Magnetism **Code: WGPS24**

Think About Magnets

Magnets produce invisible forces that can push or pull on some materials.

- In your Science Notebook, make a list of some objects that contain magnets.
- For each object on your list, write a short sentence describing how it is used.

412

Chapter 24 Planning Guide

Instructional Periods	National Standards	Lab Manual	Workbook
24.1 2 Periods	A.2, B.2, G.1, G.2, G.3; A.2, B.4, F.3, G.1, G.2, G.3; UCP.2, UCP.5	**Lab 24A: p. 138** Magnetic Forces **Lab 24B: pp. 139–140** Observing Magnetic Fields	Key Concept Review p. 151 Vocabulary Review p. 152 Interpreting Diagrams p. 153 Reading Comprehension p. 154 Curriculum Connection p. 155 Science Challenge p. 156
24.2 2 Periods	A.2, B.2, E.1, F.5, G.1, G.2; A.2, B.4, E.1, F.6, G.1, G.2; UCP.3		
24.3 2 Periods	A.1, B.1, B.2, D.1, E.2, F.3, F.5, G.1, G.2, G.3; A.1, B.2, B.4, B.6, D.1, E.2, F.1, F.5, F.6, G.1, G.2, G.3; UCP.1, UCP.3, UCP.4	**Lab 24C: pp. 141–142** The Strength of Magnetic Fields	

Middle School Standard; High School Standard; Unifying Concept and Principle

24.1 The Nature of Magnets

Before You Read

Begin a concept map in your Science Notebook for the term *Magnet*. Preview the Learning Goals, headings, and visuals in the lesson. Predict what you will learn about magnets, and record your predictions in your concept map.

Learning Goals

• Describe the origin and behavior of a magnetic field.

• Explain how magnetic fields interact with one another.

• Define *magnetic domain*.

New Vocabulary

magnetism
magnetic field
magnetic field line
magnetic pole
magnetic domain

You use magnets every day. They are inside stereo speakers and telephone receivers. They are found in televisions and computers. They store information on credit and ATM cards. They keep your refrigerator closed, and they let you mount things on the refrigerator door. What is magnetism, and what are some of the physical properties of magnets?

Figure 24.1 Magnets are part of many everyday items.

What Is Magnetism?

More than 2,000 years ago, Greeks living in a part of Turkey called Magnesia discovered deposits of a mineral that could attract pieces of iron. The Greeks named the mineral *magnetic*, for their homeland. The mineral is now called magnetite. Magnetite is a natural magnet.

A magnet produces a force that can attract or repel other magnets and can attract certain other substances. You can feel this by holding two magnets near each other. Depending on how you hold the magnets, you can feel them push or pull on each other. The physical properties and interactions of magnets are referred to as **magnetism.**

Magnetic Fields   Magnetism is produced by moving electrons. In addition to moving in their energy levels, electrons also spin. As an electron moves in these two ways, it creates a tiny magnetic field. A **magnetic field** consists of the forces of a magnet exerted in a region surrounding the magnet. A magnetic field is strongest close to the magnet, and it gets weaker farther away from it.

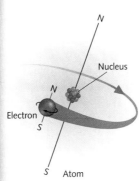

Figure 24.2
Moving electrons produce magnetic fields.

ELL Strategy

Discuss Arrange students in pairs or groups of three. When possible, group students with peers who speak the same native language. Have each group discuss and respond to the Learning Goals for the lesson. Students should write their responses in English in their Science Notebooks.

24.1 Introduce

ENGAGE Provide a variety of magnets with which students can experiment. Magnets should be of different sizes and shapes. Encourage students to write observations about how magnets interact and hypotheses about magnet behavior in their Science Notebooks.

Vocabulary terms are listed on the first student page of each lesson. You may wish to preview the terms before introducing each lesson. Strategies for teaching the vocabulary appear on the pages where the terms are introduced.

Before You Read

Model the concept map on the board. *Magnet* should be the main topic. Preview aloud the Learning Goals and add subtopics that relate to those ideas.

Have students create the concept maps in their Science Notebooks. Encourage them to preview the lesson thoroughly as they draw their maps.

Teach

EXPLAIN Ask students to describe what happened when they held magnets near each other. Reinforce the use of the words *attract* and *repel* in students' descriptions. Explain that the attraction and repulsion are magnetic forces. The overall phenomenon is known as magnetism.

Vocabulary

magnetism Tell students that the suffix *-ism* denotes a quality or state. Explain to students that a magnet is a piece of metal, often iron, that can attract or repel iron and other metals.

magnetic field Have students brainstorm common uses of the word *field*. Responses might include an area of land used to grow crops, an area of land used for playing sports, or an activity or subject that is a person's specialty or interest. Review with students the meaning of the word *magnetic*. Explain that objects experience magnetic forces in the magnetic field of a magnet.

Teach

Provide pairs of students with iron filings in a plastic bag and a bar magnet. Ask students to place all the iron filings in a clump on a flat surface and then move the magnet closer to the filings. Have students explore the movement of the filings as they move the magnet in different ways. Then have students use the filings to map out the magnetic field lines of the magnet. Students should sketch the results in their Science Notebooks.

 Vocabulary

magnetic field line Have students brainstorm common uses of the word *line*. Responses might include a long narrow mark, a row of people awaiting something, a boundary or division between two locations, a length of rope, a rail/sea/air route served by a specific company, or a perfectly straight curve. Review with students the meanings of the words *magnetic* and *field,* and then have students infer the meaning of the term.

magnetic pole Ask students to list common uses of the word *pole*. Responses might include references to Earth's north and south poles or a cylindrical rod. Review with students the meaning of the word *magnetic*. Then have students find the meaning of the term using these literal definitions.

As You Read

Give students a few minutes to update and revise their concept maps.

ANSWER The magnetic field will move from the north pole to the south pole of the magnet. Arrows on the concept map should point from the left side of the drawing to the right. Check students' drawings for understanding.

As You Read

Draw a rectangular box around the term *Magnet* in your Science Notebook. Then draw a set of magnetic field lines around the box. Label the magnetic field and the magnetic poles. Indicate which direction the magnetic field moves if the north pole of the magnet is on the left side of the drawing.

A magnetic field can be visualized by sprinkling iron filings around a magnet. The magnetic field pushes and pulls on all the bits of iron. These forces make the iron filings line up in a specific way. The filings become a picture of the magnetic field's shape, strength, and direction.

The lines that represent the shape, strength, and direction of the magnetic field around a magnet are called **magnetic field lines,** or lines of magnetic force. Magnetic field lines can be drawn to map out the magnetic field, as shown in **Figure 24.3.** Where the magnetic field is stronger, the lines are drawn closer together. The arrows on the magnetic field lines show the direction of the field.

Figure 24.3
A magnet is surrounded by a magnetic field, which can be represented by magnetic field lines. Every magnetic field starts at one end of the magnet and moves toward the other end.

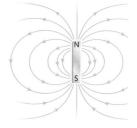

Magnetic Poles Every magnet has a magnetic field stretched between two magnetic poles. The **magnetic poles** are the regions where the magnetic field exerted by a magnet is the strongest. The north and south poles are at opposite ends of a bar magnet. A magnetic field is curved, and it moves from one end of a magnet to the other. It always starts at the north pole and moves to the south pole. Magnetic field lines are closest together at a magnet's poles. When two magnets are brought close together, their magnetic fields interact with each other. The north pole of one magnet will repel the north pole of another magnet. South poles also repel each other. The north pole of one magnet and the south pole of the other magnet, however, attract each other and stick together.

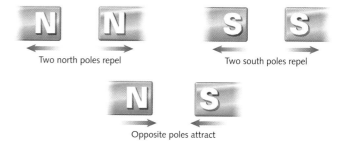

Two north poles repel   Two south poles repel

Opposite poles attract

Figure 24.4 Each magnet has a north pole and a south pole. Two north poles or two south poles repel each other. A north pole and a south pole attract each other.

Differentiate Instruction

Visual Have students make a collage of items that contain magnets or use magnets to function. Students should use magazines, pictures from the Internet, and hand-drawn illustrations.

When two magnets interact, their magnetic fields combine. Iron filings can be used to map the combined magnetic field, as shown in **Figure 24.5.** The field lines curve toward each other when opposite poles are brought close together, and they curve away from each other when like poles are brought close together. Magnetic field lines that curve away from each other show repulsion. Magnetic field lines that curve toward each other show attraction.

Figure 24.5 What do the magnetic field lines from the two magnets in each photo indicate about the interaction of like and opposite poles?

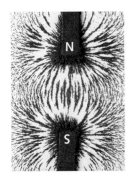 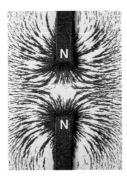

Magnets can be different shapes and sizes. A bar magnet has a pole at each of its ends. A horseshoe magnet is *U*-shaped and has a pole at each end of the *U*. A disk magnet has a pole on each of its flat sides. Each type of magnet produces a magnetic field with a different shape. The magnetic field of a bar magnet is shown in **Figure 24.3** on page 414. Compare it with the magnetic fields of the magnets shown in **Figure 24.6.**

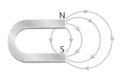 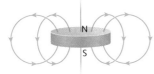

Figure 24.6 Horseshoe magnets and disk magnets produce magnetic fields with different shapes.

If a small magnet is moved into a larger magnetic field, the small magnet will rotate until its magnetic field aligns with the larger field. The north pole of the small magnet is attracted toward the south pole of the larger magnet. Although the two magnetic fields are lined up, they move in opposite directions. The north pole of one magnet is aligned with the south pole of the other magnet.

Figure It Out

1. Where is the magnetic field of the disk magnet weakest?

2. Predict what will happen when a bar magnet is placed next to the poles of the horseshoe magnet.

Teach

Provide a horseshoe magnet, disk magnet, and iron filings in plastic bags to pairs of students. Have students observe the differences in magnetic fields of the different magnets.

Next, ask students to sketch the magnetic fields in their Science Notebooks. Discuss with students the differences among the magnetic fields of the different types of magnets.

Use the Visual: Figure 24.5

[ANSWER] Opposite poles attract (magnetic field lines curve toward each other) and like poles repel (magnetic field lines curve away from each other).

Figure It Out: Figure 24.6

[ANSWER] **1.** The magnetic field is weakest at the sides of the disk magnet. **2.** When a bar magnet and a horseshoe magnet are placed near each other, the north pole of the bar magnet will stick to the south pole of the horseshoe magnet, and vice versa.

Background Information

The strength of magnetic fields can be measured using a gauss meter. Webers (Wb) are the unit of measure for magnetic lines of force or flux. The density of the flux, the strength of the magnetic field, is measured in Tesla (T) or gauss (G). Another common way to measure field strength is in Webers per square meter.

Teach

EXPLAIN to students that magnetic domains are produced when a majority of electrons spin in the same direction and cause groups of atoms to align with their magnetic poles in the same direction. When enough domains align in the same direction, a magnetic field results.

 Vocabulary

magnetic domain Have students brainstorm common uses of the word *domain*. Ask students to relate the common uses of the words to the scientific definition of the term.

 Explain It!

Because the magnetic domains are all aligned in one direction, a magnet will always have a north and south pole regardless of the size of the pieces into which it is broken.

CONNECTION: Materials Science

Give students the scientific names of different magnets and have them work with partners to research the elements of which these magnets are comprised. Examples include:

ferric magnets: iron oxide in a ceramic composite

alnico magnets: aluminum, nickel, and cobalt

Assess

Use the After You Read questions and the Alternative Assessment to help you evaluate students' understanding of the lesson.

After You Read

1. The magnetic domain should be placed inside the box representing a magnet.
2. One magnet's north pole will attract the other's south pole. Opposite poles attract.
3. It is strongest at the magnet's poles.
4. The magnetic domains are not lined up, and their random organization cancels out their magnetic fields.

 Explain It!

If you cut a magnet in half, you create two smaller magnets, each of which has a north pole and a south pole. Use what you have learned about magnetic domains to explain why you cannot make a magnet with only one pole.

CONNECTION: Materials Science

Magnets can be made out of iron, but they can also be made out of nickel, cobalt, and ceramics that contain any of these metals.

Magnets and Materials

An electron's spin creates a magnetic field. All matter contains atoms that have spinning electrons. Yet not all forms of matter are magnetic. A magnet sticks to metals such as iron, cobalt, and nickel, and to the alloy steel. A magnet does not stick to metals such as aluminum, gold, or copper. Nor does it stick to your skin or the pages of this book.

Why are some things magnetic and others not? Electrons can spin in one of two directions. In most materials, the electrons spin in different directions and cancel one another. Magnetic materials contain more electrons spinning in one direction than in the other direction. This makes each atom in the material a tiny magnet. Groups of atoms line up with their magnetic poles pointing in the same direction. Organized groups of atoms lined up with their magnetic poles pointing in the same direction are called **magnetic domains.** Although each domain contains a huge number of atoms, the domains are too small to be observed with the unaided eye. Because the magnetic poles of the individual atoms in a domain are lined up in the same direction, each domain in a magnetic material behaves like a magnet with a north pole and a south pole.

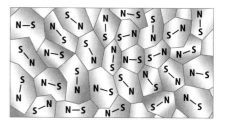

Figure 24.7 Magnetic domains are microscopic areas inside some materials that can act like tiny magnets. These domains are normally arranged randomly, and their magnetic fields cancel one another.

Most of the materials that form magnetic domains still do not become magnetic. These materials contain many magnetic domains, but each domain points in a different direction. The magnetic fields created by the domains are cancelled out. However, if something can make the magnetic domains line up, the material develops a magnetic field.

After You Read

1. Review the concept map you drew in your Science Notebook. Place the label *Magnetic Domain* correctly on the map.
2. What will happen if you bring the north pole of one magnet near the south pole of another? Why?
3. Where is a magnetic field strongest?
4. Explain why many materials that contain magnetic domains are still not magnetic.

Alternative Assessment

Have students use their concept maps to compare a magnetic field to a magnetic domain. They should use the terms *magnetic poles* and *magnetic field lines* in their comparisons. Students can use sketches to illustrate their comparisons.

Background Information

In the atoms of cobalt, iron, nickel, oxygen, and gadolinium, the spins of some electrons are not paired. Therefore, each atom is an atomic dipole; that is, it has a magnetic field and acts as a magnet. When exposed to an external magnetic field, the atoms will line up parallel to the field. This event is called paramagnetism and results in the atoms being attracted to magnets.

Before You Read

In your Science Notebook, draw a T-chart. Label one column *Natural Magnet* and the other column *Induced Magnet*. Record any facts you already know about these magnets in the appropriate columns. As you read the lesson, add information about each kind of magnet to your chart.

Try picking up some paper clips with a strong magnet. When one paper clip sticks to the magnet, it becomes a magnet, too. More paper clips stick to the first one, and those paper clips become magnets, as well. You can build a chain of paper-clip magnets that dangles from the magnet, held together by magnetic attraction only.

Figure 24.8 This magnet has magnetized the paper clips hanging from it. Each paper clip becomes a bar magnet with a north pole and a south pole.

When you separate the magnet and the paper clips, the magnet stays magnetized but the clips quickly lose their magnetic fields. What makes one magnet permanent and the others temporary?

Natural Magnets

Some materials are naturally magnetic. One of these materials is called **magnetite.** It is a form of iron ore that contains two slightly different iron atoms. Some of the iron atoms in magnetite are missing two electrons (Fe^{2+}), and some are missing three electrons (Fe^{3+}). Both types of iron are called ions, or charged atoms. Electrons are constantly passed from one type of iron ion to the other. The moving electrons create aligned magnetic domains, and the magnetic domains give the mineral a strong magnetic field.

Magnetite is also called lodestone. This name is derived from the fact that the Greeks who first discovered the mineral's attractive properties also noticed another interesting phenomenon. They observed that if they allowed a piece of the mineral to swing freely from a string, the same part would always face in the same direction. That direction was toward a northern star called the leading star, or lodestar.

Learning Goals

- Identify the origin of the magnetic field in a natural magnet.
- Explain how magnetic induction works.
- Name two ways in which a magnetic field is disrupted.

New Vocabulary

magnetite
magnetic induction

Figure It Out

1. Where are the north poles of the paper clips that are touching the magnet? Explain.
2. Describe the orientation of the magnetic domains in the magnetized paper clips.

Figure 24.9
Magnetite is a naturally magnetic mineral.

ENGAGE Provide a strong bar magnet and 10 to 20 small paper clips to each pair of students. Ask students to make a chain of paper clip magnets as long as possible, with the paper clips held together by magnetism. Have students sketch their chains in their Science Notebooks, labeling the north and south poles of the bar magnet and paper clips.

Before You Read

Draw the T-chart on the board, labeling the columns as directed. Discuss with students the terms *natural* and *induced*. Thinking aloud, write in the *Natural Magnet* column *magnetite* and a *mineral*. Have students draw their T-charts in their Science Notebooks and add their known facts.

Teach

EXPLAIN to students that while some materials (such as magnetite) are naturally magnetic, others can be made magnetic. In this lesson, students will learn how this occurs.

Figure It Out: **Figure 24.8**

ANSWER **1.** The south pole of the paper clip is at the top of the clip because it is being attracted by the north pole of the magnet. **2.** The magnetic domains in the paper clips are all pointing from the top of the clips toward the bottom of the clips.

Vocabulary

magnetite Explain to students that the suffix *-ite* denotes a mineral. Magnetite is a shiny, black, strongly magnetic mineral form of iron oxide.

ELL Strategy

Model Supply students with index cards or 2" × 2" squares and have them draw an arrow (pointing one way) on each card. The arrows represent the spin of an electron. Students should then use the cards to model magnetic induction and temporary and permanent magnets.

Key Concept Review
Workbook, p. 151

Review with students the result of the paper clip activity. Ask students to hypothesize how the paper clips became magnetized and were able to form a chain. Explain to students that the magnetic domains in the paper clips aligned to create a magnetic field. Have students use their arrow cards from the ELL Strategy on the previous page to display the process of magnetic induction in the paper clip activity.

Vocabulary

magnetic induction Tell students that the root of the word *induction, induce,* is derived from Latin and means "to lead in." Magnetic induction occurs when a material's magnetic domains are "led," or aligned.

As You Read

Give students a few minutes to add facts from the lesson to their T-charts.

ANSWER Magnetic induction is the process by which a magnetic field is created in a material as a result of aligning the material's magnetic domains.

PEOPLE IN SCIENCE

Paul C. Lauterbur was born in Ohio in 1929. Lauterbur went on to study at Case Institute of Technology in Cleveland, where he earned a degree in chemistry in 1951. Through his studies of rubber technology, he learned about nuclear magnetic resonance (NMR). In 2003, he was awarded the Nobel Prize in Physiology or Medicine.

As You Read

Read the entries you have made in the T-chart in your Science Notebook to a partner. After listening to your partner's entries, add to or correct the information in your T-chart.

What is magnetic induction?

Magnetic Induction

How do the paper clips attached to the bar magnet become magnets themselves? Remember that magnetic materials such as iron and steel contain many microscopic magnetic domains. Each magnetic domain acts like a tiny magnet. Because the domains normally point in random directions, their magnetic fields cancel out. When a magnet touches these materials, however, all of the magnetic domains swing around and line up with the magnetic field of the magnet. When all of the magnetic domains point in the same direction, the material develops a magnetic field of its own. The process by which a magnetic field is created in a material as a result of aligning the material's magnetic domains is called **magnetic induction.**

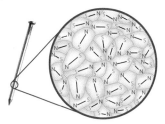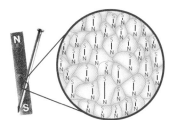

Figure 24.10 The magnetic domains inside the nail normally point in many directions (*left*). The magnetic fields cancel each other, so the nail does not act like a magnet. When a magnet is brought near the nail, the nail's magnetic domains line up with the magnet's magnetic field (*right*). The nail's magnetic domains do not cancel each other, and the nail becomes a magnet.

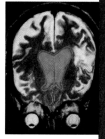

PEOPLE IN SCIENCE Paul C. Lauterbur (1929–2007)

MRI, or magnetic resonance imaging, is a revolutionary tool that allows doctors to get detailed pictures of the insides of their patients without surgery. It has led to better diagnoses and has reduced the need for exploratory surgeries. In 2003, Paul Lauterbur shared the Nobel Prize in Medicine for his part in developing MRI technology.

In the 1940s, scientists had discovered that if they surrounded a material with a strong magnetic field, they could manipulate how fast the material's atomic nuclei spun. Removing the field made the nuclei emit radio waves, which were analyzed to determine the material's chemical structure. During the early 1950s, Lauterbur became an expert in this process, which is known as nuclear magnetic resonance, or NMR.

For years, Lauterbur used the NMR equipment to study biologically active molecules. However, differences in the strength of the magnetic field blurred the radio waves emitted by the sample and made them hard to interpret. In 1971, Lauterbur realized that the blurring was the result of all of the radio waves coming out of the sample at once. By breaking the radio waves into smaller sections, he created a two-dimensional picture of the material he was imaging. It was the first step toward an MRI machine.

Differentiate Instruction

<u>Interpersonal</u> Have students talk with different types of doctors in their community about the use of MRIs. In preparation, brainstorm a class list of questions that students might ask a doctor. Students might visit a hospital, lab, or doctor's office to discover how MRI technology is used on a daily basis.

Background Information

Most organs of the body can be examined using MRI technology. It has been shown to be very effective in diagnosing strokes, some types of cancer, and spinal cord injuries.

Temporary and Permanent Magnets

Some materials stay magnetic for only a short time after magnetic induction. For example, a nail, which is made of soft iron, might act like a magnet while it is next to a stronger magnet. However, when the stronger magnet is removed, the nail's magnetic field disappears. This happens because atoms inside the nail are constantly vibrating. When the external magnetic field is removed, the atomic vibrations bump the nail's magnetic domains out of alignment. When the magnetic domains are arranged randomly, the magnetism disappears. Magnets made of materials that are easy to magnetize but lose their magnetism easily are called temporary magnets.

Some materials, including iron, nickel, and cobalt, can stay magnetic for a long time after magnetic induction. When the magnetic domains of such metals are lined up, they hold one another in place so they do not fall out of alignment. These materials become permanent magnets. Permanent magnets are more difficult to magnetize, but they tend to retain their magnetism. Many permanent magnets are made of alnico, which is a mixture of aluminum, nickel, cobalt, and iron.

A permanent magnet can lose its magnetic field if it gets very hot. When a permanent magnet is heated, its atoms move faster. If the magnet gets hot enough, its faster-moving atoms will bump the magnetic domains out of alignment. When the magnetic domains are arranged randomly, the magnetism is lost. Permanent magnets can also become demagnetized if they are dropped or struck too hard. These actions knock the domains out of alignment, and the magnet loses some or all of its magnetism.

After You Read

1. What is lodestone?
2. Explain how a steel nail can become a magnet.
3. Compare and contrast temporary magnets and permanent magnets.
4. In your Science Notebook, write a well-developed paragraph hypothesizing whether a natural magnet can lose its magnetism. Be sure to include key concepts and supporting details from this lesson.

 Explore It!

Gather objects made of the following materials: paper, copper, steel, nickel, aluminum, plastic, iron, and glass. Predict which objects are magnetic. Then use a permanent magnet to test your predictions.

Write your results in your Science Notebook.

● Teach

EXPLAIN to students that magnetic induction is often a temporary state for most materials. Some materials, such as iron, nickel, and cobalt, retain their magnetism for longer periods of time.

 **Explore It!**

Provide a sample of each of the materials and a permanent magnet to each pair of students. Students should understand that if a material is magnetic, it will be attracted to the permanent magnet. Have each student create a table with eight rows and two columns in his or her Science Notebook. Students should list one material in each row and write *Yes* or *No* in the columns labeled *Magnetic* and *Not Magnetic*.

● Assess

Use the After You Read questions and the Alternative Assessment to help you evaluate students' understanding of the lesson.

After You Read

1. Lodestone is another name for magnetite, a naturally magnetic material.
2. Descriptions will vary, but students should demonstrate an understanding of magnetic induction.
3. Both temporary magnets and permanent magnets become magnetized as a result of magnetic induction. The magnetic domains in both types of magnets are aligned. A temporary magnet is easy to magnetize, but it loses its magnetism easily. Permanent magnets are more difficult to magnetize, but they tend to retain their magnetism.
4. Even a natural magnet can lose its magnetism if it is heated enough to disrupt the alignment of the magnetic domains inside the material.

Alternative Assessment

Have students use the T-charts to compare and contrast natural and induced magnets.

Teacher Alert

Electromagnets can also be considered temporary; their magnetic fields only exist when electric current flows. Permanent magnets may also be called hard magnets, and temporary magnets are also known as soft magnets.

Background Information

Electron pairs spin in opposite directions, and their magnetic fields have a net zero effect. However, atoms of ferromagnetic elements have unpaired electrons with the same spin. The unpaired electrons create a phenomenon known as an orbital magnetic moment. This moment is a vector quantity (it has both magnitude and direction). Individual magnetic moments add together to produce the macroscopic effect of magnetism.

24.3 Introduce

ENGAGE Provide each student with a world map that has a compass rose on it showing cardinal directions. Ask students to find various locations on the map, such as the state in which your school is located, a student's native country, the north and south poles, the equator, and two or three other easily identified countries. Then ask students to work with partners to write three to five comparison statements based on these observations, such as *California is north of the equator.*

Have each pair share one statement, and write the responses on the board. Point out that students' understanding of the world is based upon knowledge of the directions north and south. Tell students that Earth has magnetic poles in addition to having geographic poles.

Before You Read

Read aloud the lesson title and subheadings from this page. Tell students that they will learn about the ways in which Earth is a magnet. Have students continue to preview the subheadings and ask them to write additional predictions in their Science Notebooks.

● Teach

EXPLAIN to students that Earth's geographic poles are not the same as the planet's magnetic poles; in fact, the poles are different by about 11 degrees. Have students draw on their maps where they estimate that the magnetic poles are.

Learning Goals

- Describe Earth's magnetic field.
- Name two ways in which Earth's magnetic field has changed over time.
- Explain how a compass works.
- Understand that Earth's magnetic field extends into space.

New Vocabulary

compass
magnetosphere
aurora

Figure 24.11 William Gilbert (1544–1603) was the royal physician to Queen Elizabeth I and James I. His experiments with magnets led him to conclude that Earth was magnetic.

24.3 Earth as a Magnet

Before You Read

Read the lesson title and the headings and look at the pictures. Predict what you think you will learn in this lesson. Write your predictions in two or three sentences in your Science Notebook.

Before 1600, a compass was considered to be magical. No one knew why a magnetized needle pointed north. There were many explanations, including that the compass pointed to veins in Earth and that the North Star pulled on the needle. In 1600, William Gilbert showed that compass needles point north because Earth is a giant magnet.

Gilbert used experiments to test the ideas people had about magnets. Many of his experiments used a model of Earth built out of a large lodestone. He placed tiny compasses on his model and observed that they behaved exactly like compasses on Earth. The miniature compasses aligned themselves with the north and south poles of the lodestone. Gilbert concluded that Earth must be a giant spherical magnet with magnetic poles at the north and south ends of the planet.

Magnetic Planet

William Gilbert was right—Earth is a giant magnet. The planet is surrounded by a magnetic field. Its field lines leave the area near the south pole and return to an area near the north pole. Earth's magnetic field is tilted about 11° from its rotational axis, which is defined by the north and south geographic poles. **Figure 24.12** shows this difference.

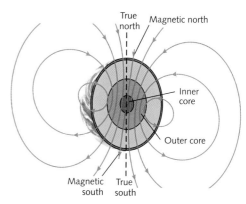

Figure 24.12 Earth's magnetic field has two poles at opposite ends of the planet. The magnetic poles are at a slight angle relative to the geographic poles.

E L L Strategy

Activate Prior Knowledge Have students discuss their experience with using cardinal directions, maps, and compasses to navigate. Encourage students to think about times when they might have traveled by car, boat, or foot and relied upon those tools to find their way.

Field Study

Show students how to navigate using a compass. Students should walk to various rooms and locations around the school and note the direction of north in each location. Students can then use their notes to draw a map of the school with correctly labeled cardinal directions.

Gilbert hypothesized that the metal making up Earth was a giant lodestone. However, scientific evidence indicates that Earth's inner core is much too hot to allow magnetic domains to form in iron. The explanation for Earth's magnetic field is based on the composition and movement of the innermost layers of the planet. The huge mass of solid iron and nickel that makes up Earth's inner core spins faster than the rest of the planet. Earth's outer core is a mass of electrically charged liquid iron. Scientists hypothesize that interactions of the liquid outer core with the fast-spinning solid inner core produce Earth's magnetic field.

Changes in Earth's Magnetic Field

The poles on a bar magnet are always in the same place. However, Earth's magnetic field is dynamic. It changes over time. The locations of the magnetic poles drift over the surface of the planet. The magnetic north pole is not in the same location now as it was 100 years ago. **Figure 24.13** shows how the location of the north magnetic pole changed between 1831 and 1997.

Figure 24.13 The location of Earth's magnetic poles drifts over time.

The polarity of Earth's magnetic field also reverses direction over time. When the field reverses itself, the magnetic north pole becomes the magnetic south pole, and vice versa. After one of these shifts, a compass that pointed north would start to point south.

Evidence of these reversals is preserved in rocks. Some types of magma, or molten rock, contain iron. When the magma cools and becomes rock, the magnetic domains in the iron line up with Earth's magnetic field. When the rock solidifies, the magnetic iron is frozen in place. It becomes a snapshot of the magnetic field at the time the rock formed. The change does not occur in regular intervals. Sometimes the field reverses itself after a few million years; sometimes after tens of millions of years. Each reversal takes about 2,000 years to complete!

As You Read

In your Science Notebook, list the facts you have learned about Earth's magnetic field. Compare those facts with your predictions. Correct your predictions as needed.

How has Earth's magnetic field changed over the past century?

Figure It Out

1. Where was the north magnetic pole in 1904, relative to its position in 1962?

2. Predict in which direction the north magnetic pole will move over the next few decades.

 CONNECTION: Astronomy

Other planets in our solar system, including Jupiter, Saturn, and Mercury, have magnetic fields, but Mars and Venus do not.

● Teach

EXPLAIN to students that many properties of Earth are dynamic. Its magnetic field and the polarity of the magnetic field both change (slowly) over time. Ask students to think of other examples of change on Earth. Examples might include erosion, plate tectonics, global warming, or the ice ages.

As You Read

Give students a few minutes to list their facts and revise their predictions. Then have them work with partners to review their predictions.

ANSWER Students should show that they understand the different time frames of the changes in Earth's magnetic field. Over the past few decades, the magnetic pole has changed its position, but there have been no magnetic field reversals.

Figure It Out: Figure 24.13

ANSWER **1.** In 1904, the north magnetic pole was south of its position in 1962.
2. Answers will vary, but students should predict a general movement northward.

CONNECTION: Astronomy

Have students label a diagram of the planets with the names of the planets, magnetic fields, size (radius) of each, and rotation. Ask students to include other observations about the planets, especially in relation to Earth.

Differentiate Instruction

Kinesthetic Have students make a model of Earth using a plastic foam ball or other three-dimensional craft material. Have students draw and label the continents, oceans, and north and south poles. Then ask students to label the locations of the magnetic poles from 1831 to the present.

Background Information

The magnetic dynamo theory states that the magnetic field in planets is created by swirling motions of liquid conducting material within the planet's body. In this liquid form, some of the electrons are squeezed out of the atoms and can move freely. A moving charge can produce a magnetic field. If a planet rotates quickly enough, the liquid within the planet will move freely and produce a magnetic field.

Teach

Tie a piece of thread around the middle of a bar magnet. In front of the class, tie the end of the thread around an object so that the magnet is suspended freely. Leave the magnet undisturbed until it stops moving. After the magnet stops moving, ask students to tell which way the ends of the magnet are pointing. Ask students how they know that one end points north and the other end points south. Explain that a device in which a magnet is free to align with Earth's magnetic field is known as a compass.

 Vocabulary

compass Ask students to list common definitions of the word *compass*. Their lists might include a tool used to draw circles or a device for finding direction. Ask students to relate the common definition to the scientific definition.

magnetosphere Tell students that the word *sphere* is derived from the Greek word *sphaira,* meaning "a globe." Review with students the meaning of the word *magnet.* Have students place the two words together and relate the literal meaning of the parts to the scientific definition of the term.

aurora Explain to students that the word *aurora* is derived from Latin and means "dawn." Ask students to relate the derivation to the scientific definition of the term.

 Explore It!

Provide students with the materials necessary for the activity. Suggest that students use a small piece of tape to secure the needle on the cork. Remind them to place the dish on a table that is level and to refrain from bumping the table throughout the activity. English language learners should be encouraged to use the vocabulary words to explain what they have observed.

ANSWER The magnetized needle will point to Earth's magnetic field until a permanent magnet is brought close to it; then the needle will align with the magnet's field.

Figure 24.14 A compass contains a magnetized needle that aligns with larger magnetic fields. As the compass is moved around the bar magnet, its needle rotates to point along the magnetic field lines.

 Explore It!

Partially fill a small nonmetal dish with water. Magnetize a needle by placing it on a permanent bar magnet in line with the north and south poles for at least one minute.

Use a cork to carefully float the needle. Turn the dish slowly and note the direction in which the needle points. Bring the permanent magnet near the needle and observe the needle's behavior. Record your observations in your Science Notebook.

422 MAGNETISM

The Compass

A **compass** is an instrument containing a magnetized needle that can swing around in a circle. The needle is a small bar magnet with a north magnetic pole and a south magnetic pole. When the needle is brought near a larger magnet, it rotates until it lines up with the magnetic field in that location. **Figure 24.14** shows how a compass needle rotates when it is placed near a larger bar magnet.

If a compass needle is not near a magnet, it lines up with Earth's magnetic field. One end of the needle will point toward the magnetic north pole; the other end will point toward the magnetic south pole.

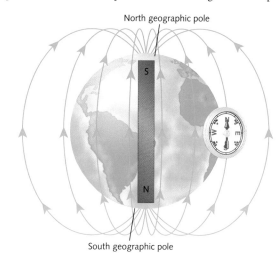

Figure 24.15 Compass needles line up with the north-south axis of Earth's magnetic field.

The north end of the compass needle always points to the north part of Earth. Yet if you place another magnet near the compass, the north end of that magnet repels the north end of the needle. Only the north and south poles of two magnets are attracted to each other. This means that the magnetic pole in the north part of Earth is really the south pole of the planet's magnetic field.

The Magnetosphere

Earth's magnetic field stretches away from the planet into space, forming the **magnetosphere** (mag NEE toh sfihr). Earth's magnetosphere extends as far as 11 Earth radii into space on the side of the planet facing the Sun, and it stretches out more than 200 Earth radii on the side of the planet facing away from the Sun.

Background Information

The ancient Chinese found that a steel needle would point north and south when freely suspended. Later, Columbus used a magnetic compass when he crossed the Atlantic Ocean and compared the process to navigating by stars. He noticed that the compass reading deviated slightly from exact north throughout the voyage. In 1600, Queen Elizabeth's personal physician, William Gilbert, theorized that Earth was a giant magnet.

Interpreting Diagrams Workbook, p. 153

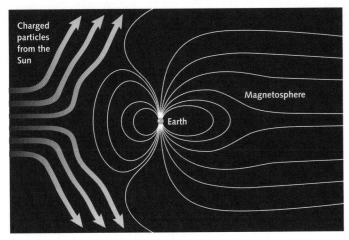

Figure 24.16 Earth's magnetic field extends into space and deflects the charged particles released by the Sun.

The Sun is constantly releasing energetic charged particles that could be dangerous to living things. The magnetosphere deflects most of these particles away from Earth. The particles that are not deflected are attracted to Earth's magnetic poles, where they crash into atoms in the atmosphere. These tiny, high-energy crashes release light. When the Sun is releasing large numbers of particles, the particles crashing into atoms in the atmosphere produce ribbons of greenish and purple light called an **aurora** (uh ROR uh). Auroras are easiest to see near the northern and southern ends of the planet, and they are also called the northern and southern lights.

After You Read

1. If Earth is like a bar magnet, where is its north magnetic pole?
2. Name two ways in which Earth's magnetic field has changed over time.
3. Why are auroras seen only near the north and south poles?
4. Review the predictions and any corrections you recorded in your Science Notebook. Use that information to compose a well-developed paragraph describing how a compass behaves when it is placed near a strong magnet.

CHAPTER 24   423

Extend It!

Charged particles from the Sun that penetrate Earth's magnetic field are forced to continually spiral around the field lines, moving back and forth between magnetic poles. These charged particles are generally found in two large regions known as the Van Allen radiation belts. Use library and internet resources to find out about these belts. Include information about their locations in the solar system, their effects on the solar system, and the derivations of their names.

Figure 24.17 An aurora is produced when charged solar particles attracted to Earth's magnetic poles crash into atoms in the atmosphere.

● Teach

EXPLAIN to students that an aurora behaves similarly to a neon sign. The differences are that the conducting gas is in the ionosphere rather than a glass tube and the current travels along magnetic field lines rather than copper wires.

Extend It!

Provide students with a variety of reference materials and Web sites about the Van Allen belts. Encourage students to think about the effect of the radiation belts on space flights, as well. It might be helpful for students to sketch Earth and the location of both belts in order to better visualize the locations.

● Assess

Use the After You Read questions and the Alternative Assessment to help you evaluate students' understanding of the lesson.

After You Read

1. Earth's north magnetic pole is near the south geographic (rotational) pole.
2. Earth's magnetic field has reversed itself, and the position of the poles has changed over time.
3. The high-energy solar particles that produce auroras are attracted to the strongest parts of Earth's magnetic field, which are at the poles.
4. Near a strong magnet, a compass needle aligns itself with the magnet's magnetic field. The needle's north pole points toward the magnet's south pole.

Alternative Assessment

Students should use the predictions in their Science Notebooks to describe Earth's magnetic field and how the field has changed over time.

Background Information

The Sun's corona, like Earth's atmosphere, is held down by gravity. However, heat is conducted through the Sun's atmosphere in such a way that the upper layers are blown away from the Sun at high velocity. This flow of high-energy particles has been named the solar wind, and it constantly shapes Earth's magnetosphere. When conditions are just right, particles leak into the magnetosphere, causing auroras or radiation belts.

The Van Allen radiation belts are named after James Van Allen, designer of Explorer I. The inner belt is centered at about 3,000 km above Earth, and it has a thickness of about 5,000 km. The outer region is located at about 15,000 to 20,000 km above Earth, and its thickness is 6,000 to 10,000 km. When manned space flights travel through the radiation belts, they are well-shielded to protect both the people and instrumentation.

Chapter 24 Summary

Check students' sentences or paragraphs to make sure they understand the meaning of each vocabulary term.

Evaluate students' essays using the following criteria:

1. The topic sentence, or main idea, should restate the Key Concept.

2. The supporting paragraphs should incorporate the answers to the Learning Goal questions students have written and include details, facts, and examples they have recorded in their Science Notebooks.

3. The concluding sentence should sum up the main idea of the chapter and restate the Key Concept.

MASTERING CONCEPTS

True or False

1. False, south
2. False, electrons
3. True
4. True
5. False, different
6. False, weaker

Short Answer

7. The history of field reversals is preserved by magnetic domains in ancient rocks. Reversals are seen as a series of stripes containing iron with reversed polarity.

8. The magnets have like poles facing each other, producing a repulsive force.

9. Anything that disrupts the alignment of the magnetic domains (random atomic movements, heat, sharp blows) can disrupt a magnetic field.

10. After a magnetic field reversal, the compass needle would point south.

11. The north pole of the nail will be touching the magnet.

Chapter
24

Summary

KEY CONCEPTS

24.1 The Nature of Magnets

- Spinning electrons create magnetic fields.
- The lines that represent the shape, strength, and direction of the magnetic field around a magnet are called magnetic field lines.
- A magnetic field is curved and moves from the north pole of a magnet to its south pole.
- Like poles repel each other, but opposite poles attract.
- A material is magnetic when it contains aligned magnetic domains.

24.2 Making Magnets

- Naturally magnetic materials contain aligned magnetic domains that are stable.
- A magnet can make some materials magnetic by aligning their magnetic domains.
- An object loses magnetism when its magnetic domains are brought out of alignment. This can happen when the object is heated or dropped. It can also happen because of the object's random atomic movements.

24.3 Earth as a Magnet

- Earth produces its own magnetic field.
- Earth's magnetic field is constantly changing.
- A compass contains a small magnet that lines up with Earth's magnetic field.
- Earth's magnetic field extends into space to form the magnetosphere.
- The magnetosphere deflects most solar particles away from Earth. Those that are not deflected are attracted to Earth's magnetic poles, where they crash into atoms in the atmosphere and produce ribbons of greenish and purple light called auroras.

VOCABULARY REVIEW

Write each term in a complete sentence or write a paragraph relating several terms.

24.1
magnetism, p. 413
magnetic field, p. 413
magnetic field line, p. 414
magnetic pole, p. 414
magnetic domain, p. 416

24.2
magnetite, p. 417
magnetic induction, p. 418

24.3
compass, p. 422
magnetosphere, p. 422
aurora, p. 423

PREPARE FOR CHAPTER TEST

To prepare for the chapter test, create a question from each Learning Goal. Use the information in your Science Notebook to answer each question. Then use these answers to write a well-developed essay about the chapter. Use the Key Concept on the first page of this chapter as your topic sentence.

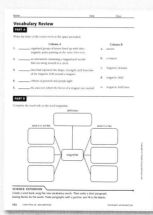

Vocabulary Review
Workbook, p. 152

Reading Comprehension
Workbook, p. 154

MASTERING CONCEPTS

True or False
If the statement is true, write "true." If it is false, change the underlined word or words to make the statement true.

1. The <u>north</u> end of a magnet is attracted to the north end of another magnet.

2. Spinning <u>neutrons</u> produce magnetic fields.

3. Earth's magnetic field <u>changes</u> over time.

4. <u>Magnetic induction</u> occurs when one magnet makes another material magnetic.

5. Earth's magnetic and geographic poles are <u>identical</u>.

6. Magnetic fields get <u>stronger</u> farther away from a magnet.

Short Answer
Answer each of the following in a sentence or brief paragraph.

7. What preserves the record of Earth's magnetic field reversals?

8. When two bar magnets are placed next to each other on a bed of iron filings, the filings form lines that bend away from one another. What can you tell about the poles of the magnets?

9. Explain how a magnet can lose its magnetic field.

10. What would happen to a compass needle if Earth's magnetic field completed a reversal tomorrow?

11. If you touch the south pole of a bar magnet to a nail to magnetize it, which pole of the nail is touching the magnet?

Critical Thinking
Use what you have learned in this chapter to answer each of the following.

12. **Infer** Cobalt atoms have 27 electrons and are magnetic. Carbon atoms have six electrons and are not. Use your knowledge of how electrons cause magnetism to infer why cobalt is magnetic and carbon is not.

13. **Hypothesize** It is possible to magnetize an iron bar by placing it on the ground pointing toward the north magnetic pole and hitting it with a hammer. Hypothesize how hammering can produce a magnetic field.

14. **Predict** When sunspot activity increases, the Sun sends more charged particles toward Earth. Predict what will happen to the auroras at these times.

Standardized Test Question
Choose the letter of the response that correctly answers the question.

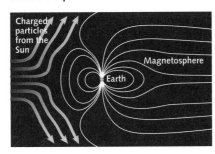

15. Which of the following statements is always true?
   A. Earth's magnetosphere is largest on the side of Earth facing the Sun.
   B. Earth's magnetosphere is weakest at the poles.
   C. Earth's magnetosphere pushes charged particles away from Earth.
   D. Earth's magnetosphere looks the same on the day and night sides of the planet.

Test-Taking Tip

Remember that qualifying words such as *only, always, all,* and *never* mean that the statement has **no** exceptions.

Critical Thinking

12. Magnetic fields are produced by spinning electrons. In atoms with an even number of electrons, such as carbon, each electron's spin is cancelled by an electron spinning in the opposite direction. Atoms containing an odd number of electrons do not cancel out and thus generate a small magnetic field.

13. Hitting the iron bar jars the magnetic domains and allows them to realign with Earth's magnetic field as they settle down.

14. When sunspot activity increases, auroral activity increases.

Standardized Test Question

15. C

Reading Links

Driving Force: The Natural Magic of Magnets

As a challenge for motivated readers, this book is sure to reward: Livingston, an MIT physicist specializing in magnetic research, explains with enthusiasm the power and scope of magnetism (touching on everything from toys to hospitals to national defense).

James D. Livingston. Harvard University Press. 320 pp. Illustrated. Trade ISBN 978-0-674-21645-7.

Northern Lights: The Science, Myth, and Wonder of Aurora Borealis

The spectacular photographs in this book—over one hundred unenhanced images taken from locations all over Alaska—bring readers closer than ever to the northern lights while teaching about the magnetic principles responsible for the phenomenon.

George Bryson, Calvin Hall, and Daryl Pederson. Sasquatch Books. 128 pp. Illustrated. Trade ISBN 978-1-570-61290-9.

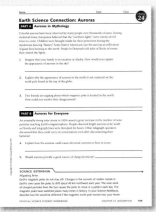

Curriculum Connection
Workbook, p. 155

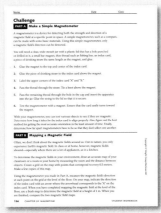

Science Challenge
Workbook, p. 156

24A Magnetic Forces

This prechapter introduction activity is designed to determine what students already know about magnetic forces and magnets by engaging them in observing, illustrating, and drawing conclusions about magnetic fields.

Objectives

- observe magnetic forces
- compare and contrast the magnetic fields
- record data in a suitable way
- communicate conclusions

Planning

 15–20 minutes   groups of 3–4 students

Materials (per group)

- horseshoe magnet
- bar magnet
- iron filings
- sheet of clear transparency film

Advance Preparation

- The sheets of transparency film should be 8½" × 11". Standard plastic page protectors can be used.
- Warn students not to place the magnets directly in the iron filings—removing the filings can be difficult.

You might want to perform the activity in advance to become familiar with the pattern of field lines that will form around each magnet.

Keep one set of magnets marked as the ones used in direct proximity to the magnet. These magnets will no longer point directly at the magnetic north.

Engagement Guide

- Challenge students to think about magnets and magnetic fields by asking:
  - *How do you know that a magnet exerts a field of magnetic force around the magnet?* (Students will likely mention experiences in which a magnet made another object move even though it was not touching it.)
  - *Is the force from a magnet always attractive?* (No, magnetic force can be attractive or repulsive.)
  - *What will the pattern of iron filings around the bar magnet look like? What will the pattern look like around the horseshoe magnet?* (Answers will vary, but might include that lines of force decrease with increasing distance from the magnet, and that lines will form related to the north and south poles of the magnet.)
  - *Where will the north and south poles of a horseshoe magnet be located?* (at each end)
- Encourage students to communicate their own experiences with magnets.

Going Further

Encourage students to repeat this activity using other kinds of magnets, such as ring magnets and refrigerator magnets. Have students make drawings of the patterns they observe and present their drawings to the class.

24B Observing Magnetic Fields

Objectives

- observe the effect of magnetic force on a compass
- illustrate the magnetic force lines around a magnet
- draw conclusions

Skill Set

observing, illustrating, drawing conclusions

Planning

 40–45 minutes   groups of 3–4 students

Materials

Materials for this activity are listed in the Student Laboratory Manual.

Advance Preparation

- You may wish to demonstrate the procedure for the activity to help students become familiar with using a compass.
- While one magnet is being used in the activity, the other should be placed away from the work area so its magnetic field will not interfere with that of the magnet in use. The poles of the magnets should be marked, so students can see how the direction of the field lines relate to the poles.

Answers to Observations: Illustrations

Illustrations will vary somewhat.
Bar magnet: lines from the center of the north pole point straight away; lines toward the sides of the north-pole end begin to curve away from the central straight line; lines from center of south pole point straight inward; lines toward the sides of the south-pole end begin to curve away from the central straight line; lines on the sides of the magnet form arcing elliptical-shaped patterns.

Horseshoe magnet: lines form an arcing elliptical pattern from the north pole to the south pole.

Answers to Analysis and Conclusions

1. Answers will vary, but students should observe that the field lines emanate from the north pole and arc toward the south pole, forming a curving elliptical pattern.

2. The compass needle points away from the north pole and toward the south pole.

3. The field lines radiate away from the north pole. When the north poles of two magnets are brought near, the field lines from each push the other lines away, creating a repulsive force.

4. Earth is a large magnet. Earth's magnetic north pole is located very close to its geographic north pole.

24C The Strength of Magnetic Fields

Objectives

- observe magnetic forces acting on objects
- record and analyze data
- assess magnetic field strength
- identify regions of maximum force
- draw conclusions

Skill Set

observing, recording and analyzing data, evaluating, illustrating, stating conclusions

Planning

 40–45 minutes   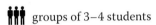 groups of 3–4 students

Materials

Materials for this activity are listed in the Student Laboratory Manual.

Advance Preparation

Provide each group with 20 paper clips. Make sure that the paper clips do not have a plastic coating on them. It is likely that the paper-clip chains will become detached from the magnet when an additional paper clip is linked on; if this happens, instruct students to reattach the chain in the same location and see if the magnet can lift it.

Going Further

Have student groups extend the experiment using a second identical bar magnet. Have them observe the effect on the field lines when one bar magnet, with the same pole orientation, is placed on top of the first bar magnet, and when like poles are directly opposite each other with only a short distance separating them. Have students share their results with other groups.

Answers to Observations: Illustrations

Actual numbers will vary, but students' data should show the ends of each magnet held up the largest number of paper clips.

Answers to Analysis and Conclusions

1. Results will vary depending on the magnets used. The results are based on the particular magnets used; either a bar magnet or a horseshoe magnet could have been the stronger magnet.

2. The ends of each magnet hold the greatest number of paper clips. The ends of the magnets are the poles.

3. Students should observe that the poles of each magnet contain the largest magnetic force. If one magnet is stronger that the other, students may observe a difference in the number of paper clips attracted to the poles of each magnet.

4. The locations of maximum magnetic strength would not change. The number of paper clips that could be supported would decrease greatly because the plastic coating decreases the magnetic attraction to the metal paper clip.

Going Further

Have students repeat this activity using other kinds of magnets, such as the magnetic rock magnetite, ring magnets, refrigerator magnets, and powerful, rare earth magnets. Have students present diagrams of their results to the class.

25.1 Magnetism from Electricity

25.2 Electricity from Magnetism

Introduce Chapter 25

As a starting activity, use Lab 25A on page 143 of the Laboratory Manual.

ENGAGE Ask students to name individual items that combine to make a new entity. If students have trouble, provide examples such as a hybrid car or a crossbred plant or animal, such as a cockapoo. Explain to students that electricity and magnetism have special properties that allow them to combine in such a way that they can do useful work.

Think About Electromagnetism

ENGAGE Talk with students about windmills and waterwheels and how they move. List locations on the board where students have seen waterwheels and windmills working, and provide pictures of each, if possible. Have students complete the bulleted items in their Science Notebooks. After students write their responses, talk with them about why scientists and others are finding ways to generate electricity using alternative resources.

• Answers will vary, but students should mention that an external energy source is used to spin a turbine. The wind is the energy source in wind power. Moving water is the energy source for hydroelectric power.

• Answers will vary, but allow students to discuss how energy from rotating tires, engine pulleys, or the driveshaft could be used to turn a device to generate electricity.

Chapter
25 Electromagnetism

KEY CONCEPT Electric and magnetic phenomena are closely related.

Do you know someone who drives a hybrid automobile? Hybrid cars run on a gasoline or diesel engine, an electric motor, and batteries. The electric motor propels, or powers, the car at low speeds. At higher speeds, the gasoline engine takes over.

A hybrid car uses electric and magnetic devices to generate electric power and recharge its batteries while the car is being driven. This chapter explores the relationship between electricity and magnetism and describes how the electromagnetic devices in a hybrid car work.

Think About Electromagnetism

Some parts of the country generate electricity from wind. In other areas, electricity is generated by moving water. Think about what you already know about these two sources of electric power.

• In your Science Notebook, describe how each source generates electricity.

• Devices that spin have mechanical energy. Think about the many spinning and moving parts of an automobile. Write one or two sentences explaining how mechanical energy might be used to generate electric power.

NSTA
SCLINKS.
THE WORLD'S A CLICK AWAY
www.scilinks.org
Electromagnetism **Code: WGPS25**

426

Chapter 25 Planning Guide

Instructional Periods	National Standards	Lab Manual	Workbook
25.1 1 period	B2, B3, E1, E2, F5, G1; B4, B6, E1, E2, F6, G1; UCP2, UCP3, UCP5	**Lab 25A: p. 143** What Makes an Electromagnet Work? **Lab 25B: pp.144–145** Generating and Detecting an Electric Current **Lab 25C: pp.146–147** Inductance Coils	Key Concept Review p. 157 Vocabulary Review p. 158 Interpreting Diagrams p. 159 Reading Comprehension p. 160 Curriculum Connection p. 161 Science Challenge pp. 162–163
25.2 1 period	A2, B2, B3, E2, F5, G1, G2, G3; A2, B4, B5, B6, E2, F6, G1, G2, G3; UCP1, UCP5		

Middle School Standard; High School Standard; Unifying Concept and Principle

25.1 Magnetism from Electricity

Before You Read

Write the vocabulary terms for this lesson in your Science Notebook. As you read the lesson, use each term in a sentence of your own. Make sure that your sentences show the meaning of each term.

In 1820, Hans Oersted, a Danish professor of science at Copenhagen University, was demonstrating electric current to students and friends. A magnetic compass, a device that normally points north, rested near one of the wires. When the circuit was connected, electric current flowed as expected. However, Oersted observed something quite unexpected, as well. The flowing electric current changed the direction of the nearby compass.

Moving Charges and Magnetic Fields

Oersted was the first person to observe that an electric current creates a magnetic field. It is now known that a magnetic field is produced by any moving electric charge. As shown in **Figure 25.1,** magnetic field lines form circles around a current-carrying wire. The direction of the field lines depends on the direction of the current. As you might expect, larger currents produce stronger magnetic fields. The strength of the magnetic field decreases as the distance from the wire increases.

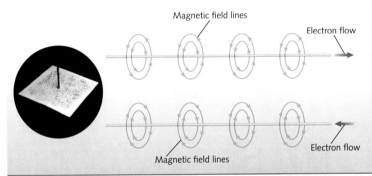

Magnetic field lines

Electron flow

Magnetic field lines

Electron flow

Figure 25.1 Iron particles are forced into a circular pattern around a current-carrying wire. The pattern matches the magnetic field lines produced by the moving electric charge.

ELL Strategy

Model Have students make diagrams that illustrate Oersted's experiment. Students should then illustrate how the direction in which the compass points changes as the compass is moved around the circuit. For further practice, students can later work with a partner to model similar concepts they learn about in the lesson.

Teacher Alert

If you allow students to experiment on their own with Oersted's discovery, warn them not to connect two ends of a wire to a battery for more than an instant. The wire will draw a large current from the battery because it offers little resistance. As a result, the wire will heat up and become dangerous for students to handle.

25.1 Introduce

ENGAGE Model for students the phenomenon that Oersted observed. Place a compass on a table or desk and wait for it to point north. Lay a thin insulated wire across the compass in the north-south direction. Bend the exposed ends of the wire so that they are close together. Attach one end of the wire to one terminal of a C or D battery. Momentarily touch the other end of the wire to the other terminal of the battery. Quickly disconnect the wire so that it does not continue to draw current from the battery.

Have students observe the compass needle when you touch the wire to the battery. Repeat several times. (Each time, the compass needle will swing 90 degrees.) Challenge students to predict any changes in the movement of the compass if you reverse the direction of the current in the wire. Reverse the connections to the battery and repeat to verify their predictions. (The compass needle will swing 90 degrees in the opposite direction.) Ask students to hypothesize about why the compass behaves as it does when current flows through the wire. Write some responses on the board. Have students revise their ideas as they encounter information in the lesson.

Vocabulary terms are listed on the first student page of each lesson. You may wish to preview the terms before introducing each lesson. Strategies for teaching the vocabulary appear on the pages where the terms are introduced.

Before You Read

Write the word *magnet* on the board and ask students to work with a partner to use it in a sentence that describes its meaning. Tell students to skim this lesson and write the vocabulary terms in their Science Notebooks, leaving a few lines between each term.

● Teach

EXPLAIN Review with students the idea that an electric current sets up a magnetic field. Ask them how they think the direction of the magnetic field is related to the direction of the electric current (they are at right angles to one another).

● Teach

Obtain an inexpensive solenoid. Use thin insulated wire to attach one end of the solenoid to one terminal of a battery. Use wire to momentarily connect the other end of the solenoid to the other terminal of the battery. (If a switch is available, add a switch into the circuit.) Quickly close the circuit again, but this time, move the solenoid near a small pile of paper clips. Allow students to observe that the paper clips are attracted to the solenoid. Use a compass to show that a magnetic field is set up around the coiled wire. Explain that the magnetic field around the coiled wire that is carrying electric current is much like the magnetic field around a bar magnet.

 Vocabulary

solenoid Explain to students that the root *solen* is derived from Greek and means "tube." The prefix *-oid* signifies something similar to or in the form of. Ask students why this is an appropriate description for the structure of a solenoid.

electromagnet Point out to students that *electromagnet* is a compound word formed by combining *electric* and *magnet*. Explain that *electric* means "relating to or caused by electricity." Review the definition of *magnet*: a piece of metal (often iron) that attracts and repels iron. Have students infer the meaning of the term *electromagnet* by combining the definitions.

Explain It!

Discuss with students the steps involved in the car-lifting process. Then have students list these steps and identify the action of the electromagnet for each step. Students should use the lists to write their paragraphs.

[ANSWER] Paragraphs will vary, but students should note that a strong electric current flows through the large electromagnet when it picks up the car. To release the car, the electromagnet is switched off. Examples of other uses will vary.

Use the Visual: Figure 25.2

[ANSWER] The direction of the magnetic field lines would reverse.

 Explain It!

Write a short, well-developed paragraph explaining how a crane equipped with an electromagnet can lift a heavy car in a salvage yard, move it, and then release it. Then identify two other uses of electromagnets.

Solenoids and Electromagnets

The strength of the magnetic field around a wire depends on the wire's shape. When a wire is bent into a loop, the magnetic field inside the loop is stronger than the magnetic field surrounding a straight wire.

Solenoids If the wire is bent into a series of loops, a coil known as a **solenoid** (SOL uh noid) is formed. **Figure 25.2** shows the magnetic field lines around and inside a solenoid. As a result of the solenoid's shape, the magnetic field lines inside the solenoid add together. Thus, the magnetic field inside a solenoid is stronger than the magnetic field inside one loop.

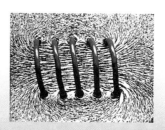 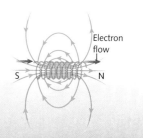

Figure 25.2 A solenoid is a coil, or a series of wire loops. The magnetic field lines from each loop overlap and add, increasing the strength of the field inside the solenoid. How would the magnetic field change if the current changed direction?

Electromagnets **Figure 25.3** shows a wire that has been coiled around an iron nail. This forms a solenoid with an iron core. When current flows through the wire, a magnetic field forms in the coil. The field magnetizes the iron core (the nail) and further strengthens the magnetic field inside the solenoid. A current-carrying wire coiled around an iron core is called an **electromagnet** (ih lek troh MAG net).

Unlike regular magnets, electromagnets are only magnetic when a current flows. When magnetized, an electromagnet has north and south poles. A stronger electromagnet can be made by increasing the current through the wire or by increasing the number of wire loops making up the solenoid.

 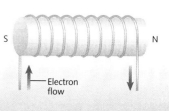

Figure 25.3 A solenoid wrapped around an iron core forms an electromagnet. When current flows, the iron core becomes magnetized.

Differentiate Instruction

Kinesthetic Provide students with iron nails and wire. Have students create three simulated solenoids: one weak, one intermediate, and one strong. Students should label each solenoid and share their models with partners.

Using Electromagnets

Electromagnets are useful because they are easily controlled. Their strength can be adjusted by changing the amount of current flowing through the wire. Their poles can be reversed by changing the direction of the current. Electromagnets can be used to make other objects move. When an electromagnet is no longer needed, it can be turned off.

Electric Doorbell   An electromagnet is used to make the doorbell in **Figure 25.4** ring. When the doorbell button is pressed, an electric circuit is completed. Electric current flows through the electromagnet and magnetizes it. The metal hammer is pulled toward the electromagnet, causing it to strike the bell. The motion of the hammer breaks the circuit, causing the electromagnet to become demagnetized. A spring pulls the hammer back to its original position. This process repeats as long as the doorbell button is pressed.

Bell

When the hammer strikes the bell, the circuit is open, and the electromagnet is turned off.

The electromagnet attracts the hammer that strikes the bell.

A spring pulls the hammer back, closing the circuit and starting the cycle over.

When the circuit is closed, an electromagnet is turned on.

Pressing the button closes the circuit.

Power source

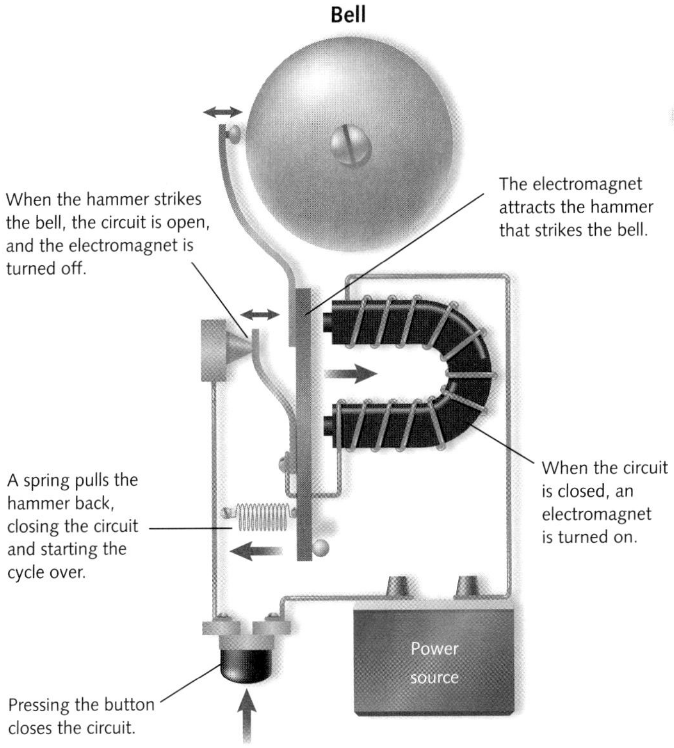

Figure 25.4 An electromagnet is used to make a doorbell ring. When the doorbell button is pressed, the electromagnet cycles on and off.

Figure It Out

1. Describe the general shape of the electromagnet shown in the illustration. How many loops does the electromagnet have?

2. Predict what will happen if the spring breaks while the doorbell button is pressed.

Teach

EXPLAIN to students that an electric circuit is a closed loop. In the demonstration with the solenoid, when both wires touch the battery, the circuit is closed. The current in an open circuit is unable to make a complete loop. One of the advantages of an electromagnet is that unlike a permanent magnet, the magnetic field of an electromagnet can be turned on and off.

As You Read

Give students a few minutes to review and revise their sentences. Have students conduct quick peer reviews to check for accuracy and understanding.

ANSWER   A solenoid that is wrapped around an iron core and has a current flowing through it forms an electromagnet.

Figure It Out: Figure 25.4

ANSWER   **1.** The electromagnet has a U shape. There are approximately 11 to 12 loops. **2.** The hammer must be in its starting position in order to complete the circuit. If the spring is broken, the hammer cannot return to its starting position and the circuit cannot be completed. The doorbell will not ring.

Science Notebook EXTRA

Have students research home security systems that use electromagnets. Ask students to compare the home security systems to the electric doorbell by writing a paragraph describing the different devices in their Science Notebooks. Students' responses will vary but should mention that the security system is a closed circuit until a door or window is opened. A doorbell is an open circuit until the button is pressed.

Background Information

Solenoids are integral components of starters in automobiles, trucks, locomotives, airplanes, and other vehicles. When the driver of the vehicle turns the key in the ignition, electric current flows to the solenoid from the battery. The current creates a magnetic field and pulls in a plunger. The plunger connects the battery with the motor. The motor then cranks the engine so that the piston moves downward. As it does so, it creates a suction that draws a mixture of fuel and air into the cylinder. A spark created by the ignition system then ignites this mixture to start the engine.

● Teach

Review with students the idea that opposite poles of magnets attract and like poles repel. Explain that the attracting and repelling forces can cause continued motion. When an electromagnet is on a rotating shaft and is between the ends of a magnet, the electromagnet rotates.

 Vocabulary

galvanometer Tell students that *galvanism* refers to an electric current produced by chemical means. Then tell students that the word *meter* is derived from Greek and means "a measure." Have students determine the literal definition of *galvanometer* and compare it to the term's scientific definition.

electric motor Review with students the meaning of *electric:* relating to or caused by electricity. Explain that *motor* comes from the Latin word *movere* and means "to move." Have students relate the common definition to the scientific definition.

Use the Visual: Figure 25.5

ANSWER a south pole

Galvanometers Many electromagnets are connected to a rotating shaft. As shown on the left in **Figure 25.5,** a rotating electromagnet can be placed between the poles of a fixed, or permanent, magnet. When the electromagnet is magnetized, its poles attract and repel the poles of the fixed magnet. These forces cause the electromagnet to rotate. The electromagnet rotates until its poles are positioned across from the opposite poles of the fixed magnet, as shown on the right in Figure 25.5.

When a current flows into the solenoid, like poles of the electromagnet are repelled by and attracted to the poles of the permanent magnet. This causes the electromagnet to rotate.

The magnetic forces on the electromagnet cause it to rotate until it is aligned along the field lines of the permanent magnet.

Figure 25.5 The electromagnet can rotate about its shaft. Forces of attraction and repulsion between the fixed magnet and the electromagnet cause the electromagnet to rotate. What type of magnetic pole is attracted to the fixed magnet's north pole?

Rotating electromagnets are used in devices called galvanometers. A **galvanometer** (gal vuh NAH muh tur) is used to measure electric current. These devices are very common—you likely see them every day. As **Figure 25.6** shows, the fuel gauge in an automobile is a galvanometer.

Look at the fuel gauge galvanometer in Figure 25.6. The electromagnet's rotating shaft is attached to a spring and a needle. An electric current from a device in the car's fuel tank flows through the electromagnet. The current rotates the electromagnet between the poles of the fixed magnet. Note, however, that the spring acts against the rotation. The electromagnet and needle stop where the force of the spring cancels the rotational force acting on the electromagnet. A scale positioned under the needle is used to read the fuel level.

Figure 25.6 In a galvanometer, the movement of the electromagnet is opposed by the force of the spring. Larger currents produce stronger forces, greater rotation, and larger scale readings. Larger currents correspond to greater amounts of fuel in the tank.

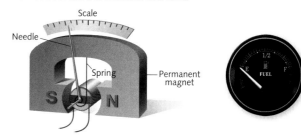

Background Information

The work of three scientists contributed to the invention of the galvanometer. In 1820, Hans Christian Oersted demonstrated the effect of electric currents on magnetic needles. Later that same year, Johann Schweigger made the first galvanometer. In 1882, the galvanometer as we know it today was created by Jacques Arsene d'Arsonval.

Key Concept Review
Workbook, p. 157

Electric Motors

Rotating electromagnets are part of one of the most common and important devices ever developed—the electric motor. An **electric motor** converts electric energy into mechanical energy. Electric motors have seemingly countless uses. Hair dryers use electric motors, as do many portable digital music players. Electric motors are also essential to hybrid cars. Electric motors propel the car up to speeds of approximately 20 miles per hour. A simple electric motor is shown in **Figure 25.7.**

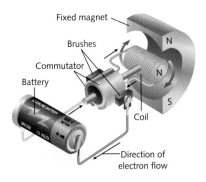

Step 1 When a current flows in the coil, the magnetic forces between the permanent magnet and the coil cause the coil to rotate.

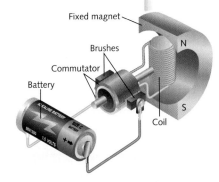

Step 2 The brushes are not in contact with the commutator and no current flows in the coil. The coil's inertia keeps it rotating.

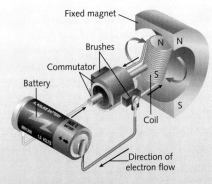

Step 3 The commutator reverses the direction of the current in the coil. This flips the north and south poles of the magnetic field around the coil.

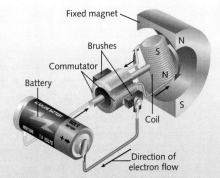

Step 4 The coil rotates until its poles are nearly opposite the poles of the fixed magnet. As the coil continues to spin, it will demagnetize as in Step 2, and then reenergize with an opposite current as in Step 3.

Figure 25.7 The motor has a rotating wire coil that becomes an electromagnet when energized. To keep the electromagnet spinning, the electric current changes direction twice during each rotation.

● Teach

EXPLAIN to students that electric motors contain rotating electromagnets. Ask students to list all the devices they know that use electric motors. Write their responses on the board. Examples could include can openers, mixers, weed trimmers, and pumps.

EXPLORE Have students make flow charts to diagram the process of converting electric energy into mechanical energy. Students could create their own symbols to signify the flow of the current, magnetic forces, and the rotation of the coil. Encourage students to include all steps in this abbreviated description. English language learners can collaborate to create and label their diagrams. Then, they can present their charts to the class, explaining the process.

Differentiate Instruction

Interpersonal Have students talk with a mechanic or someone who repairs electric motors. As a class, brainstorm a list of questions that students might ask about the work that relate to the lesson. Students might also visit a repair facility to observe the tools and techniques used.
Give English language learners the opportunity to share their discoveries with the class and to describe the tools and techniques they discovered.

Interpreting Diagrams
Workbook, p. 159

Teach

EXPLAIN to students that an electric motor works by the repetition of the steps in **Figure 25.7.** The current in the coil turns the electromagnet on and off as the current flows, stops, and changes direction.

✏ CONNECTION: Particle Physics

Explain to students that some present-day applications of particle physics include investigating the structure of the atomic nucleus, producing transistors on computer chips, and studying atoms of chemical elements heavier than uranium. Tell students that another important use is in medicine as computed tomography, also known as CT and CAT.

EXTEND Have students work with partners to research how CT works and what the benefits of it are for patients.

Assess

Use the After You Read questions and the Alternative Assessment to help you evaluate students' understanding of the lesson.

After You Read

1. increasing the current; increasing the number of loops

2. similarities: both are magnetic and have poles; differences: an electromagnet can be turned off, whereas a bar magnet is always magnetic; the strength of an electromagnet can be adjusted, whereas a bar magnet has a constant field strength

3. electric motor: A motor spins when current flows through it and creates forces that make the electromagnet rotate. As the electromagnet rotates, it continuously goes through periods where it is not energized and periods during which the current flowing through it reverses. The reversal of the current and the on-and-off switching make the motor spin.

Alternative Assessment

Have students use their sentences to describe how an electric motor works. They should use the term *electromagnet* and provide two examples of electric motors.

Parts of the Motor An electric motor is made up of a rotating wire coil, a fixed magnet, brushes, a commutator, and a power supply. The battery provides the current that energizes the coil into an electromagnet. The brushes conduct the current into a split metal ring, known as a commutator. Each half of the commutator is connected to one of the ends of the coil.

How a Motor Works Look at Step 1 in Figure 25.7 on the previous page. As current flows through the circuit, the magnetized coil begins to rotate. The circuit is broken, however, when the coil reaches the position shown in Step 2. Here, the brushes do not touch the commutator; no current flows, and the coil demagnetizes. Inertia keeps the coil spinning, however. When the coil reaches the position shown in Step 3, the brushes touch the other half of the commutator. A current again flows, but this time in the opposite direction. This reversed current flips the polarity of the energized coil. The coil now accelerates away from the like-magnetized poles and toward the opposite poles of the fixed magnet. As the motor runs, this process repeats over and over again.

⊙ CONNECTION: Particle Physics

Particle physicists, who are also known as high-energy physicists, use particle accelerators to smash apart atoms. Inside an accelerator, particles of matter are made to collide at incredibly high speeds—nearly the speed of light. To achieve these speeds, powerful electromagnets are used. In some ways, these electromagnets operate similarly to those in an electric motor. In both devices, the poles of the electromagnets are switched back and forth. In a motor, the spinning electromagnet accelerates toward the oppositely-charged pole and away from the like-charged pole. In a linear particle accelerator (linac), particles are accelerated through a series of charged plates. The particles accelerate toward an oppositely-charged plate, then pass through a hole in the plate. The polarity of the plate is then switched, and the particles are accelerated away from the like-charged plate.

After You Read

1. Describe two ways in which the strength of a magnetic field inside a solenoid can be increased.

2. Compare and contrast a bar magnet and an electromagnet.

3. Review the sentences you wrote in your Science Notebook. Which term describes a device that converts electric energy into mechanical energy? In a well-developed paragraph, explain how the device works.

Differentiate Instruction

Kinesthetic Have students act out the parts of a motor. Arrange students in groups of five and have each group decide how to simulate the motor, ideally assigning one student to each part. Groups should present their motor simulations to the class.

Background Information

Medical experts use computed tomography (CT) or computerized axial tomography (CAT) to view parts of the body in order to diagnose illnesses. Images are created when a patient lies on a table that goes through a gantry, or scanning machine, which has a tube that beams X rays through the patient's body. Images are taken at different angles, and a computer processes the information to produce a cross-section image.

25.2 Electricity from Magnetism

Before You Read

Create a working definition of the term *electric transformer*. Write what you know about the term before you begin the lesson. Then add to the definition as you read and discuss the information.

Once it was known that an electric current produced magnetism, physicists began to wonder if the opposite was also true. Could magnetism be used to produce electricity? The answer was yes. In 1831, the English physicist Michael Faraday and the American physicist Joseph Henry each demonstrated that moving a magnet through a wire coil produced an electric current.

This discovery was another breakthrough in science. The ability to easily generate electricity would change the world. Today, electricity is inexpensive and readily available.

Producing Electricity

You can generate an electric current using a magnet and a piece of wire. As shown in **Figure 25.8,** a current is produced when a magnet moves through a single loop of wire. If a moving loop of wire passes over a stationary magnet, the result is the same. In other words, relative motion between the magnet and the wire loop produces the current.

Moving the magnet faster through the wire loop increases the current produced, as does increasing the number of wire loops. As the figure shows, four loops produce twice as much voltage as two loops, and six loops produce triple the voltage of two loops.

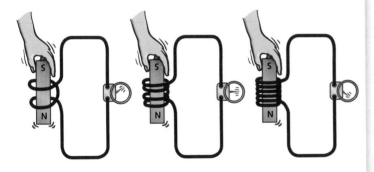

Figure 25.8 The meter shows the voltage produced as the magnet moves through the wire loops. Increasing the number of wire loops increases the voltage of the current produced.

Learning Goals

- Describe electromagnetic induction.
- Compare and contrast an electric generator and an electric motor.
- Identify step-up and step-down transformers by the number of turns on their primary and secondary coils.

New Vocabulary

electromagnetic induction
generator
alternating current (AC)
direct current (DC)
transformer

Recall Vocabulary

voltage, p. 398
electric power, p. 406
electric energy, p. 408

25.2 Introduce

ENGAGE Provide students with an insulated wire and a battery. Remind students how electricity can produce magnetism. Tell them that the reverse can also happen: magnetism can produce an electric current. Have students work with partners and challenge them to hypothesize what materials would be needed to create an electric current. Have students share their hypotheses and their reasons. Write responses on the board and review and revise them throughout the lesson.

Before You Read

Have students use a word map to organize their thoughts about the term *electric transformer*. Students should include their knowledge about each word in the term. Model the process by drawing a word map on the board and writing *electric transformer* in the middle. Add the phrase *electricity is a flowing of charge* to the map. Have students use their word maps to draft a working definition of *electric transformer* in their Science Notebooks.

● Teach

EXPLAIN to students that electricity can be created by moving a magnet through a loop of wire. Just as more loops created more magnetism, more loops will increase the strength, or voltage, of the current.

ELL Strategy

Ask and Answer Questions Have students work with partners to create two to three questions (with answers) for each page of the lesson. Encourage students to write questions related to the Learning Goals rather than focusing on minor details. Use the bank of student-created questions to help students review the information from the lesson.

Background Information

The voltage produced when moving a magnet through a coil is directly related to the rate at which the magnetic field lines are traversed.

Teach

EXPLAIN to students that the process of creating electricity from magnetism is known as electromagnetic induction.

 Vocabulary

electromagnetic induction Review with students the meaning of *electromagnet*. Explain to students that induction is the process of persuading or causing something to happen. Have students relate these meanings to the full term's scientific definition.

generator Explain to students that the verb *generate* means "to produce or create something." The suffix *-or* denotes a person or thing that performs an action or function. The literal definition of this term is "a person or thing who produces something."

alternating current (AC) Encourage students to think of common uses of the word *alternate*. Explain to students that the word *current* comes from Latin and means "to run." Have students relate the common definitions to the scientific definition of the term.

direct current (DC) Ask students to list common uses of the word *direct*. Examples might include the act of telling others what to do, the quality of being straight, being responsible for the production of a performance, or an open and honest manner.

 CONNECTION: Technology

Have students examine the contents of their pockets and bags to determine which items would set off the alarm of a metal detector. Have students make a list of items that are acceptable and items that are not acceptable for airline travel and suggest alternatives for the unacceptable items. (You may or may not choose to include items related to safety.)

Figure 25.9 As a wire moves through a magnetic field, forces push electrons through the wire. The moving electrons produce a current.

 CONNECTION: Technology

When you walk through a metal detector at an airport, you are walking through a large wire loop that carries a small current. The current creates a magnetic field inside the loop. Carrying anything through the loop that contains iron changes the field and sets off an alarm.

Figure 25.10 A generator uses an energy source to spin a wire loop or coil inside a magnetic field.

Electromagnetic Induction The magnetic field inside a wire loop changes as the magnet and wire move past each other. It is the changing magnetic field that produces the current. The generation of a current by a changing magnetic field is called **electromagnetic induction** (ih lek troh mag NEH tik • in DUHK shun).

The current produced by induction results from forces that act on the charges in the wire. Imagine a wire moving through a magnetic field, as shown in **Figure 25.9**. Electrons in the wire are free to move. As the wire moves, the magnetic field exerts force on the electrons. The exerted force is perpendicular to the wire's motion—that is, the force is along the wire. The force moves electrons through the wire and forms a current.

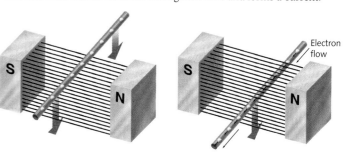

Electron flow

Electric Generators A **generator** (jen uh RAY tur) is a device that converts mechanical energy into electricity. The current is produced by electromagnetic induction. A generator is nearly opposite in function to an electric motor. A motor uses electric energy to produce mechanical energy. A generator uses mechanical energy to produce electric energy.

A simple generator is shown in **Figure 25.10**. A generator consists of a wire loop or coil that rotates between the poles of a fixed magnet. As the loop turns, magnetic forces push electrons through the wire, creating a current. It is important to note that an energy source is required to overcome the resistance that acts on the loop as it turns. More electricity is produced by generators with larger coils that spin at higher speeds.

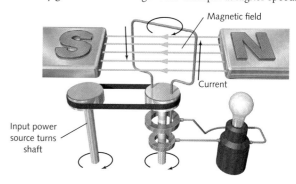

Magnetic field

Current

Input power source turns shaft

Background Information

Most airport metal detectors function based on pulse induction (PI). A coil of wire located on one side of the arch acts as the transmitter and receiver. Pulses of current are sent through the coil.

Field Study

Have students walk through various parts of the school and make note of the items that require electricity. Encourage students to note which items are in use and which items are not. Ask students to brainstorm ways in which the school's electricity use could be decreased.

Types of Current Look again at the motion of the wire loop in the generator in Figure 25.10 on page 434. As the loop rotates, each half of the loop enters and exits the magnetic field. This causes the direction of the current in the wire to alternate, or change back and forth. The current changes direction every half-turn. A current whose direction changes back and forth is called an **alternating current** (AC). Electric outlets in the United States supply alternating current.

The current from chemical batteries, such as those used in automobiles and flashlights, does not alternate. Instead, the current flows in one direction only. In a **direct current** (DC), the electrons flow in one direction. Generators can be designed to produce direct current.

Uses of Generators

Car generators, which are called alternators, are powered by belts driven by the engine. The electricity produced by the generator is used to recharge the battery and power other devices. Energy that would otherwise be wasted is converted into electricity. The energy is stored in a battery and can later be used to power the car's electric motor.

Most of the electricity used in the world is produced by generators. A variety of energy sources are used to drive generators. Power plants that produce steam use it to drive turbines that are connected to generators.

Figure 25.11 Each of these power sources uses generators to produce electricity. What supplies the energy used by each?

Extend It!

Research the various designs of generators used in power plants. How do these generators produce relative motion between the coil and the magnet? What power output can they produce?

● Teach

EXPLAIN to students that currents can be alternating or direct. Most appliances that are plugged into outlets require alternating current. Items that use battery power use direct current.

EXPLORE Have students examine items at home and note what type of current and voltage each item uses. Suggest that students examine a variety of items, such as electronic games, small kitchen appliances, and larger household appliances. Then have students note similarities and differences between the types of items and required current and voltage.

Extend It!

Have students use scientific journals, encyclopedias, or Web sites to research generators. You might also contact your local electric utility company and have a representative visit the class.

Emphasize to students that generators require fuel such as wood, coal, oil, natural gas, or nuclear energy.

The generators used in power plants often have fixed coils and rotating magnets. Outputs of single generators can exceed 100,000 kW.

Use the Visual: Figure 25.11

ANSWER   wind turbine/wind power: wind; dam/hydroelectric power: moving water; nuclear power plant: fission of uranium; coal-burning power plant: burning coal (a fossil fuel)

Background Information

Alternating current differs between the United States and European countries. In the U.S., the direction of the current reverses or alternates 60 times per second (60 Hz and 110 or 120 volts). In Europe, the rate is 50 times per second (50 Hz and 220 volts).

Scientists have found that producing ethanol from corn for car fuel uses much less petroleum than producing gasoline does. Researchers are still uncertain about greenhouse gas emissions and secondary environmental effects, such as soil erosion.

● Teach

 EXPLAIN to students that transformers change voltages of electricity. Step-up transformers increase the amount of voltage; step-down transformers decrease the amount of voltage.

💿 Vocabulary

transformer Explain to students that *trans-* comes from Latin and means "across." Ask students to brainstorm common uses of the word *form*. Responses might include the way something appears to be, the shape or appearance of a thing, a document that one completes to provide information, or a way of doing something. Tell students the suffix *-er* denotes the thing or person performing the action of the verb (in this case, *transform*). Have students compare the term's literal definition to its scientific definition.

As You Read

Have students add to their word maps and revise their definitions of *electric transformer*. Check students' work for understanding.

[ANSWER] A step-up transformer increases voltage.

Figure It Out: Figure 25.12

[ANSWER] **1.** a ratio less than 1 reduces voltage; a ratio greater than 1 increases voltage;

top transformer:

$\dfrac{\text{turns on secondary coil}}{\text{turns on primary coil}} = \dfrac{20}{10} = 2;$

the transformer doubles the voltage;
60 V × 2 = 120 V

bottom transformer:

$\dfrac{\text{turns on secondary coil}}{\text{turns on primary coil}} = \dfrac{20}{40} = \dfrac{1}{2};$

the transformer halves the voltage;
240 V × ½ = 120 V

2. A changing magnetic field in the primary coil is needed in order to produce a current in the secondary coil. Because a direct current does not change, there is no changing magnetic field and no output voltage.

As You Read

Add information related to your working definition of an electric transformer. Be sure to include supporting information in your definition.

Which type of transformer is used to increase voltage?

Figure It Out

1. How does the ratio

$\dfrac{\text{turns on secondary coil}}{\text{turns on primary coil}}$

relate to the voltage change? Explain, using data from the figure.

2. Explain why a direct current used as the input will produce an output voltage of zero.

436 ELECTROMAGNETISM

Changing Voltage

Voltage is a measure of the energy carried by the electric charges in a current. Voltages vary widely. Electricity is carried from power plants to cities at voltages ranging from about 150,000 volts to more than 750,000 volts. A hair dryer, however, requires only 120 volts. Devices called transformers make this range of voltages possible. A **transformer** is a device used to change the voltage of an alternating current.

How a Transformer Works   As shown in **Figure 25.12,** a transformer is made up of two wire coils. Both coils are wrapped around the same iron core. An alternating current is connected to the input, or primary, coil. The current produces a changing magnetic field in the primary coil and the iron core. This changing field induces an alternating current in the output, or secondary, coil. The frequency of the alternating current is not changed by the transformer.

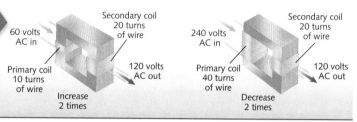

Figure 25.12 Transformers are used to increase or decrease voltage.

Step-Up and Step-Down Transformers   The number of wire loops, or turns, on each coil determines how the voltage changes. For example, an output coil with twice as many turns as the input coil doubles the output voltage. Likewise, an output coil with half the number of turns as the input coil halves the voltage.

Look at the two transformers in Figure 25.12. The transformer shown on the left has more turns on its secondary (output) coil than on its primary (input) coil. This is a step-up transformer—a transformer that increases voltage. The transformer shown on the right is a step-down transformer. A step-down transformer decreases the voltage because it has fewer turns on its secondary coil than on its primary coil.

Figure 25.13 shows a common sight—step-down transformers mounted high up on power poles. These step-down transformers are used to decrease the voltage of high-voltage power lines to the level used in homes and businesses.

Figure 25.13 Step-down transformers such as these often decrease the line voltage from about 6,000 volts to 110 volts.

Differentiate Instruction

Visual, Mathematical Have each student create a graph showing the voltage amounts of power plants, power lines, and household appliances. Students can use the information in their surveys from the Explore It! activity on page 437.

Field Study

Have students walk around a residential area near the school or their neighborhood at home and make note of the power lines at each house. Ask students to observe how many lines go to each house and to notice other lines or items on the poles.

Transmitting Electricity

Have you ever wondered why the voltage of high-power lines is so high? The answer is related to efficiency. As a wire's current increases, so does the amount of heat generated. The generated heat results in lost energy and lost efficiency. By increasing the voltage, the current is drastically reduced. The power that is wasted is also reduced. A low-current line produces little heat and wastes little energy. High-voltage lines are very efficient at transferring alternating current electricity.

Transformers are also very efficient. They change voltages with little energy loss. Transformers and high voltages are used to transmit electric power to cities far from power plants. **Figure 25.14** illustrates the process used to transmit power across large distances.

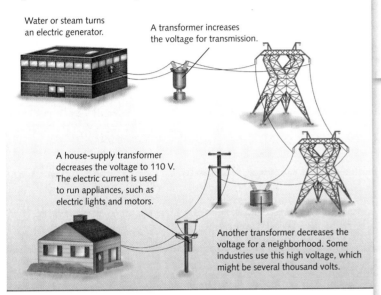

Water or steam turns an electric generator.

A transformer increases the voltage for transmission.

A house-supply transformer decreases the voltage to 110 V. The electric current is used to run appliances, such as electric lights and motors.

Another transformer decreases the voltage for a neighborhood. Some industries use this high voltage, which might be several thousand volts.

Figure 25.14 Generators produce electricity at a power plant. Step-up transformers increase the voltage so the electricity can be transmitted with little loss. Step-down transformers decrease the voltage for use in the home.

After You Read

1. Describe how you could use a magnet and a wire to create electromagnetic induction. Identify what is produced.

2. What type of energy conversion occurs in a generator?

3. Review the working definition of an electric transformer recorded in your Science Notebook. Describe how to distinguish between a step-up transformer and a step-down transformer.

Explore It!

Trace the electric power lines that come into your school back to the nearest local power substation. Record the path of the power lines on a diagram that shows the location of step-up transformers. If needed, use the Internet or contact your local power company to find out what a substation does and where the nearest one is located.

Background Information

Power equals current times voltage. If the power remains the same in the line and the voltage increases, the current has to decrease ($I = P/V$). Power loss is calculated from the formula $PL = I2R$. Power loss is directly proportional to the square of the current. Thus, less current results in less power loss.

At a pole servicing a house, there will also be a transformer drum that reduces the 7,200 volts of the line to 240 volts going to the house. All utility poles have a grounding wire (a bare wire) running down them. Two insulated wires run from the transformer to the house and connect at a meter.

Chapter 25 Summary

MASTERING CONCEPTS

True or False

1. False, Moving
2. False, weaker
3. False, rotates
4. True
5. True
6. True
7. False, doubles
8. False, increases

Short Answer

9. To increase current, move the magnet faster or increase the number of loops.

10. The magnetic strength of the electromagnet decreases.

11. Magnetic forces of attraction and repulsion will cause the electromagnet to rotate. The rotation will stop when the electromagnet is aligned with the opposite poles of the fixed magnet.

12. If the current direction did not change, the electromagnet would just align itself with the opposite poles of the fixed magnet and no longer move. Switching the direction of the current keeps the electromagnet spinning.

13. A motor converts electric energy to mechanical energy. A generator converts mechanical energy to electric energy.

KEY CONCEPTS

25.1 Magnetism from Electricity

- An electric current produces a magnetic field. A current in a wire creates circular magnetic field lines around the wire.

- A wire formed into a series of loops is called a solenoid. The magnetic field inside a solenoid is stronger than the field inside a single wire loop.

- An electromagnet is a solenoid wrapped around an iron core. When current flows through the solenoid, the electromagnet becomes magnetized.

- The magnetic field strength of an electromagnet can be altered by changing the current through it.

- A galvanometer uses a rotating electromagnet to measure current.

- Electric motors convert electric energy to mechanical energy.

25.2 Electricity from Magnetism

- An electric current is produced when there is relative movement between a wire loop and a magnetic field.

- Electromagnetic induction occurs when a changing magnetic field produces forces that push electrons though a wire, creating a current.

- A generator converts mechanical energy to electric energy. An energy source is required to turn the generator.

- Generators can produce alternating current (AC) or direct current (DC).

- Transformers are used to change voltage. Step-up transformers increase voltage; step-down transformers reduce voltage.

- Electric power is transmitted at high voltages to minimize energy losses.

VOCABULARY REVIEW

Write each term in a complete sentence or write a paragraph relating several terms.

25.1
solenoid, p. 428
electromagnet, p. 428
galvanometer, p. 430
electric motor, p. 431

25.2
electromagnetic induction, p. 434
generator, p. 434
alternating current (AC), p. 435
direct current (DC), p. 435
transformer, p. 436

PREPARE FOR CHAPTER TEST

To prepare for the chapter test, create a question from each Learning Goal. Use the information in your Science Notebook to answer each question. Then use these answers to write a well-developed essay about the chapter. Use the Key Concept on the first page of this chapter as your topic sentence.

Vocabulary Review
Workbook, p. 158

Reading Comprehension
Workbook, p. 160

MASTERING CONCEPTS

True or False
If the statement is true, write "true." If it is false, change the underlined word or words to make the statement true.

1. <u>Stationary</u> electric charges produce magnetic fields.

2. The magnetic field inside a single loop of wire is <u>stronger</u> than the field inside a coil of wire.

3. The electromagnet in a galvanometer <u>does not move</u>.

4. The current inside an electric motor changes <u>direction</u> as the motor runs.

5. A magnet moving through two loops of wire produces <u>twice</u> the voltage of a similar magnet moving through a single loop of wire.

6. Household electrical outlets supply <u>alternating</u> current.

7. A transformer with two times as many turns on its secondary coil than on its primary coil <u>halves</u> the output voltage.

8. Increasing the speed with which a magnet moves through a wire coil <u>decreases</u> the amount of current produced.

Short Answer
Answer each of the following in a sentence or brief paragraph.

9. Identify two ways to increase the amount of current induced by the movement of a magnet through a wire coil.

10. How does decreasing the current through an electromagnet affect the electromagnet's magnetic properties?

11. Describe what happens when an electromagnet connected to a shaft is placed between the poles of a fixed magnet.

12. Why must the current in a motor change direction?

13. Describe the energy conversions that occur in a motor and a generator.

14. Describe how an alternating current in the primary coil of a transformer affects the secondary coil.

Critical Thinking
Use what you have learned in this chapter to answer each of the following.

15. **Explain** Why is the magnetic field inside a wire coil greater than the field inside a single loop?

16. **Hypothesize** A bar magnet is pushed away when an electromagnet is brought near it. What would happen if the direction of the current in the electromagnet was reversed? What would happen if the bar magnet was flipped end-to-end?

17. **Apply Concepts** Small generators are sometimes used on bicycles to power a small headlight. A rotating head on the generator turns when it is held against the tire. Does using the generator make it harder to pedal the bicycle? Explain your answer.

Standardized Test Question
Choose the letter of the response that correctly answers the question.

18. A transformer's primary coil is connected to a 120-volt electrical outlet. A light is plugged into the transformer's secondary coil. The primary coil has 20 turns, and the secondary coil has two turns. What is the output voltage?

120 V

A. 12 volts
B. 18 volts
C. 102 volts
D. 1,200 volts

Test-Taking Tip
If you don't understand the directions, you can usually ask the teacher to explain them better. When the directions are clear enough for you to understand the question completely, you are less likely to pick the wrong answer.

14. The alternating current in the primary coil produces a changing magnetic field in the primary coil and in the iron core. The changing field in the core induces an alternating current in the secondary coil.

Critical Thinking

15. The magnetic field lines around each portion of the wire are the same, but the fields combine when the wire is formed into a series of loops.

16. In both cases, the ends of the bar magnet and the electromagnet would have opposite poles and would be attracted to each other.

17. Yes, the bicycle will be harder to pedal. Turning the generator's coil within the magnetic field requires energy. This required energy comes from the force applied to the pedals.

Standardized Test Question

18. A

Reading Links

Electricity and Magnetism
In everyday language, this book presents a solid and engaging overview of the principles covered in this chapter and the concepts that they build upon. Its coverage emphasizes historical background and concludes with a glossary, time line, and list of resources for further investigation.

Peter Fairley. Twenty First Century Books. Library ISBN 978-0-8225-6605-2.

The New Way Things Work
The countless applications of the principles of electricity and magnetism, in addition to many other scientific concepts students have encountered throughout the year, are explored and winningly dissected in this comprehensive and highly visual guide to the function of machines of all sorts.

David Macaulay. Houghton Mifflin. 400 pp. Illustrated. Trade ISBN 978-0-395-93847-8.

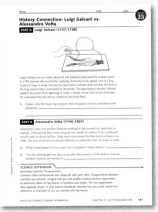

Curriculum Connection
Workbook, p. 161

Science Challenge
Workbook, pp. 162–163

25A **What Makes an Electromagnet Work?**

This prechapter introduction activity is designed to determine what students already know about electromagnetism by engaging them in observing, examining, comparing, recording data, and making conclusions.

Objectives

- predict factors that affect electromagnetic strength
- build several electromagnets
- compare and contrast electromagnets
- communicate conclusions

Planning

 25–35 minutes   groups of 3–4 students

Materials (per group)

- 30-cm length of enameled copper wire, 24–26 gauge
- 60-cm length of enameled copper wire, 24–26 gauge
- 2 equal-length bolts of various diameters, at least 10 mm thick
- switch with terminal connections
- 6-V lantern battery
- large metal washer
- spring scale

Advance Preparation

- Cut the wire lengths before class and strip the insulation from each end. Instruct students to use the shorter length wire to connect the switch to the battery.
- Tell students that the switch should only be engaged while the electromagnet is being tested. This extends the battery life and minimizes heating of the wire.

- Ask students to carefully unwind the wire after each test, without damaging the enamel. The wire can then be used in another electromagnet.
- Before students develop their experimental procedures, remind them to only change one electromagnet property at a time. They should measure the effect of one change at a time. For example, determining the effect of different numbers of wire turns on the same size bolt.

Engagement Guide

- Challenge students to think about electromagnets and how they work by asking:
  - *Have you ever seen the electromagnet that surrounds a small motor? What does it look like?* (If possible, show an electromagnet from a small motor to the class. Students should note the large number of windings.)
  - *How do you think that increasing the number of winds of wire on the electromagnet will affect its strength?* (Students will likely suggest that the greater the number of winds, the greater the electromagnetic strength will be.)
  - *How do you think that increasing the size of the iron core of the electromagnet will affect its strength?* (Students will likely suggest that the larger and more iron in the core, the greater the electromagnetic strength will be.)
- Encourage students to predict the results of the experiment that they devise and discuss their results with other groups.

Going Further

Encourage students to test how other factors affect the strength of an electromagnet. Suggest that they investigate the effects of current strength, wire gauge, and spacing the wire turns over a longer bolt. Have students record and report their results to the class.

25B Generating and Detecting Electric Current

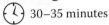

Objectives

- use electromagnetic induction to generate electric current
- build a simple galvanometer to detect current
- draw conclusions

Skill Set

observing, analyzing data, stating conclusions

Planning

30–35 minutes   groups of 3–4 students

Materials

Materials for this activity are listed in the Student Laboratory Manual.

Advance Preparation

- Make sure the bar magnet fits inside the cardboard tube.
- Use 24–26 gauge enameled copper wire and strip the insulation off each end before class.

Answers to Observations: Figures A and B

Students should find that the movement of the magnet through the round coil causes the compass needle to deflect in one direction, and the movement in the opposite direction causes the needle to deflect in the opposite direction.

Answers to Analysis and Conclusions

1. Yes. The current produced was detected by the compass; the deflection of the compass needle occurred because a current was produced.
2. The orientation of the magnetic poles as they move through the coil determines the direction the compass needle moves.

Going Further

Encourage student groups to repeat the experiment with a sensitive DC ammeter to test the current produced. Students can then experiment to discover how the current produced is affected by more turns of wire, or stronger or weaker magnets. Have groups summarize their results and present them to the class.

 25C Inductance Coils

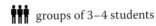

Objectives

- build an induction coil
- build a simple galvanometer to detect current
- observe induced currents in coils
- draw conclusions

Skill Set

observing, analyzing data, stating conclusions

Planning

35–45 minutes   groups of 3–4 students

Materials

Materials for this activity are listed in the Student Laboratory Manual.

Advance Preparation

- Use 24–26 gauge enameled copper wire and strip the insulation off each end before class.
- Ask students to connect the push button switch between the battery and galvanometer. Explain that the switch should only be engaged momentarily. This will extend the battery life and minimize heating of the wire.

Answers to Observations: Data Table 1

Students should observe that the needle deflects immediately when the switch is closed or released, but not while the switch is held down. When the battery is reversed, the direction of the needle deflection will be reversed.

Answers to Analysis and Conclusions

1. When the switch was opened and closed, the needle moved, but in different directions. When the battery terminals were switched, the direction of the needle deflections also switched. When the switch remained closed, there was no needle movement.
2. The current was only induced in the secondary coil immediately when the switch was closed or opened.
3. A current is induced when the magnetic field is changing. Because an alternating current is always changing, a changing current is always being induced in the secondary coil.

Going Further

Have students repeat the experiment with different types of cores, such as nonconducting and nonferric cores. Have students place a sensitive DC ammeter in place of the compass and coil and measure the differences in current produced with different cores. Ask students to record and analyze their results and present them in class.

Introduce Chapter 26

As a starting activity, use Lab 26A on page 148 of the Laboratory Manual.

ENGAGE In their Science Notebooks, have students list everything they did in the morning before coming to school today. Make a list on the board as a model for your students.

Then have students identify all the listed tasks that included the use of an electronic device. Ask students to share the devices they used, and make a class list on the board. Add to the list throughout the chapter as students encounter or remember additional electronic devices they use on a daily basis.

Think About Electronic Technology

ENGAGE Remind students that the telephone was not used to communicate until the 1870s. It might be useful to provide a model of the can telephone. Students could use the telephone to talk with partners. Have students complete the bulleted items in their Science Notebooks.

• Answers will vary. News would most likely come from newspapers, mail, town meetings, and stories passed from person to person. Some students might mention the use of a telegraph to communicate over large distances.

• Students might or might not correctly explain how the string-and-can telephone works. Evaluate answers for effort and completeness.

Chapter
26 Electronic Technology

KEY CONCEPT Electronic devices use electricity to process, transmit, and store information.

Today, electronic devices are everywhere, and communication is easier than ever. For example, when you need a ride home from school, you might use a cell phone to call or send a text message to a parent. If these options are not available, you might make a call from a pay phone.

It seems appropriate to say that this is the age of electronics and telecommunications. This chapter explores the electronic devices people use to send and receive information and communicate with one another.

Think About Electronic Technology

What would life be like if these communication technologies did not exist?

• Imagine it is 1850, and you have traveled west from Pennsylvania to search for gold in California. In your Science Notebook, describe how you would obtain news from far away and communicate with people in other cities.

• Children sometimes construct simple telephones using two empty metal cans and string. In your Science Notebook, explain how you think this simple device works, identifying each of the following: the transmitter, the receiver, and the material (or medium) through which the voice signal travels.

NSTA

SCLINKS.
THE WORLD'S A CLICK AWAY

www.scilinks.org
Electronic Circuits **Code: WGPS26**

440

Middle School Standard; High School Standard; Unifying Concept and Principle

26.1 Electronic Signals and Devices

Before You Read

In your Science Notebook, create a chart with three columns. Label the columns *Analog Signals*, *Digital Signals*, and *Semiconductors*. In the appropriate columns, write anything you already know about these devices. As you read the lesson, describe how each device operates and identify its functions or uses.

Most cities have one or more stores that sell nothing but electronic devices. Likewise, the Internet provides countless Web sites that offer almost every electronic device imaginable. These products include computers, video recorders, cameras, televisions, music players, car stereos, and much more. All of these **electronic devices** use electricity to process, transmit, and store information.

Electronic Signals

Electronic devices convert data to and from electric currents. The type of data varies. It might be the images and sounds of a school play, a sports event, or your favorite band. As shown in **Figure 26.1**, many people use digital video recorders to record important events. The video recorder converts the moving images into a changing electric current. A changing electric current used to carry information (data) is called an **electronic** (ih lek TRON ik) **signal.**

Electronic signals are stored on electronic storage media. When someone watches the video of a school play or sports event, the stored data are converted back into moving images. Sometimes the same device that recorded the video can be used to view it; other times a separate electronic device is used to play back the recording.

Figure 26.1 The video recorder converts moving images into a varying electric current that is stored. Later, the stored signal is converted back into the moving images.

Learning Goals

- Differentiate between analog and digital signals.
- Identify the types of functions performed by diodes and transistors.
- Explain how semiconductors are used in electronic devices.

New Vocabulary

electronic device
electronic signal
analog signal
digital signal
semiconductor
doping
transistor
diode
integrated circuit

Recall Vocabulary

atom, p. 392
electron, p. 392

26.1 Introduce

ENGAGE List the following terms on the board: *telephone, record player, mp3 player, GPS navigator, cassette player, transistor radio,* and *satellite radio.*

Have students work with partners to identify each device as using an analog signal, digital signal, or semiconductor. Write students' responses on the board, and check them for accuracy.

Vocabulary terms are listed on the first student page of each lesson. You may wish to preview the terms before introducing each lesson. Strategies for teaching the vocabulary appear on the pages where the terms are introduced.

Before You Read

Draw the three-column chart on the board. Thinking aloud, write in the *Analog Signal* column that the clock on the classroom wall is analog. Explain that your alarm clock at home is digital, and note that in the *Digital Signal* column. Tell students that analog clocks often depend on small motors, and digital clocks use electronics. Give students a few minutes to complete their three-column charts in their Science Notebooks.

Teach

EXPLAIN to students that they will learn about different types of electronic devices. All devices use analog signals, digital signals, or semiconductors to process, send, and store information.

 Vocabulary

electronic device Ask students to explain what *electronic* means. If needed, explain that *electronic* refers to something operated by means of electrical circuits, often several very small ones, which handle very low levels of electric current. Tell students that a device is a tool or instrument.

electronic signal Review with students the meaning of *electronic*. Have students list common uses of the word *signal*. Responses might include an action or gesture used to communicate or something used to send a message, such as railway lights. Ask students to relate these meanings to the term's scientific definition.

Teach

 EXPLAIN to students that electronic devices can use analog or digital signals. Ask students to speculate which type of signal is more accurate and why they think that. Discuss students' responses. Ask the same question again after the Explore It! activity on page 443.

Vocabulary

analog signal Tell students that an analog system represents changing values as continuously variable physical quantities. Have students compare telling time on an analog clock and a digital clock. Point out that the analog clock is always moving and changing, whereas the digital clock changes periodically.

digital signal Explain to students that the word *digital* is derived from Latin and relates to a finger or toe. The word *digit* can also refer to any of the numbers from zero to nine. Ask students to relate the derivation and common meaning to the scientific definition of the term.

Use the Visual: Figure 26.3

(ANSWER) The fluid expands with increasing temperature; thus, its density decreases. Note that most Galileo thermometers are filled with alcohol.

Figure 26.3 A Galileo thermometer produces a smooth, or continuous, measure of the temperature— it is an analog device. Weighted spheres, each with a different density, correspond to specific temperatures. They float at different levels depending on the temperature of the liquid. How does the density of liquid in the thermometer change as the liquid's temperature increases?

Types of Electronic Signals

Electronic signals can be analog or digital. Devices that use analog signals are analog devices. Likewise, digital signals are used by digital devices.

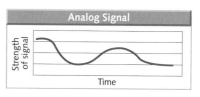

Figure 26.2 Analog signals vary smoothly over time.

Analog Signals For many years, most electronic devices used analog signals. As shown in **Figure 26.2**, an **analog** (AN uh log) **signal** changes smoothly over time. Many devices produce analog data. A liquid-filled thermometer is an analog device. The fluid inside the thermometer expands when it absorbs additional thermal energy. As the liquid expands, its level inside the thermometer rises. The rise or fall of the fluid level occurs smoothly—it does not jump abruptly. Another analog device is the Galileo thermometer shown in **Figure 26.3**. As the temperature inside the sealed glass tube changes, glass spheres carrying temperature reading tags slowly rise and fall.

During the 1980s and 1990s, many people listened to music recorded on cassette tapes. These small plastic cassettes contained magnetic tape upon which analog voice data were recorded. A tape player was used to play back the data. To do so, it converted the analog signal into a varying electric current. The current was then amplified and used to power speakers.

Digital Signals Audio cassettes declined in popularity when the compact disc, or CD, was introduced. The CD was the first popular music format to use digital data instead of analog data. Many modern electronic devices process digital signals. As shown in **Figure 26.4**, a **digital** (DIH juh tal) **signal** is made up of a series of distinct values over time. Note how the change from one value to the next occurs as a jump or step, not as a smooth, continuous change.

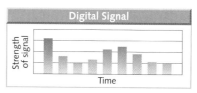

Figure 26.4 Digital signals consist of a set of distinct values. The values change in a steplike manner over time.

Differentiate Instruction

Music Have students listen to music from cassette tapes, CDs, MP3 players, and, if possible, record albums. Students should identify which storage device provided the best quality of music playback. Students should also compare the four formats to identify the strengths of each.

Background Information

The Galileo thermometer works on the premise that the water's temperature will match the temperature of the air outside the thermometer. The density of water changes along with the temperature. Each bubble has a different density that is close to the density of water and will float or sink, depending on the water's density. The temperature on the bubble that sinks the lowest is the temperature of the water, and thus of the air outside.

Producing Digital Signals

When small amounts of data from an analog device are recorded over time, a digital signal is produced. This is shown in **Figure 26.5**. The graph was produced by using a nondigital thermometer and recording the air temperature at one-hour intervals. The result—a set of distinct values over time—is a digital signal. Note that the digital signal is not smooth. Instead, it changes in a steplike manner.

Sampling Converting a continuous analog signal to a digital signal is known as sampling, or digitization. Each recorded value of the analog signal is a sample. By sampling at a very high rate, a digital signal that is nearly identical to the original analog signal can be produced. Sampling rates can exceed several million times per second. Look again at Figure 26.2 and Figure 26.4 on page 442. Figure 26.4 is a sampled, or digitized, approximation of the analog signal in Figure 26.2. Increasing the sampling rate would produce a more accurate digital signal.

Why Digital and Not Analog?

In the past several decades, there has been a major shift to digital signals and digital devices. This might seem like an odd shift, because digitized signals contain less information than do analog signals. However, the nature of the digital signal is the key to its usefulness. Digital signals are just bunches of numbers. As such, they are easily stored, manipulated, and transmitted by computers and other devices. The digital camera in **Figure 26.6** is a good example of the shift to digital technologies. The digital image files are easy to store, edit, and transmit.

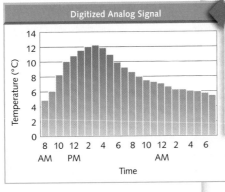

Digitized Analog Signal

Figure It Out

1. Describe the fluctuation in temperature throughout the day.
2. What is the sampling rate of the data?

Figure 26.5 A fluid-filled thermometer (an analog device) is used to record the air temperature at one-hour intervals. The resulting set of data, a set of distinct values over time, is a digital signal.

Figure 26.6 After the camera digitizes the scene, the digital information is easily processed and altered using a computer.

Explore It!

Create a graph with an x-axis numbered from 0 to 10 and a y-axis numbered from 0 to 20. Draw a smooth, upward-sloping line on the graph. How does it represent analog data? Now, approximate the curve by plotting a bar graph with four bars. Explain how this represents digital data. Is the bar graph a good approximation of the curve? Would the accuracy improve if you used 20 bars instead of four?

Teach

 EXPLAIN to students that digital signals are a compilation of data from analog devices. Digital devices are becoming increasingly popular due to their flexibility and ease of use.

Figure It Out: Figure 26.5

ANSWER **1.** The temperature is increasing fairly rapidly until about 3 P.M., and then it decreases slowly for the rest of the day. **2.** The data are sampled once an hour.

Explore It!

Provide students with graph paper and review how to draw a smooth curve. It might be helpful to draw the curve on the board. Then demonstrate how to draw one or two bars on the curve graph. Ask students to consider what the graph might represent (one possible data source is the temperature of air as the weather changes). Then ask students to imagine the data-gathering processes for the curve and for the bars, and reinforce the concept of sampling.

The curve is smooth and continuous, like an analog signal. The bars create a set of distinct values over time, like a digital signal. The analog signal carries much more information. As more bars are used, the digital signal begins to accurately approximate the analog signal.

Background Information

The amount of detail that a digital camera can capture is called the resolution, and it is measured in pixels. Resolution is often identified by the width and height of the image as well as the total number of pixels in the image. For example, an image that is 2,048 pixels wide and 1,536 pixels high (2,048 × 1,536) contains a total of 3,145,728 pixels (or 3.1 megapixels). As the number of pixels increases, more details are captured and larger photographs can be printed without blurriness. While specifics vary from one camera to another, generally, if the resolution is 1,024 × 768, the largest photo that should be printed is 4 × 6. If the resolution jumps to 1,600 × 1,200, an 8 × 10 photo can be printed clearly.

Teach

Review with students what a circuit is. Explain that most electric circuits are complex circuits, which consist of both series and parallel types.

Vocabulary

semiconductor Explain to students that the prefix *semi-* means "half." A conductor is a material that allows electricity to flow through it. The literal definition of *semiconductor* is "a material that partly allows electricity to flow."

doping Tell students that in electronics, *doping* refers to making a pure substance impure by adding another material to it. Explain that the substance being added is called the dopant.

Use the Visual: Figure 26.7

Ask students to identify the vacuum tubes in the photo. If needed, point out that they are mounted on the top of the amplifier.

Figure 26.7 Though largely replaced by semiconductor components, some audio amplifiers still use vacuum tubes. Some people like the warmer, richer sound produced by tube amplifiers.

Electronic Devices

Electronic devices use electronic signals to perform jobs. For instance, a calculator performs mathematical calculations using electronic signals. Electronic devices contain numerous circuits—sometimes thousands of them. Recall that a circuit is a path along which a current is carried. The currents flowing through these circuits are the electronic signals you just read about. Each electronic signal carries information in the form of a varying electric current.

Small devices called electronic components control the current within the circuits. There are many types of these components. Early radios and televisions used components called vacuum tubes. As shown in **Figure 26.7,** vacuum tubes are rather large. The tubes glow when in use and produce a lot of heat. As a result, early electronic devices were bulky, used a lot of electricity, and were not as reliable as those in use today. Most modern electronics do not use vacuum tubes. Instead, they rely on various components made from semiconductor materials.

Semiconductors

Modern electronic devices rely on semiconductors. A **semiconductor** is an element or compound that has properties between those of metals and nonmetals—they are neither excellent conductors nor excellent insulators. Semiconductors are tremendously important because their electrical conductivity can be altered and controlled. Semiconductor materials are used to make devices that control current flow in circuits. Semiconductors include, but are not limited to, silicon, germanium, and lead sulfide.

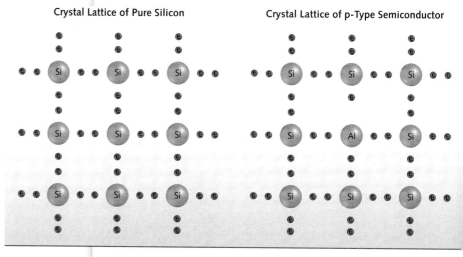

Crystal Lattice of Pure Silicon   Crystal Lattice of p-Type Semiconductor

444 ELECTRONIC TECHNOLOGY

Background Information

Microprocessor chips and transistors rely on semiconductors to work. Additionally, anything that depends on radio waves or is computerized relies on semiconductors.

Differentiate Instruction

Interpersonal Have students work with partners to interview adults and describe how semiconductor technology has influenced their work. Students could choose a school principal, secretary, cafeteria worker, custodian, coach, teacher, or bus driver. Have students focus their questions on the ways in which modern technology has changed the interviewee's work, the resulting challenges, and the positive outcomes.

444 ELECTRONIC TECHNOLOGY

Doping a Semiconductor

The arrangement of atoms in a semiconductor material makes it useful. When melted and cooled, the atoms form a repeating pattern called a lattice. A silicon lattice is shown on the left in **Figure 26.8.** Note that the nucleus of each silicon (Si) atom is surrounded by four electrons. The electrons form chemical bonds with the other silicon atoms.

p-Type Semiconductors   Replacing atoms in the lattice with atoms of other elements is known as **doping.** The middle portion of Figure 26.8 shows a doped lattice containing an aluminum (Al) atom. Because aluminum has three electrons instead of four, the lattice structure is broken. The "hole" in the lattice greatly increases its electrical conductivity. A semiconductor containing holes is a p-type semiconductor.

n-Type Semiconductors   The lattice on the right in Figure 26.8 contains an atom of arsenic (As). Because arsenic has five electrons instead of four, the lattice contains an extra electron that has nowhere to bond. The extra electron greatly increases the conductivity of the lattice. The extra electron also gives the lattice a negative charge. Thus, a semiconductor containing extra electrons is known as an n-type semiconductor.

Electron Flow   Something interesting happens where n- and p-type crystals come together. The junction allows electrons to flow in one direction only. Flow in the opposite direction is blocked. The allowed electron flow is from n-type to p-type.

Crystal Lattice of n-Type Semiconductor

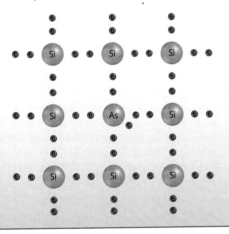

Figure 26.8 A silicon lattice (*left*) has a highly ordered, repeating pattern. Pure silicon is a poor conductor. The conductivities of the p-type semiconductor material (*center*) and the n-type semiconductor material (*right*) are much greater as a result of doping. How is each type of semiconductor produced?

As You Read

Review the chart in your Science Notebook and make sure that the sentences you wrote about analog signals, digital signals, and semiconductors are accurate. Explain your chart to a partner. Add to or modify your chart as needed.

Describe the flow of electrons through a diode.

Did You Know?

Solar panels that convert sunlight directly into electricity are basically large p-n junctions. The n-type material is exposed to the sunlight. Energy from the Sun drives electrons from the n-region to the p-region through a circuit. The electric current produced is used to power electric devices.

● Teach

EXPLAIN to students that a doped semiconductor is much more like a conductor than an undoped semiconductor. Discuss that "holes" are also charge carriers: electrons flow in one direction and holes flow in the opposite direction.

Science Notebook EXTRA

Have students study the names of the doped semiconductors and infer the origins of the names. Ask students to write sentences describing their conclusions in their Science Notebooks. (P-type semiconductors have a *positive* charge due to fewer electrons in the middle; n-type semiconductors have a *negative* charge because of an extra electron.) Then ask students to add notes describing the placement of silicon, aluminum, and arsenic on the periodic table. Students should include the atomic number of each as well as the period and family to which it belongs.

As You Read

Give students about five minutes to review and revise their three-column charts. Have students work with peers to share sentences and receive feedback.

ANSWER   Electrons flow in one direction, from the n-type material to the p-type material.

Use the Visual: Figure 26.8

ANSWER   A p-type semiconductor is doped with aluminum to create a hole due to fewer electrons. An n-type semiconductor is doped with arsenic, which gives it an excess of negative charge (electrons).

Differentiate Instruction

Kinesthetic   Provide students with modeling clay or small plastic foam balls. Have students work with a partner to make models of p-type and n-type semiconductors. Students should label the atoms in the lattice and the doping atoms.

Background Information

Many common items operate on solar or photovoltaic cells. Calculators, emergency road signs or call boxes, buoys, parking lot lights, and satellites can be powered by solar energy. On a sunny day, sunlight provides about 1,000 watts of energy per square meter of the planet's surface.

Teach

EXPLAIN to students that diodes and transistors are types of semiconductors that control the current. Integrated circuits, also known as chips, are miniature circuits that can be made of diodes, resistors, and capacitors.

 Vocabulary

diode Explain to students that the prefix *di-* means "twice." The word *hodos* is Greek and means "way." A diode contains two electrodes and only allows electrons to flow one way.

transistor Tell students that the word *transistor* is a combination of the words *transfer* and *resistor*. Ask students what the word *transfer* means. If needed, remind them that it refers to movement from one place to another.

integrated circuit Ask students to brainstorm common uses of the word *integrate*. Examples might include becoming an accepted member of a group or joining two objects into a larger unit. Explain to students that the word *circuit* comes from Latin and means "round trip" or "revolution."

Assess

Use the After You Read questions and the Alternative Assessment to help you evaluate students' understanding of the lesson.

After You Read

1. Both analog and digital signals use a varying electric current to carry information. Analog signals are smooth and continuous, whereas digital signals consist of a series of specific values that change in a step-like fashion.

2. diodes: to convert AC to DC, to provide a one-way current path; transistors: for signal amplification and modulation, current switching, voltage regulation, and as oscillators

3. Integrated circuits are miniature electronic circuits made up of numerous diodes, transistors, and other devices manufactured onto the surface of a semiconductor material.

Figure 26.9 Light-emitting diodes (LEDs) produce light from the movement of electrons in the semiconductor material. The lightbulb in the flashlight shown uses 150 LEDs to produce the same light output as a 70-W incandescent bulb, yet it only uses 9 W of power.

Figure 26.10 Transistors are used for signal amplification and modulation, current switching, voltage regulation, and as oscillators. Together with diodes, they also make up integrated circuits. The current-carrying pathways produced during the manufacturing process of an integrated circuit are easily seen when magnified.

Electronic Components

Semiconductors make up the electronic components used to control the flow of current through a circuit. By layering n-type and p-type materials in different ways, devices that amplify and switch currents, convert sunlight to electricity, and produce light from electricity can be made. Semiconductor devices are also called solid-state devices. The name dates back to the time when electronics began using semiconductors instead of vacuum tubes.

Diodes A **diode** (DIE ohd) is a semiconductor device that allows current to flow in one direction only. Think of a diode as a one-way door that allows you to enter a room but not leave. Diodes are made by creating an interface, or junction, between an n-type material and a p-type material. Diodes are often used to convert alternating current (AC) to direct current (DC). As shown in **Figure 26.9**, light-emitting diodes (LEDs) show great promise as highly efficient lightbulbs.

Transistors A **transistor** (tran ZIS ter) is a semiconductor device that can be used as a switch or to amplify currents. Transistors are one of the most important inventions in modern history. They are the key component in almost all electronic devices. Transistors are made of three sandwiched layers of semiconductor material, either n-p-n or p-n-p. Individual, or discrete, transistors are shown in **Figure 26.10**. Unlike those pictured, most transistors are now fabricated into integrated circuits.

Integrated Circuits An **integrated circuit** is a miniaturized electronic circuit. It contains diodes, resistors, capacitors (devices used to store charge in a circuit), and other electronic components that have been manufactured into the surface of a thin sheet of semiconductor material. The cost to produce an integrated circuit is low, because the components are formed at once during several passes through a light- and chemical-based process. The short distance between components greatly improves the performance of the integrated circuit. A modern computer chip like the one shown in Figure 26.10 can contain thousands of electronic components.

After You Read

1. How are analog and digital signals similar? How are they different?

2. List several uses of diodes and transistors.

3. Review the information you have recorded in your Science Notebook. Describe an integrated circuit.

Alternative Assessment

Have students use their three-column charts to write a three- to five-sentence description of analog signals, digital signals, and semiconductors. Students should include examples of each type in their descriptions.

Background Information

In 1974, Intel made the first chip (8080) to be placed in home computers; this chip was an eight-bit and held 6,000 transistors. Almost 20 years later, in 1993, the Pentium chip was introduced. The 32-bit Pentium chip contained 3,100,000 transistors. Recently, the Pentium 4 was introduced; this 32-bit chip contains 125,000,000 transistors. The Pentium 4 runs 5,000 times faster than the original 8080 chip.

26.2 Telecommunication

Before You Read

Look at the six main headings in this lesson. Fold a sheet of paper from your Science Notebook into six sections. Write one heading in each section. Then write a sentence summarizing what you know about each one. Add information to your chart as you read.

The Greek root *tele-* means "far off." The word *communication* means "the exchange of information." From these comes the term **telecommunication** (tel i kuh myoo ni KAY shun), which is the use of signals transmitted over a distance for communication purposes. Telecommunication is not new. People have communicated across distances for thousands of years. The methods of telecommunication, however, have changed. In the past, people used smoke signals, drums, lights, and flags to transmit signals. Today, the process almost always involves the transmission of electromagnetic signals.

The Telegraph

In 1825, the British physicist William Sturgeon demonstrated a device called an electromagnet. The device led to the development of electronic communication. By 1830, American Joseph Henry had demonstrated the electromagnet's communication potential. Henry connected an electromagnetic bell to a wire and rang it from over a mile away. In 1837, Samuel Morse patented a version of the electric telegraph, a communication device that uses an electromagnet. The telegraph can be considered the beginning of electronic communication.

The telegraph was the first widespread electrical communication device. The telegraph operator used an electric sending device like the one shown in **Figure 26.11** to type messages letter-by-letter. The letters were transmitted as a series of dots and dashes according to a code known as Morse code. The electric signal traveled through a wire to a distant receiving station in another city. Here, the dots and dashes were recorded on a long paper tape. After the transmission was complete, the tape was decoded and read. By 1866, a telegraph cable connected the United States to Europe, allowing for transatlantic telecommunication.

Figure 26.11 A telegraph operator used this sending device to tap out messages one letter at a time. For example, the distress signal SOS would be sent as *dot dot dot, dash dash dash, dot dot dot.*

Read Aloud Students will encounter many of these concepts in their everyday lives. Have students work in groups of three: each student should read aloud two of the six sections in the lesson. Students should then discuss their experiences with each of the telecommunication tools.

Learning Goals

- Describe the operation of various telecommunication devices.
- Describe the reception advantages of digital television signals.

New Vocabulary

telecommunication

Recall Vocabulary

electromagnet, p. 428
transformer, p. 436

26.2 Introduce

ENGAGE Have students reflect on the ways in which they communicate with their friends. Have them list in their Science Notebooks all the ways they communicate. Their lists might include instant messaging (via computer), text-messaging (on cell phones), emailing, talking at school, talking on the telephone, and using online chat rooms. Next, have students place the items in order of most commonly used to least commonly used. Discuss the advantages and challenges of the different methods. Point out that many of these methods rely on electromagnetic signals and thus depend on electricity.

Before You Read

Review the six main headings in the lesson and model the chart on the board. After you read the section about the telegraph, discuss with students how to summarize the information. Highlight the importance of being brief and of including key words and phrases. Have students work with partners to summarize the section in a sentence. Discuss students' examples and create a class summary. Have students complete their charts in their Science Notebooks.

● Teach

EXPLAIN to students that the first electronic communication occurred via the telegraph. Remind students of all the ways that electronics are involved in their present-day communications.

Vocabulary

telecommunication Explain to students that the prefix *tele-* is derived from Greek and means "far." The word *communicate* is derived from Latin and means "to share." The literal definition of *telecommunication* is "to share from afar."

● Teach

Review with students what a transmitter is (a source that sends information to a receiver) and what a receiver is (an electronic circuit that receives a signal and converts the signal into sound, pictures, or other information).

Extend It!

Provide students with resources such as encyclopedias, reference books related to sending messages, and relevant Web sites. Have students work with partners to conduct further investigation about World War II. Students should create an outline organizing their research on secret codes and Navajo code talkers. Navajo speakers were used to transmit secret messages during World War II. The Navajo language, which is an unwritten language, was a code never broken by the Germans.

Extend It!

Research Morse code and create a poster-sized chart showing the code used for each letter and number. Use the code to write a message to your class. For further research, investigate the use of secret codes used during World War II. Write a short report on the valuable role played by Navajo code talkers.

Figure 26.13 Users of early phone systems did not dial their own calls. Instead, they spoke to an operator at a switching office who manually connected their wire to the proper circuit in order to complete the call.

The Telephone

Another major advancement in telecommunications came with the invention and widespread use of the telephone. Whereas the lines of the telegraph ran from office to office, the lines of the telephone ran directly into people's homes. For the first time, it was easy for two people to talk to each other across vast distances. The conventional telephone was invented by Alexander Bell in 1876.

A conventional telephone system requires a network of transmitters and receivers that are connected by wires. The telephone acts as both the transmitter and the receiver. Because today's telephone network is worldwide, nearly anyone anywhere can be reached by phone. This is an amazing accomplishment when one considers that just 100 years ago, a hand-written note might have taken weeks to get to its destination.

A simplified diagram of a telephone system is shown in **Figure 26.12.** When you speak into a telephone, a microphone converts the pressure exerted by the sound waves into a varying electric current. The varying current is transmitted through a transformer to the receiving telephone. The transformer is connected to an output diaphragm, or speaker. The varying current creates a changing magnetic field in the transformer. The changing magnetic field moves the diaphragm, reproducing the speaker's voice. Portions of a phone call's journey are now likely to be digitized. The digital signals are converted back to analog signals before reaching the receiving telephone.

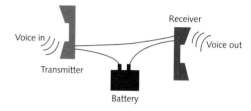

Figure 26.12 The telephone is an electric device used to transmit and receive data.

The telephone system requires little power and uses its own power source, as shown in Figure 26.12. This explains why a wired, or landline, telephone works even when a local power outage occurs. The number of wires and cables making up the telephone network is hard to imagine. As shown in **Figure 26.13,** telephone connections were originally made manually by telephone operators. Now, automated switching equipment connects and routes calls.

Differentiate Instruction

Kinesthetic Collect a variety of old or broken telecommunication devices and provide students with safety goggles, screwdrivers, pliers, and gloves. Be sure that the devices are unplugged. Ask students to take apart and observe the devices. Have students note the electronic components within the telecommunication devices.

Broadcast Media

The average American watches about four hours and 30 minutes of television a day. Many of these same people also listen to the radio throughout the day. Transmitting everything from sporting events to news to entertainment, radio and television broadcasts are a significant part of people's everyday lives.

Like the telephone system, radio and television rely on networks of transmitters and receivers. Originally, radio and television signals were transmitted only through the air. As shown in **Figure 26.14,** large transmission towers are still used to broadcast radio and television signals. Over time, however, other methods for delivering radio and television signals have been developed.

Currently, it is possible to receive radio and television signals through the air from Earth-based broadcast towers and Earth-orbiting satellites, through dedicated cable lines, and, increasingly, through telephone wires and cables used to carry internet traffic. The number of ways to receive the signals will likely continue to increase. **Figure 26.15** shows some of the devices used to receive the signals.

Figure 26.14 Radio and television transmission towers are usually tall and located on hills to maximize the range of the signal.

Figure 26.15 Different types of receiving devices are used for each type of signal. Large outdoor antennas are often used for television signals. Small outdoor dishes are used for satellite signals. Digital cable boxes decode incoming digital television signals.

Radio

Radio signals contain audio data only. The signals can be analog or digital. Radios decode the electromagnetic radio signals traveling through the air. These waves are broadcast from Earth-based transmission towers. Recall that electromagnetic waves are electric and magnetic fields that reproduce each other as they move through space. As the waves travel, they pass over a radio's receiving antenna. The changing electric and magnetic fields cause electrons in the antenna to vibrate back and forth, producing a varying current. The current is then amplified and used to drive loudspeakers.

Teach

EXPLAIN to students that television displays can be produced by cathode-ray tubes, liquid crystal, or plasma. Each display type has advantages and disadvantages.

As You Read

Give students a few minutes to revise their summaries of cathode-ray tube television. Have students share their sentences with partners and exchange constructive feedback.

[ANSWER] The phosphors emit colored light when struck by electronic devices; the phosphors produce the image on the screen.

As You Read

Review the sentences you have written in your Science Notebook. Summarize how a cathode-ray tube television works. Be sure to include important facts and supporting details.

What is the function of the phosphors?

Television

Television signals contain audio and video data. The signals can be analog or digital. Newer TVs with digital tuners are able to process high-definition, or HD, signals. HD signals contain much more video data than do older analog signals.

CRT TVs For about 75 years, all TVs used cathode-ray tubes, or CRTs, to produce images. A CRT produces an electron beam that strikes the inside of a phosphor-coated screen. Phosphors are chemicals that glow when struck by electrons. The screen is covered with three phosphor sheets: red, green, and blue. The CRT produces three beams, one aimed at each phosphor sheet. When the beam strikes the phosphor sheet, color is produced. For example, blue is created when a beam strikes the blue phosphor sheet. White is created when all three beams strike all three phosphor sheets. Colors other than red, blue, and green are created by mixing different amounts of red, blue, and green. **Figure 26.16** shows a close-up view of a CRT television screen.

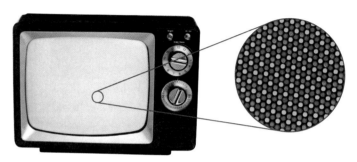

Figure 26.16 When viewed up close, the individual phosphor dots, called pixels, can be seen. The light from each group of red, blue, and green pixels combines to form different colors.

LCD TVs Many TVs use liquid crystal display, or LCD, technology. LCD TVs work by blocking light. An LCD screen is made up of a crystal-containing solution sandwiched between two flat sheets of glass. The crystal orientations are controlled electronically to block a portion of the light striking the back side of the screen. By altering the light passing through each screen pixel, different colors are formed.

Plasma TVs Plasma TVs use pockets of gas to produce color images. Each gas pixel contains three subpixels made up of red, green, and blue phosphors. Electronic devices vary the current applied to each subpixel. The current causes the gas to form plasma and emit ultraviolet light. The light reacts with a phosphor-coated screen to produce color.

Background Information

The quality of image portrayed by LCD televisions versus plasma televisions is being debated. LCDs are usually less expensive, have a higher resolution (more pixels on the screen), use less power, have a longer life, and are not as susceptible to screen burn. However, plasma is considered better for very large-screened televisions, such as those 50 inches and larger.

Problems with Airborne Signals Many things can interfere with airborne television signals. For analog signals, this results in common problems such as ghosting, or a double image onscreen, and snow, or white dots onscreen. Airborne digital signals do not suffer from these problems. Digital signals represent numbers. Part of a digital signal might be [0, 1, 1, 0]. Imagine that interference causes the signal to arrive at the television as [0.1, 0.9, 1.2, 0.1]. The television electronic devices "know" the signal can only contain ones and zeros and correct the signal back to [0, 1, 1, 0].

Cellular Phones

Cellular phones allow people to communicate from almost anywhere while doing almost anything. The name *cellular phone* comes from the network of transmission towers known as cells, shown in **Figure 26.17.**

Each cell in the network covers a roughly circular area. When a cell phone is turned on, it connects to the nearest transmission tower. The phone acts both as a transmitter and a receiver. When a call is made, the signal travels from the phone to the tower. The tower transmits the signal to other towers or to landline phone systems as needed to complete the call. If the caller or receiver is traveling, the call is "handed off" from one cell to the next.

The data, which are usually voice data but might also include video, are transmitted as a digital signal. The data are transmitted to and from the cell phone as microwaves. Microwaves are electromagnetic waves.

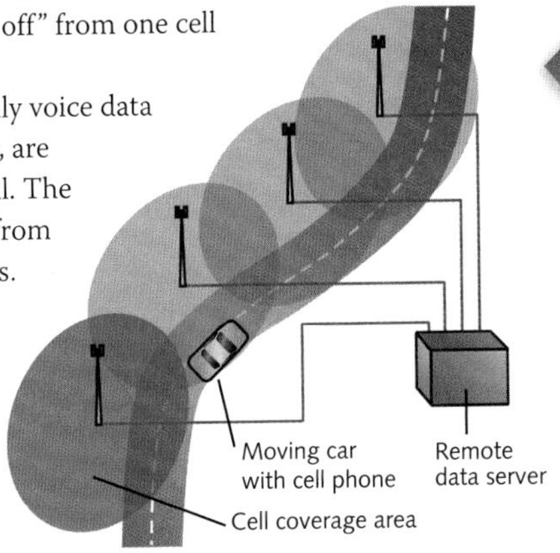

Moving car with cell phone
Remote data server
Cell coverage area

Figure 26.17 As the caller travels, the cell phone signal is switched from one cell tower to the next.

Did You Know?

Airborne digital signals also suffer from interference. However, the nature of a digital signal is that the data are either correct or missing. Missing digital data result in dropped cell phone calls and pixilated or incomplete TV images.

Figure It Out

1. Why do the coverage areas overlap?
2. What might cause a cell phone call to be dropped as the caller travels?

After You Read

1. Describe how telegraph messages were sent, received, and recorded.
2. Which telecommunication devices rely on transmitters and receivers?
3. Review the notes in your Science Notebook. Explain why digital television signals don't suffer from poor reception problems such as ghosting and snow.

Background Information

Multiple providers often share cell phone towers. At the base of the tower, each provider has its own equipment, often in a box, which includes radio transmitters and receivers. The tower, cables, and equipment are heavily grounded (copper can be used as a grounding agent).

Teach

EXPLAIN to students that video and audio data can be transmitted digitally through the air. Analog signals can suffer from interference; digital signals are more stable. Cellular phones transmit information via microwaves, a type of electromagnetic wave.

Figure It Out: Figure 26.17

ANSWER **1.** The electromagnetic signals do not stop at a predetermined distance; instead, they gradually weaken. To ensure good signal quality, the coverage areas are made to overlap. **2.** Atmospheric interference from weather and electromagnetic events such as solar flares can interfere. So, too, can the local topography (hills, mountains, etc.) or passing through a tunnel.

Assess

Use the After You Read questions and the Alternative Assessment to help you evaluate students' understanding of the lesson.

After You Read

1. Each letter of the message was sent as a series of dots and dashes. The signal traveled over wires to the receiving station, where it was recorded as a series of imprints on a paper tape.
2. all of them
3. The digital signal is either received and decoded perfectly or cannot be decoded at all. The result is that a digital signal is either perfect or missing; it does not suffer from ghosting and snow as analog signals do.

Alternative Assessment

Have each student choose two telecommunication devices to compare and contrast in a well-written paragraph. Students should include a description of how the device operates and its reception advantages and disadvantages.

ENGAGE Have students brainstorm a list of everything they use a computer to do. Lists could include the following tasks: write reports, download music, listen to music, email friends, create videos, manage and print photos, and instant-message friends. Make a class list of tasks, and ask students to organize the list in a way that makes sense. For instance, they might suggest categories such as homework, friends, and entertainment. Organize the tasks into the categories and write the list on the board to reference throughout the lesson.

Before You Read

Write the word *computer* on the board. Have students write a sentence that uses *computer*. Have students share their sentences and ask them to identify those that include the definition of the word. Write those sentences on the board and encourage students to follow those examples as they complete the task. Give students a few minutes to write the vocabulary terms for the lesson in their Science Notebooks.

Teach

EXPLAIN to students that they will learn about computers and the components that make them work.

Vocabulary

computer Tell students that the root *compute* is from Latin and means "to calculate." Ask students how the derivation relates to the scientific definition.

software program Explain to students that software programs can be classified into three types: operating systems, applications, and programming.

binary number Remind students that the prefix *bi-* means "two." A binary number is a number expressed in base-2 notation.

Learning Goals

- Explain the use of binary numbers by computers.
- Identify the parts of a computer and describe their functions.
- Distinguish between types of computer memory.

New Vocabulary

computer
software program
binary number
computer hardware
central processing unit
random-access memory
read-only memory

26.3 Computers

Before You Read

Write the vocabulary terms for this lesson in your Science Notebook. As you read the lesson, use each term in a sentence of your own. Make sure that your sentences show the meaning of each term.

You might be wondering why computers were not discussed in the previous lesson on telecommunications. After all, computers are used for video conferences, email, instant messages, and accessing the Internet. The reason is that although computers have become a powerful telecommunication device, they also do many other things.

What Is a Computer?

A **computer** is an electronic device designed to carry out a set of instructions. A set of instructions that the computer runs is known as a **software program.** By running different programs, the computer can do different tasks. For example, a laboratory software program could be used to allow the computer to collect data from a temperature probe. After the lab work was completed, a word processing program could be used to write a laboratory report. If needed, another program could be used to email a file of the report to others. Computers are versatile devices capable of performing many jobs.

The history of the computer is relatively short. **Figure 26.18** shows the ENIAC, one of the first computers, which was built in 1946. Computer technology has advanced rapidly. The small notebook computers common today weigh virtually nothing compared with the ENIAC, use far less power, and can execute millions more instructions per second.

Figure 26.18 The ENIAC, short for Electronic Numerical Integrator and Computer, weighed more than 27 metric tons, required more than 150,000 watts of power, and executed about 5,000 simple instructions per second. A modern laptop computer weighs about 2.2 kilograms, can run for hours on rechargeable batteries, and can execute millions of instructions per second.

ELL Strategy

Paraphrase Have students work in groups of three. Each student should paraphrase two of the six pages of the lesson, summarizing the important concepts and sharing their work with the other group members. Each group should then create a list of the most important concepts of the lesson. Have the class work to synthesize the concepts into three or four "big ideas."

How Computers Process Information

Computers process numbers. Everything a computer does is done by processing numbers. Even the words and letters in an email message are converted and stored as numbers. Recall that data consisting of numbers are called digital data. Computers are extremely efficient at processing digital data.

Binary Numbers The words *yes* and *no* and *on* and *off* are very direct and effective words for communicating with others. Computers use a similar and extremely limited language to process data. As shown in **Figure 26.19,** all digital information is expressed as a combination of the numbers 0 and 1. A number comprised only of the numbers 0 and 1 is known as a **binary** (BI neh ree) **number.** For example, a piece of data might be represented by the binary number 1010. Each 0 and 1 in the binary number is called a bit. Thus, the first bit in 1010 is 1.

Representing Data With Binary Numbers
Binary numbers with a small number of bits can represent a large number of possible values. Consider a single-bit binary number. It can represent two possible values, 1 or 0. Likewise, a two-bit binary number has four possible values: 00, 01, 10, and 11. Each additional bit greatly increases the number of possible values. A binary number with 16 bits has 65,536 possibilities. **Figure 26.20** shows the possible values for one-, two-, and three-bit binary numbers.

Figure 26.19
No matter what its input, this is all a computer "sees."

Computers often use eight-bit binary numbers to represent letters and numbers. There are 256 possible values for an eight-bit binary number. Using this system, the letter *A* is 01000001, the letter *a* is 01100001, and a question mark is 00111111. An eight-bit binary number is also known as a byte.

Combinations of Binary Digits

Number of Binary Digits	Possible Combinations
1	0 1
2	00 01 10 11
3	000 001 010 011 100 101 110 111

Figure 26.20 Each bit in a binary number has two possible values, 0 and 1. Thus, the number of possible combinations increases quickly as the number of bits in the binary number increases.

As You Read

Use the sentence you have written in your Science Notebook to describe a binary number.

How does a two-digit binary number compare with a two-digit number in the number system you usually use?

Figure It Out

1. What are the possible values of any bit?

2. How many possible combinations does a four-bit number have? Write out all of the combinations.

• Teach

EXPLAIN to students that all digital data are represented by the numbers 1 and 0. Data could be photographic, video, or audio.

As You Read

Have students share their sentences with partners. Then have each student create a new sentence using the best of both of sentences.

ANSWER A binary number is a number comprised only of the numbers 1 and 0. A two-digit number in the regular number system has two possible combinations. A two-digit binary number has four possible combinations.

Figure It Out: Figure 26.20

ANSWER **1.** 0 or 1 **2.** There are 16 possible combinations: 0000, 0001, 0010, 0100, 1000, 0011, 0110, 1100, 0111, 1110, 1111, 1001, 0101, 1010, 1101, 1011

Differentiate Instruction

Visual Have students create symbols to represent 1 and 0. They should then use the symbols to show the possible combinations, as done in **Figure 26.20.** For instance, a student could choose a red circle to represent 1 and a blue square to represent 0. Students' charts should include all the possible combinations of the red circle and blue square.

Teach

EXPLAIN to students that computer hardware includes devices that send information to and from the computer and that save information.

Vocabulary

computer hardware Ask students if they are familiar with any other meanings of the word *hardware*. Discuss these meanings and encourage students to identify any relationships between the meanings and the definition of the term provided in this lesson.

central processing unit Explain to students that the word *central* is the adjective form of the noun *center*. Review the definitions of *center*, *process*, and *unit*. Have students combine these definitions and relate the literal definition to the scientific definition of the term.

Use the Visual: Figure 26.21

ANSWER A scanner is an input device.

Computer Hardware

The physical parts of a computer are known as **computer hardware.** A typical setup of computer hardware is shown in **Figure 26.21.** There are three types of hardware: input devices, output devices, and storage devices.

Input Devices A device that sends data or instructions to the computer is an input device. Input devices are usually directly controlled by the computer operator. For example, to move the pointer or cursor across the screen, the operator moves the mouse. The mouse is an input device. So is the keyboard. Typing on the keyboard sends information to the computer.

Output Devices A device that displays data sent from the computer is an output device. The image on a computer monitor is produced from image data sent from the computer. Thus, the monitor is an output device. Speakers that play audio data and printers that print text and graphic data are also output devices.

Storage Devices Although computers have some amount of built-in memory, additional storage devices are also needed. CD and DVD drives, flash-memory drives, and hard-disk drives are all used to store and retrieve data.

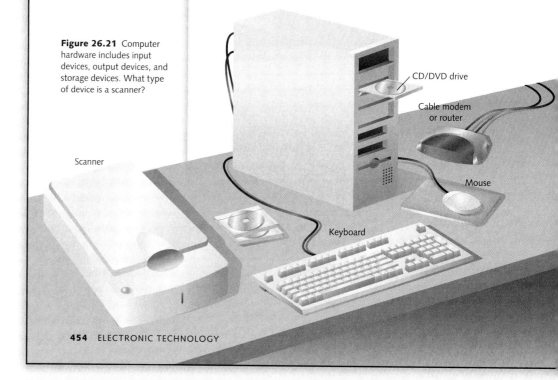

Figure 26.21 Computer hardware includes input devices, output devices, and storage devices. What type of device is a scanner?

454 ELECTRONIC TECHNOLOGY

Background Information

A variety of assistive technologies provide alternative ways for computer users to input and output data. Output technologies consist of screen magnifiers, screen readers, speech synthesizers, and Braille interface and displays. Input devices include trackballs, micromouse, touchscreens, use of sticky keys, microphones, and switches. Newer operating system software often has built-in assistive technologies.

Teacher Alert

People with special needs might use assistive technologies to input data. These devices could include larger or different keyboards, track balls, and microphones. If possible, enable students to try such devices or share their experiences if they know friends or family members who require one of these devices.

The CPU

The controlling "brain" of a computer is its **central processing unit,** or CPU. Central processing units are also called microprocessors. CPUs are very complex devices containing millions of diodes, transistors, and other electronic devices. In spite of their complexity, however, CPUs are very small, as shown in **Figure 26.22.**

The CPU receives, processes, and outputs data. This activity controls what the computer and the hardware devices are doing. For example, imagine writing a report using a word processing program. To type words on the screen, you press the keys on the keyboard. Electronic signals from the keyboard travel to the CPU. The CPU uses the software program that is running to process the signal. The CPU responds by sending a signal to the monitor, which displays the information.

A 1965 prediction stated that the capabilities of CPUs would double about every 18 months. The prediction, now known as Moore's law, has proven surprisingly accurate. The complexity, processing speed, and capability of CPUs increase each year. Faster CPUs are able to run larger, more complicated software applications.

Figure 26.22
This central processing unit has dimensions of about 2 cm by 2 cm.

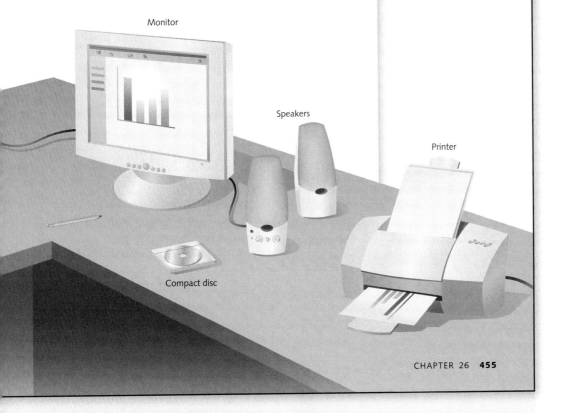

Monitor

Speakers

Printer

Compact disc

● **Teach**

EXPLAIN to students that the central processing unit does the work of the computer; it receives, processes, and outputs data.

EXTEND Have students work in pairs to create a time line of technological advances and inventions in communications. Students should include items mentioned in this chapter as well as other items of interest related to telecommunications and the computer.

Background Information

In 1965, co-founder of Intel Gordon Moore made the prediction that CPU capability would double about every 18 months. Moore's law does not refer to CPU speed but to the number of transistors on integrated circuit boards. Moore's law is used to refer to the rapid advances in computing power per unit cost, because an increase in transistor quantity is roughly equivalent to an increase in computer processing power.

Key Concept Review
Workbook, p. 164

● Teach

EXPLAIN to students that a computer's memory can be short-term (RAM) or long-term (ROM).

 Vocabulary

random-access memory Ask students if they are familiar with the meanings of the words *random* ("occurring without a pattern"), *access* ("means of approaching"), and *memory* ("ability to retain information"). Discuss these meanings and then ask students to compare the literal definition of the term to its scientific definition.

read-only memory Talk with students about the meaning of *read-only*. Explain that the opposite concept is "read and write." Review with students the meaning of the word *memory*. Read-only memory is intended to perform a specific function and cannot be changed.

 Explain It!

Each 0 or 1 in the binary number is called a bit. An eight-bit binary number is known as a byte.

ANSWER To calculate the number of bytes contained in a 128-megabyte RAM memory chip, multiply 128 MB by 1,048,576 bytes. To convert this number of bytes to bits, multiply by 8.

PEOPLE IN SCIENCE

Grace Hopper developed the first compiler. The compiler translated symbolic mathematical code into machine code. Using call numbers, the computer could retrieve commands stored on tape and then perform them. Hopper's compiler laid the foundation for modern programming languages.

EXTEND Have students conduct research on a technology pioneer of their choice, such as Bill Gates, Steve Jobs, or Larry Page. Students should write in their Science Notebooks a one- to two-paragraph summary of the pioneer's contributions.

Representing Binary Digits

Binary Number	Switches
0000	
0001	
0010	
0011	
0100	
1010	

Figure 26.23 Binary numbers can be thought of as switches that are either ON or OFF.

Explain It!

Write a few sentences explaining what a bit and a byte are. Then, knowing that 1 megabyte = 1,048,576 bytes, describe how you would calculate the number of bytes contained in a 128-megabyte RAM memory chip. Your answer should be 134,217,728 bytes. How many bits is this?

Computer Memory

In a computer, binary numbers relate to OFF and ON states of electric charge. To understand this, imagine a light switch on a wall. The switch can only be ON or OFF, just as a bit can only be a 1 or a 0. When the switch is OFF, no charge flows to the light. This corresponds to a bit value of 0. If the switch is ON, current flows. This corresponds to a bit value of 1. **Figure 26.23** shows how OFF and ON switches relate to four-bit binary numbers.

Storing Data A computer's memory is made of integrated circuits, such as the one shown in **Figure 26.24**. These devices contain millions of electronic circuits. In a computer memory chip, each circuit can either be charged (ON) or uncharged (OFF). These charged and uncharged states directly correspond to the ON and OFF switch positions and the bit values of 1 and 0. That is, a charged circuit is represented by a 1, and an uncharged circuit is represented by a 0. Because computer memory chips contain millions of circuits, they can store millions of binary values.

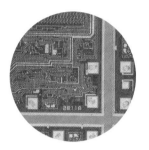

Figure 26.24 Integrated circuits contains millions of microscopic circuits.

Random-Access Memory Computers store data that are currently being used in **random-access memory,** or RAM. For example, the instructions of a software program are stored in RAM while the program is running. When a computer is turned off, all the data stored in RAM are lost. Thus, RAM cannot store data that will be needed at a later date.

Read-Only Memory Computers can store data permanently in **read-only memory,** or ROM. Basic instructions that a computer needs in order to function are stored in ROM. Data stored in ROM are not lost when the power is turned off. Because ROM data can only be read, it is not possible to accidentally alter or erase the information. This protects valuable instructions and data.

Teacher Alert

Students might be confused about the difference between RAM and ROM. RAM is read-write and ROM is read-only. Since RAM is an acronym for random-access memory, students might believe that ROM is not random access. Actually, any location can be read in any order from ROM; it *is* random access.

Differentiate Instruction

Mathematical Have students calculate the number of bytes and bits contained in a 256-megabyte RAM memory chip.

Storage Devices

Data that need to be stored so that they can be revised at a later date must be stored on a storage device. Storage devices are needed because data stored in RAM are lost when the power is turned off, and data in ROM can only be read. Storage devices include disk drives, flash memory cards, CDs, and DVDs, as shown in **Figure 26.25.** Each of these devices uses a different technology to store and retrieve data. Each has advantages and disadvantages.

Hard drives are capable of storing huge amounts of data magnetically. Access is slower on a hard drive than on a flash memory card. Flash cards are small and very fast, but they store limited amounts of data. CDs and DVDs store large amounts of data, and like flash cards, they are portable.

Figure 26.25 There are many ways to store data.

PEOPLE IN SCIENCE Grace Hopper (1906–1992)

Grace Hopper was an American computer scientist and United States Navy officer. She was born in New York City. She earned bachelor's and master's degrees in mathematics and physics and a doctorate in mathematics.

In 1943, Hopper joined the U.S. Naval Reserve, where she worked on the Mark I, II, and III line of calculators—some of the first computers. In 1949, Hopper went to work for a company developing the UNIVAC I, which would become

the first commercial computer made in the United States. She developed the first compiler for a computer programming language. Hopper later returned to the U.S. Navy, where she continued to work on computer compilers and languages. In the 1970s, she pioneered the implementation of standards for testing computer systems and components. After retiring from the Navy, she became a senior consultant to the Digital Equipment Company, a job she kept until her death in 1992.

After You Read

1. What are RAM and ROM? How are they different?
2. Explain why computers use binary numbers to store data.
3. Review the sentences you wrote in your Science Notebook describing the new vocabulary terms. Which term describes devices used to input and output data? List several of the devices and describe their purposes.

CONNECTION: Technology

The Internet is an amazing resource. Information on almost any topic is available in seconds. Where does all of this information come from? It comes from computers with huge storage devices known as servers. A server manages and delivers information to other computers. The information of the Internet is stored on millions of interconnected servers.

● Teach

EXPLAIN to students that for long-term and permanent storage of data, devices such as DVDs, CDs, flash drives, and external hard drives can be used. People also use these storage devices to back up their computers.

CONNECTION: Technology

Explain to students that HTML (hypertext markup language) programming creates text for Web pages. Then write the following on the board:

<html>

<b> This statement would be bold. </b>

</html>

Tell students that these examples contain HTML tags within the < > symbols. The HTML tags are interpreted by Web browsers such as Internet Explorer and Firefox, and then the results are displayed. The first tag, <b>, begins the bold formatting, and the second tag, </b>, ends the bold formatting.

● Assess

Use the After You Read questions and the Alternative Assessment to help you evaluate students' understanding of the lesson.

After You Read

1. RAM, or random-access memory, is where computers store data that are currently being used. ROM, or read-only memory, is where computers store data permanently. Data stored in ROM are not lost when the power is turned off.
2. Binary numbers are useful for storing data because as the number of bits in a binary number increases, so does the number of possible combinations of 0s and 1s, or uncharged and charged circuits.
3. *Computer hardware* is the term that describes input and output devices. Input devices include a mouse, a keyboard, and a scanner. Output devices include a monitor, a speaker, and a printer.

Alternative Assessment

Have each student use his or her vocabulary term sentences to write a paragraph explaining how a computer receives input and processes and stores data. Students should use at least five vocabulary terms in their paragraphs.

Interpreting Diagrams
Workbook, p. 166

Chapter 26 Summary

Check students' sentences or paragraphs to make sure they understand the meaning of each vocabulary term.

Evaluate students' essays using the following criteria:

1. The topic sentence, or main idea, should restate the Key Concept.

2. The supporting paragraphs should incorporate the answers to the Learning Goal questions students have written and include details, facts, and examples they have recorded in their Science Notebooks.

3. The concluding sentence should sum up the main idea of the chapter and restate the Key Concept.

MASTERING CONCEPTS

True or False

1. True
2. True
3. False, p-type
4. False, electromagnet
5. False, Analog
6. False, microwaves
7. False, binary
8. True

Short Answer

9. The current in a lamp is constant and continuous; the current of an electronic signal is varying.

10. A binary number has two possible values, much as a switch has two possible positions.

11. Both are lattices of a semiconductor material doped with an impurity element. P-type semiconductors have "holes" in the lattice, whereas n-type semiconductors have extra electrons.

12. As long as the digital signal is not too distorted, the TV can correct the errors by adjusting the decoded values back to the digits 0 and 1.

13. A computer can run a large number of different software programs that allow it to perform a wide range of tasks.

14. The CPU is the "brain" of the computer. CPUs contain millions of diodes, transistors, and other electronic devices.

Chapter 26

Summary

KEY CONCEPTS

26.1 Electronic Signals and Devices

- An electronic device uses electricity to process and transmit electronic signals. An electronic signal, which can be an analog or digital signal, is a varying electric current.

- Because digital signals are numbers, they are easily stored, transmitted, and processed.

- Modern electronic devices use semiconductors. The conductivity of a semiconductor is greatly increased by doping.

- Electronic devices to control currents in circuits are made from semiconductor material.

26.2 Telecommunication

- Telecommunication is the exchange of information across a distance.

- The telegraph used wires and an electromagnetic sending device to transmit coded messages from one point to another.

- The telephone system is made up of a huge network of interconnected transmitting and receiving devices.

- There are many ways to transmit and receive analog and digital signals. Many different technologies are used to reproduce television images.

- Cellular phones communicate with a network of transmission towers called cells. The network transfers the call from cell to cell as the caller moves.

26.3 Computers

- Computers are electronic devices that run software programs in order to perform various tasks.

- Computers process and store data as binary numbers. A binary digit, or bit, can have a value of 1 or 0.

- Computer hardware consists of input devices, output devices, and storage devices.

- The central processing unit, or microprocessor, is an integrated circuit that controls the function of the computer.

VOCABULARY REVIEW

Write each term in a complete sentence or write a paragraph relating several terms.

26.1
electronic device, p. 441
electronic signal, p. 441
analog signal, p. 442
digital signal, p. 442
semiconductor, p. 444
doping, p. 445
diode, p. 446
transistor, p. 446
integrated circuit, p. 446

26.2
telecommunication, p. 447

26.3
computer, p. 452
software program, p. 452
binary number, p. 453
computer hardware , p. 454
central processing unit, p. 455
random-access memory, p. 456
read-only memory, p. 456

PREPARE FOR CHAPTER TEST

To prepare for the chapter test, create a question from each Learning Goal. Use the information in your Science Notebook to answer each question. Then use these answers to write a well-developed essay about the chapter. Use the Key Concept on the first page of this chapter as your topic sentence.

Vocabulary Review
Workbook, p. 165

Reading Comprehension
Workbook, p. 167

MASTERING CONCEPTS

True or False

If the statement is true, write "true." If it is false, change the underlined word or words to make the statement true.

1. <u>Analog signals</u> change continuously.

2. An analog signal can be converted to a digital signal by <u>sampling</u>.

3. A semiconductor containing holes is called a(n) <u>n-type</u> semiconductor.

4. The invention of the <u>electric motor</u> led to the development of electronic communication.

5. <u>Digital</u> television signals are subject to reception problems known as ghosting and snow.

6. Cellular phones communicate with nearby cell transmission towers using <u>alternating current</u>.

7. Computers use <u>tertiary</u> numbers to process and store data.

8. Data stored in <u>RAM</u> are lost when the power is turned off.

Short Answer

Answer each of the following in a sentence or brief paragraph.

9. Explain how the current in a lamp and the current of an electronic signal are different.

10. Describe how a binary number is similar to a switch.

11. Describe the similarities and differences of p- and n-type semiconductors.

12. Explain why digital television signals can form perfect images even when the signal received by the television is distorted.

13. Explain how a computer can perform so many different functions.

14. Describe what a CPU is.

Critical Thinking

Use what you have learned in this chapter to answer each of the following.

15. **Explain** The basic instructions needed to run a computer are stored in an integrated circuit ROM chip. Why is this done?

16. **Apply Concepts** What are the advantages and disadvantages of using a very high sampling rate (very little time between samples) when converting an analog signal into a digital signal?

17. **Select** Which type of storage device is best for storing a huge amount of data? Which type is best for data that will travel from place to place and must be very quickly accessed? Explain.

Standardized Test Question

Choose the letter of the response that correctly answers the question.

Number of Binary Digits	Total Number of Combinations
1	2
2	4
3	8
4	16
5	?

18. Predict the total number of possible combinations for a five-bit binary number.

    A. 22

    B. 30

    C. 32

    D. 48

Test-Taking Tip

Make sure you understand what kind of answer you are being asked to provide. Pay attention to words such as *illustrate, list, define, compare, explain,* and *predict.* A graphic organizer might help you organize your thoughts if you see a word like *list* or *compare.*

Critical Thinking

15. Because the instructions cannot be overwritten or altered, the chip can always perform its basic functions.

16. A high sampling rate produces a more accurate representation of the actual signal, but it results in a tremendous amount of data that can be hard to transmit, store, and process.

17. A hard disk drive is best for storing a huge amount of data. A flash drive is best for data that will travel from place to place and must be very quickly accessed.

Standardized Test Question

18. C

Reading Links

The Telephone

It is difficult to overemphasize the social impact of the telephone, and understanding this groundbreaking invention's function and development is key to any introductory study of telecommunications. This efficient, visually rich treatment takes an interdisciplinary focus, providing readers with context and links to additional resources without overwhelming struggling learners.

Rebecca Stefoff. Benchmark Books. 127 pp. Illustrated. Library ISBN 978-0-7614-1879-5.

Exposing Electronics

This collection of essays presents the history of a vast range of devices that have had a significant impact in the electronics arena. Vintage photographs enhance the discussions, which offer challenging but thoroughly enriching reads for students interested in the history of science and technology.

Bernard Finn. Michigan State University Press. 216 pp. Illustrated. Trade ISBN 978-0-87013-658-0.

Curriculum Connection
Workbook, p. 168

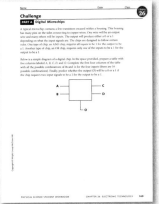

Science Challenge
Workbook, pp. 169–170

26A DC Diode Circuit

This prechapter introduction activity is designed to determine what students already know about electronic technology by engaging them in observing, examining, comparing, recording data, and making conclusions.

Objectives

* predict how a rectifier diode will act in a DC circuit
* build a circuit with a rectifier diode
* test the rectifying properties of a diode
* communicate conclusions

Planning

 25–35 minutes   groups of 3–4 students

Materials (per group)

* battery holder with 2 D battery slots and 3-V terminals
* 2 D batteries
* flashlight bulb holder with terminals
* 3-V flashlight bulb
* 1-amp rectifier diode
* 3 20-cm long test wires with alligator clips

Advance Preparation

* Show or draw the symbol for a diode for students. Explain that current flows in the direction of the triangle, or toward the minus sign or cathode, sometimes identified on the diode by a "k." Be sure to identify the appropriate indicators on the diode used for the experiment.

* Obtain battery holders from a hobby or science store. Choose a battery holder with directions on how to insert the batteries in series to produce 3-V. If there are no indicator arrows, instruct the students on how to insert the batteries. There should be wires or terminals for connecting the alligator clips.

Engagement Guide

* Challenge students to think about DC circuits and current flow by asking:
  * *In how many directions does the current flow in a direct current, or DC, circuit?* (The current flows in one direction only.)
  * *Do you think the orientation of the diode in the DC circuit will affect whether or not the bulb lights?* (Yes, because the diode allows current to flow in one direction only, only one orientation of the diode will complete the circuit and light the bulb.)
* Encourage students to predict how a diode would affect an alternating current (AC).

Going Further

Encourage students to research a simple diode bridge rectifier circuit that converts AC to DC. This circuit has four diodes in a square and directs current on both the positive and negative sweeps of an AC circuit to the same wire. Ask students to draw the conventional four-diode circuit and explain how it works to the class.

26B Telegraphing Messages

Objectives

* build a working telegraph system
* translate a simple message into Morse code
* use Morse code to communicate a simple message
* draw conclusions

Skill Set

observing, analyzing data, stating conclusions

Planning

 45–60 minutes   groups of 3–4 students

Materials

Materials for this activity are listed in the Student Laboratory Manual.

Advance Preparation

* The bases for the sending and receiving units should be about 20 cm square, 2 cm thick, and made of soft wood such as pine. Pre-drill holes in the wood to accept the screws. The holes should be slightly smaller than the screws.

* To make the receiving unit you need two 9-cm long pan head screws, four 2-cm long pan head screws, two small steel washers, wooden base, a 20-cm length of perforated metal strap, and 1 m of 24–26 gauge enameled wire with insulation stripped from ends. Locate holes A and B 10 cm apart and 5 cm from the bottom edge. Insert a 2-cm screw through a small metal washer and partially screw it into hole A. Repeat for hole B. Drill a hole located near the center of the wood and 6 cm in from the right edge. Label the hole *Coil*. Wrap the wire in tightly around a 9-cm pan head screw, leaving a 15-cm length of wire free at each end. Do not wrap coils around the bottom 2 cm of the screw. Tape the coil in place and then screw the coil about 1.5-cm

deep into the hole labeled *Coil*. Wrap the bare ends of the wires from the coil around the screws at A and B. Wrap the wires so they are under the washers and then tighten the screws. Bend the 20-cm metal strap into a Z shape, with a 4-cm horizontal foot, an 8-cm vertical portion, and an 8-cm horizontal top portion. Locate two screw holes C and D for the foot of the Z-bracket so that the top of the bracket extends about 1 cm past the coil. Insert screws at C and D through the Z-bracket and tighten. Screw the other 9 cm-pan head screw into the wood so the outer edge of the screw head just catches the top of the Z-strap. Check that the top of the strap is free to move to the coil.

- To make the sending unit, you need four 2-cm long pan head screws, four small steel washers, a wooden base, 20-cm length of perforated metal strap, and 1 m of 24–26 gauge enameled wire with insulation stripped from ends. Locate holes E and F 10 cm apart and 5 cm from the top edge. Insert a 2-cm screw through a small metal washer and partially screw it into the hole labeled E. Repeat for hole F. Locate holes G and H 5 cm from the bottom edge and 6 cm apart. Bend an 8-cm long metal strap so it has a 2-cm horizontal foot, and a 6-cm upwardly bent portion. The bend should be gentle. Cut three 20-cm lengths of bell wire and strip their ends. Insert a 2-cm screw through a small washer, and then wrap one end of a bell wire around the screw. Insert the screw into hole G and tighten. Insert another 2-cm screw through a small washer, and then wrap the other end of the bell wire (the wire attached at G) around the screw. Insert the screw in hole E and tighten. Insert another 2-cm screw through a small washer, and then wrap one end of a bell wire around the screw. Insert the screw in hole F and tighten. Leave the other end

unattached. Insert another 2-cm screw through a small washer, and then wrap one end of a bell wire around the screw. Insert the screw through the metal bracket and into hole H and tighten. The free end of the metal strap should be just above the contact screw at G. When pressed, the metal bracket should touch the screw at G. Leave the other end of the bell wire unattached.

- Supply each group with the Morse code alphabet.

Answers to Observations

Answers will vary depending on the secret message.

Answers to Analysis and Conclusions

1. Answers will vary. Many students likely had problems sending or receiving all of the transmission. User error in tapping out the messages is common, as are equipment problems.

2. When the switch is pressed, current flows and the coil becomes an electromagnet. The electromagnet attracts the metal strap of the sounder and makes a click. By connecting the sending and receiving units by wire, signals could be sent over long distances.

3. Both communicate one character or symbol at a time. Modern communications are wireless, whereas telegraph sending and receiving units had to be connected by wires.

Going Further

Encourage students to think about how they could create a two-way telegraph for sending and receiving messages. Ask them if they can design one that used one pair of wires between two groups.

26C Binary Logic Circuit

Objectives

- model a three-bit binary logic circuit
- communicate a set of binary numbers using LEDs
- read a binary number set displayed by LEDs
- draw conclusions

Skill Set

modeling, observing, analyzing data, stating conclusions

Planning

 35–45 minutes   groups of 3–4 students

Materials

Materials for this activity are listed in the Student Laboratory Manual.

Advance Preparation

- Cut the aluminum foil into strips that are half the width of the masking tape. Center the aluminum strips within pieces of masking tape of the same length; the sticky tape edges should extend on both sides of the aluminum foil strips. Make

sure the battery holder is wired to supply 3 V.

- Provide the following binary code chart for numbers 0–7: (0, 000) (1, 001) (2, 010) (3, 011) (4, 100) (5, 101) (6, 110) (7, 111) The "secret numbers" should only use numbers 0–7 (i.e., 241536).

Answers to Observations

Answers will vary depending on the secret message you give to each group.

Answers to Analysis and Conclusions

1. The three-digit positions would be reversed if viewed from the opposite side, and the numbers would read incorrectly.

2. The experiment shows AND-gate switches because the on position results in the output of the LED lighting.

3. A 4-bit number is needed. To represent the number 8, another binary digit is needed; thus, a 4-digit number must be used.

Going Further

Encourage students to think about how they could devise an experiment that demonstrated OR-gates. An OR-gate would light an LED no matter which of several switches was closed. Have the students build their design, test it, and communicate their results.

Unit 7

Case Study 1: Animal Magnetism

Gather More Information

Have students use the following key terms to aid their searches:

- animal migration
- Earth's magnetic field
- homing pigeon
- magnetite
- monarch butterflies
- whale migration

Research the Big Picture

- Have students work in groups to further research the migration patterns of an animal. To focus their research, each group should pick a particular species, such as gray whales or arctic terns. Students should map the journeys of the chosen animals and look for any scientific studies correlating these migration pathways to Earth's magnetic field.

- Have students work in pairs to find out more about Earth's magnetic field. Pairs of students should create labeled diagrams and describe what causes the magnetic field and how it functions.

Case Study 2: Hydro Power

Have students use the following key terms to aid their searches:

- dam
- electricity
- generator
- hydroelectric power
- turbine

Research the Big Picture

- Have students work in groups to create detailed diagrams or simple models of a hydroelectric power project. Each project should include a dam, water source, water delivery system, turbine, and generator.

- Help students understand that hydroelectric power is a clean, renewable energy source, but it also impacts the environment in various ways. Have students work in pairs to research a hydroelectric power project, past or present, somewhere in the world. Pairs should find out what alterations to the landscape were necessary to create the plant, and how it affects the local environment. Students should look at effects on habitat, species diversity, local agriculture, water supplies,

Animal Magnetism

Monarch butterflies migrate thousands of kilometers each year between the United States and central Mexico. Young butterflies make the trip north each spring and south each autumn, knowing where to go. Spiny lobsters roam over large distances each night in dark ocean waters, yet they manage to find their way back to their dens. Sea turtles born in Florida can migrate around the Atlantic Ocean and Caribbean Sea for years, ending up back in Florida to lay their eggs.

Humans would need maps or other landmarks to navigate over such long distances. How can these animals do it so well? The answer seems to involve a type of compass inside their bodies. The monarch butterfly, the lobster, the pigeon, and the turtle all have tiny bits of a mineral called magnetite inside them. So do whales, bees, dolphins, and even some bacteria.

Magnetite is a magnetic mineral. It's used in compass needles because it lines up with Earth's magnetic field. Scientists think that animals use magnetite in their bodies to orient themselves with Earth's magnetic field, too. A homing pigeon might use this internal compass to fly in a particular direction. The magnetite might also help the bird find its position on Earth's surface by responding to Earth's magnetic field. The field is parallel to Earth's surface at the equator. It dips straight down to the surface at the magnetic poles. In between, the magnetic lines of force slant at different angles to Earth's surface. The bird might know its location by sensing the magnetic field's orientation. It's as if the bird has a built-in GPS sensor.

Sea animals, such as whales, migrate over thousands of kilometers of open ocean. Scientists think that magnetism is involved in their navigational abilities, as

well. They might follow magnetic cues on the seafloor. Lava containing magnetic minerals pours out of cracks in the seafloor. As the lava hardens into rock, the magnetic minerals in it line up with Earth's magnetic field. Because Earth's magnetic field reverses every few thousand years, much of the seafloor is made of parallel strips of rock, with magnetic particles oriented in alternating directions. Some scientists think that migrating sea animals use their bodies' magnetite to follow these strips like cars following an interstate highway.

Animals might also use other tactics to get around, such as birds using the Sun's position to navigate. But magnetism is certainly an important tool that helps many animals find their way.

CAREER CONNECTION GAFFER

If you watch the credits at the end of a movie, you've likely seen the job title "gaffer." Gaffers are also called Chief Lighting Technicians. For TV programs, a gaffer is often called the Lighting Director. By any name, a gaffer is the person who controls how the sets and actors are illuminated in movies and on TV shows.

If a scene takes place in a dimly lit room, the gaffer must make the room appear dark while still creating enough light for the actors to be seen. If the script calls for a scene in a sunny kitchen, the gaffer must make it look as if the room is lit by sunlight streaming in the window—even if the set is inside a closed warehouse.

A TV show or movie's gaffer works with the director and maybe with a lighting designer. He or she knows who or what is supposed to be in a scene, the time of

day, and the mood the director wants. The gaffer must know the type of film and lenses used and how the scene will be shot. The gaffer determines the electricity requirements, checks the power sources available, and supervises the electricians who operate the lights and maintain the equipment.

Gaffers often learn their trade on the job. They usually start as riggers, setting up the lights around the set. Many people compete for the few jobs in this field. Providing lighting for movies and TV shows is exciting and creative work.

CAREER CONNECTION: Gaffer

As students read the article, have them list in their Science Notebooks the skills a gaffer would need to possess. Then show a TV program or movie in class that involves lighting changes, or assign students to watch one at home. Have them write everything in the show they think a gaffer would have been responsible for. Afterward, discuss how gaffers might alter existing lighting to create the effects students saw. If your school puts on any theatrical productions, find out if there is someone who serves as a gaffer (even if that title is not used). If so, invite him or her to speak to the class.

Hydro **Power**

When you turn on a light or your computer, it probably does not occur to you that the electricity powering the device just might be generated by falling water. About seven percent of the electricity produced in the United States comes from hydroelectric dams. These dams use falling water to produce electric power.

How does falling water become electricity? Hydroelectric dams have internal machinery that converts mechanical energy into electric energy. The process starts when a dam is built across a river. Water backs up behind the dam, forming an artificial lake

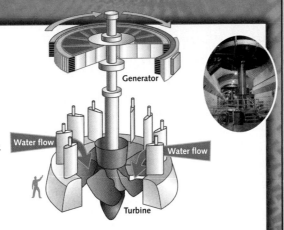

Generator

Water flow   Water flow

Turbine

Research and Report

The electricity Americans use is produced by a variety of energy sources, such as oil, coal, nuclear, wind, natural gas, solar, and geothermal. With a partner, find out how much electricity is produced by each source. Draw a circle graph to report your findings. Then write a short paragraph that summarizes the data in the graph.

called a reservoir. The surface of the reservoir is higher than the surface of the river below the dam.

To produce power, gates open to let water flow down from the reservoir through pipes in the dam. As the water rushes down, it enters machinery inside the dam's wall. The rushing water pushes on the blades of a machine called a turbine. The turbine is like a pinwheel, but water makes it spin instead of air.

The spinning turbine turns the attached shaft of a generator. It's the generator that generates electricity. The shaft has coils of copper wire wound around it. An electromagnet surrounds the coiled wires. In one design, the magnet moves electrons (electric current) in the wire as the shaft spins. This electric current moves from the generator through transmission wires to homes, schools, and businesses in the community.

Stay Safe with Electricity

Electricity is one of the most useful energy resources. However, electricity can be dangerous if it is not used properly and carefully. Here are some essential rules to follow when using electricity.

• Do not handle electric plugs, switches, cords, or appliances with wet hands. Don't turn on appliances on wet counters. Water is a good conductor of electricity. You could get a shock.

• Do not unplug an appliance by pulling on the cord. Always use the plug. Pulling

on the cord could damage it. A damaged cord could allow electric current to pass directly to you.

• Do not plug a lot of appliances into an outlet or extension cord. Each electric circuit is designed to carry a certain amount of current safely.

• Never run wires under carpets. Frays in the wires, which could cause short-circuit fires, may go unnoticed.

• Never stick your fingers or other objects in an electric socket or a plugged-in appliance. Electricity could be conducted into your hand. Exposure to electricity with both hands could create a circuit that goes through one arm, across the heart, and out the other arm.

• Never come close to wires on power poles or fallen wires. These wires often carry dangerously high currents.

461

and fishing. Students should also find out how much electricity the plant generates (or will generate) and how much this reduces (or will reduce) pollution and/or offset the region's dependence on fossil fuels. At the end of the project, pairs should assess whether they support the plant as an alternative to other available energy sources.

Case Study 3: Stay Safe with Electricity

Have students use the following key terms to aid their searches:

circuit
conduction
electric appliance
electric current
electricity safety

Research the Big Picture

• As a class, conduct an electric safety audit of your classroom or school. Search for any currently unsafe situations and look for ways to make your classroom or school safer. You might divide the class into groups to survey different areas. Have groups record their findings and determine if their examined area deserves a safety "seal of approval." Ask students to draw diagrams to accompany any descriptions of violations.

• Explain to students that in 1971, the United States Department of Labor founded the Occupational Safety and Health Administration (OSHA) to protect people from unhealthy or unsafe working conditions. Have students research the history of OSHA regulations and compare conditions before and after their implementation. Encourage students to find examples of OSHA regulations related to electrical workers or those working with wiring and electric machinery.

LAB SAFETY

Safety Symbols

These safety symbols are used in laboratory and field investigations in this book to indicate possible hazards. Learn the meaning of each symbol and refer to this page often. *Remember to wash your hands thoroughly after completing laboratory procedures.*

Safety Symbols	Hazard	Examples	Precaution	Remedy
Disposal	Special disposal procedures need to be followed.	certain chemicals, living organisms	Do not dispose of these materials in the sink or trash can.	Dispose of wastes as directed by your teacher.
Biological	Organisms or other biological materials that might be harmful to humans	bacteria, fungi, blood, unpreserved tissues, plant materials	Avoid skin contact with these materials. Wear mask or gloves.	Notify your teacher if you suspect contact with material. Wash hands thoroughly.
Extreme Temperature	Objects that can burn skin by being too cold or too hot	boiling liquids, hot plates, dry ice, liquid nitrogen	Use proper protection when handling.	Go to your teacher for first aid.
Sharp Object	Use of tools or glassware that can easily puncture or slice skin	razor blades, pins, scalpels, pointed tools, dissecting probes, broken glass	Practice common-sense behavior and follow guidelines for use of the tool.	Go to your teacher for first aid.
Fume	Possible danger to respiratory tract from fumes	ammonia, acetone, nail polish remover, heated sulfur, moth balls	Make sure there is good ventilation. Never smell fumes directly. Wear a mask.	Leave foul area and notify your teacher immediately.
Electrical	Possible danger from electrical shock or burn	improper grounding, liquid spills, short circuits, exposed wires	Double-check setup with teacher. Check condition of wires and apparatus.	Do not attempt to fix electrical problems. Notify your teacher immediately.
Irritant	Substances that can irritate the skin or mucous membranes of the respiratory tract	pollen, moth balls, steel wool, fiberglass, potassium permanganate	Wear dust mask and gloves. Practice extra care when handling these materials.	Go to your teacher for first aid.
Chemical	Chemicals that can react with and destroy tissue and other materials	bleaches such as hydrogen peroxide; acids such as sulfuric acid, hydrochloric acid; bases such as ammonia, sodium hydroxide	Wear goggles, gloves, and an apron.	Immediately flush the affected area with water and notify your teacher.
Toxic	Substance may be poisonous if touched, inhaled, or swallowed.	mercury, many metal compounds, iodine, poinsettia plant parts	Follow your teacher's instructions.	Always wash hands thoroughly after use. Go to your teacher for first aid.
Open Flame	Open flame may ignite flammable chemicals, loose clothing, or hair.	alcohol, kerosene, potassium permanganate, hair, clothing	Tie back hair. Avoid wearing loose clothing. Avoid open flames when using flammable chemicals. Be aware of locations of fire safety equipment.	Notify your teacher immediately. Use fire safety equipment if applicable.

Eye Safety	Clothing Protection	Animal Safety	Radioactivity
Proper eye care should be worn at all times by anyone performing or observing science activities.	This symbol appears when substances could stain or burn clothing.	This symbol appears when safety of animals and students must be ensured.	This symbol appears when radioactive materials are used.

METRIC SYSTEM AND SI UNITS

The International System of Measurement, or SI, is accepted as the standard for measurement throughout most of the world. The SI is a modernized version of the metric system, which is a system of measurement based on units of ten. In the United States, both the metric system and the standard system are used.

The SI system contains seven base units. All other units of measurement can be derived from these base units by multiplying or dividing the units by a factor of ten or by combining units.

- When you change from a smaller unit to a larger unit, you divide.
- When you change from a larger unit to a smaller unit, you multiply.

Prefixes are added to the base unit to identify the new unit created by multiplying or dividing by a factor of ten.

SI Base Units

Measurement	Unit	Symbol
length	meter	m
mass	kilogram	kg
time	second	s
electric current	ampere	A
temperature	Kelvin	K
amount of substance	mole	mol
intensity of light	candela	cd

Frequently Used Non-SI Base Units

Measurement	Unit	Symbol
volume	liter, cubic centimeter	L, cm³
density	grams/cubic centimeter, grams/liter	g/cm³, g/L

Common SI Prefixes

Prefix	Symbol	Equivalents
mega-	M	1,000,000
kilo-	k	1,000
hecto-	h	100
deka-	da	10
deci-	d	0.1 or 1/10
centi-	c	0.01 or 1/100
milli-	m	0.001 or 1/1,000
micro-	μ	0.000001 or 1/1,000,000
nano-	n	0.000000001 or 1/100,000,000,000
pico-	p	0.000000000001 or 1/100,000,000,000,000

Appendix C

EQUATIONS

Chapter 1 Studying Physical Science

volume of a rectangular solid =
length × width × height (p. 15)
$v = l \times w \times h$

density of an object = mass/volume (p. 16)
$d = \frac{m}{v}$

temperature in kelvin = degrees Celsius + 273 (p. 16)
$K = °C + 273$

Chapter 5 The Atom

number of neutrons in an atom's nucleus =
mass number − atomic number (p. 86)

Chapter 7 Bonding

maximum number of electrons in an energy level =
$2n^2$, where n is the number of the energy level (p. 113)

Chapter 8 Chemical Reactions

synthesis reaction (p. 135)
$A + B \rightarrow AB$

decomposition reaction (p. 135)
$AB \rightarrow A + B$

single-displacement reaction (p. 136)
$A + BC \rightarrow AC + B$

double-displacement reaction (p. 137)
$AX + CY \rightarrow AY + CX$

Chapter 12 What Is Motion?

speed = distance/time (p. 196)

acceleration = $\frac{\text{(final velocity − initial velocity)}}{\text{time}}$ (p. 200)

momentum = mass × velocity (p. 202)

Chapter 13 Nature of Forces

newton = kilogram × m/s² (p. 208)

gravitational force $F = \frac{Gm^1m^2}{r^2}$ (p. 213)

weight = mass × acceleration due to gravity (p. 215)
$w = mg$

Newton's second law of motion (p. 218)
acceleration = net force/mass
$a = \frac{F_{net}}{m}$

Chapter 14 Forces in Fluids

pressure = force/area (p. 224)
$P = F/A$

Bernoulli's principle (p. 233)
pressure$_1$ − pressure$_2$ = $\frac{\text{(density of fluid)(velocity}_2{}^2 - \text{velocity}_1{}^2)}{2}$

$P_1 - P_2 = \frac{D(V_2{}^2 - V_1{}^2)}{2}$

Chapter 15 Work, Power, and Simple Machines

work = force × distance (p. 241)
$W = Fd$

power = work/time (p. 242)
$p = \frac{W}{t}$

power = work/time = (force × distance)/time =
force × distance/time = force × velocity (p. 243)

power = energy transferred/time (p. 243)

mechanical advantage = output force/input force (p. 247)
$MA = \frac{F_{out}}{F_{in}}$

efficiency = output work/input work × 100% (p. 248)

IMA (inclined plane) = length of inclined plane/height
of slope (p. 250)

IMA (lever) = length of input arm/length of output arm
(p. 252)

IMA (wheel and axle) = radius of wheel/radius of axle
(p. 255)

Chapter 16 Nature of Energy

kinetic energy (p. 263)
$KE = ½ mv^2$

gravitational potential energy (p. 264)
$GPE = mgh$

Einstein's equation (p. 269)
$E = mc^2$

Chapter 17 Thermal Energy and Heat

temperature conversions (p. 283)
$°C = (°F − 32) \times 5/9$
$°F = (°C \times 9/5) + 32$
$K = °C + 273$

heat of a chemical reaction (p. 289)

heat gained or lost = mass of water × temperature
change × specific heat of water

Chapter 19 Waves and Energy

wave frequency and period (p. 324)
frequency = 1/period
period = 1/frequency
wave speed = frequency × wavelength (p. 325) (p. 357)
$v = f \times \lambda$

Chapter 23 Electric Charges and Currents

Ohm's law (p. 401)
voltage = current × resistance
$V = IR$

electric power = current × voltage difference (p. 406)
$P = IV$

electric energy = electric power × time (p. 408)
$E = Pt$

Chapter 25 Electromagnetism

voltage change of a transformer (p. 436)

$\frac{\text{turns on secondary coil}}{\text{turns on primary coil}}$

464

LAB EQUIPMENT

The tools shown here are important in conducting scientific investigations in the laboratory. Make sure you know how to use each tool, and practice often to make careful and correct measurements.

Metric ruler

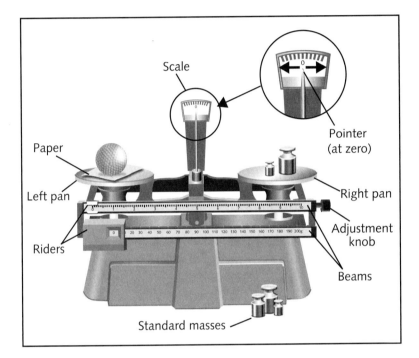

Double-pan balance

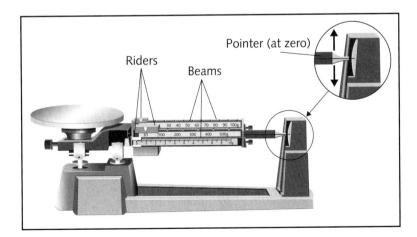

Triple-beam balance

Graduated cylinder

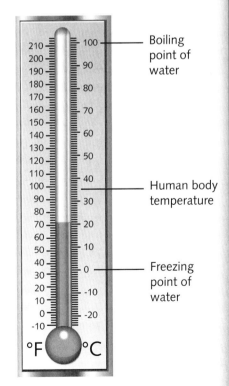

Celsius/Fahrenheit thermometer

B

primary pigment colors, 378–379
refracted in glass prism, 373
refraction and, 328

Combustion reaction a type of chemical reaction in which a substance combines with elemental oxygen, 136

Comets, 83
sublimation and, 66
Communication(s)
electronics and, 440
optical fibers in, 384
telecommunication and, 447–451

Compass an instrument containing a magnetized needle that can swing around in a circle, 420, 422

electromagnetism and, 427
gyroscopic, 427
shifts in Earth's magnetic poles and, 421
Complex carbohydrates, polysaccharides as, 172
Components, electronic, 446

Compound machine a machine made up of two or more simple machines that can operate together, 255

Compound a pure substance in which the atoms of two or more elements combine, 22, 23, 27–29, 112

atoms combined as, 112
carbon, 162
chemical formulas of, 124
composition of, 28
ions in, 117, 119
law of constant composition and, 76
list of common, 28
mixtures compared with, 30
molecular, 121
molecules in, 29
organic, 163
properties of, 27
separating, 29

Compressed squeezed together, 61

Compression solidity; in science, an area in which molecules are very close together, 320

Compressional wave a wave in which the medium moves back and forth parallel to the direction in which the wave travels, 320, 322

amplitude of, 326
sound waves as, 334, 335, 339
wavelength of, 336

Computer an electronic device designed to carry out a set of instructions, 452–457

ENIAC as, 452
information processing with, 453
memory for, 456
Computer chips, 446

Computer hardware the physical parts of a computer, 454

Computer processing, hertz as measure of speed in, 323

Concave lens a lens that is thicker at its edges than at its center, 375

for nearsightedness, 382

Concave mirror a mirror with a reflecting surface that curves in on itself, 372

Concentration the amount of solute that is dissolved in a quantity of solvent, 152

of reactants, 141
Concert pitch (frequency), 335

Conclusion a statement that uses evidence from an experiment to indicate whether the hypothesis is supported, 11

Condensation polymers, 170

Condensation the change of state from a gas to a liquid, 66, 154

Conduction the transfer of thermal energy between particles that collide with each other, 283, 396

Conductor a material that allows heat to travel through it, 284, 396

in circuit, 403
metals as, 97
Cones, in eye, 382
Conservation of energy, 268, 276
law of, 241
Conservation of mass, 76, 131
Conservation of momentum, law of, 203
Constant composition, law of, 76
Constructive interference, 330
Contact forces, 207

Control group group in an experiment in which all variables are kept the same, 9

Controlled experiment an experiment in which only one variable is changed at a time, 8

Convection the transfer of thermal energy by the movement and mixing of molecules, 285

Conversion factor a ratio of equal values used to express the same quantity in different units, 17

Conversion, among energy forms, 269–270

Convex lens a lens that is thicker at its center than at its edges, 374

for farsightedness, 381

Convex mirror a mirror whose reflecting surface curves outward, 370–371

Coolants
in cars, 288
in refrigerator, 304
Cooling
heat pumps and, 305
measuring, 295
Cooling systems, 303–305
chemicals used in, 305
Copernicus, Nicolai, 83
Copper, as element, 24
Core, of Earth, 421

Cornea a tough, transparent layer of cells in the eye, 380, 381

Covalent bond when two atoms share electrons, 120, 122

of carbon atoms, 164
electrons in, 147
CPU. *See* Central processing unit (CPU)

Crest a peak in a transverse wave, 319

Critical angle the angle at which a refracted beam skims the surface, 376

Crookes, William, 77
CRT TV, 450

Crystal a solid in which atoms or ions are arranged in a regularly repeating pattern, 119

Crystalline solid a solid in which the particles are arranged in a repeating pattern of rows, 57

crystals in, 119
dissolving, 147
Curie, Marie and Pierre, 177

Glossary/Index

O

P

United States, flag of, 45
Units of measurement, 13
  of density, 16
UNIVAC I, 457
Universe
  expansion of, 341

Unsaturated contains less than the maximum amount of dissolved solute possible, **152**

Uranium, 177
  radon gas as decay product of, 180
Uranium-235, 184
Uranium-238, 182
  isotope of, 180

Vacuum
  electromagnetic waves and, 353
  speed of light in, 356
Vacuum tubes, 444

Valence electron an electron in the outermost energy level of an atom, **114, 123, 164**

  in chlorine atom, 117
  electronegativity and, 118
  in oxygen atom, 120
Valence shells, electrons in, 115
Value
  in digital signals, 442
  of elements, 26
Van Allen radiation belts, 423
Van de Graff generator, 396
Van Gogh, Vincent, 56
Vapor, water, 61, 290
  heat of, 291
  of water, 291

Vaporization the change of state from a liquid to a gas, **65**

Variable a factor that can be changed, **8**

Velocity both the spe n object and the direction of its motion, **198**

  acceleration and, 199
  adding and subtracting, 198
  centripetal acceleration and, 200
  of electron, 83
  of fluid, 233
  kinetic energy and, 263
  momentum and, 202
  power and, 242
  terminal, 216
Vibration
  electromagnetic waves formed by, 353
  of musical instrument strings, 345
  sound waves and, 335, 336
  structural engineering and, 331
  waves and, 316
  of woodwinds, 345
Video recorder, 441
Vinegar, 112
  as homogeneous mixture, 31
Violin, resonance of, 345

Virtual image an image that is formed by diverging light rays, **371**

Viscosity a liquid's resistance to flow, **59, 223**

Visible light electromagnetic waves that the human eye can detect, **181, 357, 360, 368**

  colors and, 378
  Doppler effect and, 341
  frequency of, 323
Vision
  eye and, 380
  process of, 380–382
Vitamin D, ultraviolet waves and, 360
Volcanoes, 280

Volt the voltage of a circuit, **398**

Voltage a difference in electric energy on each end of a circuit that pulls on the electrons in the wire, **398, 406**

  changing, 436
  of high-power lines, 437
  in series circuits, 403

Volume the amount of space an object takes up, **15–16**

  displacement and, 232
  as extensive property, 43
  of liquids, 58
Voyager 1 space probe, electromagnetic signals from, 318

Walkie-talkies, radio signals and, 358
Walking, friction and, 211
Wasps, evaporation by, 292
  water as, 147
Water
  atoms in, 120
  in cells, 146
  as compound, 22, 112
  on Earth, 154
  electrolysis of, 29, 135
  elements in, 27
  expansion during freezing, 294
  as fluid, 222
  as gas (water vapor), 61
  heating to boiling, 291
  heat of fusion in, 292
  physical properties of, 43
  as polar molecule, 147
  separation into atoms, 29
  solution process sand, 147
  sound waves in, 336
  specific heat of, 288
  state changes of, 67
  suspension in, 37
  thermal expansion and, 294
Water cycle, 67
"Waterfall" (Escher), 270
Water heater, waste heat for, 305
Water pollution, 273
Water pressure, 229
  by depth, 229
Water vapor, 290
  condensation and, 66
  steam compared with, 66
Watt, James, 242
Watts, 406
  horsepower and, 242

Art Credits
McGraw-Hill and Garry Nichols

Photo Credits
Cover ©David Mack/Photo Researchers; **2** (t) ©Gary Retherford/Photo Researchers, (l) ©Eric Lundberg, (r) ©Charles D. Winters/Photo Researchers, (b) ©Royalty-Free/Corbis; **3** ©W.A. Sharman; **4** ©Bruno Vincent/Getty; **5** (t, l-r) ©Royalty-Free/Corbis, ©Creatas/PunchStock, ©Studio Photogram/Alamy, (bl) ©U.S. Dept. of Commerce, (br) ©Creatas/PunchStock; **7** ©Giovanni Rinaldi; **9** ©NASA, STS-103; **12** ©Courtesy NSSDC Goddard Space Flight Center; **13** ©Juan Silva; **19** ©Creatas/PunchStock; **20** ©Elizabeth C. Novak; **21** ©Elena Aliaga; **22** (t, l-r) ©iStockphoto.com, ©Photodisc/Getty Images, ©Steve Hamblin/Alamy, (b) ©Comstock Images/Alamy; **24** (l-r) ©Imgram Publishing/Alamy, ©Damon Davison, ©The McGraw-Hill Companies Inc./Ken Cavanagh, photographer; **25** ©The Print Collecter/Alamy; **27** (l-r) ©Andraz Cerar, Leslie Garland Picture Library/Alamy, Royalty-Free/Corbis; **28** ©Stockdisc/PunchStock; **29** ©The McGraw-Hill Companies Inc./Stephen Frisch, photographer; **30** ©Alberto Pomares; **31** (t) ©Klaus Guldbrandsen/Photo Researchers, (m) ©Brian Adducci, (bl) ©Westend61/Alamy, (br) ©C Squared Studios/Getty Images; **32** (l-r) ©Andrew Lambert Photography/Photo Researchers, ©The McGraw-Hill Companies, Inc./Stephen Frisch, photographer, ©The McGraw-Hill Companies Inc./Stephen Frisch, photographer, ©Russell Illig/Getty Images, ©Charles D. Winters/Photo Researchers; **33** ©Andrea Gingerich; **34** ©Digital Vision, (i) ©blickwinkel/Alamy; **35** (t) ©Wolfgang Schaller, (b) ©Royalty-Free/Corbis; **36** (tl) ©iStockphoto/Suzannah Skelton, (tr) ©Jonelle Weaver/Getty Images, (m) ©C Squared Studios/Getty Images, (bl) ©1985 Kip Peticolas–Fundamental Photographs, (br) ©Bojan Tezak; **37** ©Charles D. Winters/Photo Researchers; **39** (l) ©iStockphoto.com, (r) ©The McGraw-Hill Companies Inc./Ken Cavanagh, photographer; **40** ©David Virster; **41** (m) ©C. Paquin, (tr) ©Neil Roy Johnson, (br) ©Ewa Brozek; **42** (t) ©Jim and Tania Thomson/Painet, (r) ©Perennou Nuridsany/Photo Researchers; **43** ©bobo/Alamy, (i) ©R. Gino Santa Maria; **44** (l) ©Frances Roberts/Alamy, (r) ©Suhendri Utet; **45** (t) ©2005 Getty Images, (b, l-r) ©Jacom Stephens, ©Robert Crook, ©Lois Siegel; **46** (tl) ©Pixland/PunchStock, (m) ©iStockphoto/Hedda Gjerpen, (bl) ©Charles D. Winters/Photo Researchers, (r) ©Phil Jason/Getty; **47** ©Denise Cashmore; **48** (t, l-r) ©Terekhov Igor, ©Marc Dietrick, ©Gene Lee, ©ajt, (b) ©2005 Getty Images; **49** (l-r) ©V. J. Matthew, ©Charles D. Winters/Photo Researchers; **50** ©Jake Hellback; **51** (t-b) ©Moritz Frei, ©Cheryl Hill, ©Andrey Plis; **52** ©Charles D. Winters/Photo Researchers; **53** (t-b) ©The Final Image, ©Alexander Shingarev, ©Royalty-Free/Corbis, ©Ari Edlin; **54** ©Kendrick Erikson; **55** ©Gemini Observatory-GMOS Team; **56** (t) ©Vincent van Gogh/Getty, (b) ©Falguni Sarkar/www.snbose.org; **57** (l) ©Roberto de Gugliemo/Photo Researchers, (r) ©C Squared/Getty; **58** (l) ©iStockphoto/koch valerie, (r) ©Laura Bolesta; **59** (l-r) ©Pali A/Fotolia, ©Shutterstock, Inc.; **60** (l) ©Royalty-Free/Corbis, (r) ©Copyright by Autoliv Inc., (i) ©Phil Degginger/Alamy; **61** ©Royalty-Free/Corbis; **64** (t) ©Michael Klenetsky, (l) ©Steve Sant/Alamy; **65** ©Becky Luigart-Stayner/Corbis; **66** (tl) ©David Chasey/Getty, (tr) ©Janis Christie/Getty, (m) ©Dusan Po, (bl) ©StockTrek/Getty; **68** ©Royalty-Free/Corbis; **70** (t) ©NASA, (b) ©NASA Marshall Space Flight Center (NASA-MSFC); **71** ©JP Laffont/Sygma/Corbis, (i) ©Courtesy National Park Service; **72** (t) ©Mitsuo Ohtsuki/Photo Researchers, (b) ©Corbis; **73** ©David Brownell/Photographers Direct; ©Vario Images GmbH & Co.KG/Alamy; **75** ©SPL/Photo Researchers; **76** ©The Print Collecter/Alamy; **84** ©Science VU/IBMRL/Visuals Unlimited; **85** (t) ©iStockphoto.com, (b) ©Robert Kyllo; **89** ©Science VU/IBMRL/Visuals Unlimited; **90** ©Robert Rushton; **92** (t) ©SPL/Photo Researchers, (b) ©Science Source; **93** (l) ©Chris Harvey, (r) ©Wikipedia; **97** (l, t-b) ©Royalty-Free/Corbis, ©Andraz Cerar, ©Brian Chase, (r, t-b) ©Kari Mattila/Alamy, ©iStockphoto.com; **98** (l-r) ©Courtesy USGS, ©Courtesy of the Smithsonian Institution, ©Gusto/Photo Researchers; **99** (tr) ©Charles D. Winters/Photo Reserachers, (br) ©E.R. Degginger/Photo Researchers; **100** (l) ©Brand X Pictures/PunchStock, (b) ©Zephyr/Photo Researchers; **102** (l) ©Phil Degginger/Alamy, (b) ©Chad Littlejohn; **103** (t) ©Jim Varney/Photo Researchers, (b) ©Andre Nantel; **104** (l-r) ©The McGraw-Hill Companies, Inc./Stephen Frisch, photographer, ©Charles D. Winters/Photo Researchers, ©Phototake Inc./Alamy; **105** (l) ©Charles Shapiro, (r) ©Kent Knudson/PhotoLink/Getty Images; **106** ©Andraz Cerar; **108** ©iStockphoto.com/Hans F. Meier; **109** (l-r) ©Elemental Imaging, ©R. Sullivan/Wikipedia, ©iStockphoto.com/Simon Edwin; **110** (t) ©Brand X Pictures/PunchStock, (l) ©US Department of Energy/Photo Researchers, (r) ©Bruce Heinemann, (b) ©Dr. Tim Evans/Photo Researchers; **111** ©Ben Blankenburg; **112** (l-r) ©Slawomir Fajer, Burke/Triolo Productions/Getty Images, ©Travis Manley; **119** (l-r) ©E. R. Degginger/Photo Researchers, ©Charles Falco/Photo Researchers, ©Wikipedia; **121** ©Lawrence Berkeley Nat'l Lab; **127** ©E. R. Degginger/Photo Researchers; **128** ©NASA; **129** ©Mariusz Szachowski; **130** (t, l-r) ©Charles D. Winters/Photo Researchers, Radlund & Associates/Getty Images, ©Charles D. Winters/Photo Researchers; **131** ©North Wind/North Wind Picture Archives; **134** ©David Young-Wolff/Photo Edit; **135** ©Charles D. Winters/Photo Researchers; **136** ©Royalty-Free/Corbis; **137** (t) ©Charles D. Winters/Photo Researchers, (b) ©Andrew Lambert Photography/Photo Researchers; **138** ©Design Pics/age fotostock; **139** ©Peter David/Getty Images; **140** ©Jamie McDonald/Getty Images; **143** ©Royalty-Free/Corbis; **144** ©Jarvis Gray; **145** ©Royalty-Free/Corbis; **146** ©Brand X Pictures/PunchStock; **148** (t) ©1986 Richard Megna–Fundamental Photographs, (b) ©PhotoAlto/SuperStock; **150** ©Stuart Monk; **152** (tl) ©The McGraw-Hill Companies/Jacques Cornell, photographer, (tr) ©C. Paxton & J. Farrow/Photo Researchers, (b) ©Richard Megna/Fundamental Photographs; **153** ©Bill Curssinger/Getty Images; **155** ©sciencephotos/Alamy; **158** (t, l-r) ©Ed Isaacs, ©CreativEye99, ©Juha Tuomi; ©D. Hurst/Alamy, ©The McGraw-Hill Companies, Inc./Jacques Cornell, photographer, ©Felicia Martinez/Photo Edit, (b, l-r) ©Nicholas Sutcliffe, ©Felicia Martinez/Photo Edit, (l) ©Gusto Images/Science Photo Library; **159** Susumu Nishinaga/Photo Researchers; **161** © Richard Megna/Fundamental Photographs; **162** ©iStockphoto.com/Christine Glade; **163** (l-r) ©iStockphoto.com/Susan Trigg, ©The McGraw-Hill Companies, Inc./Janette Beckman, photographer, ©John C. Hooten; **165** ©Science Source; **167** (l-r) ©fStop/Alamy, ©iStockphoto.com/Justin Allfree, ©Royalty-Free/Corbis; **168** ©Aiti, (i) ©rj lerich; **175** ©iStockphoto.com/Christine Glade; **176** ©CERN/Photo Researchers; **185** ©Phil Degginger/Getty Images; **186** ©StockTrek/Getty Images; **187** (t) ©M. Kulyk/Photo Researchers, (b) ©ISM/Phototake; **188** ©CERN/Photo Researchers; **190** (t) ©Courtesy Washington State Department of Health, (b) ©Pascal Goetgheluck/Photo Researchers; **191** (t) ©Alexander Tsiaras/Photo Researchers, (b) ©Petrolium Technology Researcher Centre; **192** (t-b) ©Edward Kinsman/Photo Researchers, ©1998 Copyright IMS Communications Ltd./Capstone Design, ©iStockphoto.com/Luke Daniek; **193** ©David Schrader; **194** (tl) ©Creatas/PunchStock, (bl) ©Mandy Godbehear, (r) ©U.S. Air Force photo by Tech. Sgt. Keith Brown; **195** ©Jon Sullivan/PDPhoto.org; **196** (l) ©Max Earey, (r) ©Andrew Johnson; **198** ©David Pedre; **199** (t) ©George Burba, (b, l-r) ©Jim Parkin, ©NASA/Getty Images, ©dwphotos; **200** (tl) ©Royalty-Free/Corbis, (tr) ©iStockphoto.com; **202** ©Caruntu; **203** ©Amanita pictures; **204** ©Jon Sullivan/PDPhoto.org; **206** ©Clint Spencer; **207** ©Chris Harvey; **208** (t) ©Horizons Companies, (b) ©David Young-Wolff/PhotoEdit; **209** ©Dan Brandenburg, (i) Michael W. Davidson/Photo Researchers; **210** (m) ©Steve Cole, (b) ©Davide Fiorenzo De Conti; **211** (t, l-r) ©iStockpoto.com, ©FogStock/Alamy, ©Stephen Coburn, (bl) ©iStockphoto.com/Muran Sen, (br) ©Alloy Photography/Veer; **215** (l) ©Steve Pepple, (r) ©Tony Freeman, (b) ©Courtesy Library of Congress, Photograph and Print Collection; **216** (tl) ©Fundamental Photographs, (b) ©Sergiy Dontsov; **217** (r, t-b) ©Arthur Kwiatkoowski, ©Stockbyte, (bl) ©Romilly Lockyer/Getty Images, (br) ©by Leo Mason/Alamy; **218** ©Peter Cade/Getty Images; **219** (t-b) ©iStockphoto.com, ©Stephen Dalton/Photo Researchers, ©Royalty-Free/Corbis; **221** ©Royalty-Free/Corbis; **222** ©Jan Kranendonk; **224** ©Matt Meadows; **226** ©Laura Bolesta; **231** ©Matt Meadows; **232** ©dani92026; **233** ©Bob Daemmrich; **235** (l-r) ©Royalty-Free/Corbis, Nicholas Bergkessel, Jr./Photo Researchers, ©Steve Hamblin/Alamy, ©Jose Gil, ©Creatas/PunchStock; **237** ©Jose Gil; **238** ©David W. Hamilton/Getty Images; **239** (t) ©Chris Schmidt, (b) ©Piotr Sikora; **240** (t) ©Richard Hutchings, (b) ©Kenneth C. Zirkel; **242** (t-b) ©Danny Warren, ©Brand X Pictures, ©Royalty-Free/Corbis; **243** (t) ©Getty Images, (m) ©Photodisc; **244** ©Serdar Yagci; **245** (t) ©Michael Newman/Photo Edit, Inc., (m, l-r) ©Jan Kranendonk, ©Richard A. McGuirk, ©Robert Fried/Alamy; **246** (t-b) ©Jorge Gonzalez/Fotolia, ©Niels Laan, ©Adam Zander/Alamy; **247** (l-r) ©Burke/Triolo Productions/Getty Images, ©Mikael Damkier, ©Losevsky Pavel; **250** (l) ©C Squared Studios/Getty Images, (r) ©John Campos; **251** ©Marilyn Barbone; **252** (l-r) ©Rob Cruse, ©Ole Graf/zefa/Corbis, ©budgetstockphoto.com/iStockphoto.com; **253** (tl) ©Ingram

(t) top, (b) bottom, (l) left, (r) right, (m) middle, (i) inset

Lab Materials List

This table of lab equipment and materials can help you prepare for your physical science classes for the year. Quantities listed for the labs are per year and based on a class size of 30 students. A classroom supply of the following materials will be needed: balances, colored pencils, glue sticks, graduated cylinders, hole-punch, masking tape, markers, matches, measuring cups, medicine droppers, spring scales, test tubes, thermometers, water, and white paper.

Material	Lab(s)	Amount Per Class
Acrylic plastic sheets, 20 cm × 20 cm	18C	10
Aluminum beverage cans, 12-oz	14A	5
Aluminum foil, heavy-duty	4A, 26C	two 200 ft² rolls
Aluminum pie pans	4B	10
Apple juice for monosaccharide solution	10C	1 qt
Baking soda	8A	50 g
Baking trays, large	11B	10
Balloons	17A	30
Bandanas or handkerchiefs	20C	10
Batteries, size D	26A, 26C	40
Batteries, 6-V lantern	23B, 23C, 25A, 25C, 26B	30
Battery holders configured for 3 V	26A, 26C	10
Bells	20C	10
Binary number conversion chart	26C	1
Boards (to be used as ramps)	12C	10
Books (for use as props)	4A	30
Bromothymol blue solution	10A	500 mL
Bubble wrap	18A	enough to fill ten 30-cm² boxes
Calculators	21B	10
Candleholders, or foil-cupcake pan liners half-filled with sand	3A	10
Candles, small	3A	10
Cardboard boxes, approximately 30 cm²	18A, 21C	50
Cardboard circles	23A	10
Cardboard or poster board, 2 ft × 2 ft	4A	10
Cardboard tubes from rolls of paper towels	25B, 25C	10
Cardboard viewing box	11A	1
Catsup	4A	700 g
Ceramic mugs	17B	10
Clay "atoms"	5B	10
Clear transparency film	24A	10 pieces

Material	Lab(s)	Amount Per Class
Cloth towels, small	16C	10
Cloth, corduroy, about 30 cm wide × 2 m long	16B	10 pieces
Cloth, cotton, about 30 cm wide × 2 m long	16B	10 pieces
Cloth, polyester, about 30 cm wide × 2 m long	16B	10 pieces
Coffee filters, cone-shaped	2C	10
Coiled spring toys	19B	10
Coins	23B	10
Colored ribbons	19B	10
Compact discs (CDs)	21A	10
Compasses	24B, 25B	10
Copper wire, bare	14B	1 m
Corks	19A	10
Corn syrup	4A, 10C	470 mL
Cornstarch	10B	10 tbs
Corrugated cardboard, 150 cm × 75 cm	16C	10 sheets
Corrugated cardboard, 23 cm × 30 cm	22C	10 sheets
Corrugated cardboard, brown, 20 cm × 20 cm	18C	100 sheets
Corrugated cardboard, white, 20 cm × 20 cm	18C	10 sheets
Cotton rags	18A	enough to fill ten 30-cm² boxes
Crumpled newspaper	18A	enough to fill ten 30-cm² boxes
Cups, paper or foam	8A, 10B	100
Dark fabric	2A	20 small pieces
Dried split peas	11B	10 bags
Drums with drumsticks	20B	10
Effervescent tablets	3C, 4B	20
Enameled copper wire, 24–26 gauge, 20-cm lengths	25C	10
Enameled copper wire, 24–26 gauge, 3-m lengths	25C	10
Enameled copper wire, 24–26 gauge, 30-cm lengths	25A	10

Material	Lab(s)	Amount Per Class
Enameled copper wire, 24–26 gauge, 60-cm lengths	25A	10
Enameled copper wire, 24–26 gauge, 4-m length	25B	20
Equal-length bolts of various diameters, at least 10 mm thick	25A	20
Felt sheets, small	16C	10
Filter paper, 10-cm long strips	2B	30
Flashlight bulbs with holders	23B, 23C, 26A	30
Flashlights	21A, 21B, 22B	30
Flint igniter or matches	17C	1 or one pack
Fluorescent lightbulbs	21C	10
Foam packing popcorn	18A	enough to fill ten 30-cm² boxes
Food coloring	1A, 17C	1 bottle
Funnels	2C	20
Glass coffee carafes with heatproof handles	17B	10
Graph paper	11B	30 sheets
Half-liter water bottles filled three-quarters full with ice	18A	50
Heat-resistant potholders	17B	10
Heavy whipping cream	4C	5 cups
Honey	4A, 10C	1 pint
Hydrogen peroxide (5–6% concentration)	2A	1 bottle
Incandescent lightbulbs	21C	10
Infrared lamps on stands	18C	10
Insulated copper wire	23B, 23C	80 pieces
Iodine	10B, 10C	500 mL
Iron filings	24A	12 oz
Iron nails	23B	10
Irradiated seeds	11C	60
Knives (plastic)	5B	10
LEDs with wire leads	26C	30
Light sockets or lamps without shades	21C	10
Magnets, bar	24A, 24B, 24C	10
Magnets, bar (strong)	25B	10

Material	Lab(s)	Amount Per Class
Magnets, horseshoe	24A, 24B, 24C	10
Magnifying glasses	2C, 21A	10
Marbles	1C, 12B, 12C	30
Marbles of different masses	13A	20
Metal washers, large	25A	10
Metal weights	15C	10
Milk	4A, 4C	1 gallon
Mirrors, small	22C	10
Modeling clay	22C	20 small pieces
Morse code chart	26B	5
Mousetraps	11A	9
Non-irradiated seeds	11C	60
Oats for polysaccharide solution	10C	1 cup
Pans of water	19A	10
Paper towels	23B	10 pieces
Pennies, loose	1B	100
Pennies, rolls of 50	1B	10
Periodic table	5C	10 copies
Plastic beverage bottles, small	4B	10
Plastic bucket, large	14A	1
Plastic cups	2A, 2B, 2C, 4A, 4C, 14B	140
Plastic drink bottles with lids, 1-liter	14B	10
Plastic plates	4A	10
Plastic spoons	2C, 4C, 10B, 23B	70
Plastic zip-type bags	8A	10
Potting soil	11C	10 qts
Prisms	21A, 21B	10
Protective gloves	14A	30 pairs

Material	Lab(s)	Amount Per Class
Protractors	22C	10
Pulleys	15C	10
Push-button switches with wire leads	26C	30
Racquetballs	16C	10
Rectifier diodes, 1-amp	26A	10
Red cabbage juice	8A	about 3 L
Red, green, and blue cellophane	22B	10 ft² of each color
Red, orange, yellow, green, blue, violet, white, and black paper	5C, 7A, 21B	50 sheets each
Resealable plastic bags, gallon-size	4C	10
Resealable plastic bags, quart-size	4C	10
Resealable plastic sandwich bags	19C	50
Resistors, 100-Ω	26C	30
Rice solution	10C	250 mL
Rock salt	2C, 4C	6 cups
Rolling toy cars	16B	10
Round pencils	13C	50
Rubber bands	22B	30
Rubbing alcohol	3B	16 oz
Salt water	3B	300 mL
Sand	2C	10 tbs
Screwdrivers	23B	10
Shiny metal spoons	22A	10
Silk cloth	23A	10 pieces
Small containers or plant boxes	11C	60
Steel bolts or iron rods	25C	10
Steel wool	3C	10 pieces
Stirring rods	18B	10
Straws	10A	30

Material	Lab(s)	Amount Per Class
String	15A, 15C, 17A	50 m
Sugar, table	4C, 10C	4 cups
Sugar, powdered, for disaccharide solution	10C	1 cup
Sunscreens with different SPFs	19C	3 bottles
Switches with terminal connections	25A, 25C	10
Table-tennis balls	11A, 16C	10
Telegraph receiving units	26B	10
Telegraph sending units	26B	10
Tennis ball (for instructor use)	13B	1
Test wires with alligator clips, 20 cm long	26A	20
Three-ring binders	12B, 16B	16
Thumbtacks	22C	40
Tissue paper	23A	10 pieces
Trays	11C	10
Two-liter containers of cold water	18B	10
Two-liter containers of hot water	18B	10
UV beads	19C	pack of 1,000
Vanilla	4C	2 ½ tsp
Vinegar	3C, 8A	1 gallon
Wax paper	4B, 21C	2 boxes
White grape juice	10C	1 qt
White rice	11B	10 small bags
Wire test leads with alligator clips	26B	20
Wood blocks with eye hooks	13C, 15B	10
Wood or rigid plastic, 20 cm × 20 cm	26C	10 pieces
Zinc oxide cream	19C	16 oz

Suppliers

Carolina Biological Supply Company, Burlington, NC, 27215
www.carolina.com

Delta Education, Nashua, NH, 03061
www.deltaeducation.com

Edmund Scientific Co., Barrington, NJ, 08007
www.scientificsonline.com

Flinn Scientific, Inc., Batavia, IL, 60510
www.flinnsci.com

Frey Scientific, Mansfield, OH, 44903
www.freyscientific.com

Learning Things, Inc., St. Petersburg, FL, 33711
www.learningthings.us

National Science Resources Center, Washington, DC, 20024
www.nsrconline.org

Parco Scientific Co., Vienna, OH, 44473
www.parcoscientific.com

Science Kit, Inc., Tonawanda, NY, 14150
http://sciencekit.com

Ward's Natural Science Establishment, Inc., Rochester, NY, 14603
www.wardsci.com

Chapter 1 Answer Key

Key Concept Review, p. 1

PART A   **1.** hypothesis; **2.** independent variable;
3. control group; **4.** prediction; **5.** volume

PART B   **6.** Ask questions. **7.** controlled **8.** A safety symbol
warns you about possible dangers involved in scientific
experiments. **9.** Divide the object's mass by its volume.

SCIENCE EXTENSION   Answers will vary but should
accurately detail the steps of the scientific method as it
applies to students' examples.

Vocabulary Review, p. 2

PART A   **1.** scientific method; **2.** observation; hypothesis;
3. variable; independent variable; dependent variable;
4. control group; experimental group; **5.** conclusion; data;
hypothesis

PART B   **6.** mass; **7.** volume; **8.** measurement

SCIENCE EXTENSION   Answers will vary but should
accurately compare and contrast one pair of terms.

Graphic Organizer, p. 3

PART A   **1.** meter; **2.** m; **3.** metric ruler; **4.** A door is
about 2.5 m high. **5.** Mass; **6.** kg; **7.** triple-beam balance;
8. A bag of soil has a mass of 25 kg. **9.** Temperature;
10. Kelvin; **11.** thermometer; **12.** Water boils at 373K.
13. Time; **14.** second; **15.** s; **16.** It took 3 s for the ball to
reach the ground. **17.** one-hundredth; **18.** cm, cg;
19. 100 centimeters = 1 meter; **20.** *milli*; **21.** mm, mg;
22. 1,000 millimeters = 1 meter; **23.** one thousand;
24. kg; **25.** 1,000 meters = 1 kilometer; **26.** g/cm^3, g/L;
27. divide mass by volume; **28.** the density of gold is
19.3 g/cm^3; **29.** L, cm^3; **30.** multiply length × width × height;
31. volume of a 4 m cube = 64 m^3

PART B   **32.** 2.5×10^{-4} m; **33.** 4.34×10^6 kg; **34.** 0.43 kg;
35. 108,000 m

SCIENCE EXTENSION   Student diagrams will vary.

Reading Comprehension, p. 4

PART A   **1.** Observations; **2.** begins; **3.** answered; testing;
4. guess; knowledge; **5.** Experiment; **6.** variables;
7. Collecting; **8.** organize; graph; **9.** hypothesis; **10.** repeat;
11. Theories; **12.** predictions

PART B   **13.** Check students' answers. **14.** Sample answer:
to take a look to see what happened.

SCIENCE EXTENSION   **1.** The temperature of the pot of
water that did not have salt put in it; **2.** the salt added to the
water; the temperature of the boiling water

Sports Connection, p. 5

PART A   **1.** Running times are slow on the Sycamore
course, runners are unusually tired or complaining about the
length of the course. **2.** Highland: the course is longer than
5 km, Sycamore: the course is accurate as measured;
3. Answers will vary; could be measuring a known distance

with the wheel, comparing the measurement of this course
with an accurate course; **4.** Answers will vary; **5.** Compare
experimental results to 5 km stated distance of course and
inform both coaches.

PART B   **6.** 5 km x 1 mile/1.6 km = 3.1 miles

SCIENCE EXTENSION   Student answers will vary.

Challenge, p. 6

PART A   (Some of these answers are examples only):
1. 28 cm; **2.** 3 m; **3.** 355 mL; **4.** 2,500,000 L; **5.** 20°C;
6. 315,569,260 sec

PART B   Answers will vary depending on students'
estimated values.

SCIENCE EXTENSION   Answers will vary but should show
evidence of student research.

Chapter 2 Answer Key

Key Concept Review, p. 7

PART A   **1.** The materials in a heterogeneous mixture can
be distinguished easily, while the materials in a
homogeneous mixture are uniformly spread out. **2.** Water is
a compound, so it does not have the same properties as the
elements that form it. **3.** The purpose of blending metals
into alloys is that it gives metals properties that they do not
have alone, such as hardness or strength.

PART B   **4.** suspension; **5.** elements; **6.** compound

SCIENCE EXTENSION   Students' answers will vary.

Vocabulary Review, p. 8

PART A   **1.** d; **2.** b; **3.** f; **4.** c; **5.** e; **6.** a

PART B   **7.** true; **8.** electrolysis; **9.** distillation; **10.** atom

SCIENCE EXTENSION   Answers will vary but should
reflect an understanding of chapter terms.

Graphic Organizer, p. 9

PART A

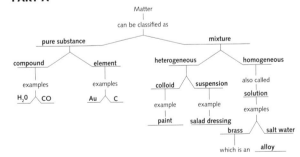

PART B   **1a.** The elements in compounds always combine
in the same ratio, but the substances in mixtures can exist in
different ratios, even within the same sample. **1b.** The
properties of a compound are different than the properties
of its elements, but the properties in a mixture are the same
as the properties of its components. **1c.** Elements in a
compound cannot be separated physically, but the

substances in a mixture can be physically separated.
2. It is a heterogeneous mixture, a colloid, and an emulsion.
3. It is a compound in which 6 atoms of carbon, 12 atoms of hydrogen, and 6 atoms of oxygen form each molecule of glucose.

SCIENCE EXTENSION Student answers will vary but should reflect an understanding of chapter content.

Reading Comprehension, p. 10

PART A **1.** separated; **2.** Can; **3.** Pure Substances; **4.** Mixtures; **5.** broken down; **6.** Cannot; **7.** evenly; **8.** Particles; **9.** Compounds; **10.** Elements; **11.** Heterogeneous mixtures; **12.** Homogeneous mixtures; **13.** water; **14.** hydrogen; **15.** salsa; **16.** seawater

PART B **17.** solvent: water; solute: carbon dioxide; **18.** solvent: water; solute: sucrose; **19.** solvent: water; solute: ammonium nitrate; **20.** There is heavy smoke from the grill and wet paint on the tables

SCIENCE EXTENSION a carton of milk, a ham sandwich with mayonnaise, and salad with salad dressing

Philosophy Connection, p. 11

PART A **1.** False. So far, 117 elements have been discovered or created. Earth, air, fire, and water are not elements. **2.** True. Atoms, molecules, mixtures, and solutions are all made of combinations of elements. **3.** True. The tiny particles are atoms, which are too small to see in small numbers.

PART B **4.** 3; **5.** 6; **6.** *compound, molecule;* Magnesium sulfate is a pure substance made up of more than one atom and more than one element.

SCIENCE EXTENSION Students' answers will vary.

Challenge, p. 12

PART A **1.** 0.1 g/g; 0.1 g/mL; 0.051 mL/mL; **2.** 3.64 g; **3.** 790 mL

PART B **4.** 55 parts per billion (ppb); **5.** 999,997 to 3

SCIENCE EXTENSION Students' answers will vary depending on the chemicals that are researched.

Chapter 3 Answer Key

Key Concept Review, p. 13

PART A **1.** mass; **2.** volume; **3.** density; **4.** texture; **5.** size; **6.** bending; **7.** folding; **8.** crushing; **9.** melting; **10.** freezing; **11.** flammability; **12.** ability to rust; **13.** ability to tarnish; **14.** burning; **15.** rusting; **16.** tarnishing

PART B **17.** specific gravity; **18.** Intensive properties do not depend upon the amount of matter present. Extensive properties depend upon the amount of matter present. **19.** change in energy, formation of a gas, production of a solid, color change, and release of an odor

SCIENCE EXTENSION Students' answers will vary but should demonstrate comprehension of chapter content.

Vocabulary Review, p. 14

PART A **1.** c; **2.** b; **3.** d; **4.** a; **5.** e

PART B **6.** the temperature at which a liquid changes into a gas; **7.** the boiling point of water is 100°C; **8.** matter that can burn easily and quickly; **9.** gasoline and oxygen are flammable; **10.** mass is neither created nor destroyed during a chemical change; **11.** mass of a burned

log = mass of ashes + mass of escaped gases; **12.** the temperature at which a solid changes into a liquid; **13.** the melting point of ice is 0°C; **14.** a physical property that tells whether a sample is a solid, liquid, gas, or plasma; **15.** H_2O as ice is a solid, as water is a liquid, and as steam is a gas

SCIENCE EXTENSION Student diagrams will vary.

Graphic Organizer, p. 15

PART A **1.** Physical property; **2.** Physical change; **3.** Chemical property; **4.** Chemical property; **5.** Physical change; **6.** Chemical change

PART B **7.** the grass is being cut into smaller pieces; the bush is being reshaped; water in the birdbath is changing states from a liquid to a gas; **8.** gasoline and oxygen are burning in the mower; the charcoal is burning and turning to ash; leaves are decomposing in the compost bin

SCIENCE EXTENSION Student answers will vary but should reflect an understanding of chapter content.

Reading Comprehension, p. 16

PART A **1.** physical change; **2.** chemical change; **3.** chemical change

PART B **4.** extensive; **5.** intensive; **6.** intensive

SCIENCE EXTENSION **1.** A chemical change means that the candle has been changed into another type of matter with different properties. **2.** Since some of the mass of the candle is converted into heat and light energy, I would design an experiment that could capture and measure the amount of heat and light energy and convert this number back to mass. I would then compare the mass before and after to ensure it has remained the same or changed.

Biology Connection, p. 17

PART A **1.** PP; **2.** CC; **3.** PP; **4.** PP; **5.** PC

PART B **6.** It describes physical properties and changes. Properties such as shortness can be observed without changing the composition of the plant. Bending hairs and closing leaves do not change the plant's composition either.

SCIENCE EXTENSION Answers will vary but should include three each of physical changes, chemical changes, and physical properties.

Challenge, p. 18

PART A **1.** Mass and volume are extensive properties because they are dependent on the amount of matter. Density is an intensive property because both mass and volume contribute to it. When more matter is present, both the mass and volume increase such that the density stays constant. **2.** The volume of the plastic bag is greater, so it is less dense. **3.** The mass of the glass is larger, so it is denser. **4.** You increase your body's volume with air, not solids and liquids like the rest of your body. The air in your lungs has a lot less mass, so your body's overall density decreases. **5.** The salt in the salt water increases the density of the water. Since the swimmer's density is not changing, the difference between the densities of the swimmer and the salt water is larger than in the fresh water. This means that there is more salt water "sinking" beneath the swimmer, which causes them to float higher.

PART B **6–7.** Students' paragraphs will vary but should reflect an understanding of how oil and mercury can be detrimental.

SCIENCE EXTENSION Answers will vary but should reflect research and understanding of the topic.

Chapter 4 Answer Key

Key Concept Review, p. 19

PART A **1.** plasma; **2.** crystalline solids; **3.** surface tension;
4. pressure; **5.** condensation

PART B **6.** They are classified according to the arrangement of their
particles. **7.** A solid has a definite shape, while a liquid takes the shape
of the container it is in. **8.** Viscosity is a liquid's resistance to flow.
9. Diffusion is the spreading of particles throughout a given volume
until they become uniformly distributed. **10.** Thermal energy is the
total energy of all the particles in a sample.

Vocabulary Review, p. 20

PART A **1.** pascal; **2.** force; **3.** thermal energy; **4.** Boyle's Law;
5. viscosity

PART B **6.** endothermic process, boiling, melting, evaporation,
sublimation, vaporization; **7.** An endothermic process is a process that
absorbs energy. Vaporization, of which boiling and evaporation are
examples, is the change of state from a liquid to a gas and sublimation
is the change of state from a solid to a gas. Both involve the absorption
of energy when matter is heated. **8.** exothermic process, condensation,
freezing; **9.** An exothermic process is a process that releases energy.
Condensation is the change of state from a gas or vapor to a liquid and
freezing is the change of state from a liquid to a solid. Both involve the
release of energy when matter is cooled.

SCIENCE EXTENSION Students' paragraphs will vary but should
illustrate comprehension of the chosen terms.

Interpreting Diagrams, p. 21

PART A Solid diagram (left): c, f, h, k; Liquid diagram (middle):
a, e, i, l; Gas diagram (right): b, d, g, j

PART B

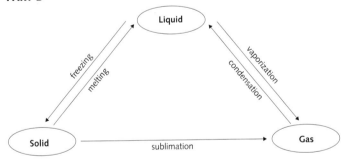

Reading Comprehension, p. 22

PART A **1.** vaporization; **2.** endothermic; **3.** Liquid water boils and
then vaporizes into steam at 100°C. **4.** gas; **5.** exothermic; **6.** Steam
condenses into liquid water at 100°C. **7.** solid; gas; **8.** Solid dry ice
sublimes into a gas at temperatures below the freezing point.
9. freezing; **10.** solid; **11.** Liquid water freezes into ice at 0°C.
12. melting; **13.** solid; **14.** endothermic; **15.** Ice melts into liquid
water at temperatures above 0°C.

PART B K-W-L-S-H charts will vary.

SCIENCE EXTENSION **1.** The state of matter is determined by how
fast the particles that make up the matter move and how strongly they
are attracted to one another. **2.** The atmospheric pressure is lower at
higher elevations than it is at sea level. **3.** Sample answer: You could
put a tablespoon of both liquids on a board, tilt the board, then watch
to see which starts to run down the board first. Honey is more viscous
than ketchup.

Engineering Connection, p. 23

PART A **1.** dust; **2.** paper; **3.** blood; **4.** honey; **5.** water vapor;
6. carbon dioxide; **7.** stars; **8.** lightning

PART B **9.** gas; no definite volume or shape, particles moving rapidly
and spread apart from each other; **10.** liquid; definite volume but not
definite shape, flows, takes shape of container, particles move past each
other; **11.** solid; definite volume and definite shape, particles vibrate
but do not move around each other

SCIENCE EXTENSION Student paragraphs will vary.

Challenge, p. 24

PART A **1.** Illustrations will vary. **2.** Illustrations will vary; The
difference between these two locations is that the Rocky Mountains are
at a higher elevation than the east coast, which means that there is less
air and lower air pressure. This also means that there are fewer
collisions occurring between the air particles and a person's skin.

PART B **3.** Boyle's law. Lying on the mattress reduces its volume,
which increases the pressure of the gas inside. The boy doesn't reduce
the volume as much as the man does, so the pressure inside is lower for
the boy than it is for the man. **4.** Charles's law. Because the air inside is
being heated, the volume is increasing. Some of the air will escape out
of the bottom of the balloon. This makes the balloon less dense because
there is less air inside. So, the balloon floats. **5.** Charles's law. Because
the evening air was cold, the volume of the air inside the bicycle tire
decreased overnight.

Chapter 5 Answer Key

Key Concept Review, p. 25

PART A Democritus, 440 B.C.; John Dalton, 1803;
J.J. Thompson, 1906; Niels Bohr, 1913; James Chadwick, 1932

PART B **1.** It is a subatomic particle that is electrically neutral.
2. According to Dalton's model, atoms cannot be created or destroyed,
but they can be combined, separated, and rearranged. **3.** a positive
charge **4.** It is the sum of the number of protons and neutrons in an
atom's nucleus. **5.** They are located in a region called an electron cloud,
which surrounds the nucleus.

SCIENCE EXTENSION Student essays will vary but should reflect an
understanding of isotopes and their properties.

Vocabulary Review, p. 26

PART A **1.** neutron; **2.** model; **3.** subatomic particle; **4.** proton;
5. isotopes; **6.** electron; **7.** atomic mass; **8.** electron cloud

PART B

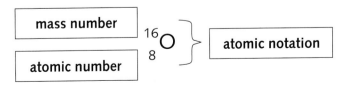

Atomic notation is a shorthand method to describe the number of protons and neutrons in the nucleus of an atom. The mass number is the total number of protons and neutrons in the nucleus and the atomic number is the number of protons. To find the number of neutrons in the atom, subtract the atomic number from the mass number. So, an atom of oxygen has 8 protons and 16 – 8, or 8, neutrons.

SCIENCE EXTENSION   Student presentations will vary.

Interpreting Diagrams, p. 27
PART A

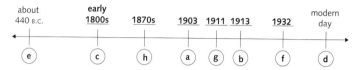

about 440 B.C. (e) early 1800s (c) 1870s (h) 1903 (a) 1911 (g) 1913 (b) 1932 (f) modern day (d)

PART B   **1.** 13; **2.** 14; **3.** 13; **4.** 4; **5.** 5; **6.** 4; **7.** 25; **8.** 30; **9.** 25

SCIENCE EXTENSION   Descriptions will vary but should reflect understanding of chapter content.

Reading Comprehension, p. 28
PART A   **1.** 3; center or nucleus; **2.** 1; Democritus; matter; **3.** 2; Thompson; electrons; **4.** 4; Chadwick; neutron; nucleus

PART B   **5.** atoms; **6.** physical; chemical; **7.** created; destroyed

SCIENCE EXTENSION   **1.** protons, neutrons, and electrons; **2.** No charge, they are neutral. **13.** Yes, these forms of an element are called isotopes. **14.** The number of protons in an element is constant, but since the neutron number may vary, the mass number, found by adding protons and neutrons, can vary.

Math Connection, p. 29
PART A   **1.** Answers in chart will vary.

PART B   **2.** carbon-12; **3.** nitrogen-14; **4.** boron-11

SCIENCE EXTENSION   Answers will vary.

Challenge, pp. 30–31
PART B   **1.** Since each metal emits certain wavelengths of light, fireworks manufacturers can choose which metal salts to include in the fireworks that will produce the desired colors when heated. **2.** Lights that use excited gases rather than incandescence have a variety of gases that can be used to produce the specific color of light that is desired. For example, neon and other noble gases are used to produce bright colors.

SCIENCE EXTENSION   Essays will vary.

Chapter 6 Answer Key

Key Concept Review, p. 32
PART A   **1.** e; **2.** g; **3.** c; **4.** b; **5.** f

PART B   **6.** periodic law; **7.** group; **8.** nonmetals

SCIENCE EXTENSION   Student answers will vary.

Vocabulary Review, p. 33
PART A   **1.** can be cut with a knife, silver color, shiny, low density, one valence electron, reacts by losing the electron; **2.** Group 1, such as lithium, sodium, potassium, rubidium; **3.** alkaline earth metal;

4. generally hard, gray-white, good conductor of electricity, two valence electrons, reacts by losing the two elections; **5.** nonmetal, seven valence electrons and generally gain or share one electron with other elements, making them very reactive; **6.** Group 17: fluorine, chlorine, bromine, iodine, astatine; **7.** noble gas; **8.** Group 18: helium, neon, argon, krypton, xenon, and radon; **9.** too many protons or too few neutrons are in the nucleus and as the nucleus decays it releases particles that can be harmful to living cells; **10.** radium in Group 2; **11.** representative element; **12.** Groups 1, 2, 13 through 18; **13.** behavior is less predictable and often depends on the conditions of a reaction; most are hard, shiny, good conductors of electricity

PART B   **14.** metal; **15.** ductile; **16.** semiconductor; **17.** nonmetal; **18.** malleable; **19.** diatomic molecule; **20.** metalloid

SCIENCE EXTENSION   Diagrams will vary.

Interpreting Diagrams, p. 34
PART A

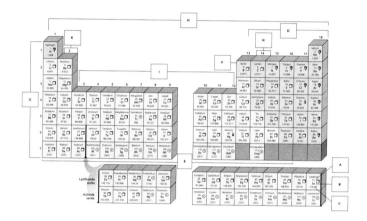

PART B   **1.** greater than; **2.** noble gases; stable; **3.** hydrogen; abundant

Reading Comprehension, p. 35
PART A   **1.** False; metals; **2.** False; With the exception of hydrogen; **3.** True

PART B   **4.** Na; **5.** 19; **6.** Rb; **7.** Cesium; **8.** Fr; **9.** Francium **10.** 1; **11.** soft; silver colored; shiny; low density

SCIENCE EXTENSION   **1.** Hydrogen is made up of only 1 proton and 1 electron. **2.** Hydrogen is the only element that does not fit into any other group. However, hydrogen combines with most of the other elements to form many compounds, so it is rarely alone. **3.** Hydrogen is an extremely flammable gas. **4.** Hydrogen is the fuel that stars use to produce energy. **5.** Hydrogen is colorless, odorless, and tasteless.

Health Connection, p. 36
PART A   **1.** Period 5, Group 12; **2.** Period 4, Group 6; **3.** Period 6, Group 12; **4.** Period 6, Group 14; **5.** Arsenic is a metalloid and selenium is a nonmetal.

PART B   **6.** barium, strontium; **7.** rubidium, cesium; **8.** arsenic

SCIENCE EXTENSION   The amount of toxic metals in seaweed is very low. At these low levels, many elements help sustain life rather than poison it.

Challenge, pp. 37–38

PART A   **1.** lithium, beryllium, boron, carbon, nitrogen, oxygen, fluorine, and neon; **2.** tin; **3.** sulfur; **4.** calcium; **5.** hydrogen; **6.** boron, carbon, fluorine, hydrogen, iodine, potassium, nitrogen, oxygen, phosphorus, sulfur, uranium, vanadium, yttrium; **7.** tellurium, polonium; **8.** sodium, potassium, iron, silver, tin, antimony, tungsten, gold, mercury, lead

PART B   Students' paragraphs will vary.

SCIENCE EXTENSION   Answers will vary.

Chapter 7 Answer Key

Key Concept Review, p. 39

PART A   **1.** e; **2.** f; **3.** c; **4.** d; **5.** m; **6.** l; **7.** k; **8.** g; **9.** i; **10.** j; **11.** h; **12.** b **13.** a

PART B   **14.** It is the energy required to pull an electron away from an atom. **15.** Their charges cancel each other out. **16.** a polyatomic ion is an ion formed of many atoms.

SCIENCE EXTENSION   Student answers will vary.

Vocabulary Review, p. 40

PART A   **1.** energy levels; electron cloud; **2.** valence electrons; electron cloud; **3.** chemical bond; valence electrons; electron-dot diagram; **4.** ion; oxidation number; **5.** Electronegativity; ionization energy

PART B   *chemical bond:* a bond between atoms; *covalent bond:* an atomic bond in which two atoms share electrons; *ionic bond:* when one atom loses one or more electrons and another atom gains one or more electrons; *metallic bond:* when metal ions share their pooled valence electrons

Interpreting Diagrams, p. 41

PART A   **1.** sodium, 7; **2.** nitrogen, 3; **3.** sulphur, 2

4. Ba

5. P

6. Br

PART B   **7.** Covalent; **8.** Ionic; **9.** Metallic; **10.** Covalent, Metallic;

SCIENCE EXTENSION   Diagrams will vary but should reflect understanding of chapter content.

Reading Comprehension, p. 42

PART A   **1.** The atoms of each element in Group 18 have 8 valence electrons. Add ten to eight and you get 18. Helium has only 2 valence electrons. **2.** The atoms of elements in Group 1 have 1 valence electron. This makes them very reactive. **3.** The atoms of elements in Group 2 have 2 valence electrons. This makes them reactive but not as

reactive as those in Group 1.

SCIENCE EXTENSION   **1.** A: true; B: true; B is not a good explanation for A because the atomic weight does not indicate how reactive an element is. **2.** A: false, gaining an electron makes the atom negatively charged; B: true

Art Connection, p. 43

PART A   **1.** ionic compound; **2.** solid, crystal, conducts electricity when dissolved in water, electrically neutral, high melting and boiling points

PART B   **3.** copper, carbon, oxygen, hydrogen; **4.** copper: 2, carbon: 1, oxygen: 5, hydrogen: 2; **5.** 10

SCIENCE EXTENSION   Answers will vary. Examples could include frying eggs, lighting a candle, etc.

Challenge, pp. 44–45

PART A   **1.** N; **2.** P; **3.** P; **4.** N; **5.** P; **6.** P

PART B   **7.** Polar; **8.** Nonpolar; **9.** Polar

SCIENCE EXTENSION   Paragraphs will vary based upon research.

Chapter 8 Answer Key

Key Concept Review, p. 46

PART A   **1.** products; **2.** coefficients; **3.** single-displacement reaction

PART B   **4.** A balanced chemical equation is an equation in which the number of atoms of each element is the same on both sides of the equation. **5.** Most synthesis reactions produce one product. **6.** a decomposition reaction

SCIENCE EXTENSION   Answers will vary but should reflect understanding of chapter content.

Vocabulary Review, p. 47

PART A   **1.** c; **2.** b; **3.** d; **4.** a

PART B   **5.** S-D; **6.** D; **7.** O-R; **8.** S **9.** describes chemical reactions; above shows that hydrogen and oxygen are the reactants and water is the product; **10.** the original substances in a chemical reaction; H_2 and O_2; **11.** the new substance(s) formed in a chemical reaction; H_2O

SCIENCE EXTENSION   Answers will vary.

Interpreting Diagrams, p. 48

PART A   **1.** d; **2.** f; **3.** i; **4.** l; **5.** e; **6.** i; **7.** k; **8.** n; **9.** b; **10.** g; **11.** i; **12.** j; **13.** c; **14.** h; **15.** i; **16.** m; **17.** a; **18.** i; **19.** l; **20.** o

PART B   **21.** $2N_2 + O_2 = 2N_2O$; **22.** $Zn + 2HCl = ZnCl_2 + H_2$

SCIENCE EXTENSION   Answers will vary.

Reading Comprehension, p. 49

PART A   **1.** A coefficient is a number written in front of a chemical formula; it is used to balance a chemical equation. A subscript is a number written behind and lower than the chemical symbol that indicates the number of atoms in one molecule of a compound. **2.** Reactants are shown on the left of a chemical equation; products are shown on the right.

PART B   First card: 3; coefficients; subscripts; Second card: 2; atoms; products; name; Third card: 4; equation; atoms; Fourth card: 1; reactants; left; right

SCIENCE EXTENSION **1.** increases the speed; **2.** happen together; **3.** double-displacement reaction

Kitchen Connection, p. 50

PART A **1.** Circle $NaHCO_3$ (aq) + $HC_2H_3O_2$ (aq) and underline H_2CO_3 (aq) + $NaC_2H_3O_2$ (aq); **2.** the reaction is endothermic, or energy-absorbing; **3.** in aqueous solution, or dissolved in water; **4.** Heat the reactants, stir the reactants, use more concentrated acetic acid.

PART B **5.** This is a decomposition reaction in which one substance breaks down into two products. **6.** a catalyst

SCIENCE EXTENSION Answers will vary. Examples of inhibiting spoilage could be refrigeration, sealing out air, adding preservatives, and canning. Rotting could be accelerated by warming the fruit, chopping it, adding other spoiled food to it, and stirring the fruit.

Challenge, pp. 51–52

PART A **1.** 58.443 g; **2.** 57.212 g (1.3 × 44.009 g); **3.** 56.028 g (2.0 × 28.014 g); **4.** 240.128 g (4 × 60.032 g); **5.** 3.406 g (0.2 × 17.031 g)

PART B **6.** $HCl + NaOH Ù H_2O + NaCl$; **7.** 1.5 mol; **8.** $CH_4 + 2O_2 Ù CO_2 + 2H_2O$; **9.** It takes 2 moles of O_2 to react with 1 mole of CH_4. If only 1.8 moles of O_2 is present, then all of the CH_4 will not react. So, the O_2 is the limiting reactant **10.** 2.0 mol; **11.** 1.2 mol/2.0 mol = 60%

Chapter 9 Answer Key

Key Concept Review, p. 53

PART A Numbering order: 3, 5, 2, 4, 6, 1

PART B **1.** It refers to the fact that polar and ionic solutes will only dissolve in polar solvents and nonpolar solutes will only dissolve in nonpolar solvents. **2.** Stirring a solution, increasing the surface area of a solute, and increasing the temperature of a solvent. **3.** If a solute has a high solubility, a large amount of the solute can dissolve in the solvent under the given conditions. If a solute has a low solubility, only a small amount of the solute can dissolve in the solvent under the given conditions.

SCIENCE EXTENSION Student descriptions will vary.

Vocabulary Review, p. 54

PART A **1.** concentration; **2.** unsaturated; **3.** true; **4.** pH; **5.** salt

PART B **6.** solubility curve; **7.** neutralization reaction; **8.** electrolyte; **9.** aqueous solution; **10.** hydronium ion

SCIENCE EXTENSION Questions will vary.

Interpreting Diagrams, p. 55

PART A **1.** copper; **2.** tin; **3.** solid; **4.** water; **5.** carbon dioxide; **6.** liquid; **7.** water; **8.** salt; **9.** liquid; **10.** water; **11.** stirred, heated, or its surface area is increased; **12.** increasing pressure

PART B **13.** basic; **14.** neutral; **15.** acidic; **16.** N; **17.** A; **18.** A; **19.** A

SCIENCE EXTENSION Answers will vary but should reflect understanding of chapter content.

Reading Comprehension, p. 56

PART A **1.** solution; **2.** dissolve; **3.** interaction; **4.** liquid; **5.** gases; **6.** solids; **7.** solvent; **8.** solute; **9.** seawater; **10.** bronze

PART B **11.** High temperature: increased solubility of solid solutes in water and decreased solubility of gas solutes in water. **12.** Low temperature: decreased solubility of solid solutes in water and increased solubility of gas solutes in water.

SCIENCE EXTENSION **1.** Dip a piece of blue litmus paper into some vinegar. Blue litmus is an indicator that turns red when placed in acids. **2.** Dip a piece of red litmus paper into some milk of magnesia. Red litmus is an indicator that turns blue when placed in a base.

Cultural Connection, p. 57

PART A **1.** The positive and negative ions in salt dissociate. Each ion is surrounded by polar water molecules and dissolved. **2.** Heat the water, stir the water, use more water or change it, chop up the fish into small pieces. **3.** physical change

PART B Answers will vary.

SCIENCE EXTENSION Answers will vary.

Challenge, p. 58

PART A **1.** HCl is an Arrhenius acid because it dissociates into H^+ and Cl^- in H_2O. HCl is a Bronsted-Lowry acid because it donates an H^+ to H_2O to form the H_3O^+ ion. HCl is a Lewis acid because it accepts a pair of electrons from the oxygen on H_2O.

2. H_2O is a Bronsted-Lowry base because it accepts a proton from HCl and it is a Lewis base because it donates electrons to HCl. It is not an Arrhenius base because it does not produce OH- ions in water. It is water!

PART B Answers will vary.

Chapter 10 Answer Key

Key Concept Review, p. 59
PART A

10.1: Nature of Carbon Compounds
    A. Organic Compounds
    B. Bonding of Carbon
    C. Groups of Carbon Compounds
10.2: Polymers
    A. Monomers and Polymers
    B. Natural Polymers
    C. Synthetic Polymers
    D. Polymerization
10.3: Living Things and Organic Compounds
    A. Proteins, Lipids, and Carbohydrates
    B. Nucleic Acids

PART B **1.** inorganic compound; **2.** space-filling model; **3.** hydrocarbons

SCIENCE EXTENSION Answers will vary.

Vocabulary Review, p. 60

PART A **1.** organic compound made up of carbon, hydrogen, and oxygen atoms; sugars, starches, and cellulose; **2.** the body's main source of energy; **3.** saccharide; **4.** made of one, two, or many molecules, such as fructose, sucrose, and starch; **5.** lipids; **6.** helps body store energy; is a large part of the structure of cell membranes; **7.** building block of lipids with a long carbon chain; **8.** can be saturated or unsaturated; **9.** nucleic acids; **10.** DNA: genetic code, and RNA:

enables cells to use the information coded in DNA; **11.** nucleotide;
12. the monomer that makes up a nucleic acid

PART B

13.

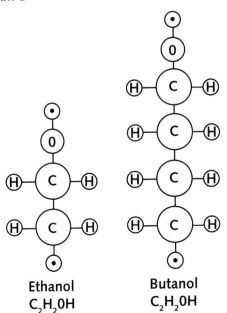

15. hydrocarbon; hydrocarbons are made up of hydrogen and carbon
atoms only and benzene has six carbon and six hydrogen atoms only

Graphic Organizer, p. 61

PART A   **1.** Substituted Hydrocarbon; **2.** Polymer; **3.** Hydrocarbon;
4. Substituted Hydrocarbon; **5.** Hydrocarbon; **6.** Polymer; **7.** Polymer;
8. Substituted Hydrocarbon; **9.** Hydrocarbon

PART B   **10.** four; four; **11.** straight chains; branched chains; rings

Reading Comprehension, p. 62

PART B   **1.** Each carbon atom can form four covalent bonds with
atoms of carbon or with atoms of other elements. This large number of
bonds that each carbon atom can form is one reason why so many
carbon compounds exist. Plus, carbon atoms can form single, double,
or triple covalent bones with other carbon atoms. **2.** The covalent
bonds between carbon atoms are particularly stable and nonpolar.
They also tend to be nonelectrolytes. **3.** If the hydrocarbon is a solid,
like a piece of coal, you could carry it in your pocket.

SCIENCE EXTENSION   **1.** Sample answer: protective clothing for
firefighters **2.** Sample answer: diapers and potting soil

Life Science Connection, p. 63

PART A   **1.** decomposition; **2.** Yeast is a catalyst and would be written
above the arrow.

PART B

3.

Ethanol
C_2H_2OH

Butanol
C_2H_2OH

4. No, the functional groups could be rearranged or the carbons could
form a branching chain.

SCIENCE EXTENSION   Silicon and carbon are both in Group 4 of the
Periodic Table. Group 4 elements have four valence electrons and can
make four bonds per atom. Without long chains or multiple bonds,
silicon cannot form many of the types of compounds essential to life.
A solvent other than water would be needed to transport silicon-based
compounds.

Challenge, pp. 64–65

PART A   **1.** octane; **2.** pentene; **3.** decyne; **4.** ethane; **5.** six; single

PART B   **6.** propylhexane; **7.** 4-octyne

SCIENCE EXTENSION   chlorine: -Cl, chloro-, example: chloroheptane;
bromine: -Br, bromo-, example: bromomethane; amine: -NH2, -amine,
example: nonylamine; cyclohexane: $-C_6H_{11}$, cyclohexyl-, example:
cyclohexylbutane; benzene: $-C_6H_5$, -benzene, example: ethylbenzene

Chapter 11 Answer Key

Key Concept Review, p. 66

PART A   **1.** radioisotopes; **2.** mass number; **3.** alpha particle;
4. artificial transmutation; **5.** nuclear fission

PART B   **6.** Radioactivity is a process in which materials emit, or give
off, particles and energy. **7.** It pulls the neutrons and protons together
in the nucleus. **8.** They are usually described in terms of number of
neutrons and protons.

Vocabulary Review, p. 67

PART A   **1.** d; **2.** b; **3.** a; **4.** c

PART B   **5.** reaction that involves changes in nuclei; **6.** a chemical
reaction that changes electrons; **7.** obeys the law of conservation of
mass; **8.** U-238 decays by emitting an alpha particle which forms
TH-234; **9.** occurs if the products of the reaction have less mass than
the reactants; **10.** involves radioactive decay; **11.** in nuclear fission, a
nucleus splits into several smaller nuclei

SCIENCE EXTENSION   Questions will vary.

Graphic Organizer, p. 68

PART A   **1.** Beta; **2.** Alpha; **3.** Beta; **4.** Gamma; **5.** Alpha and Beta

PART B   **6.** 3/1, check; **7.** 54/26; **8.** 10/5; **9.** 95/36, check; **10.** fusion;
11. fission; **12.** fission **13.** fusion

SCIENCE EXTENSION   Answers will vary but should reflect
understanding of chapter content.

Reading Comprehension, p. 69

PART B   **1.** the distance between particles in a nucleus is small;
2. the strong force is very strong; **3.** the distance between particles in a
nucleus increases; **4.** the strength of the strong force becomes
insignificant. **5.** as the nuclei become larger (as the number of protons
increases); **6.** the neutron-to-proton ratio of stable nuclei changes;
7. if the neutron-to-proton ratio of stable nuclei changes;
8. the element is radioactive

Health Connection, p. 70

PART A   **1.** 53 protons, 78 neutrons, 53 electrons; **2.** 54 protons,
77 neutrons, 54 electrons

PART B **3.** 25 million atoms of I-131 and almost 100 million atoms of I-129; **4.** I-131 because it decays much faster, releasing harmful gamma radiation. **5.** The properties will be identical; all isotopes of an element have the same chemical properties.

SCIENCE EXTENSION Answers will vary.

Challenge, pp. 71–72

PART A **1.** a piece of paper; **2.** a plastic sheet; **3.** thorium-230

PART B **4.** He could stand behind plastic as far away from the spill as possible. **5.** She should remove the latex glove as soon as possible and dispose of it appropriately.

Chapter 12 Answer Key

Key Concept Review, p. 73

PART A **1.** Speed; **2.** kilometers per hour; **3.** how fast or slow an object moves; **4.** distance/time; **5.** Velocity; **6.** an object's speed and direction; **7.** added together if in the same direction; **8.** subtracted when in the opposite direction; **9.** Acceleration; **10.** speeds up, slows down, or changes direction; **11.** rate of change in an object's speed or direction; **12.** (final velocity – initial velocity)/time; **13.** Momentum; **14.** mass × velocity; **15.** kilogram-meters per second; **16.** increases as mass increases

PART B **17.** a distance-time graph; **18.** Velocity measures not only the distance an object travels over time, but its direction as well. The measure of speed does not include direction.

SCIENCE EXTENSION Students' answers will vary but should reflect an understanding of chapter content.

Vocabulary Review, p. 74

PART A **1.** reference point; **2.** motion; **3.** speed; **4.** Displacement
PART B **5.** average speed; **6.** average speed = total distance/ total time; **7.** the rate of change in velocity as an object speeds up, slows down, or changes direction; **8.** acceleration = (final velocity – initial velocity)/time; **9.** momentum; **10.** momentum = mass × velocity

SCIENCE EXTENSION Answers will vary.

Interpreting Diagrams, p. 75

PART A **1.** The slope is slanting downward, so the object shows negative acceleration and is slowing down or decelerating.
2. The slope is zero and the acceleration is zero, so the object is neither slowing down nor speeding up and is at constant speed.
3. The slope is slanting upward, so the object shows positive acceleration and is speeding up or accelerating.

PART B **4.** 11.5 mph east; **5.** 20 mph; **6.** Bus A

SCIENCE EXTENSION Answers will vary but should reflect an understanding of chapter content.

Reading Comprehension, p. 76

PART A **1.** Stationary means not moving. **2.** meters per second; **3.** An equal length is marked off from one point to the next along the entire distance.

PART B **4.** formula for calculating acceleration; -0.5 m/s^2; **5.** formula for calculating momentum; 160 kg 5 m/s westward; formula for calculating speed; 63 miles per hour

SCIENCE EXTENSION The butterflies flew at the same speed for the same amount of time, but they did not end up at the same flower because they flew in different directions. Their velocity was different, i.e. their speed was the same but their direction was different.

Music Connection, pp. 77–78

PART A **1.** The music starts at 120 beats per minute, slows down, and then speeds back up to 120 bpm. **2.** Acceleration is zero when the tempo is steady, negative while slowing down and positive while speeding up. **3.** Reference points could the beginning or end of the piece of music.

PART B **4.** 0.29 s; **5.** The sound maintains a constant speed. The velocity keeps the same magnitude but changes in direction when the sound bounces off the back of the hall.
6. 0.29 s

SCIENCE EXTENSION Answers will vary.

Challenge, p. 79

PART A Answers will vary.
PART B Answers will vary.

Chapter 13 Answer Key

Key Concept Review, p. 80
PART A

13.1: What is Force?
    A. Types of Forces
    B. Combining Forces
13.2: Friction
    A. Factors Affecting Friction
    B. Types of Friction
    C. Using Friction
    D. Reducing Friction
13.3: Gravity
    A. The Study of Gravity
    B. Law of Universal Gravitation
    C. Falling Objects
    D. Weight Versus Mass
    E. Air Resistance
13.4: Newton's Laws of Motion
    A. Newton's First Law of Motion
    B. Newton's Second Law of Motion
    C. Newton's Third Law of Motion

PART B **1.** balanced forces; **2.** static friction; **3.** air resistance

SCIENCE EXTENSION Student answers will vary.

Vocabulary Review, p. 81
PART A **1.** d; **2.** a; **3.** b; **4.** e; **5.** f; **6.** c

PART B **7.** A force is a push or a pull, so in A, the force is a push of one arm against another arm. **8.** In A, the combination of the forces of each arm pushing against the other is the net force, which in this case, is the difference of the forces. **9.** In A, the forces are balanced because they cancel each other when they are combined, and have a net force of zero. **10.** In B, the forces acting on one arm result in a net force and the arms moves. The forces are unbalanced.

SCIENCE EXTENSION Answers will vary.

Interpreting Diagrams, p. 82

PART A **1a.** The oars push the water backwards; **1b.** The water exerts a reaction force on the boat, propelling it forward; **2a.** Exhaust gases produce a downward force; **2b.** An equal and opposite force is produced on the rocket.

PART B **3a.** rolling; **3b.** sliding; **3c.** static; **3d.** fluid

SCIENCE EXTENSION Answers will vary but should reflect understanding of chapter content.

Reading Comprehension, p. 83

PART A **1.** contact; **2.** Two interacting objects are physically touching each other. **3.** action at a distance; **4.** Two interacting objects are not physically touching each other. **5.** balanced forces; **6.** two or more forces exerted on an object that cancel each other when they are combined. Balanced forces do not change the motion of an object. **7.** unbalanced forces; **8.** Multiple forces that result in a net force on an object. It causes an object to accelerate. **9.** Static; **10.** The friction that acts on objects that are not moving. **11.** sliding; **12.** Is kinetic friction, because two surfaces are sliding past each other. **13.** fluid; **14.** The force that resists motion when a fluid is involved. **15.** rolling; **16.** The frictional force between a rolling object and the surface on which it rolls.

PART B **17.** acceleration; Second Law; **18.** equal; opposite; Third Law; **19.** unbalanced; First Law

SCIENCE EXTENSION The toy is not in free fall since air resistance acts on it as it falls.

Sports Connection, p. 84

PART A **1a.** The force of gravity pulls the ball down toward Earth. **1b.** Friction forces between the ball, air, and surface of the ground slow the ball. **1c.** When a force (a foot) acts on a ball, the ball exerts an equal force on the foot. **2.** No, gravity is always acting on the ball, as well as other forces such as air pressure, the force of the ground upon the ball, etc. **3.** Acceleration is force divided by mass. The soccer ball has less mass so it accelerates more.

PART B **4.** Mass would remain the same but weight would be 1/6 as much. **5.** The ball would travel much farther on the Moon because there is less air resistance to slow it and less gravity to pull it downward.

SCIENCE EXTENSION Answers will vary.

Challenge, p. 85

PART A **1.** When a raindrop hits a windshield, the windshield hits back. Because the water is not solid material, the force from the windshield causes the matter in the raindrop to rearrange. This makes the raindrop break apart and splatter. When a rock hits the windshield, the force from the rock causes the matter in the windshield to rearrange, which creates a crack or shatters it. **2.** In both cases, the force of gravity pulls the object down. The force of friction from the carpet is the same. The difference is that pushing an object requires different muscles in your body to create a force than pulling does. **3.** The hammer thrower pulls the hammer towards him while spinning around, but the hammer also pulls the hammer thrower towards itself too. The hammer thrower must lean back to balance this force. The planets are pulled into the Sun by gravity while they revolve, but they pull back on the Sun as well. The difference is that the difference between the masses of the hammer and hammer thrower is much smaller than the difference in the masses between the planets and the Sun. The planets' gravitational pull on the Sun is negligible, so the Sun doesn't move too much. **4.** A raw egg and a hard-boiled egg have almost the same mass. A raw egg will crush with less force than a hard-boiled egg because the inside of the egg pushes back with a lower force in the raw egg than in the hard-boiled egg.

PART B **5.** The probes don't need fuel if they aren't accelerating. They can travel fast without a force pushing them along.

Chapter 14 Answer Key

Key Concept Review, p. 86

PART A **1.** viscosity; **2.** Archimedes' principle; **3.** barometer; **4.** density; **5.** lift

PART B **6.** A fluid's viscosity depends on the attractions between its particles. **7.** They use fluid to transmit and amplify, or increase, forces. **8.** atmospheric pressure

Vocabulary Review, p. 87

PART A **1.** neutral buoyancy; **2.** hydraulic device; **3.** viscosity; **4.** barometer; **5.** lift

PART B **6.** B; **7.** P; **8.** A

Interpreting Diagrams, p. 88

PART A **1.** Archimedes' principle: The buoyant force of an object is the same as the weight of the fluid that the object displaces. **2.** Pascal's principle: When a force is applied to a fluid in a closed container, an increase in pressure is transmitted equally to all parts of the fluid. **3.** Bernoulli's principle: As the velocity of a fluid increases, the pressure the fluid exerts decreases.

PART B **4.** sink; **5.** decreases

Reading Comprehension, p. 89

PART A **1.** Effect: An increase in pressure is transmitted equally to all parts of the fluid. Principle: Pascal's principle; **2.** Effect: A buoyant force equal to the fluid displaced is experienced. Principle: Archimedes' principle; **3.** Effect: A fluid's pressure drops. Principle: Bernoulli's principle

PART B **4.** Thrust moves the disc through the air. Lift counteracts gravity, causing an upward force. **5.** The shape of the toys must be very different. The shape of the toy that floats must have a density less than that of water.

SCIENCE EXTENSION **1.** Area = $\frac{\text{Force}}{\text{Pressure}}$, Force = Area × Pressure; **2.** Use the formula $V = \frac{4}{3}\pi r^3$ to find the volume of the ball (a sphere), V equals about 0.004 m³. Using $m = DV$, you get the mass equal to about (7800 kg/m³)(0.004 m³) = 31.2 kg.

Transportation Connection, p. 90

PART A **1.** The submarine is filled with air inside and in tanks that makes it more buoyant. **2.** pump out air and let in water to increase the density of the submarine

PART B **3.** It will reduce the volume of water displaced, reducing buoyancy. **4.** Water pressure pushing down, gravity pulling toward the center of Earth, the buoyant force pushing up, and water resistance (friction) pushing back against the submarine.

SCIENCE EXTENSION Answers will vary.

Challenge, p. 91

PART A **1.** The submarine is able to float because it is less dense than the water that surrounds it because the ballast tanks are full of air. The flood ports open, allowing water to enter into the ballast tanks, which causes the sub to sink. Air in the tanks is forced out of the main vents at the top. The sub has negative buoyancy. When it stops sinking, the sub has neutral buoyancy because the force of gravity and the force of buoyancy are balanced. To rise, or have positive buoyancy, the ballast tanks must be filled with air from the compressed air tanks, which forces water out of the flood ports. **2.** The submarine's ballast tanks fill with air or water, which changes the sub's buoyancy. The air in a fish's swim bladder becomes compressed when it dives and the air expands when it rises. So, the fish has the same amount of air inside it while the sub releases air to dive and fills the ballast tanks with air from tanks when it rises.

PART B **3.** When the water balloon is thrown, a force is exerted from your hand onto the balloon. In a long thin balloon, the water is pushed to the ends of the balloon, causing it to wobble. In a spherical balloon, the force is evenly distributed over all the water and the pressure is equal everywhere. It travels as a sphere through the air. **4.** First, the balloon falls because it is slightly heavier than air due to the balloon material. Air that is blown directly on the balloon acts as a force to push it upwards. Second, the air travels around the balloon from the bottom to the top and creates lower pressure in the air on the upper part of the balloon. According to Bernoulli's principle, this helps it to float.

Chapter 15 Answer Key

Key Concept Review, p. 92

PART A **1.** Inclined Plane; **2.** c; **3.** h; **4.** Wedge; **5.** g; **6.** i; **7.** Screw; **8.** j; **9.** l; **10.** Lever; **11.** d; **12.** k; **13.** Pulley; **14.** a; **15.** f; **16.** Wheel and Axle; **17.** b; **18.** e

PART B **19.** when a force is exerted on an object that moves the object some distance in the direction of the force; **20.** They make it easier to perform.

Vocabulary Review, p. 93

PART A **1.** e; **2.** d; **3.** a; **4.** b; **5.** c

PART B **6.** work done using a machine; **7.** input work = input force × distance over which the input force is exerted; **8.** output work; **9.** output work = output force × distance over which the output force is exerted; **10.** input force; **11.** the input force is greater than the output force if the machine multiplies distance, such as a third-class lever

SCIENCE EXTENSION Answers will vary.

Interpreting Diagrams, p. 94

PART A inclined plane pointing to the ramp and stairs; wheel and axle pointing to the wheel on the cart; pulley pointing to the pulley used to raise the flag; lever pointing to the rake and wheelbarrow; screw pointing to the jug lid; wedge pointing to shovel

PART B **1.** The rake is a third-class lever because the fulcrum is at the end of the lever, which makes work easier by increasing the distance over which the force is applied. **2.** Fixed pulley; this type of pulley is attached to something that does not move. **3.** 12; 6 m / 0.5 m = 12

SCIENCE EXTENSION Answers will vary.

Reading Comprehension, p. 95

PART A Answer will vary

PART B **1.** *Efficiency* is the agility to do something well without wasted energy or effort. **2.** joule; **3.** Levers must be rigid to move objects and do work.

SCIENCE EXTENSION **4.** arrow up; **5.** arrow up; **6.** Yes; **7.** arrow to the side; **8.** arrow to the side; **9.** Yes; **10.** arrow up; **11.** arrow to the side; **12.** No

Home Connection, p. 96

PART A **1.** possibilities: can-opener turner, oven knobs, binocular focusing knob; **2.** hammer; **3.** window blinds; **4.** The blade that cuts into the metal is a wedge, the knob is a wheel and axle, and the handle is a second-class lever.

PART B **5.** The hands and their arrows represent input force, the triangles represent fulcrum, and the other arrows represent the output force. **6.** Sometimes a lever is used to multiply distance, not force. Examples could include shovel, broom, staple remover, etc.

SCIENCE EXTENSION Answers will vary. Examples of wheels could include dials, knobs, vehicle wheels, can openers, nondigital clocks, and screwdrivers.

Challenge, pp. 97–98

PART A **1a.** Since the baseball bat is a third-class lever, it shortens the length of the lever arm. This means that the force of the bat against the baseball will be smaller. **1b.** A shovel and a door are also third-class levers. By applying the force closer to the middle, the force is lowered significantly. So, it makes it harder to dig and harder to close a door. **2a.** Extending the ramp 1 m will mean a low mechanical advantage for the ramp, which requires greater force to be exerted by those carrying the boxes. But the ramp is shorter, so it will take less time overall to unload the truck. The fully extended ramp has the best mechanical advantage, but the family will have to carry the boxes a much longer distance, which also requires more time. **2b.** There is no way to tell which approach is the fastest because the rate at which the boxes are unloaded depends both on how much strength and stamina each family member has. The shorter ramp requires more strength while the longer ramp requires more stamina.

PART B Answers will vary.

Chapter 16 Answer Key

Key Concept Review, p. 99
PART A

16.1: What Is Energy?
    A. Energy Makes Everything Happen
    B. Kinetic Energy
    C. Potential Energy
    D. Forms of Energy
16.2: Energy Conversions
    A. Kinetic and Potential Energy Conversions
    B. Conservation of Energy
    C. Conversions Among Energy Forms
    D. Machines as Energy Converters
16.3: Energy Resources

A. Making Electricity
B. Energy Resources from the Sun
C. Energy from Atoms
D. Energy from Earth
16.4: Energy Choices
A. Fossil Fuel Problems
B. Energy Alternatives
C. Conservation Options

PART B   **1.** kinetic energy; **2.** chemical energy; **3.** mechanical energy

SCIENCE EXTENSION   Students answers will vary.

Vocabulary Review, p. 100

PART A   **1.** d; **2.** i; **3.** c; **4.** a; **5.** h; **6.** e; **7.** f; **8.** b; **9.** g

PART B   kinetic energy + potential energy = mechanical energy; Kinetic energy is the energy of movement. It depends on an object's mass and/or how fast it is moving. An object with greater mass and/or greater velocity than another object has more kinetic energy. Potential energy is the energy stored when something moves against a force. Examples of the forms it can take are elastic potential energy when a rubber band is stretched or gravitational potential energy when an object is raised above the ground. Mechanical energy is the sum of an object's kinetic energy and its potential energy of position. For example, a roller coaster converts potential energy at the top of a hill to kinetic energy as it goes down a hill. The sum of the energies of the conversion is mechanical energy.

SCIENCE EXTENSION   Descriptions will vary but should show an understanding of the chapter content.

Interpreting Diagrams, p. 101
PART A

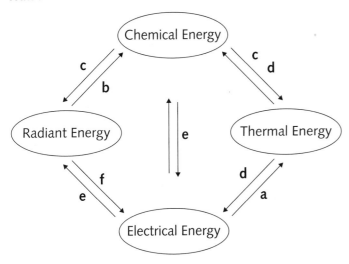

PART B   **1.** the potential energy of the bonds between the atoms of a substance; **2.** the energy stored in wood that is released through combustion; **3.** Kinetic; **4.** a moving car has kinetic energy; **5.** radiant energy released from the nucleus of an atom; **6.** used to make smoke detectors; **7.** energy that is stored when something moves against a force; **8.** an object raised above ground has this energy; **9.** Radiant; **10.** X rays

SCIENCE EXTENSION   Diagrams will vary but should reflect understanding of chapter content.

Reading Comprehension, p. 102

PART A   **1.** Nuclear Energy; **2.** Electrical Energy; **3.** Chemical Energy; **4.** Radiant Energy; **5.** Thermal Energy

PART B   **6.** False; geothermal heat comes from hot rocks just below Earth's surface. **7.** False; its potential energy is increased. **8.** False; An object with less mass can have more kinetic energy if it is moving faster. **9.** False; energy can change form, but cannot be created or destroyed. **10.** True

SCIENCE EXTENSION   Paragraphs but should state that fossil fuels will eventually run out. Conservation ideas might include reduce, reuse, recycle, use energy efficient appliances, and carpool.

Business Connection, p. 103

PART A   **1.** Best choices will vary. **1a.** clean power but not enough sunny days; **1b.** Good transportation lines but city already polluted. Price of fuel may increase as supplies become more scarce. **1c.** Possible, but wind is light and area is crowded. **1d.** Good possibility due to underground volcanic activity. Little space is needed and no pollution produced. **1e.** Lots of precipitation to produce rivers but requires large area to flood behind dam. **1f.** Clean and renewable but could be opposed in crowded area by people worried about accidents.

PART B   **2.** No, the law of conservation of energy states that energy can be transformed but not created or destroyed. **3.** Chemical potential energy is changed into thermal energy. **4.** Thermal energy is changed into kinetic energy.

SCIENCE EXTENSION   Answers will vary.

Challenge, pp. 104–105

PART A   **1.** example: 1700; 1700/30 = 56.7kWh/day; **2.** example: $175; $5.83/day; **3.** $175/1700 = $0.10

PART B   **4.** 4 × 0.15 = 0.6; **5.** 56.7 × 0.25 = 14.2 **6.** 14.2/0.6 = 23.6

Chapter 17 Answer Key

Key Concept Review, p.106

PART A   **1.** thermometer; **2.** Kelvin temperature scale; **3.** insulators; **4.** convection; **5.** heat of vaporization

PART B   **6.** the law of conservation of energy; **7.** Heat is the flow of thermal energy between objects at different temperatures. **8.** Each degree on the Celsius scale represents 1/100th of the distance between the freezing point and boiling point of water.

Vocabulary Review, p. 107

PART A   **1.** conductor; **2.** calorie; **3.** specific heat; **4.** calorimeter; **5.** insulator

PART B

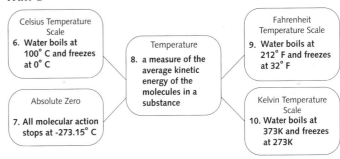

Interpreting Diagrams, p. 108

PART A **1.** radiation; c; e; h; **2.** convection; a; d; g; **3.** conduction; b; f

PART B **4.** white shirt; **5.** metal spoon; **6.** Styrofoam; **7.** water

SCIENCE EXTENSION Answers will vary.

Reading Comprehension, p. 109

PART A **1.** Warmer air around the ice cream transfers energy to the ice cream, the increased energy causes its temperature to rise. **2.** The higher energy in the water transfers to the lower energy in the air resulting in a drop of temperature in the water. **3.** Warmer liquid around the ice cube transfers energy to the ice cube, the increased energy causes the ice cube's temperature to rise.

PART B **4.** A conductor is any material that allows heat to travel through it. An insulator is a material that slows the flow of heat. **5.** Convection is the transfer of thermal energy by the movement and mixing of molecules. Conduction is the transfer of thermal energy between particles that collide with each other. **6.** Heat is the flow of thermal energy from one place to another. Temperature is a measure of the thermal energy of the molecules in a substance.

SCIENCE EXTENSION 4.9C/min × 15 min = 73.5C; 6.6C/min × 15 min = 99C; 2(73.5C + 99C) = 345C; Sample foods: 100 g of: fried eggs, baked potato, and oranges make a total of 201C + 89C + 47C = 337C.

Space Science Connection, p. 110

PART A **1.** Answers will vary, but Antarctica is sure to be much colder. **2.** Pluto is much colder at −235°C to −210°C. **3.** Energy from the Sun radiates through space to reach Pluto. Some of the energy is absorbed by the planet, raising its temperature. **4.** Heat would flow toward outer space because heat travels from warmer to colder matter.

PART B **5.** El Azizia was slightly higher at 136°F. **6.** Yes, Mars gets up to 80°F. **7.** Mars: −133°C to 27°C, for a range of 160°C. Earth: −89°C to 58°C, for a range of 147°C. Mars has the greater range.

SCIENCE EXTENSION An increase in temperature of 1°C or 1 K is equivalent to 1.6°F. Therefore, global warming would be much more extreme at 6°C or 6 K than 6°F.

Challenge, p. 111

PART A **1.** The ice cube is heated by being in direct contact with your skin. The thermal energy leaves your skin and melts the ice, which is why water forms. **2.** The water in the pool comes into direct contact with the skin of your whole body. The thermal energy easily leaves your skin and warms up the water in the pool. Since your whole body is exposed, it cools you down quickly. **3.** An electric fan speeds air up. Because it is going faster, more air particles will hit your skin than the still air around it. When these air particles hit, your skin heats them up. With more air particles hitting you, more energy can be transferred away.

PART B **4–6.** Answers will vary.

Chapter 18 Answer Key

Key Concept Review, p. 112

PART A **1.** Heating Systems; **2.** fireplaces and stoves; **3.** furnace powered by electricity or burning fuel; **4.** radiator; **5.** forced-air system; **6.** geothermal system; **7.** Cooling Systems; **8.** blocks of ice; **9.** heat movers; **10.** refrigerator; **11.** liquid coolant; **12.** air conditioner

PART B **13.** An active solar system uses the radiant energy from the Sun to heat water to be pumped through the house. A passive solar system uses materials that heat up from the radiant energy of the Sun and then release that heat into the house directly. **14.** natural gas and heating oil; **15.** They extract heat from under the ground and use it to heat a home.

Vocabulary Review, p. 113

PART A **1.** e; **2.** c; **3.** b; **4.** d; **5.** a

PART B

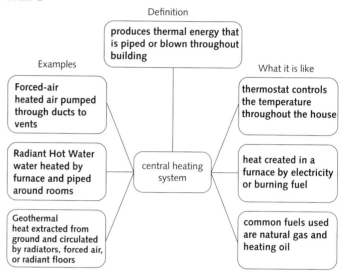

SCIENCE EXTENSION Answers will vary.

Interpreting Diagrams, p. 114

PART A **1.** external combustion engine; **2.** internal combustion engine; **3.** internal; **4.** external; **5.** internal; **6.** internal; **7.** both

PART B **8.** radiant hot-water system; **9.** heat pump; **10.** room heater

SCIENCE EXTENSION Answers will vary, but should reflect understanding of chapter content.

Reading Comprehension, p. 115

PART A **1.** Heat energy naturally flows from hot to cool. By circulating hot air or liquid, the heat is transferred to cooler areas. **2.** Cooling systems are heat movers that absorb heat from one place, carry it to another, and transfer it to the surrounding air or water. **3.** Heat engines convert thermal energy into mechanical energy that can perform useful work. For example, a car burns fuel and produces heat.

PART B **4.** geothermal system; **5.** passive solar system; **6.** radiant hot-water system; **7.** central heating system; **8.** active solar system; **9.** forced-air system

SCIENCE EXTENSION **1.** When fuel is converted from liquid to gas it wastes energy in the form of heat energy. **2.** When the steam passes through a turbine, it expands. When it no longer has enough energy to do useful work in the engine it is released through "smoke stacks."

Agriculture Connection, p. 116

PART A **1.** The tractor is a heat engine because it converts thermal energy into mechanical energy. The engine burns fuel to create heat. The heat turns the parts of the engine which drive the tractor and its attachments. **2.** The tires increase friction, giving the tractor better traction on rough or wet ground. **3.** diesel engine

PART B **4.** forced-air; **5.** Use a thermometer. **6.** Yes, radiant energy passing through the windows is absorbed by the interior, warming it.

SCIENCE EXTENSION Answers will vary. Some possible sources of waste heat: friction between wheels and ground, air resistance, friction between engine parts, hot exhaust gases. Some possible improvements: lubricate parts, use hybrid engine to recapture some energy, turn off engine when not in use, streamline design of tractor to reduce air resistance.

Challenge, pp. 117–118

PART A **1.** a picture showing heat flowing from the sunlight to the carpet, the window, the air in the room; **2.** a picture showing heat transferring from the air in the hot oven to the cold chicken and the dish it is in as well as the sides of the oven; **3.** a picture showing heat transferring from the air in the refrigerator to the ice cubes, since the refrigerator is warmer than ice; **4.** a picture showing students' bodies heating the room

PART B **5.** Carbon dioxide molecules with kinetic energy move from a high-pressure to a low-pressure area and disperse throughout the room. **6.** The ice pieces spread out, which increases entropy, and then the molecules gain kinetic energy by undergoing a phase change, which increases the motion of the particles. **7.** The milk and especially the syrup molecules become more dispersed, as does their energy. **8.** The chemical energy in the bonds of the gasoline and oxygen are released.

Chapter 19 Answer Key

Key Concept Review, p. 119
PART A

19.1: The Nature of Waves
    A. Waves and Vibration
    B. Waves and Energy
    C. Waves and Matter
    D. Mechanical Waves
    E. Electromagnetic Waves
19.2: Types of Waves
    A. Transverse Waves
    B. Compressional Waves
    C. Sound Waves
    D. Seismic Waves
19.3: Properties of Waves
    A. The Parts of a Wave
    B. Wavelength
    C. Frequency
    D. Frequency and Period
    E. Frequency and Wavelength
    F. Wave Speed
    G. Amplitude
19.4: The Behavior of Waves
    A. Reflection
    B. Refraction
    C. Diffraction
    D. Interference
    E. Resonance
PART B **1.** electromagnetic waves; **2.** compressional wave; **3.** Period

Vocabulary Review, p. 120
PART A **1.** true; **2.** medium; **3.** rarefaction; **4.** true; **5.** refraction; **6.** frequency

PART B

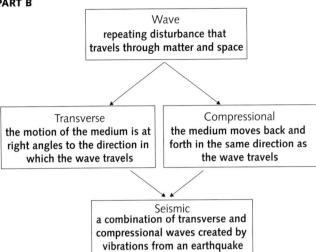

Interpreting Diagrams, p. 121
PART A

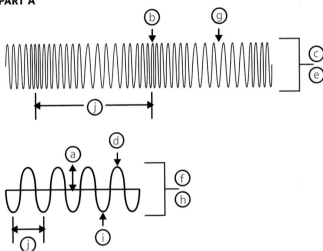

PART B **1.** gases; **2.** increases; **3.** decreases; **4.** 0.25 s

SCIENCE EXTENSION Answers will vary.

Reading Comprehension, p. 122
PART A transverse wave; right angle: In a transverse wave, the motion of the medium is at a right angle to the direction in which the wave travels. electromagnetic wave; X rays: X rays are one type of electromagnetic waves that make up the electromagnetic spectrum. seismic wave; earthquake: The energy-carrying seismic waves cause earthquakes. frequency; hertz (Hz): The frequency of a wavelength is measured in units of hertz (Hz). compressional wave; echo: A sound wave is a compressional wave, and an echo is a reflected sound wave.

PART B **1.** A wavelength is the distance between a specific point on a wave and the identical point on the next wave. **2.** light waves, sound waves, ocean waves; **3.** 10 cycles/second, or 10 Hz; **4.** 0.04 s;

SCIENCE EXTENSION **1.** Sound waves require matter, such as air, to travel. A vacuum has no air in it. **2.** Sound waves have long wavelengths about the size of the door's opening and are able to diffract around corners. He cannot see into the room while outside the door. Because the wavelengths of the light waves are very small compared to the size of the door opening, the light waves undergo almost no diffraction.

Engineering Connection, p. 123

PART A **1.** The waves were mechanical, with the bridge as a medium. **2.** The waves were transverse. They traveled perpendicular to the up-and-down direction of the bridge movement. **3.** Period = 1/0.2 Hz = 5 seconds

PART B **4.** The forced vibrations of the earthquake caused large-amplitude waves in the mud due to resonance at the mud's natural frequency. The freeway had the same natural frequency so it also began to vibrate wildly. **5.** Energy increases with amplitude.

SCIENCE EXTENSION Answers will vary.

Challenge, p. 124

PART A Answers will vary.

PART B A swinging chandelier, a guitar string, the blades of an electric shaver, an electric knife, the shocks of an automobile, etc. The motion is dampened because the energy of the oscillation is transferred to the air that is surrounding the object.

Chapter 20 Answer Key

Key Concept Review, p. 125

PART A **1.** 1; **2.** 8; **3.** 3; **4.** 2; **5.** 4; **6.** 5; **7.** 7; **8.** 6

PART B **9.** Particles in elastic media are tightly packed together, so the collisions that allow sound waves to spread happen faster. **10.** The pitch also increases. **11.** Sound travels through a series of collisions, and the wave loses energy and intensity with each collision.

Vocabulary Review, p. 126

PART A **1.** decibel; **2.** beat; **3.** eardrum; **4.** pitch; **5.** loudness; **6.** echo; **7.** elastic; **8.** ultrasonic

PART B **9.** natural frequency; **10.** fundamental frequency; **11.** intensity; **12.** overtones; **13.** fundamental frequency; **14.** sound quality

SCIENCE EXTENSION Diagrams will vary depending on the word the student chose. Diagrams should show use of resources, for example beat, overtone and pitch have homonyms.

Interpreting Diagrams, p. 127
PART A

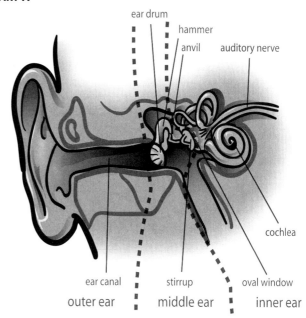

PART B **1.** 85 dB; **2.** solids; **3.** 70°F; **4.** increases; **5.** piano

SCIENCE EXTENSION Answers will vary. For example Doppler is used in weather forecasting, ultrasound has medical uses, infrasound can be used to detect catastrophic natural events such as volcanic eruptions.

Reading Comprehension, p. 128

PART A Answers will vary.

PART B **The Outer Ear:** visible part, ear canal, funnel, narrow passage, collects sound; **The Middle Ear:** eardrum, amplify sound, hammer, anvil, stirrup, oval window; **The Inner Ear:** nerve impulses, cochlea, hair-tipped sensory cells, fluid-filled, auditory nerve, interprets sound

SCIENCE EXTENSION **1.** amplitude; **2.** rarefactions; **3.** intensity; **4.** collisions; **5.** decibel; **6.** correct; **7.** Doppler effect

Biology Connection, p. 129

PART A **1.** cats, elephants, dogs; **2.** bats; **3.** tuna hears lowest and mouse hears highest; **4.** Bats and dolphins can hear these high pitches, which they use for echolocation. **5.** humans and elephants

PART B **6.** 1,000 times louder; **7.** Faster on the hot, wet night. The speed of sound is faster at higher temperatures and in denser media.

SCIENCE EXTENSION Answers will vary.

Challenge, p. 130

PART A A common example is an electric fan. It produces many different sound waves making it hard to distinguish someone's voice from the sounds of the fan. The plot looks like a bunch of differently shaped waves overlapping.

PART B Answers will vary but inventions should show an understanding of the chapter content.

Chapter 21 Answer Key

Key Concept Review, p. 131

PART A **1.** photons; **2.** microwaves; **3.** gamma rays; **4.** incandescent light; **5.** coherent light

PART B **6.** They produce the same interference patterns when passing through a small opening. **7.** The radio waves cause the electrons in the antenna to vibrate, which produces an alternating current in the antenna and can be converted into audio or video. **8.** Radio detecting and ranging; radio waves reflect off objects and return to the station broadcasting the waves.

SCIENCE EXTENSION Paragraphs should show an understanding of the workings of each type of bulb discussed in the chapter.

Vocabulary Review, p. 132

PART A **1.** ultraviolet waves; **2.** photoelectric effect; **3.** luminous object; illuminated object; **4.** Fluorescent lights; **5.** electromagnetic spectrum

PART B **6.** incoherent light; Incoherent light waves have various frequencies whose crests and trough are not aligned. The waves spread apart as they travel. A lightbulb produces incoherent light. **7.** coherent light; Coherent light waves have the same frequency and travel with their crests and troughs aligned. Coherent light does remains focused in a small-diameter beam. A laser produces coherent light.

SCIENCE EXTENSION Answers will vary but should show an understanding of the chapter.

Interpreting Diagrams, p. 133

PART A **1.** radio waves; **2.** microwaves; **3.** infrared waves; **4.** visible light; **5.** ultraviolet waves; **6.** X rays; **7.** gamma rays; **8.** increasing frequency; **9.** increasing wavelength

PART B **10.** M; **11.** V; **12.** I, V, U; **13.** R; **14.** G; **15.** U; **16.** I; **17.** R; **18.** V

SCIENCE EXTENSION Answers will vary, but should reflect understanding of the different kinds of light discussed in the chapter.

Reading Comprehension, p. 134

PART A **1.** Luminous objects produce visible light while a visible object that is not a light source is being illuminated. **2.** Incandescent light is light produced by hot objects. Florescent light is a visible light that is called a cool light because it produces less thermal energy than an incandescent light. **3.** Neon lights contain a gas, usually neon, in a clear glass tube. Electrodes energize the gas, and collisions between electrons and gas molecules release visible light. Tungsten-halogen lights are used when extremely bright light is required. The light is produced by a very hot tungsten filament inside a halogen-gas-filled quartz tube. **4.** Coherent light waves all have the same frequency and travel with their crests and troughs aligned. Incoherent light waves have various frequencies whose crests and troughs are not aligned.

PART B **5.** Its energy increases also. **6.** It is absorbed by Earth's ozone layer.

SCIENCE EXTENSION Sun: infrared waves, ultraviolet waves, visible waves; radar gun: radio waves; microwave: radio waves, microwaves; cell phone: radio waves, microwaves; reflective vest: light wave; match: infrared wave; lit candle: visible light wave; remote control: near-infrared waves; cable TV: radio waves, microwaves; radio: radio waves

Math Connection, p. 135

PART A **1.** Answers will vary. **2.** Calculations will vary but all products should be approximately 10^8 m/s.

PART B **3.** No. Such a low frequency would have a very long wavelength and require an enormous antenna. **4.** AM radio; **5.** The waves could interfere with each other, causing static on the television.

SCIENCE EXTENSION General process will involve rubbing the rod with the cloth to produce a static charge, then waving the rod back and forth to produce a radio wave. Wavelength will be the length of the rod, and frequency will be around 10^8 Hz.

Challenge, pp. 136–137

PART A **1.** Radio waves travel at the speed of light. It would take much longer to hear the message and for the astronaut to hear it. **2.** Since laser beams cannot be visibly seen unless there are particles of dust in the air, a laser beam pulse would only be visible as a dot on the other ship just like a laser pointer only shows a dot on the wall. **3.** X rays work by passing through solid objects and striking a sensor to show a shadowy black-and-white image. If the superhero is the X-ray source, then the sensor is on the other side. If the superhero's eyes are the sensors, then the source should be on the other side. If the superhero's eyes are both the source and the sensor, he still would only be able to see through thinner objects since X rays don't have enough energy to pass through bone. **4.** Since light travels at 300,000 km/s, it takes 35 minutes for light to travel this distance. Nothing can travel faster than the speed of light.

PART B Answers will vary, but should show an understanding of the chapter.

Chapter 22 Answer Key

Key Concept Review, p. 138

PART A

22.1: Shadows and Reflections
    A. Shadows
    B. Reflection of Light
    C. Convex Mirrors
    D. Concave Mirrors
22.2: Refraction—The Bending of Light
    A. The Index of Refraction
    B. Convex Lenses
    C. Concave Lenses
    D. Total Internal Reflection
22.3: Color
    A. Opaque, Transparent, and Translucent Objects
    B. Color
    C. Primary Light Colors
    D. Primary Pigment Colors
22.4: Vision—How You See
    A. The Eye and Vision
    B. Vision Problems
22.5: Using Light
    A. Polarized Light
    B. Optical Fibers
    C. Telescopes, Microscopes, and Cameras

PART B **1.** concave lens; **2.** regular reflection; **3.** translucent

SCIENCE EXTENSION   Answers will vary, but should include the following concepts: The RGB system is used for computer images, because monitors emit color as light. Colors seen on the monitor are a combination of the light colors in different percentages of red (R), green (G), and blue (B). The CMYK system is used for printed images: pigment colors are printed on paper, layered on top of each other in different percentages to create the colors you see on a magazine page. The colors used in magazine printing are cyan (C), magenta (M), yellow (Y), and black (B).

Vocabulary Review, p. 139

PART A   **1.** h; **2.** b; **3.** a; **4.** d; **5.** i; **6.** f; **7.** e; **8.** c; **9.** g

PART B   **10.** retina; the inner lining of the eye on which light rays come to a focus; **11.** cornea; a tough, transparent layer of cells through which light enters the eye; **12.** pupil; an opening through which light passes after it passes through the cornea; **13.** lens; after passing through the pupil, the lens bends the light so that it converges at a focal point on the back of the eye; the lens is flexible and convex

SCIENCE EXTENSION   Answers will vary but should show an understanding of the differences between each pair of words.

Interpreting Diagrams, p. 140

PART A   **1.** Convex, Plane; **2.** Concave; **3.** Convex, Plane; **4.** Convex; **5.** Concave

PART B   **6.** concave; **7.** convex; **8.** convex; **9.** concave; **10.** convex

SCIENCE EXTENSION   Answers will vary but should reflect understanding of chapter content.

Reading Comprehension, p. 141

PART A   Individual K-W-L-H Charts will vary, but be sure students are using the correct information in the Lesson.

PART B   **1.** flat; **2.** distance; **3.** front; **4.** upright; **5.** same; **6.** reversed; **7.** convex; **8.** larger; **9.** upright; **10.** reversed; **11.** larger; **12.** concave; **13.** smaller

Earth Science Connection, p. 142

PART A   **1.** Sunlight hits the Moon. Some of the light is reflected toward Earth and the eyes. The light passes through the cornea and lens of the eye and comes to a focus on the retina. Nerve cells conduct signals to the brain, which forms them into an image of the Moon. **2.** The Moon is illuminated by the Sun. **3.** Moonlight is reflected sunlight. Starlight is produced by hot stars and travels directly through space to the eyes. Both are waves of visible light. **4.** Moonlight is dim, reflected sunlight. Therefore, the health effects of moonlight would be similar to sunlight.

PART B   **5.** The Moon looks nearly white. All of the colors of visible light reach Earth. **6.** Blue and green wavelengths are absorbed or reflected by the dust in the atmosphere. Only the red wavelengths make it to the eye. **7.** Moonlight is refracted, or bent, as it passes through the water droplets in the air. Each color is refracted a different amount. The colors separate out to form a rainbow.

SCIENCE EXTENSION   Sunlight strikes the Moon at a 90° angle and bounces straight back. The Moon will be invisible (new Moon) from Earth.

Challenge, p. 143

PART A   **1.** Images are superimposed in both methods. In parallel viewing, the image that the left eye sees "moves" to the right and the image the right sees "moves" to the left so that the spheres B and C superimpose to create the combined image. In the cross-eyed method, the image that the left eye sees "moves" to the right and the image the right eye sees "moves" to the left so that the spheres A and D superimpose to create the combined image.

PART B   Images will vary depending upon what is drawn.

Chapter 23 Answer Key

Key Concept Review, p. 144

PART A   **1.** electrons; **2.** conduction; **3.** amperes; **4.** direct current; **5.** series circuit

PART B   **6.** Like charges repel one another, but opposite charges attract. **7.** by friction, conduction, or induction; **8.** It is produced by the movement of charges through a circuit.

SCIENCE EXTENSION   Answers will vary but should mention common household items such as TV, refrigerator, microwave, etc.

Vocabulary Review, p. 145

PART A   **1.** resistance; **2.** conductor; **3.** friction; **4.** open circuit; **5.** insulator; **6.** ion

PART B   **7.** the direction of the current changes over time; **8.** a house uses an alternating current; **9.** direct current; **10.** batteries produce direct current; **11.** amount of power an electric device uses over time; **12.** electric energy = electric power × time; **13.** electric power; **14.** electric power = current × voltage difference; **15.** electric field; **16.** positively-charged particles inside a positive electric field are pushed away

SCIENCE EXTENSION   Graphic organizers will vary. Webs might include friction, conduction, conductor, insulator, induction.

Interpreting Diagrams, p. 146

PART A   **1.** series circuit; open circuit; lightbulbs are off; **2.** parallel circuit; closed; circuit lightbulbs are on

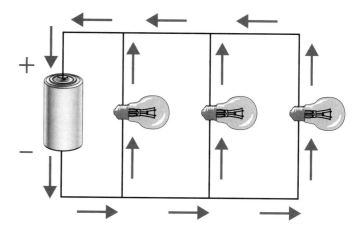

PART B   **3.** direct; **4.** amperes; **5.** voltage; **6.** ohms; **7.** longer; **8.** V = IR

SCIENCE EXTENSION   Diagrams will vary, but should reflect understanding of chapter content.

Reading Comprehension, p. 147

PART A   Answers will vary, but should include the following facts: An atom contains electrically charged particles: protons, which are positively charged, and electrons, which are negatively charged. If the atom has more protons than electrons, it is positively charged. If it has more electrons than protons, it is negatively charged. Charged particles exert force on each other through an electric field. Like charges repel one another, and unlike charges attract. When charged particles move, they create electric current.

PART B   **1.** electrons; **2.** protons; **3.** less; **4.** stripped; **5.** gains; **6.** static charges; **7.** static electricity

SCIENCE EXTENSION   **1.** Solar panels are made up of photocells. They are built of two kinds of silicon, one with a positive charge and one with a negative charge. When light hits a photocell, it frees electrons from some of the silicon atoms. The electrons are pulled into the positively-charged silicon layer. The moving electrons produce an electric current. **2.** AC, alternating current, is where the electrons move back and forth in the wire. This means that the terminals of the power source are constantly changing from positive to negative and back again. The current in your house is alternating current. **3.** A parallel circuit has branching wires that let the current follow more than one path. If one part of the circuit is opened, electrons can still flow through other parts of the circuit. A series circuit has only one path for the current to follow. **4.** You should never plug too many devices into one outlet or extension cord. This can cause a fire.

Materials Science Connection, p. 148

PART A   **1.** The negatively-charged white balls will be repelled and rise to the surface of the ink, showing a white dot. **2.** There are more electrons, giving the balls a negative charge. **3.** The paper would turn dark as the white balls were repelled.

PART B   **4.** battery, electrical outlet, solar cell, hand-powered generator, car charger, etc. **5.** The electronic ink book is "on" only when the display changes. A computer and its monitor stay on throughout the time you are using them.

SCIENCE EXTENSION   Answers will vary.

Challenge, pp. 149–150

PART A   **1a.** Feeling an object occurs from the atoms in your finger pushing up against the atoms in the book. The electrical repulsion between the electrons on the outside of the atoms is the contact force. **1b.** Example of an illustration might be:

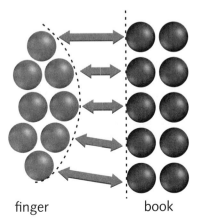

finger   book

1c. The contact force increases because more atoms are packing into a smaller space. The force of your finger against the book decreases the distance between the electrons, causing the repulsive force to increase. **2a.** The resistance is friction. The atoms in the book that are close to one another push against each other with a resistive force even at rest. When the book begins to move, the distances between those atoms decrease. To get the book to move, that resistive force must be overcome. Also, this force, which is resisted, pushes electrons from one surface to another. **2b.** Example of an illustration might be:

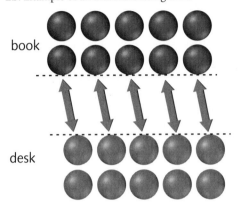

book

desk

2c. The electrical repulsion between your finger and the book is greater than the electrical repulsion between the book and the desk. **3.** Electrical resistance is friction. The only difference is that the electrons moving through a copper wire are "free" in the sense that they are moving more easily. But they still must overcome electrical repulsion.

PART B   Example of illustration:

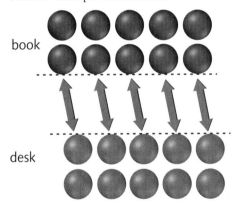

book

desk

Chapter 24 Answer Key

Key Concept Review, p. 151

PART A   **1.** iron; **2.** cobalt; **3.** nickel; **4.** steel; **5.** magnetite; **6.** Earth; **7.** copper; **8.** aluminum; **9.** gold; **10.** skin; **11.** paper; **12.** plastic

PART B   **13.** They are the lines that represent the shape, strength, and direction of the magnetic field around a magnet. **14.** when it contains aligned magnetic domains; **15.** by using a naturally magnetic material to align the magnetic domains of the second material; **16.** It is curved.

SCIENCE EXTENSION   Answers will vary.

Vocabulary Review, p. 152

PART A **1.** c; **2.** b; **3.** e; **4.** a; **5.** d

PART B Magnetite is a naturally magnetic material; It did not become a magnet through magnetic induction. It is not magnetized iron. It is not a temporary magnet that loses its magnetic field when a magnet is removed. It is a form of iron ore with a strong magnetic field. It is a permanent magnet, so its properties last a long time. It is also called lodestone from the Greeks who discovered it.

SCIENCE EXTENSION Answers will vary but might include, magnetism, magnetic field, magnetic field line, magnetic pole, magnetic domain, magnetite, magnetic induction, compass, magnetosphere, aurora.

Interpreting Diagrams, p. 153

PART A

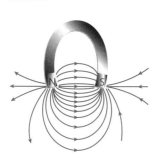
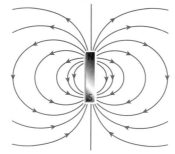

PART B

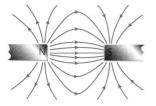
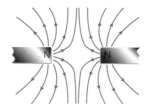

1. magnetic poles; **2.** attraction; **3.** repulsion; **4.** polar drift and reverse of polarity

Reading Comprehension, p. 154

PART A Students' K-W-L-H charts will vary.

PART B **1.** Magnetism is produced by the movement of electrons, which move in energy levels around the nucleus of an atom, and also spin. **2.** The lines are drawn closer together where the magnetic field is stronger. **3.** Magnetite contains two different types of iron atoms with different electron counts, and they pass electrons back and forth, creating a magnetic field. **4.** A permanent magnet can lose its field if it gets very hot, if it is dropped, or if it is struck very hard, taking the magnetic domains out of alignment. **5.** It is called the magnetosphere, and it extends as far as 11 Earth radii into space on the day side of the planet and more than 200 Earth radii on the night side of the planet. **6.** A compass contains a magnet that lines up with Earth's magnetic field, pointing in the direction of the north magnetic pole of the planet.

SCIENCE EXTENSION **1.** magnetic force; **2.** magnetic field lines; run from north to south

Earth Science Connection, p. 155

PART A **1.** Tiny, charged solar particles are attracted to Earth's magnetic poles. When they hit atoms in Earth's atmosphere, they give off energy as visible light. **2.** The magnetic poles are some distance from the geographic poles. **3.** The north end of a compass points toward north. Because opposite poles of a magnet attract each other, the pole in the north is physically a magnetic south pole. However, this pole has traditionally been called the magnetic "north pole."

PART B **4.** Auroras are caused by charged particles moving along the magnetic field lines of Earth's magnetosphere. Moving charges induce an electrical current. **5.** No. auroras are unpredictable and usually available only near the poles.

SCIENCE EXTENSION Compasses would point toward the new location and auroras would be visible at night. Weather and length of day would not be affected.

Challenge, p. 156

PART A Be sure that students understand the basic principles involved in making a compass.

PART B Student maps will vary.

Chapter 25 Answer Key

Key Concept Review, p. 157

PART A **1.** electromagnetic induction; **2.** generator; **3.** electric motor; **4.** galvanometer; **5.** transformer

PART B **6.** It is called a solenoid, and the magnetic field inside it is stronger than the field inside one loop. **7.** by wrapping a solenoid around an iron core; **8.** It uses a rotating electromagnet to measure current.

SCIENCE EXTENSION Answers will vary.

Vocabulary Review, p. 158

PART A **1.** alternating current (AC); **2.** direct current (DC); **3.** solenoid; solenoid; **4.** Electromagnetic induction; **5.** electromagnet

PART B **6.** converts electric energy into mechanical energy; **7.** hair dryer; **8.** common device used to measure electric current; **9.** an automobile's fuel gauge; **10.** device that converts mechanical energy into electricity; **11.** alternator in a car recharges the battery and powers other devices; **12.** device used to change the voltage of an alternating current; **13.** step-down transformers decrease voltage of power lines to homes

SCIENCE EXTENSION Answers will vary but should show an understanding of the chapter content.

Interpreting Diagrams, p. 159

PART A **1.** source of mechanical energy; **2.** shaft; **3.** coil; **4.** fixed magnet

PART B Sample answers given. **5.** A hand turns the shaft. **6.** The coil rotates between the poles of the fixed magnet. **7.** The changing magnetic field produces a current that turns on the lightbulb. **8.** G; **10.** G; **11.** G; **12.** T

SCIENCE EXTENSION Answers will vary.

Reading Comprehension, p. 160

PART A **1.** solenoid; **2.** electromagnet; **3.** galvanometer; **4.** generator; **5.** transformer

PART B **6.** decreases; **7.** stronger; **8.** weaker; decreasing

SCIENCE EXTENSION **1.** Her compass will most likely not point north because the electric current powering the radio creates a magnetic field. **2.** Her compass should most likely point north. The ladder most likely does not have an electric current flowing through it.

History Connection, p. 161

PART A **1.** Electricity traveled down the frog's nerves to the muscles in its legs, causing them to move.

PART B **2.** The electrical field of the battery would attract or repel the needle of the compass. **3.** Batteries power the camera's flash, advance film, record data, focus the camera, move the zoom lens, etc.

SCIENCE EXTENSION Answers will vary. Examples could include comparing the experimental designs, repeating the experiments, trying each other's experiments, designing a third experiment, etc.

Challenge, pp. 162–163

PART A Sample answer: 1. Attach a magnet to the door and a circuit with current flowing through it on the doorframe. When the door is opened, the magnet will move and the magnetic field will disrupt the current flow in the circuit. A device in the circuit could detect any current change. This is essentially how security systems work.
2. A device that creates a strong magnetic field could be passed close to the ground. If a metal object is present, like a coin, it will cause a current to flow in the metal. This will produce a magnetic field as well, which could be detected. This is essentially a metal detector.
3. A magnet attached to something that can vibrate like cellophane or a piece of paper is placed close to a circuit. When the bass hits the magnet, it will cause it to vibrate which will cause electrons to flow in a wire attached to a circuit. A detector could be attached to the wire that would detect when the current gets high enough.

Chapter 26 Answer Key

Key Concept Review, p. 164
PART A

26.1: Electronic Signals and Devices
    A. Electronic Signals
    B. Types of Electronic Signals
    C. Producing Digital Signals
    D. Why Digital and Not Analog?
    E. Electronic Devices
    F. Semiconductors
    G. Doping a Semiconductor
    H. Electronic Components
26.2: Telecommunication
    A. The Telegraph
    B. The Telephone
    C. Broadcast Media
    D. Radio
    E. Television
    F. Cellular Phones

26.3: Computers
    A. What is a Computer?
    B. How Computers Process Information
    C. Computer Hardware
    D. The CPU
    E. Computer Memory
    F. Storage Devices

PART B **1.** semiconductor; **2.** Telecommunication; **3.** digital signal;

SCIENCE EXTENSION Diagrams will vary depending upon the computer the student uses.

Vocabulary Review, p. 165

PART A **1.** e; **2.** f; **3.** d; **4.** c; **5.** b; **6.** a

PART B **7.** electronic device designed to carry out a set of instructions; **8.** random-access memory; **9.** receives, processes, and outputs data; also called CPU; **10.** permanently-stored data, such as instructions the computer needs to function, stored in ROM; **11.** a set of instructions that the computer runs; **12.** binary number; **13.** computer hardware

SCIENCE EXTENSION Answers will vary, but should show an understanding of the content in Section 3.

Interpreting Diagrams, p. 166

PART A **1.** c [by telegraph]; **2.** a, e, f, g [by telephone]; **3.** a, b [by radio]; **4.** a, h [by television]; **5.** a, e, h [by cellular phone]

PART B **6.** digital signal; **7.** analog signal

SCIENCE EXTENSION Answers will vary depending on the device the student chose.

Reading Comprehension, p. 167

PART A **1.** Analog signals are physical representations of data, and they change smoothly over time. Digital signals are numerical representations of data, in distinct values over time, and they jump from one value to another in steps, not smoothly. **2.** Semiconductors are used to control the flow of current in an electronic device. **3.** Telecommunication is the exchange of information across a distance. **4.** Cellular phones communicate with a network of transmission towers called cells. The network transfers the call from cell to cell as the caller moves.

PART B **5.** Dillon the Diode; **6.** Terry the Transistor; **7.** Iggy the Integrated Circuit; **8.** Ann the Analog Signal; **9.** David the Digital Signal

SCIENCE EXTENSION Answers will vary, but should include the following ideas: Stephanie could have electrocuted herself by using electric devices near water. She could have created a spark and possible fire hazard when she tripped over the cord, pulling the plug from the outlet. She created a fire hazard by putting a rug over the cord. She created a fire hazard by plugging too many devices into one outlet, and she could also overload the circuits and cause a fuse or circuit to blow or short out. Finally, she could have electrocuted herself by climbing a telephone pole with live wires and touching them to get her kite untangled.

Math Connection, p. 168
PART A **1.** CIRCUIT

PART B **2.** Babylonian. 11 is 3 in binary, 11 in decimal, or 61 in

Babylonian. **4.** There are 60 seconds in a minute and 60 minutes in an hour. **5.** $2(60^2) + 35(60) + 7 = 7200 + 2100 + 7 = 9307$ seconds

SCIENCE EXTENSION $6 \times 9 = 54$. In base 13, $54 = 4(13) + 2$, or 42.

Challenge, pp. 169–170
PART A

A	B	C	D	O
0	0	0	0	0
0	0	0	1	0
0	0	1	0	0
0	0	1	1	1
0	1	0	0	0
0	1	0	1	1
0	1	1	0	1
0	1	1	1	1
1	0	0	0	0
1	0	0	1	1
1	0	1	0	1
1	0	1	1	1
1	1	0	0	1
1	1	0	1	1
1	1	1	0	1
1	1	1	1	1

PART B

1.

I (Hz)	A	B
84	0	0
94	0	1
104	1	0
114	1	1

2.

I (Hz)	A	B	C	D
84	0	0	0	0
86	0	0	0	1
88	0	0	1	0
90	0	0	1	1
92	0	1	0	0
94	0	1	0	1
96	0	1	1	0
98	0	1	1	1
100	1	0	0	0
102	1	0	0	1
104	1	0	1	0
106	1	0	1	1
108	1	1	0	0
110	1	1	0	1
112	1	1	1	0
114	1	1	1	1

3. The first chip divides the frequency ranges in 10 Hz ranges, while the second chip divides the frequency ranges into 2 Hz a piece. The more divisions or outputs, the narrower the range becomes to break the analog signal. The second chip is superior and will resolve the signal and bring more clarity.